APA Handbook of

Clinical
Geropsychology

APA Handbooks in Psychology® Series

APA Handbooks in Psychology

APA Handbook of
Clinical
Geropsychology

VOLUME 2

Assessment, Treatment, and
Issues of Later Life

Peter A. Lichtenberg and Benjamin T. Mast, *Editors-in-Chief*

Brian D. Carpenter and Julie Loebach Wetherell, *Associate Editors*

American Psychological Association • Washington, DC

Published by
American Psychological Association
750 First Street, NE
Washington, DC 20002-4242
www.apa.org

To order
APA Order Department
P.O. Box 92984
Washington, DC 20090-2984
Tel: (800) 374-2721; Direct: (202) 336-5510
Fax: (202) 336-5502; TDD/TTY: (202) 336-6123
Online: www.apa.org/pubs/books/
E-mail: order@apa.org

In the U.K., Europe, Africa, and the Middle East, copies may be ordered from
American Psychological Association
3 Henrietta Street
Covent Garden, London
WC2E 8LU England

AMERICAN PSYCHOLOGICAL ASSOCIATION STAFF
Gary R. VandenBos, PhD, *Publisher*
Julia Frank-McNeil, *Senior Director, APA Books*
Theodore J. Baroody, *Director, Reference, APA Books*
Patricia D. Mathis, *Reference Editorial Manager, APA Books*

Typeset in Berkeley by Cenveo Publisher Services, Columbia, MD

Printer: Edwards Brothers Inc., Lillington, NC
Cover Designer: Naylor Design, Washington, DC

Library of Congress Cataloging-in-Publication Data

APA handbook of clinical geropsychology / Peter A. Lichtenberg and
Benjamin T. Mast, editors-in-chief ; Brian D. Carpenter and Julie Loebach Wetherell,
associate editors.
    volumes; cm. — (APA handbooks in psychology)
  Includes bibliographical references and index.
Contents: Volume 1. History and status of the field and perspectives on aging —
  Volume 2. Assessment, treatment, and issues of later life.
  ISBN 978-1-4338-1804-2 — ISBN 1-4338-1804-3
  1. Older people—Mental health. 2. Psychotherapy for older people. I. Lichtenberg,
Peter A., editor. II. Mast, Benjamin T., editor. III. American Psychological Association.
  RC451.4.A5A72 2015
  618.97'689—dc23
                    2014018238

British Library Cataloguing-in-Publication Data
A CIP record is available from the British Library.

Printed in the United States of America
First Edition

http://dx.doi.org/10.1037/14459-000

Contents

Volume 2: Assessment, Treatment, and Issues of Later Life

Editorial Board

Contributors: Volume 2

Rhoda Au, PhD, Department of Neurology and Framingham Heart Study, Boston University, Boston, MA

Liat Ayalon, PhD, Louis and Gabi Weisfeld School of Social Work, Bar Ilan University, Ramat-Gan, Israel

Steve Balsis, PhD, Department of Psychology, Texas A&M University, College Station

Patricia M. Bamonti, BS, Department of Psychology, West Virginia University, Morgantown

Steven Bernfeld, PhD, Department of Preventive Medicine, Rush University Medical Center, Chicago, IL

Erin D. Bigler, PhD, Department of Psychology, Brigham Young University, Provo, UT

Mark W. Bondi, PhD, VA San Diego Healthcare System; Department of Psychiatry, University of California, San Diego, La Jolla

Emily S. Bower, MS, Joint Doctoral Program in Clinical Psychology, San Diego State University/University of California, San Diego

Rebecca P. Cameron, PhD, Department of Psychology, California State University, Sacramento

Cameron J. Camp, PhD, Center for Applied Research in Dementia, Solon, OH

Brian D. Carpenter, PhD, Department of Psychology, Washington University in St. Louis, St. Louis, MO

Melissa Castro, PsyD, Department of Neurology, Dean Clinic, Madison, WI

Alexandra Clark, BS, Joint Doctoral Program in Clinical Psychology, San Diego State University/University of California, San Diego

Jiska Cohen-Mansfield, PhD, Department of Health Promotion, School of Public Health, Sackler Faculty of Medicine; Minerva Center for the Interdisciplinary Study of End of Life; and Herczeg Institute on Aging, Tel-Aviv University, Tel-Aviv, Israel

Colleen C. Cordes, PhD, Nicholas A. Cummings Behavioral Health Program, Arizona State University, Phoenix

Natalie D. Dautovich, PhD, Department of Psychology, University of Alabama, Tuscaloosa

Lisa Delano-Wood, PhD, VA San Diego Healthcare System; Department of Psychiatry, University of California, San Diego, La Jolla

Barry A. Edelstein, PhD, Department of Psychology, West Virginia University, Morgantown

Erin E. Emery-Tiburcio, PhD, Department of Behavioral Sciences, Rush University Medical Center, Chicago, IL

Amy Fiske, PhD, Department of Psychology, West Virginia University, Morgantown

Alexandra C. Geneser, PsyD, Department of Neurology, School of Medicine, University of Virginia, Charlottesville

Lindsay A. Gerolimatos, PhD, Department of Psychology, West Virginia University, Morgantown

Jeffrey J. Gregg, PhD, Department of Psychology, West Virginia University, Morgantown

Thomas Hadjistavropoulos, PhD, ABPP, Department of Psychology and Centre on Aging and Health, University of Regina, Regina, Saskatchewan, Canada

Allison R. Heid, PhD, Department of Human Development and Family Studies, Pennsylvania State University, University Park

Jennifer Ho, MS, Joint Doctoral Program in Clinical Psychology, San Diego State University/University of California, San Diego

Jason M. Holland, PhD, Department of Psychology, University of Nevada, Las Vegas

Lee Hyer, PhD, Georgia Neurosurgical Institute and Mercer Medical School, Macon

Chaya Koren, PhD, School of Social Work and Center for the Study of Society, University of Haifa, Haifa, Israel

Rebecca Lahey, LCSW, Health and Aging, Rush University Medical Center, Chicago, IL

Kenneth L. Lichstein, PhD, Department of Psychology, University of Alabama, Tuscaloosa

Peter A. Lichtenberg, PhD, ABPP, Institute of Gerontology and Merrill Palmer Skillman Institute, Wayne State University, Detroit, MI

Carol A. Manning, PhD, Department of Neurology, School of Medicine, University of Virginia, Charlottesville

Benjamin T. Mast, PhD, Department of Psychological and Brain Sciences, University of Louisville, Louisville, KY

Brent T. Mausbach, PhD, Department of Psychiatry, University of California, San Diego

Christina S. McCrae, PhD, Department of Health Psychology, University of Missouri, Columbia

Laura McKenzie, BA, Mercer University School of Medicine, Macon, GA

Cynthia K. McQuown, MAEd, University of Akron, Akron, OH

Thomas M. Meuser, PhD, Gerontology Program, School of Social Work, University of Missouri, Saint Louis

Victor Molinari, PhD, School of Aging Studies, University of South Florida, Tampa

Linda R. Mona, PhD, Behavioral Health Division, Veterans Administration Long Beach Healthcare System, Long Beach, CA

Laura Mosqueda, MD, Department of Family Medicine, Keck School of Medicine, University of Southern California, Los Angeles

Jennifer Muhaidat, PhD, Department of Physiotherapy, Faculty of Rehabilitation Sciences, University of Jordan, Amman, Jordan

Christine Mullen, Doctoral Candidate, Georgia Neurosurgical Institute and Mercer School of Medicine, Macon, GA

Lisa M. Nackers, PhD, Department of Preventive Medicine, Rush University Medical Center, Chicago, IL

Daniel A. Nation, PhD, Department of Psychology, University of Southern California, Los Angeles

Robert A. Neimeyer, PhD, Department of Psychology, University of Memphis, Memphis, TN

David Nyenhuis, PhD, Department of Clinical Neuropsychology, Hauenstein Neuroscience Center, Saint Mary's Health Care, Grand Rapids, MI

Bonnie Olsen, PhD, Department of Family Medicine, Keck School of Medicine, University of Southern California, Los Angeles

Elizabeth C. Price, MA, Department of Psychology, West Virginia University, Morgantown

Sara Honn Qualls, PhD, Gerontology Center, University of Colorado, Colorado Springs

Alicia J. Roth, Doctoral Candidate, Department of Clinical and Health Psychology, University of Florida, Gainesville

Derek D. Satre, PhD, Department of Psychiatry, University of California, San Francisco

Jamie Shouse, BA, Department of Psychological and Brain Sciences, University of Louisville, Louisville, KY

Dawn A. Skelton, PhD, School of Health and Life Sciences, Glasgow Caledonian University, Glasgow, Scotland

Glenn E. Smith, PhD, Department of Psychiatry and Psychology, Mayo Clinic, Rochester, MI

Merideth D. Smith, PhD, Psi Med Corrections, LLC, Charleston, WV

Michael A. Smyer, PhD, Office of the Provost, Bucknell University, Lewisburg, PA

Scott A. Sperling, PsyD, Department of Neurology, School of Medicine, University of Virginia, Charlottesville

Harvey L. Sterns, PhD, Department of Psychology and Institute for Life-Span Development and Gerontology, University of Akron, Akron, OH

Maggie L. Syme, PhD, MPH, Department of Psychology, San Diego State University, San Diego, CA

Julie Loebach Wetherell, PhD, Veterans Administration San Diego Healthcare System, San Diego, CA; and Department of Psychiatry, University of California, San Diego

Jennifer Price Wolf, PhD, Prevention Research Center, Oakland, CA

Roberto Zamora, BA, Department of Psychology, University of Alabama, Tuscaloosa

Steven H. Zarit, PhD, Department of Human Development and Family Studies, Pennsylvania State University, University Park

Richard A. Zweig, PhD, Ferkauf Graduate School of Psychology, Yeshiva University, New York, NY

PART I

ASSESSMENT AND TREATMENT FOR THE PSYCHOLOGICAL DISORDERS OF AGING

Chapter 1

DEPRESSION IN LATER LIFE

Barry A. Edelstein, Patricia M. Bamonti, Jeffrey J. Gregg, and Lindsay A. Gerolimatos

Major depressive disorder (MDD) affects between 1% and 5% of community-dwelling older adults (Blazer, 2009). Although MDD is less prevalent among older adults compared with younger age-groups (Gum, King-Kallimanis, & Kohn, 2009), rates of MDD are somewhat higher among medical populations (10%–15%) and older adults in long-term care (14%–42%; Blazer, 2009). The course of depression over a lifetime is unfavorable. Approximately 50%–60% of individuals with one depressive episode experience another one. Approximately 70%–80% of those individuals will experience a third episode, and approximately 90% of those individuals will experience a fourth episode (Liu & Alloy, 2010). Symptoms of depression in late life are associated with increased cognitive, social, and functional impairment as well as all-cause mortality (Blazer, 2009). Given the complexities of later life, such as cognitive changes, greater likelihood of medical comorbidity, and new social roles, late-life depression (i.e., older adult depression) presents the clinician with unique challenges. We use the term late-life depression to describe older adults with depression regardless of the time of onset of their depression. Conversely, depression that begins in later life is referred to as late-onset depression. This chapter will provide a broad overview of older adult depression, including diagnostic criteria, conceptual issues, assessment, intervention, and factors to consider in clinical application. Two case examples are presented to illustrate assessment, conceptualization, and treatment of late-life depression.

DEFINITION, DIAGNOSTIC CRITERIA, AND PRESENTATION OF LATE-LIFE DEPRESSION

In the *Diagnostic and Statistical Manual of Mental Disorders, Fifth Edition* (*DSM–5*; American Psychiatric Association, 2013), MDD is a mood disorder characterized by depressed mood or loss of interest or pleasure in activities. These symptoms must coincide with at least four additional symptoms for a minimum of 2 weeks, including insomnia or hypersomnia, weight or appetite change, thoughts of death or suicide, fatigue, psychomotor agitation or retardation, difficulty thinking or concentrating, and feelings of worthlessness or guilt (American Psychiatric Association, 2013). These depressive episodes may be singular or recurrent (American Psychiatric Association, 2013). Individuals also may present with dysthymic disorder, which is characterized by depressed mood nearly all day for more days than not. The depressed mood must occur for a minimum of 2 years and be accompanied by at least two additional symptoms, such as poor appetite or overeating, insomnia or hypersomnia, fatigue, low self-esteem, feelings of hopelessness, and difficulty thinking or concentrating (American Psychiatric Association, 2013).

With the *DSM–5* (American Psychiatric Association, 2013), diagnostic criteria better reflect the influence of developmental (i.e., age-related), gender, and cultural issues on the presentation of symptoms (Kupfer, Kuhl, & Regier, 2013). For example, bereavement was removed as an exclusion for major depression, and memory impairment is acknowledged as a common feature of depression among older

http://dx.doi.org/10.1037/14459-001
APA Handbook of Clinical Geropsychology: Vol. 2. Assessment, Treatment, and Issues of Later Life,
P. A. Lichtenberg and B. T. Mast (Editors-in-Chief)

adults, although it may be mistaken for early signs of dementia (American Psychiatric Association, 2013). The *DSM–5* also includes a mixed anxiety–depression syndrome as a condition requiring further research. The inclusion of a mixed anxiety–depression condition in the *DSM–5* is important, as many older adults present with features of both anxiety and depression (Almeida et al., 2012). The *DSM–5* also includes a dimensional approach, placing emphasis on such factors as the frequency and severity of symptoms and conceptualizing disorders along a continuum, which is more consistent with medical models (Kupfer et al., 2013). The dimensional approach also is more appropriate for older adults, as older adults are more likely to present with subsyndromal depression (T. W. Meeks, Vahia, Lavretsky, Kulkarni, & Jeste, 2011). One final significant change in the *DSM–5* is its organization, with greater similarity to the *International Classification of Diseases, 10th Edition* (*ICD–10*; World Health Organization [WHO], 1992; see also Kupfer et al., 2013).

In the *ICD–10* (WHO, 1992), depression is categorized according to severity (mild, moderate, or severe) and chronicity (single episode or recurrent). Individuals typically present with depressed mood, diminished interest or pleasure in activities, or fatigue. Other possible symptoms include reduced concentration, low self-esteem, feelings of guilt or worthlessness, pessimistic views of the future, thoughts of suicide, poor sleep, and diminished appetite. Another depressive disorder, dysthymia, is marked by chronic depressed mood that never meets criteria for recurrent depressive disorder (WHO, 1992). Although diagnostic criteria for depression in the *ICD–10* and *DSM–5* are similar, a key difference is that the *ICD–10* specifies different thresholds for mild, moderate, and severe depression (Gruenberg, Goldstein, & Pincus, 2005).

MDD is less prevalent among older than younger adults (Kessler et al., 2010). Moreover, the presentation and experience of depressive symptoms among older adults differs from depression among other age-groups (Fiske, Wetherell, & Gatz, 2009). Compared with young adults, older adults are less likely to endorse feelings of guilt (Hegeman, Kok, van der Mast, & Giltay, 2012) and suicidal ideation (Blazer, Bachar, & Hughes, 1987), although suicidal ideation tends to increase across older adulthood (Cukrowicz et al., 2009). Relative to younger age-groups, older adults report more psychomotor changes (e.g., psychomotor slowness or agitation; Fiske et al., 2009; Hegeman et al., 2012) and somatic symptoms (e.g., appetite disturbance, loss of interest in sex; Hegeman et al., 2012; Hybels, Landerman, & Blazer, 2012). Sleep disturbances are more common with late-life depression and are more likely to precipitate depression than with younger adults (Fiske et al., 2009). Additionally, older adults are more likely than members of other age-groups to present with melancholic features of depression (American Psychiatric Association, 2000; Lee et al., 2012), which include loss of pleasure or reactivity to events, early morning awakenings, poor mood in the morning, weight loss or loss of appetite, and psychomotor changes.

Older adults tend to de-emphasize depressed mood and other ideational symptoms (e.g., suicidal ideation; Blazer et al., 1987; Fountoulakis et al., 2003). Various conceptualizations of this nondysphoric depression in later life have been proposed, including "depression without sadness" (Gallo, Rabins, & Anthony, 1999), "masked depression" (M. D. Blumenthal, 1980), or "depletion syndrome" (Newmann, Engel, & Jensen, 1991). In any event, nondysphoric depression in late life prospectively is associated with increased functional impairment, psychological distress, cognitive impairment, and mortality (Gallo, Rabins, Lyketsos, Tien, & Anthony, 1997).

Depression also presents differently among older adults depending on age of onset. Roughly half of older adults with depression experienced their first depressive episode after old age (i.e., late-onset depression; Fiske et al., 2009). Older adults with late-onset depression report less guilt and suicidal ideation than do older adults with early-onset depression (i.e., those for whom depression is a continuation of symptoms from younger ages). Older adults with late-onset depression are less likely than older adults with early-onset depression to endorse family histories of depression, suggesting a greater genetic component for early-onset depression (Gallagher et al., 2010). A magnetic resonance imaging (MRI) study examining older adults with late-onset depression without history of stroke, neurodegenerative disorders, head injury, or substance misuse found greater hippocampal reductions and memory loss relative to those with early onset depression (Hickie et al., 2005), which suggests greater risk for dementia among those with late-onset depression. Similarly, research indicates that late-onset depression may be associated more closely with vascular risk factors than early-onset depression (see Jellinger, 2013). In regards to treatment, a comparison study of older adults with early-onset and late-onset depression found no differences in terms of response, remission, relapse, and termination rates for weekly interpersonal therapy and open-label paroxetine (Driscoll et al., 2005). Although there are some key differences between late-onset and early onset depression, age of onset of depressive symptoms can be difficult to ascertain, in part because of limitations of memory and self-report and uncertainty as to the definition of onset of depression (i.e., onset may be the presence of any depressive symptoms or a well-defined syndrome; K. R. Krishnan et al., 2004).

Older adults may be more likely than other age-groups to present with subsyndromal symptoms of depression that do not meet criteria for MDD. Subsyndromal depression is associated with increased incidence of physical disability, cognitive impairment, health care use, and suicidal ideation (T. W. Meeks et al., 2011). It also is two to three times more prevalent among older adults than MDD (T. W. Meeks et al., 2011). Thus, although symptoms of depression among older adults may not meet diagnostic criteria for depression, older adults may experience depressive symptoms that are clinically significant and functionally and socially impairing.

Recent studies have suggested that late-life depression also presents differently in individuals with cognitive impairment. Among individuals with vascular dementia, depression is associated with less dysphoria (Fiske et al., 2009) but more vegetative symptoms, such as fatigue and weight loss (J. H. Park et al., 2007). Because of symptom overlap between depression and cognitive impairment (e.g., difficulty thinking or concentrating), researchers have recommended that depression syndromes among individuals with cognitive impairment be diagnosed independent of these overlapping symptoms. Among individuals with Alzheimer's disease,

Olin et al. (2002) proposed that only three symptoms instead of five be required to make a diagnosis of depression. Olin et al. also suggested that symptoms, such as increased irritability and social withdrawal, be used as additional criteria for diagnosing depression in Alzheimer's disease. Depression affects approximately 58% of patients with Parkinson's disease (Quelhas & Costa, 2009). Depressed older adults with Parkinson's disease may not exhibit dysphoria and anhedonia, which can result in the underdiagnosis of depression in Parkinson's disease. Marsh, McDonald, Cummings, and Ravina (2006) have proposed an inclusive diagnostic approach, in which all symptoms, even those that overlap with symptoms of Parkinson's disease, are used to diagnose depression.

THEORIES AND CONCEPTUAL ISSUES

Several theories of depression have been advanced over the years; however, few specifically have addressed late-life depression. Although theories and models of young adult depression may be applicable to older adults, late-life depression is a more diverse phenomenon than that of young adults, symptoms and etiologies of late-life depression can diverge from those of young adults (see Jellinger, 2013), and diagnostic comorbidities often can complicate diagnosis and treatment.

Major conceptual issues regarding late-life depression have centered around its etiology and risk factors, and to a lesser degree, the maintenance of depression. The next section addresses a few of the neurobiological, social, and psychological factors that contribute to late-life depression.

Biological Risk Factors

Advances in neurobiology, genetics, pharmacology, and imaging technology have enhanced our understanding of the possible etiologies and risk factors for older adult depression. In general, biological diathesis-stress models have described the interaction of genetic risks and environmental factors. These two factors, however, leave a considerable amount of variance that V. Krishnan and Nestler (2010) have noted may be attributed to a third nongenetic and nonenvironmental factor: epigenetic modifications that regulate gene expression. Epigenetic modification refers to modification of the chromosome without changes in the underlying DNA sequence. Several hypotheses have been advanced to explain the biological bases of depression across the life span (Disabato & Sheline, 2012).

Genetic factors. There is an extensive literature on the genetics of depression, although genetic risk is considerably greater among younger than among older adults (Fiske et al., 2009). Genes that have been investigated include, for example, the serotonin transporter gene (5HTTLPR), Apolipoprotein E gene (APOE), and brain-derived neurotrophic factor gene (BDNF; Naismith, Norrie, Mowscowski, & Hickie, 2012). Most of the attempts to identify genes that could account for late-life depression have focused primarily on genes related to cardiovascular risk (Naismith et al., 2012). A discussion of the genetics of late-life depression is beyond the scope of this chapter. The interested reader is referred to Naismith et al. (2012) for a thoughtful review and discussion of genetic risk factors and the various polymorphisms that have been implicated in the etiology of late-life depression.

Nongenetic neurobiological risk factors. New insights into the neurobiology of older adult depression have been gained through advances in genetics, neuroimaging, neuropsychology, pathology, and intervention studies in recent years (Naismith et al., 2012). The mechanisms through which various associated factors contribute to these symptoms, however, are not entirely clear (Jellinger, 2013).

Neurodegenerative risk factors. Neurodegenerative changes associated with older adult depression are revealed through imaging studies (e.g., positron emission tomography and functional MRI) that form the foundation of hypotheses regarding the biological bases of depression. These findings also are supported by postmortem studies, which tend to be focused on cortical and hippocampal regions of the brain. Numerous studies suggest that depressed older adults are more likely than are depressed young adults to have structural changes in the gray matter of the fronto–limbic pathway (e.g., Disabato & Sheline,

2012), which are involved in emotional processing and cognitive control.

Neuropsychological research supports neurodegenerative hypotheses through evidence of impaired performance on episodic memory, executive functioning, and processing speed tasks (e.g., Butters et al., 2004; Jellinger, 2013; Köhler, Thomas, Barnett, & O'Brien, 2010) among depressed older adults. Importantly, impaired performance is not necessarily equivalent to neurodegeneration. Several sources of variance (e.g., diminished effort resulting from depressed mood) could contribute to impaired performance. Recent evidence suggests that impaired episodic memory and language skills may be influenced by impaired executive functioning and processing speed in older adult depression (Sexton et al., 2012).

Cardiovascular risk factors. Cardiovascular disease is a risk factor for older adult depression and also can precipitate or prolong depression (Alexopoulos et al., 1997). In a recent systematic review and meta-analysis, Valkanova and Ebmeier (2013) found strong, reciprocal relationships between vascular diseases (cardiovascular disease, diabetes, and stroke) and late-life depression. These findings are at the heart of the vascular depression hypothesis (Alexopoulos et al., 1997), which suggests that cardiovascular disease causes lesions in small blood vessels that affect functioning of the frontal–subcortical circuits associated with mood regulation (Naismith et al., 2012). Structural neuroimaging studies provide support for this hypothesis linking depression with cerebrovascular lesions, particularly white matter hyperintensities. Jellinger (2013) noted that "vascular depression" has been complemented more recently by the depression–executive dysfunction syndrome (Alexopoulos, 2005) and "subcortical ischemic depression" (K. R. Krishnan et al., 2004). The vascular depression hypothesis posits that cerebrovascular disease can place individuals at risk for depression, can precipitate it, or can maintain it. The diagnosis of depressive–executive dysfunction syndrome is based on the hypothesis that frontal striatal dysfunction contributes to the development and course of depression (Alexopoulos, Kiosses, Klimstra, Kalayam, & Bruce, 2002). Subcortical ischemic depression is similar to MRI-defined vascular depression (K. R. Krishnan et al., 2004), but is conceptualized as a more specific form of vascular depression and lies along a continuum of disorders related to subcortical ischemic disease.

Psychological and Social Risk Factors

Psychosocial risk factors for older adult depression include, among other factors, demographic variables (e.g., socioeconomic status [SES]), stressful life events, lack of social support, ruminative and avoidant coping styles, gender, ethnicity, loss and disability, subsyndromal depression, neuroticism, rumination, and sleep disturbance (Areán & Reynolds, 2005; Blazer, Steffens, & Koenig, 2009; Fiske et al., 2009). Individuals at risk for depression typically have more than one risk factor (Areán & Reynolds, 2005). We briefly discuss a few of the more commonly studied risk factors.

Stress. The relation between stress and depression is a longstanding finding in the research literature, with evidence supporting the relationship across acute, chronic, and episodic stresses (Liu & Alloy, 2010). Karg, Burmeister, Shedden, and Sen (2011) found substantial evidence that the relationship between stress and depression is moderated by the serontonin transporter promoter polymorphism (5-HTTLPR). Historically, the relationship between stress and depression has been viewed as unidirectional, but new evidence suggests a reciprocal relation (Liu & Alloy, 2010). Moreover, this relation can begin with early-life stressful events that cause hypothalamic-pituitary-adrenal (HPA) axis changes resulting in susceptibility to stressful events that continue into adulthood. These changes include hyperactivity of the HPA axis and increased activity of circuits containing adrenocorticotrophic hormone-releasing factor, which resembles changes revealed in depressed adults (Pariante & Lightman, 2008). Thus, stress increases the risk of developing depression, and depression increases the vulnerability to stress (Liu & Alloy, 2010).

Sleep. Insomnia has become regarded as a primary disorder, distinct from psychiatric and medical diseases (Baglioni et al., 2011). The prevalence of insomnia increases with age. Insomnia is a well-established risk factor for older adult depression (Pigeon et al., 2008). Individuals with insomnia who are not depressed are at a twofold risk of developing depression when compared with individuals without insomnia who are not depressed (Baglioni et al., 2011). Insomnia not only accompanies depression but also appears to perpetuate the disorder in some older adults (Pigeon et al., 2008). In addition, insomnia can be an independent risk factor for older adult depression recurrence (Cho et al., 2008). In their meta-analysis of risk factors for older adult depression in community-dwelling older adults, Cole and Dendukuri (2003) found a combined odds ratio of 2.6 for sleep disturbances.

If insomnia is a risk factor, then the treatment of insomnia (e.g., cognitive–behavioral therapy for insomnia [CBT–I]) before the onset of depression could prevent its onset (Riemann, 2009). We have brief effective treatments for older adult with insomnia (Buysse et al., 2011), but whether improving sleep quality can prevent late-life depression remains to be seen (Reynolds et al., 2012). Pigeon et al. (2008) suggested that we need to determine the most depression-vulnerable insomnia subtypes with the goal of determining whether interventions for insomnia also can prevent late-life depression.

Personality. The relationship between personality traits and depression is well established, as there is the evidence, for example, that very high neuroticism (i.e., the tendency to experience negative emotions) and low conscientiousness are risk factors for the development of depression in young adults (Klein, Kotov, & Bufferd, 2011). The literature on late-life depression, although limited, also supports the conclusion that personality traits are significant predictors of the onset of late-life depression (Steunenberg, Braam, Beekman, Deeg, & Kerkhof, 2009). In a study of 1,511 older adults over a 6-year period, Steunenberg, Beekman, Deeg, and Kerkhof (2006) found that low mastery (the extent to which individuals feel in control of their own lives) and high neuroticism were strongly related to the onset of late-life depression. Moreover, these personality traits were stronger predictors than were physical health and social resources (size of social contact network and exchange of instrumental and emotional support). In a study of centenarians, Margrett et al. (2010) found neuroticism and cognitive impairment to be predictors of late-life depression symptoms.

Neuroticism also is a risk factor for poor recovery from late-life depression (Steunenberg, Beekman, Deeg, Breemer, & Kerkhof, 2007; Steunenberg, Beekman, Deeg, & Kerkhof, 2010) and the recurrence of depression (Steunenberg et al., 2009). Assessment of personality, with a focus on neuroticism, may inform the treatment of depression among individuals with high neuroticism who are at risk for recurrent depression.

Epigenetic studies of personality and depression suggest the relation between personality and late-life depression may be moderated by environmental events (e.g., traumatic or stressful events). The studies of older adults are limited, however, and their findings are mixed, suggesting that the relation among genes, personality traits, and depression is complex (Weber, Giannakopoulos, & Canuto, 2011).

Social support. Low levels of various forms of social support (e.g., social network size, network composition, instrumental and emotional support, social contact frequency, satisfaction of social support) are associated with older adult depression (Chi & Chou, 2001). In a study of more than 10,000 Japanese older adults, Kaji et al. (2010) found strong

relations between symptoms of depression and "having no one to talk to." Analyzing data from the Longitudinal Aging Study Amsterdam, Sonnenberg et al. (2013) found that low social support among men and women, and a high need for affiliation among women, were related to late-life depression. Although women were more likely to be depressed than men, the relations among social support and depression were stronger for men than women. Similarly, in a study of Brazilian older men and women, Alexandrino-Silva, Alves, Tofoli, Wang, and Andrade (2011) found that perceived lack of social support was related to "old age symptomatic depression" (p. 235) for men, but not for women.

Integrative Model

The evidence is clear that multiple factors contribute to the vulnerability, presentation, and maintenance of late-life depression. Several authors have argued for the need for integrative models of depression that incorporate multiple contributing factors (e.g., Brown & Harris, 1978; Steunenberg et al., 2006; Weber et al., 2011). These models have become more sophisticated as researchers have identified risk factors and the manner in which they contribute. Fiske et al. (2009) integrated many of the previously discussed risk factors into a compelling diathesis-stress model of late-life depression, as illustrated in Figure 1.1. They argued that regardless

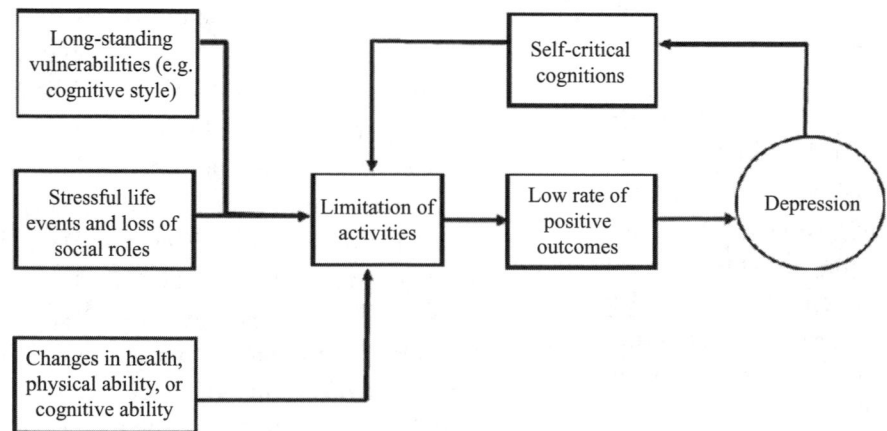

FIGURE 1.1. Behavioral model depicting onset and maintenance of depression in late life. From "Depression in Older Adults," by A. Fiske, J. L. Wetherell, and M. Gatz, 2009, *Annual Review of Clinical Psychology, 5,* p. 369. Copyright 2009 by Annual Reviews. Reprinted with permission.

of the predisposing factors, their common pathway may be a reduction in daily activities. Their model incorporates the behavioral model of depression advanced by Lewinsohn, Munoz, Youngren, and Zeiss (1986). The authors suggested that the onset and maintenance of late-life depression results from the interaction of vulnerabilities (e.g., genetic factors, age-associated neurobiological changes, negative schema) and late-life stressful events (e.g., loss of social roles, changes in health, diminished physical, and cognitive abilities), which all contribute to a reduction in activities. Automatic self-critical negative thoughts (cognitive diathesis) exacerbate and extend depressive episodes by reducing the likelihood of the older adult engaging in activities, and also result from the depression.

ASSESSMENT

Accurate assessment and detection of late-life depression is crucial, as prognosis is poor when late-life depression goes undetected (Licht-Strunk, Beekman, de Haan, & van Marwijk, 2009). Unfortunately, rates of nondetection for depression are higher among older adults compared with younger adults (Mitchell, Rao, & Vaze, 2010). This section reviews assessment methods and some of the more commonly used instruments for assessing late-life depression and also addresses the challenges associated with assessing late-life depression.

Assessment Methods

Clinicians can draw from a number of different assessment methods, including self-report, proxy report (report by others), direct observation, and physiological recording. Each approach has strengths and weaknesses. Clinicians are encouraged to use multiple methods so that the limitations of any one method are compensated by the strengths of others (e.g., Eid & Diener, 2006).

Self-report is a convenient and expedient method for obtaining assessment information. Multiple factors, however, can influence the reliability and accuracy of self-report, particularly with older adults. One must consider age-related differences in the possible influences and limitations posed by cognitive deficits and physical disabilities, and age-related differences in how older adults characterize their problems. For example, older adults tend to minimize or deny depressive symptoms (Blazer, 2009), are more hesitant than younger adults when responding to interview questions, may demonstrate a tendency to agree with the interviewer, and often provide uncertain responses (Edelstein, Woodhead, Bower, & Lowery, 2006). Clinicians should be careful regarding the nature and content of their questions, including wording (e.g., "spirits down?" versus "feeling depressed?") and format (e.g., closed-versus open-ended questions).

Given the potential limitations associated with older adults' self-report, obtaining additional information via proxy report of family, caregivers, or staff members may be critical. In some instances, self-report may be especially unreliable or difficult to obtain, as in the case of a nonverbal older adult client. Proxy reports are still subject to some of the same limitations as self-report. For instance, reports from family members, caregivers, or nursing home staff also may be unreliable and may be based only on limited interaction with the older adult client.

Formal direct observation, which often involves proxy reporting, can be useful when self-reports are unavailable or undesirable. The method is particularly useful in inpatient and other institutional settings where residents can be observed directly by staff well trained in this method, on a regular schedule using various time-sampling methods. Direct observation of older adult clients in natural settings typically is difficult at best because of the limited access to their behavior. As with the other methods, direct observation rarely can stand alone as a satisfactory assessment method.

Assessment Tools

Many assessment instruments, including semistructured interviews, self-report measures, and clinician rating scales, can assist clinicians in assessing late-life depression. This section reviews several of the more commonly used and widely researched measures. Table 1.1 includes an overview of the instruments reviewed in this section.

Structured interviews. The primary purpose of structured and semistructured interviews is to arrive

TABLE 1.1

Overview of Depression Assessment Instruments Used With Older Adults

Instrument	Designed for older adults?	Psychometric data with older adults?	Use for those with myocardial infarction?	Use for those with dementia?	Pros	Cons
Structured interviews						
SCID		✓			Yields highly reliable *DSM* diagnoses.	Time intensive. Based on diagnostic criteria that are questionable for OA. Limited psychometric data with OA.
GMS	✓	✓	✓	✓	Diagnostic criteria are age-appropriate. Select subsections may be administered to reduce time burden.	Diagnostic system is somewhat dated.
Self-report instruments						
BDI–II		✓				Guttman format difficult for CI.
CES–D		✓	✓		Validated in diverse samples. Available in many languages. Likert format appealing to non-CI.	Frequency recall and Likert format difficult for CI.
GDS	✓	✓	✓	✓	Dichotomous format easier for CI.	Dichotomous format frustrating for non-CI. Excludes somatic content that could be valuable.
PHQ-9		✓	✓	✓	Observational version available for CI.	Not yet examined in ethnically diverse populations.
BASDEC	✓	✓	✓		Card-sorting method less demanding for CI.	Limited psychometric data available.
HADS		✓			Collects information on anxiety and depression.	High degree of false positives.
Clinician rating scales						
MADRS	✓	✓	✓	✓	Higher sensitivity than CSDD in a memory clinic population.	Does not include a proxy interview.

| HRSD | ✓ | | | | | Poor psychometric performance often cited. Limited data with OA. |
| CSDD | ✓ | ✓ | ✓ | ✓ | Includes a proxy interview. | May not be sensitive in detection of subsyndromal or minor depression. |

Note. CI = individuals with cognitive impairment; SCID = Structured Clinical Interview for *DSM*; GMS = Geriatric Mental State Schedule; BDI–II = Beck Depression Inventory—Second Edition; CES–D = Center for Epidemiologic Studies—Depression Scale; GDS = Geriatric Depression Scale; PHQ–9 = Patient Health Questionnaire—9 Item Depression Scale; BASDEC = Brief Assessment Schedule Depression Cards; HADS = Hospital Anxiety and Depression Scale; MADRS = Montgomery–Åsberg Depression Rating Scale; HRSD = Hamilton Rating Scale for Depression; CSDD = Cornell Scale for Depression in Dementia.

at the appropriate psychiatric diagnosis (or diagnoses) for a given client. Historically, the Structured Clinical Interview for DSM (SCID; First, Spitzer, Gibbon, & Williams, 1997) and the Schedule for Affective Disorders and Schizophrenia (SADS; Endicott & Spitzer, 1978) have been two of the most commonly employed structured interviews. Unfortunately, neither the SCID nor the SADS was developed specifically for use with older adults. Limited evidence supports the reliability of the SCID for late-life depression (Segal, Hersen, Van Hasselt, Kabacoff, & Roth, 1993). These instruments also are lengthy (roughly 90 min to administer) and can be particularly taxing for older adults with comorbid medical illness or physical disabilities. Most important, both instruments are based on diagnostic criteria that may be inappropriate for older adults, for example, the instruments fail to capture subsyndromal depression, which is prevalent among older adults.

The Geriatric Mental State Schedule (GMS; Copeland et al., 1976) was designed specifically for older adults though the diagnostic classification system utilized by the GMS (known as AGECAT) is somewhat dated. The AGECAT system evaluates eight psychiatric syndromes, including *neurotic* and *psychotic* depression, terms that denote increasing levels of severity (Copeland, Dewey, & Griffiths-Jones, 1986). Nonetheless, the AGECAT

criteria are more inclusive compared with the *DSM* diagnoses of major or minor depression (Newman, Sheldon, & Bland, 1998). Specifically, the GMS–AGECAT criteria are more likely to detect subsyndromal symptoms of depression (Newman et al., 1998). Selected subsections of the GMS may be administered in lieu of the entire interview, which may increase its utility with frail older adults.

Self-report instruments. Self-report instruments are typically quick and easy to administer, and they can be useful in case conceptualization as well as in treatment planning and monitoring. Although countless self-report depression instruments are available, this section reviews four of the most commonly employed tools.

The Beck Depression Inventory—Second Edition (BDI–II; Beck, Steer, & Brown, 1996) is one of the most widely used depressive assessment instruments. It includes 21 items and utilizes a four-point Guttman-type response format. Emerging literature suggests that the BDI–II has strong psychometric properties with older adults (e.g., Segal, Coolidge, Cahill, & O'Riley, 2008). Despite this evidence, several important limitations of the BDI have been noted. The Guttman response format can be troublesome for older adults with cognitive impairment (e.g., Olin, Schneider, Eaton, Zemansky, & Pollock, 1992). One study found high rates of nonresponse for the "sexual interest" item among older women (Jefferson, Powers, & Pope, 2001). Furthermore, inclusion of somatic items may limit its utility with physically ill older adults (Clark, Cavanaugh, & Gibbons, 1983). Despite the consistent finding that somatic symptoms of depression are at least somewhat confounded with medical illness, Thombs et al. (2010) found that the BDI–II did not artificially inflate severity scores among heart attack patients (mean age = 58.9).

The Center for Epidemiologic Studies—Depression Scale (CES–D; Radloff, 1977) is a free, 20-item screening measure for depressive symptomatology that has been translated into several languages. It utilizes a four-point Likert-type response scale and asks respondents to rate each item based on their feelings and experiences during the past 7 days. The CES–D was not developed specifically for use with older adults but has been evaluated thoroughly with older adults and is measurement equivalent across the life span (Gatz, Johansson, Pederson, Berg, & Reynolds, 1993). Psychometric studies with various populations of older adults have attested to its internal consistency, test–retest reliability, and construct validity (e.g., Fiske, Gatz, & Pedersen, 2003; Lewinsohn, Seeley, Roberts, & Allen, 1997; Schein & Koenig, 1997).

The response format of the CES–D is both a strength and a weakness; the Likert-type rating scale may be less confusing than the Guttman scale items of the BDI–II, yet not as restrictive or simplistic as the dichotomous yes–no format of the Geriatric Depression Scale (GDS; Yesavage et al., 1982–1983). A strength is its psychometric support with ethnically diverse older adults worldwide (e.g., Coman, Iordache, Schensul, & Coiculescu, 2013; Zhang et al., 2011). A potential limitation is that it requires recall of the frequency of depressive symptoms over the past week, which may decrease its utility among cognitively impaired older adults (Edelstein et al., 2010). Its consistently low specificity at a cutoff score of 16 (e.g., Haringsma, Engels, Beekman, & Spinhoven, 2004) suggests it is better supported for screening, case conceptualization, and treatment planning rather than as a diagnostic tool (Edelstein et al., 2010).

Shorter forms of the CES–D are available (e.g., 10-item version; Andresen, Malmgren, Carter, & Patrick, 1994), as is a revised version that more closely reflects current diagnostic criteria for MDD (Eaton et al., 2004). There is preliminary support for the internal consistency and construct validity (e.g., Friedlander, Nazem, Fiske, Nadorff, & Smith, 2012).

The GDS (Yesavage et al., 1982–1983) was designed specifically for use with older adults. It contains 30 items and utilizes a dichotomous yes–no format, which is intended to reduce cognitive demand. In addition, the scale excludes somatic content because of the potential confound of somatic symptoms with physical illness. The GDS has strong psychometric properties, including internal consistency, test–retest reliability, and construct validity, in various populations of older adults (e.g., Kieffer & Reese, 2002; Marty, Pepin, June, & Segal, 2011). Numerous shorter versions of the GDS have been developed. Not all of these shorter versions have been evaluated thoroughly, although initial evidence supports their utility and diagnostic validity in medical settings (Mitchell, Bird, Rizzo, & Meader, 2010), where time may be more limited.

Despite being tailored for use with older adults, the response format and other aspects of the GDS can be problematic for some older adults. Olin et al. (1992) found that a significant number of community-dwelling older adults endorsed both "yes" and "no" on at least one item and failed to complete at least one item. Results from one survey also suggested low acceptability among respondents regarding the forced choice aspect of the GDS (Fischer, Rolnick, Jackson, Garrard, & Luepke, 1996). Even though the GDS was constructed to be more useful with cognitively impaired older adults, findings have been mixed in this population (Kørner et al., 2006). Most evidence suggests that the GDS performs well among those with mild cognitive impairment (e.g., Ott & Fogel, 1992). Evidence of reliability and validity among older adults with moderate-to-severe levels of cognitive impairment is less consistent. Some studies using the GDS suggest diminished reliability and validity in this population (e.g., Bédard et al., 2003; Ott & Fogel, 1992); however, at least one well-designed study demonstrated that the severity of cognitive impairment did not affect reliability and validity of self-reported depression with the GDS (Snow et al., 2005). Rather, lack of deficit awareness was related to poorer reliability of self-reported depression.

The Patient Health Questionnaire—9 Item Depression Scale (PHQ–9) is a brief, self-report assessment instrument of depressive symptomology that functions as both a screening and diagnostic measure (Kroenke, Spitzer, & Williams, 2001). The PHQ–9 assesses each of the nine *Diagnostic and Statistical Manual of Mental Disorders, Fourth Edition* (*DSM–IV*; American Psychiatric Association, 2000) symptoms of MDD using a four-point Likert-type response scale. Respondents are asked to recall the frequency of symptoms over the past 2 weeks. Numerous studies have attested to the strong psychometric performance of the PHQ–9 in various populations, including primary care patients, stroke victims, nursing home residents, community-dwelling older adults, and the general population (Kroenke, Spitzer, Williams & Löwe, 2010; C. Li, Friedman, Conwell, & Fiscella, 2007; Saliba, DiFilippo, et al., 2012). A two-item version of the PHQ (PHQ–2; Kroenke, Spitzer, & Williams, 2003) has been validated with community-dwelling older adults and nursing home residents (C. Li et al., 2007; Saliba, DiFilippo, et al., 2012). Unlike the nine-item measure, the PHQ–2 is not designed to function as a diagnostic measure.

The PHQ–9 is now included in the Minimum Data Set assessment (MDS 3.0), which is a mandated periodic clinical assessment for long-term care residents at facilities certified by the Centers for Medicare and Medicaid Services (CMS; Saliba, Jones, et al., 2012). The PHQ–9 had superior psychometric support compared with the GDS-15 (e.g., internal consistency across variable levels of cognitive functioning, correlation with standard psychiatric interview) among nursing home residents. Furthermore, nursing home staff rated the utility of the instrument highly. An observational version of the PHQ–9 (PHQ–9 OV), which has strong psychometric properties, is available for residents with significant cognitive impairment. Although the evidence suggests that PHQ–9 has enhanced the MDS 3.0 assessment, limitations for its use in nursing home settings have been identified (e.g., Simons et al., 2012). For instance, the PHQ–9 OV may not include depressive symptoms specific to dementia patients. Also, the PHQ–9 has not been examined extensively in ethnically diverse populations of older adults.

Several other self-report instruments are available that may warrant consideration for use with older adult clients. The Brief Assessment Schedule Depression Cards (Adshead, Cody, & Pitt, 1992) was designed specifically for older adults in nursing home settings. It uses a card-sorting method, which may be easier than having the questions read aloud (i.e., in the case of hearing impairment or noisy environments). The Hospital Anxiety and Depression Scale (Bjelland, Dahl, Haug, & Neckelmann, 2002) simultaneously provides information about anxiety and depression, and it was designed for individuals in hospital settings. Depressive symptoms related to physical illness are excluded. The California Older Persons Pleasant Events Schedule (COPPES; Rider, Gallagher-Thompson, & Thompson, 2004) includes 66 items regarding the frequency of pleasant events and the enjoyment (or would-be enjoyment) associated with each. Although this self-report instrument does not directly assess depressive symptomology, the COPPES frequency and pleasure-obtained scores are highly associated with depression severity. Furthermore, it may be useful in depression treatments in which behavioral activation is employed.

Clinician rating scales. Rating instruments can offer several advantages over self-report instruments. They are useful when response burden of a self-report measure is a concern, when moderate-to-severe cognitive impairment is suspected, or when visual or education deficits preclude the use of self-report instruments.

The Hamilton Rating Scale for Depression (HRSD; Hamilton, 1960) has been widely considered the gold-standard depression rating scale for more than 40 years (Bagby, Ryder, Schuller, & Marshall, 2004). The original version of the HRSD includes 17 clinician-rated items that assess depressive symptoms, including sad mood, guilt, insomnia, and suicidality. Several versions of the HRSD also are available, including 6-item, 21-item, and 24-item rating scales (see O'Sullivan, Fava, Agustin, Baer, & Rosenbaum, 1997). Despite being considered the gold standard for depression assessment, the HRSD has been criticized frequently for its poor psychometric performance, including (but not limited to) poor content validity, interrater reliability, and test–retest reliability (Bagby et al., 2004). Although little research has evaluated the performance of the HRSD specifically in older adults, there is some psychometric support for its use with related groups (e.g., patients with Parkinson's disease; Leentjens, Verhey, Lousberg, Spitsbergen, & Wilmink, 2000).

The Cornell Scale for Depression in Dementia (CSDD) is widely considered the gold standard for the assessment of depression in patients with dementia (Alexopoulos, Abrams, Young, & Shamoian, 1988). It is a 19-item clinician-administered scale that includes a patient interview and a proxy interview. It has strong internal consistency, interrater reliability, and construct validity when used with older adults with and without dementia (Alexopoulos et al., 1988). A cutoff score of 6 yields strong sensitivity and specificity for detecting depression. In terms of limitations, the CSDD did not differentiate between no depression and minor depression among older adults in its initial validation study (Alexopoulos et al., 1988) and requires approximately 30 min to administer. For a more comprehensive review of late-life depression assessment instruments, see Edelstein, Drozdick, & Ciliberti (2010).

The Montgomery–Åsberg Depression Rating Scale (MADRS; Montgomery & Åsberg, 1979) includes 10 items and is weighted toward the cognitive symptoms of depression, which may improve its usefulness among those with comorbid physical illness. Although it was not designed specifically for use with older adults, it has stronger psychometric properties than the HRSD among medically ill older adults (Hammond, 1998). In addition, it has psychometric support for detecting depression among nursing home residents with dementia (Leontjevas, Gerritsen, Vernooij-Dassen, Smalbrugge, & Koopmans, 2012) and is more sensitive than the CSDD in identifying depression in memory clinic patients (Knapskog, Barca, & Engedal, 2013).

Controversies and Contemporary Issues in Assessment of Late-Life Depression

Assessment of late-life depression is complicated by numerous factors, including but not limited to differential presentations of depression in old age, medical and physical comorbidities, polypharmacy, and age-related cognitive decline. Given the plethora of extenuating factors, an optimal approach to assessment of late-life depression is not always clear. This section highlights several prominent and ongoing controversies in the assessment of late-life depression.

The inclusion of questions and items that assess somatic symptoms of depression has long been a topic of research and discussion among clinical geropsychologists, as somatic symptoms of depression may mimic physical health problems. In light of this overlap, some researchers have argued that physical and somatic symptoms of depression should be omitted in the assessment of older adults (e.g., Bolla-Wilson & Bleecker, 1989). This notion likely has contributed to the widespread use of the GDS and other instruments that exclude somatic content. In contrast, older adults are less likely than are younger adults to endorse depressed mood and related affective symptoms (Hybels et al., 2012) and are more likely to endorse somatic presentations of depression (Hegeman et al., 2012). If clinicians rely solely on affective symptoms such as depressed mood, older adults with clinically relevant depressive symptoms may go undetected (Gregg, Fiske, & Gatz, 2013). In addition, most studies have found that the presence of physical illness and comorbidities does not account for the positive association between somatic symptoms of depression and age (e.g., Nguyen & Zonderman, 2006). For instance, even in cases of poststroke depression, when one would expect a high degree of overlap between somatic symptoms of depression and physical symptoms of stroke, somatic symptoms (i.e., reduced appetite, psychomotor retardation, fatigue) have been found to discriminate between stroke victims with and without depression (de Coster, Leentjens, Lodder, & Verhey, 2005). These findings suggest that somatic symptoms in late life are often actual symptoms of depression, rather than artifacts of poorer health. A conservative approach would be to include somatic symptoms as a standard part of late-life depression assessment, but to interpret these symptoms with caution and in light of other available data (e.g., medical records).

Another ongoing controversy centers around the routine use of instruments that have not been validated with older adults or were not designed for use with this population. Given that the nature of depression differs in older compared with younger adulthood (i.e., with regard to presentation, severity, consequences, etc.), it is possible that assessment instruments designed and validated with younger age-groups may not adequately detect or characterize depression in older adults. Research on the clinical assessment of other psychological disorders has demonstrated the importance of incorporating developmentally sensitive content into late-life assessment tools (e.g., social anxiety disorder; Ciliberti, Gould, Smith, Chorney, & Edelstein, 2011). The omission of age-relevant content in depression assessment instruments may increase the risk of not detecting depression in older adults when it is present. Unfortunately, only a handful of assessment measures were designed specifically for older adults and even these have been evaluated using current diagnostic criteria for depression, which may be inappropriate for older adults (e.g., requiring too many symptoms for diagnosis; T. W. Meeks et al., 2011).

Other dilemmas also exist in the assessment of late-life depression. For instance, experts disagree on the issue of scaling in self-report depression instruments. Some argue for dichotomous response options (yes–no or agree–disagree) to decrease cognitive demand (e.g., Yesavage et al., 1982–1983). Some researchers, however, have found that older adults often are frustrated by this forced-choice format (e.g., Fischer et al., 1996). These unresolved issues (and many others) highlight the need for ongoing research in the assessment of late-life depression.

INTERVENTION

For the most part, interventions that are effective with younger adults are effective with older adults as well. We initially describe a few issues associated with the client–therapist therapeutic relationship and discuss common controversies and dilemmas, treatment approaches, and implementation issues. This information is followed by discussions of various evidence-based and promising treatment and preventive interventions for late-life depression.

Client-Provider Issues Related to Intervention

The establishment of rapport and a therapeutic alliance with the client is important in light of the positive relation between the therapeutic alliance and outcome in therapy (Elvins & Green, 2008). Trust is particularly important to establish a helping relationship (Cormier, Nurius, & Osborn, 2013). Research on the placebo effect has shown that trusting a clinician and believing that therapy can be effective can result in neurophysiological and neurochemical activity in the brain that can alter the course of a disorder (Benedetti, 2012). Moreover, there is considerable evidence that client expectations of benefit from therapy can influence its success (Constantino, Castonguay, & Schut, 2002). Mohlman et al. (2012) offered strategies that can help build rapport and establish trust with older adults, for example, alternating between more and less sensitive questions. These authors also suggest that if the interviewer is younger than the older adult being interviewed, then that the interviewer should identify a subject that the older adult and interviewer have in common (e.g., appreciation of classical music) to reduce the novelty and formality of the situation.

Older adults may be less familiar with the mental health system than are young adults. Apprehension may be experienced during the initial interaction between the clinician and client (Mohlman et al., 2012). A therapist may attenuate apprehension by offering the client the opportunity to ask questions as soon as possible (Mohlman et al., 2012). By doing so, the client, and perhaps the client's family, can explore the nature of the services that will be provided, the clinician's approach to assessment and treatment, the duration of assessment and treatment, and what might be anticipated with regard to help with the client's problem. This strategy also provides an opportunity to disabuse the client or family members of depression myths. For example, it is not uncommon for adults to believe that depression is an inevitable consequence of aging.

Particular attention should be paid to the language of the client, in part because older adults may not characterize their symptoms of depression as might young adults. For example, older adults with MDD are more likely to report a loss of appetite and loss of interest in sex and less likely to report sadness, fearfulness, and crying spells (Hybels et al., 2012). In contrast, there is evidence that depressed older adults who are high in neuroticism will over-report affective symptoms (Duberstein & Heisel, 2007). The clinician may best communicate an understanding of the presenting problems through use of the client's descriptive terms and accurate paraphrasing and summarizing of client statements, which may contribute to the establishment of rapport and help build confidence in the competence of the clinician (e.g., Cormier et al., 2013).

Treatment Approaches

Several effective treatments are available for late-life depression, including biological (e.g., pharmacotherapy, electroconvulsive therapy [ECT], electrical stimulation) and psychosocial interventions. Biological treatments are thought to work by altering levels of neurotransmitters in the brain associated with depression, including serotonin and norepinephrine. Psychosocial interventions target modifiable factors associated with the precipitation and maintenance of depressed mood, including engagement in pleasant events, negative cognitions, interpersonal conflict, coping, and problem solving around life events and life-stage issues. Neuroimaging findings also suggest that psychosocial interventions produce changes in brain metabolism and activity (e.g., Linden, 2006).

Several factors influence treatment modality selection, including severity of depression, success with past treatments, insurance coverage, and patient preferences, among others. The majority of older adults are treated with antidepressant medication or benzodiazepines (Blazer, 2009; Valenstein et al., 2004). Benzodiazepines, unlike antidepressants, have not demonstrated efficacy in the treatment of depression as a monotherapy for depression in older adults (Alexopoulos, 2011). Nonetheless, benzodiazepines continue to be prescribed for late-life depression, with rates estimated at 40% or more (Bartels, Horn, Sharkey, & Levine, 1997; Valenstein et al., 2004). Note, however, that Valenstein et al. (2004) found that benzodiazepines were almost always prescribed in combination with antidepressants. Combination therapy of an antidepressant plus benzodiazepine has demonstrated improved depression outcomes in mixed-age samples compared with antidepressants alone, although not without potential risks (e.g., Furukawa, Streiner, & Young, 2001).

Older adults prefer psychotherapy or counseling over medication for depression (Gum et al., 2006). Greater access to psychosocial treatments is needed given their demonstrated acute and long-term efficacy and low potential for side effects (Scogin, Welsh, Hanson, Stump, & Coates, 2005). Expert consensus guidelines recommend combination therapy in the treatment of MDD in older adults (Alexopoulos et al., 2001); Reynolds et al. (2012) recommended the use of learning-based treatments (e.g., problem-solving therapy [PST], CBT) over pharmacological interventions, particularly for mild depression. In recent years, collaborative care models in which older adults are provided pharmacological and psychological treatment in primary care settings have been investigated (Skultety & Zeiss, 2006). Results of such studies are promising and suggest superior treatment outcomes when compared with treatment as usual over a 1- and 2-year follow-up period (Alexopoulos et al., 2009; Unützer et al., 2002).

Controversies and Dilemmas in Treatment

Several issues related to pharmacological and psychosocial treatments for late-life depression remain. First, the translation of efficacy studies to real-world settings continues to be a challenge (M. Park & Unützer, 2011). Many depressed older adults, after having being diagnosed with depression, do not receive adequate treatment (Akincigil et al., 2011; Gaboda, Lucas, Siegel, Kalay, & Crystal, 2011). This is especially true among racial minorities (Akincigil et al., 2011; Gaboda et al., 2011). Moreover, older adults in primary care rarely are offered psychosocial interventions (Akincigil et al., 2011; Skultety & Zeiss, 2006), despite older adults' preference for psychosocial interventions in primary care (Gum et al., 2006). Second, the extent to which health care providers monitor treatment outcomes is lacking (Charney et al., 2003). The initial patterns of recovery predict subsequent response to acute and maintenance therapy (Andreescu et al., 2008), highlighting the need to adequately monitor patient outcomes early in treatment. Monitoring treatment outcomes for depression in late life in real-world settings is limited (Charney et al., 2003) even though evidence has suggested that initial treatment response predicts acute recovery as well as response to maintenance therapy for depression (Andreescu et al., 2008).

Clear disparities are evident in the receipt of treatment among certain subgroups, including racial minorities, individuals with physical disability, individuals who are cognitively impaired (including those with dementia), and older adults with comorbid medical conditions (Gaboda et al., 2011). Older African Americans with depression receive treatment less often than non-Hispanic Whites, even after controlling for disease severity and differences in symptoms, sociodemographic characteristics, perceived access to care, and global health (Akincigil et al., 2012).

Intervention studies aimed at increasing physician guideline-driven treatment have demonstrated limited improvement in depression outcomes. Whooley, Stone, and Soghikian (2000) found that providing physicians with depression inventory scores, along with treatment recommendations based on the severity of depressive symptoms, failed to demonstrate change in the diagnosis of depression or antidepressant prescription behavior among physicians. After 2 years, no differences were found between patients who were treated by physicians receiving case-finding information versus those who did not receive case-finding information. Callahan (2001) noted that although interventions to improve care for late-life depression in primary care may increase detection and diagnosis of depression, upon study completion, old patterns of care generally reemerge. Thus, the implementation of new models of depression treatment based in primary care settings is needed (e.g., Hegel et al., 2002; Skultety & Zeiss, 2006).

For many years, depression was underdetected and undertreated in long-term care facilities (Gaboda et al., 2011). However, the use of antidepressants for long-term care residents with depression has increased from 21.9% in 1996 to 47.5% in 2006 (Hanlon, Handler, & Castle, 2010). The dilemma faced by physicians is balancing poor tolerance for medications by many older adults and adverse effects (e.g., falls, hyponatremia) against the need for depression treatment. Of course, psychosocial interventions are not prone to such adverse effects. In 2006, the CMS issued guidelines regarding the use of antidepressants in nursing homes, and

in 2008, the Long Term Care Professional Leadership Council issued recommendations regarding their judicious use and tapering. Nevertheless, overuse of antidepressants remains a potential problem that warrants monitoring.

Evidence-Based Treatments

To be considered an evidenced-based treatment (EBT) there must be at least two randomized controlled trials (RCTs) from independent research teams in which the treatment has demonstrated superiority to pill or psychological placebo, or to another treatment. Alternatively, the treatment can be considered an EBT if it has demonstrated equivalent efficacy when compared with an established EBT. The sample sizes of each group should be sufficient to provide adequate power to detect findings. Alternatively, efficacy can be demonstrated via a series of single-subject design experiments with sound methodology, in which the treatment is compared with another treatment (Chambless & Hollon, 1998). It is with these criteria in mind that we summarize current EBTs for depression in older adults.

Six treatments have met criteria as EBT for the treatment of depression in older adults: behavior therapy (BT), CBT, PST, cognitive bibliotherapy (CB), reminiscence therapy (RT), and brief psychodynamic therapy (BPT; Areán & Cook, 2002; Kiosses, Leon, & Areán, 2011; Scogin et al., 2005). The next section includes a brief overview of the treatment components and a summary of the evidence base. Generally, studies were included if they were tested in RCTs.

Behavior therapy. BT is grounded in the behavioral model of depression, which emphasizes the connection between mood and behavior. The therapist role is to guide the patient through the main components of BT, including (a) increasing engagement in pleasant and masterful events, (b) decreasing engagement in events that maintain depressed mood (e.g., withdrawal), and (c) developing problem-solving skills around barriers to achieving the first two aims (Dimidjian, Barrera, Martell, Muñoz, & Lewinsohn, 2011).

BT has demonstrated efficacy in older adults with MDD and minor depression

(Gallagher & Thompson, 1982; Haringsma, Engels, Cuijpers, & Spinhoven, 2006; S. Meeks, Looney, Haitsma, & Teri, 2008; Thompson & Gallagher, 1984; Thompson, Gallagher, & Breckenridge, 1987). BT has been found to be equivalent in efficacy to CBT (Gallagher & Thompson, 1982; Rokke, Tomhave, & Jocic, 1999). BT also has demonstrated efficacy when compared with treatment as usual (S. Meeks et al., 2008; Snarski et al., 2011), wait-list control (Haringsma et al., 2006; Rokke et al., 1999; Thompson et al., 1987), and no-treatment control conditions (Lichtenberg, Kimbarow, Morris, & Vangel, 1996). BT has been tested with a variety of older adult samples, including inpatient psychiatric patients (e.g., Snarski et al., 2011), psychiatric outpatients (e.g., Thompson & Gallagher, 1984), nursing home residents (e.g., S. Meeks et al., 2008), medically ill older adults (e.g., Lichtenberg et al., 1996), and community-dwelling older adults (e.g., Haringsma et al., 2006; Rokke et al., 1999). In addition, BT has demonstrated efficacy in patients with mild to moderate cognitive impairment (Snarski et al., 2011). Overall, BT is an appealing stand-alone treatment for depression or adjunct to other therapies discussed in the following section. BT has been adapted for use with caregivers of individuals with dementia and an array of other health care professionals (e.g., community consultants; Lichtenberg et al., 1996; S. Meeks et al., 2008; Teri, McCurry, Logsdon, & Gibbons, 2005).

Cognitive–behavioral therapy.   CBT is the most widely researched treatment for depression in older adults. CBT combines behavioral strategies (e.g., behavioral activation, relaxation exercises) with cognitive restructuring. Treatment duration and length of sessions are similar to that of BT. The evidence base for CBT in older adults is well established. CBT is efficacious in both individual (Scogin et al., 2005) and group formats (e.g., Steuer et al., 1984). CBT is efficacious in the treatment of both MDD (Campbell, 1992; Gallagher & Thompson, 1982; Gallagher-Thompson & Steffen, 1994; Laidlaw et al., 2008; Serfaty et al., 2009; Steuer et al., 1984; Thompson, Coon, Gallagher-Thompson, Sommer, & Koin, 2001; Thompson et al., 1987) and minor depression (Gallagher-Thompson & Steffen,

1994). CBT has demonstrated equivalent efficacy compared with other EBTs, including BT (mentioned in the previous section) and BPT (Gallagher-Thompson & Steffen, 1994; Thompson et al., 1987). One study found CBT to be superior to CB on a self-report measure of depression symptoms (Floyd et al., 2004). CBT has demonstrated efficacy when compared with treatment as usual (Laidlaw et al., 2008; Serfaty et al., 2009), attention placebo (Campbell, 1992), wait-list control (Floyd et al., 2004; Rokke et al., 1999; Thompson et al., 1987), and no-treatment control conditions (Campbell, 1992). One study found CBT to be superior to psychodynamic therapy in reducing depressive symptoms (Steuer et al., 1984). Also, CBT has demonstrated efficacy in various older adult samples, including community-dwelling older adults (Floyd et al., 2004; Rokke et al., 1999; Steuer et al., 1984; Thompson et al., 1987), outpatients (Gallagher & Thompson, 1982), distressed caregivers (Gallagher-Thompson & Steffen, 1994), and primary care patients (Serfaty et al., 2009; Laidlaw et al., 2008). Treatment gains have been maintained 1 year (Rokke et al., 1999) and 2 years posttreatment (Floyd et al., 2006).

Problem-solving therapy.   The primary aim of PST is to enhance the patient's ability to manage daily stressors and problems thought to maintain depressed mood. The structured and concrete nature of PST is especially appropriate for older adults, particularly those with comorbid executive dysfunction. PST also routinely involves behavioral activation. PST has demonstrated efficacy in older adults with both MDD (Alexopoulos, Raue, & Areán, 2003; Areán, Hegel, Vannoy, Fan, & Unutzer, 2008; Areán et al., 1993, 2010; Ciechanowski et al., 2004) and subsyndromal depression (Areán et al., 2008; Gellis & Bruce, 2010). PST has been found to produce significantly greater improvement in depression symptoms compared with RT (Areán et al., 1993). In addition, PST has demonstrated efficacy when compared with treatment as usual (Areán et al., 2008; Ciechanowski et al., 2004; Gellis & Bruce, 2010), supportive therapy (Alexopoulos et al., 2003; Areán et al., 2010), and wait list control conditions (Areán et al., 1993).

Older adults with MDD and comorbid executive dysfunction have demonstrated significant reductions in depressive symptoms after receiving PST (Alexopoulos et al., 2003; Areán et al., 2010). PST also has been delivered and demonstrated to be efficacious in multiple settings, including primary care (Areán et al., 2008) and home-based interventions (Ciechanowski et al., 2004; Gellis, McGinty, Horowitz, Bruce, & Misener, 2007; Gellis et al., 2008; Kiosses et al., 2011). Treatment effects have been maintained from 3 to 24 months (Areán et al., 2008; Ciechanowski et al., 2004; Gellis et al., 2007, 2008).

Cognitive bibliotherapy.   CB (Burns, 1999) is essentially traditional CBT in a self-help format. Patients follow a structured reading- and writing-based format that typically takes 4 weeks to complete. CB is best-suited for individuals with mild to moderate severity depression who have adequate motivation to engage in the self-directed nature of the treatment. The role of the therapist is minimal, typically involving weekly phone calls lasting 5–15 min. The appeal of the treatment includes the ability of patients who, for whatever reason (e.g., stigma, physical disability, geography, etc.), do not have access or the desire to receive traditional therapy. The advent of more sophisticated computer-based self-help treatments is likely to make CB an increasingly appealing treatment option for older adults with depression. The most frequently used self-help books for the treatment of depression include *Feeling Good* (Burns, 1999) and *Control Your Depression* (Lewinsohn et al., 1986).

Several studies support the use of CB in older adults with MDD and minor or subsyndromal depression (Floyd, Scogin, McKendree-Smith, Floyd, & Rokke, 2004; Landreville & Bissonnette, 1997) and mild to moderate depressive symptoms (Scogin, Hamblin, & Beutler, 1987; Scogin, Jamison, & Gochneaur, 1989). CB has been found to have equivalent efficacy compared with behavioral bibliotherapy (Scogin et al., 1989). CB also has demonstrated superior efficacy compared with attention placebo (Scogin et al., 1987) and wait-list control groups (Floyd et al., 2004; Landreville & Bissonnette, 1997; Scogin et al., 1987, 1989). Equally important is the finding that treatment effects of CB

have been maintained over 2 years (Floyd et al., 2006; Landreville & Bissonnette, 1997).

Reminiscence therapy.   RT was first proposed by Butler (1974). RT is based on the idea that in late life, recollection of life events is normative and part of resolving the last conflict in late life: ego integrity versus despair (Butler, 1963; Erikson, 1950). There are several types of RT, including simple reminiscence (e.g., unstructured autobiographical storytelling and spontaneous reminiscing), life review (e.g., evaluation of past negative and positive events), and life-review therapy (e.g., structured, focuses on cognitive restructuring of past events and using reminiscing as a pleasant event; Webster, Bohlmeijer, & Westerhof, 2010). Unstructured life review is typically only conducted in group format and serves a recreational and social function. The goal of unstructured reminiscence is to simply enhance social relations and is not designed as an individual intervention to reduce psychological distress (Webster, Bohlmeijer, & Westerhof, 2010). Treatment studies with older adults have focused primarily on structured reminiscence interventions, including life review (e.g., Wang, 2007) and life review therapy (e.g., Serrano, Latorre, Gatz, & Montanes, 2004). The main goal of life review is to use reminiscence to integrate past events, without changing the storyline or an individual's self-identity. Life review therapy, however, specifically aims to modify an individual's storyline and self-identify. Others have made the distinction between integrative and instrumental life review (Karimi et al., 2010; Watt & Cappeliez, 2000). Integrative life review uses cognitive restructuring to reappraise past interpretations of events and emotions, whereas instrumental life review has the client recall past successful coping strategies and assess appropriate coping strategies to use at the present time (Karimi et al., 2010; Watt & Cappeliez, 2000).

RT using life review and life review therapy has demonstrated efficacy in the treatment of older adults with clinically significant depressive symptoms (Karimi et al., 2010; Pot et al., 2010; Preschl et al., 2012; Serrano et al., 2004; Watt & Cappeliez, 2000; Westerhof, Bohlmeijer, van Beljouw, & Pot, 2010). RT has been demonstrated to be efficacious when compared with wait-list control (Areán et al., 1993; Preschl et al., 2012), attention placebo (Karimi et al., 2010; Pot et al., 2010; Watt & Cappeliez, 2000; Westerhof et al., 2010), social services as usual (Serrano et al., 2004), and no-treatment control (Wang, 2005, 2007). Karimi et al. (2010) confirmed findings by Watt & Cappeliez (2000) who found group-based integrative RT was associated with greater improvement in depressive symptoms in older adults compared with instrumental RT. Klausner et al. (1998) found that although RT and goal-focused therapy produced improvement in depressive symptoms among older adults with MDD, goal-focused therapy produced significantly greater improvement in depressive symptoms. One study found that RT reduced depressive symptoms in institutionalized older adults with dementia compared with supportive therapy and no-treatment control groups (Goldwasser, Auerbach, & Harkins, 1987). Several studies also have demonstrated the efficacy of RT in reducing depressive symptoms among community-dwelling older adults (e.g., Chiang et al., 2010; Hsu & Wang, 2009; Su, Wu, & Lin, 2012; Wang, 2005, 2007).

Brief psychodynamic therapy.   BPT is based on the therapeutic principles of psychodynamic therapy (Blagys & Hilsenroth, 2000), including a focus on the therapeutic alliance and positive transference (Leichsenring, Rabung, & Leibing, 2004) and unresolved issues and conflicts (Rose & DelMaestro, 1990). Two research studies have demonstrated the efficacy of BPT in the treatment of major and minor depressive disorder in older adults (Thompson et al., 1987) and distressed caregivers (Gallagher-Thompson & Steffen, 1994). BPT has been found to be comparable in efficacy to CBT (Gallagher-Thompson & Steffen, 1994). Thompson et al. (1987) found BT, cognitive therapy, and BPT to be comparable in efficacy in the treatment of MDD with no significant improvement found for the wait-list control group.

Promising Psychosocial Treatments

A variety of interventions have been attempted for the treatment of late-life depression. Some of these have limited empirical support or, in some cases, may be close to meeting criteria as evidence-based treatments. Two of the more promising of these interventions are interpersonal psychotherapy and exercise.

Interpersonal psychotherapy.   Interpersonal psychotherapy (IPT; Weissman, Markowitz, & Klerman, 2007) is a time-limited therapy for depression that focuses on the connection between interpersonal conflicts and depressive symptoms. Sessions are typically 60 min in length with approximately 14–16 sessions (Hinrichsen, 2008). Although IPT is considered a well-established treatment for depression in younger adults (de Mello, de Jesus Mari, Bacaltchuk, Verdeli, & Neugebauer, 2005) the number of RCTs of IPT in older adults to be considered well established is insufficient. Most studies examining IPT in older adults support its use in the treatment of geriatric depression.

Exercise.   Exercise interventions have been found to reduce depressive symptoms in older adults with MDD, minor depression, and dysthymia compared with controls (e.g., education group; J. A. Blumenthal et al., 2007; Bridle, Spanjers, Patel, Atherton, & Lamb, 2012; Chou et al., 2004; Mather et al., 2002; Singh et al., 2005). Exercise appears to be as efficacious as antidepressant therapy in the treatment of MDD and superior to placebo (J. A. Blumenthal et al., 2007; Brenes et al., 2007). Mixed results have been found for older adults with depression with some studies demonstrating positive results (Penninx et al., 2002) or no benefit associated with exercise compared with controls (Chin A Paw, van Poppel, Twisk, & van Mechelen, 2004; Conradsson, Littbrand, Lindelöf, Gustafson, & Rosendahl, 2010; Emery & Gatz, 1990; McMurdo & Burnett, 1992). The most common types of exercise examined include aerobic, mixed aerobic and resistance, or progressive resistance training (e.g., Sjösten & Kivelä, 2006). More research is needed comparing exercise interventions to EBTs.

Pharmacotherapy.   The most commonly used medications for the treatment of late-life depression are the selective serontonin reuptake inhibitors (SSRIs) and other second-generation antidepressants (Nelson, Delucchi, & Schneider, 2008). In 2001, the Expert Consensus Panel Pharmacotherapy of Depressive Disorders in Older Patients (Alexopoulos et al., 2001) recommended the combination of antidepressant medication, particularly SSRIs, and psychotherapy for the treatment of late-life depression. Two classes of second-generation antidepressant medications, SSRIs and serontonin norepinephrine reuptake inhibitors (SNRIs), have been recommended by experts (Alexopoulos, 2011). The recommendation notwithstanding, a review of randomized, double-blind, placebo-controlled trials (Tedeschini et al., 2011) suggested that they are not as effective with older adults as they are with young adults. A recent meta-analysis (Nelson, Delucchi, & Schneider, 2013), however, revealed that antidepressants offered no better treatment response than placebo when used with older adults whose depression duration was less than 2 years. In contrast, those with a longer duration of illness (i.e., more than 10 years) appeared to benefit from antidepressant therapy when compared with placebo.

Tricyclic antidepressants (TCAs) have been used for many years with effectiveness that is comparable to that of the SSRIs (I. M. Anderson, 2000). The side effect burden of the TCAs, however, is substantially greater than with the SSRIs for frail older adults, older adults with significant comorbid medical problems, and those taking multiple medications (Miller, Reynolds, Gildengers, Whyte, & Andreescu, 2013). The more common anticholinergic side effects with older adults include, for example, orthostatic hypotension, dry mouth, drowsiness, dizziness, constipation, confusional states, blurred vision, and lethargy. TCAs also are not advised for older adults with cardiac problems, as the TCAs can produce slowed cardiac conduction (Roose & Devanand, 2013). In addition, the discontinuation rate is higher for TCAs (Miller et al., 2013).

Two reviews of the treatment literature have been published since the Consensus Guidelines were issued. Rajji, Mulsant, Lotrich, Lokker, and Reynolds (2008) reviewed the literature (from 1996 to 2007) on the treatment of late-life depression using antidepressants. Among other findings, the authors failed to find consistent evidence that antidepressants of any particular class were any more effective than others. A more recent reexamination of the treatment literature (Alexopoulos, 2011) revealed that the use of SSRIs and SNRIs remain the best first-line treatments. The addition of atypical antipsychotic medications is recommended for individuals who exhibit psychotic or agitated behavior as well as for individuals whose MDD has not remitted following SSRI or SNRI treatment. Alexopoulos also concluded that few studies of pharmacological treatment of older adults have been published since publication of the 2001 Guidelines and that the results have been mixed, with high placebo response rates.

The duration of pharmacological treatment for maximal recovery from late-life depression is approximately 4–6 months (Rajji et al., 2008). Support for maintenance pharmacotherapy of up to 3 years has been established, particularly for older adults with recurrent and more severe forms of depression (Rajji et al., 2008).

Electroconvulsive therapy. Electroconvulsive therapy (ECT) is efficacious and safe in the treatment of late-life depression, including for older adults with comorbid medical illness and dementia (Salzman, Wong, & Wright, 2002; van der Wurff, Stek, Hoogendijk, & Beekman, 2003). ECT treatment typically is administered two to three times per week for a total of 6–12 sessions. The placement of electrodes in ECT is associated with treatment efficacy (Kellner et al., 2010). For example, bitemporal electrode placement has demonstrated superior immediate treatment effects compared with bifrontal or right unilateral electrode placement, and cognitive side effects did not differ by electrode placement site in a mixed-age sample (Kellner et al., 2010).

Older adults typically are referred for ECT after unsuccessful response to antidepressants or when comorbid physical illnesses (e.g., cardiovascular disease) make antidepressant treatment especially risky. The rapid treatment response of ECT is preferred over other depression treatments in emergency situations (e.g., psychosis, suicidality) in which immediate treatment effects are essential.

An extensive review of studies examining the efficacy and safety of ECT in older adults found that approximately 55%–85% of older adults achieved remission of depression (van der Wurff et al., 2003).

Follow-up remission rates over a period ranging from 6 months to 4 years varied from 46%–79.3%. Relapse rates also varied across studies, with 25%–67% of participants relapsing following ECT. Older adults have superior ECT response compared with younger adults (O'Connor et al., 2001). Past research suggests that ECT has greater efficacy compared with antidepressants in the treatment of depression in older adults (e.g., Salzman et al., 2002). The main limitation of ECT, however, is the greater potential for cognitive side effects as compared with antidepressants (American Psychiatric Association, 2001) and psychotherapy, although side effects have been found to be independent of age (Brodaty, Berle, Hickie, & Mason, 2001). A review of cognitive functioning in older adults treated with ECT revealed mixed findings that also were limited by methodological weaknesses (e.g., exclusive reliance on global screener instruments; Tielkes, Comijs, Verwijk, & Stek, 2008). Careful cognitive testing before and after ECT administration, and over a longer follow-up period, is recommended (Tielkes et al., 2008).

Brain Stimulation Therapies

Recently, other brain stimulation therapies have been examined in the treatment of depression in older adults. Repetitive transcranial magnetic stimulation (rTMS) applies magnetic stimulation to the brain and is less invasive than ECT. At present, research is limited examining the efficacy of rTMS in late-life depression. Available research suggests that rTMS has produced mixed findings in regards to treatment efficacy (Abraham et al., 2007; Narushima, McCormick, Yamada, Thatcher, & Robinson, 2010). More research is needed to further examine the effects of TMS, including the effect of higher stimulation intensities in older adults who may require more intense stimulation compared with younger adults due to cortical atrophy (Nahas et al., 2004).

Deep brain stimulation is efficacious in the treatment of treatment-resistant depression in mixed-age samples; however, no studies have focused exclusively on older adults (R. J. Anderson et al., 2012). In addition, studies have been limited by small sample sizes. Vagus nerve stimulation also has been examined as an intervention for treatment-resistant depression, but studies with older adults are limited. At present, results with young adult samples appear promising (e.g., Aaronson et al., 2012).

Combined Therapies

Although several monotherapies exist for the treatment of depression in older adults, less is known about the efficacy of combined pharmacological and psychotherapy treatment. Thompson et al. (2001) examined the efficacy of CBT alone, desipramine (a tricyclic antidepressant) alone, or a combination of CBT and desipramine in the older adults with MDD. Significant reduction in depressive symptoms was demonstrated for all treatments; however, the combined treatment condition demonstrated superior treatment effects compared with the desipramine-only condition. In addition, older adults with greater severity of depressive symptoms had greater rate of change in symptoms in the combined treatment compared with either of the monotherapies, suggesting that combined treatment was most efficacious in older adults with greater severity of depressive symptoms.

One IPT study has examined acute treatment of MDD in older adults using combination therapy (Reynolds, Miller, et al., 1999), and two studies have been conducted examining whether maintenance therapy that included a combination IPT condition resulted in superior treatment effects. Combination therapy failed to result in superior treatment effects for acute depression treatment (Reynolds, Miller, et al., 1999). Conflicting findings were found for maintenance therapy (Reynolds et al., 2006; Reynolds, Frank, et al., 1999). More research, including studies using forms of therapy other than IPT, is needed to elucidate the potential additive effects of combination therapy.

Treatment-Resistant Depression

Initial antidepressant or psychosocial treatment for late-life depression is unsuccessful with approximately 30% of young and older adults (Cooper et al., 2011). This treatment-resistant depression has been termed refractory depression, although the definition of refractory varies in the literature. Cooper et al. suggested that optimal treatment of older adults might differ from that of young adults in light of older adults presenting with more comorbid cognitive and physical disorders, multiple medication regimens, age-related differences in pharmacodynamics and pharmacokinetics, and a greater likelihood of drug interactions.

There is a paucity of literature on the treatment of refractory depression with older adults. Cooper et al. (2011) found only three randomized trials and one placebo-controlled medication trial; most were small, open-label trials. Moreover, no ECT, TMS, vagal stimulation, or psychotherapy studies met their inclusion criteria. Depression was considered refractory when it failed to respond to one adequate treatment. Approximately 50% of older adults with refractory depression improved with treatment. The outcomes could have been better had the trial durations been longer, as 50% of the studies had durations of less than 12 weeks (Cooper et al., 2011).

A meta-analysis of late-life depression studies (Bottino, Barcelos-Ferreira, & Ribeiz, 2012) revealed that of the individuals who were unresponsive to a single trial of antidepressant, 50% responded to a change to another antidepressant or augmentation with another medication. Augmentation usually refers to the addition of a nonantidepressant medication (e.g., lithium, atypical antipsychotics) to antidepressant medication (Whyte et al., 2004). The addition of individual CBT, recommended by the National Institute for Health and Clinical Excellence (2009), is effective and reduces relapse and dropout rates (Bottino et al., 2012).

Prevention

More than 50 years ago, Albee (1959) argued for the importance of prevention of mental disorders, and this objective has become even more important in subsequent years with evidence that many individuals experiencing depression never achieve remission, even when the current guidelines for treatment are followed meticulously (e.g., Baldwin, 2010). The prevention of depression is particularly important in light of its health and mental health burden over the life span and its association with increased mortality (Reynolds et al., 2012).

Hindi, Dew, Albert, Lotrich, and Reynolds (2011) suggested that clinicians identify individuals who are at risk for major depression and individuals

with subsyndromal symptoms in an effort to preempt the disorder. Subsyndromal depression may be more reversible than the full-blown disorder, as the neurobiological changes associated with subsyndromal depression may be more modifiable (Hindi et al., 2011). Individuals with functional limitations resulting from stroke, with limited social support, and with subsyndromal symptoms may be the best targets for preventive interventions (e.g., Salter, Foley, Zhu, Jutai, & Teasell, 2013; Schoevers et al., 2006). This also may prove to be the case with other conditions that limit functioning (e.g., chronic obstructive pulmonary disease, macular degeneration, hip fracture). In their review of the literature on poststroke depression prevention, Salter et al. (2013) found that early initiation of antidepressant therapy for stroke patients without depression can reduce the odds for development of poststroke depression.

There are few studies of psychological interventions for the prevention of late-life depression. In their meta-analysis of psychological interventions for the prevention of depressive disorder, Cuijpers, van Straten, Smit, Mihalopoulos, and Beekman (2008) concluded that prevention of new cases of depressive disorders appeared possible; however, of the 19 studies cases they reviewed, only one (Rovner, Casten, Hegel, Leiby, & Tasman, 2007) focused on older adults. Researchers have identified numerous risk factors. The evidence to support the efficacy of interventions to prevent late-life depression is weak but promising. Cuijpers et al. (2008) concluded their meta-analytic review of psychological interventions by stating that because of the brief follow-up periods of most of the studies, "it is not clear whether the preventive interventions actually reduced the incidence or only delayed onset" (p. 1278). Consistent with that view, Reynolds et al. (2012) suggested follow-up periods of at least 12 months and preferably 24 months.

Recent prevention studies by van't Veer-Tazelaar et al. (2009, 2011) and Dozeman et al. (2012) have shown considerable promise. These authors have demonstrated stepped-care prevention programs to be effective in reducing the cumulative incidence of depression among older adults who were considered at risk for depression based on subsyndromal symptoms of depression. van't Veer-Tazelaar et al. (2011), for example, halved the 2-year cumulative incidence of depressive disorders. Briefly, the four steps of the program, each lasting 3 months, include watchful waiting (step one), CB (step two), PST (step three), and referral to a primary care physician. The stepped-care program is consistent with the suggestion of Reynolds et al. (2012), who encouraged the use of brief, learning-based approaches that have proven effective with affective disorders and insomnia. When intervention efforts focus on individuals with subsyndromal depression, Reynolds et al. argued that psychological interventions are preferable to antidepressants because antidepressants have demonstrated little efficacy with mild depression, and they have several potential adverse effects when used with older adults. The authors also noted that nutriceuticals (e.g., vitamin D, omega-3 fatty acids) are promising for the prevention of late-life depression.

Implementation Issues Surrounding Evidence-Based Treatments

The structure and content of EBTs (e.g., agenda setting, skills training, collaboration) work well for clients of all ages; however, older adults may require treatment adaptations due to age-related cognitive changes. In general, the choice of depression treatment should be made on the basis of the client's ability to participate in and meet the demands of the intervention. For example, problem-solving therapy has been recommended for older adults with depression and executive dysfunction because of the intervention's concrete approach and focus on problem-solving steps that are particularly challenging for individuals with executive dysfunction (e.g., planning, initiating, etc.). Researchers have begun to develop algorithms to predict which patients are likely to respond to depression treatment (Andreescu et al., 2008). Andreescu et al. (2008) found that among a pooled sample of older adults receiving acute pharmacological treatment for depression (12 weeks), under a low-sensitivity model in which the risk of false positives (e.g., that the participant will respond to treatment when they do not) was maximized, the main predictors of treatment response were initial treatment response,

lower baseline anxiety, and older age of onset of depressive episode. Under a high-sensitivity model, in which the risk of false negatives (e.g., that the participant will be a nonresponder) was minimized, the predictors were initial treatment response, baseline anxiety level, and baseline sleep disturbance. Alexopoulos (2008) has issued several guidelines for personalizing treatment for late-life depression, which emphasized attending to patient (e.g., predictors of adverse outcomes) and system factors (e.g., coordinating services with other health providers).

When working with older adult clients, treatment adaptations often are needed (Knight & Satre, 1999; Zeiss & Steffen, 1996). Older adults may have greater difficulty learning new material. As such, clinicians are encouraged to present material in multiple modes (e.g., verbal instruction, by example, written), and provide handouts to the client or audio and video recordings of sessions. The pace of therapy is typically slower with an older adult client. Repeating new information throughout the session and following up by asking clients whether they understand the material is encouraged. Older adult clients may be more likely than their younger counterparts to become distracted in session. Redirecting the client to the main topic of the session may be necessary. In cases in which cognitive impairment is more severe, involving a caregiver in therapy may be necessary (e.g., Haight et al., 2003). Discussing this with the client before involving a caregiver is required to obtain the client's consent and discuss the limits of confidentiality. Caregivers can assist the client in completing homework assignments outside of session as well as providing a proxy report of mood over the past week. Therapy in nursing home settings also can involve staff members, for example, by providing reports of mood and prompting engagement in pleasant events (e.g., S. Meeks et al., 2008).

It is also important to consider that older adults have unique strengths. For example, older adults have rich life experiences that can be a source of strength in therapy. Recalling past experiencing in which the older adult successfully navigated a challenging event can enhance self-efficacy and feelings of control in the present moment; it also can serve to remind the client of skills that were successfully used in the past. In addition, Knight and Satre (1999) recommended considering how emotionality differs in older adults compared with younger adults and how this may influence therapy. For example, older adults have more complex emotions, such that an event may precipitate both positive and negative emotions. Focusing on both the positive and negative aspects of the client's emotional experience may help the client gain perspective on the event (Knight & Satre, 1999).

The content and structure of EBTs do not require modifications, although adaptations to the presentation and pacing of material may be necessary. Not all older adults require adaptations; thus, assessing cognitive functioning before therapy is recommended.

CLINICAL APPLICATIONS

This section describes some of the more salient factors that are important for the clinician to consider in the context of assessment and treatment.

Gender

Gender is important to consider during assessment and interventions for late-life depression, as the disorder is more common among women than men (Fiske et al., 2009). Symptoms of depression may present differently as a function of gender. Specifically, older women are more likely to endorse depressed affect, whereas men are more likely to present with an irritable or angry mood (Lynch & Kilmartin, 1999). Suicide often is attributable to depressive disorders, and suicide rates are highest among older males (Conwell, Van Orden, & Caine, 2011), necessitating thorough suicide assessment when working with older adults, especially men (see Chapter 6 in this volume).

Although stigma associated with mental illness is common among older adults irrespective of gender (Conner et al., 2010), older men may attach greater stigma to depression than older women do and are less apt to recognize and report symptoms of depression (Hinton, Zweifach, Oishi, Tang, & Unützer, 2006). Treatment outcomes also may differ between genders. Women are more likely to present for

treatment and continue with treatment than are men (Unützer et al., 2003; Zivin & Kales, 2008). That fewer men participate in treatment than women may be the result of underdiagnosis of depression among older males (Unützer et al., 2003). Although there is a paucity of research comparing older men and women on outcomes for psychosocial treatments for depression, studies generally show no gender differences (e.g., Bosworth, Hays, George, & Steffens, 2002; Rokke et al., 1999).

Culture and Ethnicity

Depressive symptoms may present differently across ethnic groups. For example, somatization is more common in some ethnic minority groups (Kirmayer, 2001). Moreover, older adults with depression from various cultural backgrounds have significantly more medically unexplained somatic symptoms compared with older adults without depression (Yu & Lee, 2012). Compared with Whites, Hispanics and African Americans are more likely to receive diagnoses of psychotic disorders rather than mood disorders especially if psychotic features are present (see Marin & Escobar, 2007). Coping strategies for depressive symptoms may differ across cultures. Among African Americans, older adults may cope with depression through prayer or by distracting themselves from their symptoms (Conner et al., 2010). Clinicians working with ethnic minority older adults should be mindful of potential culture-related differences in symptoms, but they also should avoid stereotyping based on ethnicity, as there is considerable variability in depression within cultures.

Few research studies have examined the efficacy of depression treatment separately among racially and ethnically diverse older adults, although the impetus for such research is a public health priority (U.S. Department of Health and Human Services, 2001). In their critical review of the literature, Fuentes and Aranda (2012) concluded that older adult minorities benefit from treatment. In particular, they identified collaborative care models as demonstrating the strongest evidence.

Much of the research examining older adult minority groups has focused on racial and ethnic minorities; however, other subgroups of older adults, such as lesbian, gay, bisexual, transgender, and queer

(LGBTQ) individuals, are beginning to become a focus of research efforts (Satterfield & Crabb, 2010). Although research in this area remains in its infancy, some noteworthy findings have emerged. Nearly one third of LGBTQ older adults have clinically significant depressive symptoms (Fredriksen-Goldsen et al., 2011), and they may be more likely than their heterosexual peers to report a history of discrimination and negative life events (e.g., antigay violence, family problems; Grossman, D'Augelli, & O'Connell, 2002), which may contribute to depressive symptomatology. Case studies (e.g., Satterfield & Crabb, 2010) also have provided support for adapting current depression treatments to meets the needs of LGBTQ older adults. Nonetheless, more empirical work examining the treatment of depression among older adult LGBTQ individuals is needed given the increasing number of sexual minorities expected in the coming decades.

Physical Health and Disability

Clinicians are encouraged to consider the reciprocal relation between depression and physical illness and disability. Symptoms of medical disorders may mimic symptoms of depression (e.g., hypothyroidism; Fountoulakis, Iacovides, Grammaticos, St. Kaprinis, & Bech, 2004). Depression also is a risk factor for disability and other medical problems (e.g., Schillerstrom, Royall, & Palmer, 2008), and, for some individuals, may represent a prodromal feature of dementia (Brommelhoff et al., 2009). In addition, several medical disorders are associated with subsequent depressive symptomology, including stroke, Parkinson's disease, myocardial infarction, and chronic obstructive pulmonary disease (Aarsland, Påhlhagen, Ballard, Ehrt, & Svenningsson, 2011; Barth, Schumacher, & Herrmann-Lingen, 2004; Kouwenhoven, Kirkevold, Engedal, & Kim, 2011; Yohannes, Baldwin, & Connolly, 2000). Moreover, medical patients with significant depressive symptoms are more likely to experience increased symptom burden, greater functional impairment, increased medical costs, and poorer outcomes (e.g., death; Katon & Ciechanowski, 2002).

Many of the somatic symptoms associated with depression overlap with symptoms of normal aging, medical illness, or adverse effects of medication (e.g., fatigue, difficulty concentrating, sleep disturbance). Therefore, disentangling the contributions of late-life depression, physical disease, and medications is an onerous, but necessary task.

Cognitive Functioning

Cognitive impairment can complicate diagnostic efforts, as many symptoms overlap, and depression and cognitive impairment are often comorbid (e.g., difficulty concentrating, impaired acquisition of new information, apathy; Pariante & Lightman, 2008). Comorbid psychiatric symptoms, such as depression, anxiety, agitation, and psychosis, often accompany dementia (Lopez et al., 2003). The prevalence of depressive symptoms in adults with dementia ranges between 30% and 50% (Steffens & Potter, 2008). There are several possible explanations for this comorbidity. Depression may be a reaction to a dementia diagnosis (Jha, Tabet, & Orrell, 2001) or a reaction to the progressive loss of cognitive abilities (Bassuk, Berkman, & Wypij, 1998). Similarly, dementia may interfere with problem-solving skills needed to cope with depression. Social networks may be influenced negatively by dementia, which may exacerbate depressive symptoms. Depression also may be a prodromal symptom of dementia (Schweitzer, Tuckwell, O'Brien, & Ames, 2002). The co-occurrence of depression and dementia is of particular clinical concern because it is also associated with adverse health outcomes such as increased mortality (Mehta et al., 2003) and functional impairment (Logsdon, McCurry, & Teri, 2008).

Clinical Settings

Older adults present with depression in a variety of settings (Segal, June, & Marty, 2010), each of which has significant implications for assessment and intervention. Older adults most frequently present with depression in primary care (Karlin, Duffy, & Gleaves, 2008). Clinically significant depressive symptoms affect more than 10% of older primary care patients, but less than half of cases are accurately identified (Mitchell, Rao, & Vaze, 2010). In primary care, assessments (Segal et al., 2010) and interventions tend to be briefer, necessitating prioritization of treatment goals (Schulberg, Katon, Simon, & Rush, 1998). Given the limited number of sessions, follow-up after completion of treatment is especially important to ensure that treatment gains have been maintained (Schulberg et al., 1998).

Older adults often present with depression in residential settings, such as long-term care facilities. Approximately 44% of long-term care patients experience clinically significant symptoms of depression (Teresi, Abrams, Holmes, Ramirez, & Eimicke, 2001) and are more likely to be depressed than their community-dwelling counterparts (Blazer, 2009). Detection rates traditionally have been low in long-term care settings (37%–45%; Teresi et al., 2001), where roughly 11% of individuals over the age of 85 years in the United States reside (Administration on Aging, 2012). Fortunately, long-term care facilities certified by the Centers for Medicare and Medicaid now require periodic depression screening (PHQ–9) as part of the MDS; however, whether this has translated into increased access to mental health services or reduced rates of depression in long-term care is unclear.

Older adults also present for mental health services in outpatient mental health facilities, psychiatric hospitals, and general hospital settings. Approximately 37% of older adults admitted to an acute care facility reported clinically significant depressive symptoms (Ciro et al., 2012), with slightly higher rates of depression among older adults in inpatient psychiatric facilities (38%–46%; T. W. Meeks et al., 2008) and outpatient mental health settings (approximately 45%; Wetherell et al., 2007). Older adults historically have accounted for a disproportionately large percentage of psychiatric inpatients, while simultaneously utilizing outpatient mental health services at much lower rates compared with younger adults (Qualls, Segal, Norman, Niederehe, & Gallagher-Thompson, 2002). Whereas most depressed older adults benefit from inpatient treatment, less than 5% seek treatment with outpatient mental health specialists following discharge (H. Li, Proctor, & Morrow-Howell, 2005).

CASE EXAMPLES

Assessment and treatment of late-life depression can be challenging. We present two case examples that illustrate the complexities of assessing and treating depression among older adults.

Case Example 1

Gertrude is a 78-year-old resident of a long-term care facility who was referred for psychological evaluation by the social worker. She was diagnosed with congestive heart failure a few years earlier and transferred to the facility because her daughter could not care for her in the home. Gertrude uses a wheelchair and needs assistance with transferring. Her husband died several years earlier and her three children comprise her primary social support. Gertrude has resided at the long-term care facility for 2 months and she spends much of her time in her room. She often refuses to go to meals or activities. Some days, Gertrude asks to return to bed following lunch and argues with staff members when encouraged to attend afternoon activities instead. Gertrude's daughter expressed concern to the social worker that her mother is more forgetful than usual. She also reported that Gertrude becomes tearful whenever her daughter leaves the nursing home, and the social worker has observed Gertrude sobbing in her room when alone. The social worker is concerned that Gertrude may have difficulty adjusting to the nursing home and may be depressed.

Assessment. Gertrude presents a complicated, but not uncommon, clinical picture. Gertrude has congestive heart failure (CHF), which may account for her refusal to attend activities, as CHF is marked by fatigue and functional limitations (Skotzko et al., 2000). There is a question of cognitive impairment, as her daughter said that Gertrude's memory is poorer than usual. However, memory problems can be a symptom of depression. Finally, Gertrude is new to the long-term care facility and her symptoms may reflect difficulty adjusting to the new living arrangement.

A clinical interview with Gertrude was completed in her room. Gertrude endorsed experiencing depressed mood and anhedonia for several weeks.

She began feeling depressed before she moved to the facility, when she realized she was a burden to her daughter, but noticed that her mood has worsened since arriving at the facility. She noted experiencing fatigue nearly every day, despite the fact she reported sleeping well during the night. She reported that she avoids activities primarily due to fatigue but that she also does not like the available group activities. When asked about solitary activities, Gertrude stated that she no longer enjoys certain activities, such as watching television and reading books. Gertrude mentioned that she has had periods of depression in the past. As examples, she recounted experiencing depression when her husband died and when she was diagnosed with CHF. Gertrude denied current and past thoughts of suicide, stating "I could never do that to my children."

With Gertrude's permission, an interview was also completed with her daughter. Her daughter expressed concern about her mother's tearfulness and believed her mother to be lonely. She acknowledged that her mother had been feeling sad some time before moving to the nursing home. Additionally, she noted that her mother had problems with memory before moving to the facility but argued her memory has deteriorated considerably in the past 2 months. The nurse that provides care to Gertrude also supplied information. The nurse echoed that Gertrude appears sad and anhedonic. The nurse stated that Gertrude is argumentative when staff members do not help her to bed in the afternoon. The nurse examined Gertrude's medical chart and noted that her oxygen levels have remained stable and adequate recently. Her medications for CHF, which included an angiotensin-converting-enzyme inhibitor and a beta-blocker, were noted. The potential adverse effects of these medications (e.g., dizziness, weakness, difficulty breathing) were ruled out as contributors to her presenting problem, as Gertrude started taking these medications before the onset of depressive symptoms.

During a second visit, Gertrude completed several assessment measures. First, she completed the Montreal Cognitive Assessment (Nasreddine et al., 2005) to screen for cognitive impairment. Gertrude scored a 19/30, which suggests mild cognitive impairment. She exhibited particular problems with memory although she performed adequately on tasks assessing attention. Additional assessments of her memory were performed to further elucidate the nature of her memory problems, which revealed poor short-term memory but adequate recognition memory. She then completed the GDS (Yesavage et al., 1982–1983) to assess for depressive symptoms. She scored a 16/30 on the measure, which suggests depression of mild severity.

Conceptualization. Gertrude exhibits depressed mood, anhedonia, fatigue, and short-term memory problems. Her CHF appears stable and her medications do not appear to be producing side effects and therefore do not explain her current symptoms of fatigue and anhedonia. Her poor memory cannot be completely explained by her depression, although it remains uncertain whether her memory has worsened further due to depression. Because she performed well on tasks measuring attention, her poor memory performance may not be due to impaired attention or poor motivation. Gertrude's depressive symptoms appeared before she relocated to the nursing home when she realized she was a burden to her daughter, but they have worsened as she now has less contact with her primary support system. Gertrude has a history of depression and this current episode appears to have been triggered by belief that she was a burden to her daughter.

Gertrude does not appear to meet criteria for major depression based on *DSM–5* diagnostic criteria, as she endorsed only four symptoms of major depression. Yet she experiences significant social impairment as she spends much of her time alone and idle and has less contact with her family members. Depression can exacerbate symptoms of CHF (Skotzko et al., 2000), suggesting that her depressive symptoms may impair her health. It appears Gertrude is experiencing subsyndromal depression that nonetheless warrants clinical attention. Given Gertrude's symptom presentation, cognitive problems, and functional limitations due to CHF, problem-solving therapy (Gellis & Bruce, 2010) is a prudent course of treatment. Included in problem solving is behavioral activation to address anhedonia, which can be implemented easily with individuals who have cognitive impairment (Crowther, Scogin, & Norton, 2010).

Intervention.   At the first session, the clinician provided the rationale for problem-solving therapy and explained that Gertrude would learn new skills to help her negotiate stressful events that may arise at the nursing home. Early sessions helped Gertrude identify her goals and obstacles to these goals. Gertrude remarked that major obstacles to leaving the facility are her health and the need for skilled care. The clinician helped her recognize that some problems may be beyond her control.

Subsequent sessions dealt with learning problem-solving skills. Gertrude identified ongoing problems, for example, that she dislikes when staff members tell her she cannot do something. The clinician helped Gertrude identify various solutions to this problem, and to state the pros and cons of each option, and select the best option. Gertrude decided that expressing her feelings with staff members was ideal. The clinician and Gertrude practiced assertive communication through role-plays and the clinician provided Gertrude with feedback. After sufficient practice, a trusted staff member was invited into the session and Gertrude practiced the skill with the staff member.

Behavioral activation was incorporated into problem-solving therapy to increase Gertrude's engagement with pleasant activities. For the first session addressing behavioral activation, Gertrude asked her daughter to be present. Gertrude, with the assistance of her daughter and the clinician, developed a list of activities that she enjoys and created a schedule for these activities (e.g., gardening, caring for potted plants in her room, playing the piano, listening to music). With Gertrude's permission, the clinician spoke with direct-care staff members to explain the intervention and to ask them to track her participation in these activities. The clinician also helped Gertrude develop and schedule less strenuous yet enjoyable activities, such as listening to music, which could be accomplished on days in which her symptoms of CHF may be worse and therefore more impairing. Gertrude met with her clinician for twelve 1-hr sessions and completed the GDS at the beginning of each session so that treatment progress could be monitored. At the last session she obtained a score of 7/30, suggesting that her depressive symptoms had improved. With her increase in activities, Gertrude reported that she was not as burdensome as she initially had thought. Performing these activities showed her that she could function independently, and by engaging in therapy, she learned that she had more control over her circumstances than she may have realized.

The final session focused on relapse prevention. Gertrude and the clinician reviewed the skills learned in session and created a plan for preventing future depressive episodes. Gertrude was worried that needing therapy in the future indicated failure. The clinician reminded her that asking for help could be part of the relapse prevention plan. The plan was written on a piece of paper and given to Gertrude.

Case Example 2

Eugene is a 66-year-old man referred to a psychologist by his primary care physician. Eugene retired from his job as a construction worker 1 year earlier. Since that time, he has gained several pounds. His wife complains that he has not found other activities to fill his day and that he spends much of his time alone at home while his wife is at work. Eugene admits that he usually spends his day drinking beer and watching TV. Eugene's wife has also noticed that he has become more irritable and they have had many verbal arguments. Their fights often center on Eugene's alcohol use. He also described feeling tired most of the time; he reported taking naps during the day and having a difficult time falling asleep at night. Eugene mentioned to his physician during a routine physical examination that he has been feeling worthless lately, and his physician is concerned he may be experiencing depression and problematic alcohol use. Eugene, with much resistance, has agreed to see a mental health professional at the insistence of his wife and primary care physician.

Assessment.   In Eugene's case, a critical goal of assessment was to disentangle the relation between potential depressive symptoms and his alcohol use. The possible influence of Eugene's gender on his presentation of depression symptoms was considered.

A clinical interview was initially conducted. Eugene requested that his wife be present for the interview. When asked about his mood, Eugene denied feeling depressed, specifying that he does not feel sad. He acknowledged feeling more irritable. His wife corroborated this statement by adding that he seems to have a "short fuse." She noted that they fight more than usual, though Eugene claimed he did not notice they have been fighting more often. His wife asserted that they tend to fight about his drinking.

When asked about his alcohol use, Eugene said he drinks one or two beers per day. His wife disagreed with this statement, as she noticed several cans of beer in the trash each day. Reluctantly, Eugene confessed that he drinks between six and twelve beers per day. He added that he started drinking shortly after retiring because of boredom. When he was still working, Eugene stated that he often worked 6 days per week and tended to use his 1 day off to relax and catch up on television shows. Now that he is retired, "I'm all caught up on television." Similarly, Eugene said he naps throughout the day because he has little else to do. Eugene described feeling "worthless" because he does not work and spends most of the day drinking beer, napping, and watching television. He has gained weight, which further adds to his feelings of low self-worth. He said he started to feel worthless shortly after retiring and began drinking alcohol to cope with his negative feelings. Eugene said he feels hopeless about the future and recently has started to think about death. He denied active suicidal ideation, emphasizing that he merely thinks about what it would be like if he were no longer alive. His wife stated that she has encouraged him to participate in local clubs, such as the construction workers' union retirement club, but he has refused. Eugene denied a history of previous depressive episodes. Eugene is prescribed no medications, and no physical health problems were revealed during his physical examination.

Eugene completed the CES–D (Radloff, 1977) to assess depressive symptoms. He scored 26/60, suggesting clinically significant depression. He also completed the Michigan Alcoholism Screening Test—Geriatric Version (MAST–G; Blow et al., 1992) and scored 7/24, suggesting significant alcohol use problems. Because he and his wife argue frequently, his anger and anger regulation skills also were assessed. An anxiety screener was administered, which indicated that Eugene was not experiencing significant anxiety symptoms. At the end of the session, Eugene was scheduled for a follow-up appointment at the clinician's office adjacent to the offices of his primary care provider.

Conceptualization.   Since retiring, Eugene has felt worthless, noting that he feels he has no purpose in life. Without a daily routine, Eugene spends much of his time idle. He sleeps more than usual and participates in few activities, such as watching television. Given his clean bill of health, the weight gain may be related to his inactivity and increased alcohol consumption. To cope with his feelings of worthlessness and lack of activities, Eugene started using alcohol. His alcohol use has escalated and is now causing problems in his marriage. Eugene does not endorse depressed mood. He reported feeling irritable, however, which can be characteristic of depression in males (Lynch & Kilmartin, 1999). He endorsed several other symptoms of major depression that have been present for several months: anhedonia, changes in sleep patterns, weight gain, thoughts of death, and feelings of worthlessness.

Eugene's alcohol use appears to be secondary to the depression, suggesting that the main crux of treatment will be to treat his depressive symptoms. He used alcohol as a means of coping with depressive symptoms, and the intervention should emphasize alternative coping strategies. He also engages in few activities during the day and is experiencing marital conflict, which will be additional targets for the intervention. In light of these goals, CBT for older adults is a suitable treatment for Eugene.

Intervention.   Eugene was reluctant to see a mental health professional and initially minimized his drinking. The clinician was concerned he may not participate in treatment. To enhance the likelihood that Eugene would accept the treatment, early sessions of CBT focused on psychoeducation about depression and alcohol use. The clinician described major depression and shared with Eugene the conceptualization of his depression and alcohol use. The clinician also articulated the nature of CBT for older adults with a focus on learning new skills through various modalities, such as role-playing and practicing skills in and outside of sessions.

A critical component of CBT was to address Eugene's maladaptive thoughts, particularly those related to feelings of worthlessness. The clinician helped Eugene identify unhelpful thoughts, for example, that Eugene believes he is worthless and "less of a man" because he no longer works. The clinician helped Eugene challenge these thoughts and identify alternative thoughts. Because Eugene appears to have largely identified himself in terms of his occupation, therapy also addressed Eugene's self-concept in light of his role change (i.e., retirement). The clinician helped Eugene identify things he could do that could create meaning and purpose in his life. Eugene noted that it is important for him to be a provider for his family and identified activities he can do to provide for his family.

Another important component of treatment included behavioral activation to increase Eugene's participation in pleasant, reinforcing events that do not involve alcohol. The clinician helped Eugene identify activities that he enjoys but may not engage in frequently. The clinician then assisted Eugene with scheduling these activities throughout the day. Eugene was asked to keep a log of his daily activities and his mood throughout the week and these logs were reviewed at each subsequent session. He also completed the CES–D and MAST–G at the beginning of each session so that progress could be monitored. Eugene recorded his daily alcohol use on his mood log. Throughout each session, Eugene's alcohol use was discussed. For example, Eugene described that, at first, using alcohol was a pleasant event. The clinician helped Eugene understand that by engaging in other pleasant activities, he may not feel he needs to use alcohol.

Because of growing marital issues, the clinician encouraged Eugene to invite his wife to participate in a few of the sessions. Eugene's wife accompanied him to the psychoeducation session, which helped her understand the nature of his depression and alcohol use. She also attended some of the behavioral activation sessions, and she was encouraged to help Eugene follow through with the pleasant activities.

After twelve weekly, 1-hr sessions, Eugene completed the CES–D and the MAST–G. He scored a 9 on the CES–D, indicating a decrease in depressive symptoms. On the MAST–G, he scored a 2/25, indicating he is not experiencing clinically significant problems with alcohol use. Given his success, Eugene and the clinician decided that treatment would be terminated. At the following session, all of the skills learned in session were reviewed with Eugene and his wife. A booster session, to ensure treatment goals were maintained (Schulberg et al., 1998), was scheduled for 1 month posttermination.

CONCLUSION

The role of the clinical geropsychologist undoubtedly will continue to expand. More geropsychologists will become members of multidisciplinary and interdisciplinary teams, particularly as mental health services expand in the primary care settings where most older adults seek treatment for late-life depression. The interested reader is referred to Chapter 4 in this volume and Skultety and Rodriguez (2008) for discussions of research examining mental health providers on integrated teams. A critical review of English-language publications (Skultety & Zeiss, 2006) found that the integrated health care models in primary care settings provided greater reductions in depressive symptoms among older adults compared with usual care. An excellent model is provided by the Department of Veterans Affairs (VA) Health Care System, which has done an admirable job of integrating mental health and primary care services (e.g., Zeiss & Karlin, 2008). Advocacy for such programs outside the VA system, including national and state-level policies to provide financial support for evidence-based collaborative care models in primary care, is sorely needed (M. Park & Unützer, 2011).

Continued development and testing of theories of late-life depression that inform assessment and treatment is an important next step. Understanding of the factors that contribute to late-life depression and particularly the manner in which they interact remains an issue that certainly warrants our attention in future research. Greater understanding hopefully will lead to improved prevention, detection, and interventions.

The assessment and diagnostic issues raised in this chapter call for further research. Specifically, the shortcomings of our diagnostic criteria and assessment measures for major depression among older adults continue to be a concern. Neither the diagnostic criteria nor the assessment measures based on these criteria may adequately capture the nature and range of depressive systems experienced by older adults. Current assessment measures may require modifications or new measures may be created to better account for older adult–specific depression presentations.

Examination of the long-term outcomes for all psychosocial, pharmacological, ECT, and brain stimulation therapies is needed. Studies typically follow patients for weeks or months posttreatment, but the effects of these treatments for longer periods of time remains largely unknown.

The number of efficacy studies far outweighs the number of effectiveness studies. In the context of effectiveness studies, we need more research that informs us on how to best personalize treatments for late-life depression. This might include information on predictors of treatment response and optimum duration of a given treatment before switching or augmenting treatments. Relatedly, brain imaging can enhance our understanding of brain abnormalities that resolve or remain after depression remits. This is important because older adults who continue to present with brain abnormalities after depression remission may be at increased risk for recurrence of depression (Alexopoulos, 2008).

Large-scale public health efforts are needed to increase older adults' knowledge of available evidence-based treatments. As outlined by M. Park and Unützer (2011), public health campaigns may include consumer activation via public education efforts, in which the range of treatments available in the treatment of depression is presented.

Outcome studies on late-life depression would benefit from including ethnically and culturally diverse, low SES, poorly educated, and rural older adults. Many participant samples tend to be dominated by young-old adults, with very few old-old adults. The study of old-old adults is particularly important, as depression rates tend to be higher in this group, and cognitive, functional, and health issues may contribute to depressive symptoms.

More research that examines interventions that are effective with younger adults but lack sufficient support as effective and efficacious for older people are needed (e.g., DBT for individuals with comorbid personality disorder and depression, and interpersonal therapy for depression). For all types of interventions, the effective elements remain largely undiscovered with older adults. Specifically, identifying therapist–client factors as they relate to treatment outcomes may be an important next step in improving late-life depression treatment. The dismantling of treatment packages would be particularly important for work in primary care settings where the duration of sessions is limited.

A significant issue with treatment of late-life depression involves access to care. There is a need to enhance detection of depression in primary care settings, where most older adults seek depression treatment. This goal can be reached in many ways, such as increased staff training on detecting depression, integration of mental health professionals into primary care, and incorporation of routine depression screenings into medical practice. Historically, detection of late-life depression in primary care did not necessarily lead to treatment, which further underscores the need for these suggestions. It also may be worthwhile to adapt alternative methods for implementing psychological treatments, such as use of home-based primary care, which has been very successful in the VA Healthcare System (Zeiss & Karlin, 2008), or telehealth. A related issue may be a shortage of professionals to deliver interventions for depression, which could be alleviated by using learning-based interventions that can be easily taught to non–mental health professionals (cf., Reynolds, 2009).

Finally, there is a growing need for programs aimed at prevention of depression among older adults. Research by Reynolds and colleagues (e.g., Reynolds, 2009; Reynolds et al., 2012) has suggested that psychosocial interventions may be more beneficial in treating subsyndromal depression among older adults than pharmacological interventions, although more research is needed. Reynolds (2009) identified several challenges facing depression prevention researchers. First, there is dearth of efficacy studies with specific groups at risk for depression (e.g., low SES groups, ethnic minorities, family caregivers). Second, better models of depression prevention are needed that can inform treatments. Third, more study of the cost-effectiveness of prevention programs is needed. Fourth, more study of dissemination of preventive interventions via the Internet, particularly with underserved populations, is needed.

For preventive interventions to be successful, theories of late-life depression that inform treatment (Reynolds, 2009) and research aimed at identifying risk factors for developing depression are needed. The development and evaluation of the efficacy and effectiveness of preventive interventions is an integral next step.

Although our knowledge of late-depression has expanded in recent years, much remains unexplored. Some of what we know about young adult depression is certainly relevant for our understanding of late-life depression. There is considerable evidence, however, that late-life depression, in at least some forms, is sufficiently different for older adults to require the development of new etiological models of depression, revised diagnostic criteria, content-valid and age period–specific assessment instruments, and further research on the most effective interventions across service delivery settings. This is an exciting time to be a late-life depression researcher and clinician.

References

Aaronson, S. T., Carpenter, L. L., Conway, C. R., Reimherr, F. W., Lisanby, S. H., Schwartz, T. L., . . . Bunker, M. (2012). Vagus nerve stimulation therapy randomized to different amounts of electrical charge for treatment-resistant depression: Acute and chronic effects. *Brain Stimulation.* Advance online publication. doi.org/10.1016/j.brs.2012.09.013

Aarsland, D., Påhlhagen, S., Ballard, C. G., Ehrt, U., & Svenningsson, P. (2011). Depression in Parkinson disease: Epidemiology, mechanisms and management. *Nature Reviews: Neurology, 8,* 35–47. doi:10.1038/nrneurol.2011.189

Abraham, G., Milev, R., Lazowski, L., Jokic, R., du Toit, R., & Lowe, A. (2007). Repetitive transcranial magnetic stimulation for treatment of elderly patients with depression—An open label trial. *Neuropsychiatric Disease and Treatment, 3,* 919–924.

Administration on Aging. (2012). *Profile of older Americans.* Retrieved from http://www.aoa.gov/AoARoot/Aging_Statistics/Profile/2012/6.aspx

Adshead, F., Cody, D. D., & Pitt, B. (1992). BASDEC: A novel screening instrument for depression in elderly medical inpatients. *British Medical Journal, 305,* 397. doi:10.1136/bmj.305.6850.397

Akincigil, A., Olfson, M., Siegel, M., Zurlo, K. A., Walkup, J. T., & Crystal, S. (2012). Racial and ethnic disparities in depression care in community-dwelling elderly in the United States. *American Journal of Public Health, 102,* 319–328. doi:10.2105/AJPH.2011.300349

Akincigil, A., Olfson, M., Walkup, J. T., Siegel, M. J., Kalay, E., Amin, S., . . . Crystal, S. (2011). Diagnosis and treatment of depression in older community-dwelling adults: 1992–2005. *Journal of the American Geriatrics Society, 59,* 1042–1051. doi:10.1111/j.1532-5415.2011.03447.x

Albee, G. W. (1959). *Mental health manpower trends.* New York, NY: Basic Books.

Alexandrino-Silva, C., Alves, T. F., Tofoli, L. F., Wang, Y., & Andrade, L. H. (2011). Psychiatry life events and social support in late life depression. *Clinics, 66,* 233–238. doi:10.1590/S1807-59322011000200009

Alexopoulos, G. S. (2005). Depression in the elderly. *Lancet, 365,* 1961–1970. doi:10.1016/S0140-6736(05)66665-2

Alexopoulos, G. S. (2008). Personalizing the care of geriatric depression. *American Journal of Psychiatry, 165,* 790–792. doi:10.1176/appi.ajp.2008.08040461

Alexopoulos, G. S. (2011). Pharmacotherapy for late-life depression. *Journal of Clinical Psychiatry, 72,* e4. doi:10.4088/JCP.7085tx2cj

Alexopoulos, G. S., Abrams, R. C., Young, R. C., & Shamoian, C. A. (1988). Cornell scale for depression in dementia. *Biological Psychiatry, 23,* 271–284. doi:10.1016/0006-3223(88)90038-8

Alexopoulos, G. S., Katz, I. R., Reynolds, C. F., III, Carpenter, D., Docherty, J. P., & Ross, R. W. (2001). Pharmacotherapy of depression in older patients: A summary of the expert consensus guidelines. *Journal of Psychiatric Practice, 7,* 361–376. doi:10.1097/00131746-200111000-00003

Alexopoulos, G. S., Kiosses, D. N., Klimstra, S., Kalayam, B., & Bruce, M. L. (2002). Clinical presentation of the "depression-executive dysfunction syndrome" of late life. *American Journal of Geriatric Psychiatry, 10,* 98–106.

Alexopoulos, G. S., Meyers, S., Young, R. C., Campbell, S., Silbersweig, D., & Charlson, M. (1997). Vascular depression hypothesis. *Archives of General Psychiatry, 54*, 915–922. doi:10.1001/archpsyc.1997.01830220033006

Alexopoulos, G. S., Raue, P., & Areán, P. (2003). Problem-solving therapy versus supportive therapy in geriatric major depression with executive dysfunction. *American Journal of Geriatric Psychiatry, 11*, 46–52. doi:org/10.1097/00019442-200301000.

Alexopoulos, G. S., Reynolds, C. F., III, Bruce, M. L., Katz, I. R., Raue, P. J., Mulsant, B. H., . . . Ten Have, T. (2009). Reducing suicidal ideation and depression in older primary care patients: 24-month outcomes of the PROSPECT study. *American Journal of Psychiatry, 166*, 882–890. doi:10.1176/appi.ajp.2009.08121779

Almeida, O. P., Draper, B., Pirkis, J., Snowdon, J., Lautenschlager, N. T., Byrne, G., . . . Pfaff, J. J. (2012). Anxiety, depression, and comorbid anxiety and depression: Risk factors and outcome over two years. *International Psychogeriatrics, 24*, 1622–1632. doi:10.1017/S104161021200107X

American Psychiatric Association. (2000). *Diagnostic and statistical manual of mental disorders* (4th ed., text revision). Washington, DC: Author.

American Psychiatric Association. (2001). *The practice of electroconvulsive therapy: Recommendations for treatment, training, and privileging* (2nd ed.). Washington, DC: Author.

American Psychiatric Association. (2013). *Diagnostic and statistical manual of mental disorders* (5th ed.). Washington, DC: Author.

Anderson, I. M. (2000). Selective serotonin reuptake inhibitors versus tricyclic antidepressants: A meta-analysis of efficacy and tolerability. *Journal of Affective Disorders, 58*, 19–36. doi:10.1016/S0165-0327(99)00092-0

Anderson, R. J., Frye, M. A., Abulseoud, O. A., Lee, K. H., McGillivray, J. A., Berk, M., & Tye, S. J. (2012). Deep brain stimulation for treatment-resistant depression: Efficacy, safety and mechanisms of action. *Neuroscience and Biobehavioral Reviews, 36*, 1920–1933. doi:10.1016/j.neubiorev.2012.06.001

Andreescu, C., Mulsant, B. H., Houck, P. R., Whyte, E. M., Mazumdar, S., Dombrovski, A. Y., . . . Reynolds, C. (2008). Empirically derived decision trees for the treatment of late-life depression. *American Journal of Psychiatry, 165*, 855–862. doi:10.1176/appi.ajp.2008.07081340

Andresen, E. M., Malmgren, J. A., Carter, W. B., & Patrick, D. L. (1994). Screening for depression in well older adults: Evaluation of a short form of the CES–D. *American Journal of Preventive Medicine, 10*, 77–84.

Areán, P. A., & Cook, B. L. (2002). Psychotherapy and combined psychotherapy/pharmacotherapy for late life depression. *Biological Psychiatry, 52*, 293–303. doi:10.1016/S0006-3223(02)01371-9

Areán, P. A., Hegel, M., Vannoy, S., Fan, M. Y., & Unutzer, J. (2008). Effectiveness of problem-solving therapy for older, primary care patients with depression: Results from the IMPACT project. *The Gerontologist, 48*, 311–323. doi:10.1093/geront/48.3.311

Areán, P. A., Perri, M. G., Nezu, A. M., Schein, R. L., Christopher, F., & Joseph, T. X. (1993). Comparative effectiveness of social problem-solving therapy and reminiscence therapy as treatments for depression in older adults. *Journal of Consulting and Clinical Psychology, 61*, 1003–1010. doi:10.1037/0022-006X.61.6.1003

Areán, P. A., Raue, P., Mackin, R. S., Kanellopoulos, D., McCulloch, C., & Alexopoulos, G. S. (2010). Problem-solving therapy and supportive therapy in older adults with major depression and executive dysfunction. *American Journal of Psychiatry, 167*, 1391–1398. doi:10.1176/appi.ajp.2010.09091327

Areán, P. A., & Reynolds, C. F. (2005). The impact of psychosocial factors on late-life depression. *Biological Psychiatry, 58*, 277–282. doi:10.1016/j.biopsych.2005.03.037

Bagby, R. M., Ryder, A. G., Schuller, D. R., & Marshall, M. B. (2004). The Hamilton Depression Rating Scale: Has the gold standard become a lead weight? *American Journal of Psychiatry, 161*, 2163–2177. doi:10.1176/appi.ajp.161.12.2163

Baglioni, C., Battagliese, G., Feige, B., Spiegelhalder, K., Nissen, C., Voderholzer, U., . . . Riemann, D. (2011). Insomnia as a predictor of depression: A meta-analytic evaluation of longitudinal epidemiological studies. *Journal of Affective Disorders, 135*, 10–19. doi:10.1016/j.jad.2011.01.011

Baldwin, R. C. (2010). Preventing late-life depression: A clinical update. *International Psychogeriatrics, 22*, 1216–1224. doi:10.1017/S1041610210000864

Bartels, S. J., Horn, S., Sharkey, P., & Levine, K. (1997). Treatment of depression in older primary care patients in health maintenance organizations. *International Journal of Psychiatry in Medicine, 27*, 215–231. doi:10.2190/VKBR-1AR6-9NBD-0N25

Barth, J., Schumacher, M., & Herrmann-Lingen, C. (2004). Depression as a risk factor for mortality in patients with coronary heart disease: A meta-analysis. *Psychosomatic Medicine, 66*, 802–813. doi:10.1097/01.psy.0000146332.53619.b2

Bassuk, S. S., Berkman, L. F., & Wypij, D. (1998). Depressive symptomatology and incident cognitive decline in an elderly community sample. *Archives of General Psychiatry, 55,* 1073–1081. doi:10.1001/archpsyc.55.12.1073

Beck, A. T., Steer, R. A., & Brown, G. K. (1996). *Beck Depression Inventory—II manual.* San Antonio, TX: Psychological Corporation.

Bédard, M., Squire, L., Minthorn-Biggs, M. B., Molloy, D. W., Dubois, S., O'Donnell, M., & Lever, J. A. (2003). Validity of self-reports in dementia research: The Geriatric Depression Scale. *Clinical Gerontologist, 26,* 155–163. doi:10.1300/J018v26n03_13

Benedetti, F. (2012). The placebo response: Science versus ethics and the vulnerability of the patient. *World Psychiatry; Official Journal of the World Psychiatric Association (WPA), 11,* 70–72. doi:10.1016/j.wpsyc.2012.05.003

Bjelland, I., Dahl, A. A., Haug, T. T., & Neckelmann, D. (2002). The validity of the Hospital Anxiety and Depression Scale-An updated literature review. *Journal of Psychosomatic Research, 52,* 69–77. doi:10.1016/S0022-3999(01)00296-3

Blagys, M. D., & Hilsenroth, M. J. (2000). Distinctive features of short-term psychodynamic-interpersonal psychotherapy: A review of the comparative psychotherapy process literature. *Clinical Psychology: Science and Practice, 7,* 167–188. doi:10.1093/clipsy.7.2.167

Blazer, D., Bachar, J. R., & Hughes, D. C. (1987). Major depression with melancholia: A comparison of middle-aged and elderly adults. *Journal of the American Geriatrics Society, 35,* 927–932.

Blazer, D. G. (2009). Depression in late life: Review and commentary. *Focus: The Journal of Lifelong Learning in Psychiatry, 7,* 118–136.

Blazer, D. G., Steffens, D. C., & Koenig, H. G. (2009). Mood disorders. In D. G. Blazer & D. C. Steffens (Eds.), *American Psychiatric Publishing textbook of psychiatry* (4th ed., pp. 275–299). Washington, DC: American Psychiatric Publishing.

Blow, F. C., Brower, K. J., Schulenberg, J. E., Demo-Dananberg, L. M., Young, J. P., & Beresford, T. P. (1992). The Michigan Alcoholism Screening Test—Geriatric Version (MAST–G): A new elderly-specific screening instrument. *Alcoholism, Clinical and Experimental Research, 19,* 372.

Blumenthal, J. A., Babyak, M. A., Doraiswamy, P. M., Watkins, L., Hoffman, B. M., Barbour, K. A., . . . Sherwood, A. (2007). Exercise and pharmacotherapy in the treatment of major depressive disorder. *Psychosomatic Medicine, 69,* 587–596. doi:10.1097/PSY.0b013e318148c19a

Blumenthal, M. D. (1980). Depressive illness in old age: Getting behind the mask. *Geriatrics, 35,* 34–43.

Bolla-Wilson, K., & Bleecker, M. L. (1989). Absence of depression in elderly adults. *Journal of Gerontology, 44,* P53–P55. doi:10.1093/geronj/44.2.P53

Bosworth, H. B., Hays, J. C., George, L. K., & Steffens, D. C. (2002). Psychosocial and clinical predictors of unipolar depression outcome in older adults. *International Journal of Geriatric Psychiatry, 17,* 238–246. doi:10.1002/gps.590

Bottino, C. M. C., Barcelos-Ferreira, R., & Ribeiz, S. R. I. (2012). Treatment of depression in older adults. *Current Psychiatry Reports, 14,* 289–297. doi:10.1007/s11920-012-0281-z

Brenes, G. A., Williamson, J. D., Messier, S. P., Rejeski, W. J., Pahor, M. M., Ip, E. E., & Penninx, B. H. (2007). Treatment of minor depression in older adults: A pilot study comparing sertraline and exercise. *Aging and Mental Health, 11,* 61–68. doi:10.1080/13607860600736372

Bridle, C., Spanjers, K., Patel, S., Atherton, N. M., & Lamb, S. E. (2012). Effect of exercise on depression severity in older people: Systematic review and meta-analysis of randomized controlled trials. *British Journal of Psychiatry, 201,* 180–185. doi:10.1192/bjp.bp.111.095174

Brodaty, H., Berle, D., Hickie, I., & Mason, C. (2001). Side effects' of ECT are mainly depressive phenomena and are independent of age. *Journal of Affective Disorders, 66,* 237–245. doi:10.1016/S0165-0327(00)00314-1

Brommelhoff, J. A., Gatz, M., Johansson, B., McArdle, J. J., Fratiglioni, L., & Pedersen, N. L. (2009). Depression as a risk factor or prodomal feature for dementia? Findings in a population-based sample of Swedish twins. *Psychology and Aging, 24,* 373–384. doi:10.1037/a0015713

Brown, G. W., & Harris, T. O. (1978). *Social origins of depression.* London, England: Tavistock.

Burns, D. D. (1999). *Feeling good: The new mood therapy.* New York, NY: William Morrow.

Butler, R. N. (1963). The life review: An interpretation of reminiscence in the aged. *Psychiatry, 26,* 65–76.

Butler, R. N. (1974). Successful aging and the role of the life review. *Journal of the American Geriatrics Society, 22,* 529–535.

Butters, M. A., Whyte, E. M., Nebes, R. D., Begley, A. E., Dew, M. A., Mulsant, B. H., . . . Becker, J. T. (2004). The nature and determinants of neuropsychological functioning in late-life depression. *Archives of General Psychiatry, 61,* 587–595. doi:10.1001/archpsyc.61.6.587

Buysse, D. J., Germain, A., Moul, D. E., Franzen, P. L., Brar, L. K., Fletcher, M. E., . . . Monk, T. H. (2011). Efficacy of brief behavioral treatment for chronic insomnia in older adults. *Archives of Internal Medicine, 171,* 887–895. doi:10.1001/archinternmed.2010.535

Callahan, C. M. (2001). Quality improvement research on late life depression in primary care. *Medical Care, 39,* 772–784. doi:10.1097/00005650-200108000-00004

Campbell, J. M. (1992). Treating depression in well older adults: Use of diaries in cognitive therapy. *Issues in Mental Health Nursing, 13*, 19–29. doi:10.3109/01612849209006882

Chambless, D. L., & Hollon, S. D. (1998). Defining empirically supported therapies. *Journal of Consulting and Clinical Psychology, 66*, 7–18. doi:10.1037/0022-006X.66.1.7

Charney, D. S., Reynolds, C. F., III, Lewis, L., Lebowitz, B. D., Sunderland, T., Alexopoulos, G. S., . . . Young, R. C. (2003). Depression and Bipolar Support Alliance consensus statement on the unmet needs in diagnosis and treatment of mood disorders in late life. *Archives of General Psychiatry, 60*, 664–672. doi:10.1001/archpsyc.60.7.664

Chi, I., & Chou, K. (2001). Social support and depression among elderly Chinese people in Hong Kong. *International Journal of Aging and Human Development, 52*, 231–252. doi:10.2190/V5K8-CNMG-G2UP-37QV

Chiang, K. J., Chu, H., Chang, H. J., Chung, M. H., Chen, C. H., Chiou, H. Y., & Chou, K. R. (2010). The effects of reminiscence therapy on psychological well-being, depression, and loneliness among the institutionalized aged. *International Journal of Geriatric Psychiatry, 25*, 380–388. doi:10.1002/gps.2350

Chin A Paw, M. J., van Poppel, M. N., Twisk, J. W., & van Mechelen, W. (2004). Effects of resistance and all-round, functional training on quality of life, vitality and depression of older adults living in long-term care facilities: A randomized controlled trial. *BMC Geriatrics, 4*(5). doi:10.1186/1471-2318-4-5

Cho, H. J., Lavretsky, H., Olmstead, R., Levin, M. J., Oxman, M. N., & Irwin, M. R. (2008). Sleep disturbance and depression recurrence in community-dwelling older adults: A prospective study. *American Journal of Psychiatry, 165*,1543–1550. doi:10.11.76/appi.ajp.2008.07121882

Chou, K. L., Lee, P. W., Yu, E. C., Macfarlane, D., Cheng, Y. H., Chan, S. S., & Chi, I. (2004). Effect of Tai Chi on depressive symptoms amongst Chinese older patients with depressive disorders: a randomized clinical trial. *International Journal of Geriatric Psychiatry, 19*, 1105–1107.

Ciechanowski, P., Wagner, E., Schmaling, K., Schwartz, S., Williams, B., Diehr, P., . . . LoGerfo, J. (2004). Community-integrated home-based depression treatment in older adults: A randomized controlled trial. *JAMA, 291*, 1569–1577. doi:10.1001/jama.291.13.1569

Ciliberti, C., Gould, C., Smith, M., Chorney, D., & Edelstein, B. (2011). A preliminary investigation of developmentally sensitive items for the assessment of social anxiety in late life. *Journal of Anxiety Disorders, 25*, 686–689. doi:10.1016/j.janxdis.2011.03.003

Ciro, C. A., Ottenbacher, K. J., Graham, J. E., Fisher, S., Berges, I., & Ostir, G. V. (2012). Patterns and correlates of depression in hospitalized older adults. *Archives of Gerontology and Geriatrics, 54*, 202–205. doi:10.1016/j.archger.2011.04.001

Clark, D. C., Cavanaugh, S. V., & Gibbons, R. D. (1983). The core symptoms of depression in medical and psychiatric patients. *Journal of Nervous and Mental Disease, 171*, 705–713. doi:10.1097/00005053-198312000-00001

Cole, M. G., & Dendukuri, N. (2003). Risk factors for depression among elderly community subjects: A systematic review and meta-analysis. *American Journal of Psychiatry, 160*, 1147–1156. doi:10.1176/appi.ajp.160.6.1147

Coman, E. N., Iordache, E., Schensul, J. J., & Coiculescu, I. (2013). Comparisons of CES–D depression scoring methods in two older adults ethnic groups. The emergence of an ethnic-specific brief three-item CES–D scale. *International Journal of Geriatric Psychiatry.* doi:10.1002/gps.3842

Conner, K. O., Lee, B., Mayers, V., Robinson, D., Reynolds, C. F., Albert, S., & Brown, C. (2010). Attitudes and beliefs about mental health among African American older adults suffering from depression. *Journal of Aging Studies, 24*, 266–277. doi:10.1016/j.jaging.2010.05.007

Conradsson, M., Littbrand, H., Lindelöf, N., Gustafson, Y., & Rosendahl, E. (2010). Effects of a high-intensity functional exercise programme on depressive symptoms and psychological well-being among older people living in residential care facilities: A cluster-randomized controlled trial. *Aging and Mental Health, 14*, 565–576. doi:10.1080/13607860903483078

Constantino, M. J., Castonguay, L. G., & Schut, A. J. (2002). The working alliance: A flagship for the "scientist–practitioner" model in psychotherapy. In G. S. Tryon (Ed.), *Counseling based on process research: Applying what we know* (pp. 81–131). Boston, MA: Allyn & Bacon.

Conwell, Y., Van Orden, K., & Caine, E. (2011). Suicide in older adults. *Psychiatric Clinics of North America, 34*, 451–468. doi:10.1016/j.psc.2011.02.002

Cooper, C., Katona, C., Lyketsos, K., Blazer, D., Brodaty, H., Rabins, P., . . . Livingston, G. (2011). A systematic review of treatments for refractory depression in older people. *American Journal of Psychiatry, 168*, 681–688. doi:10.1176/appi.ajp.2011.10081165

Copeland, J. R. M., Dewey, M. E., & Griffiths-Jones, H. M. (1986). A computerised psychiatric diagnostic system and case nomenclature for elderly subjects: GMS and AGECAT. *Psychological Medicine, 16*, 89–99. doi:10.1017/S0033291700057779

Copeland, J. R. M., Kelleher, M. J., Kellett, J. M., Gourlay, A. J., Gurland, B. J., Fleiss, J. L., & Sharpe, L. (1976).

A semi-structured clinical interview for the assessment of diagnosis and mental state in the elderly: The Geriatric Mental State Schedule: I. Development and reliability. *Psychological Medicine, 6,* 439–449. doi:10.1017/S0033291700015889

Cormier, S., Nurius, P. S., & Osborn, C. J. (2013). *Interviewing and change strategies for helpers* (7th ed.). Belmont, CA: Brooks/Cole.

Crowther, M. R., Scogin, F., & Norton, M. J. (2010). Treating the ages in rural communities: The application of cognitive-behavior therapy for depression. *Journal of Clinical Psychology, 66,* 502–512. doi:10.1002/jclp.20678

Cuijpers, P., van Straten, A., Smit, F., Mihalopoulos, C., & Beekman, A. (2008). Preventing the onset of depressive disorders: A meta-analytic review of psychological interventions. *American Journal of Psychiatry, 165,* 1272–1280. doi:10.1176/appi.ajp.2008.07091422

Cukrowicz, K. C., Duberstein, P. R., Vannoy, S. D., Lynch, T. R., McQuoid, D. R., & Steffens, D. C. (2009). Course of suicide ideation and predictors of change in depressed older adults. *Journal of Affective Disorders, 113,* 30–36. doi:10.1016/j.jad.2008.05.012

de Coster, L., Leentjens, A. G., Lodder, J., & Verhey, F. J. (2005). The sensitivity of somatic symptoms in post-stroke depression: A discriminant analytic approach. *International Journal of Geriatric Psychiatry, 20,* 358–362. doi:10.1002/gps.1290

de Mello, M. F., de Jesus Mari, J., Bacaltchuk, J., Verdeli, H., & Neugebauer, R. (2005). A systematic review of research findings on the efficacy of interpersonal therapy for depressive disorders. *European Archives of Psychiatry and Clinical Neuroscience, 255,* 75–82. doi:10.1007/s00406-004-0542-x

Dimidjian, S., Barrera, M., Jr., Martell, C., Muñoz, R. F., & Lewinsohn, P. M. (2011). The origins and current status of behavioral activation treatments for depression. *Annual Review of Clinical Psychology, 7,* 1–38. doi:10.1146/annurev-clinpsy-032210-104535

Disabato, B. M., & Sheline, Y. I. (2012). Biological basis of late life depression. *Current Psychiatry Reports, 14,* 273–279. doi:10.1016/0146-6402(84)90007-9

Dozeman, E., van Marwijk, H. W. J., van Schaik, D. J. F., Smit, F., Stek, M. L., van der Horst, H. E., . . . Beekman, A. T. F. (2012). Contradictory effects for prevention of depression and anxiety in residents in homes for the elderly: A pragmatic randomized controlled trial. *International Psychogeriatrics, 24,* 1242–1251. doi:10.1017/S1041610212000178

Driscoll, H. C., Basinski, J., Mulsant, B. H., Butters, M. A., Dew, M. A., Houck, P. R., . . . Reynolds, C. F. (2005). Late-onset major depression: Clinical and treatment-response variability. *International Journal of Geriatric Psychiatry, 20,* 661–667. doi:10.1002/gps.1334

Duberstein, P. R., & Heisel, M. J. (2007). Personality traits and the reporting of affective disorder symptoms in depressed patients. *Journal of Affective Disorders, 103,* 165–171. doi:10.1016/j.jad.2007.01.025

Eaton, W. W., Smith, C., Ybarra, M., Muntaner, C., & Tien, A. (2004). Center for Epidemiologic Studies Depression Scale: Review and Revision (CESD and CESD-R). In M. E. Maruish (Ed.), *The use of psychological testing for treatment planning and outcomes assessment: Vol. 3. Instruments for adults* (3rd ed.; pp. 363–377). Mahwah, NJ: Erlbaum.

Edelstein, B., Drozdick, L., & Ciliberti, C. (2010). Assessment of depression and bereavement in older adults. In P. Lichtenberg (Ed.), *Handbook on geriatric assessment* (2nd ed., pp. 337–351). New York, NY: Wiley. doi:10.1016/B978-0-12-374961-1.10001-6

Edelstein, B. A., Woodhead, E. L., Bower, E. H., & Lowery, A. H. (2006). Evaluating older adults. In M. Hersen (Ed.), *Clinician's handbook of adult behavioral assessment* (pp. 497–527). New York, NY: Academic Press. doi:10.1016/B978-012343013-7/50022-7

Eid, M., & Diener, E. (Eds.). (2006). *Handbook of multimethod measurement in psychology.* Washington, DC: American Psychological Association. doi:10.1037/11383-000

Elvins, R., & Green, J. (2008). The conceptualization and measurement of therapeutic alliance: An empirical review. *Clinical Psychology Review, 28,* 1167–1187. doi:10.1016/j.cpr.2008.04.002

Emery, C. F., & Gatz, M. (1990). Psychological and cognitive effects of an exercise program for community-residing older adults. *Gerontologist, 30,* 184–188. doi:10.1093/geront/30.2.184

Endicott, J., & Spitzer, R. L. (1978). A diagnostic interview. The schedule for affective disorders and schizophrenia. *Archives of General Psychiatry, 35,* 837–844. doi:10.1001/archpsyc.1978.01770310043002

Erikson, E. H. (1950). Growth and crises of the healthy personality. In M. E. Senn (Ed.), *Symposium on the healthy personality* (pp. 91–146). Oxford, England: Josiah Macy, Jr. Foundation.

First, M. B., Spitzer, R. L., Gibbon, M., & Williams, J. B. W. (1997). *User's guide for the Structured Clinical Interview for DSM–IV Axis I Disorder—Clinician Version (SCID–CV).* Washington, DC: American Psychiatric Press.

Fischer, L., Rolnick, S. J., Jackson, J., Garrard, J., & Luepke, L. (1996). The Geriatric Depression Scale: A content analysis of respondent comments. *Journal of Mental Health and Aging, 2,* 125–135.

Fiske, A., Gatz, M., & Pedersen, N. L. (2003). Depressive symptoms and aging: The effects of illness and non-health-related events. *The Journals of Gerontology, Series B: Psychological Sciences and Social Sciences, 58,* 320–328. doi:10.1093/geronb/58.6.P320

Fiske, A., Wetherell, J. L., & Gatz, M. (2009). Depression in older adults. *Annual Review of Clinical Psychology, 5,* 363–389. doi:10.1146/annurev.clinpsy.032408.153621

Floyd, M., Rohen, N., Shackelford, J. A., Hubbard, K. L., Parnell, M. B., Scogin, F., & Coates, A. (2006). Two-year follow-up of bibliotherapy and individual cognitive therapy for depressed older adults. *Behavior Modification, 30,* 281–294. doi:10.1177/0145445503261176

Floyd, M., Scogin, F., McKendree-Smith, N. L., Floyd, D. L., & Rokke, P. D. (2004). Cognitive therapy for depression: A comparison of individual psychotherapy and bibliotherapy for depressed older adults. *Behavior Modification, 28,* 297–318. doi:10.1177/0145445503259284

Fountoulakis, K., Iacovides, A., Grammaticos, P., St Kaprinis, G., & Bech, P. (2004). Thyroid function in clinical subtypes of major depression: An exploratory study. *BMC Psychiatry, 4,* 6. doi:10.1186/1471-244X-4-6

Fountoulakis, K. N., O'Hara, R. O., Iacovides, A., Camilleri, C. P., Kaprinis, S., Kaprinis, G., & Yesavage, J. (2003). Unipolar late-onset depression: A comprehensive review. *Annals of General Hospital Psychiatry, 2*(11). doi:10.1186/1475-2832-2-11

Fredriksen-Goldsen, K. I., Kim, H. J., Emlet, C. A., Muraco, A., Erosheva, E. A., Hoy-Ellis, C. P., . . . Petry, H. (2011). *The aging and health report: Disparities and resilience among lesbian, gay, bisexual, and transgender older adults.* Seattle, WA: Institute for Multigenerational Health. Retrieved from http://caringandaging.org/wordpress/wp-content/uploads/2012/10/Full-report10-25-12.pdf

Friedlander, A., Nazem, S., Fiske, A., Nadorff, M. R., & Smith, M. D. (2012). Self-concealment and suicidal behaviors. *Suicide and Life-Threatening Behavior, 42,* 332–340. doi:10.1111/j.1943-278X.2012.00094.x

Fuentes, D., & Aranda, M. P. (2012). Depression interventions among racial and ethnic minority older adults: A systematic review across 20 years. *American Journal of Geriatric Psychiatry, 20,* 915–931. doi:10.1097/JGP.0b013e31825d091a

Furukawa, T. A., Streiner, D. L., & Young, L. T. (2001). Is antidepressant–benzodiazepine combination therapy clinically more useful? A meta-analytic study. *Journal of Affective Disorders, 65,* 173–177. doi:10.1016/S0165-0327(00)00254-8

Gaboda, D., Lucas, J., Siegel, M., Kalay, E., & Crystal, S. (2011). No longer undertreated? Depression diagnosis and antidepressant therapy in elderly long-stay nursing home residents, 1999 to 2007. *Journal of the American Geriatrics Society, 59,* 673–680. doi:10.1111/j.1532-5415.2011.03322.x

Gallagher, D., Mhaolain, A. N., Greene, E., Walsh, C., Denihan, A., Bruce, I., . . . Lawlor, B. A. (2010). Late life depression: A comparison of risk factors and symptoms according to age of onset in community dwelling older adults. *International Journal of Geriatric Psychiatry, 25,* 981–987. doi:10.1002/gps.2438

Gallagher, D. E., & Thompson, L. W. (1982). Treatment of major depressive disorder in older adult outpatients with brief psychotherapies. *Psychotherapy: Theory, Research, Practice, Training, 19,* 482–490. doi:10.1037/h0088461

Gallagher-Thompson, D., & Steffen, A. M. (1994). Comparative effects of cognitive-behavioral and brief psychodynamic psychotherapies for depressed family caregivers. *Journal of Consulting and Clinical Psychology, 62,* 543–549. doi:10.1037/0022-006X.62.3.543

Gallo, J. J., Rabins, P. V., & Anthony, J. C. (1999). Sadness in older persons: 13-year follow-up of a community sample in Baltimore, Maryland. *Psychological Medicine, 29,* 341–350. doi:10.1017/S0033291798008083

Gallo, J. J., Rabins, P. V., Lyketsos, C. G., Tien, A. Y., & Anthony, J. C. (1997). Depression without sadness: Functional outcomes of nondysphoric depression in later life. *Journal of the American Geriatrics Society, 45,* 570–578.

Gatz, M., Johansson, B., Pedersen, N., Berg, S., & Reynolds, C. (1993). A cross-national self-report measure of depressive symptomatology. *International Psychogeriatrics, 5,* 147–156. doi:10.1017/S1041610293001486

Gellis, Z. D., & Bruce, M. L. (2010). Problem-solving therapy for subthreshold depression in home health-care patients with cardiovascular disease. *American Journal of Geriatric Psychiatry, 18,* 464–474. doi:10.1097/JGP.0b013e3181b21442

Gellis, Z. D., McGinty, J., Horowitz, A., Bruce, M. L., & Misener, E. (2007). Problem-solving therapy for late-life depression in home care: A randomized field trial. *American Journal of Geriatric Psychiatry, 15,* 968–978. doi:10.1097/JGP.0b013e3180cc2bd7

Gellis, Z. D., McGinty, J., Tierney, L., Jordan, C., Burton, J., & Misener, E. (2008). Randomized controlled trial of problem-solving therapy for minor depression in home care. *Research on Social Work Practice, 18,* 596–606. doi:10.1177/1049731507309821

Goldwasser, A. N., Auerbach, S. M., & Harkins, S. W. (1987). Cognitive, affective, and behavioral effects of reminiscence group therapy on demented elderly. *International Journal of Aging and Human Development, 25,* 209–222. doi:10.2190/8UX8-68VC-RDYF-VK4F

Gregg, J. J., Fiske, A., & Gatz, M. (2013). Physicians' detection of late-life depression: The roles of dysphoria and cognitive impairment. *Aging and Mental Health, 17,* 1030–1036. doi:10.1080/13607863.2013.805403

Grossman, A. H., D'Augelli, A. R., & O'Connell, T. S. (2002). Being lesbian, bay, bisexual, and 60 or older in North America. *Journal of Gay and Lesbian Social Services, 13,* 23–40. doi:10.1300/J041v13n04_05

Gruenberg, A. M., Goldstein, R. D., & Pincus, H. A. (2005). Classification of depression: Research and diagnostic criteria: *DSM–IV* and *ICD–10.* In J. Licinio & M. Wong (Eds.), *Biology of depression: From novel insights to therapeutic strategies* (pp. 1–12). Weinheim, Germany: Wiley. doi:10.1002/9783527619672.ch1

Gum, A. M., Arean, P. A., Tang, L., Katon, W., Hitchcock, P., Steffens, D. C., . . . Unutzer, J. (2006). Depression treatment preferences in older primary care patients. *Gerontologist, 46,* 14–22. doi:10.1093/geront/46.1.14

Gum, A. M., King-Kallimanis, B, & Kohn, R. (2009). Prevalence of mood, anxiety, and substance-abuse disorders for older Americans in the national comorbidity survey-replication. *American Journal of Geriatric Psychiatry, 17,* 769–781. doi:10.1097/JGP.0b013e3181ad4f5a.

Haight, B. K., Bachman, D. L., Hendrix, S., Wagner, M. T., Meeks, A., & Johnson, J. (2003). Life review: Treating the dyadic family unit with dementia. *Clinical Psychology and Psychotherapy, 10,* 165–174. doi:10.1002/cpp.367

Hamilton, M. (1960). A rating scale for depression. *Journal of Neurology, Neurosurgery, and Psychiatry, 23,* 56–62. doi:10.1136/jnnp.23.1.56

Hammond, M. F. (1998). Rating depression severity in the elderly physically ill patient: Reliability and factor structure of the Hamiltor and the Montgomery–Åsberg Depression Rating Scales. *International Journal of Geriatric Psychiatry, 13,* 257–261. doi:10.1002/(SICI)1099-1166(199804)13:4<257::AID-GPS773>3.0.CO;2-U

Hanlon, J. T., Handler, S. M., & Castle, N. G. (2010). Antidepressant prescribing in US nursing homes between 1996 and 2006 and its relationship to staffing patterns and use of other psychotropic medications. *Journal of the American Medical Directors Association, 11,* 320–324. doi:10.1016/j.jamda.2010.01.007

Haringsma, R., Engels, G. I., Beekman, A. F., & Spinhoven, P. h. (2004). The criterion validity of the Center for Epidemiological Studies Depression Scale (CES–D) in a sample of self-referred elders with depressive symptomatology. *International Journal of Geriatric Psychiatry, 19,* 558–563. doi:10.1002/gps.1130

Haringsma, R., Engels, G. I., Cuijpers, P., & Spinhoven, P. (2006). Effectiveness of the Coping With Depression (CWD) course for older adults provided by the community-based mental health care system in the Netherlands: A randomized controlled field trial. *International Psychogeriatrics, 18,* 307–326. doi:10.1017/S104161020500253X

Hegel, M. T., Imming, J., Cyr-Provost, M., Noel, P., Arean, P. A., & Unutzer, J. (2002). Role of behavioral health professionals in a collaborative stepped care treatment model for depression in primary care: Project IMPACT. *Families, Systems, and Health, 20,* 265–277. doi:10.1037/h0089475

Hegeman, J. M., Kok, R. M., van der Mast, R. C., & Giltay, E. J. (2012). Phenomenology of depression in older compared with younger adults: Meta-analysis. *British Journal of Psychiatry, 200,* 275–281. doi:10.1192/bjp.bp.111.095950

Hickie, I., Naismith, S., Ward, P. B., Turner, K., Scott, E., Mitchell, P., . . . Parker, G. (2005). Reduced hippocampal volumes and memory loss in patients with early- and late-onset depression. *British Journal of Psychiatry, 186,* 197–202. doi:10.1192/bjp.186.3.197

Hindi, F., Dew, M. A., Albert, S. M., Lotrich, F. E., & Reynolds, C. F., III. (2011). Preventing depression in later life: State of the art and science circa 2011. *Psychiatric Clinics of North America, 34,* 67–78. doi:10.1016/j.psc.2010.11.008

Hinrichsen, G. A. (2008). Interpersonal psychotherapy as a treatment for depression in later life. *Professional Psychology: Research and Practice, 39,* 306–312. doi:10.1037/0735-7028.39.3.306

Hinton, L., Zweifach, M., Oishi, S., Tang, L., & Unützer, J. (2006). Gender disparities in the treatment of late-life depression: Qualitative and quantitative findings from the IMPACT trial. *American Journal of Geriatric Psychiatry, 14,* 884–892. doi:10.1097/01.JGP.0000219282.32915.a4

Hsu, Y. C., & Wang, J. J. (2009). Physical, affective, and behavioral effects of group reminiscence on depressed institutionalized elders in Taiwan. *Nursing Research, 58,* 294–299. doi:10.1097/NNR.0b013e3181a308ee

Hybels, C. F., Landerman, L. R., & Blazer, D. G. (2012). Age differences in symptom expression in patients with major depression. *International Journal of Geriatric Psychiatry, 27,* 601–611. doi:10.1002/gps.2759

Jefferson, A. L., Powers, D. V., & Pope, M. (2001). Beck Depression Inventory—II (BDI–II) and the Geriatric Depression Scale (GDS) in older women. *Clinical Gerontologist, 22,* 3–12. doi:10.1300/J018v22n03_02

Jellinger, K. A. (2013). The organic bases of late-life depression: A critical update. *Journal of Neural Transmission, 120,* 1109–1125. doi:10.1007.S00702-012-0945-1

Jha, A., Tabet, N., & Orrell, M. (2001). To tell or not to tell—Comparison of older patients' reaction to their diagnosis of dementia and depression. *International Journal of Geriatric Psychiatry, 16,* 879–885. doi:10.1002/gps.412

Kaji, T., Mishima, K., Kitamura, S., Enomoto, M., Hagase, Y., Li, L., . . . Uchiyama, M. (2010). Relationship between late-life depression and life stressors: Large-scale cross-sectional study of a representative sample of the Japanese general population. *Psychiatry and Clinical Neurosciences, 64,* 426–434. doi:10.1111/j.1440-1819.2010.02097.x

Karg, K., Burmeister, M., Shedden, K., & Sen, S. (2011). The serotonin transporter promoter variant (5-HTTLPR), stress, and depression meta-analysis revisited: Evidence of genetic moderation. *Archives of General Psychiatry, 68,* 444–454. doi:10.1001/archgenpsychiatry.2010.189

Karimi, H., Dolatshahee, B., Momeni, K., Khodabakhshi, A., Rezaei, M., & Kamrani, A. A. (2010). Effectiveness of integrative and instrumental reminiscence therapies on depression symptoms reduction in institutionalized older adults: An empirical study. *Aging and Mental Health, 14,* 881–887. doi:10.1080/13607861003801037

Karlin, B. E., Duffy, M., & Gleaves, D. H. (2008). Patterns and predictors of mental health service use and mental illness among older and younger adults in the United States. *Psychological Services, 5,* 275–294. doi:10.1037/1541-1559.5.3.275

Katon, W., & Ciechanowski, P. (2002). Impact of major depression on chronic medical illness. *Journal of Psychosomatic Research, 53,* 859–863. doi:10.1016/S0022-3999(02)00313-6

Kellner, C. H., Knapp, R., Husain, M. M., Rasmussen, K., Sampson, S., Cullum, M., . . . Petrides, G. (2010). Bifrontal, bitemporal and right unilateral electrode placement in ECT: Randomised trial. *British Journal of Psychiatry, 196,* 226–234. doi:10.1192/bjp.bp.109.066183

Kessler, R. C., Birnbaum, H., Bromet, E., Hwang, I., Sampson, N., & Shahly, V. (2010). Age differences in major depression: Results from the National Comorbidity Survey Replication (NCS-R). *Psychological Medicine, 40,* 225–237. doi:10.1017/S0033291709990213

Kieffer, K. M., & Reese, R. J. (2002). A reliability generalization study of the Geriatric Depression Scale. *Educational and Psychological Measurement, 62,* 969–994. doi:10.1177/0013164402238085

Kiosses, D. N., Leon, A. C., & Areán, P. A. (2011). Psychosocial interventions for late-life major depression: Evidence-based treatments, predictors of treatment outcomes, and moderators of treatment effects. *Psychiatric Clinics of North America, 34,* 377–401. doi:10.1016/j.psc.2011.03.001

Kirmayer, L. J. (2001). Cultural variations in the clinical presentation of depression and anxiety: Implications for diagnosis and treatment. *Journal of Clinical Psychiatry, 62,* 22–28.

Klausner, E. J., Clarkin, J. F., Spielman, L., Pupo, C., Abrams, R., & Alexopoulos, G. S. (1998). Late-life depression and functional disability: The role of goal-focused group psychotherapy. *International Journal of Geriatric Psychiatry, 13,* 707–716. doi:10.1002/(SICI)1099-1166(1998100)13:10<707::AID-GPS856>3.0.CO;2-Q

Klein, D. N., Kotov, R., & Bufferd, S. J. (2011). Personality and depression: Explanatory models and review of the evidence. *Annual Review of Clinical Psychology, 7,* 269–295. doi:10.1146/annurev-clinpsy-032210-104540

Knapskog, A. B., Barca, M. L., & Engedal, K. (2013). A Comparison of the Cornell Scale for Depression in Dementia and the Montgomery-Åsberg Depression Rating Scale in a memory clinic population. *Dementia and Geriatric Cognitive Disorders, 35,* 256–265. doi:10.1159/000348345

Knight, B. G., & Satre, D. D. (1999). Cognitive behavioral psychotherapy with older adults. *Clinical Psychology: Science and Practice, 6,* 188–203. doi:10.1093/clipsy.6.2.188

Köhler, S., Thomas, A. J., Barnett, N.A., & O'Brien, J. T. (2010). The pattern and course of cognitive impairment in late-life depression. *Psychological Medicine, 40,* 591–602. doi:10.1017/S0033291709990833.

Kørner, A., Lauritzen, L., Abelskov, K., Gulmann, N., Brodersen, A., Wedervang, T., & Kjeldgaard, K. (2006). The Geriatric Depression Scale and the Cornell Scale for Depression in Dementia. A validity study. *Nordic Journal of Psychiatry, 60,* 360–364. doi:10.1080/08039480600937066

Kouwenhoven, S. E., Kirkevold, M., Engedal, K., & Kim, H. S. (2011). Depression in acute stroke: Prevalence, dominant symptoms and associated factors. A systematic literature review. *Disability and Rehabilitation, 33,* 539–556. doi:10.3109/09638288.2010.505997

Krishnan, K. R., Taylor, W. D., McQuoid, D. R., MacFall, J. R., Payne, M. E., Provenzale, J. M., & Steffens, D. C. (2004). Clinical characteristics of magnetic resonance imaging-defined subcortical ischemic depression. *Biological Psychiatry, 55,* 390–397. doi:10.1016/j.biopsych.2003.08.014

Krishnan, V., & Nestler, E. J. (2010). Linking molecules to mood: New insight into the biology of depression. *American Journal of Psychiatry, 167,* 1305–1320. doi:10.1176/appi.ajp.2009.10030434

Kroenke, K., Spitzer, R. L., & Williams, J. B. (2001). The PHQ-9. *Journal of General Internal Medicine, 16,* 606–613. doi:10.1046/j.1525-1497.2001.016009606.x

Kroenke, K., Spitzer, R. L., & Williams, J. B. (2003). The Patient Health Questionnaire—2: Validity of a two-item depression screener. *Medical Care, 41,* 1284–1292. doi:10.1097/01.MLR.0000093487.78664.3C

Kroenke, K., Spitzer, R. L., Williams, J. B., & Löwe, B. (2010). The patient health questionnaire somatic, anxiety, and depressive symptom scales: A systematic review. *General Hospital Psychiatry, 32,* 345–359. doi:10.1016/j.genhosppsych.2010.03.006

Kupfer, D. J., Kuhl, E. A., & Regier, D. A. (2013). *DSM–5*—The future arrived. *JAMA.* doi:10.1001/jama.2013.2298

Laidlaw, K., Davidson, K., Toner, H., Jackson, G., Clark, S., Law, J., . . . Cross, S. (2008). A randomised controlled trial of cognitive behaviour therapy vs treatment as usual in the treatment of mild to moderate late life depression. *International Journal of Geriatric Psychiatry, 23,* 843–850. doi:10.1002/gps.1993

Landreville, P., & Bissonnette, L. (1997). Effects of cognitive bibliotherapy for depressed older adults with a disability. *Clinical Gerontologist, 17,* 35–55. doi:10.1300/J018v17n04_05

Lee, C. T., Leoutsakos, J., Lyketsos, C. G., Steffens, D. C., Breitner, J. C., & Norton, M. C. (2012). Latent class-derived subgroups of depressive symptoms in a community sample of older adults: The Cache County Study. *International Journal of Geriatric Psychiatry, 27,* 1061–1069. doi:10.1002/gps.2824

Leentjens, A. F. G., Verhey, F. J., Lousberg, R., Spitsbergen, H., & Wilmink, F. W. (2000). The validity of the Hamilton and Montgomery–Åsberg depression rating scales as screening and diagnostic tools for depression in Parkinson's disease. *International Journal of Geriatric Psychiatry, 15,* 644–649. doi:10.1002/1099-1166(200007)15:7<644::AID-GPS167>3.0.CO;2-L

Leichsenring, F., Rabung, S., & Leibing, E. (2004). The efficacy of short-term psychodynamic psychotherapy in specific psychiatric disorders: A meta-analysis. *Archives of General Psychiatry, 61,* 1208–1216. doi:10.1001/archpsyc.61.12.1208

Leontjevas, R., Gerritsen, D. L., Vernooij-Dassen, M. J., Smalbrugge, M., & Koopmans, R. T. (2012). Comparative validation of proxy-based Montgomery-Åsberg Depression Rating Scale and Cornell Scale for Depression in Dementia in nursing home residents with dementia. *American Journal of Geriatric Psychiatry, 20,* 985–993. doi:10.1097/JGP.0b013e318233152b

Lewinsohn, P. M., Munoz, R. F., Youngren, M. A., & Zeiss, A. M. (1986). *Control your depression.* New York, NY: Prentice-Hall.

Lewinsohn, P. M., Seeley, J. R., Roberts, R. E., & Allen, N. B. (1997). Center for Epidemiologic Studies Depression Scale (CES–D) as a screening instrument for depression among community-residing older adults. *Psychology and Aging, 12,* 277–287. doi:10.1037/0882-7974.12.2.277

Li, C., Friedman, B., Conwell, Y., & Fiscella, K. (2007). Validity of the Patient Health Questionnaire—2 (PHQ–2) in identifying major depression in older people. *Journal of the American Geriatrics Society, 55,* 596–602. doi:10.1111/j.1532-5415.2007.01103.x

Li, H., Proctor, E., & Morrow-Howell, N. (2005). Outpatient mental health service use by older adults after acute psychiatric hospitalization. *Journal of Behavioral Health Services and Research, 32,* 74–84. doi:10.1007/BF02287329

Lichtenberg, P. A., Kimbarow, M. L., Morris, P., & Vangel, S. J., Jr. (1996). Behavioral treatment of depression in predominantly African-American medical patients. *Clinical Gerontologist, 17,* 15–33. doi:10.1300/J018v17n02_03

Licht-Strunk, E., Beekman, A., de Haan, M., & van Marwijk, H. (2009). The prognosis of undetected depression in older general practice patients. A one year follow-up study. *Journal of Affective Disorders, 114,* 310–315. doi:10.1016/j.jad.2008.06.006

Linden, D. E. J. (2006). How psychotherapy changes the brain—The contribution of functional neuroimaging. *Molecular Psychiatry, 11,* 528–538. doi:10.1038/sj.mp.4001816

Liu, R. T., & Alloy, L. B. (2010). Stress generation in depression: A systematic review of the empirical literature and recommendations for future study. *Clinical Psychology Review, 30,* 582–593. doi:10.1016/j.cpr.2010.04.010

Logsdon, R. S., McCurry, S. M., & Teri, L. (2008). Assessment and treatment of dementia-related affective disturbances. In K. Laidlaw & B. Knight (Eds.), *Handbook of emotional disorders in later life: Assessment and treatment* (pp. 345–362). New York, NY: Oxford University Press.

Lopez, O. L., Becker, J. T., Sweet, R. A., Klunk, W., Kaufer, D. I., Saxton, J., . . . DeKosky, S. T. (2003). Psychiatric symptoms vary with the severity of dementia in probable Alzheimer's Disease. *Journal of Neuropsychiatry and Clinical Neurosciences, 15,* 346–353. doi:10.1176/appi.neuropsych.15.3.346

Lynch, J., & Kilmartin, C. T. (1999). *The pain behind the mask: Overcoming masculine depression.* Binghamton, NY: Haworth.

Margrett, J., Jartin, P., Woodard, J. L., Miller, L. S., McDonald, M., Baenziger, J., . . . Poon, L. (2010). Depression among centenarians and the oldest old: Contributions of cognition and personality. *Gerontology, 56,* 93–99. doi:10.1159/000272018

Marin, H., & Escobar, J. I. (2007). Issues in the diagnosis and assessment of mood disorders in minorities. In

S. Loue & M. Sajatovic (Eds.), *Diversity issues in the diagnosis, treatment and research of mood disorders* (pp. 17–31). New York, NY: Oxford University Press.

Marsh, L., McDonald, W. M., Cummings, J., & Ravina, B., & the NINDS/NIMH Work Group on Depression and Parkinson's Disease. (2006). Provisional diagnostic criteria for depression in Parkinson's disease: Report of an NINDS/NIMH Work Group. *Movement Disorders, 21,* 148–158. doi:10.1002/mds.20723

Marty, M. A., Pepin, R., June, A., & Segal, D. L. (2011). Geriatric Depression Scale. In M. T. Abou-Saleh, C. L. E. Katona, & A. Kumar (Eds.), *Principles and practice of geriatric psychiatry* (3rd ed., pp. 152–156). New York, NY: Wiley.

Mather, A. S., Rodriguez, C., Guthrie, M. F., McHarg, A. M., Reid, I. C., & McMurdo, M. E. (2002). Effects of exercise on depressive symptoms in older adults with poorly responsive depressive disorder Randomised controlled trial. *British Journal of Psychiatry, 180,* 411–415. doi:10.1192/bjp.180.5.411

McMurdo, M. E. T., & Burnett, L. (1992). Randomised controlled trial of exercise in the elderly. *Gerontology, 38,* 292–298. doi:10.1159/000213343

Meeks, S., Looney, S. W., Van Haitsma, K., & Teri, L. (2008). BE-ACTIV: A staff-assisted behavioral intervention for depression in nursing homes. *Gerontologist, 48,* 105–114. doi:10.1093/geront/48.1.105

Meeks, T. W., Dunn, L. B., Kim, D. S., Golshan, S., Sewell, D. D., Atkinson, J. H., & Lebowitz, B. D. (2008). Chronic pain and depression among geriatric psychiatry inpatients. *International Journal of Geriatric Psychiatry, 23,* 637–642. doi:10.1002/gps.1954

Meeks, T. W., Vahia, I. V., Lavretsky, H., Kulkarni, G., & Jeste, D. V. (2011). A tune in "a minor" can "be major": A review of epidemiology, illness course, and public health implications of subthreshold depression in older adults. *Journal of Affective Disorders, 129,* 126–142. doi:10.1016/j.jad.2010.09.015

Mehta, K. M., Yaffe, K., Langa, K. M., Sands, L., Whooley, M. A., & Covinsky, K. E. (2003). Additive effects of cognitive function and depressive symptoms on mortality in elderly community-living adults. *The Journals of Gerontology, Series A: Biological Sciences and Medical Sciences, 58,* 461–467. doi:10.1093/gerona/58.5.M461

Miller, M. D., Reynolds, C. F., III, Gildengers, A., Whyte, E. M., & Andreescu, C. (2013). Late-life depression: Evidence-based treatment. In M. D. Miller & L. K. Solai (Eds.), *Geriatric psychiatry* (pp. 195–218). New York, NY: Oxford University Press.

Mitchell, A. J., Bird, V., Rizzo, M., & Meader, N. (2010). Which version of the Geriatric Depression Scale is most useful in medical settings and nursing homes? Diagnostic validity meta-analysis. *American Journal*

of Geriatric Psychiatry, 18, 1066–1077. doi:10.1097/JGP.0b013e3181f60f81

Mitchell, A. J., Rao, S., & Vaze, A. (2010). Do primary care physicians have particular difficulty identifying late-life depression? A meta-analysis stratified by age. *Psychotherapy and Psychosomatics, 79,* 285–294. doi:10.1159/000318295

Mohlman, J., Sirota, K. G., Papp, L. A., Staples, A. M., King, A., & Gorenstein, E. E. (2012). Clinical interviewing with older adults. *Cognitive and Behavioral Practice, 19,* 89–100. doi:10.1016/j.cbpra.2010.10.001

Montgomery, S. A., & Åsberg, M. (1979). A new depression scale designed to be sensitive to change. *British Journal of Psychiatry, 134,* 382–389. doi:10.1192/bjp.134.4.382

Nahas, Z., Li, X., Kozel, F. A., Mirzki, D., Memon, M., Miller, K., . . . George, M. S. (2004). Safety and benefits of distance-adjusted prefrontal transcranial magnetic stimulation in depressed patients 55–75 years of age: A pilot study. *Depression and Anxiety, 19,* 249–256. doi:10.1002/da.20015

Naismith, S. L., Norrie, L. M., Mowscowski, L., & Hickie, I. B. (2012). The neurobiology of depression in later-life: Clinical, neuropsychological, neuroimaging, and pathophysiological features. *Progress in Neurobiology, 98,* 99–143. doi:10.1016/j.pneurobio.2012.05.009

Narushima, K., McCormick, L., Yamada, T., Thatcher, R., & Robinson, R. (2010). Subgenual cingulate theta activity predicts treatment response of repetitive transcranial magnetic stimulation in participants with vascular depression. *Journal of Neuropsychiatry and Clinical Neurosciences, 22,* 75–84. doi:10.1176/appi.neuropsych.22.1.75

Nasreddine, Z. S., Phillips, N. A., Bédirian, V., Charbonneau, S., Whitehead, V., Collin, I., . . . Chertkow, H. (2005). The Montreal Cognitive Assessment, MoCA: A brief screening tool for mild cognitive impairment. *Journal of the American Geriatrics Society, 53,* 695–699. doi:10.1111/j.1532-5415.2005.53221.x

National Institute for Health and Clinical Excellence. (2009). *Depression in adults: The treatment and management of depression in adults.* Retrieved from http://www.nice.org.uk/guidance/CG90/chapter/1-Guidance#continuation-and-relapse-prevention

Nelson, J. C., Delucchi, K., & Schneider, L. S. (2008). Efficacy of second generation antidepressants in late-life depression: A meta-analysis of the evidence. *American Journal of Geriatric Psychiatry, 16,* 558–567. doi:10.1097/01.JGP.0000308883.64832.ed

Nelson, J. C., Delucchi, K. L., & Schneider, L. S. (2013). Moderators of outcome in late-life depression: A patient-level meta-analysis. *American Journal of Psychiatry, 170,* 651–659. doi:10.1176/appi.ajp.2012.12070927

Newman, S. C., Sheldon, C. T., & Bland, R. C. (1998). Prevalence of depression in an elderly community sample: A comparison of GMS-AGECAT and *DSM–IV* diagnostic criteria. *Psychological Medicine, 28*, 1339–1345. doi:10.1017/S0033291798007442

Newmann, J. P., Engel, R. J., & Jensen, J. E. (1991). Age differences in depressive symptoms experiences. *Journal of Gerontology, 46*, P224–P235. doi:10.1093/geronj/46.5.P224

Nguyen, H. T., & Zonderman, A. B. (2006). Relationship between age and aspects of depression: Consistency and reliability across two longitudinal studies. *Psychology and Aging, 21*, 119–126. doi:10.1037/0882-7974.21.1.119

O'Connor, M. K., Knapp, R., Husain, M., Rummans, T. A., Petrides, G., Smith, G., . . . Kellner, C. (2001). The influence of age on the response of major depression to electroconvulsive therapy: A CORE Report. *American Journal of Geriatric Psychiatry, 9*, 382–390. doi:10.1097/00019442-200111000-00006

Olin, J. T., Schneider, L. S., Eaton, E. M., Zemansky, M. F., & Pollock, V. E. (1992). The Geriatric Depression Scale and the Beck Depression Inventory as screening instruments in an older adult outpatient population. *Psychological Assessment, 4*, 190–192. doi:10.1037/1040-3590.4.2.190

Olin, J. T., Schneider, L. S., Katz, I. R., Meyers, B. S., Alexopoulos, G. S., Breitner, J. C., . . . Lebowitz, B. D. (2002). Provisional diagnostic criteria for depression of Alzheimer disease. *American Journal of Geriatric Psychiatry, 10*, 125–128. doi:10.1097/00019442-200203000-00003

O'Sullivan, R. L., Fava, M. M., Agustin, C. C., Baer, L. L., & Rosenbaum, J. F. (1997). Sensitivity of the six-item Hamilton Depression Rating Scale. *Acta Psychiatrica Scandinavica, 95*, 379–384. doi:10.1111/j.1600-0447.1997.tb09649.x

Ott, B. R., & Fogel, B. S. (1992). Measurement of depression in dementia: Self vs clinician rating. *International Journal of Geriatric Psychiatry, 7*, 899–904. doi:10.1002/gps.930071209

Pariante, C. M., & Lightman, S. L. (2008). The HPA axis in major depression: Classical theories and new developments. *Trends in Neurosciences, 31*, 464–468. doi:10.1016/j.tins.2008.06.006

Park, J. H., Lee, S. B., Lee, T. J., Jhoo, J. H., Youn, J. C., Choo, I. H., . . . Kim, K. W. (2007). Depression in vascular dementia is quantitatively and qualitatively different from depression in Alzheimer's disease. *Dementia and Geriatric Cognitive Disorders, 23*, 67–73. doi:10.1159/000097039

Park, M., & Unützer, J. (2011). Geriatric depression in primary care. *Psychiatric Clinics of North America, 34*, 469–487. doi:10.1016/j.psc.2011.02.009

Penninx, B. W., Rejeski, W. J., Pandya, J., Miller, M. E., Di Bari, M., Applegate, W. B., & Pahor, M. (2002). Exercise and depressive symptoms: A comparison of aerobic and resistance exercise effects on emotional and physical function in older persons with high and low depressive symptomatology. *The Journals of Gerontology, Series B: Psychological Sciences and Social Sciences, 57*, 124–132. doi:10.1093/geronb/57.2.P124

Pigeon, W. R., Hegel, M., Unutzer, J., Fan, M., Sateia, M. J., Lyness, J. M., . . . Perlis, M. L. (2008). Is insomnia a perpetuating factor for late-life depression in the IMPACT cohort? *Sleep: Journal of Sleep and Sleep Disorders Research, 31*, 481–488.

Pot, A. M., Bohlmeijer, E. T., Onrust, S., Melenhorst, A., Veerbeek, M., & De Vries, W. (2010). The impact of life review on depression in older adults: A randomized controlled trial. *International Psychogeriatrics, 22*, 572–581. doi:10.1017/S104161020999175X

Preschl, B., Maercker, A., Wagner, B., Forstmeier, S., Baños, R. M., Alcañiz, M., . . . Botella, C. (2012). Life-review therapy with computer supplements for depression in the elderly: A randomized controlled trial. *Aging and Mental Health, 16*, 964–974. doi:10.1080/13607863.2012.702726

Qualls, S. H., Segal, D. L., Norman, S., Niederehe, G., & Gallagher-Thompson, D. (2002). Psychologists in practice with older adults: Current patterns, sources of training, and need for continuing education. *Professional Psychology: Research and Practice, 33*, 435–442. doi:10.1037/0735-7028.33.5.435

Quelhas, R., & Costa, M. (2009). Anxiety, depression, and quality of life in Parkinson's disease. *Journal of Neuropsychiatry and Clinical Neurosciences, 21*, 413–419. doi:10.1176/appi.neuropsych.21.4.413

Radloff, L. S. (1977). The CES–D Scale: A self-report depression scale for research in the general population. *Applied Psychological Measurement, 1*, 385–401. doi:10.1177/014662167700100306

Rajji, T. K., Mulsant, B. H., Lotrich, F. E., Lokker, C., & Reynolds III, C. F. (2008). Use of antidepressants in late-life depression. *Drugs and Aging, 25*, 841–853. doi:1170-229X/08/0010-0841

Reynolds, C. F., III. (2009). Prevention of depressive disorders: A brave new world. *Depression and Anxiety, 26*, 1062–1065. doi:10.1002/da.20644

Reynolds, C. F., Cuijpers, P., Patel, V., Cohen, A., Dias, A., Chowdhary, N., . . . Albert, S. M. (2012). Early intervention to reduce the global health and economic burden of major depression in older adults. *Annual Review of Public Health, 33*, 123–135. doi:10.1146/annurev-publhealth-031811-124544

Reynolds, C. F., III, Dew, M. A., Pollock, B. G., Mulsant, B. H., Frank, E., Miller, M. D., . . . Kupfer, D. J. (2006). Maintenance treatment of major depression in old age. *New England Journal of Medicine, 354,* 1130–1138. doi:10.1056/NEJMoa052619

Reynolds, C. F., III, Frank, E., Perel, J. M., Imber, S. D., Cornes, C., Miller, M. D., . . . Kupfer, D. J. (1999). Nortriptyline and interpersonal psychotherapy as maintenance therapies for recurrent major depression. *JAMA, 281,* 39–45. doi:10.1001/jama.281.1.39

Reynolds, C. F., Miller, M. D., Pasternak, R. E., Frank, E., Perel, J. M., Cornes, C., . . . Kupfer, D. J. (1999). Treatment of bereavement-related major depressive episodes in later life: A controlled study of acute and continuation treatment with nortriptyline and interpersonal psychotherapy. *American Journal of Psychiatry, 156,* 202–208. doi:10.1001/jama.281.1.39

Rider, K. L., Gallagher-Thompson, D., & Thompson, L. W. (2004). *California older person's pleasant events schedule: Manual.* Retrieved from http://www. stanford.edu/group/oafc/Ken/Manual2.pdf

Riemann, D. (2009). Does effective management of sleep disorders reduce depressive symptoms and the risk of depression? *Drugs, 69*(Suppl. 2), 43–64. doi:10.2165/11531130-000000000-00000

Rokke, P. D., Tomhave, J. A., & Jocic, Z. (1999). The role of client choice and target selection in self-management therapy for depression in older adults. *Psychology and Aging, 14,* 155–169. doi:10.1037/0882-7974.14.1.155

Roose, S. P., & Devanand, D. P. (2013). Treatment of mood disorders in late life. In J. J. Mann, P. McGrath, & S. P. Roose (Eds.), *Clinical handbook for the management of mood disorders* (pp. 119–132). New York, NY: Cambridge University Press. doi:10.1017/CBO9781139175869.009

Rose, J. M., & DelMaestro, S. (1990). Separation-individuation conflict as a model for understanding distressed caregivers: Psychodynamic and cognitive case studies. *Gerontologist, 30,* 693–697. doi:10.1093/geront/30.5.693

Rovner, B. W., Casten, R. J., Hegel, M. T., Leiby, B. E., & Tasman, W. S. (2007). Preventing depression in age-related macular degeneration. *Archives of General Psychiatry, 64,* 886–892. doi:10.1001/archpsyc.64.8.886

Saliba, D., DiFilippo, S., Edelen, M. O., Kroenke, K., Buchanan, J., & Streim, J. (2012). Testing the PHQ–9 interview and observational versions (PHQ–9 OV) for MDS 3.0. *Journal of the American Medical Directors Association, 13,* 18–25. doi:10.1016/j.jamda.2012.06.003

Saliba, D., Jones, M., Streim, J., Ouslander, J., Berlowitz, D., & Buchanan, J. (2012). Overview of significant changes in the Minimum Data Set for nursing homes version 3.0. *Journal of the American Medical Directors Association, 13,* 595–601. doi:10.1016/j.jamda.2012.06.001

Salter, K. L., Foley, N. C., Zhu, L., Jutai, J. W., & Teasell, R. W. (2013). Prevention of poststroke depression: Does prophylactic pharmacotherapy work? *Journal of Stroke and Cerebrovascular Diseases, 22,* 1243–1251. doi:10.1016/j.jstrokecerebrovasdis.2012.03.013

Salzman, C., Wong, E., & Wright, B. C. (2002). Drug and ECT treatment of depression in the elderly, 1996–2001: A literature review. *Biological Psychiatry, 52,* 265–284. doi:10.1016/S0006-3223(02)01337-9

Satterfield, J. M., & Crabb, R. (2010). Cognitive-behavioral therapy for depression in an older gay man: A clinical case study. *Cognitive and Behavioral Practice, 17,* 45–55. doi.org/10.1016/j.cbpra.2009.04.008 doi:10.1016/j.cbpra.2009.04.008

Schein, R. L., & Koenig, H. G. (1997). The Center for Epidemiological Studies-Depression (CES–D) Scale: Assessment of depression in the medically ill elderly. *International Journal of Geriatric Psychiatry, 12,* 436–446. doi:10.1002/(SICI)1099-1166(199704)12:4<436::AID-GPS499>3.0.CO;2-M

Schillerstrom, J. E., Royall, D. R., & Palmer, R. F. (2008). Depression, disability and intermediate pathways: A review of longitudinal studies in elders. *Journal of Geriatric Psychiatry and Neurology, 21,* 183–197. doi:10.1177/0891988708320971

Schoevers, R. A., Smit, F., Deeg, D. J. H., Cuijpers, P., Dekker, J., van Tilburg, W., & Beekman, A. T. (2006). Prevention of late-life depression in primary care: Do we know where to begin? *American Journal of Psychiatry, 163,* 1611–1621. doi:10.1176/appi.ajp.163.9.1611

Schulberg, H. C., Katon, W., Simon, G. E., & Rush, A. J. (1998). Treating major depression in primary care practice: An update of the Agency for Health Care Policy and Research practice guidelines. *Archives of General Psychiatry, 55,* 1121–1127. doi:10.1001/archpsyc.55.12.1121

Schweitzer, I., Tuckwell, V., O'Brien, J., & Ames, D. (2002). Is late onset depression a prodrome to dementia? *International Journal of Geriatric Psychiatry, 17,* 997–1005. doi:10.1002/gps.525

Scogin, F., Hamblin, D., & Beutler, L. (1987). Bibliotherapy for depressed older adults: A self-help alternative. *Gerontologist, 27,* 383–387. doi:10.1093/geront/27.3.383

Scogin, F., Jamison, C., & Gochneaur, K. (1989). Comparative efficacy of cognitive and behavioral bibliotherapy for mildly and moderately depressed older adults. *Journal of Consulting and Clinical Psychology, 57,* 403–407. doi:10.1037/0022-006X.57.3.403

Scogin, F., Welsh, D., Hanson, A., Stump, J., & Coates, A. (2005). Evidence-based psychotherapies for depression in older adults. *Clinical Psychology: Science and Practice, 12,* 222–237. doi:10.1093/clipsy.bpi033

Segal, D. L., Coolidge, F. L., Cahill, B. S., & O'Riley, A. A. (2008). Psychometric properties of the Beck Depression Inventory—II (BDI–II) among community-dwelling older adults. *Behavior Modification, 32,* 3–20. doi:10.1177/0145445507303833

Segal, D. L., Hersen, M., Van Hasselt, V. B., Kabacoff, R. I., & Roth, L. (1993). Reliability of diagnosis in older psychiatric patients using the Structured Clinical Interview for *DSM–III–R. Journal of Psychopathology and Behavioral Assessment, 15,* 347–356. doi:10.1007%2FBF00965037

Segal, D. L., June, A., & Marty, M. A. (2010). Basic issues in interviewing and the interview process. In D. L. Segal & M. Hersen (Eds.), *Diagnostic interviewing* (4th ed., pp. 1–21). New York, NY: Springer. doi:10.1007/978-1-4419-1320-3_1

Serfaty, M. A., Haworth, D., Blanchard, M., Buszewicz, M., Murad, S., & King, M. (2009). Clinical effectiveness of individual cognitive behavioral therapy for depressed older people in primary care: A randomized controlled trial. *Archives of General Psychiatry, 66,* 1332–1340. doi:10.1001/archgenpsychiatry.2009.165

Serrano, J. P., Latorre, J., Gatz, M., & Montanes, J. (2004). Life review therapy using autobiographical retrieval practice for older adults with depressive symptomatology. *Psychology and Aging, 19,* 270–277. doi:10.1037/0882-7974.19.2.272

Sexton, C. E., McDermott, L., Kalu, U. G., Herrmann, L. L., Bradley, K. M., Allan, C., . . . Ebmeier, K. P. (2012). Exploring the pattern and neural correlates of neuropsychological impairment in late-life depression. *Psychological Medicine, 42,* 1195–1202. doi:10.1017/S0033291711002352

Simons, K., Connolly, R. P., Bonifas, R., Allen, P. D., Bailey, K., Downes, D., & Galambos, C. (2012). Psychosocial assessment of nursing home residents via MDS 3.0: Recommendations for social service training, staffing, and roles in interdisciplinary care. *Journal of the American Medical Directors Association, 13,* 190.e9–190.e15. doi:10.1016/j.jamda.2011.07.005

Singh, N. A., Stavrinos, T. M., Scarbek, Y., Galambos, G., Liber, C., & Singh, M. A. F. (2005). A randomized controlled trial of high versus low intensity weight training versus general practitioner care for clinical depression in older adults. *The Journals of Gerontology, Series A: Biological Sciences and Medical Sciences, 60,* 768–776. doi:10.1093/gerona/60.6.768

Sjösten, N., & Kivelä, S. L. (2006). The effects of physical exercise on depressive symptoms among the aged: A systematic review. *International Journal of Geriatric Psychiatry, 21,* 410–418. doi:10.1002/gps.1494

Skotzko, C. E., Krichten, C., Zietowski, G., Alves, L., Freudenberger, R., Robinson, S., . . . Gottlieb, S. S. (2000). Depression is common and precludes accurate assessment of functional status in elderly patients with congestive heart failure. *Journal of Cardiac Failure, 6,* 300–305. doi:10.1054/jcaf.2000.19222

Skultety, K. M., & Rodriguez, R. L. (2008). Treating geriatric depression in primary care. *Current Psychiatry Reports, 10,* 44–50. doi:10.1007/s11920-008-0009-2

Skultety, K. M., & Zeiss, A. (2006). The treatment of depression in older adults in the primary care setting: An evidence-based review. *Health Psychology, 25,* 665–674. doi:10.1037/0278-6133.25.6.665

Snarski, M., Scogin, F., DiNapoli, E., Presnell, A., McAlpine, J., & Marcinak, J. (2011). The effects of behavioral activation therapy with inpatient geriatric psychiatry patients. *Behavior Therapy, 42,* 100–108. doi.org/10.1016/j.beth.2010.05.001 doi:10.1016/j.beth.2010.05.001

Snow, A. L., Kunik, M., Molinari, V., Orengo, C., Doody, R., Graham, D., & Norris, M. (2005). Accuracy of self-reported depression in persons with dementia. *Journal of the American Geriatrics Society, 53,* 389–396. doi:10.1111/j.1532-5415.2005.53154.x

Sonnenberg, C. M., Deeg, D. J., van Tilburg, T. G., Vink, D., Stek, M. L., & Beekman, A. T. (2013). Gender differences in the relation between depression and social support in later life. *International Psychogeriatrics, 25,* 61–70. doi:10.1017/S1041610212001202

Steffens, D. C., & Potter, G. G. (2008). Geriatric depression and cognitive impairment. *Psychological Medicine, 38,* 163–175. doi:10.1017/S003329170700102X

Steuer, J. L., Mintz, J., Hammen, C. L., Hill, M. A., Jarvik, L. F., McCarley, T., . . . Rosen, R. (1984). Cognitive-behavioral and psychodynamic group psychotherapy in treatment of geriatric depression. *Journal of Consulting and Clinical Psychology, 52,* 180–189. doi:10.1037/0022-006X.52.2.180

Steunenberg, B., Beekman, A. T. F., Deeg, D. J. H., Bremmer, M. A., & Kerkhof, A. J. F. M. (2007). Mastery and neuroticism predict recovery of depression in later life. *American Journal of Geriatric Psychiatry, 15,* 234–242. doi:10.1097/01.JGP.0000236595.98623.62

Steunenberg, B., Beekman, A. T. F., Deeg, D. J. H., & Kerkhof, A. J. F. M. (2006). Personality and the onset of depression in late life. *Journal of Affective Disorders, 92,* 243–251. doi:10.1016/j.jad.2006.02.003

Steunenberg, B., Beekman, A. T. F., Deeg, D. J. H., & Kerkhof, A. J. F. M. (2010). Personality predicts recurrence of late-life depression. *Journal of Affective Disorders, 123,* 164–172. doi:10.1016/j.jad.2009.08.002

Steunenberg, B., Braam, A. W., Beekman, A. T. F., Deeg, D. J. H., & Kerkhof, A. J. F. M. (2009). Evidence for an association of the Big Five personality factors with recurrence of depressive symptoms in later life. *International Journal of Geriatric Psychiatry, 24,* 1470–1477. doi:10.1002/gps.2291

Su, T. W., Wu, L. L., & Lin, C. P. (2012). The prevalence of dementia and depression in Taiwanese institutionalized leprosy patients, and the effectiveness evaluation of reminiscence therapy—A longitudinal, single-blind, randomized control study. *International Journal of Geriatric Psychiatry, 27,* 187–196. doi:10.1002/gps.2707

Tedeschini, E., Levkovitz, Y., Lovieno, N., Ameral, V. E., Nelson, C., & Papakostas, G. L. (2011). Efficacy of antidepressants for late-life depression: A meta-analysis and metaregression of placebo-controlled randomized trials. *Journal of Clinical Psychiatry, 72,* 1660–1668. doi:10.4088/JCP.10r06531

Teresi, J., Abrams, R., Holmes, D., Ramirez, M., & Eimicke, J. (2001). Prevalence of depression and depression recognition in nursing homes. *Social Psychiatry and Psychiatric Epidemiology, 36,* 613–620. doi:10.1007/s127-001-8202-7

Teri, L., McCurry, S. M., Logsdon, R., & Gibbons, L. E. (2005). Training community consultants to help family members improve dementia care: A randomized controlled trial. *Gerontologist, 45,* 802–811. doi:10.1093/geront/45.6.802

Thombs, B. D., Ziegelstein, R. C., Pilote, L., Dozois, D. A., Beck, A. T., Dobson, K. S., . . . Abbey, S. E. (2010). Somatic symptom overlap in Beck Depression Inventory—II scores following myocardial infarction. *British Journal of Psychiatry, 197,* 61–66. doi:10.1192/bjp.bp.109.076596

Thompson, L. W., Coon, D. W., Gallagher-Thompson, D., Sommer, B. R., & Koin, D. (2001). Comparison of desipramine and cognitive/behavioral therapy in the treatment of elderly outpatients with mild-to-moderate depression. *American Journal of Geriatric Psychiatry, 9,* 225–240. doi:10.1097/00019442-200108000-00006

Thompson, L. W., & Gallagher, D. (1984). Efficacy of psychotherapy in the treatment of late-life depression. *Advances in Behaviour Research and Therapy, 6,* 127–139. doi:10.1016/0146-6402(84)90007-9

Thompson, L. W., Gallagher, D., & Breckenridge, J. S. (1987). Comparative effectiveness of psychotherapies for depressed elders. *Journal of Consulting and Clinical Psychology, 55,* 385–390. doi:10.1037/0022-006X.55.3.385

Tielkes, C. E., Comijs, H. C., Verwijk, E., & Stek, M. L. (2008). The effects of ECT on cognitive functioning in the elderly: A review. *International Journal of Geriatric Psychiatry, 23,* 789–795. doi:10.1002/gps.1989

Unützer, J., Katon, W., Callahan, C. M., Williams, J. W., Jr., Hunkeler, E., Harpole, L., . . . Langston, C. (2002). Collaborative care management of late-life depression in the primary care setting. *JAMA, 288,* 2836–2845. doi:10.1001/jama.288.22.2836

Unützer, J., Katon, W., Callahan, C. M., Williams, J. W., Hunkeler, E., Harpole, L., . . . Oishi, S. (2003). Depression treatment in a sample of 1,801 depressed older adults in primary care. *Journal of the American Geriatrics Society, 51,* 505–514. doi:10.1046/j.1532-5415.2003.51159.x

U.S. Department of Health and Human Services. (2001). *Mental health: Culture, race, and ethnicity—A supplement to mental health: A report of the Surgeon General.* Rockville, MD: U.S. Department of Health and Human Services, Substance Abuse and Mental Health Services Administration, Center for Mental Health Services.

Valenstein, M., Taylor, K. K., Austin, K., Kales, H. C., McCarthy, J. F., & Blow, F. C. (2004). Benzodiazepine use among depressed patients treated in mental health settings. *American Journal of Psychiatry, 161,* 654–661. doi:10.1176/appi.ajp.161.4.654

Valkanova, V., & Ebmeier, K. P. (2013). Vascular risk factors and depression in later life: A systematic review and meta-analysis. *Biological Psychiatry, 73,* 406–413. doi:10.1016/j.biopsych.2012.10.028

van der Wurff, F. B., Stek, M. L., Hoogendijk, W. J. G., & Beekman, A. T. F. (2003). The efficacy and safety of ECT in depressed older adults: A literature review. *International Journal of Geriatric Psychiatry, 18,* 894–904. doi:10.1002/gps.944

van't Veer-Tazelaar, P. J., van Marawijk, H. W. J., van Oppen, P., van der Horst, H. E., Smit, F., Cuijpers, P., & Beekman, A. T. F. (2011). Prevention of late-life anxiety and depression has sustained effects over 24 months: A pragmatic randomized trial. *American Journal of Geriatric Psychiatry, 19,* 230–239. doi:10.1097/JGP.0b013e3181faee4d

van't Veer-Tazelaar, P. J., van Marwijk, H. W. J., van Oppen, P., van Hout, H. P. J., van der Horst, H. E., Cuijpers, P., . . . Beekman, A. T. F. (2009). Stepped-care prevention of anxiety and depression in late life: A randomized controlled trial. *Archives of General Psychiatry, 66,* 297–304. doi:10.1001/archgenpsychiatry.2008.555

Wang, J. (2005). The effects of reminiscence on depressive symptoms and mood status of older institutionalized adults in Taiwan. *International Journal of Geriatric Psychiatry, 20,* 57–62. doi:10.1002/gps.1248

Wang, J. J. (2007). Group reminiscence therapy for cognitive and affective function of demented elderly in Taiwan. *International Journal of Geriatric Psychiatry, 22,* 1235–1240. doi:10.1002/gps.1821

Watt, L. M., & Cappeliez, P. (2000). Integrative and instrumental reminiscence therapies for depression in older adults: Intervention strategies and treatment effectiveness. *Aging and Mental Health, 4,* 166–177. doi:10.1080/13607860050008691

Weber, K., Giannakopoulos, P., & Canuto, A. (2011). Exploring the impact of personality dimensions in late-life depression: From group comparisons to individual trajectories. *Current Opinion in Psychiatry, 24,* 478–483. doi:10.1097/YCO.0b013e32834a349f

Webster, J. D., Bohlmeijer, E. T., & Westerhof, G. J. (2010). Reminiscence and mental health: A review of recent progress in theory, research and interventions. *Research on Aging, 32,* 527–564. doi:10.1177/0164027510364122

Weissman, M., Markowitz, J., & Klerman, G. L. (2007). *Clinician's quick guide to interpersonal psychotherapy.* New York, NY: Oxford University Press.

Westerhof, G. J., Bohlmeijer, E. T., van Beljouw. I. M. J., & Pot, A. (2010). Improvement in personal meaning mediates the effects of a life review intervention on depressive symptoms in a randomized controlled trial. *Gerontologist, 50,* 541–549. doi:10.1093/geront/gnp168

Wetherell, J. L., Kim, D. S., Lindamer, L. A., Thorp, S. R., Hawthorne, W., Kim, K., . . . Jeste, D. V. (2007). Anxiety disorders in a public mental health system: Clinical characteristics and service use patterns. *Journal of Affective Disorders, 104,* 179–183. doi:10.1016/j.jad.2007.02.021

Whooley, M. A., Stone, B., & Soghikian, K. (2000). Randomized trial of case-finding for depression in elderly primary care patients. *Journal of General Internal Medicine, 15,* 293–300. doi:10.1046/j.1525-1497.2000.04319.x

Whyte, E. M., Basinski, J., Farhi, P., Dew, A. M., Begley, A., Mulsant, B. H., & Reynolds, C. F., III. (2004). Geriatric depression treatment in non responders to selective serotonin reuptake inhibitors. *Journal of Clinical Psychiatry, 65,* 1634–1641. doi:10.4088/JCP.v65n1208

World Health Organization. (1992). *The ICD–10 classification of mental and behavioural disorders: Clinical descriptions and diagnostic guidelines.* Geneva, Switzerland: Author.

Yesavage, J. A., Brink, T. L., Rose, T. L., Lum, O., Huang, V., Adey, M., & Leirer, V. O. (1982–1983). Development and validation of a geriatric depression rating scale: A preliminary report. *Journal of Psychiatric Research, 17,* 37–49. doi:10.1016/0022-3956(82)90033-4

Yohannes, A. M., Baldwin, R. C., & Connolly, M. J. (2000). Depression and anxiety in elderly outpatients with chronic obstructive pulmonary disease: Prevalence, and validation of the BASDEC screening questionnaire. *International Journal of Geriatric Psychiatry, 15,* 1090–1096. doi:10.1002/1099-1166(200012)15:12<1090::AID-GPS249>3.0.CO;2-L

Yu, D. S., & Lee, D. T. (2012). Do medically unexplained somatic symptoms predict depression in older Chinese? *International Journal of Geriatric Psychiatry, 27,* 119–126. doi:10.1002/gps.2692

Zeiss, A. M., & Karlin, B. E. (2008). Integrating mental health and primary care services in the Department of Veterans Affairs Health Care System. *Journal of Clinical Psychology in Medical Settings, 15,* 73–78. doi:10.1007/s10880-008-9100-4

Zeiss, A. M., & Steffen, A. (1996). Treatment issues with elderly clients. *Cognitive and Behavioral Practice, 3,* 371–389. doi:10.1016/S1077-7229(96)80024-1

Zhang, B., Fokkema, M., Cuijpers, P., Li, J., Smits, N., & Beekman, A. (2011). Measurement invariance of the Center for Epidemiological Studies Depression Scale (CES–D) among Chinese and Dutch elderly. *BMC Medical Research Methodology, 11*(74). doi:10.1186/1471-2288-11-74

Zivin, K., & Kales, H. C. (2008). Adherence to depression treatment in older adults: A narrative review. *Drugs and Aging, 25,* 559–571. doi:10.2165/00002512-200825070-00003

CHAPTER 2

LATE-LIFE ANXIETY DISORDERS

Emily S. Bower and Julie Loebach Wetherell

Anxiety disorders in later life are associated with increased risk for disability and poor quality of life (Porensky et al., 2009), yet older adults with anxiety are two to three times less likely to seek mental health services than are middle-age or younger adults (Mackenzie, Reynolds, Cairney, Streiner, & Sareen, 2012). Although prevalence rates decline somewhat with age, anxiety disorders are common in older adults, and there is an urgent need to develop and disseminate evidence-based treatments for late-life anxiety.

EPIDEMIOLOGY

Anxiety disorders are the most prevalent psychiatric disorder in community-dwelling older adults, yet prevalence estimates vary across studies. Table 2.1 summarizes epidemiological research. Multiple factors may influence prevalence estimates and contribute to the variations found in the literature. Methodological differences in defining age cutoffs and diagnostic criteria represent a significant source of variation within the epidemiology literature (Bryant, Jackson, & Ames, 2008). When comparing rates, careful consideration should be given to the time frame of the estimate since 1-month rates will be inherently lower than 6- or 12-month rates. Similarly, incidence rates should be differentiated from prevalence rates, as the former represents the number of new cases in the population over a given time, whereas the latter is the rate of having the disease at any one time. Despite these differences, it is clear that late-life anxiety is a significant public health concern.

Prevalence in Community-Dwelling Older Adults

On the basis of findings from the National Comorbidity Survey Replication (NCS-R), the 12-month prevalence rate of any anxiety disorder is 11.6% in community-dwelling older adults (Byers, Yaffe, Covinsky, Friedman, & Bruce, 2010) with a lifetime prevalence of 15.3% (Kessler et al., 2005). Findings from the NCS-R are in line with other epidemiological studies, which place the rate of anxiety in community populations, including those in Latin America, Australia, Europe, Canada, and the United States, between 1.2% and 15% (El-Gabalawy, Mackenzie, Shooshtari, & Sareen, 2011; Prina, Ferri, Guerra, Brayne, & Prince, 2011; Regier et al., 1988; Ritchie et al., 2004; Trollor, Anderson, Sachdev, Brodaty, & Andrews, 2007).

Rates of anxiety are highest in women and the youngest old (Byers et al., 2010). Byers et al. (2010) examined age and gender trends in adults age 55 years and older and found that women were approximately two times as likely to suffer from an anxiety disorder as were men. Although the mechanism underlying this gender difference is unknown, it is most likely due to both biological and psychosocial factors that differentially affect men and women (McLean, Asnaani, Litz, & Hofmann, 2011). In both men and women, 16.6% of young-old adults (55–64 years) met criteria for an anxiety disorder in the past year compared with 6% in the old-old (75–84 years). Although rates of anxiety declined with age, they remained high at 8.1% even in those age 85 years and older (Byers et al., 2010). This

http://dx.doi.org/10.1037/14459-002
APA Handbook of Clinical Geropsychology: Vol. 2. Assessment, Treatment, and Issues of Later Life,
P. A. Lichtenberg and B. T. Mast (Editors-in-Chief)

TABLE 2.1

Epidemiological Studies That Document Prevalence Rates for Anxiety Disorders

Authors	Sample	Diagnostic measure	All anxiety	GAD	Panic	Agoraphobia	Specific phobia	Social phobia	PTSD	OCD	Comorbid MDD
Almeida et al. (2012)	Primary care (Australia); 60+ years	PHQ-9 and HADS-A ≥ 11	Current 4.7%	—	—	—	—	—	—	—	Current 1.8%
Beekman et al. (1998)	Community-dwelling and nursing home (Amsterdam); 55–84 years	DIS *DSM–III*	6-month 10.2%	6-month 7.3%	6-month 1.0%	—	6-month 3.1%	—	—	6-month 0.6%	—
Byers et al. (2010)	Nationally-representative community-dwelling (United States); 55+ years	CIDI *DSM–IV*	12-month 11.6%	12-month 2.0%	12-month 1.3%	12-month 0.8%	12-month 6.5%	12-month 3.5%	12-month 2.1%	—	12-month 2.8%
Cairney et al. (2007)	Nationally-representative community-dwelling (Canada); 55+ years	CIDI *DSM–IV*	—	—	—	—	—	12-month 1.3%; Lifetime 4.9%	—	—	—
Chou et al. (2011)	Nationally-representative community-dwelling (United States); 60+ years	AUDADIS–IV	—	3-year incidence 1.63%	3-year incidence 0.76%	—	3-year incidence 1.35%	3-year incidence 0.58%	—	—	—
Creamer and Parslow (2008)	Probability sample community-dwelling (Australia); 65+ years	CIDI *DSM–IV*	—	—	—	—	—	—	12-month 0.2% (52% lifetime exposure)	—	—
El-Gabalawy et al. (2011)	Nationally-representative community-dwelling (Canada); 55+ years	CIDI *DSM–IV*	12-month 7.7%	—	12-month 1.5%	12-month 0.6%	—	—	12-month 1.0%	—	—
Gonçalves et al. (2011)	Probability sample community-dwelling (Australia); 55–85 years	CIDI *DSM–IV*	—	12-month 2.8%	—	—	—	—	—	—	—
Grenier et al. (2011)	Probability sample community-dwelling (Canada); 65+ years	ESA-Q *DSM–IV*	—	—	—	—	12-month 2.0%	—	—	—	—
Gum et al. (2009)	Nationally-representative community-dwelling (United States); 65+ years	CIDI *DSM–IV*	12-month 7.0%	12-month 1.2%	12-month 0.7%	12-month 0.4%	12-month 4.7%	12-month 2.3%	12-month 0.4%	—	—
Hek et al. (2011)	Prospective population-based (the Netherlands); 55+ years	M-CIDI *DSM–IV* and SCAN *DSM–IV*	1-month 8.2%	12-month 2.2%	—	12-month 4.0%	—	—	—	—	17.9% of anxiety cases

Study	Sample	Instrument								
Kessler et al. (2005)	Nationally-representative community-dwelling (United States); 60+ years	CIDI DSM-IV	Lifetime 15.3%	Lifetime 3.6%	Lifetime 2.0%	Lifetime 1.0%	Lifetime 7.5%	Lifetime 6.6%	Lifetime 2.5%	Lifetime 0.7%	—
Mackenzie et al. (2011)	Nationally-representative community-dwelling (United States); 55+ years	AUDADIS DSM-IV	—	12-month 2.8%	—	—	—	—	—	—	12-month 1.2%
Pietrzak, Van Ness, et al. (2012)	Nationally-representative community-dwelling (United States); 60+ years	AUDADIS-IV	—	—	—	—	—	—	Lifetime 4.5%	—	—
Prina et al. (2011)	Cross-sectional survey of 11 catchment sites (7 "low-income" countries); 65+ years	GMS/AGECAT	1-month 0.1%–9.6%	—	—	—	—	—	—	—	1-month 0.3–4.5%
Regier et al. (1988)	Probability sample community-dwelling (United States); 65+ years	DIS DSM-III	1-month 5.5%	—	1-month 0.1%	—	1-month 4.8%	—	—	1-month 0.8%	—
Ritchie et al. (2004)	Community-dwelling (France); 65+ years	MINI DSM-IV	12-month 14.2%; Lifetime 29.4%	12-month 4.6%; Lifetime 10.8%	12-month 0.3%; Lifetime 2.0%	See specific phobia	12-month 10.1%; Lifetime 17.6%	12-month 1.2%; Lifetime 6.0%	—	12-month 0.5%; Lifetime 1.0%	—
C. Spitzer et al. (2008)	Population-based community-dwelling (Germany); 65+ years	SCID DSM-IV	12-month 22.0%	12-month 12.5%	12-month 8.9%	12-month 1.5%	12-month 4.8%	12-month 2.0%	1-month 1.5%; Lifetime 3.1% (Lifetime Exposure 76.5%;)	—	—
Trollor et al. (2007)	Probability sample community-dwelling (Australia); 65+ years	CIDI DSM-IV (ICD-10 diagnoses also assessed)	1-month 1.3%; 12-month 1.7%	1-month 0.8%; 12-month 0.9%	1-month 0.3%; 12-month 0.7%	See Panic Disorder	—	1-month 0.1%; 12-month 0.2%	1-month 0.2%; 12-month 0.2%	1-month 0%; 12-month 0%	—
Wells et al. (2006)	Nationally-representative community-dwelling (New Zealand); 65+ years	CIDI DSM-IV	12-month 6.0%	12-month 1.0%	12-month 0.6%	12-month 0.2%	12-month 3.2%	12-month 1.4%	12-month 1.7%	12-month 0.1%	—

Note. AUDADIS–IV = Alcohol Use Disorder and Associated Disabilities Interview Schedule—*DSM–IV*; CIDI = Composite International Diagnostic Interview; DIS = Diagnostic Interview Schedule; *DSM–IV* = *Diagnostic and Statistical Manual of Mental Disorders, Fourth Edition*; GAD = generalized anxiety disorder; GMS/AGECAT = Geriatric Mental State Examination and Automated Geriatric Examination for Computer Assisted Taxonomy; HADS–A = Hospital Anxiety Scale; *ICD–10* = *International Classification of Diseases, 10th Edition*; M–CIDI = Munich CIDI; MINI = Mini International Neuropsychiatric Interview; MDD = major depressive disorder; OCD = obsessive–compulsive disorder; PHQ–9 = Patient Health Questionnaire; PTSD = posttraumatic stress disorder; SCAN = Schedules for Clinical Assessment of Neuropsychiatry; SCID = Structured Clinical Interview for *DSM–IV*.

finding is in contrast to Beekman et al. (1998) who found consistently high rates of anxiety across subgroups of older adults ages 55–85 years. The few longitudinal studies that have examined change in anxiety over time in older samples suggest that symptom severity does decline with age but that significant subclinical symptoms often persist (Ramsawh, Raffa, Edelen, Rende, & Keller, 2009). Furthermore, some support suggests that subclinical symptoms increase in the oldest-old and continue to cause significant impairment (Teachman, 2006). Given the early age of onset and effects of chronicity for most anxiety disorders (Kessler et al., 2005), it is also possible that older adults with a history of anxiety have higher rates of mortality, hospitalization, and long-term care needs that might have excluded them from many of the large epidemiologic studies to date.

One of the most prevalent anxiety disorders in older adults is specific phobia. Past-year prevalence estimates range from 2% to 10.1% (Byers et al., 2010; Grenier et al., 2011; Gum, King-Kallimanis, & Kohn, 2009; Ritchie et al., 2004; C. Spitzer et al., 2008; Wells et al., 2006). Strikingly, more than half of older adults who meet criteria for a specific phobia do not recognize the excessiveness of their fears despite reporting avoidant behaviors and significant functional impairment (Grenier et al., 2011). Furthermore, prevalence estimates for phobia are highly influenced by the type of measure that is used (Bryant et al., 2008). For example, estimated rates of fear of falling, which may be the most common fear in older adults, range from 3% to 85% depending on how fear of falling is operationally defined (Scheffer, Schuurmans, van Dijk, van der Hooft, & de Rooij, 2008). Thus, it is likely that estimates of phobia prevalence are conservative.

Generalized anxiety disorder (GAD) is highly prevalent in older adults. Prevalence rates range from 1% to 12.5%, with higher rates seen in women and the youngest-old (Byers et al., 2010; Gonçalves, Pachana, & Byrne, 2011; Mackenzie, Reynolds, Chou, Pagura, & Sareen, 2011; C. Spitzer et al., 2008; Wells et al., 2006). Late-life GAD is associated with significant impairment in quality of life, a high rate of psychiatric comorbidity, and chronic illness (Gonçalves et al., 2011; Mackenzie et al., 2011).

A high proportion of older adults with GAD suffer from comorbid major depressive disorder (MDD; Chou, 2009), and differentiating the two disorders can be difficult. Indeed, prevalence estimates vary depending on whether or not diagnostic algorithms exclude GAD in the presence of MDD and other psychiatric disorders (i.e., with hierarchy). Mackenzie et al. (2011) estimated 2.8% of adults age 55 years and older experienced GAD in the past year when hierarchy rules were not used, whereas only 0.5% of older adults were diagnosed with GAD when hierarchy rules were used. The high comorbidity of GAD with other psychiatric disorders illustrates the complexity of anxiety presentation in older adults.

Other anxiety disorders are less prevalent in older adults, although estimates vary. Panic disorder, agoraphobia, and obsessive–compulsive disorder (OCD) are relatively rare, with most estimates lower than 1% (Beekman et al., 1998; Byers et al., 2010; Gum et al., 2009; Hek et al., 2011; Regier et al., 1988). Although many older epidemiological studies did not measure posttraumatic stress disorder (PTSD) in the community, recent estimates suggest the current rate is approximately 2% (Byers et al., 2010; Creamer & Parslow, 2008; C. Spitzer et al., 2008; Wells et al., 2006). Finally, social phobia estimates vary from 0.2% to 3.5% (Byers et al., 2010; Cairney et al., 2007; Trollor et al., 2007).

Prevalence in Institutional Populations

In relation to epidemiologic studies in community-dwelling older adults, relatively little attention has been given to the prevalence of anxiety in institutional populations (Seitz, Purandare, & Conn, 2010). This represents an important area for future research because rates of anxiety disorders may be higher in long-term care settings and hospitals given the association between anxiety and comorbid disorders, health problems, and lower quality of life (Comer et al., 2011). In a review of the literature on psychiatric disorders in long-term care settings, prevalence estimates of anxiety disorders ranged from 3.5% to 11%, while the presence of subthreshold anxiety symptoms was about twice as high (Seitz et al., 2010). These estimates do not include hospital settings where rates may be higher than in community samples (Bryant et al., 2008). Among those receiving nursing home care, comorbidity with depression is high and is most prevalent in those with severe anxiety (Smalbrugge, Jongenelis, Pot, Beekman, & Eefsting, 2005).

Comorbidity and Correlates

Anxiety disorders frequently present with other psychiatric and medical conditions in older adults. Among psychiatric comorbidities, depression and other anxiety disorders are most common, but personality disorders also co-occur with anxiety (Mackenzie et al., 2011). Within the general population, rates of comorbid anxiety and depression range from 1.2% to 4.5% (Byers et al., 2010; Hek et al., 2011; Mackenzie et al., 2011; Prina et al., 2011). Approximately one half of older adults with GAD report lifetime comorbidity with depression, but lifetime rates of comorbid anxiety and depression are also high for those with panic disorder, social phobia, and PTSD (Gonçalves et al., 2011; King-Kallimanis, Gum, & Kohn, 2009). Three quarters of older adults with comorbid anxiety and depression reported experiencing the anxiety disorder before the onset of depression (King-Kallimanis et al., 2009). This is consistent with the fact that the age of onset for anxiety disorders is much younger than that of MDD (Kessler et al., 2005). Byers et al. (2010) found no difference in rates of comorbid anxiety and depression between men and women in a nationally representative population study, whereas Gonçalves et al. (2011) found that older women with GAD were more likely to have comorbid depression than were men.

Somatic symptoms are a hallmark component of anxiety disorders in older adults, and older adults frequently present with comorbid medical conditions. Cardiovascular disease, chronically painful conditions (e.g., arthritis, migraine), lung disease, and gastrointestinal problems have all been found to be significantly associated with anxiety disorders (El-Gabalawy et al., 2011). Conversely, hypertension, cancer, diabetes, and being obese or overweight do not increase the odds of having an anxiety disorder (El-Gabalawy et al., 2011). Importantly, older adults with comorbid anxiety and physical illness rate their health as poorer than do those with anxiety or physical illness alone, indicating the importance of assessing for and treating anxiety in physically ill older adults (El-Gabalawy et al., 2011). Anxiety, and particularly GAD, is also associated with greater disability and functional impairment, lower health-related quality of life, and more medications and health care utilization (Gonçalves et al., 2011; Porensky et al., 2009).

Some socioeconomic factors are associated with higher rates of anxiety in older adults. Having lower income, lower education, a family history of anxiety, and early childhood abuse are all associated with greater risk of late-life anxiety disorders (Almeida et al., 2012; Prina et al., 2011). Beekman et al. (1998) found that the effect of family history of anxiety declined with age in older adults. One explanation for this finding could be that the impact of family history (which includes factors such as genetics and social learning) may become attenuated in the oldest-old. Alternately, the authors noted that family histories may be less salient to older adults than to younger adults, which may lead to underreporting (Beekman et al., 1998). Factors that may protect against anxiety in older adults include being married or living with someone, having more family contact, being more physically active, and having better self-assessed health (Almeida et al., 2012; Chou, Mackenzie, Liang, & Sareen, 2011). Byers et al. (2010) did not find differences in prevalence of late-life anxiety for race and ethnicity; however, low power may have affected findings, and non-English-speaking older adults were not included in the sample. Similar to findings from the United States and Western European countries, Prina et al. (2011) found that in Latin American and Asian countries late-life anxiety was associated with younger age, female gender, lower education, and physical impairment. The same study, however, found that in some countries higher anxiety also was associated with food insecurity, dementia diagnosis, and living in an urban environment. Interestingly, prevalence rates in China were significantly lower than those in other countries. The same diagnostic criteria were used for each country in this study, yet idioms of distress vary across cultures and may have contributed to differences in prevalence (Prina et al., 2011). Thus, although the experience of late-life anxiety may be similar across cultures, differences do exist and cultural factors should be considered when assessing late-life anxiety. More cross-cultural studies within the United States that include non-English-speaking older adults are needed to clarify the effects of culture on late-life anxiety.

DIAGNOSIS OF ANXIETY IN LATE LIFE

With the development of the *Diagnostic and Statistical Manual of Mental Disorders, Fifth Edition* (*DSM–5*; American Psychiatric Association, 2013) and the 11th edition of the *International Classification of Diseases*, there has been renewed inquiry regarding the definition of late-life anxiety (Mohlman, Bryant, et al., 2012; Wolitzky-Taylor, Castriotta, Lenze, Stanley, & Craske, 2010). Much has been written about the need for specific guidelines for diagnosing anxiety in the presence of depression, dementia, and physical illness (Bryant et al., 2013). Clinicians may incorrectly attribute signs of anxiety in older adults to side effects of medication, medical disorders, or normal aging processes. Anxiety, however, is not a normal part of aging, and identification and treatment of anxiety can significantly improve health outcomes in older adults (El-Gabalawy et al., 2011). Accurate diagnosis is essential for developing and implementing the best course of treatment. Therefore, assessment tools and diagnostic criteria must be sensitive to the unique anxiety experiences of older adults.

Although symptoms of anxiety tend to be similar across age-groups, qualitative differences in the emotional experience of older adults can complicate the detection of anxiety (Jeste, Blazer, & First, 2005). Older adults are more likely than younger adults to attend to positive over negative information (Mather & Carstensen, 2005). Conversely, older adults with high worry do not display the typical positivity bias, and in fact, they attend more to negative than to positive stimuli on attention tests (Lee & Knight, 2009; Price, Siegle, & Mohlman, 2012). Furthermore, older adults tend to experience lower emotional arousal and are better at regulating emotions than younger adults (for review, see Scheibe & Carstensen, 2010). Age-related changes in emotion regulation correspond with

neurobiological differences between healthy young and older adults. For example, younger adults display similar amygdala activation to both negative and positive emotional images, whereas older adults have stronger amygdala activation to positive than negative emotional images (Mather et al., 2004). These findings suggest that age-related neurobiological changes may contribute to differential emotional experiences in younger and older adults. In contrast to the age differences seen in healthy adults, evidence from imaging studies suggests that older adults with GAD suffer from a deficit in top-down control processes similar to that seen in younger adults with GAD (Price, Eldreth, & Mohlman, 2011).

Exploring the effect of age-related changes in emotion and arousal on pathophysiology is an important focus for future research and is consistent with a growing push to realign mental health research along dimensional rather than categorical diagnostic criteria (Morris & Cuthbert, 2012). Mapping behavior onto neural, molecular, and physiological circuits will improve diagnostic validity and clarify the role of pathological aging processes on behavioral manifestations of anxiety. Yet although research is moving toward a dimensional approach, categorical classification remains the basis of diagnostic criteria in clinical settings. Thus, it is important that professionals who work with older adults be aware of age-related differences in symptom reporting that may mask anxiety in older adults. For example, older adults may use or respond to different language to describe symptoms (e.g., "concerns" instead of "worry") and may misattribute their somatic anxiety symptoms to medical causes (Bryant et al., 2013). Similarly, older adults who present with anxiety symptoms but who do not meet the full criteria for an anxiety disorder (i.e., anxiety disorder not otherwise specified) often experience clinically significant distress that interferes with their health and well-being, and thus they would benefit from treatment (Wolitzky-Taylor et al., 2010; Teachman, 2006).

Generalized Anxiety Disorder

Almost half of older adults with current or lifetime GAD experienced their first onset after the age of 50 years (Chou, 2009; Le Roux, Gatz, & Wetherell,

2005). Those who develop GAD later in life report more functional impairment and poorer health than those with earlier-onset GAD. Despite this finding, some research suggests that late-life GAD is associated with less severe worry than early-onset GAD (Le Roux et al., 2005). An integral diagnostic criterion for GAD is the presence of excessive and uncontrollable worry, yet across studies, older adults generally report less worry than do younger adults (Babcock, MaloneBeach, Hou, & Smith, 2012; C. E. Gould & Edelstein, 2010). Several confounding factors make it difficult to determine whether this finding represents an actual age-related decline in worry, a cohort effect, or a qualitative change in worry presentation.

In general, findings suggest that worry content is age dependent. Older adults tend to report worrying more about the health and welfare of loved ones and world concerns but less about work or school and relationships than younger adults (Gonçalves & Byrne, 2013). Assessment instruments vary in terms of the worry content domains included, potentially introducing measurement bias. For example, Babcock et al. (2012) found that younger adults reported more worry than older adults across all content domains of the Worry Domains Questionnaire. Hunt, Wisocki, and Yanko (2003), however, found that older adults endorsed the same or more worry than younger adults across all domains of the Worry Scale for Older Adults, which was developed specifically to assess worries relevant to older adults. Thus, a single measure may not accurately assess the content of worry across all age-groups.

In addition to qualitative differences, social and demographic factors may influence assessment of worry. There is some support for a gender by age interaction, which could complicate interpretation. C. E. Gould and Edelstein (2010) found that younger women reported significantly more worry and less emotional control than younger men, but the gender differences were attenuated in older adults. Thus, men and women may experience different patterns of change in worry as they age. The experience of worry also may vary across cultures, and the effect of culture on worry is conditional on age (Babcock et al., 2012). Unfortunately, many studies comparing anxiety across age-groups fail to assess these factors.

Obsessive–Compulsive Disorder and Hoarding Disorder

Few studies have compared younger and older adults with OCD, and thus relatively little is known about the characteristics of OCD in later life. Some research suggests that older adults are more likely to have hand-washing compulsions and obsessional fears of having sinned than younger adults (Kohn, Westlake, Rasmussen, Marsland, & Norman, 1997). In comparison with other anxiety disorders, OCD in later life is more likely to present in men than in women and is associated with greater impairment in social functioning (Grenier, Preville, Boyer, & O'Connor, 2009).

Compulsive hoarding was classified under OCD in the *Diagnostic and Statistical Manual of Mental Disorders, Fourth Edition, Text Revision* (*DSM–IV–TR*; American Psychiatric Association, 2000), but has been reclassified as "Hoarding Disorder" in the *DSM–5* (American Psychiatric Association, 2013). The disorder is characterized by long-standing (i.e., persistent) difficulty and distress associated with discarding possessions, regardless of actual value. The hoarding behavior results in the accumulation of possessions to the degree that living areas are compromised by clutter, and the behavior causes significant distress or functional impairment. Although onset of hoarding symptoms typically occurs earlier in life, symptom severity tends to increase with age and often the disorder goes untreated (Ayers, Saxena, Golshan, & Wetherell, 2010). Because of the paucity of research on hoarding disorder to date, the impact of cohort and cultural factors is unclear. Comorbidity with other anxiety and mood disorders is high (55%), yet although many older adults with hoarding symptoms receive treatment for comorbid psychiatric disorders, hoarding symptoms frequently go undetected (Ayers et al., 2010). Hoarding disorder in late life is associated with significant functional impairment and health risk (Diefenbach, Dimauro, Frost, Steketee, & Tolin, 2013). Given the chronic, progressive course of the disorder, clinicians should be educated about the characteristics and risk factors of hoarding disorder to improve detection and treatment.

Specific Phobias

Fear content differs between young and older cohorts, and this leads to the underdetection of specific phobia in later life. Older adults report more situational fears (e.g., heights) than younger adults (Wolitzky-Taylor et al., 2010). Importantly, the prevalence of fear of falling increases with age and is common in older adults (Arfken, Lach, Birge, & Miller, 1994), yet it is not specifically addressed in the *DSM–5* (American Psychiatric Association, 2013). Although fear of falling could be classified as a specific phobia, diagnosis often is confounded by the fact that older adults with fear of falling have poor insight into the excessiveness of their fear and thus do not endorse criterion C (i.e., the person recognizes that the fear is excessive or unreasonable; Gagnon, Flint, Naglie, & Devins, 2005). Furthermore, signs associated with fear of falling, such as avoidance of activities and social withdrawal, may be attributed incorrectly to physical limitations resulting from age-related changes or co-occurring medical disorders. Thus, clinicians should compare the perceived risk of falling with the actual risk of falling rather than rely on self-report to determine the excessiveness of fear of falling (LeBeau et al., 2010).

Posttraumatic Stress Disorder

The majority of older adults have been exposed to at least one potentially traumatic event in their lifetime (Pietrzak, Goldstein, Southwick, & Grant, 2012b). In those who develop PTSD after an early-life trauma, symptom severity tends to decline with age (Böttche, Kuwert, & Knaevelsrud, 2012). A subgroup of individuals, however, experience delayed-onset symptoms, which are associated with increasing avoidance and hyperarousal symptoms over time (Böttche et al., 2012). Compared with those who experience a traumatic event but do not develop PTSD, lifetime PTSD is associated with poorer physical and mental health as well as higher risk of developing cardiovascular disease, gastrointestinal problems, arthritis, mood disorders, and other anxiety disorders (Pietrzak, Goldstein, Southwick, & Grant, 2012a; Pietrzak, Goldstein, et al., 2012b). Furthermore, cognitive performance is worse in older adults with a lifetime diagnosis of PTSD compared with those without PTSD, particularly in the domain

of memory (Schuitevoerder et al., 2013). More research is needed to clarify the acute impact of trauma on older adults. Böttche et al. (2012) reviewed research comparing symptom severity in young and older adults following natural disasters but were unable to reconcile inconsistencies across studies because of widespread methodological differences. Thus, it remains unclear whether symptom severity and profiles differ with age.

Important differences in the content of worries and fears between younger and older adults are not specifically described in current diagnostic criteria. Furthermore, co-occurring psychiatric and medical illnesses are common in older adults and can lead to poorer prognosis and perceived health or even mask signs of anxiety. Finally, positivity biases, cultural differences, and variations in how anxiety is assessed influence the detection of anxiety in older adults. Thus, clinicians and researchers should be sensitive to the different experiences of older adults and adapt the assessment process as needed.

ASSESSMENT OF ANXIETY IN OLDER ADULTS

Comprehensive assessment is the first step in diagnosing and providing evidence-based treatment. Many older adults with anxiety do not seek care from a mental health specialist (Mackenzie et al., 2012) so accurate detection of late-life anxiety in primary care settings is important. Unfortunately, many of the tools used for assessing anxiety in older adults were developed with younger samples and lack both psychometric evidence and norms for use with older adults (Therrien & Hunsley, 2012). Another frequently cited limitation of many commonly used anxiety assessment tools is that they rely heavily on somatic symptoms, which overlap with medical symptoms or age-related physiological changes making differential diagnosis difficult (Lauderdale & Sheikh, 2003). The following sections discuss general considerations for assessment of anxiety in older adults and provide a brief overview of currently available evidence-based assessment tools. The focus will be on scales developed specifically for use in geriatric populations. A summary of these scales appears in Table 2.2.

TABLE 2.2

Anxiety Assessment Instruments

Measure	Authors	Indication	Response format	Reliability and validity in older adults	Pros	Cons
Anxiety in Cognitive Impairment and Dementia (ACID)	Gerolimatos et al. (2013)	Anxiety symptoms in dementia	Caregiver- and patient-report (13-item)	Adequate internal consistency, weak correlation between patient and caregiver ratings, good convergent and discriminant validity	Simple response format; includes both caregiver and patient ratings	Strong association with depression symptoms
Beck Anxiety Inventory (BAI)	A. T. Beck et al. (1988)	Anxiety symptom severity	Self-report (21-item)	Mixed; adequate reliability and convergent validity, poor discriminant validity (Wetherell & Gatz, 2005)	Assesses symptoms over past month	Somatic items may be confounded by medical illness
Clinician-Administered PTSD Scale (CAPS)	Blake et al. (1995)	PTSD diagnosis and symptom severity	Clinician-rated (30–60 min)	Adequate internal consistency, convergent and divergent validity; discriminates older combat veterans with PTSD (Hyer et al., 1996)	Considered the "gold standard" PTSD assessment	Lengthy; training required
Empirical Behavioral Pathology in Alzheimer's Disease (E-BEHAVE-AD)	Auer, Monteiro, and Reisberg (1996)	Behavioral symptoms in dementia	Clinician-rated (20 min)	Excellent interrater reliability, moderate correlation between caregiver and clinician ratings	Combine with caregiver-rated BEHAVE-AD to improve symptom assessment	Only two items assess anxiety symptoms specifically.
Fear Questionnaire (FQ)	Marks and Mathews (1979)	Severity of fears and avoidance	Self-report (15-item)	Poor reliability and validity in older adults; modified version that does not assess avoidance demonstrates adequate psychometric properties (Stanley et al., 2001)	Modified version without avoidance items should be used	Poor psychometric properties in older adults
GAD-7	R. L. Spitzer et al. (2006)	GAD symptom severity	Self-report (7-item)	Adequate reliability and validity in initial validation study, but more research is needed	Brief	Only assesses past 2 weeks (6 month history needed for diagnosis)
Generalized Anxiety Disorder Severity Scale (GADSS)	Shear et al. (2006)	GAD symptom severity	Clinician-rated	Adequate reliability and concurrent validity; mixed discriminant validity; poor predictive validity (Weiss et al., 2009)	GAD-specific; sensitive to change	Overlaps with depression symptoms, poor diagnostic ability

(continues)

TABLE 2.2 (*Continued*)

Anxiety Assessment Instruments

Measure	Authors	Indication	Response format	Reliability and validity in older adults	Pros	Cons
Geriatric Anxiety Inventory (GAI)	Pachana et al. (2007)	Anxiety symptoms	Self-report (20-item)	Preliminary: adequate reliability and concurrent validity; needs more research on discriminant validity	Developed with older adults; easy response format may be ideal for use with cognitively impaired older adults	Strong emphasis on worry
Geriatric Anxiety Scale (GAS)	Segal et al. (2010)	Anxiety symptoms (cognitive, affective, somatic)	Self-report (30-item)	Preliminary: adequate reliability and convergent validity; mixed discriminant validity	Developed with older adults; assesses *DSM*-based symptoms	Strong association with depression symptoms
Geriatric Mental State Exam (GMSE)	Copeland et al. (1976)	Anxiety diagnosis	Semistructured interview	Adequate reliability and validity	Developed for older adults; computerized diagnostic algorithm	Education bias
Hamilton Anxiety Rating Scale (HAM-A)	Hamilton (1959)	Anxiety symptom severity	Clinician-rated	Adequate interrater reliability, good classification of GAD, poor discriminant validity; more research in older adults needed (J. G. Beck et al., 1999)	Frequently used in pharmacological research	Poor discrimination with depression
Hospital Anxiety Scale (HADS-A)	Zigmond and Snaith (1983)	Anxiety symptom severity	Self-report (7-item)	Adequate internal consistency, construct validity, poor predictive validity (Spinhoven et al., 1997)	Does not include somatic symptoms	High correlation with depression subscale
Neuropsychiatric Inventory (NPI)	Cummings et al. (1994)	Anxiety symptoms in dementia (subscale)	Caregiver report (8 anxiety items)	Excellent interrater reliability, moderate test–retest reliability; strong association with other anxiety caregiver rating scales	Obtains information about frequency and severity of symptoms	Score based only on caregiver rating
Older Adult Social Evaluative Scale (OASES)	C. E. Gould et al. (2012)	Social anxiety and avoidance severity	Self-report (37-item)	Preliminary evidence of adequate reliability and validity in a community-dwelling sample	Age-relevant social stimuli	Needs to be validated in clinical and diverse samples
Penn State Worry Questionnaire (PSWQ/PSWQ-A)	Hopko et al. (2003); Meyer et al. (1990)	Trait worry	Self-report (16- or 8-item)	Mixed reliability, adequate validity; sensitive to change	Discriminates from depression	Reverse-scored items on the 16-item version may be difficult for some older adults

Posttraumatic Stress Disorder Checklist (PCL)	Blanchard et al. (1996)	PTSD symptoms	Self-report (17-item)	Adequate reliability and convergent validity in civilian and combat veterans (Pietrzak, Van Ness, et al., 2012)	Civilian and Military version available	Clinical cut-point needs to be adjusted down for civilians
Rating for Anxiety in Dementia (RAID)	Shankar, Walker, and Frost (1999)	Anxiety symptoms in dementia	Clinician-rated (20-item)	Adequate reliability and validity	Scores based on reports from multiple sources	Strong correlation with depression measures
State Trait Anxiety Inventory (STAI)	Spielberger et al. (1983)	State and trait anxiety	Self-report (40-item)	Adequate internal consistency, mixed test–retest reliability, mixed concurrent validity, limited discriminant validity (Stanley et al., 2001)	Norms available for older adults (Himmelfarb & Murrell, 1984; Potvin et al., 2013)	Poor discrimination from depression
Worry Scale (WS)	Wisocki et al. (1986)	Worry severity (financial, health, social)	Self-report (35-item)	Adequate reliability; minimal validity research available (Stanley et al., 2001)	Developed for older adults; more content-specific than PSWQ	Has not been tested with diverse samples
Yale-Brown Obsessive Compulsive Scale (Y-BOCS)	Goodman, Price, Rasmussen, Mazure, Fleischmann, et al. (1989)	OCD symptom severity	Clinician-rated	Adequate reliability and validity in general adult samples; research needed with older adults (Goodman, Price, Rasmussen, Mazure, Delgado, et al., 1989)	Not obsession- or compulsion-specific	Psychometric studies with older adults needed

Note. GAD = generalized anxiety disorder; OCD = obsessive–compulsive disorder; PTSD = posttraumatic stress disorder.

General Considerations

There are currently no guidelines for evidence-based assessment practices, but several articles provide general recommendations for assessing anxiety in older adults (Antony & Rowa, 2005; Lauderdale & Sheikh, 2003; Mohlman, Sirota, et al., 2012). In general, accurate and thorough assessment should include a variety of instruments cutting across multiple modalities. As mentioned previously, older adults may use different language to describe their symptoms and may lack insight into the excessiveness of their symptoms; thus, they are less likely to endorse such words as *worry*, *excessive*, or *uncontrollable*, instead preferring the terms *issues* and *concerns* (Mohlman, Sirota, et al., 2012). Thus, using a comprehensive assessment protocol with multiple modalities and response options will improve detection of anxiety in the elderly.

In primary care settings, Lauderdale and Sheikh (2003) have recommended using clinical interviews, rating scales, and laboratory tests to diagnose anxiety and rule out other medical causes. Obtaining a thorough history of the problem from the patient and another informant, if available, with a focus on determining the onset of symptoms relative to any cognitive impairment, medical illness, medication use, and other substance use (e.g., alcohol, caffeine, recreational drugs) is necessary for differential diagnosis (Lauderdale & Sheikh, 2003). Furthermore, obtaining an accurate record of treatment history, including information about treatment response, will help guide the treatment plan (Antony & Rowa, 2005). To assist with this process, it often is helpful to request that the patient compile medical history information to bring with them to the appointment (Mohlman, Sirota, et al., 2012).

In addition to general psychiatric assessment, clinicians should assess for a number of specific conditions that may be particularly relevant to older adults with anxiety. Late-life GAD is associated with higher suicide risk (Lenze et al., 2000), and thus evaluation of suicidal ideation is an important component of anxiety assessment in older adults. Fear of falling (Arfken et al., 1994) and compulsive hoarding (Ayers et al., 2010) are both associated with functional disability in older adults, yet these conditions typically are not assessed in general anxiety measures and likely will go undiagnosed if not directly addressed.

Assessment Tools

Evidence of strong psychometric properties in older adults is a key issue to consider when determining which assessment tool to use with an elderly client. Evidence-based anxiety assessment tools for older adults are relatively scarce, but research is improving in this area. Therrien and Hunsley (2012) surveyed the literature and identified 91 different measures across 213 articles used to assess anxiety in elderly adults. This considerable lack of agreement across studies was disconcerting; however, especially disappointing was the finding that the majority of the scales used were not validated adequately for use in older adults. The authors concluded that only three of the commonly used assessment tools had adequate psychometric evidence to warrant using with older adults. These included the Beck Anxiety Inventory (BAI; A. T. Beck, Epstein, Brown, & Steer, 1988), the Penn State Worry Questionnaire (PSWQ; Meyer, Miller, Metzger, & Borkovec, 1990), and the Geriatric Mental State Exam (GMSE; Copeland, Kelleher, Duckworth, & Smith, 1976), which is not used widely in the United States. Only the GMSE includes a diagnostic algorithm, while the BAI and PSWQ are more adequate as measures of symptom severity. Furthermore, Therrien and Hunsley (2012) discouraged the use of two commonly used measures with older adults, namely the State-Trait Anxiety Inventory (STAI; Spielberger, Gorsuch, Lushene, Vagg, & Jacobs, 1983) and the Hospital Anxiety and Depression Scale (Zigmond & Snaith, 1983) because of mixed results and a lack of psychometric evidence with older adults.

Except for the GMSE, all of these assessment instruments were developed for use with younger and middle-age samples. Equivalence of scores in younger and older adults does not rule out the possibility of age bias (Corral & Landrine, 2010); thus, when assessing elderly patients, it is ideal to use tools that were developed specifically for use in older adults. In addition to the GMSE, several anxiety measures have been developed with older adults, including the Worry Scale (WS; Wisocki, Handen, & Morse, 1986), the Geriatric Anxiety Inventory (GAI; Pachana et al., 2007), the Geriatric Anxiety Scale (GAS; Segal, June, Payne, Coolidge, & Yochim, 2010), and the Older Adult Social-Evaluative Situations Questionnaire (OASES; C. E. Gould, Gerolimatos, Ciliberti, Edelstein, & Smith, 2012).

The WS is a 35-item, self-report questionnaire that was designed to assess worries salient to older adults within financial, health, and social domains (Wisocki et al., 1986). Norms are available for community-dwelling and homebound elderly (Powers, Wisocki, & Whitbourne, 1992; Wisocki et al., 1986), and there is some evidence for the reliability and convergent validity of scores in samples of older adults with and without GAD (Stanley, Novy, Bourland, Beck, & Averill, 2001). The WS may be a more useful self-report measure than the PSWQ when assessment of specific worry content is the purpose of the evaluation. More research is needed, however, to evaluate discriminant validity and to determine the validity of the WS in ethnically diverse samples.

The GAI is a 20-item, self-report questionnaire that was designed specifically to measure anxiety symptoms in older adults while minimizing cognitive demands and somatic items that might overlap with symptoms of medical illness (Pachana et al., 2007). In the initial validation study, scores on the GAI demonstrated good reliability and convergent validity, and discriminated between GAD and non-GAD samples; however, discrimination between other diagnoses needs to be evaluated (Pachana et al., 2007). Unlike most anxiety scales, the GAI uses a simple dichotomous response format that requires respondents to endorse the presence or absence of a symptom. Scores demonstrated predictive validity of anxiety in older adults with cognitive impairment living in a residential care setting

(Boddice, Pachana, & Byrne, 2008). Thus, the GAI has been recommended for detecting anxiety in older adults with mild cognitive impairment and others who have difficulty with dimensional scales or longer formats (C. E. Gould, Beaudreau, & Huh, 2013).

The GAS is a 30-item, self-report questionnaire designed to assess cognitive, affective, and somatic anxiety symptoms along a dimensional scale (Segal et al., 2010). Norms are available for community-dwelling and psychiatric outpatient older adults (Segal et al., 2010). In initial validation studies, scores on the GAS demonstrated good reliability and convergent validity but showed mixed discriminant validity due to high correlations with scores on the Geriatric Depression Scale (Segal et al., 2010; Yochim, Mueller, June, & Segal, 2010). Symptom overlap between depression and anxiety, however, contributes to a lack of discriminative ability between scales designed to assess these constructs. Yochim et al. (2010) found lower correlations with depression scales for the BAI than for the GAI or GAS; however, the BAI does not measure somatic symptoms, which are a hallmark of *DSM* diagnostic criteria for anxiety. Therefore, the BAI may be more useful than the GAS to differentiate depression from anxiety, while the GAS may be more useful than the BAI when assessment of somatic symptoms is necessary. Further research is needed to confirm the psychometric properties of the scale in additional samples, but preliminary evidence suggests that the scale may be useful for measuring anxiety in older adults.

The OASES is a 37-item self-report questionnaire that recently was developed to assess social anxiety in older adults (C. E. Gould et al., 2012). An initial validation study suggested that the measure may be sensitive to situations that are uniquely anxiety provoking to older adults with social anxiety (C. E. Gould et al., 2012). Further studies are needed to assess the psychometric properties of the OASES with diverse, independent samples.

Additionally, a number of self-report measures demonstrate good psychometric properties in the elderly. Although not originally developed with geriatric samples, an abbreviated version of the PSWQ was developed for use with older adults (PSWQ-A; Hopko et al., 2003). The PSWQ-A demonstrates adequate reliability, convergent validity,

discriminant validity, and predictive validity of late-life GAD (Hopko et al., 2003). Evidence suggests the BAI has adequate psychometric properties in older adults, although discriminant validity with measures of depression are poor (Wetherell & Gatz, 2005). The GAD-7 (R. L. Spitzer, Kroenke, Williams, & Lowe, 2006) is a brief self-report scale for diagnosing and assessing symptom severity of GAD. The GAD-7 initially was validated with a sample that included older adults ($M = 47.5$ years; range 18–95 years) and demonstrated excellent reliability and validity in a primary care cohort (R. L. Spitzer et al., 2006). The PTSD Checklist (Blanchard, Jones-Alexander, Buckley, & Forneris, 1996) has been validated with older adults (Pietrzak, Van Ness, Fried, Galea, & Norris, 2012). Finally, to assess OCD, the Yale-Brown Obsessive Compulsive Scale (Goodman, Price, Rasmussen, Mazure, Fleischmann, et al., 1989) has been used with older adults, but validation studies are needed. Evidence for the reliability and construct validity of both the STAI and the Fear Questionnaire (Marks & Mathews, 1979) with older adults is mixed, and thus it is not recommended for assessing late-life anxiety (Stanley et al., 2001).

Several clinician-rated measures originally developed with younger samples may be useful for assessing older adults. The Generalized Anxiety Disorder Severity Scale (GADSS; Shear, Belnap, Mazumdar, Houck, & Rollman, 2006) identifies target worries and assesses associated GAD symptom severity. Evidence suggests the GADSS has good reliability, has convergent validity, and is sensitive to change in elderly GAD patients; however, the GADSS strongly correlated with measures of depression symptoms and had poor diagnostic accuracy in older adults (Weiss et al., 2009). The Hamilton Anxiety Rating Scale (HAM-A; Hamilton, 1959) is another potentially useful clinician-rated anxiety measure. The HAM-A frequently is used in pharmacological trials and demonstrates good interrater reliability in older adults, but it does not discriminate well from depression (J. G. Beck, Stanley, & Zebb, 1999). Finally, the Clinician-Administered PTSD Scale (CAPS; Blake et al., 1995) has been shown to discriminate older veterans with PTSD from those without PTSD (Hyer, Summers, Boyd, Litaker, & Boudewyns, 1996).

Case Example

Mrs. D is an 82-year-old woman who enrolled in a research study on treating late-life GAD. She was referred by her daughter, who heard about the study on the radio. Mrs. D was Caucasian, widowed for 4 years, lived alone, and had a high school education. She had never worked outside of the home after her marriage. She had three adult children, one of whom (eldest daughter) provided assistance and support. Her worries, which she described as "on her mind from morning to night," included her family's health and well-being, her own health, and her finances as well as routine home maintenance tasks. She also endorsed restlessness, sleep disturbance, fatigue, and muscle tension but denied irritability and trouble concentrating. She reported that she had stopped attending church several months ago because she did not want to confront a member of the church who was acting inappropriately toward her; furthermore, she had not felt comfortable enough to return calls from the minister who was concerned about her absence (and whom Mrs. D reported had been very supportive at the time of her husband's death).

Mrs. D was evaluated using a structured diagnostic interview and found to meet *DSM–IV* criteria for social phobia in addition to GAD. She scored in the cognitively intact range on a screening test and was not experiencing significant symptoms of depression. As per the research protocol, Mrs. D was initially started on escitalopram, which she tolerated well. After 12 weeks on the medication, she began a course of cognitive–behavioral therapy (CBT) with an experienced therapist who had not done a lot of work with older adults.

Although Mrs. D appeared to benefit from the relaxation training, when they moved on to cognitive restructuring, the therapist became concerned that she was not fully understanding the material. He felt that he spent a lot of time going over the rationale and the exercises and even so was not sure that she was getting much out of the process. Because the treatment was manualized but flexible, he opted to spend additional time on both the cognitive restructuring and the problem-solving skills training modules rather than to add exposure therapy to address her social phobia. He repeatedly relayed his concerns about her mental status to the research team.

Approximately three quarters through the treatment, Mrs. D surprised him by announcing that she had returned to church and set some limits with the intrusive church member. When he asked what had happened to bring about that change, she stated that she realized she had developed some unrealistic thoughts about the situation but challenged them successfully, and then she used problem-solving skills to brainstorm, evaluate, and implement a solution. The therapist praised her and told the research staff that he learned something important about doing therapy with older people—they may learn more slowly, but they do learn.

Having done well in 16 sessions of CBT, Mrs. D was gradually tapered off the selective serotonin reuptake inhibitors (SSRI) medication. She continued to do well for approximately 2 months, at which point she reported during a routine assessment that she was starting to have trouble sleeping because she was worrying about some plumbing problems in her home. She was offered three booster sessions of CBT, which she accepted, but her worry and anxiety scores remained elevated, so the escitalopram was resumed. Her worry, anxiety, and sleep disturbance quickly abated, and she remained well on the medication for the 56-week duration of the trial.

TREATMENTS FOR ANXIETY IN OLDER ADULTS

The first challenge of treating older adults for anxiety disorders is recognizing that treatment is needed. Older adults are less likely than younger adults to recognize symptoms of anxiety and to seek treatment (Mackenzie et al., 2012; Wetherell et al., 2009). Byers, Areán, and Yaffe (2012) found that 72.6% of older adults who meet *DSM–IV* criteria for an anxiety disorder did not seek treatment, citing barriers such as feelings of discomfort discussing mental health problems with professionals and a belief that mental health treatment would be ineffective. Furthermore, the authors found that older adults with mild anxiety or mood disorders were five times less likely to seek mental health services than those with severe symptoms, and ethnic minorities were significantly less likely to seek treatment than non-Hispanic White older adults were (Byers et al., 2012). Overall, there is a pressing need for primary care physicians to assess for anxiety in older patients and to address minor complaints that may be a sign of more serious psychopathology. Educating older adults about the signs of anxiety, as well as available treatment options, may help reduce barriers to treatment seeking.

Evidence-based pharmacological and psychotherapeutic options are available for treating anxiety in older adults. Although many older adults prefer psychological over pharmacological treatments (Mohlman, 2012), pharmacological treatments appear to have slightly greater effects than currently available psychotherapeutic interventions (Gonçalves & Byrne, 2012; Schuurmans et al., 2009). There are several excellent recent reviews on evidence-based treatments for anxiety in older adults (e.g., Ayers, Strickland, & Wetherell, 2015; Ghaed, Ayers, & Wetherell, 2012; Gonçalves & Byrne, 2012; R. L. Gould, Coulson, & Howard, 2012; Stoddard, Barmann, Lenze, & Wetherell, in press; Wetherell, Ruberg, & Petkus, 2011). The following sections provide an outline of available treatments, recent advances, and current recommendations.

Pharmacological Treatments

The most commonly used pharmacological treatments for anxiety include antidepressants, such as SSRIs (e.g., citalopram, escitalopram, paroxetine) or serotonin-norepinephrine reuptake inhibitors (SNRIs; e.g., venlafaxine, duloxetine), and benzodiazepines (e.g., lorazepam, diazepam, alprazolam). Although effective at reducing anxiety symptoms in the short term (Gonçalves & Byrne, 2012), benzodiazepines should not be used as a first-line treatment in older adults because of the increased risk for falls and fractures (Pariente et al., 2008; van der Hooft et al., 2008).

Several factors should be considered when using pharmacological treatment for elderly patients with anxiety. Comorbid medical conditions, current pharmacological regimen, and medication adherence can affect the safety and effectiveness of certain medications. Hepatic and renal changes in old age also can impact the pharmacokinetics of medications, so

dosing should be monitored closely (Jackson, 1995). Furthermore, the use of multiple central nervous system medications and high dosages are associated with cognitive decline in older adults (Moore & O'Keeffe, 1999). Patients with chronic anxiety may have tried multiple treatments in the past, so discuss treatment preferences with your patient and obtain a thorough history of past treatment response to determine the best course of treatment. A few sessions of motivational interviewing may be helpful in overcoming reluctance to try psychotropics. For a description of how to use motivational interviewing to encourage medication use and promote medication adherence among older adults with anxiety, see Wetherell, Ruberg, and Petkus (2011).

Psychotherapeutic Treatments

Although evidence suggests that pharmacotherapy should be the first-line treatment for most geriatric anxiety diagnoses (Gonçalves & Byrne, 2012), evidence-based psychotherapeutic treatments for anxiety in older adults include CBT and behavioral interventions (e.g., relaxation training, exposure), both of which are effective compared with waitlist control conditions (Gonçalves & Byrne, 2012; Thorp et al., 2009). Although less effective than CBT and relaxation training, supportive therapy (Barrowclough et al., 2001), and to a lesser degree cognitive therapy (DeBerry, Davis, & Reinhard, 1989), have been shown to be effective at reducing anxiety symptoms in older adults compared with waitlist. Some evidence suggests that acceptance and commitment therapy (ACT) also may be effective with older adults (Wetherell, Afari, et al., 2011). Finally, bibliotherapy and problem-solving therapy (components of CBT) may be effective at preventing the onset of anxiety disorders in older adults with subthreshold anxiety symptoms (van't Veer-Tazelaar et al., 2009).

Psychosocial interventions are effective at reducing anxiety symptoms in older adults, but the effect is more modest than that for younger adults (Wetherell, Petkus, Thorp, et al., 2013). Modifications such as shortening sessions, presenting material at a slower rate, providing extra psychoeducation, and including caregivers and family members in the treatment plan may be necessary with older adults

(Stanley et al., 2003; Wetherell, Gatz, & Craske, 2003). Group CBT may improve outcome for those who have a limited social support network (Stanley et al., 2003). Although randomized trials are needed, there is preliminary support for an Internet-delivered CBT in reducing anxiety symptoms in older adults with GAD and comorbid psychiatric disorders (Zou et al., 2012). Thus, multiple options are available for personalizing treatment to the individual needs of the client.

Generalized Anxiety Disorder

For late-life GAD, SSRIs and SNRIs are effective at reducing symptoms, are safer than benzodiazepines, and often are recommended as a first line of treatment for older adults who are willing and able to manage their symptoms pharmacologically (Katz, Reynolds, Alexopoulos, & Hackett, 2002; Lenze et al., 2009). Although some studies suggest there can be long-term effects of pharmacological treatments (e.g., Schuurmans et al., 2009), incomplete response is common (Gonçalves & Byrne, 2012). For patients who do not respond completely to SSRIs, augmenting treatment with CBT may improve treatment response and reduce worry symptoms (Wetherell, Petkus, White, et al., 2013). Furthermore, for those who wish to taper off medication, providing CBT with medication management may improve outcomes over medication taper alone (Gorenstein et al., 2005).

Although a growing body of evidence is supporting the effectiveness of CBT over treatment as usual, less intensive therapeutic options such as supportive therapy, relaxation training, and worry discussion groups have similar effects (Stanley et al., 2003; Thorp et al., 2009; Wetherell et al., 2003). In general, CBT for GAD in older adults has not proven to be as effective as for younger adults (see Hofmann, Asnaani, Vonk, Sawyer, & Fang, 2012). There is preliminary support for the effectiveness of ACT for GAD in older adults, but randomized controlled trials are needed (Wetherell, Afari, et al., 2011).

Panic Disorder

Although most of the evidence for pharmacological treatment effectiveness is based on studies considering older adults with GAD, SSRIs appear to be effective for treating late-life panic disorder with or without agoraphobia (Hendriks et al., 2010). CBT is also effective for treating later-life panic disorder with or without agoraphobia (Hendriks et al., 2010). Some evidence suggests that medication management may be best suited to those with earlier onset and long duration of symptoms, whereas psychotherapeutic interventions may be more effective for those with shorter duration, late-onset panic disorder (Hendriks, Keijsers, Kampman, Hoogduin, & Oude Voshaar, 2012).

Specific Phobias

Treatments for specific phobia in older adults are understudied. In younger and middle-age adults, pharmacotherapy has limited support and primarily involves benzodiazepines or sedatives, which are not recommended for use in older adults because of safety issues (Choy, Fyer, & Lipsitz, 2007). In younger adult populations, CBTs, specifically exposure, are recommended as the first-line treatment for specific phobia (Wolitzky-Taylor, Horowitz, Powers, & Telch, 2008).Unfortunately, whether CBT is effective for treating specific phobias in older adults is unclear given the lack of research in this area.

Although not classified as a specific phobia, fear of falling is a related condition in older adults that is receiving a growing amount of attention in the treatment literature. Older adults with fear of falling typically do not meet criteria for a specific phobia because they do not endorse the excessiveness of their fear (Gagnon et al., 2005); however, they may cope by avoiding physical activity, which increases their risk for future falls (Arfken et al., 1994; Bertera & Bertera, 2008). Randomized controlled trials suggest that balance training and exercise programs are effective at improving physical performance and reducing the number of falls in elderly participants; the effects on psychological measures of fear of falling, however, are mixed (Freiberger, Haberle, Spirduso, & Zijlstra, 2012; Halvarsson et al., 2011). Preliminary evidence suggests that a combination treatment involving exercise, psychoeducation, and exposure therapy can reduce fear of falling and behavioral avoidance in older adults who have an excessive fear of falling (Wetherell, Johnson, et al., 2013).

Posttraumatic Stress Disorder

The evidence base for treatment of PTSD in older adults is primarily limited to case studies and a few small trials. Preliminary evidence for exposure treatments is promising (Gamito et al., 2010; Thorp, Stein, Jeste, Patterson, & Wetherell, 2012). In an open-label trial of prolonged exposure (PE) for PTSD in elderly veterans, Thorp et al. (2012) found that subjects who completed PE had significant reductions in PTSD symptoms (clinician-rated and self-reported). Furthermore, the authors found that treatment effects for PE were large and that clinician-rated symptom reduction was almost double that of a comparison treatment-as-usual group. Although they should be interpreted cautiously until results from a randomized controlled study are available, these findings from Thorp et al. (2012) are encouraging.

In regards to pharmacological treatment, research suggests that SSRI are effective for treating PTSD in the general population (Jonas et al., 2013), but no controlled trials have been conducted specifically with older adults. One open-label trial of prazosin (an antihypertensive medication) for reducing nightmares in older men with PTSD found that the drug was well-tolerated and nightmares were reduced significantly in eight of the nine subjects; however, the nightmares returned when the medication was discontinued, so long-term administration of the drug was necessary to maintain nightmare suppression (Peskind, Bonner, Hoff, & Raskind, 2003). Moreover, effects of overall PTSD symptoms as measured by the CAPS did not differ between prazosin and placebo (Raskind et al., 2007). Larger randomized controlled trials are needed to confirm the safety and effectiveness of SSRIs and prazosin for treating PTSD in older adults.

Obsessive–Compulsive Disorder

Although treatment outcome studies for older adults with OCD are sparse, exposure and response prevention (ERP) is the recommended front-line treatment for late-life OCD (Carmin, Pollard, & Ownby, 1999). The available evidence from case studies and small open-label trials suggests that ERP is an effective method of treatment for adults over the age of 60 years (e.g., Jones, Wootton, & Vaccaro, 2012).

Clinicians should assess whether modifications to the standard treatment plan are needed to account for comorbid medical conditions, cognitive ability, physical limitations, or level of caregiver support (Carmin et al., 1999). For example, an elderly patient with limited familial support may need additional therapeutic support to realize long-term maintenance of treatment gains.

Pharmacological treatment, either alone or in combination with CBT, is also an option for older adults with OCD. Similar to psychotherapy, evidence for pharmacotherapy is limited to case studies and small trials; however, the use of SSRIs to treat OCD in elderly patients is supported (Austin, Zealberg, & Lydiard, 1991; Jackson, 1995). The tricyclic antidepressant clomipramine also is approved for treatment of OCD in adults, but SSRIs are considered the first-line treatment based on safety profiles (Greist et al., 2003; Jackson, 1995).

Compulsive Hoarding

Although compulsive hoarding is more prevalent in older than younger adults, treatment trials with geriatric populations are limited. Steketee and Frost (2007) developed a manualized treatment of CBT for compulsive hoarding that was shown to be effective in middle-age adults (Steketee, Frost, Tolin, Rasmussen, & Brown, 2010; Tolin, Frost, & Steketee, 2007). In the first treatment study for geriatric compulsive hoarders, Ayers, Wetherell, Golshan, and Saxena (2011) conducted an open-label trial using the Steketee and Frost protocol but found mixed results. Of the 12 older adults included in the study, only 3 responded to treatment, and they did not maintain treatment gains at follow-up. Treatment outcome was correlated strongly with homework compliance across studies, and improving compliance through additional skills training and cognitive rehabilitation strategies may improve outcome (Ayers et al., 2011, 2014).

Although there are effective pharmacological and psychological interventions for treating anxiety in older adults, response rates are variable and effects are not as robust as those seen in younger adults (Wolitzky-Taylor et al., 2010). Behavioral techniques such as exposure and relaxation training are helpful for some subtypes of anxiety (e.g., PTSD, panic disorder, fear of falling), whereas other cognitive-behavioral components are less effective. Thus, pharmacological treatments are recommended frequently as a primary therapy for anxiety in older adults.

ANXIETY IN DEMENTIA

Given the association between anxiety and cognitive impairment, it is perhaps not surprising that there is a unique relationship between anxiety and dementia. The interaction between anxiety and neurobiological systems may reduce neurological and cognitive reserves over time, thereby increasing the risk of developing Alzheimer's disease (AD) and other dementias (Sapolsky, 1992). Although anxiety symptoms are common in patients with dementia, the issue has received little attention in the research literature until recently. The following section briefly describes the prevalence and characteristics as well as assessment, diagnostic, and treatment issues related to anxiety and dementia.

Prevalence and Course

One fifth of adults with dementia have clinically significant anxiety, and another 22%–52% have subclinical symptoms of anxiety based on caregiver and clinician ratings (Ferretti, McCurry, Logsdon, Gibbons, & Teri, 2001; Gonfrier, Andrieu, Renaud, Vellas, & Robert, 2012; Hynninen, Breitve, Rongve, Aarsland, & Nordhus, 2012). Among adults with dementia residing in assisted-living facilities, rates of clinically significant anxiety range from 11% to 18%, with approximately 50% reporting at least one symptom of anxiety (Neville & Teri, 2011; Wetzels, Zuidema, de Jonghe, Verhey, & Koopmans, 2010). Prevalence may be lower (16.5%) in those with onset of AD before age 65 years compared with late-onset AD (van Vliet et al., 2012), although severity of symptoms may be greater in younger-onset patients (Porter et al., 2003). Finally, when GAD is diagnosed formally in patients with dementia, estimates tend to be higher (5–15%) than those from population-based studies; diagnostic differences, however, preclude direct comparison between those with dementia and cognitively healthy older adults (Ferretti et al., 2001; Starkstein, Jorge, Petracca, & Robinson, 2007).

There is discrepancy as to whether the prevalence of anxiety symptoms differs across dementia subtypes, with some studies finding no difference (e.g., Hynninen et al., 2012), some finding higher rates in AD compared with other dementias (e.g., Wetzels et al., 2010), and some finding lower rates in AD compared with other dementias (e.g., Porter et al., 2003). A recent study compared neuropsychiatric symptoms between AD and vascular dementia patients with diagnoses confirmed through autopsy and found no difference in anxiety prevalence. Presence of symptoms, however, was determined through medical chart review rather than with standard neuropsychiatric assessment, which may have affected estimates.

Findings from several prospective studies suggest that anxiety symptoms decline over time in patients with dementia (Bierman, Comijs, Jonker, Scheltens, & Beekman, 2009; Wetzels et al., 2010). At least one study found that anxiety remained stable over time, but the course of anxiety in individual patients is unclear because the researchers only examined point prevalence (Gonfrier et al., 2012). Furthermore, these findings are limited by difficulties identifying and accurately assessing anxiety as dementia progresses, which will be discussed in more detail in the following sections. More prospective studies are needed to clarify the course of anxiety symptoms over time.

Characteristics and Correlates

Anxiety strongly correlates with depression, and 50% of those with anxiety and dementia have comorbid depression (Hynninen et al., 2012; Neville & Teri, 2011). Even when controlling for depression, anxiety is associated with higher caregiver stress, behavioral disturbance, and functional impairments in daily activities (Hynninen et al., 2012; Neville & Teri, 2011). Anxiety also predicts nighttime awakenings and impaired activities of daily living in community-dwelling AD patients, which may lead to institutionalization (McCurry, Gibbons, Logsdon, & Teri, 2004). Unlike patterns observed in the general population, female gender is not associated significantly with anxiety in patients with dementia (Porter et al., 2003).

Anxiety and agitation are related but distinct constructs. In patients with mild dementia, anxiety and agitation do not correlate (Hynninen et al., 2012). Studies that included adults with more severe cognitive impairment, however, found that agitation was associated significantly with anxiety (Ferretti et al., 2001; Twelftree & Qazi, 2006).

Assessment, Diagnosis, and Treatment

Assessing, diagnosing, and treating anxiety in adults with dementia represent a significant challenge due to discrepancies regarding the characteristics of anxiety in this population, heterogeneity of dementia subtypes, and a lack of standardization for diagnosing and assessing anxiety in patients with dementia. Sampling methods, sources of information (i.e., family vs. caregiver vs. patient), and operational definitions of anxiety and dementia vary widely across studies, contributing to differences in findings (Seignourel, Kunik, Snow, Wilson, & Stanley, 2008).

Diagnosis. Overlapping symptoms among anxiety, depression, and dementia complicate differential diagnosis. The use of American Psychiatric Association diagnostic criteria to assess anxiety disorders in patients with dementia is further complicated when the patient is unable to communicate cognitive symptoms that are essential for diagnosis (e.g., excessive worry). Some researchers suggest that anxiety in dementia may be better conceptualized as subsyndromal depression or a disinhibition syndrome based on findings that GAD diagnosis in patients with AD is explained primarily by the presence of delusions, pathological crying, and aggressive behavior (Seignourel et al., 2008). Recent attempts to differentiate GAD from dementia, however, found that those with GAD and dementia endorse muscle tension, fatigue, and restlessness more frequently than dementia patients without GAD (Calleo et al., 2011; Starkstein et al., 2007). Thus, the presence of these symptoms warrants further assessment of anxiety disorders in patients with dementia.

Assessment. Although several measures have been developed for assessing anxiety symptoms in patients with dementia, there is no recognized gold-standard assessment. Thus anxiety estimates vary across studies in terms of reference time points used, source of information (i.e., caregiver or patient), whether severity ratings are included, and which symptoms are rated (Gibbons, Teri, Logsdon, & McCurry, 2006). Seignourel et al. (2008) provided an excellent review of the available instruments, and although none meet all their requirements of an adequate measure, they recommended the use of the Neuropsychiatric Inventory (Cummings et al., 1994), Empirical Behavioral Pathology in Alzheimer's Disease Scale (Auer, Monteiro, & Reisberg, 1996), and the Rating for Anxiety in Dementia (RAID; Shankar, Walker, & Frost, 1999).

In general, multiple sources of information should be used when assessing anxiety in patients with dementia (Hynninen et al., 2012). The RAID is the only one of the three scales mentioned previously that includes information from multiple sources. A promising new scale developed by Gerolimatos et al. (2013), the Anxiety in Cognitive Impairment and Dementia (ACID) scale, includes both caregiver and patient report. More research on the psychometrics of the ACID is needed, but initial findings suggest that the scale has strong internal consistency as well as adequate convergent and discriminant validity.

Treatment. On the basis of patient reports, sources of anxiety include coming to terms with the diagnosis of dementia, loss of skills, environmental stressors (e.g., loud noise, crowds), relationships with others, and unknown triggers (Qazi, Spector, & Orrell, 2010). For the most part, these factors are modifiable and represent promising targets for treatment development. Adapted CBT programs are being developed to address these issues (Paukert et al., 2013; Spector et al., 2012). Other nonpharmacological treatments include emotion-oriented therapies, brief psychotherapies, sensory stimulation therapies, and person-centered therapies (for review, see McClive-Reed & Gellis, 2011). Anxiolytics and antipsychotics are effective at reducing symptoms in some patients (Cooper, 2003; Mintzer, Faison, Street, Sutton, & Breier, 2001), but their use is limited because of potential side effects and interactions with other medications.

Furthermore, both patients and caregivers feel that medication should be used as a last resort (Qazi et al., 2010). More large-scale randomized trials are needed to improve treatment options and quality of life for patients with dementia who have anxiety.

Anxiety as a Predictor of Dementia

An important question is whether anxiety increases the risk of developing dementia. Older adults with anxiety are more than two times as likely to develop dementia than those with low or no anxiety, independent of age, gender, and depression (Burton, Campbell, Jordan, Strauss, & Mallen, 2013). Furthermore, the risk of developing AD increases by 79% for older adults with high vulnerability to stress compared with those with low vulnerability (Wilson, Begeny, Boyle, Schneider, & Bennett, 2011). These findings are in line with a recent prospective autopsy study, which found that those with AD neuropathology who remained asymptomatic were more likely to have lower neuroticism scores, including lower anxiety and lower vulnerability to stress than those who were diagnosed with AD (Terracciano et al., 2013). In patients with mild cognitive impairment, it is unclear whether anxiety is associated with conversion to AD. Although some studies have found no association between anxiety and conversion to AD (e.g., Devier et al., 2009), others have found such an association (e.g., Gallagher et al., 2011). Unfortunately, these studies frequently utilize different tools for measuring anxiety, making it difficult to compare findings.

Further complicating the issue is the discrepancy over whether cognitive impairment is associated with anxiety in older adults both with and without dementia. In some studies, no associations were found between anxiety and cognitive impairment (Hynninen et al., 2012; Twelftree & Qazi, 2006), whereas other studies found that higher anxiety was associated with greater impairments in cognitive ability (Ferretti et al., 2001). The relationship is likely more complex than a strictly linear association and may be different for those with dementia compared with those without. Indeed, there is some support for a curvilinear relationship in cognitively impaired patients without dementia such that

prevalence rates of anxiety increase from mild to moderate impairment and then decline in those who have the most severe impairment (Bierman, Comijs, Jonker, & Beekman, 2007). Conversely, in patients with dementia, anxiety was lower than expected given the pattern of association, suggesting that other factors such as reduced insight may contribute to estimates of anxiety in this population (Bierman et al., 2007; Calleo et al., 2011).

CONCLUSION

Innovations in the detection and treatment of anxiety disorders in older adults are forthcoming as we unravel the complex neurobiological relationships among anxiety, depression, health, and cognition. The heterogeneity inherent in the course of late-life anxiety requires a varied and creative approach to treatment. Current evidence-based treatments include both psychotherapeutic and pharmacological options, yet there is much room for improvement. Given the high prevalence and associated burden on health and quality of life, late-life anxiety represents a significant public health concern in our aging society. Research efforts focusing on associations between aging and the domains of worry, physiological arousal, and neurological networks are promising. Research in this domain will inform clinical practice through improved understanding of symptom course and treatment response in older adults with anxiety.

References

Almeida, O. P., Draper, B., Pirkis, J., Snowdon, J., Lautenschlager, N. T., Byrne, G., . . . Pfaff, J. J. (2012). Anxiety, depression, and comorbid anxiety and depression: Risk factors and outcome over two years. *International Psychogeriatrics, 24,* 1622–1632. doi:10.1017/S104161021200107X

American Psychiatric Association. (2000). *Diagnostic and statistical manual of mental disorders* (4th ed., text revision). Washington, DC: Author.

American Psychiatric Association. (2013). *Diagnostic and statistical manual of mental disorders* (5th ed.). Washington, DC: Author.

Antony, M. M., & Rowa, K. (2005). Evidence-based assessment of anxiety disorders in adults. *Psychological Assessment, 17,* 256–266. doi:10.1037/1040-3590.17.3.256

Arfken, C. L., Lach, H. W., Birge, S. J., & Miller, J. P. (1994). The prevalence and correlates of fear of falling in elderly persons living in the community. *American Journal of Public Health, 84,* 565–570. doi:10.2105/AJPH.84.4.565

Auer, S. R., Monteiro, I. M., & Reisberg, B. (1996). The Empirical Behavioral Pathology in Alzheimer's Disease (E-BEHAVE-AD) Rating Scale. *International Psychogeriatrics, 8,* 247–266. doi:10.1017/S1041 610296002621

Austin, L. S., Zealberg, J. J., & Lydiard, R. B. (1991). Three cases of pharmacotherapy of obsessive–compulsive disorder in the elderly. *Journal of Nervous and Mental Disease, 179,* 634–635. doi:10.1097/00005053-199110000-00009

Ayers, C. R., Saxena, S., Espejo, E., Twamley, E. W., Granholm, E., & Wetherell, J. L. (2014). Novel treatment for geriatric hoarding disorder: An open trial of cognitive rehabilitation paired with behavior therapy. *American Journal of Geriatric Psychiatry, 22,* 248–252. doi:10.1016/j.jagp.2013.02.010

Ayers, C. R., Saxena, S., Golshan, S., & Wetherell, J. L. (2010). Age at onset and clinical features of late life compulsive hoarding. *International Journal of Geriatric Psychiatry, 25,* 142–149. doi:10.1002/gps.2310

Ayers, C. R., Strickland, K., & Wetherell, J. L. (2015). Evidence-based treatment for late-life generalized anxiety disorder. In P. A. Areán (Ed.), *Treatment of late-life depression, anxiety, and substance abuse* (pp. 103–132). Washington, DC: American Psychological Association.

Ayers, C. R., Wetherell, J. L., Golshan, S., & Saxena, S. (2011). Cognitive-behavioral therapy for geriatric compulsive hoarding. *Behaviour Research and Therapy, 49,* 689–694. doi:10.1016/j.brat.2011.07.002

Babcock, R. L., MaloneBeach, E. E., Hou, B., & Smith, M. (2012). The experience of worry among young and older adults in the United States and Germany: A cross-national comparison. *Aging and Mental Health, 16,* 413–422. doi:10.1080/13607863.2011.615736

Barrowclough, C., King, P., Colville, J., Russell, E., Burns, A., & Tarrier, N. (2001). A randomized trial of the effectiveness of cognitive-behavioral therapy and supportive counseling for anxiety symptoms in older adults. *Journal of Consulting and Clinical Psychology, 69,* 756–762. doi:10.1037/0022-006X.69.5.756

Beck, A. T., Epstein, N., Brown, G., & Steer, R. A. (1988). An inventory for measuring clinical anxiety: Psychometric properties. *Journal of Consulting and Clinical Psychology, 56,* 893–897. doi:10.1037/0022-006X.56.6.893

Beck, J. G., Stanley, M., & Zebb, B. (1999). Effectiveness of the Hamilton Anxiety Rating Scale with older generalized anxiety disorder patients. *Journal of Clinical Geropsychology, 5,* 281–290. doi:10.1023/A:1022962907930

Beekman, A. T., Bremmer, M. A., Deeg, D. J., van Balkom, A. J., Smit, J. H., de Beurs, E., . . . van Tilburg, W. (1998). Anxiety disorders in later life: A report from the Longitudinal Aging Study Amsterdam. *International Journal of Geriatric Psychiatry, 13,* 717–726. doi:10.1002/(SICI)1099-1166(1998100)13 :10<717::AID-GPS857>3.0.CO;2-M

Bertera, E. M., & Bertera, R. L. (2008). Fear of falling and activity avoidance in a national sample of older adults in the United States. *Health and Social Work, 33,* 54–62. doi:10.1093/hsw/33.1.54

Bierman, E. J., Comijs, H. C., Jonker, C., & Beekman, A. T. (2007). Symptoms of anxiety and depression in the course of cognitive decline. *Dementia and Geriatric Cognitive Disorders, 24,* 213–219. doi:10.1159/000107083

Bierman, E. J., Comijs, H. C., Jonker, C., Scheltens, P., & Beekman, A. T. (2009). The effect of anxiety and depression on decline of memory function in Alzheimer's disease. *International Psychogeriatrics, 21,* 1142–1147. doi:10.1017/S1041610209990512

Blake, D. D., Weathers, F. W., Nagy, L. M., Kaloupek, D. G., Gusman, F. D., Charney, D. S., & Keane, T. M. (1995). The development of a Clinician-Administered PTSD Scale. *Journal of Traumatic Stress, 8,* 75–90. doi:10.1002/jts.2490080106

Blanchard, E. B., Jones-Alexander, J., Buckley, T. C., & Forneris, C. A. (1996). Psychometric properties of the PTSD Checklist (PCL). *Behaviour Research and Therapy, 34,* 669–673. doi:10.1016/0005-7967(96)00033-2

Boddice, G., Pachana, N. A., & Byrne, G. J. (2008). The clinical utility of the geriatric anxiety inventory in older adults with cognitive impairment. *Nursing Older People, 20,* 36–39. doi:10.7748/nop2008.10.20.8.36.c6809

Böttche, M., Kuwert, P., & Knaevelsrud, C. (2012). Posttraumatic stress disorder in older adults: An overview of characteristics and treatment approaches. *International Journal of Geriatric Psychiatry, 27,* 230–239. doi:10.1002/gps.2725

Bryant, C., Jackson, H., & Ames, D. (2008). The prevalence of anxiety in older adults: Methodological issues and a review of the literature. *Journal of Affective Disorders, 109,* 233–250. doi:10.1016/j.jad.2007.11.008

Bryant, C., Mohlman, J., Gum, A., Stanley, M., Beekman, A. T., Wetherell, J. L., . . . Lenze, E. J. (2013). Anxiety disorders in older adults: Looking to *DSM–5* and beyond. *American Journal of Geriatric Psychiatry, 21,* 872–876. doi:10.1016/j.jagp.2013.01.011

Burton, C., Campbell, P., Jordan, K., Strauss, V., & Mallen, C. (2013). The association of anxiety and depression with future dementia diagnosis: A case-control study in primary care. *Family Practice, 30*, 25–30. doi:10.1093/fampra/cms044

Byers, A. L., Areán, P. A., & Yaffe, K. (2012). Low use of mental health services among older Americans with mood and anxiety disorders. *Psychiatric Services, 63*, 66–72. doi:10.1176/appi.ps.201100121

Byers, A. L., Yaffe, K., Covinsky, K. E., Friedman, M. B., & Bruce, M. L. (2010). High occurrence of mood and anxiety disorders among older adults: The National Comorbidity Survey Replication. *Archives of General Psychiatry, 67*, 489–496. doi:10.1001/archgenpsychiatry.2010.35

Cairney, J., McCabe, L., Veldhuizen, S., Corna, L. M., Streiner, D., & Herrmann, N. (2007). Epidemiology of social phobia in later life. *American Journal of Geriatric Psychiatry, 15*, 224–233. doi:10.1097/01.JGP.0000235702.77245.46

Calleo, J. S., Kunik, M. E., Reid, D., Kraus-Schuman, C., Paukert, A., Regev, T., . . . Stanley, M. (2011). Characteristics of generalized anxiety disorder in patients with dementia. *American Journal of Alzheimer's Disease and Other Dementias, 26*, 492–497. doi:10.1177/1533317511426867

Carmin, C. N., Pollard, C. A., & Ownby, R. L. (1999). Cognitive behavioral treatment of older adults with obsessive–compulsive disorder. *Cognitive and Behavioral Practice, 6*, 110–119. doi:10.1016/S1077-7229(99)80019-4

Chou, K. L. (2009). Age at onset of generalized anxiety disorder in older adults. *American Journal of Geriatric Psychiatry, 17*, 455–464. doi:10.1097/JGP.0b013e31818f3a93

Chou, K. L., Mackenzie, C. S., Liang, K., & Sareen, J. (2011). Three-year incidence and predictors of first-onset of *DSM–IV* mood, anxiety, and substance use disorders in older adults: Results from Wave 2 of the National Epidemiologic Survey on Alcohol and Related Conditions. *Journal of Clinical Psychiatry, 72*, 144–155. doi:10.4088/JCP.09m05618gry

Choy, Y., Fyer, A. J., & Lipsitz, J. D. (2007). Treatment of specific phobia in adults. *Clinical Psychology Review, 27*, 266–286. doi:10.1016/j.cpr.2006.10.002

Comer, J. S., Blanco, C., Hasin, D. S., Liu, S. M., Grant, B. F., Turner, J. B., & Olfson, M. (2011). Health-related quality of life across the anxiety disorders: Results from the national epidemiologic survey on alcohol and related conditions (NESARC). *Journal of Clinical Psychiatry, 72*, 43–50. doi:10.4088/JCP.09m05094blu

Cooper, J. P. (2003). Buspirone for anxiety and agitation in dementia. *Journal of Psychiatry and Neuroscience, 28*, 469.

Copeland, J., Kelleher, M., Duckworth, G., & Smith, A. (1976). Reliability of psychiatric assessment in older patients. *International Journal of Aging and Human Development, 7*, 313–322. doi:10.2190/3DR2-7H3C-GG9L-AQC3

Corral, I., & Landrine, H. (Eds.). (2010). *Methodological and statistical issues in research with diverse samples: The problem of measurement equivalence.* New York, NY: Springer.

Creamer, M., & Parslow, R. (2008). Trauma exposure and posttraumatic stress disorder in the elderly: A community prevalence study. *American Journal of Geriatric Psychiatry, 16*, 853–856. doi:10.1097/01.JGP.0000310785.36837.85

Cummings, J. L., Mega, M., Gray, K., Rosenberg-Thompson, S., Carusi, D. A., & Gornbein, J. (1994). The Neuropsychiatric Inventory: Comprehensive assessment of psychopathology in dementia. *Neurology, 44*, 2308–2314. doi:10.1212/WNL.44.12.2308

DeBerry, S., Davis, S., & Reinhard, K. E. (1989). A comparison of meditation-relaxation and cognitive/behavioral techniques for reducing anxiety and depression in a geriatric population. *Journal of Geriatric Psychiatry, 22*, 231–247.

Devier, D. J., Pelton, G. H., Tabert, M. H., Liu, X., Cuasay, K., Eisenstadt, R., . . . Devanand, D. P. (2009). The impact of anxiety on conversion from mild cognitive impairment to Alzheimer's disease. *International Journal of Geriatric Psychiatry, 24*, 1335–1342. doi:10.1002/gps.2263

Diefenbach, G. J., Dimauro, J., Frost, R., Steketee, G., & Tolin, D. F. (2013). Characteristics of hoarding in older adults. *American Journal of Geriatric Psychiatry.* doi:10.1016/j.jagp.2013.01.028

El-Gabalawy, R., Mackenzie, C. S., Shooshtari, S., & Sareen, J. (2011). Comorbid physical health conditions and anxiety disorders: A population-based exploration of prevalence and health outcomes among older adults. *General Hospital Psychiatry, 33*, 556–564. doi:10.1016/j.genhosppsych.2011.07.005

Ferretti, L., McCurry, S. M., Logsdon, R., Gibbons, L., & Teri, L. (2001). Anxiety and Alzheimer's disease. *Journal of Geriatric Psychiatry and Neurology, 14*, 52–58. doi:10.1177/089198870101400111

Freiberger, E., Haberle, L., Spirduso, W. W., & Zijlstra, G. A. (2012). Long-term effects of three multicomponent exercise interventions on physical performance and fall-related psychological outcomes in community-dwelling older adults: A randomized controlled trial. *Journal of the American Geriatrics Society, 60*, 437–446. doi:10.1111/j.1532-5415.2011.03859.x

Gagnon, N., Flint, A. J., Naglie, G., & Devins, G. M. (2005). Affective correlates of fear of falling in elderly persons [United States.]. *American*

Journal of Geriatric Psychiatry, 13, 7–14. doi:10.1097/00019442-200501000-00003

Gallagher, D., Coen, R., Kilroy, D., Belinski, K., Bruce, I., Coakley, D., . . . Lawlor, B. A. (2011). Anxiety and behavioural disturbance as markers of prodromal Alzheimer's disease in patients with mild cognitive impairment. *International Journal of Geriatric Psychiatry, 26*, 166–172. doi:10.1002/gps.2509

Gamito, P., Oliveira, J., Rosa, P., Morais, D., Duarte, N., Oliveira, S., & Saraiva, T. (2010). PTSD elderly war veterans: A clinical controlled pilot study. *Cyberpsychology, Behavior, and Social Networking, 13*, 43–48. doi:10.1089/cyber.2009.0237

Gerolimatos, L. A., Ciliberti, C. M., Nazem, S., Gregg, J. J., Hackney, K., & Bamonti, P. . . . Edelstein, B. (2013, November). *Development and initial evaluation of the Anxiety in Cognitive Impairment and Dementia (ACID) scale*. Paper presented at the meeting of The Gerontological Society of America, New Orleans, LA.

Ghaed, S. H., Ayers, C. R., & Wetherell, J. L. (2012). Evidence-based psychological treatment for geriatric anxiety. In F. Scogin & A. Shah (Eds.), *Making evidence-based psychological treatments work with older adults* (pp. 9–46). Washington, DC: American Psychological Association. doi:10.1037/13753-002

Gibbons, L. E., Teri, L., Logsdon, R. G., & McCurry, S. M. (2006). Assessment of anxiety in dementia: An investigation into the association of different methods of measurement. *Journal of Geriatric Psychiatry and Neurology, 19*, 202–208. doi:10.1177/0891988706292758

Gonçalves, D. C., & Byrne, G. J. (2012). Interventions for generalized anxiety disorder in older adults: Systematic review and meta-analysis. *Journal of Anxiety Disorders, 26*, 1–11. doi:10.1016/j.janxdis.2011.08.010

Gonçalves, D. C., & Byrne, G. J. (2013). Who worries most? Worry prevalence and patterns across the lifespan. *International Journal of Geriatric Psychiatry, 28*, 41–49. doi:10.1002/gps.3788

Gonçalves, D. C., Pachana, N. A., & Byrne, G. J. (2011). Prevalence and correlates of generalized anxiety disorder among older adults in the Australian National Survey of Mental Health and Well-Being. *Journal of Affective Disorders, 132*, 223–230. doi:10.1016/j.jad.2011.02.023

Gonfrier, S., Andrieu, S., Renaud, D., Vellas, B., & Robert, P. H. (2012). Course of neuropsychiatric symptoms during a 4-year follow up in the REAL-FR cohort. *Journal of Nutrition, Health and Aging, 16*, 134–137. doi:10.1007/s12603-011-0147-9

Goodman, W. K., Price, L. H., Rasmussen, S. A., Mazure, C., Delgado, P., Heninger, G. R., & Charney, D. S. (1989). The Yale-Brown Obsessive Compulsive Scale. II. Validity. *Archives of General Psychiatry,* 46, 1012–1016. doi:10.1001/archpsyc.1989.01810110054008

Goodman, W. K., Price, L. H., Rasmussen, S. A., Mazure, C., Fleischmann, R. L., Hill, C. L., . . . Charney, D. S. (1989). The Yale-Brown Obsessive Compulsive Scale. I. Development, use, and reliability. *Archives of General Psychiatry, 46*, 1006–1011. doi:10.1001/archpsyc.1989.01810110048007

Gorenstein, E. E., Kleber, M. S., Mohlman, J., Dejesus, M., Gorman, J. M., & Papp, L. A. (2005). Cognitive-behavioral therapy for management of anxiety and medication taper in older adults. *American Journal of Geriatric Psychiatry, 13*, 901–909. doi:10.1176/appi.ajgp.13.10.901

Gould, C. E., Beaudreau, S. A., & Huh, J. W. T. (2013). A Veterans Health Administration imperative: Recommendations for detecting anxiety in older adults. *Federal Practitioner, 30*, 35–42.

Gould, C. E., & Edelstein, B. A. (2010). Worry, emotion control, and anxiety control in older and young adults. *Journal of Anxiety Disorders, 24*, 759–766. doi:10.1016/j.janxdis.2010.05.009

Gould, C. E., Gerolimatos, L. A., Ciliberti, C. M., Edelstein, B. A., & Smith, M. D. (2012). Initial evaluation of the Older Adult Social-Evaluative Situations Questionnaire: A measure of social anxiety in older adults. *International Psychogeriatrics, 24*, 2009–2018. doi:10.1017/S1041610212001275

Gould, R. L., Coulson, M. C., & Howard, R. J. (2012). Efficacy of cognitive behavioral therapy for anxiety disorders in older people: A meta-analysis and metaregression of randomized controlled trials. *Journal of the American Geriatrics Society, 60*, 218–229. doi:10.1111/j.1532-5415.2011.03824.x

Greist, J. H., Bandelow, B., Hollander, E., Marazziti, D., Montgomery, S. A., Nutt, D. J., . . . Zohar, J. (2003). WCA recommendations for the long-term treatment of obsessive–compulsive disorder in adults. *CNS Spectrums, 8*(8, Suppl. 1), 7–16.

Grenier, S., Preville, M., Boyer, R., & O'Connor, K. (2009). Prevalence and correlates of obsessive–compulsive disorder among older adults living in the community. *Journal of Anxiety Disorders, 23*, 858–865. doi:10.1016/j.janxdis.2009.04.005

Grenier, S., Schuurmans, J., Goldfarb, M., Preville, M., Boyer, R., O'Connor, K., . . . Hudon, C. (2011). The epidemiology of specific phobia and subthreshold fear subtypes in a community-based sample of older adults. *Depression and Anxiety, 28*, 456–463. doi:10.1002/da.20812

Gum, A. M., King-Kallimanis, B., & Kohn, R. (2009). Prevalence of mood, anxiety, and substance-abuse disorders for older Americans in the national comorbidity survey-replication. *American Journal of Geriatric Psychiatry, 17*, 769–781. doi:10.1097/JGP.0b013e3181ad4f5a

Halvarsson, A., Oddsson, L., Olsson, E., Faren, E., Pettersson, A., & Stahle, A. (2011). Effects of new, individually adjusted, progressive balance group training for elderly people with fear of falling and tend to fall: A randomized controlled trial. *Clinical Rehabilitation, 25,* 1021–1031. doi:10.1177/0269215511411937

Hamilton, M. (1959). The assessment of anxiety states by rating. *British Journal of Medical Psychology, 32,* 50–55. doi:10.1111/j.2044-8341.1959.tb00467.x

Hek, K., Tiemeier, H., Newson, R. S., Luijendijk, H. J., Hofman, A., & Mulder, C. L. (2011). Anxiety disorders and comorbid depression in community dwelling older adults. *International Journal of Methods in Psychiatric Research, 20,* 157–168. doi:10.1002/mpr.344

Hendriks, G. J., Keijsers, G. P., Kampman, M., Hoogduin, C. A., & Oude Voshaar, R. C. (2012). Predictors of outcome of pharmacological and psychological treatment of late-life panic disorder with agoraphobia. *International Journal of Geriatric Psychiatry, 27,* 146–150. doi:10.1002/gps.2700

Hendriks, G. J., Keijsers, G. P., Kampman, M., Oude Voshaar, R. C., Verbraak, M. J., Broekman, T. G., & Hoogduin, C. A. (2010). A randomized controlled study of paroxetine and cognitive-behavioural therapy for late-life panic disorder. *Acta Psychiatrica Scandinavica, 122,* 11–19. doi:10.1111/j.1600-0447.2009.01517.x

Himmelfarb, S., & Murrell, S. A. (1984). The prevalence and correlates of anxiety symptoms in older adults. *Journal of Psychology, 116,* 159–167. doi:10.1080/00223980.1984.9923632

Hofmann, S. G., Asnaani, A., Vonk, I. J., Sawyer, A. T., & Fang, A. (2012). The efficacy of cognitive behavioral therapy: A review of meta-analyses. *Cognitive Therapy and Research, 36,* 427–440. doi:10.1007/s10608-012-9476-1

Hopko, D. R., Stanley, M. A., Reas, D. L., Wetherell, J. L., Beck, J. G., Novy, D. M., & Averill, P. M. (2003). Assessing worry in older adults: Confirmatory factor analysis of the Penn State Worry Questionnaire and psychometric properties of an abbreviated model. *Psychological Assessment, 15,* 173–183. doi:10.1037/1040-3590.15.2.173

Hunt, S., Wisocki, P., & Yanko, J. (2003). Worry and use of coping strategies among older and younger adults. *Journal of Anxiety Disorders, 17,* 547–560. doi:10.1016/S0887-6185(02)00229-3

Hyer, L., Summers, M. N., Boyd, S., Litaker, M., & Boudewyns, P. (1996). Assessment of older combat veterans with the clinician-administered PTSD scale. *Journal of Traumatic Stress, 9,* 587–593. doi:10.1002/jts.2490090314

Hynninen, M. J., Breitve, M. H., Rongve, A., Aarsland, D., & Nordhus, I. H. (2012). The frequency and correlates of anxiety in patients with first-time diagnosed mild dementia. *International Psychogeriatrics, 24,* 1771–1778. doi:10.1017/S1041610212001020

Jackson, C. W. (1995). Obsessive–compulsive disorder in elderly patients. *Drugs and Aging, 7,* 438–448. doi:10.2165/00002512-199507060-00004

Jeste, D. V., Blazer, D. G., & First, M. (2005). Aging-related diagnostic variations: Need for diagnostic criteria appropriate for elderly psychiatric patients. *Biological Psychiatry, 58,* 265–271. doi:10.1016/j.biopsych.2005.02.004

Jonas, D. E., Cusack, K., Forneris, C. A., Wilkins, T. M., Sonis, J., Middleton, J. C., . . . Gaynes, B. N. (2013). *Psychological and pharmacological treatments for adults with posttraumatic stress disorder (PTSD)* Rockville, MD: Agency for Healthcare Research and Quality. Retrieved from http://www.effectivehealthcare.ahrq.gov/reports/final.cfm

Jones, M. K., Wootton, B. M., & Vaccaro, L. D. (2012). The efficacy of exposure and response prevention for geriatric obsessive–compulsive disorder: A clinical case illustration. *Case Reports in Psychiatry, 2012,* 1–5. doi:10.1155/2012/394603

Katz, I. R., Reynolds, C. F., III, Alexopoulos, G. S., & Hackett, D. (2002). Venlafaxine ER as a treatment for generalized anxiety disorder in older adults: Pooled analysis of five randomized placebo-controlled clinical trials. *Journal of the American Geriatrics Society, 50,* 18–25. doi:10.1046/j.1532-5415.2002.50003.x

Kessler, R. C., Berglund, P., Demler, O., Jin, R., Merikangas, K. R., & Walters, E. E. (2005). Lifetime prevalence and age-of-onset distributions of *DSM–IV* disorders in the National Comorbidity Survey Replication. *Archives of General Psychiatry, 62,* 593–602. doi:10.1001/archpsyc.62.6.593

King-Kallimanis, B., Gum, A. M., & Kohn, R. (2009). Comorbidity of depressive and anxiety disorders for older Americans in the national comorbidity survey-replication. *American Journal of Geriatric Psychiatry, 17,* 782–792. doi:10.1097/JGP.0b013e3181ad4d17

Kohn, R., Westlake, R. J., Rasmussen, S. A., Marsland, R. T., & Norman, W. H. (1997). Clinical features of obsessive–compulsive disorder in elderly patients. *American Journal of Geriatric Psychiatry, 5,* 211–215. doi:10.1097/00019442-199700530-00004

Lauderdale, S. A., & Sheikh, J. I. (2003). Anxiety disorders in older adults. *Clinics in Geriatric Medicine, 19,* 721–741. doi:10.1016/S0749-0690(03)00047-8

LeBeau, R. T., Glenn, D., Liao, B., Wittchen, H. U., Beesdo-Baum, K., Ollendick, T., & Craske, M. G. (2010). Specific phobia: A review of *DSM–IV* specific phobia and preliminary recommendations for *DSM–5. Depression and Anxiety, 27,* 148–167. doi:10.1002/da.20655

Lee, L. O., & Knight, B. G. (2009). Attentional bias for threat in older adults: Moderation of the positivity bias by trait anxiety and stimulus modality. *Psychology and Aging, 24,* 741–747. doi:10.1037/a0016409

Lenze, E. J., Mulsant, B. H., Shear, M. K., Schulberg, H. C., Dew, M. A., Begley, A. E., . . . Reynolds, C. F., III. (2000). Comorbid anxiety disorders in depressed elderly patients. *American Journal of Psychiatry, 157,* 722–728. doi:10.1176/appi.ajp.157.5.722

Lenze, E. J., Rollman, B. L., Shear, M. K., Dew, M. A., Pollock, B. G., Ciliberti, C., . . . Reynolds, C. F., III. (2009). Escitalopram for older adults with generalized anxiety disorder: A randomized controlled trial. *JAMA, 301,* 295–303. doi:10.1001/jama.2008.977

Le Roux, H., Gatz, M., & Wetherell, J. L. (2005). Age at onset of generalized anxiety disorder in older adults. *American Journal of Geriatric Psychiatry, 13,* 23–30. doi:10.1097/00019442-200501000-00005

Mackenzie, C. S., Reynolds, K., Cairney, J., Streiner, D. L., & Sareen, J. (2012). Disorder-specific mental health service use for mood and anxiety disorders: Associations with age, sex, and psychiatric comorbidity. *Depression and Anxiety, 29,* 234–242. doi:10.1002/da.20911

Mackenzie, C. S., Reynolds, K., Chou, K. L., Pagura, J., & Sareen, J. (2011). Prevalence and correlates of generalized anxiety disorder in a national sample of older adults. *American Journal of Geriatric Psychiatry, 19,* 305–315. doi:10.1097/JGP.0b013e318202bc62

Marks, I. M., & Mathews, A. M. (1979). Brief standard self-rating for phobic patients. *Behaviour Research and Therapy, 17,* 263–267. doi:10.1016/0005-7967(79)90041-X

Mather, M., Canli, T., English, T., Whitfield, S., Wais, P., Ochsner, K., . . . Carstensen, L. L. (2004). Amygdala responses to emotionally valenced stimuli in older and younger adults. *Psychological Science, 15,* 259–263. doi:10.1111/j.0956-7976.2004.00662.x

Mather, M., & Carstensen, L. L. (2005). Aging and motivated cognition: The positivity effect in attention and memory. *Trends in Cognitive Sciences, 9,* 496–502. doi:10.1016/j.tics.2005.08.005

McClive-Reed, K. P., & Gellis, Z. D. (2011). Anxiety and related symptoms in older persons with dementia: Directions for practice. *Journal of Gerontological Social Work, 54,* 6–28. doi:10.1080/01634372.2010.524284

McCurry, S. M., Gibbons, L. E., Logsdon, R. G., & Teri, L. (2004). Anxiety and nighttime behavioral disturbances. Awakenings in patients with Alzheimer's disease. *Journal of Gerontological Nursing, 30,* 12–20.

McLean, C. P., Asnaani, A., Litz, B. T., & Hofmann, S. G. (2011). Gender differences in anxiety disorders: Prevalence, course of illness, comorbidity and burden of illness. *Journal of Psychiatric Research, 45,* 1027–1035. doi:10.1016/j.jpsychires.2011.03.006

Meyer, T. J., Miller, M. L., Metzger, R. L., & Borkovec, T. D. (1990). Development and validation of the Penn State Worry Questionnaire. *Behaviour Research and Therapy, 28,* 487–495. doi:10.1016/0005-7967(90)90135-6

Mintzer, J., Faison, W., Street, J. S., Sutton, V. K., & Breier, A. (2001). Olanzapine in the treatment of anxiety symptoms due to Alzheimer's disease: A post hoc analysis. *International Journal of Geriatric Psychiatry, 16*(Suppl. 1), S71–S77. doi:10.1002/1099-1166(200112)16:1+<::AID-GPS568>3.0.CO;2-M

Mohlman, J. (2012). A community based survey of older adults' preferences for treatment of anxiety. *Psychology and Aging, 27,* 1182–1190. doi:10.1037/a0023126

Mohlman, J., Bryant, C., Lenze, E. J., Stanley, M. A., Gum, A., Flint, A., . . . Craske, M. G. (2012). Improving recognition of late life anxiety disorders in *Diagnostic and Statistical Manual of Mental Disorders, Fifth Edition:* Observations and recommendations of the Advisory Committee to the Lifespan Disorders Work Group. *International Journal of Geriatric Psychiatry, 27,* 549–556. doi: 10.1002/gps.2752

Mohlman, J., Sirota, K. G., Papp, L. A., Staples, A. M., King, A., & Gorenstein, E. E. (2012). Clinical interviewing with older adults. *Cognitive and Behavioral Practice, 19,* 89–100. doi:10.1016/j.cbpra.2010.10.001

Moore, A. R., & O'Keeffe, S. T. (1999). Drug-induced cognitive impairment in the elderly. *Drugs and Aging, 15,* 15–28. doi:10.2165/00002512-199915010-00002

Morris, S. E., & Cuthbert, B. N. (2012). Research domain criteria: Cognitive systems, neural circuits, and dimensions of behavior. *Dialogues in Clinical Neuroscience, 14,* 29–37.

Neville, C., & Teri, L. (2011). Anxiety, anxiety symptoms, and associations among older people with dementia in assisted-living facilities. *International Journal of Mental Health Nursing, 20,* 195–201. doi:10.1111/j.1447-0349.2010.00724.x

Pachana, N. A., Byrne, G. J., Siddle, H., Koloski, N., Harley, E., & Arnold, E. (2007). Development and validation of the Geriatric Anxiety Inventory. *International Psychogeriatrics, 19,* 103–114. doi:10.1017/S1041610206003504

Pariente, A., Dartigues, J. F., Benichou, J., Letenneur, L., Moore, N., & Fourrier-Reglat, A. (2008). Benzodiazepines and injurious falls in community dwelling elders. *Drugs and Aging, 25,* 61–70. doi:10.2165/00002512-200825010-00007

Paukert, A. L., Kraus-Schuman, C., Wilson, N., Snow, A. L., Calleo, J., Kunik, M. E., & Stanley, M. A. (2013). The peaceful mind manual: A protocol for treating anxiety in persons with dementia. *Behavior Modification, 37,* 631–664. doi:10.1177/0145445513477420

Peskind, E. R., Bonner, L. T., Hoff, D. J., & Raskind, M. A. (2003). Prazosin reduces trauma-related nightmares in older men with chronic posttraumatic stress disorder. *Journal of Geriatric Psychiatry and Neurology, 16,* 165–171.

Pietrzak, R. H., Goldstein, R. B., Southwick, S. M., & Grant, B. F. (2012a). Physical health conditions associated with posttraumatic stress disorder in U.S. older adults: Results from wave 2 of the National Epidemiologic Survey on Alcohol and Related Conditions. *Journal of the American Geriatrics Society, 60,* 296–303. doi:10.1111/j.1532-5415.2011.03788.x

Pietrzak, R. H., Goldstein, R. B., Southwick, S. M., & Grant, B. F. (2012b). Psychiatric comorbidity of full and partial posttraumatic stress disorder among older adults in the United States: Results from wave 2 of the National Epidemiologic Survey on Alcohol and Related Conditions [United States]. *American Journal of Geriatric Psychiatry, 20,* 380–390. doi:10.1097/JGP.0b013e31820d92e7

Pietrzak, R. H., Van Ness, P. H., Fried, T. R., Galea, S., & Norris, F. (2012). Diagnostic utility and factor structure of the PTSD Checklist in older adults. *International Psychogeriatrics, 24,* 1684–1696. doi:10.1017/S1041610212000853

Porensky, E. K., Dew, M. A., Karp, J. F., Skidmore, E., Rollman, B. L., Shear, M. K., & Lenze, E. J. (2009). The burden of late-life generalized anxiety disorder: Effects on disability, health-related quality of life, and healthcare utilization. *American Journal of Geriatric Psychiatry, 17,* 473–482. doi:10.1097/JGP.0b013e31819b87b2

Porter, V. R., Buxton, W. G., Fairbanks, L. A., Strickland, T., O'Connor, S. M., Rosenberg-Thompson, S., & Cummings, J. L. (2003). Frequency and characteristics of anxiety among patients with Alzheimer's disease and related dementias. *Journal of Neuropsychiatry and Clinical Neurosciences, 15,* 180–186. doi:10.1176/appi.neuropsych.15.2.180

Potvin, O., Bergua, V., Meillon, C., Le Goff, M., Bouisson, J., Dartigues, J. F., & Amieva, H. (2013). State anxiety and cognitive functioning in older adults. *American Journal of Geriatric Psychiatry, 21,* 915–924. doi:10.1016/j.jagp.2013.01.029

Powers, C. B., Wisocki, P. A., & Whitbourne, S. K. (1992). Age differences and correlates of worrying in young and elderly adults. *Gerontologist, 32,* 82–88. doi:10.1093/geront/32.1.82

Price, R. B., Eldreth, D. A., & Mohlman, J. (2011). Deficient prefrontal attentional control in late-life generalized anxiety disorder: An fMRI investigation. *Translational Psychiatry, 1,* e46. doi:10.1038/tp.2011.46

Price, R. B., Siegle, G., & Mohlman, J. (2012). Emotional stroop performance in older adults: Effects of habitual worry. *American Journal of Geriatric Psychiatry, 20,* 798–805. doi:10.1097/JGP.0b013e318230340d

Prina, A. M., Ferri, C. P., Guerra, M., Brayne, C., & Prince, M. (2011). Prevalence of anxiety and its correlates among older adults in Latin America, India and China: Cross-cultural study. *British Journal of Psychiatry, 199,* 485–491. doi:10.1192/bjp.bp.110.083915

Qazi, A., Spector, A., & Orrell, M. (2010). User, carer and staff perspectives on anxiety in dementia: A qualitative study. *Journal of Affective Disorders, 125,* 295–300. doi:10.1016/j.jad.2009.12.015

Ramsawh, H. J., Raffa, S. D., Edelen, M. O., Rende, R., & Keller, M. B. (2009). Anxiety in middle adulthood: Effects of age and time on the 14-year course of panic disorder, social phobia and generalized anxiety disorder. *Psychological Medicine, 39,* 615–624. doi:10.1017/S0033291708003954

Raskind, M. A., Peskind, E. R., Hoff, D. J., Hart, K. L., Holmes, H. A., Warren, D., . . . McFall, M. E. (2007). A parallel group placebo controlled study of prazosin for trauma nightmares and sleep disturbance in combat veterans with post-traumatic stress disorder. *Biological Psychiatry, 61,* 928–934. doi:10.1016/j.biopsych.2006.06.032

Regier, D. A., Boyd, J. H., Burke, J. D., Jr., Rae, D. S., Myers, J. K., Kramer, M., . . . Locke, B. Z. (1988). One-month prevalence of mental disorders in the United States. Based on five epidemiologic catchment area sites. *Archives of General Psychiatry, 45,* 977–986. doi:10.1001/archpsyc.1988.01800350011002

Ritchie, K., Artero, S., Beluche, I., Ancelin, M. L., Mann, A., Dupuy, A. M., . . . Boulenger, J. P. (2004). Prevalence of *DSM–IV* psychiatric disorder in the French elderly population. *British Journal of Psychiatry, 184,* 147–152. doi:10.1192/bjp.184.2.147

Sapolsky, R. M. (1992). *Stress, the aging brain, and the mechanisms of neuron death.* Cambridge, MA: MIT Press.

Scheffer, A. C., Schuurmans, M. J., van Dijk, N., van der Hooft, T., & de Rooij, S. E. (2008). Fear of falling: Measurement strategy, prevalence, risk factors and consequences among older persons. *Age and Ageing, 37,* 19–24. doi:10.1093/ageing/afm169

Scheibe, S., & Carstensen, L. L. (2010). Emotional aging: Recent findings and future trends. *The Journals of Gerontology, Series B: Psychological Sciences and Social Sciences, 65,* 135–144. doi:10.1093/geronb/gbp132

Schuitevoerder, S., Rosen, J. W., Twamley, E. W., Ayers, C. R., Sones, H., Lohr, J. B., . . . Thorp, S. R. (2013). A meta-analysis of cognitive functioning in older adults with PTSD. *Journal of Anxiety Disorders, 27*, 550–558. doi:10.1016/j.janxdis.2013.01.001

Schuurmans, J., Comijs, H., Emmelkamp, P. M., Weijnen, I. J., van den Hout, M., & van Dyck, R. (2009). Long-term effectiveness and prediction of treatment outcome in cognitive behavioral therapy and sertraline for late-life anxiety disorders. *International Psychogeriatrics, 21*, 1148–1159. doi:10.1017/S1041610209990536

Segal, D. L., June, A., Payne, M., Coolidge, F. L., & Yochim, B. (2010). Development and initial validation of a self-report assessment tool for anxiety among older adults: The Geriatric Anxiety Scale. *Journal of Anxiety Disorders, 24*, 709–714. doi:10.1016/j.janxdis.2010.05.002

Seignourel, P. J., Kunik, M. E., Snow, L., Wilson, N., & Stanley, M. (2008). Anxiety in dementia: A critical review. *Clinical Psychology Review, 28*, 1071–1082. doi:10.1016/j.cpr.2008.02.008

Seitz, D., Purandare, N., & Conn, D. (2010). Prevalence of psychiatric disorders among older adults in long-term care homes: A systematic review. *International Psychogeriatrics, 22*, 1025–1039. doi:10.1017/S1041610210000608

Shankar, K. K., Walker, M., & Frost, D. (1999). The development of a valid and reliable scale for rating anxiety in dementia (RAID). *Aging and Mental Health, 3*, 39–49. doi:10.1080/13607869956424

Shear, K., Belnap, B. H., Mazumdar, S., Houck, P., & Rollman, B. L. (2006). Generalized anxiety disorder severity scale (GADSS): a preliminary validation study. *Depression and Anxiety (1091-4269), 23*, 77–82. doi: 10.1002/da.20149

Smalbrugge, M., Jongenelis, L., Pot, A. M., Beekman, A. T., & Eefsting, J. A. (2005). Comorbidity of depression and anxiety in nursing home patients. *International Journal of Geriatric Psychiatry, 20*, 218–226. doi:10.1002/gps.1269

Spector, A., Orrell, M., Lattimer, M., Hoe, J., King, M., Harwood, K., . . . Charlesworth, G. (2012). Cognitive behavioural therapy (CBT) for anxiety in people with dementia: Study protocol for a randomised controlled trial. *Trials, 13*, 197. doi:10.1186/1745-6215-13-197

Spielberger, C. D., Gorsuch, R. L., Lushene, R., Vagg, P. R., & Jacobs, G. A. (1983). *Manual for the State-Trait Anxiety Inventory.* Palo Alto, CA: Consulting Psychologists Press.

Spinhoven, P., Ormel, J., Sloekers, P. P., Kempen, G. I., Speckens, A. E., & Van Hemert, A. M. (1997). A validation study of the Hospital Anxiety and Depression Scale (HADS) in different groups of Dutch subjects. *Psychological Medicine, 27*, 363–370. doi:10.1017/S0033291796004382

Spitzer, C., Barnow, S., Volzke, H., John, U., Freyberger, H. J., & Grabe, H. J. (2008). Trauma and posttraumatic stress disorder in the elderly: Findings from a German community study. *Journal of Clinical Psychiatry, 69*, 693–700. doi:10.4088/JCP.v69n0501

Spitzer, R. L., Kroenke, K., Williams, J. B., & Lowe, B. (2006). A brief measure for assessing generalized anxiety disorder: The GAD-7. *Archives of Internal Medicine, 166*, 1092–1097. doi:10.1001/archinte.166.10.1092

Stanley, M. A., Beck, J. G., Novy, D. M., Averill, P. M., Swann, A. C., Diefenbach, G. J., & Hopko, D. R. (2003). Cognitive-behavioral treatment of late-life generalized anxiety disorder. *Journal of Consulting and Clinical Psychology, 71*, 309–319. doi:10.1037/0022-006X.71.2.309

Stanley, M. A., Novy, D. M., Bourland, S. L., Beck, J. G., & Averill, P. M. (2001). Assessing older adults with generalized anxiety: A replication and extension. *Behaviour Research and Therapy, 39*, 221–235. doi:10.1016/S0005-7967(00)00030-9

Starkstein, S. E., Jorge, R., Petracca, G., & Robinson, R. G. (2007). The construct of generalized anxiety disorder in Alzheimer disease. *American Journal of Geriatric Psychiatry, 15*, 42–49. doi:10.1097/01.JGP.0000229664.11306.b9

Steketee, G., & Frost, R. O. (2007). *Compulsive hoarding and acquiring: Therapist guide.* New York, NY: Oxford University Press.

Steketee, G., Frost, R. O., Tolin, D. F., Rasmussen, J., & Brown, T. A. (2010). Waitlist-controlled trial of cognitive behavior therapy for hoarding disorder. *Depression and Anxiety, 27*, 476–484. doi:10.1002/da.20673

Stoddard, J. A., Barmann, C., Lenze, E. J., & Wetherell, J. L. (in press). Combining medication and psychotherapy for late life anxiety and mood disorders. In N. Pachana & K. Laidlaw (Eds.), *Oxford handbook of clinical geropsychology: International perspectives.* New York, NY: Oxford University Press.

Teachman, B. A. (2006). Aging and negative affect: The rise and fall and rise of anxiety and depression symptoms. *Psychology and Aging, 21*, 201–207. doi:10.1037/0882-7974.21.1.201

Terracciano, A., Iacono, D., O'Brien, R. J., Troncoso, J. C., An, Y., Sutin, A. R., . . . Resnick, S. M. (2013). Personality and resilience to Alzheimer's disease neuropathology: A prospective autopsy study. *Neurobiology of Aging, 34*, 1045–1050. doi:10.1016/j.neurobiolaging.2012.08.008

Therrien, Z., & Hunsley, J. (2012). Assessment of anxiety in older adults: A systematic review of commonly used measures. *Aging and Mental Health, 16*, 1–16. doi:10.1080/13607863.2011.602960

Thorp, S. R., Ayers, C. R., Nuevo, R., Stoddard, J. A., Sorrell, J. T., & Wetherell, J. L. (2009). Meta-analysis comparing different behavioral treatments for late-life anxiety. *American Journal of Geriatric Psychiatry, 17*, 105–115. doi:10.1097/JGP.0b013e31818b3f7e

Thorp, S. R., Stein, M. B., Jeste, D. V., Patterson, T. L., & Wetherell, J. L. (2012). Prolonged exposure therapy for older veterans with posttraumatic stress disorder: A pilot study. *American Journal of Geriatric Psychiatry, 20*, 276–280. doi:10.1097/JGP.0b013e3182435ee9

Tolin, D. F., Frost, R. O., & Steketee, G. (2007). An open trial of cognitive-behavioral therapy for compulsive hoarding. *Behaviour Research and Therapy, 45*, 1461–1470. doi:10.1016/j.brat.2007.01.001

Trollor, J. N., Anderson, T. M., Sachdev, P. S., Brodaty, H., & Andrews, G. (2007). Prevalence of mental disorders in the elderly: The Australian National Mental Health and Well-Being Survey. *American Journal of Geriatric Psychiatry, 15*, 455–466. doi:10.1097/JGP.0b013e3180590ba9

Twelftree, H., & Qazi, A. (2006). Relationship between anxiety and agitation in dementia. *Aging and Mental Health, 10*, 362–367. doi:10.1080/13607860600638511

van der Hooft, C. S., Schoofs, M. W., Ziere, G., Hofman, A., Pols, H. A., Sturkenboom, M. C., & Stricker, B. H. (2008). Inappropriate benzodiazepine use in older adults and the risk of fracture. *British Journal of Clinical Pharmacology, 66*, 276–282. doi:10.1111/j.1365-2125.2008.03185.x

van't Veer-Tazelaar, P. J., van Marwijk, H. W., van Oppen, P., van Hout, H. P., van der Horst, H. E., Cuijpers, P., . . . Beekman, A. T. (2009). Stepped-care prevention of anxiety and depression in late life: A randomized controlled trial. *Archives of General Psychiatry, 66*, 297–304. doi:10.1001/archgenpsychiatry.2008.555

van Vliet, D., de Vugt, M. E., Aalten, P., Bakker, C., Pijnenburg, Y. A., Vernooij-Dassen, M. J., . . . Verhey, F. R. (2012). Prevalence of neuropsychiatric symptoms in young-onset compared to late-onset Alzheimer's disease—Part 1: Findings of the two-year longitudinal NeedYD-study. *Dementia and Geriatric Cognitive Disorders, 34*, 319–327. doi:10.1159/000342824

Weiss, B. J., Calleo, J., Rhoades, H. M., Novy, D. M., Kunik, M. E., Lenze, E. J., & Stanley, M. A. (2009). The utility of the Generalized Anxiety Disorder Severity Scale (GADSS) with older adults in primary care. *Depression and Anxiety, 26*, E10–E15. doi:10.1002/da.20520

Wells, J. E., Browne, M. A., Scott, K. M., McGee, M. A., Baxter, J., & Kokaua, J. (2006). Prevalence, interference with life and severity of 12 month *DSM–IV* disorders in Te Rau Hinengaro: The New Zealand Mental Health Survey. *Australian and New Zealand Journal of Psychiatry, 40*, 845–854. doi:10.1080/j.1440-1614.2006.01903.x

Wetherell, J. L., Afari, N., Ayers, C. R., Stoddard, J. A., Ruberg, J., Sorrell, J. T., . . . Patterson, T. L. (2011). Acceptance and commitment therapy for generalized anxiety disorder in older adults: A preliminary report. *Behavior Therapy, 42*, 127–134. doi:10.1016/j.beth.2010.07.002

Wetherell, J. L., & Gatz, M. (2005). The Beck Anxiety Inventory in older adults with generalized anxiety disorder. *Journal of Psychopathology and Behavioral Assessment, 27*, 17–24. doi:10.1007/s10862-005-3261-3

Wetherell, J. L., Gatz, M., & Craske, M. G. (2003). Treatment of generalized anxiety disorder in older adults. *Journal of Consulting and Clinical Psychology, 71*, 31–40. doi:10.1037/0022-006X.71.1.31

Wetherell, J. L., Johnson, K. J., Chang, D. G., Ward, S. R., Merz, C. C., Petkus, A. J., & Bower, E. S. (2013, March). *Activity, Balance, Learning, and Exposure (ABLE): A new intervention for excessive fear of falling.* Paper presented at the American Association for Geriatric Psychiatry, Los Angeles, CA.

Wetherell, J. L., Petkus, A. J., McChesney, K., Stein, M. B., Judd, P. H., Rockwell, E., . . . Patterson, T. L. (2009). Older adults are less accurate than younger adults at identifying symptoms of anxiety and depression. *Journal of Nervous and Mental Disease, 197*, 623–626. doi:10.1097/NMD.0b013e3181b0c081

Wetherell, J. L., Petkus, A. J., Thorp, S. R., Stein, M. B., Chavira, D. A., Campbell-Sills, L., . . . Roy-Byrne, P. (2013). Age differences in treatment response to a collaborative care intervention for anxiety disorders. *British Journal of Psychiatry.* doi:10.1192/bjp.bp.112.118547

Wetherell, J. L., Petkus, A. J., White, K. S., Nguyen, H., Kornblith, S., Andreescu, C., . . . Lenze, E. J. (2013). Antidepressant medication augmented with cognitive-behavioral therapy for generalized anxiety disorder in older adults. *American Journal of Psychiatry.* doi:10.1176/appi.ajp.2013.12081104

Wetherell, J. L., Ruberg, J. L., & Petkus, A. J. (2011). Generalized anxiety disorder. In K. H. Sorocco & S. Lauderdale (Eds.), *Cognitive behavior therapy with older adults: Innovations across care settings* (pp. 157–188). New York, NY: Springer.

Wetzels, R. B., Zuidema, S. U., de Jonghe, J. F., Verhey, F. R., & Koopmans, R. T. (2010). Course of neuropsychiatric symptoms in residents with dementia in nursing homes over 2-year period. *American Journal of Geriatric Psychiatry, 18*, 1054–1065. doi:10.1097/JGP.0b013e3181f60fa1

Wilson, R. S., Begeny, C. T., Boyle, P. A., Schneider, J. A., & Bennett, D. A. (2011). Vulnerability to stress, anxiety, and development of dementia in old age. *American Journal of Geriatric Psychiatry, 19,* 327–334. doi:10.1097/JGP.0b013e31820119da

Wisocki, P. A., Handen, B., & Morse, C. K. (1986). The Worry Scale as a measure of anxiety among homebound and community active elderly. *Behavior Therapist, 9,* 91–95.

Wolitzky-Taylor, K. B., Castriotta, N., Lenze, E. J., Stanley, M. A., & Craske, M. G. (2010). Anxiety disorders in older adults: A comprehensive review. *Depression and Anxiety, 27,* 190–211. doi:10.1002/da.20653

Wolitzky-Taylor, K. B., Horowitz, J. D., Powers, M. B., & Telch, M. J. (2008). Psychological approaches in the treatment of specific phobias: A meta-analysis. *Clinical Psychology Review, 28,* 1021–1037. doi:10.1016/j.cpr.2008.02.007

Yochim, B. P., Mueller, A. E., June, A., & Segal, D. L. (2010). Psychometric properties of the Geriatric Anxiety Scale: Comparison to the Beck Anxiety Inventory and Geriatric Anxiety Inventory. *Clinical Gerontologist, 34,* 21–33. doi:10.1080/07317115.2011.524600

Zigmond, A. S., & Snaith, R. P. (1983). The hospital anxiety and depression scale. *Acta Psychiatrica Scandinavica, 67,* 361–370. doi:10.1111/j.1600-0447.1983.tb09716.x

Zou, J. B., Dear, B. F., Titov, N., Lorian, C. N., Johnston, L., Spence, J., . . . Sachdev, P. (2012). Brief internet-delivered cognitive behavioral therapy for anxiety in older adults: A feasibility trial. *Journal of Anxiety Disorders, 26,* 650–655. doi:10.1016/j.janxdis.2012.04.002

CHAPTER 3

PERSONALITY DISORDERS
IN LATER LIFE

Steve Balsis, Richard A. Zweig, and Victor Molinari

People with personality disorders (PDs) have disturbed patterns of thinking and poorly formed self-concepts. They often display rigid and inflexible responses in social settings that compromise their abilities to develop relationships. To make matters worse, people with PDs are typically unaware of or have limited insight into these problems. Much of what we know about PDs comes from research and clinical examinations of PDs in relatively young adults. This chapter reviews an emerging area of focus on PDs in later life. We consider theoretical and conceptual issues, provide solid practical advice on assessment, and offer our best professional recommendations regarding treatment. Throughout the chapter, we present many questions that we are unable to fully answer at this point in time. But our hope is that these questions might help to stimulate future research on PDs in later life. This chapter begins with a section on theory that emphasizes the importance of studying PDs in later life, highlighting several theoretical and conceptual issues.

THEORY

PDs can cause problems for people at all ages (Segal, Zweig, & Molinari, 2012). People with PDs have significant problems with relationships. They have difficulty maintaining close ties with family members and friends, and they have trouble getting along with coworkers. People with PDs are also more likely than those without PDs to develop Axis I disorders, such as depression or anxiety disorders (Segal, Coolidge, & Rosowsky, 2006). Despite the importance of PDs, we know relatively little about the consequences of PDs in later life. We also know relatively little about the long-term course of PDs. Do they increase or decrease with age, or do they stay the same? Do they present the same in later life? Considering the nature of PDs and their effects on younger adults, one would hypothesize that PDs should have dire consequences in later life. After all, PDs are long-enduring styles of interacting with others and viewing oneself that lead to key social dysfunctions (American Psychiatric Association, 2000). In later life, individuals find themselves in a double bind—they need more help for their physical limitations, and they are forced to rely on smaller social networks to get that help. Having a PD and henceforth a compromised social support system in later life could be particularly limiting.

We turn first to some of the theoretical issues about personality that can be, we think, best answered by examining PDs in later life. We consider whether PDs change across the life span. Do they increase, decrease, or stay the same? Do they present in the same way or do they present differently in earlier and later life? We also consider what effect PDs may have on functional outcomes, such as health. As we discuss these issues, we highlight conceptual problems regarding the measurement of PDs and emphasize the implications of these measurement problems for interpreting the presentation and effect of PDs in later life.

The results from many cross-sectional studies indicate that PDs are less prevalent in older adults than they are in younger adults (e.g., Casey &

http://dx.doi.org/10.1037/14459-003
APA Handbook of Clinical Geropsychology: Vol. 2. Assessment, Treatment, and Issues of Later Life,
P. A. Lichtenberg and B. T. Mast (Editors-in-Chief)

Schrodt, 1989; Cohen et al., 1994; Fogel & Westlake, 1990; Gutiérrez et al., 2012; Samuels et al., 2002; Zimmerman & Coryell, 1989), suggesting that PDs diminish or "burn out" with age. In each of these studies, either PD diagnoses or PD traits were found to be less frequent or less severe in older adults compared with younger adults. This general finding was most pronounced among the externalizing Cluster B disorders of narcissistic, borderline, histrionic, and antisocial PDs (e.g., Cohen et al., 1994; Ferro, Klein, Schwartz, Kasch, & Leader, 1998; Gutiérrez et al., 2012; Samuels et al., 2002; Segal, Hook, & Coolidge, 2001).

Several alternate explanations for these cross-sectional findings, however, could lead one to question whether PDs really decline with age. One possibility is that PDs either do not change or may even increase with age, but they are not well-detected in later life by current personality diagnostic criteria (see Mroczek, Hurt, & Berman, 1999). Many PDs may go undetected in later life because the items used to assess PDs do not work equally well for younger and older adults primarily because the criteria for meeting each PD were created with younger adults in mind (Mroczek et al., 1999; Segal, Zweig, & Molinari, 2012). For example, one obvious problematic item comes from the criteria for avoidant PD. This item queries whether the person "avoids occupational activities . . ." (American Psychiatric Association, 2000, p. 721). Clearly, this item is not appropriate for a retired older adult. Indeed, patterns of endorsement across multiple items can reflect something about the age context of the patient rather than the patient's standing along a dimension of personality pathology. One can see how this measurement problem would make it difficult to determine, for example, whether avoidant PD really changes across the life span (Balsis, Woods, Gleason, & Oltmanns, 2007). This is just one example from the avoidant PD items. There are problems with face validity across many of the 79 PD diagnostic items (Segal et al., 2006). A recent study revealed that approximately half of the PD criteria may contain measurement bias across younger and older age-groups (Balsis, Gleason, Woods, & Oltmanns, 2007).

Problems with face validity clearly get to deeper issues with construct validity and can lead to failures to diagnose personality pathology in older adults (Balsis, Woods, et al., 2007; Zweig & Parchi, 2010). If, for example, four of the seven criteria for avoidant PD are needed for a person to be eligible for a diagnosis, and one or two key criteria are irrelevant for an older, retired person, then even if this older adult had a significant degree of avoidance, the criteria might not be able to capture it. The older adult might meet just three of the criteria and the diagnosis could be missed improperly. The opposite can happen as well. An older adult with subthreshold levels of schizoid personality might be improperly diagnosed as having schizoid PD because the schizoid items describe the context of aging in addition to the schizoid construct. The item "has little interest in sexual experiences," for example, may apply to an older adult whether or not he has diagnosable levels of schizoid pathology. In this case, a slightly schizoid older adult might meet four of the seven schizoid criteria (the diagnostic threshold for schizoid PD) and be diagnosed improperly. Older adults may have less interest or receive less pleasure from sexual experiences for a variety of reasons, including partner availability, health, and medication side effects. Thus, one can see how these problems with face validity can lead to failures to diagnose older adults properly and hence can give rise to inaccurate data and ultimately inaccurate theory about the change or stability of PDs across the life span.

Noticeably, these deep problems with validity can lead to other measurement errors. For example, measures that include items with poor validity will have poor internal consistency. If the PD criteria have high face validity for younger adults, then the ratings across items likely will reflect the core dimension of interest and internal consistency may be relatively high. If, however, the PD criteria have relatively poor face validity, as is the case for older adults, then ratings across items will be less likely to reflect the core dimension of interest. Some ratings may reflect the core PD dimension of interest, whereas others may reflect age-associated factors, such as the social or occupational context of aging. If this is the case, then the reliability of the measure will be lower. Indeed, research shows that as individuals age the diagnostic criteria become less specified for detecting PDs in those individuals (see Zweig, 2008). Here again we see that the lack of consistency of the criteria for older adults may make patterns of responding difficult to interpret.

With these measurement challenges in mind, we can consider the findings from a recent study that examined all PD diagnostic criteria across the adult life span (Gutiérrez et al., 2012). This study reported the endorsement of all *Diagnostic and Statistical Manual of Mental Disorders, Fourth Edition, Text Revision* (*DSM–IV–TR*; American Psychiatric Association, 2000) PD criteria in a sample that ranged generally between 20 and 50 years old. The overall findings were consistent with previous research showing a general decrease in PD pathology with age. Inspection of the items, however, suggests that all of the items that changed the most appeared to have measurement bias for indicating PD pathology in relatively older adults. Consider the PD item that showed the biggest decrease in endorsement with age, the narcissistic PD item, "Fantasizes about unlimited success." Notice that this item is future oriented. It is possible that this feature of narcissism declines with age. But it is very possible that it presents differently with age as people's time horizons shrink. In this case, the item may not capture narcissism as well in older people who may be less future oriented than younger people. Older adults might be less likely to endorse this item than younger adults, simply because they are less likely to focus on the future because of their advanced age. Rather, older narcissists may spend more time reliving past conquests or reinterpret their current life situation as ideal.

Thus, despite the fact that several cross-sectional studies, including the one just described, report that PDs generally decline across the life span, we suggest that measurement problems with the items, particularly with the face validity, construct validity, and the internal consistency of the items, may contribute substantially to this trend. This is problematic because measurement bias in the items can lead to an incorrect understanding of PDs across the life span. Believing that PDs mellow or subside entirely in later life can create an idea in researchers' minds (and in the minds of clinicians who conduct evidence-based practice) that PDs are not important in later life. This may be an incorrect assumption that may have the unfortunate consequence of keeping researchers from examining PDs in later life. We contend that the multiple pieces of evidence, including evidence of measurement errors in the personality criteria, and the emerging set of case studies and anecdotal evidence suggest that PDs are alive and well in later life.

In addition, evidence indicates that PDs actually can increase with age. This evidence shows that PDs can "emerge" or become functionally problematic for the first time in later adulthood (see Oltmanns & Balsis, 2011). This is not to suggest that a PD emerges in later life out of nowhere, but rather that people with latent personality pathology can meet criteria for a diagnosis for the first time in later life because of a new stressor or a context change. Later life presents many stressors. A person might have to deal with the death of a spouse, the loss of financial resources, increased physical challenges, and other major life changes, such as retirement or moving into an assisted living facility. Many people have subthreshold levels of PD pathology, and a stressor might be sufficient to move them to meet diagnostic criteria. For example, a younger man might have latent narcissistic PD, but his career success could fulfill many of his narcissistic needs (the need for power, control, ego confirmation). After retirement, however, his subthreshold narcissism might become dysfunctional. He may begin seeking reinforcement through other means, perhaps by denigrating others within the confines of his small social circle. So a subthreshold level of narcissism might in younger age have been beneficial and even socially acceptable, but in later life, it might become dysfunctional and could lead to diagnosis.

As we have described, later life brings with it many changes that can increase the presentation of PDs. These later life changes can be the very things that allow for the emergence of an officially diagnosable PD. Even though the PD traits might have existed all along, they simply were not above threshold. Thus, there is evidence and reason to believe that PDs exist in later life. What effect do they have on important outcomes? We turn now to this understudied, but important, issue.

On this issue, we may have a bias—we think that linking PDs to important outcomes should be a primary goal for personality researchers. PDs are characterized by disturbed patterns of thinking, feeling, behaving, and relating to others. People with PDs are typically rigid and unable to adapt to personal or environmental circumstances, and they lack self-awareness of their difficulties. What are the cumulative and long-term effects of these dysfunctional thoughts and behaviors? Determining how PDs contribute to disease and mortality allows researchers to examine the consequences of PDs on important health outcomes in later life, as this is a time when people typically experience serious health conditions, including most cancers, heart disease, Alzheimer's disease, and death.

Research is beginning to identify personality pathology as a risk factor for adverse physical (e.g., heart disease, arthritis, obesity; Pietrzak, Wagner, & Petry, 2007; Powers & Oltmanns, 2013; Stanley, Laugharne, Addis, & Sherwood, 2013) and mental health problems and outcomes (e.g., Segal, Marty, Meyer, & Coolidge, 2012; Stek, Van Exel, Van Tilburg, Westendorp, & Beekman, 2002) in both middle-age and older samples. Recent research also has begun to link PDs in older samples to hospital readmission (Stevenson, Brodaty, Boyce, & Byth, 2012) and to increased health care use and reduced health-related quality of life (Powers & Oltmanns, 2012). At the time of this writing, one major study is beginning to comprehensively examine the effect of PDs in later life. The St. Louis Personality and Aging Network (SPAN) study (see Oltmanns & Gleason, 2011) is a prospective, longitudinal study that is examining personality stability and change over time as well as the impact of personality pathology on later life outcomes. The main goals of the project are to determine the connections between PDs, health, and social adjustment in a large, representative, community-based sample of people between the ages at intake of 55 and 64 years. The participants in the sample are just entering late life and many will have to adjust to various late-life challenges to their social status, their financial status, and their health. Results from the SPAN study are likely to reveal ways in which PDs and PD traits influence older adults' ability to adapt to

important life transitions and serious health consequences. For example, forthcoming results indicate that PDs are associated with serious medical problems such as diabetes and heart disease, and life stressors (Gleason, Weinstein, Balsis, & Oltmanns, in press). Although the results from the SPAN study demonstrate a link between PDs and later life health outcomes, several research questions remain to be answered. For example, *how* do PDs lead to poor health outcomes, and which health outcomes are most affected by PDs? What is the cost of PDs to society? How do PDs affect the families of older adults, especially if they are called on to help with caregiving or late-life decision making? Finally, are there effective treatments for older adults with PDs that can improve their well-being and health outcomes?

We have raised theoretical issues regarding the measurement of PDs in later life, whether PDs change in later life, and how these disorders may lead to important health outcomes in later life. With these theoretical issues in mind and partially unresolved, we turn to a practical discussion of the assessment of PDs in late life.

ASSESSMENT

Psychologists who work with older adults in varied clinical settings often observe a familiar paradox. Not infrequently, health care professionals confronted with the difficult behavior of an older adult attribute this to the individual's personality rather than to the environment or another cause, engaging in the well known *fundamental attribution error* (Follett & Hess, 2002), without the benefit of any formal personality assessment. Were it not for the serious consequences of this omission, this frequent attribution and studious avoidance of assessing personality in older adults might be viewed in a manner akin to Mark Twain's observation that everybody talks about the weather but nobody does anything about it.

Although consensus regarding the precise definition of PD and the diagnostic system to assess it is currently lacking, there is ample evidence to warrant assessment, Research in clinical samples finds comorbid PD in 5% to 55% of older patients (Segal et al., 2006) and rates in older patients with carefully diagnosed depression range from 24% to 67% (Zweig & Agronin, 2011). Because base rates provide one rationale for assessment, clinicians may have a high index of suspicion for the presence of personality pathology in older patients in mental health settings. Additionally, because research has established that personality is a powerful predictor of well-being (divorce, occupational attainment, mortality) throughout the life cycle, some have argued for its routine evaluation in both adults (Roberts, Kuncel, Shiner, Caspi, & Goldberg, 2007) and older adults (Hooker & McAdams, 2003).

Approaches to Assessing Personality Pathology

Clinicians who strive to assess personality pathology in older patients currently face several challenges. Controversy abounds as to the conceptual underpinnings of the construct of PD, the relevance and clinical utility of categorical versus dimensional models of personality pathology, and the appropriate ways to bridge methods developed to assess normal and pathological personality variants. To outline the relevant domains for assessment, the process of assessing personality pathology in an older patient begins with consideration of the conceptual model of personality that undergirds the assessment, and with an appreciation of broader guidelines for assessing older adults.

Aligning the assessment approach to a conceptual model in measure selection.   When an older adult is referred for an assessment of personality pathology, the selection of appropriate assessment methods and measures depends in part on the conceptual model of normal personality and personality pathology that is foundational to the assessment endeavor. For example, McAdams and Pals (2006) offered an integrative dimensional model that defines personality as "an individual's unique variation on the general evolutionary design for human nature, expressed as a developing pattern of dispositional traits, characteristic adaptations, and integrative life stories complexly and differentially situated in culture" (p. 212). Such a model calls for a multimethod, integrative assessment approach that would incorporate personality trait measures, interview-based measures (to capture

narrative life stories), performance-based measures of characteristic adaptations (motivational goals, coping, defenses, relational patterns, etc.), and a consideration of the cultural context within which the individual resides.

In contrast, recent iterations of the *DSM–IV–TR* (American Psychiatric Association, 2000) define personality pathology as "an enduring pattern of inner experience and behavior that deviates markedly from the expectations of an individual's culture" (p. 681). The *DSM–V–TR* "General Criteria for PD" (American Psychiatric Association, 2000), which exemplify the categorical approach, hold that these experiences and behaviors (which manifest across domains of mental representations of self and others, affective regulation, interpersonal functioning, and impulse control) constitute a PD when they are inflexible, are pervasive, impair functioning, and are not a result of another mental or physical disorder. An assessment approach aligned with the *DSM* model of personality pathology would draw on varied methods and measures, including semistructured interviews for PD (to assess specific criteria and the degree to which these are pervasive, inflexible, and impairing) and self-report measures (to identify prominent traits and differentiate these from clinical states), and ultimately it requires a clinician's judgment as to the cultural context and whether another physical or mental disorder better explain symptoms.

Recently proposed unifying models of personality pathology, which as of this writing are works in progress, seek to bridge taxonomies derived from the study of normal and deviant personality and combine categorical and dimensional models into a hybrid diagnostic approach. Supporters of a dimensional model (e.g., Clark, 2007) argue that dimensional trait models derived from the study of normal personality (such as the Five-Factor Model) best explain personality variability in both personality-disordered and nondisordered populations and that the high comorbidity of PDs with other mental disorders argue for a common substrate in temperament. Furthermore, categorical diagnoses of PD are surprisingly unstable over time and have been found to lack predictive validity, whereas dimensional assessments, and particularly those that calibrate severity of personality pathology, are predictive of relevant outcomes (Clark, 2007; Pulay et al., 2008; Stevenson et al., 2012). An assessment approach aligned with dimensional or hybrid models might incorporate measures that evaluate personality trait factors purported to underlie personality pathology (e.g., neuroticism, introversion, antagonism, conscientiousness; Clark, 2007), as these are likely to be stable over time, as well as measures capable of capturing both the severity and functional impairment attributable to this pathology.

Aligning the assessment approach with guidelines for assessing older adults.   The assessment of personality pathology in an older adult, which includes the selection, administration, and interpretation of measures and the communication of findings, is framed by general principles that undergird the psychological assessment of older adults. This requires, first and foremost, the selection of methods and measures that ideally have been developed, normed, validated, and shown to be psychometrically appropriate for older populations. Second, the assessment approach should incorporate consideration of demographic (e.g., cohort, educational and cultural background), clinical (e.g., Axis I symptomatology, current medications, medical illness and sensory or functional disability, level of cognitive functioning), and contextual factors (e.g., demand characteristics of the measures or the setting of assessment) as each of these may be potent moderators of performance. Third, a multimethod approach is suggested that incorporates assessments of cognition, emotion, and behavior as well as personality; draws on self-report, interview-based, and observational methods; and incorporates informant or interdisciplinary team data.

Considering the relevance of the social history and of clinical judgment.   Because most conceptualizations of personality and personality pathology emphasize characteristic inner experiences, behaviors, adaptations, and interpersonal patterns that have an enduring and pervasive quality, the individual's social history or life narrative is an essential source of information. The approach to assessing personality pathology in older adults begins with recognition of the need to incorporate a method, such as a structured interview for assessing PDs or an unstructured clinical interview, which captures

the social history. For example, some structured interviews begin with open-ended questions regarding the major events or episodes that individuals have experienced, how they would describe themselves or how others would describe them, or how they have observed themselves functioning in work and other roles. Additionally, the social history of older adults can be a particularly rich source of information regarding how the individual traversed normative developmental events such as launching from the family of origin, establishing stable work and family roles, and contending with transitions in these roles (e.g., retirement, widowhood, etc.).

It is in the elicitation of the social history that the clinician often first detects demographic and clinical indicators that suggest risk factors for personality pathology and the adverse consequences this pathology has had on health, mental health, and well-being throughout the life course. In regard to sociodemographic indicators, studies of mixed-age adults find that those with PDs disproportionately report marital discord and are more likely to be divorced, to never have married, or to have had several marriages but few children. They also disproportionately report lower levels of educational achievement and downward occupational change compared with adults without PDs (Ames & Molinari, 1994; Samuels et al., 2002). The social and clinical histories of adults with PDs disproportionately reflect experiences of physical and sexual trauma, relatively early onset of psychiatric disorder, prior suicide attempts, and the current presence of two or more co-occurring Axis I syndromes (Livesley, 2001). Studies of depressed older adults with PDs have identified similar clinical correlates, including more frequent early onset and recurrent episodes of depression, prior suicide attempts, and co-occurring Axis I disorders than those without PDs (Abrams, Rosendahl, Card, & Alexopoulos, 1994; Kunik et al., 1993). Although clinicians should exert caution in drawing causal relationships between PDs and these demographic and clinical correlates, their presence may alert clinicians to the likelihood of PD and the need for further evaluation.

Ultimately the process of assessing personality pathology in older adults requires the clinician to utilize clinical judgment to confront several diagnostic challenges common to this population. The *DSM–IV–TR* "General Criteria for PD" (American Psychiatric Association, 2000) require that the clinician sort out features of PDs from major psychiatric syndromes, medical and neurological disorders, situational behaviors or coping styles, and social or cultural roles. Many clinicians struggle with four primary diagnostic challenges that require them to differentiate PDs from (a) persisting Axis I disorders, (b) context-dependent roles and behaviors, (c) subtle neurocognitive impairment, and (d) a difficult doctor–patient relationship.

PD versus persisting Axis I disorder. Older adults with persisting Axis I syndromes may exhibit abrasive symptoms and behaviors (e.g., irritability, dependency) that offend or exhaust their caregivers, causing others to assume that such behaviors are longstanding and attributable to personality pathology. Although personality pathology is a risk factor for poorer treatment outcomes and persisting impairment of social functioning in older adults (Morse, Pilkonis, Houck, Frank, & Reynolds, 2005), this conclusion may confuse personality pathology with illness duration and treatment responsiveness. Such situations call for a careful review of the clinical history, supplemented by dimensional measures of personality and Axis I symptoms as well as informant reports, to sort out the temporal relationship between the onset of Axis I and Axis II symptoms. In clinical practice, the persistence of symptoms and behavioral features of a PD following maximal treatment of an Axis I disorder is suggestive of personality pathology.

PD versus context-dependent roles and behaviors. In other situations, it is the nature of the stressor or context that gives rise to misattributions of personality pathology. For example, some older adults confronted with chronic medical illness or disability or admission to a long-term care environment initially demonstrate interpersonal behaviors, such as excessive demands for care or efforts to rigidly control their care, in a manner that may suggest personality pathology. Although Sadavoy and Fogel (1992) and others have argued that changing contexts or chronic stressors in late life could prompt underlying PD features to emerge, it also is plausible that such behaviors are situational or mediated by environmental factors. A careful clinical history supplemented by collateral information in addition to formal assessment measures may clarify whether interpersonal behaviors are long standing or situational.

PD versus personality change resulting from neurological illness. Recent evidence suggests that prodromal symptoms of dementia and other neurological illnesses may include personality changes, such as a lack of empathy, dysregulated affect, apathy, or rigidity (Balsis, Carpenter, & Storandt, 2005). When these changes in personality have a gradual onset, appear to represent an exacerbation of a preexisting trait, or are so prominent as to be superimposed upon more subtle neurocognitive changes, they may be mistaken for PD pathology. An appropriate clinical strategy in such cases includes a careful historical review of the onset of medical or neurological and personality symptoms, the inclusion of a neuropsychological evaluation, and the obtaining of collateral information from other health professionals (if available) to clarify the diagnosis.

PD versus a difficult doctor–patient relationship. Older patients whom clinicians find challenging to treat owing to their mistrust, anger, or fearfulness; their limited insight into their condition and tendencies to express their distress through bodily complaints; or their tendency to violate "expected rules" of the doctor–patient relationship often are perceived by their clinicians as manifesting signs of personality pathology. At times, this is indeed the case. At other times, however, clinicians encounter a difficult doctor–patient relationship when contending with the challenges of a patient's Axis I condition, such as an anxiety, substance use, or somatization disorder (Hahn, 2000; Hahn et al., 1996). Thus, although such countertransference experiences provide relevant data, they are likely nonspecific as to the presence of personality pathology. In practice settings, clinicians would be advised to weigh their experiential observations against data derived from evidence-based measures, supplemented by collateral information, to reach valid conclusions as to the presence of personality pathology.

Selected Measures for the Assessment of Personality Pathology

A variety of methods that use self-report, interview-based, and clinician-report formats have been developed for the assessment of personality and personality pathology in adults (see Exhibit 3.1). The Gerontological Personality Disorders Scale (van Alphen, van Engelen, Kuin, Hoijtink, & Derksen, 2004) is the sole measure developed for use with older adults with personality pathology, but several scales have been the subject of empirical inquiry and thus have preliminary evidence of validity for use in older populations (for a review, see Edelstein & Segal, 2011). In general, self-report measures of personality and personality pathology (such as the

---

Exhibit 3.1
Selected Measures for the Assessment of Personality Pathology

---

Self-Report Measures of Personality and Personality Pathology
Minnesota Multiphasic Personality Inventory—2 (MMPI–2; Butcher, Dahlstrom, Graham, Tellegen, & Kaemmer, 1989)[a]
NEO Personality Inventory (NEO–PI–R; Costa & McCrae, 1992)[a]

Multiscale Self-Report Inventories
Coolidge Axis II Inventory (Coolidge & Merwin, 1992)[a]
Gerontological Personality Disorders Scale (van Alphen, van Engelen, Kuin, Hoijtink, & Derksen, 2004)[a]
Millon Clinical Multiaxial Inventory (MCMI–III; Millon, Davis, & Millon, 1997)
Personality Assessment Inventory (PAI; Morey, 2007)
Schedule for Nonadaptive and Adaptive Personality (SNAP–2; Clark, 2009)
Wisconsin Personality Disorders Inventory (Klein et al., 1993)

Structured Clinical Interviews
International Personality Disorder Examination (IPDE; World Health Organization, 1995)[a]
Personality Disorder Interview—IV (Widiger, Mangine, Corbitt, Ellis, & Thomas, 1995)
Structured Clinical Interview for *DSM–IV* Axis II Personality Disorders (SCID–II; First, Gibbon, Spitzer, Williams, & Benjamin, 1997)[a]
Structured Interview for *DSM–IV* Personality (SIDP–IV; Pfohl, Blum, & Zimmerman, 1995)[a]

Prototype Matching Clinician-Report Instruments
Personality Assessment Form (PAF; Pilkonis & Frank, 1988)
Shedler–Westen Assessment Procedure (SWAP–200; Westen & Shedler, 2007)

Domain-Specific Self-Report Measures
Inventory of Interpersonal Problems (IIP; Horowitz, Rosenberg, Baer, Ureño, & Villaseñor, 1988)[a]
Social Adjustment Scale—Self Report (SAS–SR; Weissman & Bothwell, 1976)[a]

Note. [a]Instrument validated in studies of older adults.

Minnesota Multiphasic Personality Inventory [Butcher, Dahlstrom, Graham, Tellegen, & Kaemmer, 1989] and the Neuroticism–Extraversion–Openness Personality Inventory [Costa & McCrae, 1992]) have utility in both nonclinical and clinical populations, but they were not developed specifically to evaluate PD pathology, whereas most multiscale self-report inventories (e.g., Coolidge Axis II Inventory [Coolidge & Merwin, 1992], Millon Clinical Multiaxial Inventory [Millon, Davis, & Millon, 1997], Personality Assessment Inventory [Morey, 2007]) were developed for that purpose but vary as to their conceptual model of PD. Domain-specific self-report measures (e.g., Inventory of Interpersonal Problems [Horowitz, Rosenberg, Baer, Ureño, & Villaseñor, 1988]) have the advantages of brevity as they target specific domains (interpersonal problems) or functional impairments attributable to personality pathology, but they are often insufficient for diagnosis. Most structured clinical interviews to assess PD (e.g., International Personality Disorder Examination [World Health Organization, 1995], Structured Clinical Interview for *DSM–IV* Axis II Personality Disorders [First, Gibbon, Spitzer, Williams, & Benjamin, 1997]) were developed for use in clinical populations and possess items that correspond closely to the *DSM* criteria sets for PDs. Most, however, require specialized training and are lengthy to administer, and some have shown age bias in item response theory analyses (Balsis, Gleason, et al., 2007), which may limit their use in older samples. Other instruments that utilize a prototype matching approach based on clinician report (e.g., Shedler–Westen Assessment Procedure [Westen & Shedler, 2007]) may have considerable utility but remain untested in clinical samples of older adults.

Stepwise Approaches for Assessing Personality Pathology

What overall strategy should psychologists seeking to assess personality pathology in an older patient employ? Widiger and Samuel (2005) suggest a two-step approach, in which a dimensional measure serves as the screening tool, and a structured interview measure is employed to diagnose PD type. Although both approaches have merit, it is likely that an initial assessment approach that (a) permits a potentially broad interpretation of relevant domains (mental representations of self and others, affective regulation, interpersonal functioning, and impulse control) common to personality pathology across the life cycle and (b) requires the clinician to consider the impact of persisting Axis I disorders, context-dependent roles and behaviors, and personality change resulting from neurological illness will enhance diagnostic accuracy and maximize clinical utility in older adult samples (Zweig, 2008). Rather than provide a case example using either the Livesley or the Widiger and Samuel procedures, we emphasize the two-step approach—first a screen, and then a more granular characterization within the context of the older adult's life. There are three key questions to ask: Does this person have a PD? How can it be best characterized? What is the impact of the PD in the person's life?

INTERVENTION

Younger Adults

Over the past decade, an increasing number of studies have suggested that there is an evidence base for interventions with at least some types of PDs. In an early review of 15 studies that included pre–post treatment effects and follow-up, the authors concluded that PDs can be treated successfully with psychological interventions and documented a sevenfold faster recovery rate compared with those not receiving such treatment (Perry, Banon, & Ianni, 1999). Unfortunately, most of the controlled research on PDs has been conducted with Borderline PDs, and the effectiveness of these interventions with other PDs has not been validated.

Recently, the National Institute for Health and Clinical Excellence (2011) summarized the research regarding treatment for borderline PD and concluded that a variety of approaches including interpersonal therapy and varied forms of cognitive–behavioral therapy (CBT), such as schema-focused therapy, manual-assisted cognitive therapy, and dialectical behavior therapy (DBT) are effective. In their review of the literature, Bateman and Tyrer (2004) also determined that the evidence base is encouraging regarding the treatment of borderline PD

and identified psychodynamic therapy as the most effective treatment. Adding support to this claim, Clarkin, Levy, Lenzenweger, and Kernberg (2007) compared DBT, transference-focused therapy, and a supportive treatment influenced by dynamic principles. The authors found that all three treatments improved outcomes for depression, anxiety, global functioning, and social adjustment, but that transference-focused psychotherapy was associated with the most overall change including reductions in suicidality, anger, and impulsivity. The authors propose that the use of the relationship between the therapist and client to explore themes with high emotion may help to integrate self-representations, leading to greater self-control.

A review of research on the treatment of borderline PD by the Cochrane Database of Systematic Reviews that was published in 2006 and updated in 2012 noted that DBT was the only intervention with enough studies to be able to conclude that it was efficacious. DBT attenuates inappropriate anger and self-harm, while enhancing general functioning by integrating Eastern mindfulness approaches with Western behavioral change principles. DBT regulates the emotions of clients by engaging them in exercises that help them to accept the world as it is, while improving their competence via behavioral skills training. Structuring the environment by case management and family interventions maintains the motivation of clients, while consultation and supervision with other professionals helps prevent therapist burnout dealing with the high-intensity symptoms of those with borderline PD (Salsman & Linehan, 2006). There are a variety of components in DBT, and it is unclear which of them are the active therapeutic ingredients necessary for change (Bateman & Tyrer, 2004).

As noted, few treatment strategies have targeted other types of PDs in controlled trials, and the evidence base to treat PDs other than borderline PD is therefore very thin. Nonetheless, clinicians are confronted with treating a variety of individuals with PDs in their practice, frequently because Axis I symptoms and Axis II behaviors often are comorbid, with clinical theory and professional experience directing their interventions in the absence of empirical data.

Later Life

Given the paucity of research on PD interventions with adults in general, and older adults specifically, most geropsychologists integrate their knowledge of life-span development and aging theories with an understanding of preferred models of psychological change to address the variety of problems with which older adults with PDs may present. As van Alphen, Derksen, Sadavoy, and Rosowsky (2012) noted, practitioners must adapt the skills they have gained in working with younger adults while also addressing the gerontological themes of losses, social support, and cohort influences so prominent in late life. Although confronted by uncertainty, some insightful pioneering clinicians have accepted the challenge and generated some basic principles that are compatible with the evidence base for treatment of younger adults with borderline PD and for the treatment of older adults with Axis I symptomatology. These principles are postulated to be generalizable to the wide variety of PD in older adults.

Before we can fully understand the major tenets of working with older adults with PD, it is important to identify the most frequent reasons why geropsychologists are called on to consult on their mental health problems. As indicated earlier in this chapter, increases in maladaptive behavioral patterns associated with PDs often are precipitated by the losses of aging. Those with PDs are unable to modulate or adapt their responses to the necessities of environmental contingencies attendant on deterioration in functioning because of medical conditions, loss of social support because of deaths of relatives or friends, loss of gainful employment, and perhaps loss of prestige because of forced retirement.

Interpersonal losses may be particularly difficult to bear because by definition those with PDs already have difficulties with relationships, and decreases in already limited "social capital" may exacerbate their problems because their annoying interpersonal styles and poor social skills are ineffective in garnering the support necessary to buffer aging stressors. Unfortunately, some medical problems may eventuate in forced contact with institutional systems such as hospitals, rehabilitation centers, nursing homes, or assisted living facilities with resultant interpersonal tension for both people with PDs and their

treatment providers. Cluster B PDs, in particular, will grate on institutional staff and generate frequent mental health consultation requests because of conflict. Some individuals with Cluster A PDs, however, are guarded and prefer staying to themselves and may be less likely to cause concern in nursing homes, so their conditions thereby go untreated.

Given the frequent necessity of mental health consultation with older adults, especially because of the havoc caused in institutional settings, Sadavoy and Fogel (1992) proposed some basic principles for working with older adults with PDs. These include containing and limiting pathological behavior; establishing a working alliance between the client, family, and staff; utilizing a coordinated team approach to prevent "splitting" and unwarranted countertransferential reactions; and in the long-term, helping the client reduce the interpersonal strain triggering the PD behavior. In like manner, Mordekar and Spence (2008) have outlined principles for treating PDs, including fostering the therapeutic relationship, treating comorbid Axis I disorders, being consistent, using supportive CBT, developing good ties with other professionals, and involving family and friends.

It seems that most geropsychologists agree that one must exert every effort to accept the person but enforce negative consequences for PD behavior. Limit-setting is not easy to do, but it is ageistic (and poor clinical practice) to believe that older adults' obnoxious behavior should be tolerated more than the bad behavior of young adults. More important, professionals must adhere to boundaries to maintain a therapeutic framework in which progress can be achieved. In institutional settings, the treatment team must promote integrated and cohesive care by meeting regularly to outline short- and long-term treatment goals, thereby ensuring consistency and constancy in their relationships with the client, which may be a novel experience for those with PDs. Rather than reacting as a nontrained layperson to the provocative and baiting behavior of those with PDs, the idea is to use countertransference to understand the person and to respond in ways that advance the therapeutic relationship, reduce stress, and promote treatment goals. These axioms of clinical management are consistent with the evidence-based approaches developed with younger adults, including the importance of the therapeutic alliance, use of family as adjuncts, exploration of countertransference, the need to teach skills to reduce tension, and a coordinated team approach.

Unfortunately, only recently have attempts been made to go beyond general principles of treatment and delineate particular interventions with older adults based on specific criteria. In a recent study, van Alphen, Derksen, et al. (2012) used the Delphic consensus methodology to explore diagnostic and treatment issues with 35 Dutch and Belgian experts on PDs in older adults. The authors observed that proposed interventions fall on a continuum from those aimed at intrapsychic change to those emphasizing environmental manipulation. Four different treatment levels were differentiated based on treatment indications and exclusions. Treatments directed at personality change are lengthy (e.g., transference-focused psychodynamic therapy, DBT, etc.) and only suitable for motivated individuals who are capable of self-reflection and do not have significant cognitive impairment. Treatments emphasizing adaptation enhancement (e.g., interpersonal psychotherapy, social skills training, and CBT) are aimed at motivated individuals who may have less internal resources needed to change. Treatments that provide structure and support are for those with severe cognitive disorders who require a "surrogate support system." Examples include geriatric daycare or psychoeducation for caregivers. Finally, the experts noted that pharmacotherapy should be considered with the proper precautions for those with serious behavior problems who are not motivated or who do not respond to psychotherapy.

One problem in the gerontological field that has affected the development of innovative treatments of older adults with PDs is the dearth of overarching frameworks to integrate developmental research with clinical theory to guide practice activity (Segal, Zweig, & Molinari, 2012). Recently several models have been proposed to assist clinicians in working with older adults. Zweig and Agronin (2011) have described a "common factors approach" that utilizes a variety of modalities that are individualized based on the presenting problems of older adults with

PDs. Different types of individual and group psychotherapies combined with pharmacological treatment may be employed based on an evaluation of the varied personality characteristics and symptomatology in older adults. Such treatment addresses the traditional goals for those with PD of cohering disparate elements of their self-concepts that fuel maladaptive interpersonal behavior, but adds the novel element of working through traumatic experiences that are so often part of their early life histories, which may be rekindled by aging losses.

Molinari, Kier, and Rosowsky (2006) used Baltes' Selection, Optimization, Compensation (SOC) model to draw out practical implications for working with PD elders in long-term care settings. They argued that the SOC model cultivates the idea of a comprehensive bio-psycho-social assessment that focuses on the internal strengths of the person with PD rather than just emphasizing personality deficits. Intensive evaluation of personality characteristics upon admission will allow staff–resident agreement on selected individualized goals to be pursued via treatment planning. Optimization of the adaptive aspects of their exaggerated personality characteristics can be complemented by flexibility in environmental planning to compensate for interpersonal weaknesses and to create a fit between individuals with PDs and their communal living conditions.

One of the most comprehensive frameworks to guide PD treatment has been proposed by Segal et al. (2006), who employ a *Goodness-of-Fit* model in planning interventions for those older adults with PDs. The Goodness-of-Fit model is undergirded by four basic premises: (a) each personality trait lies along a continuum, (b) composites of these traits establish a profile, (c) care providers like or dislike different personality traits, and (d) whether or not a personality trait is labeled as a problem and a disorder depends on whether a personality trait is favored or not by the provider or setting. Interventions based on the Goodness-of-Fit model would be categorized broadly as (a) changing the demand on the client with the PD so that the PD trait is not exacerbated, (b) promoting the traits favored by the care provider, (c) reducing non-therapeutic responses by staff that can exacerbate maladaptive behaviors, and (d) helping to replace the loss that precipitated the increased use of maladaptive defenses.

The following vignette reflects how the common core elements of all these models guide interventions for older adults with PD. A man with a predominant narcissistic PD with psychopathic traits was admitted to a nursing home because of heart disease, mild memory problems, and the death of his wife who had been a caregiver for him. He has an exaggerated need for attention and a strong personality, annoying the members of a resident support group by constantly drawing attention to himself by reciting over and over the same apocryphal stories of his exploits as a younger man. When he is told by a staff member to please be quiet and let others speak, he becomes enraged and turns over a table in the community room. The staff convenes a special treatment team meeting and decides to maintain consistency and control not only by keeping him out of the residents' group but also by using his personal strength as a raconteur to his advantage by asking him to narrate his adventures to students from different high schools who visit the nursing home regularly. The staff member who is irritated by the client's constant need for attention is reassigned to other residents, while a low-key staff member who barely knows English allows him to tell his stories to her in order to teach her how to use words properly. Given that this resident was admitted to the nursing home because of the death of his long-suffering wife who bore his constant need for approval, one of the female residents with a mixed-dependent and avoidant PD is assigned to his dining table so that she can have much-needed company and lean on the resident with the PD, who is more than willing to direct her and who indulges his own need to be the dominant one to buttress his self-esteem.

Although as noted, some of the basic principles of clinical management for older adults are congruent with the evidence-based approaches that have been found effective with younger adults, controlled studies of DBT, CBT, and psychodynamic therapy must be validated with this age-group. Some research suggests that mindfulness-based acceptance therapies might be particularly useful for older adults who so often are unable to modify their functional or social

conditions in significant ways. DBT has been found to enhance the positive effects of medication in depressed older adults (Lynch, Morse, Mendelson, & Robins, 2003) and has shown promise in treating depressed older adults with concomitant PD (Lynch et al., 2007). Certainly more studies investigating CBT interventions with older adults with PDs need to be initiated, especially because distorted cognitive frameworks for viewing others may spawn interpersonal discord and could be a prime target for social skills training. Furthermore, although long-term psychoanalytic treatment is not appropriate for the great majority of those with PDs in old age because of its length and cost, variants of transference-based psychodynamic therapy might remain helpful for adults in later life stages, particularly if the treatment fosters intensive feedback regarding how their interpersonal style negatively affects the therapist and how it also may be upsetting to others, thereby reducing their chances of achieving needed social support and personal goals in late life. Given the complexity of the problems with which older adults with PD present, an integrative individualized approach will most probably be optimal.

CONCLUSION

Later life holds both challenges and opportunities for those interested in studying and treating PDs. PDs in later life can mask or exacerbate comorbid Axis I symptoms and medical conditions; their diagnosis is also critical to psychotherapy treatment decisions and prognostic considerations. When we consider later life in a broader context, we can identify the shortcomings of the current diagnostic criteria, which ultimately may lead us to develop better strategies regarding how best to measure PDs for people of all ages. When we consider later life, we also are offered the opportunity to examine the impact of these life-long disorders on the most important outcomes (disease, mortality). Finally, when we consider later life, we are required to reexamine basic theories and assumptions about PDs. Studying PDs in later life might provide us with good leverage to help improve PD assessment for patients of all ages, which is the first step toward effective treatment, and will enhance theory development.

References

Abrams, R. C., Rosendahl, E., Card, C., & Alexopoulos, G. S. (1994). Personality disorder correlates of late and early onset depression. *Journal of the American Geriatrics Society, 42,* 727–731.

American Psychiatric Association. (2000). *Diagnostic and statistical manual of mental disorders* (4th ed., text revision). Washington, DC: Author.

Ames, A., & Molinari, V. (1994). Prevalence of personality disorders in community-living elderly. *Journal of Geriatric Psychiatry and Neurology, 7,* 189–194. doi:10.1177/089198879400700311

Balsis, S., Carpenter, B., & Storandt, M. (2005). Personality change precedes clinical diagnosis of dementia of the Alzheimer type. *The Journals of Gerontology, Series B: Psychological Sciences and Social Sciences, 60,* 98–101. doi:10.1093/geronb/60.2.P98

Balsis, S., Gleason, M. E. J., Woods, C. M., & Oltmanns, T. F. (2007). An item response theory analysis of *DSM–IV* personality disorder criteria across younger and older age groups. *Psychology and Aging, 22,* 171–185. doi:10.1037/0882-7974.22.1.171

Balsis, S., Woods, C. M., Gleason, M. E. J., & Oltmanns, T. F. (2007). Overdiagnosis and underdiagnosis of personality disorders in older adults. *American Journal of Geriatric Psychiatry, 15,* 742–753. doi:10.1097/JGP.0b013e31813c6b4e

Bateman, A. W., & Tyrer, P. (2004). Psychological treatment for personality disorders. *Advances in Psychiatric Treatment, 10,* 378–388. doi:10.1192/apt.10.5.378

Butcher, J. N., Dahlstrom, W. G., Graham, J. R., Tellegen, A., & Kaemmer, B. (1989). *Minnesota Multiphasic Personality Inventory—2 (MMPI–2): Manual for administration and scoring.* Minneapolis: University of Minnesota Press.

Casey, D. A., & Schrodt, C. J. (1989). Axis II diagnoses in geriatric inpatients. *Journal of Geriatric Psychiatry and Neurology, 2,* 87–88. doi:10.1177/089198878900200206

Clark, L. A. (2007). Assessment and diagnosis of personality disorder: Perennial issues and an emerging reconceptualization. *Annual Review of Psychology, 58,* 227–257. doi:10.1146/annurev.psych.57.102904.190200

Clark, L. A. (2009). *Schedule for nonadaptive and adaptive personality—Second edition (SNAP–2).* Minneapolis: University of Minnesota Press.

Clarkin, J. F., Levy, K. N., Lenzenweger, M. F., & Kernberg, O. K. (2007). Evaluating three treatments for borderline personality disorder: A multiwave study. *American Journal of Psychiatry, 164,* 922–928. doi:10.1176/appi.ajp.164.6.922

Cohen, B. J., Nestadt, G., Samuels, J. F., Romanoski, A. J., McHugh, P. R., & Rabins, P. V. (1994). Personality disorder in later life: A community study. *British Journal of Psychiatry, 165,* 493–499. doi:10.1192/bjp.165.4.493

Coolidge, F. L., & Merwin, M. M. (1992). Reliability and validity of the Coolidge Axis II Inventory: A new inventory for the assessment of personality disorders. *Journal of Personality Assessment, 59,* 223–238. doi:10.1207/s15327752jpa5902_1

Costa, P. T., Jr., & McCrae, R. R. (1992). *Revised NEO Personality Inventory (NEO–PI–R) and NEO Five-Factor Inventory (NEO–FFI) professional manual.* Odessa, FL: Psychological Assessment Resources.

Edelstein, B. A., & Segal, D. L. (2011). Assessment of emotional and personality disorders in older adults. In K. W. Schaie & S. L. Willis (Eds.), *Handbook of the psychology of aging* (7th ed., pp. 325–337). San Diego, CA: Elsevier Academic Press. doi:10.1016/B978-0-12-380882-0.00021-8

Ferro, T., Klein, D. N., Schwartz, J. E., Kasch, K. L., & Leader, J. B. (1998). 30-month stability of personality disorder diagnoses in depressed outpatients. *American Journal of Psychiatry, 155,* 653–659.

First, M. B., Gibbon, M., Spitzer, R. L., Williams, J. B., & Benjamin, L. S. (1997). *Structured Clinical Interview for DSM–IV Axis II Personality Disorders (SCID–II).* Washington, DC: American Psychiatric Association Press.

Fogel, B. S., & Westlake, R. (1990). Personality disorder diagnoses and age in inpatients with major depression. *Journal of Clinical Psychiatry, 51,* 232–235.

Follett, K. J., & Hess, T. M. (2002). Aging, cognitive complexity, and the fundamental attribution error. *The Journals of Gerontology, Series B: Psychological Sciences and Social Sciences, 57,* 312–323. doi:10.1093/geronb/57.4.P312

Gleason, M. E. J., Weinstein, Y., Balsis, S., & Oltmanns, T. F. (in press). The enduring impact of maladaptive personality traits on relationship quality and health in later life. *Journal of Personality.*

Gutiérrez, F., Vall, G., Peri, J. M., Baillés, E., Ferraz, L., Gárriz, M., & Caseras, X. (2012). Personality disorder features through the life course. *Journal of Personality Disorders, 26,* 763–774. doi:10.1521/pedi.2012.26.5.763

Hahn, S. R. (2000). The difficult doctor–patient relationship questionnaire. In M. E. Maruish (Ed.), *Handbook of psychological assessment in primary care settings* (pp. 653–683). Mahwah, NJ: Erlbaum.

Hahn, S. R., Kroenke, K., Spitzer, R. L., Brody, D., Williams, J. B. W., Linzer, M., & deGruy, III, F. V. (1996). The difficult patient: Prevalence, psychopathology, and functional impairment. *Journal of General Internal Medicine, 11,* 1–8.

Hooker, K., & McAdams, D. (2003). Personality reconsidered: A new agenda for aging research. *The Journals of Gerontology, Series B: Psychological Sciences and Social Sciences, 58,* 296–304. doi:10.1093/geronb/58.6.P296

Horowitz, L. M., Rosenberg, S. E., Baer, B. A., Ureño, G., & Villaseñor, V. S. (1988). Inventory of interpersonal problems: Psychometric properties and clinical applications. *Journal of Consulting and Clinical Psychology, 56,* 885–892. doi:10.1037/0022-006X.56.6.885

Klein, M. H., Benjamin, L. S., Rosenfeld, R., Treece, C., Husted, J., & Greist, J. H. (1993). The Wisconsin Personality Disorders Inventory: Development, reliability, and validity. *Journal of Personality Disorders, 7,* 285–303. doi:10.1521/pedi.1993.7.4.285

Kunik, M. E., Mulsant, B. H., Rifai, A. H., Sweet, R., Pasternak, R., Rosen, J., & Zubenko, G. S. (1993). Personality disorders in elderly inpatients with major depression. *American Journal of Geriatric Psychiatry, 1,* 38–45. doi:10.1097/00019442-199300110-00006

Livesley, W. J. (2001). Conceptual and taxonomic issues. In W. J. Livesley (Ed.), *Handbook of personality disorders: Theory, research, and treatment* (pp. 3–38). New York, NY: Guilford Press.

Lynch, T. R., Cheavens, J. S., Cukrowicz, K. C., Thorp, S. R., Bronner, L., & Beyer, J. (2007). Treatment of older adults with co morbid personality disorder: A dialectical behavior therapy approach. *International Journal of Geriatric Psychiatry, 22,* 131–143. doi:10.1002/gps.1703

Lynch, T. R., Morse, J. Q., Mendelson, T., & Robins, C. J. (2003). Dialectical behavior therapy for depressed older adults: A randomized pilot study. *American Journal of Geriatric Psychiatry, 11,* 33–45. doi:10.1097/00019442-200301000-00006

McAdams, D. P., & Pals, J. L. (2006). A new big five: Fundamental principles for an integrative science of personality. *American Psychologist, 61,* 204–217. doi:10.1037/0003-066X.61.3.204

Millon, T., Davis, R. D., & Millon, C. (1997). *MCMI–III manual* (2nd ed.). Minneapolis, MN: National Computer Systems.

Molinari, V., Kier, F., & Rosowsky, E. (2006). SOC, personality, and long term care. In L. Hyer & R. Intrieri (Eds.), *Geropsychological interventions in long-term care* (pp. 139–155). New York, NY: Springer.

Mordekar, A., & Spence, S. A. (2008). Personality disorder in older people: How common is it and what can be done? *Advances in Psychiatric Treatment, 14,* 71–77. doi:10.1192/apt.bp.107.003897

Morey, L. C. (2007). *The Personality Assessment Inventory professional manual.* Lutz, FL: Psychological Assessment Resources.

Morse, J. Q., Pilkonis, P. A., Houck, P. R., Frank, E., & Reynolds, C. F., III. (2005). Impact of cluster C personality disorders on outcomes of acute and maintenance treatment in late-life depression. *American Journal of Geriatric Psychiatry, 13,* 808–814. doi:10.1097/00019442-200509000-00010

Mroczek, D. K., Hurt, S. W., & Berman, W. H. (1999). Conceptual and methodological issues in the assessment of personality disorders in older adults. In E. Rosowsky, R. C. Abrams, & R. A. Zweig (Eds.), *Personality disorders in older adults: Emerging issues in diagnosis and treatment* (pp. 135–150). Mahwah, NJ: Erlbaum.

National Institute for Health and Clinical Excellence. Centre for Clinical Practice. (2011). *Review of Clinical Guideline (CG78): Borderline personality disorder.* Retrieved from http://www.nice.org.uk/nicemedia/live/12125/57625/57625.pdf

Oltmanns, T. F., & Balsis, S. (2011). Personality disorders in later life: Questions about the measurement, course, and impact of disorders. *Annual Review of Clinical Psychology, 7,* 321–349. doi:10.1146/annurev-clinpsy-090310-120435

Oltmanns, T. F., & Gleason, M. E. J. (2011). Personality, health, and social adjustment in later life. In L. B. Cottler (Ed.), *Mental health in public health: The next 100 years* (pp. 151–179). New York, NY: Oxford University Press.

Perry, J. C., Banon, E., & Ianni, F. (1999). Effectiveness of psychotherapy for personality disorders. *American Journal of Psychiatry, 156,* 1312–1321.

Pfohl, B., Blum, N., & Zimmerman, M. (1995). *Structured Interview for DSM–IV Personality (SIDP–IV).* Iowa City: University of Iowa.

Pietrzak, R. H., Wagner, J. A., & Petry, N. M. (2007). *DSM–IV* personality disorders and coronary heart disease in older adults: Results from the national epidemiologic survey on alcohol and related conditions. *The Journals of Gerontology, Series B: Psychological Sciences and Social Sciences, 62,* 295–299. doi:10.1093/geronb/62.5.P295

Pilkonis, P. A., & Frank, E. (1988). Personality pathology in recurrent depression: Nature, prevalence and relationship to treatment response. *American Journal of Psychiatry, 145,* 435–441.

Powers, A. D., & Oltmanns, T. F. (2012). Personality disorders and physical health: A longitudinal examination of physical functioning, healthcare utilization, and health-related behaviors in middle-aged adults. *Journal of Personality Disorders, 26,* 524–538. doi:10.1521/pedi.2012.26.4.524

Powers, A. D., & Oltmanns, T. F. (2013). Borderline personality pathology and chronic health problems in later adulthood: The mediating role of obesity. *Personality Disorders: Theory, Research, and Treatment, 4,* 152–159.

Pulay, A. J., Dawson, D. A., Ruan, W. J., Pickering, R. P., Huang, B., Chou, S. P., & Grant, B. F. (2008). The relationship of impairment to personality disorder severity among individuals with specific axis I disorders: Results from the National Epidemiologic Survey on Alcohol and Related Conditions. *Journal of Personality Disorders, 22,* 405–417. doi:10.1521/pedi.2008.22.4.405

Roberts, B. W., Kuncel, N. R., Shiner, R., Caspi, A., & Goldberg, L. R. (2007). The power of personality: The comparative validity of personality traits, socioeconomic status, and cognitive ability for predicting important life outcomes. *Perspectives on Psychological Science, 2,* 313–345. doi:10.1111/j.1745-6916.2007.00047.x

Sadavoy, J., & Fogel, B. (1992). Personality disorders in old age. In J. E. Birren, R. B., Sloane, & G. D. Cohen (Eds.), *Handbook of mental health and aging* (2nd ed., pp. 433–462). San Diego, CA: Academic Press.

Salsman, N. L., & Linehan, M. M. (2006). Dialectical–behavioral therapy for borderline personality disorder. *Primary Psychiatry, 13,* 51–58.

Samuels, J., Eaton, W. W., Bienvenu, O. J., III, Brown, C. H., Costa, P. T., Jr., & Nestadt, G. (2002). Prevalence and correlates of personality disorders in a community sample. *British Journal of Psychiatry, 180,* 536–542. doi:10.1192/bjp.180.6.536

Segal, D. L., Coolidge, F. L., & Rosowsky, E. (2006). *Personality disorders and older adults: Diagnosis, assessment, and treatment.* Hoboken, NJ: Wiley.

Segal, D. L., Hook, J. N., & Coolidge, F. L. (2001). Personality dysfunction, coping styles, and clinical symptoms in younger and older adults. *Journal of Clinical Geropsychology, 7,* 201–212. doi:10.1023/A:1011391128354

Segal, D. L., Marty, M. A., Meyer, W. J., & Coolidge, F. L. (2012). Personality, suicidal ideation, and reasons for living among older adults. *The Journals of Gerontology, Series B: Psychological Sciences and Social Sciences, 67,* 159–166. doi:10.1093/geronb/gbr080

Segal, D. L., Zweig, R., & Molinari, V. (2012). Personality disorders in later life. In S. K. Whitbourne & M. J. Sliwinski (Eds.), *The Wiley–Blackwell handbook of adulthood and aging* (pp. 312–330). Oxford, England: Wiley–Blackwell. doi:10.1002/9781118392966.ch16

Stanley, S. H., Laugharne, J. D., Addis, S., & Sherwood, D. (2013). Assessing overweight and obesity across mental disorders: Personality disorders at high risk. *Social Psychiatry and Psychiatric Epidemiology, 48,* 487–492. doi:10.1007/s00127-012-0546-1

Stek, M. L., Van Exel, E., Van Tilburg, W., Westendorp, R. G. J., & Beekman, A. T. F. (2002). The prognosis of depression in old age: Outcome six to eight years after clinical treatment. *Aging and Mental Health, 6,* 282–285. doi:10.1080/13607860220142413

Stevenson, J., Brodaty, H., Boyce, P., & Byth, K. (2012). Does age moderate the effect of personality disorder on coping style in psychiatric inpatients? *Journal of Psychiatric Practice, 18,* 187–198. doi.org/10.1097/01.pra.0000415075.20873.0d

van Alphen, S. P. J., Derksen, J. J. L., Sadavoy, J., & Rosowsky, E. (2012). Features and challenges of personality disorders in late life. *Aging and Mental Health, 16,* 805–810. doi:10.1080/13607863.2012.667781

van Alphen, S. P. J., van Engelen, G. J. J. A., Kuin, Y., Hoijtink, H. J. A., & Derksen, J. J. L. (2004). Construction of an instrument to measure personality disorders in the elderly. *Tijdschrift voor Gerontologie en Geriatrie, 35,* 186–195.

Weissman, M. M., & Bothwell, S. (1976). Assessment of social adjustment by patient self-report. *Archives of General Psychiatry, 33,* 1111–1115. doi:10.1001/archpsyc.1976.01770090101010

Westen, D., & Shedler, J. (2007). Personality diagnosis with the Shedler–Westen Assessment Procedure (SWAP): Integrating clinical and statistical measurement and prediction. *Journal of Abnormal Psychology, 116,* 810–822. doi:10.1037/0021-843X.116.4.810

Widiger, T. A., Mangine, S., Corbitt, E. M., Ellis, G., & Thomas, G. V. (1995). *Personality Disorder Interview—IV: A semistructured interview for the assessment of personality disorders.* Odessa, FL: Psychological Assessment Resources.

Widiger, T. A., & Samuel, D. B. (2005). Evidence-based assessment of personality disorders. *Psychological Assessment, 17,* 278–287. doi:10.1037/1040-3590.17.3.278

World Health Organization. (1995). *The International Personality Disorder Examination (IPDE) DSM–IV module.* Washington, DC: American Psychiatric Association Press.

Zimmerman, M., & Coryell, W. (1989). *DSM–III* personality disorder diagnoses in a nonpatient sample: Demographic correlates and comorbidity. *Archives of General Psychiatry, 46,* 682–689. doi:10.1001/archpsyc.1989.01810080012002

Zweig, R. (2008). Personality disorder in older adults: Assessment challenges and strategies. *Professional*

Psychology: Research and Practice, 39, 298–305. doi:10.1037/0735-7028.39.3.298

Zweig, R. A., & Agronin, M. E. (2011). Personality disorders in late life. In M. E. Agronin & G. J. Maletta (Eds.), *Principles and practice of geriatric psychiatry* (pp. 523–543). Philadelphia, PA: Wolters Kluwer/ Lippincott Williams & Wilkins.

Zweig, R. A., & Parchi, D. S. (2010). Diagnostic and treatment issues regarding personality disorder in older adults. In M. T. Abou-Saleh, C. Katona, & A. Kumar (Eds.), *Principles and practice of geriatric psychiatry* (3rd ed., pp. 655–662). Chichester, England: Wiley. doi:10.1002/9780470669600. ch105

CHAPTER 4

SCHIZOPHRENIA IN LATE LIFE

Brent T. Mausbach and Jennifer Ho

According to the U.S. Census Bureau, the 21st century will see an exponential growth in the number and proportion of older adults (Day, 1996). Because of this aging trend, the number of older individuals with mental illnesses, including schizophrenia, is expected to increase accordingly, necessitating the need for mental health professionals with expertise in providing quality care that considers the interaction of age and illness. At the outset of this chapter, it is important to note the definition of *aging* in the context of schizophrenia. It has been noted that there is a shorter average life span for individuals diagnosed with schizophrenia, and "old age" may have different cutoffs in this population. Specifically, individuals with schizophrenia appear to have life expectancies that are 20% shorter than the general population (E. C. Harris & Barraclough, 1998; Newman & Bland, 1991), suggesting that old age in this population may require a different cutoff than typically is used. Thus, for the purposes of this chapter, readers should recalibrate their thinking on old age in this population, even considering individuals with schizophrenia age 45 or 50 years to be older adults. Within this framework, the current chapter will discuss schizophrenia in the context of aging, including important issues of symptoms, assessment, psychosocial functioning, and treatment. We will begin with a definition of the illness, including key symptoms and diagnostic considerations, followed by important assessment consideration, and finishing with the current status of psychosocial treatments for older adults with schizophrenia.

DEFINITIONS

In the sections that follow, we provide a definition of the disease of schizophrenia, including areas of symptoms, duration, effects of the illness on social and occupational function, and other common effects of the illness not specific to its diagnosis (e.g., cognitive function). We also present information on the prevalence of schizophrenia in the general population.

Symptoms

According to the *Diagnostic and Statistical Manual of Mental Disorders*, *Fourth Edition, Text Revision* (*DSM–IV–TR*; American Psychiatric Association, 2000), schizophrenia is a serious mental illness that typically is characterized by at least two of the following features: (a) delusions; (b) hallucinations; (c) disorganized speech; (d) negative symptoms such as affective flattening, poverty of speech, or lack of motivation; or (e) grossly disorganized or catatonic behavior (American Psychiatric Association, 2000). If present, symptoms must be evident for a significant portion of time over a 1-month period. Although the *DSM–IV–TR* states that two of these symptoms typically are used to make a diagnosis, a diagnosis also can be made if the only symptom is delusions or hallucinations as long as the delusions are "bizarre," or if hallucinations consist of a voice (or voices) keeping up a running conversation. These latter criteria (i.e., bizarre delusions or hallucinations; voices having a running conversation) were eliminated for the *DSM–5* (American Psychiatric Association, 2013). Instead, two of the five symptoms must be present, and one of them must

http://dx.doi.org/10.1037/14459-004
APA Handbook of Clinical Geropsychology: Vol. 2. Assessment, Treatment, and Issues of Later Life,
P. A. Lichtenberg and B. T. Mast (Editors-in-Chief)

be hallucinations, delusions, or disorganized speech. A discussion of these symptoms across all age-groups, will be followed by a discussion about the specifics of the various symptoms and aging.

As discussed above, three symptom classes are common to schizophrenia. These include positive symptoms, negative symptoms, and disorganized thinking. Positive symptoms refer to the psychotic symptoms of the illness, such as delusions (i.e., false beliefs) and hallucinations. Common delusions include (a) the belief that one is being persecuted, (b) beliefs that one is under the influence or control of others (e.g., one's thoughts are being influenced by others), (c) beliefs of grandiosity (e.g., believing he or she is a famous or powerful person such as Jesus or the president), and (d) somatic delusions (e.g., believing one's body or brain is deteriorating). Delusions are experienced commonly by people with schizophrenia, with 84% of individuals experiencing persecutory delusions, 75% experiencing delusions of body–mind control, approximately 50% experiencing delusions of grandiosity, and about 10% experiencing somatic delusions (Appelbaum, Robbins, & Roth, 1999). Hallucinations, which are estimated to occur in 70% of individuals with schizophrenia (Sartorius et al., 1986), can be auditory, visual, tactile, olfactory, or gustatory. Research suggests that auditory hallucinations are most common, occurring in 83% of cases, followed by visual (55%), tactile and olfactory (27% each), and gustatory (14%; Thomas et al., 2007). Disorganized thinking manifests in a variety of ways, typically with the individual being unable to stay on track in a conversation. For example, he or she may jump from one topic of conversation to another. Other manifestations include making up words or writing that is disorganized and unintelligible.

Duration. In addition, symptoms or disturbance are expected to last for a period of at least 6 months. This disturbance should include the 1-month time period in which symptoms occur for a significant portion of time, and it can include a period in which the individual experiences symptoms in an attenuated form, or only experiences residual symptoms of the condition (e.g., negative symptoms).

Social or occupational dysfunction. Individuals experiencing symptoms of schizophrenia are expected to have disturbance in one or more major areas of functioning. These typically include social or occupational functioning, such that the individual is unable to (or experience significant disruption to) work, impairment in social functioning (e.g., interpersonal relationships), or disruption to self-care. In a longitudinal study of cognitive and functional impairment in institutionalized patients with schizophrenia, Friedman et al. (2001) found that cognitive and functional decline was stable until late life, at which point individuals with schizophrenia demonstrated significant decline relative to healthy older adults and those with Alzheimer's disease. Other reports, however, have indicated that among community-dwelling schizophrenics, cognitive functioning remains stable across the life span (Kurtz, 2005). These findings have implications for social and occupational functioning because cognitive function is the strongest predictor of functioning in schizophrenia.

In a separate review of social functioning in older adults with schizophrenia, Meesters et al. (2010) reported that compared with individuals with no psychiatric illness, those with schizophrenia were more likely never to have been married, although this appeared to be moderated by age of onset. Specifically, those with early onset were more likely to never marry than those with late-onset symptoms. In addition, marital status is correlated with living status, with never married individuals more likely to reside in nursing homes or assisted-care settings. Interestingly, as individuals with schizophrenia age, there appears to be improvement in mental-health related quality of life relative to similarly aged individuals without psychiatric illness (Folsom et al., 2009).

Additional characteristics of schizophrenia. In addition to the diagnostic criteria presented in the *DSM–IV–TR* (American Psychiatric Association, 2000), cognitive impairment is common to many individuals with schizophrenia (Bowie & Harvey, 2005). Generally, moderate to severe cognitive impairment appears to be a common feature of schizophrenia (Fioravanti, Bianchi, & Cinti, 2012; Fioravanti, Carlone, Vitale, Cinti, & Clare, 2005) that appears before a first psychotic episode (Davidson et al., 1999) and persists throughout the course of the illness (Heaton et al., 2001). Meta-analyses on cognition in schizophrenia suggest that cognitive impairment is global, affecting both short- and long-term memory, verbal and language functioning, attention and concentration, and executive functioning roughly equally (Fioravanti et al., 2005, 2012). In sum, moderate to severe global cognitive impairment has been considered a core feature of the illness that has a negative impact on one's ability to adequately function or reach functional milestones (Green, 1996). With regard to cognitive functioning and aging in schizophrenia, the preponderance of evidence suggest that although significant cognitive impairment is evident at all phases of life relative to healthy individuals, individuals with schizophrenia do not show greater deterioration of cognitive functioning with age relative to healthy adults (Kurtz, 2005). The one exception noted by Kurtz (2005) is among individuals who experienced early institutionalization. This subgroup of individuals with schizophrenia appears to evidence significant deterioration of cognitive functioning in the fifth or sixth decade of life.

Prevalence. Numerous studies have investigated the prevalence of schizophrenia. Because of differences in diagnostic criteria, prevalence rates vary from study to study. Saha, Chant, Welham, and McGrath (2005), however, reviewed 1,721 prevalence estimates encompassing 188 studies from 46 countries and reported point, period, lifetime, and lifetime morbid risk of schizophrenia. Point prevalence, defined as the proportion of individuals with schizophrenia at a given point in time (i.e., in the past month), was estimated as 4.6 per 1,000 individuals (0.46%). Period prevalence differs from point prevalence in that it represents the proportion of individuals who have schizophrenia during a specified period of time (e.g., 1 calendar year). Using this criteria, Saha et al. reported a period prevalence of 3.3 per 1,000 individuals (0.33%). Lifetime prevalence is the proportion of individuals who have ever had schizophrenia that are alive on a given day. Thus, a person who is no longer living is not included in the lifetime prevalence estimate. The estimate for lifetime prevalence was 4 per 1,000 individuals (0.4%). In contrast to lifetime prevalence, *lifetime morbid risk*

is an estimate based on all individuals from a specific cohort, and thus includes individuals who may have had the disorder but are now deceased. Using this definition, the lifetime morbid risk was reported as 7.2 per 1,000 individuals (0.72%). Saha et al. further reported no significant difference between males and females, or between urban and rural settings. Studies of developing countries, however, had prevalence estimates that were lower than those from emerging and industrial countries. Also, when rating the quality of the estimates, studies with more stringent methodology (e.g., diagnostic interview vs. chart review) reported higher estimates, underscoring the need for thorough assessment in making a diagnosis.

Symptoms in the Context of Aging

For the majority of individuals with schizophrenia, a diagnosis usually is made before the age of 30 years (Mueser & McGurk, 2004). Evidence from two epidemiologic studies indicated that 77% of people with schizophrenia evidence the first signs of schizophrenia before the age of 30 years, and 41% show signs before the age of 20 years, making the risk of onset greatest from ages 15–30 years (an der Heiden & Hafner, 2000). In the majority of cases (68%) the onset of the disease is insidious, whereby the earliest signs of the illness last for 1 year before individuals experience maximum psychotic symptoms. An additional 18% evidence acute onset (i.e., maximum psychotic symptoms occur within 1 month of onset), and 15% evidence subacute onset (i.e., earliest onset lasts more than 1 month but less than 1 year before maximum symptoms appear). For 73% of individuals, negative or nonspecific symptoms appear first, compared with just 7% who experience positive symptoms first. The remaining 20% of individuals experience both positive and negative symptoms simultaneously (an der Heiden & Hafner, 2000).

Late-onset schizophrenia, historically defined as an onset after the age of 40 years (Bleuler, 1943; Howard, Rabins, Seeman, & Jeste, 2000), is now more accepted by clinicians as not fixed to an arbitrary cutoff age (Howard & Jeste, 2011). Yet it is generally believed that late-onset schizophrenia is relatively uncommon, manifesting in less than 5% of people over the age of 40 years (Howard & Jeste, 2011). Clinically, the sum of evidence suggests that individuals with late-onset schizophrenia are clinically similar to those with early-onset schizophrenia (Hafner, Hambrecht, Loffler, Munk-Jorgensen, & Riecher-Rossler, 1998; Jeste et al., 1995). Notable clinical and demographic differences, however, appear between these groups. For example, women appear more likely to evidence late-onset schizophrenia, with one study reporting 67.2% of late-onset cases (i.e., after age 45 years) were women, compared with 42% of early-onset cases (Howard, Castle, Wessely, & Murray, 1993). Various authors have suggested that these sex differences in early versus late-onset schizophrenia may be due to a higher susceptibility to neurodevelopmental disorders among males (e.g., Dyslexia, Autism, Asperger's syndrome), possible higher rates of nonspecific stressors among males during adolescence, and possible biological protective factors among women (e.g., dopaminergic inhibition by estrogens; M. J. Harris & Jeste, 1988; Seeman, 1996). In addition, individuals with late-onset schizophrenia appear more likely to have been married and have an occupational history (Jeste et al., 1995).

Various studies suggest that symptoms of schizophrenia appear to change over the course of the illness. Schultz et al. (1997) conducted a cross-sectional study of 391 individuals with schizophrenia, schizoaffective disorder, or schizophreniform disorder and evaluated the relationship between age and both psychotic and disorganized symptoms. Results of their study indicated that hallucinations, delusions, and disorganized symptoms all demonstrated reduced severity with aging. Negative symptoms, however, did not evidence significant change with age. Another study by Davidson et al. (1995) reported similar results among chronically institutionalized persons with schizophrenia. In this study, positive symptoms became less severe as individuals aged. These authors, however, found that negative symptoms became more severe with age. This discrepancy between trajectories for positive and negative symptoms also was reported by Gur, Petty, Turetsky, and Gur (1996).

ASSESSMENT

In the sections that follow, we provide an overview of instruments useful for assessing individuals with schizophrenia. These are broadly categorized as either tools that measure symptoms of psychosis (e.g., positive and negative symptoms) or tools that measure functioning or functional capacity. We discuss the reliability and validity of each measure as well as the relevant scientific research supporting its use in this population.

Assessment Approaches, Tools, and Instruments

Assessment of patients with schizophrenia must take into account multiple issues, most notably the assessment of symptoms that are treatment targets as well as assessments designed to determine functional ability, including but not limited to employability and residential placement. The following measures commonly are used for these purposes.

Symptoms of Psychosis

Positive and Negative Syndromes Scale. The Positive and Negative Syndromes Scale (PANSS; Kay, Fiszbein, & Opler, 1987) is administered in a structured interview format with interviews designed to last approximately 30–40 min. Although the PANSS traditionally has been used as a research tool, the Remission in Schizophrenia Working Group has recommended its use as a clinical tool in identifying remission in schizophrenia (Andreasen et al., 2005). A structured clinical interview manual (SCI-PANSS) is available to ensure reliable ratings of symptoms (Kay, 1991). The structured format of the interview helps interviewers ascertain whether or not a variety of symptoms is present as well as determine the severity of the symptoms. On the basis of responses to the interview questions, interviewers rate patients on 30 symptoms. Ratings are made according to a detailed rating manual (Kay, 2006), and training is required to ensure reliability of ratings. Seven items assess positive symptoms (e.g., hallucinations, delusions, grandiosity) and seven assess negative symptoms (e.g., blunted affect, emotional withdrawal, poor rapport). The remaining 16 items assess general symptoms, such as anxiety, depression, poor attention, and judgment or insight. All items are scored on a seven-point scale, with 1 indicating the absence of the symptom and 7 indicating extreme manifestation of the symptom. Scores for each subscale are summed, with higher scores indicating more severe expression of symptoms.

Reliability and validity of the PANSS are very good. The scale, on which individual symptoms are rated by the interviewer, has shown excellent interrater reliability. Interrater correlations for the four subscales range from 0.83 for the positive syndrome subscale to 0.87 for the general psychopathology subscale (Kay, Opler, & Lindenmayer, 1988). Overlap in scores among the PANSS and other psychosis rating scales (e.g., scale for the assessment of positive symptoms, scale for the assessment of negative symptoms) is also high, with correlations exceeding 0.70 (Kay et al., 1988). Internal reliability is 0.73 for the positive subscale, 0.83 for the negative subscale, and 0.79 for the general subscale. Test–retest reliability (3–6 months) was also high for the positive ($r = 0.80$), negative ($r = 0.68$), and general subscales ($r = 0.60$).

Brief Psychiatric Rating Scale. One of the earlier psychiatric rating scales for schizophrenia, the Brief Psychiatric Rating Scale (BPRS) was developed with a balance of speed and accuracy in mind. The original scale consisted of 16 symptoms rated by an interviewer on a seven-point scale (1 = not present, 7 = very severe; Overall & Gorham, 1962). Symptom ratings are made by the interviewer based on a combination of the patient's self-report and on observed behaviors and speech. More recent versions include an 18-item scale (Overall, 1976) and an expanded version (BPRS–E) containing 24 symptoms (Lukoff, 1986; Ventura, Nuechterlein, Subotnik, & Gilbert, 1993) that also are rated on a seven-point scale.

The 18-item version is one of the most utilized instruments in measuring psychiatric symptoms in schizophrenia. As for reliability and validity, Bell, Milstein, Beam-Goulet, Lysaker, and Cicchetti (1992) found the BPRS positive symptoms subscale to have an internal reliability (alpha) of 0.69, while the negative symptoms subscale had a reliability of 0.68. For the general subscale, reliability was 0.46. For individual items on the BPRS evaluated using intraclass correlations, coefficients ranged from 0.52 for the emotional withdrawal item to 0.92 for hallucinations. The overall scale had an excellent intraclass correlation of 0.87. Also, correlations between the BPRS and PANSS subscales were high: 0.82 for positive syndromes and 0.92 for negative syndromes. When examining correlations between BPRS scores and multiple aspects of work performance, negative symptoms were correlated significantly with work quality, measured by the Minnesota Satisfactoriness Scale (Gibson, Weiss, & Dawis, 1970), as well as work skills and social skills, measured by the Work Personality Profile (Bolton & Roessler, 1986).

Functioning

The task of judging an individual's functioning is not an easy one for health care professionals. Functioning, in this case, involves an individual's ability to perform daily activities that are necessary for self-maintenance (e.g., earning an income; maintaining a residence; developing and maintaining social relationships). Using clinical judgment alone may not be enough because clinicians are not embedded into the natural environment of those they work with, thereby making it difficult to know how an individual functions in the real world. Clinicians therefore rely on additional measures for assessing functioning. These additional measures may be used before treatment to help develop an intervention plan, during treatment to "shift course" or to determine progress, and at the conclusion of treatment to aid in a discharge or follow-up plan. Indeed, increasing one's accuracy in predicting one's ability to self-maintain would be of great value for determining whether functional recovery has or is occurring. Along these lines, this section examines existing measures to assess functioning among individuals with psychosis.

UCSD Performance-Based Skills Assessment. The UCSD Performance-based Skills Assessment (UPSA; Patterson, Goldman, McKibbin, Hughs, & Jeste, 2001). The conceptual reasoning behind its development arose from clinical observation that people with schizophrenia often had cognitive deficits that made it difficult to learn or perform tasks necessary to function independently. Rather than asking the individual to perform abstract tasks, the UPSA is a role-play test requiring individuals to perform tasks similar to those in the real world. The UPSA consists of five subtests assessing the individual's ability in the following domains: (a) planning and organization (i.e., planning a trip to the beach or zoo), (b) finances (i.e., counting change; writing a check), (c) communication (i.e., calling information to request a phone number; calling the doctor to reschedule an appointment), (d) travel (i.e., reading a bus route map), and (e) household (i.e., completing a shopping list; reading a recipe). On the basis of their performance, individuals receive scores ranging from 0 to 20 for each of the five domains, with the five domain scores summed to create a total score (range = 0–100).

The UPSA contains a number of props, including grocery items, maps of bus schedules, and a telephone. Individuals who administer the UPSA do not need any specific academic credentials, but they do require a brief training to learn proper prompts, how to use props and testing materials, and proper scoring techniques. Once trained, administration of the test takes approximately 30 min (Green et al., 2011). Importantly, Green et al. (2011) found that compared with a variety of tests of functioning, the UPSA was rated best by testers in terms of practicality (i.e., ease of setup, administration, and scoring).

Reliability and validity of the UPSA has been very good. Specifically, interrater and 2-week test–retest reliability are .91 and .93, respectively (Harvey, Velligan, & Bellack, 2007), and 4-week test–retest reliability is .70 (Green et al., 2008). In a large, multisite study of functional outcome measures, Green et al. (2011) found the UPSA's intraclass correlation coefficient was 0.74, and 4-week test–retest was 0.75.

A variety of studies have evaluated the usefulness of the UPSA for determining real-world outcomes, such as community involvement, ability to live independently, and work outcomes. One study demonstrated a high correlation between UPSA performance and level of residential independence (Twamley et al., 2002). Another study of middle-age and older adults with schizophrenia found that optimal sensitivity and specificity occurred when UPSA scores were 75 or higher, at which cutoff point the UPSA was able to accurately identify 68% of individuals in terms of independent living status (Mausbach, Bowie, et al., 2008). In a sample of middle-age and older Latinos with schizophrenia, Cardenas et al.

(2008) demonstrated that higher scores on the UPSA were associated with achievement in more functional milestones, such as working for pay, doing volunteer work, and going to school. Two additional studies found that performance on the UPSA was highly correlated with proxy reports (i.e., individuals familiar with the person) of an individual's daily functional and work abilities. (Bowie et al., 2008; Bowie, Reichenberg, Patterson, Heaton, & Harvey, 2006).

Clinical trials increasingly are using the UPSA as a primary or coprimary measure of improvement in functional ability. The first trial to use the UPSA for assessing functioning in middle-age and older adults with schizophrenia was the Functional Adaptation and Skills Training (FAST) study (Patterson et al., 2006). FAST was designed to compare a behavioral skills-training intervention with a support group intervention. The FAST condition, which was based on social-cognitive theory (Bandura, 1986), taught participants specific functional skills, such as social skills, organizational skills, transportation, and medication management. Change in the UPSA was measured at baseline and again at posttreatment (24 weeks). Change over the treatment period was significantly greater for FAST participants than for those in the support group condition. A related study demonstrated similar results in a small sample of Latinos with schizophrenia, in which change from pre- to posttreatment was significantly greater in those receiving skills-training versus the support group (Patterson et al., 2005). A third study examined whether individuals receiving 24 weeks of cognitive–behavioral social skills training (CBSST) showed significantly greater improvement in the UPSA than individuals receiving 24 weeks of treatment as usual (TAU), which consisted primarily of visiting a physician regarding medication management (Granholm et al., 2005). Results indicated that UPSA scores were not significantly different for individuals receiving CBSST, although the effect size (Cohen's d) was 0.48 and favored CBSST. The sum of these articles suggests the UPSA is amenable to change via targeted, skills-training interventions.

To date, the UPSA has been applied almost exclusively in a research context. The status of this research, however, has suggested that its greatest clinical benefits would be to aid in discharge planning in the context of acute hospitalization and as a tool for evaluating the benefits of treatments to improve overall functional ability. Specifically, clinicians seeking to determine whether patients should be discharged to independent, semi-independent, or supervised housing arrangements may consider using the UPSA to determine the most appropriate setting based on current functional status. Clinically, awareness is increasing that improvement in symptoms does not translate to improvements in functioning and to community adaptation specifically (Green et al., 2011). Practitioners may consider the UPSA as a leading tool for evaluating the effectiveness of psychosocial treatments for improving overall functioning, with scores of 75 or higher serving as a target for adequate community functioning.

Brief UCSD Performance-Based Skills Assessment. As described previously, the UPSA consists of a number of props, including bus maps and a mock pantry containing a number of real food items. Because these props can be wieldy to transport and set up, the original UPSA can be challenging to administer in field settings where patients often are visited. In addition, the administration time may serve as a challenge for field professionals who may not have the recommended time to administer the full test. In recognition of these limitations, Mausbach, Harvey, Goldman, Jeste, and Patterson (2007) introduced the Brief UCSD Performance-Based Skills Assessment (UPSA–Brief), which narrowed the original UPSA from five subtests to two. Specifically, the UPSA–Brief consisted of a subtests measuring communication (e.g., calling to reschedule a doctor's appointment) and finance skills (e.g., making change; interpreting and paying a utility bill). The UPSA–Brief requires only 10–15 min to administer.

Reliability of the UPSA–Brief also appears very good. In a sample of adults ages 18–60 years (mean = 43.9 years), Green et al. (2011) reported that intraclass and 4-week test–retest reliability coefficients were both 0.69. In a study involving 211 individuals with schizophrenia-spectrum disorders (age-range = 23–74 years; mean age = 49 years), Olsson, Helldin, Hjarthag, and Norlander (2012) found the 1-year test–retest reliability was 0.73, with

lower reliability for individuals in remission at both assessments ($r = 0.58$) compared with those who were not in remission at both assessments ($r = 0.83$). Another study (Leifker, Patterson, Bowie, Mausbach, & Harvey, 2010) examined test–retest reliability in two unique samples of participants in the United States. The first subsample, consisting of 133 older adults with schizophrenia, found the 18-month test–retest reliability to be 0.75 and the 36-month test–retest reliability was 0.73. The second subsample, consisting of 101 older adults, found the 6-, 12-, and 18-month test–retest reliability was 0.79, 0.81, and 0.66, respectively. This consistency from three unique samples across a broad range of test–retest intervals suggests the UPSA–Brief has excellent test–retest reliability.

Validity for the UPSA–Brief appears similar to that of the full version. Concurrent validity has been assessed by examining correlations between scores on the UPSA–Brief and functional ratings of patients by health care professionals and relatives. In the Olsson et al. study (2012), UPSA–Brief scores were related significantly to functional ratings made by health care professionals and family members. In addition, ratings of the patients' ability to work, made through chart reviews and interviews with the patients and family members, were related significantly to UPSA–Brief scores.

Olsson et al. (2012) found that the UPSA–Brief adequately differentiates individuals who are in remission from those who are not, suggesting that level of psychosis is associated with functional level. In addition, scores on the UPSA–Brief appear to be related to residential independence and level of community responsibility. For example, Mausbach et al. (2011) found that scores on the UPSA–Brief significantly differentiated individuals who were living independently from those who were not, with scores of 60 or higher achieving the greatest sensitivity and specificity. Another study, which included 367 individuals with schizophrenia, found that the UPSA was able to accurately identify 78% of individuals who were residing independently and 74% who worked 20 hours per week or more (Mausbach et al., 2011). In addition, the UPSA was able to accurately identify nearly 91% of individuals who had achieved both milestones (vs. only one or the other). A third study found that individuals with a greater number of community responsibilities (e.g., working for pay, attending school) performed significantly better on the UPSA–Brief relative to those engaging in fewer responsibilities (Mausbach, Depp, Cardenas, Jeste, & Patterson, 2008). This relationship, however, did not exist in individuals residing in assisted living facilities such as board-and-care homes, suggesting that environmental factors may limit the availability of or motivation to achieve these functional milestones.

Social Skills Performance Assessment. Another performance-based assessment measure that has garnered increased attention is the Social Skills Performance Assessment (SSPA), which is a role-play test designed to determine an individual's ability to engage socially with others (Patterson, Moscona, McKibbin, Davidson, & Jeste, 2001). Administration of the test involves the test-taker role-playing two separate social scenarios in which he or she is required to demonstrate mastery of social skills. In the first scenario, individuals are told they are meeting a new neighbor (who is role-played by the person administering the test) for the first time. The individual is to hold a friendly and infor-mative conversation with this new neighbor for a period of 3 min. The conversation is audio recorded and later scored by two separate raters, using a scale from 1 (worse) to 5 (better), on seven criteria: (a) interest or disinterest (i.e., willingness to engage in the interaction), (b) fluency (i.e., participant's overall flow of conversation), (c) clarity (i.e., ability and willingness to express self clearly and directly), (d) focus (i.e., ability to concentrate on and track the role play), (e) affect (e.g., tone of voice, body posture), (f) social appropriateness, and (g) over-all conversation. An additional score for grooming and physical appearance is provided by the person administering the test, using the same five-point scale. This score then is added to the other seven items to provide an overall score. The second sce-nario involves a situation in which the test-taker needs to speak to his or her landlord (played by the interviewer) and indicate that a leak has occurred in the home and needs to be fixed. An added com-ponent of the role-play is that the test-taker is told he or she previously had complained about the leak,

but it has yet to be fixed. The objective therefore is to have the leak repaired immediately. In this scenario, the test administer (i.e., the landlord) is to display reluctance to fix the leak, thus requiring that the test-taker be persistent in requesting a fix. Conversations are audio-recorded and rated by two separate or independent raters on the following factors: (a) interest or disinterest, (b) fluency, (c) clarity, (d) focus, (e) affect, (f) negotiation ability (i.e., ability to generate solutions and make compro-mises), (g) submissive-persistent (i.e., ability and willingness to stick firmly to the goal of reaching a solution), (h) overall argument, and (i) social appro-priateness. Similar to the first role-play, the individ-ual is scored from 1 (worse) to 5 (better). Properly trained paraprofessionals can administer the SSPA in approximately 20 min.

Reliability of the SSPA appears solid. Patterson, Goldman, et al. (2001) found interrater reliability was 0.91 and 1-week test–retest reliability was 0.92. In a separate study of 152 middle-age and older adults with serious mental illness, Pratt et al. (2007) reported interrater reliability of 0.99 but did not report test–retest reliability for this sample.

Fewer publications report the SSPA's validity compared with the UPSA and UPSA–Brief. Higher scores on the SSPA, however, appear to be signifi-cantly correlated with a variety of other measures of functioning (Pratt et al., 2007). For example, Bowie et al. (2008) administered the SSPA to 222 individu-als with schizophrenia and examined whether scores were correlated with proxy ratings of interpersonal behavior (e.g., initiating, accepting, and maintaining social contacts; effectively communicating), com-munity activities (e.g., shopping, using telephone, paying bills, use of leisure time, use of public trans-portation), and work skills (e.g., employable skills, level of supervision required to complete tasks, abil-ity to stay on task, punctuality). Results indicated significant correlations between the SSPA and each of these "real-world" outcomes. Another study by Patterson, Moscona, et al. (2001) found the SSPA was able to adequately differentiate individuals with schizophrenia from those without.

A few studies have examined whether individual performance on the SSPA changes as a function of psychosocial interventions targeting social skills.

The first study to examine change in SSPA performance was conducted by Patterson et al. (2006), which randomized 240 individuals with schizophrenia or schizoaffective disorder to 24 weeks of skills training or 24 weeks of group support classes. A key component of the skills training intervention was to teach social and communication skills via role-plays and homework assignments. As expected, participants enrolled in the skills training intervention showed significant improvement in SSPA scores relative to those in the support condition. Another study by Bowie, McGurk, Mausbach, Patterson, and Harvey (2012) replicated these findings by showing that a modified, 12-week version of the skills training intervention produced significant change in social skills from pre- to posttreatment.

Test of Adaptive Behavior in Schizophrenia.
Another performance-based test that has garnered good reliability and validity is the Test of Adaptive Behavior in Schizophrenia (TABS; Velligan et al., 2007). Similar to the UPSA and UPSA–Brief, the TABS is a role-play test, containing a variety of props, designed to capture an individual's ability to perform important everyday functional tasks. Specifically, the TABS contains the following five role-play tasks: (a) medication management (i.e., taking three types of medication as directed, identifying that the pills would run out prior to the end of the week, and generating a solution to this problem), (b) empty bathroom (i.e., identify what items are needed in an empty bathroom so they could use it every day), (c) shopping (i.e., using a map to get to a store, shop for items by viewing pictures of supermarket aisles, and identify when they have not received correct change), (d) clothes closet (i.e., selecting appropriate clothes for various circumstances), (e) work and productivity (i.e., correctly collate flyers), and (f) social skills (i.e., tester rating of testee's eye contact, speech, etc. during the test). For each test, participants receive a percent correct score for each of the six domains, with the average of the six domain scores serving as a total score (range = 0–100). Administration of the test takes approximately 30–40 min (Green et al., 2011; Velligan et al., 2007). In a survey of test administers (Green et al., 2011), practicality (e.g.,

ease of administration, scoring) was rated 5.2 on a seven-point scale, in which 7 is the best score.

Reliability of the TABS is excellent. Velligan et al. (2007) reported internal consistency (i.e., Cronbach's alpha) was 0.84. Intraclass and 3-month test–retest reliability were both 0.80. In a separate study, Green et al. (2011) reported intraclass and 4-week test–retest coefficients of 0.69 and 0.71, respectively. The Green et al. (2011) sample consisted of adults ages 18–60 years, with a mean age of approximately 44 years and an average duration of illness of 20.3 years.

There appears to be a lack of studies reporting the validity of the TABS for predicting real-world outcomes, such as employment, residential independence, or other social milestones. The TABS successfully differentiates individuals with schizophrenia from those without, with effect size estimates showing that approximately 96% of individuals with schizophrenia would score lower than the average (healthy) nonschizophrenia subject. Furthermore, convergent and divergent validity appear strong. For example, the TABS has been shown to be significantly correlated with other measures of functional ability, including the Multnomah Community Ability scale, the Social and Occupational Functioning scale, and the Independent Living scales (Velligan et al., 2007). As for its relation to symptoms of schizophrenia, some discrepancies exist across studies. Velligan et al. (2007) reported that TABS scores are related significantly to negative symptoms but not positive symptoms, whereas Green et al. (2011) reported that the TABS was not significantly correlated with either positive or negative symptoms.

Independent Living Skills Survey. The Independent Living Skills Survey (ILSS; Wallace, Liberman, Tauber, & Wallace, 2000) is administered via one of two versions; an informant report form (ILSS-I) and a self-report form (ILSS-SR). The ILSS-I contains 103 items assessing functioning across 12 domains: (a) *appearance and clothing* (e.g., washed clothes by hand or machine using the proper amount of detergent [without prompting]), (b) *personal hygiene* (e.g., bathed/showered with soap at least twice/week [without prompting]), (c) *care of personal possessions* (e.g., kept room clean [without prompting]), (d) *food preparation/storage* (e.g., prepared simple foods such as sandwiches, cold cereal, etc. that did not require cooking), (e) *health maintenance* (e.g., self-administered medication), (f) *money management* (e.g., paid bills such as rent, utilities, phone, and transportation [without prompting]), (g) *transportation* (e.g., used public buses, trains, or subway [without prompting]), (h) *leisure and community* (e.g., worked regularly on a hobby [without prompting]), (i) *job seeking* (e.g., read classified ads one or more times per week to look for jobs [without prompting]), (j) *job maintenance* (e.g., when last employed, got along with co-workers), (k) *eating* (e.g., drank neatly [without prompting]), and (l) *social relations* (e.g., communicated with coherent, comprehensible speech). This scale is completed by an informant familiar with the person's functioning (e.g., family member, case manager, community agency). The scale can be completed in person, by phone, or by mail. Informants rate the individual in terms of how often he or she performed each behavior over the past 30 days, with responses on a five-point scale (0 = never, 1 = sometimes, 2 = often, 3 = usually, and 4 = always). To account for the possibility that all behaviors may not be observed by the informant, a sixth option of "no opportunity" is available. Once rated, average item responses are calculated for each subscale, unless three items are rated "no opportunity." Total time for completing the scale is approximately 20–35 min.

Reliability of the ILSS-I is very good. In three separate samples encompassing 448 participants, internal consistency was greater than 0.90 for six subscales (personal hygiene, appearance and clothing, care of personal possessions, food preparation and storage, money management, and job seeking), greater than 0.80 for two subscales (leisure and community, transportation), and greater than 0.70 for one subscale (health maintenance; Wallace et al., 2000). Internal consistency was not calculated for the job maintenance or social relations subscales. Six-month test–retest for the ILSS-I was also very high, with all scales having coefficients greater than 0.70 except for job seeking and job maintenance (0.60 and 0.34, respectively).

Validity for the ILSS-I was measured primarily through correlation with theoretically similar con-

structs. In their original manuscript, Wallace et. al (2000) found the ILSS-I total score to be significantly correlated with global functioning, as measured by Global Assessment Scale (GAS; Endicott, Spitzer, Fleiss, & Cohen, 1976) and symptoms of psychosis, as measured by the BPRS. Unfortunately, no studies specifically address the validity of the ILSS-I among middle-age and older adults with schizophrenia.

A self-report version of the ILSS (ILSS-SR) consists of 70 items assessing 10 similar domains of functioning: (a) personal hygiene, (b) appearance and care of clothing, (c) care of personal possessions and living space, (d) food preparation, (e) care of personal health and safety, (f) money management, (g) transportation, (h) leisure and recreational activities, (i) job seeking, and (j) job maintenance. This version was developed to navigate the reality that some patients have limited contact with individuals who are familiar with their level of functioning. The ILSS-SR differs from the informant version in that respondents indicate whether or not they performed each behavior over the past month ("yes" or "no"). For each domain in which three or more items were answered, a total score is created by summing the "yes" responses. The ILSS-SR takes approximately 20–30 min to administer.

As with the informant version, the ILSS-SR was initially validated on three samples encompassing a total of 448 individuals with severe mental illnesses (Wallace et al., 2000). Internal reliability for the 10 subscales was mixed; one scale had a reliability coefficient more than 0.90 (job seeking), 3 scales had coefficients more than 0.70 (personal hygiene, care of personal possessions and living space, and job maintenance), and 6 scales had coefficients less than 0.70 (range = 0.43–0.63). Perivoliotis, Granholm, and Patterson (2004) examined reliability coefficients in middle-age and older adults with psychosis and reported internal reliability coefficients and found that 6 of the 10 subscales had reliability estimates less than 0.70. Six-month test–retest reliability coefficients showed stability of responses, ranging from 0.42 for the leisure and recreational activities subscale to 0.90 for the job maintenance subscale.

Key tests of the validity of the ILSS-SR were conducted by examining correlations with similar constructs. Results of these tests indicated that the ILSS-SR total score was moderately correlated with scores on the GAS ($r = 0.375$) and the BPRS ($r = -0.318$), suggesting that individuals who rated themselves as more functional had higher functional ratings on the GAS and fewer symptoms of psychosis (Wallace et al., 2000). Similarly, in a sample consisting of individuals with schizophrenia, major mood disorder, or substance abuse, the ILSS-SR was the best predictor of employability, defined as working at least 1 month with a minimum income of $300 per month. The ILSS-SR was better than all but the BPRS in predicting "sustained employability," which was defined as working at the same income level for 6 continuous months (Wallace et al., 2000). In a separate study, Perivoliotis et al. (2004) compared ILSS-SR scores of 57 middle-age and older adults with psychosis to a sample of 40 nonpsychiatric participants of similar age. The psychiatric sample scored significantly worse than the nonpsychiatric sample on 8 of 10 subscales, and the two samples did not significantly differ on the care of personal possessions and job maintenance subscales. Also, participants with psychosis had significantly lower ILSS-SR Total scores.

TREATMENT APPROACHES

Impairments associated with schizophrenia have a profound impact on multiple domains of the lives of those affected. These include but are not limited to quality of life, social functioning, emotional stability, vocational outcomes, and ability to live independently. Consequently, clinicians and clinical researchers have committed to the task of creating interventions that can help to reduce psychotic symptoms and improve the life outcomes of individuals with schizophrenia. A mainstay of treatment remains pharmacotherapy to reduce the frequency and intensity of psychotic symptoms (Lehman, Steinwachs, & Coinvestigators of the PORT Project, 1998; Moore, 2011). According to Fenton, Blyler, and Heinssen (1997), however, there are many reasons why patients with schizophrenia exhibit nonadherence in taking their medication, including the extent of a patient's illness, self-perceived well-being, comorbid drug use, the complexity of medication instructions, and environmental supports and barriers. Unfortunately, the efficacy of drug therapies is not sustained if patients decide to discontinue, as evidenced by increased symptoms, rate of hospitalizations, and emergency room visits (Lacro, Dunn, Dolder, Leckband, & Jeste, 2002). Additionally, some patients' symptoms are resistant to pharmacotherapy, and thus they may require additional treatments such as adjunctive medications, electroconvulsive therapy, and psychosocial treatments (Elkis, 2007). As electroconvulsive therapy involves a highly invasive procedure with potentially severe side effects, many psychosocial treatments have been created to target the reduction of psychotic symptoms as well as the distress affiliated with these symptoms, rehospitalization, and relapses. These include routine care (RC), cognitive–behavioral therapy (CBT), supportive therapy (ST), and family therapy (FT).

In reaction to the myriad treatments available, several bodies of experts and researchers came together to provide recommendations for "best practice" in treating schizophrenia. Thus, the American Psychiatric Association's (2004) *Practice Guideline for the Treatment of Patients With Schizophrenia*, the Texas Medication Algorithm Project (TMAP; Miller et al., 2004), and the Schizophrenia Patient Outcomes Research Team (PORT) were created (Lehman et al., 2004). PORT is unique from the other two in that it combines expert opinion with empirical review of available research to provide recommendations for treatment, and TMAP is concerned primarily with decision making with regards to prescribing medications to people with schizophrenia. This chapter summarizes the treatments described and recommended by the 2009 PORT report (Dixon et al., 2010) and provides information on the efficacy of the treatments for specific outcomes. Of note regarding the PORT report, no recommendations were made regarding psychosocial treatments for older adults with schizophrenia. Thus, it is unknown how generalizable these findings are to older adults. Yet, where relevant, we will report findings from specific studies relevant to older adults with schizophrenia.

A meta-analysis conducted by Eack and Newhill (2007) illustrated that greater severity of negative, positive, and general psychopathological symptoms were associated with reduced objective indicators of quality of life, including observer-reported or self-reported social and material attainment (e.g., number of friends, income, housing). This study compiled 190 effect sizes from 56 studies and created mean effect sizes weighted by degrees of freedom and 95% confidence intervals. The effect sizes fell in the small to medium range ($r = -.18$ to $r = -.26$) for positive and general psychopathological symptoms. They were in the medium to large range, however, for negative symptoms ($r = -.47$). A caveat to keep in mind when interpreting these findings is that self-reported outcomes may be influenced by a patient's current level of symptomatology and insight (Doyle et al., 1999). These findings suggest that despite achieving a reduction of certain psychotic symptoms and distress affiliated with symptoms either through medications or other means, people with schizophrenia may continue to have impairments in the domains of social relationships, vocational attainment, self-care, and independent living, to name a few. Thus, a new wave of psychosocial approaches was developed in an attempt to bolster the quality of life of and life outcomes of individuals with schizophrenia. These more functioning-oriented treatments include skills training, cognitive rehabilitation (CR), assertive community treatment (ACT), and supported employment (SE). A third wave of treatments for persons with schizophrenia targets comorbid health problems, including substance abuse and overweight.

Although many variations of treatments exist, the main categories that have been empirically tested include RC, CBT for schizophrenia, ST, FT, ACT, SE, skills training, and token economy (TE). We will first describe and define these treatments and then provide a review of the literature regarding their efficacy and effectiveness for treating specific outcomes: positive and negative symptoms, independent living, social functioning, relapse, and hospitalization. When considering the question of which interventions show efficacy and in persons with schizophrenia, it is imperative to contextualize this question by clarifying the outcomes of interest. For example, certain interventions seem efficacious for reducing homelessness but have little effect on the severity of

psychotic symptoms. Thus, this chapter specifies the specific outcomes for which the treatments show efficacy. According to PORT, the premier treatment of positive, negative, and disorganized symptoms in schizophrenia is psychopharmacology. Despite available psychopharmacological treatment, however, many clients fail to adhere to their medications once they feel that they are getting better and then relapse. Moreover, certain individuals with schizophrenia seem to have symptoms that are resistant to medications or experience impairments that cannot solely be addressed by medications (Rector & Beck, 2001). Thus, the psychosocial treatments described in this chapter are meant to be adjunctive to ongoing pharmacotherapy, in line with the 2009 PORT recommendations (Dixon et al., 2010).

The evidence presented here encompasses trials of all age-groups. As noted by others (Bartels et al., 2003), the evidence supporting psychosocial interventions for schizophrenia in older persons has fallen behind that of the general schizophrenia population. Recent studies, however, are lending support for rehabilitation efforts in older adults with schizophrenia, particularly in the area of cognition and functional outcomes. We will touch on those interventions in the latter part of this section but first will present the evidence-based interventions for schizophrenia in general.

Routine Care or Treatment as Usual

RC is defined by Tarrier and colleagues (2000) as case management of mental health. The aim of RC is to reduce the frequency and severity of relapses and rehospitalizations in individuals with schizophrenia. Key components of RC include services such as medication management, monitoring and follow-up in the community, identifying patients' mental health needs, connecting them with social services, creating and modifying care plans, and communicating with family members and other individuals who provide care for patients. Variations of RC, however, may incorporate only some of the features listed. RC can be provided by a wide range of mental health professionals in the community, including social workers, case managers, and psychologists (Tarrier et al., 2000).

RC commonly is used as a reference treatment, that is, a placebo or control, in many intervention studies, and has demonstrated smaller effects in terms of reducing symptoms and improving outcomes in patients with schizophrenia. In particular, Rector and Beck (2001) reported Cohen's *d* effect sizes of treatment outcomes for six randomized controlled trials. All six trials enrolled participants of all age-groups and thus were not exclusive to older adults. A Cohen's *d* can range from -3.00 to 3.00, with a 0 suggesting no change between baseline and posttreatment, a 1.00 suggesting that scores in outcome measures were one standard deviation better at posttreatment, and a -1.00 suggesting that scores on the outcome measure were 1 standard deviation worse at posttreatment. According to Cohen (1988), a small effect size is equal to 0.2, a moderate effect size is 0.5, and a large effect size is 0.8 and higher. The review from Rector and Beck (2001) found that patients in the RC condition exhibited treatment effect sizes of $d = -0.09$ to $d = 0.24$ for positive, negative, and total symptoms as measured by the BPRS and present state examination. Thus, it appears that RC led to small decreases in symptoms of schizophrenia at best and led to small increases in symptoms of schizophrenia at worst. Otherwise, RC seemed to lead to almost no change in symptoms posttreatment.

Cognitive–Behavioral Therapy for Schizophrenia

Although mental health practitioners provide varying forms of cognitive therapy (CT) and CBT, certain shared features distinguish these treatments from other therapeutic techniques. CT for schizophrenia, as defined by Beck and Rector (2000), aims to help individuals with schizophrenia understand their hallucinations and delusions by identifying their triggers, content, and reactions to these symptoms. This is otherwise known as the psychoeducational component of CBT, and it often includes attempts to normalize and destigmatize the diagnosis of schizophrenia. Specifically with sensory hallucinations, a therapist may ask questions about when they tend to occur, where, how often, how intense they are, what exacerbates or mitigates them, and whether or not they vary. Furthermore, CBT aims to decrease the frequency of hallucinations and delusions as well as the distress that stems from these

experiences. This is achieved via behavioral and cognitive interventions. A behavioral intervention, for example, may include listening to music on headphones to reduce the distress associated with auditory hallucinations. A cognitive intervention is composed of nonconfrontational questioning and empirical testing to evaluate the reality of hallucinations and delusions. Relapse prevention is another important component of CBT. It often includes addressing emotional problems that accompany schizophrenia. To accomplish these goals, it is essential to foster a sense of trust and collaboration with the patient. CBT primarily is provided by doctoral-level clinical psychologists with the appropriate training (Gould, Mueser, Bolton, Mays, & Goff, 2001). Treatment formats vary from 6–50 sessions or more (Dixon et al., 2010).

CBT repeatedly has been shown to reduce severity of positive symptoms including delusions and hallucinations (Bouchard, Vallieres, Roy, & Maziade, 1996; Dickerson, 2000; Dixon et al., 2010; Rector & Beck, 2001). Zimmermann, Favrod, Trieu, and Pomini (2005) conducted a meta-analysis using Hedge's *g* to capture effect size of CBT treatment gains. They reported that when CBT was compared with "nonspecific treatments" (i.e., supportive psychotherapies), CBT significantly improved positive symptoms with a small to moderate effect ($g = 0.30$). When CBT was compared with TAU (Zimmermann et al., 2005), CBT significantly reduced positive symptoms with a moderate effect ($g = 0.42$). CBT also has demonstrated efficacy in reducing negative symptoms with small to large effects, showing Glass's Δ ranging from small to large effects: $\Delta = 0.20$ to $\Delta = 1.26$ (Gould, Mueser, Bolton, Mays, & Goff, 2001). CBT also has been compared with ST and RC. Rector and Beck (2001) reviewed several articles that found that individuals in the CBT generally showed larger treatment gains than individuals who received ST and that both of these treatments showed larger treatment gains than individuals who received RC. According to the 2009 PORT report (Dixon et al., 2010), however, a few studies also indicated that CBT did not improve outcomes in hallucinations, positive symptoms, negative symptoms, and social functioning. When interpreting these results, it must be borne in mind that none of the studies were exclusive to middle-age and older adults with schizophrenia and some of the studies reviewed had issues related to methodology, including whether or not the outcomes rater was blind to treatment condition, and whether or not an active comparison treatment condition was used. These issues can have an unknown impact on treatment outcomes and comparison of treatment conditions, especially as they pertain to age-related issues.

Symptoms that often are comorbid with schizophrenia include depression, suicidality, hopelessness, illness insight, relapse, and rehospitalizaton. Although CBT may have an effect on these general psychological outcomes, the evidence is unclear at this point (Dixon et al., 2010); CBT has demonstrated improved social functioning in people with schizophrenia (Dixon et al., 2010).

Supportive Therapy

As described by Penn and colleagues (2004), ST aims to improve outcomes in schizophrenia by building a supportive relationship with patients and treating them with unconditional positive regard. Clinicians use basic counseling skills in discussing the patients' problems, but they do not focus specifically on any symptoms. ST often involves reflective listening, in which the clinician functions as a sounding board by restating what the patient has said and fosters a supportive relationship with the patient. Compared with other treatments that emphasize the importance of having an agenda (e.g., CBT), ST sessions are relatively unstructured. Penn et al. (2004) reviewed several studies that used ST for people with schizophrenia and proposed that the active components involved in improved treatment outcomes were social support and its positive ties with health, the therapeutic alliance, and social cognition. In particular, because people with schizophrenia often have limited social connections, having a therapeutic relationship with a clinician may reintegrate them into the "social world" and help to improve their social confidence. Moreover, social support may improve health outcomes by buffering against perceived stress or by providing information via advice and modeling on how to navigate life's problems. With regards to the therapeutic alliance, Penn et al. (2004) identified the importance of intervention-related tasks, the sense of attachment and trust between therapist and client, and the mutual goals of treatment in reducing patients' symptoms and improving functioning in the real world. Last, the authors explained that ST can address social cognition and interpersonal concerns, providing patients with a positive social relationship that boosts their confidence and changes how they view themselves and others in a social environment.

As reported by Rector and Beck (2001), ST seems to lead to improved symptoms in comparison to RC. When compared with CBT, however, it appears that ST may not have as large of an effect in reducing schizophrenia-related and general psychopathological symptoms. Moreover, a review conducted by Penn et al. (2004) corroborated these findings showing that CBT may be better at treating positive symptoms as compared with ST. It appears that ST also may contribute to better outcomes relating to relapse, vocation, and social impairment as compared with RC (Penn et al., 2004), but this finding requires further study.

Family Therapy

FT comes in many forms, including behavioral management, psychoeducation, multifamily groups, groups including relatives, consultation of the family, and short-term family psychoeducation led by professionals (McFarlane, Dixon, Lukens, & Luckstead, 2003). The aim of FT is to build the resiliency and strengths of a family in coping with having a family member who is dealing with schizophrenia. The rationale for focusing on families in treatment comes from the idea that family systems and dysfunction can meaningfully impact patients' outcomes. For example, families are often responsible for providing various forms of services and support to individuals with schizophrenia, such as financial support, emotional support, medication management, and advocacy. Families' abilities to provide support to relatives with schizophrenia can be limited by a lack of access to necessary information and resources. Thus, FT attempts to provide the tools that a family needs to deal with the issues that arise in their relatives with schizophrenia. FTs can have significant variation in who delivers them, the format of the sessions, and the focus. For example, multifamily groups pair families together to share effective strategies that have been successful for each family, whereas short-term family psychoeducation can be led by a professional clinician. The goal of FT is primarily to reduce the rate of relapse and rehospitalization in persons with schizophrenia.

Family interventions have shown efficacy in terms of improved vocational outcomes, symptom reduction, and treatment adherence as well as improved family relationships (Dixon et al., 2010). It is possible that symptom reduction is achieved through increased medication adherence (Dixon et al., 2010). According to the PORT 2009 report, several meta-analyses have suggested that longer treatment, such as 6–9 months of FT, can significantly reduce the number of relapse and hospitalizations compared with individuals in RC (Dixon et al., 2010). According to this review, this seems especially true in those who have had a recent acute episode of symptoms. According to PORT, however, other studies also have suggested that brief family interventions (at least 4 months in duration) also can improve various patient outcomes. McFarlane et al. (2003) found that 50% of the participants relapsed in the RC condition, whereas only 20% of the participants relapsed in the FT condition. Family interventions also may reduce self-report burden and distress from the family as well as strengthen relationships among family members. Additionally, it was reported that family members who partake in family interventions have a greater sense of professional and social support. In terms of patients' perceptions, those who participated in family interventions tended to experience greater satisfaction with treatment (Dixon et al., 2010).

Therapies Focusing on Improving Social and Vocational Outcomes

Despite the benefits of CBT, ST, and FT in reducing severity of psychotic and general psychopathological symptoms, people with schizophrenia continue to struggle in completing everyday tasks that are required to adequately function in the real world (Penn et al., 2004). Specifically, they tend to have marked impairments in social, vocational, self-care, and other realms as a result of their illness.

Consequently, people with schizophrenia often depend on others to help them with functions of daily living, including self-care and personal hygiene, housing, money management, medication management, food preparation, and transportation. These fundamental capabilities are necessary to become self-sufficient. On a higher level of functioning is one's ability to interact with and relate to others as well as the ability to participate in society through employment or community engagement. Thus, there has been an impetus toward a rehabilitation model in schizophrenia treatment, the goal of which is to increase level of independence and functioning in society. The therapies that have resulted from this shift include ACT, skills training (including self-care and social skills), SE, TE, and CR.

Assertive Community Treatment

As described by the 2009 PORT report (Dixon et al., 2010), ACT was created in an attempt to help persons with schizophrenia coordinate care among providers and create continuity of care. ACT emphasizes patients' strengths to help them partake in community life. Treatment is carried out by a multidisciplinary team of individuals who provide different services, such as medication prescription, and includes the following key components: having low staff-to-patient ratios, maintaining frequent contact with the patient, and providing outreach to patients in the community. Moreover, it seeks to cooperate with existing support systems and to provide outreach to bolster medication adherence and continued participation in treatment programs to maintain stability and prevent crises.

ACT has shown efficacy in improving several domains of functioning in persons with schizophrenia, including reduced hospitalizations, reduced homelessness, reduction of time hospitalized, increased use of outpatient services (e.g., housing programs), and reduced use of inpatient services (e.g., emergency room visits). In particular Coldwell and Bender (2007), reported that ACT contributed to a greater reduction in homelessness and symptom severity by 37% and 26%, respectively, when compared with RC. There have been mixed findings on the potential benefits of ACT on symptom reduction, increased medication adherence, increased contact with the treatment team, increased time in stable housing, and increased self-reported satisfaction with treatment (Dixon et al., 2010). It was posited that ACT helps to reduce rates of homelessness by increasing the length of time people with schizophrenia spend in stable housing, but further investigation will be needed to support this hypothesis.

Supported Employment

Many individuals with schizophrenia are unemployed and depend on support from their families or government assistance programs. Twamley, Jeste, and Lehman (2003) reported that only 15% of people with schizophrenia have paid competitive employment in the community. SE programs have a prescribed focus on helping individuals with schizophrenia gain employment. SE targets individuals whose symptoms have been stabilized by treatment and are now interested in finding jobs. It is characterized by the following components: emphasis on community employment, a circumscribed search for a job, coordinating mental health services with employment, emphasis on the patient's preferences, integrating patients into typical work settings, and providing ongoing job support after obtaining employment (Dixon et al., 2010; Twamley, Jeste, & Lehman, 2003).

SE programs have been shown empirically to aid individuals in obtaining a job, earning higher wages, and recording more hours worked (Dixon et al., 2010). These outcomes are in contrast to typical vocational interventions and services. In particular, approximately 50% of study participants who received both psychiatric services and SE obtained some form of "competitive employment" at follow-up (Dixon et al., 2010). Furthermore, Twamley et al. (2003) found that when SE programs were compared with more traditional vocational programs, people with severe mental illness had better job outcomes, with a large effect size ($d = .79$). Although these findings indicate promise for SE, according to the 2009 PORT report, at this point it is unclear whether the gains made by SE translate to long-term benefits of economic self-sufficiency and ability to retain a job. Thus, future studies are needed to understand the mechanisms underlying

sustained change toward vocational stability in persons with schizophrenia.

Skills Training

Skills training interventions can encompass a wide range of skills that are necessary for self-sufficiency and independence, including interpersonal skill (e.g., communication skills), interpreting affect, and daily living skills (e.g., purchasing food; Kopelowicz, Liberman, & Zarate, 2006; Eckman et al., 1992). These skills are built through behavioral modeling, positive reinforcement, and finding a way to integrate what is learned into their everyday lives (Dixon et al., 2010).

ST has demonstrated efficacy in measures featuring role-play of skills as well as measures of actual community functioning (Dixon et al., 2010). A meta-analysis conducted by Kurtz and Mueser (2008) revealed that ST displayed moderate effects ($d = .52$) on performance-based measures of social skills and living skills as well as level of functioning in the community (Kurtz & Mueser, 2008). Findings have been mixed, however, on ST's impact on general psychpathological symptoms and relapse (Dixon et al., 2010).

Token Economy

TE interventions are comprehensive programs that are designed to increase the frequency of desirable behaviors while decreasing the frequency of undesirable behaviors. Essentially TE involves providing positive reinforcement when individuals partake in desired behaviors and punishment when they avoid engaging in the positive behaviors. According to the 2009 PORT report, it is recommended specifically for patients who reside in community living settings or those who spend a substantial amount of time in day programs (Dixon et al., 2010).

Individuals with schizophrenia have demonstrated an increase in desirable and adaptive behaviors as a result of TE programs. In particular, they show improvements in personal hygiene, interpersonal interactions, and work tasks in the hospital (Dixon et al., 2010). According to the 2009 PORT report (Dixon et al., 2010), however, these findings should be interpreted with the caveat that many studies using TE were conducted several decades ago, during which time different diagnostic criteria for schizophrenia existed.

Cognitive Remediation

It has been well-established that cognitive impairment is a core feature that affects functional outcomes and everyday functioning in people with schizophrenia (Harvey, Green, Keefe, & Velligan, 2004). As a result, CR has been developed to target specific cognitive abilities, with the eventual goal of improving everyday functioning. CR typically involves treatment for improving specific cognitive functions, such as attention, memory, reasoning, and both verbal and visual abilities (Dixon et al., 2010; McGurk, Twamley, Sitzer, McHugo, & Mueser, 2007).

According to the summary of recommendations provided by PORT, CR and its impact on everyday functioning in people with schizophrenia has been tested for several decades. In particular, McGurk et al. (2007) conducted a meta-analysis and found that schizophrenia patients who underwent CR displayed lower moderate to moderate effect sizes for improvements in overall cognition and on seven of eight specific cognitive abilities. Moreover, they reviewed six studies and found that effect sizes at follow-up were in the moderate range. In terms of the impact of CR on symptoms and functioning, McGurk et al. (2007) found small effects ($d = .28$) for symptoms and small-to-moderate effects for everyday functioning ($d = .35$). This meta-analysis, however, found significant variation among the effect sizes for functioning, which speaks to the fact that CR has mixed effects on functioning. Despite these findings, the 2009 PORT report (Dixon et al., 2010) argued that there is a dearth of rigorous randomized controlled trials involving CR and that previous studies have not clarified which specific components of the treatment may be underlying treatment outcomes. Moreover, the authors claimed that vast differences among the various models of CR make it difficult to identify shared elements. At this point, it seems that there may be potential for CR to improve cognitive abilities and everyday functioning, but more rigorous randomized controlled trials are necessary to investigate this further.

Treatments for Managing Weight and Substance Abuse

In the wake of developing treatments for people with schizophrenia that address vocational outcomes, social relationships, and overall quality of life, there has been a recent movement toward improving physical health outcomes. In particular, persons with schizophrenia seem to be at increased risk for physical health problems (e.g., cardiovascular disease) and shortened life spans (Hennekens, Hennekens, Hollar, & Casey, 2005), a pattern that may be related to the higher incidence of substance abuse and weight problems in this group. In particular, Hennekens et al. (2005) found that smoking and weight problems are highly prevalent in individuals with schizophrenia, both of which heighten the risk of developing cardiovascular disease. Thus began an impetus toward improving physical health in this population through targeting weight and substance use. As reported by the 2009 PORT report (Dixon et al., 2010), interventions for substance abuse include motivational enhancement (ME) and CBT, whereas interventions for weight management include ME, psychoeducation about nutrition and weight, health behavior monitoring (e.g., food and activity logs), and health behavior change.

Faulkner, Soundy, and Lloyd (2003) conducted a systematic review of 16 studies on weight management interventions for schizophrenia. They found that pharmacological treatment, behavioral weight management, and nutrition-related interventions were able to achieve weight reductions with small effects. There is a dearth of studies, however, testing the specific weight management interventions. Regarding substance abuse, Drake, Mercer-McFadden, Mueser, McHugo, and Bond (1998) conducted a review of 26 studies that identified the following components as instrumental in improving substance abuse outcomes in persons with schizophrenia: assertive outreach, case management, and a motivational approach that builds in stages over time. This review found that patients who participated in integrated, comprehensive outpatient programs had better outcomes in terms of remission and reduced substance abuse compared with individuals who received RC. Moreover, these gains seemed to be maintained at follow-up, which was not the case for intensive inpatient care for substance abuse. Integrated comprehensive outpatient programs for substance abuse in schizophrenia seemed to have mixed effects on hospitalizations and psychopathological symptoms. There is speculation that substance abuse treatments for schizophrenia also may reduce homelessness (Dixon et al., 2010), but this relationship is not yet clearly established.

TREATMENT CONSIDERATIONS FOR AGING

It has been well-established that earlier onset of psychotic symptoms is linked with poorer prognosis throughout one's life span. Specifically, a longitudinal study following patients with chronic schizophrenia demonstrated that individuals who have experienced longer illness had greater increases in negative symptoms and overall symptoms than individuals who had a shorter duration of illness (Breier, Schreiber, Dyer, & Pickar, 1991). Thus, individuals who have earlier onset may exhibit more severe symptomatology and outcomes. Jeste et al. (2003), however, conducted a study suggesting that aging was affiliated with decreases in psychopathology after controlling for illness duration. They also found that compared with normal controls, aging in people with schizophrenia did not result in an acceleration of impairments in the domains of psychopathology, quality of life, everyday functioning, and movement abilities. It is posited, however, that deficits originate during times of exacerbated symptoms. It appears that functioning does not necessarily deteriorate over time as previously expected, but that there is a plateau effect in which existing deficits are maintained and stabilized throughout aging. In particular, Jeste et al. (2003) found that people with schizophrenia continued to demonstrate marked impairments in these domains when compared with controls.

An important consideration in evaluating treatment outcomes for individuals of an aging population is in how functional outcomes are defined. Not surprisingly, activities of daily living and abilities fluctuate throughout the life span (Berkman et al., 1993). Thus, the definition of what functional

outcomes are in older populations may have to be modified in accordance with age. For example, vocational status and independent living are important indicators that a person is capable of taking care of himself or herself and is capable of being self-sufficient. As individuals reach a certain age, however, they accrue both physical and cognitive limitations, and thus, they are less likely to keep a regular job and be able to live independently. Accordingly, treatments may need to be tailored and individualized such that older individuals with schizophrenia are supported based on their current level of impairment.

Cognitive–Behavioral Social Skills Training

One of the most studied psychosocial interventions for older adults with schizophrenia, CBSST is a manualized intervention that entails combining elements of CBT with those of social skills training, consisting of three modules. Earlier trials of CBSST included four classes per module (2 hr each), whereas later trials consisted of six classes lasting 2 hr each. In addition, each class is designed to be completed twice, making the entire CBSST treatment a total of 24 or 36 sessions, respectively. The first module teaches Thought Challenging, which consists of training individuals on the use of simplified thought challenging skills and behavioral experiment activities. The primary technique used to challenge thoughts is called the 3Cs: (a) catch it, (b) check it, and (c) change it. Thought challenging targets the experience of symptoms (e.g., "Spirits will harm me") as well as use of social skills. Specific examples of thought challenging of functional skills include challenging expectancy beliefs (e.g., "It won't be fun"), self-efficacy beliefs (e.g., "I always fail"), and ageist beliefs (e.g., "I'm too old to change"; Granholm, Holden, Link, McQuaid, & Jeste, 2013).

The second module consists of social skills training. As with traditional social skills training, this consists of improving social skills through the use of role plays. Specific examples of role plays include practicing communication skills with a doctor or health care provider; interacting with roommates (e.g., in a board-and-care setting); interacting with friends and family; and effectively discussing treatment-related issues or needs with case managers, doctors, or other treatment providers. In addition, participants learn effective communication strategies and methods of using assertive communication style versus other, less effective styles of communicating (e.g., aggressive, passive).

The final module focused on teaching problem-solving skills. In this module, participants are taught the SCALE technique, in which they (a) specify the problem, (b) consider the possible solutions, (c) assess the best solution, (d) lay out a plan, and (e) execute and evaluate the outcome. As described by Granholm et al. (2013), the primary purpose of the module was to help participants develop and execute plans to solve real-world problems, including scheduling pleasant events, improving living situations, improving financial circumstances and living situations, using public transportation (e.g., to attend therapy or go shopping), and finding a volunteer or paid job or attend school.

The first full-scale randomized trial of CBSST was conducted by Granholm et al. (2005) from 1999 to 2003. In this trial, 76 middle-age and older adults with schizophrenia were randomized to receive either 24 weeks of CBSST ($n = 37$) or TAU ($n = 39$), which primarily consisted of medication management. The primary treatment outcomes included social functioning (measured with the ILSS) and functional capacity (measured with the UPSA). Results indicated that CBSST outperformed TAU for improving frequency of social activities (i.e., social functioning), with a Cohen's *d* effect size of .64. CBSST, however, did not significantly outperform TAU in changing functional capacity, although the effect size was medium ($d = .48$), suggesting the study was underpowered to detect change. Granholm et al. (2007) later reported that the benefits of CBSST for social functioning were maintained at a long-term (12-month) follow-up.

This earlier study, while demonstrating the benefits of CBSST, did not control for the effects of therapeutic contact. Thus, in a later trial, Granholm et al. (2013) examined the efficacy of CBSST by comparing it to a supportive group therapy they called goal-focused supportive contact (GFSC). Specifically, GFSC was an enhanced supportive contact

intervention that helped participants set and work toward functioning goals in a support group format. In this trial, 76 middle-age and older (age range = 45–78 years) participants were randomized to receive either 36 sessions of CBSST or GFSC. Relative to GFSC participants, those who received CBSST demonstrated significant improvements in skill mastery and improved functioning, particularly among those with more severe defeatist attitudes, which was measured using the Defeatist Attitude Scale, which is a 15-item subscale of the Dysfunctional Attitude Scale (DAS; Cane, Olinger, Gotlib, & Kuiper, 1986). Furthermore, changes in defeatist attitudes appeared to mediate the effect of CBSST on functional outcomes.

Functional Adaptation Skills Training

The FAST program was developed to address deficits in functional skills among middle-aged and older adults with schizophrenia. The intervention, which is based on social-cognitive theory (Bandura, 1989) and the Social and Independent Living Skills Program of Liberman and colleagues (Psychiatric Rehabilitation Consultants, 1991), is a group-based, 24-week intervention that targets six areas of everyday functioning. These six modules consist of medication management, social skills, communication skills, organization and planning, transportation, and financial management. Each module consists of four sessions that are 2 hr in length and occur once per week. Psychoeducation is used to teach the basic functional skills. After psychoeducation, behavioral modeling of the various functional skills is used. Students then practice skills via role-playing. Continued practice of skills in the real world, through homework assignments, is used to reinforce learning the skills.

The medication management module consists of teaching individuals to track medication administration, monitor psychiatric symptoms and drug side effects, communicate with health care providers regarding symptoms and needs, and solve day-to-day problems. In the social skills module, participants learn to engage in appropriate conversations (e.g., initiation, maintenance, termination, and active listening). The communication skills module teaches different styles of communication (i.e., passive, assertive, and aggressive). The organization and planning module helps individuals to plan for outings or events (e.g., scheduling health care or other appointments, items required to take, or items that one needs to provide or obtain). In the transportation module, students learn to read maps and transportation schedules and to identify appropriate persons to ask for help. Finally, the financial management module helps students to count money, write checks, and read account statements.

Patterson et al. (2006) conducted a randomized controlled trial assessing the efficacy of the FAST intervention. In this trial, 240 middle-age and older adults with schizophrenia (minimum age = 40 years) were randomized to receive either the FAST intervention or an attention control (AC) intervention, which consisted of 24 weekly support group sessions that allowed individuals to address personal problems. The primary outcomes were ability to perform everyday functional skills (as measured by the UPSA) and social skills (as measured by the SSPA). At the end of the 24-week therapy, participants randomized to the FAST condition showed greater improvement than AC participants on both functional and social skills ability. Cohen's *d* effect sizes were .32 for functional ability and .46 for social skills.

CONCLUSION

The 21st century will see an exponential growth in the number and proportion of older adults with schizophrenia. This growth will require greater knowledge of aging-related issues on the part of psychologists, particularly in the assessment and care of these individuals. This chapter noted that aging in the context of schizophrenia is unique, in that the average life span of an individual with schizophrenia is 20% shorter than the average adult. Thus, the definition of old age in this population is likely different than that of other populations. We also demonstrated that research on the assessment and treatment of older adults with schizophrenia is lacking. Most of the research on these topics is housed within the broader context of the illness, often including individuals throughout the life span rather than focusing on only middle-age and older adults. This may be due to the low base rates of

schizophrenia, thereby presenting unique challenges in studying a subpopulation of older adults, but more recent research has included only middle-age and older adults, demonstrating an awareness of the importance of this growing subpopulation. From the little research that is available, it appears clear that assessment of cognitive and functional abilities are important in understanding the ability of persons with schizophrenia for residing independently and even obtaining employment. Likewise, in addition to standard treatments such as CBT and ACT, novel treatments appear to be targeting cognition and functional skills with the goal of enhancing recovery. Yet, much work is still needed to understand the evidence base for these treatments in older adults. It is our hope that more research will be conducted providing this evidence before the rapid expansion of older individuals with schizophrenia takes effect.

References

American Psychiatric Association. (2000). *Diagnostic and statistical manual of mental disorders* (4th ed., text revision). Washington, DC: Author.

American Psychiatric Association. (2004). *Practice guidelines for the treatment of patients with schizophrenia* (2nd ed.). Retrieved from http://psychiatryonline. org/content.aspx?bookid=28&sectionid=1665359

American Psychiatric Association. (2013). *Diagnostic and statistical manual of mental disorders* (5th ed.). Arlington, VA: Author.

an der Heiden, W., & Hafner, H. (2000). The epidemiology of onset and course of schizophrenia. *European Archives of Psychiatry and Clinical Neuroscience, 250*, 292–303. doi:10.1007/s004060070004

Andreasen, N. C., Carpenter, W. T., Jr., Kane, J. M., Lasser, R. A., Marder, S. R., & Weinberger, D. R. (2005). Remission in schizophrenia: Proposed criteria and rationale for consensus. *American Journal of Psychiatry, 162*, 441–449. doi:10.1176/appi.ajp.162.3.441

Appelbaum, P. S., Robbins, P. C., & Roth, L. H. (1999). Dimensional approach to delusions: Comparison across types and diagnoses. *American Journal of Psychiatry, 156*, 1938–1943.

Bandura, A. (1986). *Social foundations of thought and action: A social cognitive theory*. Englewood Cliffs, NJ: Prentice-Hall.

Bandura, A. (1989). Perceived self-efficacy. In V. Mays, G. Albee, & S. Schneider (Eds.), *Prevention of AIDS: Psychological Approaches* (pp. 128–141). Newbury Park, CA: Sage.

Bartels, S. J., Dums, A. R., Oxman, T. E., Schneider, L. S., Arean, P. A., Alexopoulos, G. S., & Jeste, D. V. (2003). Evidence-based practices in geriatric mental health care: An overview of systematic reviews and meta-analyses. *Psychiatric Clinics of North America, 26*, 971–990. doi:10.1016/S0193-953X(03)00072-8

Beck, A. T., & Rector, N. A. (2000). Cognitive therapy of schizophrenia: A new therapy for the new millennium. *American Journal of Psychotherapy, 54*, 291–300.

Bell, M., Milstein, R., Beam-Goulet, J., Lysaker, P., & Cicchetti, D. (1992). The Positive and Negative Syndrome Scale and the Brief Psychiatric Rating Scale. Reliability, comparability, and predictive validity. *Journal of Nervous and Mental Disease, 180*, 723–728. doi:10.1097/00005053-199211000-00007

Berkman, L. F., Seeman, T. E., Albert, M., Blazer, D., Kahn, R., Mohs, R., . . . Rowe, J. (1993). High, usual and impaired functioning in community-dwelling older men and women: Findings from the MacArthur Foundation Research Network on Successful Aging. *Journal of Clinical Epidemiology, 46*, 1129–1140. doi:10.1016/0895-4356(93)90112-E

Bleuler, M. (1943). Die spatschizophrenen krankheitsbilder. *Fortschritte der Neurologie-Psychiatrie, 15*, 259–290.

Bolton, B., & Roessler, R. (1986). *Manual for the work personality profile.* Fayetteville: Arkansas Research and Training Center in Vocational Research.

Bouchard, S., Vallieres, A., Roy, M., & Maziade, M. (1996). Cognitive restructuring in the treatment of psychotic symptoms in schizophrenia: A critical analysis. *Behavior Therapy, 27*, 257–277. doi:10.1016/S0005-7894(96)80017-7

Bowie, C. R., & Harvey, P. D. (2005). Cognition in schizophrenia: Impairments, determinants, and functional importance. *Psychiatric Clinics of North America, 28*, 613–633. doi:10.1016/j.psc.2005.05.004

Bowie, C. R., Leung, W. W., Reichenberg, A., McClure, M. M., Patterson, T. L., Heaton, R. K., & Harvey, P. D. (2008). Predicting schizophrenia patients' real-world behavior with specific neuropsychological and functional capacity measures. *Biological Psychiatry, 63*, 505–511. doi:10.1016/j.biopsych.2007.05.022

Bowie, C. R., McGurk, S. R., Mausbach, B., Patterson, T. L., & Harvey, P. D. (2012). Combined cognitive remediation and functional skills training for schizophrenia: Effects on cognition, functional competence, and real-world behavior. *American Journal of Psychiatry, 169*, 710–718. doi:10.1176/appi.ajp.2012.11091337

Bowie, C. R., Reichenberg, A., Patterson, T. L., Heaton, R. K., & Harvey, P. D. (2006). Determinants of real-world functioning performance in schizophrenia: Correlations with cognition, functional capacity, and symptoms. *American Journal of Psychiatry, 163*, 418–425. doi:10.1176/appi.ajp.163.3.418

Breier, A., Schreiber, J. L., Dyer, J., & Pickar, D. (1991). National Institute of Mental Health longitudinal study of chronic schizophrenia: Prognosis and predictors of outcome. *Archives of General Psychiatry, 48*, 239–246. doi:10.1001/archpsyc.1991.01810270051007

Cane, D. B., Olinger, L. J., Gotlib, I. H., & Kuiper, N. A. (1986). Factor structure of the Dysfunctional Attitude Scale in a student population. *Journal of Clinical Psychology, 42*, 307–309. doi:10.1002/1097-4679(198603)42:2<307::AID-JCLP2270420213>3.0.CO;2-J

Cardenas, V., Mausbach, B. T., Barrio, C., Bucardo, J., Jeste, D., & Patterson, T. (2008). The relationship between functional capacity and community responsibilities in middle-aged and older Latinos of Mexican origin with chronic psychosis. *Schizophrenia Research, 98*, 209–216. doi:10.1016/j.schres.2007.09.008

Cohen, J. (1988). *Statistical power analysis for the behavioral sciences* (rev. ed.). Hillsdale, NJ: Erlbaum.

Coldwell, C. M., & Bender, W. (2007). The effectiveness of assertive community treatment for homeless populations with severe mental illness: A meta-analysis. *American Journal of Psychiatry, 164*, 393–399. doi:10.1176/appi.ajp.164.3.393

Davidson, M., Harvey, P. D., Powchik, P., Parrella, M., White, L., Knobler, H. Y., . . . Frecska, E. (1995). Severity of symptoms in chronically institutionalized geriatric schizophrenic patients. *American Journal of Psychiatry, 152*, 197–207.

Davidson, M., Reichenberg, A., Rabinowitz, J., Weiser, M., Kaplan, Z., & Mark, M. (1999). Behavioral and intellectual markers for schizophrenia in apparently healthy male adolescents. *American Journal of Psychiatry, 156*, 1328–1335.

Day, J. C. (1996). *Population projections of the United States by age, sex, race, and Hispanic origin: 1995 to 2050.* Washington, DC: U.S. Bureau of the Census.

Dickerson, F. (2000). Cognitive–behavioral psychotherapy for schizophrenia: A review of recent empirical studies. *Schizophrenia Research, 43*, 71–90. doi:10.1016/S0920-9964(99)00153-X

Dixon, L. B., Dickerson, F., Bellack, A. S., Bennett, M., Dickinson, D., Goldberg, R. W., . . . Kreyenbuhl, J. (2010). The 2009 schizophrenia PORT psychosocial treatment recommendations and summary statements. *Schizophrenia Bulletin, 36*, 48–70. doi:10.1093/schbul/sbp115

Doyle, M., Flanagan, S., Browne, S., Clarke, M., Lydon, D., Larkin, C., & O'Callaghan, E. (1999). Subjective and external assessments of quality of life in schizophrenia: Relationship to insight. *Acta Psychiatrica Scandinavica, 99*, 466–472. doi:10.1111/j.1600-0447.1999.tb00994.x

Drake, R. E., Mercer-McFadden, C., Mueser, K. T., McHugo, G. J., & Bond, G. R. (1998). Review of integrated mental health and substance abuse treatment for patients with dual disorders. *Schizophrenia Bulletin, 24,* 589–608. doi:10.1093/oxfordjournals. schbul.a033351

Eack, S. M., & Newhill, C. E. (2007). Psychiatric symptoms and quality of life in schizophrenia: A meta-analysis. *Schizophrenia Bulletin, 33,* 1225–1237. doi:10.1093/schbul/sbl071

Eckman, T. A., Wirshing, W. C., Marder, S. R., Liberman, R. P., Johnston-Cronk, M. S., Zimmermann, K., & Mintz, J. (1992). Technique for training schizophrenic patients in illness self-management: A controlled trial. *American Journal of Psychiatry, 149,* 1549–1555.

Elkis, H. (2007). Treatment-resistant schizophrenia. *Psychiatric Clinics of North America, 30,* 511–533. doi:10.1016/j.psc.2007.04.001

Endicott, J., Spitzer, R. L., Fleiss, J. L., & Cohen, J. (1976). The global assessment scale. A procedure for measuring overall severity of psychiatric disturbance. *Archives of General Psychiatry, 33,* 766–771. doi:10.1001/archpsyc.1976.01770060086012

Faulkner, G., Soundy, A. A., & Lloyd, K. (2003). Schizophrenia and weight management: A systematic review of interventions to control weight. *Acta Psychiatrica Scandinavica, 108,* 324–332. doi:10.1034/j.1600-0447.2003.00218.x

Fenton, W. S., Blyler, C. R., & Heinssen, R. K. (1997). Determinants of medication compliance in schizophrenia. *Schizophrenia Bulletin, 23,* 637–651. doi:10.1093/schbul/23.4.637

Fioravanti, M., Bianchi, V., & Cinti, M. E. (2012). Cognitive deficits in schizophrenia: An updated meta-analysis of the scientific evidence. *BMC Psychiatry, 12*(64). doi:10.1186/1471-244X-12-64

Fioravanti, M., Carlone, O., Vitale, B., Cinti, M. E., & Clare, L. (2005). A meta-analysis of cognitive deficits in adults with a diagnosis of schizophrenia. *Neuropsychology Review, 15,* 73–95. doi:10.1007/s11065-005-6254-9

Folsom, D. P., Depp, C., Palmer, B. W., Mausbach, B. T., Golshan, S., Fellows, I., . . . Jeste, D. V. (2009). Physical and mental health-related quality of life among older people with schizophrenia. *Schizophrenia Research, 108,* 207–213. doi:10.1016/j.schres.2008.12.008

Friedman, J. I., Harvey, P. D., Coleman, T., Moriarty, P. J., Bowie, C., Parrella, M., . . . Davis, K. L. (2001). Six-year follow-up study of cognitive and functional status across the lifespan in schizophrenia: A comparison with Alzheimer's disease and normal aging. *American Journal of Psychiatry, 158,* 1441–1448. doi:10.1176/appi.ajp.158.9.1441

Gibson, D. R., Weiss, D. J., & Dawis, P. (1970). *Manual for the Minnesota Satisfactoriness Scales.* Minneapolis: Vocational Psychology Research, University of Minnesota.

Gould, R. A., Mueser, K. T., Bolton, E., Mays, V., & Goff, D. (2001). Cognitive therapy for psychosis in schizophrenia: An effect size analysis. *Schizophrenia Research, 48,* 335–342. doi:10.1016/S0920-9964(00)00145-6

Granholm, E., Holden, J., Link, P. C., McQuaid, J. R., & Jeste, D. V. (2013). Randomized controlled trial of cognitive–behavioral social skills training for older consumers with schizophrenia: Defeatist performance attitudes and functional outcome. *American Journal of Geriatric Psychiatry, 21,* 251–262. doi:10.1016/j.jagp.2012.10.014

Granholm, E., McQuaid, J. R., McClure, F. S., Auslander, L. A., Perivoliotis, D., Pedrelli, P., . . . Jeste, D. V. (2005). A randomized, controlled trial of cognitive–behavioral social skills training for middle-aged and older outpatients with chronic schizophrenia. *American Journal of Psychiatry, 162,* 520–529. doi:10.1176/appi.ajp.162.3.520

Granholm, E., McQuaid, J. R., McClure, F. S., Link, P. C., Perivoliotis, D., Gottlieb, J. D., . . . Jeste, D. V. (2007). Randomized controlled trial of cognitive–behavioral social skills training for older people with schizophrenia: 12-month follow-up. *Journal of Clinical Psychiatry, 68,* 730–737. doi:10.4088/JCP.v68n0510

Green, M. F. (1996). What are the functional consequences of neurocognitive deficits in schizophrenia? *American Journal of Psychiatry, 153,* 321–330.

Green, M. F., Nuechterlein, K. H., Kern, R. S., Baade, L. E., Fenton, W. S., Gold, J. M., . . . Marder, S. R. (2008). Functional co-primary measures for clinical trials in schizophrenia: Results from the MATRICS Psychometric and Standardization Study. *American Journal of Psychiatry, 165,* 221–228. doi:10.1176/appi.ajp.2007.07010089

Green, M. F., Schooler, N. R., Kern, R. S., Frese, F. J., Granberry, W., Harvey, P. D., . . . Marder, S. R. (2011). Evaluation of functionally meaningful measures for clinical trials of cognition enhancement in schizophrenia. *American Journal of Psychiatry, 168,* 400–407. doi:10.1176/appi.ajp.2010.10030414

Gur, R. E., Petty, R. G., Turetsky, B. I., & Gur, R. C. (1996). Schizophrenia throughout life: Sex differences in severity and profile of symptoms. *Schizophrenia Research, 21,* 1–12. doi:10.1016/0920-9964(96)00023-0

Hafner, H., Hambrecht, M., Loffler, W., Munk-Jorgensen, P., & Riecher-Rossler, A. (1998). Is schizophrenia a disorder of all ages? A comparison of first episodes and early course across the life-cycle. *Psychological Medicine, 28,* 351–365. doi:dx.doi.org/10.1017/S0033291797006399

Harris, E. C., & Barraclough, B. (1998). Excess mortality of mental disorder. *British Journal of Psychiatry, 173,* 11–53. doi:10.1192/bjp.173.1.11

Harris, M. J., & Jeste, D. V. (1988). Late-onset schizophrenia: An overview. *Schizophrenia Bulletin, 14,* 39–55. doi:10.1093/schbul/14.1.39

Harvey, P. D., Green, M. F., Keefe, R. S. E., & Velligan, D. I. (2004). Cognitive functioning in schizophrenia: A consensus statement on its role in the definition and evaluation of effective treatments for the illness. *Journal of Clinical Psychiatry, 65,* 361–372. doi:10.4088/JCP.v65n0312

Harvey, P. D., Velligan, D. I., & Bellack, A. S. (2007). Performance-based measures of functional skills: Usefulness in clinical treatment studies. *Schizophrenia Bulletin, 33,* 1138–1148. doi:10.1093/schbul/sbm040

Heaton, R. K., Gladsjo, J. A., Palmer, B. W., Kuck, J., Marcotte, T. D., & Jeste, D. V. (2001). Stability and course of neuropsychological deficits in schizophrenia. *Archives of General Psychiatry, 58,* 24–32. doi:10.1001/archpsyc.58.1.24

Hennekens, C. H., Hennekens, A. R., Hollar, D., & Casey, D. E. (2005). Schizophrenia and increased risks of cardiovascular disease. *American Heart Journal, 150,* 1115–1121. doi:10.1016/j.ahj.2005.02.007

Howard, R., Castle, D., Wessely, S., & Murray, R. (1993). A comparative study of 470 cases of early-onset and late-onset schizophrenia. *British Journal of Psychiatry, 163,* 352–357. doi:10.1192/bjp.163.3.352

Howard, R., & Jeste, D. (2011). Late-onset schizophrenia. In D. R. Weinberger & P. J. Harrison (Eds.), *Schizophrenia* (pp. 47–61). Hoboken, NJ: Wiley–Blackwell.

Howard, R., Rabins, P. V., Seeman, M. V., & Jeste, D. V. (2000). Late-onset schizophrenia and very-late-onset schizophrenia-like psychosis: An international consensus. *American Journal of Psychiatry, 157,* 172–178. doi:10.1176/appi.ajp.157.2.172

Jeste, D. V., Harris, M. J., Krull, A., Kuck, J., McAdams, L. A., & Heaton, R. (1995). Clinical and neuropsychological characteristics of patients with late-onset schizophrenia. *American Journal of Psychiatry, 152,* 722–730.

Jeste, D. V., Twamley, E. W., Eyler Zorrilla, L. T., Golshan, S., Patterson, T. L., & Palmer, B. W. (2003). Aging and outcome in schizophrenia. *Acta Psychiatrica Scandinavica, 107,* 336–343. doi:10.1034/j.1600-0447.2003.01434.x

Kay, S. R. (1991). *Positive and negative syndromes in schizophrenia: Assessment and research.* New York, NY: Brunner/Mazel.

Kay, S. R. (2006). *Positive and Negative Syndrome Scale (PANSS): Technical manual.* Toronto, Ontario, Canada: Multi-Health Systems.

Kay, S. R., Fiszbein, A., & Opler, L. A. (1987). The Positive And Negative Syndrome Scale (PANSS) for schizophrenia. *Schizophrenia Bulletin, 13,* 261–276. doi:10.1093/schbul/13.2.261

Kay, S. R., Opler, Lewis A., & Lindenmayer, J.-P. (1988). Reliability and validity of the positive and negative syndrome scale for schizophrenics. *Psychiatry Research, 23,* 99–110. doi:10.1016/0165-1781(88)90038-8

Kopelowicz, A., Liberman, R. P., & Zarate, R. (2006). Recent advances in social skills training for schizophrenia. *Schizophrenia Bulletin, 32*(Suppl. 1), S12–S23. doi:10.1093/schbul/sbl023

Kurtz, M. M. (2005). Neurocognitive impairment across the lifespan in schizophrenia: An update. *Schizophrenia Research, 74,* 15–26. doi:10.1016/j.schres.2004.07.005

Kurtz, M. M., & Mueser, K. T. (2008). A meta-analysis of controlled research on social skills training for schizophrenia. *Journal of Consulting and Clinical Psychology, 76,* 491–504. doi:10.1037/0022-006X.76.3.491

Lacro, J. P., Dunn, L. B., Dolder, C. R., Leckband, S. G., & Jeste, D. V. (2002). Prevalence of and risk factors for medication nonadherence in patients with schizophrenia: A comprehensive review of recent literature. *Journal of Clinical Psychiatry, 63,* 892–909. doi:10.4088/JCP.v63n1007

Lehman, A. F., Lieberman, J. A., Dixon, L. B., McGlashan, T. H., Miller, A. L., Perkins, D. O., . . . Steering Committee on Practice Guidelines. (2004). Practice guideline for the treatment of patients with schizophrenia, second edition. *American Journal of Psychiatry, 161*(Suppl. 2), 1–56.

Lehman, A. F., Steinwachs, D. M., & Coinvestigators of the PORT Project. (1998). At issue: Translating research into practice: The schizophrenia Patient Outcomes Research Team (PORT) treatment recommendations. *Schizophrenia Bulletin, 24,* 1–10. doi:10.1093/oxfordjournals.schbul.a033302

Leifker, F. R., Patterson, T. L., Bowie, C. R., Mausbach, B. T., & Harvey, P. D. (2010). Psychometric properties of performance-based measurements of functional capacity: Test-retest reliability, practice effects, and potential sensitivity to change. *Schizophrenia Research, 119,* 246–252. doi:10.1016/j.schres.2010.03.021

Lukoff, D. (1986). Manual for the expanded BPRS. *Schizophrenia Bulletin, 12,* 594–602.

Mausbach, B. T., Bowie, C. R., Harvey, P. D., Twamley, E. W., Goldman, S. R., Jeste, D. V., & Patterson, T. L. (2008). Usefulness of the UCSD Performance-Based Skills Assessment (UPSA) for predicting residential independence in patients with chronic schizophrenia. *Journal of Psychiatric Research, 42,* 320–327. doi:10.1016/j.jpsychires.2006.12.008

Mausbach, B. T., Depp, C. A., Bowie, C. R., Harvey, P. D., McGrath, J. A., Thronquist, M. H., . . . Patterson,

T. L. (2011). Sensitivity and specificity of the UCSD Performance-based Skills Assessment (UPSA–B) for identifying functional milestones in schizophrenia. *Schizophrenia Research, 132,* 165–170. doi:10.1016/j.schres.2011.07.022

Mausbach, B. T., Depp, C. A., Cardenas, V., Jeste, D. V., & Patterson, T. L. (2008). Relationship between functional capacity and community responsibility in patients with schizophrenia: Differences between independent and assisted living settings. *Community Mental Health Journal, 44,* 385–391. doi:10.1007/s10597-008-9141-z

Mausbach, B. T., Harvey, P. D., Goldman, S. R., Jeste, D. V., & Patterson, T. L. (2007). Development of a brief scale of everyday functioning in persons with serious mental illness. *Schizophrenia Bulletin, 33,* 1364–1372. doi:10.1093/schbul/sbm014

McFarlane, W. R., Dixon, L., Lukens, E., & Luckstead, A. (2003). Family psychoeducation and schizophrenia: A review of the literature. *Journal of Marital and Family Therapy, 29,* 223–245. doi:10.1111/j.1752-0606.2003.tb01202.x

McGurk, S. R., Twamley, E., Sitzer, D., McHugo, G., & Mueser, K. (2007). A meta-analysis of cognitive remediation in schizophrenia. *American Journal of Psychiatry, 164,* 1791–1802. doi:10.1176/appi.ajp.2007.07060906

Meesters, P. D., Stek, M. L., Comijs, H. C., de Haan, L., Patterson, T. L., Eikelenboom, P., & Beekman, A. T. (2010). Social functioning among older community-dwelling patients with schizophrenia: A review. *American Journal of Geriatric Psychiatry, 18,* 862–878. doi:10.1097/JGP.0b013e3181e446ff

Miller, A. L., Crismon, M. L., Rush, A. J., Chiles, J., Kashner, T. M., Toprac, M., . . . Shon, S. (2004). The Texas medication algorithm project: Clinical results for schizophrenia. *Schizophrenia Bulletin, 30,* 627–647. doi:10.1093/oxfordjournals.schbul.a007111

Moore, T. A. (2011). Schizophrenia treatment guidelines in the United States. *Clinical Schizophrenia and Related Psychoses, 5,* 40–49. doi:10.3371/CSRP.5.1.6

Mueser, K. T., & McGurk, S. R. (2004). Schizophrenia. *Lancet, 363,* 2063–2072. doi:10.1016/S0140-6736(04)16458-1

Newman, S. C., & Bland, R. C. (1991). Mortality in a cohort of patients with schizophrenia: A record linkage study. *Canadian Journal of Psychiatry, 36,* 239–245.

Olsson, A. K., Helldin, L., Hjarthag, F., & Norlander, T. (2012). Psychometric properties of a performance-based measurement of functional capacity, the UCSD Performance-Based Skills Assessment—Brief Version. *Psychiatry Research, 197,* 290–294. doi:10.1016/j.psychres.2011.11.002

Overall, J. E. (1976). *The Brief Psychiatric Rating Scale.* Rockville, MD: National Institute of Mental Health.

Overall, J. E., & Gorham, D. R. (1962). The Brief Psychiatric Rating Scale. *Psychological Reports, 10,* 799–812. doi:10.2466/pr0.1962.10.3.799

Patterson, T. L., Bucardo, J., McKibbin, C. L., Mausbach, B. T., Moore, D., Barrio, C., . . . Jeste, D. V. (2005). Development and pilot testing of a new psychosocial intervention for older Latinos with chronic psychosis. *Schizophrenia Bulletin, 31,* 922–930. doi:10.1093/schbul/sbi036

Patterson, T. L., Goldman, S., McKibbin, C. L., Hughs, T., & Jeste, D. V. (2001). UCSD Performance-Based Skills Assessment: Development of a new measure of everyday functioning for severely mentally ill adults. *Schizophrenia Bulletin, 27,* 235–245. doi:10.1093/oxfordjournals.schbul.a006870

Patterson, T. L., Mausbach, B. T., McKibbin, C., Goldman, S., Bucardo, J., & Jeste, D. V. (2006). Functional Adaptation Skills Training (FAST): A randomized trial of a psychosocial intervention for middle-aged and older patients with chronic psychotic disorders. *Schizophrenia Research, 86,* 291–299.

Patterson, T. L., Moscona, S., McKibbin, C. L., Davidson, K., & Jeste, D. V. (2001). Social skills performance assessment among older patients with schizophrenia. *Schizophrenia Research, 48,* 351–360. doi:10.1016/S0920-9964(00)00109-2

Penn, D. L., Mueser, K. T., Tarrier, N., Gloege, A., Cather, C., Serrano, D., & Otto, M. W. (2004). Supportive therapy for schizophrenia: Possible mechanisms and implications for adjunctive psychosocial treatments. *Schizophrenia Bulletin, 30,* 101–112. doi:10.1093/oxfordjournals.schbul.a007055

Perivoliotis, D., Granholm, E., & Patterson, T. L. (2004). Psychosocial functioning on the Independent Living Skills Survey in older outpatients with schizophrenia. *Schizophrenia Research, 69,* 307–316. doi:10.1016/j.schres.2003.09.012

Pratt, S. I., Kelly, S. M., Mueser, K. T., Patterson, T. L., Goldman, S., & Bishop-Horton, S. (2007). Reliability and validity of a performance-based measure of skills for communicating with doctors for older people with serious mental illness. *Journal of Mental Health, 16,* 569–579. doi:10.1080/09638230701494894

Psychiatric Rehabilitation Consultants. (1991). *Modules in the UCLA social and independent living skill series.* Camarillo, CA: Psychiatric Rehabilitation Consultants.

Rector, N. A., & Beck, A. T. (2001). Cognitive–behavioral therapy for schizophrenia: An empirical review. *Journal of Nervous and Mental Disease, 189,* 278–287. doi:10.1097/00005053-200105000-00002

Saha, S., Chant, D., Welham, J., & McGrath, J. (2005). A systematic review of the prevalence of schizophrenia. *PLoS Medicine, 2,* e141. doi:10.1371/journal.pmed.0020141

Sartorius, N., Jablensky, A., Korten, A., Ernberg, G., Anker, M., Cooper, J. E., & Day, R. (1986). Early manifestations and first-contact incidence of schizophrenia in different cultures. A preliminary report on the initial evaluation phase of the WHO Collaborative Study on determinants of outcome of severe mental disorders. *Psychological Medicine, 16*, 909–928. doi:10.1017/S0033291700011910

Schultz, S. K., Miller, D. D., Oliver, S. E., Arndt, S., Flaum, M., & Andreasen, N. C. (1997). The life course of schizophrenia: Age and symptom dimensions. *Schizophrenia Research, 23*, 15–23. doi:10.1016/S0920-9964(96)00087-4

Seeman, M. V. (1996). The role of estrogen in schizophrenia. *Journal of Psychiatry and Neuroscience, 21*, 123–127.

Tarrier, N., Kinney, C., McCarthy, E., Humphreys, L., Wittkowski, A., & Morris, J. (2000). Two-year follow-up of cognitive–behavioral therapy and supportive counseling in the treatment of persistent symptoms in chronic schizophrenia. *Journal of Consulting and Clinical Psychology, 68*, 917–922. doi:10.1037/0022-006X.68.5.917

Thomas, P., Mathur, P., Gottesman, I. I., Nagpal, R., Nimgaonkar, V. L., & Deshpande, S. N. (2007). Correlates of hallucinations in schizophrenia: A cross-cultural evaluation. *Schizophrenia Research, 92*, 41–49. doi:10.1016/j.schres.2007.01.017

Twamley, E. W., Doshi, R. R., Nayak, G. V., Palmer, B. W., Golshan, S., Heaton, R. K., . . . Jeste, D. V. (2002). Generalized cognitive impairments, ability to perform everyday tasks, and level of independence in community living situations of older patients with psychosis. *American Journal of Psychiatry, 159*, 2013–2020. doi:10.1176/appi.ajp.159.12.2013

Twamley, E. W., Jeste, D. V., & Lehman, A. F. (2003). Vocational rehabilitation in schizophrenia and other psychotic disorders: A literature review and meta-analysis of randomized controlled trials. *Journal of Nervous and Mental Disease, 191*, 515–523. doi:10.1097/01.nmd.0000082213.42509.69

Velligan, D. I., Diamond, P., Glahn, D. C., Ritch, J., Maples, N., Castillo, D., & Miller, A. L. (2007). The reliability and validity of the Test of Adaptive Behavior in Schizophrenia (TABS). *Psychiatry Research, 151*, 55–66. doi:10.1016/j.psychres.2006.10.007

Ventura, J., Nuechterlein, K. H., Subotnik, K. L., & Gilbert, E. (1993). Training and quality assurance with the Brief Psychiatric Rating Scale: The drift busters. *International Journal of Methods in Psychiatric Research, 3*, 221–244.

Wallace, C. J., Liberman, R. P., Tauber, R., & Wallace, J. (2000). The Independent Living Skills Survey: A comprehensive measure of the community functioning of severely and persistently mentally ill individuals. *Schizophrenia Bulletin, 26*, 631–658. doi:10.1093/oxfordjournals.schbul.a033483

Zimmermann, G., Favrod, J., Trieu, V. H., & Pomini, V. (2005). The effect of cognitive–behavioral treatment on the positive symptoms of schizophrenia spectrum disorders: A meta-analysis. *Schizophrenia Research, 77*, 1–9. doi:10.1016/j.schres.2005.02.018

CHAPTER 5

ALCOHOL ABUSE AND SUBSTANCE MISUSE IN LATER LIFE

Derek D. Satre and Jennifer Price Wolf

Substance use assessment and intervention are important components of clinical practice for geropsychologists. Alcohol is the most commonly used substance among older adults, and drinking may lead to a number of medical (Finlayson & Hurt, 1998; Meyerhoff et al., 2005), functional (Moore, Endo, & Carter, 2003), and psychiatric problems (Blow, Walton, Barry, et al., 2000). In addition to alcohol, recent studies showing the increased use of cannabis and prescription drugs with potential for abuse (especially pain medications; Simoni-Wastila & Yang, 2006) demonstrate the importance of substance use awareness in clinical geropsychology practice. As will be described, a substantial percentage of older adults seeking mental health services also report use of alcohol and drugs. Psychology has an important role to play in providing appropriate care for these patients. To inform clinical work with older adults, this chapter summarizes what is currently known regarding alcohol and drug use patterns and strategies for effective assessment and intervention.

DEFINITION AND CLINICAL CRITERIA

The *Diagnostic and Statistical Manual of Mental Disorders, Fifth Edition* (*DSM–5*; American Psychiatric Association, 2013) is the current standard for diagnostic appraisal in the United States and includes a rubric that differentiates between alcohol and drug dependence and alcohol abuse. Although utilized by most mental health professionals, hospitals, and insurance companies, overreliance on *DSM* criteria may be problematic in diagnosing and

conceptualizing substance use problems among older adult populations. For example, older adults may be more likely than younger adults to encounter significant alcohol problems necessitating specialized chemical dependency services, yet they may not meet *DSM* diagnostic criteria for alcohol use disorder (AUDs) and other substance use disorders (SUDs; Blow, 1998; Satre, Mertens, Arean, & Weisner, 2003). One study of a large outpatient treatment program found that 19% of adults age 55 years and older who were enrolled in the program did not meet dependence criteria (versus 14% of adults ages 40–54 years and 10% of adults ages 18–39 years; Satre, Mertens, et al., 2003). Older adults may have alcohol-related problems without developing tolerance or physiological dependence, may have fewer activities to give up because of substance use (e.g., fewer family, social, or work obligations), and may attribute physical symptoms to age-related changes instead of substance use (Blow, 1998; Moore, Beck, Babor, Hays, & Reuben, 2002). As a result, the screening instruments typically used by research studies and clinical psychologists might be less effective at capturing alcohol abuse or dependence in older adults than they would be in other populations.

Some of these problems potentially could be addressed once the criteria established by the *DSM–5* come into general use. Eliminating both Substance Abuse and Substance Dependence, the *DSM–5* includes only one substance-related diagnosis, Substance Use Disorder (American Psychiatric Association, 2013). To be diagnosed with an SUD, individuals will need to have a problematic pattern of substance use leading to impairment or distress as well as two or more additional factors such as the following: (a) using in larger amounts or over a longer period than intended, (b) unsuccessful efforts to cut down or control use, (c) spending significant amounts of time in activities to obtain the substance or recover from its effects, (d) failure to fulfill role obligations, (e) continued use in spite of social or interpersonal problems associated with use, (f) giving up or reducing important activities, (g) recurrent use in hazardous situations, (h) continued use in spite of physical or psychological problems associated with use, (i) tolerance as indicated by either a need for markedly increased amounts of the substance or diminished effect with continued use of the same amount of the substance, (j) withdrawal when substance use is stopped (or avoidance of withdrawal by continued use), (k) or craving or strong desire for the substance.

The new diagnosis potentially is less stigmatizing than the old ones, especially for those who may have developed dependence based on long-term use of medically indicated substance use (e.g., pain medications) and for whom a psychiatric diagnosis may be unwarranted. In spite of the elimination of substance abuse and dependence as separate diagnoses, however, there are several similarities between the proposed criteria and those in the previous edition of the *Diagnostic and Statistical Manual of Mental Disorders, Fourth Edition, Text Revision* (DSM–IV–TR; American Psychiatric Association, 2000), including tolerance and failure in social or other role obligations, both of which may be less meaningful in older age (Blow, 1998; Moore et al., 2002). Consequently, it is unknown whether adoption of these proposed criteria will improve diagnostic validity in older adults.

Regardless of how diagnostic categories evolve, quantity and frequency of use, patterns of use and substance-related problems are critical to consider in screening and assessment. Clinical geropsychologists, with specialized training and experience in evaluating older adults, are well positioned to take a comprehensive approach to determining the presence and extent of substance-related problems (including risk for future adverse consequences) in this population.

Alcohol continues to be the most commonly used substance among older patients. There are several issues to consider when screening and assessing alcohol use and related disorders among older adults. First, maladaptive use patterns conceptualized as "hazardous drinking and use" or "at-risk drinking and use" (consuming greater quantities of alcohol than is recommended, which puts patients at risk of alcohol-related problems) and "problem drinking and use" (having adverse consequences) should be targeted for screening and intervention even among individuals who do not meet diagnostic criteria for substance abuse or dependence (Blow, 1998). As will be described, screening and treatment models such as the public health–based Screening, Brief Intervention, and Referral to Treatment (SBIRT; Academic ED SBIRT Research Collaborative, 2007) have successfully used this broader approach to addressing problematic drinking among older as well as younger adults (Blow & Barry, 2002). Second, there are circumstances when any alcohol consumption in older age is risky, such as with concurrent use of alcohol-interactive prescription drugs. Alcohol can interact with prescription drugs in two ways (Weathermon & Crabb, 1999). Pharmacokinetic interactions occur when heavy or chronic alcohol consumption affects how the body metabolizes a prescription drug. As a result, older adults may not receive the full benefits of their prescribed medication. Pharmacodynamic interactions occur when acute alcohol consumption enhances negative side effects of a prescription medication, for example, leading to dizziness or drowsiness. Certain medical conditions also enhance risks of drinking (e.g., liver disease, pancreatitis, gout, and depression, or use in combination with medications that could have an adverse interaction; Barnes et al., 2010). Because approximately 70% of older adults regularly use alcohol-interactive medication (Wolf, 2012), any use of alcohol has the potential to be problematic.

In consideration of these issues, alcohol use limits modified for older adults have been proposed. The National Institute on Alcohol Abuse and Alcoholism (NIAAA) has current guidelines that recommend that adults older than 65 years have no more than three drinks on any one day and no more than seven drinks a week (NIAAA, 2010). Some have argued, however, that these guidelines are too high for older adults and particularly for older women, who can experience alcohol's effect at lower doses due to lower body mass. These researchers have categorized women 65 years and over as overlimit drinkers if they reported drinking either more than one drink per day or more than seven drinks per week, and men 65 years and older overlimit drinkers if they consumed either more than two drinks per day or more than 14 drinks per week (Adams, Barry, & Fleming, 1996; Satre, Gordon, & Weisner, 2007). Moos, Brennan, Schutte, and Moos (2004) found that drinking problems among men were substantial at the lower as well as the higher cutoff, and that increased problems were associated with higher number of drinks consumed. This finding indicates that recommended drinking limits should probably be no higher among men than among women to reduce risk.

Epidemiological studies indicate that a substantial number of older adults are affected by hazardous or overlimit drinking. Approximately one third of older men and one tenth of older women drink above recommend NIAAA guidelines, with a population average of 10%–13% overall (Blazer & Wu, 2009a; Sacco, Bucholz, & Spitznagel, 2009). A recent study of community-dwelling Medicare beneficiaries age 65 years and older found that 9% of participants reported either monthly use exceeding 30 drinks per typical month or heavy episodic drinking of four or more drinks in any single day during a typical month in the previous year (Merrick et al., 2008). Another study found that among older adults who drink, almost one half of older men and one third of older women drinkers consumed more than two drinks per day or seven drinks per week (Moos, Schutte, Brennan, & Moos, 2009). Thus, hazardous drinking among older adults appears to be a significant public health problem, strengthening the case for enhanced detection and intervention training for clinical psychologists in a variety of community, gerontology, and medical settings.

Although older adults in general should be screened for hazardous drinking, variations based on gender and ethnicity are also relevant on an epidemiological level. Demographic shifts indicate that larger numbers of older adults in these subgroups will be affected in the future. For example, the percentages of older Hispanic and Black adults in the population are expected to increase at more than twice the rate of Whites between 2004 and 2030 (Administration on Aging, 2013) and may be more likely to drink in older age at the problematic levels (Blazer & Wu, 2009a; Merrick et al., 2008; Satre, Gordon, & Weisner, 2007). For these reasons, psychologists should be particularly aware of the extent and impact of alcohol consumption on members of older minority groups.

Drinking problems in late life also may increasingly affect older women, on the basis of cohort-based shifts in drinking patterns and the growth of older women as a subgroup within the U.S. population (Han, Gfroerer, Colliver, & Penne, 2009). Women's drinking and alcohol-related problems may develop later in life than those of men (Holdcraft & Iacono, 2002; Satre, Mertens, & Weisner, 2004). Although older women generally drink less than older men do (Blazer & Wu, 2009a; Merrick et al., 2008; Moore et al., 2003; Sacco et al., 2009), they potentially experience more related health problems at comparable levels of alcohol consumption (Bradley, Badrinath, Bush, Boyd-Wickizer, & Anawalt, 1998; Greenfield, Manwani, & Nargiso, 2003; Walter, Dvorak, Gutierrez, Zitterl, & Lesch, 2005). The course of women's drinking problems may be shorter and more intense than those of men (Redgrave, Swartz, & Romanoski, 2003), and because of physiological differences, women may be more vulnerable to intoxication (Blow & Barry, 2002) and alcohol-related adverse drug events (Onder et al., 2002). Alcohol use has the potential to exacerbate symptoms of depression, which is more common among women than men. These factors suggest that when working with older adults, psychologists should be especially aware of the potential for alcohol-related problems at relatively low levels among older women; should thoroughly assess patterns of alcohol use, including usual quantity and frequency; and should ask about any associated consequences.

Prescription Drug Use

Prescription drug misuse and related consequences such as overdose have gained increasing public attention as a major health problem (Bohnert et al.,

2011). Misuse of prescription medication can include using others' medication, taking a lower or higher dose than prescribed, using medication for a longer duration than prescribed, or using medication for recreational or nonmedical purposes (Blow, 1998; Simoni-Wastila & Yang, 2006). Inappropriate use can be either accidental or intentional. Unintentional misuse may be common among older adults, as a result of cognitive changes with age and the greater number of medications that older adults take, which increases the likelihood of errors.

Such variability in patterns of misuse raises measurement challenges that have not been addressed in studies of either older or younger adults. Scales have been developed to measure opiate misuse by pain patients (e.g., the 31-item Prescription Drug Use Questionnaire; P. A. Compton, Wu, Schieffer, Pham, & Naliboff, 2008). Measurement of substance use motivations also has been incorporated into the subtyping of medication misuse (e.g., recreational vs. self-treatment; McCabe, Boyd, & Teter, 2009). More rudimentary measures of drug misuse include frequency of opiate and sedative use other than as prescribed by a physician in the prior 30 days (Satre, Sterling, Mackin, & Weisner, 2011), based on the Addiction Severity Index (Weisner, McLellan, & Hunkeler, 2000). Better approaches to prescription drug misuse measurement are needed and are especially important for older adults who may be at higher risk of prescription misuse than younger adults because of polypharmacy, high prevalence of insomnia and chronic pain, and cognitive changes with age that make measurement based on self-reported patterns of use potentially less valid than they would be for younger adults.

Psychologists working with older adults in an assessment or treatment capacity should be especially aware of the medications that older adults are most likely to use or misuse. For example, prescription drugs frequently misused by older adults include sedative hypnotics (sleep aids) and opioid analgesics (pain killers), which have significant potential for abuse or dependence (Simoni-Wastila & Yang, 2006). In a study of benzodiazepine use among primary care patients adults age 60 years and older, researchers examined patterns of long-term use (Simon & Ludman, 2006). Although ongoing use

generally is not recommended, 30% of participants reported ongoing daily use 60 days after their initial prescription, putting them at risk for dependence. Substantial prior-month rates of misuse of prescription sedatives (using medication other than as prescribed) have been found in 16% of men and 9% of women age 60 years and older in depression treatment (Satre et al., 2011). These rates potentially could be explained by the high prevalence of sleeping problems among older adults and among individuals with depression.

Evidence indicates that use of pain medication among older adults has been increasing in recent years, which could put patients at risk of medication-related problems. For example, in a recent study, administrative data were used to examine age and sex trends in long-term use of prescribed opioids for chronic noncancer pain in members of two large health care plans (Campbell et al., 2010). From 1997 to 2005, there was a total increase ranging from 16% to 87% in incident long-term opioid use, and from 61% to 135% in prevalent long-term opioid use, which varied by age and sex. Older women had the highest prevalence of long-term opioid use (8%–9% in 2005). These studies indicate that psychotropic drug use with abuse potential appears to be increasing among older adults and highlight the importance of screening and assessment in mental health settings, primary care, and pain management contexts.

Patterns of Illicit Drug Use

Use of illegal drugs also appears to be increasing among older adults. On the basis of the 2005 National Survey on Drug Use and Health (NSDUH), among adults ages 50 to 59 years, illicit drug use in the prior month increased between 2002 and 2005. For those ages 50 to 54 years, the rates increased from 3.4% to 5.2%. Among those ages 55 to 59 years, the rate increased from 1.9% to 3.4%, a statistically significant increase (Substance Abuse and Mental Health Services Administration, 2006). Marijuana, the most frequently used illegal drug among all age-groups, accounted for most of the increase over time. Examining cannabis use patterns in the 2008 NSDUH sample, 2.8% of adults age 50 years and older used cannabis in the prior year. Of these participants, 23% had used marijuana on at least half the days of the year (DiNitto & Choi, 2011). On the basis of data from the National Epidemiological Study of Alcohol and Related Conditions, 0.2% of adults age 65 years and older had a 12-month *DSM–IV–TR* drug use disorder (W. M. Compton, Thomas, Stinson, & Grant, 2007). In a study of adults age 60 years and older in outpatient depression treatment in a psychiatry department, cannabis use in the prior 30 days was reported by 12% of men and 4% of women (Satre et al., 2011). These findings highlight the potential for substance problems in older psychiatric populations.

RISK FACTORS FOR ALCOHOL AND DRUG PROBLEMS

Building on developmental theories and the stress and coping model, a number of studies have examined factors associated with alcohol and drug problems among older adults (Blow, 1998). For example, stresses associated with growing older, including physical changes, retirement, and loss of a partner or close friends have been identified as potential risk factors for development or exacerbation of alcohol problems among older adults (Satre, Chi, Mertens, & Weisner, 2012). One study of adults age 55 years and older found that those who had more friends who approved of drinking, relied on substances for tension reduction, or had higher income were more likely to report high-risk alcohol consumption and to develop alcohol-related problems at 10- and 20-year follow-up time points (Moos, Brennan, Schutte, & Moos, 2010a). In another longitudinal study that examined the relationship of pain to alcohol consumption, older adults who reported problem drinking at later time points had reported more severe pain at study baseline, more disruption of daily activities because of pain, and more frequent use of alcohol to manage pain than did those who did not go on to develop alcohol-related problems (Brennan, Schutte, & Moos, 2005). These studies indicate that older adults who drink and whose pain is not well managed are at increased risk for developing alcohol-related problems over time.

Some evidence indicates that older adults who experienced alcohol problems early in life are at

greater risk for exacerbation or reemergence of heavy drinking and related problems later in life. These studies have used a stress-and-coping approach to examine vulnerabilities and protective factors that appear to influence late-life drinking patterns. For example, one study found that drinking problems by age 50 years were associated with a higher likelihood of late-life high-risk alcohol consumption and drinking problems (Moos et al., 2010a). Having tried to cut down on alcohol use and reporting participation in Alcoholics Anonymous, however, were associated with a lower likelihood of high-risk consumption and alcohol-related problems at later time points (Moos et al., 2010a). This suggests that prior intervention and treatment can have a preventative effect on substance abuse later in the life course.

Socioeconomic and demographic factors also are associated with increased risk of alcohol misuse. In a study using 2005 and 2006 NSDUH data, binge drinking (five or more drinks on the same occasion) compared with no alcohol use among men was associated with higher income and being separated, divorced, or widowed; among women, binge drinking was associated with being employed and with misuse of prescription medications. Among all respondents to the survey, binge drinking was associated with the use of tobacco and illicit drugs (Blazer & Wu, 2009a). Among women, binge drinking was associated with being African American and having less education, but race and education were not associated with binge drinking among men (Blazer & Wu, 2009a). In a survey conducted among adults age 65 years and older in Northern California, drinking over recommended limits (more than 7 drinks per week among women and more than 14 drinks per week among men) was more common among Whites and Latinos than among African Americans and Asian Americans (Satre, Gordon, & Weisner, 2007). In cross-sectional studies, overlimit drinkers are more likely than moderate drinkers to have behavioral health risks such as smoking and poor dietary practices (Blow, Walton, Barry, et al., 2000; Satre, Gordon, & Weisner, 2007). Because the analyses are not longitudinal, however, it is not clear whether these other problematic health behaviors are risk factors or consequences of hazardous drinking.

Factors associated with prescription drug misuse among older adults are somewhat different than those associated with alcohol misuse. Using NSDUH data to examine risk factors for nonprescription use of pain medication, risk for nonprescription use was associated with younger age, Native American or Alaskan Native ethnicity, and use of cannabis (Blazer & Wu, 2009b). Adults ages 50–64 years are more likely to misuse prescription drugs than adults age 65 years and older (Wu & Blazer, 2011). Among older women, use of psychotropic medication with abuse potential (e.g., benzodiazepines) is associated with being widowed or divorced, lower education, lower income, worse health, anxiety, and depression (Simoni-Wastila & Yang, 2006). Additionally, opioid use has been increasing over time, and older women may be the most at risk for using these medications for longer periods than recommended (Campbell et al., 2010). Older adults with cognitive impairment are also at risk for medication misuse (Weston, Weinstein, Barton, & Yaffe, 2010) because of memory loss or confusion regarding medication dosages and schedules. Worse memory impairment and greater number of medications prescribed both increase the risk that medications will not be taken as indicated (Thiruchselvam et al., 2012). Clinicians working with older adults should be especially alert to the possibility of accidental or intentional misuse of prescription medications.

It is anticipated that cannabis use will continue to increase among older adults as the baby boom cohort ages (Blow & Barry, 2012; Gfroerer, Penne, Pemberton, & Folsom, 2003). Yet only a small number of studies have investigated predictors of cannabis use in older adult samples. In a study of cannabis users in the 2008 NSDUH sample, prior-year users were likely to be younger (50–64 years old), Black, and not married, and they had significantly higher psychological distress scores compared with nonusers (DiNitto & Choi, 2011). Similarly, cannabis use was associated with higher depression score after controlling for other factors in a clinical sample of adults age 60 years and older in an outpatient psychiatric setting (Satre et al., 2011). Although these studies could not establish directional relationships between distress or depression and cannabis use, they imply that psychologists working with older

adults in mental health settings may find that cannabis use is not uncommon.

COURSE AND PROGRESSION

Patterns of alcohol and drug use vary over the life course. Some individuals reduce alcohol use or recover from substance use disorders as they get older. Others may develop an alcohol or drug problem for the first time in later life. Although not all cohorts demonstrate the same degree of change (Levenson, Aldwin, & Spiro, 1998), some longitudinal studies have found a decline in the quantity of alcohol consumed and an increase in abstinence with age (Fillmore, 1987; Moore et al., 2005; Shaw, Krause, Liang, & McGeever, 2011). Because alcohol can exacerbate medical conditions and has potential for adverse medication interactions, older adults with health problems who drank when they were younger may cut back over time or stop drinking completely (Krause, 1991; Moos, Brennan, Schutte, & Moos, 2005; Satre & Arean, 2005). This tendency to reduce drinking over time may help to explain why studies comparing older adults who drink heavily or moderately to those who abstain completely have found that abstainers generally have worse health status (Bridevaux, Bradley, Bryson, McDonell, & Fihn, 2004; Graham & Schmidt, 1998; Vogeltanz, Wilsnack, Vickers, & Kristjanson, 1999). For example, in a sample of men age 65 years and older, those who reported drinking alcohol in the previous year had better health (as measured by the SF-36 short-form health survey) than abstainers (Bridevaux et al., 2004). In a health plan survey in Northern California, worse self-reported health was associated with having stopped drinking in the prior year (vs. current light drinking) after controlling for other factors (Satre, Gordon, & Weisner, 2007). These studies support the theory that declines in health help motivate a reduction in alcohol consumption.

There are differences between men and women in the course of substance use over time and in treatment response (Redgrave et al., 2003). In one study, older women had higher posttreatment abstinence rates than older men, based on a 6-month follow-up interviews with alcohol-dependent patients in an outpatient program (Satre,

Mertens, & Weisner, 2004). In that study, women had a later onset of heavy drinking than men but were consuming similar amounts of alcohol at the time of treatment entry. Once in treatment, women stayed longer than men and had higher abstinence rates. In a study of patients recruited from a public clinic in an urban setting, women who stopped drinking had higher rates of hypertension and heart problems than current drinkers, whereas the same relationship was not observed among men (Satre & Arean, 2005). These studies suggest that older women may be more responsive in reducing their alcohol intake to protect their health than older men and also may be more likely to benefit from formal treatment programs.

Although older adults typically reduce drinking with age, alcohol problems increase late in life for a subset of individuals. Late onset drinking problems have been defined variously as those that appear for the first time after age 55, 60, or 65 years (Hurt, Finlayson, Morse, & Davis, 1988; Schonfeld & Dupree, 1991; Wells-Parker, Miles, & Spencer, 1983). Studies of older adults in treatment have found that approximately one third of older adults have a late-onset alcohol problem. Late-onset problems may be less severe and may have better treatment response (Schonfeld & Dupree, 1991). It has been hypothesized that bereavement, retirement, and other late-life changes in support networks contribute to problem drinking (Satre et al., 2012). In a 7-year longitudinal study of drinking among adults ages 55–65 years at baseline, compared with stable nonproblem drinkers, late-onset problem drinkers at baseline were more likely to report incipient alcohol-related problems, heavier alcohol consumption, greater friend approval of drinking, and more reliance on avoidance coping strategies; and they were more likely to smoke, were less likely to have acute medical conditions that potentially could be complicated by alcohol consumption, and had a history of responding to stressors and negative affect with increased alcohol consumption (Schutte, Brennan, & Moos, 1998). Analysis of changes in late-life drinking has found no independent effect for retirement status (Brennan, Schutte, & Moos, 2010; Satre et al., 2012). It remains possible, however, that retirement may be a disruptive life transition for

some older adults. Clinicians working with older adults experiencing retirement, loss, or other stressful live events should be aware of the potential for misuse of alcohol or other substances as a coping mechanism.

One recent study has examined gender differences in the course and outcomes of older adults with a history of opioid dependence (Grella & Lovinger, 2012). Study participants were initially sampled from methadone maintenance clinics in California in the 1970s and completed follow-up interviews in 2005–2009. Out of the original study sample ($N = 914$), 343 participants (44.3% female) were interviewed (70.6% of those not deceased). The average age was 58.3 (standard deviation [SD] = 4.9) years for men and 55 (SD = 4.1) years for women. There were no significant gender differences in past-year drug use (38% of sample) or injection drug use (19%). Women, however, reported significantly more chronic health problems and psychological distress compared with men and had overall worse health and functioning compared with general population norms. Men younger than 65 years had worse physical health and social functioning compared with population norms. Men in the study sample reporting past-year substance use also had poorer physical functioning, but less bodily pain, than nonusers, whereas women with past-year substance use had poorer mental health than other women. These data indicate that older adults with a history of heroin dependence have poorer health and functioning than older adults in the general population, and that at a younger age, women had worse overall health status and more chronic health and mental health problems than men with a history of opioid dependence.

Negative Outcomes Associated With Misuse of Alcohol and Drugs

A number of negative outcomes are associated with the misuse of alcohol and drugs among older adults. Among these, problems associated with alcohol use have received the most study. Physical systems negatively affected by heavy drinking include the gastrointestinal, cardiovascular, endocrine, hematological, and neurological systems (Gambert & Katsoyannis, 1995; National Institute on Alcohol Abuse and Alcoholism, 2000; World Health Organization, 2013).

Illnesses involving these systems are particularly prevalent and serious among older adults. Heavy drinking also has been associated with elevated risk of depression across all age-groups, and hazardous drinking is common among older adults with depression (Satre et al., 2011). Suicidality is higher in patients with depression and alcohol problems than it is among those with depression alone (Cornelius et al., 1995; Salloum et al., 1995; Waller, Lyons, & Costantini-Ferrando, 1999). Heavy alcohol consumption is associated with nonadherence to medications (Bryson et al., 2008) not obtaining preventive medical care recommended for older adults (Merrick et al., 2008), and increased emergency room visits (Cherpitel, 2007; Cherpitel & Ye, 2008) and inpatient hospitalizations (Freyer-Adam et al., 2008). As with younger adults, older adults in alcohol and drug treatment have many substance abuse–related medical conditions (Mertens, Flisher, Satre, & Weisner, 2008), in addition to chronic disorders and disabilities that increase in prevalence with age. The combination of physical illness, disability and social and psychological problems among older people with alcohol and drug problems is evidence of the complex service needs of this population (Satre, Mertens, et al., 2003; Satre & Olson, 2009). For providers working with older adults, it is important that alcohol be considered as a contributing factor to both physical and psychiatric problems.

Heavy drinking can increase the risk of injury from falling due to acute intoxication (Stenbacka, 2003) and over time can increase risk of cognitive impairment (Chan, Chiu, & Chu, 2010; Son, Lee, Oh, & Hong, 2012). Additional consequences include social isolation, increased risk of depression, and suicide (Blow, Brockmann, & Barry, 2004). Excessive alcohol consumption may be clustered with other behavioral health risks, such as smoking, poor diet (Adams et al., 1996; Ma, Betts, & Hampl, 2000; Satre, Gordon, & Weisner, 2007), and obesity (Breslow & Smothers, 2004), increasing the cumulative risk for medical problems. Drinking over recommended guidelines has been associated with increased risk of emergency room admission among Medicare recipients (Merrick, Perloff, & Tompkins, 2010). Spouses of older adults with drinking problems also experience more alcohol-related problems

themselves (Moos, Brennan, Schutte, & Moos, 2010b), highlighting the potential adverse impact of alcohol on family and social support networks.

The consequences of inappropriate psychotropic medication use (e.g., use of sedative hypnotics, anxiolytics, and opiates other than as prescribed) in older adults include confusion, increased risk of sedation, impaired motor coordination, and impaired vision and attention as well as development of dependence. Aging may result in changes to pharmacodynamics of commonly prescribed psychotropic drugs (Bowie & Slattum, 2007) and increase neurological vulnerability to the effects of drugs and alcohol, including neurotoxicity (Dowling, Weiss, & Condon, 2008). Decreased lean body mass with aging results in elevated blood serum levels and increases the potential for adverse drug reactions. Such physical changes help to explain why adults should consume smaller quantities of alcohol than younger adults, and why age is an important consideration in prescribing medications with potential for abuse or misuse.

Assessment

Among patients in mental health settings, alcohol and drug use should be part of routine screening and assessment. As part of initial screening, adults older than 65 years should be asked whether they ever had four or more drinks on any one occasion during the prior year (a lower threshold than the five or more drinks used to screen younger adults). This single-item screener has been validated in the general population as a tool for identifying alcohol use disorders (Smith, Schmidt, Allensworth-Davies, & Saitz, 2009), but it has not been examined specifically among older adults. Of the slightly longer instruments available, the four-item CAGE (cut down, annoyance, guilt, eye-opener) to screen for lifetime alcohol use disorders (Ewing, 1984) has been used widely although it is not well validated among older adults as a standalone measure (Reid, Tinetti, O'Connor, Kosten, & Concato, 2003). CAGE is an acronym representing the following four questions: (a) Have you ever felt you needed to *cut down* on your drinking? (b) Have people *annoyed* you by criticizing your drinking? (c) Have you ever felt *guilty* about drinking? (d) Have you ever felt you needed a drink first thing in the morning (*eye-opener*) to steady your nerves or to get rid of a hangover? A positive response to one or more of these questions should prompt assessment of a possible current alcohol problem.

It is important to ask about usual quantity and frequency of alcohol consumption during a typical week, keeping in mind that as with other age-groups, patients potentially may underestimate the amount they actually drink. To help improve the accuracy of reporting, it may be helpful to show patients visually what is included in a standard drink (i.e., 1.5 ounces of liquor, 5 ounces of wine, or 12 ounces of regular beer; National Institute on Alcohol Abuse and Alcoholism, 2013) using a printed card. Such visual aids are also helpful in giving feedback to patients regarding recommended drinking limits.

There are additional choices for brief screening and assessment. Comparison of a five-item version of the Alcohol Use Disorders Identification Test (AUDIT; Philpot et al., 2003) versus the full-length version (Babor, Higgins-Biddle, Saunders, & Monteiro, 2001) and the CAGE found that the five-item AUDIT performed as well as the full-length AUDIT and better than the CAGE in identifying alcohol problems among older adults. Therefore, clinicians should consider using the five-item AUDIT if they have time to ask more than one question related to drinking.

For older adult patients with a likely alcohol use problem, the Michigan Alcohol Screening Test—Geriatric Version (MAST–G) is a screening and assessment instrument that also gives an indication of severity (Blow et al., 1992) and includes items appropriate to older adults. This scale has 24 items, and five or more positive responses are indicative of an alcohol problem. Shorter versions of this instrument also have been proposed as screening instruments that show comparable validity to the longer instrument (Johnson-Greene, Adams, Gilman, & Junck, 2002), but as assessment tools, they do not provide clinicians with the same amount of information regarding the extent of alcohol related problems.

Geropsychologists also should be aware of common medical issues that could be associated with alcohol or drug use, which should prompt questions regarding possible substance involvement. These include many of the most widespread clinical problems of older adults: sleep difficulties, cognitive complaints, seizures, nutritional problems, liver abnormalities, depression or anxiety, unexplained chronic pain, incontinence, poor hygiene, vision problems, dry mouth, gastrointestinal distress, appetite changes, slurred speech, motor problems, or falls (Blow, 1998). Alcohol or drug use should be considered as a potential contributing factor if any of these problems are present. As noted earlier, older adults with alcohol or drug use problems often seek treatment in mental health settings (Satre et al., 2011) or may be seeking treatment for depression or anxiety in a primary care or social service setting that employs psychologists. Therefore, psychologists working with older patients in any health or social service context should be alert to the importance of alcohol and drug use screening and assessment, and all patients should receive routine screening.

Psychologists also should be aware of potential barriers to care for alcohol and drug use problems and be prepared to help engage patients with needed services. For example, older adults in general are less often referred to substance abuse consultations in hospitals than are younger adults, even when admitted for trauma related to substance abuse (Weintraub et al., 2001). One study found that of the 21% of adults 60 years of age or older who entered a hospital program and screened positive for alcohol dependence, only one third were identified by their physicians as having alcohol-related problems (Curtis, Geller, Stokes, Levine, & Moore, 1989). Females, Whites, and those with higher education were less likely to be identified. Other studies have also found that older women are less likely to be screened for substance use by regular health care providers (Blow & Barry, 2002; Brennan, Kagay, Geppert, & Moos, 2001). Psychologists experienced in working with older adults and trained to identify substance use problems, and who work in health care settings, are in a position to reduce the number of patients whose substance use goes unrecognized.

Screening in medical and social service settings is an especially important route for older adults to obtain formal treatment. For example, in a cross-sectional study of adults in treatment for AUDs and other SUDs in a private health maintenance organization, older patients were more likely than younger patients to report that a physician encouraged them to enter the program (Satre, Mertens, et al., 2003). Although physicians play an important role in referral, alcohol screening of older adults in primary care is inconsistent (Reid, Tinetti, Brown, & Concato, 1998). One study found that physicians were less likely to initiate discussions about alcohol with Latinos than with Whites, among older adults who drink alcohol (Duru et al., 2010). Care providers may minimize the negative impact of substance abuse in older patients, believing that older adults should be allowed to choose if they want to abuse alcohol (Klein & Jess, 2002). Therefore, geropsychologists working in medical settings have an important role to play in ensuring that older adults get the care that they need.

In addition to underrecognition among providers, older adults may be more likely to deny or minimize substance-related problems than younger adults because of the social stigma associated with substance abuse (Solomon & Stark, 1993). One study found that older adults were less likely than younger adults to perceive their substance use as problematic (Wu & Blazer, 2011). Social stigma could disproportionally affect older women (Ridlon, 1988) and older women of color (Aira, Hartikainen, & Sulkava, 2008; Herd & Grube, 1996). Mexican Americans also may view alcohol abuse as a stigmatized behavior (Gomberg, 2003), thus increasing reluctance to discuss alcohol-related problems with practitioners. This reluctance is particularly worrisome given the higher risk of problematic drinking among older Latinos compared with Asian and African Americans (Satre, Gordon, & Weisner, 2007), and it suggests that training, particularly education that emphasizes culturally appropriate practice, is needed for the range of providers working with older adults.

Client–Provider Issues Related to Intervention

Engaging older adults in treatment may have special challenges. One study investigated whether older Medicare beneficiaries utilize outpatient mental health services after being diagnosed with substance abuse during an inpatient stay, finding that less than

one half of participants ever received treatment from a formal or community source (Brennan et al., 2001). Older women were less likely to have substance-use problems identified by regular health care providers but were more likely to receive outpatient mental health care. The authors were unable to specifically identify why Medicare beneficiaries did not access treatment, but they speculated that ill health may play a role. Other factors such as difficulty affording copayments could act as a barrier to treatment (Lo Sasso & Lyons, 2002). This could be especially relevant for older adults with less disposable income.

SBIRT interventions in primary care, emergency departments, and social service organizations serving older adults are a promising approach to identifying patients in need of services. SBIRT interventions are relatively quick and effective in a variety of settings and with a variety of populations (Cherpitel, 2007; Moyer & Finney, 2004–2005; Moyer, Finney, Swearingen, & Vergun, 2002). Unless SBIRT interventions utilize screening instruments appropriate for older adults, patients who need treatment may not be identified. To address this problem, a recent randomized controlled intervention trial examined alcohol problems specifically among older adults in primary care (Moore et al., 2011). Older adults were screened for problems using an instrument designed with this population in mind. For example, in addition to alcohol quantity and frequency questions and problem assessment, the instrument asked whether older adults were taking a medication that interacts with alcohol. Although this intervention emphasizes the potential role prescription drugs play in enhancing risk, it is unlikely that older adults, particularly those with lower education levels, would be able to accurately self-report whether their medications are alcohol interactive.

Psychologists working to enhance engagement of older adults with specialized alcohol and drug programs should be aware of potential treatment access barriers. In addition to stigma and financial barriers, greater age may function as a treatment access barrier, possibly because of health, mobility, transportation problems, and the effects of cognitive impairment that become more common with age (Blow, 1998), as found in studies of older men seeking alcohol and drug treatment in a Veterans Affairs program in Southern California (Satre, Knight, Dickson-Fuhrmann, & Jarvik, 2003, 2004). Because of these potential obstacles and because outpatient programs tend to be designed with younger patients in mind, referring clinicians should actively assist patients in engaging with outpatient chemical dependency programs. For those who are unable to form a connection to such a program, individually delivered services may be a viable alternative, as described in greater detail below.

Technical Aspects of Intervention

As with other population subgroups of people with an alcohol or drug use problem, treatment approaches for older adults should be adapted to the specific needs of the individual. Important considerations include problem severity and co-occurring conditions. The recommendations described in this section are based on the limited empirical literature on older adults as well as on reviews and consensus statements from research and clinical leaders in the field (Blow, 1998). As much as possible, minimally intensive approaches should be considered first. Many older adults may drink at levels considered risky or problematic, yet they do not meet criteria for substance abuse or dependence and are unlikely to seek out formal alcohol treatment (and may not be appropriate for such programs). These adult, however, often come to the attention of health and mental health providers. For older adults that fall into this category, brief motivational interventions (one to five short sessions) focused on health risks and other potential problems associated with drinking often can be effective in reducing alcohol consumption (Blow & Barry, 2000; Schonfeld et al., 2010). In providing brief interventions to older adults, the medical risks and consequences described earlier should be conveyed in an empathic, supportive manner that acknowledges the difficulty of cutting back.

In the context of brief interventions, motivational interviewing techniques often are incorporated to elicit reasons that an older patient may have to cut back on drinking (e.g., concerns about its impact on family, health, or finances; Miller & Rollnick, 2002). Brief interventions may be conducted in primary care and other mental

health settings, avoiding the stigma associated with addiction treatment programs, and are useful in helping patients engage with specialized addiction services when needed.

Miller and Rollnick (1991) developed motivational interviewing based on work with problem drinkers, as part of a general effort to identify factors that enhance behavior change. They linked observations to existing approaches and psychological theories, including Rogers's (1961) patient-centered therapy, Bem's (1967) self-perception theory, Festinger's (1957) theory of cognitive dissonance, and Prochaska and DiClemente's (1984) transtheoretical model of stages of change. Acknowledging that change happens in stages, the focus in a motivational interviewing session is not merely to promote alcohol use reduction but also to enhance intrinsic motivation. Miller and Rollnick (1991) also have emphasized that (a) ambivalence is normal, (b) change occurs naturally, and (c) the likelihood of change is strongly influenced by relationships such as the one between the therapist and patient.

The motivational interviewing model also takes the position that when confronted or coerced, individuals tend to argue, harden their stance, or resist recommendations to change. The more a patient articulates their retrenched position (e.g., "alcohol is my only pleasure"), the less likely it is that he or she will be motivated to change. Most psychologists have encountered oppositional responses when we have moved too quickly to suggest a course of action to a patient. Patients may spend a great deal of time explaining why the suggested solution will not work or why the problem is not even worth tackling. In contrast with confrontational approaches, which increase resistance, a key goal of motivational interviewing is to evoke "change talk" from the patient. In this approach, the therapist strategically creates a series of opportunities for the patient to state the case for making a change. The more that patients verbalize a commitment to change, the more likely they are to actually make that change. Motivational interviewing includes techniques designed to strengthen or intensify clients' statements of desire, need, ability, and reasons for change –(i.e., to strengthen clients' commitment to changing a target behavior such as alcohol use).

In addition to specific techniques, it is important to adopt the overall stance of motivational interviewing, which is rooted in Rogerian-style empathy and nonpossessive warmth. Motivational interviewing builds on the idea that the quality of the working relationship between therapist and patient is key to therapeutic change and emphasizes the importance of an accurate and empathic connection. The therapist facilitates an open exploration of the pros and cons of current substance use and expresses empathy for the patient's difficulty in cutting back. Accurate empathy enables patients to explore the pros and cons of making a change, which in turn enables a deeper resolution of ambivalence. By evoking and accurately reflecting the patient's internal conflict about change, and selectively reinforcing change talk, the therapist enables patients to hear themselves in a new light.

Although we are not aware of any studies specifically examining motivational interviewing among older adults, this model has developed a strong evidence base over the past 20 years. It has been applied to a range of behavioral health problems (Dunn, Deroo, & Rivara, 2001) and extensively tested for helping individuals reduce drinking. It has been standardized in a number of treatment manuals, is adaptable for use in a variety of health care settings (Miller & Rollnick, 2002; Moyers, Martin, Manuel, Hendrickson, & Miller, 2005; Wilk, Jensen, & Havighurst, 1997), and can be delivered in person and by phone (Cosio et al., 2010; Lovejoy et al., 2011). Thus, motivational interviewing is an important skill for psychologists working with older adults with alcohol or drug use problems.

Psychologists working with older adults with alcohol and drug use problems also may need to address other problematic behaviors, and motivational interviewing is a useful tool for these target behaviors. For example, hazardous drinking often is accompanied by other behavioral health risks, such as smoking, poor diet (Adams et al., 1996; Ma et al., 2000; Satre, Gordon, & Weisner, 2007), and obesity (Breslow & Smothers, 2004), increasing cumulative risk for medical problems. Psychologists delivering brief interventions and motivational interviewing for alcohol use should be aware of these patterns and consider incorporating counseling to stop smoking

and improve eating habits. The relationship between health problems, worse self-reported health, and reduction in drinking over time suggests that medical illness and the perception of having poor health may motivate the elimination of alcohol use. Brief interventions focused on adverse drinking consequences may effectively capitalize on this inclination (Blow, Walton, Barry, et al., 2000; Mundt, French, Roebuck, Manwell, & Barry, 2005). Clinical geropsychologists, with a strong foundation in aging and health behavior, are in an excellent position to take a holistic approach to helping older adults improve their health behavior. Many individuals with alcohol or drug use problems, however, will need more extensive treatment than that which typically is included in a brief intervention.

Recommendations for adapting psychosocial interventions to older adults have been proposed, which apply to individual as well as group treatment for substance problems. For example, to accommodate hearing loss and cognitive changes of some older clients, adaptations may include using a slower tempo of speech, slower pace of therapy, speaking louder, more frequent repetition of material covered to assist in learning, and use of simpler language (Satre, Knight, & David, 2006). Although these modifications are not difficult to employ, they may require practice by clinicians not used to working with older people. On the other hand, clinical psychologists experienced in working with older adults will already be familiar with the need to make these adaptations when needed.

Further adaptation to psychosocial treatment for alcohol and drug problems may be necessary for older clients with cognitive dysfunction, including greater emphasis on behavioral intervention strategies. For example, assisting an older patient in tracking how many drinks are consumed each day is a concrete behavioral step that can help enhance motivation to cut back on the typical quantity of alcohol consumed. It is also especially important to be aware of possible stigma. Some older adults may have greater feelings of guilt or shame regarding drinking behavior. It has been suggested that this sense of shame may be particularly strong among older women with an alcohol or other substance use problem (Wilsnack, Vogeltanz, Diers, & Wilsnack,

1995). When working with such patients, it is especially important to use an empathic approach and to emphasize that alcohol and drug use problems are not unusual, that there are understandable biological and environmental reasons why people use more alcohol or drugs than is healthy, and that these problems can be addressed effectively by treatment. Alcohol and drug misuse often occurs in the context of other social and mental health problems, which providers must address concurrently. For example, common clinical issues include loss of close friends and partners to death, housing difficulties, decreased physical mobility, and health problems as well as retirement and associated financial challenges. If alcohol or drug dependence is present, withdrawal needs to be carefully monitored to avoid seizures or other adverse events (Curran et al., 2003). When possible, coordination of substance abuse treatment with medical and social services is highly desirable. Psychologists have an important role to play in such service coordination.

Older women may have special clinical needs, including higher rates of comorbid depression than men, greater social isolation (as older women are more likely than older men to be unmarried as a result of being widowed or divorced), and potentially greater guilt around substance use (Blow, 2000). As will be described, treatment retention and alcohol use outcomes may be better for older women compared with older men (Satre, Blow, Chi, & Weisner, 2007; Satre, Mertens, & Weisner, 2004). Recent studies support the potential benefits of women-only AUD and other SUD treatment (Niv & Hser, 2006; Prendergast, Messina, Hall, & Warda, 2011). Unfortunately, the literature specifically on older women in treatment remains underdeveloped at this point in time.

Treatment Outcomes

Brief interventions to reduce hazardous drinking. A small number of studies have examined brief intervention outcomes among older adults. In a primary care sample in which interventions were delivered by physicians, Fleming and Manwell (1999) compared brief advice to reduce drinking with a control group that received a general health booklet. The intervention group had greater reductions in alcohol use than the control group. In another primary care study, Blow and Barry (2000) found a reduction in overall alcohol consumption and heavy drinking compared with controls. In a controlled trial of 631 adults age 55 years and older recruited from three primary care clinics in Southern California, participants were randomized to receive either a booklet on health behaviors or an intervention condition that included personalized feedback on alcohol use risks, a drinking diary, and three telephone counseling sessions from a health educator (Moore et al., 2011). At 3 months, fewer intervention group participants reported hazardous drinking. At 12 months, rates of hazardous drinking were not significantly different, although the intervention participants reported fewer drinks in the prior 7 days.

The Florida Brief Intervention and Treatment for Elders project was a large, 3-year, state-funded pilot program of screening and brief intervention for older adults. Brief interventions were conducted among older adults screened in a range of health and service settings. Prescription medication misuse (i.e., either using medications faster than prescribed, difficulty remembering how much to take, not taking medications, borrowing someone else's prescription, or saving old medications) was the most prevalent substance use problem, followed by alcohol, over-the-counter medications, and illicit substances (Schonfeld et al., 2010). Although specific medications were not recorded, 29.5% were prescribed pain medications, 22.9% anxiolitics, 21.7% sleeping medications, and 2.7% medications for loneliness or sadness. Depression also was prevalent among those with alcohol and prescription medication problems. Brief interventions ranged from one to five sessions. Content included identification of goals to improve quality of life, potential changes in health habits (exercise and use of tobacco, alcohol, medications, and drugs), education about alcohol, medication interactions, consequences of drinking, reasons to quit or cut down drinking, how to handle risky situations for drinking, and medication management strategies. The counselors incorporated motivational interviewing techniques. Those who received the brief intervention had improvement in alcohol and medication misuse and depression measured at 90-day follow-up interviews compared with baseline (Schonfeld et al., 2010). These studies highlight the efficacy of using brief interventions, which psychologists easily can be trained to deliver in a variety of settings that provide services to older adults.

Outpatient specialty alcohol and drug treatment programs. The evidence base relevant to psychological practice with older adults also includes a limited number of studies conducted in mixed-age outpatient treatment programs. In a randomized study of outpatient psychotherapy (Rice, Longabaugh, Beattie, & Noel, 1993), 229 patients with alcohol abuse or dependence were assigned to receive up to 20 sessions of either extended cognitive–behavioral treatment, relationship enhancement, or relationship and vocational enhancement. At 6-month follow-up, there were no significant main effects for age or treatment condition in the sample. Adults age 50 years and older, however, had better alcohol use outcomes in the cognitive–behavioral group, suggesting that cognitive–behavioral treatment would be appropriate in this age-group, at least relative to treatment that incorporates relationship or vocational components.

A small number of studies have examined age-group differences in standard group-model outpatient alcohol and drug treatment programs. These programs typically do not have a single psychotherapy model, but rather participants receive a combination of 12-step–based treatment, cognitive–behavioral–informed treatment (e.g., relapse prevention strategies), and supportive individual or group psychotherapy. From a psychotherapy research perspective, it can be difficult to disentangle the most efficacious components, yet this model remains widely used.

In one such outpatient alcohol and drug treatment program based in the Kaiser Permanente Northern California Health Plan (Sacramento), treatment components included supportive group therapy, education, relapse prevention, and family-oriented therapy. Pharmacotherapy and individual counseling were available as needed. Researchers compared patients age 55 years and over to those 40–54 years and 18–40 years (Satre, Mertens, et al., 2003). At the time of entry into treatment, adults age 55 years and older were more likely to be married and 30% were employed (vs. 63% of middle-age adults and 56% of younger adults). At intake, 49% of older adults reported prior Alcoholics Anonymous attendance compared with 61% of middle-age adults. Attendance at 12-step meetings off-site was encouraged but not required. Examination of treatment retention data found that older adults remained in treatment for an average of 57 days ($SD = 69$) versus 33 days ($SD = 52$) for younger adults. At 6 months, 55% of older adults reported abstinence versus 59% of middle-age adults. An important question that remained was why older adults did not have better outcomes: Older adults had lower hostility and drug dependence, higher abstinence motivation, and longer treatment stays, each of which independently predicted abstinence in the sample as a whole, yet older adult abstinence was not significantly different (Satre, Mertens, et al., 2003).

The sample was followed over time by the research group. At 5-year follow-up (Satre, Mertens, Arean, & Weisner, 2004), differences were found in social support networks by age-group. Older adults reported having fewer people to talk to about personal problems than did younger adults. Only 19% of older adults reported ever having called a 12-step member for help compared with 42% of middle-age adults and 47% of younger adults. Yet older adults were more likely to be married and were less likely to have anyone in their social network who encouraged use of alcohol and drugs (a factor that significantly predicted relapse). This finding indicates that although older adults may have smaller social networks and are less engaged with 12-step programs, support from spouses and the absence of negative influences among friends and family potentially contribute to recovery over time.

Gender differences in clinical characteristics and outcomes among older adults also were examined in this same treatment program. At baseline, older women had later onset of heavy drinking than did men (Satre, Mertens, & Weisner, 2004), but they had similar drinking levels at the time of treatment entry (an average of 16 days consuming five or more drinks each day in the 30 days before treatment entry). At 6 months, women had higher 30-day abstinence rates than men did, but both men and women made substantial reductions in frequency of heavy drinking. This study also examined participants at 7-year follow-up to assess outcomes of women ($n = 25$) and men ($n = 59$; Satre, Blow, et al., 2007). Among women, 56% reported abstinence versus 45% of men. Findings indicated that older women had better long-term outcomes than older men did, but that treatment length was more significant than gender in predicting outcome.

Interest is growing in pharmacological treatment of alcohol and drug problems. Although psychologists may not be involved directly in prescribing these treatments, they should be aware of the potential for medications to augment psychological interventions (Jarosz, Miernik, Wachal, Walczak, & Krumpl, 2013). Outpatient pharmacological approaches to treatment have received limited research attention among older adults. In a small study of 44 veterans over 50 years of age who were enrolled in a 12-week, double-blind, placebo-controlled study of naltrexone, there were no differences in the frequency of any self-reported adverse effects between the placebo- and naltrexone-treated groups (D. Oslin, Liberto, O'Brien, Krois, & Norbeck, 1997). There were no differences between the treatment groups in the number of subjects remaining abstinent or in the number of subjects who relapsed. All placebo-treated subjects relapsed after sampling alcohol, however, whereas only three of six naltrexone-treated subjects met relapse criteria after alcohol exposure ($P = 0.024$). In a somewhat larger study examining age-group differences among alcohol dependent patients ($N = 183$), patients received naltrexone in addition to participating in an outpatient psychosocial alcohol treatment program (D. W. Oslin, Pettinati, & Volpicelli, 2002). Adults age 55 years and older had better adherence to naltrexone and lower rates of relapse than did younger adults. This limited evidence indicates that older adults may be well-positioned to benefit from the increased interest in pharmacological treatments for alcohol dependence.

No studies to date, however, have examined the relative acceptability of behavioral versus pharmacological treatments among older adults.

The recent increases in prescription opioid dependence and overdose-related mortality have raised public health alarms (Bohnert et al., 2011). Older adults are among those at high risk because of the high prevalence of chronic pain (Campbell et al., 2010). Although no studies have specifically examined the efficacy of pharmacological approaches to opioid dependence among older adults (e.g., buprenorphine, methadone), clinicians working with older adults should be aware of these treatment options and work collaboratively with physicians in addressing opioid dependence. Similarly, patients dependent on benzodiazepines and other sedatives or hypnotics require collaboration with a medical provider. The key components of treatment include gradual reduction of benzodiazepine dosage and psychological support as needed (Ashton, 2005). These medical aspects of substance use treatment provide an opportunity for geropsychologists to develop interdisciplinary collaborations to enhance integrated care.

Inpatient treatment. Inpatient treatment has become less frequently utilized in recent years because of its high cost and limited evidence for efficacy over and above outpatient treatment programs. Among older adults, few inpatient treatment outcome studies have been conducted. Blow, Walton, Chermack, Mudd, and Brower (2000) reported on an inpatient program for older adults, with 90 participants over 55 years. The program included supportive, interpersonal, and cognitive–behavioral approaches; the mean length of stay was 20 days ($SD = 7$). Clinical providers were trained to address bereavement, loneliness, and physical and cognitive disability. At 6 months posttreatment, 56% of patients were abstinent, and depression and functional status was improved among most patients. In a residential treatment study of middle-age versus older adults (D. W. Oslin, Slaymaker, Blow, Owen, & Colleran, 2005), patients participated in a 12-step-based 28-day program. The researchers found no differences in abstinence rates. Older adults were less likely to engage in aftercare appointments, although potential reasons for this (e.g., logistical barriers, patients' perceptions regarding the need for aftercare) were not measured.

Case Example

Maria is a 73-year-old, college-educated Caucasian woman who retired 7 years ago from an administrative position with the local public utility company. She has been married for 40 years, and her husband is also retired from work as an engineer. They have three grown children, one of whom has been living with them for the past 6 months because of financial stress associated with job loss. Maria was referred to a psychologist by her primary care physician because her physician was worried about Maria's recent low mood and sleep problems. Since retiring, Maria has progressively become less physically active, has gained 20 pounds, and has had a general increase in somatic complaints including intermittent back pain. Maria's current medications include over-the-counter pain medications and a benzodiazepine (temazepam) for sleep, and she reports using each of these two to three nights per week.

Maria has a long history of alcohol use, which she considers to be normal social drinking among her friends. She indicates that at one point in her 40s her husband expressed concern about her drinking level and that she reduced her consumption in response to his complaints. For the past 20 years, she typically has had a mixed drink after work, and sometimes one more with dinner. Since retiring she has stopped drinking hard alcohol, instead drinking two to three glasses of wine most nights, sometimes starting in the afternoon, and on occasion drinks as much a four to five glasses of wine.

Maria also has suffered from intermittent depressed mood for many years. She never has taken medication for depression because she does not think there is anything unusual about feeling "down" sometimes. At the suggestion of her physician, she has agreed to visit a psychologist. Maria's husband also asked her to talk to the psychologist about alcohol consumption because he is concerned about her evening sleepiness, late-night wakefulness, and occasional slurred speech. Maria enjoys her nightly wine, however, and thinks that it lifts her mood and relieves her aches and pains at the end of the day.

As with many people seeking services in a mental health setting, Maria would like to feel better but is unsure of exactly what would help. She is willing to attend psychotherapy because her physician suggested it, and because she is hopeful that her pain level and sleep also could be addressed. She describes herself as "blue" but not necessarily depressed, and does not see a connection between her drinking and low mood. Maria's physician may or may not have advised her about potential interactions between alcohol, antidepressants, and pain medication. Although Maria's husband has expressed concerns about her drinking, she does not see alcohol as an important problem.

On the basis of the initial description of this patient, there are a number of areas to assess further before implementing a treatment strategy. In the alcohol and drug use domain, important unknowns include current and past alcohol-related problems, symptoms of abuse or dependence, potential patterns of concurrent sleep and pain medication and alcohol use, and family history of substance-related problems. An instrument such as the MAST–G could be used to inquire about alcohol-related problems specific to older adults. In gathering information that may be useful in developing a motivational intervention, it also would be useful to know more about how important it is from Maria's perspective to cut back on her drinking (since it currently appears to be low) as well as her confidence that she could cut back if she wanted to. In addition, broader psychological evaluation would include mental status, depression and anxiety symptoms, sleep patterns, family relationship stressors and strengths, other sources of social support and any prior experience with mental health or substance use treatment providers, and educational and social history.

As a geropsychologist working with Maria, assuming that her current motivation to cut back on her drinking is low, a brief intervention using motivational interviewing is a reasonable strategy to try, and this approach could be integrated into a psychosocial intervention for depression (Satre, Delucchi, Lichtmacher, Sterling, & Weisner, 2013). Motivational interviewing is described in greater detail earlier in the chapter. In presenting this approach as part of the overall treatment agenda, the clinician might say upfront that in addition to addressing low mood and pain management strategies, it also is important to explore a bit further how alcohol fits into the picture and to get Maria's agreement upfront. In working to enhance Maria's motivation to reduce drinking, it would be helpful to ask about what she likes about drinking (i.e., factors maintaining her current drinking behavior), such as using it to relax or lift her mood, to fill empty time in the evenings, or to bond with her adult child living at home, or potentially as part of her pain management strategy. Conversely, it is also important to ask about any potential downsides of her current drinking pattern, such as her husband complaining about how much she drinks or how she feels the next day. The aim of this approach is to get Maria to start considering how her current alcohol consumption is affecting important aspects of her life and to start to verbalize some concern in session. Gentle incorporation of psychoeducation regarding recommended drinking limits (no more than one drink per day), the risks of mixing alcohol and medications, or the adverse impact of drinking on sleep also could be incorporated.

Assuming that Maria agrees to reduce her drinking level, a number of strategies are possible depending on what she is willing to try. One simple approach would be to ask her to write down how many drinks she has each day as part of an activity tracking log to help monitor how successful she is in cutting back. Similarly, using a weekly calendar, you could track what kinds of behavioral changes she is able to make in substituting other activities in the evening instead of drinking. In subsequent psychotherapy sessions, the success of these strategies and any barriers she encounters could be examined. For example, some patients have trouble keeping to a safe limit once they start drinking. If cutting back seems too difficult, stopping drinking altogether may be a better approach. If abstinence is Maria's goal, and it appears that she needs more intensive assistance than her psychologist can provide once a week (while simultaneously working on low mood, sleep problems, etc.), seeking specialized outpatient alcohol and drug use treatment would be an excellent option to consider and potentially could run concurrently with individual psychotherapy.

CONCLUSION

The aging of the U.S. population and rise in the proportion of older adults in the United States have led to increased interest in alcohol and drug use issues among older adults. Nationally representative epidemiologic studies have provided a better sense of alcohol and drug use patterns among older adults. This recent interest has only minimally extended to substances other than alcohol, however, and relatively little is known about the extent of illicit drug use or misuse of prescription drugs in older age as well as how to best screen and assess these problems. This is despite evidence that treatment admissions for illicit drug use and prescription drug misuse are increasing, whereas treatment admissions for alcohol use disorders may be decreasing in older age (Wu & Blazer, 2011). Although older adults can benefit from treatment in specialty care settings (Satre, Mertens, et al., 2003), most do not receive these services. As increased efforts are made to integrate behavioral health and primary care, more information on how to efficiently and effectively identify and treat substance abuse in diverse groups of older adults in a range of health and social service settings is needed.

Historically, the study of alcohol and drug use among older adults has been somewhat neglected: Within the alcohol and drug use field, greater prevalence of substance use and associated problems among younger adults than among older adults means that younger adults receive more attention. Likewise, the trend for many individuals to reduce or eliminate substance use as they age, combined with the relatively greater prevalence of problems such as dementia, depression, and anxiety in late life, has resulted in an underemphasis on substance use within clinical gerontology. As described in this chapter, however, for those older adults who are affected by alcohol and drug problems, the consequences are substantial in terms of health and well-being. Therefore, expertise in addressing alcohol and drug problems is an important component of the skill set for clinical geropsychologists.

As geropsychologists are aware, older age can be associated with certain benefits in terms of mental health. Aging is not simply a process of decline, as older adults generally tend to be happier, less angry, and less stressed than are younger adults (Stone, Schwartz, Broderick, & Deaton, 2010). Problematic drinking and substance use in older adulthood, however, has the potential to negate the benefits of aging by decreasing health and well-being. Additional research investigating drinking and substance use patterns, risk factors for the development of problems, the process of treatment initiation and engagement, and intervention strategies for older adults is needed to improve understanding, strengthen assessment efforts, and optimize treatment opportunities. As the baby boom cohort ages and the number of older adults with alcohol and drug use problems grows, geropsychologists will find increasing opportunities to contribute to this important component of late-life clinical research and mental health service provision.

References

Academic ED SBIRT Research Collaborative. (2007). The impact of screening, brief intervention, and referral for treatment on emergency department patients' alcohol use. *Annals of Emergency Medicine, 50,* 699–710.

Adams, W. L., Barry, K. L., & Fleming, M. F. (1996). Screening for problem drinking in older primary care patients. *JAMA, 276,* 1964–1967. doi:10.1001/jama.1996.03540240042028

Administration on Aging. (2013). *A profile of older Americans: 2012.* Retrieved from http://www.aoa.gov/Aging_Statistics/Profile/index.aspx

Aira, M., Hartikainen, S., & Sulkava, R. (2008). Drinking alcohol for medicinal purposes by people aged over 75: A community-based interview study. *Family Practice, 25,* 445–449. doi:10.1093/fampra/cmn065

American Psychiatric Association. (2000). *Diagnostic and statistical manual of mental disorders* (4th ed., text rev.). Washington, DC: Author.

American Psychiatric Association. (2013). *Diagnostic and statistical manual of mental disorders* (5th ed.). Washington, DC: Author.

Ashton, H. (2005). The diagnosis and management of benzodiazepine dependence. *Current Opinion in Psychiatry, 18,* 249–255. doi:10.1097/01.yco.0000165594.60434.84

Babor, T. F., Higgins-Biddle, J. C., Saunders, J. B., & Monteiro, M. G. (2001). *The Alcohol Use Disorders Identification Test (AUDIT): Guidelines for use in primary care* (2nd ed.). Geneva, Switzerland: World Health Organization.

Barnes, A. J., Moore, A. A., Xu, H., Ang, A., Tallen, L., Mirkin, M., & Ettner, S. L. (2010). Prevalence and correlates of at-risk drinking among older adults: The project SHARE study. *Journal of General Internal Medicine, 25,* 840–846. doi:10.1007/s11606-010-1341-x

Bem, D. J. (1967). Self-perception: An alternative interpretation of cognitive dissonance phenomena. *Psychological Review, 74,* 183–200. doi:10.1037/h0024835

Blazer, D. G., & Wu, L. T. (2009a). The epidemiology of substance use and disorders among middle aged and elderly community adults: National Survey on Drug Use and Health. *American Journal of Geriatric Psychiatry, 17,* 237–245. doi:10.1097/JGP.0b013e318190b8ef

Blazer, D. G., & Wu, L. T. (2009b). Nonprescription use of pain relievers by middle-aged and elderly community-living adults: National Survey on Drug Use and Health. *Journal of the American Geriatrics Society, 57,* 1252–1257. doi:10.1111/j.1532-5415.2009.02306.x

Blow, F. C. (1998). *Substance abuse among older adults. Treatment Improvement Series Protocol (TIP) Series 26.* DHHS Publication No. (SMA) 98-3179. Rockville, MD: Center for Substance Abuse Treatment, Substance Abuse and Mental Health Services Administration.

Blow, F. C. (2000). Treatment of older women with alcohol problems: Meeting the challenge for a special population. *Alcoholism: Clinical and Experimental Research, 24,* 1257–1266. doi:10.1111/j.1530-0277.2000.tb02092.x

Blow, F. C., & Barry, K. L. (2000). Older patients with at-risk and problem drinking patterns: New developments in brief interventions. *Journal of Geriatric Psychiatry and Neurology, 13,* 115–123. doi:10.1177/089198870001300304

Blow, F. C., & Barry, K. L. (2002). Use and misuse of alcohol among older women. *Alcohol Research and Health, 26,* 308–315.

Blow, F. C., & Barry, K. L. (2012). Alcohol and substance misuse in older adults. *Current Psychiatry Reports, 14,* 310–319. doi:10.1007/s11920-012-0292-9

Blow, F. C., Brockmann, L. M., & Barry, K. L. (2004). Role of alcohol in late-life suicide. *Alcoholism: Clinical and Experimental Research, 28,* 48S–56S. doi:10.1111/j.1530-0277.2004.tb03603.x

Blow, F. C., Brower, K. J., Schulenberg, J. E., Demo-Dananberg, L. M., Young, J. P., & Beresford, T. P. (1992). The Michigan Alcoholism Screening Test—Geriatric Version (MAST–G): A new elderly-specific screening instrument. *Alcoholism: Clinical and Experimental Research, 16,* 372.

Blow, F. C., Walton, M. A., Barry, K. L., Coyne, J. C., Mudd, S. A., & Copeland, L. A. (2000). The relationship between alcohol problems and health functioning of older adults in primary care settings. *Journal of the American Geriatrics Society, 48,* 769–774.

Blow, F. C., Walton, M. A., Chermack, S. T., Mudd, S. A., & Brower, K. J. (2000). Older adult treatment outcome following elder-specific inpatient alcoholism treatment. *Journal of Substance Abuse Treatment, 19,* 67–75. doi:10.1016/S0740-5472(99)00101-4

Bohnert, A. S., Valenstein, M., Bair, M. J., Ganoczy, D., McCarthy, J. F., Ilgen, M. A., & Blow, F. C. (2011). Association between opioid prescribing patterns and opioid overdose-related deaths. *JAMA, 305,* 1315–1321. doi:10.1001/jama.2011.370

Bowie, M. W., & Slattum, P. W. (2007). Pharmacodynamics in older adults: A review. *American Journal of Geriatric Pharmacotherapy, 5,* 263–303. doi:10.1016/j.amjopharm.2007.10.001

Bradley, K. A., Badrinath, S., Bush, K., Boyd-Wickizer, J., & Anawalt, B. (1998). Medical risks for women who drink alcohol. *Journal of General Internal Medicine, 13,* 627–639. doi:10.1046/j.1525-1497.1998.cr187.x

Brennan, P. L., Kagay, C. R., Geppert, J. J., & Moos, R. H. (2001). Predictors and outcomes of outpatient mental health care: a 4-year prospective study of elderly Medicare patients with substance use disorders. *Medical Care, 39,* 39–49. doi:10.1097/00005650-200101000-00006

Brennan, P. L., Schutte, K. K., & Moos, R. H. (2005). Pain and use of alcohol to manage pain: Prevalence and 3-year outcomes among older problem and non-problem drinkers. *Addiction, 100,* 777–786. doi:10.1111/j.1360-0443.2005.01074.x

Brennan, P. L., Schutte, K. K., & Moos, R. H. (2010). Retired status and older adults' 10-year drinking trajectories. *Journal of Studies on Alcohol and Drugs, 71,* 165–168.

Breslow, R. A., & Smothers, B. (2004). Drinking patterns of older Americans: National Health Interview Surveys, 1997-2001. *Journal of Studies on Alcohol, 65,* 232–240.

Bridevaux, I. P., Bradley, K. A., Bryson, C. L., McDonell, M. B., & Fihn, S. D. (2004). Alcohol screening results in elderly male veterans: Association with health status and mortality. *Journal of the American Geriatrics Society, 52,* 1510–1517. doi:10.1111/j.1532-5415.2004.52414.x

Bryson, C. L., Au, D. H., Sun, H., Williams, E. C., Kivlahan, D. R., & Bradley, K. A. (2008). Alcohol screening scores and medication nonadherence. *Annals of Internal Medicine, 149,* 795–804. doi:10.7326/0003-4819-149-11-200812020-00004

Campbell, C. I., Weisner, C., Leresche, L., Ray, G. T., Saunders, K., Sullivan, M. D., . . . Von Korff, M. (2010). Age and gender trends in long-term opioid analgesic use for non-cancer pain. *American Journal of Public Health, 100,* 2541–2547. doi:10.2105/AJPH.2009.180646

Chan, K. K., Chiu, K. C., & Chu, L. W. (2010). Association between alcohol consumption and cognitive impairment in Southern Chinese older adults. *International Journal of Geriatric Psychiatry, 25,* 1272–1279. doi:10.1002/gps.2470

Cherpitel, C. J. (2007). Alcohol and injuries: A review of international emergency room studies since 1995. *Drug and Alcohol Review, 26,* 201–214. doi:10.1080/09595230601146686

Cherpitel, C. J., & Ye, Y. (2008). Drug use and problem drinking associated with primary care and emergency room utilization in the US general population: Data from the 2005 national alcohol survey. *Drug and Alcohol Dependence, 97,* 226–230. doi:10.1016/j.drugalcdep.2008.03.033

Compton, P. A., Wu, S. M., Schieffer, B., Pham, Q., & Naliboff, B. D. (2008). Introduction of a self-report version of the Prescription Drug Use Questionnaire and relationship to medication agreement noncompliance. *Journal of Pain and Symptom Management, 36,* 383–395. doi:10.1016/j.jpainsymman.2007.11.006

Compton, W. M., Thomas, Y. F., Stinson, F. S., & Grant, B. F. (2007). Prevalence, correlates, disability, and comorbidity of *DSM–IV* drug abuse and dependence in the United States: Results from the National Epidemiologic Survey on Alcohol and Related Conditions. *Archives of General Psychiatry, 64,* 566–576. doi:10.1001/archpsyc.64.5.566

Cornelius, J. R., Salloum, I. M., Mezzich, J., Cornelius, M. D., Fabrega, H., Jr., Ehler, J. G., . . . Mann, J. J. (1995). Disproportionate suicidality in patients with comorbid major depression and alcoholism. *American Journal of Psychiatry, 152,* 358–364.

Cosio, D., Heckman, T. G., Anderson, T., Heckman, B. D., Garske, J., & McCarthy, J. (2010). Telephone-administered motivational interviewing to reduce risky sexual behavior in HIV-infected rural persons: A pilot randomized clinical trial. *Sexually Transmitted Diseases, 37,* 140–146. doi:10.1097/OLQ.0b013e3181c18975

Curran, H. V., Collins, R., Fletcher, S., Kee, S. C., Woods, B., & Iliffe, S. (2003). Older adults and withdrawal from benzodiazepine hypnotics in general practice: Effects on cognitive function, sleep, mood and quality of life. *Psychological Medicine, 33,* 1223–1237. doi:10.1017/S0033291703008213

Curtis, J. R., Geller, G., Stokes, E. J., Levine, D. M., & Moore, R. D. (1989). Characteristics, diagnosis, and treatment of alcoholism in elderly patients.

Journal of the American Geriatrics Society, 37, 310–316.

DiNitto, D. M., & Choi, N. G. (2011). Marijuana use among older adults in the U.S.A.: User characteristics, patterns of use, and implications for intervention. *International Psychogeriatrics, 23,* 732–741.

Dowling, G. J., Weiss, S. R., & Condon, T. P. (2008). Drugs of abuse and the aging brain. *Neuropsychopharmacology, 33,* 209–218. doi:10.1038/sj.npp.1301412

Dunn, C., Deroo, L., & Rivara, F. P. (2001). The use of brief interventions adapted from motivational interviewing across behavioral domains: A systematic review. *Addiction, 96,* 1725–1742. doi:10.1046/j.1360-0443.2001.961217253.x

Duru, O. K., Xu, H., Tseng, C. H., Mirkin, M., Ang, A., Tallen, L., . . . Ettner, S. L. (2010). Correlates of alcohol-related discussions between older adults and their physicians. *Journal of the American Geriatrics Society, 58,* 2369–2374. doi:10.1111/j.1532-5415.2010.03176.x

Ewing, J. A. (1984). Detecting alcoholism: The CAGE questionnaire. *JAMA, 252,* 1905–1907. doi:10.1001/jama.1984.03350140051025

Festinger, L. (1957). *A theory of cognitive dissonance.* Stanford, CA: Stanford University Press.

Fillmore, K. M. (1987). Women's drinking across the adult life course as compared to men's: A longitudinal and cohort analysis. *British Journal of Addiction, 82,* 801–811. doi:10.1111/j.1360-0443.1987.tb01547.x

Finlayson, R. E., & Hurt, R. D. (1998). Medical consequences of heavy drinking by the elderly. In E. S. L. Gomberg, A. M. Hegedus, & R. A. Zucker (Eds.), *Alcohol problems and aging* (pp. 193–212). NIH Publication 98-4163. Bethesda, MD: National Institute on Alcohol Abuse and Alcoholism.

Fleming, M., & Manwell, L. B. (1999). Brief intervention in primary care settings. A primary treatment method for at-risk, problem, and dependent drinkers. *Alcohol Research and Health, 23,* 128–137.

Freyer-Adam, J., Coder, B., Bischof, G., Baumeister, S. E., Rumpf, H. J., John, U., & Hapke, U. (2008). Predicting utilization of formal and informal help among general hospital inpatients with alcohol use disorders. *International Journal of Methods in Psychiatric Research, 17*(Suppl. 1), S70–S73. doi:10.1002/mpr.252

Gambert, S. R., & Katsoyannis, K. K. (1995). Alcohol-related medical disorders of older heavy drinkers. In T. P. Beresford & E. S. Gomberg (Eds.), *Alcohol and aging* (pp. 70–81). New York, NY: Oxford University Press.

Gfroerer, J., Penne, M., Pemberton, M., & Folsom, R. (2003). Substance abuse treatment need among older adults in 2020: The impact of the aging baby-boom cohort. *Drug and Alcohol Dependence, 69,* 127–135. doi:10.1016/S0376-8716(02)00307-1

Gomberg, E. S. (2003). Treatment for alcohol-related problems: Special populations: research opportunities. *Recent Developments in Alcoholism, 16,* 313–333. doi:10.1007/0-306-47939-7_22

Graham, K., & Schmidt, G. (1998). The effects of drinking on health of older adults. *American Journal of Drug and Alcohol Abuse, 24,* 465–481. doi:10.3109/00952999809016910

Greenfield, S. F., Manwani, S. G., & Nargiso, J. E. (2003). Epidemiology of substance use disorders in women. *Obstetrics and Gynecology Clinics of North America, 30,* 413–446. doi:10.1016/S0889-8545(03)00072-X

Grella, C. E., & Lovinger, K. (2012). Gender differences in physical and mental health outcomes among an aging cohort of individuals with a history of heroin dependence. *Addictive Behaviors, 37,* 306–312. doi:10.1016/j.addbeh.2011.11.028

Han, B., Gfroerer, J. C., Colliver, J. D., & Penne, M. A. (2009). Substance use disorder among older adults in the United States in 2020. *Addiction, 104,* 88–96. doi:10.1111/j.1360-0443.2008.02411.x

Herd, D., & Grube, J. (1996). Black identity and drinking in the US: A national study. *Addiction, 91,* 845–857. doi:10.1111/j.1360-0443.1996.tb03579.x

Holdcraft, L. C., & Iacono, W. G. (2002). Cohort effects on gender differences in alcohol dependence. *Addiction, 97,* 1025–1036. doi:10.1046/j.1360-0443.2002.00142.x

Hurt, R. D., Finlayson, R. E., Morse, R. M., & Davis, L. J., Jr. (1988). Alcoholism in elderly persons: Medical aspects and prognosis of 216 inpatients. *Mayo Clinic Proceedings, 63,* 753–760. doi:10.1016/S0025-6196(12)62354-4

Jarosz, J., Miernik, K., Wachal, M., Walczak, J., & Krumpl, G. (2013). Naltrexone (50 mg) plus psychotherapy in alcohol-dependent patients: A meta-analysis of randomized controlled trials. *American Journal of Drug and Alcohol Abuse, 39,* 144–160. doi:10.3109/00952990.2013.796961

Johnson-Greene, D., Adams, K. M., Gilman, S., & Junck, L. (2002). Relationship between neuropsychological and emotional functioning in severe chronic alcoholism. *Clinical Neuropsychologist, 16,* 300–309. doi:10.1076/clin.16.3.300.13845

Klein, W. C., & Jess, C. (2002). One last pleasure? Alcohol use among elderly people in nursing homes. *Health and Social Work, 27,* 193–203. doi:10.1093/hsw/27.3.193

Krause, N. (1991). Stress, religiosity, and abstinence from alcohol. *Psychology and Aging, 6,* 134–144. doi:10.1037/0882-7974.6.1.134

Levenson, M. R., Aldwin, C. M., & Spiro, A., III. (1998). Age, cohort and period effects on alcohol consumption and problem drinking: Findings from the Normative Aging Study. *Journal of Studies on Alcohol*, *59*, 712–722.

Lo Sasso, A. T., & Lyons, J. S. (2002). The effects of copayments on substance abuse treatment expenditures and treatment reoccurrence. *Psychiatric Services*, *53*, 1605–1611. doi:10.1176/appi.ps. 53.12.1605

Lovejoy, T. I., Heckman, T. G., Suhr, J. A., Anderson, T., Heckman, B. D., & France, C. R. (2011). Telephone-administered motivational interviewing reduces risky sexual behavior in HIV-positive late middle-age and older adults: A pilot randomized controlled trial. *AIDS and Behavior*, *15*, 1623–1634. doi:10.1007/s10461-011-0016-x

Ma, J., Betts, N. M., & Hampl, J. S. (2000). Clustering of lifestyle behaviors: The relationship between cigarette smoking, alcohol consumption, and dietary intake. *American Journal of Health Promotion*, *15*, 107–117. doi:10.4278/0890-1171-15.2.107

McCabe, S. E., Boyd, C. J., & Teter, C. J. (2009). Subtypes of nonmedical prescription drug misuse. *Drug and Alcohol Dependence*, *102*, 63–70. doi:10.1016/j.drugalcdep.2009.01.007

Merrick, E. L., Horgan, C. M., Hodgkin, D., Garnick, D. W., Houghton, S. F., Panas, L., . . . Blow, F. C. (2008). Unhealthy drinking patterns in older adults: Prevalence and associated characteristics. *Journal of the American Geriatrics Society*, *56*, 214–223. doi:10.1111/j.1532-5415.2007.01539.x

Merrick, E. L., Perloff, J., & Tompkins, C. P. (2010). Emergency department utilization patterns for Medicare beneficiaries with serious mental disorders. *Psychiatric Services*, *61*, 628–631. doi:10.1176/appi.ps.61.6.628

Mertens, J. R., Flisher, A. J., Satre, D. D., & Weisner, C. M. (2008). The role of medical conditions and primary care services in 5-year substance use outcomes among chemical dependency treatment patients. *Drug and Alcohol Dependence*, *98*, 45–53. doi:10.1016/j.drugalcdep.2008.04.007

Meyerhoff, D. J., Bode, C., Nixon, S. J., de Bruin, E. A., Bode, J. C., & Seitz, H. K. (2005). Health risks of chronic moderate and heavy alcohol consumption: How much is too much? *Alcoholism: Clinical and Experimental Research*, *29*, 1334–1340. doi:10.1097/01.ALC.0000171488.63823.09

Miller, W., & Rollnick, S. (1991). *Motivational interviewing: Preparing people to change addictive behavior*. New York, NY: Guilford Press.

Miller, W. R., & Rollnick, S. (2002). *Motivational interviewing: Preparing people for change* (2nd ed.). New York, NY: Guilford Press.

Moore, A. A., Beck, J. C., Babor, T. F., Hays, R. D., & Reuben, D. B. (2002). Beyond alcoholism: Identifying older, at-risk drinkers in primary care. *Journal of Studies on Alcohol*, *63*(Suppl.), 316–324.

Moore, A. A., Blow, F. C., Hoffing, M., Welgreen, S., Davis, J. W., Lin, J. C., . . . Barry, K. L. (2011). Primary care-based intervention to reduce at-risk drinking in older adults: A randomized controlled trial. *Addiction*, *106*, 111–120. doi:10.1111/j.1360-0443.2010.03229.x

Moore, A. A., Endo, J. O., & Carter, M. K. (2003). Is there a relationship between excessive drinking and functional impairment in older persons? *Journal of the American Geriatrics Society*, *51*, 44–49. doi:10.1034/j.1601-5215.2002.51008.x

Moore, A. A., Gould, R., Reuben, D. B., Greendale, G. A., Carter, M. K., Zhou, K., & Karlamangla, A. (2005). Longitudinal patterns and predictors of alcohol consumption in the United States. *American Journal of Public Health*, *95*, 458–464. doi:10.2105/AJPH.2003.019471

Moos, R. H., Brennan, P. L., Schutte, K. K., & Moos, B. S. (2004). High-risk alcohol consumption and late-life alcohol use problems. *American Journal of Public Health*, *94*, 1985–1991. doi:10.2105/AJPH.94.11.1985

Moos, R. H., Brennan, P. L., Schutte, K. K., & Moos, B. S. (2005). Older adults' health and changes in late-life drinking patterns. *Aging and Mental Health*, *9*, 49–59. doi:10.1080/13607860412331323818

Moos, R. H., Brennan, P. L., Schutte, K. K., & Moos, B. S. (2010a). Older adults' health and late-life drinking patterns: A 20-year perspective. *Aging and Mental Health*, *14*, 33–43. doi:10.1080/13607860902918264

Moos, R. H., Brennan, P. L., Schutte, K. K., & Moos, B. S. (2010b). Spouses of older adults with late-life drinking problems: Health, family, and social functioning. *Journal of Studies on Alcohol and Drugs*, *71*, 506–514.

Moos, R. H., Schutte, K. K., Brennan, P. L., & Moos, B. S. (2009). Older adults' alcohol consumption and late-life drinking problems: A 20-year perspective. *Addiction*, *104*, 1293–1302. doi:10.1111/j.1360-0443.2009.02604.x

Moyer, A., & Finney, J. W. (2004–2005). Brief interventions for alcohol problems: Factors that facilitate implementation. *Alcohol Research and Health*, *28*, 44–50.

Moyer, A., Finney, J. W., Swearingen, C. E., & Vergun, P. (2002). Brief interventions for alcohol problems: A meta-analytic review of controlled investigations in treatment-seeking and non-treatment-seeking populations. *Addiction*, *97*, 279–292. doi:10.1046/j.1360-0443.2002.00018.x

Moyers, T. B., Martin, T., Manuel, J. K., Hendrickson, S. M., & Miller, W. R. (2005). Assessing competence in the use of motivational interviewing. *Journal of Substance Abuse Treatment, 28,* 19–26. doi:10.1016/j.jsat.2004.11.001

Mundt, M. P., French, M. T., Roebuck, M. C., Manwell, L. B., & Barry, K. L. (2005). Brief physician advice for problem drinking among older adults: An economic analysis of costs and benefits. *Journal of Studies on Alcohol, 66,* 389–394.

National Institute on Alcohol Abuse and Alcoholism. (2000). *10th special report to the U.S. Congress on alcohol and health: Highlights from current research, June 2000.* Washington, DC: Government Printing Office.

National Institute on Alcohol Abuse and Alcoholism. (2010). *Rethinking drinking: Alcohol and your health.* Retrieved from http://rethinkingdrinking.niaaa.nih.gov

National Institute on Alcohol Abuse and Alcoholism. (2013). *What is a standard drink?* Retrieved from http://www.niaaa.nih.gov/alcohol-health/overview-alcohol-consumption/standard-drink

Niv, N., & Hser, Y. I. (2006). Women-only and mixed-gender drug abuse treatment programs: Service needs, utilization and outcomes. *Drug and Alcohol Dependence, 87,* 194–201. doi:10.1016/j.drugalcdep.2006.08.017

Onder, G., Landi, F., Della Vedova, C., Atkinson, H., Pedone, C., Cesari, M., . . . Gambassi, G. (2002). Moderate alcohol consumption and adverse drug reactions among older adults. *Pharmacoepidemiology and Drug Safety, 11,* 385–392. doi:10.1002/pds.721

Oslin, D., Liberto, J. G., O'Brien, J., Krois, S., & Norbeck, J. (1997). Naltrexone as an adjunctive treatment for older patients with alcohol dependence. *American Journal of Geriatric Psychiatry, 5,* 324–332. doi:10.1097/00019442-199700540-00007

Oslin, D. W., Pettinati, H., & Volpicelli, J. R. (2002). Alcoholism treatment adherence: Older age predicts better adherence and drinking outcomes. *American Journal of Geriatric Psychiatry, 10,* 740–747. doi:10.1097/00019442-200211000-00013

Oslin, D. W., Slaymaker, V. J., Blow, F. C., Owen, P. L., & Colleran, C. (2005). Treatment outcomes for alcohol dependence among middle-aged and older adults. *Addictive Behaviors, 30,* 1431–1436. doi:10.1016/j.addbeh.2005.01.007

Philpot, M., Pearson, N., Petratou, V., Dayanandan, R., Silverman, M., & Marshall, J. (2003). Screening for problem drinking in older people referred to a mental health service: A comparison of CAGE and AUDIT. *Aging and Mental Health, 7,* 171–175. doi:10.1080/1360786031000101120

Prendergast, M. L., Messina, N. P., Hall, E. A., & Warda, U. S. (2011). The relative effectiveness of women-only and mixed-gender treatment for substance-abusing women. *Journal of Substance Abuse Treatment, 40,* 336–348. doi:10.1016/j.jsat.2010.12.001

Prochaska, J. O., & DiClemente, C. C. (1984). *The transtheoretical approach: Crossing the traditional boundaries of therapy.* Melbourne, FL: Krieger.

Redgrave, G. W., Swartz, K. L., & Romanoski, A. J. (2003). Alcohol misuse by women. *International Review of Psychiatry, 15,* 256–268. doi:10.1080/0954026031000136875

Reid, M. C., Tinetti, M. E., Brown, C. J., & Concato, J. (1998). Physician awareness of alcohol use disorders among older patients. *Journal of General Internal Medicine, 13,* 729–734. doi:10.1046/j.1525-1497.1998.00223.x

Reid, M. C., Tinetti, M. E., O'Connor, P. G., Kosten, T. R., & Concato, J. (2003). Measuring alcohol consumption among older adults: A comparison of available methods. *American Journal on Addictions, 12,* 211–219. doi:10.1111/j.1521-0391.2003.tb00649.x

Rice, C., Longabaugh, R., Beattie, M., & Noel, N. E. (1993). Age group differences in response to treatment for problematic alcohol involvement. *Addiction, 88,* 1369–1375. doi:10.1111/j.1360-0443.1993.tb02023.x

Ridlon, F. (1988). *A fallen angel: The status insularity of the female alcoholic.* Lewisburg, PA: Bucknell University Press.

Rogers, C. (1961). *On becoming a person: A therapist's view of psychotherapy.* London, England: Constable.

Sacco, P., Bucholz, K. K., & Spitznagel, E. L. (2009). Alcohol use among older adults in the national epidemiologic survey on alcohol and related conditions: A latent class analysis. *Journal of Studies on Alcohol and Drugs, 70,* 829–838.

Salloum, I. M., Mezzich, J. E., Cornelius, J., Day, N. L., Daley, D., & Kirisci, L. (1995). Clinical profile of comorbid major depression and alcohol use disorders in an initial psychiatric evaluation. *Comprehensive Psychiatry, 36,* 260–266. doi:10.1016/S0010-440X(95)90070-5

Satre, D. D., & Arean, P. A. (2005). Effects of gender, ethnicity, and medical illness on drinking cessation in older primary care patients. *Journal of Aging and Health, 17,* 70–84. doi:10.1177/0898264304272785

Satre, D. D., Blow, F. C., Chi, F. W., & Weisner, C. (2007). Gender differences in seven-year alcohol and drug treatment outcomes among older adults. *American Journal on Addictions, 16,* 216–221. doi:10.1080/10550490701375673

Satre, D. D., Chi, F. W., Mertens, J. R., & Weisner, C. M. (2012). Effects of age and life transitions on alcohol and drug treatment outcome over nine years. *Journal of Studies on Alcohol and Drugs, 73,* 459–468.

Satre, D. D., Delucchi, K., Lichtmacher, J., Sterling, S. A., & Weisner, C. (2013). Motivational Interviewing to reduce hazardous drinking and drug use among depression patients. *Journal of Substance Abuse Treatment, 44*, 323–329. doi:10.1016/j.jsat.2012.08.008

Satre, D. D., Gordon, N. P., & Weisner, C. (2007). Alcohol consumption, medical conditions, and health behavior among older adults. *American Journal of Health Behavior, 31*, 238–248. doi:10.5993/AJHB.31.3.2

Satre, D. D., Knight, B. G., & David, S. (2006). Cognitive behavioral interventions with older adults: Integrating clinical and gerontological research. *Professional Psychology: Research and Practice, 37*, 489–498. doi:10.1037/0735-7028.37.5.489

Satre, D. D., Knight, B. G., Dickson-Fuhrmann, E., & Jarvik, L. F. (2003). Predictors of alcohol-treatment seeking in a sample of older veterans in the GET SMART program. *Journal of the American Geriatrics Society, 51*, 380–386. doi:10.1046/j.1532-5415.2003.51112.x

Satre, D. D., Knight, B. G., Dickson-Fuhrmann, E., & Jarvik, L. F. (2004). Substance abuse treatment initiation among older adults in the GET SMART program: Effects of depression and cognitive status. *Aging and Mental Health, 8*, 346–354. doi:10.1080/13607860410001709692

Satre, D. D., Mertens, J., Arean, P. A., & Weisner, C. (2003). Contrasting outcomes of older versus middle-aged and younger adult chemical dependency patients in a managed care program. *Journal of Studies on Alcohol, 64*, 520–530.

Satre, D. D., Mertens, J. R., Arean, P. A., & Weisner, C. (2004). Five-year alcohol and drug treatment outcomes of older adults versus middle-aged and younger adults in a managed care program. *Addiction, 99*, 1286–1297. doi:10.1111/j.1360-0443.2004.00831.x

Satre, D. D., Mertens, J. R., & Weisner, C. (2004). Gender differences in treatment outcomes for alcohol dependence among older adults. *Journal of Studies on Alcohol, 65*, 638–642.

Satre, D. D., & Olson, S. L. (2009). Specialty approaches to older adults. In P. Korsmeyer & H. Kranzler (Eds.), *Encyclopedia of drugs, alcohol and addictive behavior* (3rd ed., pp. 213–216). Detroit, MI: Macmillan Reference.

Satre, D. D., Sterling, S., Mackin, R. S., & Weisner, C. (2011). Patterns of alcohol and drug use among depressed older adults seeking outpatient psychiatric services. *American Journal of Geriatric Psychiatry, 19*, 695–703. doi:10.1097/JGP.0b013e3181f17f0a

Schonfeld, L., & Dupree, L. W. (1991). Antecedents of drinking for early- and late-onset elderly alcohol abusers. *Journal of Studies on Alcohol, 52*, 587–592.

Schonfeld, L., King-Kallimanis, B. L., Duchene, D. M., Etheridge, R. L., Herrera, J. R., Barry, K. L., & Lynn, N. (2010). Screening and brief intervention for substance misuse among older adults: The Florida BRITE project. *American Journal of Public Health, 100*, 108–114. doi:10.2105/AJPH.2008.149534

Schutte, K. K., Brennan, P. L., & Moos, R. H. (1998). Predicting the development of late-life late-onset drinking problems: A 7-year prospective study. *Alcoholism: Clinical and Experimental Research, 22*, 1349–1358.

Shaw, B. A., Krause, N., Liang, J., & McGeever, K. (2011). Age differences in long-term patterns of change in alcohol consumption among aging adults. *Journal of Aging and Health, 23*, 207–227. doi:10.1177/0898264310381276

Simon, G. E., & Ludman, E. J. (2006). Outcome of new benzodiazepine prescriptions to older adults in primary care. *General Hospital Psychiatry, 28*, 374–378. doi:10.1016/j.genhosppsych.2006.05.008

Simoni-Wastila, L., & Yang, H. K. (2006). Psychoactive drug abuse in older adults. *American Journal of Geriatric Pharmacotherapy, 4*, 380–394. doi:10.1016/j.amjopharm.2006.10.002

Smith, P. C., Schmidt, S. M., Allensworth-Davies, D., & Saitz, R. (2009). Primary care validation of a single-question alcohol screening test. *Journal of General Internal Medicine, 24*, 783–788. doi:10.1007/s11606-009-0928-6

Solomon, K., & Stark, S. (1993). Comparison of older and younger alcoholics and prescription drug abusers: History and clinical presentation. *Clinical Gerontologist, 12*, 41–56. doi:10.1300/J018v12n03_05

Son, S. J., Lee, K. S., Oh, B. H., & Hong, C. H. (2012). The effects of head circumference (HC) and lifetime alcohol consumption (AC) on cognitive function in the elderly. *Archives of Gerontology and Geriatrics, 54*, 343–347. doi:10.1016/j.archger.2011.05.025

Stenbacka, M. (2003). Problematic alcohol and cannabis use in adolescence--risk of serious adult substance abuse? *Drug and Alcohol Review, 22*, 277–286. doi:10.1080/0959523031000154418

Stone, A. A., Schwartz, J. E., Broderick, J. E., & Deaton, A. (2010). A snapshot of the age distribution of psychological well-being in the United States. *Proceedings of the National Academy of Sciences of the United States of America, 107*, 9985–9990. doi:10.1073/pnas.1003744107

Substance Abuse and Mental Health Services Administration. (2006). *Results from the 2005 National Survey on Drug Use and Health: National findings.* Rockville, MD: Office of Applied Studies. Retrieved from http://www.oas.samhsa.gov/nsduh/2k5nsduh/2k5results.htm#2.4

Thiruchselvam, T., Naglie, G., Moineddin, R., Charles, J., Orlando, L., Jaglal, S., . . . Tierney, M. C. (2012). Risk factors for medication nonadherence in older adults with cognitive impairment who live alone. *International Journal of Geriatric Psychiatry*, 27, 1275–1282. doi:10.1002/gps.3778

Vogeltanz, N. D., Wilsnack, S. C., Vickers, K. S., & Kristjanson, A. P. (1999). Sociodemographic characteristics and drinking status as predictors of older women's health. *Journal of General Psychology*, 126, 135–147. doi:10.1080/00221309909595357

Waller, S. J., Lyons, J. S., & Costantini-Ferrando, M. F. (1999). Impact of comorbid affective and alcohol use disorders on suicidal ideation and attempts. *Journal of Clinical Psychology*, 55, 585–595. doi:10.1002/(SICI)1097-4679(199905)55:5<585:: AID-JCLP6>3.0.CO;2-U

Walter, H., Dvorak, A., Gutierrez, K., Zitterl, W., & Lesch, O. M. (2005). Gender differences: Does alcohol affect females more than males? *Neuropsychopharmacologia Hungarica*, 7, 78–82.

Weathermon, R., & Crabb, D. W. (1999). Alcohol and medication interactions. *Alcohol Research and Health*, 23, 40–54.

Weintraub, E., Dixon, L., Delahanty, J., Schwartz, R., Johnson, J., Cohen, A., & Klecz, M. (2001). Reason for medical hospitalization among adult alcohol and drug abusers. *American Journal on Addictions*, 10, 167–177. doi:10.1080/105504901750227813

Weisner, C., McLellan, A. T., & Hunkeler, E. M. (2000). Addiction Severity Index data from general membership and treatment samples of HMO members. One case of norming the ASI. *Journal of Substance Abuse Treatment*, 19, 103–109. doi:10.1016/S0740-5472(99)00103-8

Wells-Parker, E., Miles, S., & Spencer, B. (1983). Stress experiences and drinking histories of elderly drunken-driving offenders. *Journal of Studies on Alcohol*, 44, 429–437.

Weston, A. L., Weinstein, A. M., Barton, C., & Yaffe, K. (2010). Potentially inappropriate medication use in older adults with mild cognitive impairment. *The Journals of Gerontology, Series A: Biological Sciences and Medical Sciences*, 65, 318–321. doi:10.1093/gerona/glp158

Wilk, A. I., Jensen, N. M., & Havighurst, T. C. (1997). Meta-analysis of randomized control trials addressing brief interventions in heavy alcohol drinkers. *Journal of General Internal Medicine*, 12, 274–283. doi:10.1007/s11606-006-5063-z

Wilsnack, S. C., Vogeltanz, N. D., Diers, L. E., & Wilsnack, R. W. (1995). Drinking and problem drinking in older women. In T. P. Beresford & E. S. Gomberg (Eds.), *Alcohol and Aging* (pp. 263–292). New York, NY: Oxford University Press.

Wolf, J. (2012). *Gender, ethnicity, and drinking in older age: Understanding mediators and moderators of risk.* Unpublished doctoral dissertation, University of California, Berkeley.

World Health Organization. (2013). *Status report on alcohol and health in 35 European countries, 2013.* Retrieved from http://www.euro.who.int/en/what-we-publish/abstracts/status-report-on-alcohol-and-health-in-35-european-countries-2013

Wu, L. T., & Blazer, D. G. (2011). Illicit and nonmedical drug use among older adults: A review. *Journal of Aging and Health*, 23, 481–504. doi:10.1177/0898264310386224

CHAPTER 6

SUICIDAL BEHAVIOR IN OLDER ADULTS

Amy Fiske, Merideth D. Smith, and Elizabeth C. Price

Suicidal behavior represents one of the most pressing challenges currently facing clinical geropsychologists. Rates of suicide are higher among older adults, and specifically among older men, than in any other demographic group (McIntosh & Drapeau, 2012). With the aging of the baby boom cohort, with its historically elevated propensity for suicide, rates of late-life suicide are expected to climb even further in coming decades (Conwell, Van Orden, & Caine, 2011). Although public opinion historically has viewed suicide as more acceptable among older adults than among younger individuals (Deluty, 1988–1989), evidence shows that the impact of older adult suicide on those left behind is marked by greater stigma, shame, and feelings of rejection compared with bereavement by natural causes of death (Harwood, Hawton, Hope, & Jacoby, 2002). Furthermore, there is evidence that suicide potentially can be prevented through behavioral (De Leo, Buono, & Dwyer, 2002; Oyama et al., 2008) and pharmacological interventions (Baldessarini et al., 2006). Unfortunately, most mental health professionals, including psychologists, receive little formal training in the assessment and treatment of individuals at risk for suicide (Schmitz et al., 2012). This chapter focuses on suicidal behavior in late life, reviewing theory, risk and protective factors, assessment, intervention, and clinical issues.

DEFINITIONS

There has been much discussion regarding nomenclature pertaining to suicidal behaviors. A commonly accepted definition of the term *suicide* is "a self-inflicted death with evidence (either explicit or implicit) of intent to die" (Silverman, Berman, Sanddal, O'Carroll, & Joiner, 2007, p. 273). Suicidal behavior, however, may include a wide range of covert and overt behaviors with varying levels of intent to die. A proposed nomenclature was published by Silverman et al. (2007). In this rubric, *suicide attempt* is defined as "a self-inflicted, potentially injurious behavior with a nonfatal outcome for which evidence exists (either explicit or implicit) of intent to die" (p. 273). The term *suicide-related ideations* (previously referred to as "suicidal ideation") is used to refer to suicidal thoughts, with any level of suicidal intent, which may range from casual to persistent. Thoughts of death and dying without explicit thoughts of taking one's own life, sometimes referred to as *death ideation*, are subsumed under the term suicide-related ideations. Death ideation, which occurs among 10–20% of older adults, shares some risk factors with other suicidal behavior and therefore merits clinical attention (Rurup, Deeg, Poppelaars, Kerkhof, & Onwuteaka-Philipsen, 2011). This chapter uses the Silverman et al. (2007) nomenclature.

Currently, suicide is not considered a disorder, but rather a potential consequence of a wide range of psychological disorders. The *Diagnostic and Statistical Manual for Mental Disorders, Fifth Edition* (*DSM–5*; American Psychiatric Association, 2013) emphasizes the need to assess for suicidal ideation and behavior independent of diagnosis. In addition, criteria for a proposed new diagnosis characterized by repeated suicidal behavior, suicidal

http://dx.doi.org/10.1037/14459-006
APA Handbook of Clinical Geropsychology: Vol. 2. Assessment, Treatment, and Issues of Later Life,
P. A. Lichtenberg and B. T. Mast (Editors-in-Chief)

behavior disorder, has been added to a separate section of the *DSM–5* to promote further study.

EPIDEMIOLOGY

Suicide is presently the 10th leading cause of death in the United States. In 2010, 38,364 individuals died by suicide in the United States, nearly 6,000 of whom were age 65 years or older (McIntosh & Drapeau, 2012). The rate of suicide varies with age, gender, and race or ethnicity. As in most countries internationally, the suicide rate increases dramatically for males in late life (in addition to peaks in early adulthood and middle age). The highest rates in the United States are in men over age 85 years, whose rate of suicide of 47.3 per 100,000 population is more than triple the overall rate of 12.4 (Centers for Disease Control & Prevention [CDC], 2013). In contrast, suicide rates for females peak in midlife and do not rise again in late life. As a result of the gender difference in patterns of suicidal behavior across the life span, the ratio of male to female suicide, which is approximately 4:1 overall, climbs to 7:1 in adults age 65 years and older (CDC, 2013). Among older adults, suicide rates are highest among non-Hispanic Whites (Nock et al., 2008).

The epidemiology of suicide attempts differs dramatically from that of deaths by suicide. Although there is no official mechanism for tracking suicide attempts in the United States, estimates suggest a ratio of 25 suicide attempts per death overall, with the highest ratio among youth (100–200:1) and the lowest among older adults (4:1; McIntosh and Drapeau, 2012). Suicide attempts that do not result in death are three times more frequent among females compared with males (McIntosh & Drapeau, 2012).

The greater case fatality ratio (i.e., the proportion of cases that are fatal) among older adults compared with other age groups can largely be attributed to the use of more immediately lethal means (Miller, Azrael, & Barber, 2012). Firearms were used by 78% of older men (65 years and older) compared with 49% of younger men (15–24 years old) who died by suicide in the United States in 2010 (CDC, 2013). Similarly, firearms were used by 36% of older women and 24% of younger women who died by

suicide. In contrast, the most frequently used method of nonfatal suicide attempt in all age-groups, in a study using a representative sample of emergency departments, was poisoning (59% of males; 73% of females), followed by cutting or piercing (21% of males, 18% of females; Vyrostek, Annest, & Ryan, 2004). It is also possible that the higher case fatality ratio among older adults represents greater intent to die. Older adults who die by suicide make attempts that more clearly demonstrate planning and reflect more seriousness of intent (Conwell et al., 1998).

These differences in the epidemiology of suicide versus suicide attempt should be considered when interpreting results of research on suicide-related behaviors. On the other hand, because the ratio of attempts to deaths is much smaller in older adults than in younger age groups, factors that predict suicide attempt are more likely to be useful in predicting suicide among older adults compared with other age groups (Beautrais, 2001).

THEORETICAL CONCEPTUALIZATION OF LATE-LIFE SUICIDE

Suicide has been conceptualized in theories and models that range from sociological to psychodynamic, cognitive, and behavioral. Few theories encapsulate suicide within a developmental framework. This section discusses some of the current theories and models of suicide, emphasizing those with a specific focus on explaining suicide in late life.

Emile Durkheim's (1951) theory of social integration stated primarily that communities and individuals with few social ties and more social isolation experience higher rates of suicide compared with those with more social integration. Considerable evidence suggests the importance of social forces on suicide in late life (Turvey et al., 2002).

Beck, Kovacs, and Weissman (1975) conceptualized suicide as proceeding from "hopelessness depression," a variant of depression characterized by high levels of hopelessness. Hopelessness has been found to be related to death by suicide and suicide ideation in older adults (De Leo, Draper, Snowdon, & Kõlves, 2013).

Shneidman (1993) conceptualized suicide as escape from "psychache," the intolerable psychological pain that develops from unmet psychological needs. This model has not been studied directly in older adults.

Another example of an escape theory is Baumeister's escape from self and self-regulatory theory of suicidal behavior (Vohs & Baumeister, 2000). According to this theory, when an individual makes internal attributions about failure, significant internal resources are exerted to escape from the resulting negative thoughts and feelings. As a result, the individual's time perspective becomes limited, characterized by focusing only on proximal goals and engaging in concrete thinking, in a state known as *cognitive deconstruction*. In this state, the individual may focus on the immediate consequences of suicide (i.e., escape from negative self-awareness) but cannot rationally comprehend the long-term consequences of lethal self-harm behavior or find alternative solutions. Events associated with aging, such as a decline in health, may serve as precipitating stressors, as described by Baumeister, that result in the cascade toward suicide (Reich, Newsom, & Zautra, 1996).

D. C. Clark (1993) proposed a model that specifically addresses the unique nature of late-life suicide. D. C. Clark posited that death by suicide in older adults is precipitated by life-long character traits, such as an excessive need for independence or difficulty asking for help, that lead to a suicidal crisis only when the older adult is confronted with a series of acute, aging-related life stressors, such as functional impairment, need for a caregiver, or loss of a driver's license. When confronted with the aging-related life stressor, the older adult possessing these traits is unable to successfully adapt, resulting in a "narcissistic crisis of aging." The crisis may reach a point at which the stress can no longer be tolerated, and suicide is viewed as a means to escape and gain mastery over the environment. Consistent with this theory, O'Riley and Fiske (2012) found that older adults who more strongly endorsed a cognitive style characterized by heavy emphasis on control were more likely to report suicidal ideation, whereas this pattern of results was not found in a younger adult sample.

Caine and Conwell (2001) proposed a public health model of suicide risk that takes into account the processes that alter risk over the life span. Distal factors such as personality (inflexibility), childhood events (trauma experienced as a child), social and ecological factors (presence of support network), and cultural values are present throughout the life span. Additional distal risk factors that may develop in late life include changes in role status (retirement, widowhood), onset of medical problems, and the accumulation of chronic and acute life stressors. The presence of mental health problems, such as depressive symptoms, decreased resiliency, and a decrease in help-seeking behavior are proximal factors to the development of a suicidal crisis. The onset of acute stressors interacts with the distal and proximal factors, which can result in the onset of suicidal behaviors. This model is one of the few to offer a comprehensive, developmentally informed conceptualization of late-life suicide.

One of the more recent advancements in understanding suicide comes from the interpersonal theory of suicidal behavior, which conceptualizes suicide risk as the interaction between the desire to die and the capability of engaging in lethal self-harm (Joiner, 2005). The theory asserts that desire for death arises from a sense of thwarted belonging and a sense that one is a burden to others (Van Orden et al., 2010). Nonetheless, many individuals have a desire for suicide but do not take their own lives. Joiner (2005) theorized that the difference is attributable to the ability to engage in lethal self-harm behaviors. Theoretically, to engage in these behaviors, an individual needs to have a higher threshold for pain and a lowered fear of death, which may be acquired primarily through exposure to painful and provocative experiences. These experiences lead to habituation to the factors that generally serve as barriers to self-harm (e.g., pain, fear). Painful and provocative events can include trauma, combat, repeated invasive medical procedures, or past suicide attempts. Joiner posited that older adults may acquire greater capability to engage in lethal self-harm behavior because of the increased possibility of repeated exposure to painful or provocative events over the life span. Although acquired capability for suicide is an important concept for explaining the small percentage of older adults who go on to engage in lethal self-harm behaviors, no research has been done to validate this specific component of the theory within an aging population. Understanding how risk and protective factors across the life span influence both a desire to die and increased capability for suicide can lead to a better conceptualization of the risk for death by suicide across different groups. A limitation of the interpersonal theory of suicide is that developmental factors influencing late-life suicide have not been specified fully.

This chapter conceptualizes late-life suicide within a life-span developmental framework. Like Joiner (2005), we view suicide risk as a function of both the desire to die and the capability to engage in lethal self-harm behaviors (Figure 6.1). The desire to die is influenced by vulnerabilities, stressors, and protective factors that can vary in both frequency and influence over the life span. Some risk factors, such as genetic influence, personality, and psychopathology, are present early in life and continue to influence suicide risk late in life. Other risk factors occur with greater frequency in late life, such as physical illness, functional impairment, and cognitive decline. Still other factors are present throughout the life span, but they may confer greater risk for suicide late in life. These include low openness to experience and a heavy emphasis on independence. Individuals with low openness to experience may exhibit more cognitive rigidity and may be more likely to struggle with adapting to changes in life circumstances, making this a risk factor that becomes more salient with the changes that occur in late life. Theoretically, the capability for suicide is influenced by factors that may accumulate across the life span (e.g., habituation to pain) as well as factors that may vary with age (e.g., isolation) and factors that may be independent of age (e.g., access to means). Social factors and cognitive functioning, which vary with age, are related to suicide risk in complex ways and may be related to both desire and capability for suicide. This distinction is primarily conceptual, however, as there has not been a systematic effort to verify that factors thought to contribute specifically to the capability for suicide are related to suicide or suicide attempt independent of a desire to die.

RISK AND PROTECTIVE FACTORS

This section examines risk and protective factors for suicide in late life. We primarily draw on evidence from case-control psychological autopsy studies, a retrospective method that involves interviews with informants and review of medical records and other relevant materials for individuals who have died by suicide and matched controls. Most of the research examines factors likely to influence desire to die by suicide, and we consider these findings first, followed by factors likely to influence the ability to enact lethal self-harm.

Genetics

Findings show that familial aggregation of suicides can be attributed primarily to genetic influence rather than to shared environmental experiences, such as the loss of another family member to suicide. Research using the population-based Swedish twin registry demonstrated significant genetic influence on suicide (Pedersen & Fiske, 2010). Although the heritability of suicide is significant, concordance rates are low (6% for monozygotic twins and 2% for dizygotic twins; Pedersen & Fiske, 2010), reflecting the relative rarity of suicide. These statistics reflect the probability of suicide in one twin given suicide in the co-twin. Genes may influence suicidal behavior through personality traits, vulnerability for psychopathology, propensity for impulsivity, or other factors. Further research is needed to clarify mechanisms.

Personality

Several dimensions of personality have been linked to suicide across the life span. Personality dimensions generally have been measured by retrospective report of family members on an inventory that assesses normal personality traits. Both middle-age and older adults who die by suicide are described as having higher levels of neuroticism and lower levels of extraversion than controls (De Leo et al., 2013; Duberstein, 2001). It is possible that extraversion has a protective effect by facilitating social support, although low extraversion may also reflect the presence of depression.

Other aspects of personality appear to confer greater risk for suicide in late life. Duberstein and

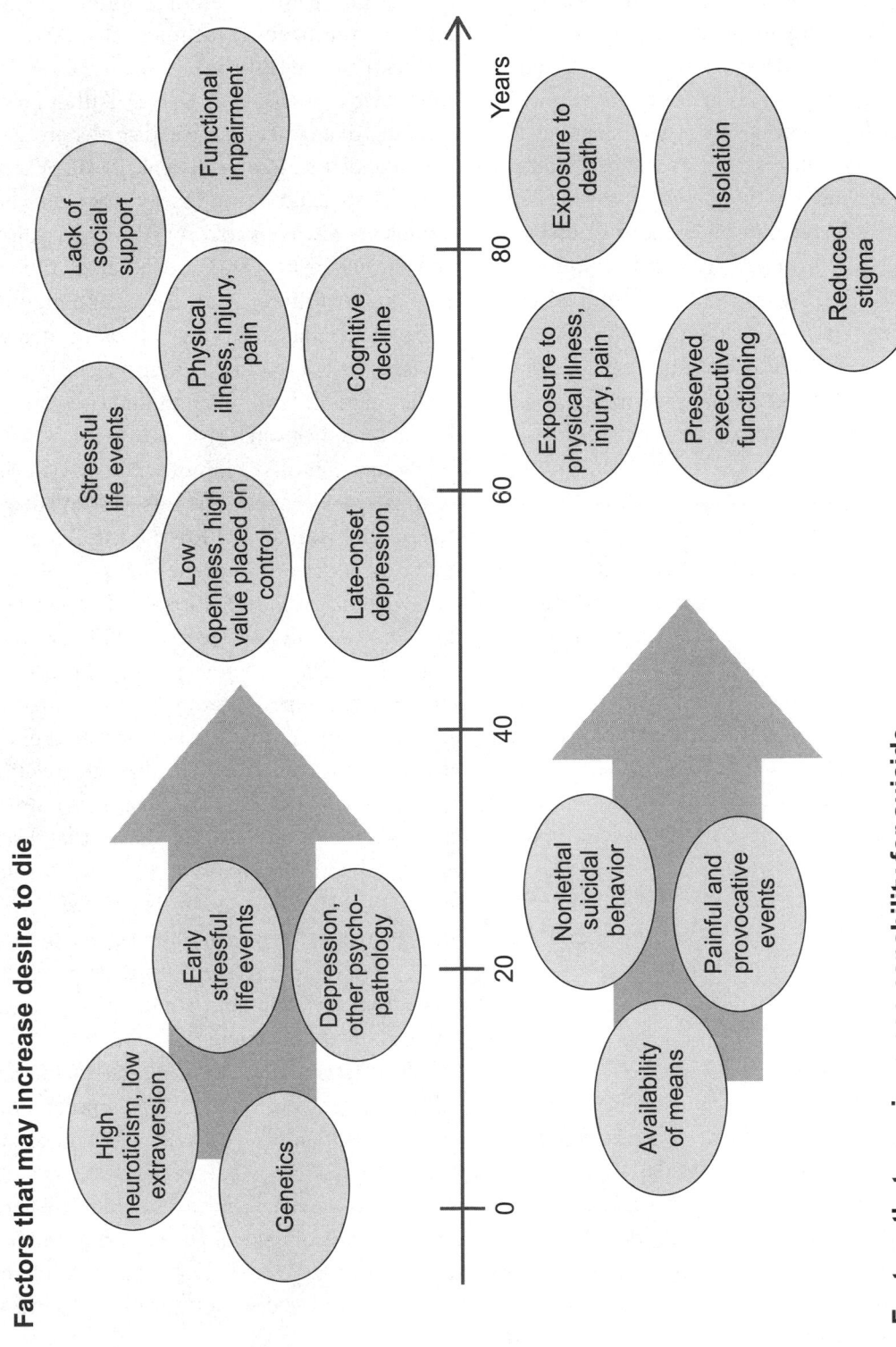

Factors that may increase desire to die

Factors that may increase capability for suicide

FIGURE 6.1. Factors that may increase risk of suicide.

colleagues found that adults age 50 years and older who died by suicide were characterized as having low levels of openness to experience (Duberstein, 2001; but see De Leo et al., 2013), and the effect was greater for older than for younger age groups (Duberstein, Conwell, & Caine, 1994). One interpretation of these findings would be that growing old requires flexibility, and individuals who are lower in openness (i.e., more rigid, conventional, and traditional) would be less likely to age successfully. It is also possible that normal age-related decrements in cognitive flexibility increase risk for suicide in this age group. Indeed, older adult suicide decedents have been described as rigid and independent (D. C. Clark, 1993). O'Riley and Fiske (2012) found that heavy emphasis on independence and control was linked to suicide-related ideations in older but not younger adults.

Psychopathology

Psychopathology is the most consistently replicated risk factor for suicide at all ages. Psychological autopsy studies show that up to 97% of older adults who die by suicide meet criteria for a diagnosable mental disorder (reviewed by Conwell et al., 2011; see also De Leo et al., 2013). Mood disorders represent the most frequent type of psychopathology in older adults who die by suicide. Even mild depressive disorders confer risk for suicide in older adults (Waern et al., 2002). Substance use disorders, anxiety disorders, and schizophrenia play a larger role in suicide among younger and middle-aged adults (De Leo et al., 2013). Evidence linking alcohol use disorder to suicide among older adults has been mixed (see Conwell et al., 2011).

Physical Health Status

Physical illness, disability, and pain have been linked to suicide in late life. Suicide in late life is related to the number (Juurlink, Herrmann, Szalai, Kopp, & Redelmeier, 2004) and severity of physical illnesses (Conwell et al., 2000; but see also Beautrais, 2002; Turvey et al., 2002). Waern, Rubenowitz, and Wilhelmson (2003) reported that burden of illness increased suicide risk for adults 75 years and older but not 65–74 years, and for men but not for women. Specific types of diseases and disorders that have been associated with increased risk of suicide among older

adults include cancer (Conwell et al., 2010; Waern et al., 2002), seizure disorder (Juurlink et al., 2004), chronic pulmonary disorder (Juurlink et al., 2004), renal failure (Kurella, Kimmel, Young, & Chertow, 2005), incontinence (Juurlink et al., 2004), congestive heart failure (Juurlink et al., 2004), and vision impairment (Waern et al., 2002). Although global measures of any neurological disorder are associated with suicide risk (Conwell et al., 2010; Waern et al., 2002), there is little evidence of risk associated with Parkinson's disease, stroke, or Alzheimer's disease (for a review, see Fiske, O'Riley, & Widoe, 2008). Poor sleep quality (Turvey et al., 2002) and nightmares (Tanskanen et al., 2001) also are associated with increased risk of suicide. Timing may be important, as studies of adults and older adults with cancer have demonstrated elevated risk during the period shortly following diagnosis (Llorente et al., 2005). Similarly, death by suicide among patients with end-stage renal disease is most likely within the first 3 months after initiation of dialysis (Kurella et al., 2005).

Depression accounts for some (Conwell et al., 2000), but not all (Waern et al., 2002), of the risk for suicide associated with physical health status. The extent to which disability, or the impairment in independently completing tasks because of the physical impairment, may mediate the relation between physical illness and suicide is not yet known, although it has been shown that disability is associated with elevated risk of suicide in late life (Conwell et al., 2000). Pain also has been shown to increase risk of suicide in older adults, independent of the effects of depression (Juurlink et al., 2004). It is not known whether pain mediates the effects of physical illness on suicide risk.

When considering physical health status and suicide risk among older adults, it is important to keep several facts in mind. The base rate of physical illness is high among older adults; as a result, physical illness is a nonspecific risk factor for suicide. Furthermore, the magnitude of risk conferred by physical health status is dwarfed by that conferred by psychological and substance use disorders, primarily depression.

Cognitive Functioning

Emerging evidence suggests that some aspects of cognitive functioning may be related to suicide in late life. Poorer global cognitive status has been linked to greater suicidal ideation in older adults without dementia (Ayalon, Mackin, Arean, Chen, & Herr, 2007) and the relation appears to be mediated by depression and hopelessness (Heisel, Flett, & Besser, 2002). It is less clear, however, whether global cognitive status is related to death by suicide. In a cohort study, scores on a cognitive screening measure did not predict suicide among older adults (Turvey et al., 2002).

Case-control psychological autopsy studies generally have found no difference in dementia status between older adults who died by suicide and controls (e.g., Waern et al., 2002). A large, national, longitudinal study did find that hospital-diagnosed dementia was associated with elevated risk of suicide, independent of depression (Erlangsen, Zarit, & Conwell, 2008). Risk was greatest in younger (50–69 years old) versus older (70 years and older) individuals and in the period shortly after diagnosis. Although findings may not generalize beyond inpatient-diagnosed cases of dementia, the study highlights conditions under which dementia may confer risk for suicide.

An accumulating body of research has examined specific types of cognitive functioning in older adults who have made suicide attempts. Evidence has shown older adult suicide attempters to have greater overall impairment in executive functioning than nonattempters (Dombrovski et al., 2008), with poorer problem-solving skills (Gibbs et al., 2009), impairments in decision making (L. Clark et al., 2011), impairments in cognitive inhibition (Richard-Devantoy et al., 2012), and poorer cognitive control, especially among those who made high lethality attempts (McGirr, Dombrovski, Butters, Clark, & Szanto, 2012). Older adult suicide attempters also display impaired social cognition compared with healthy controls, a deficit that could complicate interpersonal relationships (Szanto et al., 2012). Neuroimaging research with older adult suicide attempters has documented structural alterations in the basal ganglia (Dombrovski et al., 2012) and decreased gray-matter and white-matter volume, especially in the dorsal ventral prefrontal cortex (Hwang et al., 2010). Although findings from the study of suicide attempts may not generalize to death by suicide,

examining high lethality suicide attempts may be more generalizable. Delay discounting, a behavioral measure of impulsivity, has been shown to distinguish between low and high lethality suicide attempts among older adults (Dombrovski et al., 2011). Delay discounting involves displaying a preference for a smaller, sooner reward rather than a larger, later reward. The authors suggested that the more lethal, and better-planned, suicide attempts are associated with greater ability to delay rewards.

Taken together, findings are consistent with the notion that suicidal ideation may be associated with cognitive impairment. Risk of death by suicide, however, may be greatest among older adults when cognitive functions are relatively preserved, as in the early stages of cognitive decline and in the absence of impulsivity, such that the older adult may be capable of planning and carrying out more lethal suicidal behavior.

Social Factors

Evidence suggests that lack of social connectedness is related to suicide in late life, although findings vary (reviewed by Fässberg et al., 2012). Older adults who died by suicide were more likely than controls to live alone (De Leo et al., 2013; but see also Beautrais, 2002), less likely to live with children (Tsoh et al., 2005), and less likely to have a confidante (Turvey et al., 2002). They were described by informants as having more limited social contact (Beautrais, 2002), receiving less social support (De Leo et al., 2013), being less likely to participate in community activities (Duberstein et al., 2004) or organizations (Rubenowitz et al., 2001) or to have a hobby (Rubenowitz et al., 2001), and being more likely to be lonely (Rubenowitz et al., 2001; Waern et al., 2003). Conflict in relationships and family discord has been linked to late-life suicide in numerous studies (Beautrais, 2002; Rubenowitz et al., 2001) and may be more strongly related to suicide risk than positive social factors (Rubenowitz, Waern, Wilhelmson, & Allebeck, 2001). These results are consistent with the observation that older adult suicide attempters were characterized by social emotion recognition deficits (Szanto et al., 2012). Some studies (Conwell, Rotenberg, & Caine, 1990) have found recent bereavement to be related to suicide in late life, but widowhood appears to confer greater risk for suicide among younger adults (Luoma & Pearson, 2002).

Studies of suicidal ideation in older adults show that perceived burdensomeness is associated with suicidal ideation even after controlling for depressive symptoms (Cukrowicz, Cheavens, Van Orden, Ragain, & Cook, 2011), consistent with the interpersonal theory of suicide (Joiner, 2005). In cross-sectional analyses, perceived burdensomeness mediated the relation between depressive symptoms and suicide ideation in older adults (Jahn & Cukrowicz, 2011). Prospective research indicates that perceived burdensomeness erodes the older adult's sense of meaning in life (Van Orden, Talbot, & King, 2012). These relations have yet to be examined in relation to suicide. Social factors also may play a role in preventing suicidal intent. Perceived obligation to family members or friends often is endorsed as an important reason for living among older adults (Edelstein et al., 2009).

Hopelessness

Among the numerous other psychological variables that have been associated with suicide in late life, hopelessness may be particularly important. It predicts eventual suicide in mixed-age samples of suicide attempters (Beck, Brown, Berchick, Stewart, & Steer, 1990) and distinguishes older adults who died by suicide from sudden death controls (De Leo et al., 2013). Persistently elevated levels of hopelessness following treatment distinguish depressed older adults who attempted suicide from those with suicide ideation only and those without suicidal ideation (Szanto, Reynolds, Conwell, Begley, & Houck, 1998), suggesting that hopelessness may serve as a marker for elevated suicide risk even outside the context of a depressive episode.

Protective Factors

Many of the risk factors for suicide noted above also could be conceptualized, conversely, as protective factors (e.g., social connection and treatment for depression). In addition, Edelstein et al. (2009) have created a self-report measure of reasons for living in older adults. Compared with results from a similar measure designed for younger adults, the older adults endorsed more reasons related to family and friends and to religious beliefs, and moral objections to suicide.

Factors Associated With the Ability to Enact Lethal Self-Harm

The interpersonal theory of suicide (Joiner, 2005) posits that higher rates of suicide in late life can be explained in part by both suicide attempt history and engagement in other painful and provocative events, such as military combat, and occurrences of illness and injury, which gradually increase a person's capability of engaging in self-harm behavior. Consistent with this theory, history of suicide attempt, which dramatically increases the risk of suicide in older adults (Beautrais, 2002; De Leo et al., 2013), predicts future suicidal symptoms in older adults even after controlling for such strong suicide risk factors as symptoms of psychopathology and hopelessness (Van Orden et al., 2010).

The availability of readily lethal means should decrease barriers and thus increase the ability to enact suicide at any age. Much evidence has shown that the availability of firearms is closely linked to case fatality ratios for suicidal behavior in the United States (Miller et al., 2012). Among older adults specifically, suicide deaths decreased following legislation restricting access to firearms (Ludwig & Cook, 2000; see the section "Means Restriction" later in this chapter).

Cognitive status also may be relevant to capability for suicide in late life. Evidence that suicide risk is greatest shortly after dementia diagnosis (Erlangsen et al., 2008), and that delay discounting characterizes low-lethality but not high-lethality suicide attempts, suggests that preserved executive functioning may contribute to a person's ability to enact a highly lethal suicide plan (McGirr et al., 2012).

Exposure to death and dying also should lead to habituation and thereby increase a person's capability of enacting lethal self-harm, although this proposition remains to be tested directly. Studies using both self-report (Neimeyer, Wittkowski, & Moser, 2004) and attentional processing measures (De Raedt, Koster, & Ryckewaert, 2013) have shown reduced death anxiety in older compared with middle-age adults. Furthermore, social isolation, which consistently has been linked to late-life suicide (e.g., Beautrais, 2002), may contribute to a person's capability for suicide by reducing the likelihood that someone would be present to intervene.

Another factor that may influence capability for suicide is reduced stigma associated with suicide in late life, particularly in the context of physical illness (Canetto, 1997; Deluty, 1988–1989; Stice & Canetto, 2008). Canetto's (1997) cultural script theory of suicidal behavior proposes that cultural norms and beliefs about the acceptability of suicide influence the likelihood that an individual will engage in suicidal behavior. Normative beliefs have a small but significant effect on behavioral intentions (Ajzen, 1991), so it is conceivable that for older adults who believe that late-life suicide is viewed as acceptable, barriers to enacting lethal self-harm are reduced. Taboo enhancement has been evaluated as part of a larger intervention (Oyama et al., 2008), but it has not been tested separately.

Progression of Suicide Risk

Few studies have focused on the progression of suicide risk over time in older adults. Murphy et al. (2012) followed adults age 60 years and older after hospitalization for a suicide attempt. The 1-year incidence of suicide following the first suicide attempt after the age of 60 years that occurred during the study period was 1.5%. The only independent risk factor was use of a violent method in the initial suicide attempt (after age 60 years and during the study period). Notably, self-poisoning was used in 75% of initial suicide attempts, but half of the adults subsequently switched to violent methods. Results highlight the role capability for suicide may play in explaining late-life suicide.

ASSESSMENT OF SUICIDE RISK

The use of models can help clinicians assess an older adult's risk for suicide. The fluid vulnerability model is a diathesis stress model that describes overall suicide risk as the fluid interaction between chronic and acute risk factors (Rudd, 2006). A person's baseline risk for suicide is composed of the accumulation of chronic and acute risk factors. A confrontation with an acute stressor can result in a period of

suicidal crisis, increasing the imminent risk of engaging in suicidal behavior. The resolution of the acute stressor returns the person to the baseline level of suicide risk. In formulating an estimate of the client's risk of suicide, both baseline and current risk levels should be considered.

There are numerous clinician-administered and self-report measures to assess suicide risk. Most of these measures were not developed specifically for older adults and thus have limited content validity. Content validity is particularly important when assessing late-life suicide risk because there are differences in the presentation of suicide-related behaviors across the life span, as noted. Assessments developed utilizing younger adults may fail to detect age-specific risk factors, or they may place greater emphasis on factors that are less frequent in late life, such as previous suicide attempts. Considering the importance of utilizing content-valid suicide measures for older adults, this section discusses measures and interviews developed specifically for older adults as well as common measures of suicide ideation and behavior that have been developed in mixed-age samples and validated with older adults (see Table 6.1).

Measures of Suicide-Related Ideation and Suicide Risk

The Scale for Suicidal Ideation (SSI; Beck, Kovacs, & Weissman, 1979) is a 21-item interviewer-administered rating scale that measures preparation and motivation for suicidal behavior, including attitudes, behaviors, and plans related to suicide. This measure was designed for use in psychiatric populations and is not aging specific; however, several studies have used this measure in older adult samples. The SSI has good interitem consistency when used with psychiatric patients and participants in outpatient settings (Beck, Brown, & Steer, 1997; Beck et al., 1979). Scores on the SSI also distinguished between suicidal inpatients and depressed outpatients (Beck et al., 1979). Furthermore, SSI scores predicted death by suicide in an adult population (Brown, Beck, Steer, & Grisham, 2000). In older adults, the SSI maintained good reliability (Heisel et al., 2002; Witte et al., 2006). Witte et al. (2006) identified two factors that emerged when using this

---

TABLE 6.1

Psychometric Properties of Measures of Suicide Risk in Older Adult Populations

Measure	Description	Items	Validity	Reliability	Test–retest reliability
Scale for Suicide Ideation (SSI; Beck et al., 1979)	Clinician-administered interview; measures suicidal desire and ideation (SDI) and resolved planning and preparation for suicidal behavior (RPP)	21	Total score: GSIS $r =$ .65; SDI factor: prior attempt $r =$ .43; Beck Depression Inventory $r =$ .36; BHS $r =$ .24; RPP factor: Beck Depression Inventory $r =$ .26	Total score: $\alpha =$ .89–.93; SDI factor: $\alpha =$ .81; RPP factor: $\alpha =$ .75; Interrater reliability = .83	
Geriatric Suicide Ideation Scale (GSIS; Heisel & Flett, 2006)	Measures suicide ideation, death ideation, loss of personal and social meaning, and perceived meaning in life	31	SSI $r =$ .62; Geriatric Depression Scale $r =$ .77	Total score: $\alpha =$ .93; Suicide ideation: $\alpha =$ .82; Death ideation: $\alpha =$ .84; Loss of worth: $\alpha =$ .82; Meaning in life: $\alpha =$ .82	Total score: $r =$ .86; Suicide ideation: $r =$ .78; Death ideation: $r =$ .76; Loss of worth: $r =$ .77; Meaning in life: $r =$ .75
Suicidal Older Adult Protocol (SOAP; Fremouw et al., 2009)	Clinician administered interview; measures static and dynamic risk and protective factors for late life suicide	18			

measure with older adults: (a) suicidal desire and ideation and (b) resolved plans and preparation. Both factors were related significantly to depressive symptoms, while suicidal desire and ideation was related to prior history of suicide attempts and hopelessness.

The Geriatric Suicide Ideation Scale (GSIS; Heisel & Flett, 2006) is a 31-item self-report measure developed to assess suicide ideation, death ideation, loss of personal and social meaning, and perceived meaning of life in older adults. This measure has good interitem consistency and demonstrated reliable test–retest scores over a 1- to 2-month period. Interitem consistency scores were stable across participants with normal and impaired cognitive functioning. The GSIS was correlated significantly with other measures of suicide ideation, including the SSI total scale score, as well as depressive symptoms and hopelessness. Furthermore, the GSIS distinguished between psychiatric patients and nonpsychiatric patients.

The Suicidal Older Adult Protocol (SOAP; Fremouw, McCoy, Tyner, & Musick, 2009) is a clinician-administered semistructured interview that assesses suicide risk in older adults. This interview utilizes the fluid vulnerability model to conceptualize factors that make up a baseline risk and factors that contribute to an acute risk for suicidal behaviors. Fremouw et al. (2009) weighted both static and dynamic factors using effect sizes derived from the previous literature to identify a range of suicide risk (low risk to extreme risk). This is a useful and age-specific measure for guiding clinicians in the assessment of risk and protective factors in late life. However, the reliability and predictive validity of this measure have not been investigated, and psychometric properties have not been established.

Measures of Factors Related to Suicide

The Beck Hopelessness Scale (BHS; Beck, Weissman, Lester, & Trexler, 1974), although not aging specific, has been validated in older adult populations. A version of the BHS with expanded response options had acceptable to excellent interitem consistency and strong correlations to depressive symptoms and suicide ideation in an older adult population (Neufeld, O'Rourke, & Donnelly, 2010). The Geriatric Hopelessness Scale (GHS) does not have as strong psychometric properties as the BHS, but an 11-item suicide risk subscale of the GHS (GHS-SR) had strong correlations with other measures of hopelessness, depressive symptoms, and suicide-related ideation (Fry, 1984; Heisel & Flett, 2005).

The Reasons for Living—Older Adult (RFL–OA) scale contains 69 items and measures the level of reasons for living in older adults (Edelstein et al., 2009). The RFL–OA asks participants to rate the importance (*extremely unimportant* to *extremely important*) of each reason why they do not take their own life. Examples of reasons include "it would hurt my family too much" and "committing suicide would prevent me from going to heaven." Higher scores on the RFL–OA predicted the worst episode of suicide-related ideation and current episode of suicide-related ideation even when controlling for depressive symptoms. This measure has been used primarily as a research tool and may be difficult to administer clinically because of the length of the measure. The use of an exhaustive list of RFL that are content valid for older adults does allow for a thorough assessment of protective factors. Although not empirically tested at this time, an RFL scale also may function as an intervention by reinforcing a commitment to stay alive.

Suicide-Related Items on Depressive Symptom Measures

Several measures of depressive symptoms also contain suicide-related items. These include the Patient Health Questionairre-9 (PHQ-9; Spitzer, Kroenke, & Williams, 1999), the Beck Depression Inventory—II (BDI–II), and the Center for Epidemiologic Studies Depression Scale—Revised (CESD–R; Eaton, Smith, Ybarra, Muntaner, & Tien, 2004).

The suicide-related item on the PHQ-9 has been found to identify patients with cancer and Veterans Affairs patients who expressed suicide ideation as rated by a clinician or with additional follow-up questions assessing suicide ideation and intent (Corson, Gerrity, & Dobscha, 2004; Walker et al., 2011). Impressively, the PHQ-9 suicide-related item was predictive of suicide attempt and death by suicide 1 year later in outpatients age 13 years or older after controlling for demographics, treatment history, and depressive symptoms (Simon et al., 2013).

Five items from the Self-Rating Depression scale (Zung, 1965) were used to develop a suicide and depression screener, the Depression and Suicide Screen, for use with older adults in primary care (Fujisawa et al., 2005). Using a cutoff score of two or higher, the Depression and Suicide Screen had a sensitivity of .70 and a specificity of .69, with a positive predictive value of .32 and negative predictive value of .83 when predicting the presence or absence of suicide ideation as rated by a clinician.

The Geriatric Depression Scale (GDS; Yesavage, 1982–1983) does not have a specific suicide item, but research has shown it can identify older adults with high risk for suicide ideation (Heisel, Flett, Duberstein, & Lyness, 2005). A cutoff score of 12 on the 30-item GDS and 6 on the 15-item GDS resulted in the best balance of sensitivity and specificity when predicting GSIS and SSI scores. Heisel et al. (2005) identified five items on the GDS that had the strongest relation with the SSI. The five-item version of the GDS demonstrated good interitem reliability. A cutoff score of two yielded the best sensitivity and specificity when using the GSIS and SSI (sensitivity .81 and .71; specificity .92 and .85). In a sample of Chinese older adults, including an item assessing suicide-related ideation ("Do you wish to end your life?") when administering the GDS improved sensitivity and specificity when detecting clinician-rated suicide-related ideation in adults 75 years or older, but not for adults ages 60–74 years (Cheng et al., 2010). The BDI–II and CESD–R also may be useful in identifying older adults at risk for suicide; however, the predictive validity of these measures in identifying older adults at risk for suicide has not been established.

The use of depression measures can aid a clinician in identifying older adult patients who may be at higher risk for suicidal behavior; however, follow-up assessments are needed to understand better the severity of risk, acute risk factors, and protective factors.

Issues Related to Assessment

Assessment of suicide risk in older adults may be complicated by a clinician's attitudes regarding aging and death. Physicians rated suicide ideation as more normative and less a product of pathology, and they were less likely to recommend therapeutic interventions or encourage the patient to find reasons for living when the hypothetical patient was an older adult (Barnow, Linden, Lucht, & Freyberger, 2004; Uncapher & Areán, 2000). Clinicians' age-related biases may result in less adequate assessment and treatment in older adults compared with younger adults.

Limited clinician training and competency to manage aging patients with elevated suicide risk may further complicate this age bias. In a psychological autopsy study of older adults who died by suicide, suicide warnings were ignored or missed due to not recognizing the seriousness of such threats, feeling helpless to effect change, feeling isolated in ability to consult with colleagues, and acceptance or normalization of the desire to die because of the aging process (Kjølseth & Ekeberg, 2012). Additionally, primary care physicians with lower perceived competency in managing suicide risk indicated lower levels of willingness to assess or treat suicidal patients (Graham, Rudd, & Bryan, 2011).

Concerning assessment of available means, medicine, family medicine, and geriatric physicians were more likely to assess intent to misuse medications than access to firearms when assessing suicide risk, despite the higher prevalence of use of firearms compared with medications in deaths by suicide (Kaplan, Adamek, & Calderon, 1999). With training, however, both mental health and non–mental health providers showed improved competency and confidence in assessment and treatment skills for hypothetical older adult patients with suicide ideation (Huh et al., 2012). Confidence in assessing suicide risk in older adult patients was related to increased training during residency and continuing education as well as increased training in geriatric mental health and broadly in geriatric medicine (Kaplan, Adamek, & Martin, 2001).

Some clinicians may hesitate to assess suicide risk in older adults because of unfounded concerns about the impact of suicide assessment on the patient. In a study of members of a Human Research Ethics Committee, 65% indicated concern that the process of asking a study participant about suicide ideation would have iatrogenic effects on suicide risk by increasing distress, reinforcing suicidal ideation, and potentially normalizing suicidal behavior (Lakeman & FitzGerald, 2009). Adult research participants who made suicide attempts in the past, however, reported a decrease in suicide ideation 1 month after participating in a study that assessed suicidal behavior and exposed participants to images related to suicide (Cukrowicz, Smith, & Poindexter, 2010).

CLIENT–PROVIDER ISSUES

Expectancies About Treatment: Education of Client and Family

Regardless of age, people with persistent suicidal thoughts often do not seek treatment. The World Mental Health Survey found that only 17% of suicidal individuals in low-income countries and 56% of suicidal individuals in high-income countries sought mental health treatment in the past year (Pitman & Osborn, 2011). Older adults, specifically, are unlikely to seek mental health treatment and are more likely to seek treatment from a medical or general practitioner instead of psychiatric or specialty treatment for mental health problems (Mackenzie, Gekoski, & Knox, 2006). Lack of knowledge about treatment options may be a substantial barrier. Among older adults who perceived a need for mental health treatment, 40% believed the treatment would not work and reported a lack of knowledge about appropriate providers (Mackenzie, Pagura, & Sareen, 2010). Orienting the older adult to psychotherapy or promoting mental health literacy may result in positive but realistic expectancies about the nature of the therapy (Jorm et al., 2003). The clinician should inform the client and family members, if involved, that desire for suicide is not a normal part of aging. Family members may serve an important role in monitoring behavior and suicide risk (Erlangsen et al., 2011).

Geropsychologist–Client Relationship Issues and Controversies

Significant legal, ethical, and moral considerations surround older adult suicide. Clinical wisdom indicates that empathy and a solid therapeutic relationship are essential when treating suicidal individuals, perhaps more so than for other behavioral problems (Rudd, Joiner, & Rajab, 2001). Rudd et al., (2001) suggested that the clinician aim to treat the client "better than everyone else" (p. 43) in the client's life. They also suggested that in managing suicidal crises, clinician–client relationships can be forged and strengthened, which may increase the client's feelings of belonging and reduce the desire for suicide (Joiner et al., 2009)

Although less common in older adults, individuals who engage in chronic self-harm, make repeated suicide attempts, or display features of borderline personality disorder may be particularly challenging psychotherapy clients (Linehan, 1993; McIntosh & Drapeau, 2012). Additionally, therapists working with suicidal individuals of any age encounter the challenge of balancing safety concerns with other treatment goals. Clinicians are encouraged to reference Linehan's (1993) detailed writing on the subject of client–therapist relationships and how to prioritize safety, as other goals cannot be achieved without it. In all cases, therapists may go to greater lengths to keep suicidal individuals in therapy (Berk, Henriques, Warman, Brown, & Beck, 2004).

Regardless of age, anxiety and fear on the part of the therapist may interfere with the therapeutic process and relationship (Rudd et al., 2001). A survey of randomly selected clinical psychologists found that 97% feared a client dying by suicide while under their care (Pope & Tabachnick, 1993). Litigation is also a serious concern for therapists who work with clients of elevated suicide risk (Jobes, 2006). Consultation may be important to manage biases, stress, and reactions in the therapist. Although the vast majority of mental health practitioners will encounter a suicidal individual over the course of their practice, training for assessment, treatment, and management of suicidal behavior is often sporadic or ineffective (Schmitz et al., 2012). Challenges abound for the clinician working with suicidal clients, but training in assessment of risk, maintaining awareness of legal and ethical issues (Bongar & Sullivan, 2013), seeking consultation, and talking frankly with the older client and their family members about suicide may ameliorate some of these problems and stressors.

INTERVENTIONS

This section summarizes and discusses the existing evidence for interventions to prevent suicidal behavior in older adults. Suicide prevention may be described as falling along a continuum of universal, selected, and indicated strategies. This language was suggested by the Institute of Medicine to classify prevention efforts generally (Muñoz, Mrazek, & Haggerty, 1996) and has been applied in different ways to interventions for suicidal behavior (e.g., Conwell et al., 2011; Erlangsen et al., 2011). Universal prevention targets whole populations. Selective prevention targets groups that are at higher risk for, but do not display signs of, the outcome of interest. According to an expert consensus report on suicide prevention in late life, selective suicide interventions include monitoring and treating problems related to suicide, such as depressive symptoms or pain (Erlangsen et al., 2011). Indicated prevention, provided at the individual level, is focused on reducing acute risk among individuals with early signs or symptoms of the outcome of interest. The consensus report describes indicated suicide interventions as targeting individuals after they display serious suicidal behavior. An indicated approach may be problematic for older adults because they are much more likely to die during any single attempt, compared with younger adults (McIntosh & Drapeau, 2012). Waiting to intervene until after serious suicidal behavior is likely to be too late for older adults. Thus, universal and selected interventions may be particularly important for older adults.

Universal Preventive Interventions

Universal prevention efforts applicable to the prevention of suicide include means restriction, screenings, and education (Erlangsen et al., 2011).

Means restriction. Guns are used in most late-life suicide deaths, especially among men (Kaplan, Huguet, McFarland, & Mandle, 2012), so legislation or public health efforts that reduce the proliferation or use of guns could affect suicide deaths in this population. The Brady Handgun Violence Prevention Act, implemented in 1994, required waiting periods and background checks for handgun sales. Ludwig and Cook (2000) analyzed change in homicide and suicide rates after the implementation of the law. Although no effect was found on homicides, gun suicide rates among those over 55 years old were reduced by about 6% in states that had newly implemented the laws, controlling for age, race, poverty, income levels, urban residence, and alcohol consumption.

Screening and public education. Several large-scale screening programs have been evaluated with respect to reducing suicidal behavior. A population-based intervention on the island of Gotland, Sweden, involved training all general practitioners in the identification and treatment of depression and suicide risk (Rihmer, Rutz, & Pihlgren, 1995). The intervention had positive effects on the appropriateness of prescribed medication (i.e., more antidepressants; fewer sedatives and anxiolytics), decreases in inpatient care, and lower suicide death rates among depressed women (Rutz, 1999). A similar intervention in Hungary included education of medical professionals, the opportunity for free consultation with psychiatrists via telephone, and a newly established clinic for depression treatment (Szanto, Kalmar, Hendin, Rihmer, & Mann, 2007). Results were more modest than those found in Sweden, but similar in that there was a greater reduction in suicide deaths among females than among males. Although these screening strategies were not older adult-specific, they may be relevant to older individuals, who are overrepresented among medical patients.

Oyama et al. (2008) conducted a meta-analysis of a series of quasi-experimental studies that he and his colleagues conducted in regions of Japan with very high suicide rates for individuals over 65 years. The interventions consisted of a multistep depressive symptom screening in the community conducted by nurses and psychiatrists, with follow-up by either a psychiatrist or a general practitioner. Some trials also included education, group activities, or training focused on increasing stigma for death by suicide. Across studies, intervention by psychiatrists resulted in a 40% reduction in suicide deaths in women and

a 20% reduction in men over 6 to 10 years, compared with regions that did not receive the screenings. When general practitioners provided the follow-up treatment, however, there was a 35% reduction for women and almost no effect for men (Oyama et al., 2008). The authors also concluded that education, group activities, and referral to a general practitioner were effective for women, but men required psychiatric care to reduce their risk (Oyama et al., 2005). A subsequent study showed reductions in suicide rates that were even greater among men than women when screening with psychiatric follow-up was used (Oyama et al., 2010).

Existing evidence suggests that universal approaches can prevent suicides in older adults, but that older men may require psychiatric intervention to reduce suicide deaths.

Selected Preventive Interventions

Selected interventions include telephone-based outreach programs, treatments for depression or other psychological problems related to suicide, and pharmacological treatments. We define selected interventions to be approaches that are used for people who have a heightened risk for suicide, although the interventions themselves are not suicide specific.

Gatekeepers. Identifying individuals at increased risk for suicide is an important task to facilitate the application of selected interventions. Paul Quinnett and the QPR ("question, persuade, refer") team developed a training program for laypersons and professionals to identify people at risk for suicide (Quinnett, 2007). In the case of older adults, "gatekeepers" may be primary health care providers, mail carriers, individuals delivering meals, clergy, or various other workers who might be in a unique position of contact with older persons. No evidence yet suggests that QPR prevents suicide deaths, but a review of gatekeeping interventions across ages and settings, including some of the prevention strategies already listed in this chapter, supports the efficacy of these efforts for improving gatekeeper knowledge and attitudes and reducing suicidal outcomes (Isaac et al., 2009).

Telephone-based outreach programs. An outreach program in northern Italy, Telehelp-Telecheck, provided an emergency button to summon help, brief and informal twice-weekly phone calls, and 24-hour telephone support as-needed to a large number of older adults with psychiatric or somatic problems. Users of the service had lower than expected suicide rates over 11 years: 6 suicide deaths versus more than 20 expected suicide deaths (De Leo et al., 2002). In addition to the quasi-experimental studies in Japan (Oyama et al., 2008), this study describes one of the only interventions associated with a reduction in suicide deaths in older adults (see Table 6.2).

Phone-based crisis and supportive counseling programs have been shown to reduce hopelessness (Fiske & Arbore, 2000–2001), increase social contact, and reduce depressive symptoms (Morrow-Howell, Becker-Kemppainen, & Judy, 1998) among older adults at risk for suicide.

Treatments for depressive symptoms and disorders. Treatments for depressive symptoms are likely to be the most promising avenue for preventing suicide in older adults. Psychosocial treatments are effective for treating depressive disorders and reducing depressive symptoms among older adults (Pinquart, Duberstein, & Lyness, 2007; see also Chapter 1, this volume). Evidence linking depression treatment to reductions in suicidal outcomes is sparse. Using depression care managers in primary care has been shown to reduce suicide-related ideation (Alexopoulos et al., 2009; Unützer et al., 2002). Likewise, the population-based interventions described earlier targeted depression treatment and saw reductions in suicide rates.

Treatments for other related disorders and risk factors. Physical illness, disability or physical limitations, and pain are risk factors for suicide-related ideation or behavior in older adults (see previous section). Integrating management of medical conditions into psychotherapy could be an avenue to maximize well-being and reduce suicide risk (Bhar & Brown, 2012).

Treatment of psychological problems such as insomnia also may help to prevent suicidal behavior in older adults. Cognitive–behavioral therapy for insomnia has been shown to be associated with substantial reductions in suicide-related ideation and increases in hopefulness in adults ages 21 to 88 years (Manber et al., 2011). The Substance Abuse and Mental Health Services Administration's (2013) National Registry for Evidence-Based Programs and Practices lists interventions targeted throughout the life span for a wide variety of other problems. Reducing the burden of substance abuse or other psychological problems through empirically based treatments could have an impact on suicidal behaviors, although these relations have not been demonstrated in exclusively older adult samples.

Pharmacological treatments. No pharmacological treatments have been specifically developed to prevent suicidal behavior. Among individuals with major affective disorders, however, lithium was associated with five times fewer suicide deaths and attempted suicide compared with other treatments (Baldessarini et al., 2006). Other pharmacological treatments are associated with reduced suicidal behaviors in older adults. Among depressed adults over 60 years old, paroxetine or nortriptyline reduced the prevalence of suicide-related ideation from 77.5% to 18.4% over 12 weeks (Szanto, Mulsant, Houck, Dew, & Reynolds, 2003). Hall et al. (2003) found that an increase in the prescription of antidepressants in Australia between 1991 and 2000 was followed by reduced suicide deaths among older adults, who had the greatest exposure to antidepressants of all age groups (Hall et al., 2003). Although studies show an elevated suicide risk for young adults who use antidepressants, the opposite effect was found in adults and older adults. The odds of suicidal behavior among individuals taking antidepressants significantly decreased with age in clinical trials (Stone et al., 2009). This evidence suggests that pharmaceutical treatments can help to prevent late-life suicide deaths.

Indicated Preventive Interventions

For individuals with recurring and intense ideation or suicide attempts, it may be appropriate to focus therapy on these behaviors, instead of depression or other psychopathology (Bruce et al., 2004). Although several treatment packages have been tailored for the purpose of addressing and reducing suicide-related outcomes (e.g., Joiner, Van Orden,

TABLE 6.2

Summary of Treatments for Suicide-Related Outcomes, With Emphasis on Those Tested in Older Adults

Treatment approach	Example publication	Evidence of effectiveness for . . .	Tested in older adults?
Universal			
Physician training (screening for and treatment of depression)	Rihmer et al., 1995	Suicide deaths	No
	Oyama et al., 2008	Suicide deaths	Yes
Brady Bill (means restriction)	Ludwig and Cook, 2000	Suicide deaths	Yes
Selected			
Telephone-based outreach	De Leo et al., 2002	Suicide deaths	Yes
	Fiske and Arbore, 2000–2001	Hopelessness	Yes
	Morrow-Howell et al., 1998	Depressive symptoms, social contact	Yes
Depression care management			
1. Antidepressant medication and problem-solving therapy	Unützer et al., 2006	Suicide-related ideation	Yes
2. Citalopram and interpersonal therapy	Alexopoulos et al., 2009	Suicide-related ideation	Yes
Cognitive–behavioral therapy for insomnia	Manber et al., 2011	Suicide-related ideation	No
Lithium	Baldessarini et al., 2006	Suicide deaths, self-harm	No
Antidepressant medication	Stone et al., 2009	Suicide deaths	Yes
Indicated			
Cognitive therapy	Brown et al., 2005	Suicide attempt	No
Dialectical behavior therapy	Lynch et al., 2003	Depressive symptoms	Yes
Problem-solving therapy	Koons et al., 2001	Suicide-related ideation, self-harm	No
	Stewart et al., 2009	Suicide-related ideation, hopelessness, depressive symptoms	No
Interpersonal therapy	Heisel et al., 2009	Suicide-related ideation	Yes

Witte, & Rudd, 2009; Rudd, Joiner, & Rajab, 2001), most have not been tested in older adults.

Cognitive and cognitive–behavioral therapies.
Cognitive and cognitive–behavioral therapies (CT and CBT) provide strategies for both reducing suicidal urges and alleviating poor mood (van der Sande, Buskens, Allart, van der Graaf, & van Engeland, 1997). Targets include cognitive distortions related to suicide, namely, dichotomous thinking, ineffective problem solving, and a view of suicide as a desirable solution (Berk et al., 2004; Coon, DeVries, & Gallagher-Thompson, 2004). CT and CBT are structured and include ongoing tracking of mood and assessment of suicidal risk, agenda-setting, and homework assignments (Berk et al., 2004).

Other behavioral techniques include behavioral activation, strategies to increase social support, and safety planning. Finally, relapse prevention is an important part of CT and CBT (for a detailed description, see Berk et al., 2004).

CT and CBT have empirical support in younger samples. Randomized controlled trials in adult suicide attempters have found reduced future suicide attempts (Brown et al., 2005) and decreased suicidal ideation, hopelessness, and depressive symptoms (Stewart, Quinn, Plever, & Emerson, 2009) compared with treatment as usual. Bhar and Brown (2012) have developed a 12-session CBT protocol for older adults with depressive symptoms and suicide risk. Modifications for older adults include a focus on managing medical issues and loneliness, restoring a sense of purpose, and the use of simple, practical homework. However, data generated from the use of this intervention have not yet been published.

Dialectical behavior therapy (DBT) is an effective treatment for chronic suicidal and parasuicidal behavior in women (e.g., Koons et al., 2001). The coping skills of radical acceptance, mindfulness, distress tolerance, and opposite action are taught to the client to increase their flexible and adaptive behavior in the face of crises. Among other strategies, suicidal crises are examined for precipitating events and the resulting thoughts and behaviors that perpetuate self-harm. This technique is designed to help the client avoid self-harm by planning to use techniques learned in therapy the next time they feel suicidal. Although DBT has not been evaluated in relation to suicidal outcomes in older adults, it has been used for the treatment of depression in this group. Two randomized controlled trials including individuals over age 60 years who exhibited depressive symptoms showed that modified DBT plus antidepressant medication resulted in a higher proportion of participants reaching remission, compared with medication alone (Lynch et al., 2007; Lynch, Morse, Mendelson, & Robins, 2003). It seems likely that DBT may reduce suicide risk in older adults, but further study is needed.

Another cognitive–behavioral approach is problem-solving therapy (PST), which focuses on teaching clients to consider alternatives and approach problems in a flexible and competent way. PST may be especially valuable for older adults with inflexible cognitive styles or mild cognitive impairment. PST has been tested as part of the care management algorithm for depression used in the IMPACT trial, which was shown to reduce suicide-related ideation in older adults (Unützer et al., 2006). PST has been shown to reduce suicidal ideation, hopelessness, and depressive symptoms in a young to middle-age adult sample, compared with treatment as usual (Stewart et al., 2009).

Interpersonal therapy.   Interpersonal therapy (IPT) focuses on relationships, role changes, and grief. It was part of the care management algorithm provided in the PROSPECT trial, which reduced

suicide-related ideation in a sample of older adults receiving care for major or minor depression (Alexopoulos et al., 2009). Not all participants in that trial received IPT. Results are mixed regarding the efficacy of brief IPT for reducing suicide-related ideation in older adults (Heisel, Duberstein, Talbot, King, & Tu, 2009; Szanto et al., 2003).

Safety plans, no-harm contracts, and hospitalization.   Safety plans consist of a sequence of steps, generally developed in collaboration with the client, that the client agrees to take if they are feeling suicidal. They typically include reminders to use emotion regulation skills, people to call for help, and hotline or hospital information. Although safety planning has not been evaluated empirically as a stand-alone treatment, the technique is widely recommended (e.g., Rudd et al., 2001; Stanley & Brown, 2012). Sample safety plans can be found in Joiner et al. (2009) and Rudd et al. (2001). Joiner et al. (2009) and others also have suggested the use of a commitment-to-treatment statement, which outlines client responsibilities, including engaging fully in the therapy and using a crisis plan.

Safety plans and commitment-to-treatment contracts should not be confused with no-harm contracts, which generally are not recommended (Rudd et al., 2001). A no-harm contract may be an oral or written agreement in which the client promises not to engage in suicide-related behavior during a specified period of time. No-harm contracts may seem administrative, instead of therapeutic, to the client, and may take the place of more effective intervention strategies. They also may seem coercive if there is an implied or real threat of hospitalization if the client does not sign, for example. Furthermore, no-harm contracts may be asking the client to promise something they cannot deliver (i.e., to behave rationally in the midst of a suicidal crisis). Although common in clinical practice, "contracted for safety" is not an adequate legal documentation of the procedure, nor is it an adequate suicide prevention technique (Lewis, 2007). Instead, clinicians should establish a procedure for baseline and ongoing assessment and documentation to formalize the attention to suicide risk. The Collaborative

Assessment and Management of Suicidality (Jobes, 2006) provides an example.

Like no-harm contracts, hospitalization in a psychiatric facility does not guarantee safety. In a study of individuals who had died by suicide during or shortly after hospitalization, a large percentage of decedents had been on "15-min checks" for safety or were acting under an active no-suicide contract (Busch, Fawcett, & Jacobs, 2003). Among Danish older adults, more than half of suicide deaths occurred within 1 week of psychiatric hospital admission or discharge (Erlangsen, Zarit, Tu, & Conwell, 2006). This evidence suggests that prevention of suicide-related behavior in older individuals must consist of more than hospitalization. Simple follow-up after discharge may prevent suicides. Letters sent to a randomly selected group of young adult patients for up to 5 years after hospitalization were associated with fewer suicides compared with a no-follow-up group (Motto & Bostrom, 2001). The strategy has yet to be tested in older adults.

In summary, several comprehensive interventions have addressed the treatment of suicidal behavior, but most have not been specific to older adults or tested in older adult populations. Across age groups, intervention research regarding death by suicide is limited. As one avenue to increasing the research base, clinicians and researchers are encouraged to also consider single-case designs for examining suicide-related outcomes in individual or small groups of older adult clients (Rizvi & Nock, 2008). Overall, more research is needed on which interventions actually prevent suicide attempts and deaths among older adults.

CLINICAL APPLICATIONS

Several contextual factors should be considered when assessing or treating older adults at risk of suicide. In the sections that follow, we discuss gender and cultural factors and consider the management of suicide risk in two settings relevant to older adults: long-term care and primary care.

Gender

Although men have the highest rates of death by suicide in late life (CDC, 2013), most studies find that women benefit more from preventive interventions aimed at preventing or reducing suicidal outcomes (De Leo et al., 2002; Oyama et al., 2008; Rutz, Wålinder, Von Knorring, Rihmer, & Pihlgren, 1997). Suggested reasons for this apparent gender difference include reduced help-seeking in men as well as enhanced stigma of mental illness or surviving a suicide attempt among men (Hinton, Zweifach, Oishi, Tang, & Unützer, 2006). Men and individuals who strongly endorse a masculine gender role may also be less likely to fit the diagnostic criteria for major depressive disorder, which could contribute to difficulty in identifying men at risk (Price, Gregg, Smith, & Fiske, 2014). A heavy focus on autonomy has been found to moderate the relation between depressive symptoms and suicide risk for men but not women, providing another clue as to gender differences in suicidal behavior (Bamonti, Price, & Fiske, 2014). Men are more likely than women to use guns to die by suicide (Kaplan et al., 2012). Gun safety efforts could be one avenue for reducing suicide deaths among older men. Researchers conducting treatment research should make substantial efforts to include older men and explore ways to reach men before a suicide attempt or death.

Cultural Factors

Little is known about the treatment of suicidal behaviors in older adults of different racial and ethnic backgrounds. Non-White older adults, with the exception of Native American and Alaskan Natives, are less likely to die by suicide, but they are also less likely to seek psychological help for anxiety or mood disorders (Byers, Arean, & Yaffe, 2012; Nock et al., 2008). Coon et al. (2004) suggested that clinicians be sensitive to multiple layers of disadvantage that minority elders may face (i.e., aging and racial prejudice). In addition, culture can influence how individuals interpret the etiology and meaning of their psychological distress as well as how they respond to it.

Long-Term Care

Individuals in long-term care (LTC) tend to have several risk factors for suicidal behavior, including advanced age, functional limitations, hopelessness, and mood disorders. Researchers are just beginning to turn their attention to suicidal behaviors in this group. Current methods to deal with suicidal thoughts or behavior in LTC include initiating "15-min checks," close observation, or transferring the individuals to the emergency room or hospital. Unfortunately, none of these strategies are optimal or effective (Busch et al., 2003; O'Riley, Nadorff, Conwell, & Edelstein, 2013). O'Riley et al. (2013) have suggested that LTC staff be trained to handle suicidal crises in a structured way to keep the person in the facility and safe, without overextending resources.

A promising development in the area of LTC and suicide risk management is the inclusion of the PHQ-9 in the Minimum Data Set, a set of regular physical and psychosocial assessments required for facilities receiving Medicare or Medicaid payments. Regular assessment of suicide-related ideation could enhance detection of individuals at risk in LTC.

Primary Care

Of older adults who die by suicide, 43% to 70% have contact with a health care professional in the month before death (Luoma, Martin, & Pearson, 2002). By contrast, only a small minority of older adults who die by suicide are seen in specialty mental health care in this timeframe. The implication is that primary care may provide an opportunity for identifying older adults at risk of suicide. The U.S. Preventive Services Task Force concluded in 2005 (USPSTF, 2005) and again in 2013 (O'Connor, Gaynes, Burda, Soh, & Whitlock, 2013) that there was insufficient evidence to recommend for or against screening for suicide risk in primary care. Nonetheless, recent research provides some evidence that screening instruments can reliably predict suicidal ideation among older adults in primary care settings (Fujisawa et al., 2005; Heisel et al., 2010), and that interventions can lead to improved outcomes for identified patients (Bruce et al., 2004; Alexopoulos et al., 2009), including reduced likelihood of suicide attempt (Almeida et al., 2012) and perhaps even reduced risk of suicide (Oyama et al., 2008). No studies have tested specifically for harms associated with screening for suicide risk in primary care, although studies show no iatrogenic effects of screening for suicide risk, even among adults

(Cukrowicz et al., 2010). Primary care practices screening for suicide risk in older adults should have a plan in place for further assessment and referral or treatment when suicide risk is detected. The potential benefits of screening for suicide risk in primary care were illustrated by research conducted by Bryan, Corso, Rudd, and Cordero (2008), who reported that screening improved detection by 600% compared with reliance on patients to mention suicide-related ideations to the primary care physician.

Case Example

This case study describes assessment and intervention with a functionally impaired older man who expressed a desire to die but largely denied suicidal ideation. The case illustrates the complexities, and potential benefits, of psychological interventions in such instances.

The client was a retired professional in his mid-80s living in a skilled nursing facility for which our clinical team provides psychological services. Staff referred him after he stated that he would rather be dead than go on living in the facility, depleting financial resources that otherwise would go to his heirs. The resident had several chronic illnesses, was confined to his bed, and required assistance with basic activities of daily living. He reported significant pain, especially when being moved. He had a history of depression and insomnia. Intake assessment indicated possible cognitive dysfunction. He scored below the clinical cutoff for significant depressive symptoms. He endorsed reduced appetite, thoughts of death, and feelings of worthlessness, but denied pervasive dysphoria or anhedonia, and thus did not meet diagnostic criteria for major depressive disorder. There was no sign of other affective disorders, anxiety, psychosis, substance use disorders, or insomnia. Scores on the Geriatric Suicide Ideation Scale (GSIS) were below the level seen in clinical samples, although he did endorse items on the death ideation subscale. The resident denied current suicidal ideation or intent, spontaneously offering reasons for living (religion and family). He indicated strong social support, good relationships with facility staff, and engagement in activities he enjoyed (e.g., listening to music, solving puzzles).

We initially evaluated the resident's current risk of suicide as low and did not recommend treatment. Staff members, however, reported that he continued to express a wish that he were dead. We reconsidered his symptoms of depression in light of the evidence that even minor depression increases risk for suicide (Waern et al., 2002) and that some older adults (Gallo, Anthony, & Muthén, 1994) and men (Magovcevic & Addis, 2008) display symptoms of depression without endorsing sadness. Furthermore, the resident's disability, chronic pain, and feelings of burden placed him at increased risk for suicide (Cukrowicz et al., 2011; Juurlink et al., 2004). For these reasons, we recommended CBT to address perceived burdensomeness and persistent death ideation. When we presented this option to the resident, he indicated that he did not need treatment but would participate to help the student therapist.

The intervention consisted of weekly 30-min sessions of individual therapy using cognitive-behavioral techniques. A major focus was the resident's perception that he was a burden on his family, although he acknowledged that his family members indicated otherwise. On the basis of the norm of reciprocity, we reasoned that the resident's perception of being a burden on others would be reduced to the extent that his perception of being helpful to others increased. Therefore, we used cognitive restructuring techniques to assist the resident in recognizing the ways he was helpful to his family members and others. In addition, we used behavioral activation strategies to facilitate the resident's engagement in pleasant and meaningful activities, with a focus on introducing activities that would involve giving back to others (e.g., assisting staff in developing new activities for other residents in the facility). Although initially skeptical, the resident was cooperative and engaged fully in the psychotherapy. He participated in cognitive restructuring without apparent difficulty, in spite of slightly low scores on cognitive screening.

Evidence suggests the intervention was successful. Staff reported that the resident was no longer expressing a wish to die or indicating a perception that he was a burden on others. We observed improved affect and greater interest in his environment. Self-report measures reflected no significant change, as would be expected because of the low scores at baseline.

This case study highlights the potential for improving outcomes in older adults who express a desire to die. It is not possible to determine whether the beneficial effects of treatment can be attributed to behavioral activation generally or to facilitation of giving behavior in the resident. Volunteer activity and other forms of giving have been linked to positive mental health outcomes (Lum & Lightfoot, 2005; Wheeler, Gorey, & Greenblatt, 1998). Giving assistance to others may have reduced distress associated with accepting help and may have enhanced the resident's sense of meaning in life, even in a situation that others would consider hopeless.

A limitation of this case study is that the client did not endorse suicidal ideation. Nonetheless, even older adults who display no suicidal ideation or psychopathology may be at risk of suicide, and those who exhibit difficulties coping with stressors potentially could benefit from treatment. The older man described here appeared to have benefited from the intervention.

Finally, this case study highlights the importance of integrated psychological services within an LTC setting. The staff functioned as highly effective gatekeepers, recognizing that this resident's statements regarding a wish to be dead, although understandable, also could be a signal that he would benefit from psychological services. Their vigilance helped our team to monitor the resident's progress. In addition, the activity staff worked with us to make it possible for the resident to contribute to the life of the community.

CONCLUSION

Suicide is an important issue for clinical geropsychologists. Older men are at increased risk of suicide compared with other age groups, but it is not yet clear to what extent the increased risk stems from greater desire to die versus a greater ability to enact lethal self-harm. This is an important distinction, as these two mechanisms have different implications for prevention.

To understand suicidal behavior in late life, it is necessary to take a life-span developmental perspective. Depression is the most important risk factor for suicide in late life. Other proximal risk factors include physical health status, cognitive status, and social factors. Factors that may increase vulnerability to suicide include genetics and some aspects of personality. Hopelessness remains an important marker of suicide risk throughout the life span. Factors that specifically increase capability for suicide, rather than desire to die by suicide, among older adults have not yet been directly examined, but promising targets include past suicidal behavior, access to readily lethal means, social isolation, exposure to death and dying, and perceived acceptability of suicide.

Several suicide risk assessment measures have been developed specifically for, or validated in, older adult populations. Selected and universal suicide prevention strategies have some support in older adult samples and may be most appropriate for this group. Several individual therapy interventions have addressed the treatment of suicidal behavior, but most have not been specific to older adults or tested in older adult populations. Gender and other demographic factors may affect the efficacy of prevention efforts. Family members and LTC staff, among others, can act as gatekeepers to help older adults access treatment. Screening in primary care may be helpful, but additional research is needed. Overall, more research is needed on which interventions actually prevent suicide attempts and deaths among older adults.

References

Ajzen, I. (1991). The theory of planned behavior. *Organizational Behavior and Human Decision Processes*, *50*, 179–211. doi:10.1016/0749-5978(91)90020-T

Alexopoulos, G. S., Reynolds, C. F. I., Bruce, M. L., Katz, I. R., Raue, P. J., Mulsant, B. H., . . . Ten Have, T. (2009). Reducing suicidal ideation and depression in older primary care patients: 24-month outcomes of the PROSPECT study. *American Journal of Psychiatry*, *166*, 882–890. doi:10.1176/appi.ajp.2009.08121779

Almeida, O. P., Pirkis, J., Kerse, N., Sim, M., Flicker, L., Snowdon, J., . . . Pfaff, J. J. (2012). A randomized trial to reduce the prevalence of depression and self-harm behavior in older primary care patients. *Annals of Family Medicine*, *10*, 347–356. doi:10.1370/afm.1368

American Psychiatric Association. (2013). *Diagnostic and statistical manual of mental disorders* (5th ed.). Washington, DC: Author.

Ayalon, L., Mackin, S., Arean, P. A., Chen, H., & Herr, C. M. (2007). The role of cognitive functioning and distress in suicidal ideation in older adults. *Journal of the American Geriatrics Society*, *55*, 1090–1094. doi:10.1111/j.1532-5415.2007.01237.x

Baldessarini, R. J., Tondo, L., Davis, P., Pompili, M., Goodwin, F. K., & Hennen, J. (2006). Decreased risk of suicides and attempts during long-term lithium treatment: A meta-analytic review. *Bipolar Disorders*, *8*, 625–639. doi:10.1111/j.1399-5618.2006.00344.x

Bamonti, P. M., Price, E. C., & Fiske, A. (2014). Depressive symptoms and suicide risk in older adults: Value placed on autonomy as a moderator for men but not women. *Suicide and Life-Threatening Behavior*, *44*, 188–199. doi:10.1111/sltb.12062

Barnow, S., Linden, M., Lucht, M., & Freyberger, H. J. (2004). Influence of age of patients who wish to die on treatment decisions by physicians and nurses. *American Journal of Geriatric Psychiatry*, *12*, 258–264. doi:10.1097/00019442-200405000-00004

Beautrais, A. L. (2001). Suicide and attempted suicide: Two populations or one? *Psychological Medicine*, *31*, 837–845. doi:10.1017/S0033291701003889

Beautrais, A. L. (2002). A case control study of suicide and attempted suicide in older adults. *Suicide and Life-Threatening Behavior*, *32*, 1–9. doi:10.1521/suli.32.1.1.22184

Beck, A. T., Brown, G., Berchick, R. J., Stewart, B. L., & Steer, R. A. (1990). Relationship between hopelessness and ultimate suicide: A replication with psychiatric outpatients. *American Journal of Psychiatry*, *147*, 190–195.

Beck, A. T., Brown, G. K., & Steer, R. A. (1997). Psychometric characteristics of the Scale for Suicide Ideation with psychiatric outpatients. *Behaviour Research and Therapy*, *35*, 1039–1046. doi:10.1016/S0005-7967(97)00073-9

Beck, A. T., Kovacs, M., & Weissman, A. (1975). Hopelessness and suicidal behavior: An overview. *JAMA*, *234*, 1146–1149. doi:10.1001/jama.1975.03260240050026

Beck, A. T., Kovacs, M., & Weissman, A. (1979). Assessment of suicidal intention: The Scale for Suicide Ideation. *Journal of Consulting and Clinical Psychology*, *47*, 343–352. doi:10.1037/0022-006X.47.2.343

Beck, A. T., Weissman, A., Lester, D., & Trexler, L. (1974). The measurement of pessimism: The Hopelessness Scale. *Journal of Consulting and Clinical Psychology*, *42*, 861–865. doi:10.1037/h0037562

Berk, M. S., Henriques, G. R., Warman, D. M., Brown, G. K., & Beck, A. T. (2004). A cognitive therapy intervention for suicide attempters: An overview of the treatment and case examples. *Cognitive and Behavioral Practice, 11*, 265–277. doi:10.1016/S1077-7229(04)80041-5

Bhar, S. S., & Brown, G. K. (2012). Treatment of depression and suicide in older adults. *Cognitive and Behavioral Practice, 19*, 116–125. doi:10.1016/j.cbpra.2010.12.005

Bongar, B., & Sullivan, G. R. (2013). *The suicidal patient: Clinical and legal standards of care* (3rd ed.). Washington, DC: American Psychological Association. doi:10.1037/14184-000

Brown, G. K., Beck, A. T., Steer, R. A., & Grisham, J. R. (2000). Risk factors for suicide in psychiatric outpatients: A 20-year prospective study. *Journal of Consulting and Clinical Psychology, 68*, 371–377. doi:10.1037/0022-006X.68.3.371

Brown, G. K., Ten Have, T., Henriques, G. R., Xie, S. X., Hollander, J. E., & Beck, A. T. (2005). Cognitive therapy for the prevention of suicide attempts: A randomized controlled trial. *JAMA, 294*, 563–570. doi:10.1001/jama.294.5.563

Bruce, M. L., Ten Have, T. R., Reynolds, C. F., III, Katz, I. I., Schulberg, H. C., Mulsant, B., . . . Alexopoulos, G. S. (2004). Reducing suicidal ideation and depressive symptoms in depressed older primary care patients: A randomized controlled trial. *JAMA, 291*, 1081–1091. doi:10.1001/jama.291.9.1081

Bryan, C. J., Corso, K. A., Rudd, M. D., & Cordero, L. (2008). Improving identification of suicidal patients in primary care through routine screening. *Primary Care and Community Psychiatry, 13*, 143–147.

Busch, K. A., Fawcett, J., & Jacobs, D. G. (2003). Clinical correlates of inpatient suicide. *Journal of Clinical Psychiatry, 64*, 14–19. doi:10.4088/JCP.v64n0105

Byers, A. L., Arean, P. A., & Yaffe, K. (2012). Low use of mental health services among older Americans with mood and anxiety disorders. *Psychiatric Services, 63*, 66–72. doi:10.1176/appi.ps.201100121

Caine, E. D., & Conwell, Y. (2001). Suicide in the elderly. *International Clinical Psychopharmacology, 16*(Suppl. 2), S25–S30. doi:10.1097/00004850-200103002-00005

Canetto, S. S. (1997). Gender and suicidal behavior: Theories and evidence. In R. W. Maris, M. M. Silverman, & S. S. Canetto (Eds.), *Review of suicidology* (pp. 138–167). New York, NY: Guilford Press.

Centers for Disease Control and Prevention. (2013). *Web-based injury statistics query and reporting system.* Retrieved from http://www.cdc.gov/injury/wisqars/index.html

Cheng, S.-T., Yu, E. C. S., Lee, S. Y., Wong, J. Y. H., Lau, K. H., Chan, L. K., . . . Wong, M. W. L. (2010). The Geriatric Depression Scale as a screening tool for depression and suicide ideation: A replication and extension. *American Journal of Geriatric Psychiatry, 18*, 256–265. doi:10.1097/JGP.0b013e3181bf9edd

Clark, D. C. (1993). Narcissistic crises of aging and suicidal despair. *Suicide and Life-Threatening Behavior, 23*, 21–26.

Clark, L., Dombrovski, A. Y., Siegle, G. J., Butters, M. A., Shollenberger, C. L., Sahakian, B. J., & Szanto, K. (2011). Impairment in risk-sensitive decision-making in older suicide attempters with depression. *Psychology and Aging, 26*, 321–330. doi:10.1037/a0021646

Conwell, Y., Duberstein, P. R., Cox, C., Herrmann, J., Forbes, N., & Caine, E. D. (1998). Age differences in behaviors leading to completed suicide. *American Journal of Geriatric Psychiatry, 6*, 122–126. doi:10.1097/00019442-199805000-00005

Conwell, Y., Duberstein, P. R., Hirsch, J. K., Conner, K. R., Eberly, S., & Caine, E. D. (2010). Health status and suicide in the second half of life. *International Journal of Geriatric Psychiatry, 25*, 371–379. doi:10.1002/gps.2348

Conwell, Y., Lyness, J. M., Duberstein, P., Cox, C., Seidlitz, L., DiGiorgio, A., & Caine, E. D. (2000). Completed suicide among older patients in primary care practices: A controlled study. *Journal of the American Geriatrics Society, 48*, 23–29.

Conwell, Y., Rotenberg, M., & Caine, E. D. (1990). Completed suicide at age 50 and over. *Journal of the American Geriatrics Society, 38*, 640–644.

Conwell, Y., Van Orden, K., & Caine, E. D. (2011). Suicide in older adults. *Psychiatric Clinics of North America, 34*, 451–468. doi:10.1016/j.psc.2011.02.002

Coon, D. W., DeVries, H. M., & Gallagher-Thompson, D. (2004). Cognitive–behavioral therapy with suicidal older adults. *Behavioural and Cognitive Psychotherapy, 32*, 481–493. doi:10.1017/S1352465804001651

Corson, K., Gerrity, M., & Dobscha, S. (2004). Screening for depression and suicidality in a VA primary care setting: 2 items are better than 1 item. *American Journal of Managed Care, 10*, 839–845.

Cukrowicz, K., Smith, P., & Poindexter, E. (2010). The effect of participating in suicide research: Does participating in a research protocol on suicide and psychiatric symptoms increase suicide ideation and attempts? *Suicide and Life-Threatening Behavior, 40*, 535–543. doi:10.1521/suli.2010.40.6.535

Cukrowicz, K. C., Cheavens, J. S., Van Orden, K. A., Ragain, R. M., & Cook, R. L. (2011). Perceived burdensomeness and suicide ideation in older adults.

Psychology and Aging, 26, 331–338. doi:10.1037/a0021836

De Leo, D., Buono, M. D., & Dwyer, J. (2002). Suicide among the elderly: The long-term impact of a telephone support and assessment intervention in northern Italy. *British Journal of Psychiatry, 181,* 226–229. doi:10.1192/bjp.181.3.226

De Leo, D., Draper, B. M., Snowdon, J., & Kõlves, K. (2013). Suicides in older adults: A case-control psychological autopsy study in Australia. *Journal of Psychiatric Research, 47,* 980–988. doi:10.1016/j.jpsychires.2013.02.009

Deluty, R. H. (1988–1989). Factors affecting the acceptability of suicide. *Omega: Journal of Death and Dying, 19,* 315–326.

De Raedt, R., Koster, E. H. W., Ryckewaert, R. (2013). Aging and attentional bias for death related and general threat-related information: Less avoidance in older as compared with middle-aged adults. *The Journals of Gerontology, Series B: Psychological Sciences and Social Sciences, 68,* 41–48. doi:10.1093/geronb/gbs047

Dombrovski, A. Y., Butters, M. A., Reynolds, C. F., III, Houck, P. R., Clark, L., Mazundar, S., & Szanto, K. (2008). Cognitive performance in suicidal depressed elderly: Preliminary report. *American Journal of Geriatric Psychiatry, 16,* 109–115. doi:10.1097/JGP.0b013e3180f6338d

Dombrovski, A. Y., Siegle, G. J., Szanto, K., Clark, L., Reynolds, C. F., III, & Aizenstein, H. (2012). The temptation of suicide: Striatal gray matter, discounting of delayed rewards, and suicide attempts in late-life depression. *Psychological Medicine, 42,* 1203–1215. doi:l0.1017/50033291711002133

Dombrovski, A. Y., Szanto, K., Siegle, G. J., Wallace, M. L., Forman, S. D., Sahakian, B., . . . Clark, L. (2011). Lethal forethoughts: Delayed reward discounting differentiates high- and low-lethality suicide attempts in old age. *Biological Psychiatry, 70,* 138–144. doi:10.1016/j.biopsych.2010.12.025

Duberstein, P. R. (2001). Are closed-minded people more open to the idea of killing themselves? *Suicide and Life-Threatening Behavior, 31,* 9–14. doi:10.1521/suli.31.1.9.21309

Duberstein, P. R., Conwell, Y., & Caine, E. D. (1994). Age differences in the personality characteristics of suicide completers: Preliminary findings from a psychological autopsy study. *Psychiatry: Interpersonal and Biological Processes, 57,* 213–224.

Duberstein, P. R., Conwell, Y., Connor, K. R., Eberly, S., Evinger, J. S., & Caine, E. D. (2004). Poor social integration and suicide: Fact or artifact? A case control study. *Psychological Medicine, 34,* 1331–1337. doi:10.1017/S0033291704002600

Durkheim, E. (1951). *Suicide: A study in sociology.* New York, NY: Free Press.

Eaton, W. W., Smith, C., Ybarra, M., Muntaner, C., & Tien, A. (2004). Center for Epidemiologic Studies Depression Scale: Review and revision (CESD and CESD–R). In M. E. Maruish (Ed.), *The use of psychological testing for treatment planning and outcomes assessment: Vol. 3. Instruments for adults* (3rd ed., pp. 363–377). Mahwah, NJ: Erlbaum.

Edelstein, B. A., Heisel, M. J., McKee, D. R., Martin, R. R., Koven, L. P., Duberstein, P. R., & Britton, P. C. (2009). Development and psychometric evaluation of the Reasons for Living—Older Adults Scale: A suicide risk assessment inventory. *Gerontologist, 49,* 736–745. doi:10.1080/07317110802072108

Erlangsen, A., Nordentoft, M., Conwell, Y., Waern, M., De Leo, D., Lindner, R., . . . Lapierre, S. (2011). Key considerations for preventing suicide in older adults: Consensus opinions of an expert panel. *Crisis, 32,* 106–109. doi:10.1027/0227-5910/a000053

Erlangsen, A., Zarit, S. H., & Conwell, Y. (2008). Hospital-diagnosed dementia and suicide: A longitudinal study using prospective, nationwide data. *American Journal of Geriatric Psychiatry, 16,* 220–228. doi:10.1097/01.JGP.0000302930.75387.7e

Erlangsen, A., Zarit, S. H., Tu, X., & Conwell, Y. (2006). Suicide among older psychiatric inpatients: An evidence-based study of a high-risk group. *American Journal of Geriatric Psychiatry, 14,* 734–741. doi:10.1097/01.JGP.0000225084.16636.ec

Fässberg, M. M., Van Orden, K. A., Duberstein, P., Erlangsen, A., Lapierre, S., Bodner, E., . . . Waern, M. (2012). A systematic review of social factors and suicidal behavior in older adulthood. *International Journal of Environmental Research and Public Health, 9,* 722–745. doi:10.3390/ijerph9030722

Fiske, A., & Arbore, P. (2000–2001). Future directions in late life suicide prevention. *Omega: Journal of Death and Dying, 42,* 37–53.

Fiske, A., O'Riley, A. A., & Widoe, R. K. (2008). Physical health and suicide in late life. *Clinical Gerontologist, 31,* 31–50. doi:10.1080/07317110801947151

Fremouw, W., McCoy, K., Tyner, E. A., & Musick, R. (2009). Suicidal Older Adult Protocol—SOAP. In J. B. Allen, E. M. Wolf, & L. VandeCreek (Eds.), *Innovations in clinical practice: A 21st century sourcebook* (Vol. 1, pp. 203–212). Sarasota, FL: Professional Resource Press/Professional Resource Exchange.

Fry, P. S. (1984). Development of a geriatric scale of hopelessness: Implications for counseling and intervention with the depressed elderly. *Journal of Counseling Psychology, 31,* 322–331. doi:10.1037/0022-0167.31.3.322

Fujisawa, D., Tanaka, E., Sakamoto, S., Neichi, K., Nakagawa, A., & Ono, Y. (2005). The development of a brief screening instrument for depression and suicidal ideation for elderly: The Depression and Suicide Screen. *Psychiatry and Clinical Neurosciences*, *59*, 634–638. doi:10.1111/j.1440-1819.2005.01429.x

Gallo, J. J., Anthony, J. C., & Muthén, B. O. (1994). Age differences in the symptoms of depression: A latent trait analysis. *Journal of Gerontology*, *49*, 251–264. doi:10.1093/geronj/49.6.P251

Gibbs, L. M., Dombrovski, A. Y., Morse, J., Siegle, G. J., Houck, P. R., & Szanto, K. (2009). When the solution is part of the problem: Problem solving in elderly suicide attempters. *International Journal of Geriatric Psychiatry*, *24*, 1396–1404. doi:10.1002/gps.2276

Graham, R. D., Rudd, M. D., & Bryan, C. J. (2011). Primary care providers' views regarding assessing and treating suicidal patients. *Suicide and Life-Threatening Behavior*, *41*, 614–623. doi:10.1111/j.1943-278X.2011.00058.x

Hall, W. D., Mant, A., Mitchell, P. B., Rendle, V. A., Hickie, I. B., & McManus, P. (2003). Association between antidepressant prescribing and suicide in Australia, 1991–2000: Trend analysis. *British Medical Journal*, *326*, 1008–1010. doi:10.1136/bmj.326.7397.1008

Harwood, D., Hawton, K., Hope, T., & Jacoby, R. (2002). The grief experiences and needs of bereaved relatives and friends of older people dying through suicide: A descriptive and case-control study. *Journal of Affective Disorders*, *72*, 185–194. doi:10.1016/S0165-0327(01)00462-1

Heisel, M. J., Duberstein, P. R., Lyness, J. M., & Feldman, M. D. (2010). Screening for suicide ideation, among older primary care patients. *Journal of the American Board of Family Medicine*, *23*, 260–269. doi:10.3122/jabfm.2010.02.080163

Heisel, M. J., Duberstein, P. R., Talbot, N. L., King, D. A., & Tu, X. M. (2009). Adapting interpersonal psychotherapy for older adults at risk for suicide: Preliminary findings. *Professional Psychology: Research and Practice*, *40*, 156–164. doi:10.1037/a0014731

Heisel, M. J., & Flett, G. L. (2005). A psychometric analysis of the geriatric hopelessness scale (GHS): Towards improving assessment of the construct. *Journal of Affective Disorders*, *87*, 211–220. doi:10.1016/j.jad.2005.03.016

Heisel, M. J., & Flett, G. L. (2006). The development and initial validation of the Geriatric Suicide Ideation Scale. *American Journal of Geriatric Psychiatry*, *14*, 742–751. doi:10.1097/01.JGP.0000218699.27899.f9

Heisel, M. J., Flett, G. L., & Besser, A. (2002). Cognitive functioning and geriatric suicide ideation: Testing a mediational model. *American Journal of Geriatric Psychiatry*, *10*, 428–436. doi:10.1097/00019442-200207000-00009

Heisel, M. J., Flett, G. L., Duberstein, P. R., & Lyness, J. M. (2005). Does the Geriatric Depression Scale (GDS) distinguish between older adults with high versus low levels of suicidal ideation? *American Journal of Geriatric Psychiatry*, *13*, 876–883. doi:10.1097/00019442-200510000-00007

Hinton, L., Zweifach, M., Oishi, S., Tang, L., & Unützer, J. (2006). Gender disparities in the treatment of late-life depression: Qualitative and quantitative findings from the IMPACT trial. *American Journal of Geriatric Psychiatry*, *14*, 884–892. doi:10.1097/01.JGP.0000219282.32915.a4

Huh, J. T., Weaver, C. M., Martin, J. L., Caskey, N. H., O'Riley, A., & Kramer, B. J. (2012). Effects of a late-life suicide risk–assessment training on multidisciplinary healthcare providers. *Journal of the American Geriatrics Society*, *60*, 775–780. doi:10.1111/j.1532-5415.2011.03843.x

Hwang, J. P., Lee, T. W., Tsai, S. J., Chen, T. J., Yang, C. H., Lirng, J. F., & Tsai, C. F. (2010). Cortical and subcortical abnormalities in late-onset depression with history of suicide attempts investigated with MRI and voxel-based morphometry. *Journal of Geriatric Psychiatry and Neurology*. doi:10.1177/0891988710363713

Isaac, M., Elias, B., Katz, L. Y., Belik, S., Deane, F. P., Enns, M. W., & Sareen, J. (2009). Gatekeeper training as a preventative intervention for suicide: A systematic review. *Canadian Journal of Psychiatry*, *54*, 260–268.

Jahn, D. R., & Cukrowicz, K. C. (2011). The impact of the nature of relationships on perceived burdensomeness and suicide ideation in a community sample of older adults. *Suicide and Life-Threatening Behavior*, *41*, 635–649. doi:10.1111/j.1943-278X.2011.00060.x

Jobes, D. A. (2006). *Managing suicidal risk: A collaborative approach*. New York, NY: Guilford Press.

Joiner, T. (2005). *Why people die by suicide*. Cambridge, MA: Harvard University Press.

Joiner, T. E., Jr., Van Orden, K. A., Witte, T. K., & Rudd, M. D. (2009). *The interpersonal theory of suicide: Guidance for working with suicidal clients*. Washington, DC: American Psychological Association. doi:10.1037/11869-000

Jorm, A. F., Griffiths, K. M., Christensen, H., Korten, A. E., Parslow, R. A., & Rodgers, B. (2003). Providing information about the effectiveness of treatment options to depressed people in the community: A randomized controlled trial of effects on mental health literacy, help-seeking and symptoms. *Psychological Medicine*, *33*, 1071–1079. doi:10.1017/S0033291703008079

Juurlink, D. N., Herrmann, N., Szalai, J. P., Kopp, A., & Redelmeier, D. A. (2004). Medical illness and the risk of suicide in the elderly. *Archives of Internal Medicine, 164*, 1179–1184. doi:10.1001/archinte.164.11.1179

Kaplan, M. S., Adamek, M. E., & Calderon, A. (1999). Managing depressed and suicidal geriatric patients: Differences among primary care physicians. *Gerontologist, 39*, 417–425. doi:10.1093/geront/39.4.417

Kaplan, M. S., Adamek, M. E., & Martin, J. L. (2001). Confidence of primary care physicians in assessing the suicidality of geriatric patients. *International Journal of Geriatric Psychiatry, 16*, 728–734. doi:10.1002/gps.420

Kaplan, M. S., Huguet, N., McFarland, B. H., & Mandle, J. A. (2012). Factors associated with suicide by firearm among U.S. older adult men. *Psychology of Men and Masculinity, 13*, 65–74. doi:10.1037/a0023173

Kjølseth, I., & Ekeberg, Ø. (2012). When elderly people give warning of suicide. *International Psychogeriatrics, 24*, 1393–1401. doi:10.1017/S1041610212000312

Koons, C. R., Robins, C. J., Tweed, J. L., Lynch, T. R., Gonzalez, A. M., Morse, A. M., . . . Bastian, L. A. (2001). Efficacy of dialectical behavior therapy in women veterans with borderline personality disorder. *Behavior Therapy, 32*, 371–390. doi:10.1016/S0005-7894(01)80009-5

Kurella, M., Kimmel, P. L., Young, B. S., & Chertow, G. M. (2005). Suicide in the United States end-stage renal disease program. *Journal of the American Society of Nephrology, 16*, 774–781. doi:10.1681/ASN.2004070550

Lakeman, R., & FitzGerald, M. (2009). The ethics of suicide research: The views of ethics committee members. *Crisis, 30*, 13–19. doi:10.1027/0227-5910.30.1.13

Lewis, L. M. (2007). No-harm contracts: A review of what we know. *Suicide and Life-Threatening Behavior, 37*, 50–57. doi:10.1521/suli.2007.37.1.50

Linehan, M. M. (1993). *Cognitive–behavioral treatment of borderline personality disorder*. New York, NY: Guilford Press.

Llorente, M. D., Burke, M., Gregory, G. R., Bosworth, H. B., Grambow, S. C., Horner, R. D., . . . Olsen, E. J. (2005). Prostate cancer: A significant risk factor for late-life suicide. *American Journal of Geriatric Psychiatry, 13*, 195–201. doi:10.1097/00019442-200503000-00004

Ludwig, J., & Cook, P. J. (2000). Homicide and suicide rates associated with implementation of the Brady handgun violence prevention act. *JAMA, 284*, 585–591. doi:10.1001/jama.284.5.585

Lum, T. Y., & Lightfoot, E. (2005). The effects of volunteering on the physical and mental health of older people. *Research on Aging, 27*, 31–55. doi:10.1177/0164027504271349

Luoma, J. B., Martin, C. E., & Pearson, J. L. (2002). Contact with mental health and primary care providers before suicide: A review of the evidence. *American Journal of Psychiatry, 159*, 909–916. doi:10.1176/appi.ajp.159.6.909

Luoma, J. B., & Pearson, J. L. (2002). Suicide and marital status in the United States, 1991–1996: Is widowhood a risk factor? *American Journal of Public Health, 92*, 1518–1522. doi:10.2105/AJPH.92.9.1518

Lynch, T. R., Cheavens, J. S., Cukrowicz, K. C., Thorp, S. R., Bronner, L., & Beyer, J. (2007). Treatment of older adults with comorbid personality disorder and depression: A dialectical behavior therapy approach. *International Journal of Geriatric Psychiatry, 22*, 131–143. doi:10.1002/gps.1703

Lynch, T. R., Morse, J. Q., Mendelson, T., & Robins, C. J. (2003). Dialectical behavior therapy for depressed older adults: A randomized pilot study. *American Journal of Geriatric Psychiatry, 11*, 33–45. doi:10.1097/00019442-200301000-00006

Mackenzie, C. S., Gekoski, W. L., & Knox, V. J. (2006). Age, gender, and the underutilization of mental health services: The influence of help-seeking attitudes. *Aging and Mental Health, 10*, 574–582. doi:10.1080/13607860600641200

Mackenzie, C. S., Pagura, J., & Sareen, J. (2010). Correlates of perceived need for and use of mental health services by older adults in the collaborative psychiatric epidemiology surveys. *American Journal of Geriatric Psychiatry, 18*, 1103–1115. doi:10.1097/JGP.0b013e3181dd1c06

Magovcevic, M., & Addis, M. E. (2008). The Masculine Depression Scale: Development and psychometric evaluation. *Psychology of Men and Masculinity, 9*, 117–132. doi:10.1037/1524-9220.9.3.117

Manber, R., Bernert, R. A., Suh, S., Nawoakowski, S., Siebern, A. T., & Ong, J. C. (2011). CBT for insomnia in patients with high and low depressive symptom severity: Adherence and clinical outcomes. *Journal of Clinical Sleep Medicine, 7*, 645–652.

McGirr, A., Dombrovski, A. Y., Butters, M. A., Clark, L., & Szanto, K. (2012). Deterministic learning and attempted suicide among older depressed individuals: Cognitive assessment using the Wisconsin Card Sorting Task. *Journal of Psychiatric Research, 46*, 226–232. doi:10.1016/j.jpsychires.2011.10.001

McIntosh, J. L., & Drapeau, C. W. for the American Association of Suicidology. (2012, September). *U.S.A. suicide 2010: Official final data*. Washington, DC: American Association of Suicidology. Retrieved from http://www.suicidology.org

Miller, M., Azrael, D., & Barber, C. (2012). Suicide mortality in the United States: The importance of attending to method in understanding population-level disparities in the burden of suicide. *Annual Review of Public Health, 33*, 393–408. doi:10.1146/annurev-publhealth-031811-124636

Morrow-Howell, N., Becker-Kemppainen, S., & Judy, L. (1998). Evaluating an intervention for the elderly at increased risk of suicide. *Research on Social Work Practice, 8*, 28–46. doi:10.1177/104973159800800104

Motto, J. A., & Bostrom, A. G. (2001). A randomized controlled trial of postcrisis suicide prevention. *Psychiatric Services, 52*, 828–833. doi:10.1176/appi.ps.52.6.828

Muñoz, R. F., Mrazek, P. J., & Haggerty, R. J. (1996). Institute of Medicine report on prevention of mental disorders: Summary and commentary. *American Psychologist, 51*, 1116–1122. doi:10.1037/0003-066X.51.11.1116

Murphy, E., Kapur, N., Webb, R., Purandare, N., Hawton, K., Bergen, H., . . . Cooper, J. (2012). Risk factors for repetition and suicide following self-harm in older adults: Multicentre cohort study. *British Journal of Psychiatry, 200*, 399–404. doi:10.1192/bjp.bp.111.094177

Neimeyer, R. A., Wittkowski, J., & Moser, R. P. (2004). Psychological research on death attitudes: An overview and evaluation. *Death Studies, 28*, 309–340. doi:10.1080/07481180490432324

Neufeld, E., O'Rourke, N., & Donnelly, M. (2010). Enhanced measurement sensitivity of hopeless ideation among older adults at risk of self-harm: Reliability and validity of Likert-type responses to the Beck Hopelessness Scale. *Aging and Mental Health, 14*, 752–756. doi:10.1080/13607860903421052

Nock, M. K., Borges, G., Bromets, E. J., Cha, C. B., Kessler, R. C., & Lee, S. (2008). Suicide and suicidal behavior. *Epidemiologic Reviews, 30*, 133–154. doi:10.1093/epirev/mxn002

O'Connor, E., Gaynes, B. N., Burda, B. U., Soh, C., & Whitlock, E. P. (2013). Screening for and treatment of suicide risk relevant to primary care: A systematic review for the U.S. Preventive Services Task Force. *Annals of Internal Medicine, 158*, 741–754. doi:10.7326/0003-4819-158-10-201305210-00642

O'Riley, A. A., & Fiske, A. (2012). Emphasis on autonomy and propensity for suicidal behavior in younger and older adults. *Suicide and Life-Threatening Behavior, 42*, 394–404. doi:10.1111/j.1943-278X.2012.00098.x

O'Riley, A. A., Nadorff, M. R., Conwell, Y., & Edelstein, B. (2013). Challenges associated with managing suicide risk in long-term care facilities. *Annals of Long-Term Care, 21*, 28–34.

Oyama, H., Sakashita, T., Hojo, K., Ono, Y., Watanabe, N., Takizawa, T., . . . Tanaka, E. (2010). A community-based survey and screening for depression in the elderly: The short-term effect on suicide risk in Japan. *Crisis, 31*, 100–108. doi:10.1027/0227-5910/a000007

Oyama, H., Sakashita, T., Ono, Y., Goto, M., Fujita, M., & Koida, J. (2008). Effect of community-based intervention using depression screening on elderly suicide risk: A meta-analysis of the evidence from Japan. *Community Mental Health Journal, 44*, 311–320. doi:10.1007/s10597-008-9132-0

Oyama, H., Watanabe, N., Ono, Y., Sakashita, T., Takenoshita, Y., Taguchi, M., . . . Kumagai, K. (2005). Community-based suicide prevention through group activity for the elderly successfully reduced the high suicide rate for females. *Psychiatry and Clinical Neurosciences, 59*, 337–344. doi:10.1111/j.1440-1819.2005.01379.x

Pedersen, N. L., & Fiske, A. (2010). Genetic influence on suicide and nonfatal suicidal behavior: Twin study findings. *European Psychiatry, 25*, 264–267. doi:10.1016/j.eurpsy.2009.12.008

Pinquart, M., Duberstein, P. R., & Lyness, J. M. (2007). Effects of psychotherapy and other behavioral interventions on clinically depressed older adults: A meta-analysis. *Aging and Mental Health, 11*, 645–657. doi:10.1080/13607860701529635

Pitman, A., & Osborn, D. P. J. (2011). Cross-cultural attitudes to help seeking among individuals who are suicidal: New perspective for policy-makers. *British Journal of Psychiatry, 199*, 8–10. doi:10.1192/bjp.bp.110.087817

Pope, K. S., & Tabachnick, B. G. (1993). Therapists' anger, hate, fear, and sexual feelings: National survey of therapist responses, client characteristics, critical events, formal complaints, and training. *Professional Psychology: Research and Practice, 24*, 142–152. doi:10.1037/0735-7028.24.2.142

Price, E. C., Gregg, J., Smith, M., Fiske, A. (2014). *Masculine gender role and depressive symptom endorsement: Evaluation of the Masculine Depression Scale in younger and older adults.* Manuscript submitted for publication.

Quinnett, P. (2007). *QPR gatekeeper training for suicide prevention: The model, rationale, and theory.* Retrieved from http://www.qprinstitute.com

Reich, J. W., Newsom, J. T., & Zautra, A. J. (1996). Health downturns and predictors of suicidal ideation: An application of the Baumeister model. *Suicide and Life-Threatening Behavior, 26*, 282–291.

Richard-Devantoy, S., Jollant, F., Kefi, Z., Turecki, G., Olié, J. P., Annweiler, C., . . . Le Gall, D. (2012). Deficit of cognitive inhibition in depressed elderly: A neurocognitive marker of suicidal risk. *Journal of Affective Disorders*, *140*, 193–199. doi:10.1016/j.jad.2012.03.006

Rihmer, Z., Rutz, W., & Pihlgren, H. (1995). Depression and suicide on Gotland: An intensive study of all suicides before and after a depression-training programme for general practitioners. *Journal of Affective Disorders*, *35*, 147–152. doi:10.1016/0165-0327(95)00055-0

Rizvi, S. L., & Nock, M. K. (2008). Single-case experimental designs for the evaluation of treatments for self-injurious and suicidal behaviors. *Suicide and Life-Threatening Behavior*, *38*, 498–510. doi:10.1521/suli.2008.38.5.498

Rubenowitz, E., Waern, M., Wilhelmson, K., & Allebeck, P. (2001). Life events and psychosocial factors in elderly suicides: A case-control study. *Psychological Medicine*, *31*, 1193–1202. doi:10.1017/S0033291701004457

Rudd, M. D. (2006). Fluid vulnerability theory: A cognitive approach to understanding the process of acute and chronic suicide risk. In T. E. Ellis (Ed.), *Cognition and suicide: Theory, research, and therapy* (pp. 355–368). Washington, DC: American Psychological Association. doi:10.1037/11377-016

Rudd, M. D., Joiner, T., & Rajab, M. H. (2001). *Treating suicidal behavior: An effective, time-limited approach.* New York, NY: Guilford Press.

Rurup, M. L., Deeg, D. J. H., Poppelaars, J. L., Kerkhof, A. J. F. M., & Onwuteaka-Philipsen, B. D. (2011). Wishes to die in older people: A quantitative study of prevalence and associated factors. *Crisis*, *32*, 194–203. doi:10.1027/0227-5910/a000079

Rutz, W. (1999). Improvement of cave for people suffering from depression: The need for comprehensive education. *International Clinical Psychopharmacology*, *14*, S27–S33. doi:10.1097/00004850-199906003-00005

Rutz, W., Wålinder, J., Von Knorring, L., Rihmer, Z., & Pihlgren, H. (1997). Prevention of depression and suicide by education and medication: Impact on male suicidality. An update from the Gotland study. *International Journal of Psychiatry in Clinical Practice*, *1*, 39–46. doi:10.3109/13651509709069204

Schmitz, W. M. J., Allen, M. H., Feldman, B. N., Gutin, N. J., Jahn, D. R., & Simpson, S. (2012). Preventing suicide through improved training in suicide risk assessment and care: An American Association of Suicidology task force report addressing serious gaps in U.S. mental health training. *Suicide and Life-Threatening Behavior*, *42*, 292–304. doi:10.1111/j.1943-278X.2012.00090.x

Shneidman, E. S. (1993). Commentary: Suicide as psychache. *Journal of Nervous and Mental Disease*, *181*, 145–147. doi:10.1097/00005053-199303000-00001

Silverman, M. M., Berman, A. L., Sanddal, N. D., O'Carroll, P. W., & Joiner, T. E. (2007). Rebuilding the Tower of Babel: A revised nomenclature for the study of suicide and suicidal behaviors Part 2: Suicide-related ideations, communications, and behaviors. *Suicide and Life-Threatening Behavior*, *37*, 264–277. doi:10.1521/suli.2007.37.3.264

Simon, G. E., Rutter, C., Peterson, D., Oliver, M., Whiteside, U., Operskalski, B., & Ludman, E. (2013). Does response on the PHQ-9 Depression Questionnaire predict subsequent suicide attempt or suicide death? *Psychiatric Services*, *64*, 1195–1202. doi:10.1176/appi.ps.201200587

Spitzer, R. L., Kroenke, K., & Williams, J. B. (1999). Validation and utility of a self-report version of PRIME-MD: The PHQ primary care study. Primary care evaluation of mental disorders. Patient Health Questionnaire. *JAMA*, *282*, 1737–1744. doi:10.1001/jama.282.18.1737

Stanley, B., & Brown, G. K. (2012). Safety planning intervention: A brief intervention to mitigate suicide risk. *Cognitive and Behavioral Practice*, *19*, 256–264. doi:10.1016/j.cbpra.2011.01.001

Stewart, C. D., Quinn, A., Plever, S., & Emerson, B. (2009). Comparing cognitive behavior therapy, problem solving therapy, and treatment as usual in a high risk population. *Suicide and Life-Threatening Behavior*, *39*, 538–547. doi:10.1521/suli.2009.39.5.538

Stice, B. D., & Canetto, S. S. (2008). Older adult suicide: Perceptions of precipitants and protective factors. *Clinical Gerontologist*, *31*, 4–30. doi:10.1080/07317110801947144

Stone, M., Laughren, T., Jones, M. L., Levenson, M., Holland, P. C., Hughes, A., . . . Rochester, G. (2009). Risk of suicidality in clinical trials of antidepressants in adults: Analysis of proprietary data submitted to US Food and Drug Administration. *British Medical Journal*, *339*, b2880. doi:10.1136/bmj.b2880

Substance Abuse and Mental Health Services Administration. (2013, June). *National registry of evidence-based programs and practices.* Retrieved from http://www.nrepp.samhsa.gov

Szanto, K., Dombrovski, A. Y., Sahakian, B. J., Mulsant, B. H., Houck, P. R., Reynolds, C. F., III, & Clark, L. (2012). Social emotion recognition, social functioning, and attempted suicide in late-life depression. *American Journal of Geriatric Psychiatry*, *20*, 257–265. doi:10.1097/JGP.0b013e31820eea0c

Szanto, K., Kalmar, S., Hendin, H., Rihmer, Z., & Mann, J. J. (2007). A suicide prevention program in a region with a very high suicide rate. *Archives of General Psychiatry*, *64*, 914–920. doi:10.1001/archpsyc.64.8.914

Szanto, K., Mulsant, B. H., Houck, P., Dew, M. A., & Reynolds, C. F., III. (2003). Occurrence and course of suicidality during short-term treatment of late-life depression. *Archives of General Psychiatry, 60,* 610–617. doi:10.1001/archpsyc.60.6.610

Szanto, K., Reynolds, C. F., III, Conwell, Y., Begley, A. E., & Houck, P. (1998). High levels of hopelessness persist in geriatric patients with remitted depression and a history of attempted suicide. *Journal of the American Geriatrics Society, 46,* 1401–1406.

Tanskanen, A., Tuomilehto, J., Viinamäki, H., Vartiainen, E., Lehtonen, J., & Puska, P. (2001). Nightmares as predictors of suicide. *Sleep, 24,* 845–848.

Tsoh, J., Chiu, H. F. K., Duberstein, P. R., Chan, S. S. M., Chi, I., Yip, P. S. F., & Conwell, Y. (2005). Attempted suicide in elderly Chinese persons: A multi-group, controlled study. *American Journal of Geriatric Psychiatry, 13,* 562–571. doi:10.1097/00019442-200507000-00004

Turvey, C. L., Conwell, Y., Jones, M. P., Phillips, C., Simonsick, E., Pearson, J. L., & Wallace, R. (2002). Risk factors for late-life suicide: A prospective community-based study. *American Journal of Geriatric Psychiatry, 10,* 398–406. doi:10.1097/00019442-200207000-00006

Uncapher, H., & Areán, P. A. (2000). Physicians are less willing to treat suicidal ideation in older patients. *Journal of the American Geriatrics Society, 48,* 188–192.

Unützer, J., Katon, W., Callahan, C. M., Williams, J. W. J., Hunkeler, E., Harpole, L., . . . Langston, C. (2002). Collaborative care management of late-life depression in the primary care setting: A randomized controlled trial. *JAMA, 288,* 2836–2845. doi:10.1001/jama.288.22.2836

Unützer, J., Tang, L., Oishi, S., Katon, W., Williams, J. W., Hunkeler, E., . . . Langston, C. (2006). Reducing suicidal ideation in depressed older primary care patients. *Journal of the American Geriatrics Society, 54,* 1550–1556. doi:10.1111/j.1532-5415.2006.00882.x

U.S. Preventive Services Task Force. (2005). Screening for suicide risk: Recommendation statement. *Internet Journal of Mental Health, 2*(2). Retrieved from http://ispub.com/IJMH/2/2/12801

van der Sande, R., Buskens, E., Allart, E., van der Graaf, Y., & van Engeland, H. (1997). Psychosocial intervention following suicide attempt: A systematic review of treatment interventions. *Acta Psychiatrica Scandinavica, 96,* 43–50. doi:10.1111/j.1600-0447.1997.tb09903.x

Van Orden, K. A., Talbot, N., & King, D. (2012). Using the interpersonal theory of suicide to inform interpersonal psychotherapy with a suicidal older adult. *Clinical Case Studies, 11,* 333–347. doi:10.1177/1534650112457710

Van Orden, K. A., Witte, T. K., Cukrowicz, K. C., Braithwaite, S. R., Selby, E. A., & Joiner, T. E., Jr. (2010). The interpersonal theory of suicide. *Psychological Review, 117,* 575–600. doi:10.1037/a0018697

Vohs, K. D., & Baumeister, R. F. (2000). Escaping the self consumes regulatory resources: A self-regulatory model of suicide. In T. E. Joiner & M. D. Rudd (Eds.), *Suicide science: Expanding the boundaries* (pp. 33–41). New York, NY: Kluwer Academic/Plenum Press.

Vyrostek, S. B., Annest, J. L., & Ryan, G. W. (2004). Surveillance for fatal and nonfatal injuries—United States, 2001. *MMWR. Surveillance Summaries, 53,* 1–57.

Waern, M., Rubenowitz, E., Runeson, B., Skoog, I., Wilhelmson, K., & Allebeck, P. (2002). Burden of illness and suicide in elderly people: Case-control study. *British Medical Journal, 324,* 1355–1357. doi:10.1136/bmj.324.7350.1355

Waern, M., Rubenowitz, E., & Wilhelmson, K. (2003). Predictors of suicide in the old elderly. *Gerontology, 49,* 328–334. doi:10.1159/000071715

Walker, J., Hansen, C., Butcher, I., Sharma, N., Wall, L., Murray, G., & Sharpe, M. (2011). Thoughts of death and suicide reported by cancer patients who endorsed the "suicidal thoughts" item of the PHQ-9 during routine screening for depression. *Psychosomatics, 52,* 424–427. doi:10.1016/j.psym.2011.02.003

Wheeler, J. A., Gorey, K. M., & Greenblatt, B. (1998). The beneficial effects of volunteering for older volunteers and the people they serve: A meta-analysis. *International Journal of Aging and Human Development, 47,* 69–79. doi:10.2190/VUMP-XCMF-FQYU-V0JH

Witte, T. K., Joiner, T. E., Jr., Brown, G. K., Beck, A. T., Beckman, A., Duberstein, P., & Conwell, Y. (2006). Factors of suicide ideation and their relation to clinical and other indicators in older adults. *Journal of Affective Disorders, 94,* 165–172. doi:10.1016/j.jad.2006.04.005

Yesavage, J. A. (1982–1983). Development and validation of a geriatric depression screening scale: A preliminary report. *Journal of Psychiatric Research, 17,* 37–49. doi:10.1016/0022-3956(82)90033-4

Zung, W. W. K. (1965). A self-rating depression scale. *Archives of General Psychiatry, 12,* 63–70. doi:10.1001/archpsyc.1965.01720310065008

MILD COGNITIVE IMPAIRMENT AND ALZHEIMER'S DISEASE

Melissa Castro and Glenn E. Smith

This chapter will discuss the recent reformulations of research and clinical diagnostic criteria related to mild cognitive impairment (MCI) and Alzheimer's disease (AD). The updates to research criteria have been promulgated jointly by the National Institute on Aging and the Alzheimer's Association (NIA–AA). New clinical criteria have arrived in the *Diagnostic and Statistical Manual, Fifth Edition* (*DSM–5*) of the American Psychiatric Association (2013). After an overview of each of these criteria, the focus will turn to the epidemiology, neurobiology, genetics, and neuropsychology of AD. Finally, clinical features of, and interventions for, AD will be reviewed.

DIAGNOSTIC CRITERIA

Recent scientific insights and technological advances in the field of dementia have provided compelling evidence that AD has a decade-long prodrome that includes reliably identifiable epochs preceding the manifestation of the full syndrome of dementia (see Figure 7.1). These advances in science and technology have spurred demand for new consensus diagnosis of AD that recognizes the preclinical and prodromal periods in AD development. For a summary of the evolution of diagnostic terminology for AD please refer to Table 7.1.

Research Criteria

A task force of experts from the United States and Europe empanelled by the NIA–AA convened to propose updated and revised guidelines for the evaluation of AD-related diagnoses. The two most notable differences of the new criteria relative to the AD criteria published in 1984 are the incorporation of underlying disease biomarkers and the formalization of different stages of disease: preclinical AD, MCI, and dementia.

Operational research criteria for defining preclinical AD (Sperling, Aisen, et al., 2011). On the basis of new findings that biomarkers for the disease might be detected years before symptoms arise, the guidelines propose a new definition for preclinical AD. This stage may appear well before the development of dementia or even MCI. These operational research criteria for preclinical stages rely on different biomarkers that are not yet validated for clinical use but that set the stage for future scientific investigation. These stages are described below:

Stage 1 = Biomarker evidence of amyloid-beta (Aβ) accumulation (asymptomatic cerebral amyloidosis):

a. Elevated tracer retention on positron emission tomography (PET) amyloid imaging and/or low Aβ42 on cerebrospinal fluid assay.

Parts of this work was supported by Grants P50 AG16574, 1 R01NR12419, CTSA Grant UL1 TR000135 from the National Center for Advancing Translational Science (NCATS). Its contents are solely the responsibility of the authors and do not necessarily represent the official views of the NIH. This work draws upon the book *Mild Cognitive Impairment and Dementia; Definitions, Diagnosis and Treatment* by G. Smith and M. Bondi (2013). We wish to acknowledge the indirect contributions of Dr. Mark Bondi to this chapter.

http://dx.doi.org/10.1037/14459-007
APA Handbook of Clinical Geropsychology: Vol. 2. Assessment, Treatment, and Issues of Later Life,
P. A. Lichtenberg and B. T. Mast (Editors-in-Chief)

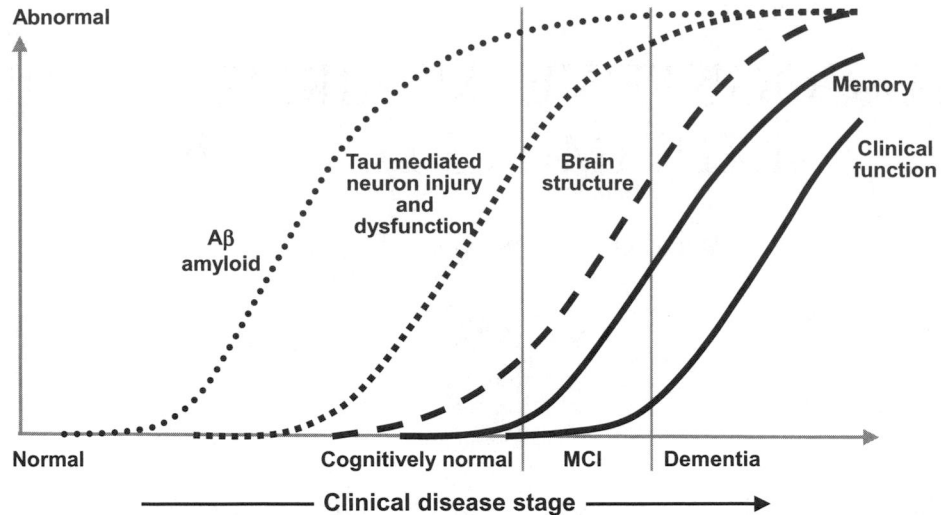

FIGURE 7.1. Dynamic biomakers of the Alzheimer's pathological cascade. From "Hypothetical Model of Dynamic Biomarkers of the Alzheimer's Pathological Cascade," by C. Jack Jr., D. Knopman, W. Jagust, L. Shaw, P. Aisen, M. Weiner, R. C. Peterson, and J. Trojanowski, 2010, *Lancet Neurology, 9*, p. 127. Copyright 2010 by Lancet Publishing Group. Reprinted with permission.

Stage 2 = Biomarker evidence of synaptic dysfunction and/or early neurodegeneration (evidence of amyloid positivity + presence of one or more additional AD markers):

a. Elevated cerebrospinal fluid tau or phospho-tau.
b. Hypometabolism in an AD-like pattern (i.e., posterior cingulate, precuneus, and/or temporo-parietal cortices) on fluorodeoxyglucose position emission tomography (FDG-PET).

c. Cortical thinning/gray-matter loss in AD-like anatomic distribution (i.e., lateral and medial parietal, posterior cingulate and lateral temporal cortices) and/or hippocampal atrophy on volumetric magnetic resonance imaging (MRI).

Stage 3 = Evidence of subtle cognitive decline, but does not meet criteria for MCI or dementia (amyloid positivity + markers of neurodegeneration + very early cognitive symptoms):

TABLE 7.1

Summary of Evolution of Alzheimer's Disease Diagnostic Terminology

Stage of AD	Research criteria		Clinical criteria	
	NIA (old)	**NIA–AA (new)**	**DSM–IV–TR**	**DSM–5**
Preclinical	—	Sperling et al., 2011	—	—
Mild cognitive impairment	Winblad et al., 2004	Albert et al., 2011	Minor neurocognitive disorder (research only)	Mild neurocognitive disorder
Alzheimer's disease dementia	McKhann et al., 1984	McKhann et al., 2011	Dementia	Major neurocognitive disorder

Note. DSM = Diagnostic and Statistical Manual of Mental Disorders; AD = Alzheimer's disease; NIA = National Institute on Aging; AA = Alzheimer's Association.

a. Demonstrated cognitive decline over time on standard cognitive tests, but not meeting criteria for MCI.

b. Subtle impairment on challenging cognitive tests, particularly accounting for level of innate ability or cognitive reserve but not meeting criteria for MCI.

Given that the newly proposed stages rely on advanced and expensive biomarker tests capable of detecting presymptomatic changes in brain anatomy and function, their utility is currently limited to research including outcome studies and possibly clinical trials. Techniques, assays, and cutoffs for these biomarkers remain to be standardized. Although these criteria provide hope for eventual prevention models, they currently have no clinical application.

Criteria for the diagnosis of MCI due to AD (Albert et al., 2011). No adequate discussion of AD can neglect the crucial prodromal phase of MCI. Directly preceding the dementia stage, this stage is characterized by mild changes in cognition that are noticeable and measureable (without biomarkers) but do not disrupt day-to-day functioning.

Generic MCI criteria. The work group in this area has proposed a two-step process in which, first, a clinical diagnosis of "generic" MCI is rendered, and then biomarker information is used to assign AD as the etiology with increasing levels of confidence. Low confidence is reflected in the term MCI with neurodegenerative etiology. Intermediate confidence is described as MCI with presumed AD, and highest confidence is termed prodromal AD. The generic criteria for MCI are as follows:

1. *Concern regarding a change in cognition.* There should be evidence of concern about a change in cognition, in comparison to the person's prior level. This concern can be obtained from the patient, from an informant who knows the patient well, or from a skilled clinician observing the patient.

2. *Impairment in one or more cognitive domains.* There should be evidence of lower performance in one or more cognitive domains that is greater than would be expected for the patient's age and educational background. If repeated assessments are available, then a decline in performance should be evident over time. This change can occur in a variety of cognitive domains, including memory, executive function, attention, language, and visuospatial skills. An impairment in episodic memory (i.e., the ability to learn and retain new information) is seen most commonly in MCI patients who subsequently progress to a diagnosis of AD (see the Cognitive Characteristics section, for further details).

3. *Preservation of independence in functional abilities.* People with MCI commonly have mild problems performing complex functional tasks they used to be able to perform, such as paying bills, preparing a meal, or shopping at the store. They may take more time, be less efficient, and make more errors at performing such activities than in the past. Nevertheless, they generally maintain their independence of function in daily life with minimal aids or assistance.

4. *Not demented.* These cognitive changes should be sufficiently mild that there is no evidence of a significant impairment in social or occupational functioning. It should be emphasized that the diagnosis of MCI requires evidence of intraindividual change. If an individual has only been evaluated once, change will need to be inferred from the history or evidence that cognitive performance is impaired beyond what would have been expected for that individual. Serial evaluations are of course optimal, but they may not be feasible in a particular circumstance.

If the generic clinical criteria for MCI are met, the clinician then endeavors to determine the cause of the MCI:

1. *MCI of a neurodegenerative etiology.* The criteria outlined for MCI with a presumed degenerative etiology represents the typical presentation of individuals who are at an increased risk of progressing to AD dementia. As noted, these individuals typically have a prominent impairment in episodic memory, but other patterns of cognitive impairment (e.g., executive dysfunction, visuospatial, or language impairment) also can progress to AD dementia over time. In the event of negative,

conflicting, or ambiguous biomarker evidence from either downstream or nonspecific biomarkers, the possibility that the patient with MCI has underlying AD pathology is unlikely but cannot entirely be ruled out (Albert et al., 2011). Thus, when MCI is present but PET, MRI, or cerebrospinal fluid (CSF) biomarkers are either negative or unavailable the research diagnosis is limited to MCI of neurodegenerative etiology.

2. *MCI of the Alzheimer type.* If the subject meets the MCI criteria but, in addition, has one or more topographic (i.e., structural/functional) biomarkers associated with the "downstream" effects of AD pathology (e.g., MRI evidence of medial temporal atrophy, or FDG PET evidence of decreased temporoparietal metabolism, adjusting for age), then the likelihood is increased that the outcome will be AD dementia. Even in the absence of molecular biomarker information (or equivocal findings from molecular biomarkers) the presentation of amnestic MCI may still be consistent with an intermediate level of certainty that the individual will progress to AD dementia over time. In instances in which MCI is present and there is structural or functional evidence for AD, but molecular confirmation is lacking, the research diagnosis would be MCI of the Alzheimer type.

3. *Prodromal Alzheimer's dementia.* If the subject meets the MCI criteria, and in addition has a positive biomarker for the molecular neuropathology of the AD (e.g., lower CSF Aß-42 and raised CSF tau measures), this provides the highest level of certainly that over time the individual will progress to AD dementia. This level of certainty would be increased even further if the individual has positive topographic biomarker evidence of AD. However, the absence of such topographic biomarker evidence (or equivocal or normal findings) is still consistent with the highest level of certainty that the individual will progress to AD dementia over time.

Dementia due to AD (McKhann et al., 2011). The dementia stage is the most recognizable because of clear impairments in memory, thinking, and behavior that affect a person's ability to function independently in everyday life. The diagnosis of AD dementia is based on the same criteria created almost three decades prior and retains the terms *probable* AD for high degree of certainty and *possible* AD for lower levels of certainty. The 2011 criteria attempt to update and clarify the diagnosis of dementia resulting from AD and to differentiate it from dementia due to other causes. The process of appraising core dementia criteria followed by exploring indicators that increase levels of certainly for AD etiology replicates the MCI approach earlier. The core dementia features include the traditional requirements of disruption of daily function, decline from a previously higher state of function, exclusion of delirium, and disruption of at least two areas of cognition or behavior. For the diagnosis of AD, the dementia should meet additional criteria, including the following:

1. Insidious onset (symptoms have a gradual onset over months to years, and the onset was not sudden over hours or days);
2. Clear-cut history of worsening of cognition by report or observation; and
3. Cognitive deficits are evident on history and examination in one of the two categories:

   a. Amnestic presentation: The most common syndromicx presentation of AD dementia. The deficits should include impairment in learning and recall of recently learned information. There should also be evidence of cognitive dysfunction in other cognitive domains as defined previously.

   b. Nonamnestic presentations:

      1. Language presentation: The most prominent deficits are in word-finding, but dysfunction in other cognitive domains should be present.
      2. Visual presentation: The most prominent deficits are in spatial cognition, including object agnosia, impaired face recognition, simultanagnosia, and alexia. Deficits in other cognitive domains should be present.
      3. Executive dysfunction: The most prominent deficits are in impaired reasoning, judgment, and problem solving. Deficits in other cognitive domains should be present.

Clinical AD dementia. Although the probable and possible qualifiers were retained (McKhann et al., 1984), the original 1984 criteria were revised and updated as outlined follows:

1. *Probable AD dementia.* Meets clinical and cognitive criteria for AD dementia given previously, and without evidence of any alternative diagnoses; in particular, no significant cerebrovascular disease (CVD). In people who meet the basic criteria for probable AD dementia, the diagnosis of probable AD dementia can be enhanced by one of these three features that increase certainty:

    a. Documented decline: Has evidence of progressive cognitive decline on subsequent evaluations based on information from informants and cognitive testing in the context of either brief mental status examinations or formal neuropsychological evaluation; or

    b. Biomarker positive: Has one or more of the following supporting biomarkers.

        1. Low cerebrospinal fluid Aβ42, elevated cerebrospinal fluid tau, or phospho tau;
        2. Positive amyloid PET imaging;
        3. Decreased FDG uptake on PET in temporoparietal cortex;
        4. Disproportionate atrophy on structural MR in medial temporal lobe (especially the hippocampus), basal and lateral temporal lobe, and medial parietal isocortex; or

    c. Mutation carrier: Meets clinical and cognitive criteria for AD dementia and has a proven AD autosomal dominant genetic mutation (presenilin 1 [PSEN1], presenilin 2 [PSEN2], amyloid precursor protein [APP]).

2. *Possible AD dementia.*

    a. Atypical course: Evidence for progressive decline is lacking or uncertain but meets other clinical and cognitive criteria for AD dementia; or

    b. Biomarkers obtained and negative: Meets clinical and cognitive criteria for AD dementia but biomarkers (cerebrospinal fluid, structural or functional brain imaging) do not support the diagnosis; or

    c. Mixed presentation: Meets clinical and cognitive criteria for AD dementia but evidence shows concomitant CVD; this would mean that there is more than one lacunar infarct, or a single large infarct, or extensive and severe white-matter hyperintensity changes, or evidence for some features of dementia with lewy bodies (DLB) that do not achieve a level of a diagnosis of probable DLB.

3. *Not AD dementia.*

    a. Does not meet clinical criteria for AD dementia; or

    b. Has sufficient evidence for an alternative diagnosis such as HIV; Huntington's disease; or others that rarely, if ever, overlap with AD.

In spite of substantial improvements in the accuracy of clinical diagnosis for AD, final diagnosis continues to occur on autopsy. The new NIA–AA criteria extended the levels of certainty approach to the postmortem diagnosis of AD with the introduction of a novel neuropathology qualifier. Discussions of these criteria are beyond the scope of this chapter other than to note that pathologically proven AD dementia meets clinical and cognitive criteria for probable AD dementia during life and is proven AD by pathological examination postmortem.

CLINICAL CRITERIA

Although the NIA–AA task forces were crafting new research criteria, the American Psychiatric Association also was seeking to capture the continuum of cognitive disturbance resulting from neurodegenerative diseases. Although the NIA–AA criteria use the term *dementia* and the previous version of the *Diagnostic and Statistical Manual of Mental Disorders, Fourth Edition, Text Revision* (DSM–IV–TR; American Psychiatric Association, 2000) devoted an entire section to dementia, the newly published *DSM–5* (American Psychiatric Association, 2013) criteria altogether eliminate the term *dementia*. Furthermore, although the term *mild neurocognitive disorder* was used in the *DSM–IV–TR* in association with criteria to be used for research purposes, the criteria could be considered analogous to MCI. The *DSM–5*, however, does not make use of the now well-accepted term MCI. The respective terms *major* and

minor neurocognitive disorder are introduced in the
DSM–5 with formal criteria outlining specific parameters of cognitive performance, thereby incorporating
the value of cognitive testing into the diagnostic process. Both criteria for major and mild neurocognitive
disorder underwent field-testing at several sites,
including one led by Glenn E. Smith.

DSM–5 Criteria for Neurocognitive Disorders

Major neurocognitive disorder. The *DSM–5*
(American Psychiatric Association, 2013) eliminates
the antiquated requirement for memory impairment,
allowing for multiple cognitive deficits. Major neurocognitive disorder is defined by significant cognitive decline from a previous level of performance in
one or more cognitive domains (e.g., enumerated as
complex attention, executive ability, learning and
memory, language, visual constructional–perceptual
ability, and social cognition) based on both subjective and objective assessment as evidenced by
(a) the concerns of the patient, a knowledgeable
informant, or the clinician; and (b) clear deficits in
formal neurocognitive assessment of the relevant
domain. Deficits typically are identified by test performance that is more than 2 standard deviations
(*SD*) below the mean (or below the 2.5th percentile)
of an appropriate reference population (e.g., adjusted
for age, gender, education, premorbid intellect, language, and culture).

The cognitive deficits must be sufficient to interfere with independence, at a minimum requiring
assistance with instrumental activities of daily living
(i.e., more complex tasks such as finances or managing medications). In addition, the cognitive deficits
must not occur exclusively in the context of a delirium and may not be primarily attributable to another
Axis I disorder (e.g., major depressive disorder,
schizophrenia).

Mild neurocognitive disorder. To diagnose mild
neurocognitive disorder (American Psychiatric
Association, 2013), there must be evidence of minor
cognitive decline from a previous level of performance in one or more of the cognitive domains
previously mentioned. Typically, this will involve
greater than usual difficulty performing these tasks,

and compensatory strategies may be required to
maintain independence. The cognitive deficits, however, should not be sufficient to interfere with independence (i.e., instrumental activities of daily living
are preserved).

Similarly, cognitive decline is based on patient
self-report, knowledgeable third-party informant, or
clinician observation as well as mild deficits on
objective cognitive assessment (typically 1–2 *SD*
below the mean [or in the 2.5–16th percentile] relative to appropriate norms). When serial measurements are available, a significant (e.g., 0.5 *SD*)
decline from the patient's own baseline would serve
as more definitive evidence of decline. Again, the
cognitive deficits should not occur exclusively in the
context of a delirium or be primarily attributable to
another Axis I disorder (e.g., major depressive disorder, schizophrenia).

Although these sets of criteria integrate objective
test data into the diagnostic process, thereby promoting standardization in clinical practice, it is
important to recall that testing is suggested but not
required, and testing alone is insufficient for diagnostic purposes. The criteria clearly require the presence of other features (subjective concern and
degree of independence in activities of daily living).
Only after determining whether a patient fulfills all
criteria for mild or major neurocognitive disorder
does the clinician specify etiological subtype from
the options provided (including vascular, frontotemporal, traumatic brain injury, LBD, Parkinson's disease (PD), Huntington's disease, HIV infection,
substance-induced, prion disease, or other medical
condition).

International Classification of Diseases

The impact of the *DSM–5* (American Psychiatric Association, 2013) changes is muted by the presence of the
NIA–AA criteria, which are likely to be co-opted into
clinical use. Moreover, the Patient Protection and
Affordable Care Act (2010) mandates the use of *International Classification of Diseases* (*ICD–10*; World
Health Organization, 1992) codes for billing diagnoses. The *ICD–10* structure for the diagnosis of AD
and MCI follows the structure of *DSM–IV–TR*
(American Psychiatric Association, 2000) more
closely than that of *DSM–5*.

CASE EXAMPLES

The following case examples portray how the finite trajectories for an individual with MCI present in real-life clinical practice and how neuropsychological assessment assists with the diagnostic process (see Figure 7.2).

Case Example: MCI With Return to Premorbid Baseline

Chief complaint.   The patient was a 63-year-old retired pastor who complained of progressive short-term memory loss after experiencing a "spell" while on a plane 6 months prior. Since then, he and his wife noted that he was more forgetful of the date, names of people he should know, shopping lists, and appointments.

History of present illness.   On the day of the spell, the patient had a meal on the plane after which he began to feel very warm and tired. He reportedly lost consciousness for a short time and subsequently vomited. He was observed by other passengers to be pallid and "tremoring." The patient denied any confusion, unilateral weakness, or speech disturbance. After getting off the plane, he saw a physician who suspected a seizure, but no further investigations were performed. He did not experience any subsequent spells and did not develop a tremor. Vascular workup came back normal, and the spell was later presumed to represent an episode of simple syncope.

Medical history.   The patient denied any previous history of seizures, meningitis, or head trauma. He was undergoing concurrent evaluation and treatment for obstructive sleep apnea (OSA) and restless leg syndrome. He also had a history of depression that was well-controlled with Wellbutrin.

Mental status examination.   His physician administered the Kokmen short test of mental status on which he obtained a score of 32/38, losing one point for attention, one for arithmetic, one for learning, and three for short-term recall. Neurological examination was otherwise normal with no evidence of Parkinsonism. MRI revealed moderate chronic white-matter small vessel ischemic changes and mild atrophy. He was suspected to have MCI and referred for cognitive testing.

Neuropsychological assessment.   Patient was right-handed with 15 years of education. On formal testing, this patient exhibited subtle difficulties in verbal memory retrieval with mild deficits in executive functions. Global cognitive functioning was intact with normal language and reasoning

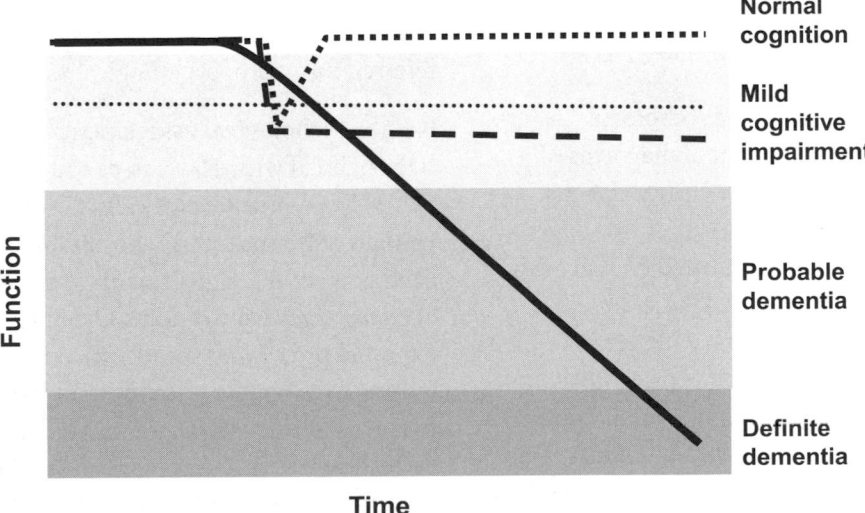

FIGURE 7.2.   Finite trajectories for an individual with MCI. From *Mild Cognitive Impairment and Dementia: Definitions, Diagnosis, and Treatment* (p. 6), by G. E. Smith and M. W. Bondi, 2013, New York, NY: Oxford University Press. Copyright 2013 by Oxford University Press. Adapted with permission.

abilities. His status was determined to be best described as MCI. Some oversight of instrumental activities, such as financial management and legal and medical decision making, was recommended and ongoing monitoring of his mental status was initiated.

Treatment plan.   The patient was initiated on VPAP (variable/bilevel positive airway pressure) therapy for OSA and recommended a trial of Aricept, which the patient declined because of concerns about adverse effects of the medication. He subsequently was enrolled in an Alzheimer's Disease Research Center program and underwent serial neuroimaging and neuropsychological assessments on a yearly basis. Over the course of 4 years, neuropsychological test results were stable and remained consistent with a diagnosis of MCI. Baseline PET scan revealed mild decreased FDG metabolism within parasagittal regions and questionably within the temporal lobes. Over subsequent years, mild generalized decreases were observed throughout the cerebral cortex, but no specific evidence was found for a neurodegenerative process. He continued to be followed by his neurologist and chose to hold off on treatment with cholinesterase inhibitors. His neurologist referred him to an intensive multicomponent memory compensation program for individuals with MCI, the Healthy Action to Benefit Independence and Thinking (HABIT), which he successfully completed.

Outcomes.   Most recent neuropsychological assessment conducted 5 years after initial diagnosis of MCI revealed improvement in cognitive deficits observed previously. The patient's OSA and depression were well managed. He indicated he had been taking multivitamins and an over-the-counter memory supplement over the past 2–3 years to which he attributed his improvement. It is more likely that cognitive recovery was related to an overall improvement in his general health and optimal management of comorbid medical conditions, which may have been playing a larger contributory role in his cognitive symptoms than originally was anticipated. Nonetheless, the patient disclosed that he now had difficulties obtaining life insurance because of his

diagnosis of MCI and inquired as to whether these new findings would provide the basis for removal of the diagnosis from his permanent medical record. This case raises important issues with regards to early diagnosis of MCI and the possibility that this condition can resolve (i.e., not all MCI is early AD or another dementia).

Case Example: MCI With Progression to Dementia

Chief complaint.   The patient was a 78-year-old retired salesman with memory concerns.

History of present illness.   At the age of 74 years, the patient initially presented with memory concerns, which were dismissed by his physician as age related without formal assessment. One year later he began to complain of word-finding difficulties and was noted to be easily confused.

Medical history.   Medical history was significant for moderately controlled atrial fibrillation, hypertension, monitoring of abdominal aortic aneurysm, mild thrombocytopenia, transient ischemic attacks, obstructive sleep apnea, and nocturia. He also had hearing loss.

Mental status examination.   When mental status finally was examined, at the age of 75 years, he scored 22/30 on the Folstein Mini-Mental Status Examination (Folstein, Folstein, & McHugh, 1975) and was unable to draw a clock. He then was referred for neuropsychological assessment.

Neuropsychological assessment.   Patient was right handed with 16 years of education. On the Mattis Dementia Rating Scale-2 (DRS-2, Jurica, Leitten, & Mattis, 2001), he obtained a score of 121 (2nd percentile). Impairments were noted in memory, language (word-finding), spatial ability, informational processing speed, and nonverbal problem solving. The results were thought to be consistent with a mild to moderate dementia, likely Alzheimer's dementia. It was recommended that he refrain from driving, and oversight of complex activities of daily living were recommended.

Treatment plan.   The patient subsequently was followed by a neurologist who administered the

Kokmen short test of mental status on which he obtained a score of 31/38, recalling only one of four words after a 5-minute delay. Although it was expected that the patient and his family were minimizing symptomology because of the perceived lack of impairment in his activities of daily living, he was diagnosed with MCI. A trial of Aricept was considered and discussed with the patient but deferred.

Outcomes. On evaluation 2 years later, it was determined that there was some slight deterioration, and he was prescribed Namenda with reported improvement. One year later, at the age of 78 year, the patient was enrolled in the memory compensation program (i.e., HABIT) for individuals with MCI. From the beginning of the program, the patient had comprehension and learning difficulties, and it was uncertain whether this was compounded by hearing and vision deficits. To clarify this issue, he underwent repeat neuropsychological assessment midway through the program. His DRS-2 score had declined to a score of 101 (<1st percentile), and it was determined that he indeed met criteria for AD and had progressed too far along to fully benefit from the intervention technique used as part of the program (calendar training). As such, the goals of the program were adjusted to better suit his level of functional ability, and the dementia diagnosis was disclosed clearly to both patient and his family. Despite being unable to engage fully in the program, the patient embraced his diagnosis and served as a role-model for others in the program. In this case, the diagnosis and communication of dementia was perhaps withheld for too long. The neuropsychological assessment results suggested an already evolved AD process as early as age 75 years, and treatment may have differed had this information been given greater consideration. For example, pharmacotherapy may have been initiated earlier on, and he may have been better able to fully participate in the HABIT program and possibly other interventions.

In both cases, brief screening of mental status resulted in similar scores, ranging from 31/38 to 32/38 on the Kokmen short test of mental status. The outcomes, however, differed considerably for each patient consistent with possible trajectories depicted in Figure 7.2. Thorough and repeated neuropsychological assessment proved crucial in determining the presence of cognitive impairment, assisting with differential diagnoses, and directing course of treatment.

EPIDEMIOLOGY

In 2010, 454,000 people received a new diagnosis of AD (Alzheimer's Association [AA], 2011; Brookmeyer, Gray, & Kawas, 1998). Data from the Rand Corporation (Hurd, Martorell, Delavande, Mullen, & Langa, 2013) combined with census data suggest that in that year 4.1 million people over age 70 years had dementia. The nearly 2:1 ratio in numbers of women to men follows almost entirely from the association of AD with aging combined with women's greater longevity. Roughly 17% of women versus 9% of men living to age 65 years will receive a diagnosis of AD before death. Unless dementia risk can be reduced, it is estimated that by 2050 the number of Americans with AD will triple, exceeding 13 million (AA, 2013). Worldwide projections are for the number of people with AD to move from 26.6 million in 2006 to 107 million in 2050 (Brookmeyer, Johnson, Ziegler-Graham, & Arrighi, 2007).

The cognitive, emotional, behavioral, and functional impact of AD is detailed through this chapter. The economic impact alone, however, can be devastating. Table 7.2 presents the average annual costs of care for a person with dementia (Hurd et al., 2013).

Note that these estimates result from spreading costs over all people with dementia in 2010, some of whom were in nursing home care, but most of whom were not. Therefore, the actual cost in each category is actually higher. For example, the estimated $81,000 annual cost for 1-year of nursing home care (MetLife, 2012) is being spread across the more than 7 out of 10 people with AD in the United States who live at home (AA, 2013). Similarly, home health and informal care costs are being averaged over the 30% who are no longer using those services. Nevertheless, Table 7.2 does provide a valid assessment of the relative contributions of various types of care. Clearly, Medicare expenditures are but a pittance relative to overall expenses, of which the greatest costs are to informal caregivers.

TABLE 7.2

Average Annual Cost of Dementia Care in U.S. Dollars Adjusted for Comorbid Health Conditions

Cost	Dollars
Out-of-pocket spending	$6,194
Medicare spending	$2,752
Formal home care	$5,678
Nursing home care	$13,876
Value of informal home care if same amount of home health care had to be purchased in marketplace	$27,789
Total	$56,290

Note. From "Monetary Costs of Dementia in the United States," by M. D. Hurd, P. Martorell, A. Delavande, K. J. Mullen, and K. M. Langa, 2013, *New England Journal of Medicine, 368*, p. 1332. Copyright 2013 by the Massachusetts Medical Society. Adapted with permission.

Approximately 90% of patients with dementia will require custodial care at some point during their illness (Smith, Kokmen, & O'Brien, 2000), with median time to placement from diagnosis at 5.3 years (Smith, O'Brien, Ivnik, Kokmen, & Tangalos, 2001). Cognitive function and functional status at diagnosis are important predictors of time to institutionalization (Smith et al., 2000, 2001). Survival time from diagnosis of AD varies with age of diagnosis and ranges from about 7 years in those with diagnosis in their 60s to 3 years for those with diagnosis in their 90s (Brookmeyer, Corrada, Curriero, & Kawas, 2002). Across ages, men's survival is about 88% of women's survival time. People with AD commonly will succumb to pneumonia or cardiovascular failure (Beard et al., 1996).

NEUROBIOLOGY

The Choline Hypothesis

Before the emergence and dominance of the amyloid hypothesis discussed in the following section, the choline hypothesis pervaded the field of dementia research. This explains why three of the four currently approved medications for the treatment of AD target the neurotransmitter acetylcholine. This hypothesis emanated from neuropathological studies that found massive loss of cholinergic cells in the basal forebrain of people with AD (Whitehouse et al., 1983). Specifically, the nucleus basalis of Meynert was found to be atrophied in autopsies of individuals

with AD. The nucleus basalis is known to be a key producer of acetylcholine in the brain. Acetylcholine is processed to generate choline, which has been found to be important to learning and memory in a variety of animal and human studies (Furey, 2011). Thus, there appeared to be a consistency between the neuropathology, the neurotransmitter, and the clinical syndrome. Because choline is degraded for reuptake by cholinesterase, research began to pursue the notion that maintaining bioavailability of choline could be neuroprotective. Several acetylcholine compounds subsequently were developed, tested, approved, and marketed (see the Pharmacologic Interventions section). It has become increasingly clear, however, that nucleus basalis degeneration and choline depletion is a late-stage issue in AD (Gilmor et al., 1999). This fact may explain why cholinesterase inhibition has not produced compelling results in the treatment of AD (Rafii, 2013; Tayeb, Yang, Price, & Tarazi, 2012).

The Amyloid Cascade Hypothesis

The amyloid hypothesis (Selkoe, 2001) currently is the most widely accepted model for explaining the development of Alzheimer's neuropathology. The model posits that misprocessing of APP leads to amyloid fragments that are insoluble in the brain. It is thought that these fragments begin to aggregate to form plaques in the extracellular space in the brain, producing a mild inflammatory response. The plaques and inflammation prove neurotoxic, especially to certain neuron populations. As these neurons die, their processes tangle (i.e., neurofibrillary tangles [NFTs] develop). Some neural fibrils also are incorporated in the plaques. Theoretically this explains why, on autopsy, the hallmark features of AD are filamentous amyloid plaques and NFTs. A dynamic time course for these developments has been proposed by Jack et al. (2010) from the landmark Alzheimer Disease Neuroimaging Initiative (ADNI) and is depicted in Figure 7.3. Components of this pathology model are nonspecific and can be seen exclusive of active AD processes. For example, amyloid plaques can be seen in people with normal cognitive aging. Tangles can occur in other supposedly unrelated conditions like frontotemporal dementia or head trauma. As a consequence, the pathological diagnosis of AD is made on a semiquantitative basis.

Braak and Braak neuropathological staging system. The movement toward the concept of preclinical AD was launched in part by the seminal work of (Braak & Braak, 1991). These neuropathologists demonstrated the presence of NFTs in the entorhinal cortex in people as young as 30 years of age. Their work led to a neuropathological staging system that depicts a progression of pathology from its initial presence in hippocampal pathways through to pervasive neocortical NFT dispersal (see Figure 7.3). This progression of pathology has obvious implications for the presentation and progression of cognitive, behavioral, and functional deficits in preclinical and clinical AD.

Insulin and other causes. Researchers recently have proposed that AD can be viewed as type III diabetes, wherein central nervous system (CNS) insulin resistance impairs Aβ regulation, leading to amyloid plaques (Baker et al., 2011). Preliminary studies of direct delivery of insulin to CNS via inhalation have provided mixed support for this hypothesis (Craft et al., 2012). Additional recent research raises hypoxia as an instigating event in the development of amyloid pathology (Orešič et al., 2011). These hypotheses are subsidiaries of the amyloid hypothesis as they merely seek to explain how amyloid plaques develop, assuming that the rest of the amyloid cascade is correct.

Critiques of the amyloid cascade hypothesis. The success of the amyloid hypothesis primarily has centered on its explicit prediction that AD relates to amyloid production and clearance, and the known deterministic gene mutations for the disease directly relate to amyloid production. Despite the prevailing evidence in support of the amyloid hypothesis on the genetics front, a number of unanswered questions remain, and there have been increasing criticisms that the amyloid hypothesis is not delivering effective therapies for the disease in the wake of a multitude of unsuccessful clinical trials. Hardy (2009) reviewed a number of problems with the amyloid hypothesis. First, according to this hypothesis, amyloid/Aβ should be toxic, but Aβ toxicity has rarely been convincingly demonstrated. While newer species of smaller soluble Aβ oligomers have shown some toxicity, "none of this amounts to convincing toxicity: these subtle alterations . . . are a far cry from the massive cell loss seen in AD" (p. 1130). Second, the amyloid hypothesis sequences the cascade of events such that amyloid/Aβ should initiate tau-related alterations and tangle dysfunction, although few data are available on the pathway linking these two molecules as of yet. Third, the most important prediction of the amyloid hypothesis is that reducing Aβ and plaques should lead to improvements in the symptoms associated with AD. The amyloid immunization trials, although unsuccessful and stopped because of vascular and other neurologic complications, seemed to show that amyloid could be cleared from the brain. On this point, Hardy (2009) has noted that the "clearance of visible plaques is remarkable and runs completely counter to the previous wisdom that amyloid plaques were forever" (p. 1130). Unfortunately, it had little to no effect on ameliorating the dementia in those few individuals who showed amyloid clearance. It remains to be seen whether amyloid clearance at more mild stages of dementia, or in MCI individuals, will have greater effects on cognition, if clinical trials eventually and safely get to that phase.

Moreover, amyloid deposition does not correlate with dementia severity or the extent of neurodegeneration, and it does not account for the role of tau in the pathophysiology of AD (Cordonnier & van der Flier, 2011). Amyloid is regarded as one of the initiating events, and other processes such as tangle formation leading to neuronal dysfunction

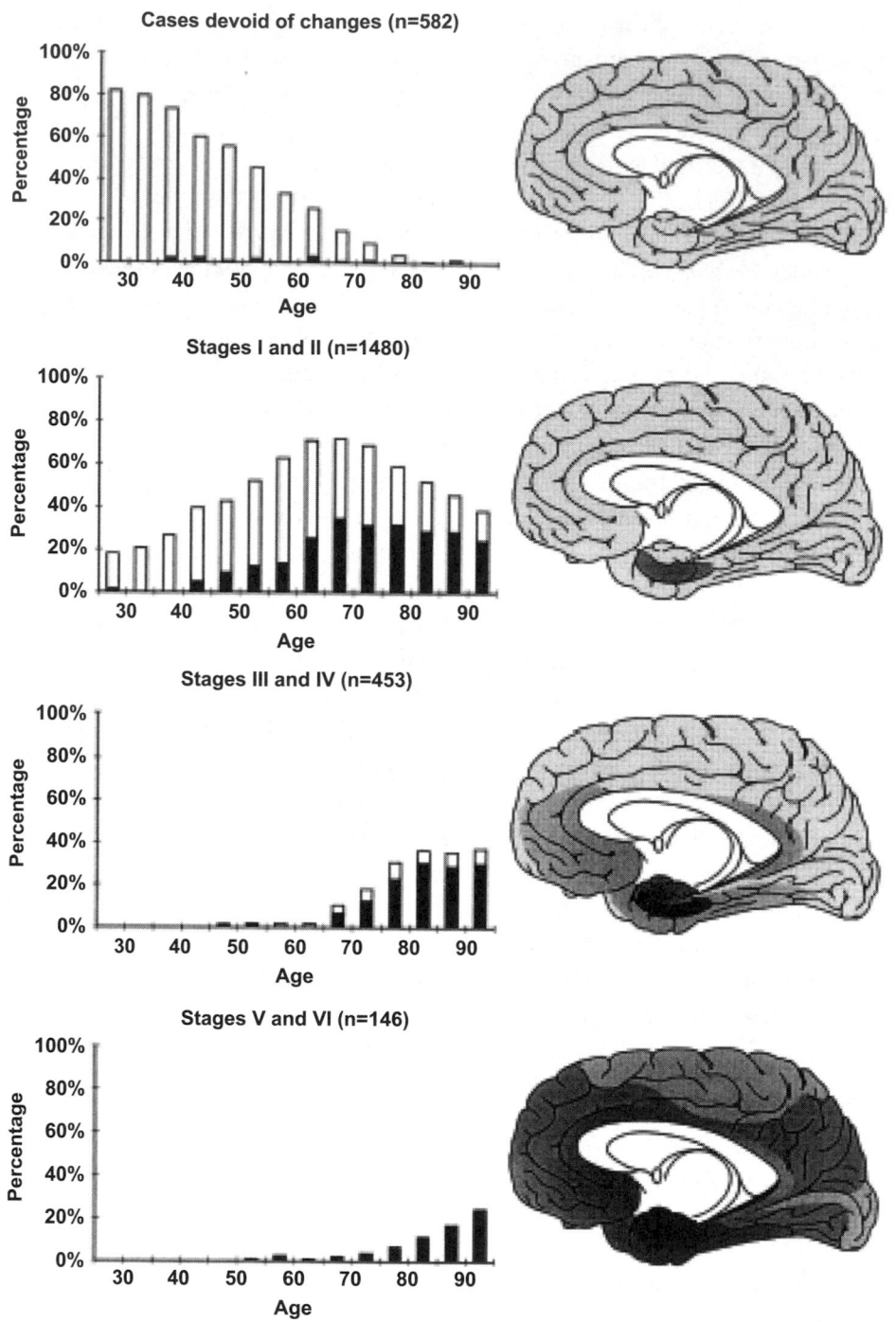

FIGURE 7.3. Distribution of neurofibrillary pathology by age at autopsy n = 2661. From "Neuropathological Staging of Alzheimer-Related Changes," by H. Braak and E. Braak, 1991, *Acta Neuropathologica, 82*, p. 246. Copyright 1991 by Springer-Verlag. Adapted with permission.

and neurodegeneration then become key pathologic processes later in the course of decline (Jack et al., 2010; Sperling, Jack, et al., 2011). The link between these two essential lesions is unknown.

The Vascular Hypothesis

Clearly the neuritic plaque and the NFTs are the best known of the lesions first recognized by Alois Alzheimer in his original 1907 publication. Within a few decades of his original observations, however, the accumulation of amyloid in the cerebrovasculature in AD also gained attention. Notably, the infiltration of small blood vessel walls by Aβ is present in all but a few cases of AD. More recent MRI studies also commonly have observed that CVD pathology (e.g., white-matter hyperintensities, lacunes) occurs more often in patients with AD than in normal aging (DeCarli, 2006). Thus, the presence of cerebral amyloid angiopathy (CAA), as well as the overrepresentation of CVD pathology in AD, has led to the vascular hypothesis, which posits that CVD plays an important role in the pathogenesis of AD (de la Torre, 2004). Critics of the vascular hypothesis point to the weak associations within CVD pathology, particularly small vessel ischemic disease and cognition. These critics argue that CVD pathology is ubiquitous in aging and does not fully explain the dementia syndrome (Bronge & Wahlund, 2007; DeCarli et al., 2004).

Other researchers offer brain microbleeds as an alternative to ischemia to explain a plausible intersection between the amyloid cascade hypothesis and the vascular hypothesis (Cordonnier & van der Flier, 2011). Given that microbleeds can be expected to occur at the site of amyloid deposition in the blood vessel wall, they are an expression of vascular damage and at the same time are related closely to amyloid deposition. Thus, cerebral microbleeds may serve as an additional argument for the notion that amyloid and CVD pathology act in synergy to cause AD. In fact, Arvanitakis et al. (2011) found that CAA pathology is associated with AD pathology and that moderate-to-severe levels of CAA were associated with cognitive deficits in perceptual speed and episodic memory—independent of the effects of AD pathology (Arvanitakis et al., 2011). These data support a separate role for CAA in lowering specific cognitive functions in older people with and without AD pathology.

There are numerous other hypothesized mechanisms for the development of AD pathology, including autoimmunity, pathogenic, and toxin models (Alzheimer Research Forum, 2011). These models have a less robust evidence base and fewer adherents, however, and thus are not reviewed here.

GENETICS

The pursuit of prevention and early detection efforts also has been spurred by the identification of genes associated with dementia. Early diagnosis in a person with some equivocal evidence of cognitive decline can be facilitated by knowledge of his or her genes (Roses, 1997). Whole populations without evidence of cognitive decline, but with genetic risk, can be studied (e.g., Reiman et al., 1996) and even entered into prevention trials. The extent to which these polymorphisms directly affect cognitive function or simply serve as markers for the underlying pathology affecting cognition remains unclear. Current evidence, however, suggests that known genes do not directly influence cognition in the absence of AD-related neuropathology (Bennett et al., 2003; Bondi, Salmon, Galasko, Thomas, & Thal, 1999a; Brainerd, Reyna, Petersen, Smith, & Taub, 2011). More genes will be found, and more ways in which genes associate with AD undoubtedly will be discovered. At this time, it is reasonable to discuss the four known genes as either causative or susceptibility genes.

Causative Genes

At the time of this writing, three genetic mutations appear to have a causative link to AD. These gene mutations are called causative because whenever a person with the genetic mutation lives to the age of risk, he or she invariably develops dementia. Moreover, members of the family who live through the age of risk without developing dementia are not carriers of the genetic mutation found in other family members. These causative mutations include anomalies in the APP gene on chromosome 21, the PSEN1 gene on chromosome 14, and the PSEN2 gene on chromosome 1. These genes all have a role in amyloid processing (Selkoe, 2001). Yet, these genetic mutations account for less than 5% of all AD cases (Campion et al., 1999). All of the AD causative gene mutations are associated with an early age of onset (i.e., AD occurring before the age of 65 years). The identification of these deterministic genes is significant because it demonstrates that AD can have a genetic cause and also that it has multiple genetic causes with a common final clinical expression. It is possible that a portion of the common late-onset form of AD will have a genetic cause as well, although no causative gene mutations have been identified.

Susceptibility Genes

In addition to genetic mutations that apparently cause AD, several genetic variations have been identified that increase AD susceptibility. The most ubiquitous and well studied of these is the apolipoprotein E (APOE) gene. The APOE gene is located on chromosome 19 (Strittmatter et al., 1993). This gene has three common isoforms labeled epsilon-2 (ε2), epsilon-3 (ε3), and epsilon-4 (ε4), and a person receives one from each parent to combine to one of six possible genotypic combinations (e.g., ε2/ε2, ε2/ε3, ε2/ε4, ε3/ε3, ε3/ε4, and ε4/ε4). People who possess the ε4 genotype are at increased risk for developing late-onset AD, whereas people who possess the ε2 genotype may be at decreased risk (Corder et al., 1993; Saunders et al., 1993). A variety of brain changes are associated with the APOE ε4 allele in AD, including increased counts of neuritic plaques and NFT pathology as well as greater depletions of cholinergic markers in a variety of regions. In older adults without dementia, the APOE ε4 allele has been associated with structural (Plassman et al., 1997; Soininen et al., 1995) and functional brain changes (Bondi, Golden, Eyler Zorrilla, Lange, & Brown, 2002; Bookheimer et al., 2000; Reiman et al., 1996) as well as with subtle neuropsychologic deficits (Bondi et al., 1995, 1999a; Smith et al., 1998), all of which presumably are deriving from the prodromal brain changes of AD.

Other genes recently identified or confirmed by a large-scale genomewide association study include common genetic variants at MS4A4/MS4A6E, CD2AP, CD33, EPHA1, CR1, CLU, BIN1, and PICALM (Naj et al., 2011). TOMM40 genetic variation (Roses et al., 2010) remains a controversial susceptibility gene. Even in combination, however, all of these newly identified genes do not approach the strength of association seen between the APOE gene and late-onset AD.

Unlike causative genes, some people with the susceptibility gene do live through the age of risk without developing AD. It is likely that some people with late-onset AD do not carry any of the known susceptibility genes. As such, these genes remain neither necessary nor sufficient for the development of AD. Still, these genes are overrepresented in AD, and inheriting one increases risk for developing dementia. For example, being a carrier of one of the APOE ε4 alleles (e.g., ε2/ε4, ε3/ε4 heterozygotes) increases risk approximately fourfold, and inheriting both ε4 alleles (e.g., ε4/ε4 heterozygote) increases risk on the order of 16 times. Identifying such a significant increased risk for AD may justify intervention with ε4 carriers before they show signs of dementia.

APOE genotype may be involved in complex interactions with nongenetic factors, such as a prior head injury (Jordan, 2000; Mayeux et al., 1993, 1995), nutritional status (Bunce, Kivipelto, & Wahlin, 2004), or endocrine function (e.g., diabetes; Dore, Elias, Robbins, Elias, & Nagy, 2009; Irie et al., 2008). These interactions may modify vulnerability to develop or display AD. A study by Bunce et al. (2004) highlighted the importance of examining for gene–environment interactions in AD. They found that low vitamin B_{12} among ε4 carriers resulted in poor free recall performance, and these results remained after removing incident dementia cases that occurred up to 6 years later. Although it is clear that gene variations, such as APOE, appear to predispose one to developing AD, a significant proportion of people who carry the risk factor do not go on to develop AD. Identifying other factors that may interact with the APOE gene to further influence one's vulnerability to developing AD clearly are needed, and Bunce et al. (2004) demonstrated that nutritional factors may be one such important influence.

Clinical and Ethical Implications

Because of the complexity of APOE as a risk factor, consensus workgroups warn against utilizing APOE genotype information for diagnostic considerations (Knopman et al., 2001; G. W. Small et al., 1997), even in symptomatic individuals. Nevertheless, others have argued that APOE genotype is useful for predicting the development of AD in individuals with MCI (Petersen et al., 1995; Petersen, Waring, Smith, Tangalos, & Thibodeau, 1996; Smith et al., 1998) and helps identify those who may benefit from treatment (Petersen et al., 2005). Green et al. (2009) have argued that in those with established familial risk, knowing APOE status may be useful.

Practice guidelines (American College of Medical Genetics/American Society of Human Genetics Working Group on APOE and Alzheimer Disease, 1995; Post et al., 1997; Hsiung & Sadovnick, 2007) recommended no use of APOE genotyping outside the research arena for asymptomatic individuals despite the fact that recent research has revealed that APOE status disclosure has been well tolerated, at least in the short-term, by cognitively intact individuals seeking AD risk assessment (Schipper, 2011). Arguments for and against genetic clinical testing for AD include discussion on such issues as consumer demand, cost–benefit analysis, risk reduction, and potential for genetic discrimination at the hands of employers and insurers. These issues highlight the need for genetic and psychosocial counseling by specialists to be readily available to the patient and their family both pre- and posttest. Regardless of disputes about the value of predictive genetic testing for AD susceptibility genes, APOE genotyping is now available in many tertiary care centers, clinical laboratories, and through direct-to-consumer (DTC) commercial services. DTC commercial services should pose a special problem because they lack follow-up to deal with the interpretation of the test results as well as reaction and adjustment to the findings over the long term (Hsiung & Sadovnick, 2007). Clinicians should be prepared to discuss general topics of genetic risk factors, such as APOE, and the utility of predictive genetic testing for individuals with and without a family history of AD.

NEUROPSYCHOLOGY OF AD

For the early identification of MCI or dementia in clinical practice, a referral for neuropsychological assessment may prove to be more useful than biomarker assessment or testing for susceptibility genes. It is rapidly becoming conventional wisdom that the pathophysiologic changes of AD begin years before the clinically evident manifestations of the disease. This delay in part is due to a much-publicized heuristic curve of preclinical AD changes presented by ADNI leaders (Jack et al., 2010; see Figure 7.1). The figure illustrates a late appearance of memory and cognitive changes in AD, well after neuroimaging changes and just before demonstrable

functional declines. This proposed late appearance of cognitive decline in AD, however, ignores the immense body of literature on preclinical episodic memory changes and its predictive power for the development of AD some years later. In fact, Jedynak et al. (2012) used the ADNI's data to show that memory changes are the first measurable biomarker for AD (see Figure 7.4).

Furthermore, as shown in Table 7.3, Smith and Bondi (2013) summarized three other studies from ADNI that compared the utility of similar biomarkers and neuropsychological measures, as well as their combinations, to predict progression from MCI to AD. In each case, cognitive, rather than neuroimaging or cerebrospinal fluid biomarkers, had the strongest predictive power for progression to dementia. These types of findings support the contention of Fields, Ferman, Boeve, and Smith (2011) that neuropsychological measures are biomarkers in their own right, worthy of equal status as indicators of AD.

Cognitive Screening and Neuropsychological Assessment for AD

The first step in early identification of AD is to recognize and identify the sometimes-subtle and nonspecific warning signs of an underlying dementing process. Fortunately, the Patient Protection and Affordable Care Act provides for Medicare reimbursement for annual well visits that are required to assess for cognitive impairment. The AA has developed recommendations for operationalizing this cognitive screening process (Cordell et al., 2013), as reflected in Figure 7.5.

This care process appears reasonable for psychologists as well as general medical practitioners. Brief assessment of cognitive status is intended only to assist the clinician in determining whether more thorough neurocognitive assessment is warranted. Unlike predictive genetic testing, the risk of adverse effects resulting from cognitive screening of apparently asymptomatic individuals is low. As mentioned earlier in this chapter, the salience of mild preclinical memory changes for the early detection of AD is in fact the basis for the original MCI criteria (Petersen et al., 1999) and more recently for MCI resulting from AD (Albert et al., 2011). Thus, screening instruments included in the AA's

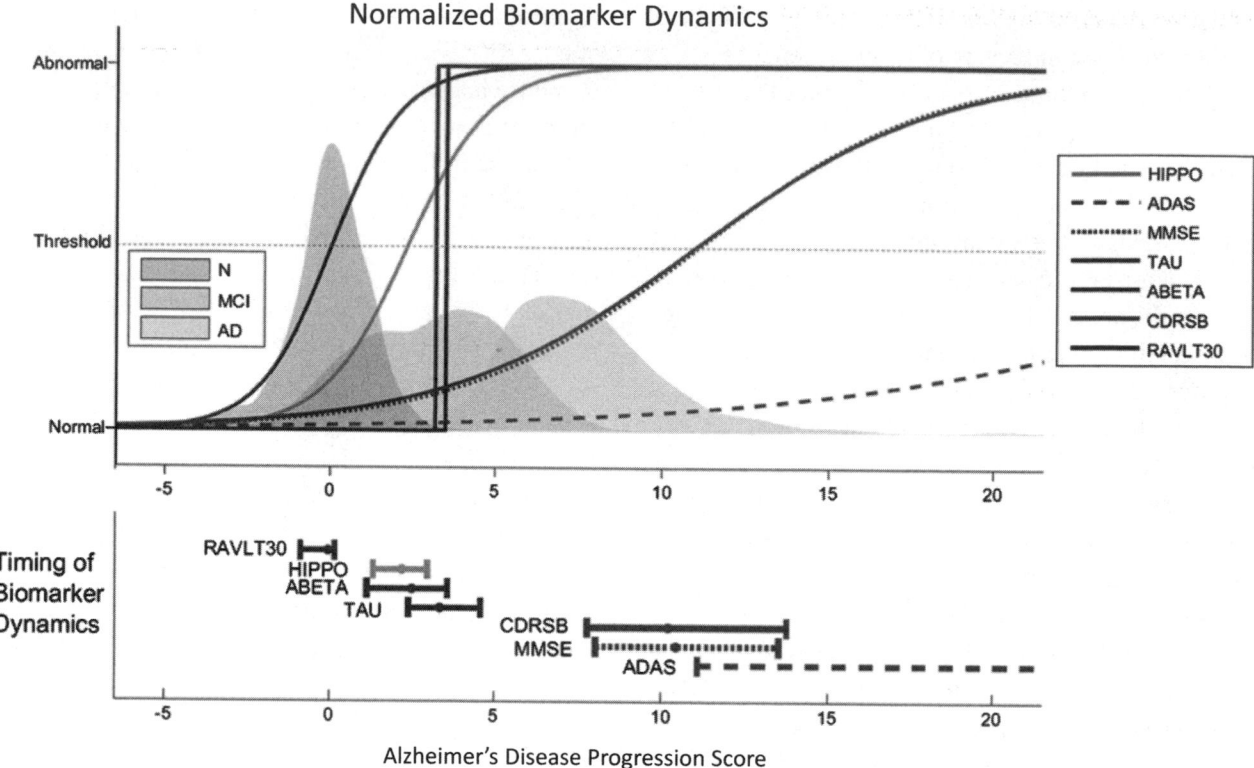

FIGURE 7.4. Estimated time course of disease progression. HIPPO = hippocampal volume; ADAS = Alzheimer's disease assessment score; MMSE = Mini-Mental State Exam; Tau and ABETA = Tau and Abeta42 levels measures in CSF; CDRSB = Clinical dementia rating sum of box scores; RAVLT30 = 30-minute delayed recall score for the Rey Auditory Verbal Learning Test. From "A Computational Neurodegenerative Disease Progression Score: Method and Results With the Alzheimer's Disease Neuroimaging Initiative Cohort," by B. M. Jedynak, A. Lang, B. Liu, E. Katz, Y. Zhang, B. T. Wyman, D. Raunig, C. P. Jedynak, B. Caffo, and J. L. Prince, 2012, *Neuroimage, 63*, p. 21. Copyright 2012 by Elsevier Inc. Adapted with permission.

recommendations (Cordell et al., 2013) place a heavy emphasis on memory assessment even though the tools are brief. Screening of cognitively intact individuals may be beneficial in that it not only provides a confirmation of normal cognitive status for the "worried-well" but also serves as a baseline measurement for future reference.

Suspicion or observation warning signs, however, merit further evaluation for cognitive decline (e.g., referral for neuropsychological assessment). Neuropsychological assessment results in an evaluation that integrates multiple sources of information from self- and collateral reports, medical data, and performance on standardized psychometric measures (Frerichs, 2004). A thorough evaluation will follow American Psychological Association (2012) guidelines for evaluation of dementia and age-related cognitive change. This evaluation should be completed by those with

documented evidence of competency in neuropsychological assessment (e.g., board certification in clinical neuropsychology). It will employ a full array of measures to assess cognitive skills across various domains, including intellectual and academic abilities, attention and concentration, processing speed, visuospatial abilities, language, learning and memory, executive functioning, and sensory–motor and perceptual abilities as well as behavior, mood, and personality variables. Testing is a rigorous and demanding process, and depending on the referral question and clinical setting, sessions can take several hours. Test selection is influenced by several factors, such as referral question and individual characteristics of the patient, including but not limited to age, education, language facility, cultural factors, and sensory and motor limitations. Test results are compared with appropriate population norms that account for age, education,

TABLE 7.3

Results of Alzheimer's Disease Neuroimaging Initiative Studies Examining the Utility of CSF, Imaging, and Neuropsychological Biomarkers, to Predict Progression from Mild Cognitive Impairment to Alzheimer's Disease

Study	Variables	Hazard ratios	ROC analyses (overall accuracy, %)	Significance
		Odds Ratio/ΔR^2	AUC	
Gomar, Bobes-Bascaran, Conejero-Goldberg, Davies, and Goldberg, 2011	Logical memory delay	1.01/.06	0.80	<.001
	Rey AVLT delay	0.80/.04	0.80	<.001
	Middle temporal lobe volume	0.02/.18	0.77	<.001
	CSF: t-tau/Aβ_{1-42} ratio	0.03/.11	0.64	<.001
	Best combination (LM + MTL + Rey AVLT)	—/.34	0.80	<.001
Heister, Brewer, Magda, Blennow, and McEvoy, 2011	Rey AVLT total learning	4.1	0.97	<.001
	CSF: p-tau/Aβ_{1-42} ratio	3.8	0.85	<.001
	CSF: t-tau/Aβ_{1-42} ratio	4.1	0.85	<.001
	Hippocampal occupancy (HOC)	3.9	0.91	<.001
	Hippocampal volume	2.3	0.90	<.001
	Best combination (Rey AVLT + HOC atrophy)	29.0		
Landau et al., 2010	Rey AVLT total learning	4.68	90%	.01/.01
	CSF: p-tau/Aβ_{1-42} ratio	3.99	78%	.03/.01
	CSF: t-tau/Aβ_{1-42} ratio	ns	81%	ns/ns
	FDG-PET	2.94	76%	.02/.04
	Hippocampal volume	2.49	81%	.04/.06
	Best combination (Rey AVLT + FDG-PET)	11.7		

Note. Average follow-up periods for examination of progression to AD ranged from 2 to 3 years. AVLT = Auditory Verbal Learning Test; AUC = area under the curve; CSF = cerebrospinal fluid; t-tau = total tau; p-tau = hyperphosphorylated tau; Aβ = amyloid beta 1-42 fragments; HOC = hippocampal occupancy score, ratio of hippocampal volume to hippocampal volume plus volume of the inferior lateral ventricle; hippocampal volume = hippocampal volume as a percent of intracranial volume; FDG-PET = [18F]fluorodeoxyglucose position emission tomography (measure of glucose metabolism). From *Mild Cognitive Impairment and Dementia: Definitions, Diagnosis, and Treatment* (pp. 161–162), by G. E. Smith and M. W. Bondi, 2013, New York, NY: Oxford University Press. Copyright 2013 by Oxford University Press. Reprinted with permission.

and ethnicity and, if available, previous test data. Serial testing can be useful in its ability to document cognitive change over time and increases the sensitivity of detecting dementia (Mitrushina & Satz, 1991). Neuropsychological assessment, although somewhat time-consuming, is cost-effective because it generates at least five crucial outcomes (Fields et al., 2011). In addition to validating the presence (or absence) of cognitive dysfunction, neuropsychological evaluation assists with the following: (a) providing a differential diagnosis, (b) describing the cognitive trajectory, (c) predicting time to dementia, (d) estimating

functional status, and (e) determining recommendations for treatment or disease management (i.e., future planning, medical decision making).

Referral for neuropsychological assessment is not necessary or appropriate in every case of positive screening for cognitive impairment. The patient's current medical status and ability to tolerate testing are important factors to evaluate when considering a referral for neuropsychological assessment. If from the onset, a medical condition is suspected to be causing the patient's cognitive symptoms, psychometric testing should be deferred until the individual

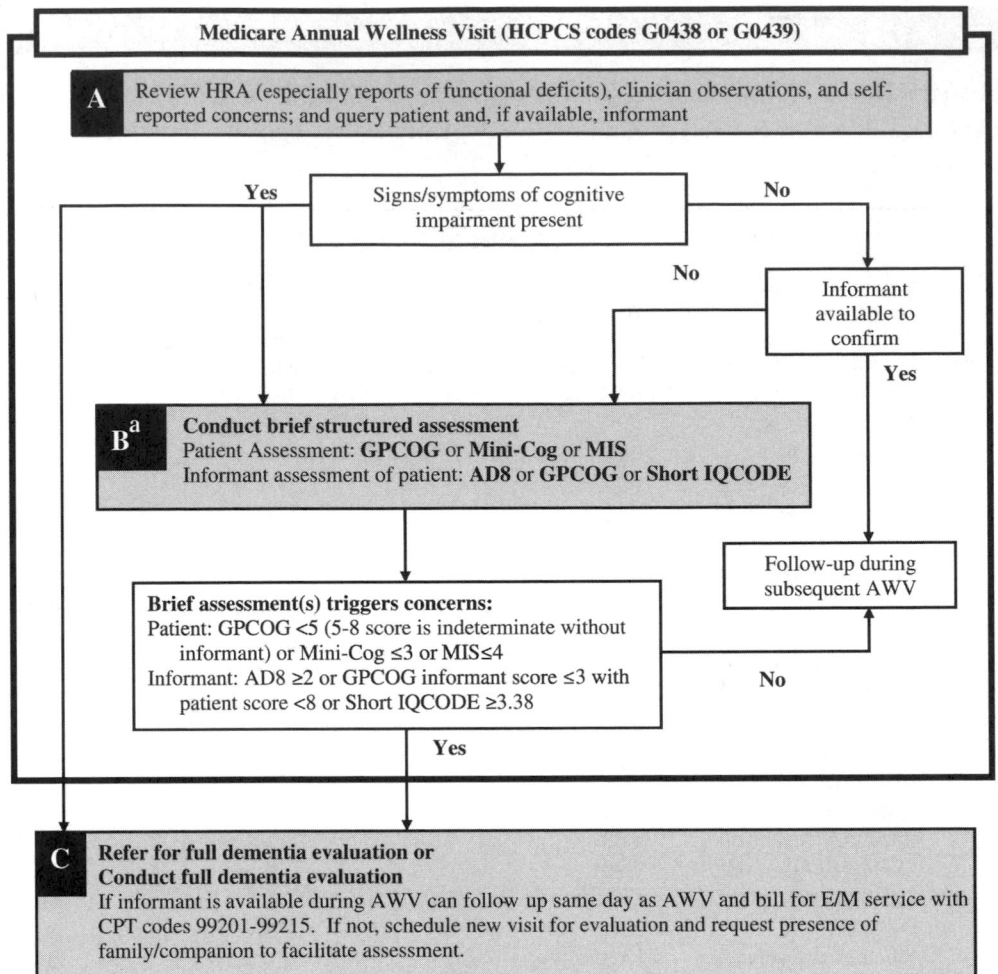

FIGURE 7.5.   Alzheimer's Association recommended operationalization of annual well visit cognitive screening. AWV = Annual Wellness Visit; GPCOG = General Practitioner Assessment of Cognition; HRA = Health Risk Assessment; MIS = Memory Impairment Screen; MMSE = Mini Mental Status Exam; MoCA = Montreal Cognitive Assessment; SLUMS = St. Louis University Mental Status Exam; Short IQCODE = short Informant Questionnaire on Cognitive Decline in the Elderly. From "Alzheimer's Association Recommendations for Operationalizing the Detection of Cognitive Impairment During the Medicare Annual Wellness Visit in a Primary Care Setting," by C. B. Cordell, S. Borson, M. Boustani, J. Chodosh, D. Reuben, J. Verghese, W. Thies, L. B. Fried, and the Medicare Detection of Cognitive Impairment Workgroup, 2013, *Alzheimer's and Dementia, 9*, p. 5. Copyright 2013 by the Alzheimer's Association. Adapted with permission.
[a]No one tool is recognized as the best brief assessment to determine if a full dementia evaluation is needed. Alternate tools (e.g., MMSE, SLUMS, or MoCA) can be used at the discretion of the clinician. Some providers use multiple brief tools prior to referral or initiation of a full dementia evaluation.

is medically stable (i.e., no infections, delirium, intoxication, or withdrawal). Brief cognitive screening is more appropriate if the individual is in the acute recovery stage following an injury, stroke, or surgery. If the patient is in too much pain, is overly fatigued, or is insufficiently motivated to participate in the testing process, the test results may not be accurate. Similarly, situations involving medication misuse, substance abuse, and recent medication

changes can interfere with an individual's ability to be assessed accurately, and testing should be avoided under these circumstances. Finally, there is little utility in referral for full neuropsychological evaluation when the degree of dementia is so substantial that scores on many measures are likely to be at the floor. In our clinical practices, we discourage most referrals when the Mini Mental State Examination (Folstein et al., 1975) score is lower than 17 or equivalent.

Serial neuropsychological assessment can be useful in charting the progression of subtle signs of concern to MCI to AD or other neurodegenerative conditions, but note that periods of stability can occur as described in the next section. Thus, lack of change over two time points does not rule out a degenerative course. Cognitive monitoring in older adults with MCI is recommended approximately every 12–18 months. Short intervals may exceed the longitudinal sensitivity of the tests. Certain clinical factors, however, may support briefer intervals between testing. For example, pre- and posttreatment assessment of cognition may provide a way to detect or exclude underlying neurodegeneration in the presence of sleep apnea, mood disturbance, or other medical conditions. If follow-up testing confirms that the cognitive impairment was situational in nature, no further testing may be required. Alternately, in cases in which MCI has progressed to a dementia and etiology seems clear, longitudinal mental status testing may be adequate to document the severity of impairment and rate of progression as well as to shed light on the impact of cognitive deficits on the patient's daily life.

The following sections provide an overview of the role of neuropsychology in identifying changes exhibited in early and late AD as well as offer some insight into the complexity of the neuropsychological interpretation of cognitive findings. A more detailed account can be found in Smith and Bondi (2013).

Earliest Neuropsychological Changes of AD

As depicted in Figure 7.3, the neurodegenerative changes associated with AD, particularly the NFTs, begin primarily in the medial temporal lobe limbic structures (e.g., hippocampus) and then spread to the association cortices of the frontal, temporal, and parietal lobes over time (Braak & Braak, 1991). As the NFTs continue to accumulate and spread, a threshold gradually is reached wherein the clinical symptoms of the disease, particularly the cognitive deficits, appear. The proposed distribution and spread of NFTs fits well with the pattern and progression of neuropsychological changes.

The pattern of these cognitive deficits in AD often has been characterized heuristically as a *cortical* dementia and distinct from the *subcortical* or frontal–subcortical dementias, PD, or vascular dementia. The general profile of impairment in the cortical dementia of AD is characterized by prominent deficits in new learning and delayed recall with additional challenges to language and semantic memory, abstract reasoning, executive functions, attention, and constructional and visuospatial abilities. Subcortical dementias, such as PD dementia, in addition to their motor disorder, usually demonstrate slowness of thought and deficits in executive functions and visuoperceptual and constructional abilities, although they often show only mild or moderate memory and language impairments that are both quantitatively and qualitatively different from those of cortical dementia patients. Although it is well understood that pathologic changes in various cortical and subcortical dementias are not restricted to either cortical or subcortical brain regions, the cortical–subcortical dementia distinction serves as a useful model for describing the profile and pattern of neuropsychological changes that are observed in these different patient groups.

Given the early appearance and prominence of pathologic changes in the medial temporal lobe, coupled with the fact that these structures are critical for learning and recall of new material, a wealth of neuropsychological evidence supports that episodic memory impairment is usually the first and most salient cognitive manifestation of AD. Salmon and Bondi (2009) reviewed various characteristics of the episodic memory changes that are quite effective in differentiating between mild AD patients and normal older adults.

The primacy of the episodic memory deficit in AD is further demonstrated in its appearance before the diagnosis of either dementia or MCI (Jedynak et al., 2012). Studies have shown that a subtle decline in episodic memory often occurs before the emergence of the obvious cognitive and behavioral changes required for a clinical diagnosis of the disease (Albert, Moss, Tanzi, & Jones, 2001; Bäckman, Small, & Fratiglioni, 2001; Bondi et al., 1994; Chen et al., 2001; Grober & Kawas, 1997; Howieson et al., 1997; Jacobs et al., 1995; Lange et al., 2002;

Masur, Sliwinski, Lipton, Blau, & Crystal, 1994) and has been shown to predict the subsequent development of AD (Albert et al., 2001; Bondi et al., 1994, 1999a; Lange et al., 2002; Smith & Ivnik, 1998).

A few studies have examined the course of episodic memory changes during the preclinical phase of AD (Bäckman et al., 2001; Chen et al., 2001; Lange et al., 2002; Rubin et al., 1998; S. A. Small, Nava, Perera, Delapaz, & Stern, 2000). These studies suggested that a long period of lowered, but stable, memory capacity in individuals with preclinical AD is followed by a relatively precipitous decline in the period immediately preceding the development of overt dementia. Supporting this idea, other studies have demonstrated a precipitous decline in episodic memory 1–3 years before the onset of the dementia syndrome (Chen et al., 2001; Lange et al., 2002). The consistent finding of an initial decline in recall followed by a plateau before a precipitous decline to dementia runs counter to the monotonic decline pattern presumed for AD. Smith et al. (2007) sought to specifically test whether a plateau

model or a monotonic model of decline better fit the longitudinal course of decline in episodic memory (and other cognitive domains) in a cohort of 199 persons followed from normal or MCI status to clinically probable AD. Modeling revealed that the plateau model (represented by the heavy line in Figure 7.6) did in fact better fit the data for memory retention. In four other cognitive domains–verbal comprehension (VC), perceptual organization, attention and concentration, and learning–decline began later than memory change, but the pattern of decline was monotonic (see Figure 7.7). The clinical importance of this finding is substantial. It suggests that a period of stability in memory function in people with MCI does not contraindicate the presence of AD. Given that other cognitive domains are deteriorating, these findings also suggest that some form of compensation, either neurobiological or psychological, is being invoked to stabilize memory function.

Mechanisms that could account for this compensatory process include the engagement of additional neural circuits and recruitment of alternate brain

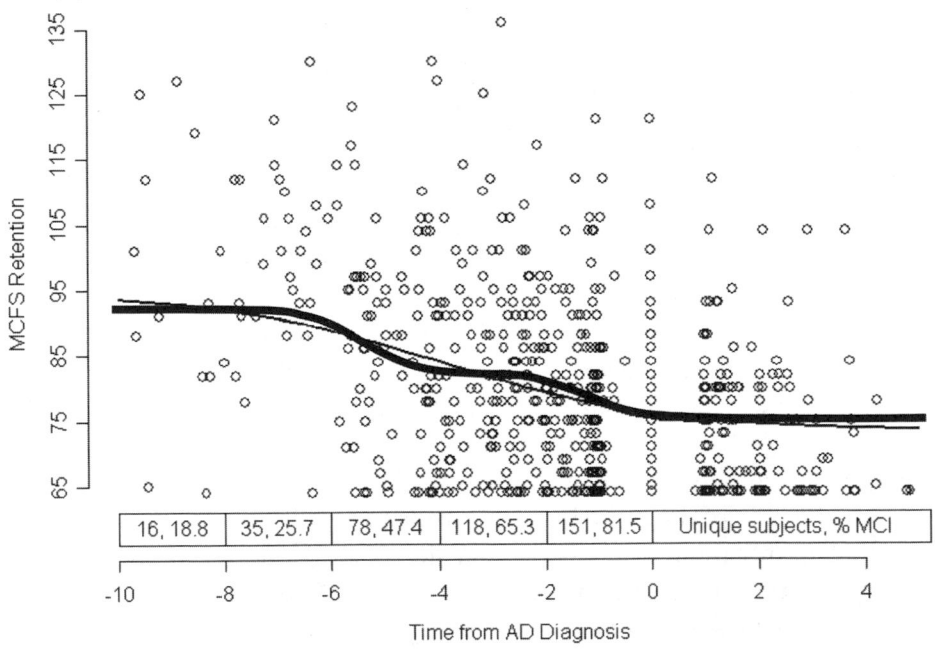

FIGURE 7.6.   Mixed effects model of memory decline in the 10 years prior to Alzheimer's disease diagnosis. The heavy thick line is the model of best fit. MCFS = Mayo Cognitive Factor Scores. From "A Plateau in Pre-Clinical Alzheimer Memory Decline: Evidence for Compensatory Mechanisms?" by G. Smith, V. Pankratz, S. Negash, M. Machulda, R. Petersen, B. Boeve, D. S. Knopman, J. A. Lucas, I. J. Ferman, N. Graff-Radford, and R. Ivnik, 2007, *Neurology, 69*, p. 137. Copyright 2007 by AAN Enterprises. Adapted with permission.

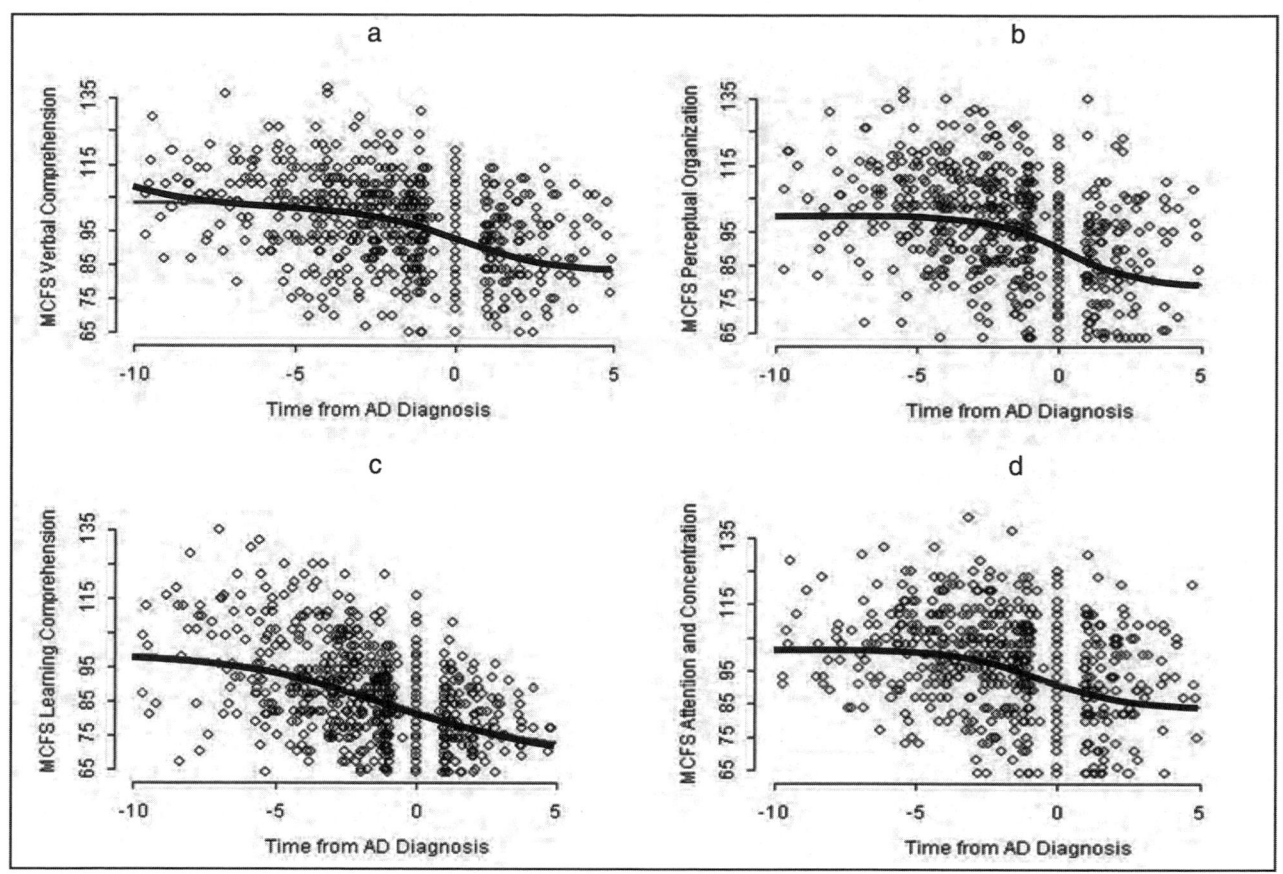

FIGURE 7.7. Mixed effect models: Other Mayo Cognitive Factor Scores. The heavy thick line is the model of best fit. (a) verbal comprehension; (b) perceptual organization; (c) learning comprehension; (d) attention and concentration. From *Mild Cognitive Impairment and Dementia: Definitions, Diagnosis, and Treatment* (p. 166), by G. E. Smith and M. W. Bondi, 2013, New York, NY: Oxford University Press. Copyright 2013 by Oxford University Press. Adapted with permission.

areas, such as the contralateral hemisphere or the prefrontal cortex, to make up for decline in dysfunctional structures (Park & Reuter-Lorenz, 2009; Peters, 2006; Smith et al., 2007). Others have postulated age-dependent homeostatic changes in the regions that subserve memory (i.e., hippocampus) through the upregulation of dendritic spines in reaction to diminished synaptic transmission (Kirov, Goddard, & Harris, 2004). Upregulation of cholinergic activity and the presence of neurotrophic factors also have been noted in preclinical and early AD, prompting Smith et al. (2007) to liken this period of stabilization to a "last gasp" of upregulation before ultimate failure of mesial temporal pathways. Neurotransmitter upregulation, synaptic modeling, and recruitment of alternative neural networks all may be manifestations of cognitive

reserve—that is, the brain's resilience or ability to cope with damage and still function adequately. The pause in memory decline allows for the possibility of neuronal rescue. Although neuroprotective attempts thus far have been met with little success (e.g., using various neuroprotective agents, apoptose inhibitors, gene mutations, immunotherapy, and other strategies to reduce brain amyloid deposits), advances in our understanding of the neuroscientific bases of neurodegenerative diseases are expected to lead to new therapeutic approaches (Nieoullon, 2011).

This period of stabilization offers a critical new window of opportunity to influence subsequent trajectory of cognitive changes (Smith et al., 2007). Explicit compensatory strategies include cognitive–behavioral attempts at adaptation that involve the use of external strategies to overcome or alleviate memory decline. Compensation occurs through four key mechanisms (Dixon, de Frias, & Bäckman, 2001): remediation (compensating by investing more time), substitution (developing or using tools to compensate), adaptation (adjusting goals to better suit current abilities), and assimilation (altering environmental demands). The integration of explicit compensatory techniques into treatment interventions for MCI and early AD has proven to be successful (Greenaway, Duncan, & Smith, 2013; Greenaway, Hanna, Lepore, & Smith, 2008). Such initiatives have been spearheaded by psychologists, perhaps as a result of their involvement in the identification of this preclinical period and through their pioneering of behavioral rehabilitation techniques.

Other Early Neuropsychological Changes of AD

Language and semantic knowledge. As the tangle pathology of AD spreads beyond the medial temporal lobes to adjacent lateral temporal cortex as well as to cortical association areas in the temporal, parietal, and frontal lobes (Salmon & Filoteo, 2007), patients with AD often develop a semantic memory deficit that is characterized by a loss of general knowledge and impairment of language abilities. The meta-analytic work by Henry, Crawford, and Phillips (2004) suggested that in general AD patients show a specific pattern of language deficits where semantic retrieval (e.g., category fluency) is affected first, naming later, and lexical (i.e., letter) fluency last. Testa, Ivnik, and Smith (2003) have noted that although early AD patients may have confrontation naming deficits, they are neither necessary nor sufficient findings for the diagnosis of early AD. Nevertheless, studies show that AD patients have a significant naming impairment that is not equaled by patients with subcortical disorders (Hodges, Salmon, & Butters, 1991). More general, overlearned, VC skills are typically thought to be spared early in the course of the disease. Yet Powell et al. (2006) showed that after memory retention scores, initial VC scores were most useful in predicting findings of AD at autopsy. This observation occurred in spite of the fact that most autopsy-confirmed AD cases in the cohort had initial scores

within the normal range. It appears that low-normal VC scores add to retention values in identifying early AD. The VC scores are more powerful than initial perceptual organization, attention, or learning index scores in making this prediction.

Executive functions. Although the Henry et al. (2004) meta-analysis argued that executive function as indexed by letter fluency is not an early feature of AD, other aspects of executive function do appear to be affected early on. Salmon and Bondi (2009) noted early impairments in cognitive processes involved in "concurrent mental manipulation of information, concept formation, problem solving, and cue-directed behavior" (p. 259–260). These deficits are expected from the relatively early encroachment of tangle pathology on frontal association areas. Executive dysfunction has been noted consistently in early AD (Albert et al., 2001; Bäckman, Jones, Berger, Laukka, & Small, 2005; Chen et al., 2001; Dickerson, Sperling, Hyman, Albert, & Blacker, 2007; Bisiacchi, Borella, Bergamaschi, Carretti, & Mondini, 2008) and may even be evident in prodromal stages. Consistent with this possibility, many studies have shown that poor performance on executive function measures added to poor episodic memory in nondemented elderly predict cognitive decline and progression to AD over as many as 6 years (Albert et al., 2001; Bäckman et al., 2005; Bondi, Salmon, Galasko, Thomas, & Thal, 1999b; Chen et al., 2001; Fine et al., 2008; Lange et al., 2002). As such, decrements in executive function, particularly on complex tasks, may be evident in prodromal AD and signal future global cognitive decline.

This is tantamount to saying deficits in executive functions are evident in MCI, and such difficulties add predictive power for identifying progression to AD in individuals with MCI. Studies comparing the development of dementia across subtypes of MCI found that concurrent declines in episodic memory and executive function may increase the accuracy of these predictions. Consistent with that notion are studies showing progression rates to AD to be higher for MCI patients with deficits in multiple cognitive domains than for those with isolated memory impairments (Ganguli et al., 2011; Mitchell

& Shiri-Feshki, 2009; Tabert et al., 2006). For example, Tabert et al. (2006) found that for progression from MCI to AD over 3 years, the predictive accuracy of combined deficits in verbal memory and executive function was 86%. This was the highest predictive value of any combination of cognitive predictors. Chapman et al. (2010) and Clark et al. (2012) also found that the combination of memory and speeded executive function measures was the strongest predictor of progression to dementia in a sample of either cognitively normal older adults or individuals with MCI.

Given the vast array of abilities and cognitive processes subsumed under the rubric of executive functions, it is not surprising that there are discrepancies in results across studies regarding the predictive utility of executive function measures (Albert et al., 2001; Aretouli, Okonkwo, Samek, & Brandt, 2011; Brandt et al., 2009; Clark et al., 2012; Elias et al., 2000). Nonetheless, the majority of studies are consistent with the notion that impairment of executive function in MCI is not global; only certain higher order domains appear to be affected. The findings at least suggest that in addition to episodic and semantic memory performance, executive dysfunction is associated with greater cortical involvement and may add to the prediction of declines in cognitive functioning in subsets of individuals at risk for progression to dementia.

Visuospatial skills.   Deficits in visuospatial skills and constructional praxis, although commonly observed in AD, tend to emerge later in the course of the disease (Locasio, Growdon, & Corkin, 1995) and do not appear to be evident in the preclinical stages or among MCI patients. A few studies have begun to show evidence for relatively subtle visual processing difficulties in amnestic MCI (Bonney et al., 2006; Bublak et al., 2011; Ferman et al., 2006; Mapstone, Steffenella, & Duffy, 2003).

A so-called visual variant–AD, known as posterior cortical atrophy (PCA), also exists. PCA could be conceptualized as a form of single-domain nonamnestic MCI because memory and language as well as judgment and insight are relatively preserved until the late stages of disease (Salmon, 2011). Neuropsychologically, PCA patients have prominent deficits in tasks requiring visual processing, including reading, writing, and object naming (McMonagle, Deering, Berliner, & Kertesz, 2006). Patients with PCA usually have prominent visual agnosia (sometimes including prosopagnosia) and constructional apraxia, and exhibit many or all of the features of Balint's syndrome, including optic ataxia, gaze apraxia, and simultanagnosia (i.e., they can detect visual details of an object but cannot organize them into a meaningful whole). They also may exhibit components of Gerstmann's syndrome, including acalculia, right-left disorientation, finger agnosia, and agraphia (Renner et al., 2004; Tang-Wai et al., 2004). A visual field defect, decreased visual attention, impaired color perception, or decreased contrast sensitivity also may occur (Della Sala, Kinnear, Spinnler, & Stangalino, 2000).

Neuropsychological Changes at Later Stages of AD

As AD progresses, deficits accumulate to extend beyond those in episodic learning and memory, loss of semantic knowledge, and executive dysfunction. AD patients can exhibit agnosia and often demonstrate a general lack of awareness of their cognitive problems, termed *anosognosia*. Deterioration in language skills (e.g., anomia, paraphasias), visuospatial impairments (e.g., clock drawing, visuoconstructional skills), apraxia, and more basic attention deficits appear. In other words, as the neuropathology and dementia advance, the distinction between AD and other cortical and subcortical dementias disappear. In advanced stages of dementia, it is difficult if not impossible to discriminate etiology, and regardless of etiology, the endpoint for all dementias is the same: terminal brain failure.

ASSOCIATED CLINICAL FEATURES

Behavioral disturbances and personality changes are common in AD and may represent a greater burden to the caregiver than do the cognitive symptoms of the disease. These symptoms can contribute to differential diagnosis. Even though delusions of infidelity were the presenting complaint of Dr. Alzheimer's original AD patient, Auguste D., often it is the absence or late onset of these symptoms that characterizes AD (Alzheimer, 1906). For example, Ferman et al. (2003) has shown that late-onset hallucinations are one feature distinguishing AD from LBD, in which hallucinations are an early phenomena. Similarly, disinhibition is often an early symptom of frontotemporal dementia but a late symptom in AD. Other behavioral disturbances that are more universal and occur throughout the different stages of the disease are wandering, repetitive questioning, shadowing, aggressiveness, apathy, sleep disorders, hoarding, and resistance to help with daily activities (see Chapter 11, this volume). These multiple troublesome behaviors can require more effort to manage than the cognitive symptoms.

Using the National Alzheimer Coordinating Centers database of nearly 2,500 cases of people with AD (Johnson, Watts, Chapin, Anderson, & Burns, 2011), reported rates of neuropsychiatric symptoms ranged from 57% for apathy to 5% for euphoria. Delusion and hallucination rates were reported as 28% and 13%, respectively. Paulsen et al. (2000) found that the incidence (i.e., onset of new cases) of psychosis increased over time. Specifically, the cumulative incidence of hallucinations and delusions was 20% at 1 year, 36% at 2 years, 50% at 3 years, and 51% at 4 years. The classification of neuropsychiatric symptoms using standard psychiatric nomenclature, however, can oversimplify the situation or mislabel behavior. Take the case in which a person with memory impairment has forgotten where he or she placed a wallet. With poor awareness of the memory impairment, the person concludes someone must have stolen it. As a consequence, she or he begins hiding other possessions and cannot remember where. Thus, a cycle arises wherein suspiciousness increases, more hiding and forgetting occurs, and in fact more possessions do go missing. To call this paranoia or delusional does not capture that the essence of this problem is memory disturbance. As another example, imagine the posterior cortical atrophy patient that misperceives coats on a coat rack as a person and begins talking to the coat rack. This is not truly a hallucination. It is a misperception. But lacking understanding of the cognitive deficits, family and health providers are likely to call these situations delusions and hallucinations (i.e., psychosis). This

may lead to inflated prevalence estimates for psychosis in AD.

Thus, behavioral disturbances of AD often can relate directly to the cognitive symptoms. A growing literature suggests that these noncognitive symptoms may be responsive to specific therapies and approaches (Rodda, Morgan, & Walker, 2009; Rovner, Steele, Shmuely, & Folstein, 1996; Schneider, Pollock, & Lyness, 1990; G. W. Small et al., 1997; Sultzer et al., 2008; Teri et al., 1992).

INTERVENTIONS

Effective dementia care starts with the diagnosis. The progressive and terminal nature of AD makes the diagnosis challenging to deliver and even more difficult to hear. In fact, evidence suggests that what people hear is only moderately consistent with the actual diagnostic impression from a dementia evaluation, even when understanding of the results was deemed to be good (Zaleta, Carpenter, Porensky, Xiong, & Morris, 2012). Discrepancies in diagnostic agreement among physicians, patient, and their companions varied according to dementia severity, with lowest agreement occurring in instances of mild dementia. This finding was thought to reflect the diagnostic complexity of diagnosing mild dementia and uncertainty is understandable. When physicians communicated that uncertainty, however, patients and companions interpreted this as absence of dementia and, in some cases, heard certainty where there was none. The use of ambiguous language by the physician was thought to contribute to this misinterpretation. By using language qualifiers (e.g., "this could be," "what we might be seeing"), either when conveying uncertainty or in an attempt to mitigate negative emotional reactions, the opportunity for potential misinterpretation is increased. It was proposed that patients and companions may be prone to hear a diagnostic outcome consistent with their hopes. Using clear language to convey the diagnosis, even when diagnosis is unclear, is described as essential to comprehension and subsequent adjustment. To achieve this, Zaleta et al. (2012) recommended that diagnostic disclosure be considered a continual process as opposed to a singular event. This allows for optimal communication and comprehension of the diagnosis, which presumably results in better adjustment and treatment planning.

Patient-centered communication techniques, such as demonstrating empathy, have been found to be associated with positive outcomes in serious diseases. When disclosing a dementia diagnosis, however, the use of these techniques among physicians was highly variable and infrequent in the case of emotional rapport building (Zaleta & Carpenter, 2010). Disclosure of a diagnosis of dementia is a highly sensitive and life-changing event. As the disease progresses and cognitive impairment becomes more severe, patient-centered communication becomes increasingly important and may be difficult to balance with a simultaneous necessity for a more authoritarian style. Psychologists, by nature of their training and focus on emotional rapport-building techniques, are particularly well equipped to engage in effective medical communication with patients and their families. Effective clinician–patient interactions include communicating in a manner that respects both the autonomy of the patient and those emotionally invested in the patient's well-being. Positive rapport building includes behaviors that aim to demonstrate a shared understanding of the situation, establish a connection with the patient's emotional experience, and facilitate and encourage patient confidence and autonomy (patient activation; Zaleta & Carpenter, 2010).

Although AD often is described as "untreatable," psychologists in fact can provide a vast array of interventions to aid the quality of life for people with dementia and their caregivers. Geropsychologists, neuropsychologists, and rehabilitation psychologists are especially well suited to develop and deliver these interventions. Table 7.4 provides a conceptual framework for these interventions.

PREVENTION

Public health professionals argue (U.S. Preventive Services Task Force & U.S. Office of Disease Prevention and Health Promotion., 1996) that there are three forms of prevention: (a) primary prevention involves interventions to the entire population to reduce risk, like fluoridating the water to reduce cavities; (b) secondary prevention involves interventions targeted to those at higher risk for a condition, like giving statins to those with high cholesterol to reduce strokes; and (c) tertiary prevention involves interventions given to those with disease to mitigate morbidity, like providing cardiac rehabilitation to reduce the functional impact of heart attack. The case for primary prevention of dementia is emerging. Nearly all primary prevention models involve lifestyle modifications that improve overall health. For example, Barnes and Yaffe (2011) recently noted that a combined 25% reduction in midlife diabetes, obesity, hypertension, and physical and cognitive inactivity potentially could prevent 500,000 cases of dementia. Moreover, the emergence of the concept and diagnosis of MCI, as a risk state for dementia, creates the opportunity for secondary prevention models aimed at delaying (or ideally preventing) progression to dementia. Tertiary models in dementia include providing person-centered care to optimize quality of life in the face of cognitive and functional loss (see Chapter 12, this volume). The

---

TABLE 7.4

A Conceptual Framework for the Prevention and Treatment Interventions in Alzheimer's Disease

Symptoms	Prevention		Treatment	
	Behavioral/psychological	Pharmacological	Behavioral/psychological	Pharmacological
Cognition	Brain fitness/physical	—	—	Acetylcholinesterase
Daily function	fitness/social	—	Compensation training	inhibitors?
Mood	engagement	—	Psychotherapy	SSRIs
Disruptive behavior	Person-centered, activity-based care	—	Person-centered, activity-based care	Neuroleptics

Note. SSRI = selective serontonin reuptake inhibitors.

following sections discuss pharmacological approaches to MCI and AD. This focus does not reflect the belief that the pharmacological approaches are most efficacious. There is little evidence for that supposition. Rather, nonpharmacological intervention approaches receive substantial treatment in later chapters of this handbook (see Chapters 11 and 12, this volume), so we limit our focus here to pharmacological interventions.

Pharmacological Interventions for MCI

Two classes of drugs currently are approved by the U.S. Food and Drug Administration (FDA) for treatment of cognitive symptoms of AD. The first of these are the cholinesterase inhibitors (ChEIs). These drugs were developed based on the now out-of-fashion choline hypothesis described previously. The three cholinesterase inhibitors commonly prescribed in the United States are donepezil (Aricept), galantamine (Razadyne), and rivastigmine (Exelon). As might well be expected, investigators have sought to determine whether these current Alzheimer's medications could improve outcomes for MCI, especially amnestic forms of MCI. The AD Cooperative Studies group undertook a large-scale trial examining the efficacy of donepezil versus vitamin E versus placebo in delaying progression from MCI to dementia. This 3-year study of nearly 800 patients found no benefit for donepezil or vitamin E at 3 years, although some interim benefit from donepezil was observed (Petersen et al., 2005). In 2007, Raschetti, Albanese, Vanacore, and Maggini (2007) reviewed the literature on this topic and concluded "the use of ChEIs in MCI was not associated with any delay in the onset of AD or dementia. Moreover, the safety profile showed that the risks associated with ChEIs are not negligible" (p. e388). A 2010 review by the British Association for Psychopharmacology (O'Brien & Burns, 2011) concurred and further added memantine to the list of medications approved for AD that do not have demonstrated efficacy in delaying or preventing dementia in people with MCI.

Pharmacological Interventions for AD

Cochrane Reviews (Birks, 2006) noted that treatment for 6 months with any of the ChEI medications produced improvements in cognitive function. Benefits of treatment extended to global clinical state, activities of daily living, and behavior; however, none of these treatment effects were deemed to be large.

The second class of medications investigated for AD is the glutamate antagonist medications, with only memantine (Namenda) having been approved by the FDA for AD. Memantine is approved for moderate to severe AD. Pooled data suggest that relative to placebo, memantine contributes to a retention of less than 1 point on the Alzheimer's Disease Assessment Scale–Cognitive Subscale over 6 months of dosing (McShane, Areosa Sastre, & Minakaran, 2006). Research examining the combination memantine and donepezil treatment has reported clinically significant benefits in reducing global decline over 24 weeks with good safety and tolerability (Atri et al., 2013). Combination therapy with memantine and any of the ChEIs is purported to be the current gold standard for treatment of moderate to severe AD (Patel & Grossberg, 2011). Although generally well tolerated, the main side effects noted for these drugs include dizziness, diarrhea, nausea, and vomiting. Little attention has been paid to whether families or patients want to delay progression in the moderate to severe dementia stage.

Relative to the overall decline in cognitive and functional status in AD, improvements with donepezil and memantine are small (Howard et al., 2012). Given that medications do not halt the deteriorating course of AD, patients continue to worsen as the disease progresses, and it can be difficult to determine whether sustained pharmacological treatment is worthwhile. Many discontinue treatment as they perceive the medications as being ineffective or experience adverse side effects. Some patients discontinue without difficulty, whereas others have shown significant worsening in cognition and mood (Fillit et al., 2010) dropping to levels below original baseline even if the drug was restarted (Doody et al., 2001). Treatment with AD drugs should be withdrawn when the patient no longer has any cognitive or functional skills left to preserve and slowing decline is no longer a goal.

Pharmacological Approaches for Behavioral Symptoms

The major clusters of disruptive behavioral symptoms include classic mood disorders of depression, mania, anxiety, and agitated behavior.

Depression, mania, and anxiety. Clinically significant depression is present in 20–30% of Alzheimer's patients cross-sectionally. Anxiety is also common with prevalence rates ranging from 5% to 21% (Seignourel, Kunik, Snow, Wilson, & Stanley, 2008). Mood disorders in AD appear to respond to standard treatments, including antidepressant, mood stabilizing, and anxiolytic medications. Use of benzodiazepines, however, is associated with further impairments in cognition and falls (Hartikainen & Lonnroos, 2010).

Agitated behavior. The large-scale Clinical Antipsychotic Trials of Intervention Effectiveness—Alzheimer's Disease (CATIE–AD) study demonstrated modest and selective efficacy for the atypical antipsychotics in treating agitated behavior in AD (Schneider et al., 2006), which, however, was offset by adverse effects. Indeed, meta-analyses have suggested that treatment with these agents is associated with increased risk for cerebrovascular events and death. This led the *Cochrane Reviews* to state:

> Evidence suggests that risperidone and olanzapine are useful in reducing aggression and risperidone reduces psychosis, but both are associated with serious adverse cerebrovascular events and extrapyramidal symptoms. Despite the modest efficacy, the significant increase in adverse events confirms that neither risperidone nor olanzapine should be used routinely to treat dementia patients with aggression or psychosis unless there is severe distress or risk of physical harm to those living and working with the patient. (Ballard, Waite, & Birks, 2006, Discussion section, para.1)

Although insufficient data were available from the considered trials, a meta-analysis conducted by the FDA of 17 placebo-controlled trials of atypical neuroleptics for the treatment of behavioral symptoms in people with dementia suggested a significant increase in mortality odds ratio ($OR = 1.7$). A peer-reviewed meta-analysis (Schneider, Dagerman, & Insel, 2005) of 15 placebo controlled studies (nine unpublished) found similarly increased risk in mortality ($OR = 1.54$, 95% confidence interval [CI] 0.004–0.02; $p = 0.01$) for the atypical neuroleptics. The FDA has placed a "black box" warning on atypical neuroleptics regarding their use in dementia. This may be advantageous overall to people with dementia as it forces more careful consideration of a full range of treatment options. Nevertheless, in some cases of dementia, neuroleptics may benefit quality of life at the expense of survival risk in the same way that narcotics improve quality of life in terminal cancer patients but add mortality risk. AD is also a terminal illness.

CONCLUSION

AD is the most common form of dementia, with a prevalence ranging from about 4% for those under the age of 65 years to about 38% of those over age 85 years (AA, 2013). Current theories suggest that it arises from the misprocessing of Aβ that generates plaque formation, which is neurotoxic. Mesial temporal and frontal brain regions are especially sensitive, producing the earliest neurofibrillary tangle accumulations. This anatomical specificity helps explain the early episodic and semantic memory deficits and executive dysfunction observed in AD, before, during, and after MCI. Neuropsychological assessment has an important role in detecting these changes. The early spread of disease to other limbic and frontal lobe structures in AD also is associated with a variety of behavioral disturbances that are as variable as the people affected.

The challenges of AD can be categorized loosely into classes involving cognition, daily function, mood, and disruptive behavior, although the overlap of these categories is great. Current FDA-approved therapies based on the cholinergic deficit hypothesis are targeted mostly toward cognitive and functional changes and are not particularly effective. Pharmacological treatment in other domains presently continues to involve primarily symptom management and caregiver education and support. Prevention models are more likely to reduce AD morbidity than are models involving treatment only after dementia is present. The lack of adequate prevention models to date is a clarion call to geropsychologists to lead initiatives to better implement current strategies and to discover better strategies to implement.

References

Albert, M. S., DeKosky, S. T., Dickson, D., Dubois, B., Feldman, H. H., Fox, N. C., . . . Phelps, C. H. (2011). The diagnosis of mild cognitive impairment due to Alzheimer's disease: Recommendations from the National Institute on Aging-Alzheimer's Association workgroups on diagnostic guidelines for Alzheimer's disease. *Alzheimer's and Dementia, 7,* 270–279. doi:10.1016/j.jalz.2011.03.008

Albert, M. S., Moss, M., Tanzi, R., & Jones, K. (2001). Preclinical prediction of AD using neuropsychological tests. *Journal of the International Neuropsychological Society, 7,* 631–639. doi:10.1017/S1355617701755105

Alzheimer, A. (1906). Über einen eigenartigen schweren Erkrankungsprozeß der Hirnrinde [A peculiar severe disease process of the cerebral cortex]. *Neurologisches Centralblatt, 23,* 1129–1136.

Alzheimer Research Forum. (2011, October). *Alzheimer's disease: Current Hypotheses.* Retrieved from http://www.alzforum.org/res/adh/cur

Alzheimer's Association. (2011). *Alzheimer's disease facts and figures.* Retrieved from http://www.alz.org/alzheimers_disease_facts_figures.asp

Alzheimer's Association. (2013). *Alzheimer's disease facts and figures.* Retrieved from http://www.alz.org/alzheimers_disease_facts_figures.asp

American College of Medical Genetics/American Society of Human Genetics Working Group on APOE and Alzheimer Disease. (1995). Statement on use of apolipoprotein E testing for Alzheimer's disease. *JAMA, 274,* 1627–1629.

American Psychiatric Association. (2000). *Diagnostic and statistical manual of mental disorders* (4th ed., text revision). Washington, DC: Author.

American Psychiatric Association. (2013). *Diagnostic and statistical manual of mental disorders* (5th ed.). Washington, DC: Author. doi:10.1176/appi.books.9780890425596.680172

American Psychological Association. (2012). Guidelines for evaluation of dementia and age-related cognitive change. *American Psychologist, 67,* 1–9. doi:10.1037/a0024643

Aretouli, E., Okonkwo, O. C., Samek, J., & Brandt, J. (2011). The fate of the 0.5s: Predictors of 2-year outcome in mild cognitive impairment. *Journal of the International Neuropsychological Society, 17,* 277–288. doi:10.1017/S1355617710001621

Arvanitakis, Z., Leurgans, S., Wang, Z., Wilson, R., Bennett, D., & Schneider, J. (2011). Cerebral amyloid angiopathy pathology and cognitive domains in older persons. *Annals of Neurology, 69,* 320–327. doi:10.1002/ana.22112

Atri, A., Molinuevo, J. L., Lemming, O., With, Y., Pulte, I., & Wilkinson, D. (2013). Memantine in patients with Alzheimer's disease receiving donepezil: New analysis of efficacy and safety for combination therapy. *Alzheimer's Research and Therapy, 5,* 6.

Bäckman, L., Jones, S., Berger, A., Laukka, E., & Small, B. (2005). Cognitive impairment in preclinical Alzheimer's disease: a meta-analysis. *Neuropsychology, 19,* 520–531. doi:10.1037/0894-4105.19.4.520

Bäckman, L., Small, B., & Fratiglioni, L. (2001). Stability of the preclinical episodic memory deficit in Alzheimer's disease. *Brain: A Journal of Neurology, 124,* 96–102. doi:10.1093/brain/124.1.96

Baker, L. D., Cross, D. J., Minoshima, S., Belonga, D., Watson, G. S., & Craft, S. (2011). Insulin resistance and Alzheimer-like reductions in regional cerebral glucose metabolism for cognitively normal adults with prediabetes or early type 2 diabetes. *Archives of Neurology, 68,* 51–57.

Ballard, C., Waite, J., & Birks, J. (2006). Atypical antipsychotics for aggression and psychosis in Alzheimer's disease. *Cochrane Database of Systematic Reviews (1),* CD003476. doi:10.1002/14651858.CD003476.pub2

Barnes, D. E., & Yaffe, K. (2011). The projected effect of risk factor reduction on Alzheimer's disease prevalence. *Lancet Neurology, 10,* 819–828. doi:10.1016/S1474-4422(11)70072-2 S1474-4422(11)70072-2

Beard, C. M., Kokmen, E., Sigler, C., Smith, G., Petterson, T., & O'Brien, P. (1996). Cause of death in Alzheimer's disease. *Annals of Epidemiology, 6,* 195–200. doi:10.1016/1047-2797(95)00068-2

Bennett, D. A., Wilson, R. S., Schneider, J. A., Evans, D. A., Aggarwal, N. T., Arnold, S. E., . . . Bienias, J. L. (2003). Apolipoprotein E epsilon 4 allele, AD pathology, and the clinical expression of Alzheimer's disease. *Neurology, 60,* 246–252. doi:10.1212/01.WNL.0000042478.08543.F7

Birks, J. (2006). Cholinesterase inhibitors for Alzheimer's disease. *Cochrane Database of Systematic Reviews (1),* CD005593. doi:10.1002/14651858.CD005593

Bisiacchi, P. S., Borella, E., Bergamaschi, S., Carretti, B., & Mondini, S. (2008). Interplay between memory and executive functions in normal and pathological aging. *Journal of Clinical and Experimental Neuropsychology, 30,* 723–733. doi:10.1080/13803390701689587

Bondi, M., Goldin, P., Eyler Zorrilla, L., Lange, K. L., & Brown, G. (2002). Novel picture learning in non-demented older adult at genetic risk for Alzheimer's disease: A functional MRI study [abstract]. *Neurobiology of Aging, 23,* S359.

Bondi, M., Monsch, A., Galasko, D., Butters, N., Salmon, D., & Delis, D. (1994). Preclinical cognitive markers of dementia of the Alzheimer type. *Neuropsychology, 8,* 374–384. doi:10.1037/0894-4105.8.3.374

Bondi, M., Salmon, D., Galasko, D., Thomas, R., & Thal, L. (1999a). Neuropsychological function and apolipoprotein E genotype in the preclinical detection of Alzheimer's disease. *Psychology and Aging, 14,* 295–303. doi:10.1037/0882-7974.14.2.295

Bondi, M., Salmon, D., Galasko, D., Thomas, R., & Thal, L. (1999b). Neuropsychological function and apolipoprotein E genotype in the preclinical detection of Alzheimer's disease. *Psychology and Aging, 14,* 295–303. doi:10.1037/0882-7974.14.2.295

Bondi, M., Salmon, D. P., Monsch, A. U., Galasko, D., Butters, N., Klauber, . . . Saitoh, T. (1995). Episodic memory changes are associated with the APOE e4 allele in nondemented older adults. *Neurology, 45,* 2203–2206. doi:10.1212/WNL.45.12.2203

Bonney, K. R., Almeida, O. P., Flicker, L., Davies, S., Clarnette, R., Anderson, M., & Lautenschlager, N. T. (2006). Inspection time in non-demented older adults with mild cognitive impairment. *Neuropsychologia, 44,* 1452–1456. doi:10.1016/j.neuropsychologia. 2005.12.002

Bookheimer, S. Y., Strojwas, M., Cohen, M., Saunders, A., Pericak-Vance, M., Mazziotta, J., & Small, G. (2000). Patterns of brain activation in people at risk for Alzheimer's disease. *New England Journal of Medicine, 343,* 450–456. doi:10.1056/NEJM200008173430701

Braak, H., & Braak, E. (1991). Neuropathological staging of Alzheimer-related changes. *Acta Neuropathologica, 82,* 239–259. doi:10.1007/BF00308809

Brainerd, C. J., Reyna, V. F., Petersen, R. C., Smith, G. E., & Taub, E. S. (2011). Is the apolipoprotein e genotype a biomarker for mild cognitive impairment? Findings from a nationally representative study. *Neuropsychology, 25,* 679–689. doi:10.1037/a0024483

Brandt, J., Aretouli, E., Neijstrom, E., Samek, J., Manning, K., Albert, M. S., & Bandeen-Roche, K. (2009). Selectivity of executive function deficits in mild cognitive impairment. *Neuropsychology, 23,* 607–618. doi:10.1037/a0015851

Bronge, L., & Wahlund, L.-O. (2007). White matter changes in dementia: Does radiology matter. *British Journal of Radiology, 80,* S115–S120. doi:10.1259/bjr/35265137

Brookmeyer, R., Corrada, M., Curriero, F., & Kawas, C. (2002). Survival following a diagnosis of Alzheimer disease. *Archives of Neurology, 59,* 1764–1767. doi:10.1001/archneur.59.11.1764

Brookmeyer, R., Gray, S., & Kawas, C. (1998). Projections of Alzheimer's disease in the United States and the public health impact of delaying disease onset. *American Journal of Public Health, 88,* 1337–1342. doi:10.2105/AJPH.88.9.1337

Brookmeyer, R., Johnson, E., Ziegler-Graham, K., & Arrighi, H. M. (2007). Forecasting the global burden of Alzheimer's disease. *Alzheimer's and Dementia, 3,* 186–191. doi:10.1016/j.jalz.2007.04.381

Bublak, P., Redel, P., Sorg, C., Kurz, A., Forstl, H., Muller, H. J., . . . Finke, K. (2011). Staged decline of visual processing capacity in mild cognitive impairment and Alzheimer's disease. *Neurobiology of Aging, 32,* 1219–1230. doi:10.1016/j.neurobiolaging.2009.07.012

Bunce, D., Kivipelto, M., & Wahlin, A. (2004). Utilization of cognitive support and episodic free recall as a function of Apolipoprotein E and vitamin B12 or folate among adults aged 75 years and older. *Neuropsychology, 18,* 362–370. doi:10.1037/0894-4105.18.2.362

Campion, D., Dumanchin, C., Hannequin, D., Dubois, B., Belliard, S., Puel, M., . . . Frebourg, T. (1999). Early-onset autosomal dominant Alzheimer disease: prevalence, genetic heterogeneity, and mutation spectrum. *American Journal of Human Genetics, 65,* 664–670. doi:10.1086/302553

Chapman, R. M., Mapstone, M., Porsteinsson, A. P., Gardner, M. N., McCrary, J. W., DeGrush, E. Reilly, L. A., Sandoval, T. C., & Guillily, M. D. (2010). Diagnosis of Alzheimer's disease using neuropsychological testing improved by multivariate analyses. *Journal of Clinical and Experimental Neuropsychology, 32,* 793–808. doi:10.1080/13803390903540315

Chen, P., Ratcliff, G., Belle, S., Cauley, J., DeKosky, S., & Ganguli, M. (2001). Patterns of cognitive decline in presymptomatic Alzheimer disease: A prospective community study. *Archives of General Psychiatry, 58,* 853–858. doi:10.1001/archpsyc.58.9.853

Clark, L. R., Schiehser, D., Weissberger, G., Salmon, D., Delis, D., & Bondi, M. (2012). Specific measures of executive function predict cognitive decline in older adults. *Journal of the International Neuropsychological Society, 18,* 118–127. doi:10.1017/S1355617711001524

Cordell, C. B., Borson, S., Boustani, M., Chodosh, J., Reuben, D., Verghese, J. . . . the Medicare Detection of Cognitive Impairment Workgroup. (2013). Alzheimer's Association recommendations for operationalizing the detection of cognitive impairment during the Medicare Annual Wellness Visit in a primary care setting. *Alzheimer's and Dementia, 9,* 141–150. doi:10.1016/j.jalz.2012.09.011

Corder, E. H., Saunders, A., Strittmatter, W., Schmechel, D., Gaskell, P., Small, W., . . . Pericak-Vance, M. (1993). Gene dose of apolipoprotein E type 4 allele and the risk of Alzheimer's disease in late onset families. *Science, 261*, 921–923. doi:10.1126/science.8346443

Cordonnier, C., & van der Flier, W. M. (2011). Brain microbleeds and Alzheimer's disease: Innocent observation or key player? *Brain: A Journal of Neurology, 134*, 335–344. doi:10.1093/brain/awq321

Craft, S., Baker, L., Montine, T., Minoshima, S., Watson, G., Claxton, A., . . . Gerton, B. (2012). Intranasal insulin therapy for Alzheimer disease and amnestic mild cognitive impairment: A pilot clinical trial. *Archives of Neurology.* doi:10.1001/archneurol.2011.233

DeCarli, C., Mungas, D., Harvey, D., Reed, B., Weiner, M., Chui, H., & Jagust, W. (2004). Memory impairment but not cerebrovascular disease, predicts progression of MCI to dementia. *Neurology, 63*, 220–227. doi:10.1212/01.WNL.0000130531.90205.EF

DeCarli, C. S. (2006). When two are worse than one: Stroke and Alzheimer disease. *Neurology, 67*, 1326–1327. doi:10.1212/01.wnl.0000244911.16867.11

de la Torre, J. C. (2004). Is Alzheimer's disease a neurodegenerative or a vascular disorder? Data, dogma, and dialectics. *Lancet Neurology, 3*, 184–190. doi:10.1016/S1474-4422(04)00683-0

Della Sala, S., Kinnear, P., Spinnler, H., & Stangalino, C. (2000). Color-to-Figure Matching in Alzheimer's Disease. *Archives of Clinical Neuropsychology, 15*, 571–585. doi:10.1016/S0887-6177(99)00047-5

Dickerson, B. C., Sperling, R., Hyman, B., Albert, M., & Blacker, D. (2007). Clinical prediction of Alzheimer disease dementia across the spectrum of mild cognitive impairment. *Archives of General Psychiatry, 64*, 1443–1450. doi:10.1001/archpsyc.64.12.1443

Dixon, R. A., de Frias, C. M., & Bäckman, L. (2001). Characteristics of self-reported memory compensation in older adults. *Journal of Clinical and Experimental Neuropsychology, 23*, 650–661.

Doody, R. S., Geldmacher, D. S., Gordon, B., Perdomo, C. A., Pratt, R. D., & the Donepezil Study Group. (2001). Open-label, multicenter, phase 3 extension study of the safety and efficacy of donepezil in patients with Alzheimer disease. *Archives of Neurology, 58*, 427–433. doi:10.1001/archneur.58.3.427

Dore, G., Elias, M., Robbins, M., Elias, P., & Nagy, Z. (2009). Presence of APOE e4 allele modifies the relationship between type 2 diabetes and cognitive performance: The Maine–Syracuse study. *Diabetologia, 52*, 2551–2560.

Elias, M. F., Beiser, A., Wolf, P. A., Au, R., White, R. F., & D'Agostino, R. B. (2000). The preclinical phase of Alzheimer disease: A 22-year prospective study of the Framingham Cohort. *Archives of Neurology, 57*, 808–813. doi:noc90027

Ferman, T., Dickson, D., Graff-Radford, N., Arvanitakis, Z., DeLucia, M., Boeve, B., . . . Brassler, S. (2003). Early onset of visual hallucinations in dementia distinguishes pathologically-confirmed Lewy body disease from AD. *Neurology, 60*, A264.

Ferman, T., Smith, G., Boeve, B., Graff-Radford, N., Lucas, J., Knopman, D., . . . Dickson, D. (2006). Neuropsychological differentiation of dementia with Lewy bodies from normal aging and Alzheimer's disease. *Clinical Neuropsychologist, 20*, 623–636. doi:10.1080/13854040500376831

Fields, J., Ferman, T., Boeve, B., & Smith, G. (2011). Neuropsychological assessment of patients with dementing illness. *Nature Reviews Neurology, 7*, 677–687. doi:10.1038/nrneurol.2011.173

Fillit, H., Hofbauer, R. K., Setyawan, J., Tourkodimitris, S., Fridman, M., Pejovic, V., . . . Lyketsos, C. (2010). Memantine discontinuation and the health status of nursing home residents with Alzheimer's disease. *Journal of the American Medical Directors Association, 11*, 636–644. doi:10.1016/j.jamda.2009.12.086

Fine, E. M., Delis, D., Wetter, S., Jacobson, M., Hamilton, J., Peavy, G., . . . Salmon, D. (2008). Identifying the "source" of recognition memory deficits in patients with Huntington's disease or Alzheimer's disease: Evidence from the CVLT-II. *Journal of Clinical and Experimental Neuropsychology, 30*, 463–470. doi:10.1080/13803390701531912

Folstein, M. F., Folstein, S. E., & McHugh, P. R. (1975). Mini-mental state: A practical method for grading the cognitive state of patients for the clinician. *Journal of Psychiatric Research, 12*, 189–198.

Frerichs, R. (2004). When should an older adult be referred to neuropsychology. *Canadian Alzheimer's Disease Review, 7*, 1–9.

Furey, M. L. (2011). The prominent role of stimulus processing: Cholinergic function and dysfunction in cognition. *Current Opinion in Neurology, 24*, 364–370. doi:10.1097/WCO.0b013e328348bda5

Ganguli, M., Snitz, B. E., Saxton, J. A., Chang, C. C., Lee, C. W., Vander Bilt, J., . . . Petersen, R. C. (2011). Outcomes of mild cognitive impairment by definition: A population study. *Archives of Neurology, 68*, 761–767. doi:10.1001/archneurol.2011.101

Gilmor, M. L., Erickson, J., Varoqui, H., Hersh, L., Bennett, D., Cochran, E., . . . Levey, A. (1999). Preservation of nucleus basalis neurons containing choline acetyltransferase and the vesicular acetylcholine transporter in the elderly with mild cognitive impairment and early Alzheimer's disease. *Journal of*

Comparative Neurology, 411, 693–704. doi:10.1002/(SICI)1096-9861(19990906)411:4<693::AID-CNE13>3.0.CO;2-D

Gomar, J., Bobes-Bascaran, M., Conejero-Goldberg, C., Davies, P., & Goldberg, T. (2011). Utility of combinations of biomarkers, cognitive markers, and risk factors to predict conversion from mild cognitive impairment to Alzheimer disease in the Alzheimer's Disease Neuroimaging Initiative. *Archives of General Psychiatry, 68*, 961–969. doi:10.1001/archgenpsychiatry.2011.96

Green, R. C., Roberts, J. S., Cupples, L. A., Relkin, N. R., Whitehouse, P. J., Brown, T., . . . Farrer, L. A. (2009). Disclosure of APOE genotype for risk of Alzheimer's disease. *New England Journal of Medicine, 361*, 245–254. doi:10.1056/NEJMoa0809578

Greenaway, M. C., Duncan, N. L., & Smith, G. E. (2013). The memory support system for mild cognitive impairment: Randomized trial of a cognitive rehabilitation intervention. *International Journal of Geriatric Psychiatry, 28*, 402–409. doi:10.1002/gps.3838

Greenaway, M. C., Hanna, S. M., Lepore, S. W., & Smith, G. E. (2008). A behavioral rehabilitation intervention for amnestic mild cognitive impairment. *American Journal of Alzheimer's Disease and Other Dementias, 23*, 451–461. doi:10.1177/1533317508320352

Grober, E., & Kawas, C. (1997). Learning and retention in preclinical and early Alzheimer's disease. *Psychology and Aging, 12*, 183–188. doi:10.1037/0882-7974.12.1.183

Hardy, J. (2009). The amyloid hypothesis for Alzheimer's disease: A critical reappraisal. *Journal of Neurochemistry, 110*, 1129–1134. doi:10.1111/j.1471-4159.2009.06181.x

Hartikainen, S., & Lonnroos, E. (2010). Systematic review: Use of sedatives and hypnotics, antidepressants and benzodiazepines in older people significantly increases their risk of falls. *Evidence-Based Medicine, 15*, 59. doi:10.1136/ebm1058

Heister, D., Brewer, J., Magda, S., Blennow, K., & McEvoy, L. (2011). Predicting MCI outcome with clinically available MRI and CSF biomarkers. *Neurology, 77*, 1619–1628. doi:10.1212/WNL.0b013e3182343314

Henry, J. D., Crawford, J., & Phillips, L. (2004). Verbal fluency performance in dementia of the Alzheimer's type: A meta-analysis. *Neuropsychologia, 42*, 1212–1222. doi:10.1016/j.neuropsychologia.2004.02.001

Hodges, J. R., Salmon, D. P., & Butters, N. (1991). The nature of the naming deficit in Alzheimer's and Huntington's disease. *Brain, 114*, 1547–1558. doi:10.1093/brain/114.4.1547

Howard, R., McShane, R., Lindesay, J., Ritchie, C., Baldwin, A., Barber, R., . . . Philips, P. (2012). Donepezil and memantine for moderate-to-severe Alzheimer's Disease. *New England Journal of Medicine, 366*, 893–903. doi:10.1056/NEJMoa1106668

Howieson, D. B., Dame, A., Camicioli, R., Sexton, G., Payami, H., & Kaye, J. (1997). Cognitive markers preceding Alzheimer's dementia in the healthy oldest old. *Journal of the American Geriatrics Society, 45*, 584–589.

Hsiung, G.-Y. R., & Sadovnick, A. D. (2007). Genetics and dementia: Risk factors, diagnosis, and management. *Alzheimer's and Dementia, 3*, 418–427. doi:10.1016/j.jalz.2007.07.010

Hurd, M. D., Martorell, P., Delavande, A., Mullen, K. J., & Langa, K. M. (2013). Monetary costs of dementia in the United States. *New England Journal of Medicine, 368*, 1326–1334. doi:10.1056/NEJMsa1204629

Irie, F., Fitzpatrick, A., Lopez, O., Kuller, L. H., Peila, R., Newman, A. B., & Launer, L. J. (2008). Enhanced risk for Alzheimer disease in persons with type 2 diabetes and APOE e4. *Archives of Neurology, 65*, 89–93. doi:10.1001/archneurol.2007.29

Jack, C., Jr., Knopman, D., Jagust, W., Shaw, L., Aisen, P., Weiner, M., . . . Trojanowski, J. (2010). Hypothetical model of dynamic biomarkers of the Alzheimer's pathological cascade. *Lancet Neurology, 9*, 119–128. doi:10.1016/S1474-4422(09)70299-6

Jacobs, D. M., Sano, M., Dooneief, G., Marder, K., Bell, K., & Stern, Y. (1995). Neuropsychological detection and characterization of preclinical Alzheimer's disease. *Neurology, 45*, 957–962. doi:10.1212/WNL.45.5.957

Jedynak, B. M., Lang, A., Liu, B., Katz, E., Zhang, Y., Wyman, B. T., . . . Prince, J. L. (2012). A computational neurodegenerative disease progression score: method and results with the Alzheimer's disease Neuroimaging Initiative cohort. *Neuroimage, 63*, 1478–1486. doi:10.1016/j.neuroimage.2012.07.059 S1053-8119(12)00789-6

Johnson, D. K., Watts, A. S., Chapin, B. A., Anderson, R., & Burns, J. M. (2011). Neuropsychiatric profiles in dementia. *Alzheimer Disease and Associated Disorders, 25*, 326–332. doi:10.1097/WAD.0b013e31820d89b600002093-201110000-00006

Jordan, B. D. (2000). Chronic traumatic brain injury associated with boxing [Review]. *Seminars in Neurology, 20*, 179–186. doi:10.1055/s-2000-9826

Jurica, P. J., Leitten, C. L., & Mattis, S. (2001). *Dementia Rating Scale-2.* Odessa, FL: Psychological Assessment Resources.

Kirov, S. A., Goddard, C. A., & Harris, K. M. (2004). Age-dependence in the homeostatic upregulation of hippocampal dendritic spine number during blocked synaptic transmission. *Neuropharmacology, 47*, 640–648. doi:10.1016/j.neuropharm.2004.07.039

Knopman, D. S., DeKosky, S., Cummings, J., Chui, H., Corey-Bloom, J., Relkin, N., . . . Stevens, J. (2001). Practice parameter: Diagnosis of dementia (an evidence-based review): Report of the Quality Standards Subcommittee of the American Academy of Neurology. *Neurology, 56,* 1143–1153. doi:10.1212/WNL.56.9.1143

Landau, S., Harvey, D., Madison, C., Reiman, E., Foster, N., Aisen, P., . . . Jagust, W. (2010). Comparing predictors of conversion and decline in mild cognitive impairment. *Neurology, 75,* 230–238. doi:10.1212/WNL.0b013e3181e8e8b8

Lange, K. L., Bondi, M., Salmon, D., Galasko, D., Delis, D., Thomas, R., & Thal, L. (2002). Decline in verbal memory during preclinical Alzheimer's disease: Examination of the effect of APOE genotype. *Journal of the International Neuropsychological Society, 8,* 943–955. doi:10.1017/S1355617702870096

Locasio, J. J., Growdon, J. H., & Corkin, S. (1995). Cognitive test performance in detecting, staging, and tracking Alzheimer's disease. *Archives of Neurology, 52,* 1087–1099. doi:10.1001/archneur.1995.00540350081020

Mapstone, M., Steffenella, T. M., & Duffy, C. J. (2003). A visuospatial variant of mild cognitive impairment: Getting lost between aging and AD. *Neurology, 60,* 802–808. doi:10.1212/01.WNL.0000049471.76799.DE

Masur, D. M., Sliwinski, M., Lipton, R., Blau, A., & Crystal, H. (1994). Neuropsychological prediction of dementia and the absence of dementia in healthy elderly persons. *Neurology, 44,* 1427–1432. doi:10.1212/WNL.44.8.1427

Mayeux, R., Ottman, R., Maestre, G., Ngai, C., Tang, M., Ginsberg, H., . . . Shelanski, M. (1995). Synergistic effects of traumatic head injury and apolipoprotein-epsilon 4 in patients with Alzheimer's disease. *Neurology, 45,* 555–557. doi:10.1212/WNL.45.3.555

Mayeux, R., Ottman, R., Tang, M. X., Noboa-Bauza, L., Marder, K., Gurland, B., & Stern, Y. (1993). Genetic susceptibility and head injury as risk factors for Alzheimer's disease among community-dwelling elderly persons and their first-degree relatives. *Annals of Neurology, 33,* 494–501.

McKhann, G., Drachman, D., Folstein, M., Katzman, R., Price, D., & Stadlan, E. (1984). Clinical diagnosis of Alzheimer's disease: Report of the NINCDS-ADRDA work group under the auspices of Department of Health and Human Services Task Force on Alzheimer's Disease. *Neurology, 34,* 939–944.

McKhann, G., Knopman, D., Chertkow, H., Hyman, B., Jack, C., Jr., Kawas, C., . . . Phelps, C. (2011). The diagnosis of dementia due to Alzheimer's disease: Recommendations from the National Institute on Aging–Alzheimer's Association workgroups on diagnostic guidelines for Alzheimer's disease.

Alzheimer's and Dementia, 7, 263–269. doi:10.1016/j.jalz.2011.03.005

McMonagle, P., Deering, F., Berliner, Y., & Kertesz, A. (2006). The cognitive profile of posterior cortical atrophy. *Neurology, 66,* 331–338. doi:10.1212/01.wnl.0000196477.78548.db

McShane, R., Areosa Sastre, A., & Minakaran, N. (2006). Memantine for dementia. *Cochrane Database of Systematic Reviews* (2), CD003154. doi:10.1002/14651858.CD003154.pub5

Met Life. (2012, November). *Market survey of long-term care costs.* Retrieved from https://www.metlife.com/assets/cao/mmi/publications/studies/2012/studies/mmi-2012-market-survey-long-term-care-costs.pdf

Mitchell, A. J., & Shiri-Feshki, M. (2009). Rate of progression of mild cognitive impairment to dementia–meta-analysis of 41 robust inception cohort studies. *Acta Psychiatrica Scandinavica, 119,* 252–265. doi:10.1111/j.1600-0447.2008.01326.x

Mitrushina, M., & Satz, P. (1991). Effect of repeated administration of a neuropsychological battery in the elderly. *Journal of Clinical Psychology, 47,* 790–801. doi:10.1002/1097-4679(199111)47:6<790::AID-JCLP2270470610>3.0.CO;2-C

Naj, A. C., Jun, G., Beecham, G., Wang, L., Vardarajan, B., Buros, J., . . . Schellenberg, G. D. (2011). Common variants at MS4A4/MS4A6E, CD2AP, CD33 and EPHA1 are associated with late-onset Alzheimer's disease. *Nature Genetics, 43,* 436–441. doi:10.1038/ng.801

Nieoullon, A. (2011). Neurodegenerative diseases and neuroprotection: Current views and prospects. *Journal of Applied Biomedicine, 9,* 173–183. doi:10.2478/v10136-011-0013-4

O'Brien, J. T., & Burns, A. (2011). Clinical practice with anti-dementia drugs: A revised (second) consensus statement from the British Association for Psychopharmacology. *Journal of Psychopharmacology, 25,* 997–1019. doi:10.1177/0269881110387547

Orešič, M., Hyötyläinen, T., Herukka, S., Sysi-Aho, M., Mattila, I., Seppänan-Laakso, T., . . . Soininen, H. (2011). Metabolome in progression to Alzheimer's disease. *Translational Psychiatry, 1,* e57. doi:10.1038/tp.2011.55

Park, D. C., & Reuter-Lorenz, E. (2009). The adaptive brain: Aging and neurocognitive scaffolding. *Annual Review of Psychology, 60,* 173–196. doi:10.1146/annurev.psych.59.103006.093656

Patel, L., & Grossberg, G. T. (2011). Combination therapy for Alzheimer's disease. *Drugs and Aging, 28,* 539–546. doi:10.2165/11591860-000000000-00000

Patient Protection and Affordable Care Act, Pub. L. No. 111-148, § 2702, 124 Stat. 119, 318-319 (2010).

Paulsen, J. S., Salmon, D., Thal, L., Romero, R., Weisstein-Jenkins, C., Galasko, D., . . . Jeste, D. (2000). Incidence of and risk factors for hallucinations and delusions in patients with probable AD. *Neurology, 54*, 1965–1971. doi:10.1212/WNL.54.10.1965

Peters, R. (2006). Ageing and the brain. *Postgraduate Medical Journal, 82*, 84–88. doi:10.1136/pgmj.2005.036665

Petersen, R. C., Smith, G., Ivnik, R., Tangalos, E., Schaid, D., Thibodeau, S., . . . Kurland, L. (1995). Apolipoprotein E status as a predictor of the development of Alzheimer's disease in memory-impaired individuals. *JAMA, 273*, 1274–1278. doi:10.1001/jama.1995.03520400044042

Petersen, R. C., Smith, G., Waring, S., Ivnik, R., Tangalos, E., & Kokmen, E. (1999). Mild cognitive impairment: Clinical characterization and outcome. *Archives of Neurology, 56*, 303–308. doi:10.1001/archneur.56.3.303

Petersen, R. C., Thomas, R., Grundman, M., Bennett, D., Doody, R., Ferris, S., . . . Thal, L. (2005). Vitamin E and donepezil for the treatment of mild cognitive impairment. *New England Journal of Medicine, 352*, 2379–2388. doi:10.1056/NEJMoa050151

Petersen, R. C., Waring, S., Smith, G., Tangalos, E., & Thibodeau, S. (1996). Predictive value of APOE genotyping in incipient Alzheimer's disease. *Annals of the New York Academy of Sciences, 802*, 58–69. doi:10.1111/j.1749-6632.1996.tb32599.x

Plassman, B. L., Welsh-Bohmer, K., Bigler, E., Johnson, S., Anderson, C., Helms, M., . . . Breitner, J. (1997). Apolipoprotein E e4 allele and hippocampal volume in twins with normal cognition. *Neurology, 48*, 985–988. doi:10.1212/WNL.48.4.985

Post, S. G., Whitehouse, P. J., Binstock, R. H., Bord, T. D., Eckert, S. K., Farrer, L. A., . . . Zinn, A. B. (1997). The clinical introduction of genetic testing for Alzheimer's disease: An ethical perspective. *JAMA, 277*, 832–836. doi:10.1001/jama.1997.03540340066035

Powell, M. R., Smith, G., Knopman, D., Parisi, J., Boeve, B., Petersen, R., & Ivnik, R. (2006). Cognitive measures predict Alzheimer's disease pathology. *Archives of Neurology, 63*, 865–868. doi:10.1001/archneur.63.6.865

Rafii, M. S. (2013). Update on Alzheimer's Disease Therapeutics. *Reviews on Recent Clinical Trials*. Advance online publication. doi:10.2174/15748871113089990045.

Raschetti, R., Albanese, E., Vanacore, N., & Maggini, M. (2007). Cholinesterase inhibitors in mild cognitive impairment: A systematic review of randomised trials. *PLoS Medicine, 4*, e338. doi:10.1371/journal.pmed.0040338

Reiman, E. M., Caselli, R., Yun, L., Chen, K., Bandy, D., Minoshima, S., . . . Osborne, D. (1996). Preclinical evidence of Alzheimer's disease in persons homozygous for the epsilon 4 allele for apolipoprotein E. *New England Journal of Medicine, 334*, 752–758. doi:10.1056/NEJM199603213341202

Renner, J. A., Burns, J. M., Hou, C. E., McKeel, D. W., Jr., Storandt, M., & Morris, J. C. (2004). Progressive posterior cortical dysfunction: A clinicopathologic series. *Neurology, 63*, 1175–1180. doi:10.1212/01.WNL.0000140290.80962.BF

Rodda, J., Morgan, S., & Walker, Z. (2009). Are cholinesterase inhibitors effective in the management of the behavioral and psychological symptoms of dementia in Alzheimer's disease? A systematic review of randomized, placebo-controlled trials of donepezil, rivastigmine and galantamine. *International Psychogeriatrics/IPA, 21*, 813–824. doi:10.1017/S1041610209990354

Roses, A. (1997). The predictive value of APOE genotyping in the early diagnosis of dementia of the Alzheimer type: Data from three independent series. In K. Iqbal, B. Winblad, T. Nishimura, M. Takeda, & H. Wisniewski (Eds.), *Alzheimer's disease: Biology, diagnosis and therapeutics* (pp. 85–91). West Sussex, England: Wiley.

Roses, A. D., Lutz, M. W., Amrine-Madsen, H., Saunders, A. M., Crenshaw, D. G., Sundseth, S. S., . . . Reiman, E. M. (2010). A TOMM40 variable-length polymorphism predicts the age of late-onset Alzheimer's disease. *Pharmacogenomics Journal, 10*, 375–384. doi:10.1038/tpj.2009.69

Rovner, B. W., Steele, C., Shmuely, Y., & Folstein, M. (1996). A randomized trial of dementia care in nursing homes. *Journal of the American Geriatrics Society, 44*, 7–13.

Rubin, E. H., Storandt, M., Miller, J., Kinscherf, D., Grant, E., Morris, J., & Berg, L. (1998). A prospective study of cognitive function and onset of dementia in cognitively healthy elders. *Archives of Neurology, 55*, 395–401. doi:10.1001/archneur.55.3.395

Salmon, D. P. (2011). *Neuropsychological features of mild cognitive impairment and preclinical Alzheimer's disease*. Berlin, Germany: Springer-Verlag. doi:10.1007/7854_2011_171

Salmon, D. P., & Bondi, M. (2009). Neuropsychological assessment of dementia. *Annual Review of Psychology, 60*, 257–282. doi:10.1146/annurev.psych.57.102904.190024

Salmon, D. P., & Filoteo, J. (2007). Neuropsychology of cortical vs subcortical dementia. *Seminars in Neurology, 27*, 7–21. doi:10.1055/s-2006-956751

Saunders, A. M., Strittmatter, W., Schmechel, D., St. George-Hyslop, P., Pericak-Vance, M., Joo, S., & Rose, A. (1993). Association of apolipoprotein E allele e4 with late-onset Alzheimer's disease. *Neurology, 43,* 1467–1472. doi:10.1212/WNL.43.8.1467

Schipper, H. M. (2011). Presymptomatic apolipoprotein E genotyping for Alzheimer's disease risk assessment and prevention. *Alzheimer's and Dementia, 7,* e118–e123. doi:10.1016/j.jalz.2010.06.003

Schneider, L. S., Dagerman, K., & Insel, P. (2005). Risk of death with atypical antipsychotic drug treatment for dementia: Meta-analysis of randomized placebo-controlled trials. *JAMA, 294,* 1934–1943. doi:10.1001/jama.294.15.1934

Schneider, L. S., Pollock, V., & Lyness, S. (1990). A meta-analysis of controlled trials of neuroleptic treatment in dementia. *Journal of the American Geriatrics Society, 38,* 553–563.

Schneider, L. S., Tariot, P. N., Dagerman, K. S., Davis, S. M., Hsiao, J. K., Ismail, M. S., . . . Lieberman, J. A. (2006). Effectiveness of atypical antipsychotic drugs in patients with Alzheimer's disease. *New England Journal of Medicine, 355,* 1525–1538. doi:10.1056/NEJMoa061240

Seignourel, P. J., Kunik, M. E., Snow, L., Wilson, N., & Stanley, M. (2008). Anxiety in dementia: A critical review. *Clinical Psychology Review, 28,* 1071–1082. doi:10.1016/j.cpr.2008.02.008

Selkoe, D. J. (2001). Alzheimer's disease: genes, proteins, and therapy. *Physiological Reviews, 81,* 741–766.

Small, G. W., Rabins, P., Barry, P., Buckholtz, N., DeKosky, S., Ferris, S., . . . Tune, L. (1997). Diagnosis and treatment of Alzheimer disease and related disorders. Consensus statement of the American Association for Geriatric Psychiatry, the Alzheimer's Association, and the American Geriatrics Society. *JAMA, 278,* 1363–1371. doi:10.1001/jama.1997.03550160083043

Small, S. A., Nava, A., Perera, G., Delapaz, R., & Stern, Y. (2000). Evaluating the function of hippocampal subregions with high-resolution MRI in Alzheimer's disease and aging. *Microscopy Research and Technique, 51,* 101–108. doi:10.1002/1097-0029(20001001)51:1<101::AID-JEMT11>3.0.CO;2-H

Smith, G. E., Bohac, D., Waring, S., Kokmen, E., Tangalos, E., Ivnik, R., & Petersen, R. (1998). Apolipoprotein E genotype influences cognitive "phenotype" in patients with Alzheimer's disease but not in healthy control subjects. *Neurology, 50,* 355–362. doi:10.1212/WNL.50.2.355

Smith, G. E., & Bondi, M. W. (2013). *Mild cognitive impairment and dementia: Definitions, diagnosis, and treatment.* New York, NY: Oxford University Press.

Smith, G. E., & Ivnik, R. (1998). Normative neuropsychology in aging and disease. In R. Petersen (Ed.), *Mild cognitive impairment: Normal aging to Alzheimer's disease* (pp. 66–88). New York, NY: Oxford UniversityPress.

Smith, G. E., Kokmen, E., & O'Brien, P. (2000). Risk factors for nursing home placement in a population-based dementia cohort. *Journal of the American Geriatrics Society, 48,* 519–525.

Smith, G. E., O'Brien, P., Ivnik, R., Kokmen, E., & Tangalos, E. (2001). Prospective analysis of risk factors for nursing home placement of dementia patients. *Neurology, 57,* 1467–1473. doi:10.1212/WNL.57.8.1467

Smith, G. E., Pankratz, V., Negash, S., Machulda, M., Petersen, R., Boeve, B., . . . Ivnik, R. (2007). A plateau in pre-clinical Alzheimer memory decline: Evidence for compensatory mechanisms? *Neurology, 69,* 133–139. doi:10.1212/01.wnl.0000265594.23511.16

Soininen, H., Partanen, K., Pitkanen, A., Hallikainen, M., Hanninen, T., Helisalmi, S., . . . Riekkinen, P. S. (1995). Decreased hippocampal volume asymmetry on MRIs in nondemented elderly subjects carrying the apolipoprotein E epsilon 4 allele. *Neurology, 45,* 391–392. doi:10.1212/WNL.45.2.391

Sperling, R., Aisen, P., Beckett, L., Bennett, D., Craft, S., Fagan, A., . . . Phelps, C. (2011). Toward defining the preclinical stages of Alzheimer's disease: recommendations from the National Institute on Aging-Alzheimer's Association workgroups on diagnostic guidelines for Alzheimer's disease. *Alzheimer's and Dementia, 7,* 280–292. doi:10.1016/j.jalz.2011.03.003

Sperling, R. A., Jack, C. R., Jr., Black, S. E., Frosch, M. P., Greenberg, S. M., Hyman, B. T., . . . Schindler, R. J. (2011). Amyloid-related imaging abnormalities in amyloid-modifying therapeutic trials: recommendations from the Alzheimer's Association Research Roundtable Workgroup. *Alzheimer's and Dementia, 7,* 367–385. doi:10.1016/j.jalz.2011.05.2351

Strittmatter, W. J., Saunders, A., Schmechel, D., Pericak-Vance, M., Enghild, J., Salvesen, G., & Roses, A. (1993). Apolipoprotein E: High avidity binding to beta-amyloid and increased frequency of type 4 allele in late-onset familial Alzheimer disease. *Proceedings of the National Academy of Sciences of the United States of America, 90,* 1977–1981. doi:10.1073/pnas.90.5.1977

Sultzer, D. L., Davis, S. M., Tariot, P. N., Dagerman, K. S., Lebowitz, B. D., Lyketsos, C. G., . . . Schneider, L. S. (2008). Clinical symptom responses to atypical antipsychotic medications in Alzheimer's disease: phase 1 outcomes from the CATIE-AD effectiveness trial. *American Journal of Psychiatry, 165,* 844–854. doi:10.1176/appi.ajp.2008.07111779

Tabert, M., Manly, J., Liu, X., Pelton, G., Rosenblum, S., Jacobs, M., . . . Devanand, D. (2006). Neuropsychological prediction of conversion to Alzheimer disease in patients with mild cognitive impairment. *Archives of General Psychiatry, 63,* 916–924. doi:10.1001/archpsyc.63.8.916

Tang-Wai, D. F., Graff-Radford, N. R., Boeve, B. F., Dickson, D. W., Parisi, J. E., Crook, R., . . . Petersen, R. C. (2004). Clinical, genetic, and neuropathologic characteristics of posterior cortical atrophy. *Neurology, 63,* 1168–1174. doi:10.1212/01. WNL.0000140289.18472.15

Tayeb, H. O., Yang, H. D., Price, B. H., & Tarazi, F. I. (2012). Pharmacotherapies for Alzheimer's disease: Beyond cholinesterase inhibitors. *Pharmacology and Therapeutics, 134,* 8–25. doi:10.1016/j.pharmthera. 2011.12.002.

Teri, L., Truax, P., Logsdon, R., Zarit, S., Uomoto, J., & Vitaliano, P. (1992). Assessment of behavioral problems in dementia: The revised memory and behavior problems checklist. *Psychology and Aging, 7,* 622–631.

Testa, J., Ivnik, R., & Smith, G. (2003). Diagnostic utility of the Boston naming test in MCI and Alzheimer's disease. *Journal of the International Neuropsychological Society, 9,* 504–512.

U.S. Preventive Services Task Force & U.S. Office of Disease Prevention and Health Promotion. (1996). *Guide to Clinical Preventive Services: Report of the U.S. Preventive Services Task Force* (2nd ed.). Washington, DC: U.S. Department of Health and Human Services, Office of Public Health and Science.

Whitehouse, P. J., Struble, R. G., Hedreen, J. C., Clark, A. W., White, C. L., Parhad, I. M., & Price, D. L. (1983). Neuroanatomical evidence for a cholinergic deficit in Alzheimer's disease. *Psychopharmacology Bulletin, 19,* 437–440.

World Health Organization. (1992). *The ICD–10 classification of mental and behavioural disorders: Clinical descriptions and diagnostic guidelines.* Geneva, Switzerland: Author.

Zaleta, A. K., & Carpenter, B. D. (2010). Patient-centered communication during the disclosure of a dementias diagnosis. *American Journal of Alzheimer's Disease and Other Dementias, 25,* 513–520.

Zaleta, A. K., Carpenter, B. D., Porensky, E. K., Xiong, C., & Morris, J. C., (2012). Agreement about diagnosis among patients, companions, and professionals following a dementia evaluation. *Alzheimer's Disease and Associated Disorders, 26,* 232–237.

Chapter 8

VASCULAR COGNITIVE IMPAIRMENT

David Nyenhuis

Vascular cognitive impairment (VCI) refers to all levels of cognitive impairment that are associated with stroke and cerebrovascular disease (CVD), from the severe cognitive and functional impairment of vascular dementia (VaD), to the less severe vascular mild cognitive impairment (vascular MCI). VCI is common in older adults. For example, VaD is the second most frequent cause of dementia confirmed by autopsy (Brunnström, Gustafson, Passant, & Englund, 2009). The goal of this chapter is for the psychologist working with older persons to improve his or her skills in identifying the cognitive, behavioral, and functional characteristics of VCI. Because of the nature of the topic, the chapter will emphasize assessment rather than intervention, although sections on pharmacotherapy and cognitive rehabilitation also are included.

CLINICAL DEFINITIONS AND CLASSIFICATIONS

VCI is one of many sources of cognitive decline and dementia among older adults. Dementia refers to relatively permanent, clinically defined, generalized cognitive impairment that is severe enough to cause significant impairment in daily function skills. By definition, dementia cannot be transient. For example, a patient with delirium associated with a urinary tract infection cannot be diagnosed with dementia unless it is demonstrated that the cognitive and functional impairment persists after the delirium lifts. Instead, dementia is long term, usually stable or progressive, and functionally debilitating.

MCI is a term coined by Petersen et al. (1999) to denote people at risk for developing dementia. Patients with MCI show and report significant cognitive impairment, often restricted to a single cognitive domain, such as memory. They do not meet dementia criteria because they do not demonstrate significant impairment in daily function skills. Approximately 5–10% of people with MCI convert to dementia annually (Mitchell & Shiri-Feshki, 2009).

The terminology to classify cognitive impairment among older adults changed significantly in the current edition of the *Diagnostic and Statistical Manual of Mental Disorders, Fifth Edition* (*DSM–5*; American Psychiatric Association, 2013). The *Diagnostic and Statistical Manual of Mental Disorders, Fourth Edition, Text Revision* (*DSM–IV–TR*; American Psychiatric Association, 2000) classified dementia as present if a person is impaired in at least two cognitive areas, one of which was memory. The cognitive impairment must be associated with impaired daily function and cannot be caused by a delirium. *DSM–IV–TR* VaD is reserved for people who meet dementia criteria that is connected with a neurovascular event, such as an ischemic or hemorrhagic stroke. *DSM–IV–TR* predated MCI and does not formally classify less severe cognitive conditions. By contrast, *DSM–5* dispenses with the term *dementia* and instead introduces the terms *major neurocognitive disorder* and *minor neurocognitive disorder*. Major neurocognitive disorder is similar to dementia, although neither memory nor any other specific cognitive area is required to be impaired. Minor neurocognitive disorder is similar to MCI in that the cognitive impairment is not severe

http://dx.doi.org/10.1037/14459-008
APA Handbook of Clinical Geropsychology: Vol. 2. Assessment, Treatment, and Issues of Later Life,
P. A. Lichtenberg and B. T. Mast (Editors-in-Chief)

enough to impair daily function. Both major and minor neurocognitive disorders are subclassified according to etiology, including vascular neurocognitive disorder. For the near term, before validation studies of *DSM–5* criteria for major and minor neurocognitive disorder are completed, *DSM–IV–TR* criteria likely will continue to be used most often.

HISTORY OF VCI TERMINOLOGY

The changes from *DSM–IV–TR* to *DSM–5* are the latest modifications in the definition and classification of terms used to define vascular-based cognitive impairment. Neurovascular disease (e.g., arteriosclerotic dementia) was viewed as the most common cause for dementia among older adults for much of the early 20th century (Román, 2003). During the 1960s and 1970s, Alzheimer's disease (AD) became recognized as the most common source of cognitive decline and dementia among older people, while neurovascular disease was relegated to a much more minor role. In 1994, Hachinski, Lassen, and Marshall (1974) coined the term *multi-infarct dementia* (MID), which emphasized the role of multiple cortical and subcortical clinical strokes in the development of dementia.

The Hachinski Ischemia Scale was introduced to help differentiate between MID and AD. The scale identified stroke risk factors and posited a stepwise progression of cognitive and functional impairment, associated with discrete stroke events. The stepwise progression was juxtaposed with the insidious onset and progression of AD. A subsequent clinicopathologic study found it to possess excellent specificity in comparison with other diagnostic criteria. This specificity, however, came at the cost of sensitivity (Gold et al., 1997). Pantoni and Inzitari (1993), in their review, opined that the scale possessed adequate sensitivity and specificity, but showed poor results in determining mixed VaD plus AD or in identifying subtypes of VaD.

During the 1990s, the term VaD gained prominence. Two sets of VaD classification criteria were created, the National Institute of Neurological Disorders and Stroke—Association Internationale Pour la Recherche et l'Enseignement en Neurosciences (NINDS–AIREN; Román et al., 1993) and ischemic vascular dementia (IVD; Chui et al., 1992).

Although both criteria introduced a role for subcortical ischemic vascular disease as a possible alternative to large artery strokes in developing VaD, there were important differences between NINDS–AIREN and the IVD criteria. For example, NINDS–AIREN required evidence of relevant CVD by brain imaging, whereas IVD accepted stroke evidence from imaging, history, or neurological signs. Also, NINDS–AIREN required an established temporal relationship between a stroke and dementia. Such an ironclad temporal relationship is not required in the IVD criteria. Instead, there must be evidence of two or more ischemic strokes, or a single stroke with a clearly documented temporal relationship between this stroke and dementia.

With the advent of MCI came a desire to move upstream from dementia to milder forms of cognitive impairment in an effort to intervene before severe cognitive debilitation. Two terms within the cerebrovascular community, *vascular cognitive impairment, no dementia* (VCIND) and *vascular MCI*, attempted to capture this less-impaired cognitive state. VCI then became the term of choice, designed to capture all severity levels of cognitive impairment, from mild impairment to fully developed dementia (O'Brien et al., 2003). In a 2011 summary statement, VCI is defined as "a syndrome with evidence of clinical stroke or subclinical vascular brain injury and cognitive impairment affecting at least one cognitive domain" (Gorelick et al., 2011, p. 2677). VCI truly captures the entire range of cognitive and behavioral deterioration associated with stroke and CVD.

Risk Factors for VCI

As with all forms of dementia and cognitive decline among older adults, age is the strongest risk factor for VCI (Gorelick et al., 2011). Other demographic factors include education (which is protective), male gender (although some studies do not find sex differences), and both African American race and Hispanic ethnicity (reviewed in Gorelick et al., 2011). Several midlife stroke risk factors are associated with later life cognitive decline and dementia, including hypertension, dyslipidemia, and diabetes mellitus (Gorelick et al., 2011). Of interest is the fact that these risk factors are associated with both increased risk of VCI and AD, suggesting potential linkages between CVD and AD (Launer et al., 2000). Although stroke risk factors are well-established predictors of dementia, later-life treatment of these factors have met with only mixed success, with several studies showing no significant cognitive results associated with tighter risk factor control (Birns & Kalra, 2009). Some have even suggested that in the case of hypertension control, later-life control of blood pressure may lead to greater cognitive impairment because of decreased cerebral perfusion in hypertensive elders (Gorelick et al., 2012).

Cerebrovascular Disease Definitions and Classifications

CVD is heterogeneous and complex. It affects the function of both large and small cerebral blood vessels, and it can result in either sudden neurobehavioral change (e.g., from large artery stroke), or chronic cognitive and behavior decline (e.g., from small-vessel disease). It can attack by itself, or in combination with other disease states, such as AD. CVD refers to any pathologic process to the blood vessels that results in brain abnormality (Ropper & Samuels, 2009). The most common forms of CVD are large artery ischemic stroke, hemorrhage, small-vessel disease, and the co-occurrence of CVD and AD (Exhibit 8.1).

Stroke

A stroke is a clinically defined, sudden, focal loss of neurologic function (Ropper & Samuels, 2009). When resulting from CVD, stroke is caused by either a blocked vessel (ischemic stroke) or a burst vessel (hemorrhagic stroke). Stroke is common, with recent incidence estimates of 750,000 new strokes occurring in the United States each year. Stroke is the third most common cause of death in the United States and is a leading cause of both physical and cognitive disability. For many years from the 1950s to the 1990s, the incidence rate of stroke declined, likely because of better treatment of stroke risk factors, such as hypertension. Stroke diagnosis has increased in recent years, perhaps because of widespread use of neuroimaging has led to greater stroke surveillance (Ropper & Samuels, 2009).

Ischemic strokes are the result of a lack of blood flow resulting from vessel blockage or vessel damage.

Exhibit 8.1
A Brief Classification of Cerebrovascular Disease

I. Stroke
   A. Ischemic: lack of blood flow due to vessel blockage or damage.
   1. Embolic: blockage by material brought to the blockage site by blood flow.
   2. Thrombotic: blockage material formed at the blockage site.
   B. Hemorrhagic: a rupture of the blood vessel.
   1. Intracerebral hemorrhage: bleeding from a ruptured vessel within the cerebrum.
   2. Subarachnoid hemorrhage: bleeding from a ruptured vessel in the subarachnoid space, usually in the ventral area around the Circle of Willis.

II. Small Vessel Disease
   A. Lacunar strokes: events caused by blockage of the small vessels (arterioles).
   B. White-matter hyperintensities: diffuse, usually subcortical areas of chronic, incomplete ischemia of small vessels.
   C. Microhemorrhages: Small vessel bleeds, either in lobar or subcortical regions.
   D. Microinfarcts: Very small lesions, usually only visible at autopsy.

III. Other
   A. Atrophy: reduction in brain parenchymal volume, often associated with small vessel disease.
   B. Transient ischemic attack: a brief, reversible stroke-like event.
   C. Silent stroke: a nonclinical stroke event.
   D. Mixed disease: a combination of cerebrovascular disease and other disease process, usually Alzheimer's disease.

They account for approximately 80–85% of stroke events. Ischemic strokes may be further divided into embolic and thrombotic events. An *embolism* is thrombotic or other intravessel material brought to a place of blockage by blood flow. For example, a cardioembolic stroke refers to a blocked brain vessel caused by thrombi formed at or near the heart, often associated with atrial fibrillation, that is transported via the arterial system to the brain. By contrast, a *thrombotic* ischemic stroke is caused by a buildup of intravessel material at the site of the blockage, often in a previously stenosed (narrowed) area.

A *transient ischemic attack* (TIA) is caused by either an embolic or a thrombotic event and is defined by its duration time rather than the severity of its symptoms. Ischemic events that last 24 hours or less are arbitrarily defined as TIAs, although most TIAs last fewer than 15 min before symptom recovery is achieved. By definition, TIAs do not result in permanent brain lesions. TIAs increase risk for subsequent stroke; approximately 5% of people who experience a TIA will experience a stroke within 1 year. Recent studies have questioned whether TIA's are actually transient. For example, Fens et al. (2013) found a high rate of cognitive or communication deficits in a sample of patients with TIA or *minor stroke*. Also, more sophisticated neuroimaging techniques have begun to show longer lasting pathologic changes after TIA. For example, Guo et al. (2014) found both cognitive impairment and whole-brain diffusion in their sample of patients after TIA.

A *silent stroke* is a nonclinical event discovered serendipitously at a later time, usually as a lesion on computed tomography (CT) or magnetic resonance imaging (MRI). One could say that silent strokes are actually neither "silent" nor "strokes." They are not strokes because of the lack of a clinical event and they are not silent because of their potent risk for subsequent stroke, cognitive impairment, and dementia (Vermeer, Longstreth, & Koudstaal, 2007). Silent strokes outnumber clinical stroke events by greater than 10 to 1 and are estimated to have occurred in 11% of healthy older adults (Vermeer et al., 2007).

Hemorrhagic strokes account for the remaining 15–20% of stroke events. Cerebral hemorrhages may be further divided into *intracerebral* and *subarachnoid* events. Spontaneous intracerebral hematomas (SICH) occur in the absence of other trauma. Hypertension is by far the leading cause of SICH, followed by arteriovenous malformations (AVMs) and aneurysms. Hemorrhages also may occur after an ischemic stroke, especially after an embolic event. They often occur from the bleeding of small-vessels, which form a hematoma, and in more severe cases, may leak into the ventricles or subarachnoid space.

Hemorrhages that originate in the subarachnoid space most often are secondary to the rupture of a saccular aneurysm at the branching or bifurcation points of large arteries in or around the Circle of Willis on the ventral surface of the brain. Subarachnoid hemorrhages (SAH) may lead to delayed ischemia caused by vasospasm, or a constriction of the blood vessels. The onset of vasospasm may occur several days after the hemorrhagic event, with peak frequency at about 5–7 days post SAH.

Cerebral Small-Vessel Disease

Whereas the clinical emphasis of CVD traditionally has focused on overt large artery stroke, more attention is now being focused on small-vessel subcortical vascular pathology and its relationship to cognition. The most common form of VCI is the subcortical type (Pantoni, 2010). Cerebral small-vessel disease (CSVD) refers to primarily subcortical gray- or white-matter pathology associated with distal penetrating arterioles most often branching from the middle, posterior, or basilar arteries. CSVD includes both focal arteriolar occlusion (lacunar infarction) and more diffuse white-matter pathology, which is seen as nonspecific white-matter hyperintensities (WMH) on T-2 weighted and fluid attenuated inversion recovery (FLAIR) MRI sequences. Lacunar infarcts most often are located in basal ganglia structures, thalamus, and the area of internal capsule or deep hemispheric white matter, and they may be associated with focal syndromes, such as a pure motor or pure sensory loss event, the co-occurrence of dysarthria, and a "clumsy hand" or hemiparesis. Multiple bilateral lacunar infarctions are associated with etat lacunaire, a syndrome marked by cognitive impairment, incontinence, dysarthria, and gait disturbance.

WMH are ubiquitous among older adults, with more than 90% of community samples showing hyperintensities on MRI (de Leeuw et al., 2001). They most often are thought to be related to chronic, incomplete ischemia (perhaps venular based) in addition to incomplete arteriole occlusion (Black, Gao, & Bilbao, 2009), but the pathology underlying WMHs also may reflect other etiologies, including glial swelling, demyelination, enlarged perivascular spaces, spongiosis, amyloid angiopathy, and cyst formation (Pantoni, 2010). Axial T-2 or FLAIR MRI often show periventricular *caps* and *bands* of WMH (Figure 8.1). Small-vessel disease also is associated with brain atrophy, which in turn may be associated independently with cognitive impairment (Jokinen et al., 2012).

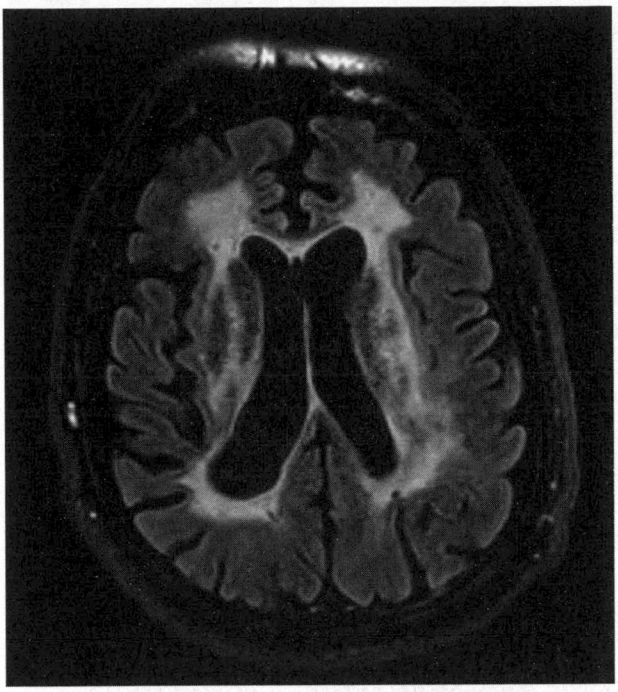

FIGURE 8.1. Axial FLAIR MRI showing perventricular caps and bands of severe white-matter hyperintensities.

Microhemorrhages and Microinfarcts

Two additional types of CSVD recently have been described. Cerebral microbleeds most often are identified via gradient-echo MRI sequences (T-2). Their etiology may depend on their location. Lobar microbleeds likely are associated with cerebral amyloid angiopathy, which in turn is associated with AD. Conversely, deep, subcortical microbleeds, primarily found in and around basal ganglia structures, are associated with stroke risk factors, most notably hypertension. Linkages between cerebral microhemorrhages and cognitive impairment are tenuous, although they are established risk factors for subsequent stroke and cognitive decline (Greenberg, Eng, Ning, Smith, & Rosand, 2004; Patel et al., 2013).

Cerebral microinfarcts are very small lesions, difficult to visualize with conventional MRI techniques and most often identified at autopsy. They have been linked with cognitive decline and dementia. For example, a clinicopathologic study that is part of the Honolulu Asia Aging Study found microinfarcts to be the most common pathology at autopsy in study subjects identified before death as

demented or possessing significant cognitive impairment (Launer, Hughes, & White, 2011).

Co-Occurrence of CVD and AD

Important linkages have been established between CVD and AD. Midlife stroke risk factors, such as hypertension and diabetes, are associated with late-life cognitive impairment and dementia (Gorelick et al., 2011). These dementia cases are not limited to VaD; instead, there is also a higher incidence of AD in persons with midlife stroke risk factors, suggesting potential common pathologic pathways for AD and VaD. In addition, the most common pathology associated with late-life dementia is a combination of AD and CVD pathology rather than either "pure" AD or "pure" CVD (James, Bennett, Boyle, Leurgans, & Schneider, 2012). Furthermore, neuropathologic study of the brains of subjects tested clinically before death has suggested an additive influence of CVD and AD pathology to produce neurocognitive impairment. Thus, in research such as the Nun Study, less AD pathology was needed for cognitive impairment and dementia in people who also showed pathologically defined CVD (Snowdon et al., 1997).

Connecting CVD to VCI

The clinical picture of patients with VCI depends on the underlying CVD pathology (Figure 8.2). When considering the relationship of CVD to cognitive and behavioral change, the clinician should consider three primary factors: infarcts (location, size, and number), small-vessel disease (lacunar infarcts and WMH), and brain atrophy. If there are one or more clinical strokes, the location, number, and volume of the brain infarctions largely determine the pattern and extent of cognitive impairment and behavior change. In a seminal study, Tomlinson, Blessed, and Roth (1970) suggested that total lesion volume plays a critical role in VaD with significant and pervasive cognitive deficits following loss of a critical volume of tissue. The results of other studies investigating the effect of total lesion volume have been mixed, however, with some finding relationships between lesion volume and dementia–cognitive impairment (e.g., Kase et al., 1998; Pohjasvaara et al., 2000), whereas others have not (e.g., Corbett, Bennett, & Kos, 1994; Gorelick et al., 1992). Lesion location appears to be at least as

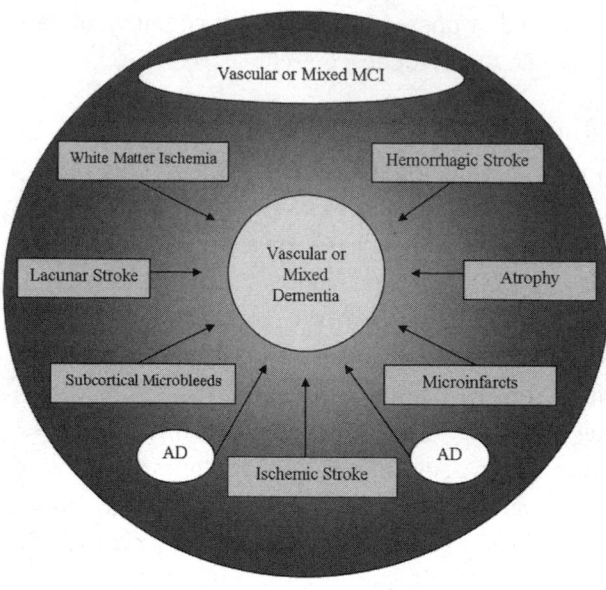

FIGURE 8.2. A VCI schematic demonstrating multiple sources of CVD, the possible co-occurrence of Alzheimer's disease, and a potential progression from vascular MCI to VaD.

important as lesion volume. Single lesions in the angular gyrus of the dominant hemisphere (Benson & Cummings, 1982) and basal frontal structures in the distribution of the anterior communicating artery (Alexander & Freedman, 1984) are associated with significant memory and other cognitive symptoms. More pervasively, lesions of the thalamus are implicated in dementia associated with stroke (e.g., Annoni et al., 2003; Katz, Alexander, & Mandell, 1987; Steinke et al., 1992), especially in the dominant (usually left) hemisphere for language. A more recent study employing voxel-based morphometry found poststroke thalamic atrophy to be associated with cognitive impairment (Stebbins et al., 2008).

Other focal cognitive deficits may be associated with specific lesion locations, such as lesions located in language (usually dominant hemisphere, fronto-temporo-parietal regions) or visuospatial (usually nondominant hemisphere, parietal region) brain regions. Executive dysfunction and behavior change often are associated with anterior lesions, such as after ruptured anterior communicating artery aneurysms. Multiple strokes may correspond with ever-deteriorating cognitive skills and are the source of so-called MID. Lesion analyses of stroke patients play a key role in this line of research.

Juxtaposed with the focal features of specific stroke-related lesions is the more diffuse pattern of cognitive impairment associated with subcortical small-vessel disease, consisting of both lacunar infarctions and WMHs. In fact, separate diagnostic criteria have been suggested to capture the clinical–cognitive and behavioral syndrome called subcortical ischemic vascular dementia (Erkinjuntti et al., 2000), including executive cognitive impairments and behavioral manifestations, such as irritability, apathy, low mood, and gait difficulties.

Although both components of small-vessel disease appear to contribute to cognitive impairment (Koga et al., 2009), lacunar infarcts likely have a stronger relationship with cognitive function than white-matter lesions, and multiple lacunar infarcts may have an additive effect with respect to cognitive and functional impairment (Viswanathan et al., 2007). Paired with the lacunar infarcts are WMHs, also known as subcortical hyperintensities and leukoarariosis. The relationship of WMHs and cognitive function is debated. There appears to be a relationship between stroke risk factors, such as hypertension, dyslipidemia, and diabetes, and WMH (Gorelick et al., 2011). But how much WMH is needed for it to affect cognitive function? Large community samples, such as in the Rotterdam Scan Study and the Cardiovascular Health Study support a threshold effect, above which WMH is associated with cognitive impairment (Longstreth et al., 1996). In this latter study, a mild degree of WMH is not related to lower scores on the Modified Mini-Mental State Examination (MMSE). Moderate and severe WMH, however, are related inversely to cognitive function. Whether the location of small-vessel disease is also important is less clear. Some studies report localized effects. For example, memory disturbance has been related to hyperintensities in the anteromedial thalamus, whereas hyperintensities involving cholinergic tracts appear to compromise executive functions (Swartz, Sahlas, & Black, 2003). Other studies report executive dysfunction independent of location (Reed et al., 2004).

Cerebral atrophy in the context of CVD also is related to cognitive impairment. Mungas et al. (2001) found cortical gray-matter volume to be a stronger predictor of cognitive function than lacunar infarct volume in normal, cognitively impaired and demented individuals with and without subcortical lacunar infarcts. In this study, white-matter lesions independently predicted selected timed measures of cognition. There is, however, an inverse relationship between brain size and the presence of white-matter lesions (Wang et al., 2013). Some investigators have begun to address this issue by quantifying both atrophy and small-vessel disease burden simultaneously. Although these studies agree that atrophy explains most of the variance for cognitive decline, lesion load also independently contributes (Swartz, Stuss, Gao, & Black, 2008). Localized atrophy also may be important. For example, Stebbins et al. (2008) used voxel-based morphometric measures (VBM) to show lower thalamic gray-matter volume in poststroke patients with MCI than in poststroke patients with normal cognitive function.

ASSESSMENT OF VASCULAR COGNITIVE IMPAIRMENT

Several factors are important when considering the assessment of persons with suspected VCI. The following sections outline the modal neuropsychological patterns in VCI, some suggested cognitive test protocols in this patient group, and specific assessment challenges when completing assessments with persons after stroke and cerebrovascular disease.

Neuropsychological Patterns in VCI

Given the heterogeneity of stroke and CVD that may lead to VCI, it is not surprising that there is no single neuropsychological pattern that is both sensitive and specific to CVD, and the clinician is cautioned not to diagnose VCI based on neuropsychological test results alone. Still, several studies have found that a pattern of slowed information processing, executive dysfunction, immediate memory deficits, and mood disturbance are common in patients with stroke and CVD (e.g., Nyenhuis et al., 2004). One of the complexities of VCI is that patients often present with focal stroke or strokes superimposed on a foundation of longstanding small-vessel disease. Thus, they show both the focal pattern of cognitive impairment dependent on the location of the infarction as well as the diffuse, subcortical pattern of

executive dysfunction; slowed processing; and memory-encoding deficits associated with the small-vessel disease. Patients also may show evidence of concurrent AD, such as anomia, rapid forgetting of newly learned information, and inconsistent orientation.

Although as in any neuropsychological examination it is important to sample all cognitive domains, two specific areas deserve special mention because of their prominence in VCI research. First, executive function, which refers to higher level cognitive skills, such as planning, organizing, and synthesizing, is seen by many as a hallmark of VCI. In fact, some have suggested that executive dysfunction be a required feature of VCI. Although tests of executive function certainly are sensitive to CVD-related impairment (Nyenhuis et al., 2004), they only inconsistently have shown to be specific to CVD, as compared with patients with AD pathology (Reed et al., 2007).

Memory is a second important cognitive domain. The NINDS–AIREN criteria for VaD require memory impairment. Perhaps in fear of the "Alzheimerization" of all dementia, subsequent groups of VCI investigators have argued that memory should not be required (Hachinski et al., 2006), and the American Heart Association—American Stroke Association criteria do not require memory impairment for diagnosis of VaD or VaMCI (Gorelick et al., 2011). Still, memory impairment is common in patients with VCI (Nyenhuis et al., 2004). The pattern of memory impairment in VCI may be qualitatively different from that of AD in that a rapid forgetting of newly learned information may not be seen in VCI patients for which there is not an AD component. Instead, patients with CVD often show inefficient encoding of new information, resulting in less information acquired.

Cognitive Test Protocols

Given the hundreds of neuropsychological tests at their disposal, the clinician may find it difficult to choose which tests to administer to their patients with potential vascular cognitive impairment. Some guidance was provided by the neuropsychology committee at the VCI harmonization conference cosponsored by the National Institute of

Neurological Disorders and Stroke and the Canadian Stroke Network in 2005 (Hachinski et al., 2006). The committee examined the literature and chose tests with acceptable psychometric properties, a track record of research in patient groups with suspected VCI, relatively little cost and equipment, and conducive to studies across different languages and cultures. A list of the tests included in their recommended 60-Min Protocol is contained in Exhibit 8.2.

Screening examinations. The MMSE, although brief, may not be as sensitive to cognitive impairment associated with CVD as newer screening tools with better psychometric properties, such as the Montreal Cognitive Assessment Test (MoCA; Nasreddine, n.d.) or, if more time is available for screening, the Repeatable Battery for the Assessment of Neuropsychological Status (RBANS). In several studies, the MoCA has been shown to be more sensitive than the MMSE to detecting cognitive impairment in patients with suspected CVD, although some have noted that the test's sensitivity may come at the expense of specificity (Godefroy et al., 2011; Rossetti, Lacritz, Cullum, & Weiner, 2011) and that there is a need for educational corrections when using the MoCA. Multiple studies also have

demonstrated the validity of the RBANS for use with patients with stroke and CVD (e.g., Larson, Kirschner, Bode, Heinemann, & Goodman, 2005). The 5-Min Protocol from the VCI Harmonization conference is designed to be administered potentially by telephone and includes the immediate and delayed five-word recall, the orientation items, and the one-letter phonemic fluency tasks from the MoCA (Hachinski et al., 2006). Its validity, however, has yet to be established.

Executive domain tests. The construct of executive dysfunction is complex and multifaceted. Speeded tests of executive function have been shown to be especially sensitive to patients with suspected VCI (Nyenhuis et al., 2004). The NINDS-CSN Protocols include several speeded executive function tests, based on Stuss and Levine's (2002) initiation–activation factor of executive function. These tests include Digit Symbol Substitution Test from the Wechsler Adult Intelligence Scale—Third Edition (WAIS–III) as well as phonemic fluency, semantic fluency, and the Trailmaking Test.

Memory domain tests. The construct of memory encompasses a wide array of subdomains, depending on the material that is to be learned and recalled (e.g., verbal versus visual memory), when it is to be recalled (e.g., immediate and delayed recall paradigms), the method of recollection (e.g., free versus cued recall), and the neural system involved (e.g., declarative versus procedural memory). Decisions of which memory test to choose will depend in part on patient characteristics, such as the severity of their cognitive impairment (e.g., choosing a 16-word versus a 9-word list learning task), the location of their stroke lesion (e.g., left versus right hemisphere), and the cognitive symptoms with which they present (e.g., spatial memory deficits). Much has been made of differences in the pattern of memory disturbance between patients with CVD and those with AD, with the former group showing the relative lack of rapid forgetting than the latter group, and the greater likelihood that patients with CVD will benefit from delayed recognition paradigms than those with AD. For these reasons, VCI neuropsychology protocols should involve memory measures that include immediate free recall, delayed free

---

Exhibit 8.2
60-Minute Protocol From the VCI Harmonization Conference

Executive/activation
- Animal Naming (semantic fluency)
- Controlled Oral Word Association Test
- WAIS–III Digit Symbol-Coding
- Trailmaking Test
- Future Use: Simple and Choice Reaction Time

Language/lexical retrieval
- Boston Naming Test, 2nd Edition, Short Form

Visuospatial
- Rey–Osterrieth Complex Figure Copy

Memory
- Hopkins Verbal Learning Test-Revised
- Alternate: California Verbal Learning Test–2

Neuropsychiatric/depressive symptoms
- Neuropsychiatric Inventory Questionnaire Version
- Center for Epidemiological Studies Depression Scale

---

recall, and delayed recognition paradigms. The VCI Harmonization committee recommended both the revised Hopkins Verbal Learning Test (HVLT) and the revised California Verbal Learning Test (CVLT), depending on the time available to complete the assessment; the HVLT takes less time than the CVLT, but it does not include potentially important components, such as cued recall and an interference list. Potential tests of visual memory include the recall condition of the Rey Complex Figure and the Brief Visual Memory Test.

Language and visuospatial domain tests. Aphasic patients provide methodological challenges to the neuropsychologist because they frequently are unable to complete formal neuropsychological testing. Aphasic patients also should be examined by the neuropsychologist or the speech pathologist with standard aphasia protocols, such as the Western Aphasia Battery or the Boston Diagnostic Aphasia Examination.

Other than in patients with focalized lesions leading to aphasia, tests that measure primary language functions (e.g., confrontation naming, auditory comprehension, repetition skills) may not be as sensitive as tests in other domains in patient groups with suspected VCI. Verbal fluency tests have been sorted into both language and executive cognitive domains, and indeed, they show aspects of both. In nonaphasic patients groups, however, the activation and working memory demands of the tasks make them ideal measures of executive function. Similarly, other than in patients with focal nondominant hemisphere frontoparietal lesions, tests of spatial function may not be as sensitive to cognitive impairment in patients with suspected VCI as tests in other domains. The VCI Harmonization committee recommended the Rey Complex Figure, in part, because it included both spatial and executive components.

Assessment Dilemmas and Challenges in Stroke and Cerebrovascular Disease

Patients with stroke and CVD may present special challenges when assessing *cognitive*, *functional*, and *psychological* issues. The cognitive challenges may require an augmentation of standardized test administration. For example, if a patient presents with focal cognitive deficits secondary to stroke, cognitive examination is often a two-step process: (a) examine for the presence and extent of focal deficits related to the stroke location and (b) examine other cognitive domains while minimizing the effects of the focal deficits. The goal of the first step is to understand the extent of the focal deficit. For example, if a patient presents with language deficits secondary to a left hemisphere middle cerebral artery ischemic stroke, the first step in the examination is to examine language, including an assessment of fluency, auditory comprehension, repetition, reading, and writing to come to an adequate understanding of the changes that likely occurred to language-based functions because of the stroke. Once the examination of the focal deficit is complete, the second step of the examination takes an opposite tack.

During this phase, the goal of the examination is to assess the remaining cognitive domains while attempting to minimize the effects of the focal deficit. Of course, this may not be completely possible (e.g., it is not possible to remove the effects of language deficits from the examination). Still, the clinician may be able to minimize language deficits by relying on tests that do not require extensive verbal output, such as recognition memory paradigms. The clinician also may wish to supplement a standard administration of a test by testing the limits of a performance. For example, he or she may wish to allow extra time on a verbal fluency task for a patient with an expressive aphasia. A traditional score is produced for production during the standard time (usually 1 min). The clinician, however, then also may obtain and record the raw score of what is achieved at 2 min to see whether additional points are achieved when more time is allowed. Other ways to test the limits of a patient's abilities include paraphrasing the directions, allowing a patient to read the directions, pantomiming the directions, or (when examining patients with unilateral neglect) drawing attention to all areas of a visual stimulus (e.g., to all four pictures on a page from the Peabody Picture Vocabulary Test) or even cutting them out and presenting them in a vertical array. Although standard scores cannot be generated when altering the test administration, valuable qualitative information may be gained using this approach.

A second challenge in examining patients with stroke and CVD occurs when examining functional impairment. Specifically, one must separate functional impairment caused by physical disability from impairment associated with cognitive changes. This is an important distinction because of the requirement of cognitively based functional decline in the diagnosis of dementia. For example, many measures of activities of daily living (ADL), such as Barthel Index (Mahoney & Barthel, 1965), the Bristol-ADL (Bucks, Ashworth, Wilcock, & Siegfried, 1996), and the Disability Assessment for Dementia (DAD; Gélinas, Gauthier, McIntyre, & Gauthier, 1999) include items such as the ability to dress, bathe, and use the telephone. Few measures, however, break down a functional action into its component parts, such as initiation, planning, and performance of the required behavior. The DAD is an exception to this and may be especially useful in examining functional impairment following stroke. For the most part, however, examining the score alone on ADL measures may not provide all of the information required when assessing for cognitive-related functional impairment. Also, many functional measures require the report of family members or close friends of the patient, and it may be difficult for these untrained raters to differentiate cognitive versus physical functional impairment.

A third challenge in examining patients with stroke and CVD is determining when to complete the assessment. Unlike other patient groups with dementia, patients with stroke often recover cognitive functions rather than show relentless cognitive decline. For this reason, it is not recommended to test patients in the first days and weeks after a stroke if the purpose of the examination is to determine the patient's long-term cognitive capability. Because recovery after stroke can be dramatic, especially during the first days and weeks, it would be better to wait until at least 4–6 months before completing such an examination. If, however, the question is the patient's capacity to make medical decisions or their ability to engage in a rehabilitation program, an examination soon after a stroke may be warranted.

Sometimes, repeated examinations are required, such as before and after a specific treatment. In such cases, the clinician should devise a protocol of tests with alternate forms, to limit practice effects. Use of alternate forms, however, does not completely counteract practice effects (Beglinger et al., 2005). Therefore, to determine whether there has been a significant change in cognitive function across the two assessments, the clinician should consider computing a reliable change index, based on known practice effects associated with the test and the measure's test–retest reliability. Several studies have determined reliable change indices on tests with stroke patients (e.g., Chen, Koh, Hsieh, & Hsueh, 2013; Koh et al., 2011).

Finally, a fourth clinical challenge in the assessment of people with stroke and CVD is the accurate assessment of depression and neurobehavior disorders. Depression is the most common poststroke psychiatric disturbance (Hackett, Yapa, Parag, & Anderson, 2005), with approximately one third of patients with stroke experiencing depression in the months following their stroke event. Self-report measures cannot diagnose depression, but they can provide a time- and cost-effective means of exploring depressive symptoms. One must be sure, however, that vegetative symptoms of depression, such as poor concentration, memory difficulties, and fatigue, are associated with a primary mood disturbance instead of simply associated with stroke-related alterations in cognition and drive. Measures such as the Chicago Multiscale Depression Inventory (Nyenhuis et al., 1998), may assist in this task by breaking down depressive symptoms into mood, vegetative, and cognitive subsets. Other studies have modified existing self-report measures, such as the Beck Depression Inventory, for use with neurological patients (Benedict, Fishman, McClellan, Bakshi, & Weinstock-Guttman, 2003). Once again, the clinician may not simply rely on the original scores generated on instruments that are standardized on populations without stroke or other neurological impairment.

Patients with stroke and CVD often present with other neurobehavior disorders. Scales such as the Frontal Systems Behavior Scale and the Neuropsychiatric Inventory, examine for the presence and severity of common neurobehavior disorders, such as disinhibition, apathy, and dysexecutive behaviors, and may be completed by either the patient or a family member. These scales often are useful in augmenting the clinician's behavior observations during the examination of stroke patients. Similarly, it is often helpful to supplement the clinician's observations with those of other team members, such as physical, occupation and speech therapists, psychiatrists, social workers, and nursing staff. In an outpatient setting, it is often helpful to speak with the patient's primary care physician or neurologist to both clarify assessment questions and to learn more about how the patient interacted with these other professionals.

TREATMENT

Pharmacotherapy

The majority of treatment studies have focused on either the effects of medications originally targeted for patients with AD or on control of stroke risk factors. Results in both areas of study have been modest and inconsistent. Currently, no medication has FDA approval for use in patients with VCI. Pivotal trials for cholinesterase inhibitors approved for use with patients with AD, such as donepezil and galantamine, have shown modest cognitive effects and inconsistent global or daily functioning differences when compared with placebo (e.g., Black et al., 2003). A similar pattern of results was found with memantine, an N-methyl D-aspartate agonist (e.g., Orgogozo, Rigaud, Stöffler, Möbius, & Forette, 2002). Several methodologic factors have made these trials difficult to complete and interpret, including the potential presence of AD in patients enrolled in the trials, the difficulty assigning cognitive versus physical cause for functional impairment, and the requirement for significant memory impairment for study entry, thus increasing the potential confound with AD. In addition, the cognitive tests used in these trials included only a limited assessment of executive function and, therefore, may not have been sensitive enough to the presence and extent of cognitive impairment (Gorelick et al., 2011).

Risk factors for stroke are well known and include many modifiable markers, such as hypertension, dyslipidemia, diabetes, smoking, and heavy alcohol use (Gorelick et al., 2011). Strong linkages are demonstrated in large observational studies between midlife stroke risk factors and late-life cognitive impairment

and dementia (Birns & Kalra, 2009). Clinical trials to date have found only inconsistent evidence that risk factor control later in life results in better cognitive outcomes (Birns & Kalra, 2009). Potential reasons for the apparent discrepancy between midlife and late-life studies include (a) cognitive test scores are often secondary endpoints to these clinical trials, with primary outcomes being other events, such as stroke or death, and trials may be halted before there is sufficient time and statistical power to test the cognitive outcome; (b) the damage, such as CSVD and cognitive decline, already may have occurred before the onset of the clinical trial; or (c) relatively weak cognitive outcome measures, such as the MMSE, commonly have been used in these studies. Current and future clinical trials may attempt to correct these shortcomings.

Cognitive Rehabilitation

It is beyond the scope of this chapter to review the breadth of research having to do with the effectiveness of cognitive rehabilitation with patients after stroke or other forms of CVD. This remains a controversial topic. For example, Cicerone et al. (2011) have published three reviews on evidence-based cognitive rehabilitation. The latest review covers the literature from 2003 to 2008 (Cicerone et al., 2011). The authors concluded that,

> there is substantial evidence to support interventions for attention, memory, social communications skills, executive function, and for comprehensive-holistic neuropsychologic rehabilitation after TBI. Evidence supports visuospatial rehabilitation after right hemisphere stroke, and interventions for aphasia and apraxia after left hemisphere stroke. . . . There is now sufficient information to support evidence-based protocols and implement empirically-supported treatments for cognitive disability after TBI and stroke. (Cicerone et al., 2011, p. 519)

Several systematic Cochrane reviews, however, do not come to the same conclusion. Reviews of cognitive rehabilitation for memory deficits following stroke (Nair & Lincoln, 2007), cognitive rehabilitation for spatial neglect following stroke (Bowen, Hazelton, Pollock, & Lincoln, 2013), cognitive rehabilitation for executive dysfunction in adults with stroke or other adult nonprogressive acquired brain damage (Chung, Pollock, Campbell, Durward, & Hagen, 2013), and occupational therapy for cognitive impairment in stroke patients (Hoffmann, Bennett, Koh, & McKenna, 2011) all conclude insufficient evidence for effectiveness of cognitive remediation for these various stroke-related cognitive deficits. A general conclusion from the reviews is that there are not enough high-quality studies (e.g., studies with randomized subject selection, well-designed control groups, and consistent outcome measures) to definitively conclude treatment effectiveness. In a recent review, Cumming, Marshall, and Lazar (2013) came to similar conclusions. They also noted that the lack of a consistent pattern of poststroke cognitive impairment complicates the research area and reported some progress in the rehabilitation of focally based cognitive impairment, whereas rehabilitation of cognitive deficits associated with more diffuse neuropathology remains elusive.

Case Example

The following case example demonstrates some of the diagnostic challenges mentioned earlier as well as the vital role of the psychologist (in this case, the neuropsychologist) in ascertaining the patient's general level of function, the probable causes of her dysfunction and some of the practical implications of her cognitive and behavioral deficits.

Ms. A. is a 76-year-old, right-handed retired secretary with a high school education referred for neuropsychological examination. Nine months before this examination, she experienced an intracerebral hemorrhage in the right inferior frontal lobe, resulting in a 5-day hospital stay; a 3-week stay at an inpatient rehabilitation facility that included physical, occupational, and speech therapy; and continued outpatient physical, occupational, and speech therapy until 7 months poststroke, at which time therapy was discontinued in light of the lack of noted continued progress. Her neurologist referred her for neuropsychological examination because of continued suspected poststroke memory problems.

Ms. A.'s past medical history is notable for a meningioma resected from the left lateral frontal lobe approximately 10 years before this examination. She and her sister, who accompanied her, did not note changes in her cognition or behavior after this resection. Her other medical history was noncontributory; she and her sister deny a history of other stroke, cancer, seizures, or traumatic brain injury. She takes medication for hypertension and dyslipidemia. She denies past or current mental health treatment.

Although Ms. A. reports no significant memory problems, her sister, who was interviewed separately, reports that Ms. A.'s memory is quite impaired. The impairment began suddenly, at the time of the hemorrhage, and has not progressed. According to her sister, Ms. A. is now unable to remember the date or time. She is easily confused. She has difficulty keeping the sequence of events correctly. Her sister has not noted changes in speech. She has noted mild, intermittent left-sided weakness of her arm and leg. Ms. A.'s sister also believes that Ms. A. is depressed. She is apathetic and more dependent than she was before the hemorrhage. She appears to lack drive and initiative and she sleeps more. Ms. A.'s sister also reports that Ms. A. has lived with her and her husband since before the event. She wonders when Ms. A. might be able to return home. Ms. A.'s sister had previously been selected by Ms. A. as her durable power of attorney for medical and financial affairs if Ms. A. became incapacitated. During Ms. A.'s hospitalization, the power of attorney was invoked due to Ms. A.'s diminished decisional capacity.

MRI was not available due to Ms. A.'s claustrophobia. CT, completed 3 months after the event, showed postoperative changes from the excised meningioma; evidence of the right, frontal hemorrhage; and diffuse, moderate to severe small-vessel disease.

Ms. A. demonstrated a mild, left-sided limp. She walked with the aid of a cane. She spoke at low volume, but her speech was fluent and well articulated. It lacked prosody. Occasional anomic pauses were noted. She appeared to lack insight into the presence and severity of her cognitive deficits. She did not appear overtly sad or anxious. Although cooperative, she appeared to lack drive and initiative and had to be reminded multiple times to stay on task.

Test findings indicated a significant discrepancy between her estimated premorbid level of functioning in the average range (based on her education and occupation history as well as her word reading skills; Wechsler Test of Adult Reading Predicted Full Scale IQ: 99) and her current general cognitive functioning (e.g., Montreal Cognitive Assessment Total Score: 10/30 correct; RBANS Total Score: 60, less than the first percentile). Significant deficits were noted in all cognitive areas, but especially in memory and executive functioning. On memory testing, she showed both deficits in acquiring new information and a rapid forgetting of the limited information she successfully learned. She did not recall a single word, story detail, or shape on four of the five delayed recall tasks that were administered. Recognition memory test performances were equally as poor and those for free recall tasks. Executive skills were severely impaired (Trailmaking Part B: discontinued; 0 Wisconsin Card Sorting Categories; 5 of 19 points on the Behavioral Dyscontrol Scale, a measure of "frontally" mediated motor sequencing and other executive tasks).

Ms. A. passed all symptom validity measures, suggesting that she put forth adequate effort during the examination. Her scores on the Hospital Anxiety and Depression Scale, the Beck Depression Inventory, and the Beck Anxiety Inventory were all below clinical limits. Her sister reported significantly increased apathy (T = 85) and executive dysfunction (T = 77) but not disinhibition (T = 46) on the Frontal Systems Behavior Scale. She also reported significant deficits in daily functioning on all complex tasks, such as financial management and medication management, as well as a decline in daily hygiene (Ms. A. needed to be reminded to change her clothing, to bathe, and to brush her teeth).

The challenges of Ms. A.'s case were to determine the sources of her cognitive impairment and behavior change. It was clear that she met *DSM–IV–TR* criteria for dementia as she showed impairment in all cognitive areas that were connected to a significant decline in daily function, and she was not in a delirium state. Following are other conclusions:

1. Based on the reported history (e.g., sudden onset) and current findings (e.g., severe, acquired dysexecutive function), it is most likely that the cognitive and behavioral changes were due to a cerebrovascular process; therefore, Ms. A. met *DSM–IV–TR* criteria for a vascular dementia.

2. Concomitant AD cannot be ruled out in any elder with significant memory problems, especially given the rapid forgetting of newly learned material that Ms. A. showed. However, the sudden nature of the cognitive deficits, the reported high level of prehemorrhage cognitive functioning, and the lack of continued cognitive decline since the event argue against an Alzheimer's process.

3. Ms. A. was not depressed. She denied most symptoms of depression or anxiety. Her lack of drive and initiative, as well as the lack of insight into her cognitive deficits, fit well with the location of the hemorrhage and is consistent with inferior, right-sided frontal lobe pathology. It is not clear what role, if any, the remote, left frontal meningioma played in Ms. A.'s symptoms. There was no report at the time of resection of cognitive or behavior change and the combination of right frontal hemorrhage and extensive small-vessel ischemic changes explained the presence and severity of her current cognitive and behavioral status without the need for additional sources of neuropathology.

4. Ms. A. was 9 months posthemorrhage and had 7 months of intensive in- and outpatient therapy. It was likely that most recovery from the hemorrhage had already occurred, although mild additional recovery often is seen 1–2 years postevent.

5. Because of her cognitive and functional impairment, Ms. A. is unlikely to ever be able to live independently. She also continues to lack decisional capacity because of the combination of cognitive deficits and the lack of insight she displayed into the presence and extent of those deficits.

Ms. A., her sister, and her brother-in-law attended a feedback session 2 weeks after the examination was completed. A hospital social worker also attended.

The test results were explained to them and a copy of her test report was provided to them. It was also explained that Ms. A. may require a guardian to make her financial and medical decisions, as she may lack decisional capacity in these areas. However, additional, specific testing would be needed to confirm this. Ms. A.'s sister explained that they did not wish to pursue guardianship, as they found that the durable power of attorney was sufficient for their needs at present. The social worker invited Ms. A. and her family members to attend a support group for stroke patients and their family members. They were encouraged to seek reexamination for Ms. A. if additional cognitive decline was noted in the future. Ms. A.'s sister and brother-in-law expressed appreciation in the information they received. They reported to have a more complete understanding of the source of her behavior change and more accurate expectations regarding Ms. A.'s long-term care requirements.

CONCLUSION

As the population in the United States and other Western countries continues to age, the number of older people with cognitive decline and dementia will increase, as will the number of persons who experience stroke and other forms of CVD. Psychologists, with their understanding of psychometrics combined with that of brain-behavior relationships, will continue to play a leading role in the assessment of these persons. Neuroimaging and other neurobiological approaches will continue to advance our knowledge of neuropathology. It will continue to fall to the psychologist, however, to interpret the cognitive, behavioral, and functional implications of newfound pathology and to do so in a reliable and valid manner.

As such, future VCI research likely will include the following three branches. First, future research in VCI will include the continued development of instruments and test protocols that are sensitive to the effects of cerebrovascular pathology. The greatest need in instrument development is in the assessment of functional impairment, which remains based on the (often limited) recollections of patient's

relatives and friends, many of whom also may have cognitive impairment. The field is very much in need of time-limited, reliable, and valid assessment of everyday functional abilities that can augment standard cognitive assessment. Second, it is clear that the largest group of older persons with cognitive decline and dementia have multiple sources of pathology, such as mixed AD and VCI (e.g., Schneider, Arvanitakis, Bang, & Bennett, 2007). More research is needed to examine potential interactions between different disease states and the clinical effects of multiple pathologies. Finally, perhaps building on mixed-pathology research, additional linkages between midlife stroke risk factors, such as hypertension, dyslipidemia, and diabetes, and late-life cognitive decline and dementia need to be made. It is likely that the underpinnings of VCI predate its clinical expression by many years, perhaps many decades. As with many diseases, the key to stopping VCI is to prevent it from occurring in the first place.

References

Alexander, M. P., & Freedman, M. (1984). Amnesia after anterior communicating artery aneurysm rupture. *Neurology, 34,* 752–757. doi:10.1212/WNL.34.6.752

American Psychiatric Association. (2000). *Diagnostic and Statistical Manual of Mental Disorders* (4th ed., text rev.). Washington, DC: Author.

American Psychiatric Association. (2013). *Diagnostic and Statistical Manual of Mental Disorders* (5th ed.). Washington, DC: Author.

Annoni, J. M., Khateb, A., Gramigna, S., Staub, F., Carota, A., Maeder, P., & Bogousslavsky, J. (2003). Chronic cognitive impairment following laterothalamic infarcts: A study of 9 cases. *Archives of Neurology, 60,* 1439–1443. doi:10.1001/archneur.60.10.1439

Beglinger, L. J., Gaydos, B., Tangphao-Daniels, O., Duff, K., Kareken, D. A., Crawford, J., . . . Siemers, E. R. (2005). Practice effects and the use of alternate forms in serial neuropsychological testing. *Archives of Clinical Neuropsychology, 20,* 517–529. doi:10.1016/j.acn.2004.12.003

Benedict, R. H., Fishman, I., McClellan, M. M., Bakshi, R., & Weinstock-Guttman, B. (2003). Validity of the Beck Depression Inventory-Fast Screen in multiple sclerosis. *Multiple Sclerosis, 9,* 393–396. doi:10.1191/1352458503ms902oa

Benson, D. F., & Cummings, J. L. (1982). Angular gyrus syndrome simulating Alzheimer's disease. *Archives of Neurology, 39,* 616–620. doi:10.1001/arch-neur.1982.00510220014003

Birns, J., & Kalra, L. (2009). Cognitive function and hypertension. *Journal of Human Hypertension, 23,* 86–96. doi:10.1038/jhh.2008.80

Black, S., Gao, F., & Bilbao, J. (2009). Understanding white matter disease: Imaging-pathological correlations in vascular cognitive impairment. *Stroke, 40*(Suppl.), S48–S52. doi:10.1161/STROKEAHA.108.537704

Black, S., Román, G. C., Geldmacher, D. S., Salloway, S., Hecker, J., Burns, A., . . . the Donepezil 307 Vascular Dementia Study Group. (2003). Efficacy and tolerability of donepezil in vascular dementia: Positive results of a 24-week, multicenter, international, randomized, placebo-controlled clinical trial. *Stroke, 34,* 2323–2330. doi:10.1161/01. STR.0000091396.95360.E1

Bowen, A., Hazelton, C., Pollock, A., & Lincoln, N. B. (2013). Cognitive rehabilitation for spatial neglect following stroke. *Cochrane Database of Systematic Reviews, 7,* CD003586.

Brunnström, H., Gustafson, L., Passant, U., & Englund, E. (2009). Prevalence of dementia subtypes: a 30-year retrospective survey of neuropathological reports. *Archives of Gerontology and Geriatrics, 49,* 146–149. doi:10.1016/j.archger.2008.06.005

Bucks, R. S., Ashworth, D. L., Wilcock, G. K., & Siegfried, K. (1996). Assessment of activities of daily living in dementia: Development of the Bristol Activities of Daily Living Scale. *Age and Ageing, 25,* 113–120. doi:10.1093/ageing/25.2.113

Chen, H. C., Koh, C. L., Hsieh, C. L., & Hsueh, I. P. (2013). Test of Everyday Attention in patients with chronic stroke: Test-retest reliability and practice effects. *Brain Injury, 27,* 1148–1154. doi:10.3109/ 02699052.2013.775483

Chui, H. C., Victoroff, J. I., Margolin, D., Jagust, W., Shankle, R., & Katzman, R. (1992). Criteria for the diagnosis of ischemic vascular dementia proposed by the State of California Alzheimer's Disease Diagnostic and Treatment Centers. *Neurology, 42,* 473–480. doi:10.1212/WNL.42.3.473

Chung, C. S., Pollock, A., Campbell, T., Durward, B. R., & Hagen, S. (2013). Cognitive rehabilitation for executive dysfunction in adults with stroke or other adult non-progressive acquired brain damage. *Cochrane Database of Systematic Reviews, 4,* CD008391.

Cicerone, K. D., Langenbahn, D. M., Braden, C., Malec, J. F., Kalmar, K., Fraas, M., . . . Ashman, T. (2011). Evidence-based cognitive rehabilitation: Updated review of the literature from 2003 through 2008. *Archives of Physical Medicine and Rehabilitation, 92,* 519–530. doi:10.1016/j.apmr.2010.11.015

Corbett, A., Bennett, H., & Kos, S. (1994). Cognitive dysfunction following subcortical infarction. *Archives of Neurology, 51,* 999–1007. doi:10.1001/arch-neur.1994.00540220045013

Cumming, T. B., Marshall, R. S., & Lazar, R. M. (2013). Stroke, cognitive deficits, and rehabilitation: Still an incomplete picture. *International Journal of Stroke, 8,* 38–45. doi:10.1111/j.1747-4949.2012.00972.x

de Leeuw, F. E., de Groot, J. C., Achten, E., Oudkerk, M., Ramos, L. M., Heijboer, R., . . . Breteler, M. M. (2001). Prevalence of cerebral white matter lesions in elderly people: A population based magnetic resonance imaging study. The Rotterdam Scan Study. *Journal of Neurology, Neurosurgery, and Psychiatry, 70,* 9–14. doi:10.1136/jnnp.70.1.9

Erkinjuntti, T., Inzitari, D., Pantoni, L., Wallin, A., Scheltens, P., Rockwood, D., & Desmond, D. W. (2000). Limitations of clinical criteria for the diagnosis of vascular dementia in clinical trials. Is a focus on subcortical vascular dementia a solution? *Annals of the New York Academy of Sciences, 903,* 262–272. doi:10.1111/j.1749-6632.2000.tb06376.x

Fens, M., van Heugten, C. M., Beusmans, G. H., Limburg, M., Haeren, R., Kaemingk, A., & Metsemakers, J. F. (2013). Not as transient: Patients with transient ischaemic attack or minor stroke experience cognitive and communication problems; an exploratory study. *European Journal of General Practice, 19,* 11–16. doi:10.3109/13814788.2012.715147

Gélinas, I., Gauthier, L., McIntyre, M., & Gauthier, S. (1999). Development of a functional measure for persons with Alzheimer's disease: The disability assessment for dementia. *American Journal of Occupational Therapy, 53,* 471–481. doi:10.5014/ajot.53.5.471

Godefroy, O., Fickl, A., Roussel, M., Auribault, C., Bugnicourt, J. M., Lamy, C., . . . Petitnicolas, G. (2011). Is the Montreal Cognitive Assessment superior to the Mini-Mental State Examination to detect poststroke cognitive impairment? A study with neuropsychological evaluation. *Stroke, 42,* 1712–1716. doi:10.1161/STROKEAHA.110.606277

Gold, G., Giannakopoulos, P., Montes-Paixao Júnior, C., Herrmann, F. R., Mulligan, R., Michel, J. P., & Bouras, C. (1997). Sensitivity and specificity of newly proposed clinical criteria for possible vascular dementia. *Neurology, 49,* 690–694. doi:10.1212/WNL.49.3.690

Gorelick, P. B., Chatterjee, A., Patel, D., Flowerdew, G., Dollear, W., Taber, J., & Harris, Y. (1992). Cranial computed tomographic observations in multi-infarct dementia. A controlled study. *Stroke, 23,* 804–811. doi:10.1161/01.STR.23.6.804

Gorelick, P. B., Nyenhuis, D., American Society of Hypertension Writing Group, Materson, B. J., Calhoun, D. A., Elliott, W. J., . . . Townsend, R. R. (2012). Blood pressure and treatment of persons with hypertension as it relates to cognitive outcomes including executive function. *Journal of the American Society of Hypertension, 6*, 309–315. doi:10.1016/j.jash.2012.08.004

Gorelick, P. B., Scuteri, A., Black, S. E., Decarli, C., Greenberg, S. M., Iadecola, C., . . . Council on Cardiovascular Surgery and Anesthesia. (2011). Vascular contributions to cognitive impairment and dementia: A statement for healthcare professionals from the American Heart Association/American Stroke Association. *Stroke, 42*, 2672–2713. doi:10.1161/STR.0b013e3182299496

Greenberg, S. M., Eng, J. A., Ning, M., Smith, E. E., & Rosand, J. (2004). Hemorrhage burden predicts recurrent intracerebral hemorrhage after lobar hemorrhage. *Stroke, 35*, 1415–1420. doi:10.1161/01.STR.0000126807.69758.0e

Guo, J., Wang, S., Li, R., Chen, N., Zhou, M., Chen, H., . . . He, L. (2014). Cognitive impairment and whole brain diffusion in patients with carotid artery disease and ipsilateral transient ischemic attack. *Neurological Research, 36*, 41–46. doi:10.1179/1743132813Y.0000000255

Hachinski, V., Iadecola, C., Petersen, R. C., Breteler, M. M., Nyenhuis, D. L., Black, S. E., . . . Leblanc, G. G. (2006). National Institute of Neurological Disorders and Stroke-Canadian Stroke Network vascular cognitive impairment harmonization standards. *Stroke, 37*, 2220–2241. doi:10.1161/01.STR.0000237236.88823.47

Hachinski, V. C., Lassen, N. A., & Marshall, J. (1974). Multi-infarct dementia. A cause of mental deterioration in the elderly. *Lancet, 304*, 207–209. doi:10.1016/S0140-6736(74)91496-2

Hackett, M. L., Yapa, C., Parag, V., & Anderson, C. S. (2005). Frequency of depression after stroke: A systematic review of observational studies. *Stroke, 36*, 1330–1340. doi:10.1161/01.STR.0000165928.19135.35

Hoffmann, T., Bennett, S., Koh, C., & McKenna, K. (2011). The Cochrane review of occupational therapy for cognitive impairment in stroke patients. *European Journal of Physical and Rehabilitation Medicine, 47*, 513–519.

James, B. D., Bennett, D. A., Boyle, P. A., Leurgans, S., & Schneider, J. A. (2012). Dementia from Alzheimer disease and mixed pathologies in the oldest old. *JAMA, 307*, 1798–1800. doi:10.1001/jama.2012.3556

Jokinen, H., Lipsanen, J., Schmidt, R., Fazekas, F., Gouw, A. A., van der Flier, W. M., . . . the LADIS Study Group. (2012). Brain atrophy accelerates cognitive decline in cerebral small vessel disease: The LADIS study. *Neurology, 78*, 1785–1792. doi:10.1212/WNL.0b013e3182583070

Kase, C. S., Wolf, P. A., Kelly-Hayes, M., Kannel, W. B., Beiser, A., & D'Agostino, R. B. (1998). Intellectual decline after stroke: The Framingham Study. *Stroke, 29*, 805–812. doi:10.1161/01.STR.29.4.805

Katz, D. I., Alexander, M. P., & Mandell, A. M. (1987). Dementia following strokes in the mesencephalon and diencephalon. *Archives of Neurology, 44*, 1127–1133. doi:10.1001/archneur.1987.00520230017007

Koga, H., Takashima, Y., Murakawa, R., Uchino, A., Yuzuriha, T., & Yao, H. (2009). Cognitive consequences of multiple lacunes and leukoaraiosis as vascular cognitive impairment in community-dwelling elderly individuals. *Journal of Stroke and Cerebrovascular Diseases, 18*, 32–37. doi:10.1016/j.jstrokecerebrovasdis.2008.07.010

Koh, C. L., Lu, W. S., Chen, H. C., Hsueh, I. P., Hsieh, J. J., & Hsieh, C. L. (2011). Test-retest reliability and practice effect of the oral-format Symbol Digit Modalities Test in patients with stroke. *Archives of Clinical Neuropsychology, 26*, 356–363. doi:10.1093/arclin/acr029

Larson, E., Kirschner, K., Bode, R., Heinemann, A., & Goodman, R. (2005). Construct and predictive validity of the repeatable battery for the assessment of neuropsychological status in the evaluation of stroke patients. *Journal of Clinical and Experimental Neuropsychology, 27*, 16–32. doi:10.1080/138033990513564

Launer, L. J., Hughes, T. M., & White, L. R. (2011). Microinfarcts, brain atrophy, and cognitive function: The Honolulu Asia Aging Study Autopsy Study. *Annals of Neurology, 70*, 774–780. doi:10.1002/ana.22520

Launer, L. J., Ross, G. W., Petrovitch, H., Masaki, K., Foley, D., White, L. R., & Havlik, R. J. (2000). Midlife blood pressure and dementia: The Honolulu-Asia aging study. *Neurobiology of Aging, 21*, 49–55. doi:10.1016/S0197-4580(00)00096-8

Longstreth, W. T., Jr., Manolio, T. A., Arnold, A., Burke, G. L., Bryan, N., Jungreis, C. A., . . . Fried, L. (1996). Clinical correlates of white matter findings on cranial magnetic resonance imaging of 3301 elderly people. The Cardiovascular Health Study. *Stroke, 27*, 1274–1282. doi:10.1161/01.STR.27.8.1274

Mahoney, F. I., & Barthel, D. W. (1965). Functional evaluation: The Barthel Index. *Maryland State Medical Journal, 14*, 61–65.

Mitchell, A. J., & Shiri-Feshki, M. (2009). Rate of progression of mild cognitive impairment to dementia-meta-analysis of 41 robust inception cohort studies. *Acta Psychiatrica Scandinavica, 119*, 252–265. doi:10.1111/j.1600-0447.2008.01326.x

Mungas, D., Jagust, W. J., Reed, B. R., Kramer, J. H., Weiner, M. W., Schuff, N., . . . Chui, H. C. (2001). MRI predictors of cognition in subcortical ischemic vascular disease and Alzheimer's disease. *Neurology, 57*, 2229–2235. doi:10.1212/WNL.57.12.2229

Nair, R. D., & Lincoln, N. B. (2007). Cognitive rehabilitation for memory deficits following stroke. *Cochrane Database of Systematic Reviews, 3*, CD002293.

Nasreddine, Z. (n.d.). *Montreal Cognitive Assessment Test.* Retrieved from http://www.mocatest.org

Nyenhuis, D. L., Gorelick, P. B., Geenen, E. J., Smith, C. A., Gencheva, E., Freels, S., & deToledo-Morrell, L. (2004). The pattern of neuropsychological deficits in vascular cognitive impairment–no dementia (Vascular CIND). *Clinical Neuropsychologist, 18*, 41–49. doi:10.1080/13854040490507145

Nyenhuis, D. L., Luchetta, T., Yamamoto, C., Terrien, A., Bernardin, L., Rao, S. M., & Garron, D. C. (1998). The development, standardization, and initial validation of the Chicago Multiscale Depression Inventory. *Journal of Personality Assessment, 70*, 386–401. doi:10.1207/s15327752jpa7002_14

O'Brien, J. T., Erkinjuntti, T., Reisberg, B., Román, G., Sawada, T., Pantoni, L., . . . DeKosky, S. T. (2003). Vascular cognitive impairment. *Lancet Neurology, 2*, 89–98. doi:10.1016/S1474-4422(03)00305-3

Orgogozo, J. M., Rigaud, A. S., Stöffler, A., Möbius, H. J., & Forette, F. (2002). Efficacy and safety of memantine in patients with mild to moderate vascular dementia: A randomized, placebo-controlled trial (MMM 300). *Stroke, 33*, 1834–1839. doi:10.1161/01.STR.0000020094.08790.49

Pantoni, L. (2010). Cerebral small vessel disease: From pathogenesis and clinical characteristics to therapeutic challenges. *Lancet Neurology, 9*, 689–701. doi:10.1016/S1474-4422(10)70104-6

Pantoni, L., & Inzitari, D. (1993). Hachinski's ischemic score and the diagnosis of vascular dementia: A review. *Italian Journal of Neurological Sciences, 14*, 539–546. doi:10.1007/BF02339212

Patel, B., Lawrence, A. J., Chung, A. W., Rich, P., Mackinnon, A. D., Morris, R. G., . . . Markus, H. S. (2013). Cerebral microbleeds and cognition in patients with symptomatic small vessel disease. *Stroke, 44*, 356–361. doi:10.1161/STROKEAHA.112.670216

Petersen, R. C., Smith, G. E., Waring, S. C., Ivnik, R. J., Tangalos, E. G., & Kokmen, E. (1999). Mild cognitive impairment: Clinical characterization and outcome. *Archives of Neurology, 56*, 303–308. doi:10.1001/archneur.56.3.303

Pohjasvaara, T., Mantyla, R., Salonen, O., Aronen, H. J., Ylikoski, R., Hietanen, M., . . . Erkinjuntti, T. (2000). MRI correlates of dementia after first clinical ischemic stroke. *Journal of the Neurological Sciences, 181*, 111–117. doi:10.1016/S0022-510X(00)00437-8

Reed, B. R., Eberling, J. L., Mungas, D., Weiner, M., Kramer, J. H., & Jagust, W. J. (2004). Effects of white matter lesions and lacunes on cortical function. *Archives of Neurology, 61*, 1545–1550. doi:10.1001/archneur.61.10.1545

Reed, B. R., Mungas, D. M., Kramer, J. H., Ellis, W., Vinters, H. V., Zarow, C., . . . Chui, H. C. (2007). Profiles of neuropsychological impairment in autopsy-defined Alzheimer's disease and cerebrovascular disease. *Brain: A Journal of Neurology, 130*, 731–739. doi:10.1093/brain/awl385

Román, G. (2003). Vascular dementia: A historical background. *International Psychogeriatrics, 15*, 11–13. doi:10.1017/S1041610203008901

Román, G. C., Tatemichi, T. K., Erkinjuntti, T., Cummings, J. L., Masdeu, J. C., Garcia, J. H., . . . Scheinberg, P. (1993). Vascular dementia: Diagnostic criteria for research studies. Report of the NINDS–AIREN International Workshop. *Neurology, 43*, 250–260. doi:10.1212/WNL.43.2.250

Ropper, A. H., & Samuels, M. A. (2009). *Adams and Victor's principles of neurology* (9th ed.). New York, NY: McGraw Hill.

Rossetti, H. C., Lacritz, L. H., Cullum, C. M., & Weiner, M. F. (2011). Normative data for the Montreal Cognitive Assessment (MoCA) in a population-based sample. *Neurology, 77*, 1272–1275. doi:10.1212/WNL.0b013e318230208a

Schneider, J. A., Arvanitakis, Z., Bang, W., & Bennett, D. A. (2007). Mixed brain pathologies account for most dementia cases in community-dwelling older persons. *Neurology, 69*, 2197–2204. doi:10.1212/01.wnl.0000271090.28148.24

Snowdon, D. A., Greiner, L. H., Mortimer, J. A., Riley, K. P., Greiner, P. A., & Markesbery, W. R. (1997). Brain infarction and the clinical expression of AD. The Nun Study. *JAMA, 277*, 813–817. doi:10.1001/jama.1997.03540340047031

Stebbins, G. T., Nyenhuis, D. L., Wang, C., Cox, J. L., Freels, S., Bangen, K., . . . Gorelick, P. B. (2008). Gray matter atrophy in patients with ischemic stroke with cognitive impairment. *Stroke, 39*, 785–793. doi:10.1161/STROKEAHA.107.507392

Steinke, W., Sacco, R. L., Mohr, J. P., Foulkes, M. A., Tatemichi, T. K., Wolf, P. A., . . . Hier, D. B. (1992). Thalamic stroke. Presentation and prognosis of infarcts and hemorrhages. *Archives of Neurology, 49*, 703–710. doi:10.1001/archneur.1992.00530310045011

Stuss, D. T., & Levine, B. (2002). Adult clinical neuropsychology: Lessons from studies of the frontal lobes. *Annual Review of Psychology, 53*, 401–433. doi:10.1146/annurev.psych.53.100901.135220

Swartz, R. H., Sahlas, D. J., & Black, S. E. (2003). Strategic involvement of cholinergic pathways and executive dysfunction: Does location of white matter signal hyperintensities matter? *Journal of Stroke and Cerebrovascular Diseases, 12,* 29–36. doi:10.1053/jscd.2003.5

Swartz, R. H., Stuss, D. T., Gao, F., & Black, S. E. (2008). Independent cognitive effects of atrophy and diffuse subcortical and thalamico-cortical cerebrovascular disease in dementia. *Stroke, 39,* 822–830. doi:10.1161/STROKEAHA.107.491936

Tomlinson, B. E., Blessed, G., & Roth, M. (1970). Observations of the brains of demented old people. *Journal of the Neurological Sciences, 11,* 205–242. doi:10.1016/0022-510X(70)90063-8

Vermeer, S. E., Longstreth, W. T., Jr., & Koudstaal, P. J. (2007). Silent brain infarcts: A systematic review. *Lancet Neurology, 6,* 611–619. doi:10.1016/S1474-4422(07)70170-9

Viswanathan, A., Gschwendtner, A., Guichard, J. P., Buffon, F., Cumurciuc, R., O'Sullivan, M., . . . Chabriat, H. (2007). Lacunar lesions are independently associated with disability and cognitive impairment in CADASIL. *Neurology, 69,* 172–179. doi:10.1212/01.wnl.0000265221.05610.70

Wang, R., Fratiglioni, L., Laveskog, A., Kalpouzos, G., Ehrenkrona, C.H., Zhang, Y., . . . Qiu, C. (2013). Do cardiovascular risk factors explain the link between white matter hyperintensities and brain volumes in old age? A population-based study. *European Journal of Neurology,* 2013 Advance online publication.

CHAPTER 9

PARKINSON'S DISEASE DEMENTIA AND DEMENTIA WITH LEWY BODIES

Scott A. Sperling, Alexandra C. Geneser, and Carol A. Manning

Parkinson's disease (PD) is a movement disorder that affects about 1 million Americans. Increasing attention and resources have been devoted to characterizing and treating the nonmotor symptoms of PD that went unrecognized for so long. References to symptoms of PD date back thousands of years to the Ayurveda, the system of medicine practiced in India as early as 5000 BC. PD was first described in James Parkinson's 1817 work, *An Essay on the Shaking Palsy* (Parkinson, 1817). More than 50 years later, Jean Martin Charcot furthered the research and knowledge base regarding PD, providing more detailed descriptions of the disease. Although PD originally was conceptualized as a motor disorder that left cognitive functions untouched, more recent research has clearly demonstrated that cognitive deficits and other nonmotor symptoms, such as alterations in mood and behavioral impairments, are common aspects of the clinical picture. As non-motor changes in PD have become more apparent, Parkinson's disease dementia (PDD) and mild cognitive impairment (MCI) in PD have become more widely recognized. Similar non-motor symptoms are seen in dementia with lewy bodies (DLB).

PARKINSON'S DISEASE

To meet criteria for PDD, an individual must first be diagnosed with PD. The four cardinal motor features of PD are bradykinesia (i.e., slowness of movement), rest tremor, rigidity, and postural instability or gait impairment. In the early stages of the disease, a mild tremor usually presents in the hand or foot on one side of the body, spreading to the other limbs over the next 1–3 years (Alves, Forsaa, Pedersen, Gjerstad, & Larsen, 2008). Tremor occurs when a person's muscles are relaxed, or at rest, hence the term "resting tremor." Rigidity can be painful and individuals with rigidity and bradykinesia tend to not to swing their arms when walking. Postural instability and gait impairment is a primary contributor to falls and typically is characterized by a stooped posture and a slow, narrow-based gait with short shuffling steps, decreased arm swing, and slow difficult turning.

PD has several secondary motor symptoms. Freezing of gait, which is marked by impaired initiation of gait at onset or when walking through doorways, is common. Other symptoms include reduced facial expression and eye blinking known as "masked facies," decreased voice volume, micrographia, olfactory sensitivity, autonomic dysfunction (e.g., orthostatic hypotension, constipation, urinary dysfunction, excessive sweating), mood and sleep disorders (e.g., insomnia, rapid eye movement [REM] sleep behavior disorder, restless legs syndrome), pain, and fatigue (Alves et al., 2008; Massano & Bhatia, 2012). Although it is common to observe these symptoms in the setting of PD, it is important to recognize that PD is a heterogeneous disorder and that symptom profiles significantly vary between and within individuals over time.

http://dx.doi.org/10.1037/14459-009
APA Handbook of Clinical Geropsychology: Vol. 2. Assessment, Treatment, and Issues of Later Life,
P. A. Lichtenberg and B. T. Mast (Editors-in-Chief)

Mild Cognitive Impairment in Parkinson's Disease

In PD, there are high rates of cognitive impairment, ranging from MCI to dementia. In 2012, the Movement Disorders Society (MDS) commissioned a task force that proposed specific criteria and standardized methods of diagnosing MCI in PD (PD–MCI; Litvan et al., 2012). The new criteria were proposed to enhance the ability of clinicians and researchers to reliably identify the clinical features of PD–MCI and identify predictors of conversion from PD–MCI to PDD.

For a diagnosis of PD–MCI to be made, an insidious cognitive decline must present in the setting of already established PD. The decline can be identified by the patient, a caregiver, or a clinician, but unlike PDD, the cognitive deficits cannot be severe enough to significantly interfere with daily functioning. Abbreviated testing (Level I) or a comprehensive neuropsychological assessment (Level II) can be utilized to assess for impairment. A Level I assessment allows a diagnosis to be made if impairment is observed using either a cognitive screening measure validated in PD or on at least two tests within a brief neuropsychological battery. For a diagnosis to be made on the basis of a Level II assessment, impairment must be observed on at least two tests, either within one or across multiple cognitive domains. Although brief evaluations are sometimes more practical, comprehensive neuropsychological testing that includes at least two tests from each of the five cognitive domains (i.e., attention, executive functioning, language, memory, and visuospatial functioning) is more reliable and sensitive. Comprehensive testing also allows for a more detailed assessment of the severity and pattern of cognitive impairment.

Parkinson's Disease Dementia

PDD is a dementia syndrome with an insidious onset and slow progression that develops in the context of established PD. In 2007, The MDS Task Force on Dementia in Parkinson's Disease established specific criteria for the assessment and diagnosis of PDD (Dubois et al., 2007). Similar to PD–MCI, PDD can be diagnosed only when the cognitive impairment is deemed attributable to underlying PD pathology. The cognitive deficits must be present in at least two of the four cognitive domains typically affected in PD (i.e., attention, executive functioning, visuospatial ability, and memory), occur in the context of declines in general cognition, and significantly interfere with activities of daily living beyond impairments attributable to motor or autonomic dysfunction. The cognitive impairments may affect one or multiple life arenas, including social functioning, occupational productivity, or personal care. Although not required to make the diagnosis, given the high prevalence of behavioral symptoms in PDD, the presence of apathy, depression, anxiety, psychosis, or excessive daytime sleepiness can be viewed as supportive evidence when making a diagnosis of PDD. Importantly, to meet criteria for PDD, the cognitive symptoms also must develop at least 1 year after the onset of PD motor symptoms, as this is an important differentiating feature between PDD and DLB.

Dementia With Lewy Bodies

Diagnostic criteria for DLB were first established in 1996 (McKeith et al., 1996). The initial criteria stipulated that a diagnosis of DLB required the presence of dementia, accompanied by at least one of three core symptoms: fluctuating cognition, visual hallucinations, and motor parkinsonism. In 2005, the DLB consortium incorporated new information about the core clinical features of DLB and revised the criteria for clinical and pathologic diagnosis and assessment (McKeith et al., 2005). This new criteria includes additional clinical signs and specific neuroimaging findings as suggestive features of DLB. Specifically, the presence of severe neuroleptic sensitivity or REM sleep behavior disorder, which is characterized by vivid dreaming and abnormal and sometimes violent physical enactment of dreams during REM sleep, can be used to support a diagnosis of DLB. As demonstrated on single-photon emission computerized tomography and positron emission tomography imaging, low-dopamine transporter uptake in basal ganglia can increase diagnostic confidence.

To make a diagnosis of probable DLB, two of the three core clinical features (i.e., fluctuations in cognition with pronounced variations in attention and alertness, recurrent and typically well-formed visual hallucinations, and spontaneous features of parkinsonism) must be present in the setting of a progressive dementia that is of a sufficient severity to cause interference with daily functioning. If only one core clinical feature is present, the presence of a suggestive feature still permits for a diagnosis of probable DLB. In the absence of any core features, a diagnosis of possible DLB can be made in a patient with dementia if at least one supportive feature is also present, including repeated falls, severe autonomic dysfunction, unexplained losses of consciousness, depression, and systematic delusions. Although these features commonly are observed in DLB, they are also typical of other neurodegenerative diseases and therefore lack diagnostic specificity. As mentioned earlier, to differentiate DLB from PDD, the former requires that cognitive symptoms develop prior to or concurrently with parkinsonism. Last, the current diagnostic criteria includes a schema for staging the pathologic features of diffuse Lewy bodies in relation to neurofibrillary tangles, thereby increasing diagnostic sensitivity and discriminating DLB from Alzheimer's disease (AD).

Parkinson's Disease Dementia and Dementia With Lewy Bodies

In general, the typical cognitive profile in both PDD and DLB reflects the underlying disruption in frontal-subcortical neural systems and includes impairments in attention, executive functioning, memory, and visuospatial abilities (Bronnick, Emre, & Lane, 2007; Collerton, Burn, McKeith, & O'Brien, 2003; Janvin, Larsen, Aarsland, & Hugdahl, 2006). Executive functions are especially impaired on tasks that require initiation, planning, mental flexibility, and conceptual reasoning. When present, the short-term memory impairments are less pronounced and in a different pattern than in AD, as they typically are constrained to deficits in retrieval-based memory, rather than in consolidation or "storage." Also in contrast to AD, core language functions generally are well preserved in PDD and DLB (Connor et al., 1998; Janvin et al., 2006). Given this cognitive profile, PDD historically has been described as a "subcortical dementia." However, with increased recognition of the heterogeneity of symptom presentation and what we now know to be the common

occurrence of neuropathology in both subcortical and cortical structures (Wu, 2011), there has been a shift away from this terminology.

In addition to a progressive cognitive decline, fluctuations in attention are common in PDD and DLB. Fluctuations in levels of alertness frequently are observed in DLB and, in fact, are characteristic of the disorder (Ballard et al., 2002). Fluctuations in alertness have been historically difficult to operationalize, as they can present as periods of unresponsiveness, excessive sleepiness, or periods of confusion with diminished awareness of the environment (Y. Huang & Halliday, 2013). They can last from several hours to days, with a return to normal or near-normal functioning upon remittance. The magnitude of the changes in cognition and daily functioning that is observed in patients with fluctuating alertness distinguishes it from the more commonly observed variations in day-to-day functioning seen in other disease processes. With that said, tracking and operationalizing fluctuations is quite difficult and remains an ongoing problem in both clinical and research realms.

Cognitive dysfunction often is accompanied by neuropsychiatric symptoms in both PDD and DLB. The majority of PDD patients show at least two psychiatric symptoms (Aarsland et al., 2007), and patients with more advanced dementia have more psychiatric symptoms. Changes in mood may occur due to either the underlying disease process or in response to the motor and functional changes inherent to the disease process. Mood disorders are associated with increased morbidity and mortality (Hughes, Ross, Mindham, & Spokes, 2004) and exacerbated cognitive impairment.

The symptoms of depression and anxiety can occur early in the disease course and even before the occurrence of dopaminergic depletion in the substantia nigra and the manifestation of motor symptoms (Postuma et al., 2012). Depression can exacerbate cognitive dysfunction, particularly in individuals with less education and other psychiatric comorbidities. Although depression occurs in upward of 40% of PD and DLB patients, it often goes unrecognized and undertreated because of the lack of assessment and the misattribution of depressive features to motor pathology, such as masked face and motor slowing. There is also an indication that depression manifests differently in the context of PD than in depressed individuals without PD. It can be marked by greater concentration difficulties, cognitive slowing, anergia, and less affective symptoms (Ehrt, Bronnick, Leentjens, Larsen, & Aarsland, 2006). Untreated depression in PDD is of particular concern, given its association with a more precipitous cognitive, motor, and functional decline, worse quality of life, and increased caregiver burden.

Depression often is confused with apathy, which instead refers to a lack of motivation, initiative, and interest in completing purposeful and even pleasurable activity as well as reduced concern about such changes. Although depression and apathy represent different disorders that individually can present in any given individual with PD (Aarsland et al., 1999), they frequently occur together (M. L. Levy et al., 1998). Apathy can manifest itself in individuals who have difficulties adjusting to progressive functional impairment, or as a complication of pathophysiological changes. The current estimates of the prevalence of apathy in PD vary between 16.5% (Aarsland et al., 1999) and 70% (Santangelo et al., 2013).

Anxiety also frequently co-occurs with depression (Menza, Robertson-Hoffman, & Bonapace, 1993) and is relatively common, occurring in up to 40% of patients with PD (Stein, Heuser, Juncos, & Uhde, 1990; Walsh & Bennett, 2001). Anxiety can manifest in several ways, including as a generalized anxiety disorder, social phobia, panic disorder, or even as obsessive–compulsive behavior (Tan, 2012). The symptoms of anxiety can exacerbate the motor symptoms of PD, but anxiety itself also can be exacerbated by parkinsonian medications. It may manifest cyclically during or immediately preceding a transition into an "off" period, during which time the efficacy of PD medications diminishes or dissipates altogether (Siemers, Shekhar, Quaid, & Dickson, 1993; Vázquez, Jimenez-Jimenez, Garcia-Ruiz, & Garcia-Urra, 1993.) Unfortunately, despite the high prevalence rate and disabling features of anxiety, particularly in patients with dementia, its presence often goes underappreciated (Marsh, 2000).

Psychotic features, such as delusions and hallucinations, also are shared features of PDD and DLB, with greater prevalence in DLB. Hallucinations occur in about 40% of individuals with PD (Aarsland, Marsh, & Schrag, 2009; Emre et al., 2007; Fenelon, Mahieux, Huon, & Ziegler, 2000) and their presence has been shown to be a significant predictor of later development of dementia (Aarsland, Andersen, Larsen, Lolk, & Kragh-Sorensen, 2003). Hallucinations are even more common in individuals with PDD and DLB, as they occur in about 45–65% and 60–80% of these individuals, respectively (Emre et al., 2007). The nature of the hallucinations in PDD and DLB tend to be similar and are typically of people, most often children, and animals. They can be benign or quite distressing to both the individual with dementia and their caregivers.

Conceptual Issues

PDD and DLB share pathological and clinical features. The commonalities between the two disorders have fostered an ongoing disagreement as to whether they are two distinct entities or if they merely represent different time points on the spectrum of Lewy body disease. Both DLB and PDD are synucleinopathies and are classified under the umbrella of Lewy body disease. *Synucleinopathies* is the term used to describe a group of neurodegenerative disorders that are marked by the presence of abnormal α-synuclein inclusion bodies in select neurons or macroglial cells (Takeda et al., 1998). In addition, both diseases result in similar end-stage pathologies, with diffuse brain involvement. Given these pathological commonalities, it is not surprising that a great deal of overlap exists between clinical expression of PDD and DLB.

Those who maintain a distinction between PDD and DLB point to subtle, but disorder-specific pathological differences, including greater neuronal loss in the substantia nigra in PDD, greater alpha-synuclein (α-synuclein) burden in the striatum in DLB, and more consistently observed beta-amyloid (Aβ) patterns in DLB (Duda, Giasson, Mabon, Lee, & Trojanowski, 2002). At the group level, the presence of subtle differences in symptom complex, prognosis, clinical course, and clinical management also are regarded by some as evidence that these reflect separate disorders, albeit with shared features. For example, patients with DLB tend to present with earlier and more severe and complex visual hallucinations.

They also may present with less resting tremor, greater symmetry of motor symptoms, and fewer parkinsonian signs, which when present tend to manifest with more significant generalized slowing and postural and gait disturbances than in PDD.

Incidence and Prevalence

PD occurs in about 0.3% of the general population of the United States and is the second most common movement disorder behind essential tremor (Alves et al., 2008; Kowal, Dall, Chakrabarti, Storm, & Jain, 2013; Massano & Bhatia, 2012; Tanner & Aston, 2000). The average age of onset is 62 years, with men being 1.5 times more likely to develop PD than women. The prevalence rate is 1–2% in individuals over 65 years and rises to 4–5% in those over 85 years (Alves et al., 2008; Kowal et al., 2013; Massano & Bhatia, 2012). Although PD often is viewed as a motor disease, cognitive dysfunction is common and can present early in the disease course. PD–MCI occurs in about 25% of individuals with PD and increases the risk for conversion to PDD, which itself develops on average 10 years after disease onset (Aarsland et al., 2010) and is prevalent in 30–40% of those with PD (Aarsland, Zaccai, & Brayne, 2005). In fact, individuals with PD are up to 6 times more likely to develop dementia than their age-matched peers (Aarsland, Andersen, et al., 2001), with longitudinal studies demonstrating a 75% incidence rate before death (Hely, Reid, Adena, Halliday, & Morris, 2008). Not unexpectedly, the incidence of PDD significantly increases with older age and longer disease duration (Aarsland, Andersen, et al., 2003).

DLB is the second most common dementia subtype in older adults, following AD (Geser, Wenning, Poewe, & McKeith, 2005; Zupancic, Mahajan, & Handa, 2011). Nevertheless, there is an indication that DLB remains grossly underdiagnosed, with more than 60% of cases going unrecognized (Palmqvist, Hansson, Minthon, & Londos, 2009). A 2005 systematic review of epidemiological studies showed a wide variation in the prevalence of DLB (Zaccai, McCracken, & Brayne, 2005). With growing awareness and standardization of diagnostic criteria, however, recognition and assessment of this disorder has improved significantly over the past decade. A 2013 review of epidemiological studies revealed the mean population prevalence of DLB in those over 65 years to be 0.36% (Vann Jones & O'Brien, 2014), with an annual incidence rate of 3.8% of new dementia diagnoses. Of those with dementia, 4.2% were found to have DLB. Prevalence rates of DLB in clinical settings dramatically increased to 7.5%, or 1 in 13 patients with dementia. This could be attributable to poor recognition of DLB in the community, biases in referral rates, or heightened awareness of DLB in specialized clinics. Although DLB historically has been thought of as more common in males, the previous review did not find clear support for differences in sex distribution.

Risk and Protective Factors

Although the etiology of PD remains unclear in most cases, interactions between genetic and environmental factors likely are involved (Alves et al., 2008; Bronstein et al., 2009; Massano & Bhatia, 2012). Increasing age, positive family history, and exposure to pesticides each have been identified as independent risk factors for PD (Alves et al., 2008; Massano & Bhatia, 2012). The incidence of PD is significantly higher in men than in women, with a disparity that increases with age (Alves et al., 2008). In addition, evidence suggests a possible association between higher intakes of poly-unsaturated fatty acids, nonsteroidal anti-inflammatory drug use, and statin use and reduced risk of PD (Bronstein et al., 2009; Gao, Chen, Schwarzschild, & Ascherio, 2011).

Although results are conflicting across studies, in aggregate, data support an increased risk of cognitive decline and dementia in PD patients with the apolipoprotein E, type epsilon-4 (ε4) allele (APOE-ε4); the microtubule-associated protein tau (MAPT) H1/H1 genotype; and glucocerebrosidase (GBA) mutations. The MAPT H1/H1 genotype and GBA mutations are both examples of genes that are associated with PD risk as well as a differential phenotype, namely greater cognitive impairment. A meta-analysis of nine studies and a more recent large prospective study found that the APOE-ε4 allele was associated with PD dementia (X. Huang, Chen, Kaufer, Troster, & Poole, 2006; Morley et al., 2012). A large prospective study of PD patients also found that MAPT H1/H1 was associated with increased risk of dementia over 5 years (Williams-Gray et al., 2009). In addition, PD patients with heterozygous GBA mutations possess greater cognitive impairment than PD subjects without mutations (Alcalay et al., 2012; Brockmann et al., 2011; Setó-Salvia et al., 2012). A similar situation exists for SNCA, the gene encoding α-synuclein. A number of single-nucleotide polymorphisms (SNPs) near SNCA have been implicated in PD risk in genome-wide association studies (GWAS), while familial PD cases caused by SNCA mutations have been associated with greater cognitive impairment.

Despite this evidence, genetic factors account for only a small portion of the risk for cognitive decline in PD. The most widely supported risk factors for cognitive decline in PD are instead older age, older age at disease onset, more severe parkinsonism, and evidence of early cognitive impairment (Aarsland, 2010; Dodel et al., 2008; Emre et al., 2007; G. Levy et al., 2002). Identification of even mild cognitive deficits early on is critical, given that more the half of individuals with PD with objective deficits on baseline neuropsychological testing will develop dementia within the following 4 years (Janvin et al., 2006). In addition, phenotypic variances in motor symptoms are correlated strongly with the malignancy of disease course, in terms of the presence, severity, and rate of decline of motor and nonmotor symptoms. Individuals with prominent postural instability, gait impairment, and akinetic rigidity, or the so-called PIGD phenotype, have a significantly greater risk for dementia than individuals with tremor-dominant presentations (Burn et al., 2006; G. Levy et al., 2002). The presence of excessive daytime sleepiness (Gjerstad, Aarsland, & Larsen, 2002) or visual hallucinations (Aarsland, 2010; Aarsland, Andersen, et al., 2003), symmetric extrapyramidal symptoms, a suboptimal response to levodopa, or dystonic dyskinesias early in the disease course also have been associated with increased risk of dementia (Emre et al., 2007).

As with dementia in general, higher education serves as a protective factor for cognitive decline in PD (Glatt et al., 1996). Physical exercise (Ahlskog et al., 2011) and participation in cognitively stimulating activities and social endeavors also may attenuate cognitive decline and reduce the risk of

dementia in general (Fratiglioni, Paillard-Borg, & Winblad, 2004). Coffee consumption has been described as a protective factor against dementia (Bronstein et al., 2009), and cigarette smoking has been associated with reduced risk for both PD and PD-related cognitive decline (Bronstein et al., 2009; Weisskopf, Grodstein, & Ascherio, 2007). Smoking, however, increases one's risk for cardiovascular disease and subsequently cerebrovascular-related cognitive decline, and the negative effects of tobacco use on overall health likely outweigh any potential benefits.

Disease Progression and Outcomes

The typical onset of dementia in PDD and DLB is in the early and mid-70s, respectively. DLB may present with earlier and more severe executive dysfunction (Wand, 2007), but the duration of dementia and rate of cognitive decline among PDD and DLB is similar (Emre et al., 2007; Horimoto et al., 2003). Although earlier reports suggested a notably faster disease progression to death in DLB (around 6 years) than AD (8–12 years) more recent studies indicate similar rates of progression (Walker, Allen, Shergill, Mullan, & Katona, 2000; Wand, 2007) on the order of 8–12 years from disease onset to mortality (Olichney et al., 1998; Walker et al., 2000; Wand, 2007; Williams, Xiong, Morris, & Galvin, 2006). The increase in disease duration seen in DLB in part may reflect increased recognition of neuroleptic sensitivity and the subsequent avoidance of prescribing such medications in DLB patients. In PD, patients with PIGD phenotypes or autonomic dysfunction have an elevated risk for dementia (Williams et al., 2006) as well as increased risk of falls and shorter survival rates (Stubendorff, Aarsland, Minthon, & Londos, 2012).

Comorbid neuropathologies also play a role in disease progression and outcome. AD pathology (i.e., Aβ and tau protein tangles) commonly is found in both PDD and DLB, with higher rates observed in DLB (Wider et al., 2012). There may be a synergistic interaction among Aβ, tau, and α-synuclein that promotes accumulation of each other and contributes to an accelerated cognitive decline (Clinton et al., 2010; Compta et al., 2011). One study examining outcomes related to comorbid AD pathology in individuals with PDD demonstrated shorter disease duration compared with individuals without AD pathology, although the presence of AD pathology also was associated with later PD onset by 10 years and older age at death (Sabbagh et al., 2009).

Impact of Progression

Studies have shown that patients with PDD and DLB and their caregivers report lower quality of life than their AD counterparts (Boström, Jonsson, Minthon, & Londos, 2007). Although both motor and nonmotor symptoms contribute to disability and impaired functional abilities, nonmotor symptoms disproportionately affect overall burden. In fact, cognitive impairment, mood disturbance, hallucinations, and fatigue are associated positively with greater disability, diminished functional abilities, poorer quality of life, increased caregiver distress, and increased nursing home placement (Aarsland, Marsh, & Schrag, 2009; Pandya, Kubu, & Giroux, 2008; M. Samuel, Maidment, Boustani, & Fox, 2006; Walker et al., 2012).

ASSESSMENT

The cognitive and neuropsychiatric symptomatology of PD and DLB varies widely among individuals. Given the high prevalence of nonmotor symptomatology in PD, formal assessment of such features early in the disease process should be incorporated into the interdisciplinary care of all patients and conducted on a consistent and ongoing basis. Most often, this necessitates the services of neurologists and neuropsychologists with expertise in movement disorders, but geropsychologists and other health care professional also can play a critical role in the evaluation of such patients.

Assessment Approaches, Tools, and Instruments

Per the recommended diagnostic criteria outlined by the MDS in 2007, a multilevel assessment approach can be used to diagnosis PDD (Dubois et al., 2007). A Level I evaluation permits a diagnosis of PDD to be made based on observed impairment in general cognition, as demonstrated on a brief screening measure (i.e., Mini-Mental Status Examination [MMSE]).

Although less sensitive, brief testing is often more practical in the clinical setting and can be completed by clinicians who lack expertise in neuropsychological assessment. An MMSE score below 26 initially was recommended as the cutoff for PDD (Dubois et al., 2007); however, subsequent studies have shown the MMSE to be fairly insensitive to cognitive impairment (Hoops et al., 2009). More recently developed cognitive screening measures, such as the Montreal Cognitive Assessment (MoCA), are better suited to assess PDD. MoCA cutoff scores of less than 21 show the best balance between sensitivity and specificity for dementia in PD, whereas MoCA scores of less than 26 can reliably detect PD–MCI (Dalrymple-Alford et al., 2010).

A Level II evaluation requires the services of a trained neuropsychologist, as it includes a more detailed assessment of a patient's cognitive and neuropsychiatric profiles. Level II assessments generally are completed to specify the pattern and severity of impairments in the setting of established PDD or when the diagnosis of PDD remains equivocal following a Level I assessment. This more thorough evaluation is particularly helpful in highly educated patients, when cognitive deficits are mild, variable, or occurring in the setting of significant neuropsychiatric symptoms. The MMSE and most other cognitive screening measures are ill equipped to distinguish PPD or DLB from other common dementia syndromes, such as AD. Moreover, comprehensive neuropsychological evaluations are required when there is a question of a comorbid diagnosis, given that the presence of mixed pathologies has important ramifications on the expected pattern of impairment and course of decline (Andersson, Zetterberg, Minthon, Blennow, & Londos, 2011), which cannot be captured adequately via cognitive screening tools.

As mentioned earlier, the typical cognitive profiles of both PDD and DLB are marked by prominent subcortical impairments, with marked attentional deficits and significant executive and visuospatial dysfunction, although cortical deficits also can present (Bronnick et al., 2007; Janvin et al., 2006). Neuropsychological testing therefore should include tests of executive functioning that encompass an assessment of planning, initiation, mental flexibility, abstract reasoning, and inhibitory control. Tests of simple and sustained attention also are useful, as are those that assess both fundamental visuoperception and higher order visuospatial abilities. In fact, simple constructional tasks, such as clock drawing and copying pentagons, are highly sensitive to PDD and DLB (Ala, Hughes, Kyrouac, Ghobrial, & Elble, 2001; Cormack, Aarsland, Ballard, & Tovee, 2004). In terms of memory, verbal and visual memory measures should both be utilized and close attention should be paid to evaluation of the specific pattern of performance demonstrated across testing. Patients with PDD and DLB typically demonstrate more significant retrieval-based impairments but intact recognition memory (Aarsland, Litvan, et al., 2003; Pillon, Deweer, Agid, & Dubois, 1993). Language testing should include measures of naming and comprehension, which often are well preserved in these disorders, as well as tests of verbal fluency. Patients with PDD and DLB show deficits in both phonemic and semantic fluency, but relative to patients with AD, patients with PDD are significantly more impaired on phonemic fluency and significantly less impaired on semantic fluency (Henry & Crawford, 2004).

Assessment Controversies and Dilemmas

Other than age at onset and possibly less rest tremor and greater levodopa responsivity, no significant differences between individuals with DLB and PDD have been shown to reliably exist. The cognitive profiles, fluctuations in attention, neuropsychiatric symptoms, prevalence of RBD and autonomic dysfunction, type and severity of parkinsonism, heightened neuroleptic sensitivity, and responsiveness to cholinesterase inhibitors all are shared clinical features of PDD and DLB (Aarsland, Ballard, Larsen, & McKeith, 2001; Aarsland, Ballard, et al., 2005; Aarsland, Ballard, McKeith, Perry, & Larsen, 2001; Aarsland, Litvan, et al., 2003; Bonelli et al., 2004; Emre et al., 2004; Molloy, McKeith, O'Brien, & Burn, 2005; Wenning et al., 1999). Despite that fact that the current zeitgeist dictates a diagnosis of DLB rather than PDD be made when dementia occurs before or concurrently with parkinsonism, this 1-year-rule serves only as an arbitrary distinction between two disorders. Moreover, differentiation between PDD and DLB based on such a recommendation becomes increasingly

difficult when reliable descriptions of the temporal sequencing of symptoms are lacking.

The assessment of PDD and DLB frequently is complicated by the dynamic interplay between the neuropsychiatric, behavioral, and cognitive features present in each disorder. Depression, anxiety, apathy, REM sleep behavior disorder, fatigue, and psychosis can cause or exacerbate underlying cognitive impairment and contribute to poor neuropsychological test performance. Medication side effects can interfere significantly with cognitive efficiency and performance on testing. When assessing cognition, careful distinction must be taken to ensure that impaired test results are indeed secondary to cognitive dysfunction, rather than other factors. Similarly, the motor symptoms inherent to both disorders can significantly affect the assessment of nonmotor symptomatology. When possible, test batteries that limit reliance on psychomotor demands are encouraged. Care should be taken to assess patients in their optimal medication state, increasing the likelihood of capturing their cognitive capacities.

Assessing the presence and severity of symptoms outside of the clinical setting is challenging. Patients may not possess the knowledge or language to appropriately communicate their symptoms. Elderly demented patients often underreport cognitive impairment and psychiatric symptoms and their caregivers may not be privy to the full nature of their internal experiences. For example, although recurrent visual hallucinations occurring early in the disease course is a cardinal symptom of DLB (McKeith et al., 1996), their presence often is underreported (Mosimann et al., 2006). Poor reliability in the assessment of fluctuations in attention and alertness also has long been reported (Cummings, 2004; Luis et al., 1999). In addition, caregivers may be in denial of the nonmotor changes, be unaware that these changes are related to the disease, or feel that they are betraying their loved one by discussing these changes with the health care team.

INTERVENTIONS

No therapies exist that cure, alter, or delay disease progression in PDD or DLB. That said, early and aggressive treatment of symptoms inherent to these disorders is important. Pharmacological therapies in conjunction with physical, occupational and speech therapy are effective in their ability to improve motor functioning and quality of life. Acetylcholinesterase inhibitors (ACHEIs) often can improve cognitive functioning and ameliorate behavioral problems in patients with either disorder (McKeith & Mosimann, 2004; Rolinski, Fox, Maidment, & McShane, 2012). Pharmacological and more recently surgical treatments, such as deep brain stimulation, can be critical for symptom relief, particularly in the motor domain, but dementia is a contraindication. Incorporation of nonpharmacological treatments—in particular, caregiver education that focuses on environmental issues—can improve the presence or severity of symptoms while reducing caregiver burden.

Treatment Approaches

The treatment of PDD and DLB varies depending on the motor and nonmotor symptom profiles. Successful management often requires an interdisciplinary approach that includes pharmacological and non-pharmacological or behavioral treatments. Addressing the underlying movement disorder, including symptoms of instability, falls, bradykinesia, and autonomic dysfunction is essential. Careful assessment and treatment of cognitive and neuropsychiatric symptoms as well as evaluation and management of sleep disorders or psychosis is also critical. These symptoms individually and in aggregate affect functional status and quality of life and all should be considered when developing an integrated treatment plan (Chaudhuri & Schapira, 2009; Hawkes, Del Tredici, & Braak, 2010; Lim, Fox, & Lang, 2009; Tolosa, Gaig, Santamaría, & Compta, 2009).

Controversies and Dilemmas in Treatment

As has been described, PDD and DLB are complex diseases with heterogeneous phenotypes. The intra-personal motor and nonmotor symptom profiles in these disorders also vary over the disease course. The treatment and management of motor symptoms is complicated by cognitive deficits and neuropsychiatric symptoms. Some therapeutic approaches to nonmotor symptoms may trigger motor deterioration and functional impairment (Breier et al., 2002;

Ford, Lynch, & Greene, 1994). Treatment of each individual symptom therefore must be addressed with consideration of the potential effects posed on the others.

Evidence-Based Treatments

Dopaminergic therapy, and levodopa in particular, remains the primary treatment for the extrapyramidal symptoms of PD and DLB (Bonelli et al., 2004). Medication often is introduced at low doses and titrated slowly to the minimum dosage needed to overcome functional disability without exacerbating behavioral or psychotic symptoms (Emre, 2003). Dopamine agonists also can be used, particularly early in the disease course and to treat dyskinesias; however, even at lower dosages, they are associated with greater side effect profiles, including drug-induced psychosis (Goldman, Vaughan, & Goetz, 2011). Other PD medications, such as amantadine and catechol-O-methyl transferase (COMT) inhibitors, have increased risks of confusion and psychosis and should be avoided if possible.

Psychopharmacological management of nonmotor deficits in PDD and DLB follows therapies developed for AD. ACHEIs frequently are used to treat PDD and DLB and, in fact, may have a more robust effect than in AD (W. Samuel et al., 2000; Weintraub, Somogyi, & Meng, 2011). The difference in the magnitude of purported improvement is thought to be secondary to the greater cholinergic deficit and added burden of striatal pathology in these disorders compared with AD (Perry et al., 1994). As a class, ACHEIs have been shown to slow the rate of generalized cognitive decline; decrease attentional fluctuations, behavioral and neuropsychiatric symptoms, and sleep disturbances; and improve activities of daily living (Rolinski et al., 2012).

In both PDD and DLB, the most widely studied medication is rivastigmine. A double-blinded random controlled trial (RCT) of rivastigmine in PDD was found to have significant benefits for cognition, behavioral symptoms, and global outcome (Emre et al., 2004). Secondary analyses showed that individuals on rivastigmine exhibited specific improvements in the domains of attention and executive functioning and in activities of daily living (Olin, Aarsland, & Meng, 2010; Schmitt, Farlow, Meng,

Tekin, & Olin, 2010; Wesnes, McKeith, Edgar, Emre, & Lane, 2005). The most common medication side effects included nausea, vomiting, and transient rest tremor that occurred during dose titration. These positive results led to the U.S. Food and Drug Administration's (FDA) approval of rivastigmine for mild to moderate dementia associated with PD in 2006. In a controlled study of the effects of rivastigmine on behavioral symptomatology in DLB, rivastigmine was found efficacious in reducing anxiety, apathy, hallucinations, and delusions (McKeith et al., 2000).

Donepezil is the most widely used ACHEI for AD, but in PDD and DLB, evidence is insufficient to support its efficacy. Although two open-label studies found that donepezil improved cognition in PDD (Müller et al., 2006; Rowan et al., 2007), the results from others studies have been conflicting (Ravina et al., 2005). Further work also needs to be completed to substantiate the benefit of galantamine in PDD and DLB. The results of preliminary studies, however, are promising in that they showed cognitive and behavioral improvements with initiation (Aarsland, Hutchinson, & Larsen, 2003; Litvinenko, Odinak, Mogil'naia, & Emelin, 2007).

In addition to cholinergic depletion, glutamate dysfunction also has been associated with cognitive impairment. The effects of memantine, an N-methyl D-aspartate (NMDA) receptor agonist that acts on the glutamatergic system by blocking NMDA receptors, only recently have been evaluated in PDD and DLB. A double-blind RCT of both PDD and DLB found significant medication benefits in the DLB group only (Emre et al., 2010). In contrast, others studies have found significant improvements on clinician measures of global change and deteriorations in functioning following memantine withdrawal in patients with PDD (Aarsland, Ballard, et al., 2009).

As has been described, mood disorders often accompany cognitive dysfunction and are common in PDD and DLB. Before resorting to pharmacologic treatment of depression in PD, close attention should be paid to when the symptoms manifest. Depression may develop solely in the context of off symptoms, when dopaminergic medications are wearing off (Storch et al., 2013). In such cases,

readjustment of dopaminergic medication may improve symptom fluctuations and ameliorate off-time depression. Pharmacologic treatment of depression in PDD typically includes use of selective serotonin reuptake inhibitors, serotonin-norepinephrine reuptake inhibitors (SNRIs), or tricyclic antidepressants. A recent systematic review of all available clinical trials found that only pramipexole, a dopamine agonist, had enough evidence to support its efficacy in treating depression, whereas the tricyclics nortriptyline and desipramine were deemed likely efficacious (Seppi et al., 2011). Although evidence was insufficient to make firm conclusions about the efficacy of other medications, a large double-blind RCT of antidepressants in PD showed that venlafaxine XR and paroxetine significantly improved depression (Richard et al., 2012). Case reports also have suggested that the dual dopamine and norepinephrine reuptake inhibitory actions of bupropion are well suited to treat depression, given the absence of serotoninergic side-effects seen in other classes of medications (Załuska & Dyduch, 2011).

Although anxiety and apathy exists in upward of 40% and 70% of patients with PD, respectively (Santangelo et al., 2013; Starkstein et al., 1992; Starkstein, Robinson, Leiguardia, & Preziosi, 1993), their presence can be even less appreciated than other nonmotor symptoms. Pharmacologically, anxiety is managed similarly to depression, with the use of antidepressants, despite clear evidence supporting their efficacy. Small open-label studies of levodopa, the SNRI atomoxetine, and the dopamine agonist ropinirole showed improvements in apathy (Czernecki et al., 2002, 2008; Weintraub et al., 2010). RCTs of agents aimed at treating apathy or anxiety, however, are lacking.

In addition to mood disorders, psychosis in the context of both PD and DLB is common. Symptoms can include visual illusions, frank hallucinations, or paranoid delusions. The latter is associated with a loss of insight and therefore tends to be quite disabling and difficult to treat. In addressing treatment, it is important to first conduct a thorough review of all potential etiologies, including medication side effects and unrelated comorbid illness. Reductions or discontinuation of over-the-counter sleep agents or bladder-control medications should first be attempted, as these can cause agitation. Anticholinergic medications and amantadine also should be reduced or discontinued, as these agents can trigger psychosis. If psychotic symptoms persist after their discontinuation, care should be taken to consider whether dopamine agonists should then be discontinued.

When pharmacological intervention of psychosis in PDD and DLB is warranted, CHEIs often are used first. In DLB specifically, visual hallucinations actually may be a good predictor of positive response to cholinesterase inhibitors (McKeith, Wesnes, Perry, & Ferrara, 2004). Open-label studies have shown CHEIs to be effective in improving hallucinations, attentional fluctuations, and associated behavioral features in both disorders. Rivastigmine specifically has been shown to improve behavioral dysfunction, hallucinations, apathy, anxiety, and sleep dysfunction in DLB (McKeith et al., 2000). Unfortunately, psychosis often persists despite medication adjustments. In such cases, treatment mirrors that in other psychiatric diseases and involves the use of antipsychotics. Clozapine has been found to alleviate psychosis, (Factor et al., 2001), but blood monitoring is mandated given the risk of neutropenia with this medication. Quetiapine is easier to manage and therefore more commonly utilized, but its efficacy remains unclear (Merims, Balas, Peretz, Shabtai, & Giladi, 2006).

Management of psychosis with neuroleptics in PDD and DLB is particularly challenging because, as dopamine antagonists, they limit the reuptake of dopamine in the brain, often resulting in exacerbation and sometimes significant deterioration in motor functioning. For this reason, utilization of typical antipsychotics and many atypical agents, such as olanzapine and risperidone, is discouraged. As has been mentioned, patients with DLB have particularly high rates of severe neuroleptic sensitivity (Wolters, 1999). A severe sensitivity reaction occurs in about 30–50% of DLB patients after initiation of antipsychotic medication (Aarsland, Ballard, et al., 2005) and is marked by deterioration in cognition, sedation, acute and sometimes irreversible onset parkinsonism (McKeith, Fairbaim, Perry, Thompson, & Perry, 1992), and in rare cases, by

symptoms representing neuroleptic malignant syndrome, which can be fatal.

Nonpharmacological therapies also can improve the symptoms of mood disorders and psychosis in PDD and DLB and should be incorporated into a comprehensive approach to treatment. Both RCTs and open-label trials have shown cognitive–behavioral therapies to be an effective treatment for depression (Dobkin et al., 2011; Secker & Brown, 2005; Teri, Logsdon, & McCurry, 2002; Teri, Logsdon, Uomoto, & McCurry, 1997). Psychotherapy, mindfulness, and relaxation techniques also can improve anxiety. Importantly, amelioration of depression and anxiety often is associated with improvements in cognition, which together can improve daily functioning and quality of life. In-home care, social–community involvement, and caregiver education also can play a vital role in reducing psychiatric symptoms and improving quality of life.

Contextual Factors and Barriers to Treatment

An interdisciplinary approach to diagnosing and managing DLB and PDD is ideal because of the complexity and range of cognitive, physical, social, and emotional problems associated with these neurodegenerative diseases. Specialized PD and movement disorders centers often include a team of neurologists, neuropsychologists, geropsychologists, nurses, physical and occupational therapists, and social workers with specific expertise in movement disorders and dementia. Unfortunately, individuals with less education and a disadvantaged socioeconomic status are less likely to seek help and have access to adequate health care. Those in rural locations commonly face the burden of limited health care access, particularly to specialized diagnostic and treatment centers. In such cases, not only is access to quality clinical care limited but so too is access to clinical trials.

Role of the Geropsychologist

Geropsychologists can play a critical role in the management of PDD and DLB. As has been described, complex cognitive and neuropsychiatric profiles are inherent to these disorders. Although pharmacological management typically is required, patients and caregivers alike can benefit tremendously from education as well as supportive and behavioral management therapies. Specifically, geropsychologists can guide patients and caregivers as they adjust to their diagnosis and cope with changes in their functioning or roles as the disease progresses. They also can play vital roles in ensuring that neuropsychiatric symptoms are recognized and treated, the living environment is safe and functional, and that appropriate long-term care has been arranged.

Patients and caregivers can play a critical role in the assessment and treatment process, and their active participation can improve functional outcome. To this end, it is vital that both patients and families receive ongoing education related to the full continuum of potential symptoms manifested in PDD and DLB. The presence of psychosis and mood changes can be particularly difficult for patients and families. As such, education regarding nonmotor symptoms as well as behavioral management strategies to minimize agitation and confusion can be particularly helpful. Education regarding the side-effect profiles of different therapeutic agents is also important, especially in cases in which neuroleptic or dopamine agonist use is required.

The geropsychologist can be important in the care of patients with PDD and DLB, but he or she may play a different role from that when treating other older individuals. A significant issue involving the geropsychologist–client relationship involves a broad definition of who the client is. Early on in the disease, the individual with the disease may have insight and be the focus of treatment. As the disease progresses, families and other caregivers are often in significant need of help, and the focus of treatment may shift to them. At times, both the patient and multiple family members may be receiving care from the geropsychologist, thus redefining the notion of one patient to one psychologist. The successful geropsychologist will become adept at recognizing and treating the needs of multiple family members.

An additional issue is the degenerative nature of these diseases, which requires constant adjustment to the inherent decline associated with the disease processes. As such, new difficulties can be expected to arise and solutions that worked last week may not be relevant the next. The ongoing changes in the individual with the disease can cause anxiety and depression, not to mention significant fatigue in caregivers.

Yet another client relationship issue involves working with patients with dementia and fluctuations in cognition. On occasion, the patient will have good insight. On others, he or she may possess a limited ability to process information. Hence, the geropsychologist must be aware of fluctuating cognitive abilities in the person with PDD or DLB and modulate treatment approaches accordingly.

Case Example 1

Mr. K was 69 years old when he noticed a tremor in his right hand. When discussing it with his wife, she noted that he moved more slowly than previously and that his face seemed generally less expressive. He had been diagnosed with depression 3 years earlier, however, and she had assumed that the changes she saw were related to his depression, which was treated with an antidepressant medication. Mr. K mentioned his tremor to his primary care physician who referred him to a neurologist. The neurologist subsequently diagnosed him with PD, which he treated with levodopa. The neurologist sent Mr. K to a neuropsychologist who found that while Mr. K had cognitive slowing associated with PD, he did not have evidence of dementia or even MCI. Approximately 5 years later, Mrs. K noticed that her husband was having increasing difficulty making decisions and she feared a decline in his memory. Repeat neuropsychological testing revealed this his cognitive abilities had declined significantly such that he was not processing information adequately and that he was not able to make decisions consistent with his educational level. Importantly, testing revealed that his recognition memory was good, but he was unable to recall information without a recognition format. Testing revealed the decline in memory retrieval seen in PDD rather than the memory consolidation difficulty seen in AD. Mr. K's course of decline and pattern of impairment was consistent with a diagnosis of PDD.

Case Example 2

Mrs. L was a 77-year-old previously healthy woman who began experiencing periods of confusion that lasted hours or days followed by periods of normal functioning. Her family worried, but she always seemed to return to her "normal self," and the family decided that her advancing age and poor sleep were the culprits. Regarding her sleep, she had become combative while dreaming, and her husband moved to another bed for fear of being hit while she was acting out her dreams. The family finally took her to the doctor when she revealed that she saw small children and animals watching her in the yard. Her husband saw only the bushes that had always been in the yard. Typical of DLB, Mrs. L. did not seem frightened or even disturbed by the hallucinations. Mrs. L was sent to a neurologist who noted that she had significant motor slowness and rigidity, which according to her husband had begun only recently and after the changes in confusion and sleep. Cognitive testing revealed significant deficits in attention, executive functioning, and visuoperceptual abilities. Mrs. L. was diagnosed with DLB. A treatment team, including a psychologist, successfully worked with Mr. and Mrs. L to help them adjust to the diagnosis and prepare for the future using both pharmacological and behavioral treatment methods.

CONCLUSION

Basic, clinical, and translation research is being conducted in institutions around the globe in efforts to advanced knowledge of the causes of PD, PDD, and DLB and speed the development of therapeutics into practice. Future studies, aimed at identifying the genetic biomarkers of PDD and DLB, will play a critical role in elucidating disease-specific mechanisms, helping to identify at-risk individuals, and developing treatments. Studies that investigate the relationship between environmental factors that affect disease risk and course, such as the effects of repeated occupational exposure to certain pesticides and regular physical exercise, also will prove important in helping researchers understand and treat these disorders.

References

Aarsland, D. (2010). Epidemiology of dementia associated with Parkinson's disease. In M. Emre (Ed.), *Cognitive impairment and dementia in Parkinson's disease* (pp. 6–14). New York, NY: Oxford University Press. doi:10.1093/med/9780199564118.003.002

Aarsland, D., Andersen, K., Larsen, J. P., Lolk, A., & Kragh-Sorensen, P. (2003). Prevalence and characteristics of dementia in Parkinson disease: An 8-year prospective study. *Archives of Neurology, 60,* 387–392. doi:10.1001/archneur.60.3.387

Aarsland, D., Andersen, K., Larsen, J. P., Lolk, A., Nielsen, H., & Kragh-Sorensen, P. (2001). Risk of dementia in Parkinson's disease: A community-based, prospective study. *Neurology, 56,* 730–736. doi:10.1212/WNL.56.6.730

Aarsland, D., Ballard, C., Larsen, J. P., & McKeith, I. (2001). A comparative study of psychiatric symptoms in dementia with Lewy bodies and Parkinson's disease with and without dementia. *International Journal of Geriatric Psychiatry, 16,* 528–536. doi:10.1002/gps.389

Aarsland, D., Ballard, C., Larsen, J. P., McKeith, I., O'Brien, J., & Perry, R. (2005). Marked neuroleptic sensitivity in dementia with Lewy bodies and Parkinson's disease. *Journal of Clinical Psychiatry, 66,* 504–514. doi:10.4088/JCP.v66n0514

Aarsland, D., Ballard, C., McKeith, I., Perry, R. H., & Larsen, J. P. (2001). Comparison of extrapyramidal signs in dementia with Lewy bodies and Parkinson's disease. *Journal of Neuropsychiatry and Clinical Neurosciences, 13,* 374–379. doi:10.1176/appi.neuropsych.13.3.374

Aarsland, D., Ballard, C., Walker, Z., Boström, F., Alves, G., Kossakowski, K., . . . Londos, E. (2009). Memantine in patients with Parkinson's disease dementia or dementia with Lewy bodies: A double-blind, placebo-controlled, multicentre trial. *Lancet Neurology, 8,* 613–618. doi:10.1016/S1474-4422(09)70146-2

Aarsland, D., Bronnick, K., Ehrt, U., De Deyn, P. P., Tekin, S., Emre, M., & Cumming, J. L. (2007). Neuropsychiatric symptoms in patients with PD and dementia: Frequency, profile and associated caregiver stress. *Journal of Neurology, Neurosurgery, and Psychiatry, 78,* 36–42. doi:10.1136/jnnp.2005.083113

Aarsland, D., Bronnick, K., Williams-Gray, C., Weintraub, D., Marder, K., Kulisevsky, J., . . . Emre, M. (2010). Mild cognitive impairment in Parkinson disease: A multicenter pooled analysis. *Neurology, 75,* 1062–1069. doi:10.1212/WNL.0b013e3181f39d0e

Aarsland, D., Hutchinson, M., & Larsen, J. P. (2003). Cognitive, psychiatric and motor response to galantamine in Parkinson's disease with dementia. *International Journal of Geriatric Psychiatry, 18,* 937–941. doi:10.1002/gps.949

Aarsland, D., Larsen, J. P., Lim, N. G., Javin, C., Karlsen, K., Tandberg, E., & Cummings, J. L. (1999).

Range of neuropsychiatric disturbances in patients with Parkinson's disease. *Journal of Neurology, Neurosurgery, and Psychiatry, 67,* 492–496. doi:10.1136/jnnp.67.4.492

Aarsland, D., Litvan, I., Salmon, D., Galasko, D., Wentzel-Larsen, T., & Larsen, J. P. (2003). Performance on the Dementia Rating Scale in Parkinson's disease with dementia and dementia with Lewy bodies: Comparison with progressive supranuclear palsy and Alzheimer's disease. *Journal of Neurology, Neurosurgery, and Psychiatry, 74,* 1215–1220. doi:10.1136/jnnp.74.9.1215

Aarsland, D., Marsh, L., & Schrag, A. (2009). Neuropsychiatric symptoms in Parkinson's disease. *Movement Disorders, 24,* 2175–2186. doi:10.1002/mds.22589

Aarsland, D., Zaccai, J., & Brayne, C. (2005). Clinical review: A systematic review of prevalence studies of dementia in Parkinson's disease. *Movement Disorders, 20,* 1255–1263. doi:10.1002/mds.20527

Ahlskog, J. E., Geda, Y. E., Graff-Radford, N. R., & Petersen, R. C. (2011). Physical exercise as a preventative or disease-modifying treatment of dementia and brain aging. *Mayo Clinic Proceedings, 86,* 876–884. doi:10.4065/mcp.2011.0252

Ala, T. A., Hughes, L. F., Kyrouac, G. A., Ghobrial, M. W., & Elble, R. J. (2001). Pentagon copying is more impaired in dementia with Lewy bodies than in Alzheimer's disease. *Journal of Neurology, Neurosurgery, and Psychiatry, 70,* 483–488. doi:10.1136/jnnp.70.4.483

Alcalay, R. N., Caccappolo, E., Mejia-Santana, H., Tang, M., Rosado, L., Orbe Reilly, M., . . . Marder, K. (2012). Cognitive performance of GBA mutation carriers with early-onset PD: The CORE-PD study. *Neurology, 78,* 1434–1440. doi:10.1212/WNL.0b013e318253d54b

Alves, G., Forsaa, E. B., Pedersen, K. F., Gjerstad, M. D., & Larsen, J. P. (2008). Epidemiology of Parkinson's disease. *Journal of Neurology, 255*(Suppl. 5), 18–32. doi:10.1007/s00415-008-5004-3

Andersson, M., Zetterberg, H., Minthon, L., Blennow, K., & Londos, E. (2011). The cognitive profile and CSF biomarkers in dementia with Lewy bodies and Parkinson's disease dementia. *International Journal of Geriatric Psychiatry, 26,* 100–105. doi:10.1002/gps.2496

Ballard, C. G., Aarsland, D., McKeith, I., O'Brien, J., Gray, A., Cormack, F., . . . Tovee, M. (2002). Fluctuations in attention: PD dementia vs DLB with parkinsonism. *Neurology, 59,* 1714–1720. doi:10.1212/01.WNL.0000036908.39696.FD

Bonelli, S. B., Ransmayr, G., Steffelbauer, M., Lukas, T., Lampl, C., & Deibl, M. (2004). L-dopa responsiveness in dementia with Lewy bodies, Parkinson disease with and without dementia. *Neurology, 63,* 376–378. doi:10.1212/01.WNL.0000130194.84594.96

Boström, F., Jonsson, L., Minthon, L., & Londos, E. (2007). Patients with dementia with Lewy bodies have more impaired quality of life than patients with Alzheimer disease. *Alzheimer Disease and Associated Disorders, 21,* 150–154. doi:10.1097/WAD.0b013e318065c4a9

Breier, A., Sutton, V. K., Feldman, P. D., Kadam, D. L., Ferchland, I., Wright, P., & Friedman, J. H. (2002). Olanzapine in the treatment of dopamimetic-induced psychosis in patients with Parkinson's disease. *Biological Psychiatry, 52,* 438–445. doi:10.1016/S0006-3223(02)01392-6

Brockmann, K., Srulijes, K., Hauser, A. K., Schulte, C., Csoti, I., Gasser, T., & Berg, D. (2011). GBA-associated PD presents with nonmotor characteristics. *Neurology, 77,* 276–280. doi:10.1212/WNL.0b013e318225ab77

Bronnick, K., Emre, M., & Lane, R. (2007). Profile of cognitive impairment in dementia associated with Parkinson's disease compared with Alzheimer's disease. *Journal of Neurology, Neurosurgery, and Psychiatry, 78,* 1064–1068. doi:10.1136/jnnp.2006.108076

Bronstein, J., Carvey, P., Chen, H., Cory-Slechta, D., MiMonte, D., Duda, J., . . . Weisskopf, M. (2009). Meeting report: Consensus statement–Parkinson's disease and the environment: Collaborative on health and the environment and Parkinson's action network (CHE PAN) conference 26-28 June 2007. *Environmental Health Perspectives, 117,* 117–121.

Burn, D. J., Rowan, E. N., Allan, L. M., Mollow, S., O'Brien, J. T., & McKeith, I. G. (2006). Motor subtype and cognitive decline in Parkinson's disease, Parkinson's disease with dementia, and dementia with Lewy bodies. *Journal of Neurology, Neurosurgery, and Psychiatry, 77,* 585–589. doi:10.1136/jnnp.2005.081711

Chaudhuri, K. R., & Schapira, A. H. (2009). Non-motor symptoms of Parkinson's disease: Dopaminergic pathophysiology and treatment. *Lancet Neurology, 8,* 464–474. doi:10.1016/S1474-4422(09)70068-7

Clinton, L. K., Blurton-Jones, M., Myczek, K., Trojanowski, J. Q., & LaFerla, F. M. (2010). Synergistic interactions between beta-amyloid, tau, and alpha-synuclein: Acceleration of neuropathology and cognitive decline. *Journal of Neuroscience, 30,* 7281–7289. doi:10.1523/JNEUROSCI.0490-10.2010

Collerton, D., Burn, D., McKeith, I., & O'Brien, J. (2003). Systematic review and meta-analysis show that dementia with Lewy bodies is a visual-perceptual and attentional-executive dementia. *Dementia and Geriatric Cognitive Disorders, 16,* 229–237. doi:10.1159/000072807

Compta, Y., Parkkinen, L., O'Sullivan, S. S., Vandrovcova, J., Holton, J. L., Collins, C., . . . Revesz, T. (2011). Lewy- and Alzheimer-type pathologies in Parkinson's disease dementia: Which is more important? *Brain: A Journal of Neurology, 134*, 1493–1505. doi:10.1093/brain/awr031

Connor, D. J., Salmon, D. P., Sandy, T. J., Galasko, D., Hansen, L. A., & Thal, L. J. (1998). Cognitive profiles of autopsy-confirmed Lewy body variant vs. pure Alzheimer disease. *Archives of Neurology, 55*, 994–1000. doi:10.1001/archneur.55.7.994

Cormack, F., Aarsland, D., Ballard, C., & Tovee, M. J. (2004). Pentagon drawing and neuropsychological performance in dementia with Lewy bodies, Alzheimer's disease, Parkinson's disease and Parkinson's disease with dementia. *International Journal of Geriatric Psychiatry, 19*, 371–377. doi:10.1002/gps.1094

Cummings, J. L. (2004). Fluctuations in cognitive function in dementia with Lewy bodies. *Lancet Neurology, 3*, 266. doi:10.1016/S1474-4422(04)00728-8

Czernecki, V., Pillon, B., Houeto, J. L., Pochon, J. B., Levy, R., & Dubois, B. (2002). Motivation, reward, and Parkinson's disease: Influence of dopatherapy. *Neuropsychologia, 40*, 2257–2267. doi:10.1016/S0028-3932(02)00108-2

Czernecki, V., Schüpbach, M., Yaici, S., Lévy, R., Bardinet, E., Yelnik, J., . . . Agid, Y. (2008). Apathy following sub-thalamic stimulation in Parkinson disease: A dopamine responsive symptom. *Movement Disorders, 23*, 964–969. doi:10.1002/mds.21949

Dalrymple-Alford, J. C., MacAskill, M. R., Nakas, C. T., Livingston, L., Graham, C., Crucian, G. P., . . . Anderson, T. J. (2010). The MoCA well-suited screen for cognitive impairment in Parkinson disease. *Neurology, 75*, 1717–1725. doi:10.1212/WNL.0b013e3181fc29c9

Dobkin, R. D., Menza, M., Allen, L. A., Gara, M. A., Mark, M. H., Tiu, J., . . . Friedman, J. (2011). Cognitive-behavioral therapy for depression in Parkinson's disease: A randomized, controlled trial. *American Journal of Psychiatry, 168*, 1066–1074. doi:10.1176/appi.ajp.2011.10111669

Dodel, R., Csoti, I., Ebersbach, G., Fuchs, G., Hahne, M., Kuhn, W., . . . Schulz, J. B. (2008). Lewy body dementia and Parkinson's disease with dementia. *Journal of Neurology, 255*(Suppl. 5), 39–47. doi:10.1007/s00415-008-5007-0

Dubois, B., Burn, D., Goetz, C., Aarsland, D., Brown, R. G., Broe, G. A., . . . Emre, M. (2007). Diagnostic procedures for Parkinson's disease dementia: Recommendations from the movement disorder society task force. *Movement Disorders, 22*, 2314–2324.

Duda, J. E., Giasson, B. I., Mabon, M. E., Lee, V. M. Y., & Trojanowsk, J. Q. (2002). Novel antibodies to synuclein show abundant striatal pathology in Lewy body diseases. *Annals of Neurology, 52*, 205–210. doi:10.1002/ana.10279

Ehrt, U., Bronnick, K., Leentjens, A. F., Larsen, J. P., & Aarsland, D. (2006). Depressive symptom profile in Parkinson's disease: A comparison with depression in elderly patients without Parkinson's disease. *International Journal of Geriatric Psychiatry, 21*, 252–258. doi:10.1002/gps.1456

Emre, M. (2003). Dementia associated with Parkinson's disease. *Lancet Neurology, 2*, 229–237. doi:10.1016/S1474-4422(03)00351-X

Emre, M., Aarsland, D., Albanese, A., Byrne, J. E., Deuschl, G., De Deyn, P. P., . . . Lane, R. (2004). Rivastigmine for dementia associated with Parkinson's disease. *New England Journal of Medicine, 351*, 2509–2518. doi:10.1056/NEJMoa041470

Emre, M., Aarsland, D., Brown, R., Burn, M., Duyckaerts, C., Mizuno, Y., . . . Dubois, B. (2007). Clinical diagnostic criteria for dementia associated with Parkinson's disease. *Movement Disorders, 22*, 1689–1707. doi:10.1002/mds.21507

Emre, M., Tsolaki, M., Bonuccelli, U., Destée, A., Tolosa, E., Kutzelnigg, A., . . . Jones, R. (2010). Memantine for patients with Parkinson's disease dementia or dementia with Lewy bodies: A randomised, double-blind, placebo-controlled trial. *Lancet Neurology, 9*, 969–977. doi:10.1016/S1474-4422(10)70194-0

Factor, S. A., Friedman, J. H., Lannon, M. C., Oakes, D., Bourgeois, K., & Parkinson, S. G. (2001). Clozapine for the treatment of drug-induced psychosis in Parkinson's disease: Results of the 12 week open label extension in the PSYCLOPS trial. *Movement Disorders, 16*, 135–139. doi:10.1002/1531-8257(200101)16:1<135::AID-MDS1006>3.0.CO;2-Q

Fenelon, G., Mahieux, F., Huon, R., & Ziegler, M. (2000). Hallucinations in Parkinson's disease: Prevalence, phenomenology and risk factors. *Brain, 123*, 733–745. doi:10.1093/brain/123.4.733

Ford, B., Lynch, T., & Greene, P. (1994). Risperidone in Parkinson's disease. *Lancet, 344*, 681. doi:10.1016/S0140-6736(94)92114-8

Fratiglioni, L., Paillard-Borg, S., & Winblad, B. (2004). An active and socially integrated lifestyle in late life might protect against dementia. *Neurology, 3*, 343–353.

Gao, X., Chen, H., Schwarzschild, M. A., & Ascherio, A. (2011). Use of ibuprofen and risk of Parkinson disease. *Neurology, 76*, 863–869. doi:10.1212/WNL.0b013e31820f2d79

Geser, F., Wenning, G. K., Poewe, W., & McKeith, I. (2005). How to diagnose dementia with Lewy bodies: State of the art. *Movement Disorders, 20*(Suppl. 12), S11–S20. doi:10.1002/mds.20535

Gjerstad, M. D., Aarsland, D., & Larsen, J. P. (2002). Development of daytime somnolence over time in Parkinson's disease. *Neurology, 58*, 1544–1546. doi:10.1212/WNL.58.10.1544

Glatt, S. L., Hubble, J. P., Lyons, K., Paolo, A., Troster, A., Hassanein, R. E., & Koller, W. C. (1996). Risk factors for dementia in Parkinson's disease: Effect of education. *Neuroepidemiology, 15*, 20–25. doi:10.1159/000109885

Goldman, J. G., Vaughan, C. L., & Goetz, C. G. (2011). An update expert opinion on management and research strategies in Parkinson's disease psychosis. *Expert Opinion on Pharmacotherapy, 12*, 2009–2024. doi:10.1517/14656566.2011.587122

Hawkes, C. H., Del Tredici, K., & Braak, H. (2010). A timeline for Parkinson's disease. *Parkinsonism and Related Disorders, 16*, 79–84. doi:10.1016/j.parkreldis.2009.08.007

Hely, M. A., Reid, W. G., Adena, M. A., Halliday, G. M., & Morris, G. L. (2008). The Sydney multicenter study of Parkinson's disease: The inevitability of dementia at 20 years. *Movement Disorders, 23*, 837–844. doi:10.1002/mds.21956

Henry, J. D., & Crawford, J. R. (2004). Verbal fluency deficits in Parkinson's disease: A meta-analysis. *Journal of the International Neuropsychological Society, 10*, 608–622. doi:0.1017S1355617704104141

Hoops, S., Nazem, S., Siderowf, A. D., Duda, J. E., Xie, S. X., Stern, M. B., & Weintraub, D. (2009). Validity of the MoCA and MMSE in the detection of MCI and dementia in Parkinson disease. *Neurology, 73*, 1738–1745. doi:10.1212/WNL.0b013e3181c34b47

Horimoto, Y., Matsumoto, M., Nakazawa, H., Yuasa, H., Morishita, M., Akatsu, H., . . . Kosaka, K. (2003). Cognitive conditions of pathologically confirmed dementia with Lewy bodies and Parkinson's disease with dementia. *Journal of the Neurological Sciences, 216*, 105–108. doi:10.1016/S0022-510X(03)00220-X

Huang, X., Chen, P., Kaufer, D. I., Troster, A. I., & Poole, C. (2006). Apolipoprotein E and dementia in Parkinson disease: A meta-analysis. *Archives of Neurology, 63*, 189–193. doi:10.1001/archneur.63.2.189

Huang, Y., & Halliday, G. (2013). Can we clinically diagnose dementia with Lewy bodies yet? *Translational Neurodegeneration, 2*, 4–9.

Hughes, T. A., Ross, H. F., Mindham, R. H., & Spokes, E. G. (2004). Mortality in Parkinson's disease and its association with dementia and depression. *Acta Neurologica Scandinavica, 110*, 118–123. doi:10.1111/j.1600-0404.2004.00292.x

Janvin, C. C., Larsen, J. P., Aarsland, D., & Hugdahl, K. (2006). Subtypes of mild cognitive impairment in Parkinson's disease: Progression to dementia. *Movement Disorders, 21*, 1343–1349. doi:10.1002/mds.20974

Kowal, S. L., Dall, T. M., Chakrabarti, R., Storm, M. V., & Jain, A. (2013). The current and projected economic burden of Parkinson's disease in the United States. *Movement Disorders, 28*, 311–318. doi:10.1002/mds.25292

Levy, G., Tang, M. X., Louis, E. D., Cote, L. J., Alfaro, B., Mejia, H., . . . Marder, K. (2002). The association of incident dementia with mortality in PD. *Neurology, 59*, 178–1713. doi:10.1212/01.WNL.0000036610.36834.E0

Levy, M. L., Cummings, J. L., Fairbanks, L. A., Masterman, D., Miller, B., Craig, A. H., . . . Litvan, I. (1998). Apathy is not depression. *Journal of Neuropsychiatry and Clinical Neurosciences, 10*, 314–319.

Lim, S. Y., Fox, S. H., & Lang, A. E. (2009). Overview of the extranigral aspects of Parkinson disease. *Archives of Neurology, 66*, 167–172. doi:10.1001/archneurol.2008.561

Litvan, I., Goldman, J. G., Troster, A. I., Schmand, A., Weintraub, D., Peterson, R. C., . . . Emre, M. (2012). Diagnostic criteria for mild cognitive impairment in Parkinson's disease: Movement disorder society task force guidelines. *Movement Disorders, 27*, 349–356. doi:10.1002/mds.24893

Litvinenko, I. V., Odinak, M. M., Mogil'naia, V. I., & Emelin, A. I. (2007). Efficacy and safety of galantamine (Reminyl) in the treatment of dementia inpatients with Parkinson's disease (open-label controlled trial). *Zhurnal Nevrologii I Psikhiatrii Imeni S.S. Korsakova, 107*, 25–33.

Luis, C. A., Barker, W. W., Gajaraj, K., Harwood, D., Petersen, R., Kashuba, A., . . . Duara, R. (1999). Sensitivity and specificity of three clinical criteria for dementia with Lewy bodies in an autopsy verified sample. *International Journal of Geriatric Psychiatry, 14*, 526–533. doi:10.1002/(SICI)1099-1166(199907)14:7<526::AID-GPS965>3.0.CO;2-0

Marsh, L. (2000). Anxiety disorders in Parkinson's disease. *International Review of Psychiatry, 12*, 307–318. doi:10.1080/09540260020002532

Massano, J., & Bhatia, K. P. (2012). Clinical approach to Parkinson's disease: Features, diagnosis, and principles of management. *Cold Spring Harbor Perspectives in Medicine, 2*, a008870. doi:10.1101/cshperspect.a008870

McKeith, I. G., Del Ser, T., Spano, P., Emre, M., Wesnes, K., Anand, R., . . . Spiegel, R. (2000). Efficacy of rivastigmine in dementia with Lewy bodies: A randomised, double-blind, placebo-controlled international study. *Lancet, 356*, 2031–2036. doi:10.1016/S0140-6736(00)03399-7

McKeith, I. G., Dickson, D. W., Lowe, J., Emre, M., O'Brien, J. T., Feldman, H., . . . Yamada, M. (2005). Diagnosis and management of dementia with

Lewy bodies: Third report of the DLB consortium. *Neurology, 65,* 1863–1872. doi:10.1212/01. wnl.0000187889.17253.b1

McKeith, I. G., Fairbaim, A., Perry, R., Thompson, P., & Perry, E. (1992). Neuroleptic sensitivity in patients with senile dementia of Lewy body type. *British Medical Journal, 305,* 673–678. doi:10.1136/bmj.305.6855.673

McKeith, I. G., Galasko, D., Kosaka, K., Perry, E. K., Dickson, D. W., Hansen, L. A., . . . Perry, R. H. (1996). Consensus guidelines for the clinical and pathologic diagnosis of dementia with Lewy bodies (DLB): Report of the consortium on DLB international workshop. *Neurology, 47,* 1113–1124. doi:10.1212/WNL.47.5.1113

McKeith, I. G., & Mosimann, U. P. (2004). Dementia with Lewy bodies and Parkinson's disease. *Parkinsonism and Related Disorders, 10*(Suppl. 1), S15–S18. doi:10.1016/j.parkreldis.2003.12.005

McKeith, I. G., Wesnes, K. A., Perry, E., & Ferrara, R. (2004). Hallucinations predict attentional improvements with rivastigmine in dementia with Lewy bodies. *Dementia and Geriatric Cognitive Disorders, 18,* 94–100. doi:10.1159/000077816

Menza, M. A., Robertson-Hoffman, D. E., & Bonapace, A. S. (1993). Parkinson's disease and anxiety: Comorbidity with depression. *Biological Psychiatry, 34,* 465–470. doi:10.1016/0006-3223(93)90237-8

Merims, D., Balas, M., Peretz, C., Shabtai, H., & Giladi, N. (2006). Rater-blinded, prospective comparison: Quetiapine versus clozapine for Parkinson's disease psychosis. *Clinical Neuropharmacology, 29,* 331–337. doi:10.1097/01.WNF.0000236769.31279.19

Molloy, S., McKeith, I., O'Brien, J. T., & Burn, D. (2005). The role of levodopa in the management of dementia with Lewy bodies. *Journal of Neurology, Neurosurgery, and Psychiatry, 76,* 1200–1203. doi:10.1136/jnnp.2004.052332

Morley, J. F., Xie, S. X., Hurtig, H. I., Stern, M. B., Colcher, A., Horn, S., . . . Siderowf, A. (2012). Genetic influences on cognitive decline in Parkinson's disease. *Movement Disorders, 27,* 512–518. doi:10.1002/mds.24946

Mosimann, U. P., Rowan, E. N., Partington, C. E., Collerton, D., Littlewood, E., O'Brien, J. T., . . . McKeith, I. G. (2006). Characteristics of visual hallucinations in Parkinson's disease dementia and dementia with Lewy bodies. *American Journal of Geriatric Psychiatry, 14,* 153–160. doi:10.1097/01.JGP.0000192480.89813.80

Müller, T., Welnic, J., Fuchs, G., Baas, H., Ebersbach, G., & Reichmann, H. (2006). The DONPAD-study—Treatment of dementia in patients with Parkinson's disease with donepezil. *Journal of Neural Transmission, 71,* 27–30.

Olichney, J. M., Galasko, D., Salmon, D. P., Hofstetter, C. R., Hansen, L. A., Katzman, R., & Thal, L. J. (1998). Cognitive decline is faster in Lewy body variant than in Alzheimer's disease. *Neurology, 51,* 351–357. doi:10.1212/WNL.51.2.351

Olin, J. T., Aarsland, D., & Meng, X. Y. (2010). Rivastigmine in the treatment of dementia associated with Parkinson's disease: Effects on activities of daily living. *Dementia and Geriatric Cognitive Disorders, 29,* 510–515. doi:10.1159/000305100

Palmqvist, S., Hansson, O., Minthon, L., & Londos, E. (2009). Practical suggestions on how to differentiate dementia with Lewy bodies from Alzheimer's disease with common cognitive tests. *International Journal of Geriatric Psychiatry, 24,* 1405–1412. doi:10.1002/gps.2277

Pandya, M., Kubu, C. S., & Giroux, M. L. (2008). Parkinson's disease: Not just a movement disorder. *Cleveland Clinic Journal of Medicine, 75,* 856–864. doi:10.3949/ccjm.75a.07005

Parkinson, J. (1817). *An essay on the shaking palsy.* London, England: Whittingham & Rowland.

Perry, E. K., Haroutunian, V., Davis, K. L., Levy, R., Lantos, P., Eagger, S., . . . McKeith, I. G. (1994). Neocortical cholinergic activities differentiate Lewy body dementia from classical Alzheimer's disease. *Neuroreport, 5,* 747–749. doi:10.1097/00001756-199403000-00002

Pillon, B., Deweer, B., Agid, Y., & Dubois, B. (1993). Explicit memory in Alzheimer's, Huntington's, and Parkinson's diseases. *Archives of Neurology, 50,* 374–379. doi:10.1001/archneur.1993.00540040036010

Postuma, R. B., Aarsland, D., Barone, P., Burn, D. J., Hawkes, C. H., Oertel, W., & Ziemssen, T. (2012). Identifying prodromal Parkinson's disease: Premotor disorders in Parkinson's disease. *Movement Disorders, 27,* 617–626. doi:10.1002/mds.24996

Ravina, B., Putt, M., Siderowf, A., Farrar, J., Gillespie, M., & Crawley, A. (2005). Donepezil for dementia in Parkinson's disease: A randomised, double blind, placebo controlled, crossover study. *Journal of Neurology, Neurosurgery, and Psychiatry, 76,* 934–939. doi:10.1136/jnnp.2004.050682

Richard, I. H., McDermott, M. P., Kurlan, R., Lyness, J. M., Como, P. G., Pearson, N., . . . McDonald, W. (2012). A randomized, double-blind, placebo-controlled trial of antidepressants in Parkinson disease. *Neurology, 78,* 1229–1236. doi:10.1212/WNL.0b013e3182516244

Rolinski, M., Fox, C., Maidment, I., & McShane, R. (2012). Cholinesterase inhibitors for dementia with Lewy bodies, Parkinson's disease dementia and cognitive impairment in Parkinson's disease. *Cochrane Database of Systematic Reviews, 3,* CD006504.

Rowan, E., McKeith, I. G., Saxby, B. K., O'Brien, J. T., Burn, D., Mosimann, U., . . . Wesnes, K. (2007). Effects of donepezil on central processing speed and attentional measures in Parkinson's disease with dementia and dementia with Lewy bodies. *Dementia and Geriatric Cognitive Disorders, 23,* 161–167. doi:10.1159/000098335

Sabbagh, M. N., Adler, C. H., Lahti, T. J., Connor, D. J., Vedders, L., Peterson, L. K., . . . Beach, T. G. (2009). Parkinson's disease with dementia: Comparing patients with and without Alzheimer pathology. *Alzheimer Disease and Associated Disorders, 23,* 295–297. doi:10.1097/WAD.0b013e31819c5ef4

Samuel, M., Maidment, I., Boustani, M., & Fox, C. (2006). Clinical management of Parkinson's disease dementia: Pitfalls and progress. *Advances in Psychiatric Treatment, 12,* 121–129. doi:10.1192/apt.12.2.121

Samuel, W., Caligiuri, M., Galasko, D., Lacro, J., Marini, M., McClure, F. S., . . . Jeste, D. V. (2000). Better cognitive and psychopathologic response to donepezil in patients prospectively diagnosed as dementia with Lewy bodies: A preliminary study. *International Journal of Geriatric Psychiatry, 15,* 794–802. doi:10.1002/1099-1166(200009)15:9<794::AID-GPS178>3.0.CO;2-1

Santangelo, G., Trojano, L., Barone, P., Errico, D., Grossi, D., & Vitale, C. (2013). Apathy in Parkinson's disease: Diagnosis, neuropsychological correlates, pathophysiology and treatment. *Behavioural Neurology, 27,* 501–513. doi:10.1155/2013/851890

Schmitt, F. A., Farlow, M. R., Meng, X. Y., Tekin, S., & Olin, J. T. (2010). Efficacy of rivastigmine on executive function in patients with Parkinson's disease dementia. *CNS Neuroscience and Therapeutics, 16,* 330–336. doi:10.1111/j.1755-5949.2010.00182.x

Secker, D. L., & Brown, R. G. (2005). Cognitive behavioural therapy (CBT) for carers of patients with Parkinson's disease: A preliminary randomized controlled trial. *Journal of Neurology, Neurosurgery, and Psychiatry, 76,* 491–497. doi:10.1136/jnnp.2004.042291

Seppi, K., Weintraub, D., Coelho, M., Perez-Lloret, S., Fox, S. H., Katzenschlager, R., . . . Sampaio, C. (2011). The movement disorder society evidence-based medicine review update: Treatments for the non-motor symptoms of Parkinson's disease. *Movement Disorders, 26,* S42–S80. doi:10.1002/mds.23884

Setó-Salvia, N., Pagonabarraga, J., Houlden, H., Pascual-Sedano, B., Dols-Icardo, O., Tucci, A., . . . Clarimon, J. (2012). Glucocerebrosidase mutations confer a greater risk of dementia during Parkinson's

disease course. *Movement Disorders, 27,* 393–399. doi:10.1002/mds.24045

Siemers, E. R., Shekhar, A., Quaid, K., & Dickson, H. (1993). Anxiety and motor performance in Parkinson's disease. *Movement Disorders, 8,* 501–506. doi:10.1002/mds.870080415

Starkstein, S. E., Mayberg, S. E., Preziosi, T. J., Andrezejewski, P., Leiguarda, R., & Robinson, R. G. (1992). Reliability, validity and clinical correlates of apathy in Parkinson's disease. *Journal of Neuropsychiatry and Clinical Neurosciences, 4,* 134–139.

Starkstein, S. E., Robinson, R. G., Leiguardia, R., & Preziosi, T. J. (1993). Anxiety and depression in Parkinson's disease. *Behavioural Neurology, 6,* 151–154. doi:10.1155/1993/539179

Stein, M. B., Heuser, I. J., Juncos, J. L., & Uhde, T. W. (1990). Anxiety disorders in patients with Parkinson's disease. *American Journal of Psychiatry, 147,* 217–220.

Storch, A., Schneider, C. B., Wolz, M., Stürwald, Y., Nebe, A., Odin, P., . . . Ebersbach, G. (2013). Nonmotor fluctuations in Parkinson disease: Severity and correlation with motor complications. *Neurology, 80,* 800–809. doi:10.1212/WNL.0b013e318285c0ed

Stubendorff, K., Aarsland, D., Minthon, L., & Londos, E. (2012). The impact of autonomic dysfunction on survival in patients with dementia with Lewy bodies and Parkinson's disease with dementia. *PLoS ONE, 7,* e45451. doi:10.1371/journal.pone.0045451

Takeda, A., Mallory, M., Sundsmo, M., Honer, W., Hansen, L., & Masliah, E. (1998). Normal accumulation of NACP/α-synuclein in neurodegenerative disorders. *American Journal of Pathology, 152,* 367–372.

Tan, L. C. (2012). Mood disorders in Parkinson's disease. *Parkinsonism and Related Disorders, 18,* S74–S76. doi:10.1016/S1353-8020(11)70024-4

Tanner, C. M., & Aston, D. A. (2000). Epidemiology of Parkinson's disease and akinetic syndromes. *Current Opinion in Neurology, 13,* 427–430. doi:10.1097/00019052-200008000-00010

Teri, L., Logsdon, R. G., & McCurry, S. M. (2002). Nonpharmacologic treatment of behavioral disturbance in dementia. *Medical Clinics of North America, 86,* 641–656. doi:10.1016/S0025-7125(02)00006-8

Teri, L., Logsdon, R. G., Uomoto, J., & McCurry, S. M. (1997). Behavioral treatment of depression in dementia patients: A controlled clinical trial. *The Journals of Gerontology, Series B: Psychological Sciences and Social Sciences, 52,* 159–166. doi:10.1093/geronb/52B.4.P159

Tolosa, E., Gaig, C., Santamaría, J., & Compta, Y. (2009). Diagnosis and the premotor phase of Parkinson disease. *Neurology, 72*(7, Suppl. 2), S12–S20. doi:10.1212/WNL.0b013e318198db11

Vann Jones, S. A., & O'Brien, J. T. (2014). The prevalence and incidence of dementia with Lewy bodies: A review of population and clinical studies. *Psychological Medicine, 44*, 673–683. doi:10.1017/S0033291713000494

Vázquez, A., Jimenez-Jimenez, F. J., Garcia-Ruiz, P., & Garcia-Urra, D. (1993). "Panic attacks" in Parkinson's disease. A long-term complication of levodopa therapy. *Acta Neurologica Scandinavica, 87*, 14–18. doi:10.1111/j.1600-0404.1993.tb04068.x

Walker, Z., Allen, R. L., Shergill, S., Mullan, E., & Katona, C. L. (2000). Three years survival in patients with a clinical diagnosis of dementia with Lewy bodies. *International Journal of Geriatric Psychiatry, 15*, 267–273. doi:10.1002/(SICI)1099-1166(200003)15:3<267::AID-GPS107>3.0.CO;2-7

Walker, Z., McKeith, I. G., Rodda, J., Qassem, T., Tatsch, K., Booij, J., . . . O'Brien, J. (2012). Comparison of cognitive decline between dementia with Lewy bodies and Alzheimer's disease: A cohort study. *British Medical Journal, 2*, e000380. doi:10.1136/bmj.2.2635.1

Walsh, K., & Bennett, G. (2001). Parkinson's disease and anxiety. *Postgraduate Medical Journal, 77*, 89–93. doi:10.1136/pmj.77.904.89

Wand, A. P. (2007). Review: Distinguishing dementia with Lewy bodies from dementia occurring in Parkinson's disease: A literature review. *Australian Journal on Ageing, 26*, 58–63. doi:10.1111/j.1741-6612.2007.00216.x

Weintraub, D., Mavandadi, S., Mamikonyan, E., Siderowf, A. D., Duda, J. E., Hurtig, H. I., . . . Stern, M. B. (2010). Atomoxetine for depression and other neuropsychiatric symptoms in Parkinson disease. *Neurology, 75*, 448–455. doi:10.1212/WNL.0b013e3181ebdd79

Weintraub, D., Somogyi, M., & Meng, X. (2011). Rivastigmine in Alzheimer's disease and Parkinson's disease dementia: An ADAS-cog factor analysis. *American Journal of Alzheimer's Disease and Other Dementias, 26*, 443–449. doi:10.1177/1533317511424892

Weisskopf, M. G., Grodstein, F., & Ascherio, A. (2007). Smoking and cognitive function in Parkinson's disease. *Movement Disorders, 22*, 660–665. doi:10.1002/mds.21373

Wenning, G. K., Scherfler, C., Granata, R., Böscha, S., Vernyb, M., Chaudhuric, K. R., . . . Litvan, I. (1999).

Time course of symptomatic orthostatic hypotension and urinary incontinence in patients with postmortem confirmed parkinsonian syndromes: A clinicopathological study. *Journal of Neurology, Neurosurgery, and Psychiatry, 67*, 620–623. doi:10.1136/jnnp.67.5.620

Wesnes, K. A., McKeith, I., Edgar, C., Emre, M., & Lane, R. (2005). Benefits of rivastigmine on attention in dementia associated with Parkinson disease. *Neurology, 65*, 1654–1656. doi:10.1212/01.wnl.0000184517.69816.e9

Wider, C., Ross, O. A., Nishioka, K., Heckman, M. G., Vilarino-Guell, C., Jasinska-Myga, B., . . . Dickson, D. W. (2012). An evaluation of the impact of MAPT, SNCA and APOE on the burden of Alzheimer and Lewy body pathology. *Journal of Neurology, Neurosurgery, and Psychiatry, 83*, 424–429. doi:10.1136/jnnp-2011-301413

Williams, M. M., Xiong, C., Morris, J. C., & Galvin, J. E. (2006). Survival and mortality differences between dementia with Lewy bodies vs Alzheimer disease. *Neurology, 67*, 1935–1941. doi:10.1212/01.wnl.0000247041.63081.98

Williams-Gray, C. H., Evans, J. R., Goris, A., Foltynie, T., Ban, M., Robbins, T. W., . . . Barker, R. A. (2009). The distinct cognitive syndromes of Parkinson's disease: 5 year follow-up of the campaign cohort. *Brain: A Journal of Neurology, 132*, 2958–2969. doi:10.1093/brain/awp245

Wolters, E. C. (1999). Dopaminomimetic psychosis in Parkinson's disease patients: Diagnosis and treatment. *Neurology, 52*(7, Suppl. 3), S10–S13.

Wu, C. K. (2011). Parkinson's disease with dementia, Lewy-body disorders and alpha-synuclein: Recent advances and a case report. *Acta Neurologica Taiwanica, 20*, 4–14.

Zaccai, J., McCracken, C., & Brayne, C. (2005). Systematic review: A systematic review of prevalence and incidence studies of dementia with Lewy bodies. *Age and Ageing, 34*, 561–566. doi:10.1093/ageing/afi190

Załuska, M., & Dyduch, A. (2011). Bupropion in the treatment of depression in Parkinson's disease. *International Psychogeriatrics, 23*, 325–327. doi:10.1017/S1041610210001687

Zupancic, M., Mahajan, A., & Handa, K. (2011). Dementia with Lewy bodies: Diagnosis and management for primary care providers. *Primary Care Companion for CNS Disorders, 13*, PCC.11r01190. doi:10.4088/PCC.11r01190

CLINICO–BEHAVIORAL AND NEUROPATHOLOGICAL SEQUELAE OF TRAUMATIC BRAIN INJURY IN THE AGING BRAIN

Lisa Delano-Wood, Erin D. Bigler, Daniel A. Nation,
Alexandra Clark, Rhoda Au, and Mark W. Bondi

Closely paralleling the unprecedented burgeoning of our aging population is the dramatic rise in the prevalence of traumatic brain injury (TBI), which has an annual incidence in the United States of 3.5 million (Coronado et al., 2012). TBI is an important public health issue that is gaining increasing attention given its high prevalence in the recent military conflicts in Iraq and Afghanistan as well as improvements in its recognition and detection in general. In the United States alone, roughly 1.7 million people per year suffer a TBI severe enough to result in the requirement for emergency care, hospital admission, or death (Faul, Xu, Wald, & Coronado, 2010), with 1–2 million being assessed in the outpatient clinic or office (Coronado et al., 2012; Mannix, O'Brien, & Meehan, 2013). Furthermore, among adults age 65 years and older, TBI is the leading cause of hospitalization and death (Faul et al., 2010; Rutland-Brown, Langlois, Thomas, & Xi, 2006). Unfortunately, long-term outcomes associated with head injury across the life span—particularly neuropsychiatric and neuropsychological sequelae—and the risk factors that potentiate and aggravate these outcomes remain poorly understood. This chapter reviews existing histopathological, imaging, genetic, and protein-based studies that, taken together, provide compelling evidence that a prior history of TBI likely represents a distal or latent risk factor for the later development of neurodegenerative disorders. Additionally, it discusses the ramifications of late-life TBI given recent evidence suggesting that older adults are especially prone to head injuries.

BIOMECHANICS AND NEUROPATHOLOGY OF TBI

Pathologic cytoskeletal changes of the axon (stretching, tearing, shearing, or deformation injuries)—collectively termed *traumatic axonal injury* (TAI)—increasingly are considered to be the primary mechanism of injury in TBI (Büki & Povlishock, 2006; Farkas & Povlishock, 2007; Scheid, Preul, Gruber, Wiggins, & von Cramon, 2003). TAI is an umbrella designation that signifies the ultimate overall pathology of TBI that may occur, including desolation of the axon, Wallerian degeneration, and cell death. At the histological level, TAI may be characterized by disruption of the axonal membranes and cytoskeletal network, leading to impaired axonal transport (Arfanakas et al., 2002). Acutely, what has been termed diffuse axonal injury (DAI; Adams, Graham, Murray, & Scott, 1982) may dominate early pathology in which axon damage results in characteristic swelling, beading, fragmentation, and degradation in which the neuropathological effects are expressed early. More recently, converging evidence has shown that when acute axonal pathology does not result in complete degradation, TAI may represent a progressive injury (Johnson et al., 2013). Thus, axonal injury likely does not occur only at the time of injury but also may manifest as progressive axonal changes continuing long after injury. These effects that follow the immediate impact-related injury often are referred to as *rolling pathology*, which is thought ultimately to lead to disconnection over time (Povlishock & Katz, 2005) and progressive degenerative pathology within the brain (Maxwell,

http://dx.doi.org/10.1037/14459-010
APA Handbook of Clinical Geropsychology: Vol. 2. Assessment, Treatment, and Issues of Later Life,
P. A. Lichtenberg and B. T. Mast (Editors-in-Chief)

Domloe, McColl, Jafari, & Graham, 2003; D. H. Smith, Hicks, & Povlishock, 2013). See Figure 10.1 for pathological characteristics and outcomes of both mild and severe TBI (DeKosky, Blennow, Ikonomovic, & Gandy, 2013).

THE POSTCONCUSSIVE SYNDROME: COGNITIVE, BEHAVIORAL, AND FUNCTIONAL SEQUELAE FOLLOWING TBI

The pathology of TBI is highly heterogeneous, with diverse manifestations resulting from both immediate (acute) and delayed (chronic) mechanisms. Whereas the majority of patients with TBI—particularly milder forms of injury—frequently show apparent complete recoveries within 1 year (Mittenberg & Strauman, 2000; Whyte, DiPasquale, & Vaccaro, 1999), several studies have shown compelling evidence that cognitive and behavioral sequelae persist for many years in some individuals (Draper, Ponsford, & Schonberger, 2007; Engberg & Teasdale, 2004; McMillan, Teasdale, & Stewart, 2012), and these findings have been corroborated by neuroimaging abnormalities (Kinnunen et al., 2011; Niogi & Mukherjee, 2010). Indeed, many patients with TBI continue to experience long-term cognitive, psychiatric, and behavioral difficulties that significantly interfere with cognitive and psychosocial functioning and, ultimately, quality of life (Bay & Liberzon, 2009; Himanen et al., 2006; Rees, 2003; Whiteneck, Gerhart, & Cusick, 2004). These findings are especially alarming in light of recent estimates showing that approximately 5.3 million people in the United States alone are living with the long-term effects of prior TBI that often can worsen with age (Langlois, Rutland-Brown, & Thomas, 2005).

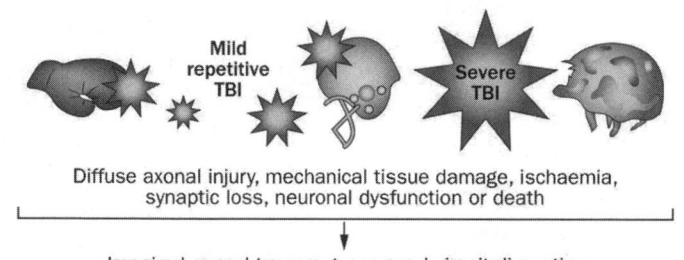

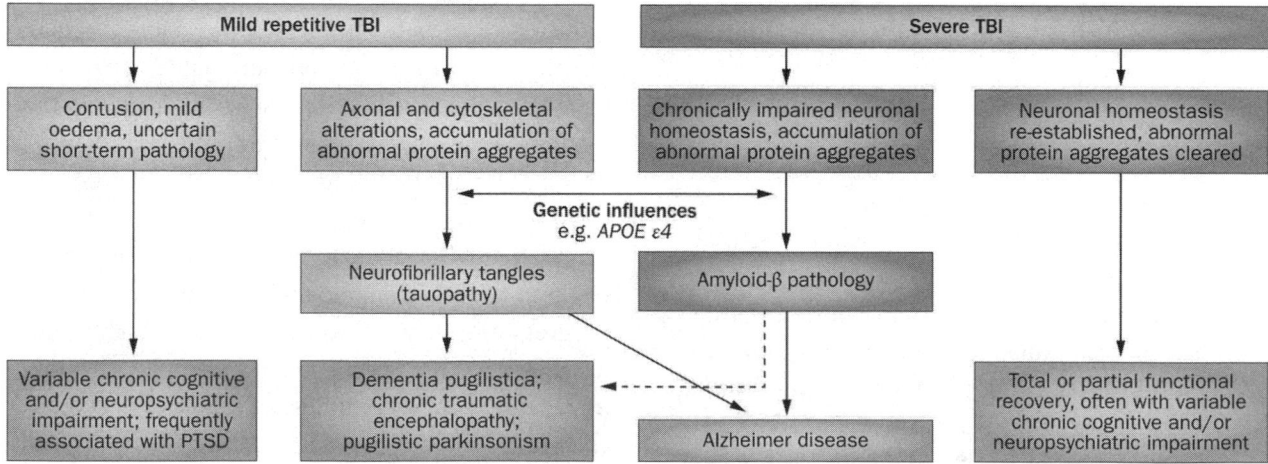

FIGURE 10.1. Pathological outcomes of mild and severe traumatic brain injury. DAI is associated with alteration in important physiological processes as well as the aggregation of abnormal protein in the brain. APOE = apoliprotein; PTSD = posttraumatic stress disorder; TBI = traumatic brain injury. From "Acute and Chronic Traumatic Encephalopathies: Pathogenesis and Biomarkers," by S. T. DeKosky, K. Blennow, M. D. Ikonomovic, and S. Gandy, 2013, *Nature Reviews Neurology, 9,* p. 194. Copyright 2013 by Macmillan Publishers. Reprinted with permission.

Cognitive and Functional Changes Related to TBI

In comparison to the often-persisting myriad of neurologic and physical symptoms resulting from TBI (e.g., chronic pain, headaches, fatigue, sleep problems, dizziness, and sensory loss; O'Connor, Colantonio, & Polatajko, 2005; Young, 2004), perceptions of changes in cognitive functioning are often more prevalent and salient. Specifically, patients with a history of TBI frequently complain about impaired concentration, problems with attention, and memory difficulties. Studies generally have shown that individuals with a history of neurotrauma frequently evidence impaired attention and concentration, reduced processing speed, and word-finding difficulties on traditional neuropsychological measures (Dikmen et al., 2009; Lezak, Howieson, Bigler, & Tranel, 2012). In addition, because the frontal lobe system is a predilection site for head injury, mild impairments of executive functions are quite common (Fortin, Godbout, & Braun, 2003; McAllister & Arciniegas, 2002). Moreover, memory difficulties sometimes are demonstrated in TBI, either because of direct effects on memory systems or secondary to disrupted attentional and executive systems (McAllister & Arciniegas, 2002; Rees, 2003). Unfortunately, the severity of perceived cognitive deficits often may not become apparent until the individual with TBI attempts to resume previous activities, such as return to work or school (McAllister & Arciniegas, 2002).

Behavioral and Psychosocial Consequences of TBI

In addition to increased cognitive difficulties, survivors of TBI consistently show much higher rates of psychological and psychosocial symptomatology when compared with the general population (Ashman et al., 2004; Koponen et al., 2002). In many cases, the severity of behavioral and psychosocial difficulties may dwarf any impairments noted on neuropsychological testing. Many of these symptoms relate to behavioral dysregulation (e.g., impulsive behavior, reduced frustration tolerance, lack of empathy, emotional lability, and apathy or aggression; Thurman, Alverson, Dunn, Guerrero, & Sniezek, 1999).

It is notable that a majority of individuals with TBI are diagnosed with one or more psychiatric diagnoses after injury, including major depression, substance abuse, posttraumatic stress disorder, and other anxiety disorders (Ashman et al., 2004; Hibbard, Uysal, Sliwinski, & Gordon, 1998; Holsinger et al., 2002; Koponen et al., 2002). Importantly, psychiatric disturbance is associated with poorer recovery from head injury (Hibbard et al., 1998; Holsinger et al., 2002), and studies have shown that the degree of psychological disturbance is not related to Glasgow Coma Scale (GCS) scores, duration of posttraumatic amnesia, or level of cognitive functioning (Jennett & Braakman, 1990; Sterr, Herron, Hayward, & Montaldi, 2006; Thompson, McCormick, & Kagan, 2006). These symptoms can complicate the picture of TBI by interfering with daily functioning and quality of life, particularly in aging patients.

TBI SUSTAINED IN OLD AGE

Of particular concern to the growing aging population is the high incidence of TBI suffered in old age. In adults age 65 years and older, each year more than 80,000 emergency department visits are the result of TBI (Faul et al., 2010), and the incidence rate (155.9 per 100,000) of hospitalization for nonfatal TBI in this cohort is nearly double that of the age-adjusted rate (60.6 per 100,000) of the general population (Coronado et al., 2012). Falls are the leading cause of all injuries in older adults (Faul et al., 2010), accounting for approximately 8% of all emergency department visits each year (King, 2003), and although other mechanisms of injury include motor vehicle accidents and assault, a large proportion of causes of injuries reportedly are unknown (Faul et al., 2010). In the United States, 90% of all head injuries are either mild or moderate in severity, with mild accounting for the vast majority of both young and elderly cases (Vollmer & Dacey, 1991). Increased risk for mortality, however, often is seen for milder injuries in the elderly (more than 65 years old) and postinjury outcomes among this group are especially poor when compared with the nonelderly (16–64 years old; Susman et al., 2002), suggesting that older age appears to negatively affect outcome following TBI. Furthermore, increased cognitive and functional limitations also have been demonstrated in older adults who sustain a TBI versus those who do not, suggesting that any existing decline because of the normal aging process may be exacerbated by such injuries. For example, Goldstein et al. (1994) found that adults over the age of 50 years that had sustained a TBI demonstrated significantly decreased cognitive performance in the domains of language, memory, and executive functioning when compared with community control patients. Furthermore, declines in both mood and interpersonal functioning have been observed in another elderly TBI sample postinjury when compared with age-matched controls (Goldstein et al., 1999). Although full recovery generally has been observed in younger adults who suffer mild injuries, the impact and response of TBI is not uniform across the life span. Instead, the impact of TBI and subsequent recovery may be influenced by a variety of physiological and medical conditions that complicate assessment and intervention within the geriatric population.

Even within normally aging populations, gray- and white-matter brain volumes decrease over time (Raz & Rodriguez, 2006), and these changes are associated with reduced synaptic density (Terry & Katzman, 2001) and lower neurotransmitter levels (Volkow et al., 1998). These age-related changes occur slowly beginning in early adulthood and then occur at hastened rates after about age 50 years (Scahill et al., 2003). Evidence from animal models suggests that the timing of cellular and genetic responses is dysregulated in the aging brain (Sandhir, Onyszchuk, & Berman, 2008). The proinflammatory and proapopotic conditions (discussed at length in the following paragraphs) already present due to the normal aging process lead to further increased vulnerability following trauma and less cognitive reserve from which to recover (Goldstein & Levin, 2001). Thus, neurological insults are particularly not well tolerated by the aged brain and explain the reduced capacity for recovery in this population. Furthermore, assessment of TBI in older adults is complicated by widespread atrophy or neuronal shrinkage, making detection of significant trauma in this cohort difficult. Increased cranial space at the time of injury allows for greater time for the pooling of blood before significant symptoms of trauma may present. Elderly patients with mild GCS scores of 13–15 have the highest rate of intracranial hemorrhaging (16%) when compared with younger adults (5%) and are more prone to subdural hematomas (Styrke, Stalnacke, Sojka, & Bjornstig, 2007). As highlighted by a 2006 case series on elderly patients with TBI, computed tomography (CT) scans and neurological examinations may first appear normal but rapid deterioration and death is possible, as all subjects were later determined to have had subdural hematomas that were undetected on original scans (Itshayek et al., 2006).

Medical comorbidities may be increasingly important in prevention and intervention strategies for TBI in old age. Approximately 80% of community-dwelling adults age 65 years and older have at least one chronic condition (Centers for Disease Control and Prevention, 2003) and nearly 73% of older adults with TBI had a prior medical condition as compared with only 28% of younger adults who sustained a TBI (Mosenthal et al., 2004). Although some studies suggest that preexisting medical conditions like diabetes, dementia, and hypertension increase the risk for TBI (Kennedy et al., 2002), the interaction of medical conditions, medications, and the physiology of the aging brain has been implicated in complicated recovery in older adults with TBI. Medication interactions potentially may affect treatment by increasing risk for secondary complications (Jacoby, Ackerson, & Richmond, 2006) and adversely affecting cerebrovascular response to injury (Thompson et al., 2006). For example, anticoagulant medications not only have been linked to increased bleeding postinjury but also to poorer outcome, longer hospital stay, and increased mortality in older adults (Itshayek et al., 2006; Reynolds, Dietz, Higgins, & Whitaker, 2003). Furthermore, medical conditions like hypertension and diabetes may affect the cerebral vasculature by altering perfusion and responsiveness (Thompson et al., 2006). Future work is needed to determine the extent to which these issues affect interventions as well as aid in establishing guidelines for care in elderly populations.

As estimates place the cost of health care utilization for TBI among older adults above $2 billion (Thompson et al., 2012), efforts should focus on prevention and efficient intervention. Reducing the overall incidence of TBI may prove most effective through primary interventions targeting older adults who are at increased risk for falls. Rapid assessment and incorporation of head CT or MRI may help in early detection of injuries in this vulnerable population, especially when no symptoms are present. Although teasing apart cognitive symptoms as a result of TBI may prove difficult, as decreased cognition also is associated with age, postinjury interventions should focus on increasing functional status and decreasing dependency. Primary and secondary interventions in those with increased risk for TBI because of medical conditions may prove useful. Current treatment guidelines for older adults who sustain TBI often are extrapolated from younger populations with TBI injuries. As such, special consideration of comorbid medical conditions, medications, and preexisting deficits that are essential to clinical management are neglected. Future research should not only focus on the prognostic significance of medical comorbidities but also establish guidelines that facilitate improving functional outcome in the presence of complex medical issues.

TBI as a Risk Factor for Poor Long-Term Outcome in the Context of Aging

It has been suggested that the biomechanics and neurobiological underpinnings of head trauma may hasten the aging process. For example, Corkin, Rosen, Sullivan, and Clegg (1989) showed that after penetrating (missile) brain injury, patients showed more neuropsychological impairment with increasing age when compared with demographically comparable orthopedic control participants. Authors of this study suggested that head injury incurred in early life may have a deleterious impact on the aging process. More recently, Senathi-Raja, Ponsford, and Schonberger (2010) also showed that the combined effects of TBI and older age had a synergistic negative effect on long-term cognitive outcome and that the level of cognitive impairment was greater with increasing years postinjury. Moreover, Colantonio, Ratcliff, Chase, and Vernich (2004) showed evidence of accelerated aging in a study of individuals treated 14 years post-TBI. Specifically, participants with histories of head trauma evidenced poorer

cognition and decreased physical and sensory function following inpatient rehabilitation. Similarly, in a study of Vietnam veterans who sustained TBI and were followed for up to 40 years postinjury, results showed a more significant drop in age-related cognitive decline in comparison with age-matched veterans, although there was no significant increase in actual rates of dementia (Raymont, Salazar, Krueger, & Grafman, 2011).

A recent cross-sectional study of 243 participants with a history of head trauma showed that years-since-TBI and age-at-injury were predictive of several poor outcomes across the aging continuum (Sendroy-Terrill et al., 2010). Specifically, increasing decades post-TBI predicted declines in physical functioning, cognitive performance, and societal participation. Similarly, increased age-at-injury significantly predicted declines in functional independence and societal participation, increases in fatigue, and decreased perceived economic barriers. A seminal 30-year longitudinal study of 84 veterans of World War II (57 participants with penetrating head injury and 27 with peripheral nerve injury) matched for age and premorbid intelligence showed that participants with a past history of neurotrauma but not those with peripheral nerve injury showed exacerbated cognitive decline (Himanen et al., 2011). Specifically, on the Army General Classification Test, the TBI group declined on average roughly 8 points during the 30-year follow-up period, whereas the control group declined on average only 0.4 points (Himanen et al., 2011). Similar to results by Sendroy-Terrill et al. (2010), accelerated cognitive decline was more pronounced for participants who were older at time of injury. Finally, Marquez de la Plata et al. (2008) showed, when compared with patients who experienced TBI at younger ages, participants who sustained head injury at older ages demonstrated greater cognitive decline as indexed by the Dementia Rating Scale (Mattis, 1988) over the first 5 years following head injury.

Taken together, although some have suggested that greater neuropsychological impairment frequently observed in older adults with a history of neurotrauma primarily is due to the normal aging process (Johnstone, Childers, & Hoerner, 1998), there is compelling evidence that prior TBI likely leads to cognitive decline that is outside of what would be expected with normal aging. In general, however, studies examining the link between prior history of TBI and long-term clinical outcome, particularly long-term longitudinal studies, are sparse. Additionally, existing studies are hampered by several confounds, including the retrospective nature of many of these studies coupled with small sample sizes and limited scope, such as the use of a single test to assess cognition (Hoofien, Gilboa, Vakil, & Donovick, 2001; Klein, Houx, & Jolles, 1996; Ponsford et al., 2008; Thomsen, 1984, 1992).

Links Between TBI and Later Development of Alzheimer-Related Neuropathological Changes

Although TBI typically is conceptualized as a static pathological event from a single insult, and from which recovery proceeds along some prototypical curve, clinically evident symptoms can arise several years postinjury, including alterations in activities of daily living that may be a harbinger for dementia such as Alzheimer's disease (AD; Marshall, Amariglio, Sperling, & Rentz, 2012). Indeed, in addition to probable interaction effects between history of TBI and aging, several epidemiological studies have shown that neurotrauma appears to represent an environmental and epigenetic risk factor for the later development of AD (Corrada, Costa, & Kawas, 1997; Fleminger, Oliver, Lovestone, Rabe-Hesketh, & Giora, 2003; Magnoni & Brody, 2010; Mayeux, Ottman, et al., 1993; Mayeux et al., 1995; Mortimer et al., 1991; Plassman et al., 2000; Rasmusson, Brandt, Martin, & Folstein, 1995; Zabar & Kawas, 2000). Although the precise nature of this relationship is still unclear, several case-control studies have reported odds ratios for AD risk following TBI ranging from 3.5 (Barclay, Kheyfets, Zemcov, Blass, & McDowell, 1986) to 13.75 (Bidzan & Ussorowska, 1995), and a meta-analytic study showed that AD risk is increased after TBI, at least for men (Fleminger et al., 2003; see Figure 10.2). Likewise, Mortimer et al. (1991) showed that the pooled relative risk for AD in patients with prior history of head trauma was 1.82 and that there were stronger associations in cases without a positive family history of dementia and in males. Finally,

another study showed that any history of brain injury increased the risk of developing AD as well as other forms of dementia, and history of severe TBI doubled the risk of developing AD (Gottlieb, 2000).

Analysis of more than 1,200 TBI survivors demonstrated that the time to onset of AD was reduced significantly in those who previously sustained TBI of any severity (Nemetz et al., 1999) and, bolstering these findings, two meta-analyses have provided support for a relationship between early head injury and acceleration of development of later dementia (Fleminger et al., 2003; Mortimer et al., 1991). Others, however, have suggested that TBI may lead to an earlier onset of dementia versus increasing the lifetime risk of developing AD (Mehta et al., 1999; Rapoport et al., 2008), and yet others have shown minimal or no association between early head trauma and later development of dementia. For example, a prospective report of military veterans followed over 50 years postinjury found that only moderate and severe TBI, but not mild head injury, was associated with two- to fourfold increased risk of AD and other dementias in late life (Plassman et al., 2000). Other studies have failed to find any association between prior history of head trauma and increased risk for AD (Bratsun, 1998; French et al., 1985). Moreover, Sayed, Culver, Dams-O'Connor, Hammond, and Diaz-Arrastia (2013) showed that in a sample of 877 individuals with dementia who had sustained TBI from the National Alzheimer's Coordinating Center Uniform Data Set, only TBI with "chronic deficit or dysfunction" was related to increased risk of dementia. It is unclear, however, how chronic deficit or dysfunction was characterized for the purposes of this study.

Although the relationship between early TBI and increased risk of developing dementia in late life remains elusive (Fleminger et al., 2003; Mayeux et al., 1996; Mehta et al., 1999; Millar, Nicoll, Thornhill, Murray, & Teasdale, 2003; Newcombe, 1996), considerable compelling data strongly suggest that there is an association between prior history of head trauma and the later development of dementia, especially AD. The neurobiological mechanisms underlying this probable link are unclear, although acceleration of underlying neurodegenerative changes and impaired cognitive reserve (discussed in the following paragraphs) are thought to

1st author	Quality*	Cs+†	Cs–‡	Cnt+†	Cnt–‡	Odds ratio	95% CI
Pre-Mortimer studies							
Mortimer (1985)	P	20	54	11	108	3.64	1.52 to 8.99
Amaducci (1986)	P	7	106	5	203	2.68	0.71 to 10.95
Chandra (1987)	Q	6	51	1	56	6.00	0.73 to 276.02
Chandra (1989)	P, Q	5	269	4	270	1.25	0.27 to 6.30
Broe (1990)	P	8	162	6	164	1.33	0.41 to 4.66
Ferini-Strambi (1990)	P	5	58	10	116	1.00	0.26 to 3.39
Graves (1990)	P, Q	19	111	8	122	2.61	1.04 to 7.15
van Duijn (1992)	P	22	176	17	181	1.33	0.65 to 2.77
Post-Mortimer studies							
Li (1992)	Q	1	69	2	138	1.00	0.09 to 11.03
Fratiglioni (1993)	P, Q	4	84	25	232	0.44	0.11 to 1.34
CSHA (1994)	P	13	149	27	393	1.27	0.58 to 2.63
Forster (1995)		22	87	16	93	1.50	0.68 to 3.41
Rasmusson (1995)	P, Q	4	64	1	33	2.06	0.19 to 104.59
O'Meara (1997)		32	317	16	326	2.06	1.07 to 4.09
Tsolaki (1997)		14	47	15	54	1.07	0.43 to 2.66

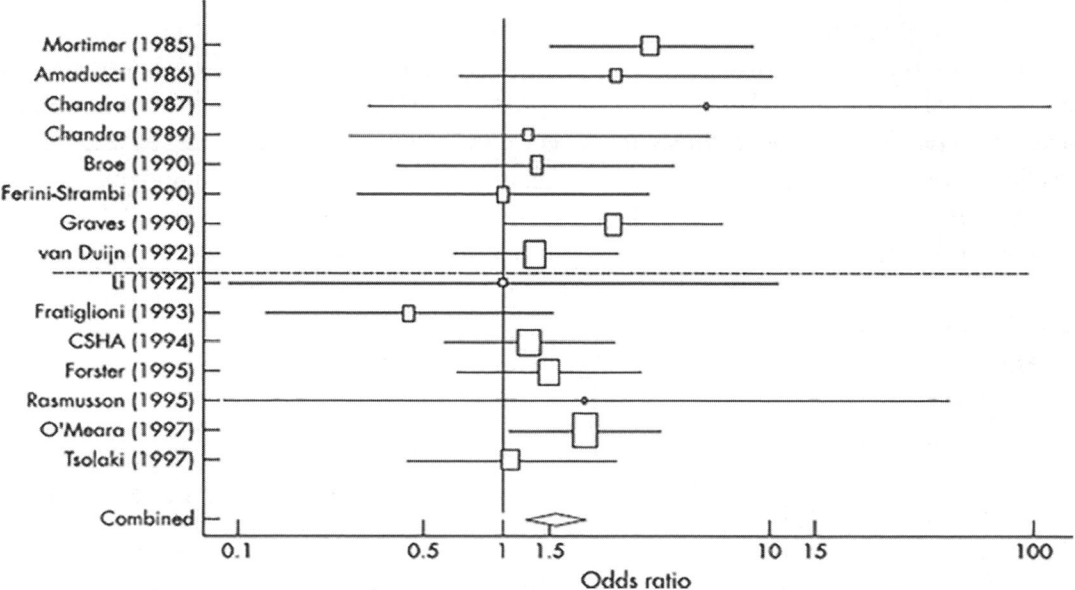

FIGURE 10.2.   Odds ratios and 95% confidence intervals for each of 15 different studies (and their combination) on the risk of developing Alzheimer's disease given a history of TBI. Odds ratio and 95% confidence intervals for each of the 15 studies and for all studies combined from the meta-analysis conducted by Fleminger et al. (2013). An odds ratio of >1 (reference line) indicates higher frequency of head injuries in the Alzheimer's cases. Pre-Mortimer studies are separated from post-Mortimer studies by the horizontal dashed line. The areas of the boxes are proportional to the inverse variances of the estimated log odds ratios. From "Head Injury as a Risk Factor for Alzheimer's Disease: The Evidence 10 Years On; A Partial Replication," by S. Fleminger, D. L. Oliver, S. Lovestone, S. Rabe-Hesketh, and A. Giora, 2003, *Journal of Neurology, Neurosurgery, and Psychiatry, 74*, p. 859. Copyright 2003 by the BMJ Publishing. Reprinted with permission.
*P, studies with head injury X years prior to Alzheimer's onset; Q, studies with matched informant type.
†Cs+/Cnl+, number of cases/controls who had sustained a head injury with loss of consciousness.
‡Cs-/Cnl-, number of cases/controls who had not sustained a head injury with loss of consciousness.

potentiate the development of progressive cognitive decline in some older adults with a history of TBI. Specifically, neurotrauma may lead to progressive and extensive neuronal loss (Johnson, Stewart, & Smith, 2010; Maxwell, MacKinnon, Stewart, & Graham, 2010; D. H. Smith et al., 1997), chronic inflammation (Gentleman et al., 2004), cytoskeletal pathology that can lead to protein accumulation (Geddes, Vowles, Robinson, & Sutcliffe, 1996; D. H. Smith, Chen, & Nonaka, 1999). As Bigler and Maxwell (2012) recently indicated, TBI itself may represent a "latent risk factor" for poor outcomes in aging insofar as the head injury event may predispose the brain to later neuroanatomical and functional changes that lead to neurodegeneration and, eventually, cognitive dysfunction. Importantly, TBI history may interact with other risk factors for cognitive decline (e.g., genetic status, frequency and age of TBI, and inflammatory factors) to increase the risk for negative outcomes. In the section that follows, specific neurobiological and neuropathological findings central to dementia in the aftermath of TBI will be described.

Chronic TBI Links to Cytoskeletal Damage, Diffuse Axonal Injury, and Neurodegeneration

Although the vast majority survives the initial impact of a concussive blow, evidence is mounting to show that TBI may initiate chronic disease processes temporally distal to the episode that ultimately may contribute to early morbidity and mortality (Masel & DeWitt, 2010). Given that neuronal death following head injury is a major cause of neurological deficits and mortality (Stoica & Faden, 2010; Yu, Zhang, Liebl, & Kernie, 2008), it has been suggested that TBI is a disease process that, in turn, perpetuates further neuronal damage and cell death over time. This continuing damage (secondary injury) is thought to involve multiple apoptotic and inflammatory mechanisms that become activated following neurotrauma (Loane et al., 2009). Specifically, following TBI, a major shift occurs in the balance between proapoptotic and antiapoptotic protein synthesis mechanics, promoting either cell death or survival (Lotocki, Alonso, Frydel, Dietrich, & Keane, 2003; Sullivan, Rabchevsky, Waldmeier, & Springer, 2005). Thus, the status of the

cerebral environment post-TBI coupled with secondary responses to the head injury largely determines long-term outcome (i.e., cell death or recovery).

The theory that impaired axonal transport leads to cell death; disconnection between brain areas; tissue loss; and, ultimately, dementia, such as AD, is receiving considerable attention in the recent literature (Chen, Johnson, Uryu, Trojanowaki, & Smith, 2009; Roy, Cohen, & Nicoll, 2005; Stokin et al., 2005). For example, Serra-Grabulosa et al. (2005) showed that severe TBI in childhood resulted in widespread white-matter loss and hippocampal atrophy 10 years post-TBI and that this hippocampal damage likely contributed to their memory impairment. The authors suggested that a number of frontal, subcortical, and limbic gray matter and white matter pathways involved in hippocampal processing and frontal-subcortical functioning may be damaged in TBI and thus may be responsible for memory and executive functioning difficulties in the aftermath of neurotrauma. Figure 10.3 shows this via a side-by-side comparison of a 14-year-old atrophic brain from a severe TBI and imaging findings from an 86-year-old patient clinically diagnosed with AD.

NEURODEGENERATIVE, GENETIC, AND NEUROINFLAMMATORY BIOMARKERS

Beta-amyloid (Aβ) which forms plaques characteristic of the AD brain has been implicated as a mechanism of AD pathology for decades, and human studies and experimental animal data have shown evidence linking TBI-related acceleration of AD-related neuropathological processes and Aβ deposition (for a review, see Honjo, Black, & Verhoeff, 2012). Indeed, studies have shown that head trauma can lead to the overexpression of the Aβ precursor protein—a well-known cell adhesion protein present in large quantities in synaptic membranes—resulting in deposition of Aβ in the brain (Graham et al., 1996). For example, several investigations have shown that Aβ plaques and intra-axonal Aβ deposits exist in the brains of roughly one third of patients with fatal neurotrauma with no preexisting diagnosis of AD or other neurological syndrome such as Down's syndrome (Gentleman et al., 1997;

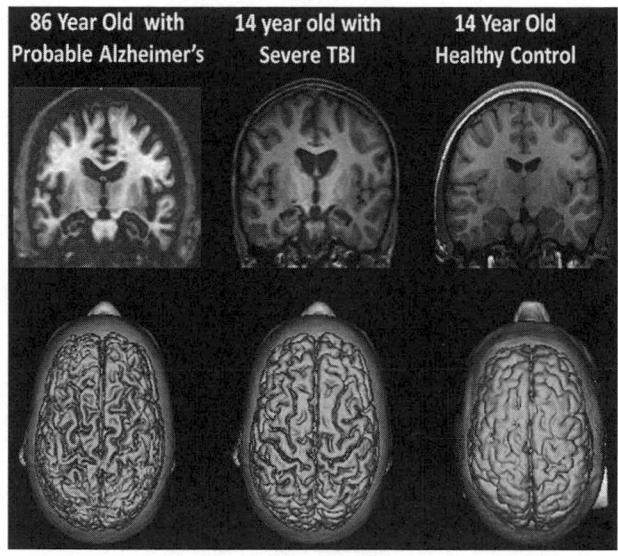

| 86 Year Old with Probable Alzheimer's | 14 year old with Severe TBI | 14 Year Old Healthy Control |

FIGURE 10.3. Side-by-side comparison of hippocampal atrophy, ventricular dilation, and sulcal widening of a 14-year-old patient with severe TBI and an 86-year-old patient diagnosed with Alzheimer's disease (AD). (Top): T1-weighted coronal images depicting hippocampal atrophy in an 86-year-old patient with Alzheimer's disease (AD) and a 14-year-old patient with severe TBI. Both patients demonstrate hippocampal atrophy, ventricular dilation, and sulcal widening. (Bottom): Three-dimensional renderings show the similarity of the diffuse pattern of atrophic change occurring in both the patients. The atrophy in the TBI adolescent is considerable, particularly when compared with the typical developing adolescent control. From "Traumatic Brain Injury, Neuroimaging, and Neurodegeneration," by E. D. Bigler, 2013, *Frontiers in Human Neuroscience, 7,* p. 9. Copyright 2013 by Frontiers Media S.A. Adapted with permission.

Gentleman, Nash, Sweeting, Graham, & Roberts, 1993; Huber, Gabbert, Kelemen, & Cervod-Navarro, 1993; Johnson et al., 2010; Loane et al., 2009; G. W. Roberts, Allsop, & Bruton, 1991; G. W. Roberts et al., 1994; D. H. Smith, Chen, Iwata, & Graham, 2003). These findings have been confirmed in biopsies of TBI survivors undergoing decompressive temporal lobectomy (DeKosky et al., 2007; Ikonomovic et al., 2004). Even in young patients with head trauma, Aβ deposits have been detected histologically within only a few hours after injury (Schwetye et al., 2010).

Although amyloid plaques develop slowly and predominantly are found in older adults (versus TBI-associated plaques that can appear rapidly after injury; G. W. Roberts et al., 1994), amyloid plaques found in patients with history of neurotrauma are strikingly histopathologically similar to those observed in the early stages of AD. Interestingly, although TBI-associated plaques largely appear in the gray matter, they also have been observed in the white matter (D. H. Smith et al., 2003). Further strengthening the evidence for a potentially causative role of TBI, experimental studies of TAI using a pig model reliably reproduced Aβ plaque pathology (Cirrito et al., 2003; D. H. Smith et al., 1999). The predominant type is Aβ42, the AD-associated form of Aβ that is prone to aggregation (DeKosky et al., 2007; Gentleman et al., 1993, 1997; Huber et al., 1993; Peavy et al., 2012; G. W. Roberts et al., 1991, 1994).

Disruption of axonal transport processes post-TBI results in the rapid and massive accumulation of amyloid precursor protein, possibly serving as the substrate for Aβ production (Gentleman et al., 1993) and subsequent tissue loss and cognitive dysfunction. D. H. Smith et al. (1999, 2003) showed in both a pig model of DAI, as well as in humans, that Aβ plaques were found in association with extensive axonal accumulations of Aβ throughout the white matter within days after injury. Thus, following neurotrauma, a mechanism may be giving rise to Aβ formation within damaged axons. As axons undergo cytoskeletal disorganization and progressive protein accumulation, there is a patchy loss of myelin staining, possibly associated with chronic death of oligodendrocytes (Shaw et al., 2001; Williams & Hammond, 2000). Given that inflammatory processes may adversely affect axonal integrity, resulting in degeneration that may persist for many years after human TBI, Chen et al. (2009) suggested that leakage of injured axons could potentiate the release of Aβ into the surrounding brain tissue, thereby leading to the formation of plaques and subsequent failed axonal transport. Although the precise role of Aβ in this pathophysiologic cascade is unknown, multiple preclinical studies have demonstrated a correlation between reduced Aβ and improved outcome (Loane et al., 2011). Given this putative role of amyloid in the chronic brain changes associated with TBI, it may be interesting to examine secondary prevention models using antiamyloid medications that are now under way in clinical trials of early and preclinical AD.

The Influence of the Apolipoprotein E Gene on Neuropsychological and Neuropathological Outcomes

A recent meta-analysis of 14 studies showed that the apolipoprotein E-4 (APOE-ε4) allele is associated with poor long-term outcome after TBI, although it does not affect initial severity of the brain injury at baseline (Zhou et al., 2008). Additionally, several case-control studies indicate that possession of APOE-ε4 coupled with an early history of TBI raises the risk of developing AD later in life (Graves et al., 1990; Lendon et al., 2003; Mayeux, Stern, et al., 1993; Mortimer, Ebbitt, Jun, & Finch, 1992; Mortimer, French, Hutton, & Schuman, 1985; Plassman et al., 2000), although several investigators have been unable to verify these findings (Chandra, Kokmen, Schoenberg, & Beard, 1989; Mehta et al., 1999; Millar et al., 2003; O'Meara et al., 1997; Raymont et al., 2008; Salib & Hillier, 1997). Mayeux et al. (1995) found a synergistic effect of head injury and APOE-ε4 genotype such that, whereas APOE-ε4 increased AD risk twofold, the co-occurrence of head injury and APOE-ε4 genotype increased the risk of AD 10-fold. There was no increased risk of dementia in participants who had TBI but were APOE-ε4 negative. Others have reported that TBI and APOE-ε4 act additively to increase the risk of AD (Katzman et al., 1996; O'Meara et al., 1997).

The specific role of APOE after brain injury is not well understood, although considerable experimental evidence indicates impairment in the clearance of lipid and cholesterol debris after insult and the recycling of these lipids to damaged cells in the repair process (Blackman, Worley, & Strittmatter, 2005). Indeed, TBI patients have a fivefold decrease in cerebrospinal fluid concentration of APOE compared with control subjects (Kay et al., 2003), suggesting that APOE may have a central role in terms of lipid delivery for growth and regeneration of axons after injury. This impaired transport and delivery of lipids then may promote the development and accrual of Aβ plaque pathology (Kim, Basak, & Holtzman, 2009).

Peripheral APOE is synthesized in the liver, but expression is also high in the central nervous system where APOE is the dominant apolipoprotein, primarily synthesized by astrocytes (Li, Fowler, Neil, Colton, & Vitek, 2010). Both animal experiments and clinical studies have shown that, following TBI, large quantities of membrane lipids are released from damaged axons and, in response, astrocytes increase APOE expression and release APOE into the extracellular space to scavenge cholesterol and other lipids for reuse during axonal and synaptic regeneration (Poirier, Baccichet, Dea, & Gauthier, 1993; Poirier, Hess, May, & Finch, 1991; Horsburgh, Cole & Yang, 2000). Indeed, a large autopsy study showed that almost half of all patients with TBI who were APOE-ε4 positive demonstrated Aβ plaque pathology compared with only 10% of TBI patients not possessing the APOE-ε4 allele (Nicoll, Roberts, & Graham, 1995). Additionally, severe TBI in humans induces cortical Aβ deposition in about 30–50% of patients (for a review, see Johnson et al., 2010). Other studies have shown that the APOE-ε4 allele is significantly overrepresented in participants with head trauma histories who display Aβ deposition (Nicoll et al., 1995; Nicoll, Roberts, & Graham, 1996). Additional multidisciplinary prospective studies are needed to more fully elucidate the role that genetic influences, such as the APOE-ε4 allele, may play in heralding cognitive impairment post-TBI, particularly in the context of accelerated aging models.

Neuroinflammation in Aging and TBI

In the context of aging, there is a slow shift over several years from the homeostatic balance of inflammatory mediators to a more proinflammatory state (Popa-Wagner, Buga, & Kokaia, 2011). The elevated level of inflammatory cytokines seen in aging has been suggested to indicate a subclinical chronic inflammatory process in older adults, referred to in the literature as "inflamm-aging" (Franceschi et al., 2007; Timaru-Kast et al., 2012). In AD, inflammatory changes have been implicated in the formation of Aβ plaques and the progression of the disease (Griffin, Sheng, Roberts, & Mrak, 1995) and, more recently, interest has been increasing in the role of neuroinflammation in the context of TBI (Morganti-Kossmann, Rancan, Stahel, & Kossmann, 2002;

Wager-Smith & Markou, 2011; Ziebell & Morganti-Kossmann, 2010).

It has been shown that within minutes of TBI, activated microglia mimic the peripheral macrophages, respond as antigen-presenting cells, and release proinflammatory cytokines (Gehrmann, Banati, Wiessner, Hossmann, & Kreutzberg, 1995). It thus has been suggested that following TBI, an initially elevated neuroinflammatory level can set the stage for an exaggerated, prolonged, and protracted inflammatory cytokine response (cytokine cycle) that eventually leads to behavioral and cognitive deficits (Badan et al., 2003; Sandhir et al., 2008). This cytokine cycle initiates early after TBI as a protective inflammatory response; in some individuals, however, this reaction may become protracted and self-perpetuating and therefore may promote blood–brain barrier breakdown and progressive neurodegenerative changes, sometimes after an initial delay (Koshinaga et al., 2000; Morganti-Kossmann, Satgunaseelan, Bye, & Kossmann, 2007; C. Smith et al., 2013). Evidence for a prolonged inflammatory response recently was found on postmortem examination in humans several years post TBI (Ramlackhansingh et al., 2011). Neuroinflammatory responses may serve as a common denominator between TBI and dementia such as AD and play a central role in mediating secondary neuronal injury in these conditions.

CHRONIC TRAUMATIC ENCEPHALOPATHY: OLD AND NEW CONCEPTUALIZATIONS

Concerns about the long-term impact of even milder forms of head injury have been amplified more recently given evidence that head injuries sustained by football players and other athletes can cause chronic traumatic encephalopathy (CTE), which was described almost 100 years ago as "punch drunk syndrome" (Martland, 1928) or "dementia pugilistica" (Millspaugh, 1937), a neurodegenerative disease thought to be caused by repeated exposure to TBI (McKee et al., 2009; Victoroff, 2013). CTE most often occurs in midlife, years or decades after exposure to multiple TBI (i.e., after one's sports career has ended). Clinical presentation varies extensively,

likely because of the different sites of damage among patients with TBI. Although controversial, CTE is thought to be characterized by a distinct tauopathy-based neuropathological profile, and it presents clinically with a history of problems with anger, rash and risky decision making, impairments of memory and attention, and substance abuse (McKee et al., 2009; Omalu, Bailes, Hammers, & Fitzsimmons, 2010; Omalu et al., 2005, 2011). Indeed, several National Football League (NFL) players have retired prematurely because of postconcussion syndrome and have described several symptoms, including but not limited to headaches, vertigo, imbalance, cognitive dysfunction, hearing and visual difficulties, fatigue, and personality and mood change (Pellman, 2003). Focusing on cognitive decline, Randolph, Karantzoulis, and Guskiewicz (2013), in a study of 513 retired NFL players, found possible cognitive impairment in 35% of this relatively young sample (64 years of age on average), which they concluded to be reflective of diminished cerebral reserve. Repetitive head trauma from contact sports over a long career may result in diminished cerebral reserve, leading to the earlier clinical expression of neurodegenerative disorders, such as AD.

Specific clinical symptoms of CTE, on the other hand, are thought to include neurologic and neuropsychological complaints coupled with various psychiatric and behavioral abnormalities (Jordan, 2000; Mendez, 1995). Early neurological symptoms often seen include speech and language problems and impaired balance and coordination, whereas later symptoms include ataxia, spasticity, coordination difficulties, and extrapyramidal symptoms, with bradykinesia and tremor (Jordan, 2000; Mendez, 1995; McKee et al., 2009; Stiller & Weinberger, 1985). Cognitive problems, such as attention deficits and memory disturbances, may become especially problematic for the patient and caregivers in the later stages of the disease (Jordan, 2000; A. H. Roberts, 1969). In addition to poor decision-making abilities, the most commonly evidenced psychiatric and behavioral changes observed in these patients are the following: lack of insight and judgment, disinhibition and euphoria, hypomania, irritability, and aggressiveness. These problems tend to surface, disappear, and then resurface at different points in time along the CTE disease continuum (Guterman & Smith, 1987; Jordan, 2000; A. H. Roberts, 1969).

Unfortunately, although CTE was first described in 1928, its actual prevalence is unknown because, despite its relatively clearly described clinical picture (e.g., personality changes, neurodegeneration, and dementia later in life), there are as yet no consensus-based criteria for clinically diagnosing this syndrome. Additionally, specific clinical phenotypes of CTE have not been delineated because individuals with a history of repeated brain injury have not been studied prospectively. Although data still are quite limited, neuropathologic data derived from autopsies of dozens of former NFL players have shown that the most severely damaged regions of the brain include the medial structures of the limbic system (e.g., hippocampal-entorhinal complex, amygdala, basal forebrain, and mammillary bodies; McKee et al., 2009) as well as hallmark abnormal progressive accumulation of a protein called high-density hyperphosphorylated tau (McKee et al., 2009), which also forms pathological tangles in people with AD and frontotemporal dementia. Importantly, this damage mirrors the location of tau protein depositions that usually are concentrated in and around the medial temporal lobe (MTL) structures.

Neurofibrillary tangles—thread-like aggregates of hyperphosphorylated tau protein—were first described histopathologically in the 1970s (Corsellis, Bruton, & Freeman-Browne, 1973). Several early postmortem studies have shown extensive tangle pathology in boxers who have sustained considerable blows to the head (Dale, Leigh, Luthert, Anderton, & Roberts, 1991; Geddes et al., 1996; Hof et al., 1992; Schmidt, Zhukareva, Newell, Lee, & Trojanowski, 2001; Tokuda, Ikeda, Yanagisawa, Ihara, & Glenner, 1991). Because these tangles also are found in the brains of patients with AD as well as in patients with other chronic neurological diseases with different etiologies (Wisniewski, Jervis, Moretz, & Wisniewski, 1979), it may be that tangles represent a more general response to neurodegenerative pathology. Tau is found intracellularly in the cytoplasm of neurons (Grundke-Iqbal et al.,

1986), and it appears to be associated with the outgrowth of neuronal processes and the development of neuronal polarity and stability (Knops et al., 1991). Tau phosphorylation seen in AD reduces microtubule binding, which causes the disassembly of microtubules and associated impaired axonal transport. This breakdown in axonal transport leads to decreased neuronal and synaptic function, increased tau aggregation, and the formation of insoluble fibrils and tangles (Mandelkow & Mandelkow, 2012). These cellular and molecular changes, particularly as they form in aggregate, further compromise neuronal function.

Although tangles observed in the context of CTE are structurally and chemically similar to those found in AD (Dale et al., 1991; Tokuda et al., 1991), they generally are found in different populations of cortical pyramidal neurons. Specifically, in CTE, tangles typically are found in the superficial neocortical layers, whereas tangles in AD generally are located within both deep and superficial layers (Corsellis et al., 1973; Hof et al., 1992; McKee et al., 2009). Furthermore, tau pathology in CTE is considerably patchy and irregularly distributed. This pattern of regional distribution is presumed to be related to the many different directions of shearing forces that physical trauma induces (McKee et al., 2009). The neurochemical disturbances that trigger tau pathology in CTE are not fully understood, but recent studies suggest that TBI-related tau pathology is not a downstream event of Aβ plaque formation (Tran, LaFerla, Holtzman, & Brody, 2011) and instead is a consequence of abnormal intraaxonal activation coupled with the accumulation of kinases that work to phosphorylate tau (Tran, Sanchez, & Brody, 2012). Figure 10.4 highlights the tau pathology and pathway thought to be central to CTE neuropathological changes.

THE ROLE OF REDUCED COGNITIVE RESERVE IN INCREASED AD RISK

The concept of cognitive reserve (Stern, 2007) posits that intelligence, education, or other life experiences are in some way protective against neurodegenerative brain changes throughout the life span (Satz, 1993). Indeed, some studies have shown

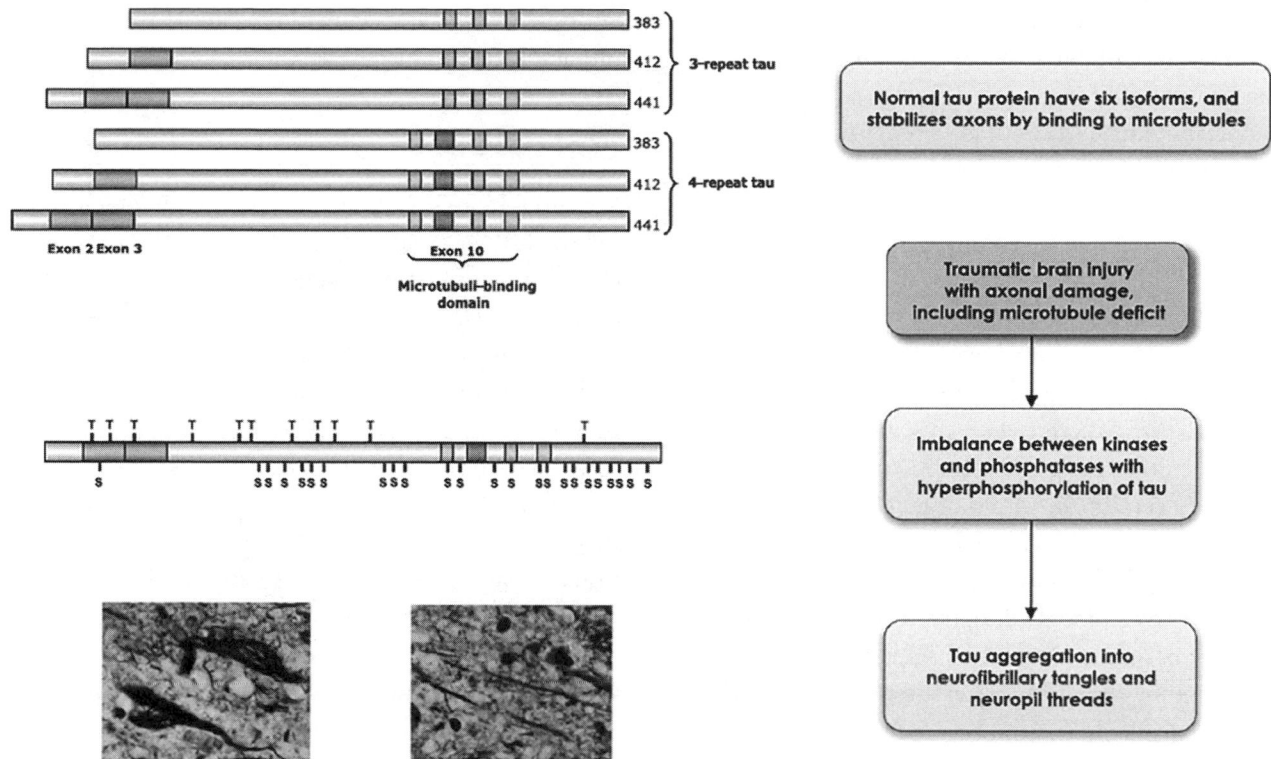

FIGURE 10.4. The tau pathway and tau pathology in chronic traumatic encephalopathy. Flow chart depicting molecular changes related to tau phosphorylation and aggregation in repeated mild TBI. Located in the neuronal axons, tau binds to the microtubules and therefore promotes microtubule assembly and stability. TBI leads to an imbalance in kinases and phosphates, resulting in tau phosphorylation and, later, neurofibrillary tangles. From "The Neuropathology and Neurobiology of Traumatic Brain Injury," by K. Blennow, J. Hardy, and H. Zetterberg, 2012, *Neuron, 76,* p. 890. Copyright 2012 by Elsevier, Inc. Adapted with permission.

a lower risk of dementia among individuals with high education and intelligence (Cervilla, Prince, Joels, Lovestone, & Mann, 2004). Even in younger participants with mild TBI (i.e., children and adolescents), results have shown that increased cognitive reserve is associated with lower levels of reported postconcussive symptomatology (Fay et al., 2010). It may be that cognitive or neuronal reserve delays the onset of clinically relevant cognitive and functional impairment.

In line with this theory, it is possible that TBI sustained earlier in life damages neurons, reduces connections between nerve cells, and subsequently diminishes the brain's capacity to function properly. Thus, later in life when AD pathology begins to accumulate, individuals with a history of TBI may demonstrate an earlier age of onset and possibly greater cognitive dysfunction and neuropathology when compared with those without a history of head trauma. Indeed, TBI may be a risk factor for AD through acceleration of AD-related pathology in tandem with reductions in cognitive reserve. These mechanisms frequently are described in the context of the margin-of-safety model, which states that the brain's organization is inherently redundant and that a considerable amount of gray and white matter can be lost without easily discernable, obvious consequences (Glassman, 1987; Raymont et al., 2008; Teuber, 1974). Thus, redundancy is decreased by the initial head injury; by the effects of aging; and, later, by the secondary effects related to the initial head injury, all of which combine to lead to the eventual appearance of new deficits and increased risk for progressive cognitive impairment years after the initial injury.

Importantly, as Stern (2006) has noted, there is not a direct relationship between amount of brain damage associated with head injury and the actual clinical manifestation of the injury. Additionally, findings are not particularly clear-cut. For example, participants with seemingly greater cognitive reserve capacity evidence a more rapid decline once dementia is detected clinically (Stern et al., 1995), given the assumption that more severe neuropathology has accumulated before clinical expression. Stern (2006) pointed to the concept of the *threshold model* (Satz, 1993) to potentially explain the apparent disconnect between degree of damage and concomitant clinical outcome. The threshold model suggests that deficits occur only when brain reserve (richly connected neuronal networks) is depleted beyond a certain threshold or level. Alternatively, the brain may cope with damage by bringing online preexisting networks in a more efficient manner (brain reserve model). Finally, it has been suggested that the brain simply compensates for any damage sustained by recruiting other alternative networks that are available (neural compensation model; Stern, 2006). Such reserve-based compensation hypotheses also have been incorporated into recent models of the pathophysiological cascade of neurodegeneration leading to the development of AD (see Jack et al., 2013).

As posited by Kolb (1995) and further underscored recently by Senathi-Raja et al. (2010), the brain may draw on similar mechanisms for recovery and adaptation to aging. This model would imply that the brain may have a limited or finite capacity for plasticity. Within this framework, Kolb and Whishaw (1998) argued that as the injured brain ages, decline may occur more swiftly and precipitously because the brain's compensatory ability already may have been depleted in response to an earlier TBI (Kolb, 1995). In line with this theory, Shimamura, Garcia, Prough, and Hellmich (2004) demonstrated that the expression of genes associated with regeneration and repair was reduced significantly in MTL regions (e.g., hippocampus) of older but not younger rodents. Interestingly, this particular gene expression differed considerably more in older versus younger rodents after neurotrauma. Similarly, Onyszchuk, He, Berman, and Brooks (2008) showed that older mice incurred greater neurodegeneration and increased functional impairment when compared with younger mice that sustained the same injury impact to the brain.

CONCLUSION

Recently, interest has been heightened in elucidating the link between neurotrauma and the later development of neurodegenerative disorders, most especially AD. Several epidemiological studies have shown that TBI is a well-documented environmental and epigenetic risk factor for the later development of AD (Fleminger et al., 2003; Magnoni & Brody, 2010), and time to disease onset of this type of dementia is reduced significantly in patients with a history of TBI (Nemetz et al., 1999). These associations are supported by the observation of both acute and chronic AD-like pathologies in autopsied brains of patients with TBI histories (Chen et al., 2009) as well as in animal models of neurotrauma (D. H. Smith et al., 1999). Although the neurobiological mechanisms underlying this link remain unclear, it is likely that acceleration of underlying neurodegeneration and impaired cognitive reserve secondary to the TBI potentiate the development of progressive cognitive decline. Specifically, extensive neuronal loss seen in AD patients with a history of TBI may be related to chronic inflammation and subsequent cytoskeletal pathology that impair the brain's ability to move and use proteins (Mannix & Whalen, 2012). Moreover, studies suggest that genetic risk factors for AD (i.e., APOE-ε4 allele) may promote the development and accrual of Aβ plaque pathology (Nicoll et al., 1995; Sivanandam & Thakur, 2012) or impair its clearance and, in turn, lead to increased brain inflammation and cognitive dysfunction.

Because of the rapid aging of the general population, the number of older adults with history of head trauma will increase dramatically. Thus, we quickly are entering an era in which an unprecedented number of older adults with a history of TBI will present for clinical care. Unfortunately, understanding the relationship between TBI and the later development of cognitive impairment in the context of aging has been especially challenging as outcome appears to be multifactorial and considerably complex. As Zappalà, Thiebaut, Schotten, and Eslinger (2012) stated,

"TBI is frequently not a 'focal' injury; it is not purely vascular nor degenerative . . . nor inflammatory . . . it escapes most of the well-known pathophysiological interpretations, rendering it difficult to understand and accept" (p. 7). Indeed, a host of genetic, inflammatory, genetic, and protein-based risk factors are thought to underlie the cognitive sequelae observed in patients with TBI; however, little is understood in terms of how these risk factors may interact to produce "rolling" pathology central to the delayed chronic phase of damage that occurs in individuals who have sustained neurotrauma. Thus, there is a critical need to better elucidate the long-term consequences of TBI as well as its interaction with the aging process and other environmental, genetic, and neuroinflammatory biomarkers to assist in the development of more effective strategies to stave off and possibly prevent TBI-related progressive cognitive decline.

References

Adams, J. H., Graham, D. I., Murray, L. S., & Scott, G. (1982). Diffuse axonal injury due to nonmissile head injury in humans: An analysis of 45 cases. *Annals of Neurology, 12,* 557–563. doi:10.1002/ana.410120610

Arfanakas, K., Haughton, V. M., Carew, J. D., Rogers, B. P., Dempsey, R. J., & Meyerand, M. E. (2002). Diffusion tensor MR imaging in diffuse axonal injury. *American Journal of Neuroradiology, 23,* 794–802.

Ashman, T. A., Spielman, L. A., Hibbard, M. R., Silver, J. M., Chandna, T., & Gordon, W. A. (2004). Psychiatric challenges in the first 6 years after traumatic brain injury: Cross-sequential analyses of axis I disorders. *Archives of Physical Medicine and Rehabilitation, 85,* S36–S42. doi:10.1016/j.apmr.2003.08.117

Badan, I., Buchhold, B., Hamm, A., Graz, M., Walker, L. C., Graz, L., . . . Popa-Wagner, A. (2003). Accelerated glial reactivity to stroke in aged rats correlates with reduced functional recovery. *Journal of Cerebral Blood Flow and Metabolism, 23,* 845–854. doi:10.1097/01.WCB.0000071883.63724.A7

Barclay, L. L., Kheyfets, S., Zemcov, A., Blass, J. P., & McDowell, F. H. (1986). Risk factors in Alzheimer's disease. In A. Fisher, I. Hanin, & C. Lauchman (Eds.), *Alzheimer's and Parkinson's disease* (pp. 141–146). New York, NY: Plenum. doi:10.1007/978-1-4613-2179-8_18

Bay, E. H., & Liberzon, I. (2009). Early stress response: A vulnerability framework for functional impairment following mild TBI. *Research and Theory for Nursing Practice, 23,* 42–61. doi:10.1891/1541-6577.23.1.42

Bidzan, L., & Ussorowska, D. (1995). Risk factors for dementia of Alzheimer type. *Psychiatria Polska, 29,* 297–306.

Bigler, E. D. (2013). Traumatic brain injury, neuroimaging, and neurodegeneration. *Frontiers in Human Neuroscience, 7,* 1–15.

Bigler, E. D., & Maxwell, W. L. (2012). Neuropathology of mild traumatic brain injury: Relationship to neuroimaging findings. *Brain Imaging and Behavior, 6,* 108–136.

Blackman, J. A., Worley, G., & Strittmatter, W. J. (2005). Apolipoprotein E and brain injury: Implications of children. *Developmental Medicine and Child Neurology, 47,* 64–70. doi:10.1111/j.1469-8749.2005.tb01042.x

Blennow, K., Hardy, J., & Zetterberg, H. (2012). The neuropathology and neurobiology of traumatic brain injury. *Neuron, 76,* 886–899. doi:10.1016/j.neuron.2012.11.021

Bratsun, A. L. (1998). Risk factors of dementia Alzheimer's type. *Zhurnal Nevrologii I Psikhiatrii Imeni S.S. Korsakova, 98,* 16–20.

Büki, A., & Povlishock, J. T. (2006). All roads lead to disconnection? Traumatic axonal injury revisited. *Acta Neurochirurgica, 148,* 181–194. doi:10.1007/s00701-005-0674-4

Centers for Disease Control and Prevention. (2003). Public health and aging: Trends in aging—United States and worldwide. *Morbidity and Mortality Weekly Report, 52*(6), 101.

Cervilla, J., Prince, M., Joels, S., Lovestone, S., & Mann, A. (2004). Premorbid cognitive testing predicts the onset of dementia and Alzheimer's disease better than independently of APOE genotype. *Journal of Neurology, Neurosurgery, and Psychiatry, 75,* 1100–1106. doi:10.1136/jnnp.2003.028076

Chandra, V., Kokmen, E., Schoenberg, B. S., & Beard, C. M. (1989). Head trauma with loss of consciousness as a risk factor for Alzheimer's disease. *Neurology, 39,* 1576–1578. doi:10.1212/WNL.39.12.1576

Chen, X. H., Johnson, V. B., Uryu, K., Trojanowaki, J., & Smith, D. A. (2009). A lack of amyloid B plaques despite persistent accumulation of amyloid b in axons of long-term survivors of traumatic brain injury. *Brain Pathology, 19,* 214–223. doi:10.1111/j.1750-3639.2008.00176.x

Cirrito, J. R., May, P. C., O'Dell, M. A., Taylor, J. W., Parsadanian, M., Cramer, J. W., . . . Holtzman, D. M. (2003). In vivo assessment of brain interstitial fluid with microdialysis reveals plaque-associated changes in amyloid-B metabolism and half-life. *Journal of Neuroscience, 23,* 8844–8853.

Colantonio, A., Ratcliff, G., Chase, S., & Vernich, L. (2004). Aging with traumatic brain injury: Long-term health conditions. *International Journal of Rehabilitation Research, 27,* 209–214. doi:10.1097/00004356-200409000-00006

Corkin, S., Rosen, T. J., Sullivan, E. V., & Clegg, R. A. (1989). Penetrating head injury in young adulthood exacerbates cognitive decline in later years. *Journal of Neuroscience, 9,* 3876–3883.

Coronado, V. G., McGuire, L. C., Sarmiento, K., Bell, J., Lionbarger, M. R., Jones, C. D., . . . Xu, L. (2012). Trends in traumatic brain injury in the US and the public health response. *Journal of Safety Research, 43,* 299–307. doi:10.1016/j.jsr.2012.08.011

Corrada, M. M., Costa, P. T., & Kawas, C. H. (1997). Head injury and the risk of developing Alzheimer's disease. *Neurology, 48,* A301.

Corsellis, J. A., Bruton, C. J., & Freeman-Browne, D. (1973). The aftermath of boxing. *Psychological Medicine, 3,* 270–303. doi:10.1017/S0033291700049588

Dale, G. E., Leigh, P. N., Luthert, P., Anderton, B. H., & Roberts, G. W. (1991). Neurofibrillary tangles in dementia pugilistica are ubiquitinated. *Journal of Neurology, Neurosurgery, and Psychiatry, 54,* 116–118. doi:10.1136/jnnp.54.2.116

DeKosky, S. T., Abrahamson, E. E., Ciallella, J. R., Paljug, W. R., Wisniewski, R., Clark, R. S., & Ikonomovic, M. D. (2007). Association of increased cortical soluble abeta42 levels with diffuse plaques after severe brain injury in humans. *Archives of Neurology, 64,* 541–544. doi:10.1001/archneur.64.4.541

DeKosky, S. T., Blennow, K., Ikonomovic, M. D., & Gandy, S. (2013). Acute and chronic traumatic encephalopathies: Pathogenesis and biomarkers. *Nature Reviews Neurology, 9,* 192–200. doi:10.1038/nrneurol.2013.36

Dikmen, S. S., Corrigan, J. D., Levin, H. S., Machamer, J., Stiers, W., & Weisskopf, M. G. (2009). Cognitive outcome following traumatic brain injury. *Journal of Head Trauma Rehabilitation, 24,* 430–438. doi:10.1097/HTR.0b013e3181c133e9

Draper, K., Ponsford, J., & Schonberger, M. (2007). Psychosocial and emotional outcomes 10 years following traumatic brain injury. *Journal of Head Trauma Rehabilitation, 22,* 278–287. doi:10.1097/01.HTR.0000290972.63753.a7

Engberg, A. W., & Teasdale, T. W. (2004). Psychosocial outcome following traumatic brain injury in adults: A long-term population-based follow-up. *Brain Injury, 18,* 533–545. doi:10.1080/02699050310001645829

Farkas, O., & Povlishock, J. T. (2007). Cellular and subcellular change evoked by diffuse traumatic brain injury: A complex web of change extending far beyond focal damage. *Progress in Brain Research, 161,* 43–59. doi:10.1016/S0079-6123(06)61004-2

Faul, M., Xu, L., Wald, M. M., & Coronado, V. G. (2010). *Traumatic brain injury in the Unites States: Emergency department visits, hospitalization, and deaths, 2002–2006.* Atlanta, GA: Centers for Disease Control and Prevention, National Center for Injury Prevention and Control.

Fay, T. B., Yeates, K. O., Taylor, H. G., Bangert, B., Dietrich, A., Nuss, K. E., . . . Wright, M. (2010). Cognitive reserve as a moderator of postconcussive symptoms in children with complicated and uncomplicated mild traumatic brain injury. *Journal of the International Neuropsychological Society, 16,* 94–105. doi:10.1017/S1355617709991007

Fleminger, S., Oliver, D. L., Lovestone, S., Rabe-Hesketh, S., & Giora, A. (2003). Head injury as a risk factor for Alzheimer's disease: The evidence 10 years on; A partial replication. *Journal of Neurology, Neurosurgery, and Psychiatry, 74,* 857–862. doi:10.1136/jnnp.74.7.857

Fortin, S., Godbout, L., & Braun, C. M. J. (2003). Cognitive structure of executive deficits in frontally lesioned head trauma patients performing activities of daily living. *Cortex, 39,* 273–291. doi:10.1016/S0010-9452(08)70109-6

Franceschi, C., Capri, M., Monti, D., Giunta, S., Olivieri, F., Sevini, F., . . . Salvioli, S. (2007). Inflammaging and anti-inflammaging: A systemic perspective on aging and longevity emerged from studies in humans. *Mechanisms of Ageing and Development, 128,* 92–105. doi:10.1016/j.mad.2006.11.016

French, L. R., Schuman, L. M., Mortimer, J. A., Hutton, J. T., Boatman, R. A., & Christians, B. (1985). A case-control study of dementia of the Alzheimer type. *American Journal of Epidemiology, 121,* 414–421.

Geddes, J. F., Vowles, G. H., Robinson, S. F., & Sutcliffe, J. C. (1996). Neurofibrillary tangles, but not Alzheimer-type pathology, in a young boxer. *Neuropathology and Applied Neurobiology, 22,* 12–16. doi:10.1111/j.1365-2990.1996.tb00840.x

Gehrmann, J., Banati, R. B., Wiessner, C., Hossmann, K. A., & Kreutzberg, G. W. (1995). Reactive microglia in cerebral ischaemia: An early mediator of tissue damage? *Neuropathology and Applied Neurobiology, 21,* 277–289. doi:10.1111/j.1365-2990.1995.tb01062.x

Gentleman, S. M., Greenberg, B. D., Savage, M. J., Newman, S. J., Roberts, G. W., Griffin, W. T., & Graham, D. I. (1997). AB42 is the predominant form of amyloid B-protein in the brains of short-term survivors of head injury. *Neuroreport, 8,* 1519–1522. doi:10.1097/00001756-199704140-00039

Gentleman, S. M., Leclercq, P. D., Moyes, L., Graham, D. I., Smith, C., Griffin, W. S., & Nicoll, J. A. (2004). Long-term intracerebral inflammatory response after traumatic brain injury. *Forensic Science International, 146,* 97–104. doi:10.1016/j.forsciint.2004.06.027

Gentleman, S. M., Nash, M. J., Sweeting, C. J., Graham, D. I., & Roberts, G. W. (1993). Beta-amyloid precursor protein (beta APP) as a marker for axonal injury after head injury. *Neuroscience Letters, 160,* 139–144. doi:10.1016/0304-3940(93)90398-5

Glassman, R. B. (1987). An hypothesis about redundancy and reliability in the brains of higher species: Analogies with genes, internal organs, and engineering systems. *Neuroscience and Biobehavioral Reviews, 11,* 275–285. doi:10.1016/S0149-7634(87)80014-3

Goldstein, F. C., & Levin, H. S. (2001). Cognitive outcome after mild and moderate traumatic brain injury in older adults. *Journal of Clinical and Experimental Neuropsychology, 23,* 739–753. doi:10.1076/jcen.23.6.739.1028

Goldstein, F. C., Levin, H. S., Goldman, W. P., Kalechstein, A. D., Clark, A., & Kenehan-Altonen, T. (1999). Cognitive and behavioral sequelae of closed head injury in older adults according to their significant others. *Journal of Neuropsychiatry and Clinical Neurosciences, 11,* 38–44.

Goldstein, F. C., Levin, H. S., Presley, R. M., Searcy, J., Colohan, A. R., Eisenberg, H. M., . . . Kusnerik-Bertolino, L. (1994). Neurobehavioral consequences of closed head injury in older adults. *Journal of Neurology, Neurosurgery, and Psychiatry, 57,* 961–966. doi:10.1136/jnnp.57.8.961

Gottlieb, S. (2000). Head injury doubles the risk of Alzheimer's disease. *British Medical Journal, 321,* 1100.

Graham, D. I., Gentleman, S. M., Nicoll, J. A. R., Royston, M. C., McKenzie, J. E., Roberts, G. W., & Griffin, W. S. (1996). Altered B-APP metabolism after head injury and its relationship to the etiology of Alzheimer's disease. *Acta Neurochirurgica, 66,* 96–102.

Graves, A. B., White, E., Koepsell, T. D., Reifler, B. V., van Belle, G., Larson, E. B., & Raskind, M. (1990). The association between head trauma and Alzheimer's disease. *American Journal of Epidemiology, 131,* 491–501.

Griffin, W. S., Sheng, J. G., Roberts, G. W., & Mrak, R. E. (1995). Interleukin-1 expression in different plaque types in Alzheimer's disease: Significant in plaque evolution. *Journal of Neuropathology and Experimental Neurology, 54,* 276–281. doi:10.1097/00005072-199503000-00014

Grundke-Iqbal, I., Iqbal, K., Tung, Y. C., Quinlan, M., Wisniewski, H. M., & Binder, L. I. (1986). Abnormal phosphorylation of the microtubule-associated protein tau (tau) in Alzheimer cytoskeletal pathology. *Proceedings of the National Academy of Sciences of the United States of America, 83,* 4913–4917. doi:10.1073/pnas.83.13.4913

Guterman, A., & Smith, R. W. (1987). Neurological sequelae of boxing. *Sports Medicine, 4,* 194–210. doi:10.2165/00007256-198704030-00004

Hibbard, M. R., Uysal, S., Sliwinski, M., & Gordon, W. A. (1998). Undiagnosed health issues individuals with traumatic brain injury living in the community. *Journal of Head Trauma Rehabilitation, 13,* 47–57. doi:10.1097/00001199-199808000-00005

Himanen, L., Portin, R., Hamalainen, P., Hurme, S., Hiekkanen, H., & Tenovuo, O. (2011). Risk factors for reduced survival after traumatic brain injury: A 30-year follow-up study. *Brain Injury, 25,* 443–452. doi:10.3109/02699052.2011.556580

Himanen, L., Portin, R., Isoniemi, H., Helenius, H., Kurki, T., & Tenovuo, O. (2006). Longitudinal cognitive changes in traumatic brain injury: A 30-year follow-up study. *Neurology, 66,* 187–192. doi:10.1212/01.wnl.0000194264.60150.d3

Hof, P. R., Bouras, C., Buee, L., Delacourte, A., Perl, D. P., & Morrison, J. H. (1992). Differential distribution of neurofibrillary tangles in the cerebral cortex of dementia pugilistica and Alzheimer's disease cases. *Acta Neuropathologica, 85,* 23–30. doi:10.1007/BF00304630

Holsinger, T., Steffens, D. C., Phillips, C., Helms, R. J., Havlik, J. C. S., Breitner, J. M., . . . Plassman, B. L. (2002). Head injury in early adulthood and the lifetime risk of depression. *Archives of General Psychiatry, 59,* 17–22. doi:10.1001/archpsyc.59.1.17

Honjo, K., Black, S. E., & Verhoeff, N. P. (2012). Alzheimer's disease, cerebrovascular disease, and the β-amyloid cascade. *Canadian Journal of Neurological Sciences, 39,* 712–728.

Hoofien, D., Gilboa, A., Vakil, E., & Donovick, P. J. (2001). Traumatic brain injury 10-20 years later: A comprehensive outcome study of psychiatric symptomatology, cognitive abilities, and psychosocial functioning. *Brain Injury, 15,* 189–209. doi:10.1080/026990501300005659

Horsburgh, K., Cole, G. M., & Yang, F. (2000). B-amyloid (Abeta) 42(43), abeta42, abeta40, and apoE immunostaining of plaques in fatal head injury. *Neuropathololgy and Applied Neurobiology, 26,* 124–132. doi:10.1046/j.1365-2990.2000.026002124.x

Huber, A., Gabbert, K., Kelemen, J., & Cervod-Navarro, J. (1993). Density of amyloid plaques in brains after head trauma. *Journal of Neurotrauma, 10,* 180.

Ikonomovic, M. D., Uryu, K., Abrahamson, E. E., Ciallella, J. R., Trojanowski, J. Q., Lee, M. V., . . . DeKosky, S. T. (2004). Alzheimer's pathology in human temporal cortex surgically excised after severe brain injury. *Experimental Neurology, 190,* 192–203. doi:10.1016/j.expneurol.2004.06.011

Itshayek, E., Rosenthal, G., Fraifeld, S., Perez-Sanchez, X., Cohen, J. E., & Spektor, S. (2006). Delayed posttraumatic acute subdural hematoma in elderly patients on anticoagulation. *Neurosurgery, 58*, E851–E856. doi:10.1227/01.NEU.0000209653.82936.96

Jack, C. R., Knopman, D. S., Jagust, W. J., Petersen, R. C., Weiner, M. W., Aisen, P. S., . . . Trojanowski, J. Q. (2013). Tracking pathophysiological processes in Alzheimer's disease: An updated hypothetical model of dynamic biomarkers. *Lancet Neurology, 12*, 207–216.

Jacoby, S. F., Ackerson, T. H., & Richmond, T. S. (2006). Outcome from serious injury in older adults. *Journal of Nursing Scholarship, 38*, 133–140. doi:10.1111/j.1547-5069.2006.00090.x

Jennett, B., & Braakman, R. (1990). Severe traumatic brain injury. *Journal of Neurosurgery, 73*, 479–480.

Johnson, V. E., Stewart, J. E., Begbie, F. D., Trojanowski, J. Q., Smith, D. H., & Stewart, W. (2013). Inflammation and white matter degeneration persist for years after a single traumatic brain injury. *Brain: A Journal of Neurology, 136*, 28–42. doi:10.1093/brain/aws322

Johnson, V. E., Stewart, W., & Smith, D. H. (2010). Traumatic brain injury and amyloid-B pathology: A link to Alzheimer's disease? *Nature Reviews Neuroscience, 11*, 361–370.

Johnstone, B., Childers, M. L., & Hoerner, J. (1998). The effects of normal ageing on neuropsychological functioning following traumatic brain injury. *Brain Injury, 12*, 569–576. doi:10.1080/026990598122331

Jordan, B. D. (2000). Chronic traumatic brain injury associated with boxing. *Seminars in Neurology, 20*, 179–185. doi:10.1055/s-2000-9826

Katzman, R., Galasko, D. R., Saitoh, R., Chen, X., Pay, M. M., Booth, A., & Thomas, R. G. (1996). Apolipoprotein-epsilon4 and head trauma: Synergistic or additive risks? *Neurology, 46*, 889–891.

Kay, A. D., Petzold, A., Kerr, M., Keir, G., Thompson, E. J., & Nicoll, J. A. (2003). Cerebrospinal fluid apolipoprotein E concentration decreases after traumatic brain injury. *Journal of Neurotrauma, 20*, 243–250. doi:10.1089/089771503321532824

Kennedy, R. L., Henry, J., Chapman, A. J., Nayar, R., Grant, P., & Morris, A. D. (2002). Accidents in patients with insulin-treated diabetes: Increased risk of low-impact falls but not motor vehicle crashes—A prospective register-based study. *Journal of Trauma, 52*, 660–666. doi:10.1097/00005373-200204000-00008

Kim, J., Basak, J. M., & Holtzman, D. M. (2009). The role of apolipoprotein E in Alzheimer's disease. *Neuron, 63*, 287–303. doi:10.1016/j.neuron.2009.06.026

King, M. B. (2003). Falls. In W. Hazzard, J. P. Blass, & J. B. Halter (Eds.), *Principles of geriatric medicine and gerontology* (pp. 1517–1529). New York, NY: McGraw Hill.

Kinnunen, K. M., Greenwood, R., Powell, J. H., Leech, R., Hawkins, P. C., Bonnelle, V., . . . Sharp, D. J. (2011). White matter damage and cognitive impairment after traumatic brain injury. *Brain: A Journal of Neurology, 134*, 449–463. doi:10.1093/brain/awq347

Klein, M., Houx, P. J., & Jolles, J. (1996). Long-term persisting cognitive sequelae of traumatic brain injury and the effect of age. *Journal of Nervous and Mental Disease, 184*, 459–467. doi:10.1097/00005053-199608000-00002

Knops, J., Kosik, K. S., Lee, G., Pardee, J. D., Cohen-Gould, L., & McConlogue, L. (1991). Overexpression of tau in nonneuronal cell induces long cellular processes. *Journal of Cell Biology, 114*, 725–733. doi:10.1083/jcb.114.4.725

Kolb, B. (1995). *Brain plasticity and behavior.* Hillsdale, NJ: Erlbaum.

Kolb, B., & Whishaw, I. Q. (1998). Brain plasticity and behavior. *Annual Review of Psychology, 49*, 43–64. doi:10.1146/annurev.psych.49.1.43

Koponen, S., Taiminen, T., Portin, R., Himanen, L., Isoniemi, H., Hinkka, S., & Tenovuo, O. (2002). Axis I and II psychiatric disorders after traumatic brain injury: A 30-year follow-up study. *American Journal of Psychiatry, 159*, 1315–1321. doi:10.1176/appi.ajp.159.8.1315

Koshinaga, M., Katayama, Y., Fukushima, M., Oshima, H., Suma, T., & Takahata, T. (2000). Rapid and widespread microglial activation induced by traumatic brain injury in rat brain slices. *Journal of Neurotrauma, 17*, 185–192. doi:10.1089/neu.2000.17.185

Langlois, J. A., Rutland-Brown, W., & Thomas, K. E. (2005). The incidence of traumatic brain injury among children in the United States; Differences by race. *Journal of Head Trauma Rehabilitation, 20*, 229–238. doi:10.1097/00001199-200505000-00006

Lendon, C. L., Harris, J. M., Pritchard, A. L., Nicoll, J. A. R., Teasdale, G. M., & Murray, G. (2003). Genetic variation of the APOE promoter and outcome after head injury. *Neurology, 61*, 683–685. doi:10.1212/01.WNL.0000078033.81925.80

Lezak, M., Howieson, D. B., Bigler, E. D., & Tranel, D. (2012). *Neuropsychological assessment.* New York, NY: Oxford University Press.

Li, F. Q., Fowler, K. A., Neil, J. E., Colton, C. A., & Vitek, M. P. (2010). An apolipoprotein E-mimetic stimulates axonal regeneration and remyelination after peripheral nerve injury. *Journal of Pharmacology and Experimental Therapeutics, 334*, 106–115. doi:10.1124/jpet.110.167882

Loane, D. J., Pocivavsek, A., Moussa, C., Thompson, E. H., Matsuoka, R., Faden, Y. A. I., . . . Burns, M. P. (2009). Amyloid precursor protein secretases as therapeutic targets for traumatic brain injury. *Nature Medicine, 15,* 377–379. doi:10.1038/nm.1940

Loane, D. J., Washington, P. M., Vardanian, L., Pocivavsek, A., Hoe, H. S., Duff, K. E., . . . Burns, M. P. (2011). Modulation of ABCA1 by an LXR agonist reduces B-amyloid levels and improves outcome after traumatic brain injury. *Journal of Neurotrauma, 28,* 225–236. doi:10.1089/neu.2010.1595

Lotocki, G., Alonso, O. F., Frydel, B., Dietrich, W. D., & Keane, R. W. (2003). Monoubiquitination and cellular distribution of XIAP in neurons after traumatic brain injury. *Journal of Cerebral Blood Flow and Metabolism, 23,* 1129–1136. doi:10.1097/01. WCB.0000086938.68719.E0

Magnoni, S., & Brody, D. L. (2010). New perspective on amyloid-beta dynamics after acute brain injury: Moving between experimental approaches and studies in the human brain. *Archives of Neurology, 67,* 1068–1073. doi:10.1001/archneurol.2010.214

Mandelkow, E. M., & Mandelkow, E. (2012). Biochemistry and cell biology of tau protein in neurofibrillary degeneration. *Cold Spring Harbor Perspectives in Medicine, 2,* a00647. doi:10.1101/ cshperspect.a006247

Mannix, R., O'Brien, M. J., & Meehan, W. P., III. (2013). The epidemiology of outpatient visits for minor head injury: 2005 to 2009. *Neurosurgery, 73,* 129–134. doi:10.1227/01.neu.0000429846.14579.41

Mannix, R. C., & Whalen, M. J. (2012). Traumatic brain injury, microglia, and beta amyloid. *International Journal of Alzheimer's Disease, 2012,* 608732. doi:10.1155/2012/608732

Marquez de la Plata, C. D., Hart, T., Hammond, F. M., Frol, A., Hudak, A., Harper, C. R., . . . Diaz-Arrastia, R. (2008). Impact of age on long-term recovery from traumatic brain injury. *Archives of Physical Medicine and Rehabilitation, 89,* 896–903. doi:10.1016/j. apmr.2007.12.030

Marshall, G. A., Amariglio, R. E., Sperling, R. A., & Rentz, D. M. (2012). Activities of daily living: Where do they fit in the diagnosis of Alzheimer's disease? *Neurodegenerative Disease Management, 2,* 483–491. doi:10.2217/nmt.12.55

Martland, H. (1928). Punch Drunk. *JAMA, 91,* 1103–1107. doi:10.1001/jama.1928.02700150029009

Masel, B. E., & DeWitt, D. S. (2010). Traumatic brain injury: A disease process, not an event. *Journal of Neurotrauma, 27,* 1529–1540. doi:10.1089/ neu.2010.1358

Mattis, S. (1988). *Dementia Rating Scale: Professional manual.* Odessa, FL: Psychological Assessment Resources.

Maxwell, W. L., Domloe, A., McColl, G., Jafari, S. S., & Graham, D. I. (2003). Post-acute alterations in the axonal cytoskeleton after traumatic axonal injury. *Journal of Neurotrauma, 20,* 151–168. doi:10.1089/08977150360547071

Maxwell, W. L., MacKinnon, M. A., Stewart, J. E., & Graham, D. I. (2010). Stereology of cerebral cortex after traumatic brain injury matched to the Glasgow outcome score. *Brain: A Journal of Neurology, 133,* 139–160. doi:10.1093/brain/awp264

Mayeux, R., Galasko, D. R., Saitoh, T., Chen, X., Pay, M. M., Booth, A., & Thomas, R. G. (1996). Apolipoprotein-E4 and head trauma: Synergistic or additive risks? *Neurology, 46,* 889–891.

Mayeux, R., Ottman, R., Maestre, G., Ngai, C., Tang, M. X., Ginsberg, H., . . . Shelanski, M. (1995). Synergistic effects of traumatic head injury and apolipoprotein-epsilon 4 in patients with Alzheimer's disease. *Neurology, 45,* 555–557. doi:10.1212/ WNL.45.3.555

Mayeux, R., Ottman, R., Tang, M. X., Noboa-Bauza, L., Marder, K., Gurland, B., & Stern, Y. (1993). Genetic susceptibility and head injury as risk factors for Alzheimer's disease among community-dwelling elderly persons and their first-degree relatives. *Annals of Neurology, 33,* 494–501. doi:10.1002/ana.410330513

Mayeux, R., Stern, Y., Ottman, R., Tatemichi, T. K., Tang, M. X., Maestre, G., . . . Ginsberg, K. (1993). The apolipoprotein (varepsilon) 4 allele in patients with Alzheimer's disease. *Annals of Neurology, 34,* 752–754. doi:10.1002/ana.410340527

McAllister, T. W., & Arciniegas, D. (2002). Evaluation and treatment of post-concussive symptoms. *Neuro Rehabilitation, 17,* 265–283.

McKee, A. C., Cantu, R. C., Nowinski, C. J., Hedley-Whyte, E. T., Gavett, B. E., Budson, A. E., . . . Stern, R. A. (2009). Chronic traumatic encephalopathy in athletes: Progressive tauopathy after repetitive head injury. *Journal of Neuropathology and Experimental Neurology, 68,* 709–735. doi:10.1097/ NEN.0b013e3181a9d503

McMillan, T. M., Teasdale, G. M., & Stewart, E. (2012). Disability in young people and adults after head injury: 12-14 Year follow-up of a prospective cohort. *Journal of Neurology, Neurosurgery, and Psychiatry, 83,* 1086–1091. doi:10.1136/jnnp-2012-302746

Mehta, K. M., Ott, A., Kalmijn, S., Slooter, A. J., van Duijn, C. M., Hofman, A., & Breteler, M. M. B. (1999). Head trauma and risk of dementia and Alzheimer's disease: The Rotterdam Study. *Neurology, 53,* 1959–1964. doi:10.1212/WNL.53.9.1959

Mendez, M. F. (1995). The neuropsychological aspects of boxing. *International Journal of Psychiatry in Medicine, 25,* 249–262. doi:10.2190/CUMK-THT1-X98M-WB4C

Millar, K., Nicoll, J. A. R., Thornhill, S., Murray, G. D., & Teasdale, G. M. (2003). Long term neuropsychological outcome after head injury: Relation to APOE genotype. *Journal of Neurology, Neurosurgery, and Psychiatry, 74*, 1047–1052. doi:10.1136/jnnp.74.8.1047

Millspaugh, J. A. (1937). Dementia pugilistica. *Naval Medical Bulletin, 35*, 297–305.

Mittenberg, W., & Strauman, S. (2000). Diagnosis of mild head injury and the postconcussion syndrome. *Journal of Head Trauma Rehabilitation, 15*, 783–791. doi:10.1097/00001199-200004000-00003

Morganti-Kossmann, M. C., Rancan, M., Stahel, P. F., & Kossmann, T. (2002). Inflammatory response in acute traumatic brain injury: A double-edged sword. *Current Opinion in Critical Care, 8*, 101–105. doi:10.1097/00075198-200204000-00002

Morganti-Kossmann, M. C., Satgunaseelan, L., Bye, N., & Kossmann, T. (2007). Modulation of immune response by head injury. *Injury, 38*, 1392–1400. doi:10.1016/j.injury.2007.10.005

Mortimer, J. A., Ebbitt, B., Jun, S. P., & Finch, M. D. (1992). Predictors of cognitive and functional progression in patients with probable Alzheimer's disease. *Neurology, 42*, 1689–1696. doi:10.1212/WNL.42.9.1689

Mortimer, J. A., French, L. R., Hutton, J. T., & Schuman, L. M. (1985). Head injury as a risk factor for Alzheimer's disease. *Neurology, 35*, 264–267. doi:10.1212/WNL.35.2.264

Mortimer, J. A., van Duijn, C. M., Chandra, V., Fratiglioni, L., Graves, A. B., Heyman, A., . . . Soininen, H. (1991). Head trauma as a risk factor for Alzheimer's disease: A collaborative reanalysis of case-control studies. *International Journal of Epidemiology, 20*, S28–S35. doi:10.1093/ije/20.Supplement_2.S28

Mosenthal, A. C., Livingston, D. H., Laverty, R. F., Knudson, M. M., Lee, S., Morabito, D., & Coimba, R. (2004). The effect of age on functional outcome in mild traumatic brain injury: 6-month report of a prospective multicenter trial. *Journal of Trauma, 56*, 1042–1048. doi:10.1097/01.TA.0000127767.83267.33

Nemetz, P. N., Leibson, C., Naessens, J. M., Beard, M., Kokmen, E., Annegers, J. F., & Kurland, L. T. (1999). Traumatic brain injury and time to onset of Alzheimer's disease: A population-based study. *American Journal of Epidemiology, 149*, 32–40. doi:10.1093/oxfordjournals.aje.a009724

Newcombe, F. (1996). Very late outcome after focal wartime brain wounds. *Journal of Clinical and Experimental Neuropsychology, 18*, 1–23. doi:10.1080/01688639608408258

Nicoll, J. A., Roberts, G. W., & Graham, D. I. (1995). Apolipoprotein E epsilon 4 allele is associated with deposition of amyloid beta-protein following head injury. *Nature Medicine, 1*, 135–137. doi:10.1038/nm0295-135

Nicoll, J. A., Roberts, G. W., & Graham, D. I. (1996). Amyloid beta-protein, APOE genotype, and head injury. *Annals of the New York Academy of Sciences, 777*, 271–275. doi:10.1111/j.1749-6632.1996.tb34431.x

Niogi, S. N., & Mukherjee, P. (2010). Diffusion tensor imaging of mild traumatic brain injury. *Journal of Head Trauma Rehabilitation, 25*, 241–255. doi:10.1097/HTR.0b013e3181e52c2a

O'Connor, C., Colantonio, A., & Polatajko, H. (2005). Long term symptoms and limitations of activity of people with traumatic brain injury: A ten-year follow-up. *Psychological Reports, 97*, 169–179. doi:10.2466/pr0.97.1.169-179

Omalu, B., Hammers, J. L., Bailes, J., Hamilton, R. L., Kamboh, M. I., Webster, G., & Fitzsimmons, R. P. (2011). Chronic traumatic encephalopathy in an Iraqi war veteran with posttraumatic stress disorder who committed suicide. *Neurosurgical Focus, 31*, E3. doi:10.3171/2011.9.FOCUS11178

Omalu, B. I., Bailes, J., Hammers, J. L., & Fitzsimmons, R. P. (2010). Chronic traumatic encephalopathy, suicides, and parasuicides in professional American athletes: The role of the forensic pathologist. *American Journal of Forensic Medicine and Pathology, 31*, 130–132. doi:10.1097/PAF.0b013e3181ca7f35

Omalu, B. I., DeKosky, S. T., Minster, R. L., Kamboh, M. I., Hamilton, R. L., & Wecht, C. H. (2005). Chronic traumatic encephalopathy in a National Football League player. *Neurosurgery, 57*, 128–134. doi:10.1227/01.NEU.0000163407.92769.ED

O'Meara, E. S., Kukull, W. A., Sheppard, L., Bowen, J. D., McCormick, W. C., Teri, L., . . . Larson, E. B. (1997). Head injury and risk of Alzheimer's disease by apolipoprotein E genotype. *American Journal of Epidemiology, 146*, 373–384. doi:10.1093/oxfordjournals.aje.a009290

Onyszchuk, G., He, Y. Y., Berman, N. E., & Brooks, W. M. (2008). Detrimental effects of aging on outcome from traumatic brain injury: A behavioral, magnetic resonance imaging, and histological study in mice. *Journal of Neurotrauma, 25*, 153–171. doi:10.1089/neu.2007.0430

Peavy, G. M., Jacobson, M. W., Salmon, D. P., Gamst, A. C., Patterson, T. L., Goldman, S., . . . Galasko, D. (2012). The influence of chronic stress on dementia-related diagnostic change in older adults. *Alzheimer Disease and Associated Disorders, 26*, 260–266. doi:10.1097/WAD.0b013e3182389a9c

Pellman, E. J. (2003). Background on the National Football League's research on concussion in professional football. *Neurosurgery, 53,* 797–798.

Plassman, B. L., Havlik, R. J., Steffens, D. C., Helms, M. J., Newman, T. N., & Drosdick, D. (2000). Documented head injury in early adulthood and risk of Alzheimer's disease and other dementias. *Neurology, 55,* 1158–1166. doi:10.1212/WNL.55.8.1158

Poirier, J., Baccichet, A., Dea, D., & Gauthier, S. (1993). Cholesterol synthesis and lipoprotein reuptake during synaptic remodelling in hippocampus in adult rats. *Neuroscience, 55,* 81–90. doi:10.1016/0306-4522(93)90456-P

Poirier, J., Hess, M., May, C., & Finch, J. C. (1991). Astrocytic apolipoprotein E mRNA and GFAP mRNA in hippocampus after entorhinal cortex lesioning. *Proceedings of the National Academy of Sciences of the United States of America, 87,* 303–307. doi:10.1073/pnas.87.1.303

Ponsford, J. L., Myles, P. D., Cooper, D. J., McDermott, F. T., Murray, L. J., Laidlaw, J., . . . Bernard, S. A. (2008). Gender differences in outcome in patients with hypotension and severe traumatic brain injury. *Injury, 39,* 67–76. doi:10.1016/j.injury.2007.08.028

Popa-Wagner, A., Buga, A. M., & Kokaia, Z. (2011). Perturbed cellular response to brain injury during aging. *Ageing Research Reviews, 10,* 71–79. doi:10.1016/j.arr.2009.10.008

Povlishock, J. T., & Katz, D. I. (2005). Update on neuropathology and neurological recovery after traumatic brain injury. *Journal of Head Trauma Rehabilitation, 20,* 76–94. doi:10.1097/00001199-200501000-00008

Ramlackhansingh, A. F., Brooks, D. J., Greenwood, R. J., Bose, S. K., Turkheimer, F. E., Kinnunen, K. M., . . . Sharp, D. J. (2011). Inflammation after trauma: Microglial activation and traumatic brain injury. *Annals of Neurology, 70,* 374–383. doi:10.1002/ana.22455

Randolph, C., Karantzoulis, S., & Guskiewicz, K. (2013). Prevalence and characterization of mild cognitive impairment in retired National Football League players. *Journal of the International Neuropsychological Society, 19,* 873–880. doi:10.1017/S1355617713000805

Rapoport, M., Wolf, U., Herrmann, N., Kiss, A., Shammi, P., Reis, M., . . . Feinstein, A. (2008). Traumatic brain injury, apolipoprotein E-4, and cognition in older adults: A two year longitudinal study. *Journal of Neuropsychiatry and Clinical Neurosciences, 20,* 68–73. doi:10.1176/appi.neuropsych.20.1.68

Rasmusson, D. X., Brandt, J., Martin, D. B., & Folstein, M. F. (1995). Head injury as a risk factor in Alzheimer's disease. *Brain Injury, 9,* 213–219. doi:10.3109/02699059509008194

Raymont, V., Greathouse, A., Reding, K., Lipsky, R., Salazar, A., & Grafman, J. (2008). Demographic, structural, and genetic predictors of late cognitive decline after penetrating head injury. *Brain: A Journal of Neurology, 131,* 543–558. doi:10.1093/brain/awm300

Raymont, V., Salazar, A. M., Krueger, F., & Grafman, J. (2011). "Studying injured minds"—The Vietnam head injury study and 40 years of brain injury research. *Frontiers in Neurology, 2,* 1–15.

Raz, N., & Rodriguez, K. M. (2006). Differential aging of the brain: Patterns, cognitive correlates and modifiers. *Neuroscience and Biobehavioral Reviews, 30,* 730–748. doi:10.1016/j.neubiorev.2006.07.001

Rees, P. M. (2003). Contemporary issues in mild traumatic brain injury. *Archives of Physical Medicine and Rehabilitation, 84,* 1885–1894. doi:10.1016/j.apmr.2003.03.001

Reynolds, F. D., Dietz, P. A., Higgins, D., & Whitaker, T. S. (2003). Time to deterioration of the elderly, anticoagulated, minor head injury patient who presents without evidence of neurologic abnormality. *Journal of Trauma, 54,* 492–496. doi:10.1097/01.TA.0000051601.60556.FC

Roberts, A. H. (1969). *Brain damage in boxers: Study of the prevalence of traumatic encephalopathy among ex-professional boxers.* London, England: Pitman.

Roberts, G. W., Allsop, D., & Bruton, C. (1991). The occult aftermath of boxing. *Journal of Neurology, Neurosurgery, and Psychiatry, 53,* 373–378. doi:10.1136/jnnp.53.5.373

Roberts, G. W., Gentleman, S. M., Lynch, A., Murray, L., Landon, M., & Graham, D. I. (1994). B-amyloid protein deposition in the brain after severe brain injury: Implications for the pathogenesis of Alzheimer's disease. *Journal of Neurology, Neurosurgery, and Psychiatry, 57,* 419–425. doi:10.1136/jnnp.57.4.419

Roy, O. W., Cohen, N. R., & Nicoll, J. A. (2005). Pathophysiology of dementias and implications for therapy. *Indian Journal of Pathology and Microbiology, 48,* 289–299.

Rutland-Brown, W., Langlois, J. A., Thomas, K. E., & Xi, Y. L. (2006). Incidence of traumatic brain injury in the United States, 2003. *Journal of Head Trauma Rehabilitation, 21,* 544–548. doi:10.1097/00001199-200611000-00009

Salib, E., & Hillier, V. (1997). Head injury and the risk of Alzheimer's disease: A case control study. *International Journal of Geriatric Psychiatry, 12,* 363–368. doi:10.1002/(SICI)1099-1166(199703)12:3<363::AID-GPS515>3.0.CO;2-F

Sandhir, R., Onyszchuk, G., & Berman, N. E. (2008). Exacerbated glial response in the aged mouse hippocampus following controlled cortical impact injury.

Experimental Neurology, 213, 372–380. doi:10.1016/j.expneurol.2008.06.013

Satz, P. (1993). Brain reserve capacity on symptom onset after brain injury: A formulation and review of evidence for the threshold theory. *Neuropsychology, 7*, 273–295. doi:10.1037/0894-4105.7.3.273

Sayed, N., Culver, C., Dams-O'Connor, K., Hammond, F., & Diaz-Arrastia, R. (2013). Clinical phenotype of dementia after traumatic brain injury. *Journal of Neurotrauma, 30*, 1117–1122. doi:10.1089/neu.2012.2638

Scahill, R. I., Frost, C., Jenkins, R., Whitwell, J. L., Rossor, M. N., & Fox, N. C. (2003). A longitudinal study of brain volume changes in normal aging using serial registered magnetic resonance imaging. *Archives of Neurology, 60*, 989–994. doi:10.1001/archneur.60.7.989

Scheid, R., Preul, C., Gruber, O., Wiggins, C., & von Cramon, D. Y. (2003). Diffuse axonal injury associated with chronic traumatic brain injury: Evidence form T2-weighted gradient-echo imaging at 3T. *American Journal of Nursing, 24*, 1049–1056.

Schmidt, M. L., Zhukareva, V., Newell, K. L., Lee, V. M., & Trojanowski, J. Q. (2001). Tau isoform profile and phosphorylation state in dementia pugilistica recapitulate Alzheimer's disease. *Acta Neuropathologica, 101*, 518–524.

Schwetye, K. E., Cirrito, J. R., Esparza, T. J., Mac Donald, C. L., Holtzman, D. M., & Brody, D. L. (2010). Traumatic brain injury reduces soluble extracellular amyloid-B in mice: A methodologically novel combined microdialysis-controlled cortical impact study. *Neurobiology of Disease, 40*, 555–564.

Senathi-Raja, D., Ponsford, J., & Schonberger, M. (2010). Impact of age on long-term cognitive function after traumatic brain injury. *Neuropsychology, 24*, 336–344. doi:10.1037/a0018239

Sendroy-Terrill, M., Whiteneck, G. G., & Brooks, C. A. (2010). Aging with traumatic brain injury: Cross-sectional follow-up of people receiving inpatient rehabilitation over more than 3 decades. *Archives of Physical Medicine and Rehabilitation, 91*, 489–497. doi:10.1016/j.apmr.2009.11.011

Serra-Grabulosa, J. M., Junque, C., Verger, K., Salgado-Pineda, P., Maneru, C., & Mercader, J. M. (2005). Cerebral correlates of declarative memory dysfunctions in early traumatic brain injury. *Journal of Neurology, Neurosurgery, and Psychiatry, 76*, 129–131. doi:10.1136/jnnp.2004.027631

Shaw, K. T., Utsuki, T., Rogers, J., Yu, Q. S., Sambamurti, K., Brossi, A., . . . Greig, N. H. (2001). Phenserine regulates translation of beta-amyloid precursor protein mRNA by a putative interleukin-1 responsive element, a target for drug development. *Proceedings of the National Academy of Sciences, USA, 98*, 7605–7610. doi:10.1073/pnas.131152998

Shimamura, M., Garcia, J. M., Prough, D. S., & Hellmich, H. L. (2004). Laser capture microdissection and analysis of amplified antisense RNA from distinct cell populations of the young and aged rat brain: Effect of traumatic brain injury on hippocampal gene expression. *Molecular Brain Research, 122*, 47–61. doi:10.1016/j.molbrainres.2003.11.015

Sivanandam, T. M., & Thakur, M. K. (2012). Traumatic brain injury: A risk factor for Alzheimer's disease. *Neuroscience and Biobehavioral Reviews, 36*, 1376–1381. doi:10.1016/j.neubiorev.2012.02.013

Smith, C., Gentleman, S. M., Leclercq, P. D., Murray, L. S., Griffin, W. S. T., Graham, D. I., & Nicoll, J. A. R. (2013). The neuroinflammatory response in humans after traumatic brain injury. *Neuropathology and Applied Neurobiology, 39*, 654–666. doi:10.1111/nan.12008

Smith, D. H., Chen, X., & Nonaka, M. (1999). Accumulation of amyloid beta and tau and the formation of neurofilament inclusions following diffuse brain injury in the pig. *Journal of Neuropathology and Experimental Neurology, 58*, 982–992. doi:10.1097/00005072-199909000-00008

Smith, D. H., Chen, X. H., Iwata, A., & Graham, D. I. (2003). A-beta accumulation in axons after TBI. *Journal of Neurosurgery, 98*, 1072–1077. doi:10.3171/jns.2003.98.5.1072

Smith, D. H., Chen, X. H., Pierce, J. E., Wolf, J. A., Trojanowski, J. Q., Graham, D. I., & McIntosh, T. K. (1997). Progressive atrophy and neuron death for one year following brain trauma in the rat. *Journal of Neurotrauma, 14*, 715–727. doi:10.1089/neu.1997.14.715

Smith, D. H., Hicks, R., & Povlishock, J. T. (2013). Therapy development for diffuse axonal injury. *Journal of Neurotrauma, 30*, 307–323. doi:10.1089/neu.2012.2825

Stern, Y. (2006). Cognitive reserve and Alzheimer disease. *Alzheimer Disease and Associated Disorders, 20*, S69–S74. doi:10.1097/00002093-200607001-00010

Stern, Y. (2007). *Cognitive reserve: Theory and applications.* New York, NY: Taylor & Francis.

Stern, Y., Alexander, G. E., Prohovnik, I., Stricks, L., Link, B., Lennon, M. C., & Mayeux, R. (1995). Relationship between lifetime occupation and parietal flow: Implications for a reserve against Alzheimer's disease pathology. *Neurology, 45*, 55–60. doi:10.1212/WNL.45.1.55

Sterr, A., Herron, K. A., Hayward, C., & Montaldi, D. (2006). Are mild head injuries as mild as we think? Neurobehavioral concomitants of chronic post-concussion syndrome. *BMC Neurology, 6*, 7.

Stiller, J. W., & Weinberger, D. R. (1985). Boxing and chronic brain damage. *Psychiatric Clinics of North America, 8,* 339–356.

Stoica, B. A., & Faden, A. I. (2010). Cell death mechanisms and modulation in traumatic brain injury. *Neurotherapeutics, 7,* 3–12. doi:10.1016/j.nurt.2009.10.023

Stokin, G. B., Lillo, C., Falzone, T. L., Brusch, R. G., Rockenstein, E., Mount, S. L., . . . Goldstein, L. S. (2005). Axonopathy and transport deficits early in the pathogenesis of Alzheimer's disease. *Science, 307,* 1282–1288. doi:10.1126/science.1105681

Styrke, J., Stalnacke, B. M., Sojka, P., & Bjornstig, U. (2007). Traumatic brain injuries in a well-defined population: Epidemiological aspects and severity. *Journal of Neurotrauma, 24,* 1425–1436. doi:10.1089/neu.2007.0266

Sullivan, P. G., Rabchevsky, A. G., Waldmeier, P. C., & Springer, J. E. (2005). Mitochondrial permeability transition in CNS trauma: Cause or effect of neuronal cell death? *Journal of Neuroscience Research, 79,* 231–239. doi:10.1002/jnr.20292

Susman, M., DiRusso, S. M., Sullivan, T., Risucci, D., Nealon, P., Cuff, S., . . . Benzil, D. (2002). Traumatic brain injury in the elderly: Increased mortality and worse functional outcome at discharge despite lower injury severity. *Journal of Trauma, 53,* 219–224. doi:10.1097/00005373-200208000-00004

Terry, R. D., & Katzman, R. (2001). Life span and synapses: Will there be a primary senile dementia? *Neurobiology of Aging, 22,* 347–348. doi:10.1016/S0197-4580(00)00250-5

Teuber, H. L. (1974). Functional recovery after lesions of the nervous system. II. Recovery of function after lesions of the central nervous system: History and prospects. *Neurosciences Research Program Bulletin, 12,* 197–211.

Thompson, H. J., McCormick, W. C., & Kagan, S. H. (2006). Traumatic brain injury in older adults: Epidemiology, outcomes, and future implications. *Journal of the American Geriatrics Society, 54,* 1590–1595. doi:10.1111/j.1532-5415.2006.00894.x

Thompson, H. J., Weir, S., Rivara, F. P., Wang, J., Sullivan, S. D., Salkever, D., & MacKenzie, E. J. (2012). Utilization and costs of health care after geriatric traumatic brain injury. *Journal of Neurotrauma, 29,* 1864–1871. doi:10.1089/neu.2011.2284

Thomsen, I. V. (1984). Late outcome of very severe blunt head trauma: A 10-15 year second follow-up. *Journal of Neurology, Neurosurgery, and Psychiatry, 47,* 260–268. doi:10.1136/jnnp.47.3.260

Thomsen, I. V. (1992). Late psychosocial outcome in severe traumatic brain injury. *Scandinavian Journal of Rehabilitation Medicine, 26*(Suppl.), 142–152.

Thurman, D. L., Alverson, C., Dunn, K., Guerrero, J., & Sniezek, J. (1999). Traumatic brain injury in the United States: A public health perspective. *Journal of Head Trauma Rehabilitation, 14,* 602–615. doi:10.1097/00001199-199912000-00009

Timaru-Kast, R., Luh, C., Gotthardt, P., Huang, C., Schafer, M., Engelhard, K., & Thal, S. C. (2012). Influence of age on brain edema formation, secondary brain damage and inflammatory response after brain trauma in mice. *PLoS ONE, 7,* e0043829. doi:10.1371/journal.pone.0043829

Tokuda, T., Ikeda, S., Yanagisawa, N., Ihara, Y., & Glenner, G. G. (1991). Re-examination of ex-boxers' brains using immunohistochemistry with antibodies to amyloid beta-protein and tau protein. *Acta Neuropathologica, 82,* 280–285. doi:10.1007/BF00308813

Tran, H. T., LaFerla, F. M., Holtzman, D. M., & Brody, D. L. (2011). Controlled cortical impact traumatic brain injury in 3xTg-AD mice causes acute intra-axonal amyloid-β accumulation and independently accelerates the development of tau abnormalities. *Journal of Neuroscience, 31,* 9513–9525. doi:10.1523/JNEUROSCI.0858-11.2011

Tran, H. T., Sanchez, L., & Brody, D. L. (2012). Inhibition of JNK by a peptide inhibitor reduces traumatic brain Injury-inducted tauopathy in transgenic mice. *Journal of Neuropathology and Experimental Neurology, 71,* 116–129. doi:10.1097/NEN.0b013e3182456aed

Victoroff, J. (2013). Traumatic encephalopathy: Review and provisional research diagnostic criteria. *NeuroRehabilitation, 32,* 211–224.

Volkow, N. D., Wang, G. J., Fowler, J. S., Ding, Y. S., Gur, R. C., Gatley, J., . . . Pappas, N. (1998). Parallel loss of presynaptic and postsynaptic dopamine markers in normal aging. *Annals of Neurology, 44,* 143–147. doi:10.1002/ana.410440125

Vollmer, D. G., & Dacey, R. G. (1991). The management of mild and moderate head injuries. *Neurosurgery Clinics of North America, 2,* 437–455.

Wager-Smith, K., & Markou, A. (2011). Depression: A repair response to stress-induced neuronal micro-damage that can grade into a chronic neuroinflammatory condition. *Neuroscience and Biobehavioral Reviews, 35,* 742–764. doi:10.1016/j.neubiorev.2010.09.010

Whiteneck, G. G., Gerhart, K. A., & Cusick, C. P. (2004). Identifying environmental factors that influence the outcomes of people with traumatic brain injury. *Journal of Head Trauma Rehabilitation, 19,* 191–204. doi:10.1097/00001199-200405000-00001

Whyte, J., DiPasquale, M. C., & Vaccaro, M. (1999). Assessment of command-following in minimally conscious brain injured patients. *Archives of Physical Medicine and Rehabilitation, 80,* 653–660. doi:10.1016/S0003-9993(99)90168-5

Williams, H. K., & Hammond, L. (2000). Multiple residual cysts containing deposits of AL-amyloid. *Histopathology, 37*, 567–569. doi:10.1046/j.1365-2559.2000.01018-4.x

Wisniewski, K., Jervis, G. A., Moretz, R. C., & Wisniewski, H. M. (1979). Alzheimer neurofibrillary tangles in diseases other than senile and presenile dementia. *Annals of Neurology, 5*, 288–294. doi:10.1002/ana.410050311

Young, J. A. (2004). Pain and traumatic brain injury. *Physical Medicine and Rehabilitation Clinics of North America, 18*, 145–163.

Yu, T. S., Zhang, G., Liebl, D. J., & Kernie, S. G. (2008). Traumatic brain injury-induced hippocampal neurogenesis requires activation of early nestin expressing progenitors. *Journal of Neuroscience, 28*, 12901–12912. doi:10.1523/JNEUROSCI.4629-08.2008

Zabar, Y., & Kawas, C. H. (2000). Epidemiology and clinical genetics of Alzheimer's disease. In C. M. Clark & J. Q. Trojanowski (Eds.), *Neurodegenerative dementias* (pp. 79–94). New York, NY: McGraw Hill.

Zappalà, G., Thiebaut, D., Schotten, M., & Eslinger, P. J. (2012). Traumatic brain injury and the frontal lobes: What can we gain with diffusion tensor imaging. *Cortex, 48*, 156–165.

Zhou, W., Xu, D., Peng, X., Zhang, Q., Jia, J., & Crutcher, K. A. (2008). Meta-analysis of APOE4 allele and outcome after traumatic brain injury. *Journal of Neurotrauma, 25*, 279–290. doi:10.1089/neu.2007.0489

Ziebell, J. M., & Morganti-Kossmann, M. C. (2010). Involvement of pro- and anti-inflammatory cytokines and chemokines in the pathophysiology of traumatic brain injury. *Neurotherapeutics, 7*, 22–30. doi:10.1016/j.nurt.2009.10.016

Chapter 11

BEHAVIORAL AND PSYCHOLOGICAL SYMPTOMS OF DEMENTIA

Jiska Cohen-Mansfield

This chapter refers to four distinct types of behavioral and psychological symptoms: (a) behavioral symptoms and agitation, (b) misinterpretations and "psychotic symptoms," (c) depressed affect, and (d) apathy and disengagement. When considering other constructs usually included in behavioral and psychological symptoms in dementia, we include "delusions" and "hallucinations" under misinterpretations and "psychotic symptoms"; agitation or aggression, anxiety, disinhibition, irritability or lability, and aberrant motor behavior are included in the different subtypes of agitation and behavior problems; "apathy and indifference" are included under apathy and disengagement; and "depression and dysphoria" are included under depressed affect. Elation and euphoria have been found to be rather rare (Steinberg et al., 2008) and when occurring do not seem to pose a problem and thus are not discussed.

The heterogeneity of the manifestations of dementia stems from three sources: predisposing characteristics, life events, and the individual's current condition. Each of these occurs in several domains: a genetic, biologic, or medical domain; a psychosocial domain; and an environmental domain (Cohen-Mansfield, 2000). Such factors affect how dementia is manifested in areas of functioning, such as self-maintenance, affect, cognition, and behavior. Mapping these sources through correlational studies has proven useful in illuminating common causes for difficulties in caring for individuals with dementia (e.g., Whall et al., 2008).

DEFINITION AND DESCRIPTION

Diagnostic criteria for dementia, also referred to as neurocognitive disorder (NCD) in the *Diagnostic and Statistical Manual of Mental Disorders, Fifth Edition* (*DSM–5*; American Psychiatric Association, 2013), includes—in addition to cognitive symptoms such as decline or impairment in memory, learning, and cognition—behavioral and psychological manifestations, ranging from depression or apathy in the mild stages; to psychotic features, irritability, and wandering in moderate cases; to dysphagia, gait disturbance, and seizures in the late stages (American Psychiatric Association, 2013). Behavioral and psychological symptoms of dementia (BPSD) have been defined as a syndrome because of pharmaceutical companies' interest in creating a medical entity that can be used as an indication for the need for medications for noncognitive symptoms in dementia. Consensus conferences funded by pharmaceutical companies and organized by the International Psychogeriatric Association were the venue through which this entity was explored and finally published in *International Psychogeriatrics*. The definition of BPSD established through this conference is a "term used to describe a heterogeneous range of psychological reactions, psychiatric symptoms, and behaviors occurring in people with dementia of any etiology" (Finkel & Burns, 2000). Because of its origin as a mechanism for drug approval rather than based on any scientific finding, the term BPSD reflects a conglomerate of generally unrelated

http://dx.doi.org/10.1037/14459-011
APA Handbook of Clinical Geropsychology: Vol. 2. Assessment, Treatment, and Issues of Later Life,
P. A. Lichtenberg and B. T. Mast (Editors-in-Chief)

potential symptoms rather than a syndrome with internal reliability or cohesive significance.

Behavioral Symptoms and Agitation

Behavioral symptoms, frequently termed *agitation*, have been defined as "inappropriate verbal, vocal, or motor activity that is not judged by an outside observer to result directly from the needs or confusion of the individual" (Cohen-Mansfield, 2008, 64). Defining behavioral symptoms in this way results in an approach that includes the following attributes:

- Range of behaviors. Behavioral symptoms include repetitive acts (e.g., walking back and forth, repetition of words), behaviors inappropriate to the social norms (e.g., entering someone else's room and handling their belongings, unbuttoning a blouse in public), and aggressive behaviors toward self or others.

- Who determines whether this is a problem behavior? The behavior is in the eyes of the beholder; in other words, behavioral symptoms are labeled problematic by those who perceive them as inappropriate. Such behaviors may or may not be inappropriate from the point of view of the older person. The older person indeed may have a need that explains the behavior, but the need is not obvious to the observer and furthermore may not be consciously known to the older person. For example, an older person who is walking incessantly may be searching for the bathroom. Not only does he or she not make this need known, but he or she may not be consciously aware of this need because of his or her dementia. An additional concern in this regard is the need to separate the problem from the person. Because these behaviors can severely challenge caregivers, and it may appear as if the person is being deliberately aggravating, there is an unfortunate tendency to think of the person, rather than the behavior, as a problem. This perspective interferes with effective caregiver problem solving and further victimizes the person with dementia (PWD).

- Not necessarily disruptive. Behavioral symptoms are not always disruptive. It is important to observe these behaviors because such observations may lead to an understanding of the internal state of the older person. Repetitious mannerisms, although not bothersome to anyone, may indicate boredom; low groans that are not disruptive, nevertheless, may indicate pain.

- Not necessarily dementia. Although behavioral symptoms are more common among PWDs, some of these behaviors also are manifested by people who are not cognitively impaired. For example, Koss et al. (1997) reported that the average scores on a measure of the frequency of behavior problems (Cohen-Mansfield Agitation Inventory [CMAI]; see the section Assessment of Behavioral Symptoms) of age-matched control participants was 3.7 as compared with scores of 15 for PWDs with a Mini-Mental State Examination (MMSE) >21 of 15 and a score of 40.7 for PWDs with an MMSE score of 0–4.

- Not a necessary outcome of dementia. Although many PWDs manifest behavioral symptoms, not all do. Furthermore, these behaviors do not refer to behaviors representative of the actual deterioration involved with dementia, such as memory problems or incontinence during the later stages of disease.

Behavioral symptoms are observable behaviors, and no underlying emotional state is assumed to cause these behaviors. In this sense, the label "agitation" is deceptive and was chosen only because it traditionally has been used by practitioners to describe these behaviors.

Behavioral symptoms in the nursing home manifest as three subtypes: aggressive behaviors (e.g., hitting, kicking, pushing, scratching, tearing things, biting, spitting, cursing, or verbal aggression), physically nonaggressive behaviors (e.g., pacing, inappropriate dressing and undressing, trying to get to a different place, handling things inappropriately, general restlessness, repetitious mannerisms), and verbal and vocal agitated behaviors (e.g., complaining, constant requests for attention, negativism, repetitious sentences or questions, screaming; Cohen-Mansfield, Marx, & Rosenthal, 1989; Husebo, Ballard, Cohen-Mansfield, Seifert, & Aarsland, 2014; Rabinowitz et al., 2005). Findings relating to the subtypes of behavioral symptoms are presented in the following sections.

Verbally and vocally agitated behaviors. Verbally and vocally agitated behaviors are manifested by individuals who suffer from more medical conditions and higher levels of pain and depressed affect, in comparison with others in the same care setting (C. Beck et al., 2011; Cohen-Mansfield, Marx, & Werner, 1992a). Verbal and vocal behavioral symptoms are more likely to manifest themselves in the evening, when people are alone, when people are physically restrained, or when they are involved in activities of daily living (ADL), especially toileting and bathing (Cohen-Mansfield, Werner, & Marx, 1990; Schreiner, Yamamoto, & Shiotani, 2000). These findings support the notion that at least some verbal behavioral symptoms are associated with discomfort, pain, or unmet social needs. Indeed, in a study of 138 nursing home residents, predictors of verbally agitated behaviors included discomfort and poor general health status (C. Beck et al., 2011). The treatment of pain has been found to affect primarily verbal–vocal behaviors (Husebo et al., 2014).

Physically nonaggressive behaviors. People who engage in physically nonaggressive behavioral symptoms have been reported to have fewer medical diagnoses and better appetites than other nursing home residents (Cohen-Mansfield et al., 1992a). Wandering and pacing, the most common forms of physically nonaggressive agitation, occur most frequently in a corridor and near the nurses' station, where other people often spend time (Cohen-Mansfield, Werner, & Marx, 1992). Wandering and pacing takes place under normal conditions of light, noise, and temperature, rather than during uncomfortable environmental conditions (Cohen-Mansfield & Werner, 1995). Relatively healthy people with advanced dementia (Cohen-Mansfield, Marx, & Rosenthal, 1990; Cohen-Mansfield, Culpepper, & Werner, 1995) may manifest these behaviors as a form of self-stimulation because opportunities for meaningful activities are limited by their dementia or the nursing home environment.

Physically aggressive disruptive behaviors. Physically aggressive disruptive behaviors are more likely to be manifested by individuals with severe cognitive impairment (Cohen-Mansfield, Marx, & Rosenthal, 1990; Cohen-Mansfield, Culpepper, & Werner, 1995; Nösman, Bucht, Eriksson, & Sandman, 1993), particularly among individuals with advanced dementia in response to uncomfortable stimuli (while performing ADLs or feeling cold) or in situations perceived to be threatening (e.g., invasion of personal space; Bridges-Parlet, Knopman, & Thompson, 1994; Cohen-Mansfield & Werner, 1995). One study found aggressive behaviors to be related to physical pain (Feldt, Warne, & Ryden, 1998). Aggressive behaviors are more likely to be manifested by males and by people with premorbid tendencies toward aggressive behavior (Ryden, 1988; W. D. Spector & Jackson, 1994).

Most of the behavioral symptoms, with the exception of pacing, have been shown to manifest more frequently under the following conditions: physical restraints are used, residents are inactive, residents are alone, staffing levels are low, or it is cold at night. Such behavioral symptoms are less likely to be demonstrated when structured activities are offered, music is playing, or residents are involved in social interaction (Cohen-Mansfield & Werner, 1995). These results concur with the hypothesis that behavioral symptoms frequently signal discomfort and unmet needs. On the basis of these findings, behavioral symptoms are conceptualized as resulting from an interaction between life-long habits and personality, current physical and mental conditions, and physical and psychological environmental factors (Cohen-Mansfield & Deutsch, 1996). More specifically, most behavioral symptoms are manifestations of unmet needs. The most common needs of PWDs are socializing and stimulating activities, both of which are limited by the combination of the effects of dementia, sensory deficits, and the monotony of the nursing home environment (Hancock, Woods, Challis, & Orrell, 2006). Other commonly unmet needs in this population are those relating to discomfort and pain (Cohen-Mansfield & Werner, 1999a). An individual with dementia is unable to independently fulfill these needs because of a combination of perceptual problems, communication difficulties, and an inability to manipulate the environment through appropriate channels. Therefore, the goal of treatment should focus on uncovering and addressing the unmet needs of these individuals. A decrease in inappropriate behaviors is likely to occur once the needs are addressed.

Psychotic Symptoms and Misinterpretations

The *DSM–5* (American Psychiatric Association, 2013) defines delusions as false, fixed beliefs that do not change, even when evidence to the contrary is presented. Types of delusions associated with dementia include "one's house is not one's home," theft, abandonment, danger, misidentification, infidelity, and nonparanoid delusions (Fischer, Bozanovic-Sosic, & Norris, 2004). An important note is that in utilizing the term delusion, the person's behavior is relegated to the domain of severe psychiatric phenomena; this leads to a nonrecognition of the importance of understanding the behavior or phenomena from the point of view of the person experiencing them and therefore may lead to a lack of understanding of the true meaning of the behavior. Furthermore, studies addressing the topic of delusions in dementia often classify the presence of delusions, hallucinations, and a misidentification syndrome under the general term of psychosis, or psychotic symptoms in dementia (Cohen-Mansfield, Golander, Ben-Israel, & Garfinkel, 2011). These phenomena, however, have distinct correlates and different etiologies (see the section Theoretical Models for the Causes of Psychotic Symptoms and Misinterpretations), which are obscured by the terminology that lumps them together. Consequently, reviews of interventions that lump all symptoms together do not inform the reader which intervention to use for which symptom.

Past research reported a large range of prevalence rates, finding that 10% to 73% of individuals with Alzheimer's disease suffer from delusions (e.g., Fernández, Gobartt, & Balañá, 2010; Scarmeas et al., 2005). Although rates of subtypes of delusions among PWDs vary across studies, most studies found delusions of theft to be most common, followed by the delusion that "one's house is not one's home" and delusions of suspicion (see Cohen-Mansfield, Golander, Ben-Israel, & Garfinkel, 2011; Reisberg, Borenstein, Salob, & Ferris, 1987; Shaji, Bose, & Kuriakose, 2009).

A hallucination (visual, auditory, or otherwise) refers to a sensory experience that occurs in the absence of actual sensory stimulation (Cummings et al., 1994), for example, seeing something that is not there. Studies reporting the prevalence of hallucinations in dementia have yielded a wide range of results (Ropacki & Jeste, 2005), possibly because of the various definitions of hallucinations used across studies (Cohen-Mansfield, Taylor, & Werner, 1998). Visual hallucinations are much more common than auditory ones, whereas tactile, gustatory, and olfactory hallucinations are rare (Ropacki & Jeste, 2005). The etiology of hallucinations in dementia has been reported in several studies. Vision loss is the most common etiology (Cohen-Mansfield et al., 1998; Holroyd, 1998; Murgatroyd & Prettyman, 2001), possibly leading to misidentifying objects (e.g., with the perceptual deficits in low-vision syndrome possibly increasing confusion, especially in unfamiliar settings such as a nursing home). Insufficient lighting, which has been linked to hallucinations (Murgatroyd & Prettyman, 2001), similarly can lead to misinterpretation of the visual environment. Following a similar notion, deafness appears to be the most consistent factor associated with auditory hallucinations, and a decrease in auditory hallucination symptoms was observed with the use of a hearing aid (Khan, Clark, & Oyebode, 1988), although concomitant neurological or psychiatric disease has been reported in a large number of cases (Keshavan, David, Steingard, & Lishman, 1992). Furthermore, "sensory deprivation," referring to the absence of the stimulation of sensory areas by external objects, can result in people experiencing hallucinations (Kempe & Reimer, 1976; Zubek, Pushkar, Sansom, & Gowing, 1961). Research concerning the onset of hallucinations and their prevalence at various stages of dementia is inconclusive. In a study of residents of adult day care centers (Cohen-Mansfield et al., 1998), hallucinations were reported to occur in the very late stages of the disease, specifically in stages 6 and 7 on the Brief Cognitive Rating Scale (Reisberg, Schneck, Ferris, Schwartz, & Deleon, 1983). Similarly, more hallucinations were reported among those with more advanced dementia (Lerner et al., 1994). In contrast, another study found that neither visual nor auditory hallucinations were related to the severity of dementia (Burns, Jacoby, & Levy, 1990).

Depressed Affect

Depressed affect is a term used to describe depressive symptoms, such as depressed mood, diminished pleasure or interest in activities, feelings of worthlessness or inappropriate guilt, and diminished ability to concentrate. Depression occurring later in life is often an early symptom of dementia (Schweitzer, Tuckwell, O'Brien, & Ames, 2002). Levels of depression are often persistent after onset in persons with Alzheimer's disease or dementia (Fritze, Ehrt, Hortobagyi, Ballard, & Aarsland, 2011). Displays of psuedobulbar affect, characterized as involuntary or uncontrollable laughing and crying, in those with Alzheimer's disease also have been associated with a presence of congruent mood disorders, such as major depression, or mood episodes (Schiffer & Pope, 2005; Starkstein et al., 1995). Additional causes of depression are discussed in the section Theoretical Models for the Causes of Depressed Affect.

Apathy and Disengagement

Apathy is characterized by a lack of motivation, interests, and emotions (Marin, 1991). Lack of motivation may be influenced by, but not solely attributed to, dementia or the emotional status of the individual (Höltta et al., 2012). In a set of diagnostic criteria for apathy in Alzheimer's disease and other neuropsychiatric disorders proposed by a task force, the main identifier of apathy is diminished motivation, with additional criteria relating to reductions in goal-directed behavior and cognitive ability, emotions, and functional impairment (Robert et al., 2009). Three subtypes of apathy—affective (indifference, lack of empathy), behavioral (inertia), and cognitive (loss of interest)—have been identified in PWDs (Chow et al., 2009). Apathy is related to disengagement (Leone, Deudon, Piano, Robert, & Dechamps, 2012) as one loses the motivation or interest to engage with stimuli. Engagement, the opposite of disengagement, refers to the act of being occupied or involved with an external stimulus, which includes concrete objects, activities, and

other people (Cohen-Mansfield, Marx, et al., 2011). In a study of 354 dementia clinic outpatients in Argentina, baseline apathy prevalence was 24%, with higher rates found in those in later stages of dementia, increasing from 14% among those with mild dementia to 61% in those with severe Alzheimer's disease (Starkstein, Jorge, Mizrahi, & Robinson, 2006). The etiology of apathy in dementia is further discussed in the section Theoretical Models for the Causes of Apathy and Disengagement.

MAJOR THEORIES

Theoretical models for the etiology of behavioral symptoms, of psychotic symptoms, of depressed affect, and of apathy are described in the following paragraphs. These theoretical frameworks vary in their specificity for PWDs. In some frameworks, general psychological theories are utilized, such as behavioral theory. In others, general theories for the psychological condition are utilized, such as cognitive and behavioral approaches to depressed affect. Yet, other theoretical approaches are based specifically on the characteristics of dementia. When general theories are used, the role of dementia in accentuating or mitigating the processes causing the behavioral or psychological syndromes should be considered.

Theoretical Models for the Causes of Behavioral Symptoms and Agitation

The consistent relationship between cognitive impairment and behavioral symptoms (e.g., for physically aggressive behaviors, Cohen-Mansfield, Culpepper, & Werner, 1995; Marx, Cohen-Mansfield, & Werner, 1990; Nösman et al., 1993) naturally gives rise to the question concerning the role of dementia in causing these behaviors. Theories that address this question can be divided into four general categories, with the first pertaining to the direct impact of dementia, and the others focusing either on factors that interact with dementia or the context of dementia. Specifically these are: (a) direct impact of dementia—biological model, (b) unmet needs model, (c) behavioral model, and (d) environmental vulnerability model. These models are not mutually exclusive and can be interactive

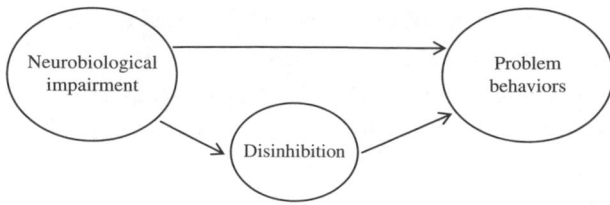

FIGURE 11.1. Direct impact of dementia model.
Copyright 1998 by Cohen-Mansfield. All rights reserved.
Reprinted by permission.

as one may cause the outcome of another. The four models are summarized as follows:

Direct impact of dementia—biological model. This model is based on two essential premises: (a) behavioral symptoms result directly from neurological changes in the brain; and (b) severe organic brain deterioration results in behavioral disinhibition (Figure 11.1).

The literature concerning this model is not reviewed in this chapter (the interested reader is referred to Borroni, Costanzi, & Padovani, 2010; Geda et al., 2013; Huang et al., 2012; Kar, 2009; Pritchard et al., 2013).

Unmet needs model. According to this model, behavioral symptoms result from an imbalance in the interaction between lifelong habits and personality, current physical and mental states, and less-than-optimal environmental conditions (Figure 11.2; Algase et al., 1996; Cohen-Mansfield et al., 1992a; Cohen-Mansfield & Werner, 1995). Most unmet needs arise because of dementia-related impairments in both communication and in the ability to utilize the environment appropriately to accommodate needs. Such needs may pertain to pain, health, and physical discomfort; mental discomfort (evident in affective states: depression, anxiety, frustration); the need for social contacts; uncomfortable environmental conditions; or an inadequate level of stimulation (too low, too high, inappropriate). The behavioral symptoms result from the unmet needs in one of several ways. The behavior may aim to meet the need, may communicate the need, or may represent the outcome of having an unmet need. An example of the first is pacing, which may provide stimulation to alleviate the unmet needs of boredom and understimulation. The second mechanism can be exemplified in some

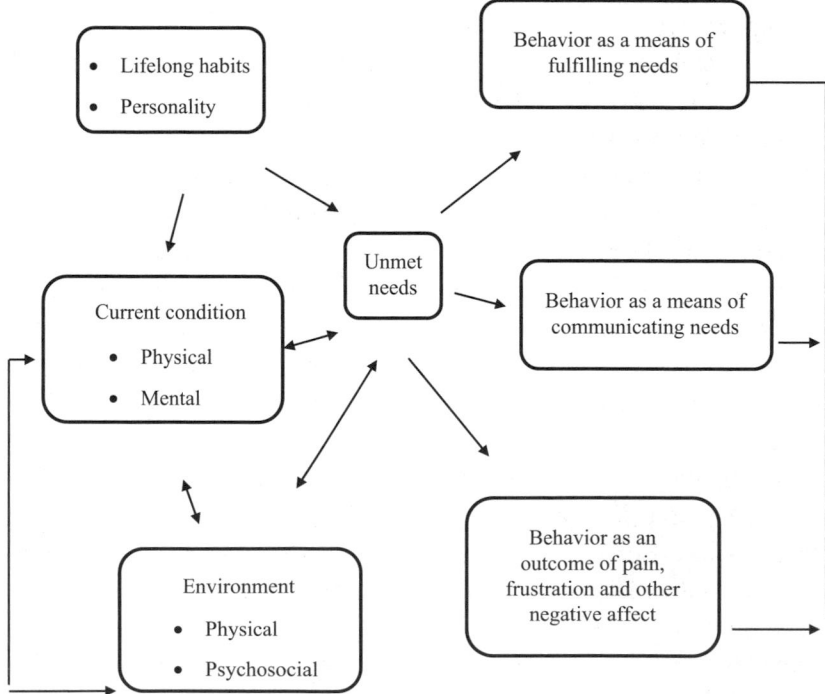

FIGURE 11.2. Unmet needs model of problem behaviors.
Copyright 1998 by Cohen-Mansfield. All rights reserved. Reprinted by permission.

repetitious vocalizations that represent an effort to communicate an unmet need, albeit a fruitless one. The third type of relationship between behavior and need can occur when the behavior, such as screaming, is an outcome of frustration or pain. Examples of specific unmet needs leading to agitation are described in the following paragraphs.

Pain, health, and physical discomfort. Physical pain and ill-health factors have been associated with verbal and vocal forms of behavior problems (Cohen-Mansfield, Billig, Lipson, Rosenthal, & Pawlson, 1990). Treatment of pain has been shown to reduce behavior problems (Husebo, Ballard, Sandvik, Nilsen, & Aarsland, 2011) and verbal–vocal behaviors in particular (Husebo et al., 2014). The behavior problem may be a direct manifestation of discomfort because vocally disruptive behaviors are a natural response to pain and may be exacerbated in people who are unable to communicate and therefore express their suffering through screaming. Alternatively, the vocally disruptive behavior may be an attempt to communicate the discomfort under circumstances in which a cognitively impaired individual is no longer able to communicate more directly. A high rate of discomfort from sources other than pain, such as uncomfortable seating or feeling cold, has been observed in PWDs (Cohen-Mansfield, Thein, Marx, Dakheel-Ali, & Jensen, 2013).

The relationship between health and aggressive behavior is inconclusive. A positive association between aggressive behavior and urinary tract infections has been reported (Ryden, Bossenmaier, & McLachlan, 1991). Other medical problems, such as dehydration and chest and dental infections, also were reported to precipitate aggressive behaviors (Cipriani, Vedovello, Nuti, & Di Fiorino, 2011). Physical pain and poor physical health predicted verbal aggression (McShane, Cohen-Mansfield, & Werner, 2000) and predicted development of aggression in those in whom it was not present initially (Kunik et al., 2010). In contrast, people who engage in physically nonaggressive behavior (e.g., pacing) have been reported to have fewer medical diagnoses than other nursing home residents and have better appetites (Cohen-Mansfield, Billig, Lipson, Rosenthal, & Pawlson, 1990). Sleep

disturbance and fatigue is another aspect of health that has been linked to behavioral symptoms (Cohen-Mansfield & Marx, 1990; Cohen-Mansfield, Werner, & Freedman, 1995). The impairment of circadian rhythms, which is characteristic of Alzheimer's disease (e.g., Bliwise, 1993), also may be related to behavior problems. In particular, an increase in behavior problems in older individuals with dementia beginning at a time near sunset has been termed "sundowning" (Bliwise, 1994).

Mental discomfort evident in affective states: depression, anxiety, and frustration. These affective processes may themselves be the result of (a) neurobiological changes, (b) lifelong problems, (c) the individual's confrontation with his or her decreasing abilities, or (d) other unmet needs. Research revealed a positive relationship between verbal–vocal behavioral symptoms and depressed affect (Cohen-Mansfield & Werner, 1998b; Cohen-Mansfield & Werner, 1999a; Majić et al., 2012), but physically nonaggressive behaviors were not correlated significantly with depressed affect (Cohen-Mansfield & Marx, 1988). This finding may be related to the fact that the same group also had more physical pain, or that this group was more cognitively intact and therefore better able to communicate their moods (via complaints or other negative comments) to caregivers than those manifesting other types of behavior problems.

Need for social contacts and social isolation. Verbal–vocal behavioral symptoms, as well as some physically nonaggressive behaviors besides pacing and wandering, tended to increase in frequency when nursing home residents manifesting these behavioral symptoms were alone and to decrease when they were with others. Similarly, such behaviors decreased when staffing levels increased (Cohen-Mansfield & Werner, 1995). These findings suggest that loneliness or the need for social contact may be at the root of these behaviors. This idea is supported by a prevention study (Cohen-Mansfield, Marx, Dakheel-Ali, Regier, Thein, & Freedman, 2010), in which social interaction was more beneficial in decreasing behavioral symptoms than the mere provision of pleasant stimuli, such as music.

Uncomfortable environmental conditions. In an observational study of the nursing home environment, most behavioral symptoms tended to increase when it was cold at night, and requests for attention increased when it was hot during the day (Cohen-Mansfield & Werner, 1995). These findings suggest that discomfort caused by the surroundings may cause some of these behaviors. Because of cognitive impairments, PWDs may not be able to understand or communicate that the environment is causing them discomfort or to alter the environment; thus, for example, thermal discomfort in a room or in a bath can precipitate behavioral symptoms (van Hoof, Kort, Hensen, Duijnstee, & Rutten, 2010). Accordingly, making environmental modifications that directly address environment-based sources of discomfort in PWDs, such as insufficient levels of light, having furniture in ones' way, and an unsupported head (Cohen-Mansfield, Thein, et al., 2013), may prevent the emergence of behavioral symptoms.

Inadequate level of stimulation (too low, too high, inappropriate) or sensory deprivation. Behavioral symptoms have been attributed to overstimulation that cannot be processed because of the dementia (e.g., Meyer et al., 1992). Other studies, however, have supported the opposite view, namely, that behavioral symptoms result from understimulation and sensory deprivation. According to this view, the PWD has a reduced ability to obtain stimulation and process it. Additionally, many of those suffering from dementia also have vision and hearing deficits that further decrease their ability to process stimuli. Finally, many of the nursing homes in which PWDs reside offer few activities or other positive stimuli. An observational study of the nursing home found that the nursing home was a relatively monotonous place (Cohen-Mansfield, Marx, & Werner, 1992b). Routine is the rule and activities and stimulation are infrequent (Cohen-Mansfield et al., 1992a). All of these factors result in a state of sensory deprivation, possibly evoking feelings of fear, loneliness, and boredom, to which the person responds with either self-stimulation or behaviors that manifest discontent because of their unmet need for stimulation. Indeed, most behavioral symptoms increased when the older person was inactive and decreased when structured activities were offered (Cohen-Mansfield & Werner, 1995). Similarly, several

studies showed that providing sensory stimulation to nursing home residents decreased behavioral disturbances in general, and vocally disruptive behaviors in particular (e.g., Bédard, Landreville, Voyer, Verreault, & Vézina, 2011; Cohen-Mansfield, Marx, Dakheel-Ali, Regier, Thein, & Freedman, 2010).

Delusions and hallucinations. Regardless of their cause, delusions and hallucinations provide inappropriate internal stimuli, which may result in problem behaviors. The relationship between problem behaviors and delusions or hallucinations has been documented repeatedly (Cohen-Mansfield et al., 1998; Lachs, Becker, Siegal, Miller, & Tinetti, 1992).

Behavioral model. According to the ABC model (Antecedents → Behavior ↔ Consequences), behavioral symptoms are controlled by their antecedents and consequences (Figure 11.3). Specifically, antecedents operate through stimulus control, and the consequences reinforce behavior, or they reinforce certain behavior related to specific antecedent stimuli. Many problem behaviors are learned through reinforcement by staff members who provide attention when the problem behavior is displayed. Within the environment of the nursing home, where social stimulation often is lacking, any attention potentially can be a potent reinforcement. Other types of learning processes, such as those involved in stimulus control, also may be operating. In a description of a 70-year-old blind woman, it was observed that she screamed more when the nurses spoke to her (Birchmore & Clague, 1983). On the other hand, other findings with nursing home populations did not support this model (e.g., Cohen-Mansfield et al., 1992; Cohen-Mansfield & Werner, 1995). In one study, most behavioral symptoms were found not to be triggered by any observable incident, and most did not receive any reaction. Aggressive behaviors

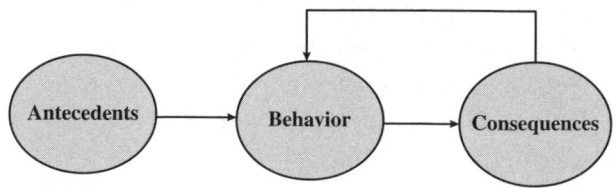

FIGURE 11.3. Behavioral model. Copyright 1998 by Cohen-Mansfield. All rights reserved. Reprinted with permission.

showed the highest rates of triggering events (26%) and reactions (43%; Cohen-Mansfield et al., 1992). Rates were less than half that for other behaviors. It is still possible that behaviors are reinforced and maintained on a low reinforcement schedule, although this would be very low for most behaviors. Furthermore, this model is based on the premise that learning can occur with dementia, when it is specifically the mechanisms responsible for learning that are impaired in dementia. Some case reports and small studies are utilizing behavioral treatments successfully (Padilla, González, Agis, Strizzi, & Rodríguez, 2013; Sato et al., 2013). Given that the behavioral treatment usually involved the older person receiving increased attention, the provision of attention (thereby fulfilling social needs), rather than the contingency of attention as a consequence of the behavior, might be the factor responsible for a change in behavior. The poor control used in most studies does not allow for proper distinction between these possibilities. Furthermore, there are unpublished reports of behavioral treatment failure or even exacerbation of behavioral problems with treatment (Lewin, 1996).

Environmental vulnerability model. According to the environmental vulnerability model, the dementia process results in greater vulnerability to the environment and a lower threshold at which stimuli affect behavior (Figure 11.4). Therefore, a stimulus that may be appropriate for a cognitively intact person may result in an overreaction from the person with cognitive impairment.

The concept of person–environment congruence (French, Rodgers, & Cobb, 1974; Kahana, 1982) and the press-competence model (Lawton & Nahemow, 1973) suggest that for optimal functioning, the demands of the environment need to be matched to the person's needs and abilities. For any level of competence, there is a range of favorable environmental demands. The environmental docility hypothesis (Lawton & Simon, 1968) states that as personal competence decreases, the environment becomes a more potent determinant of behavioral outcome. Fitting those theoretical perspectives are both the understimulation hypothesis (described in the section Unmet Needs Model, Inadequate Level of Stimulation) or the overstimulation model, which, although not supported by research, nevertheless may be represented by certain instances of inappropriate stimulation (i.e., loudspeakers in the nursing home). A related concept holds that dementia results in a progressively lowered stress threshold (Hall, 1994). Accordingly, PWDs progressively lose their coping abilities, and they therefore come to perceive their environment as increasingly stressful. At the same time, their threshold for tolerating stress decreases, resulting in anxiety and inappropriate behavior. The lowered stress threshold can result from decreased comprehension, fatigue, change in routine, or other reasons. The excess levels of stress can be caused by inappropriate environmental

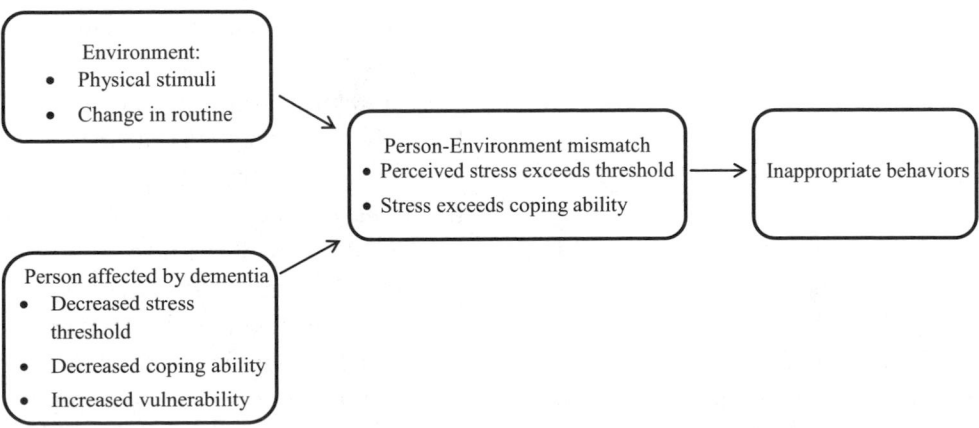

FIGURE 11.4. Environmental vulnerability and progressively lowered stress threshold model. Copyright 1998 by Cohen-Mansfield. All rights reserved. Reprinted with permission.

stimulus levels, inappropriate environmental expectations, and physical stressors, such as pain.

Theoretical Models for the Causes of Psychotic Symptoms and Misinterpretations

Various types of explanations have been proposed concerning the etiology of delusions in dementia (e.g., Ballard & Oyebode, 1995; Cohen-Mansfield, 2003; Rao & Lyketsos, 1998). Essentially, these reflect three categories: (a) Delusions may evolve from brain damage caused by dementia. (b) Delusions may evolve from the person's response to the environment, which is restricted by the impairments caused by dementia and affected by factors, such as personality and past life experience (Rao & Lyketsos, 1998), and they often present an interpretation of reality in the face of limitations, such as when a person cannot find a treasured object and assumes it was stolen. (c) Delusions may reflect a separate disorder interacting with dementia, such as sensory limitations (Cohen-Mansfield et al., 1998) or delirium, which theoretically should exclude a designation of a delusion but often is not detected (Cohen-Mansfield, 2009). Behavior that is not understood often is labeled a delusion and therefore categorized as a psychiatric symptom instead of being understood in other possible contexts. The use of the term *delusion* excludes investigation into other possible reasons for the behavior, such as cultural differences, past experiences of the PWD, misunderstandings, or drug side-effects (Cohen-Mansfield, 2009; Cohen-Mansfield, Golander, et al., 2011). Study limitations and inconsistencies in the definition and classification of delusions in dementia have led to inconclusive results regarding the frequency of experiencing delusions in dementia and their prevalence over time.

Hallucinations in dementia are associated with impaired vision or hearing (Cohen-Mansfield & Golander, 2012), which often goes undetected (Murgatroyd & Prettyman, 2001). Cataracts in particular were found to be associated with visual hallucinations (F. M. Chapman, Dickinson, McKeith, & Ballard, 1999; Jefferis, Mosimann, & Clarke, 2011). In one study, it was noted that most

visual and auditory hallucinations were not associated with negative affect (Cohen-Mansfield & Golander, 2012). Some hallucinations may be due to boredom, which exacerbates the sensory deprivation experienced by PWDs, thereby increasing the likelihood of hallucinations (Cohen-Mansfield & Golander, 2012). Many reported visual and auditory hallucinations involve talking to people who are not there, including hallucinations that seem to provide interactions with loved ones. This has been termed "comfort phenomenon" (Ballard & Oyebode, 1995), which may represent a positive coping mechanism. It also has been suggested that *hallucination* was a term staff caregivers used for the phenomena they could not explain easily, but which was not a true hallucination, thereby demonstrating their lack of understanding of the resident or of the phenomena they termed hallucination (Cohen-Mansfield & Golander, 2012).

Theoretical Models for the Causes of Depressed Affect

Cognitive and behavioral theories of depressed affect include: (a) a cognitive theory that asserts that depression is a consequence of negative and distorted cognitions about oneself (A. T. Beck, 1997; Ellis, 1994), (b) a theory that claims that depression involves learned helplessness and a sense of loss of control (Seligman, 1974; Seligman, 1975), and (c) a theory that depression relates to an insufficient level of reinforcement or pleasurable experiences (Lewinsohn & Youngren, 1976). Related to the last concept is an insufficient level of reinforcing social contacts manifested as loneliness. Depressed affect has been linked to loneliness (Cohen-Mansfield & Parpura-Gill, 2007b) and need for supportive social relationships. Depressed affect also may result from awareness of cognitive and functional decline (Amore, Tagariello, Laterza, & Savoia, 2007). Yet in a study of 92 PWDs, Ballard et al. (1993) found that people at very early stages of dementia were more likely to be depressed, but they found no significant correlation between insight into the dementia and depression.

On the basis of these theoretical frameworks, interventions to address depressed affect generally aim to increase reinforcing or pleasant events in general and social ones in particular, or to increase the sense of control of the PWD. Various models can be used to address depressed affect in PWDs, and affirmation of self also can improve affect in this population.

Theoretical Models for the Causes of Apathy and Disengagement

Whereas apathy and disengagement are symptoms of dementia and tend to increase with the progression of dementia, their course is not uniform and can be affected by environmental factors. The Comprehensive Process Model of Engagement (Cohen-Mansfield, Marx, et al., 2011) describes the factors that affect engagement in PWDs. According to the model, engagement with stimuli is influenced by environmental characteristics, personal characteristics, and stimulus attributes. Engagement can improve affect and decrease the manifestation of behavior problems (Cohen-Mansfield, Marx, et al., 2011; Cohen-Mansfield, Marx, Regier, Dakheel-Ali, Thein, & Freedman, 2010).

ASSESSMENT

The following section reviews assessment of behavioral symptoms, psychotic symptoms, depressed affect, and apathy in PWDs. Whereas the assessment of behavioral symptoms is described in the greatest detail, many of the underlying challenges of assessment in this population are invariant across assessment domains. The inability to use self-report with people with advanced dementia necessitates the use of informant ratings and observational tools. Those ratings and tools have limitations that also are described in this section. It is most important to view assessments as a first step in trying to understand the point of view of the PWD, despite the absence of self-report.

Assessment of Behavioral Symptoms

Three general methodologies have been used to assess agitation: informant ratings, observational methods, and technological devices.

Informant rating methods. Informant ratings are the most commonly used method in clinical settings, in which a caregiver rates the frequency or severity of the behaviors that constitute agitation. Many informant rating instruments have been developed and used with community-dwelling older persons, hospital patients, and nursing home residents. Some of the available assessments are listed in Table 11.1. Three informant-rating scales that represent a sample of the range of existing assessments are presented next.

One informant-rating instrument is the CMAI (Cohen-Mansfield, Marx, & Rosenthal, 1989). In the nursing home version, a nursing staff member who knows the resident well rates, on a seven-point scale ranging from "never" to "a few times an hour," the frequency of 29 behaviors (e.g., pacing, spitting, complaining) during the previous 2 weeks, as manifested by the resident. Most of the terms used in this instrument are based on reports by nursing staff and are therefore usually well understood. Another form of the CMAI includes an additional scale, namely, subjective evaluation of disruptiveness of each of the behaviors, rated on a five-point scale (1 = never, 5 = extremely). A high interrater agreement on disruptiveness is not necessarily expected, as some caregivers are bothered by agitated behaviors and others are not. Sometimes, however, change in subjective perception of disruptiveness of behavior is the main purpose of treatment, rather than a change of behavior. Furthermore, despite its subjective nature, disruptiveness is related to both the type of behavior and its frequency (Cohen-Mansfield, 2008). The final score of the CMAI usually is summarized as four scores based on the typology of behavioral symptoms described previously. Therefore, the mean frequency for each of the syndromes, physically aggressive behaviors, physically nonaggressive behaviors, verbally aggressive behaviors, and verbally agitated behaviors, is used. Findings indicate that these syndromes occur at different stages of dementia and correlate with different environmental conditions and different psychosocial characteristics (e.g., Cohen-Mansfield, Culpepper, & Werner, 1995; Cohen-Mansfield & Libin, 2005; Cohen-Mansfield et al., 1992a; Cohen-Mansfield & Werner, 1995). For example, aggressive behaviors tend to be manifested in the very late stages of dementia and to be directed at staff,

TABLE 11.1

Informant-Based Assessments for Agitation

Assessment	Authors	No. of items total (agitation)	Scale
Minimum Data Set (MDS) 3.0	(Saliba & Buchanan, 2008)	359 (3)	3-point frequency
Dementia Behavior Disturbance Scale (DBD)	(Baumgarten, Becker, & Gauthier, 1990)	28 (19)	5-point frequency
Disruptive Behavior Scale (DBS)	(J. G. Beck, 1997)	45 (all)	presence/absence 9-point severity
Cohen-Mansfield Agitation Inventory–Nursing Home version (CMAI-NH)	(Cohen-Mansfield, Werner, & Marx, 1989)	29 (all)	7-point frequency
Cohen-Mansfield Agitation Inventory–Community (CMAI-C)	(Cohen-Mansfield, Werner, Watson, & Pasis, 1995)	36 (all)	7-point frequency 7-point disruptiveness
Cohen-Mansfield Agitation Inventory–Short form (CMAI-S)	(Werner et al., 1994a)	14 (all)	5-point frequency
The Neuropsychiatric Inventory (NPI)	(Cummings et al., 1994)	83 (62)	4-point frequency 3-point severity 6-point disruptiveness
Behavioral Syndromes Scale for Dementia	(Devanand, Broekington, Moody, & Brown, 1992)	33 (all)	varies according to item: 6-point severity, yes/no occurrence
Gottfries-Brane-Steen Scale (GBS)	(Gottfries, Bråne, Gullberg, & Steen, 1982)	29 (4)	7-point severity
Cornell Scale for Depression in Dementia	(Alexopoulos et al., 1988)	19 (2)	3-point severity
Multidimensional Observation Scale for Elderly Subjects (MOSES)	(Fisman et al., 1988)	40 (10)	5-point frequency
Behavioral Pathology in Alzheimer's Disease Rating Scale (BEHAVE-AD)	(Reisberg et al., 1987)	25 (18)	4-point severity
Pittsburgh Agitation Scale (PAS)	(Rosen et al., 1995)	4 (all)	varies; 5-point severity for most
The Alzheimer's Disease Assessment Scale (ADAS)	(Mohs, 1996)	21 (4)	5-point severity
Ryden Aggression Scale (RAS)	(Ryden, 1988)	25 (all aggression)	6-point frequency
Consortium to Establish a Registry for Alzheimer's Disease Behavior Rating Scale for Dementia (CERAD)	(Blazina & Rubin, 1995)	51 (17)	3-point frequency
Revised Memory and Behavioral Problems Checklist (RMBPC)	(Teri et al., 1992)	24 (10)	5-point frequency 5-point reaction

Note. Copyright 2003 by Cohen-Mansfield. Reprinted with permission.

especially during the performance of ADLs. Verbal agitation occurs in the middle stages of the disease and is more common in people suffering from pain and discomfort. Physically nonaggressive behaviors occur more often as the dementia progresses and are not associated with discomfort. In some analyses, however, all aggressive behaviors (verbal and physical) cluster together or all verbal behaviors (aggressive and nonaggressive) correlate, and three rather than four factors emerge (Cohen-Mansfield, Werner, Watson, & Pasis, 1995). Consequently, lumping all

the behaviors together can mask the significance of the findings.

Another example of an informant rating scale is the Pittsburgh Agitation Scale (PAS; Rosen et al., 1994). The PAS rates agitated behaviors in four general behavior groups: aberrant vocalization, motor agitation, aggressiveness, and resisting care, on a scale ranging from zero, "not present", to four, an extreme manifestation of the behavior. The behaviors are rated according to intensity, which includes descriptions of disruptiveness, and ease of redirection of the person's behavior. The brevity of the PAS makes it useful for repeated measurement and for monitoring behavioral progression.

The Behavioral Pathology in Alzheimer's Disease Rating Scale (BEHAVE-AD; Reisberg et al., 1987) is yet another informant rating instrument; it is composed of 25 items assessing paranoid or delusional ideation, hallucinations, activity disturbance (e.g., wandering, purposeless activity, inappropriate activity), aggressiveness, diurnal rhythm disturbance, affective disturbance, and anxieties and phobias. Items are rated on a four-point severity scale, ranging from "not present" to "present generally with an emotional and physical component." Additionally, the BEHAVE-AD has a four-point scale of the global danger or disruptiveness of the behavior for both the patient and caregivers, ranging from "not at all troubling" to "severely troubling."

Comparing informant rating instruments. Some protocols represent a combination of methods, such as when a nursing staff member rates the behavior of the resident at the end of each hour or at the end of a nursing shift. Although commonly referred to as an observational method, this combination method does not involve the nursing staff member's observing the older person for the complete hour or nursing shift. Rather, it is a caregiver rating of behavior occurring over a short time frame, which is representative of the behaviors observed via clinical work during the hour or the shift.

Informant rating instruments (Table 11.1) often share items and are generally very similar. They do differ, however, in the domains described and the type of scale used, and consequently in sensitivity, ceiling and floor effects, setting and informant used, length and content, and the time frame considered.

Domains. An estimation of the number of items that focus on behavioral symptoms in each of the instruments can be seen in Table 11.1. Some of those instruments assess cognitive functioning, affect, and other constructs, in addition to behavioral symptoms. For example, the Neuropsychiatric Inventory (NPI) evaluates 10 behavioral domains, including delusions and hallucinations, agitation and aggression, dysphoria, anxiety, apathy, disinhibition, irritability and lability, and aberrant motor

activity. Other assessments focus specifically on assessing inappropriate behaviors and do not tap into additional constructs. Some instruments are geared to a specific behavioral syndrome, such as the Ryden Aggression Scale (Ryden, 1988), while others include a range of behavioral syndromes.

Informants. Different assessments are rated by different informants, such as nursing assistants, charge nurses, and family members. Obviously, because the assessments inquire about the frequency of behavioral symptoms, crucial factors in this form of assessment are the amount of contact the informant had with the older person during the period to be rated and the informant's ability to observe and report the behavior. Some assessments therefore use several types of informants. Informant-based data reflects the perceptions of the informant, which may be affected by the informant's level of stress (Cohen-Mansfield & Libin, 2004)—for example, a nursing staff member who has to assess residents when there are many on the unit who have an acute illness. Conversely, it may be affected by habituation to the behavior through long-term exposure. At times, informants may underreport behavior because of a concern that high levels of inappropriate behavior may reflect negatively either on the quality of care they provide or on the older person (Cohen-Mansfield & Libin, 2004).

Length and content. Scales vary from 3 to approximately 40 items, although the content of many items can overlap. Three items often are not able to capture the variability among inappropriate behaviors and do not elicit from the informant the full range of behaviors that need to be rated. Detailed and inclusive instruments are important when the most crucial behaviors for any specific condition in a given population are unknown. At other times, a very short instrument is needed, such as when behaviors need to be continuously monitored to assess fluctuation or responsiveness to treatment in a clinical setting or when items on the longer instruments are not useful. Therefore, a shorter form of the CMAI has been developed (CMAI-S; Werner, Cohen-Mansfield, Koroknay, & Braun, 1994a). This version has been useful for clinical studies (e.g., Cooke, Moyle, Shum, Harrison, & Murfield, 2010) with limited funding that need to minimize the requirements of staff members. Furthermore, some projects concentrate on specific behaviors, such as pacing and wandering or verbally disruptive behaviors, and thus may use shorter assessments that focus on only the behavior under study. Related to the issue of length is content. Generally, short instruments either concentrate on a subset of the behaviors or lump some of them into somewhat larger categories. Depending on the population treated, indicators that collapse behaviors (e.g., all physical aggression is one item on the Minimum Data Set 3.0; Saliba & Buchanan, 2008) either may be particularly useful or may be too broad for the designation of treatment and monitoring of its effects.

Scales. Different assessments use different scales to measure such characteristics as frequency and disruptiveness. Points on the scale that are well defined, for example, that record frequency of a behavior over a specified "period" that are more precise and less open to interpretation than more general categories like "a lot" or "frequently." Scales can emphasize the impact of the behavior through focus on the disruptiveness of the behavior or on reactions to the behavior. Scales also may exhibit a ceiling effect. When the population exhibits behaviors that occur much more frequently than once per day, instruments on which the highest frequency noted is "daily" may not be sufficiently sensitive. This is particularly important when a scale is being used to make decisions about the staff resources necessary to manage behaviors.

Time frames. The time frames over which the older person is rated depend on the study and on the scale used. Some studies use the last nursing shift (i.e., the previous 8 hr); others use the past month or a time frame in between. The time period chosen can vary according to the nature of the behaviors to be rated and according to the expected recall of caregivers. If the behavior is hitting or biting, raters usually remember such high-impact behaviors, even if they occurred a month before rating. If, on the other hand, the behavior is one with a low impact, such as repetitive mannerisms, it is less likely to be remembered over long periods of time.

Scoring. There are various ways to score these assessments. Items can be summed by their frequency, disruptive impact, or frequency weighted by disruptive impact; they also can be scored by syndromes; or they can be used to determine the most frequently occurring behavior or the most disruptive behavior. These different methods will yield different rates and results. As mentioned, we have found meaningful differences among the syndromes of agitation (e.g., verbal behaviors, physically nonaggressive, and physically aggressive behaviors), and therefore for most purposes, these should be scored separately. The final choice depends, however, on the purpose of the assessment.

Observational methods. Observational methods are systematic observations of the older person in his or her natural setting (e.g., home, hospital, nursing home, adult day care setting, etc.). A trained research assistant observes the older person for a given time period, examines the behaviors, and rates them on a standardized printed instrument or using portable computers or devices, or by scanning a barcode from a list. Alternatively, the behaviors can be videotaped and later rated by a trained research assistant who views the recording as in direct in vivo observations.

One major difficulty with the use of observational methods for assessing behavioral symptoms is that many behaviors occur infrequently or rarely, so either very long or multiple observations are needed to detect these behaviors. This is especially true, for example, in the case of aggressive behaviors, which are among the most important in terms of impact on others but are infrequent.

One observational tool is the Agitation Behavior Mapping Instrument (ABMI; Cohen-Mansfield, Thein, Marx, Dakheel-Ali, & Freedman, 2012; Cohen-Mansfield, Werner, & Marx, 1989; Mossello et al., 2011) in which several aspects of agitation are examined, including the frequency of occurrence of the agitated behaviors, the social environment (i.e., the identity of those in proximity), the activity in which the PWD is engaged and who initiated the activity, the location of the resident on the unit, and environmental characteristics and body position. Proper use of the ABMI requires thorough training of the observers. The types of agitated behaviors observed are similar to those covered in informant rating assessments.

Although most assessments, including the ABMI, originally have been used as paper and pencil tools, they have been computerized on various devices that allow direct computerized data entry.

Technological devices.   Technological devices can automatically measure an aspect of the older person's behavior, such as degree of movement or level of noise emitted. They have been used for assessing wandering and include instruments such as a pedometer, an actigraph, or a step sensor. These devices typically are attached at the ankle of the person and measure the amount of walking activity. Most of these devices have a demonstrated validity against an observational criterion (Algase, Beattie, Leitsch, & Beel-Bates, 2003; Bankole et al., 2012; Cohen-Mansfield, Werner, Culpepper, Wolfson, & Bickel, 1997; Greiner, Makimoto, Suzuki, Yamakawa, & Ashida, 2007). They vary in the degree to which they bother the older person, the extent to which the older person fidgets with the devices, the difficulty of putting the device on the older person, and the difficulty of transferring data from the device to a computer database for analysis (Cohen-Mansfield, Werner, Culpepper, Wolfson, & Bickel, 1997). Use of technical devices has been limited and generally has been confined to ambulatory behavior, although there are some trials of the use of devices to analyze vocal (Cohen-Mansfield, Werner, Hammerschmidt, & Newman, 2003) and aggressive (D. Chen et al., 2008) behavior.

Assessment Controversies and Dilemmas

Comparing methods of assessment.   Given that various methods are available (i.e., informant ratings, observational methods, and mechanical devices), how do we decide which methods to use? Overall, the actual choice of an assessment method will depend on the goals and resources of the user and how they match the strengths and weaknesses of each method. The choice also requires understanding of differences of the assessments on dimensions, such as time sampling, objectivity, and cost.

Time sampling.   In vivo observations and video recordings are most useful for covering very short periods of time. They require spending the actual amount of time observing a person and recording behaviors as they occur. Observations typically use time-sampling procedures (i.e., specific time-limited periods are chosen for observation, such as observing for 3 min/hr for 6 hr a day during 1 week). Informant ratings, however, report behavior based on a longer time frame, such as the last 2 weeks or month. They tap behavior as noticed by the informant during time in contact with the rated person; however, they also depend on the informant's memory of events. Longer periods can be covered using technological devices.

Regarding the appropriateness of each of these methods for assessing low-frequency behaviors, such as aggressive behavior, informant ratings are usually reasonably appropriate, although it depends on the salience of the behavior. Observations, on the other hand, generally are inappropriate for the detection of low-frequency behaviors.

Objectivity.   In terms of objectivity, informant ratings can be biased by the relationship between the informant and the person who is rated. This may cause a problem, depending on the purpose of the assessment. If the ability of the caregiver to take care of the person is the focal point, then their perception of the behavior is likely to be the target for assessment whether objective or biased. It may be useful to assess and address the bias (e.g., via a discussion on patience, empathy, expectations, tolerance, etc.), or it may be appropriate to handle the bias through an improved approach to handling of the behavior (e.g., teaching the caregiver to better engage the older person, which may alter the presentation of the behavior to an extent that it is no longer disturbing to the caregiver). If the focus is the behavior per se, then the bias is a source of concern, and other methods should be considered.

Cost.   Caregiver ratings are relatively inexpensive, but they require buy-in on the part of key stakeholders (head of facility, charge nurse, etc.) because they take caregivers' time, whereas observations are very costly. The cost of mechanical devices depends not only on the price of the device but also on costs associated with usage, ease of use, and costs of transferring data from the device to a computer.

Assessment of Psychotic Symptoms and Misinterpretations

Results of studies assessing psychosis in dementia may vary depending on the assessment tool used and its design. In a comparison study of assessment tools for psychosis in dementia, the Behavioral Pathology in Alzheimer's Disease Rating Scale (BEHAVE-AD), NPI–Nursing Homes (NPI-NH), Consortium to Establish a Registry for Alzheimer's Disease Behavior Rating Scale for Dementia, and Columbia University Scale for Psychopathology in Alzheimer's Disease were compared with their ability to detect psychotic symptoms (Cohen-Mansfield & Golander, 2011). It was found that depending on the assessment, some symptoms were missed or not at all specified. Length of the instrument or use of global questions can affect interpretations, as a short instrument may be limited in its ability to detect a range of symptoms, and global questions may lead to a misinterpretation of symptoms. All instruments have established reliability and validity (Devanand, Miller, et al., 1992; Jacobs et al., 1998; Mack et al., 1999; Patterson et al., 1997; Reisberg et al., 1996; Tariot, 1996; Tariot et al., 1995; Weiner et al., 1998; Wood et al., 2000).

Assessment of Depressed Affect

There are various measurements for depressed affect. These typically include self-report scales that are reviewed in Chapter 1 in this volume. Self-report assessments usually are appropriate only in early stages of dementia, whereas informant ratings are used to assess depressed affect in people with more advanced dementia. For example, the Raskin Depression Scale (RDS; Raskin, 1988) includes three items, verbal report, behavior, and secondary symptoms of depression, each rated on a five-point scale from not at all to very much. Cohen-Mansfield and Werner (1995) reported good interrater agreement (81%) and reliability (Cronbach's alpha [α] = .85) for the RDS.

The Cornell Scale for Depression in Dementia (Alexopoulos, Abrams, Young, & Shamoian, 1988) is a longer instrument based on a combination of interviews with informants, interviews with PWDs, and observation of PWDs. It includes 19 symptoms rated on a scale of 0 = absent, 1 = mild or intermittent, and 2 = severe. The scale has good reliability (Cronbach's α = .84) and validity (total scale scores correlate with the intensity of depressive subtypes classified according to research diagnostic criteria, r = .83; Alexopoulos et al., 1988).

Assessment of Apathy and Disengagement

The Apathy Evaluation Scale (AES) is a clinician-, informant-, and self-rated measurement composed of 18 items that tap participant's thoughts, emotions, and activities during the previous 4 weeks. Each item is rated on a four-point scale ("slightly" to "a lot"). The clinician version is administered as a semistructured interview (Marin, Firinciogullari, & Biedrzycki, 1993). The Short Version Apathy Scale (Starkstein et al., 1992) is a self-rated scale, in which the interviewer reads the questions and the participant states an answer, which includes 14 items rated on a three- or four-point scale, with a higher score indicating greater apathy. The Apathy Inventory includes ratings of apathy in general and also of emotional blunting, lack of initiative, and lack of interest (Robert et al., 2002). It has two versions: a caregiver version to be administered in the patient's absence, and a patient version. The Short-Form Lille Apathy Rating Scale consists of seven categories, with a total of 12 questions rated on a five- or three-point scale, on such topics as initiation and motivation, for an end-score ranging from −15 (no apathy) to +15 (severe apathy; Dujardin, Sockeel, Carette, Delliaux, & Defebvre, 2013). It is rated by the interviewer during a structured interview with the patient. The Apathy in Dementia, Nursing Home scale includes 26 items relating to deficit of thinking and self-generated behaviors, emotional blunting, and cognitive inertia, with each item rated on a scale from 0 points (no apathy) to 3 points (severe apathy; Agüera-Ortiz et al., 2013). It is an informant-based assessment completed by a professional caregiver who regularly works with the patient and therefore has a good familiarity with the patient.

Engagement usually is assessed through direct observations. One such assessment is the Observational Measurement of Engagement. It measures several dimensions of engagement, including rate of refusal of stimulus or activity, duration of engagement with stimulus or activity, degree of attention to the stimulus measured on a four-point scale (not attentive, somewhat attentive, attentive, and very attentive), and attitude toward the stimulus rated on a seven-point scale (very negative, negative, somewhat negative, neutral, somewhat positive, positive, and very positive; Cohen-Mansfield, Dakheel-Ali, & Marx, 2009).

Other Assessments Needed

This discussion of assessment has focused on how to assess the level of specific symptoms of dementia. To develop interventions, however, additional assessments are needed to understand the identity, preferences, habits, and abilities of PWDs. A discussion of these assessments is beyond the scope of this chapter; however, examples of those assessments are the Self-Identity in Dementia Questionnaire (Cohen-Mansfield, Parpura-Gill, & Golander, 2006b), which explores past and present self-identities of PWDs focusing on occupational role, social role, hobbies role, and important attributes, and querying about preferred activities; the Sources of Discomfort Scale (Cohen-Mansfield, Thein, et al., 2013), which delineates a methodology for ascertaining the types and sources of discomfort that a PWD may be experiencing; the Pleasant Events Schedule (Logsdon & Teri, 1997; Meeks, Shah, & Ramsey, 2009), which is an assessment that helps caregivers identify activities that may provide pleasure to PWDs; and Self-Maintenance Habits and Preferences in Elderly (SHAPE; Cohen-Mansfield & Jensen, 2007), which inquires about older persons' preferences and habits with respect to their self-care practices and daily routines and the level of importance assigned to these practices. SHAPE can be used with community-dwelling or institutional populations and includes sections dealing with sleeping, eating, dressing and grooming, and hygiene.

TYPES OF INTERVENTIONS

At the most general level, interventions for any of the syndromes described in this chapter can be divided into nonpharmacological and pharmacological interventions. In the following text, however, we describe pharmacological interventions only in the behavioral symptoms and agitation category. For depression antidepressant medications are used with PWDs; methylphenidate (Ritalin) has been tried with PWDs who manifest apathy (Rosenberg et al., 2013), while antipsychotic medication has been used for psychotic symptoms. Whereas the efficacy of all these approaches is under debate, that discussion is beyond the scope of this chapter.

Interventions for Behavioral Symptoms and Agitation

Nonpharmacological interventions. Nonpharmacological approaches to care for PWDs are based on a wide range of theoretical orientations and represent a broad array of methodologies. Rather than viewing the patient's disease as the problem, this perspective considers the interactions among the patient, caregiver, environment, and system of care, and ascertains treatment accordingly (Figure 11.5). Nonpharmacological interventions have been used to enhance cognition, affect, and ADL performance; to reinforce a positive sense of self; and to reduce agitation or behavior problems and psychotic symptoms. A variety of nonpharmacological interventions have been described in the literature and summarized in multiple reviews (Bates, Boote, & Beverley, 2004; Brodaty & Arasaratnam, 2012; Cohen-Mansfield, 2001; Cohen-Mansfield, 2003; Cohen-Mansfield, 2004; Cohen-Mansfield, 2013; Cooper et al., 2012; Gräsel, Wiltfang, & Kornhuber, 2003; Seitz et al., 2012; Siders et al., 2004).

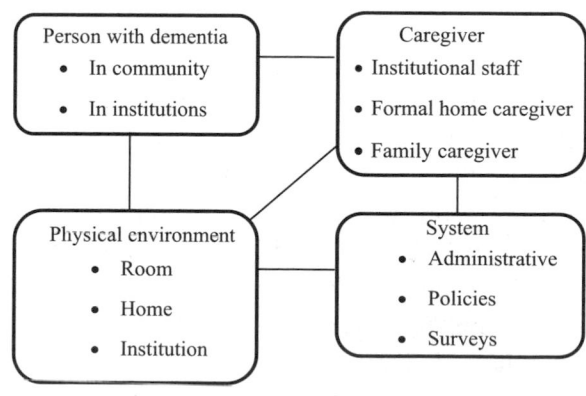

FIGURE 11.5.   Who should be treated? Copyright 2013 by Cohen-Mansfield. Reprinted with permission.

Nonpharmacological treatments of behavioral symptoms for older persons include adjusting the physical environment, redirecting when distressed, improving communication, and promoting social-ization interactions, sometimes consisting of simu-lated socialization (e.g., pet therapy), structured activities (e.g., reminiscence therapy), or behavioral interventions. Interventions should be combined with caregiver education and support (Cohen-Mansfield, 2006; Cohen-Mansfield, 2001; Cohen-Mansfield, 2003; Cohen-Mansfield, 2005; Lavretsky & Nguyen, 2006; Salzman et al., 2008). Studies on the effectiveness of training for nursing home caregivers (e.g., training in communication with PWDs and colleagues; training aimed at reduc-ing agitation and use of restraint in the interaction with residents with dementia) showed improvement in patients' symptoms, lessened the need for restraints by changing the way nursing home caregivers con-ceptualize and intervene with problem behaviors (Haberstroh, Neumeyer, Schmitz, & Pantel, 2009; Testad, Ballard, Bronnick, & Aarsland, 2010), and increased the quality of medical care (Mitchell et al., 2009).

A number of questions must be answered before decision makers commit to any treatment plan, including the following: What is the goal of treat-ment? Who needs to be treated? Whose problem is being treated? Whose reality is being considered? Whose needs and preferences take precedence? Answers to these questions will determine the treat-ment's ultimate goal, which then will dictate the selection of intervention.

The goal of treatment is important when dealing with conflicts of interest. For example, when a PWD says he needs to meet with his father, reminding him of his father's death may improve his grasp of reality but will conflict with the goal of patient com-fort. Cleanliness may at times be at odds with per-sonal autonomy, which is extremely important, as an individual with dementia may prefer not to take a bath, but at times this preference may need to be compromised to prevent pain and suffering resulting from infection. Sometimes it is possible to accom-plish both goals or to minimally compromise both, but in other instances, a choice must be made. Com-fort and positive life experiences are often more

relevant for PWDs than is perceiving a reality that is consistent with that of caregivers; for example, when PWDs experience life as if it is taking place when they are children, it often is preferable to accept their perception rather than continually try to orient them to the present. The approach under-lying this current discussion assumes that a positive life experience, or at least the absence of negative experiences, is a goal that takes priority over improved function.

Preliminary requirements for nonpharmacological interventions. Providing information to caregivers of PWDs is essential to the provision of nonpharma-cological interventions. Knowledge of the disease, as well as of specific symptoms and their etiology, meaning, and management, will allow caregiv-ers to better understand the individual's behaviors rather than attributing them to resistance, difficult personality, malicious intent, or indifference. A sec-ond prerequisite for nonpharmcological interven-tions is communication training. Communication skills are crucial for maintaining quality of life and for understanding the perspective of the PWD, despite the decline in the ability to communicate in advanced dementia. Caregivers therefore must be taught to observe, listen, speak, ask questions, and offer alternatives in ways that will maximize the PWD's ability to receive and transmit information. Communication training programs are instrumental in advancing the knowledge and communication skills of both professional and family caregivers. A review of 12 studies published between the years 1994 and 2009 concluded that communication skills training has significant benefits for caregiver com-munication skills, competencies, and knowledge, including increased awareness of the perspective of the PWD as well as improvement of PWD's qual-ity of life and well-being (Eggenberger, Heimerl, & Bennett, 2012). Detailed information on caregiver training programs can be found in the section Education of Staff and Family Members.

Another condition necessary for successful implementation of nonpharmacological interven-tions is a positive practice style by the intervener (usually a caregiver). This practice style requires respect for the patient as a person, empathy, willing-ness to enhance the person's autonomy, flexibility in addressing both care and environmental issues, and compassion toward the individual. In targeting the system, caregiver, or environment for intervention, the nonpharmacological approach imparts a greater significance to the patient's point of view. Providing maximal autonomy to the PWD is a central guiding principle and bestows greater importance to the person's habits or preferences rather than to the convenience of the caregiving system. Understanding this point of view is an important stage in the determination of treatment. In accord with this framework, a nursing home may be expected to adapt meal times to residents' habits and wishes rather than to the convenience of the kitchen staff.

An intervention targeting specific behaviors should follow a thorough assessment, including a functional analysis examining the nature of the behaviors (assessment of specific symptoms), an evaluation of the interaction of symptoms with the environment (antecedents, consequences), and clarification of who is affected negatively by the symptom. Systematic observation often is useful for this assessment. In addition to information about physical and mental health, the assessment taps into the topics of identity, habits and preferences, and past stress, thus guiding the understanding of the etiology of symptoms presented as well as determining realistic goals and options for treatment. In ascertaining the etiology of symptoms, the assessor examines a multitude of issues to try to elucidate their causes, including when and where the behavior occurs, what seems to trigger it, whether relationships between the caregiver and recipient affect the behavior, whether the caregiver has the resources necessary to perform his or her tasks, whether the PWD understands the intent of the caregiver, and whether the person has sufficient activities and social contacts.

Following this assessment, an intervention is chosen to match the hypothesized etiology of symptoms, the individual's prior habits and preferences, and his or her current abilities and limitations. The intervention may target a change in the environment, the behavior of the staff member or caregiver, the system of care, or the PWD. After the intervention is implemented, another evaluation is performed to determine whether the approach was helpful or should be changed. A change may require a different intervention entirely or may focus on a specific aspect of the intervention, such as timing, dosage, or presentation style.

Nonpharmacological interventions to treat inappropriate behaviors. Nonpharmacological interventions to treat inappropriate behaviors can be organized according to the needs they address, most of which pertain to social contact, engaging activities, and relief from discomfort (Figures 11.6, 11.7, and 11.8). Many interventions address more than a single unmet need—for example, meaningful social contact may alleviate both loneliness and boredom.

Providing social support and contact. At the most basic level, providing social support and contact involves talking to the PWD, even if it is the caregiver who provides the majority of the conversation. One-on-one interaction is a potent intervention that can be implemented by relatives, paid caregivers, or volunteers. There are two major difficulties in providing positive social contact for PWDs: (a) these individuals may prefer socializing with loved ones rather than formal caregivers, and (b) providing one-on-one interaction with staff members can become costly. A successful intervention that addresses both of these issues is simulated presence therapy. In this intervention, family members interact with their relative with dementia by means of videotapes (Cohen-Mansfield & Werner, 1997; O'Connor, Smith, Nott, Lorang, & Mathews, 2011; Werner, Cohen-Mansfield, Fischer, & Segal, 2000) or audiotapes (the family member audiotapes his or her side of a telephone conversation, which is then played for the older person; Camberg et al., 1999; Cheston, Thorne, Whitby, & Peak, 2007). Intervention variants include training staff members to view all interactions with individuals in their care as opportunities for social contact (including during ADLs) and commercially produced videos for PWDs. These interactive videotapes often incorporate remembrances from the past and invite viewers to sing along to familiar music. Animal-assisted interventions are another option (Bernabei et al., 2013) and may include visits with dogs, cats, fish, or even plush stuffed animals or robotic pets (Libin & Cohen-Mansfield, 2004; Marx et al., 2010). In addition to interaction with the animal, animal-assisted

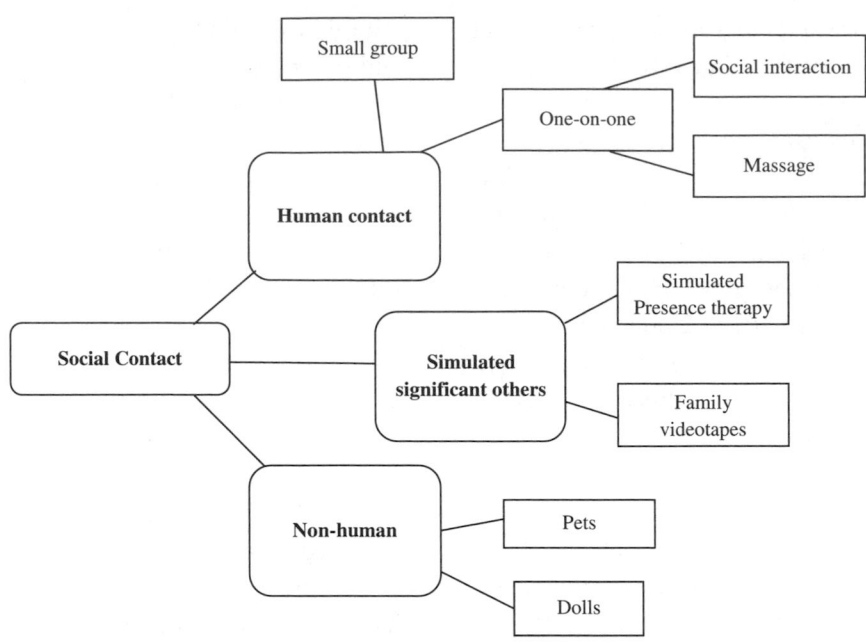

FIGURE 11.6.   Nonpharmacological interventions for behavioral problems. Examples of treatment by need: social contact. Copyright 2013 by Cohen-Mansfield. Reprinted wih permission.

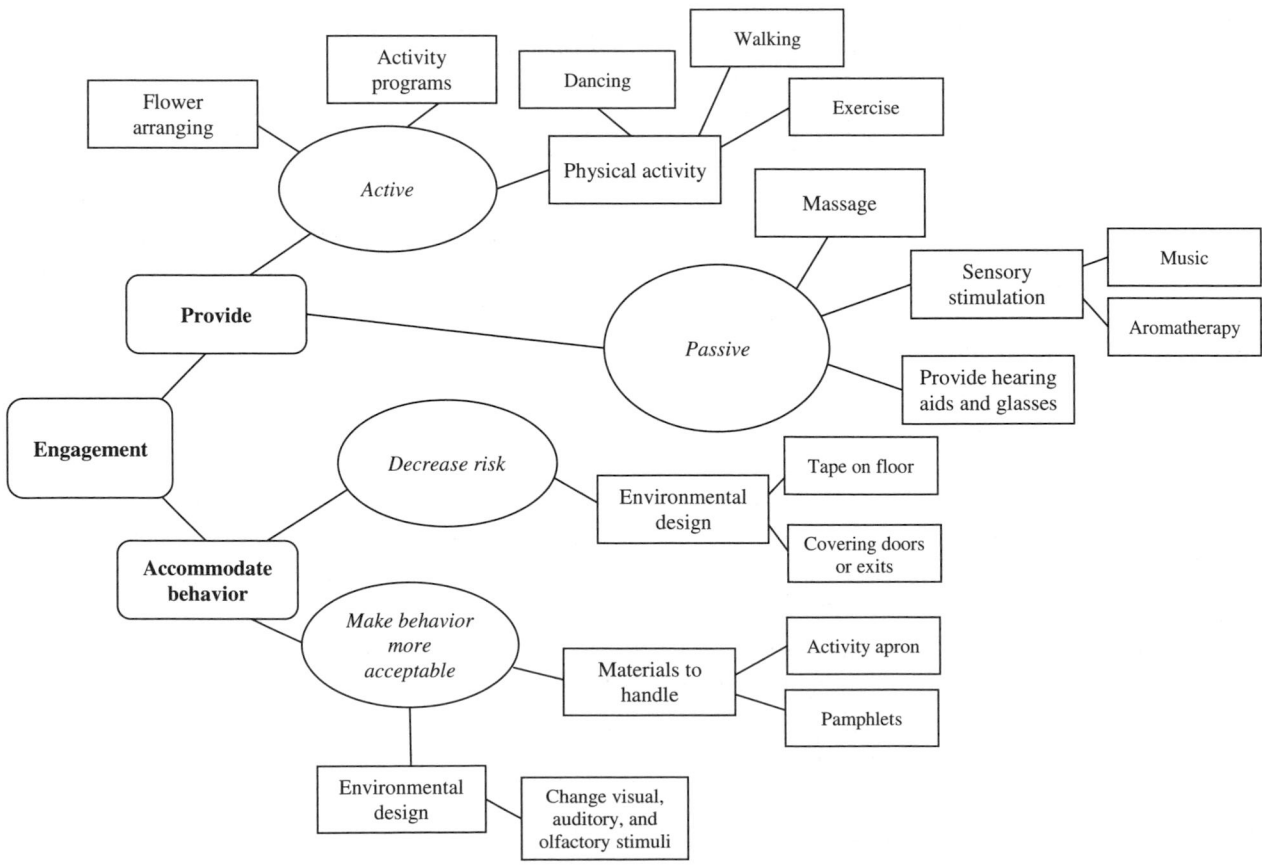

FIGURE 11.7.   Nonpharmacological interventions for behavioral problems. Examples of treatment by need: engagement. Copyright 2013 by Cohen-Mansfield. Reprinted with permission.

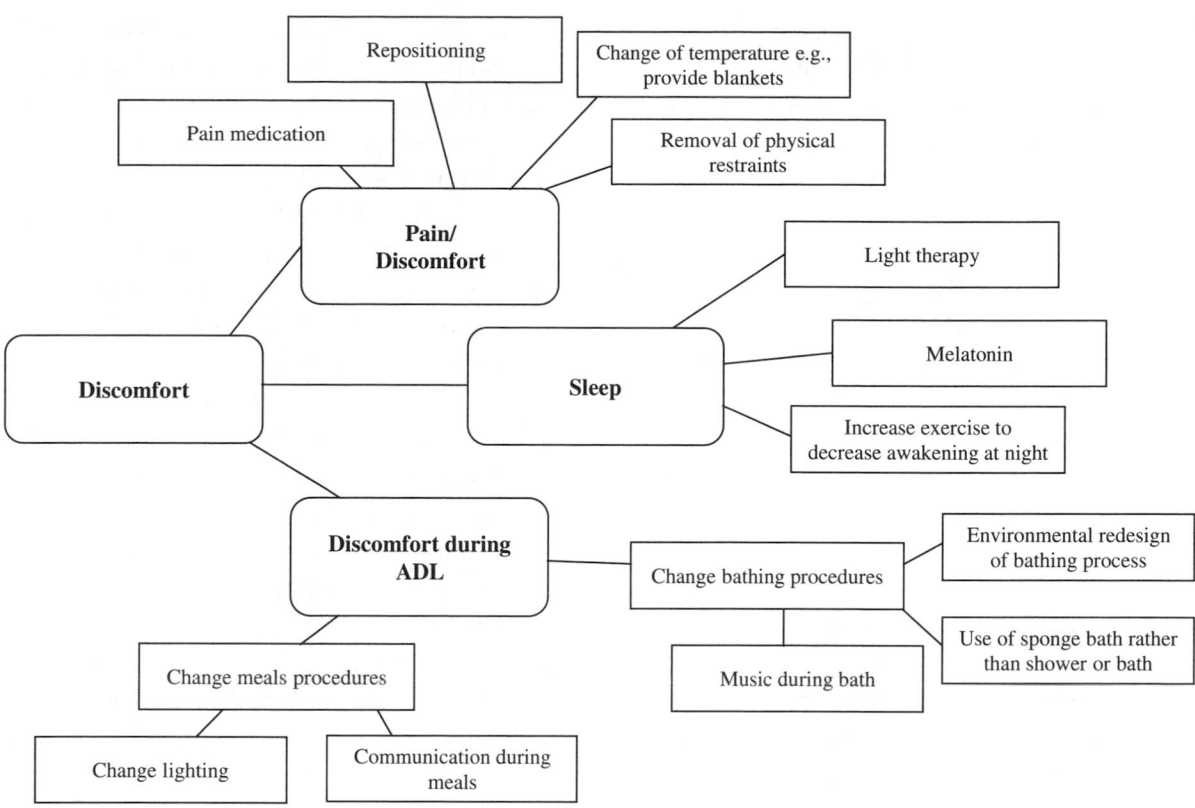

FIGURE 11.8. Nonpharmacological interventions for behavioral problems. Examples of treatment by need: discomfort. Copyright 2013 by Cohen-Mansfield. Reprinted with permission.

interventions provide a topic for interaction with other people. Dolls have been used to simulate companions and babies (Higgins, 2010), and massage (Moyle, Johnston, & O'Dwyer, 2011) may be an effective mechanism for social contact with nonverbal people with advanced dementia.

Providing engaging activities.   Engaging PWDs can be accomplished by providing them with stimulation (passive engagement), providing activities (active engagement), and allowing self-stimulation by accommodating inappropriate behaviors (Figure 11.7). Stimulation that can be provided includes the use of music, which should be tailored to the person's preferences (Gerdner, 2000), and other sensory stimulation, such as aromatherapy (Fung, Tsang, & Chung, 2012) or touch therapy (Weiser, Gegenheimer, & Klein, 2009). Music interventions take many forms, including listening to recorded music, playing musical games, dancing or moving to music, and singing. Considerations before initiating music therapy include testing hearing and

using an amplifier, headphone, or hearing aid, if necessary. One example of sensory stimulation is the "snoezelen" program, which was developed in Holland and includes a variety of relaxing stimuli (Baillon et al., 2004).

Active engagement usually is offered in the form of structured activities, including group and individual activities. Activity interventions may include tasks (e.g., flower arrangement), reading stimuli (e.g., being presented with a large-print magazine), manipulative stimuli (e.g., a tetherball), individually tailored activities matched to the individual's past preferences or identity, and work-like activities (e.g., stamping envelopes; Cohen-Mansfield, Marx, Dakheel-Ali, Regier, & Thein, 2010). Another approach is the use of Montessori-based activities derived from the principles of Maria Montessori (Camp, Cohen-Mansfield, & Capezuti, 2002); they involve task breakdown, immediate feedback, and use of everyday, real-world materials. Alternatively, the content of activities may be based on information obtained regarding "pleasant activities"—that is, activities that have been or are presently reinforcing to the individual (Teri & Logsdon, 1991), or using information about the individual's past or present role-identity (Cohen-Mansfield, Parpura-Gill, & Golander, 2006a; Cohen-Mansfield, Thein, Dakheel-Ali, & Marx, 2010; Parpura-Gill & Cohen-Mansfield, 2006). Activities can involve dance (Guzmán-García, Hughes, James, & Rochester, 2013) and exercise (Thuné-Boyle, Iliffe, Cerga-Pashoja, Lowery, & Warner, 2012), or they may incorporate an adaptation of ADLs, such as setting the table or cooking (Marsden, Meehan, & Calkins, 2001).

Cognitive tasks are activities that stimulate cognitive and memory skills (Livingston, Johnston, Katona, Paton, & Lyketsos, 2005). An example of a group activity is "Question Asking Readings," in which a group reads a script accompanied by questions typed on cards that encourage participants to discuss related topics (Camp, Foss, O'Hanlon, & Stevens, 1996). An individual cognitive task is sorting cards or objects by category (additional examples of activities for PWDs are available elsewhere; see Milders, Bell, Lorimer, MacEwan, & McBain, 2013; Quayhagen & Quayhagen, 2001; Woods, Aguirre, Spector, & Orrell, 2012).

Interventions for accommodating pacing or wandering behavior include outdoor walks (Cohen-Mansfield & Werner, 1998c) and the use of wandering areas. Outdoor walks may take place in the company of a caregiver, in which case they also involve a social component, or they may occur in secure outdoor wandering areas (Cohen-Mansfield & Werner, 1999b; Namazi & Johnson, 1992). A benefit of accommodating pacing and wandering is the prevention of trespassing while wandering, protecting both the wanderer and others. Another technique to prevent trespassing into another person's room or through emergency exit doors is to camouflage doors and doorknobs with cloth panels or murals (Kincaid & Peacock, 2003). When disguising doors, safety regulations should be kept in mind as well as ethical considerations such as making sure other doors are visible, preventing residents from feeling trapped. Additionally, providing alternative doors, which can be controlled by the PWD and permit movement into another secured area, can be useful in reducing trespassing (Namazi, Rosner, & Calkins, 1989) and behavioral symptoms (Namazi & Johnson, 1992).

Inappropriate handling or the constant manipulation of objects can be accommodated by providing appropriate and safe-to-handle materials, such as suitable books and pamphlets (Cohen-Mansfield & Werner, 1998a) and activity aprons with buttons, zippers, and other articles sewn on. Similarly, rocking chairs and gliding swings have been used to accommodate restless behavior and improve relaxation (see Snyder et al., 2001).

Providing relief from discomfort.   Interventions addressing discomfort target pain, hearing and vision problems, positioning problems, difficulties adjusting to ADLs, and unmet ADL-related needs. Although these can be considered medical and nursing care interventions rather than "nonpharmacological" interventions, these interventions address negative affect or behavioral problems that are detected by the behavioral assessment of the underlying etiology of the symptoms manifested and thus are included here. Interventions such as pain management, light therapy to improve sleep, reduction of discomfort by improved seating or positioning, and removal of physical restraints all have been related to improvement in behavior. Once needs have been identified, straightforward medical or nursing interventions may be called for, whereas other needs may require more complex approaches, such as assessment of pain. Many articles have described the difficulties involved in assessing pain in this population (Cohen-Mansfield & Lipson, 2002), and strategies for approaching these complexities have been suggested (Cohen-Mansfield & Lipson, 2008; Feldt, 2000). Individualized pain medication treatment was found to significantly reduce behavioral symptoms in intervention participants when compared with controls (Husebo et al., 2011). A number of methods have been used to improve sleep and thereby decrease agitation, including the use of bright-light therapy (BLT; Mishima et al., 1994; Sloane et al., 2007), although the results are controversial and may even exacerbate behavioral symptoms (Barrick et al., 2010); increased exercise

(Thuné-Boyle et al., 2012); continuous activity programming (Volicer, Simard, Pupa, Medrek, & Riordan, 2006); and a decrease in nighttime interruptions. Improvement in eating or drinking, resulting from the use of enhanced light during meals, has been linked with a decrease in inappropriate behaviors (Koss & Gilmore, 1998), as has the use of hearing aids (Palmer, Adams, Bourgeois, Durrant, & Rossi, 1999). Physical restraints have been shown to result in increased levels of behavioral symptoms (Werner, Cohen-Mansfield, Braun, & Marx, 1989), and the removal of physical restraints may eliminate those behaviors (Werner, Cohen-Mansfield, Koroknay, & Braun, 1994b; Yeh et al., 2001). Changes in the methods and environment of providing ADLs also have been associated with a reduction in inappropriate behaviors. For example, person-centered showering (i.e., individualizing the bathing experience by techniques, such as using no-rinse soap and providing choices) and towel bath (i.e., an in-bed bathing method that keeps the resident covered at all times and uses a gentle body massage) significantly decreased aggressive behavioral symptoms in nursing home residents (Sloane et al., 2004). Improving ADL care and increasing comfort may involve a multitude of factors as illustrated in a case study documenting decreases in aggression during bathing (Cohen-Mansfield & Parpura-Gill, 2007a). These factors include environmental factors (e.g., facilitating access to the bathroom and making temperature during bathing more comfortable), caregiver behavior (e.g., type of touch during care and responses to PWD's behavior), and institutional resources and regulations (e.g., degree of flexibility allowed in timing and type of bathing, or materials used during bathing). Similarly, changing location of meals from central dining to dining on the unit was effective in reducing patient-to-patient assaults on an Alzheimer's and related dementias unit (Negley & Manley, 1990).

Other types of interventions. Additional categories of nonpharmacological intervention studies include (a) staff training and education programs (Livingston et al., 2005), in which staff members are trained in communication, in providing ADLs, or in techniques to handle inappropriate behaviors (see

the section Education of Staff and Family Members); (b) behavioral interventions (Doyle, Zapparoni, O'Connor, & Runci, 1997), which can employ several techniques, including differential reinforcement (providing positive reinforcement contingent on nonagitated behavior), time out (moving the person to a quiet area when agitated), restriction (denying the person goods, activities, etc. when agitated), or stimulus control (changing the properties of the stimuli that tend to trigger a behavior); and (c) interventions employing a combination of treatments (Doyle et al., 1997). These interventions include those that utilize algorithms to address a diverse range of unmet needs (Bédard et al., 2011; Cohen-Mansfield, Thein, Marx, Dakheel-Ali, & Freedman, 2012).

To illustrate the approach of tailoring nonpharmacological interventions to PWDs, a few experience-based examples are presented.

Case Example 1

Mr. A. is a former accountant diagnosed with vascular dementia, with an MMSE score of 15. He was especially agitated in the morning hours, manifesting screaming, complaining, groaning, nonsense talk, and hallucinations. On the basis of these observations, we hypothesized that his agitation resulted from a combination of discomfort and boredom. The Self-Identity in Dementia Questionnaire (Cohen-Mansfield et al., 2006b) revealed that he loved history, and swimming used to be his favorite sport. The interventions that were successful with him were as follows: (a) providing a neck pillow that supported his neck when sleeping in a chair; (b) history movies, for example, one about the history of Jamestown, Virginia; (c) a sports video with Olympic swimming that includes Michael Phelps; and (d) an interactive respite video. The impact of the interventions was such that his son was so impressed with his father's condition that he bought a DVD to show the videos whenever his father was bored.

Case Example 2

Mrs. B. is 85 years old from Turkey and a former housewife, diagnosed with probable Alzheimer's disease, with an MMSE score of 0, who was observed cursing, hitting, grabbing, pushing, scratching, manifesting restlessness, making strange noises, and repeating the same sentences or questions. She was restrained most of the time because the staff was having difficulties with her. On the basis of these observations, she was considered to be both lonely and bored. A number of interventions were successful with Mrs. B, including the following: (a) she enjoyed flower arranging, although she needed prompting; (b) old Turkish songs were played for her; (c) she enjoyed folding towels; and (d) a family audiotape sent via e-mail by her daughter seemed to work, but only for a few days.

Case Example 3

Mrs. C. is an 86-year-old housewife diagnosed with Alzheimer's disease, with an MMSE score of 1. During the afternoons and evenings, she presented physical and verbal–vocal problem behaviors, including making strange noises, complaining, negativism, and repetitious mannerisms. She was considered to be lonely. The interventions used with her were as follows: (a) She was given a baby doll. She said to the baby doll "Hello, look at you," hummed to her, and ran her fingers over the doll's face, touching her eyes and the pacifier. She was so happy with the doll, she said to the staff "baby, baby likes me," and told them the doll was her grandchild. She loved keeping the baby doll with her, and at the end of the study, we left the baby with her. (b) She listened to a singing respite video, which she enjoyed. She continued to hum the song even after the video stopped. (c) She enjoyed sewing, despite vision difficulties.

Case Example 4

Ms. D. was 81 years old with a diagnosis of probable Alzheimer's disease and an MMSE score of 11. Ms. D was moved to the locked unit and became more and more agitated. Many of the interventions that worked earlier were ineffective. We decided to try something new and wrote a letter with lots of spelling and grammar mistakes in it (she had been an editor). We asked her to correct the letter and that activity engaged her and calmed her.

These four case examples illustrate the range of interventions that can be used, the importance of the particular type of intervention and of matching those particulars to the specific person and to one's needs, abilities, preferences, personal history, and cultural background. They also point to the need to identify multiple solutions that can be used for each individual. Although most of these case examples focus on the need for activities and social contact, addressing the needs that arise from discomfort is equally important. Interventions addressing discomfort may involve taking the person to bed upon request, attending to a crying person and investigating whether they have had an injury, removing physical restraints, providing food or drink to those who request it, providing a favorite food to those who are not eating the regular food, and providing blankets and sweaters to those who either complain of being cold or feel cold when touched.

Efficacy, effectiveness, and utility.   Two basic questions about nonpharmacological interventions concern their effectiveness and their costs. Research is insufficient to fully address either issue, although partial answers have been suggested. Validation therapy is an intervention that encourages communication with PWDs and provides respect for and acceptance of their perceptions of reality. Reality orientation therapy is an intervention focusing on providing PWDs with information on spatial and temporal orientation, thus potentially strengthening their cognitive function. Several studies (Baldelli et al., 1993; Toseland et al., 1997) reported that validation therapy and reality orientation therapy reduce aggressive behaviors and depressed affect, while increasing scores on cognitive functioning tests in comparison with control groups. Two reviews (Gagnon, 1996; Livingston et al., 2005), however, concluded that reality orientation and validation therapy are not effective, and thus, according to one review (Gagnon, 1996), they do not justify their costs. Other reviews report insufficient information or limited evidence (Neal & Briggs, 2003; A. Spector, Davies, Woods, & Orrell, 2000; Woods, Spector, Jones, Orrell, & Davies, 2005). Cohen-Mansfield (2001) reviewed 83 studies of nonpharmacological interventions for inappropriate behaviors in dementia and described the majority as reporting a positive, although not always significant, impact. Many of the studies included small samples and other methodological limitations, most often resulting from limited funding for this type of research.

Despite the lack of conclusive evidence regarding the efficacy of nonpharmacological interventions, the research shows that despite many difficulties associated with conducting research in this population, a wide variety of approaches have been used successfully. Indeed, a recent review of the field supports this notion (Cohen-Mansfield, 2013). Many nonpharmacological approaches resulted in a statistically and clinically meaningful improvement in the manifestation of behavior problems, ADL, and affect according to some of the studies. For some problems, however, such as delusions and hallucinations, no studies were found regarding the efficacy of nonpharmacologic approaches. It is likely that a paradigm change is needed in the approach to examining the efficacy of nonpharmacological approaches (Cohen-Mansfield et al., 2014). The idea that each of the potential interventions will be validated with a full randomized controlled trial (RCT) probably is not practical for several reasons. First, there are a very large number of potential interventions. Each intervention type can be presented in a multitude of ways. For example, consider the following questions for music: —Which type of music? Which specific song or melody? Is it provided with an amplifier, personally, or in the room? Is it played with a music therapist? It is played with dance?

For how long is it presented?. All these factors could affect the response to the music. Given the enormous costs of clinical trials, it may be more important to understand the impact of specific parameters on the efficacy of an intervention rather than conduct a separate trial for each intervention. Furthermore, because responses to treatment often are affected by past habits and preferences as well as cognitive and sensory abilities, many interventions are not appropriate or optimal for many of the participants in a trial. Rather than the current approach of favoring RCTs for any type of intervention, we suggest that initial studies of nonpharmacological interventions need to demonstrate feasibility and positive trends. RCTs should focus on the use of algorithms that match specific treatments to behavioral manifestations and to personal and environmental characteristics.

Pharmacological Interventions

Rates of use of pharmacological interventions in nursing homes and long-term care facilities vary (e.g., Azermai, Elseviers, Petrovic, Van Bortel, & Stichele, 2011; Y. Chen et al., 2010; Olsson et al., 2010; Taipale, Bell, Soini, & Pitkälä, 2009), with rates of prescribed psychotropic drugs for older nursing home residents reaching as high as 92.5% (Cohen-Mansfield, Juravel-Jaffe, Cohen, Rasooly, & Golander, 2013). In contrast, evidence of the utilization of nonpharmacological interventions is scant. Although physicians report rates of use ranging from 60% to 95%, (Cohen-Mansfield & Jensen, 2008a; Cohen-Mansfield, Juravel-Jaffe, et al., 2013; Cornegé-Blokland, Kleijer, Hertogh, & van Marum, 2012), they often are not administering the nonpharmacological intervention themselves; therefore, rates of actual use and quality are not reported. Physicians in nursing homes have noted reservations regarding the implementation of nonpharmacological interventions with residents because resources were deemed insufficient or the staff wanted to prescribe medication, which served as barriers to implementation (Cohen-Mansfield & Jensen, 2008b). Such attitudes may be beginning to change. In a U.S. survey in 1996 the use of medication was recommended more than twice as often when compared with nonpharmacological interventions in treating agitation in patients with dementia (Colenda, Rapp, Leist, & Poses, 1996). More recently, surveys have found that the majority of physicians have reported using both pharmacological and nonpharmacological methods (Cohen-Mansfield & Jensen, 2008a; Cornegé-Blokland et al., 2012), with only slightly higher rates for prescribing medication than for the use of nonpharmacological practices as a single modality (Cohen-Mansfield & Jensen, 2008a). The actual input of physicians, however, into the utilization of nonpharmacological interventions may be questioned, as their role is much less clear than it is in the use of pharmacological agents. In a report of use of pharmacological versus nonpharmacological treatment, physicians' personal characteristics, including age, gender, and specialty (Colenda, Leist, & Rapp, 1996), as well as factors such as being pressured and perceiving a lack of other options, were found to affect their decision (Cornegé-Blokland et al., 2012).

The effectiveness of atypical antipsychotics, the most commonly prescribed pharmacological intervention, is modest (Schneider, Dagerman, & Insel, 2006; Sink, Holden, & Yaffe, 2005), and side effects pose a serious concern (e.g., Ames, 2005; Ballard, Waite, & Birks, 2006; Schneider et al., 2006; Sink et al., 2005). The risk of side effects with other antipsychotics, such as haloperidol, may be even higher, including increased mortality rates (Huybrechts et al., 2012; Kales et al., 2012). Consensus statements and guidelines recommend treating agitation first with nonpharmacological methods, and only if these fail, to resort to medication therapy (American Geriatrics Society & American Association for Geriatric Psychiatry, 2003). It has been stressed that genuine efforts to limit the use of antipsychotics in all settings should be made because of their questionable efficacy and risk of negative side effects (American Psychiatric Association, 2007; Salzman et al., 2008).

Education of Staff and Family Members

In supporting caregivers to properly care for persons with behavioral symptoms, training is often helpful. Many such programs, outlined in the following paragraphs (e.g., Staff Training in Assisted Living

Residences [STAR] program; Teri, Huda, Gibbons, Young, & van Leynseele, 2005), focus on improved understanding of the older person and the impact of dementia. Changing caregiver behavior through training is a complex and difficult challenge and often requires ongoing instruction, modeling, monitoring, feedback, and support for the caregiver. Therefore, in institutional settings, staff training is closely tied to management.

Staff training. It is thought that with staff training, nursing home staff will come to better understand the needs of the PWD and, therefore, be able to better meet those needs; it also potentially may decrease staff burnout rates. Most staff training programs focus on communication or knowledge related to caregiving of PWDs.

Communication training for caregivers of PWDs focuses on environmental aspects of communication (e.g., approaching slowly, communicating at eye level), content, phrasing, and interpreting nonverbal or confused verbal communication. Recommendations for implementing the following techniques have been made in this regard: nonverbal communications, such as eye contact, smiling, and affective touch (Levy-Storms, 2008); phrasing sentences in a short and clear way and using a moderate rate of speed (Hopper, 2001; Small, Gutman, Makela, & Hillhouse, 2003) on a level compatible with the person's understanding (Hart & Wells, 1997); paying attention to phrases used by the PWD and repeating them in future communications (Davis & Smith, 2009); and asking yes–no and choice questions (preferably not more than two options; Hopper, 2001). In line with these recommendations, caregivers' clear, concise, and feasible commands resulted in higher compliance rates among PWDs (Christenson, Buchanan, Houlihan, & Wanzek, 2011), and caregivers' elderspeak (i.e., infantilizing communication) has been associated with an increased probability of care resistance compared with normal talk and silence (K. N. Williams, Herman, Gajewski, & Wilson, 2009). Others have advised using broad opening sentences, treating the PWD as an equal, sharing experiences and feelings, and finding topics that are meaningful (Tappen, Williams-Burgess, Edelstein, Touhy, & Fishman, 1997). Finally, caregivers must be aware that even when individuals with dementia do not speak in coherent sentences, their individual words may be meaningful and their messages may be embedded in those words. Most essential is to not ignore, discount, or negate the verbalizations of PWDs, but rather to view these as insights into their perspectives and to use them to improve their situations whenever possible (Cohen-Mansfield & Parpura-Gill, 2008; Jootun & Mcghee, 2011; Ripich, 1994; Ripich, Wykle, & Niles, 1995; Small & Gutman, 2002).

A review of methods to improve caregiver–PWD verbal communication concluded that caregiver communication programs may benefit from incorporating the use of memory aids (Egan, Bérubé, Racine, Leonard, & Rochon, 2010). In line with this, a video-based communication and memory training program significantly improved knowledge of caregivers (Broughton et al., 2011; Liddle et al., 2012); significantly increased qualified nurse caregiver satisfaction (Broughton et al., 2011); and on a level approaching statistical significance, increased caregivers' positive perceptions of caregiving and reduced behavioral symptoms, according to caregiver's reports (Liddle et al., 2012). In a study of communication and conflict-resolution training with both staff members and family members of PWDs in special care units, residents' behavioral symptoms decreased (Robison et al., 2007). The Calming Aggressive Reactions in the Elderly (CARE) program (Mentes & Ferrario, 1989) involved six staff training sessions that emphasized risk factors for aggression, preventive and calming techniques, and protective intervention. Sessions utilized videotaped vignettes, discussions, and role-play and emphasized nonverbal communications. The authors reported a decline from 11 to 9 incidence reports of staff abuse by residents over the 3-month period of the intervention (Mentes & Ferrario, 1989). The Nursing Assistant Communication Skill Program (McCallion, Toseland, Lacey, & Banks, 1999) included five group training sessions and four individual conferences with nursing assistants. The program emphasized enhancing residents' ability to utilize sensory input, effective and ineffective communication styles, utilization of memory aids, and addressing residents' needs. This

resulted in a significant decrease in verbal agitation and in physically nonaggressive behaviors at the end of 3 months, relative to a control group. Results were less compelling at 6 months, suggesting that ongoing training may be necessary. Indeed, evidence from multiple studies supports the need for repeated ongoing training to alter staff behavior (e.g., Chrzescijanski, Moyle, & Creedy, 2007; McCabe, Davison, & George, 2007; Testad, Ballard, et al., 2010). In line with this, a one-session training on understanding and treating physically nonaggressive behaviors showed no improvement in staff or resident behavior (Cohen-Mansfield, Werner, Culpepper, & Barkley, 1997).

Educational training programs focus on caregivers' understanding of the behaviors and needs of PWDs and on improving methods of addressing these needs. The STAR program focuses on increasing knowledge of dementia, improving verbal and nonverbal communication skills, introducing and maintaining pleasant events for residents, improving staff–family communication, and using a behavioral approach to reduce resident distress (Teri et al., 2005). The program included two 4-hr workshops as well as four individualized consultations and three leadership sessions. An exploratory trial with no control group found that the STAR program significantly reduced behavioral disorders in 32 assisted living residents with dementia. The abilities-focused program of morning care (Wells, Dawson, Sidani, Craig, & Pringle, 2000) included a five-session educational program about the impact of dementia on social and self-care abilities, methods of assessing abilities, and interventions to maintain or compensate for those abilities. At postintervention, agitation was significantly decreased in comparison with the control group. ADLs were also a major focus in a staff training program that emphasized the adaptation of ADLs to the person's level of function based on Piaget's stages (Matteson, Linton, Cleary, Barnes, & Lichtenstein, 1997). A further program utilized lectures, instruction cards, and individual and iterative sessions on how to handle behavioral symptoms. In addition, the trainers provided training and advice to staff members at designated times. In a controlled study of this program, significantly reduced behavioral disorders were found (Deudon et al., 2009). Finally, a program focused on providing caregivers with a practical framework to reduce agitation and use of restraints and involved a 2-day seminar with monthly group follow-ups over 6 months. The intervention engendered a reduction in the severity of behavioral symptoms and in the frequency of initiating new use of restraints (Testad, Ballard, et al., 2010). Nevertheless, in spite of this evidence, a review of the literature concluded that removal of restraints requires a systemic approach and an educational program is likely to be insufficient (Möhler, Richter, Köpke, & Meyer, 2011).

When analyzing staff training and its effects on burnout, one study found that although the staff had perceived a benefit from the training and felt confident in their skills, burnout levels remained unchanged (Visser et al., 2008). In this study and others, speculations were made that this could be due to system barriers; specifically, a lack of ability or support of the nursing home to enable the staff to utilize and incorporate their learning (Kuske et al., 2007; Visser et al., 2008).

Family caregivers. When being cared for by a family caregiver, the behavior of the key caregiver directly affects the quality of care for the PWD. For example, nonadapting strategies (i.e., lack of understanding of the PWD or lack of acceptance of the situation) by informal caregivers were associated with higher levels of behavioral and psychological problems for the PWD at 6- and 12-month followups when compared with supporting strategies (i.e., adjusting the care to the person's level of functioning and stimulating the person's abilities; de Vugt et al., 2004). Similarly, high levels of emotional expression (e.g., criticism, emotional involvement) by family caregivers were related to an increase in negative behaviors over time (Vitaliano, Young, Russo, Romano, & Magana-Amato, 1993). Knowledge of effective coping strategies and how to train family caregivers of PWDs is limited and warrants further research (Li, Cooper, Austin, & Livingston, 2013; Samia, Hepburn, & Nichols, 2012).

Interventions for family caregivers can include instructing family members to provide for unmet needs. For example, the Tailored Activities

Program (TAP) involved occupational therapist visits to identify appropriate activities for PWDs as well as instructions to caregivers in use of those activities. This program resulted in significant decreases in behavior problems among PWDs in comparison with a control group (Gitlin, Winter, Burke, Chernett, Dennis, & Hauck, 2008). A more global approach addressing multiple unmet needs utilized home and phone contacts made by health professionals who focused on identifying triggers to behavior; examining medical, communication, and environmental conditions; and training family caregivers to modify those triggers. This approach also resulted in significant reductions in problem behaviors in PWDs at 4-month follow-up (Gitlin, Winter, Dennis, Hodgson, & Hauck, 2010).

Interventions for Psychotic Symptoms and Misinterpretations

No studies of nonpharmacologic interventions for psychotic symptoms and misinterpretations were found. An analysis of their sources and meanings, however, may suggest avenues for potential interventions. When addressing psychotic symptoms, several points must be considered: Is the behavior a symptom of actual psychosis? Are there alternative explanations? What is the severity of consequences for the PWD and his or her caregiver? Is an intervention necessary due to potential benefit or harm? Following is a brief review of such considerations.

Misinterpretation of stimuli. At times, the diagnosed "delusion" or "hallucination" is triggered by an environmental stimulus. For example, a loudspeaker system may sound like voices from outside, or an image seen through a mirror may be interpreted as someone being in the room. This is facilitated by the combination of sensory deficits and cognitive limitations that occur with dementia, raising an incorrect interpretation of an initially vague or unclear stimulus. Interventions to minimize this confusion could include removing or changing the stimulus to avoid eliciting the mistaken interpretation.

Disturbing stimuli. Stimuli in the person's environment may exacerbate sensory limitations, resulting in presentation of psychotic symptoms. In a small study of BLT and its effects on patients with dementia, one individual began hallucinating after 8 days of treatment, and her eyes became markedly red. The hallucinations stopped 1 day after discontinuing BLT (Schindler, Graf, Fischer, Tölk, & Kasper, 2002).

Delusion as a reflection of reality. At times, it is possible that the "delusion" is an actual representation of reality. Examples are delusions of theft, as theft is common in many nursing homes, or the delusion of abandonment that may occur when a person enters a nursing home. Whether this reflects reality from the point of view of the caregiver is irrelevant, as the move into a strange environment may represent abandonment from the point of view of the PWD. Indeed, in a qualitative analysis of descriptions of delusions in 74 PWDs, themes identified included reality (i.e., the delusion represents a true reality from the perspective of the PWD) and loneliness and insecurity (Cohen-Mansfield, Golander, Ben-Israel, & Garfinkel, 2011). The goal of interventions in this case should be to alleviate these feelings and establish trust in the relationship with the caregiver. Residents eventually may change their perceptions when they become comfortable with their care and when they sense continued and consistent caring by the family. Positive frequent contact with family members, either real or simulated (e.g., family members on videotape or audiotape), phone calls, and items from home may provide a sense of love and familiarity, thus countering the feelings of abandonment and betrayal.

Delusion as confabulation in the face of memory loss. Many delusions are misinterpretations of actual events in the environment. When a PWD complains that an object has been stolen, she may be forgetting where she has placed her personal belongings and interpreting her inability to find them as theft. In line with this, delusions of theft were changed immediately once the missing object had been presented to the PWD (Cohen-Mansfield, Golander, et al., 2011). A number of potential solutions can be offered to residents, including marking personal belongings in clear ways so that they are easily identifiable, attaching a finder such as a KeyRinger™ to a personal belonging, or purchasing

multiple inexpensive copies of personal articles so they may be replaced easily when necessary. Similarly, the delusion that a caregiver is an imposter is often the result of an individual's inability to recognize the caregiver. In that case, an intervention should work toward improving the individual's relationship with the caregiver.

Delirium. Delirium is a disorder characterized by acute changes in cognition, perception, and attention due to an underlying medical condition. Delusions can be a symptom of delirium that should be treated for the underlying medical condition. For example, in a study of 504 women age 85 years and older, dementia and urinary tract infections were associated with delirium. The infection was considered to be the cause of the delirium (Eriksson, Gustafson, Fagerström, & Olofsson, 2011). Similarly, delusions resulting from opioid-induced delirium have been described in a case study by Ito and Kanemoto (2013).

Depressed affect. Delusions have been linked to depressed affect in many studies (Bassiony et al., 2002; Cohen-Mansfield et al., 1998). It is unclear whether the delusions lead to depression, or whether the depression leads to delusions (e.g., through inactivity and isolation), or if both are caused by other factors. Delusions may be reduced by treating the depression nonpharmacologically, such as by increasing levels of reinforcing events or activities, by enhancing an individual's sense of control, or by other nonpharmacological psychotherapeutic methodologies (see section on interventions for depressed affect and Table 11.2).

Pleasant psychotic symptoms. At times hallucinations are pleasurable. Some people talk with deceased relatives and derive happiness from these encounters. As mentioned earlier, such symptoms that provide the person experiencing them with a sense of security have been referred to as "comfort phenomenon" (Ballard & Oyebode, 1995). If a person seems to enjoy such hallucinations and does not suffer any ill effects, an optimal intervention may be to explain this situation to caregivers in a manner that will make the practice acceptable to them.

Visual and auditory problems and sensory deprivation. Hallucinations are more likely to occur

	TABLE 11.2

Nonpharmacological Interventions by Purpose: Examples

Purpose	Examples
Cognitive	Memory books; Spaced retrieval; Cognitive remediation; Reality orientation; Cognitive tasks (e.g., sorting) and games (e.g., bingo); Signs to improve orientation
Affect/Self-affirming	Providing pleasurable/meaningful activities; Enhancing control; Provide social contacts (Figure 11.6); Reminiscence therapy; Validation therapy; Self-identity activities/use of objects that were meaningful in the past; Cognitive restructuring for persons with mild dementia
Functional	Enhanced communication; Use of prompts (physical and/or verbal); Equipment; Environmental intervention (e.g., cues, enhanced lighting); Staffing and staff training; Technology; Music to promote relaxation during task
Psychotic symptoms	Remove, cover or change stimulus that is misinterpreted, such as a reflecting mirror or window;
	Delusion of theft, investigate the possibility of real theft, if the person misplaces the object, either try to teach the person to always place the object in the same place (possibly through spaced retrieval), or provide multiple copies of object, or use technology to locate the object;
	For delusion of abandonment, utilize techniques to promote trust;
	If the person has delirium or depression, treat those conditions;
	If the person hallucinating has severe sensory impairment, examine options to correct the impairment or use aides to compensate for it, or otherwise provide sensory stimulation;
	If the hallucination does not bother anyone, and provides stimulation or positive affect, or if it fits with the person's cultural habits, allow it to continue

Note. This is not a comprehensive list, but a list that provides examples of the types of available interventions. Note that some interventions may belong to several categories. Copyright 2003 by Cohen-Mansfield. Reprinted with permission.

in people with visual problems (F. M. Chapman et al., 1999; Cohen-Mansfield et al., 1998; Forsell, 2000; Holroyd, 1998) and may be linked to sensory deprivation (Holroyd & Sheldon-Keller, 1995; Zubek et al., 1961) as well as hearing difficulties (Khan et al., 1988). Additionally, evidence suggests that a lack of the stimulation of sensory areas by external objects can result in hallucinations (Zubek et al., 1961). Correction of visual problems through medical intervention or through aids, such as eyeglasses, enhanced contrast, larger type or object, or improved lighting, is a first step in addressing hallucinations among people with visual impairments. Similarly, hearing aids can be helpful in decreasing auditory hallucination. To the extent that sensory deprivation may be a contributing cause of hallucinations, sensory stimulation, such as music, massage, and aromatherapy, may be beneficial.

Cultural differences between caregivers and PWDs. In some cultures, "talking" to the dead is a fairly common practice (Howland, 1984; MacDonald, 1992), yet the intentions of people who speak to deceased loved ones may be misunderstood, and they may be diagnosed as hallucinating.

In addition, someone who is heard speaking aloud in a certain way, or singing, could in fact be praying or invoking a higher power based on religious beliefs or practices or self-stimulating in an environment that is lacking appropriate stimuli.

Interventions for Depressed Affect

Cognitive interventions. Cognitive interventions based on Beck's and Ellis's work have been used to treat depressed persons with mild levels of dementia. These interventions involve cognitive restructuring, that is, challenging or changing distorted thought processes and thoughts that cause depressed affect. Similarly, cognitive behavior interventions decreased depressed affect in people with mild to moderate dementia and their caregivers in comparison to controls (Graff, Vernooij-Dassen, Thijssen, Dekker, Hoefnagels, & Olderikkert, 2007).

Increasing sense of control and decreasing helplessness. Helplessness has been shown to relate to depressed affect, whereas control is associated with well-being. Providing opportunities for PWDs to exercise control, such as making decisions about meals, clothes, bath-time procedures, or caring for a plant, may be used to target depression in this population (Cohen-Mansfield & Parpura-Gill, 2007a; Mallers, Claver, & Lares, 2014).

Increasing levels of pleasant activities or noncontingent reinforcements.

Pleasant activities. Individualizing activities based on knowledge of what experiences are reinforcing for PWDs has been used to treat depressed affect in this population (Teri & Logsdon, 1991; Teri, Logsdon, Uomoto, & McCurry, 1997).

Social contact interventions. Loneliness is highly correlated with depressed affect, and being alone has been shown to relate to behavioral problems. Therefore, social interaction and social contact interventions are appropriate for improving affect. The best intervention for loneliness is a positive interaction with a person who is meaningful to the older person (Cohen-Mansfield & Werner, 1997; Cohen-Mansfield, Marx, et al., 2012; Phinney, Chaudhury, & O'Connor, 2007). In this vein, therapeutic conversation resulted in significant decrease in sad mood in PWDs in comparison with control participants (Tappen & Williams, 2009). Because such interventions often are not feasible, a variety of alternative social interventions have been developed, including simulated interaction and most group activities (including cognitive activities), which can be used as vehicles to promote social contacts. Animal-assisted therapy has been found to decrease sad mood (Mossello et al., 2011). These interventions, discussed in detail in the section Providing Social Support and Contact, are presented in Figure 11.6.

Self-affirming interventions. Self-affirming interventions also target the improvement of affect. These include reminiscence therapy, which encourages PWDs to talk about their pasts and may utilize audiovisual aids, such as old family photos and objects. Reminiscence can enhance an individual's sense of identity, sense of worth, or general well-being (Brooker & Duce, 2000; Dempsey et al., 2014) and may stimulate memory processes. Validation therapy, in which a therapist accepts the disorientation of a PWD and validates his or her feelings, was developed by Naomi Feil (1982). This self-affirming intervention is based on the assumption that people return to unfinished conflicts in their pasts, thereby providing a background for meaningful conversations addressing their emotions. The utility of validation therapy is questionable, as discussed in the section Efficacy, Effectiveness, Utility. Self-maintenance therapy is an intervention that aims to help the person maintain a sense of self and meaning. It includes four components of psychotherapeutic support, in which the therapist helps the PWD understand the disease and maintain a sense of meaning and goals; self-knowledge training in which the therapist establishes what the person remembers about his or her past and identity and uses tools, such as a memory book, to help the person continue to remember them; facilitation of pleasant daily activities; and training caregivers to validate the PWD in communications. This intervention was found to reduce depressed affect in a pre–post study (Romero & Wenz, 2001).

Other interventions: Exercise, crisis intervention, and treatment of pain.

An exercise program and a walking program have been found to reduce depressed affect as compared to preintervention levels (C. L. Williams & Tappen, 2008). A program combining exercise training for PWDs with behavioral management training for caregivers resulted in decreased levels of depression for the PWDs (Teri et al., 2003). Also, the Bridge Project, a crisis support intervention project provided for PWDs and their caregivers, has been found to reduce levels of depression in PWDs (Johnson et al., 2013).

Several studies have found a link between pain and depressed affect (e.g., Cohen-Mansfield & Marx, 1993; Walid & Zaytseva, 2009). Pain scores were predictive of behavioral problems and of depressed affect 4 months later (Snow et al., 2009). Therefore, it stands to reason that treatment of pain may improve mood in PWDs. Pain, however, often is undetected because PWDs may not be able to communicate that they are experiencing pain because of impaired cognition and language (Cohen-Mansfield & Lipson, 2002). Understanding the optimal methodology for assessing pain in this population (see Cohen-Mansfield & Lipson, 2008) therefore is crucial for proper treatment of pain and depressed affect.

Interventions for Apathy and Disengagement

Studies have shown that it is possible to engage PWDs with activities and stimuli (Cohen-Mansfield, Marx, Dakheel-Ali, Regier, & Thein, 2010), and interventions have been found to decrease apathy and disengagement among PWDs (Leone et al., 2013; Leone et al., 2012). Activity kits done together with a therapist and during one-on-one time with a therapist had comparable efficacy in reducing apathy (Politis et al., 2004). Similarly, therapeutic conversation significantly decreased apathy in PWDs in comparison with control participants (Tappen & Williams, 2009). Live interactive music was shown to have a positive impact on apathy throughout the duration of the activity, although further studies are necessary to evaluate long-term impact (Holmes, Knights, Dean, Hodkinson, & Hopkins, 2006). These interventions had a social component, corroborating the finding that social stimuli are particularly effective with PWDs (Cohen-Mansfield, Thein, Dakheel-Ali, Regier, & Marx, 2010). When using simulated social stimuli, realistic stimuli (e.g., a doll that looks like a baby rather than a doll) and animated stimuli (e.g., robotic animal vs. stuffed animal) resulted in higher levels of engagement of PWDs than exhibited when presented with their counterpart stimuli (Cohen-Mansfield, Thein, Dakheel-Ali, Regier, & Marx, 2010). Human and live stimuli also resulted in significantly more engagement than their counterparts (Cohen-Mansfield, Thein, Dakheel-Ali, Regier, & Marx, 2010). In addition, stimuli that are individualized and have meaning to the person—that is, that relate to the PWD's past roles or preferences, result in more engagement than nonindividualized stimuli (Cohen-Mansfield, Thein, Dakheel-Ali, & Marx, 2010). Engagement is increased when PWDs are guided in the use of stimuli (S. B. Chapman, Weiner, Rackley, Hynan, & Zientz, 2004; Leone et al., 2012).

Implementation Issues

Once assessments, based on theoretical framework, lead to the identification of an intervention, a stage of implementation and monitoring of the intervention and its impact is to follow. This stage requires an effective infrastructure. Such infrastructure requires a skilled management and sufficient, competent, and compassionate staff as well as a shared conceptualization of care and priorities. Concurrently, aligned procedures, including accountability for following through and monitoring the change, are needed. The physical environment, including space, décor, and resources is a necessary, although not sufficient, condition for implementation of nonpharmacological interventions. Deficiencies in any of these domains result in barriers to successful implementation of nonpharmacological interventions.

Environmental, staff, and managerial issues. The ability to provide quality care for people with behavioral symptoms can be affected by factors in the environment. Many studies stress the need for individual treatment plans for the PWD. With time and budget constraints, however, and the physical demands of the work itself, this can be difficult to achieve (Stone & Dawson, 2008).

Staff turnover is one concern when providing quality care in the nursing home. Many nursing home staff have limited English language skills, have low levels of education, receive little training, and earn low wages with few benefits; therefore, the rate of turnover is high and recruitment is difficult (Stone & Dawson, 2008). In one study, flexible management and staff schedules were found to improve the environment for the nursing home staff and thus for residents (Cohen-Mansfield & Bester, 2006). Not only was it found that workplace flexibility improved staff retention and decreased levels of burnout, but such flexibility, as provided by Adards Nursing Home in Australia, also allowed for a more homelike environment, where staff eat with residents and can bring their children to work. In contrast, in cases in which caregivers are not well supported, the quality of care is lower. If the workplace or other family members are not able to care for and support caregivers to do their job, it is the caregiver and, consequently, the PWD, who suffer.

In a study on bathing using the Treatment Routes for Exploring Agitation as a tool for assessing behavioral problems and creating person-centered treatment plans, making environmental changes was found to help address the needs of the PWD as well as the caregiver, and thus to improve the bathing process (Cohen-Mansfield & Parpura-Gill, 2007a). This speaks to the importance of allowing for structural and environmental changes to support the PWD as well as and his or her caregiver.

Consideration of management style, the setting and environment of care, physical design of the area where caregiving takes place, availability of training, and accessibility of devices and technology to assist in caregiving can greatly affect the ability of the caregiver to provide quality care (Stone, 2001). Where these conditions are favorable, the quality of care is likely to improve.

Barriers to practice of nonpharmacological interventions in dementia. The actual utilization of nonpharmacological interventions in dementia falls far short of its potential. A number of systemic issues are responsible for this gap. Funding is lacking both for the practice of nonpharmacological interventions and for the acquisition of relevant knowledge through systematic research. The commonly used alternative intervention of psychoactive medication is reimbursed, and the underlying structure for its delivery, such as physicians, medicine aids, pharmacies, and monitoring and quality control systems, is largely in place. In contrast, the provision of nonpharmacological interventions generally is not reimbursed, and a system for providing these interventions often is absent. No one in the care system is currently responsible for assessing, observing, and analyzing inappropriate behavior or psychotic symptoms to determine their etiology and impact on individuals' lives. The ability of caregivers to provide nonpharmacological interventions is further limited by lack of staff knowledge, insufficient staffing levels, and stressful experiences within and outside the care situation. Indeed, staff-related barriers to the implementation of nonpharmacological interventions, such as denial of unmet need, refusal to provide for a need, or lack of access to a physician, have been identified (Cohen-Mansfield, Thein, Marx, & Dakheel-Ali, 2012).

As mentioned previously, there are several prerequisites to good nonpharmacological care for PWDs. To provide nonpharmacological interventions, the system of care must promote an atmosphere and practice of caring that goes beyond what currently is found in most care settings. A practice style that includes good communication skills and compassion and empathy by caregivers, as well as a high level of flexibility of direct care staff and of the larger organization, is needed but often is lacking. To allow for alternative interventions, the system of care must promote autonomy and respect for the PWD and maximize flexibility in all procedures.

CONCLUSION

Greater monetary resources must be allocated to allow research to develop the knowledge necessary for optimizing nonpharmacological care and for understanding behavioral symptoms in diverse populations. There is an urgent need to improve our ability to answer basic questions: Which interventions are efficacious for which individuals? Which aspects of an intervention are necessary for it to be efficacious? What are the active ingredients, or principles at work, in different interventions? Which personal characteristics (gender, culture, prior stress) should be considered in matching an intervention with an individual? What is the impact of the person delivering the intervention and the manner in which it is delivered? Only once these basic questions are answered can the issues of effectiveness and costs be properly addressed.

Nonpharmacological interventions generally provide more personalized care for PWDs by addressing their individual needs and thereby preventing or treating inappropriate behaviors or declines in function. To increase the use of nonpharmacological interventions in dementia care, there is a need for public education and advocacy concerning the importance of such interventions and their support.

References

Agüera-Ortiz, L., Gil-Ruiz, N., Cruz-Orduña, I., Ramos-García, I., Osorio, R. S., Valentí-Soler, M., . . . Martínez-Martín, P. (2013). A novel rating scale for the measurement of apathy in institutionalized persons with dementia: The APADEM–NH. *American Journal of Geriatric Psychiatry.* Advance online publication. doi:10.1016/j.jagp.2013.01.079

Alexopoulos, G. S., Abrams, R. C., Young, R. C., & Shamoian, C. A. (1988). Cornell scale for depression in dementia. *Biological Psychiatry, 23*, 271–284. doi:10.1016/0006-3223(88)90038-8

Algase, D. L., Beattie, E. R., Leitsch, S. A., & Beel-Bates, C. A. (2003). Biomechanical activity devices to index wandering behaviour in dementia. *American Journal of Alzheimer's Disease and Other Dementias, 18*, 85–92. doi:10.1177/153331750301800202

Algase, D. L., Beck, C., Kolanowski, A., Whall, A., Berent, S., Richards, K., & Beattie, E. (1996). Need-driven dementia-compromised behavior: An alternative view of disruptive behavior. *American Journal of Alzheimer's Disease and Other Dementias, 11*, 10–19. doi:10.1177/153331759601100603

American Geriatrics Society, & American Association for Geriatric Psychiatry. (2003). Consensus statement on improving the quality of mental health care in U.S. nursing homes: Management of depression and behavioral symptoms associated with dementia. *Journal of the American Geriatrics Society, 51*, 1287–1298. doi:10.1046/j.1532-5415.2003.51415.x

American Psychiatric Association. (2007). *Practice guideline for the treatment of patients with Alzheimer's disease and other dementias* (2nd ed.). Washington, DC: Author.

American Psychiatric Association. (2013). *Diagnostic and statistical manual of mental disorders* (5th ed.). Washington, DC: Author.

Ames, D. (2005). For debate: Should novel antipsychotics ever be used to treat the behavioral and psychological symptoms of dementia (BPSD)? *International Psychogeriatrics, 17*, 3–29. doi:10.1017/S104161020521102X

Amore, M., Tagariello, P., Laterza, C., & Savoia, E. M. (2007). Subtypes of depression in dementia. *Archives of Gerontology and Geriatrics, 44*, 23–33. doi:10.1016/j.archger.2007.01.004

Azermai, M., Elseviers, M., Petrovic, M., Van Bortel, L., & Stichele, R. V. (2011). Geriatric drug utilisation of psychotropics in Belgian nursing homes. *Human Psychopharmacology: Clinical and Experimental, 26*, 12–20. doi:10.1002/hup.1160

Baillon, S., Van Diepen, E., Prettyman, R., Redman, J., Rooke, N., & Campbell, R. (2004). A comparison of the effects of Snoezelen and reminiscence therapy on the agitated behaviour of patients with dementia. *International Journal of Geriatric Psychiatry, 19*, 1047–1052. doi:10.1002/gps.1208

Baldelli, M. V., Pirani, A., Motta, M., Abati, E., Mariani, E., & Manzi, V. (1993). Effects of reality orientation therapy on elderly patients in the community. *Archives of Gerontology and Geriatrics, 17*, 211–218. doi:10.1016/0167-4943(93)90052-J

Ballard, C. G., Cassidy, G., Bannister, C., & Mohan, R. N. C. (1993). Prevalence, symptom profile, and aetiology of depression in dementia sufferers. *Journal of Affective Disorders, 29*, 1–6. doi:10.1016/0165-0327(93)90111-V

Ballard, C., Waite, J., & Birks, J. (2006). Atypical antipsychotics for aggression and psychosis in Alzheimer's disease [Review]. *Cochrane Database of Systematic Reviews, 1*, 1–48.

Ballard, C., & Oyebode, F. (1995). Psychotic symptoms in patients with dementia. *International Journal of Geriatric Psychiatry, 10*, 743–752. doi:10.1002/gps.930100904

Bankole, A., Anderson, M., Smith-Jackson, T., Knight, A., Oh, K., Brantley, J., . . . Lach, J. (2012). Validation of noninvasive body sensor network technology in the detection of agitation in dementia. *American Journal of Alzheimer's Disease and Other Dementias, 27*, 346–354. doi:10.1177/1533317512452036

Barrick, A. L., Sloane, P., Williams, C., Mitchell, M., Connell, B., Wood, W., . . . Zimmerman, S. (2010). Impact of ambient bright light on agitation in dementia. *International Journal of Geriatric Psychiatry, 25*, 1013–1021. doi:10.1002/gps.2453

Bassiony, M. M., Warren, A., Rosenblatt, A., Baker, A., Steinberg, M., Steele, C. D., . . . Lyketsos, C. G. (2002). The relationship between delusions and depression in Alzheimer's disease. *International Journal of Geriatric Psychiatry, 17*, 549–556. doi:10.1002/gps.641

Bates, J., Boote, J., & Beverley, C. (2004). Psychosocial interventions for people with a milder dementing illness: A systematic review. *Journal of Advanced Nursing, 45*, 644–658. doi:10.1046/j.1365-2648.2003.02959.x

Baumgarten, M., Becker, R., & Gauthier, S. (1990). Validity and reliability of the dementia behavior disturbance scale. *Journal of the American Geriatrics Society, 38*, 221–226.

Beck, A. T. (1997). The past and future of cognitive therapy. *Journal of Psychotherapy Practice and Research, 6*, 276–284.

Beck, C., Richards, K., Lambert, C., Doan, R., Landes, R. D., Whall, A., . . . Feldman, Z. (2011). Factors associated with problematic vocalizations in nursing home residents with dementia. *Gerontologist, 51*, 389–405. doi:10.1093/geront/gnq129

Beck, J. G. (1997). Mental health in the elderly: Challenges for behavior therapy. introduction to the special series. *Behavior Therapy, 28*, 1–2. doi:10.1016/S0005-7894(97)80030-5

Bédard, A., Landreville, P., Voyer, P., Verreault, R., & Vézina, J. (2011). Reducing verbal agitation in people with dementia: Evaluation of an intervention based on the satisfaction of basic needs. *Aging and*

Mental Health, 15, 855–865. doi:10.1080/13607863. 2011.569480

Bernabei, V., De Ronchi, D., La Ferla, T., Moretti, F., Tonelli, L., Ferrari, B., . . . Atti, A. (2013). Animal-assisted interventions for elderly patients affected by dementia or psychiatric disorders: A review. *Journal of Psychiatric Research, 47*, 762–773. doi:10.1016/j. jpsychires.2012.12.014

Birchmore, T., & Clague, S. (1983). A behavioural approach to reduce shouting. *Nursing Times, 79*, 37–39.

Blazina, L., & Rubin, E. (1995). The behavior rating scale for dementia of the consortium to establish a registry for Alzheimer's disease. *American Journal of Psychiatry, 152*, 1349–1357.

Bliwise, D. L. (1993). Sleep in normal aging and dementia. *Sleep, 16*, 40–81.

Bliwise, D. L. (1994). What is sundowning? *Journal of the American Geriatrics Society, 42*, 1009–1011.

Borroni, B., Costanzi, C., & Padovani, A. (2010). Genetic susceptibility to behavioural and psychological symptoms in Alzheimer disease. *Current Alzheimer Research, 7*, 158–164. doi:10.2174/156720510 790691173

Bridges-Parlet, S., Knopman, D., & Thompson, T. (1994). A descriptive study of physical aggressive behavior in dementia by direct observation. *Journal of the American Geriatrics Society, 42*, 192–197.

Brodaty, H., & Arasaratnam, C. (2012). Meta-analysis of nonpharmacological interventions for neuropsychiatric symptoms of dementia. *American Journal of Psychiatry, 169*, 946–953. doi:10.1176/appi. ajp.2012.11101529

Brooker, D., & Duce, L. (2000). Wellbeing and activity in dementia: A comparison of group reminiscence therapy, structured goal-directed group activity and unstructured time. *Aging and Mental Health, 4*, 354–358. doi:10.1080/713649967

Broughton, M., Smith, E. R., Baker, R., Angwin, A. J., Pachana, N. A., Copland, D. A., . . . Chenery, H. J. (2011). Evaluation of a caregiver education program to support memory and communication in dementia: A controlled pretest–posttest study with nursing home staff. *International Journal of Nursing Studies, 48*, 1436–1444. doi:10.1016/j.ijnurstu.2011.05.007

Burns, A., Jacoby, R., & Levy, R. (1990). Behavioral abnormalities and psychiatric symptoms in Alzheimer's disease: Preliminary findings. *International Psychogeriatrics, 2*, 25–36. doi:10.1017/ S1041610290000278

Camberg, L., Woods, P., Hurley, A., Volicer, L., Ashley, J., Odenheimer, G., & McIntyre, K. (1999). Evaluation of simulated presence: A personalized approach to enhance well-being in persons with Alzheimer's disease. *Journal of the American Geriatrics Society, 47*, 446–452.

Camp, C. J., Cohen-Mansfield, J., & Capezuti, E. (2002). Nonpharmacological interventions for dementia: Enhancing and maintaining mental health in long-term care residents. *Psychiatric Services, 53*, 1397–1404. doi:10.1176/appi.ps.53.11.1397

Camp, C. J., Foss, J. W., O'Hanlon, A. M., & Stevens, A. B. (1996). Memory interventions for persons with dementia. *Applied Cognitive Psychology, 10*, 193–210. doi:10.1002/(SICI)1099-0720(199606)10:3<193:: AID-ACP374>3.0.CO;2-4

Chapman, F. M., Dickinson, J., McKeith, I., & Ballard, C. (1999). Association among visual hallucinations, visual acuity, and specific eye pathologies in Alzheimer's disease: Treatment implications. *American Journal of Psychiatry, 156*, 1983–1985.

Chapman, S. B., Weiner, M. F., Rackley, A., Hynan, L. S., & Zientz, J. (2004). Effects of cognitive-communication stimulation for Alzheimer's disease patients treated with donepezil. *Journal of Speech, Language, and Hearing Research, 47*, 1149–1163. doi:10.1044/1092-4388(2004/085)

Chen, D., Wactlar, H., Chen, M., Gao, C., Bharucha, A., & Hauptmann, A. (2008). Recognition of aggressive human behavior using binary local motion descriptors. *Engineering in Medicine and Biology Society, 2008. EMBS 2008. 30th Annual International Conference of the IEEE*, 5238-5241.

Chen, Y., Briesacher, B. A., Field, T. S., Tjia, J., Lau, D. T., & Gurwitz, J. H. (2010). Unexplained variation across US nursing homes in antipsychotic prescribing rates. *Archives of Internal Medicine, 170*, 89–95. doi:10.1001/archinternmed.2009.469

Cheston, R., Thorne, K., Whitby, P., & Peak, J. (2007). Simulated presence therapy, attachment and separation amongst people with dementia. *Dementia, 6*, 442–449. doi:10.1177/1471301207006003703

Chow, T. W., Binns, M. A., Cummings, J. L., Lam, I., Black, S. E., Miller, B. L., . . . van Reekum, R. (2009). Apathy symptom profile and behavioral associations in frontotemporal dementia vs dementia of Alzheimer type. *Archives of Neurology, 66*, 888–893. doi:10.1001/archneurol.2009.92

Christenson, A. M., Buchanan, J. A., Houlihan, D., & Wanzek, M. (2011). Command use and compliance in staff communication with elderly residents of long-term care facilities. *Behavior Therapy, 42*, 47–58. doi:10.1016/j.beth.2010.07.001

Chrzescijanski, D., Moyle, W., & Creedy, D. (2007). Reducing dementia-related aggression through a staff education intervention. *Dementia, 6*, 271–286. doi:10.1177/1471301207080369

Cipriani, G., Vedovello, M., Nuti, A., & Di Fiorino, M. (2011). Aggressive behavior in patients with dementia: Correlates and management. *Geriatrics and Gerontology International, 11,* 408–413. doi:10.1111/j.1447-0594.2011.00730.x

Cohen-Mansfield, J. (2000). Heterogeneity in dementia: Challenges and opportunities. *Alzheimer Disease and Associated Disorders, 14,* 60–63. doi:10.1097/00002093-200004000-00002

Cohen-Mansfield, J. (2001). Nonpharmacologic interventions for inappropriate behaviors in dementia: A review, summary, and critique. *American Journal of Geriatric Psychiatry, 9,* 361–381. doi:10.1097/00019442-200111000-00005

Cohen-Mansfield, J. (2003). Nonpharmacologic interventions for psychotic symptoms in dementia. *Journal of Geriatric Psychiatry and Neurology, 16,* 219–224. doi:10.1177/0891988703258665

Cohen-Mansfield, J. (2004). Cognitive and behavioral interventions for persons with dementia. In C. Spielberger (Ed.), *Encyclopedia of applied psychology* (Vol. 1, pp. 377–385). Boston, MA: Elsevier.

Cohen-Mansfield, J. (2005). Nonpharmacological interventions for persons with dementia. *Alzheimer's Care Today, 6,* 129–145.

Cohen-Mansfield, J. (2006). Nonpharmacological approaches to the care of dementia with Lewy bodies. In J. O'Brien, I. McKeith, D. Ames, & E. Chui E, *Dementia with Lewy bodies* (pp. 193–206). Oxon, England: Taylor and Francis. doi:10.4324/9780203313909_chapter_15

Cohen-Mansfield, J. (2008). Agitated behavior in persons with dementia: The relationship between type of behavior, its frequency, and its disruptiveness. *Journal of Psychiatric Research, 43,* 64–69. doi:10.1016/j.jpsychires.2008.02.003

Cohen-Mansfield, J. (2009). Hallucinations in dementia. *Geriatrics and Aging, 12,* 70–76.

Cohen-Mansfield, J. (2013). Nonpharmacologic treatment of behavioral disorders in dementia. *Current Treatment Options in Neurology, 15,* 765–785. doi:10.1007/s11940-013-0257-2

Cohen-Mansfield, J., & Bester, A. (2006). Flexibility as a management principle in dementia care: The Adards example. *Gerontologist, 46,* 540–544. doi:10.1093/geront/46.4.540

Cohen-Mansfield, J., Billig, N., Lipson, S., Rosenthal, A. S., & Pawlson, L. G. (1990). Medical correlates of agitation in nursing home residents. *Gerontology, 36,* 150–158. doi:10.1159/000213191

Cohen-Mansfield, J., Buckwalter, K., Beattie, E., Rose, K., Neville, C., & Kolanowski, A. (2014). Expanded review criteria: The case of nonpharmacological interventions in dementia. *Journal of Alzheimer's Disease, 41,* 15–28. doi:10.3233/JAD-132357

Cohen-Mansfield, J., Culpepper, W. J., & Werner, P. (1995). The relationship between cognitive function and agitation in senior day care participants. *International Journal of Geriatric Psychiatry, 10,* 585–595. doi:10.1002/gps.930100709

Cohen-Mansfield, J., Dakheel-Ali, M., & Marx, M. S. (2009). Engagement in persons with dementia: The concept and its measurement. *American Journal of Geriatric Psychiatry, 17,* 299–307. doi:10.1097/JGP.0b013e31818f3a52

Cohen-Mansfield, J., & Deutsch, L. H. (1996). Agitation: Subtypes and their mechanisms. *Seminars in Clinical Neuropsychiatry, 1,* 325–339.

Cohen-Mansfield, J., & Golander, H. (2011). The measurement of psychosis in dementia: A comparison of assessment tools. *Alzheimer Disease and Associated Disorders, 25,* 101–108. doi:10.1097/WAD.0b013e3181f811f4

Cohen-Mansfield, J., & Golander, H. (2012). Analysis of caregiver perceptions of "hallucinations" in people with dementia in institutional settings. *American Journal of Alzheimer's Disease and Other Dementias, 27,* 243–249. doi:10.1177/1533317512446475

Cohen-Mansfield, J., Golander, H., Ben-Israel, J., & Garfinkel, D. (2011). The meanings of delusions in dementia: A preliminary study. *Psychiatry Research, 189,* 97–104. doi:10.1016/j.psychres.2011.05.022

Cohen-Mansfield, J., & Jensen, B. (2007). Self-maintenance habits and preferences in elderly (SHAPE): Reliability of reports of self-care preferences in older persons. *Aging Clinical and Experimental Research, 19,* 61–68. doi:10.1007/BF03325212

Cohen-Mansfield, J., & Jensen, B. (2008a). Assessment and treatment approaches for behavioral disturbances associated with dementia in the nursing home: Self-reports of physicians' practices. *Journal of the American Medical Directors Association, 9,* 406–413. doi:10.1016/j.jamda.2008.02.010

Cohen-Mansfield, J., & Jensen, B. (2008b). Nursing home physicians' knowledge of and attitudes toward nonpharmacological interventions for treatment of behavioral disturbances associated with dementia. *Journal of the American Medical Directors Association, 9,* 491–498. doi:10.1016/j.jamda.2008.04.009

Cohen-Mansfield, J., Juravel-Jaffe, A., Cohen, A., Rasooly, I., & Golander, H. (2013). Physicians' practice and familiarity with treatment for agitation associated with dementia in Israeli nursing homes. *International Psychogeriatrics, 25,* 236–244. doi:10.1017/S104161021200172X

Cohen-Mansfield, J., & Libin, A. (2004). Assessment of agitation in elderly patients with dementia: Correlations between informant rating and direct observation. *International Journal of Geriatric Psychiatry, 19,* 881–891. doi:10.1002/gps.1171

Cohen-Mansfield, J., & Libin, A. (2005). Verbal and physical agitation in cognitively impaired elderly with dementia: Robustness of syndromes. *Journal of Psychiatric Research, 39,* 325–332. doi:10.1016/j.jpsychires.2004.08.009

Cohen-Mansfield, J., & Lipson, S. (2002). Pain in cognitively impaired nursing home residents: How well are physicians diagnosing it? *Journal of the American Geriatrics Society, 50,* 1039–1044. doi:10.1046/j.1532-5415.2002.50258.x

Cohen-Mansfield, J., & Lipson, S. (2008). The utility of pain assessment for analgesic use in persons with dementia. *Pain, 134,* 16–23. doi:10.1016/j.pain.2007.03.023

Cohen-Mansfield, J., & Marx, M. S. (1988). Relationship between depression and agitation in nursing home residents. *Comprehensive Gerontology. Section B, Behavioural, Social, and Applied Sciences, 2,* 141–146.

Cohen-Mansfield, J., & Marx, M. S. (1990). The relationship between sleep disturbances and agitation in a nursing home. *Journal of Aging and Health, 2,* 42–57. doi:10.1177/089826439000200104

Cohen-Mansfield, J., & Marx, M. S. (1993). Pain and depression in the nursing home: Corroborating results. *Journal of Gerontology, 48,* 96–97. doi:10.1093/geronj/48.2.P96

Cohen-Mansfield, J., Marx, M. S., Dakheel-Ali, M., Regier, N. G., & Thein, K. (2010). Can persons with dementia be engaged with stimuli? *American Journal of Geriatric Psychiatry, 18,* 351–362. doi:10.1097/JGP.0b013e3181c531fd

Cohen-Mansfield, J., Marx, M. S., Dakheel-Ali, M., Regier, N. G., Thein, K., & Freedman, L. (2010). Can agitated behavior of nursing home residents with dementia be prevented with the use of standardized stimuli? *Journal of the American Geriatrics Society, 58,* 1459–1464. doi:10.1111/j.1532-5415.2010.02951.x

Cohen-Mansfield, J., Marx, M. S., Freedman, L. S., Murad, H., Regier, N. G., Thein, K., & Dakheel-Ali, M. (2011). The comprehensive process model of engagement. *American Journal of Geriatric Psychiatry, 19,* 859–870. doi:10.1097/JGP.0b013e318202bf5b

Cohen-Mansfield, J., Marx, M. S., Freedman, L. S., Murad, H., Thein, K., & Dakheel-Ali, M. (2012). What affects pleasure in persons with advanced stage dementia? *Journal of Psychiatric Research, 46,* 402–406. doi:10.1016/j.jpsychires.2011.12.003

Cohen-Mansfield, J., Marx, M. S., & Rosenthal, A. S. (1989). A description of agitation in a nursing home. *Journal of Gerontology, 44,* 77–84.

Cohen-Mansfield, J., Marx, M. S., & Rosenthal, A. S. (1990). Dementia and agitation in nursing home residents: How are they related? *Psychology and Aging, 5,* 3–8. doi:10.1037/0882-7974.5.1.3

Cohen-Mansfield, J., Marx, M. S., & Werner, P. (1992a). Agitation in elderly persons: An integrative report of findings in a nursing home. *International Psychogeriatrics, 4,* 221–240. doi:10.1017/S1041610292001285

Cohen-Mansfield, J., Marx, M. S., & Werner, P. (1992b). Observational data on time use and behavior problems in the nursing home. *Journal of Applied Gerontology, 11,* 111–121. doi:10.1177/073346489201100109

Cohen-Mansfield, J., & Parpura-Gill, A. (2007a). Bathing: A framework for intervention focusing on psychosocial, architectural and human factors considerations. *Archives of Gerontology and Geriatrics, 45,* 121–135. doi:10.1016/j.archger.2006.09.001

Cohen-Mansfield, J., & Parpura-Gill, A. (2007b). Loneliness in older persons: A theoretical model and empirical findings. *International Psychogeriatrics, 19,* 279–294. doi:10.1017/S1041610206004200

Cohen-Mansfield, J., & Parpura-Gill, A. (2008). Practice style in the nursing home: Dimensions for assessment and quality improvement. *International Journal of Geriatric Psychiatry, 23,* 376–386. doi:10.1002/gps.1888

Cohen-Mansfield, J., Parpura-Gill, A., & Golander, H. (2006a). Salience of self-identity roles in persons with dementia: Differences in perceptions among elderly persons, family members and caregivers. *Social Science and Medicine, 62,* 745–757. doi:10.1016/j.socscimed.2005.06.031

Cohen-Mansfield, J., Parpura-Gill, A., & Golander, H. (2006b). Utilization of self-identity roles for designing interventions for persons with dementia. *The Journals of Gerontology, Series B: Psychological Sciences and Social Sciences, 61,* 202–212. doi:10.1093/geronb/61.4.P202

Cohen-Mansfield, J., Taylor, L., & Werner, P. (1998). Delusions and hallucinations in an adult day care population: A longitudinal study. *American Journal of Geriatric Psychiatry, 6,* 104–121.

Cohen-Mansfield, J., Thein, K., Dakheel-Ali, M., & Marx, M. S. (2010). The underlying meaning of stimuli: Impact on engagement of persons with dementia. *Psychiatry Research, 177,* 216–222. doi:10.1016/j.psychres.2009.02.010

Cohen-Mansfield, J., Thein, K., Dakheel-Ali, M., Regier, N. G., & Marx, M. S. (2010). The value of social attributes of stimuli for promoting engagement in persons with dementia. *Journal of Nervous and Mental Disease, 198,* 586–592. doi:10.1097/NMD.0b013e3181e9dc76

Cohen-Mansfield, J., Thein, K., Marx, M. S., & Dakheel-Ali, M. (2012). What are the barriers to performing nonpharmacological interventions for behavioral symptoms in the nursing home? *Journal of the*

American Medical Directors Association, 13, 400–405. doi:10.1016/j.jamda.2011.07.006

Cohen-Mansfield, J., Thein, K., Marx, M. S., Dakheel-Ali, M., & Freedman, L. (2012). Efficacy of nonpharmacologic interventions for agitation in advanced dementia: A randomized, placebo-controlled trial. *Journal of Clinical Psychiatry, 73*, 1255–1261. doi:10.4088/JCP.12m07918

Cohen-Mansfield, J., Thein, K., Marx, M. S., Dakheel-Ali, M., & Jensen, B. (2013). Sources of discomfort in persons with dementia. *JAMA Internal Medicine, 173*, 1378–1379.

Cohen-Mansfield, J., & Werner, P. (1995). Environmental influences on agitation: An integrative summary of an observational study. *American Journal of Alzheimer's Disease and Other Dementias, 10*, 32–39. doi:10.1177/153331759501000108

Cohen-Mansfield, J., & Werner, P. (1997). Management of verbally disruptive behaviors in nursing home residents. *The Journals of Gerontology, Series A: Biological Sciences and Medical Sciences, 52*, 369–377. doi:10.1093/gerona/52A.6.M369

Cohen-Mansfield, J., & Werner, P. (1998a). The effects of an enhanced environment on nursing home residents who pace. *Gerontologist, 38*, 199–208. doi:10.1093/geront/38.2.199

Cohen-Mansfield, J., & Werner, P. (1998b). Predictors of aggressive behaviors: A longitudinal study in senior day care centers. *The Journals of Gerontology, Series B: Psychological Sciences and Social Sciences, 53*, 300–310. doi:10.1093/geronb/53B.5.P300

Cohen-Mansfield, J., & Werner, P. (1998c). Visits to an outdoor garden: Impact on behavior and mood of nursing home residents who pace. In B. Vellas, J. Fitten, & G. Frisoni (Eds.), *Research and practice in Alzheimer's disease* (pp. 419–436). Paris, France: Serdi.

Cohen-Mansfield, J., & Werner, P. (1999a). Longitudinal predictors of non-aggressive agitated behaviors in the elderly. *International Journal of Geriatric Psychiatry, 14*, 831–844. doi:10.1002/(SICI)1099-1166(199910)14:10<831::AID-GPS29>3.0.CO;2-A

Cohen-Mansfield, J., & Werner, P. (1999b). Outdoor wandering parks for persons with dementia: A survey of characteristics and use. *Alzheimer Disease and Associated Disorders, 13*, 109–117. doi:10.1097/00002093-199904000-00009

Cohen-Mansfield, J., Werner, P., Culpepper, W. J., & Barkley, D. (1997). Evaluation of an inservice training program on dementia and wandering. *Journal of Gerontological Nursing, 23*, 40–47.

Cohen-Mansfield, J., Werner, P., Culpepper, W., Wolfson, M., & Bickel, E. (1997). Assessment of ambulatory behavior in nursing home residents who

pace or wander: A comparison of four commercially available devices. *Dementia and Geriatric Cognitive Disorders, 8*, 359–365. doi:10.1159/000106656

Cohen-Mansfield, J., Werner, P., & Freedman, L. (1995). Sleep and agitation in agitated nursing home residents: An observational study. *Sleep, 18*, 674–680.

Cohen-Mansfield, J., Werner, P., Hammerschmidt, K., & Newman, J. D. (2003). Acoustic properties of vocally disruptive behaviors in the nursing home. *Gerontology, 49*, 161–167. doi:10.1159/000069173

Cohen-Mansfield, J., Werner, P., & Marx, M. S. (1989). An observational study of agitation in agitated nursing home residents. *International Psychogeriatrics, 1*, 153–165. doi:10.1017/S1041610289000165

Cohen-Mansfield, J., Werner, P., & Marx, M. (1990). Screaming in nursing home residents. *Journal of the American Geriatrics Society, 38*, 785–792.

Cohen-Mansfield, J., Werner, P., & Marx, M. S. (1992). The social environment of the agitated nursing home resident. *International Journal of Geriatric Psychiatry, 7*, 789–798. doi:10.1002/gps.930071104

Cohen-Mansfield, J., Werner, P., Watson, V., & Pasis, S. (1995). Agitation among elderly persons at adult day-care centers: The experiences of relatives and staff members. *International Psychogeriatrics, 7*, 447–458. doi:10.1017/S1041610295002195

Colenda, C. C., Leist, J. C., & Rapp, S. R. (1996). Survey of physician practices for community-dwelling agitated dementia patients. *International Journal of Geriatric Psychiatry, 11*, 635–644. doi:10.1002/(SICI)1099-1166(199607)11:7<635::AID-GPS363>3.0.CO;2-Z

Colenda, C. C., Rapp, S. R., Leist, J. C., & Poses, R. M. (1996). Clinical variables influencing treatment decisions for agitated dementia patients: Survey of physician judgments. *Journal of the American Geriatrics Society, 44*, 1375–1379.

Cooke, M. L., Moyle, W., Shum, D. H., Harrison, S. D., & Murfield, J. E. (2010). A randomized controlled trial exploring the effect of music on agitated behaviours and anxiety in older people with dementia. *Aging and Mental Health, 14*, 905–916. doi:10.1080/13607861003713190

Cooper, C., Mukadam, N., Katona, C., Lyketsos, C. G., Ames, D., Rabins, P., . . . Livingston, G. (2012). Systematic review of the effectiveness of non-pharmacological interventions to improve quality of life of people with dementia. *International Psychogeriatrics, 24*, 856–870. doi:10.1017/S1041610211002614

Cornegé-Blokland, E., Kleijer, B. C., Hertogh, C. M., & van Marum, R. J. (2012). Reasons to prescribe antipsychotics for the behavioral symptoms of dementia: A survey in Dutch nursing homes among physicians, nurses, and family caregivers. *Journal of the American Medical Directors Association, 13*, 80.e1–80.e6.

Cummings, J. L., Mega, M., Gray, K., Rosenberg-Thompson, S., Carusi, D. A., & Gornbein, J. (1994). The neuropsychiatric inventory comprehensive assessment of psychopathology in dementia. *Neurology, 44,* 2308–2314. doi:10.1212/WNL.44.12.2308

Davis, B. H., & Smith, M. K. (2009). Infusing cultural competence training into the curriculum: Describing the development of culturally sensitive training on dementia communication. *Kaohsiung Journal of Medical Sciences, 25,* 503–509. doi:10.1016/S1607-551X(09)70557-1

de Vugt, M. E., Stevens, F., Aalten, P., Lousberg, R., Jaspers, N., Winkens, I., . . . Verhey, F. R. (2004). Do caregiver management strategies influence patient behaviour in dementia? *International Journal of Geriatric Psychiatry, 19,* 85–92. doi:10.1002/gps.1044

Dempsey, L., Murphy, K., Cooney, A., Casey, D., O'Shea, E., Devane, D., . . . Hunter, A. (2014). Reminiscence in dementia: A concept analysis. *Dementia, 13,* 176–192.

Deudon, A., Maubourguet, N., Gervais, X., Leone, E., Brocker, P., Carcaillon, L., . . . Robert, P. H. (2009). Non-pharmacological management of behavioural symptoms in nursing homes. *International Journal of Geriatric Psychiatry, 24,* 1386–1395. doi:10.1002/gps.2275

Devanand, D. P., Broekington, C., Moody, B. J., & Brown, R. P. (1992). Behavioral syndromes in Alzheimer's disease. *International Psychogeriatrics, 4,* 161–184.

Devanand, D. P., Miller, L., Richards, M., Marder, K., Bell, K., Mayeux, R., & Stern, Y. (1992). The Columbia University scale for psychopathology in Alzheimer's disease. *Archives of Neurology, 49,* 371. doi:10.1001/archneur.1992.00530280051022

Doyle, C., Zapparoni, T., O'Connor, D., & Runci, S. (1997). Efficacy of psychosocial treatments for noisemaking in severe dementia. *International Psychogeriatrics, 9,* 405–422. doi:10.1017/S1041610297004547

Dujardin, K., Sockeel, P., Carette, A., Delliaux, M., & Defebvre, L. (2013). Assessing apathy in everyday clinical practice with the short-form Lille apathy rating scale. *Movement Disorders, 28,* 2014–2019.

Egan, M., Bérubé, D., Racine, G., Leonard, C., & Rochon, E. (2010). Methods to enhance verbal communication between individuals with Alzheimer's disease and their formal and informal caregivers: A systematic review. *International Journal of Alzheimer's Disease,* 1–12. doi:10.4061/2010/906818

Eggenberger, E., Heimerl, K., & Bennett, M. I. (2012). Communication skills training in dementia care: A systematic review of effectiveness, training content, and didactic methods in different care settings. *International Psychogeriatrics, 25,* 345–358.

Ellis, A. (1994). *Reason and emotion in psychotherapy.* Secaucus, NJ: Carol Publishing Group.

Eriksson, I., Gustafson, Y., Fagerström, L., & Olofsson, B. (2011). Urinary tract infection in very old women is associated with delirium. *International Psychogeriatrics, 23,* 496–502. doi:10.1017/S1041610210001456

Feil, N. (1982). *Validation: The Feil method.* Cleveland, OH: Feil Productions.

Feldt, K. (2000). Improving assessment and treatment of pain in cognitively impaired nursing home residents. *Annals of Long-Term Care, 8,* 36–46.

Feldt, K. S., Warne, M. A., & Ryden, M. B. (1998). Examining pain in aggressive cognitively impaired older adults. *Journal of Gerontological Nursing, 24,* 14–22.

Fernández, M., Gobartt, A., & Balañá, M. (2010). Behavioural symptoms in patients with alzheimer's disease and their association with cognitive impairment. *BMC Neurology, 10,* 87–95. doi:10.1186/1471-2377-10-87

Finkel, S., & Burns, A. (2000). Introduction. *International Psychogeriatrics, 12*(Suppl. 1), 9–12. doi:10.1017/S1041610200006694

Fischer, C., Bozanovic-Sosic, R., & Norris, M. (2004). Review of delusions in dementia. *American Journal of Alzheimer's Disease and Other Dementias, 19,* 19–23. doi:10.1177/153331750401900104

Fisman, M., Gordon, B., Feleki, V., Helmes, E., McDonald, T., & Dupre, J. (1988). Metabolic changes in Alzheimer's disease. *Journal of the American Geriatrics Society, 36,* 298–300.

Forsell, Y. (2000). Predictors for depression, anxiety and psychotic symptoms in a very elderly population: Data from a 3-year follow-up study. *Social Psychiatry and Psychiatric Epidemiology, 35,* 259–263. doi:10.1007/s001270050237

French, J. R. P., Rodgers, W., & Cobb, S. (1974). Adjustment as person-environment fit. In G. V. Coelho, D. A. Hamburg, & J. E. Adams (Eds.), *Coping and adaptation* (pp. 316–333). New York, NY: Basic Books.

Fritze, F., Ehrt, U., Hortobagyi, T., Ballard, C., & Aarsland, D. (2011). Depressive symptoms in Alzheimer's disease and Lewy body dementia: A one-year follow-up study. *Dementia and Geriatric Cognitive Disorders, 32,* 143–149. doi:10.1159/000332016

Fung, J. K. K., Tsang, H. W., & Chung, R. C. (2012). A systematic review of the use of aromatherapy in treatment of behavioral problems in dementia. *Geriatrics and Gerontology International, 12,* 372–382. doi:10.1111/j.1447-0594.2012.00849.x

Gagnon, D. (1996). A review of reality orientation (RO), validation therapy (VT), and reminiscence therapy (RT) with the Alzheimer's client. *Physical and Occupational Therapy in Geriatrics, 14*, 61–77. doi:10.1080/J148v14n02_05

Geda, Y. E., Schneider, L. S., Gitlin, L. N., Miller, D. S., Smith, G. S., Bell, J., . . . Lyketsos, C. G. (2013). Neuropsychiatric symptoms in Alzheimer's disease: Past progress and anticipation of the future. *Alzheimer's and Dementia, 9*, 602–608. doi:10.1016/j.jalz.2012.12.001

Gerdner, L. A. (2000). Effects of individualized versus classical "relaxation" music on the frequency of agitation in elderly persons with Alzheimer's disease and related disorders. *International Psychogeriatrics, 12*, 49–65. doi:10.1017/S1041610200006190

Gitlin, L. N., Winter, L., Burke, J., Chernett, N., Dennis, M. P., & Hauck, W. W. (2008). Tailored activities to manage neuropsychiatric behaviors in persons with dementia and reduce caregiver burden: A randomized pilot study. *American Journal of Geriatric Psychiatry, 16*, 229–239. doi:10.1097/01. JGP.0000300629.35408.94

Gitlin, L. N., Winter, L., Dennis, M. P., Hodgson, N., & Hauck, W. W. (2010). A biobehavioral home-based intervention and the well-being of patients with dementia and their caregivers. *JAMA, 304*, 983–991. doi:10.1001/jama.2010.1253

Gottfries, C. G., Brâne, G., Gullberg, B., & Steen, G. (1982). A new rating scale for dementia syndromes. *Archives of Gerontology and Geriatrics, 1*, 311–321. doi:10.1016/0167-4943(82)90031-0

Graff, M. J., Vernooij-Dassen, M. J., Thijssen, M., Dekker, J., Hoefnagels, W. H., & Olderikkert, M. G. (2007). Effects of community occupational therapy on quality of life, mood, and health status in dementia patients and their caregivers: A randomized controlled trial. *The Journals of Gerontology, Series A: Biological Sciences and Medical Sciences, 62*, 1002–1009. doi:10.1093/gerona/62.9.1002

Gräsel, E., Wiltfang, J., & Kornhuber, J. (2003). Non-drug therapies for dementia: An overview of the current situation with regard to proof of effectiveness. *Dementia and Geriatric Cognitive Disorders, 15*, 115–125. doi:10.1159/000068477

Greiner, C., Makimoto, K., Suzuki, M., Yamakawa, M., & Ashida, N. (2007). Feasibility study of the integrated circuit tag monitoring system for dementia residents in Japan. *American Journal of Alzheimer's Disease and Other Dementias, 22*, 129–136. doi:10.1177/1533317507299414

Guzmán-García, A., Hughes, J., James, I., & Rochester, L. (2013). Dancing as a psychosocial intervention in care homes: A systematic review of the literature. *International Journal of Geriatric Psychiatry, 28*, 914–924. doi:10.1002/gps.3913

Haberstroh, J., Neumeyer, K., Schmitz, B., & Pantel, J. (2009). Development and evaluation of a training program for nursing home professionals to improve communication in dementia care. [Evaluation eines Kommunikationstrainings fur Altenpfleger in der stationaren Betreuung demenzkranker Menschen (Tandem im Pflegeheim)]. *Zeitschrift für Gerontologie und Geriatrie, 42*, 108–116. doi:10.1007/s00391-008-0527-x

Hall, G. R. (1994). Caring for people with Alzheimer's disease using the conceptual model of progressively lowered stress threshold in the clinical setting. *Nursing Clinics of North America, 29*, 129–141.

Hamel, M., Gold, D. P., Andres, D., Reis, M., Dastoor, D., Grauer, H., & Bergman, H. (1990). Predictors and consequences of aggressive behavior by community-based dementia patients. *Gerontologist, 30*, 206–211. doi:10.1093/geront/30.2.206

Hancock, G. A., Woods, B., Challis, D., & Orrell, M. (2006). The needs of older people with dementia in residential care. *International Journal of Geriatric Psychiatry, 21*, 43–49. doi:10.1002/gps.1421

Hart, B. D., & Wells, D. L. (1997). The effects of language used by caregivers on agitation in residents with dementia. *Clinical Nurse Specialist CNS, 11*, 20–23. doi:10.1097/00002800-199701000-00015

Higgins, P. (2010). Using dolls to enhance the wellbeing of people with dementia in residential care. *Nursing Times, 106*, 18–20.

Holmes, C., Knights, A., Dean, C., Hodkinson, S., & Hopkins, V. (2006). Keep music live: Music and the alleviation of apathy in dementia subjects. *International Psychogeriatrics, 18*, 623–630. doi:10.1017/S1041610206003887

Holroyd, S. (1998). Hallucinations and delusions in Alzheimer's disease. In B. Vellas, J. Fitten, & G. Frisconi (Eds.), *Research and practice in Alzheimer's disease* (pp. 213–222). Paris, France: Serdi.

Holroyd, S., & Sheldon-Keller, A. (1995). A study of visual hallucinations in Alzheimer's disease. *American Journal of Geriatric Psychiatry, 3*, 198–205. doi:10.1097/00019442-199522330-00003

Hölttä, E. H., Laakkonen, M., Laurila, J. V., Strandberg, T. E., Tilvis, R. S., & Pitkälä, K. H. (2012). Apathy: Prevalence, associated factors, and prognostic value among frail, older inpatients. *Journal of the American Medical Directors Association, 13*, 541–545. doi:10.1016/j.jamda.2012.04.005

Hopper, T. (2001). Indirect interventions to facilitate communication in Alzheimer's disease. *Seminars in Speech and Language, 22*, 305–316. doi:10.1055/s-2001-17428

Howland, L. G. (1984). Spirit communication at the Carib Dugu. *Language and Communication, 4*, 89–103. doi:10.1016/0271-5309(84)90001-6

Huang, Y. J., Lin, C. H., Lane, H. Y., & Tsai, G. E. (2012). NMDA neurotransmission dysfunction in behavioral and psychological symptoms of alzheimer's disease. *Current Neuropharmacology, 10*, 272–285. doi:10.2174/157015912803217288

Husebo, B. S., Ballard, C., Cohen-Mansfield, J., Seifert, R., & Aarsland, D. (2014). The response of agitated behavior to pain management in persons with dementia. *American Journal of Geriatric Psychiatry, 22*, 708–717. doi:10.1016/j.jagp.2012.12.006

Husebo, B. S., Ballard, C., Sandvik, R., Nilsen, O. B., & Aarsland, D. (2011). Efficacy of treating pain to reduce behavioural disturbances in residents of nursing homes with dementia: Cluster randomised clinical trial. *British Medical Journal, 2011*, 343.

Huybrechts, K., Gerhard, T., Crystal, S., Olfson, M., Avorn, J., Levin, R., . . . Schneeweiss, S. (2012). Differential risk of death in older residents in nursing homes prescribed specific antipsychotic drugs: Population based cohort study. *British Medical Journal (Clinical Research Ed.), 344*, 977–989. doi:10.1136/bmj.e977

Ito, G., & Kanemoto, K. (2013). A case of topical opioid-induced delirium mistaken as behavioural and psychological symptoms of dementia in demented state. *Psychogeriatrics, 13*, 118–123. doi:10.1111/psyg.12007

Jacobs, M. R., Strauss, M. E., Patterson, M. B., & Mack, J. L. (1998). Characterization of depression in Alzheimer's disease by the CERAD Behavior Rating Scale for Dementia (BRSD). *American Journal of Geriatric Psychiatry, 6*, 53–58.

Jefferis, J. M., Mosimann, U. P., & Clarke, M. P. (2011). Cataract and cognitive impairment: A review of the literature. *British Journal of Ophthalmology, 95*, 17–23. doi:10.1136/bjo.2009.165902

Johnson, D. K., Niedens, M., Wilson, J. R., Swartzendruber, L., Yeager, A., & Jones, K. (2013). Treatment outcomes of a crisis intervention program for dementia with severe psychiatric complications: The Kansas bridge project. *Gerontologist, 53*, 102–112. doi:10.1093/geront/gns104

Jootun, D., & Mcghee, G. (2011). Effective communication with people who have dementia. *Nursing Standard, 25*, 40–46. doi:10.7748/ns2011.02.25.25.40.c8347

Kahana, E. (1982). A congruence model of person-environment interaction. In M. P. Lawton, P. G. Windley, & T. O. Byerts (Eds.), *Aging and the environment: Theoretical approaches* (pp. 97–121). New York, NY: Springer.

Kales, H. C., Kim, H. M., Zivin, K., Valenstein, M., Seyfried, L. S., Chiang, C., . . . Blow, F. C. (2012). Risk of mortality among individual antipsychotics in patients with dementia. *American Journal of Psychiatry, 169*, 71–79. doi:10.1176/appi.ajp.2011.11030347

Kar, N. (2009). Behavioral and psychological symptoms of dementia and their management. *Indian Journal of Psychiatry, 51*, 77–86.

Kempe, P., & Reimer, C. (1976). Hallucinatory phenomenona during the withdrawal of stimuli. [Halluzinatorische Phanomene bei Reizentzug]. *Der Nervenarzt, 47*, 701–707.

Keshavan, M., David, A., Steingard, S., & Lishman, W. (1992). Musical hallucinations: A review and synthesis. *Cognitive and Behavioral Neurology, 5*, 211–223.

Khan, A. M., Clark, T., & Oyebode, F. (1988). Unilateral auditory hallucinations. *British Journal of Psychiatry, 152*, 297–298. doi:10.1192/bjp.152.2.297

Kincaid, C., & Peacock, J. R. (2003). The effect of a wall mural on decreasing four types of door-testing behaviors. *Journal of Applied Gerontology, 22*, 76–88. doi:10.1177/0733464802250046

Koss, E., & Gilmore, G. (1998). Environmental interventions and functional ability of AD patients. In B. Vellas, J. Fritten, & G. Frisoni (Eds.), *Research and practice in Alzheimer's disease* (pp. 185–192). Paris, France: Serdi.

Koss, E., Weiner, M., Ernesto, C., Cohen-Mansfield, J., Ferris, S. H., Grundman, M., . . . Thomas, R. (1997). Assessing patterns of agitation in Alzheimer's disease patients with the Cohen-Mansfield agitation inventory. *Alzheimer Disease and Associated Disorders, 11*, 45–50. doi:10.1097/00002093-199700112-00007

Kunik, M. E., Snow, A. L., Davila, J. A., Steele, A. B., Balasubramanyam, V., Doody, R. S., . . . Morgan, R. O. (2010). Causes of aggressive behavior in patients with dementia. *Journal of Clinical Psychiatry, 71*, 1145–1152. doi:10.4088/JCP.08m04703oli

Kuske, B., Hanns, S., Luck, T., Angermeyer, M. C., Behrens, J., & Riedel-Heller, S. G. (2007). Nursing home staff training in dementia care: A systematic review of evaluated programs. *International Psychogeriatrics, 19*, 818–841. doi:10.1017/S1041610206004352

Lachs, M. S., Becker, M., Siegal, A., Miller, R., & Tinetti, M. (1992). Delusions and behavioral disturbances in cognitively impaired elderly persons. *Journal of the American Geriatrics Society, 40*, 768–773.

Lavretsky, H., & Nguyen, L. (2006). Innovations: Geriatric psychiatry: Diagnosis and treatment of neuropsychiatric symptoms in Alzheimer's disease. *Psychiatric Services, 57*, 617–619. doi:10.1176/appi.ps.57.5.617

Lawton, M. P., & Nahemow, L. (1973). Ecology and the aging process. In C. Eisdorfer & M. P. Lawton (Eds.), *The psychology of adult development and aging* (pp. 619–674). Washington, DC: American Psychological Association. doi:10.1037/10044-020

Lawton, M. P., & Simon, B. (1968). The ecology of social relationships in housing for the elderly. *Gerontologist, 8,* 108–115. doi:10.1093/geront/8.2.108

Leone, E., Deudon, A., Bauchet, M., Laye, M., Bordone, N., Lee, J., . . . Delva, F. (2013). Management of apathy in nursing homes using a teaching program for care staff: The STIM-EHPAD study. *International Journal of Geriatric Psychiatry, 28,* 383–392. doi:10.1002/gps.3836

Leone, E., Deudon, A., Piano, J., Robert, P., & Dechamps, A. (2012). Are dementia patient's engagement using tailored stimuli the same? The apathy dilemma in nursing home residents. *Current Gerontology and Geriatrics Research, 2012,* 1–11. doi:10.1155/2012/942640

Lerner, A., Koss, E., Patterson, M., Ownby, R., Hedera, P., Friedland, R., & Whitehouse, P. (1994). Concomitants of visual hallucinations in Alzheimer's disease. *Neurology, 44,* 523. doi:10.1212/WNL.44.3_Part_1.523

Levy-Storms, L. (2008). Therapeutic communication training in long-term care institutions: Recommendations for future research. *Patient Education and Counseling, 73,* 8–21. doi:10.1016/j.pec.2008.05.026

Lewin, L. (1996, August). *Disruptive vocalizations in nursing home residents: Treatment, successes, and failure.* Paper presented at the 104th Annual Meeting of the American Psychological Association, Toronto, Ontario, Canada.

Lewinsohn, P. M., & Youngren, M. A. (1976). The symptoms of depression. *Comprehensive Therapy, 2,* 62–69.

Li, R., Cooper, C., Austin, A., & Livingston, G. (2013). Do changes in coping style explain the effectiveness of interventions for psychological morbidity in family carers of people with dementia? A systematic review and meta-analysis. *International Psychogeriatrics, 25,* 204–214. doi:10.1017/S1041610212001755

Libin, A., & Cohen-Mansfield, J. (2004). Therapeutic robocat for nursing home residents with dementia: Preliminary inquiry. *American Journal of Alzheimer's Disease and Other Dementias, 19,* 111–116. doi:10.1177/153331750401900209

Liddle, J., Smith-Conway, E. R., Baker, R., Angwin, A. J., Gallois, C., Copland, D. A., . . . Chenery, H. J. (2012). Memory and communication support strategies in dementia: Effect of a training program for informal caregivers. *International Psychogeriatrics, 24,* 1927–194216.

Livingston, G., Johnston, K., Katona, C., Paton, J., & Lyketsos, C. G. (2005). Systematic review of psychological approaches to the management of neuropsychiatric symptoms of dementia. *American Journal of Psychiatry, 162,* 1996–2021. doi:10.1176/appi.ajp.162.11.1996

Logsdon, R. G., & Teri, L. (1997). The pleasant events schedule-AD: Psychometric properties and relationship to depression and cognition in Alzheimer's disease patients. *Gerontologist, 37,* 40–45. doi:10.1093/geront/37.1.40

MacDonald, W. L. (1992). Idionecrophanies: The social construction of perceived contact with the dead. *Journal for the Scientific Study of Religion, 31,* 215–223. doi:10.2307/1387010

Mack, J. L., Patterson, M. B., & Tariot, P. N. (1999). Behavior Rating Scale for Dementia: Development of test scales and presentation of data for 555 individuals with Alzheimer's disease. *Journal of Geriatric Psychiatry and Neurology, 12,* 211–223. doi:10.1177/089198879901200408

Majić, T., Pluta, J. P., Mell, T., Treusch, Y., Gutzmann, H., & Rapp, M. A. (2012). Correlates of agitation and depression in nursing home residents with dementia. *International Psychogeriatrics, 24,* 1779–1789. doi:10.1017/S104161021200066X

Mallers, M. H., Claver, M., & Lares, L. A. (2013). Perceived control in the lives of older adults: The influence of Langer and Rodin's work on gerontological theory, policy, and practice. *Gerontologist, 54,* 67–74.

Marin, R. S. (1991). Apathy: A neuropsychiatric syndrome. *Journal of Neuropsychiatry and Clinical Neurosciences, 3,* 243–254.

Marin, R. S., Firinciogullari, S., & Biedrzycki, R. C. (1993). The sources of convergence between measures of apathy and depression. *Journal of Affective Disorders, 28,* 117–124. doi:10.1016/0165-0327(93)90040-Q

Marsden, J. P., Meehan, R. A., & Calkins, M. P. (2001). Therapeutic kitchens for residents with dementia. *American Journal of Alzheimer's Disease and Other Dementias, 16,* 303–311. doi:10.1177/153331750101600509

Marx, M. S., Cohen-Mansfield, J., & Werner, P. (1990). A profile of the aggressive nursing home resident. *Behavior, Health, and Aging, 1,* 65–73.

Marx, M. S., Cohen-Mansfield, J., Regier, N. G., Dakheel-Ali, M., Srihari, A., & Thein, K. (2010). The impact of different dog-related stimuli on engagement of persons with dementia. *American Journal of Alzheimer's Disease and Other Dementias, 25,* 37–45. doi:10.1177/1533317508326976

Matteson, M. A., Linton, A. D., Cleary, B. L., Barnes, S. J., & Lichtenstein, M. J. (1997). Management of problematic behavioral symptoms associated with dementia: A cognitive developmental approach. *Aging, 9,* 342–355.

McCabe, M. P., Davison, T., & George, K. (2007). Effectiveness of staff training programs for behavioral problems among older people with dementia. *Aging and Mental Health, 11*, 505–519. doi:10.1080/13607860601086405

McCallion, P., Toseland, R. W., Lacey, D., & Banks, S. (1999). Educating nursing assistants to communicate more effectively with nursing home residents with dementia. *Gerontologist, 39*, 546–558. doi:10.1093/geront/39.5.546

McShane, R., Cohen-Mansfield, J., & Werner, P. (2000). Predictors of aggressive behaviors. *Research and Practice in Alzheimer's Disease, 3*, 183–188.

Meeks, S., Shah, S. N., & Ramsey, S. K. (2009). The pleasant events Schedule–Nursing home version: A useful tool for behavioral interventions in long-term care. *Aging and Mental Health, 13*, 445–455. doi:10.1080/13607860802534617

Mentes, J. C., & Ferrario, J. (1989). Calming aggressive reactions: A preventive program. *Journal of Gerontological Nursing, 15*, 22–27.

Meyer, D. L., Dorbacker, B., O'Rourke, J., Dowling, J., Jacques, J., & Nicholas, M. (1992). Effects of a 'quiet week' intervention on behavior in an Alzheimer boarding home. *American Journal of Alzheimer's Disease and Other Dementias, 7*, 2–7. doi:10.1177/153331759200700402

Milders, M., Bell, S., Lorimer, A., MacEwan, T., & McBain, A. (2013). Cognitive stimulation by caregivers for people with dementia. *Geriatric Nursing, 34*, 267–273. doi:10.1016/j.gerinurse.2013.03.003

Mishima, K., Okawa, M., Hishikawa, Y., Hozumi, S., Hori, H., & Takahashi, K. (1994). Morning bright light therapy for sleep and behavior disorders in elderly patients with dementia. *Acta Psychiatrica Scandinavica, 89*, 1–7. doi:10.1111/j.1600-0447.1994.tb01477.x

Mitchell, S. L., Teno, J. M., Kiely, D. K., Shaffer, M. L., Jones, R. N., Prigerson, H. G., . . . Hamel, M. B. (2009). The clinical course of advanced dementia. *New England Journal of Medicine, 361*, 1529–1538. doi:10.1056/NEJMoa0902234

Möhler, R., Richter, T., Köpke, S., & Meyer, G. (2011). Interventions for preventing and reducing the use of physical restraints in long-term geriatric care. *Cochrane Database of Systematic Reviews, 2*, 1–26.

Mohs, R. C. (1996). The Alzheimer's disease assessment scale. *International Psychogeriatrics, 8*, 195–203. doi:10.1017/S1041610296002578

Mossello, E., Ridolfi, A., Mello, A. M., Lorenzini, G., Mugnai, F., Piccini, C., . . . Marchionni, N. (2011). Animal-assisted activity and emotional status of patients with Alzheimer's disease in day care. *International Psychogeriatrics, 23*, 899–905. doi:10.1017/S1041610211000226

Moyle, W., Johnston, A. N. B., & O'Dwyer, S. T. (2011). Exploring the effect of foot massage on agitated behaviours in older people with dementia: A pilot study. *Australasian Journal on Ageing, 30*, 159–161. doi:10.1111/j.1741-6612.2010.00504.x

Murgatroyd, C., & Prettyman, R. (2001). An investigation of visual hallucinosis and visual sensory status in dementia. *International Journal of Geriatric Psychiatry, 16*, 709–713. doi:10.1002/gps.426

Namazi, K. H., & Johnson, B. D. (1992). Pertinent autonomy for residents with dementias: Modification of the physical environment to enhance independence. *American Journal of Alzheimer's Disease and Other Dementias, 7*, 16–21. doi:10.1177/153331759200700105

Namazi, K. H., Rosner, T. T., & Calkins, M. P. (1989). Visual barriers to prevent ambulatory Alzheimer's patients from exiting through an emergency door. *Gerontologist, 29*, 699–702. doi:10.1093/geront/29.5.699

Neal, M. and Briggs, M. (Directors). (2003). *Validation therapy for dementia* [Video/DVD]. Wiley Online Library.

Negley, E. N., & Manley, J. T. (1990). Environmental interventions in assaultive behavior. *Journal of Gerontological Nursing, 16*, 29–33.

Nösman, B., Bucht, G., Eriksson, S., & Sandman, P. (1993). Behavioural symptoms in the institutionalized elderly: Relationship to dementia. *International Journal of Geriatric Psychiatry, 8*, 843–849. doi:10.1002/gps.930081007

O'Connor, C. M., Smith, R., Nott, M., Lorang, C., & Mathews, R. (2011). Using video simulated presence to reduce resistance to care and increase participation of adults with dementia. *American Journal of Alzheimer's Disease and Other Dementias, 26*, 317–325. doi:10.1177/1533317511410558

Olsson, J., Bergman, Å., Carlsten, A., Oké, T., Bernsten, C., Schmidt, I. K., & Fastbom, J. (2010). Quality of drug prescribing in elderly people in nursing homes and special care units for dementia. *Clinical Drug Investigation, 30*, 289–300. doi:10.2165/11534320-000000000-00000

Padilla, D. V., González, M. T. D., Agis, I. F., Strizzi, J., & Rodríguez, R. A. (2013). The effectiveness of control strategies for dementia-driven wandering, preventing escape attempts: A case report. *International Psychogeriatrics, 25*, 500–504. doi:10.1017/S1041610212001810

Palmer, C. V., Adams, S. W., Bourgeois, M., Durrant, J., & Rossi, M. (1999). Reduction in caregiver-identified problem behaviors in patients with Alzheimer disease post-hearing-aid fitting. *Journal of Speech, Language, and Hearing Research, 42*, 312.

Parpura-Gill, A., & Cohen-Mansfield, J. (2006). Utilization of self-identity roles in individualized activities designed to enhance well-being in persons with dementia. In L. Hyer & R. C. Intrieri (Eds.), *Geropsychological interventions in long-term care* (pp. 157–184). New York, NY: Springer.

Patterson, M. B., Mack, J. L., Mackell, J. A., Thomas, R., Tariot, P., Weiner, M., & Whitehouse, P. J. (1997). A longitudinal study of behavioral pathology across five levels of dementia severity in Alzheimer's disease: The CERAD Behavior Rating Scale for Dementia. *Alzheimer Disease and Associated Disorders, 11,* 40–44. doi:10.1097/00002093-199700112-00006

Phinney, A., Chaudhury, H., & O'Connor, D. L. (2007). Doing as much as I can do: The meaning of activity for people with dementia. *Aging and Mental Health, 11,* 384–393. doi:10.1080/13607860601086470

Politis, A. M., Vozzella, S., Mayer, L. S., Onyike, C. U., Baker, A. S., & Lyketsos, C. G. (2004). A randomized, controlled, clinical trial of activity therapy for apathy in patients with dementia residing in long-term care. *International Journal of Geriatric Psychiatry, 19,* 1087–1094. doi:10.1002/gps.1215

Pritchard, A. L., Ratcliffe, L., Sorour, E., Haque, S., Holder, R., Bentham, P., & Lendon, C. L. (2009). Investigation of dopamine receptors in susceptibility to behavioural and psychological symptoms in Alzheimer's disease. *International Journal of Geriatric Psychiatry, 24,* 1020–1025. doi:10.1002/gps.2214

Quayhagen, M. P., & Quayhagen, M. (2001). Testing of a cognitive stimulation intervention for dementia caregiving dyads. *Neuropsychological Rehabilitation, 11,* 319–332. doi:10.1080/09602010042000024

Rabinowitz, J., Davidson, M., De Deyn, P. P., Katz, I., Brodaty, H., & Cohen-Mansfield, J. (2005). Factor analysis of the Cohen-Mansfield agitation inventory in three large samples of nursing home patients with dementia and behavioral disturbance. *American Journal of Geriatric Psychiatry, 13,* 991–998. doi:10.1097/00019442-200511000-00010

Rao, V., & Lyketsos, C. G. (1998). Delusions in Alzheimer's disease: A review. *Journal of Neuropsychiatry and Clinical Neurosciences, 10,* 373–382.

Raskin, A. (1988). Three area severity of depression scales. In A. S. Bellack & M. Herson (Eds.), *Dictionary of behavioral assessment techniques* (pp. 476–477). New York, NY: Pergamon Press.

Reisberg, B., Auer, S. R., & Monteiro, I. M. (1996). Behavioral Pathology in Alzheimer's Disease (BEHAVE-AD) Rating Scale. *International Psychogeriatrics, 8,* 301–308. doi:10.1017/S1041610297003529

Reisberg, B., Schneck, M. K., Ferris, S. H., Schwartz, G. E., & Deleon, M. J. (1983). The brief cognitive rating-scale (BCRS): Findings in primary degenerative dementia (PDD). *Psychopharmacology Bulletin, 19,* 47–50.

Reisberg, B., Borenstein, J., Salob, S. P., & Ferris, S. H. (1987). Behavioral symptoms in Alzheimer's disease:

Phenomenology and treatment. *Journal of Clinical Psychiatry, 48,* 9–15.

Ripich, D. N. (1994). Functional communication with AD patients: A caregiver training program. *Alzheimer Disease and Associated Disorders, 8,* 95–109. doi:10.1097/00002093-199404000-00011

Ripich, D. N., Wykle, M., & Niles, S. (1995). Alzheimer's disease caregivers: The FOCUSED program: A communication skills training program helps nursing assistants to give better care to patients with Alzheimer's disease. *Geriatric Nursing, 16,* 15–19. doi:10.1016/S0197-4572(05)80073-4

Robert, P., Clairet, S., Benoit, M., Koutaich, J., Bertogliati, C., Tible, O., . . . Bedoucha, P. (2002). The apathy inventory: Assessment of apathy and awareness in Alzheimer's disease, Parkinson's disease and mild cognitive impairment. *International Journal of Geriatric Psychiatry, 17,* 1099–1105. doi:10.1002/gps.755

Robert, P., Onyike, C., Leentjens, A., Dujardin, K., Aalten, P., Starkstein, S., . . . Drapier, D. (2009). Proposed diagnostic criteria for apathy in Alzheimer's disease and other neuropsychiatric disorders. *European Psychiatry, 24,* 98–104. doi:10.1016/j.eurpsy.2008.09.001

Robison, J., Curry, L., Gruman, C., Porter, M., Henderson, C. R., & Pillemer, K. (2007). Partners in caregiving in a special care environment: Cooperative communication between staff and families on dementia units. *Gerontologist, 47,* 504–515. doi:10.1093/geront/47.4.504

Romero, B., & Wenz, M. (2001). Self-maintenance therapy in Alzheimer's disease. *Neuropsychological Rehabilitation, 11,* 333–355. doi:10.1080/09602010143000040

Ropacki, S. A., & Jeste, D. V. (2005). Epidemiology of and risk factors for psychosis of Alzheimer's disease: A review of 55 studies published from 1990 to 2003. *American Journal of Psychiatry, 162,* 2022–2030. doi:10.1176/appi.ajp.162.11.2022

Rosen, J., Burgio, L., Kollar, M., Cain, M., Allison, M., Fogleman, M., . . . Zubenko, G. S. (1994). The Pittsburgh agitation scale: A user-friendly instrument for rating agitation in dementia patients. *American Journal of Geriatric Psychiatry, 2,* 52–59. doi:10.1097/00019442-199400210-00008

Rosenberg, P. B., Lanctôt, K. L., Drye, L. T., Herrmann, N., Scherer, R. W., Bachman, D. L., Mintzer, J. E., & ADMET Investigators. (2013). Safety and efficacy of methylphenidate for apathy in Alzheimer's disease: A randomized, placebo-controlled trial. *Journal of Clinical Psychiatry, 74,* 810–816. doi:10.4088/JCP.12m08099

Ryden, M. B. (1988). Aggressive behavior in persons with dementia who live in the community. *Alzheimer*

Disease and Associated Disorders, 2, 342–355. doi:10.1097/00002093-198802040-00003

Ryden, M. B., Bossenmaier, M., & McLachlan, C. (1991). Agressive behavior in cognitively impaired nursing home residents. *Research in Nursing and Health, 14,* 87–95. doi:10.1002/nur.4770140203

Saliba, D., & Buchanan, J. (2008). *Development and validation of a revised nursing home assessment tool: MDS 3.0.* Santa Monica: Rand Corporation Health.

Salzman, C., Jeste, D., Meyer, R. E., Cohen-Mansfield, J., Cummings, J., Grossberg, G., . . . Maslow, K. (2008). Elderly patients with dementia-related symptoms of severe agitation and aggression: Consensus statement on treatment options, clinical trials methodology, and policy. *Journal of Clinical Psychiatry, 69,* 889–898. doi:10.4088/JCP.v69n0602

Samia, L. W., Hepburn, K., & Nichols, L. (2012). "Flying by the seat of our pants": What dementia family caregivers want in an advanced caregiver training program. *Research in Nursing and Health, 35,* 598–609. doi:10.1002/nur.21504

Sato, J., Nakaaki, S., Torii, K., Oka, M., Negi, A., Tatsumi, H., . . . Mimura, M. (2013). Behavior management approach for agitated behavior in Japanese patients with dementia: A pilot study. *Neuropsychiatric Disease and Treatment, 9,* 9–14.

Scarmeas, N., Brandt, J., Albert, M., Hadjigeorgiou, G., Papadimitriou, A., Dubois, B., . . . Marder, K. (2005). Delusions and hallucinations are associated with worse outcome in Alzheimer disease. *Archives of Neurology, 62,* 1601–1608. doi:10.1001/archneur.62.10.1601

Schiffer, R., & Pope, L. E. (2005). Review of pseudobulbar affect including a novel and potential therapy. *Journal of Neuropsychiatry and Clinical Neurosciences, 17,* 447–454. doi:10.1176/appi.neuropsych.17.4.447

Schindler, S. D., Graf, A., Fischer, P., Tölk, A., & Kasper, S. (2002). Paranoid delusions and hallucinations and bright light therapy in Alzheimer's disease. *International Journal of Geriatric Psychiatry, 17,* 1071–1072. doi:10.1002/gps.497

Schneider, L. S., Dagerman, K., & Insel, P. S. (2006). Efficacy and adverse effects of atypical antipsychotics for dementia: Meta-analysis of randomized, placebo-controlled trials. *American Journal of Geriatric Psychiatry, 14,* 191–210. doi:10.1097/01.JGP.0000200589.01396.6d

Schreiner, A. S., Yamamoto, E., & Shiotani, H. (2000). Agitated behavior in elderly nursing home residents with dementia in Japan. *The Journals of Gerontology, Series B: Psychological Sciences and Social Sciences, 55,* 180–187. doi:10.1093/geronb/55.3.P180

Schweitzer, I., Tuckwell, V., O'Brien, J., & Ames, D. (2002). Is late onset depression a prodrome to dementia? *International Journal of Geriatric Psychiatry, 17,* 997–1005. doi:10.1002/gps.525

Seitz, D. P., Brisbin, S., Herrmann, N., Rapoport, M. J., Wilson, K., Gill, S. S., . . . Conn, D. (2012). Efficacy and feasibility of nonpharmacological interventions for neuropsychiatric symptoms of dementia in long-term care: A systematic review. *Journal of the American Medical Directors Association, 13,* 503–506. doi:10.1016/j.jamda.2011.12.059

Seligman, M. E. P. (1974). Depression and learned helplessness. In R. J. Friedman & M. M. Katz (Eds.), *The psychology of depression: Contemporary theory and research.* Washington, DC: Halsted Press.

Seligman, M. E. P. (1975). *Helplessness: On depression, development, and death.* San Francisco, CA: WH Freeman.

Shaji, S., Bose, S., & Kuriakose, S. (2009). Behavioral and psychological symptoms of dementia: A study of symptomology. *Indian Journal of Psychiatry, 51,* 38–41. doi:10.4103/0019-5545.44903

Siders, C., Nelson, A., Brown, L. M., Joseph, I., Algase, D., Beattie, E., & Verbosky-Candena, S. (2004). Evidence for implementing non-pharmacological interventions for wandering. *Rehabilitation Nursing, 29,* 195–206.

Sink, K. M., Holden, K. F., & Yaffe, K. (2005). Pharmacological treatment of neuropsychiatric symptoms of dementia. *JAMA, 293,* 596–608. doi:10.1001/jama.293.5.596

Sloane, P. D., Hoeffer, B., Mitchell, C. M., McKenzie, D. A., Barrick, A. L., Rader, J., . . . Zink, R. C. (2004). Effect of person-centered showering and the towel bath on bathing-associated aggression, agitation, and discomfort in nursing home residents with dementia: A randomized, controlled trial. *Journal of the American Geriatrics Society, 52,* 1795–1804. doi:10.1111/j.1532-5415.2004.52501.x

Sloane, P. D., Williams, C. S., Mitchell, C. M., Preisser, J. S., Wood, W., Barrick, A. L., . . . Edinger, J. (2007). High-intensity environmental light in dementia: Effect on sleep and activity. *Journal of the American Geriatrics Society, 55,* 1524–1533. doi:10.1111/j.1532-5415.2007.01358.x

Small, J. A., & Gutman, G. (2002). Recommended and reported use of communication strategies in Alzheimer caregiving. *Alzheimer Disease and Associated Disorders, 16,* 270–278. doi:10.1097/00002093-200210000-00009

Small, J. A., Gutman, G., Makela, S., & Hillhouse, B. (2003). Effectiveness of communication strategies used by caregivers of persons with Alzheimer's disease during activities of daily living. *Journal of Speech, Language, and Hearing Research, 46,* 353–367. doi:10.1044/1092-4388(2003/028)

Snow, A. L., Chandler, J. F., Kunik, M. E., Davila, J. A., Balasubramanyam, V., Steele, A. B., & Morgan, R. O. (2009). Self-reported pain in persons with dementia predicts subsequent decreased psychosocial functioning. *American Journal of Geriatric Psychiatry, 17,* 873–880. doi:10.1097/JGP.0b013e3181ad4f73

Snyder, M., Tseng, Y., Brandt, C., Croghan, C., Hanson, S., Constantine, R., & Kirby, L. (2001). A glider swing intervention for people with dementia. *Geriatric Nursing, 22,* 86–90. doi:10.1067/mgn.2001.115197

Spector, A., Davies, S., Woods, B., & Orrell, M. (2000). Reality orientation for dementia: A systematic review of the evidence of effectiveness from randomized controlled trials. *Gerontologist, 40,* 206–212. doi:10.1093/geront/40.2.206

Spector, W. D., & Jackson, M. E. (1994). Correlates of disruptive behaviors in nursing homes A reanalysis. *Journal of Aging and Health, 6,* 173–184. doi:10.1177/089826439400600203

Starkstein, S. E., Jorge, R., Mizrahi, R., & Robinson, R. G. (2006). A prospective longitudinal study of apathy in Alzheimer's disease. *Journal of Neurology, Neurosurgery, and Psychiatry, 77,* 8–11. doi:10.1136/jnnp.2005.069575

Starkstein, S. E., Mayberg, H. S., Preziosi, T., Andrezejewski, P., Leiguarda, R., & Robinson, R. (1992). Reliability, validity, and clinical correlates of apathy in Parkinson's disease. *Journal of Neuropsychiatry and Clinical Neurosciences, 4,* 134–139.

Starkstein, S. E., Migliorelli, R., Teson, A., Petracca, G., Chemerinsky, E., Manes, F., & Leiguarda, R. (1995). Prevalence and clinical correlates of pathological affective display in Alzheimer's disease. *Journal of Neurology, Neurosurgery, and Psychiatry, 59,* 55–60. doi:10.1136/jnnp.59.1.55

Steinberg, M., Shao, H., Zandi, P., Lyketsos, C. G., Welsh-Bohmer, K. A., Norton, M. C., . . . Tschanz, J. T. (2008). Point and 5-year period prevalence of neuropsychiatric symptoms in dementia: The cache county study. *International Journal of Geriatric Psychiatry, 23,* 170–177. doi:10.1002/gps.1858

Stone, R. I. (2001). Research on frontline workers in long-term care. *Generations, 25,* 49–57.

Stone, R. I., & Dawson, S. L. (2008). The origins of better jobs better care. *Gerontologist, 48*(Suppl. 1), 5–13. doi:10.1093/geront/48.Supplement_1.5

Taipale, H. T., Bell, J. S., Soini, H., & Pitkälä, K. H. (2009). Sedative load and mortality among residents of long-term care facilities. *Drugs and Aging, 26,* 871–881. doi:10.2165/11317080-000000000-00000

Tappen, R. M., & Williams, C. L. (2009). Therapeutic conversation to improve mood in nursing home residents with Alzheimer's disease. *Research in Gerontological Nursing, 2,* 267–275. doi:10.3928/19404921-20090428-02

Tappen, R. M., Williams-Burgess, C., Edelstein, J., Touhy, T., & Fishman, S. (1997). Communicating with individuals with Alzheimer's disease: Examination of recommended strategies. *Archives of Psychiatric Nursing, 11,* 249–256. doi:10.1016/S0883-9417(97)80015-5

Tariot, P. N. (1996). CERAD behavior rating scale for dementia. *International Psychogeriatrics, 8,* 317–320.

Tariot, P. N., Mack, J. L., Patterson, M. B., ... (1995). The behavior rating scale for dementia of the Consortium to Establish a Registry for Alzheimer's Disease. *American Journal of Psychiatry, 152,* 1349–1357.

Teri, L., Gibbons, L. E., McCurry, S. M., Logsdon, R. G., Buchner, D. M., Barlow, W. E., . . . Larson, E. B. (2003). Exercise plus behavioral management in patients with Alzheimer disease. *JAMA, 290,* 2015–2022. doi:10.1001/jama.290.15.2015

Teri, L., Huda, P., Gibbons, L., Young, H., & van Leynseele, J. (2005). STAR: A dementia-specific training program for staff in assisted living residences. *Gerontologist, 45,* 686–693.

Teri, L., & Logsdon, R. G. (1991). Identifying pleasant activities for Alzheimer's disease patients: The pleasant events schedule-AD. *Gerontologist, 31,* 124–127. doi:10.1093/geront/31.1.124

Teri, L., Logsdon, R. G., Uomoto, J., & McCurry, S. M. (1997). Behavioral treatment of depression in dementia patients: A controlled clinical trial. *The Journals of Gerontology, Series B: Psychological Sciences and Social Sciences, 52,* 159–166. doi:10.1093/geronb/52B.4.P159

Teri, L., Truax, P., Logsdon, R., Uomoto, J., Zarit, S., & Vitaliano, P. P. (1992). Assessment of behavioral problems in dementia: The revised memory and behavior problems checklist. *Psychology and Aging, 7,* 622–631. doi:10.1037/0882-7974.7.4.622

Testad, I., Auer, S., Mittelman, M., Ballard, C., Fossey, J., Donabauer, Y., & Aarsland, D. (2010). Nursing home structure and association with agitation and use of psychotropic drugs in nursing home residents in three countries: Norway, Austria and England. *International Journal of Geriatric Psychiatry, 25,* 725–731. doi:10.1002/gps.2414

Testad, I., Ballard, C., Bronnick, K., & Aarsland, D. (2010). The effect of staff training on agitation and use of restraint in nursing home residents with dementia: A single-blind, randomized controlled trial. *Journal of Clinical Psychiatry, 71,* 80–86. doi:10.4088/JCP.09m05486oli

Thuné-Boyle, I. C., Iliffe, S., Cerga-Pashoja, A., Lowery, D., & Warner, J. (2012). The effect of exercise on behavioral and psychological symptoms of dementia: Towards a research agenda. *International*

Psychogeriatrics, 24, 1046–1057. doi:10.1017/S1041610211002365

Toseland, R. W., Diehl, M., Freeman, K., Manzanares, T., Naleppa, M., & McCallion, P. (1997). The impact of validation group therapy on nursing home residents with dementia. *Journal of Applied Gerontology, 16,* 31–50. doi:10.1177/073346489701600102

van Hoof, J., Kort, H., Hensen, J., Duijnstee, M., & Rutten, P. (2010). Thermal comfort and the integrated design of homes for older people with dementia. *Building and Environment, 45,* 358–370. doi:10.1016/j.buildenv.2009.06.013

Visser, S. M., Mccabe, M., Hudgson, C., Buchanan, G., Davison, T., & George, K. (2008). Managing behavioural symptoms of dementia: Effectiveness of staff education and peer support. *Aging and Mental Health, 12,* 47–55. doi:10.1080/13607860701366012

Vitaliano, P. P., Young, H. M., Russo, J., Romano, J., & Magana-Amato, A. (1993). Does expressed emotion in spouses predict subsequent problems among care recipients with Alzheimer's disease? *Journal of Gerontology, 48,* 202–209. doi:10.1093/geronj/48.4.P202

Volicer, L., Simard, J., Pupa, J. H., Medrek, R., & Riordan, M. E. (2006). Effects of continuous activity programming on behavioral symptoms of dementia. *Journal of the American Medical Directors Association, 7,* 426–431. doi:10.1016/j.jamda.2006.02.003

Walid, M. S., & Zaytseva, N. (2009). Pain in nursing home residents and correlation with neuropsychiatric disorders. *Pain Physician, 12,* 877–880.

Weiner, M. F., Koss, E., Patterson, M., Jin, S., Teri, L., Thomas, R., . . . Whitehouse, P. (1998). A comparison of the Cohen-Mansfield agitation inventory with the CERAD behavioral rating scale for dementia in community-dwelling persons with Alzheimer's disease. *Journal of Psychiatric Research, 32,* 347–351. doi:10.1016/S0022-3956(98)00027-2

Weiser, M., Gegenheimer, H., & Klein, P. (2009). The effect of therapeutic touch on behavioral symptoms and cortisol in persons with dementia. *Forschende Komplementärmedizin/Research in Complementary Medicine, 16,* 181–189.

Wells, D. L., Dawson, P., Sidani, S., Craig, D., & Pringle, D. (2000). Effects of an abilities-focused program of morning care on residents who have dementia and on caregivers. *Journal of the American Geriatrics Society, 48,* 442–449.

Werner, P., Cohen-Mansfield, J., Braun, J., & Marx, M. S. (1989). Physical restraints and agitation in nursing home residents. *Journal of the American Geriatrics Society, 37,* 1122.

Werner, P., Cohen-Mansfield, J., Fischer, J., & Segal, G. (2000). Characterization of family-generated videotapes for the management of verbally disruptive behaviors. *Journal of Applied Gerontology, 19,* 42–57. doi:10.1177/073346480001900103

Werner, P., Cohen-Mansfield, J., Koroknay, V., & Braun, J. (1994a). The impact of a restraint-reduction program on nursing home residents. *Geriatric Nursing, 15,* 142–146. doi:10.1016/S0197-4572(09)90040-4

Werner, P., Cohen-Mansfield, J., Koroknay, V., & Braun, J. (1994b). Reducing restraints: Impact on staff attitudes. *Journal of Gerontological Nursing, 20,* 19–24.

Whall, A. L., Colling, K. B., Kolanowski, A., Kim, H., Hong, G. S., DeCicco, B., . . . Beck, C. (2008). Factors associated with aggressive behavior among nursing home residents with dementia. *Gerontologist, 48,* 721–731. doi:10.1093/geront/48.6.721

Williams, C. L., & Tappen, R. M. (2008). Exercise training for depressed older adults with Alzheimer's disease. *Aging and Mental Health, 12,* 72–80. doi:10.1080/13607860701529932

Williams, K. N., Herman, R., Gajewski, B., & Wilson, K. (2009). Elderspeak communication: Impact on dementia care. *American Journal of Alzheimer's Disease and Other Dementias, 24,* 11–20. doi:10.1177/1533317508318472

Wood, S., Cummings, J. L., Hsu, M. A., Barclay, T., Wheatley, M. V., Yarema, K. T., & Schnelle, J. F. (2000). The use of the neuropsychiatric inventory in nursing home residents: Characterization and measurement. *American Journal of Geriatric Psychiatry, 8,* 75–83. doi:10.1097/00019442-200002000-00010

Woods, B., Aguirre, E., Spector, A. E., & Orrell, M. (2012). Cognitive stimulation to improve cognitive functioning in people with dementia [Review]. *Cochrane Database of Systematic Reviews, 2,* 1–51.

Woods, B., Spector, A., Jones, C., Orrell, M., & Davies, S. (2005). Reminiscence therapy for dementia. *Cochrane Database of Systematic Reviews, 2,* 1–21.

Yeh, S. H., Lin, L. W., Wang, S. Y., Wu, S. Z., Lin, J. H., & Tsai, F. M. (2001). The outcomes of restraint reduction program in nursing homes [abstract, article in Chinese] [Nursing Research]. *Hu Li Yan Jiu, 9,* 183–193.

Zubek, J. P., Pushkar, D., Sansom, W., & Gowing, J. (1961). Perceptual changes after prolonged sensory isolation (darkness and silence). *Canadian Journal of Psychology, 15,* 83–100. doi:10.1037/h0083205

CHAPTER 12

PERSON-CENTERED ASSESSMENT AND INTERVENTION FOR PEOPLE WITH DEMENTIA

Benjamin T. Mast, Jamie Shouse, and Cameron J. Camp

The world of dementia research and practice is evolving quickly. Within the past several years, new diagnostic guidelines have been proposed by a working group convened by the National Institute on Aging and the Alzheimer's Association. These are notable for their inclusion of and emphasis upon biomarkers in the diagnosis of Alzheimer's disease and its hypothesized precursor, mild cognitive impairment (MCI; Albert et al., 2011; McKhann et al., 2011). Perhaps more striking are the proposed guidelines for diagnosing Alzheimer's disease before the onset of clinically detectable changes in cognition using amyloid imaging combined with analysis of beta-amyloid and tau in cerebrospinal fluid (Sperling et al., 2011). Another piece of the changing landscape is that the newest edition of the *Diagnostic and Statistical Manual, Fifth Edition* (American Psychiatric Association, 2013) no longer uses the term *dementia* and proposes the new terms *major cognitive* and *minor cognitive* disorders (see Volume 1, Chapter 21, this handbook and Chapter 7, this volume).

As important as understanding the underlying disease process and proper diagnosis may be, considerable work still needs to be done to understand people living with dementia, the impact of the cognitive changes on them and their family, and the ways in which they live their remaining years after receiving a diagnosis. Millions of people are living with cognitive changes for years after the diagnosis is delivered, and as of yet, there is no cure or effective treatment for either the underlying neuropathological changes or the resulting cognitive symptoms. Within this context, earlier detection fuels an increasing need for the science of clinical geropsychology to consider how we can help people live well after they receive a dementia (major neurocognitive disorder) diagnosis (Camp, Zeisel, & Antenucci, 2011).

This chapter describes assessment and intervention approaches to dementia that fall within the realm of person-centered care. The focus of this chapter is to enhance understanding of the person through broader assessment of the person and with the goal of developing and implementing interventions that are tailored to the individual and that can improve quality of life, optimize functioning and enhance well-being.

HISTORY AND CONTEXT FOR PERSON-CENTERED CARE

Person-centered care has become an important and increasingly central concept for defining best practices in the treatment of dementia. It represents, in essence, a rebellion against attempts to objectify a truly human experience. Person-centered care, therefore, is the opposite of reductionism and a mechanistic worldview regarding dementia:

> It asserts that patients are persons and should not be reduced to their disease alone, but rather that their subjectivity and integration within a given environment, their strengths, their future plans and their rights should also be taken into account. (Ekman et al., 2011, p. 249)

http://dx.doi.org/10.1037/14459-012
APA Handbook of Clinical Geropsychology: Vol. 2. Assessment, Treatment, and Issues of Later Life,
P. A. Lichtenberg and B. T. Mast (Editors-in-Chief)

Person-centered care has a variety of origins. Humanistic psychology in the works of Rogers and Maslow emphasized a holistic approach to understanding human health and behavior, emphasizing the multifaceted nature of causality and focusing on optimal conditions for living. Kitwood (1997) emphasized the concept of personhood in dementia care: "Standing or status that is bestowed upon one human by others in the context of relationship and social being. Personhood implies recognition, respect and trust" (Kitwood, 1997, p. 8). He introduced a number of important new ideas to consider when discussing dementia, including that of the "malignant social psychology" of toxic care systems that dehumanized care, along with "excess disability" created when social and physical environments disengage the person with dementia (PWD). Complementary to these ideas was the concept of "rementing"—the capacity for PWD to improve when care systems change to provide person-centered care.

Ekman et al. (2011) emphasized the difference between patient-centered care and person-centered care. Patient-centered care examines individual exceptions to responses to standardized care. The patient is still the relatively passive recipient of medical treatment. Person-centered care "highlights the importance of knowing the person behind the patient—as a human being with reason, will, feelings, and needs—in order to engage the person as an active partner in his/her care and treatment" (Ekman et al., 2011, p. 249).

In the United States, the National Citizens' Coalition for Nursing Home Reform in the 1980s, with support from organizations such as the Robert Wood Johnson Foundation and what are now known as the Centers for Medicare and Medicaid Services and AARP (formerly the American Association of Retired Persons), held focus groups with nursing home residents on quality of care. Residents reported that quality of care was strongly linked to quality of life (being shown respect and dignity), and published results in turn were incorporated into the 1986 publication by the Institute of Medicine entitled, "Improving the Quality of Care in Nursing Homes." This publication led to legislation requiring reforms in nursing homes known as the Nursing Home Reform Act, which was incorporated into the Omnibus Budget Reconciliation Act (1987). The law mandates what is now known as person-centered care in nursing homes (Koren, 2010).

This set of actions represents a paradigm change, which generally goes under the rubric of the culture change movement. The Pioneer Network was formed in 1997 to advocate for person-centered care in nursing homes. It has been a leading advocate for culture change in the United States. Its approach emphasizes making nursing homes more home-like, "away from institutional provider-driven models to more humane consumer-driven models that embrace flexibility and self-determination" (Pioneer Network, n.d., para. 1). The organization promotes changing organizational culture, exemplified by honoring rights of residents, empowering direct care staff, and creating more flexible organizational structures. One example of this is the "first person care plan," with such entries as "when I am anxious I need to be able to walk around." Today, an "ideal facility" would be viewed as having these features: resident direction, homelike atmosphere, close relationships, staff empowerment, collaborative decision making, and ongoing quality-improvement process (Koren, 2010). More recently, the Pioneer Network has expanded its scope to include all care settings for older adults.

DISABILITY AND CHRONIC ILLNESS FRAMEWORK

Society views phenomena through a variety of prisms, or paradigmatic lenses. At present, because Alzheimer's disease is the prototype for dementia and cannot be cured, a huge amount of society's resources has been focused on finding treatments that will reverse or at least halt the progress of a disease. A long-term goal is the eventual discovery of a cure.

Viewing dementia through the lens of a medical model thus has led to viewing PWDs as "diseased." Fortunately, the disease does not appear to be contagious (in most instances), although it can run in families (for a review, see Goldman et al., 2011).

An alternative prism or model is that of disability. In U.S. society, people who are disabled have their civil rights protected. This protection has been provided through federal legislation, most recently by the Americans With Disabilities Act Amendments of 2008. A person with a disability is defined as having a condition that "substantially limits . . . major life activities." Examples of major life activities specifically mentioned in this law include caring for oneself, performing manual tasks, seeing, hearing, eating, sleeping, walking, speaking, breathing, learning, reading, concentrating, thinking, communicating, and working. Considering how these activities are affected when a person has dementia, one might make a strong case that people with Alzheimer's disease and related disorders may be considered disabled.

The law prohibits discrimination on the basis of disability in language similar to that of the Civil Rights Act of 1964. The Americans With Disabilities Act of 1990 legislated creation of environmental features (e.g., ramps) to accommodate people with disabilities. If we take the view that a person with dementia is disabled, and consider current practices regarding the care and treatment of these individuals, another case could be made that in U.S. society, these individuals have been systematically denied their basic civil and human rights. Where are the cognitive ramps for PWDs?

In some European communities, shop windows display signs with a symbol on them—a handkerchief with a knot tied in it. Tying a knot in a handkerchief was used in the past as a mnemonic—an external aid to remind the owner of the handkerchief not to forget something. One would think of the piece of information to remember while tying the knot. A shop with this symbol in the window indicates that staff in this establishment are dementia friendly, in that they have been trained to accommodate people with memory impairment.

Bruges, Belgium (population 117,000), is defining itself as a dementia-friendly city. Throughout the town, shop owners have installed the knotted-handkerchief signs to highlight places where people with dementia can be served by staff trained to work with people with memory impairment. Started in 2010, this program involves a 2-hr training program regarding how to interact effectively with PWDs, along with a film about right and wrong scenarios of how to interact with these people. Counselors provide practical advice for those with dementia and

therapy for their caregivers. Additionally, police have developed a database of vulnerable citizens, including their home and work addresses as well as other information that could expedite a search when someone goes missing.

If existing thinking and regulatory systems could be adapted and applied to dementia care, we could build on past experience and tap into a reserve of support for people with disabilities within our society. Although we may not be able to cure a disability, we certainly can make efforts to accommodate a disability in our physical and social environments. Taking this approach is a logical extension of the movement toward person-centered care. It shifts the emphasis from an impairment to the person, and from focusing on deficits to focusing on abilities that remain as the basis for remediation. This approach also emphasizes aspects of the person's life that are, in some ways, less cognitive and that are more resistant to the effects of dementia-related declines.

This movement to view dementia through the lens of disability informs assessment and intervention. Within the assessment context, the person-centered and disability frameworks suggest reconsidering what is important to assess throughout the stages of dementia and what the source of the data should be. In the following sections, we review models describing aspects of quality of life and psychological well-being with the goal of highlighting what and how to assess people with dementia, how to assess remaining strengths, and how to consider the person's input to develop and implement person-centered interventions.

ASSESSMENT IN PERSON-CENTERED CARE

Person-centered perspectives, consistent with Ekman et al.'s (2011) definition of person-centered care, recognize that assessment should not be reduced to evaluation of potential disease but should include an emphasis on understanding the person more broadly. Person-centered assessment and intervention, by definition, must seek the input of the person. Historically, there has been concern about the reliability and validity of self-reports in dementia; the current literature, however, indicates that individuals with dementia can provide valuable and clinically useful reports of their own quality of life and well-being, although this may vary based on the domain measured.

Individuals with dementia and MCI have been noted to give self-ratings for depression that correlate well with clinician ratings of the individual's depression (Arlt et al., 2008), but they may have a tendency to underreport relative to caregivers and clinicians (Snow et al., 2005). Other studies have found that caregivers tended to be less accurate in rating the individual with dementia's quality of life and values, suggesting this is an area in which self-report might be especially important (Arlt et al., 2008; Reamy, Kim, Zarit & Whitlatch, 2011). A study by Snow et al. (2005) assessed the extent to which older adults with dementia could report on symptoms of depression, which then were compared with both caregiver and clinician reports. Results indicated that deficit awareness was a better predictor of an individual's ability to correctly self-report depression than dementia diagnosis alone.

Clark, Tucke, and Whitlatch (2008) reported results supporting reliable self-report in individuals with dementia. They interviewed 213 individuals with dementia and their caregivers with questions that were either fact based or state dependent. Generally consistent responses were observed from individuals with dementia on both state-dependent questions and fact-based questions, although this varied somewhat according to severity of impairment. One caveat is that when individuals with dementia are asked about quality of life, their reports may be influenced by their current and fluctuating mood (Berwig, Leicht, Hartwig, & Gertz, 2011).

Inconsistency has been noted in the literature regarding self-report versus proxy report, implying that each type of report might be evaluating slightly different constructs. Both self-report and proxy reports have been used in the literature described in the following sections, and differences in self-report versus caregiver or family report underscore the complexity clinicians face when making decisions and highlight the importance of integrating multiple perspectives in assessment.

Quality of Life and Well-Being in Dementia

Psychological assessment in clinical geropsychology draws on the utilization of psychometrically sound instruments to help understand the older person and their presenting problems. Research and scholarship has grown in relation to assessing geropsychological problems in a variety of settings (Lichtenberg, 2010). Traditionally, however, the assessment of people with suspected dementia has focused almost exclusively on detecting and defining a pattern of deficits for the purposes of differential diagnosis. As noted at the start of this chapter, this is certainly important, but it allows the clinician to understand only a portion of the person (Mast, 2011). If a dementia diagnosis led to a specific and clinically significant treatment, this would grow in importance. At present, however, the existing pharmacological treatments do not reverse or stabilize the cognitive and functional changes observed in PWDs (Birks, 2006; Birks & Flicker, 2006; Rodda & Walker, 2009).

The deficit detection approach leaves the clinician with little data to rely on to make specific recommendations and initiate interventions that might improve the quality of life and well-being of the PWD and the family. Indeed, it is difficult to take steps in this direction without a better understanding of the person more broadly, including values and preferences (Whitlatch, Feinberg, & Tucke, 2005), activity levels and preferred activity (Logsdon & Teri, 1997), quality of life (Logsdon, Gibbons, McCurry, & Teri, 1999, 2002), quality of caring relationships (Sebern & Whitlatch, 2007), and life story (Haight et al., 2003). These latter components provide the clinician with a framework for offering tailored interventions that provide continuity for people and their families during a period of considerable change. In a time when cognition is changing, the geropsychologist can look for stability and continuity, building on the person's remaining strengths particularly in domains of life that are less cognitive in nature.

The developing research literature has demonstrated that although cognition is important, it is not a consistent predictor of well-being in dementia. For instance, in a study assessing quality of life in individuals with dementia, Banerjee et al. (2006) noted that neither cognition nor functional abilities were associated significantly with quality of life. On the other hand, behavioral and psychological symptoms of dementia (BPSD), such as agitation, depression, anxiety, disinhibition, and irritability, were associated with lower quality of life. Similarly, in a longitudinal study of quality of life in individuals with dementia, both depression and anxiety were associated with quality of life at follow-up, but cognition was not (Selwood, Thorgrimsen, & Orrell, 2005).

Such findings suggest that factors beyond cognition are most influential for quality of life and well-being in individuals with dementia. These studies suggest that BPSD are important predictors of low well-being and quality of life. Although there are clear links between BPSD and well-being (see Chapter 11, this volume), recent studies have begun to investigate factors that promote well-being in dementia, recognizing that flourishing or living well in the context of dementia reflects more than the absence of BPSD, just as models from positive psychology and successful aging reflect more than the avoidance of disease, disability, and psychopathology (see Volume 1, Chapters 12 and 13, this handbook).

Purpose, Meaning, and Continuity

Living well with dementia relies on (a) an ongoing sense of purpose and meaning in life and (b) continuity within identity and life experience (Mak, Sörensen, & Camp, 2014; Mast, 2011). Preston, Marshall, and Bucks (2007) asked individuals with dementia about strategies they use to cope with cognitive changes. Although some participants experienced dementia as foreign and frightening, others appeared to integrate their experiences into their ongoing story, linking their dementia-related experiences to things they had done prior to the onset of dementia. These efforts reflect attempts to manage identity and maintain a sense of continuity and making sense of the dementia process.

In another qualitative study, Menne, Kinney, and Morhardt (2002) interviewed six older adults with dementia or cognitive impairment about their adjustment to cognitive changes. Responses were evaluated using Atchley's continuity theory (Atchley, 1989) and Park and Folkman's (1997) model of meaning-making as theoretical frameworks. Consistent with these theories, each older adult reported the importance of developing a sense of meaning and also of maintaining a sense of continuity (in particular, continuity of lifestyle).

Continuing to maintain one's way of living has been identified as especially critical, and this coincides with the expected fit of Atchley's (1989) continuity theory to adaptation to dementia. Additionally, from the interviews Menne et al. (2002) identified two activities that are important and meaningful to older adults in U.S. society: driving and helping others. The choices each participant made regarding driving and helping behavior differed according to their own personal meaning. Some made alterations in behavior and their environment to attempt to continue to drive, whereas others decided to stop driving altogether. The choice in each case was dependent on the meaning the individual ascribed to the activity, with some individuals choosing to give up driving for concern of hurting other drivers and others attempting to modify driving behavior to maintain independence. Regarding helping others, individuals in the study emphasized that continuing to feel needed and able to contribute in ways similar to their lives before diagnosis was of critical importance. Inability to identify a sense of continuity in helping behavior in some of the participants appeared to cause them a high level of stress.

A study by Mak (2011) demonstrated the extent to which using meaningful activity can improve a sense of purpose in PWDs. Individuals with dementia were assigned to either a meaningful activity (creating a card for a soldier or a sick child) or an undirected one (creating a picture). Results indicated that people with a greater sense of goal pursuit also have a greater sense of purpose, and those who were assigned to the meaningful activity condition reported feeling a greater sense of purpose afterward, compared with those in the undirected activity.

These findings are consistent with a qualitative study in which PWDs were interviewed about their life and experience with dementia. Their responses reflected a need to feel valued and to be viewed by others as a person who has something to contribute (Steeman, Godderis, Grypdonck, De Bal, & De Casterle, 2007). Their responses indicate that this need is particularly strong when the person feels devalued by an excessive focus on their memory problems. As individuals experience the declines and losses of dementia, the need remains to contribute, to have a sense of purpose and meaning, and to have their views heard and considered.

Stress Process Model of Well-Being in Dementia

The stress process model (SPM) originally was developed to understand well-being and burden in dementia caregivers (see Chapter 20, this volume), but recently it has been applied to individuals with dementia (Judge, Menne, & Whitlatch, 2010). This model incorporates the objective stressors (e.g., cognitive impairment, functional limitations) as well as subjective experience of the PWD and considers multiple domains that can contribute to personal well-being reflected as quality of life and levels of depression and anxiety. The SPM is useful for individuals with dementia because its multifactorial nature allows for consideration of the complexities involved in understanding how people live with dementia as well as an appreciation for the observation that objective stressors may not predict well-being as well as subjective stressors. It may not be sufficient to understand the person's cognitive status; clinicians also must understand the way cognitive impairment is experienced by the person on a daily basis. This model includes potential mediators that influence the way the changes of dementia are experienced by the person. These mediators can be aspects of the person (personality, spirituality, values) or their environment (social support, knowledge of the illness). The advantage of this type of model is that it provides a blueprint for assessing (a) aspects of the person and his or her life that can provide the basis living well with dementia and (b) domains that might be fruitful for further development of assessment measures and interventions.

Using this model, Dawson, Powers, Krestar, Yarry, and Judge (2013) found that different aspects of the experience of dementia were associated with well-being outcomes. Lower difficulties performing instrumental activities of daily living (IADLs) and a greater sense of self-efficacy were associated with better quality of life. Embarrassment about memory problems was associated with greater anxiety, and health strains and feelings of dependence on the caregiver were associated with greater depression. Consistent with the studies discussed previously, cognitive status was not predictive of anxiety, depression, or quality of life.

Assessment of Strengths

Camp and his colleagues (Camp, Koss, & Judge, 1999; Camp, Skrajner, Lee, & Judge, 2010) have been developing an assessment approach for PWDs based on Montessori-Based Dementia Programming. This assessment approach (the Myers-Menorah Park/Montessori Assessment System [MMP/MAS]) involves providing a series of activities designed to assess the remaining capabilities of PWDs and to translate results into individualized programming. For example, one component of the MMP/MAS involves both the ability to read large-printed pages of a story aloud and to follow along as the assessor reads pages aloud. People capable of doing this can be placed into reading and discussion groups that use this approach. The capacity to place objects into categories is assessed (e.g., land and water; lake—mountain). People capable of categorization can be given category-sorting activities that are individualized (e.g., baseball teams—National League or American League; sorting pictures of different grandchildren). The capacity to imitate actions can be translated into learning to measure the amount of malt to be used in a beer-making activity or to cleaning materials used by the beer-making club (a real example, by the way). This approach represents a cognitive rehabilitation model for both assessment and development of interventions.

A key point to this approach is that assessment of remaining abilities should accomplish two very important goals. First, it should allow for the creation of activity that is personally meaningful to individuals with dementia. Second, it should encourage development of meaningful social roles that the individual can fulfill as part of a group and community. Camp et al. (2011) highlighted the need to extend person-centered care from providing individualized activity to providing group activities designed to create community and providing opportunities to connect with larger social networks outside of residences. Creating a fan club for a local minor league sports team, visiting museums, making jam to be entered into a county fair contest (and winning a blue ribbon), or collecting funds for a charity at a stand outside of a supermarket (all actual activities by PWDs) enhance quality of life by promoting a sense of purpose, value, meaningfulness, and personal connectedness. The capacity to remain connected to the "outside" world, to be present in it, and to create new connections should be emphasized as key components of person-centered care. By both assessing competencies and translating results into provision of meaningful social roles, psychologists can become key players in the culture change movement.

Considering the Preferences of the Person

Empirical research repeatedly has demonstrated that individuals with dementia can continue to reliably report their values and preferences regarding their life and care (Whitlatch et al., 2005). Menne, Johnson, Whitlatch, and Schwartz (2012) emphasized the importance of preferences and values in activity selection with individuals with dementia. The authors suggested that engaging in activities considered enjoyable for the individual is more important than the sheer quantity of activities. Two hundred sixteen individuals with dementia were asked about the sorts of activities they enjoyed and responses were coded into 18 different categories. Engaging in a greater number of enjoyed activities was tied to decision-making involvement and lower depression. Selection of the particular activities should involve input from the PWD and take into account their longstanding interests (Menne et al., 2012).

Involvement in the care planning process is important for quality of life in dementia. In light of this, enhancing our understanding of differences between the individual's care preferences and values and those perceived by the caregiver is a priority.

Reamy et al. (2011) interviewed 266 caregiving dyads about care preferences related to family, safety, burden, control, and autonomy. The authors found that caregivers tended to perceive that the care receiver would rate each value lower than the care receiver actually did, with the greatest difference noted in perceptions of the care receiver's rating of involvement in making decisions. In other words, individuals with dementia rated each value as more important, generally, than caregivers perceived they would.

Similarly, when clinician and staff reports of perceived preferences of individuals with dementia are compared with actual self-reported preferences, they appear to be fairly inaccurate, further highlighting the value of incorporating the input of people with dementia into daily caregiving (Mesman, Buchanan, Husfeldt, & Berg, 2011).

Taken together, these studies demonstrate that individuals with dementia seek to find meaning and continuity despite changes and that this can be facilitated by considering their preferences and perspective. As such, it is important to assess the individual with dementia's prior activities and interests to ensure some continuity in these activities (perhaps with adjustment) as a way to encourage better quality of life.

WHAT SHOULD WE ASSESS?

Assessment should be focused broadly on understanding the person so that interventions can be tailored to the individual. Understanding the person's values and preferences, activities they find enjoyable and meaningful, and perceptions of key relationships are critical because they are closely tied with well-being and quality of life, as noted previously. Moreover, when individuals experience continuity within their life, routine, and activity, they demonstrate both better emotional functioning and fewer BPSD that interfere with well-being and quality of life (see Cohen-Mansfield, Parpura-Gill, & Golander, 2006).

Table 12.1 includes a list of measures that are relevant to the assessment of PWDs for the purposes of better understanding of the PWD and for more tailored planning of intervention strategies. Each of the instruments has demonstrated strong evidence of reliability and validity for use with PWDs.

TABLE 12.1

Measures Used to Assess People With Dementia

Measure	Use	Reliability and validity
Predictors of well-being		
Values and Preferences Scale (Whitlatch, Feinberg, & Tucke, 2005)	Assesses care preferences and can be completed by both care receiver and caregiver Two factors: environmental and social network as well as personal autonomy	**Reliability** α = .70 to .82 **Validity** Factors associated with the care receiver feeling included in decision making and with care receiver quality of life ratings
Stigma Impact Scale (SIS; Burgener & Burger, 2008)	Assesses four factors of stigma associated with living with a progressive neurological condition: social isolation, financial insecurity, internalized shame, and social rejection	**Reliability** α = .87 for both Alzheimer's disease (AD) and Parkinson's disease (PD) samples; however, while all four subscales demonstrated acceptable reliability with PD, only social rejection and internalized shame had adequate reliability in the AD sample **Validity** Scores associated with mental status (in Alzheimer's sample), personal control, depression, and self-esteem
Fears of Alzheimer's Disease Scale (FAD; French, Floyd, Wilkins, & Osato, 2012)	Assesses anticipatory dementia or fear of developing Alzheimer's disease Three factors: general fear, physical symptoms, and catastrophic attitude	**Reliability** α = .94 **Validity** Significantly correlated with the State-Trait Anxiety Inventory-Form Y, particularly with trait anxiety
Knowledge of Alzheimer's Disease Scale (Carpenter, Balsis, Otilingam, Hanson, & Gatz, 2009)	30-item true–false scale designed to measure knowledge of Alzheimer's disease in the following domains: risk factors, assessment and diagnosis, symptoms, course, life impact, caregiving, and treatment and management	**Test–retest reliability** = .81 over a period between 2 and 50 hr **Internal consistency** α = .71 **Validity** Comparing self-reported knowledge about AD with scores on the AD Knowledge Scale yielded a correlation of .5, $p < .001$ Those with the highest scores were professionals involved in dementia care or research; scores on the measure improved for undergraduates after taking a course on aging
Dyadic Relationship Scale (Sebern & Whitlatch, 2007)	Assesses negative dyadic strain and positive dyadic interaction and can be administered to both care receiver and caregiver	**Reliability** Internal consistency was adequate for both caregiver and care receiver scores on negative dyadic strain and positive dyadic interaction **Validity** Dyadic strain was significantly associated with depression scores for both the caregiver and care receiver
Decision-Making Involvement Scale (Menne, Tucke, Whitlatch, & Feinberg, 2008)	Assesses the individual with dementia's daily decision making	**Reliability** As a single factor, 15-item measure yielded α = .85 **Validity** Correlated with measures of well-being for both care receiver and caregiver

Pleasant Events Scale–AD (Logsdon & Teri, 1997)	Offers a baseline of the individual's engagement in pleasant activities Consists of a list of 20 activities an individual with dementia might endorse as pleasant The individual reports how often the activity was engaged in and the level of enjoyment obtained from the activity	**Reliability** Coefficient α values ranged from .86 to .95 among the subscales **Validity** In older adults with Alzheimer's disease, depression was associated with a greater reduction in the regularity with which they engaged in pleasant activities

Measures of well-being

Alzheimer's Disease and Related Dementias Mood Scale (Tappen & Williams, 2008)	Assesses both positive and negative mood in older adults with mild to severe AD Five total subscales, two positive subscales (spirited and contented) and three negative mood subscales (hostile, apathetic, and sad)	**Test–retest reliability** Spirited subscale $r = .73$ Hostile subscale $r = .73$ Contented subscale $r = .63$ Apathetic $r = .72$ Sad subscale $r = .77$ **Internal consistency** Subscales demonstrated adequate consistency, with two exceptions: apathetic with moderately impaired individuals and sad with significantly impaired individuals **Validity** Significantly different scores were observed on all five subscales when the sample was divided into those who were depressed and those who were not depressed Comparisons with other mood measures yield significant results in the expected directions
Rating Anxiety in Dementia (RAID; Shankar, Walker, & Frost, 1999)	Assesses anxiety in older adults with dementia, including items addressing worry in specific domains and somatic symptoms Utilizes patient and caregiver report, in additional to clinical observations and medical records	**Reliability** Internal consistency is adequate $α = .83$ **Validity** Scores are higher for patients who qualify for a diagnosis of generalized anxiety disorder according to *DSM–IV* criteria, and are associated with selected measures of anxiety; also has been significantly associated with specific measures of depression (Gibbons, Teri, Logsdon, & McCurry, 2006)
Rating Anxiety in Dementia— Structured Interview (RAID–SI; Snow et al., 2012)	Provides assessment similar to RAID but with an attempt to improve standardization of administration	**Reliability** Adequate internal consistency and interrater reliability were demonstrated **Validity** Significantly associated with other measures of anxiety (both patient and collateral report), with higher scores observed in people with a *DSM–IV* anxiety diagnosis; scores were not associated with measures of depression or quality of life

(*continues*)

TABLE 12.1 (*Continued*)

Measures Used to Assess People With Dementia

Measure	Use	Reliability and validity
Quality of Life in Alzheimer's Disease (QoL-AD; Logsdon, Gibbons, McCurry, & Teri, 1999)	Assesses the patient's and caregiver's perception of quality of life in the following domains: physical condition, mood, interpersonal relationships, participation in meaningful activities, financial situation, and overall self	In a community sample of 77 older adults **Internal consistency** Overall coefficient α for caregiver = .87 Overall coefficient α for care receiver = .88 **Test–retest reliability** For person with dementia = .76 For caregiver = .92 **Validity** Scores from caregiver and care receiver linked with a measure of activities of daily living (ADL) performance, Geriatric Depression Scale (GDS) score (assessed by both care receiver and caregiver) and the Pleasant Events Schedule Composite QOL-AD score associated with patient depression, pleasant events and ADL ability, but not correlated with Mini-Mental State Examination (MMSE), IADLs, or caregiver depression Additionally, demonstrated reliability and validity in older adults with an MMSE score of 3–11, but did not appear useful to those with a score below 3 (Hoe, Katona, Roch, & Livingston, 2005)
Geriatric Depression Scale (GDS Short Form; Brink, 1982; Yesavage et al., 1982–1983)	Offers a depression screen for older adult in a shorter form, 15-item scale with questions selected from the original 30-item GDS	**Reliability** Adequate internal consistency has been established (Parmelee, Lawton, & Katz, 1989) **Validity** Higher scores have been associated with impairment in functional activities for individuals with dementia (Espiritu et al., 2001) Successfully differentiated older adults with depressions from older adults without depressions in a sample of community-dwelling normal elderly and elderly in treatment for depression (Sheikh & Yesavage, 1986)

General Intervention Issues

Expectancies regarding intervention. A study by Wald et al. (2003) demonstrated a discrepancy between what families expect regarding treatment and what the clinician has to offer. They found that although caregivers generally wanted as much information as possible at the time of diagnosis, what people wanted to know varied as a function of time since diagnosis. Whereas at the time of diagnosis, caregivers wanted information on dementia,

medications for it, and BPSD, by 2 years postdiagnosis, they wanted information on psychological interventions. Their desire for information on psychological interventions came later, after information on support groups, financial aspects, and legal issues.

Therefore, one challenge for clinical geropsychologists armed with an array of psychosocial interventions is to determine what needs individuals and families are seeking to address. These findings may suggest that early in the dementia process there may be a mismatch between what individuals and families want versus what geropsychologists are seeking to deliver. The modern health care system has been driven by a biomedical approach that emphasizes a diagnosis-treatment paradigm in which the treatment typically reduces the symptoms and maybe even removes the underlying pathological process. But, as discussed earlier, dementia fits better into a chronic illness and disability model in which intervention is focused more on maintaining functioning, reducing excess disability, and enhancing a range of quality-of-life outcomes. The psychologist must focus on early education regarding dementia progression and care, which might result in earlier acceptability of the psychosocial interventions discussed in the following section.

Evidence base for nonpharmacologic interventions. Curyto, Trevino, Ogland-Hand, and Lichtenberg (2012) reviewed evidence-based nonpharmacologic treatments for behavioral disturbances in PWDs. They described three major theoretical frameworks to classify such treatments. One is the need-driven behavior model, in which disruptive behaviors are assumed to be caused by unmet human needs. Treatment therefore focuses on adjusting the physical and social environment based on the abilities, personality, and preferences of the individual to meet these unmet needs. Cohen-Mansfield's Treatment Routes for Exploring Agitation (TREA) strategy is cited as an exemplar of this model.

A second is the person–environment fit model, which is based on the premise that having dementia results in a greater reliance on the environment and a lower threshold at which stimuli affect behavior (Lawton & Nahemow, 1973). A poor fit between a PWD's abilities and the demands of the environment results in disruptive behavior. Treatment involves matching environmental demands to the abilities of the PWD, thus optimizing levels of stimulation and decreasing excess disability. Gitlin et al.'s (2008) research is cited and an exemplar of this model.

A third model is the learning behavior model, which focuses on the learned relationship between behaviors and their antecedents and consequences. Behavior change is achieved by manipulating the antecedents and consequences of disruptive behaviors to promote more adaptive behaviors and reduce disruptive behaviors. Linda Teri and colleagues' (Teri et al., 2003; Teri, Logsdon, Uomoto, & McCurry, 1997; Teri, McCurry, Logsdon, & Gibbons, 2005) research is cited as an exemplar of this model.

A final model not covered in Curyto et al.'s (2012) review is that of cognitive rehabilitation, reviewed in the following, with the research of Camp and his colleagues (Brush & Camp, 1998; Camp, 2006; Camp & Foss, 1997; Camp, Foss, O'Hanlon, & Stevens, 1996; Camp, Foss, Stevens, & O'Hanlon, 1996; Camp & Nasser, 2003), along with others in this field representing this approach. Intervention is designed to circumvent cognitive deficits in dementia by utilizing remaining learning and other abilities available to PWDs.

For a general overview of nonpharmacologic interventions for dementia see Chapter 11 in this volume. This section focuses on intervention for a specific but highly salient issue in providing care to PWDs—repetitive disruptive behaviors (RDBs). RDBs are among the most common and stressful symptoms of dementia, and they represent the most common spontaneous complaint of family members of the PWD (Coen, Duane, Coakley, & Lawlor, 2001; Ready, Ott, & Grace, 2003). Cullen et al. (2005) noted that RDBs often are subsumed under more general categories of BPSD, such as agitation or vocal disruptions. Hwang, Tsai, Yang, Liu, and Lirng (2000) found that 56% of their sample of 141 inpatients with dementia exhibited some type of repetitive behavior. Of these 75% had repetitive speech, 59% had repetitive actions, and 35% had both.

Repetitive questioning is seen as the most frequent repetitive speech pattern, and has been reported as being highly prevalent in samples of PWD—for example, 67% (Baumgarten, Becker, & Gautier, 1990), 68% (Cullen et al., 2005), 90% (Teri et al., 1992), and 91% (Coen et al., 2001). Cullen et al. (2005) found that 87% of their outpatient sample of people with probable AD had at least one repetitive behavior. Using a revision of Hope and Fairburn's (1992) present behavioral examination, they found that repetitive questioning was the most common repetitive behavior (68% of the sample), followed by repetitive statements and stories (61%). Almost half (48%) of their sample had one or more repetitive motor actions, including searching (28%), plucking (11%), and moving (11%) as well as lesser frequencies of behaviors such as rubbing body parts and paper-tearing. They found that repetitive questions were associated with poor episodic memory and generally had themes (89% of cases), most commonly concerning temporal orientation, family news or well-being, and the whereabouts of another person.

Repeated statements and stories also generally had themes (86% of cases), most commonly concerning stories of childhood or early adulthood and a preoccupation with current affairs or weather. Repetitive statements and stories were not related to memory measures, but instead were related to measures of executive dysfunction and younger age. The researchers noted that the presence of themes indicates that such behaviors may serve a function for the PWD and should be dealt with sensitively. Executive dysfunction, longer duration of illness, and higher depression scores were predictive of repetitive motor actions. The key points from the extant literature show that RDBs are as follows:

1. very frequent in PWD and are seen as a major source of stress by family caregivers,
2. heterogeneous and should not be seen as a single class of behaviors (e.g., agitation),
3. patterned and may serve a functional purpose, and
4. related to a heterogeneity of causal factors.

With regard to the third key point, Casby and Holm (1994) examined the use of music as a treatment for repetitive verbalizations not related to information seeking and that resembled a stereotypic behavior pattern, similar to a repetitive motor action. Such behavior, they noted, might enable the PWD to either withdraw from aversive stimuli or to provide additional sensory input. Using either classical music or favorite music, they were able to relatively extinguish repetitive verbalizations that had been occurring at a rate from 15 to 45 times within a 10-min period.

The fourth key point is further emphasized in the fact that even a specific behavior such as repetitive questioning could be caused by a variety of factors, including episodic memory deficits, feelings of

insecurity or anxiety about one's ability to cope, boredom, and anxiety about future events (Bourgeois et al., 2003; Camp & Foss, 1997). Camp and Foss (1997) stated the case this way:

> Researchers working in real-world settings soon learn that knowledge about memory functioning is, by itself, inadequate if one wishes to be truly effective. It quickly becomes apparent that knowledge of behavioral technology, physiological changes associated with normal and pathological aging, neuroscience, behavioral ecology, human factors, and developmental psychology are extremely useful and indeed necessary. (p. 323)

Problematic RDBs in PWD are pervasive and cause extensive suffering. Available evidence on RDBs strongly suggests that an intervention for RDBs must be tailored to the specific PWD-caregiver dyads, to the specific behavior, and to the underlying cause of the behavior. It is also critical that any intervention be relevant and applicable to PWD across a wide range of cognitive and functional abilities.

A variety of nonpharmacologic interventions for RDBs have been examined. Bourgeois, Burgio, Schultz, Beach, and Palmer (1997) demonstrated decreased frequency of repeated verbalizations when caregivers were trained to direct patients with dementia to read a memory book page (or written message on a memo board or index card) when they asked a question repeatedly. Caregivers expressed satisfaction with both their ability to redirect the PWD to an external stimulus and the speed with which the PWD learned to use the external aid independently. Repeated verbalizations included repetitive questioning and other forms of repetitive verbalization.

Camp and colleagues (Bourgeois et al., 2003; Brush & Camp, 1998; Camp, 2006; Camp & Foss, 1997; Camp & Nasser, 2003) and others (Bird, 2001; Bird & Kinsella, 1996) have used a technique called spaced retrieval (SR) to address challenging behaviors in PWDs. SR is an evidence-based memory intervention that gives individuals practice at successfully recalling information over progressively longer intervals of time (Brush & Camp, 1998; Camp, 2006).

The goal of SR is to enable individuals to remember important information for clinically meaningful periods of time. Specific techniques like SR have been shown to significantly improve functional skills in people with dementia. We know that it is possible for older people with AD and related disorders, when treated with SR, to successfully learn and utilize new compensatory strategies (Camp, Foss, O'Hanlon, & Stevens, 1996; Camp, Foss, Stevens, & O'Hanlon, 1996; Stevens, O'Hanlon, & Camp, 1993) and to use external cues and assistive devices (Bourgeois et al., 2003; Brush & Camp, 1998). As such, SR represents the use of an innovative cognitive prosthesis to overcome or circumvent deficits associated with dementia and other cognitive disorders. Furthermore, SR can significantly increase the ability of PWDs to benefit from assistive devices and other technologies by training such individuals to use these devices effectively in spite of their short-term memory deficits. Finally, several authors have demonstrated SR's effectiveness as a cognitive intervention for relieving dementia-related symptoms (Buschert, Bokde, & Hampel, 2010); for learning new information (Bier et al., 2008; Cherry, Hawley, Jackson, & Boudreaux, 2009; Cherry, Simmons, & Camp, 1999; Cherry, Walvoord, & Hawley, 2010); for adhering to medication regimens, keeping doctor's appointments, and remembering to pay bills (Vance, Struzick, & Farr, 2010); and for generally maintaining their functional independence and, therefore, their autonomy (Ozgis, Rendell, & Henry, 2009; Thivierge, Simard, Jean, & Grandmaison, 2008).

A pilot study demonstrated that when trained adequately, family members can successfully implement SR in home settings while caring for relatives (McKitrick & Camp, 1993). Another study examined the use of SR with PWDs who were exhibiting behavior problems (Bird, Alexopoulos, & Adamowicz, 1995). After initial SR training by staff, SR was reinforced by family members. Negative behaviors were extinguished and after the training had ceased, this improvement continued. Hunter, Ward, and Camp (2012) successfully illustrated that SR can be implemented by caregiving staff in a nursing home to effectively maintain gains and improve outcomes for both staff and residents. In this study, staff responded that their training and the chance to maintain SR resulted in an increased sense of achievement in their work.

Bourgeois et al. (2003) discussed the use of SR with external aids as a means of increasing conversation and social interaction, increasing ADLs (e.g., safe swallowing, toileting, hair brushing, etc.), increasing activity participation, decreasing repetitive behaviors (e.g., repetitive questioning), and increasing specific adaptive behaviors, such as use of names, call buttons, guest books to determine when visitors have come and will come again, and so on. Small (2012) investigated how SR could be applied effectively in helping people with Alzheimer's disease improve their recall of recent events. Ptak, der Linden, and Schnider (2010) noted that SR can be used with individuals with varying degrees of memory impairment. Hopper et al. (2005) reviewed and developed evidence-based practice guidelines for speech-language pathologists who work with clients with dementia. The authors summarized scientific evidence related to clinical interventions using SR training and noted expected outcomes of SR as improvement in the acquisition, retention, and generalization of trained information or skills; retention of learned information or skills; and generalization of learned information or skills to specific contexts and situations.

With regard to the treatment efficacy of SR, Bourgeois et al. (2003) conducted a study in which 25 PWDs received an SR intervention and an alternative cognitive intervention (a modified cueing hierarchy [CH]), 48% of whom were living at home and attending adult day centers. Trainers primarily were students in a speech-language pathology program who had not used SR previously. For each PWD, one goal was trained using SR and another goal using CH, with order of treatment condition randomized. Goal mastery was defined as provision of the appropriate goal response at the first prompt on three consecutive training sessions, with a minimum 24-hr interval between sessions. Twenty-three participants (92%) mastered their SR goal, while 18 participants (72%) mastered their CH goal, a statistically significant difference. No participant mastered a CH goal without also mastering a SR goal. A subsample of each treatment condition was retested 1 week and 4 months posttraining. For SR, 70% of goals and 50% of goals were maintained at 1-week and 4-month posttraining intervals, respectively. Corresponding percentages for CH were 45% and 9%, respectively, each of which represented a significant difference from SR. Thus, SR is an extremely useful training paradigm that could be used by caregivers to implement interventions across a variety of problematic behaviors seen in PWD, including the three categories of RDBs described earlier.

Clare et al. (2000) reported the use of external aids and errorless-learning techniques from neuropsychological rehabilitation to reduce repetitive questions in a series of single-case studies. This was conducted in home settings by researchers. Interventions were tailored to specific PWDs and their specific questions. SR can be considered a form of errorless-learning training (Camp, 2006). The use of external aids, errorless-learning procedures, and application of learning techniques still available to PWDs, such as SR, represents a cognitive rehabilitation approach to treating dementia.

Cohen-Mansfield, Dakheel-Ali, Jensen, Marx, and Thein (2012) evaluated the implementation of the TREA intervention in a randomized, placebo-controlled clinical trial. This study involved a systematic approach to creating individualized nonpharmacologic interventions for nursing home residents with dementia who were exhibiting agitation. Selection of an intervention began with an assessment of the PWD, including physical status, structured interviews, and direct observations. In addition, personal histories, preferences, and abilities were assessed. The cause of agitation was hypothesized to reflect an unmet need (e.g., loneliness or depression, boredom, or discomfort). Standardized interventions using a manualized approach were used to tailor interventions to specific needs of specific residents. For example, if the unmet need was hypothesized to be boredom, standardized interventions were from the categories *activities* and *stimulation*. Examples of activities included physical activities (such as exercise), reading large-print magazines, and work activities (such as sorting envelopes). Specific activities and specific examples of a particular activity (e.g., the magazine to be read, the work task) were selected to be meaningful to the specific PWD and adapted to that person's ability level. Primary outcomes included significant

reductions in verbal and physical agitation compared with the placebo-control condition, representing two of the three categories of RDBS.

Gitlin et al. (2008) created a Tailored Activities Program (TAP) for at-home dementia patients to test whether caregivers could implement TAP, reduce neuropsychiatric behaviors, and through this intervention reduce caregiver burden. They conducted a prospective, two-group randomized controlled trial (RCT) with 60 PC-PWD dyads randomly assigned to either treatment or wait-list control conditions. The intervention consisted of an eight-session, manualized occupational therapy intervention involving neuropsychological and functional assessments, from which activities were customized for specific PWDs and instructions on the use of the activities provided to caregivers. At 4 months posttest, compared with controls, caregivers receiving and implementing TAP reported reduced frequency of problematic behaviors, specifically for shadowing and repetitive questioning compared with controls. Caregiver benefits included a greater sense of mastery and self-efficacy. Wait-list control participants showed similar benefits for behavioral frequency following intervention for their group. This study demonstrates that caregivers can be trained to implement personalized interventions for RDBs (a motor behavior as well as repetitive questioning) that can be effective in reducing frequency of the RDBs. Importantly, all caregivers receiving the TAP intervention demonstrated an understanding of the strategies used. Most (85%) caregivers found the intervention very useful, while 15% found it somewhat useful. Thus, it was demonstrated that caregivers could understand intervention strategies when appropriately trained and that the great majority of them found the intervention helpful.

Teri and her colleagues (Teri et al., 1997, 2003, 2005) conducted RCTs in home settings, primarily using the Seattle Protocol, which trains caregivers in treating behavior and depression in PWDs. Interventions included increasing frequencies of pleasant events, behavior management techniques, and exercise. Intervention sessions with caregivers either were delivered face-to-face or over the telephone. Control conditions involved routine medical care. Frequency and severity of behavior problems and caregiver reactivity to such problems decreased as a result of the intervention, and at 6-month follow-up, caregivers in the treatment condition reported fewer memory-related behavior problems than in the control condition.

In any attempt at intervention, it will be critical to keep in mind the tenets of person-centered care. To understand the cause of a challenging behavior, one must understand the person—his or her background, needs, culture, and physical and social environment. Goals must be meaningful to the person, and to ensure this, it is important to establish goals in collaboration with the person. For example, a clinician can train a PWD to look at a calendar for things to do. But if "take out the trash" is not seen as appropriate or worthwhile, the action will not be performed.

In addition, the person's physical and social environment must be prepared and maintained so that goals are maintained once reached. Intervention, therefore, must work across levels of systems, from the individual to the primary family caregiver or staff member to the family or unit supervisor, and so on. As a result, it becomes necessary to be involved in organizational change to ensure that interventions are both efficacious and effective. As a result, both supporting and taking part in culture change are useful and necessary for successful intervention.

Case Example

Whereas traditional dementia assessment has focused primarily on detecting cognitive impairment associated with underlying disease, person-centered assessment takes a broader perspective, seeking to better understand aspects of the person and their life that can be drawn on to plan and implement person-centered, nonpharmacological interventions.

Mr. A reluctantly came to the memory care clinic at the urging of his wife and longtime primary care physician. He was understandably hesitant to have an evaluation of his memory, partly because he feared a loss of independence (i.e., driving) and because he was afraid to face the possibility of Alzheimer's disease. He had failed a cognitive screening test a couple weeks prior to this assessment (for a discussion of screening tests, see Volume 1, Chapter 21, this handbook), and now he

was quite anxious about what this assessment would involve and what it would be like.

Although some of the testing was unpleasant, he found that the psychologist also asked him questions about his life, what he liked to do, and what was important to him, and he didn't seem to shy away from difficult questions about how he would like to be taken care of if he found that he needed more help. The psychologist had administered a brief battery of neuropsychological tests that evaluated his memory and other cognitive abilities, and she also incorporated the Pleasant Events Schedule, the Values and Preferences Scale, and the Quality of Life in Alzheimer's Disease (see Table 12.1 for a description of these measures). They also discussed aspects of his life story, including key events and relationships. Finally, they spent time discussing his fears related to Alzheimer's disease, cognitive decline and loss of independence and the stigma associated with Alzheimer's disease.

The psychologist also spent time with his wife to better understand how Mr. A was functioning in his daily life and how the changes were affecting her. She reported that Mr. A had been growing increasingly forgetful over the last 2 years, but they had both been reluctant to seek help, thinking, and sometimes wishing, that it was just "normal aging." But over the past few months, things seemed to be worse. In particular, she had noticed that he would become increasingly upset and would repeatedly ask questions over and over, until she would get so frustrated that she would snap at him (followed by guilt). This was beginning to affect their relationship and she was experiencing growing feelings of burden. Using the learning behavior model, she asked Mrs. A to track when and where this behavior was likely to occur, which she did over the next week.

At the follow-up meeting, the psychologist reviewed the assessment results with Mr. and Mrs. A. She spent time explaining his strengths and weaknesses on cognitive testing and discussed how these fit with the team's diagnosis of Alzheimer's disease. She not only explained how the memory problems might influence his repetitive questions but also pointed out that these were much more likely to occur in the late afternoon and early evening.

In response, Mr. A noted that he often feels bored and restless, and his wife suggested that might be the case in the afternoon. The psychologist suggested that his boredom and his unmet need for activity and stimulation led him to seek out his wife asking questions over and over, to which she would initially answer, but as her frustration would grow, she would tend to angrily tell him that she already answered the question many times. These responses led him to worry further about his memory, which increased his anxiety and fueled further agitation and worry. Together they discussed Mr. A's need for greater activity during the afternoon hours and explained that these activities should be those that he finds meaningful and enjoyable. By addressing the antecedents of the behavior and unmet needs, they planned to try to reduce the frequency and intensity of this behavior. They also developed, with Mr. A's input, an organizational system that helped support reminding about the schedule of the day and the next day. Over time, this combination led to less agitation, and they both felt that they had more energy to plan additional activities that were meaningful and which they could do together. They elected to begin a walking program while the weather allowed and planned to either join a gym or walk in the local shopping mall during the winter months. This provided an activity they could do together, and his wife found that this allowed her to focus on her friendship with her husband, rather than just focusing on the tasks of caregiving.

Finally, Mr. A wanted to find a way to continue to contribute to his church, which had been a long-standing value within his life. Using his cognitive test results to highlight his remaining strengths, he decided to try writing letters of encouragement to people who were in the hospital or were in some other difficult situation. His wife would support him in helping him with the names and circumstances, but the act of writing and helping others met his need for meaningful and purposeful activity.

Role of Geropsychologist
In a health care system that increasingly focuses on identification of deficits and biomarkers that promise to predict the onset of disease before symptoms, the geropsychologist fills several critical roles in assessing and caring for PWDs and their families. In addition to assessing cognitive changes, the geropsychologist plays a role in helping the health care team remember that the pathology and associated cognitive changes are just one aspect of the person and that other outcomes beyond cognition deserve consideration in care planning, including quality of life, well-being, and a sense of meaning and purpose. Second, the geropsychologist helps assess other aspects of the person's life and experience that can be drawn on to help present the individual to the health care team as a whole person, not just a set of symptoms and pathologies (Mast, 2011). Finally, the geropsychologist plays a key role in making the team more aware of nonpharmacological options for addressing both core symptoms (cognitive change) and interventions to improve quality of life and psychological functioning.

References
Albert, M. S., DeKosky, S. T., Dickson, D., Dubois, B., Feldman, H. H., Fox, N. C., . . . Phelps, C. H. (2011). The diagnosis of mild cognitive impairment due to Alzheimer's disease: Recommendations from the National Institute on Aging-Alzheimer's Association workgroups on diagnostic guidelines for Alzheimer's disease. *Alzheimer's and Dementia, 7,* 270–279. doi:10.1016/j.jalz.2011.03.008

American Psychiatric Association. (2013). *Diagnostic and statistical manual of mental disorders* (5th ed.). Washington, DC: Author.

Americans With Disabilities Act of 1990, Pub. L. No. 101-336, § 2, 104 Stat. 328 (1991).

Americans With Disabilities Amendments Act of 2008, Pub. L. No. 110-325, § 2(b)(1), 122 Stat. 3553 (2008).

Arlt, S., Hornung, J., Eichenlaub, M., Jahn, H., Bullinger, M., & Petersen, C. (2008). The patient with dementia, the caregiver and the doctor: Cognition, depression and quality of life from three perspectives. *International Journal of Geriatric Psychiatry, 23,* 604–610. doi:10.1002/gps.1946

Atchley, R. C. (1989). A continuity theory of normal aging. *Gerontologist, 29,* 183–190. doi:10.1093/geront/29.2.183

Banerjee, S., Smith, S. C., Lamping, D. L., Harwood, R. H., Foley, B., Smith, P., . . . Knapp, M. (2006). Quality of life in dementia: More than just cognition. An analysis of associations with quality of life in dementia. *Journal of Neurology, Neurosurgery, and Psychiatry, 77,* 146–148. doi:10.1136/jnnp.2005.072983

Baumgarten, M., Becker, R., & Gautier, S. (1990). Validity and reliability of the Dementia Behavior Disturbance scale. *Journal of the American Geriatrics Society, 38,* 221–226.

Berwig, M., Leicht, H., Hartwig, K., & Gertz, H. J. (2011). Self-rated quality of life in mild cognitive impairment and Alzheimer's disease: The problem of affective distortion. *GeroPsych, 24,* 45–51. doi:10.1024/1662-9647/a000029

Bier, N., Van Der Linden, M., Gagnon, L., Derosiers, J., Adam, S., Louveaux, S., & Saint Mleux, J. (2008). Face–name association learning in early Alzheimer's disease: A comparison of learning methods and their underlying mechanisms. *Neuropsychological Rehabilitation, 18,* 343–371. doi:10.1080/09602010701694723

Bird, M. (2001). Behavioural difficulties and cued recall of adaptive behaviour in dementia: Experimental and clinical evidence. *Neuropsychological Rehabilitation, 11,* 357–375. doi:10.1080/09602010042000042

Bird, M., Alexopoulos, P., & Adamowicz, J. (1995). Success and failure in five case studies: Use of cued recall to ameliorate behaviour problems in senile dementia. *International Journal of Geriatric Psychiatry, 10,* 305–311. doi:10.1002/gps.930100407

Bird, M., & Kinsella, G. (1996). Long-term cued recall of tasks in senile dementia. *Psychology and Aging, 11,* 45–56. doi:10.1037/0882-7974.11.1.45

Birks, J. (2006). Cholinesterase inhibitors for Alzheimer's disease. *Cochrane Database of Systematic Reviews, 2006*(1), CD005593. doi:10.1002/14651858. CD005593

Birks, J., & Flicker, L. (2006). Donepezil for mild cognitive impairment. *Cochrane Database of Systematic Reviews, 2006*(3), CD006104. doi:10.1002/14651858. CD00610

Bourgeois, M. S., Burgio, L. D., Schultz, R., Beach, S., & Palmer, B. (1997). Modifying repetitive verbalizations of community-dwelling patients with AD. *Gerontologist, 37,* 30–39. doi:10.1093/geront/37.1.30

Bourgeois, M. S., Camp, C., Rose, M., White, B., Malone, M., Carr, J., & Rovine, M. (2003). A comparison of training strategies to enhance use of external aids by persons with dementia. *Journal of Communication Disorders, 36,* 361–378. doi:10.1016/S0021-9924(03)00051-0

Brink, T. L. (1982). Screening tests for geriatric depression. *Clinical Gerontologist, 1,* 37–43. doi:10.1300/J018v01n01_06

Brush, J. A., & Camp, C. J. (1998). Using spaced-retrieval as an intervention during speech-language therapy. *Clinical Gerontologist, 19,* 51–64. doi:10.1300/J018v19n01_05

Burgener, S. C., & Burger, B. (2008). Measuring perceived stigma in persons with progressive neurological disease. *Dementia, 7,* 31–53. doi:10.1177/1471301207085366

Buschert, V., Bokde, A. L. W., & Hampel, H. (2010). Cognitive intervention in Alzheimer disease. *Nature Reviews Neurology, 6,* 508–517.

Camp, C. J. (2006). Spaced retrieval: A case study in dissemination of a cognitive intervention for persons with dementia. In D. K. Attix & K. A. Welsch-Bohmner (Eds.), *Geriatric neuropsychological assessment and intervention* (pp. 275–292). New York, NY: Guilford Press.

Camp, C. J., & Foss, J. W. (1997). Designing ecologically valid memory interventions for persons with dementia. In D. G. Payne & F. G. Conrad (Eds.), *Intersections in basic and applied memory research* (pp. 311–325). Mahwah, NJ: Erlbaum.

Camp, C. J., Foss, J. W., O'Hanlon, A. M., & Stevens, A. B. (1996). Memory interventions for persons with dementia. *Applied Cognitive Psychology, 10,* 193–210. doi:10.1002/(SICI)1099-0720(199606)10:3<193::AID-ACP374>3.0.CO;2-4

Camp, C. J., Foss, J. W., Stevens, A. B., & O'Hanlon, A. M. (1996). Improving prospective memory task performance in persons with Alzheimer's disease. In M. McDaniel & G. Einstein (Eds.), *Prospective memory: Theory and application* (pp. 351–367). Hillsdale, NJ: Erlbaum.

Camp, C. J., Koss, E., & Judge, K. S. (1999). Cognitive assessment in late stage dementia. In P. A. Lichtenberg (Ed.), *Handbook of assessment in clinical gerontology* (pp. 442–467). New York, NY: Wiley.

Camp, C. J., & Nasser, E. H. (2003). Nonpharmacological aspects of agitation and behavioral disorders in dementia: Assessment, intervention, and challenges to providing care. In P. A. Lichtenberg. D. L. Murman, & A. M. Mellow (Eds.), *Handbook of dementia: Psychological, neurological, and psychiatric perspectives* (pp. 359–401). New York, NY: Wiley.

Camp, C. J., Skrajner, M. J., Lee, M. M., & Judge, K. S. (2010). Cognitive assessment in late stage dementia. In P. A. Lichtenberg (Ed.), *Handbook of assessment in clinical gerontology* (2nd ed., pp. 531–555). New York, NY: Wiley. doi:10.1016/B978-0-12-374961-1.10020-X

Camp, C. J., Zeisel, J., & Antenucci, V. (2011). Implementing the "I'm Still Here Approach": Montessori methods for engaging persons with dementia. In P. E. Hartman-Stein & A. La Rue (Eds.), *Enhancing cognitive fitness in adults* (pp. 401–417). New York, NY: Springer. doi:10.1007/978-1-4419-0636-6_23

Carpenter, B. D., Balsis, S., Otilingam, P. G., Hanson, P. K., & Gatz, M. (2009). The Alzheimer's Disease Knowledge Scale: Development and psychometric properties. *Gerontologist, 49*, 236–247. doi:10.1093/geront/gnp023

Casby, J. A., & Holm, M. B. (1994). The effect of music on repetitive disruptive vocalizations of persons with dementia. *American Journal of Occupational Therapy, 48*, 883–889. doi:10.5014/ajot.48.10.883

Cherry, K. E., Hawley, K. S., Jackson, E. M., & Boudreaux, E. O. (2009). Booster sessions enhance the long-term effectiveness of spaced retrieval in older adults with probable Alzheimer's disease. *Behavior Modification, 33*, 295–313. doi:10.1177/0145445509333432

Cherry, K. E., Simmons, S. S., & Camp, C. J. (1999). Spaced-retrieval enhances memory in older adults with probably Alzheimer's disease. *Journal of Clinical Geropsychology, 5*, 159–175. doi:10.1023/A:1022983131186

Cherry, K. E., Walvoord, A. G., & Hawley, K. S. (2010). Spaced retrieval enhances memory for a name-face occupation association in older adults with probable Alzheimer's disease. *Journal of Genetic Psychology, 171*, 168–181. doi:10.1080/00221320903548118

Civil Rights Act of 1964, Pub. L. No. 88-352, 78 Stat. 241.

Clare, L., Wilson, B. A., Carter, G., Breen, K., Gosses, A., & Hodges, J. R. (2000). Intervening with everyday memory problems in dementia of the Alzheimer's type: An errorless learning approach. *Journal of Clinical and Experimental Neuropsychology, 22*, 132–146. doi:10.1076/1380-3395(200002)22:1;1-8;FT132

Clark, P. A., Tucke, S. S., & Whitlatch, C. J. (2008). Consistency of information from persons with dementia: An analysis of differences by question type. *Dementia, 7*, 341–358. doi:10.1177/1471301208093288

Coen, R. F., Duane, Y., Coakley, D., & Lawlor, B. A. (2001). Behavioural symptoms in Alzheimer's disease: Evaluation and frequency of occurrence and caregiver tolerability. *Irish Journal of Medical Science, 170*(Suppl. 3), 98.

Cohen-Mansfield, J., Dakheel-Ali, M., Jensen, B., Marx, M. S., & Thein, K. (2012). An analysis of the relationships among engagement, agitated behavior, and affect in nursing home residents with dementia. *International Psychogeriatrics, 24*, 742–752. doi:10.1017/S1041610211002535

Cohen-Mansfield, J., Parpura-Gill, A., & Golander, H. (2006). Utilization of self-identity roles for designing interventions for persons with dementia. *The Journals of Gerontology, Series B: Psychological Sciences and Social Sciences, 61*, 202–212. doi:10.1093/geronb/61.4.P202

Cullen, B., Coen, R. F., Lynch, C. A., Cunningham, C. J., Coakley, D., Robertson, I. A., & Lawlor, B. A. (2005). Repetitive behaviour in Alzheimer's disease: Description, correlates and functions. *International Journal of Geriatric Psychiatry, 20*, 686–693. doi:10.1002/gps.1344

Curyto, K. J., Trevino, K. M., Ogland-Hand, S., & Lichtenberg, P. (2012). Evidence-based treatments for behavioral disturbances in long-term care. In F. Scogin & A. Shah (Eds.), *Making evidence-based treatments work with older adults* (pp. 167–223). Washington, DC: American Psychological Association. doi:10.1037/13753-006

Dawson, N. T., Powers, S. M., Krestar, M., Yarry, S. J., & Judge, K. S. (2013). Predictors of self-reported psychosocial outcomes in individuals with dementia. *Gerontologist, 53*, 748–759. doi:10.1093/geront/gns137

Ekman, I., Swedberg, K., Taft, C., Lindseth, A., Norberg, A., Brink, E., . . . Sunnerhagen, K. S. (2011). Person-centered care—Ready for prime time. *European Journal of Cardiovascular Nursing, 10*, 248–251. doi:10.1016/j.ejcnurse.2011.06.008

Espiritu, D. A. V., Rashid, H., Mast, B. T., Fitzgerald, J., Steinberg, J., & Lichtenberg, P. A. (2001). Depression, cognitive impairment and function in Alzheimer's Disease. *International Journal of Geriatric Psychiatry, 16*, 1098–1103. doi:10.1002/gps.476

French, S. L., Floyd, M., Wilkins, S., & Osato, S. (2012). The fear of Alzheimer's disease scale: A new measure designed to assess anticipatory dementia in older adults. *International Journal of Geriatric Psychiatry, 27*, 521–528. doi:10.1002/gps.2747

Gibbons, L. E., Teri, L., Logsdon, R. G., & McCurry, S. M. (2006). Assessment of anxiety in dementia: An investigation into the association of different methods of measurement. *Journal of Geriatric Psychiatry and Neurology, 19*, 202–208. doi:10.1177/0891988706292758

Gitlin, L. N., Winter, L., Burke, J., Chernett, N., Marie, P., Dennis, M. P., & Hauck, W. W. (2008). Tailored activities to manage neuropsychiatric behaviors in persons with dementia and reduce caregiver burden: A randomized pilot study. *American Journal of Geriatric Psychiatry, 16*, 229–239. doi:10.1097/01.JGP.0000300629.35408.94

Goldman, J. S., Hahn, S. E., Catania, J. W., Larusse-Eckert, S., Butson, M. B., Rumbaugh, M., . . . Bird, T. (2011). Genetic counseling and testing for Alzheimer disease: Joint practice guidelines of the American College of Medical Genetics and the National Society of Genetic Counselors. *Genetics in Medicine, 13*, 597–605. doi:10.1097/GIM.0b013e31821d69b8

Haight, B. K., Bachman, D. L., Hendrix, S., Wagner, M. T., Meeks, A., & Johnson, J. (2003). Life review: Treating the dyadic family unit with dementia. *Clinical Psychology and Psychotherapy, 10*, 165–174. doi:10.1002/cpp.367

Hoe, J., Katona, C., Roch, B., & Livingston, G. (2005). Use of the QOL–AD for measuring quality of life in people with severe dementia: The LASER–AD study. *Age and Ageing, 34,* 130–135. doi:10.1093/ageing/afi030

Hope, T., & Fairburn, C. G. (1992). Present Behavioural Examination: A semi-structured interview for assessing the behaviour of patients with dementia. *Psychological Medicine, 22,* 223–230. doi:10.1017/S0033291700032888

Hopper, T., Mahendra, N., Kim, E., Azuma, T., Bayles, K., Cleary, S., & Tomoeda, C. (2005). Evidence-based practice recommendations for working with individuals with dementia: Spaced-retrieval training. *Journal of Medical Speech-Language Pathology, 13,* xxvii–xxxiv.

Hunter, C. E. A., Ward, L., & Camp, C. J. (2012). Transitioning spaced retrieval training to care staff in an Australian residential aged care setting for older adults with dementia: A case study approach. *Clinical Gerontologist, 35,* 1–14. doi:10.1080/07317115.2011.626513

Hwang, J. P., Tsai, S., Yang, C., Liu, K., & Lirng, J. (2000). Repetitive phenomena in dementia. *International Journal of Psychiatry in Medicine, 30,* 165–171. doi:10.2190/2QDA-YAL3-2E69-PYJW

Institute of Medicine. (1986). *Improving the quality of care in nursing homes.* Washington, DC: National Academies Press.

Judge, K. S., Menne, H. L., & Whitlatch, C. J. (2010). Stress process model for individuals with dementia. *Gerontologist, 50,* 294–302. doi:10.1093/geront/gnp162

Kitwood, T. (1997). *Dementia reconsidered: The person comes first.* Berkshire, England: Open University Press.

Koren, M. J. (2010). Person-centered care for nursing home residents: The Culture-Change Movement. *Health Affairs, 29,* 312–317. doi:10.1377/hlthaff.2009.0966

Lawton, M. P., & Nahemow, L. (1973). Ecology and the aging process. In L. Eisdorfer & M. P. Lawton (Eds.), *The psychology of adult development and aging* (pp. 619–674). Washington, DC: The American Psychological Association. doi:10.1037/10044-020

Lichtenberg, P. A. (2010). *Handbook of assessment in clinical gerontology* (2nd ed.). San Diego, CA: Academic Press.

Logsdon, R. G., Gibbons, L. E., McCurry, S. M., & Teri, L. (1999). Quality of life in Alzheimer's disease: Patient and caregiver reports. *Journal of Mental Health and Aging, 5,* 21–32.

Logsdon, R. G., Gibbons, L. E., McCurry, S. M., & Teri, L. (2002). Assessing quality of life in older adults with cognitive impairment. *Psychosomatic Medicine, 64,* 510–519. doi:10.1097/00006842-200205000-00016

Logsdon, R. G., & Teri, L. (1997). The Pleasant Events Schedule-AD: Psychometric properties and relationship to depression and cognition in Alzheimer's disease patients. *Gerontologist, 37,* 40–45. doi:10.1093/geront/37.1.40

Mak, W. (2011). Self-reported goal pursuit and purpose in life among people with dementia. *The Journals of Gerontology, Series B: Psychological Sciences and Social Sciences, 66,* 177–184. doi:10.1093/geronb/gbq092

Mak, W., Sörensen, S., & Camp, C. J. (2014). Dementia and self-reported purpose in life. In A. C. Michalos (Ed.), *Encyclopedia of quality of life and well-being research* (pp. 1498–1503). New York, NY: Springer. doi:10.1007/978-94-007-0753-5_3871

Mast, B. T. (2011). *Whole person dementia assessment.* Baltimore, MD: Health Professions Press.

McKhann, G. M., Knopman, D. S., Chertkow, H., Hyman, B. T., Jack, C. R., Kawas, C. H. . . . Phelps, C. H. (2011). The diagnosis of dementia due to Alzheimer's disease: Recommendations from the National Institute on Aging-Alzheimer's Association workgroups on diagnostic guidelines for Alzheimer's disease. *Alzheimer's and Dementia, 7,* 263–269. doi:10.1016/j.jalz.2011.03.005

McKitrick, L. A., & Camp, C. J. (1993). Relearning the names of things: The spaced-retrieval intervention implemented by a caregiver. *Clinical Gerontologist, 14,* 60–62.

Menne, H. L., Johnson, J. D., Whitlatch, C. J., & Schwartz, S. M. (2012). Activity preferences of persons with dementia. *Activities, Adaptation and Aging, 36,* 195–213. doi:10.1080/01924788.2012.696234

Menne, H. L., Kinney, J. M., & Morhardt, D. J. (2002). Trying to continue to do as much as they can do: Theoretical insights regarding continuity and meaning making in the face of dementia. *Dementia, 1,* 367–382. doi:10.1177/147130120200100308

Menne, H. L., Tucke, S. S., Whitlatch, C. J., & Feinberg, L. F. (2008). Decision-making involvement scale for individuals with dementia and family caregivers. *American Journal of Alzheimer's Disease and Other Dementias, 23,* 23–29. doi:10.1177/1533317507308312

Mesman, G. R., Buchanan, J. A., Husfeldt, J. D., & Berg, T. M. (2011). Identifying preferences in persons with dementia: Systematic preference testing vs. caregiver and family member report. *Clinical Gerontologist, 34,* 154–159. doi:10.1080/07317115.2011.539516

Omnibus Budget Reconciliation Act of 1987, Pub. L. No. 100-203, 101 Stat. 1330, 42 U.S.C. §§ 4201–4218 (1987).

Ozgis, S., Rendell, P. G., & Henry, J. D. (2009). Spaced retrieval significantly improves prospective memory performance of cognitively impaired older adults. *Gerontology, 55,* 229–232. doi:10.1159/000163446

Park, C. L., & Folkman, S. (1997). Meaning in the context of stress and coping. *Review of General Psychology, 1,* 115–144. doi:10.1037/1089-2680.1.2.115

Parmelee, P. A., Lawton, M. P., & Katz, I. R. (1989). Psychometric properties of the Geriatric Depression Scale among the institutionalized aged. *Psychological Assessment, 1,* 331–338. doi:10.1037/1040-3590.1.4.331

Pioneer Network. (n.d.). *About us.* Retrieved from http://www.pioneernetwork.net/AboutUs

Preston, L., Marshall, A., & Bucks, R. S. (2007). Investigating the ways that older people cope with dementia: A qualitative study. *Aging and Mental Health, 11,* 131–143. doi:10.1080/13607860600844572

Ptak, R., der Linden, M. V., & Schnider, A. (2010). Cognitive rehabilitation of episodic memory disorders: From theory to practice. *Frontiers in Human Neuroscience, 4,* 1–11.

Ready, R. E., Ott, B. R., & Grace, J. (2003). Amnestic behavior in dementia: Symptoms to assist in early detection and diagnosis. *Journal of the American Geriatrics Society, 51,* 32–37. doi:10.1034/j.1601-5215.2002.51006.x

Reamy, A. M., Kim, K., Zarit, S. H., & Whitlatch, C. J. (2011). Understanding discrepancy in perceptions of values: Individuals with mild to moderate dementia and their family caregivers. *Gerontologist, 51,* 473–483. doi:10.1093/geront/gnr010

Rodda, J., & Walker, Z. (2009). Ten years of cholinesterase inhibitors. *International Journal of Geriatric Psychiatry, 24,* 437–442. doi:10.1002/gps.2165

Sebern, M. D., & Whitlatch, C. J. (2007). Dyadic relationship scale: A measure of the impact of the provision and receipt of family care. *Gerontologist, 47,* 741–751. doi:10.1093/geront/47.6.741

Selwood, A., Thorgrimsen, L., & Orrell, M. (2005). Quality of life in dementia—A one-year follow-up study. *International Journal of Geriatric Psychiatry, 20,* 232–237. doi:10.1002/gps.1271

Shankar, K. K., Walker, M., & Frost, D. (1999). The development of a valid and reliable scale for rating anxiety in dementia (RAID). *Aging and Mental Health, 3,* 39–49. doi:10.1080/13607869956424

Sheikh, J. I., & Yesavage, J. A. (1986). Geriatric Depression Scale (GDS) recent evidence and development of a shorter form. *Clinical Gerontologist, 5,* 165–172. doi:10.1300/J018v05n01_09

Small, J. A. (2012). A new frontier in spaced retrieval memory training for persons with Alzheimer's disease. *Neuropsychological Rehabilitation, 22,* 329–361. doi:10.1080/09602011.2011.640468

Snow, A. L., Huddleston, C., Robinson, C., Kunik, M. E., Bush, A. L., Wilson, N., . . . Stanley, M. A. (2012). Psychometric properties of a structured interview guide for the rating for anxiety in dementia. *Aging and Mental Health, 16,* 592–602. doi:10.1080/13607863.2011.644518

Snow, A. L., Kunik, M. E., Molinari, V. A., Orengo, C. A., Doody, R., Graham, D. P., & Norris, M. P. (2005). Accuracy of self-reported depression in persons with dementia. *Journal of the American Geriatrics Society, 53,* 389–396. doi:10.1111/j.1532-5415.2005.53154.x

Sperling, R. A., Aisen, P. S., Beckett, L. A., Bennett, D. A., Craft, S., Fagan, A. M., . . . Phelps, C. H. (2011). Toward defining the preclinical stages of Alzheimer's disease: Recommendations from the National Institute on Aging-Alzheimer's Association workgroups on diagnostic guidelines for Alzheimer's disease. *Alzheimer's and Dementia, 7,* 280–292. doi:10.1016/j.jalz.2011.03.003

Steeman, E., Godderis, J., Grypdonck, M., De Bal, N., & De Casterle, B. D. (2007). Living with dementia from the perspective of older people: Is it a positive story? *Aging and Mental Health, 11,* 119–130. doi:10.1080/13607860600963364

Stevens, A. B., O'Hanlon, A. M., & Camp, C. J. (1993). Strategy training using the spaced-retrieval method: A case study. *Clinical Gerontologist, 13,* 106–109.

Tappen, R. M., & Williams, C. L. (2008). Development and testing of the Alzheimer's Disease and Related Dementias Mood Scale. *Nursing Research, 57,* 426–435. doi:10.1097/NNR.0b013e31818c3dcc

Teri, L., Gibbons, L. E., McCurry, S. M., Logsdon, R. G., Buchner, D. M., Barlow, W. E., . . . Larson, E. B. (2003). Exercise plus behavioral management in patients with Alzheimer's disease: A randomized control trial. *JAMA, 290,* 2015–2022. doi:10.1001/jama.290.15.2015

Teri, L., Logsdon, R. G., Uomoto, J., & McCurry, S. M. (1997). Behavioral treatment of depression in dementia patients: A controlled clinical trial. *The Journals of Gerontology, Series B: Psychological Sciences and Social Sciences, 52,* 159–166.

Teri, L., McCurry, S. M., Logsdon, R. G., & Gibbons, S. E. (2005). Training community consultants to help family members improve dementia care: A randomized controlled trial. *Gerontologist, 45,* 802–811. doi:10.1093/geront/45.6.802

Teri, L., Truax, P., Logsdon, R., Uomoto, J., Zarit, S., & Vitaliano, P. P. (1992). Assessment of behavioral problems in dementia: The Revised Memory and

Behavior Problems Checklist. *Psychology and Aging, 7*, 622–631. doi:10.1037/0882-7974.7.4.622

Thivierge, S., Simard, M., Jean, L., & Grandmaison, E. (2008). Errorless learning and spaced retrieval techniques to relearn instrumental activities of daily living in mild Alzheimer's disease: A case report study. *Neuropsychiatric Disease and Treatment, 4*, 987–999.

Vance, D. E., Struzick, T., & Farr, K. (2010). Spaced retrieval technique—A cognitive tool for social workers and their clients. *Journal of Gerontological Social Work, 53*, 148–158. doi:10.1080/01634370903409745

Wald, C., Fahy, M., Walker, Z., & Livingston, G. (2003). What to tell dementia caregivers: The rule of threes.

International Journal of Geriatric Psychiatry, 18, 313–317. doi:10.1002/gps.828

Whitlatch, C. J., Feinberg, L. F., & Tucke, S. S. (2005). Measuring the values and preferences for everyday care of persons with cognitive impairment and their family caregivers. *Gerontologist, 45*, 370–380. doi:10.1093/geront/45.3.370

Yesavage, J. A., Brink, T. L., Rose, T. L., Lum, O., Huang, V., Adey, M., & Leirer, V. O. (1982–1983). Development and validation of a geriatric depression screening scale: A preliminary report. *Journal of Psychiatric Research, 17*, 37–49. doi:10.1016/0022-3956(82)90033-4

CHAPTER 13

COGNITIVE TRAINING FOR MILDLY IMPAIRED OLDER ADULTS

Lee Hyer, Christine Mullen, and Laura McKenzie

Society has now reached the era in which cognitive training (CT) is being applied liberally to older adults. In 2010, Americans spent $265 million on brain fitness software and web-based programs on adults that claim to boost brainpower (Owen et al., 2010). This trend is on the rise. Cognitive decline, particularly in late adulthood, is becoming one of the nation's top public health problems. In fact, distinct cognitive deficits are now recognized as part of the broader phenotype of many late life problems and clearly many late life psychiatric disorders. Given that as many 5.1 million Americans have Alzheimer's disease (AD; Hebert, Scherr, Bienias, Bennett, & Evans, 2003) and that the prevalence of mild cognitive impairment (MCI) is even higher, a core question for researchers and clinicians alike is, how can the harmful aspects leading to impaired cognition at later life be prevented (Le Couteur & Sinclair, 2010)?

It is now reasonably well accepted that CT improves function of younger adults (e.g., Busch-kuehl et al., 2008; Dahlin, Neely, Larsson, Bäck-man, & Nyberg, 2008; Mahncke et al., 2006) and many healthy older adults (e.g., Small & Vorgan, 2011). Consensus guidelines on the value of CT for healthy older adults are mildly encouraging. Recent findings from the National Institute of Health (NIH; 2011) Conference for Alzheimer's Disease and Cognitive Decline, assessing 6,713 studies on risks and protective factors for factors related to cognitive decline examined by the NIH, found CT and behavioral factors to be most associated with sizable risk reduction for cognitive decline. In *Lancet Neurology* (Nitrini, 2012), engagement in cognitively stimulating activities along with seven other factors accounted for a 10% to 25% reduction in the incidence of AD. In addition, the Centers for Disease Control and Prevention's (2011) Healthy Brain Initiative was updated and emphasized the importance of maintaining a healthy brain as a key component in the staving off dementia. The initiative outlined a road map for healthy brains that highlighted engagement in cognitively stimulating activities, physical activity, and the fostering of a healthy vascular system.

The extent to which CT can make a difference as a neuroprotective or compensatory method for better functioning currently is being explored. This chapter discusses overall aging issues as they relate to brain health as well as the constructs of MCI and dementia. It continues by discussing extant taxonomies on CT as applied to older adults and presents numerous CT studies. It starts with important reviews regarding CT and impaired older adults. Following this discussion, it addresses CT interventions involving and not involving the use of computers. We then briefly discuss lifestyle factors, a critical topic for cognitive health for older adults, and addresses special problems in the assessment of outcomes for CT, especially as it applies to a core feature on memory training, working memory (WM). This is followed by a brief consideration on typical assessment measures applied in CT. The chapter ends with a summary of one intervention, Cogmed, used on an older impaired group (MCI).

http://dx.doi.org/10.1037/14459-013
APA Handbook of Clinical Geropsychology: Vol. 2. Assessment, Treatment, and Issues of Later Life,
P. A. Lichtenberg and B. T. Mast (Editors-in-Chief)

THEORIES ABOUT COGNITION

In the past 30 years, geropsychology has been steeped in the importance of the "life span developmental" perspective. Development is embedded in multiple contexts and is conceived as a dynamic process in which the individual interacts with the social environment; a set of interconnected social settings, including cultural considerations. These influences occur as the brain develops, creating new neural connections, sometimes labeled *scaffolds*. This scaffolding protects cognitive functioning and may be strengthened by cognitive engagement as well as positive lifestyles (Park & Reuter-Lorenz, 2009). The normal aging brain adapts to these factors.

In recent years, four areas of cognitive functioning have been special targets of CT (Park & Reuter-Lorenz, 2009). These include memory (WM especially), reasoning, speed of processing, and executive functioning. Each domain appears to predict function in different ways and to different degrees. For example, reasoning tends to be the best predictor of initial functioning and memory is the best predictor of changes in everyday functioning over time (Gross, Rebok, Unverzagt, Willis, & Brandt, 2011).

Assessment of these areas is important as it has been estimated that at least 22% of people greater than 70 have memory impairment (Alzheimer's Association, 2012). Increasingly, it is accepted that degenerative problems start early in life in selected areas of the brain and progress to syndromes in which behavioral problems become noticeable (Jack et al., 2010). These factors increase or decrease in the cerebrospinal fluid (CSF) across the years and cause problems in the brain with oxidative stress, inflammation, insulin signaling components, size and frequency of infarcts, concentration of growth factors, cortisol, and other hormones (Hyer, 2014). Recently, we have come to understand that over the 10 years before a formal diagnosis of dementia, cognition declines at a steady pace and then accelerates on average approximately 2 years before the actual diagnosis (Wilson et al., 2012). Although the process is variable, disability in old age is associated with accelerated cognitive decline (Rajan, Hebert, Scherr, Mendes de Leon, & Evans, 2013). The accelerated cognitive decline associated with MCI and dementia suggests that something organic is rapidly occurring. Importantly, these can be reflected in cognitive markers and assessed (see Smith & Bondi, 2013).

As an overview, the extent to which CT (or simply experience) prevents decompensating as a function of aging in later life, or due to a degenerative disease, is unknown (Mayr, 2008). Targeting cognitive tasks like executive functioning that are more encompassing, especially the effects of set shifting, inhibition, and updating (Dahlin et al., 2008), seem to improve cognitive outcomes. Additionally, more "holistic" CT involving various aspects of later life and socialization seems to provide benefits that extend beyond simple training in attention and WM (Basak, Boot, Voss, & Kramer, 2008; Stine-Morrow, Parisi, Morrow, & Park, 2008). Environmental enrichment and an emphasis on health, as well as cognitive skill training and physical exercise, also are helpful for cognitive functioning. The effects of these factors have been labeled brain or cognitive reserve, which prevents cognitive decline.

Mild Cognitive Impairment

Although several models and constructs have been proposed over the years, the cognitive decline distribution at later life ranges from normalcy to age-associated memory impairment and benign senescent forgetfulness, to the more forgetful and declining states of the forgetting spectrum, MCI, and eventually dementia. At a clinical level, MCI has been defined as either amnestic (memory deficits) or nonamnestic (other cognitive areas impaired; Jak et al., 2009). It is a loose stage of cognitive functioning between normal aging and a dementia that may or may not be associated with biomarkers of dementia. The definition of MCI also may depend on the specific cognitive targets or number of cognitive tests that reveal impairment. Loewenstein (2011), for example, has suggested that usual clinical history and evaluation of memory decline generally is not as sensitive or specific as formal psychological testing, especially when two or more tests are applied for a memory marker of 1.5 standard deviations (*SD*) below the norm.

MCI thus can be seen as a strategic construct allowing health care providers the luxury of placing the identified patient into a category in which time (and perhaps CT) can lead to an eventual degenerative diagnosis or not. Conversion rates of MCI to dementia have been estimated for more than a decade to be approximately 12%–15% per year. As implied, conversion rates depend heavily on the sample and the measures involved. For example, Morris, one of the original researchers on MCI, noted that 100% of MCI subjects in one Memory Disorders Clinic progressed to dementia over 9.5 years; 84% met neuropathological criteria for AD (Morris et al., 2001). Comparatively, a review of epidemiological studies (Brooks & Loewenstein, 2010) has shown that as many as 30% of individuals identified as MCI are reclassified as normal based on follow-up evaluation. One other problem is the fact that older "normal" community adults often have dementia biomarkers as well (Jak et al., 2009).

Several other problems are caused by the complexity of aging and the degenerative process. Autopsy studies, for example, have found that up to 90% of patients with AD exhibited cerebrovascular pathology and about one third of vascular dementia patients showed AD pathology (Kalaria, 2000). Given that most definitions of MCI require memory impairment or involvement of another cognitive domain, the memory requirement has the potential to produce false negatives when assessing any cognitive impairment associated with vascular causes—that is, vascular cognitive impairment. The earliest cognitive manifestations of vascular disease are changes in executive function, such as planning, organizing, and decision making, rather than memory per se (Smith & Bondi, 2013).

There is increasing appreciation that the traditional definition of dementia is imperfect (see discussion in the *Diagnostic and Statistical Manual of Mental Disorders, Fifth Edition* [*DSM–5*]; American Psychiatric Association, 2013). It is categorical, exclusive, and arbitrary. Creating a dichotomy between dementia and nondementia ignores the spectrum of cognitive impairment. Converting soft data into hard categories fails to capture the complexity of the common coexistence and probable interaction of cerebrovascular disease and AD.

Although it is time to shift the focus from thresholds to a continuum of cognitive impairment, from the late to the early stages, and from effects to causes, this may not be helpful to health care providers on the frontlines who need immediate clarity.

Recently the *DSM–5* (American Psychiatric Association, 2013) advocated for changes; MCI is now labeled minor neurocognitive disorder and dementia is labeled major neurocognitive disorder. The *DSM–5* criteria for minor neurocognitive disorder involve cognitive decline from a previous level, concern of the person or a significant other, modest impairment in cognition, lower performance on standard tests, reasonable independence, a problem not attributed to a delirium, and one that is not better explained by other mental disorder. Although not formally endorsed, more emphasis too has been placed on biomarkers, such as serum, blood, and CSF, using position emission tomography (PET) with a radiolabeled glucose analogue (fluorodeoxyglucose-PET; Sperling, 2011). Combining diagnostic markers may provide the most useful approach to identifying those who will progress to an AD diagnosis. For example, Prestia et al. (2013) assessed for hippocampal atrophy, decreased CSF amyloid, and decreased brain glucose metabolism in 73 patients with MCI. Among those with no positive biomarkers, just 4% went on to develop AD. Of the patients positive for all three biomarkers, 100% ultimately progressed to AD. Still, although AD biomarker profiles are increasingly common in academic and research settings, the limited availability, cost, and not yet fully validated efficacy of current therapies has largely kept them out of clinics.

MCI and its variants are useful concepts in that they have generated interest in studying dementing diseases in their early stages. Although MCI is not a necessary precursor to AD, it has been shown to be a useful marker. MCI and its etiological underpinnings, however, must be established through comprehensive clinical evaluation and neuropsychological testing. We may infer that certain cognitive profiles and biomarkers related to MCI increase the probability of an underlying AD process. Although researchers may be ready to make a diagnosis of AD at an MCI stage based on cognitive and biomarker data, clinicians typically are not.

In sum, the combination of cognitive dysfunction and neural circuitry plays a key role in understanding the etiology of behavioral and psychiatric symptoms. Distinct memory and cognitive deficits increasingly are recognized as part of the broader phenotype of many psychiatric illnesses (e.g., depression and anxiety), and cognitive dysfunction is perceived as a significant risk factor for the development of psychiatric illnesses, particularly in older adults. These cognitive impairments offer a potentially effective target for addressing psychiatric illness through CT.

Taxonomies

There is no set taxonomy of CT (Clare, Wilson, Carter, & Hodges, 2003; Eschen, 2012; Huckans et al., 2013; Mowszowski, Batchelor, & Naismith, 2010; Rebok et al., 2012; Sitzer, Twamley, & Jeste, 2006). Huckans et al. (2013) reviewed 14 studies in which participants met strict criteria for MCI and divided CT into cognitive rehabilitation approaches directly or indirectly to target key outcomes involving restorative CT (targeting cognitive compromise), compensatory CT (targeting functional compromise), lifestyle interventions, and psychotherapeutic techniques. This group outlined a model of CT moving from a spectrum of normal cognition to MCI to dementia, and noted that the progression is modified by protective factors (e.g., diet and exercise) and risk factors (e.g., tobacco and alcohol). Results indicate that improvement in objective cognitive domains is notable but inconsistent; more clarity is required to yield practical advice for clinicians.

Rebok et al. (2012) added to these findings. His group examined the complexity of CT among older adults. They noted that training differs by population (community dwelling or impaired) and goals (immediate vs. long term, specific vs. broader training, improvement in functional competence, and quality of life) and by self-guided or formally guided training as well as by specific type of training. The type of training can be simple (association, categorization, visual imagery, rehearsal) or more complex (method of loci, face name recognition, number and story mnemonics). Training also is available for types of memory, including procedural (spaced

retrieval, errorless), external aids, and reality orientation. All methods provided some benefit.

More generally, CT and its methods can be categorized by their purpose (Bryck & Fisher, 2012). Laboratory-based training often is applied in clinics with special programs and involves computers and targets specific cognitive domains. General cognitive stimulation approaches with mnemonic strategies are popular. Neurobiologically informed interventions actually may strengthen compensatory processes. These authors also address self-regulation. Neurorehabilitation involves the rehabilitation of brain-injured patients and addresses neural systems that still function. The bulk of CT involves generic approaches, including reality orientation as well as external assists in life (e.g., sticky notes). Group-based cognitive stimulation also can be helpful as this applies to dementia patients and includes stimulation and structure. As we have intimated, most of these methods provide some cognitive benefit for impaired older adults but the extent and conditions involved need to be assessed or cross-validated (see Exhibit 13.1).

Exhibit 13.1
Types of Cognitive Training

---

1. Laboratory-based training often involves repeated performance, typically computer training or speed choice tasks. These approaches tend to target a particular cognitive domain rather than take a domain-general approach aimed at overall improvement with well-being, improved symptoms, and better behaviors.
2. General cognitive stimulation, mnemonic strategies, or games on older adults who are normal but show aging-associated memory problems.
3. Neurobiologically informed ecological interventions address social emotional skills that are based on executive function. Skills include self-regulation and effortful control.
4. Neurorehabilitaion therapies for patients with traumatic brain injury are aimed at improving cognitive functioning by using strategic training techniques to offset rather than restitute lost functionality. The rerouting of neural connections enable individuals to learn new methods of handling older problems or goals.
5. Generic approaches include reminiscence, reality orientation, and cognitive stimulation therapy. Reality orientation, has been largely superseded by cognitive stimulation, which uses more implicit methods, with activities or games.

Reviews

There are several reviews of the effects of CT on healthy older adults (e.g., Valenzuela & Sachdev, 2009). Reviews of studies of impaired older adults (Acevedo & Loewenstein, 2007; Belleville, 2008; Buschert et al., 2011; Clare, 2008; Huckans et al., 2013; Jak, Seelye, & Jurick, 2013; Melby-Lervåg & Hulme, 2013; Mowszowski et al., 2010; Rebok et al., 2012; Simon, Yokomizo, & Bottino, 2012; Sitzer et al., 2006; Stott & Spector, 2011) and at least one meta-analysis have reported largely beneficial effects for patients with MCI.

Additional reviews have focused on specific training methods. One group (De Werd, Boelen, Rikkert, & Kessels, 2013) evaluated errorless learning (EL) on everyday tasks in people with dementia. A review of 26 studies ($n = 70$) showed that people with minimal to moderate dementia can (re)learn meaningful daily life tasks or relevant knowledge using an error-reducing teaching approach. Five controlled studies and 12 single-case studies obtained significantly superior effects using EL. Many of the studies conducted follow-ups spanning months after training. Additionally, training in these studies lasted 20 min to 2.5 hr in 6 to 21 sessions. Tasks included daily life behaviors like use of electronic devices and household appliances, orientation skills, face–name association, and definitions and uses of objects. Although results were most impressive for MCI or the earlier stages of dementia, results applied to both procedural and nonprocedural tasks at various times.

Several of the tabled reviews are worth highlighting. Rebok et al. (2012) found that CT was valuable for MCI and dementia, and highlighted the strategies reported previously. Simon et al. (2012) evaluated types of CT and amnestic-MCI in 20 studies, highlighting the importance of other aspects of cognition, including self-evaluation of memory, mood, daily life activities, and quality of life. All studies that were evaluated addressed episodic memory as training goals, including training strategies of EL, spaced-retrieval training, visual imagery, face–name associations, cueing, categorization, and method of loci. The overall conclusion was that amnestic-MCI patients are capable of learning new information and memory strategies.

Olazarán et al. (2010) also carefully assessed high-quality studies. Evaluating just 13 out of a universe of 179 studies that met strict methodological standards, the authors found favorable results associated with many techniques. Many studies, however, had small samples or the methods applied were flawed (e.g., lack of blinding, nonspecific definitions of population). Favorable intervention categories included CT, behavioral interventions, cognitive stimulation, transcutaneuous electrical stimulation, physical exercise, music, caregiver interventions (education, support, respite, multi-component), other integrative therapies, and targeted aspects of cognition, including activities of daily living (ADLs), mood, and quality of life for patients and caregivers. The most effective interventions for delay of institutionalization were multi-component caregiver interventions. Improvement in cognition was particularly associated with small and individual CT sessions. Cognitive stimulation in conjunction with other therapies also demonstrated benefits relative to treatment as usual, most often involving basic care support. ADL, cognitive stimulation, and behavioral management improved outcomes specific to these techniques. Mood interventions improved mood and quality of life. Multicomponent training positively influenced environmental tasks. In a review by Mowszowski et al. (2010), the authors emphasized the importance of multiple interventions (e.g., episodic and procedural training) for memory, attention, and functioning. Such interventions included computerized training, practical problem solving, assertiveness training, stress management, and exercise. Not enough follow-up data exist to make conclusive statements about preventive care. This group recommended that some form of CT should be applied early in the life cycle, by at least age 50 years.

Additional reviews also have targeted various methods of enhancing cognition but highlight more limits on study outcomes. It was been noted in one careful review (Melby-Lervåg & Hulme, 2013) that CT has limits and may be oversold. Acevedo and Loewenstein (2007) lamented the lack of high-quality randomized controlled trials in the evaluation of single-domain and multimodal interventions, as methodologies are ill-defined among studies.

Rebok et al. (2012) reviewed CT and found many positive results for MCI but fewer for dementia. Jak et al. (2013) evaluated technology-based interventions and found positive results for tasks in which training was applied directly (specific training for specific tasks; near transfer) but not more general tasks (far transfer).

For many years, clinicians have recommended external supports, such as white boards, paper pads, and the like, to their memory-impaired patients (e.g., Clare et al., 2003), or interventions targeting nonepisodic memory in dementia patients, such as procedural memory (e.g., Camp, 2005), reminiscence, or reality orientation (repetitive training on basic orientation; Hyer, 2013). More recently, nonepisodic memory interventions also have been applied in the form of strategy acquisition in this population (Gonzalez Rothi et al., 2009; Souchay, 2007). There has been some interest in the combination of psychosocial interventions along with cognitive enhancers (Gonzalez Rothi et al., 2009; Meguro et al., 2008). Interestingly, Rozzini et al. (2007) showed positive follow-up results over 3 months with the combined use of cognitive enhancers (cholinesterase inhibitors [ChEIs]) and CT. This latter study was mildly positive but has not been replicated to any degree.

In sum, cognitive decline is the result of a dynamic tension between a progressive disease and the brain's limited ability to adapt, react, and regenerate. There is a complex interaction between cognitive reserve factors (e.g., education) and biomarkers of neuronal injury and neurodegeneration that moderates the benefits of cognitive interventions. Although promising, these reviews suggest that the exact CT technique applicable for a particular person has yet to be identified. Unfortunately, only moderate evidence suggests that CT can generalize to untrained cognitive abilities, but the complexity of the program of CT as well as individual factors play a large role. Jak et al. (2013) firmly noted that generalizability of improvements on trained tasks or untrained cognitive abilities to ecologically valid tasks of everyday cognitive and functional status have not been routinely examined or proven. Huckans et al. (2013), too, labeled the efficacy of CT as promising but inconclusive.

Noncomputer- and Computer-Based Programs

Increasing research is indicating that older adults who are *impaired* can benefit from CT (Akhtar, Moulin, & Bowie, 2006; Backman & Dixon, 1992; Barnes et al., 2009; Belleville, 2008; Belleville et al., 2006, 2011; Boripuntakul, Kothan, Methapatara, Munkhetvit, & Sungkarat, 2012; Bourgeois et al., 2003; Buschert et al., 2011; Camp, 2005; Clare, 2008; De Vreese, Neri, Fioravanti, Belloi, & Zanetti, 2001; Finn & McDonald, 2011; Gagnon & Belleville, 2012; Gatz, 2005; Grandmaison & Simard, 2003; Greenaway, Duncan, & Smith, 2013; Greenaway, Hanna, Lepore, & Smith, 2008; Günther, Schäfer, Holzner, & Kemmler, 2003; Hampstead, Sathian, Moore, Nalisnick, & Stringer, 2008; Hampstead et al., 2012; Hutchens et al., 2012; Jean, Bergeron, Thivierge, & Simard, 2010; Jean, Simard, van Reekum, & Bergeron, 2007; Jean, Simard, et al., 2010; Joosten-Weyn Banningh et al., 2013; Kinsella et al., 2009; Kurz, Pohl, Ramsenthaler, & Sorg, 2009; Lim et al., 2012; Little, Volans, Hemsley, & Levy, 1986; Loewenstein, Acevedo, Czaja, & Duara, 2004; Londos et al., 2008; Olazarán et al., 2004; Olchik, Farina, Steibel, Teixeira, & Yassuda, 2013; Rapp, Brenes, & Marsh, 2002; Rozzini et al., 2007; Talassi et al., 2007; Troyer, Murphy, Anderson, Moscovitch, & Craik, 2008; Unverzagt et al., 2007, 2012; Yesavage et al., 2008).

Most of these studies targeted episodic memory, but many addressed other cognitive domains, including attention, speed of processing, language, visual spatial abilities, and executive functioning. Table 13.1 includes only more recent studies of CT in MCI patients. We highlight these studies because they represent newer perspectives in CT for MCI, and include one of the following: more intensive training programs, inclusion of booster sessions postintervention, the addition of outcome variables beyond specific training domains, or combining CT with caregiver interventions.

Table 13.1 identifies recent major studies of patients with an MCI or mild AD, and all but one (Rapp et al., 2002) have shown positive effects for CT on elements of cognition, mood, or functioning. Current research centers around determining whether internal aids, such as teaching method of

TABLE 13.1

Noncomputer-Based Training

Author	Sample and groups	Sessions and time	Pilot	RCT	Interventions used in experimental condition	Conclusions
Boripuntakul et al. (2012)	10 aMCI patients; experimental or control group	18 sessions, 6 weeks	X	X	Episodic memory: Method of loci; short story memory Attention: Differentiating similar pictures, identifying target stimuli from distractors Executive function: IADL practice, categorize objects by function	Memory, attention span, and executive function were positively affected and training executive function through practical application may help generalize training.
Buschert et al. (2011)	39 aMCI or Mild AD patients; cognitive intervention or active control group	20 units, 6 months	X	X	Cognitive: Face–name associations, errorless learning, visual imagery Behavioral: External aids (calendars, notes), behavioral activation	This model was effective for aMCI patients, but only showed positive trends for mild AD patients.
Greenaway et al. (2013)	40 aMCI patients and program partners; intervention or control group	12 sessions, 6 weeks		X	Memory support system: Three-part calendar, with use and practice during sessions Appointments: Time sensitive tasks To-do items: List format Journal: Note life events, thoughts	Functioning and self-efficacy improved more readily than cognitive status, suggesting possibilities for increasing quality of life.
Hampstead et al. (2012)	29 aMCI patients and 23 matched controls	5 sessions, 2 weeks	X		Mnemonic devices: Participants were trained to remember locations of distinct stimuli in digital "rooms," and asked to choose among location choices in a recall phase; those randomized to mnemonic devices learned cues to aid in locating the stimuli along with the simple location association	aMCI patients may improve as much as healthy adults with the aid of mnemonics, but will likely still exhibit reduced functioning overall.
Jean, Simard, et al. (2010)	22 aMCI patients; experimental or control (errorful learning) groups	6 sessions, 3 weeks		X	Face–name associations: Goal of learning five unknown and five famous associations Errorless learning: No guesses, only "Don't know," added Spaced retrieval Errorful learning: Guesses encouraged, at least one error per trial	There was not a significant difference between the techniques for increasing correct associations, thus structured practice may aid in learning regardless of type.

(continues)

TABLE 13.1 *(Continued)*

Noncomputer-Based Training

Author	Sample and groups	Sessions and time	Pilot	RCT	Interventions used in experimental condition	Conclusions
Kinsella et al. (2009)	52 aMCI patients and primary caregivers; intervention or waitlist control groups	5 sessions, 5 weeks	X	X	Coping skills, compensatory strategies, and attention training: Applied to everyday tasks and problems and practiced in sessions	Easily implemented strategies are useful but may require refresher sessions.
Lim et al. (2012)	20 MCI patients, all received intervention	10 sessions, 10 weeks			Cognitive stimulation: Encoding a story, method of loci; Memory training: Focused on daily tasks, visual imagery for steps	Memory tasks help improve cognition, but may not directly translate to improved functioning.
Loewenstein et al. (2004)	44 probable or possible AD, cholinesterase inhibitors; cognitive rehabilitation or mental stimulation	24 sessions, 12 weeks			Cognitive rehabilitation: Face–name association task, orientation task, continuous performance test, making-change-for-a-purchase task, bill paying; Mental stimulation: Computer games based on memory, hangman-like games, reviewing articles	Improved cognitive functioning at postintervention and 3 months postintervention.
Olchik et al. (2013)	47 aMCI, 65 normal adults, intervention or control (education only) groups	8 sessions, 8 weeks		X	Memory training: Active attention, categorization, association, and visual imagery	aMCI patients benefit more from training than normal adults.
Rapp et al. (2002)	19 MCI patients with MMSE >24; intervention or control groups	6 sessions, 6 weeks	X	X	Psychoeducation and relaxation (systematic breathing); Memory training: Cueing, categorization, chunking, method of loci	Improved patient perception of memory, and may be beneficial for increasing motivation.
Troyer et al. (2008)	54 aMCI patients; intervention or waitlist control groups	10 sessions, 10 weeks		X	Memory training: Creating a memory book, spaced retrieval for names, memory for actions	Functional gains from practical memory training are promising.
Unverzagt et al. (2012)	2802 ACTIVE study participants; 3 intervention groups or control	10 sessions, 5–6 weeks		X	Memory training, reasoning, and speed of processing training	Training did not reduce incident of dementia, but there are now more than 20 ACTIVE studies available.

Note. AD = Alzheimer's disease; aMCI = amnestic mild cognitive impairment; IADLs = instrumental activities of daily living; MMSE = Mini-Mental State Examination.

loci, focused practice on face–name associations, and manipulating learning strategies, can help patients regain cognitive vigor more robustly than other popular external aids, such as using notebooks (Greenaway et al., 2013; Kinsella et al., 2009). The hope for these studies is that relying on internal compensatory strategies may help improve cognition rather than encouraging dependence on external prompts. For internal methods, research is unclear as to how much more effective one strategy of learning is over another. Patients with an MCI appear to benefit from various types of training. Of interest, is that the number of training sessions can be limited (less than 6 months), but the exact mixture of internal or external strategies is still uncertain. What seems reasonable is that sessions that target both cognition and the practical application of strategies tend to help patients maintain higher levels of cognition and functioning (Hampstead et al., 2012; Troyer et al., 2008). It is also true that older adults who perform better in training tend to be more motivated, to have a higher baseline score, and to complete the training.

We now direct attention to computer-based interventions. The studies outlined in the following paragraphs vary based on degree of cognitive dysfunction, cognitive domains targeted in CT, and rigor of study. The majority of these computer-based studies report positive gains. The only study that did not report positive gains had a potential ceiling effect given that participants were recruited from a memory clinic and already were receiving CT (Gaitán et al., 2013). Some of these studies showed improvements in both control and treatment groups (Barnes et al., 2009; Gagnon & Belleville, 2012; Gaitán et al., 2013) that can be attributed to the control group interventions being similar to treatment group interventions or placebo. Improvement in cognition was shown to be maintained from 3 to 12 months posttreatment (Cipriani, Bianchetti, & Trabucchi, 2006; Eckroth-Bucher & Siberski, 2009; Gaitán et al., 2013; Günther et al., 2003; Johansson & Tornmalm, 2012; Loewenstein et al., 2004; Rozzini et al., 2007). The two studies that investigated CT, computer and noncomputer based, with individuals already taking ChEIs (Loewenstein et al., 2004; Rozzini et al., 2007) revealed positive effects in cognitive functioning.

In contrast, generalization of cognitive gains from computer-based CT was observed in only a few studies (Herrera, Chambon, Michel, Paban, & Alescio-Lautier, 2012; Johansson & Tornmalm, 2012; Westerberg et al., 2007), while not occurring in others (Ackerman, Kanfer, & Calderwood, 2010; Gagnon & Belleville, 2012). Authors who did not observe generalizations recommended that maintenance of cognitive abilities may require more long-term effort (Ackerman et al., 2010), and metacognition pertaining to training could assist with self-perception, goal setting, and attention (Gagnon & Belleville, 2012). Barnes et al. (2009) also suggested that motivation is a key factor in benefiting from CT.

Additionally, among studies that assessed affect, treatment groups demonstrated a decrease in depressive symptoms (Belleville et al., 2006; Rozzini et al., 2007), anxiety (Gaitán et al., 2013; Rozzini et al., 2007), apathy (Rozzini et al., 2007), and isolation (Belleville et al., 2006). There were also nonsignificant effects on mood (Günther et al., 2003). Overall, the utilization of computer-based CT demonstrated long-term positive changes in cognitive functioning for different levels of dysfunction, and positively influenced affect, with mixed results regarding generalization. Given that many newer computer-based CT programs are self-maintained, easily accessible to the public, and relatively affordable, this form of CT may be the wave of the future (see Table 13.2).

As might be expected, these studies are varied in method and rigor. Many have found changes in cognitive, affective, or function areas but not all (e.g., Finn & McDonald, 2011). Absolute conclusions cannot be made: Many techniques were taught as a package, making individual identification of effects impossible. Many also applied external techniques, suggesting that MCI patients can benefit from both internal and external techniques. In addition, many studies are nonrandomized or reviews. By way of summary, Jak et al. (2013) indicated that the available peer-reviewed literature suggests that computer and video game–based cognitive enhancement programs yield the most significant and robust improvements on trained tasks, for processing speed in particular. These results may generalize to untrained cognitive abilities; however, the complexity of the game or program as well as individual

TABLE 13.2

Computer-Based Training

Author	Population	Program	Intervention cognitive domains	Time frame	Results
Cipriani, Bianchetti, & Trabucchi, 2006	Adults: AD (10), MCI (10), Multiple System Atrophy (MSA) (2)	Multidimensional Software, NeuroPsychological Training (NPT) Software	Attention, memory, perception, visuospatial cognition, language, and nonverbal intelligence	13- to 45-min session, 4 d/wk, 4 weeks, completed twice	AD: most significant improvements in memory, perception, and attention at 3 month follow-up. MCI: significantly improved in working memory and psychomotor learning. MSA: no significant improvement.
Rozzini et al., 2007	59 Adults with MCI; TNP and Cholinesterase inhibitor [ChEIs] (n = 15), ChEIs only (n = 22), No treatment (n = 22), ra	Multidimensional Software, NeuroPsychological Training (NPT) Software	Memory, attention, language, abstract reasoning, visuospatial abilities	3 blocks of sessions spaced by 2-month break. Blocks: 20 sessions, 1 hr, 5 d/wk, 4 weeks	The group treated with ChEIs and TNP demonstrated improvement in episodic memory, abstract reasoning, depression, anxiety, and apathy at postintervention and at 3-month follow-up. The ChEIs group only demonstrated moderate improvements in depression.
Johansson & Tornmalm, 2012	18 Adults with acquired brain injury (TBI, Stroke, Tumor)	Cogmed QM	Attention, working memory; also includes coaching, peer support, and education	30–45 mins/d, 3 sessions/wk, 7–8 weeks	Improved occupational performance and decreased cognitive failures. Results were still present at 6-month follow-up. All had significant improvement on trained tasks. Socialization and peer support may have produced positive observed effects.
Westerberg et al., 2007	18 Adult stroke victims, TxG (n = 9), Passive CG group (n = 9), ra	TxG: Cogmed QM, CG: No intervention	Attention, working memory; also includes coaching, peer support, and education	40 mins/d, 5 d/wk, 5 weeks	TxG demonstrated improved working memory and attention; intervention affected the subjective experience of cognitive functioning in daily living.
Barnes et al., 2009	36 Adults with MCI, TxG (n = 17), CG (n = 19), ra	TxG: CBCT developed by Posit Science Corporation; CG: audio books, online newspapers, visuospatially oriented videogame	Attention, processing speed, verbal memory, visual processing	TxG: 90–100 mins/d, 5 d/wk until asymptotic performance or 80% of training material completed over several days; CG: 30 mins/task/day, 5 d/wk, ~2 months	All outcomes favored TxG, excluding language/visuospatial and visuospatial domains; no findings were statistically significant. CG tasks were similar between groups; potential confounded results.
Rosen, Sugiura, Kramer, Whitfield-Gabrieli, & Gabrieli, 2011	12 Adults with MCI, TxG (n = 6), CG (n = 6), ra	TxG: CBCT developed by Posit Science Corporation; CG: audio books, online newspapers, visuospatially oriented computer game	Attention, concentration, processing speed	TxG: 100 mins/d, 5 d/wk until asymptotic performance or 80% of training material completed over several days; CG: 30 mins/task/day, 5 d/wk, ~2 months	TxG had significant improvement in memory performance compared with CG. Left hippocampal activation gains were demonstrated in the TxG compared with the consistent loss of activation in the CG. Significant interaction between group, session, and specific location observed in the hippocampus. Functional MRI changes postintervention correlated with psychometric changes.

Citation	Sample	Intervention	Domains	Dosage	Results
Eckroth-Bucher & Siberski, 2009	32 Adults: impairment ranging from none to moderate; TxG (n = 15); waitlist CG (n = 17), ra	Cognitive Stimulation and Training Program (Sound Smart and Captain's Log), augmented with pencil-and-paper exercises	Attention, concentration, visuomotor, processing speed, memory, visual spatial processing, executive functioning	45 mins, 2 d/wk, 6 weeks	Significant improvement in dementia rating scores, short-term and delayed-memory, and verbal delayed recall with TxG. Effects were maintained 8 months postintervention
Haimov & Shatil, 2013	51 Older adults with insomnia; Cognitive training group (n = 34), Active control group (n = 17), ra	TxG: CogniFit; CG: computer exercises, no high-level cognitive engagement (Word and Paint)	Divided attention, concentration, processing speed, recognition, eye-hand coordination, short-term memory, contextual memory, long-term memory, naming, executive functioning, visual perception	Both groups: 20–30 min/session, 3 sessions/wk, 8 weeks	CBCT improved cognitive functioning and sleep quality. These improvements were not observed in the CG. Improvements in cognitive functioning predicted improvement in sleep quality. CBCT demonstrated improvement in avoiding distractions, naming, and memory. The CG demonstrated a significant decline in working memory.
Finn & McDonald, 2011	25 Adults with MCI, TxG (n = 8), waitlist CG (n = 8), ra	Lumosity	Attention, processing speed, visual memory, and cognitive control	4–5 sessions/wk, 30 sessions	Improved performance on trained tasks over time. Significant improvement in visual sustained attention that generalized outside of training.
Ackerman, Kanfer, & Calderwood, 2010	78 Middle-age adults (<70) with age-related cognitive decline	Wii Big Brain Academy (15 mini games), Reading activities (4 packets of newspaper and magazine articles)	Attention, concentration, recognition, processing speed, perceptual speed, visual working memory, working memory, categorical matching, spatial visualization, numerical computation, spatial orientation and integration, and psychomotor skills	Wii Big Brain Academy: 5 hr/wk, 4 weeks; Reading: 5 hr/d, 1 hr/d; Reading: 5 hr/wk, 4 weeks, different topic each week; 2 groups counterbalanced over 2-month period alternating interventions	Participants had significant improvement in Wii Big Brain Academy mini games. Topic knowledge based on readings was temporarily increased; attributed to participants' being highly engaged in acquiring and maintaining knowledge in the topics of the study. Practice effects were present in cognitive testing. No evidence of generalization.
Günther et al., 2003	19 Adults with age-associated memory impairment	Cognition I	Attention, visuomotor, reaction time, concentration, memory, verbal performance, general knowledge; mimic real-life tasks	One 45-min sessions/wk, 14 weeks	Significant improvement posttraining: verbal and visual, secondary and delayed memory, processing speed, learning, and interference tendency. Significant improvement in interference tendency and learning observed at 5 months postintervention. Self-rating of mood and subjective aging experience did not have significant effects.

(continues)

351

TABLE 13.2 (Continued)

Computer-Based Training

Author	Population	Program	Intervention cognitive domains	Time frame	Results
Gaitán et al., 2013	Adults with MCI/Mild AD, CBCT plus traditional cognitive training (TCT) (n = 23), TCT only (n = 15), ra	TCT: pencil-and-paper exercises; CBCT: FESKITS_Estimulacion Cognitiva, Version 2.5	TCT: attention, concentration, memory, language, calculation, gnosias and praxis, orientation; CBCT: attention, concentration, memory, executive function, perception and recognition, language, orientation	TCT: 1 hr, 2–3 d/wk, 12 weeks; CBCT: 1 hr (targeting each cognitive domain), 2–3 sessions/wk, 12 weeks, 30 sessions	CBCT + TCT group demonstrated to have larger effects on anxiety and decision-making ability at 12-month follow-up. The combined group did not demonstrate any significant effects in comparison to the TCT group. Effect sizes for all cognitive domains favored the combined group but were not statistically significant.
Herrera, Chambon, Michel, Paban, & Alescio-Lautier, 2012	22 Adults with MCI; Performance Training (PT) (n = 11); Simulating cognitive activities (SCA) (n = 11), ra	TxG (PT): CBCT developed on Java; CG (SCA): paper-and-pencil cognitive tasks	Both groups: attention, information processing, memory; treatment group: processing speed	24 1-hr training sessions	TxG had positive effects in memory and attention at varying levels based on time task performed (i.e., with or without distractions for recall tasks) that was not clinically significant. Level of cognitive functioning was maintained 6-months postintervention.
Gagnon & Belleville, 2012	24 Adults with MCI Variable Priority (VP) (n = 12), Fixed Priority (FP) (n = 12), ra	VP: attentional control, divided attention task, visual monitoring, performance feedback self-regulation strategy; FP: rote practice on the same divided attention task of VP training	Attention, concentration, processing speed	6 1-hr sessions, 3 sessions/wk, 2 weeks	Both training groups improved performance in focused and divided attention conditions. VP group demonstrated higher accuracy for divided attention. Effects did not generalize outside of training.
Belleville et al., 2006	25 Adults with MCI, 17 Healthy Adults, TxG (n = 17 MCI, 9 Healthy); Waitlist CG (n = 8 MCI, 8 Healthy)	Assigned to groups of 4–5 participants to complete an unspecified CBCT that included pretraining on stress, self-efficacy, or imagery	Attention, processing speed, memory	120 min sessions, 8 weekly sessions (first session was an overview)	Significant intervention effect in delayed list recall and face–name association; significant improvement in subjective memory and well-being. TxG had reduction in depression and isolation levels. Subjects recruited from memory clinics.

Note. CBCT = computer-based cognitive training; TxG = treatment group; CG = control group; MCI = mild cognitive impairment; AD = Alzheimer's disease; mins/d = minutes per day, d/wk = days per week; ra = random assignment.

factors play a large role. In sum, one can say that the data are promising regarding computer-based CT and any side effects are minimal, but any commercial claims of the efficacy of computerized cognitive enhancement systems is perhaps premature (Jak et al., 2013).

Lifestyle

Perhaps the biggest component of positive change in late life is engagement in intellectually and socially stimulating activities (e.g., reading books, puzzles, volunteer work, traveling, card games, etc.). These activities have been shown to enhance thinking and memory, and attention control processes, thereby increasing brain reserve capacity (e.g., Carlson et al., 2009; Fabrigoule et al., 1995; Schooler, Mulatu, & Oates, 1999; Staff, Murray, Deary, & Whalley, 2004; Wang, Karp, Winblad, & Fratiglioni, 2002). Using data from the Cache County Dementia Progression Study, Treiber et al. (2011) showed an interaction between dementia duration and number of activities in predicting cognitive decline. This is one of several studies that suggest that older adults with a dementia can have the trajectory of the disease "improved" over time with cognitive stimulation. In a 6-week program addressing not only memory but also healthy lifestyle issues, Miller et al. (2012) showed that encoding and recall of new verbal information had improved as well as self-perceptions of memory ability in older adults with memory problems residing in the community.

Other programs have been applied with success with more impaired older adults, including those with dementia. Notably, these studies involved caregivers (Carlson et al., 2008; Logsdon et al., 2010; Zarit, Femia, Kim, & Whitlack, 2010). A growing body of research seems to show that support groups for patients in early stages of the disease can be beneficial (e.g., Goldsilver & Gruneir, 2001; Snyder, Bower, Arneson, Sheperd, & Quayhagen, 1994; Snyder, Jenkins, & Joosten, 2007). Logsdon et al. (2010) demonstrated the utility of a holistic approach in overall cognitive health. This approach involves the caregiver, as well as other family members, and focuses on psychoeducation, behavioral activation, and monitoring of targeted problem areas. These more "holistic" approaches often

provide benefits that extend beyond attention and WM if applied to complex goal-directed activity (Basak et al., 2008; Stine-Morrow et al., 2008). In addition, general environmental enrichment (occupation, leisure, complexity in life, mental training) and a health focus, notably enhanced cardiovascular health and neurocognitive function (Hertzog, Kramer, Wilson, & Linderberger, 2008), as well as exercise (Kramer, Erickson, & Colcombe, 2006), can have a large impact. Several years ago, Albert et al. (1995) in the MacArthur Studies of Successful Aging noted that genetics may account for only a third of AD risk, with the rest dependent on nongenetic factors, suggesting a major role for lifestyle modification in preventing AD. Lifestyle factors influence brain health and aging. Human studies show that chronic stress, leads to an increased risk for dementia, depression, and poorer health (Small, 2013). Lavretsky (2013) showed that relaxation or meditation affects biomarkers of inflammation and telomerase activity. Mediterranean diets high in omega-3 fatty acids improve WM (Narendran, Frankle, Mason, Muldoon, & Moghaddam, 2012) and reduce the risk for MCI (Scarmeas, Stern, et al., 2009) and AD (Scarmeas, Luchsinger, & Schupf, 2009). Antioxidant-rich fruits and vegetables improve cognition while refined sugars and transfats impair it (Parrott & Greenwood, 2007). Moderate alcohol use—defined in many studies as up to one drink per day for women and up to two drinks per day for men—also is associated with better brain health, possibly due to both relaxation effects and, in the case of red wine, high levels of the antiaging compound resveratrol (Small, 2013). Finally, weight management also plays a major role in brain health. Several studies support an association between being overweight and increased dementia risk, including a recent twin study that controlled for sex, education, diabetes, hypertension, stroke, and heart disease (Xu et al., 2011). This same conclusion applies to brain injuries across the life span (Small et al., 2013).

In our clinic we place special emphasis on diet, exercise, meditation and relaxation, stress reduction, and religion or socialization, in addition to a focus on memory (Hyer, Scott, Lyles, Dhabliwala, & McKenzie, 2014). We applied a holistic CT model to a variety of older adults with abilities ranging from normal cognition to mild dementia. We targeted memory as the core issue and taught a concentration method in the style of Small et al. (2013), while adding one of the lifestyle components in Table 13.3 for each group. Older adults universally appreciated these tasks and, given assistance, were able to comply with the memory intervention and one or more of the lifestyle components. Results were positive for cognition, affect, and quality of life. We identify representative and often-cited articles or summaries on the major areas of lifestyle input for healthy living and cognitive benefit (see Table 13.3).

Special Issues

Several issues related to CT with older adults are difficult to assess or control for. This especially applies to the training of WM, perhaps the most sensitive marker of cognitive decline and identified as one of the main factors underlying cognitive impairment in old age and in dementia (Bäckman, Jones, Berger, Laukka, & Small, 2005; Bäckman & Small, 2007; Baddeley, Bressi, Della Sala, Logie, & Spinnler, 1991; Craik & Bialystok, 2006; Salthouse & Babcock, 1991). WM previously was defined as a mental workspace that is capacity limited (Morrison & Chein, 2011). Early models of WM posited the existence of material-specific slave systems under the management of an active manipulation component (Baddeley & Hitch, 1974). More recent models have proposed a single memory store in which specific information can be brought up into WM (e.g., Cowan, 2005). WM generally refers to active "online" and short-term maintenance of information in the service of more complex tasks, such as mental arithmetic, language comprehension, planning, or problem solving (Cowan, 2005; Shah & Miyake, 1999).

Whatever the case, WM asserts a general influence over other cognitive spheres. Training in WM affects individual differences in executive function (Engle, Kane, & Tuholski, 1999), language acquisition (Baddeley, 2003), reading comprehension (Chein & Morrison, 2010; Daneman & Carpenter, 1980), problem solving (Logie, Gilhooly, & Wynn, 1994), reasoning (Kane et al., 2004), cognitive control (Klingberg et al., 2005; Klingberg, Forssberg, & Westerberg, 2002), speed of processing (Ball et al.,

2002), attention (e.g., Bherer et al., 2008; Smith et al., 2009), and fluid intelligence (Jaeggi, Buschkuehl, Jonides, & Perrig, 2008). In a few studies, WM training extended beyond the context of cognitive performance and translated into benefits in ADLs (e.g., Willis et al., 2006). To date, only a few studies have investigated the effects of WM training in older adults, generally healthy subjects (see Borella, Carretti, Zanoni, Zavagnin, & De Beni, 2013). On the basis of the type of task used in training, the nature of the training (verbal, visual, spatial, combined), the duration of training, the condition of subjects (age and health), and use of an active control group, results vary. Virtually all studies, however, reported gains in the trained task and some (e.g., Borella, Carretti, Riboldi, & De Beni, 2010; Borella et al., 2013) showed gains in transfer tasks.

WM then may serve as a domain-general cognitive resource that modulates ability in a number of seemingly disparate areas of cognitive performance. Exhibit 13.2 summarizes four problem areas involving CT and impaired older adults. Although most of these areas have been applied to WM, they all involve episodic and semantic memory. Each of these areas represents complications in CT outcome research to varying degrees and by itself can be a topic for further study.

ASSESSMENT

The holy grail of assessment for MCI and dementia is the identification of patients in the earliest stage of a disorder (e.g., MCI or prior) before the clinical manifestation of a dementia to provide effective early intervention to delay significant impairment. Of course, a definitive diagnosis of AD requires a detailed postmortem microscopic examination of the brain. That said, AD can be diagnosed with more than 95% accuracy in living patients by using a combination of tools. These include taking a careful history from patients and their families, magnetic resonance imaging scans, functioning assessment, and an evaluation of cognitive function by neuropsychological tests (Hyer, 2013; Smith & Bondi, 2013). Other causes of cognitive impairment must be ruled out, such as low thyroid function, vitamin deficiencies, infections, cancer, and depression. It is

TABLE 13.3

Lifestyle Components

Lifestyle area	Author	Population	Findings
Mediterranean diet	Solfrizzi et al., 2011	Alzheimer's and MCI	The critical review of the literature that included 84,041 participants, demonstrated that individuals who had higher adherence to the Mediterranean diet have a trend for reduced risk of developing MCI and progression from MCI to Alzheimer's disease. The diet also is associated with slower cognitive decline and lowered risk of mortality in AD patients. Findings are inconsistent in relation to protectant agents of specific components within the diet.
Physical activity	Hamer & Chida, 2009	Neurodegenerative disease	The systematic review included 163,797 participants who presented to be free of neurodegeneration at baseline; of which 3,219 cases developed. Results showed relative risk factor of dementia diagnosis, including AD, that was clinically significant when the highest level of physical activity was compared with lowest level. The findings were more robust for men. Physical activity was found to reduce the risk of dementia and AD by 28% and 45%, respectively.
Physical activity	Sofi et al., 2011	Cognitive decline	The meta-analysis included 33,816 participants without dementia at baseline who were followed for 1–12 years; 3,210 participants demonstrated cognitive decline at follow-up. Those who had a high level of physical activity were as well as low-to-moderate levels of exercise had significant protection compared to those with sedentary lifestyles. Effects of physical activity demonstrated to be stronger for women.
Meditation	Zeidan, Johnson, Diamond, David, & Goolkasian, 2010	Attention and executive functioning	Prior research has demonstrated the positive effects of long-term mediation in areas including attention and executive functioning. Brief mindfulness in as little as four sessions in the current study resulted in positive effects in mood, mindfulness, reduction in anxiety, and fatigue. The brief mindfulness significantly improved visuospatial processing, working memory, and executive functioning.
Spirituality and meditation	Newberg, 2011	Aging	Neurophysiological studies have shown that changes in brain functioning are associated with religious and spiritual practices. The specific tasks associated with these activities require sustained attention that stimulates specific areas of the brain. Practices also produce higher rates of neurotransmitters that improve mood. The literature review states those who participate in these practices have higher rates of hope, self-monitoring, and reasoning and have a reduction in anxiety, depression, anger, and fatigue. Results also show improved attention, cognitive flexibility, and memory and increased efficiency in executive attention.
Religion	Kaufman, Anaki, Binns, & Freeman, 2007	Alzheimer's disease	The study analyzed 70 individuals with probable Alzheimer's disease. A slower rate of cognitive decline was associated with higher levels of spirituality and private religious practices when level of cognition, age, sex, and education were controlled for. The results showed that attendance of religious services was not associated with the rate of AD progression; possibly due to difficulties with mobility. Spirituality was nonsignificantly correlated with quality of life.

(continues)

TABLE 13.3 (*Continued*)

Lifestyle Components

Lifestyle area	Author	Population	Findings
Social network	Crooks, Lubben, Petitti, Little, & Chiu, 2008	Dementia	Previous research suggests social support networks may have positive effects on cognition and could serve as a protective factor in the development of dementia. The study analyzed 2,249 members of a health maintenance organization who were free of dementia. Over the course of 1 year, 12% of individuals developed dementia at follow-up. Those with daily social contact and larger social networks had lower rates of dementia diagnoses. The lowered risk was maintained after controlling for age, education, depression, and other health conditions.
Social network	Bennett, Schneider, Tang, Arnold, & Wilson, 2006	Alzheimer's disease	Medical findings support findings that social networks have an inverse relationship with cognitive decline. The present study analyzed individuals postmortem to confirm Alzheimer's disease diagnosis. The participants did not present with dementia at baseline and were thoroughly assessed each year for cognitive functioning. The study analyzed premorbid social networks in relation to pathology and cognition. Results demonstrated social network size altered cognitive functioning, most notably for semantic and working memory.
Stress	Depp, Vahia, & Jeste, 2010	Elderly adults	This in-depth annual review of the literature discusses the mechanisms of aging and the heightened responsiveness to stress in brain functioning in elderly adults that can lead to overactivation of the hypothalamic-pituitary-adrenal (HPA) axis. When chronically overactivated, the HPA produces neurochemicals that can result in damage to critical brain regions that can affect memory. Dysregulation of the HPA has been found to be correlated with decreased cognitive functioning and increases in anxiety and depression. Stress can lead to inflammation and the diminishment of immune system functioning. Chronic stress has the potential to alter chromosomes that protect against cell death. Low levels of stress produced by activities, such as exercising, cognitive stimulation, caloric restriction, have resulted in positive changes in the brains of elderly adults, including neuroplasticity.

crucial to differentiate AD from other neurodegenerative dementias.

Whatever the amalgam of biomarkers or psychological tests given, memory and function add incremental validity and perhaps encompass the most variance accounting for later brain assays in determining a dementia (see Hyer, 2014). Neuropsychological testing of cognitive problems for diagnosis or use of CT is important. Importantly, testing should not be lengthy, (except for a research protocol). Table 13.4 presents a partial listing of typical screens. All of these measures possess acceptable levels of correct classification ratios for normal function versus dementia. The

psychometric markers for MCI are less robust. Efficacy increases measurably in combination with other scales, interviews, biomarkers, and function evaluations.

TREATMENT

We summarize the results of one study using a computer-based intervention, Cogmed, conducted at our clinic (Hyer, 2014). Cogmed training is a software product (Cogmed QM) that can be used at a clinic or at home on a computer. The intervention software involves intense and adaptive computerized training on various verbal and nonverbal WM tasks. All tasks involve the following: (a) maintenance of

---

Exhibit 13.2
Special Problems of Cognitive Training

Durability: Studies of older adults have shown promise as long as 2 years (Ball et al., 2002) and extending out to 5 years (Oswald, Gunzelmann, Rupprecht, & Hagen, 2006; Wolinsky et al., 2009). Unverzagt et al. (2007) revealed the effects of CT on speed of processing after 2 years. This occurred with booster sessions. Minor effects were noted for specific training in memory over time (Jean et al., 2007). Simon et al. (2012) trained amnestic MCI (aMCI) participants showing effects over time, using booster sessions.

Function: CT can have a beneficial impact on function and neuropsychiatric symptoms. Sitzer et al. (2006) found that CT has a medium effect size in multiple functional domains, including activities of daily living (ADLs) and self-rated general functioning. Other studies (Kurz et al., 2009; Rozzini et al., 2007) have supported this finding as well as for quality of life (Belleville et al., 2006) and goal attainment changes (Clare et al., 2010). Performance-based tasks are recommended (Acevedo & Loewenstein, 2007).

Self-regulation: Self-regulatory factors in training improvement (Bissig & Lustig, 2007; Lachman Weaver, Bandura, Elliott, & Lewkowicz, 1992; Rebok & Balcerak, 1989; Valentijn et al., 2005). West and Hastings (2011) emphasized that successful training outcomes depend on self-regulation. Largely, this involves aspects of self-control and self-efficacy.

Brain reserve: This represents protective brain areas due to life skills, like intelligence, occupational complexity, "thick" leisure, computer games, less stress, and healthy living. Adults with more education, for example, can have more brain problems (degeneration) to show the same level of cognitive burden as someone with less education (or less brain reserve). Required for brain reserve are markers of brain deterioration, cognition assessment, and a marker of reserve.

---

multiple stimuli at the same time, (b) short delays during which the representation of stimuli should be held in WM, (c) unique sequencing of stimuli order in each trial, and (d) the difficulty level adapting as a function of individual performance.

The present study is representative of other similar clinical trials but directly addresses MCI in older adults. Currently, more than 40 studies are published on Cogmed (see http://www.cogmed.com). These studies largely have addressed attention deficit problems, mostly in children. Recent studies using Cogmed or Cogmed-like tasks have shown that training on WM leads to improvements on trained tasks and, for some studies, also generalizes to improvements on tasks that are not part of the training. Research on older adults, however, has been limited to only a few studies on community samples (Brehmer, Westerberg, & Bäckman, 2012; McNab et al., 2009; Olesen, Westerberg, & Klingberg, 2004), on adults after stroke (Westerberg et al., 2007), or cognitive problems as a result of brain injury (Johansson & Tornmalm, 2012; Westerberg et al., 2007).

Older adults ($N = 68$) living in the community were assessed. All participants had memory complaints and demonstrated memory impairment during initial screening (Delayed Recall Memory Index, Repeatable Battery for the Assessment of Neuropsychological Status; Randolph, 1998), but they had normal Mini-Mental State Examination (Folstein, Folstein, & McHugh, 1975), ADLs, and instrumental ADLs (IADLs). They met criteria for MCI—that is, they were a standard deviation below the mean on Delayed Recall. Other neuropsychological domains were generally in the average range. Participants were randomized to either Cogmed or to a sham cognitive program. The sham training involved training with the same software but with no adaptivity—the difficulty level remained constant across the intervention period. A total of twenty-five 45-min sessions were completed over 5–7 weeks.

Importantly, both groups (Cogmed and the sham) had a coach, a person who ensured that the tasks were being done properly and who used verbal rewards as part of the process. Coaches were a spouse or significant other (82%), an adult child (16%), or a good friend (2%). Both groups also had a study coach who assisted the caregiver coach, and monitored the results daily, allowing an immediate response to the day's results. This study coach generally interacted with the significant other coach on a weekly basis, ensuring that the tasks were complied with and that the data markers uploaded were accurate.

Pre-, post-, and 3-month follow-up measures included a battery of cognitive and functional markers. Table 13.5 presents data on three core cognitive measures that represent more difficult cognitive tasks and a functional scale that addresses more complex problem solving. The three cognitive scales were Trail Making B (Reitan & Wolfson, 1993),

---

TABLE 13.4

Assessments

Assessment	Cognitive domains assessed	Description
Cognistat (Kiernan, Mueller, & Langston, 1995)	Global cognition, orientation, attention, visuospatial or perceptual ability, language fluency and expression, auditory memory, executive functioning	The assessment typically takes 10–30 min to complete, dependent on the individual's level of cognitive functioning. This screening measure is broken down into 10 different subsections in which the individual's level of functioning can be interpreted separately. Each subsection has a screening measure that has the most difficult tasks presented first. If answered correctly, the subsequent tasks are credited. Several of the separate domains are similar to neuropsychological assessments: Digit Span, Similarities, and a three-step command. One particular benefit of this assessment is the inclusion of the Judgment subsection, not typical of screening measures. This can be utilized to assess cognitive changes.
Dementia Rating Scale-2 (Mattis, 2001)	Global cognition, attention, initiation/perseveration, construction, conceptualization, memory	The measure takes 15–30 minutes to administer that is used to assess cognitive changes over time. Each domain presents with a screening measure with the most difficult task of that domain. If answered correctly, subsequent tasks on the subscale are credited to shorten administration time.
MiniCog (Borson et al., 2000)	Visuoperceptual or perceptual ability, language fluency & expression	This is a brief tool used to assess presence of cognitive dysfunction that would warrant further testing. The 3 min measure consists of a three-item recall and a clock-drawing test. Anything other than a perfect score on recall warrants further assessment.
Montreal Cognitive Assessment (MoCA; Nasreddine et al., 2005)	Global cognition, orientation, attention, visuospatial or perceptual ability, language fluency and expression, auditory memory, executive functioning	The screen was developed to assess for mild cognitive impairment. The test takes approximately 10 min to administer, dependent of the individual's level of cognitive functioning. The MoCA includes features of popular screening instruments including a shortened form of Trail Making B and the Clock-Drawing test. The assessment is separated by cognitive domain, but can only be interpreted based on the total score. This can be utilized to assess cognitive changes.
Repeatable Battery for the Assessment for Neuropsychological Status (Randolph, 1998)	Global cognition, attention, visuospatial or perceptual ability, language fluency and expression, auditory memory, visual memory, executive functioning	The screening instrument was originally developed to assess potential dementia, but has since been utilized for more general practice. The 10 subsections contribute to 5 index scores and a total score. Each index is interpreted as a standard score and comparable to the normative data. The measure typically can be completed within 30 min. The assessment includes several facets found in neuropsychological assessments, including the Judgment Line Orientation, Complex Figure, Digit Span, and Coding. This can be utilized to assess cognitive changes.
Saint Louis University Mental Status (Tariq, Tumosa, Chibnall, Perry, & Morley, 2006)	Global cognition, orientation, attention, visuospatial or perceptual ability, auditory memory, language fluency and expression, executive functioning	The assessment typically takes 10–15 min to administer and was developed to assess potential mild cognitive impairment and dementia. The SLUMS also includes the Clock-Drawing test. The total score categorizes individuals into one of three cognitive domains based on education level; those below the normal range are to be further assessed for proper diagnosis. The measure has been found to be more sensitive than the MMSE.
Trail Making Test— Part B (Army Individual Test Battery, 1944)	Attention, visuospatial or perceptual ability, executive functioning	This is a brief assessment of executive functioning that requires the individual to connect dots in ascending order switching back and forth from number to letter. Norms have been developed to determine cognitive dysfunction. On the basis of higher times of completion, further assessment would be warranted to develop a thorough understanding of the dysfunction. This is a reliable measure of several neuropsychological markers of cognition, including speed of processing, sequencing, and general executive functioning.

Note. MMSE = Mini-Mental State Examination.

	TABLE 13.5		
Means and Standard Deviations of Core Cognitive Measures			
	Mean Scores Over Time		
Scales	**Pre (SD)**	**Post (SD)**	**3-month Follow-up (SD)**
Trails B			
Cogmed	132.38 (47.92)	118.92 (43.49)	102.92 (32.98)
Sham	133.97 (41.56)	112.57 (39.74)	112.87 (32.15)
WAIS–III LNS			
Cogmed	9.63 (3.13)	10.90 (2.38)	10.83 (3.02)
Sham	10.00 (2.85)	10.53 (2.46)	10.37 (2.50)
WMS–III Span Board			
Cogmed	8.79 (2.48)	11.54 (3.37)	12.13 (3.46)
Sham	9.73 (3.10)	10.77 (3.07)	10.63 (3.12)
FAQ			
Cogmed	1.72 (3.59)	1.83 (3.47)	1.33 (3.18)
Sham	2.06 (2.49)	1.82 (2.79)	3.12 (4.53)

Note. FAQ = Functional Adjustment Sale; LNS = Letter Number Sequencing; WAIS–III = Wechsler Adult Intelligence Scale; WMS = Wechsler Memory Scale

Wechsler Memory Scale–Third Edition Span Board (Wechsler, 1997b), and Wechsler Adult Intelligence Scale–Third Edition Letter Number Sequencing (Wechsler, 1997a), and the functional scale was the Functional Adjustment Questionnaire (FAQ; Pfeffer, Kurosaki, Harrah, Chance, & Filos, 1982).

The intervention groups had similar scores before treatment. Both improved over time. Cogmed was superior to sham at posttest (3 months) on the core WM measures. However, only on the Span Board was there a significant interaction at posttest, suggesting that Cogmed outperformed sham due to the Cogmed training itself. Importantly, Cogmed was superior to sham on adjustment (FAQ). FAQ was significant because Cogmed remained the same while the sham group declined in adjustment. Interestingly, although both groups liked their intervention, Cogmed subjects liked their intervention more than those assigned to the sham group. Means and standard deviations are given in Table 13.5.

In the first study using Cogmed with an MCI population, we found that the intervention was superior to an active control condition on one WM task and on adjustment. Adjustment is considered a "far transfer" indicator in CT and indicates improvement in important IADLs. Participants in the control condition improved as well, which is consistent with other research on MCI patients (Rebok et al., 2012). The fact that between-group differences were not evident until 3 months following the end of treatment suggests that the mechanism may involve learning as opposed to the effects of attention.

Noteworthy is that some type of CT made a difference to subjects who had MCI, a difficult study group. Perhaps any structured CT, given some belief and acceptance, can make a difference. When analyses were run controlling for occupation and education, the pattern of results did not change, suggesting that cognitive reserve was probably not a factor in these findings. Thus, overall, this study provides additional evidence that CT can have a positive effect on older adults with MCI.

CONCLUSION

Scientists are not going to solve the problem of recovery from brain damage to the brain with cellular, molecular or pharmaceutical treatments alone. We're going to have to figure out how to get learning to occur in combination with that, whether it is cognitive, sensory, or motor learning.

Elissa Newport (2013)

Overall, CT appears to show some benefit for cognitively impaired older adults. Although all forms of CT appear to have some impact, CT targeting WM appears to achieve the best results, as does CT used with less impaired older adults (i.e., those with MCI rather than dementia). Furthermore, older adults seem to appreciate CT. In an important summary, Valenzuela and Sachdev (2009) placed some perspective here: Activities that combine cognitive, social, and physical exercise are likely to be the most appealing combination of interventions leading to a reduction in dementia risk. The cognitive tasks would include a broad array of cognitive domains including drill and practice approach.

Moderators include education and social, mental, or physical stimulation, such that individuals with these factors appear to respond better to CT than those with lower levels of education or stimulation. Mediators and mechanisms of CT include complex learning engagement (Nyberg et al., 2012). The appropriate dosage of CT has not been determined; many studies with shorter trainings have proven to be as effective as those with more extensive training periods (see Buschkuehl et al., 2008). On the basis of previous studies it is reasonable to speculate further that caregivers who are engaged in the active support of the patient can make a significant difference. An ecosystem of positive lifestyle support, especially involving CT, optimizes compliance and possible success. It may take a village to keep older adults healthy and active.

Implied in this chapter is the importance of a geropsychologist. The roles of this person have changed over time and now are expanding as well as intermixing with other professions. Competencies have expanded and now have a wide birth and a long view. The geropsychologist is a key person with a vision of health care and skills in the core components for the care of older adult, including assessment, treatment, consultation, and research. Older adults come with a panorama of problems, such as depression, anxiety, cognitive impairment, poor health, and problems in daily living. Each person possesses a profile of these issues. We (Hyer, 2014) have promulgated the "watch and wait" model in which the

geropsychologist practices in a broad manner, slowly organizing care, and monitoring change. The belief is that a careful and slow process of care—assessment, psychoeducation, trust building, team application, and focused psychosocial modules—can make a difference in the unique profile of each older adult. CT is a necessary part of this process.

Increasing evidence has suggested that several techniques can make a difference in the outcomes of older adults with impairment. CT is certainly in this mix and seems to be helpful for older adults with MCI (or early dementia). Time and research will unfold the full story and impact. For now, the picture looks more upbeat.

References

Acevedo, A., & Loewenstein, D. A. (2007). Non-pharmacological cognitive interventions in aging and dementia. *Journal of Geriatric Psychiatry and Neurology, 20,* 239–249. doi:10.1177/08919887 07308808

Ackerman, P. L., Kanfer, R., & Calderwood, C. (2010). Use it or lose it? Wii brain exercise practice and reading for domain knowledge. *Psychology and Aging, 25,* 753–766. doi:10.1037/a0019277

Akhtar, S., Moulin, C. J., & Bowie, P. C. (2006). Are people with mild cognitive impairment aware of the benefits of errorless learning? *Neuropsychological Rehabilitation, 16,* 329–346. doi:10.1080/09602010 500176674

Albert, M. S., Jones, K., Savage, C. R., Berkman, L., Seeman, T., Blazer, D., & Rowe, J. W. (1995). Predictors of cognitive change in older persons: MacArthur studies of successful aging. *Psychology and Aging, 10,* 578–589. doi:10.1037/0882-7974.10. 4.578

Alzheimer's Association. (2012). *Alzheimer's disease facts and figures.* Retrieved from http://www.alz.org/downloads/facts_figures_2012.pdf

American Psychiatric Association. (2013). *Diagnostic and statistical manual of mental disorders* (5th Ed.). Washington, DC: Author.

Army Individual Test Battery. (1944). *Manual of directions and scoring.* Washington, DC: War Department, Adjutant General's Office.

Bäckman, L., & Dixon, R. A. (1992). Psychological compensation: A theoretical framework. *Psychological Bulletin, 112,* 259–283. doi:10.1037/0033-2909.112. 2.259

Bäckman, L., Jones, S., Berger, A. K., Laukka, E. J., & Small, B. J. (2005). Cognitive impairment in preclinical

Alzheimer's disease: A meta-analysis. *Neuropsychology*, *19*, 520–531.

Bäckman, L., & Small, B. J. (2007). Cognitive deficits in preclinical Alzheimer's disease and vascular dementia: Patterns of findings from the Kungsholmen Project. *Physiology and Behavior*, *92*, 80–86. doi:10.1016/j.physbeh.2007.05.014

Baddeley, A. D. (2003). Working memory and language: An overview. *Journal of Communication Disorders*, *36*, 189–208. doi:10.1016/S0021-9924(03)00019-4

Baddeley, A. D., Bressi, S., Della Sala, S., Logie, R., & Spinnler, H. (1991). The decline of working memory in Alzheimer's disease. A longitudinal study. *Brain: A Journal of Neurology*, *114*, 2521–2542. doi:10.1093/brain/114.6.2521

Baddeley, A. D., & Hitch, G. J. (1974). Working memory. In G. H. Bower (Ed.), *The psychology of learning and motivation* (Vol. 8, pp. 47–89). London, England: Academic Press.

Ball, K., Berch, D. B., Helmers, K. F., Jobe, J. B., Leveck, M. D., Marsiske, M., . . . Willis, S. L. (2002). Effects of cognitive training interventions with older adults: A randomized controlled trial. *JAMA*, *288*, 2271–2281. doi:10.1001/jama.288.18.2271

Barnes, D. E., Yaffe, K., Belfor, N., Jagust, W., Decarli, C., Reed, B., . . . Kramer, J. (2009). Computer-based cognitive training for mild cognitive impairment: Results from a pilot randomized controlled trial. *Alzheimer Disease and Associated Disorders*, *23*, 205–210. doi:10.1097/WAD.0b013e31819c6137

Basak, C., Boot, W. R., Voss, M. W., & Kramer, A. F. (2008). Can training in a real-time strategy video-game attenuate cognitive decline in older adults? *Psychology and Aging*, *23*, 765–777. doi:10.1037/a0013494

Belleville, S. (2008). Cognitive training for persons with mild cognitive impairment. *International Psychogeriatrics*, *20*, 57–66. doi:10.1017/S104161020700631X

Belleville, S., Clément, F., Mellah, S., Gilbert, B., Fontaine, F., & Gauthier, S. (2011). Training-related brain plasticity in subjects at risk of developing Alzheimer's disease. *Brain: A Journal of Neurology*, *134*, 1623–1634. doi:10.1093/brain/awr037

Belleville, S., Gilbert, B., Fontaine, F., Gagnon, L., Ménard, É., & Gauthier, S. (2006). Improvement of episodic memory in persons with mild cognitive impairment and healthy older adults: Evidence from a cognitive intervention program. *Dementia and Geriatric Cognitive Disorders*, *22*, 486–499. doi:10.1159/000096316

Bennett, D. A., Schneider, J., Tang, Y., Arnold, S., & Wilson, R. (2006). The effect of social networks on the relation between Alzheimer's disease pathology and level of cognitive function in old people: A longitudinal cohort study. *Lancet Neurology*, *5*, 406–412. doi:10.1016/S1474-4422(06)70417-3

Bherer, L., Kramer, A. F., Peterson, M. S., Colcombe, S., Erickson, K., & Becic, E. (2008). Transfer effects in task-set cost and dual-task cost after dual-task training in older and younger adults: Further evidence for cognitive plasticity in attentional control in late adulthood. *Experimental Aging Research*, *34*, 188–219. doi:10.1080/03610730802070068

Bissig, D., & Lustig, C. (2007). Who benefits from psychological training? *Psychological Science*, *18*, 720–726. doi:10.1111/j.1467-9280.2007.01966.x

Borella, E., Carretti, B., Riboldi, F., & De Beni, R. (2010). Working memory training in older adults: Evidence of transfer and maintenance effects. *Psychology and Aging*, *25*, 767–778.

Borella, E., Carretti, B., Zanoni, G., Zavagnin, M., & De Beni, R. (2013). Working memory training in old age: An examination of transfer and maintenance effects. *Archives of Clinical Neuropsychology*, *28*, 331–347. doi:10.1093/arclin/act020

Boripuntakul, S., Kothan, S., Methapatara, P., Munkhetvit, P., & Sungkarat, S. (2012). Short-term effects of cognitive training program for individuals with amnestic mild cognitive impairment: A pilot study. *Physical and Occupational Therapy in Geriatrics*, *30*, 138–149. doi:10.3109/02703181.2012.657822

Borson, S., Scanlan, J., Brush, M., Vitaliano, P., & Dokmak, A. (2000). The Mini-Cog: A cognitive "vital signs" measure for dementia screening in multilingual elderly. *International Journal of Geriatric Psychiatry*, *15*, 1021–1027.

Bourgeois, M. S., Camp, C., Rose, M., White, B., Malone, M., Carr, J., . . . Rovine, M. (2003). A comparison of training strategies to enhance use of external aids by persons with dementia. *Journal of Communication Disorders*, *36*, 361–378. doi:10.1016/S0021-9924(03)00051-0

Brehmer, Y., Westerberg, H., & Bäckman, L. (2012). Working-memory training in younger and older adults: Training gains, transfer, and maintenance. *Frontiers in Human Neuroscience*, *6*, 1–7. doi:10.3389/fnhum.2012.00063

Brooks, L. G., & Loewenstein, D. A. (2010). Assessing the progression of mild cognitive impairment to Alzheimer's disease: Current trends and future directions. *Alzheimer's Research and Therapy*, *2*, 28. doi:10.1186/alzrt52

Bryck, R. L., & Fisher, P. A. (2012). Training the brain: Practical applications of neural plasticity from the intersection of cognitive neuroscience, developmental psychology, and prevention science. *American Psychologist*, *67*, 87–100. doi:10.1037/a0024657

Buschert, V. C., Friese, U., Teipel, S. J., Schneider, P., Merensky, W., Rujescu, D., . . . Buerger, K. (2011). Effects of a newly developed cognitive intervention in amnestic mild cognitive impairment and mild Alzheimer's disease: A Pilot Study. *Journal of Alzheimer's Disease, 25*, 679–694.

Buschkuehl, M., Jaeggi, S. M., Hutchison, S., Perrig-Chiello, P., Däpp, C., Müller, M., . . . Perrig, W. J. (2008). Impact of working memory training on memory performance in old-old adults. *Psychology and Aging, 23*, 743–753. doi:10.1037/a0014342

Camp, C. J. (2005). Spaced retrieval: A model for dissemination of cognitive intervention for persons with dementia. In D. K. Attix & K. A. Welsh-Bohmer (Eds.), *Geriatric Neuropsychology: Assessment and Intervention* (pp. 275–292). New York, NY: Guilford Press.

Carlson, M. C., Saczynski, J. S., Rebok, G. W., Seeman, T., Glass, T. A., McGill, S., . . . Fried, L. (2008). Exploring the effects of an "everyday" activity program on executive function and memory in older adults: Experience Corps. *Gerontologist, 48*, 793–801. doi:10.1093/geront/48.6.793

Carlson, M. C., Erickson, K. I., Kramer, A. F., Voss, M. W., Bolea, N., Mielke, M., . . . Fried, L. P. (2009). Evidence for neurocognitive plasticity in at-risk older adults: The experience corps program. *The Journals of Gerontology, Series A: Biological Sciences and Medical Sciences, 64*, 1275–1282. doi:10.1093/gerona/glp117

Centers for Disease Control and Prevention. (2011). *Healthy brain initiative.* Retrieved from http://www.cdc.gov/aging/healthybrain/roadmap.htm

Chein, J. M., & Morrison, A. (2010). Expanding the mind's workspace: Training and transfer effects with a complex working memory span task. *Psychonomic Bulletin and Review, 17*, 193–199. doi:10.3758/PBR.17.2.193

Cipriani, G., Bianchetti, A., & Trabucchi, M. (2006). Outcomes of a computer-based cognitive rehabilitation program on Alzheimer's disease patients compared with those on patients affected by mild cognitive impairment. *Archives of Gerontology and Geriatrics, 43*, 327–335. doi:10.1016/j.archger.2005.12.003

Clare, L. (2008). Cognitive rehabilitation and cognitive training for early-stage Alzheimer's disease and vascular dementia. *Cochrane Database of Systematic Reviews, 4*, CD003260. doi:10.1002/14651858.CD003260

Clare, L., Linden, D., Woods, R., Whitaker, R., Evans, S., Parkinson, C., . . . Rugg, M. (2010). Goal-oriented cognitive rehabilitation for people with early-stage Alzheimer disease: A single-blind randomized controlled trial of clinical efficacy. *American Journal of Geriatric Psychiatry, 18*, 928–939. doi:10.1097/JGP.0b013e3181d5792a

Clare, L., Wilson, B. A., Carter, G. G., & Hodges, J. R. (2003). Cognitive rehabilitation as a component of early intervention in Alzheimer's disease: A single case study. *Aging and Mental Health, 7*, 15–21. doi:10.1080/1360786021000045854

Cowan, N. (2005). Working-memory capacity limits in a theoretical context. In C. Izawa & N. Ohta (Eds.), *Human learning and memory: Advances in theory and application: The 4th Tsukuba International Conference on Memory* (pp. 155–175). Mahwah, NJ: Erlbaum.

Craik, F. I., & Bialystok, E. (2006). Cognition through the lifespan: Mechanisms of change. *Trends in Cognitive Sciences, 10*, 131–138. doi:10.1016/j.tics.2006.01.007

Crooks, V. C., Lubben, J., Petitti, D., Little, D., & Chiu, V. (2008). Social network, cognitive function, and dementia incidence among elderly women. *American Journal of Public Health, 98*, 1221–1227. doi:10.2105/AJPH.2007.115923

Dahlin, E., Neely, A. S., Larsson, A., Bäckman, L., & Nyberg, L. (2008). Transfer of learning after updating training mediated by the striatum. *Science, 320*, 1510–1512. doi:10.1126/science.1155466

Daneman, M., & Carpenter, P. (1980). Individual differences in working memory and reading. *Journal of Verbal Learning and Verbal Behavior, 19*, 450–466. doi:10.1016/S0022-5371(80)90312-6

De Vreese, L. P., Neri, M., Fioravanti, M., Belloi, L., & Zanetti, O. (2001). Memory rehabilitation in Alzheimer's disease: A review of progress. *International Journal of Geriatric Psychiatry, 16*, 794–809. doi:10.1002/gps.428

Depp, C., Vahia, I. V., & Jeste, D. (2010). Successful aging: Focus on cognitive and emotional health. *Annual Review of Clinical Psychology, 6*, 527–550. doi:10.1146/annurev.clinpsy.121208.131449

De Werd, M., Boelen, D., Rikkert, M., & Kessels, R. (2013). Errorless learning of everyday tasks in people with dementia. *Clinical Interventions in Aging, 20*, 1177–1190.

Eckroth-Bucher, M., & Siberski, J. (2009). Preserving cognition through an integrated cognitive stimulation and training program. *American Journal of Alzheimer's Disease and Other Dementias, 24*, 234–245. doi:10.1177/1533317509332624

Engle, R. W., Kane, M. J., & Tuholski, S. W. (1999). Individual differences in working memory capacity and what they tell us about controlled attention, general fluid intelligence and functions of the prefrontal cortex. In A. Miyake & P. Shah (Eds.), *Models of working memory: Mechanisms of active maintenance and executive control* (pp. 102–134). New York, NY: Cambridge University Press. doi:10.1017/CBO9781139174909.007

Eschen, A. (2012). The contributions of cognitive trainings to the stability of cognitive, everyday, and brain functioning across adulthood. *Geropsych: Journal of Gerontopsychology and Geriatric Psychiatry, 25,* 223–234.

Fabrigoule, C., Letenneur, L., Dartigues, J. F., Zarrouk, M., Commenges, D., & Barberger-Gateau, P. (1995). Social and leisure activities and risk of dementia: A prospective longitudinal study. *Journal of the American Geriatrics Society, 43,* 485–490.

Finn, M., & McDonald, S. (2011). Computerised cognitive training for older persons with mild cognitive impairment: A pilot study using a randomised controlled trial design. *Brain Impairment, 12,* 187–199. doi:10.1375/brim.12.3.187

Folstein, M. F., Folstein, S. E., & McHugh, P. R. (1975). "Mini-mental state": A practical method for grading the cognitive state of patients for the clinician. *Journal of Psychiatric Research, 12,* 189–198.

Gagnon, L. G., & Belleville, S. (2012). Training of attentional control in mild cognitive impairment with executive deficits: Results from a double-blind randomised controlled study. *Neuropsychological Rehabilitation, 22,* 809–835. doi:10.1080/09602011. 2012.691044

Gaitán, A., Garolera, M., Cerulla, N., Chico, G., Rodriguez-Querol, M., & Canela-Soler, J. (2013). Efficacy of an adjunctive computer-based cognitive training program in amnestic mild cognitive impairment and Alzheimer's disease: A single-blind, randomized clinical trial. *International Journal of Geriatric Psychiatry, 28,* 91–99. doi:10.1002/gps.3794

Gatz, M. (2005). Educating the brain to avoid dementia: Can mental exercise prevent Alzheimer's disease? *PLoS Medicine, 2,* e7. doi:10.1371/journal. pmed.0020007

Goldsilver, P. M., & Gruneir, M. R. (2001). Early stage dementia group: An innovative model of support for individuals in the early stages of dementia. *American Journal of Alzheimer's Disease and Other Dementias, 16,* 109–114. doi:10.1177/153331750101600206

Gonzalez Rothi, L. J., Fuller, R., Leon, S. A., Kendall, D., Moore, A., Wu, S. S., . . . Nadeau, S. E. (2009). Errorless practice as a possible adjuvant to donepezil in Alzheimer's disease. *Journal of the International Neuropsychological Society, 15,* 311–322. doi:10.1017/S1355617709090201

Grandmaison, E., & Simard, M. (2003). A critical review of memory stimulation programs in Alzheimer's disease. *Journal of Neuropsychiatry and Clinical Neurosciences, 15,* 130–144. doi:10.1176/appi. neuropsych.15.2.130

Greenaway, M. C., Duncan, N. L., & Smith, G. E. (2013). The memory support system for mild cognitive impairment: Randomized trial of a cognitive rehabilitation intervention. *International Journal of Geriatric Psychiatry, 28,* 402–409. doi:10.1002/gps.3838

Greenaway, M. C., Hanna, S. M., Lepore, S. W., & Smith, G. E. (2008). A behavioral rehabilitation intervention for amnestic mild cognitive impairment. *American Journal of Alzheimer's Disease and Other Dementias, 23,* 451–461. doi:10.1177/1533317508320352

Gross, A., Rebok, G., Unverzagt, F., Willis, S., & Brandt, J. (2011). Cognitive predictors of everyday functioning in older adults: Results from the ACTIVE cognitive Intervention trial. *The Journals of Gerontology, Series B: Psychological Sciences and Social Sciences, 66,* 557–566.

Günther, V. K., Schäfer, P., Holzner, B., & Kemmler, G. (2003). Long-term improvements in cognitive performance through computer-assisted cognitive training: A pilot study in a residential home for older people. *Aging and Mental Health, 7,* 200–206. doi:10.1080/1360786031000101175

Haimov, I., & Shatil, E. (2013). Cognitive training improves sleep quality and cognitive function among older adults with insomnia. *PLoS ONE, 8,* e61390. doi:10.1371/journal.pone.0061390

Hamer, M., & Chida, Y. (2009). Physical activity and risk of neurodegenerative disease: A systematic review of prospective evidence. *Psychological Medicine, 39,* 3–11. doi:10.1017/S0033291708003681

Hampstead, B. M., Sathian, K., Moore, A. B., Nalisnick, C., & Stringer, A. Y. (2008). Explicit memory training leads to improved memory for face–name pairs in patients with mild cognitive impairment: Results of a pilot investigation. *Journal of the International Neuropsychological Society, 14,* 883–889. doi:10.1017/S1355617708081009

Hampstead, B. M., Sathian, K., Phillips, P. A., Amaraneni, A., Delaune, W. R., & Stringer, A. Y. (2012). Mnemonic strategy training improves memory for object location associations in both healthy elderly and patients with amnestic mild cognitive impairment: A randomized, single-blind study. *Neuropsychology, 26,* 385–399. doi:10.1037/a0027545

Hebert, L. E., Scherr, P. A., Bienias, J. L., Bennett, D. A., & Evans, D. A. (2003). Alzheimer disease in the U.S. population: Prevalence estimates using the 2000 census. *Archives of Neurology, 60,* 1119–1122. doi:10.1001/archneur.60.8.1119

Herrera, C., Chambon, C. C., Michel, B. F., Paban, V. V., & Alescio-Lautier, B. B. (2012). Positive effects of computer-based cognitive training in adults with mild cognitive impairment. *Neuropsychologia, 50,* 1871–1881. doi:10.1016/j.neuropsychologia.2012. 04.012

Hertzog, C., Kramer, A. F., Wilson, R. S., & Linderberger, U. (2008). Enrichment effects on adult cognitive development: Can the functional capacity of older adults be preserved and enhanced? *Psychological Science in the Public Interest, 9*, 1–65.

Huckans, M., Hutson, L., Twamley, E., Jak, A., Kaye, J., & Storzbach, D. (2013). Efficacy of cognitive rehabilitation therapies for mild cognitive impairment (MCI) in older adults: Working toward a theoretical model and evidence-based interventions. *Neuropsychology Review, 23*, 63–80. doi:10.1007/s11065-013-9230-9

Hutchens, R. L., Kinsella, G., Ong, B., Pike, K., Parsons, S., Storey, E., . . . Clare, L. (2012). Knowledge and use of memory strategies in amnestic mild cognitive impairment. *Psychology and Aging, 27*, 768–777. doi:10.1037/a0026256

Hyer, L. (2014). *Treatment of older adults: A holistic approach*. New York, NY: Springer Press.

Hyer, L., Scott, C., Lyles, J., Dhabliwala, J., & McKenzie, L. (2014). Memory intervention: The value of a holistic program for older adults with memory impairments. *Aging and Mental Health, 18*, 169–178.

Jack, C. R., Jr., Knopman, D. S., Jagust, W. J., Shaw, L. M., Aisen, P. S., Weiner, M. W., . . . Trojanowski, J. Q. (2010). Hypothetical model of dynamic biomarkers of the Alzheimer's pathological cascade. *Lancet Neurology, 9*, 119. doi:10.1016/S1474-4422(09)70299-6

Jaeggi, S. M., Buschkuehl, M., Jonides, J., & Perrig, W. J. (2008). Improving fluid intelligence with training on working memory. *Proceedings of the National Academy of Sciences of the United States of America, 105*, 6829–6833. doi:10.1073/pnas.0801268105

Jak, A. J., Bondi, M. W., Delano-Wood, L., Wierenga, C., Corey-Bloom, J., Salmon, D. P., & Delis, D. C. (2009). Quantification of five neuropsychological approaches to defining mild cognitive impairment. *American Journal of Geriatric Psychiatry, 17*, 368–375. doi:10.1097/JGP.0b013e31819431d5

Jak, A. J., Seelye, A., & Jurick, S. (2013). Crosswords to computers: A critical review of popular approaches to cognitive enhancement. *Neuropsychology Review, 23*, 13–26. doi:10.1007/s11065-013-9226-5

Jean, L., Bergeron, M., Thivierge, S., & Simard, M. (2010). Cognitive intervention programs for individuals with mild cognitive impairment: Systematic review of the literature. *American Journal of Geriatric Psychiatry, 18*, 281–296. doi:10.1097/JGP.0b013e3181c37ce9

Jean, L., Simard, M., van Reekum, R., & Bergeron, M. (2007). Towards a cognitive stimulation program using an errorless learning paradigm in amnestic mild cognitive impairment. *Neuropsychiatric Disease and Treatment, 3*, 975–985.

Jean, L., Simard, M., Wiederkehr, S., Bergeron, M., Turgeon, Y., Hudon, C., . . . van Reekum, R. (2010). Efficacy of a cognitive training programme for mild cognitive impairment: Results of a randomised controlled study. *Neuropsychological Rehabilitation, 20*, 377–405. doi:10.1080/09602010903343012

Johansson, B., & Tornmalm, M. (2012). Working memory training for patients with acquired brain injury: Effects in daily life. *Scandinavian Journal of Occupational Therapy, 19*, 176–183. doi:10.3109/11038128.2011.603352

Joosten-Weyn Banningh, L., Roelofs, S. F., Vernooij-Dassen, M. J., Prins, J. B., Olde Rikkert, M., & Kessels, R. C. (2013). Long-term effects of group therapy for patients with mild cognitive impairment and their significant others: A 6- to 8-month follow-up study. *Dementia, 12*, 81–91. doi:10.1177/1471301211420332

Kalaria, R. N. (2000). The role of cerebral ischemia in Alzheimer's disease. *Neurobiology of Aging, 21*, 321–330. doi:10.1016/S0197-4580(00)00125-1

Kane, M. J., Hambrick, D., Tuholski, S., Wilhelm, O., Payne, T., & Engle, R. (2004). The generality of working memory capacity: A latent-variable approach to verbal and visuospatial memory span and reasoning. *Journal of Experimental Psychology: General, 133*, 189–217. doi:10.1037/0096-3445.133.2.189

Kaufman, Y., Anaki, D., Binns, M., & Freeman, M. (2007). Cognitive decline in Alzheimer disease: Impact of spirituality, religiosity, and QOL. *Neurology, 68*, 1509–1514. doi:10.1212/01.wnl.0000260697.66617.59

Kiernan, R. J., Mueller, J., & Langston, J. W. (1995). *Cognistat (Neurobehavioral Cognitive Status Examination)*. Lutz, FL: Psychological Assessment Resources.

Kinsella, G. J., Mullaly, E., Rand, E., Ong, B., Burton, C., Price, S., . . . Storey, E. (2009). Early intervention for mild cognitive impairment: A randomised controlled trial. *Journal of Neurology, Neurosurgery, and Psychiatry, 80*, 730–736. doi:10.1136/jnnp.2008.148346

Klingberg, T., Fernell, E., Olesen, P. J., Johnson, M., Gustafsson, P., Dahlström, K., . . . Westerberg, H. (2005). Computerized training of working memory in children with ADHD—A randomized, controlled trial. *Journal of the American Academy of Child and Adolescent Psychiatry, 44*, 177–186. doi:10.1097/00004583-200502000-00010

Klingberg, T., Forssberg, H., & Westerberg, H. (2002). Training of working memory in children with ADHD. *Journal of Clinical and Experimental Neuropsychology, 24*, 781–791. doi:10.1076/jcen.24.6.781.8395

Kramer, A. F., Erickson, K. I., & Colcombe, J. (2006). Exercise, cognition, and the aging brain. *Journal of Applied Physiology, 101,* 1237–1242.

Kurz, A., Pohl, C., Ramsenthaler, M., & Sorg, C. (2009). Cognitive rehabilitation in patients with mild cognitive impairment. *International Journal of Geriatric Psychiatry, 24,* 163–168. doi:10.1002/gps.2086

Lachman, M. E., Weaver, S. L., Bandura, M., Elliott, E., & Lewkowicz, C. J. (1992). Improving memory and control beliefs through cognitive restructuring and self-generated strategies. *The Journals of Gerontology, Series B: Psychological Sciences and Social Sciences, 47,* 293–299.

Lavretsky, H. (2013, May). *Lifestyle behaviors, integrative therapies, and mental health across the lifespan.* Program and abstracts of the 2013 American Psychiatric Association Annual Meeting, San Francisco, California, Symposium 33.

Le Couteur, D. G., & Sinclair, D. A. (2010). A blueprint for developing therapeutic approaches that increase healthspan and delay death. *The Journals of Gerontology, Series A: Biological Sciences and Medical Sciences, 65,* 693–694. doi:10.1093/gerona/glq048

Lim, M. X., Liu, K. Y., Cheung, G. F., Kuo, M. C., Ruijie, L., & Choy-Ying, T. (2012). Effectiveness of a multifaceted cognitive training programme for people with mild cognitive impairment: A one-group pre- and posttest design. *Hong Kong Journal of Occupational Therapy, 22,* 3–8. doi:10.1016/j.hkjot.2012.04.002

Little, A., Volans, P., Hemsley, D., & Levy, R. (1986). The retention of new information in senile dementia. *British Journal of Clinical Psychology, 25,* 71–72.

Loewenstein, D. (2011, October). *Value of brain reserve in adults.* Presentation at Annual Meeting of the National Association of Neuropsychology, Marco Island, Florida.

Loewenstein, D. A., Acevedo, A., Czaja, S., & Duara, R. (2004). Cognitive rehabilitation of mildly impaired Alzheimer's disease patients on cholinesterase inhibitors. *American Journal of Geriatric Psychiatry, 12,* 395–402. doi:10.1097/00019442-200407000-00007

Logie, R. H., Gilhooly, K., & Wynn, V. (1994). Counting on working memory in arithmetic problem solving. *Memory and Cognition, 22,* 395–410. doi:10.3758/BF03200866

Logsdon, R. G., Pike, K. C., McCurry, S. M., Hunter, P., Maher, J., Snyder, L., & Teri, L. (2010). Early-stage memory loss support groups: Outcomes from a randomized controlled clinical trial. *The Journals of Gerontology, Series B: Psychological Sciences and Social Sciences, 65,* 691–697. doi:10.1093/geronb/gbq054

Londos, E., Boschian, K. K., Lindén, A. A., Persson, C. C., Minthon, L. L., & Lexell, J. J. (2008). Effects of a goal-oriented rehabilitation program in mild cognitive impairment: A pilot study. *American Journal of Alzheimer's Disease and Other Dementias, 23,* 177–183. doi:10.1177/1533317507312622

Mahncke, H. W., Connor, B. B., Appelman, J., Ahsanuddin, O. N., Hardy, J. L., Wood, R. A., . . . Merzenich, M. M. (2006). Memory enhancement in healthy older adults using a brain plasticity-based training program: A randomized, controlled study. *Proceedings of the National Academy of Sciences of the United States of America, 103,* 12523–12528. doi:10.1073/pnas.0605194103

Mayr, U. (2008). Introduction to the special section on cognitive plasticity in the aging mind. *Psychology and Aging, 23,* 681–683. doi:10.1037/a0014346

Mattis, S. (2001). *Dementia Rating Scale (DRS-2).* Odessa, FL: Psychological Assessment Resources.

McNab, F., Varrone, A., Farde, L., Jucaite, A., Bystritsky, P., Forssberg, H., & Klingberg, T. (2009). Changes in cortical dopamine D1 receptor binding associated with cognitive training. *Science, 323,* 800–802. doi:10.1126/science.1166102

Meguro, M., Kasai, M., Akanuma, K., Ishii, H., Yamaguchi, S., & Meguro, K. (2008). Comprehensive approach of donepezil and psychosocial interventions on cognitive function and quality of life for Alzheimer's disease: The Osaki-Tajiri Project. *Age and Ageing, 37,* 469–473. doi:10.1093/ageing/afn107

Melby-Lervåg, M., & Hulme, C. (2013). Is working memory training effective? A meta-analytic review. *Developmental Psychology, 49,* 270–291. doi:10.1037/a0028228

Miller, K., Siddarth, P., Gaines, J., Parrish, J., Ercoli, L., Marx, K., . . . Small, G. W. (2012). The memory fitness program: Cognitive effects of a healthy again population. *American Journal of Geriatric Psychology, 20,* 514–523. doi:10.1097/JGP.0b013e318227f821

Morris, J. C., Storandt, M., Miller, J., McKeel, D. W., Price, J. L., Rubin, E. H., & Berg, L. (2001). Mild cognitive impairment represents early-stage Alzheimer disease. *Archives of Neurology, 58,* 397–405. doi:10.1001/archneur.58.3.397

Morrison, A. B., & Chein, J. M. (2011). Does working memory training work? The promise and challenges of enhancing cognition by training working memory. *Psychonomic Bulletin and Review, 18,* 46–60. doi:10.3758/s13423-010-0034-0

Mowszowski, L., Batchelor, J., & Naismith, S. (2010). Early intervention for cognitive decline: Can cognitive training be used as a selective prevention technique? *International Psychogeriatrics, 22,* 537–548. doi:10.1017/S1041610209991748

Narendran, R., Frankle, W. G., Mason, N. S., Muldoon, M. F., & Moghaddam, B. (2012). Improved working memory but no effect on striatal vesicular mono-amine transporter type 2 after omega-3 polyun-saturated fatty acid supplementation. *PLoS ONE, 7*, e46832. doi:10.1371/journal.pone.0046832

Nasreddine, Z. S., Phillips, N. A., Bedirian, V., Charbonneau, S., Whitehead, V., Collin, I., . . . Chertkow, H. (2005). The Montreal Cognitive Assessment, MoCA: A brief screening tool for mild cognitive impairment. *Journal of the American Geriatric Society, 53*, 695–699.

National Institutes of Health. (2011). *NIH state of the science conference: Preventing Alzheimer's Disease and Cognitive Decline*. Bethesda, MD: Author.

Newberg, A. B. (2011). Spirituality and the aging brain. *Generations, 35*, 83–91.

Newport, E. (2013). In DeAngelis, T. (2013, May). New hope for the damaged brain. *Monitor on Psychology, 44*, 40–43.

Nitrini, R. (2012). Dementia incidence in middle-income countries. *Lancet, 380*, 1470. doi:10.1016/S0140-6736 (12)61838-8

Nyberg, L., Lovden, M., Riklund, K., Lindenberger, U., & Backman, L. (2012). Memory aging and brain maintenance. *Trends in Cognitive Sciences, 16*, 292–305.

Olazarán, J., Reisberg, B., Clare, L., Cruz, I., Peña-Casanova, J., del Ser, T., . . . Muñiz, R. (2010). Nonpharmacological therapies in Alzheimer's disease: A systematic review of efficacy. *Dementia and Geriatric Cognitive Disorders, 30*, 161–178. doi:10.1159/000316119

Olazarán, J. J., Muñiz, R., Reisberg, B. B., Peña-Casanova, J. J., del Ser, T. T., Cruz-Jentoft, A. J., . . . Sevilla, C. C. (2004). Benefits of cognitive-motor intervention in MCI and mild to moderate Alzheimer disease. *Neurology, 63*, 2348–2353. doi:10.1212/01. WNL.0000147478.03911.28

Olchik, M. R., Farina, J., Steibel, N., Teixeira, A., & Yassuda, M. (2013). Memory training (MT) in mild cognitive impairment (MCI) generates change in cognitive performance. *Archives of Gerontology and Geriatrics, 56*, 442–447. doi:10.1016/j. archger.2012.11.007

Olesen, P. J., Westerberg, H., & Klingberg, T. (2004). Increased prefrontal and parietal activity after training of working memory. *Nature Neuroscience, 7*, 75–79. doi:10.1038/nn1165

Oswald, W. D., Gunzelmann, T., Rupprecht, R., & Hagen, B. (2006). Differential effects of single versus combined cognitive and physical training with older adults: The SimA study in a 5-year perspective. *European Journal of Ageing, 3*, 179–192. doi:10.1007/ s10433-006-0035-z

Owen, A. M., Hampshire, A., Grahn, J. A., Stenton, R., Dajani, S., Burns, A. S., . . . Ballard, C. G. (2010). Putting brain training to the test. *Nature, 465*, 775–778. doi:10.1038/nature09042

Park, D. C., & Reuter-Lorenz, P. (2009). The adaptive brain: Aging and neurocognitive scaffolding. *Annual Review of Psychology, 60*, 173–196. doi:10.1146/ annurev.psych.59.103006.093656

Parrott, M. D., & Greenwood, C. E. (2007). Dietary influences on cognitive function with aging: From high-fat diets to healthful eating. *Annals of the New York Academy of Sciences, 1114*, 389–397. doi:10.1196/ annals.1396.028

Pfeffer, R. I., Kurosaki, T. T., Harrah, C. H., Chance, J. M., & Filos, S. (1982). Measurement of functional activities in older adults in the community. *Journal of Gerontology, 37*, 323–329.

Prestia, A., Caroli, A., Wiesje, M., Ossenkoppele, R., Van Berckel, B., Barkhof, F., . . . Frisoni, G. (2013). Prediction of dementia in MCI patients based on core diagnostic markers for Alzheimer disease. *Neurology, 80*, 1048–1056. doi:10.1212/ WNL.0b013e3182872830

Rajan, K. B., Hebert, L. E., Scherr, P. A., Mendes de Leon, C. F., & Evans, D. A. (2013). Disability in basic and instrumental activities of daily living is associated with faster rate of decline in cognitive function of older adults. *The Journals of Gerontology, Series A: Biological Sciences and Medical Sciences, 68*, 624–630. doi:10.1093/gerona/gls208

Randolph, C. (1998). *Repeatable battery for the assessment of neuropsychological status (RBANS)*. San Antonio, TX: Psychological Corporation.

Rapp, S., Brenes, G., & Marsh, A. P. (2002). Memory enhancement training for older adults with mild cognitive impairment: A preliminary study. *Aging and Mental Health, 6*, 5–11. doi:10.1080/136078601 20101077

Rebok, G. W., & Balcerak, L. J. (1989). Memory self-efficacy and performance differences between younger and older adults: Effects of mnemonic training. *Developmental Psychology, 25*, 714–721. doi:10.1037/0012-1649.25.5.714

Rebok, G. W., Parisi, J. M., Gross, A. L., Sipra, A. P., Ko, J., Samus, Q. M., . . . Holtzman, R. E. (2012). Evidence-based psychological treatments for improving memory function among older adults. In F. R. Scogin & A. Shah (Eds.), *Making evidence-based psychological treatments work with older adults* (pp. 131–165). Washington, DC: American Psychological Association. doi:10.1037/13753-005

Reitan, R. M., & Wolfson, D. (1993). *The Halstead–Reitan neuropsychological test battery: Theory and clinical interpretation* (2nd ed.). Tucson, AZ: Neuropsychology Press.

Rosen, A. C., Sugiura, L., Kramer, J. H., Whitfield-Gabrieli, S., & Gabrieli, J. D. (2011). Cognitive training changes hippocampal function in mild cognitive impairment: A pilot study. *Journal of Alzheimer's Disease, 26*(Suppl. 3), 349–357.

Rozzini, L., Costardi, D., Chilovi, B., Franzoni, S., Trabucchi, M., & Padovani, A. (2007). Efficacy of cognitive rehabilitation in patients with mild cognitive impairment treated with cholinesterase inhibitors. *International Journal of Geriatric Psychiatry, 22,* 356–360. doi:10.1002/gps.1681

Salthouse, T. A., & Babcock, R. L. (1991). Decomposing adult age differences in working memory. *Developmental Psychology, 27,* 763–776. doi:10.1037/0012-1649.27.5.763

Scarmeas, N., Luchsinger, J. A., & Schupf, N. (2009). Physical activity, diet, and risk of Alzheimer disease. *JAMA, 302,* 627–637. doi:10.1001/jama.2009.1144

Scarmeas, N., Stern, Y., Mayeux, R., Manly, J. J., Schupf, N., & Luchsinger, J. A. (2009). Mediterranean diet and mild cognitive impairment. *Archives of Neurology, 66,* 216–225.

Schooler, C., Mulatu, M. S., & Oates, G. (1999). The continuing effects of substantively complex work on the intellectual functioning of older workers. *Psychology and Aging, 14,* 483–506. doi:10.1037/0882-7974.14.3.483

Shah, P., & Miyake, A. (1999). Toward unified theories of working memory: Emerging general consensus, unresolved theoretical issues, and future research directions. In A. Miyake & P. Shah (Eds.), *Models of working memory: Mechanisms of active maintenance and executive control* (pp. 442–482). New York, NY: Oxford University Press.

Simon, S. S., Yokomizo, J. E., & Bottino, C. M. C. (2012). Cognitive intervention in amnestic Mild cognitive impairment: A systematic review. *Neuroscience and Biobehavioral Reviews, 36,* 1163–1178. doi:10.1016/j.neubiorev.2012.01.007

Sitzer, D. I., Twamley, E. W., & Jeste, D. V. (2006). Cognitive training in Alzheimer's disease: A meta-analysis of the literature. *Acta Psychiatrica Scandinavica, 114,* 75–90. doi:10.1111/j.1600-0447.2006.00789.x

Small, G., & Vorgan, G. (2011). *The Alzheimer's prevention program: Keep your brain healthy for the rest of your life.* New York, NY: Workman.

Small, G. W. (2013, May). *Brain health and Alzheimer's prevention.* Program and abstracts of the 2013 American Psychiatric Association Annual Meeting, San Francisco, California, Lecture 11.

Small, G. W., Kepe, V., Siddarth, P., Ercoli, L. M., Merrill, D. A., Donoghue, N., . . . Barrio, J. R. (2013). PET scanning of brain tau in retired national football league players: Preliminary findings. *American Journal of Geriatric Psychiatry, 21,* 138–144. doi:10.1016/j.jagp.2012.11.019

Smith, G. E., & Bondi, M. (2013). *Mild cognitive impairment and dementia: Definitions, diagnosis, and treatment.* New York, NY: Oxford Workshop Series.

Smith, G. E., Housen, P., Yaffe, K., Ruff, R., Kennison, R. F., Mahncke, H. W., . . . Zelinski, E. M. (2009). A cognitive training program based on principles of brain plasticity: Results from the Improvement in Memory With Plasticity-Based Adaptive Cognitive Training (IMPACT) study. *Journal of the American Geriatrics Society, 57,* 594–603. doi:10.1111/j.1532-5415.2008.02167.x

Snyder, L., Bower, D., Arneson, S., Sheperd, S., & Quayhagen, M. (1994). *Coping with Alzheimer's disease and related disorders: An educational support group for early stage individuals and their families.* San Diego, CA: UCSD Alzheimer's Disease Research Center.

Snyder, L., Jenkins, C., & Joosten, L. (2007). The effectiveness of support groups for people with mild-to-moderate Alzheimer's disease—An evaluative survey. *American Journal of Alzheimer's Disease and Other Dementias, 22,* 14–19. doi:10.1177/1533317506295857

Sofi, F., Valecchi, D. D., Bacci, D. D., Abbate, R. R., Gensini, G. F., Casini, A. A., & Macchi, C. C. (2011). Physical activity and risk of cognitive decline: A meta-analysis of prospective studies. *Journal of Internal Medicine, 269,* 107–117. doi:10.1111/j.1365-2796.2010.02281.x

Solfrizzi, V., Panza, F., Frisardi, V., Seripa, D., Logroscino, G., Imbimbo, B., & Pilotto, A. (2011). Diet and Alzheimer's disease risk factors or prevention: The current evidence. *Expert Review of Neurotherapeutics, 11,* 677–708. doi:10.1586/ern.11.56

Souchay, C. (2007). Metamemory in Alzheimer's disease. *Cortex, 43,* 987–1003. doi:10.1016/S0010-9452(08)70696-8

Sperling, R. (2011). The potential of functional MRI as a biomarker in early Alzheimer's disease. *Neurobiology of Aging, 32*(Suppl. 1), S37–S43. doi:10.1016/j.neurobiolaging.2011.09.009

Staff, R. T., Murray, A. D., Deary, I. J., & Whalley, L. J. (2004). What provides cerebral reserve? *Brain: A Journal of Neurology, 127,* 1191–1199. doi:10.1093/brain/awh144

Stine-Morrow, E. A. L., Parisi, J. M., Morrow, D. G., & Park, D. C. (2008). The effects of an engaged lifestyle on cognitive vitality: A field experiment. *Psychology and Aging, 23,* 778–786. doi:10.1037/a0014341

Stott, J., & Spector, A. (2011). A review of the effectiveness of memory interventions in mild cognitive impairment (MCI). *International Psychogeriatrics, 23,* 526–538. doi:10.1017/S1041610210001973

Talassi, E., Guerreschi, M. M., Feriani, M. M., Fedi, V. V., Bianchetti, A. A., & Trabucchi, M. M. (2007). Effectiveness of a cognitive rehabilitation program in mild dementia (MD) and mild cognitive impairment (MCI): A case control study. *Archives of Gerontology and Geriatrics, 44*(Suppl. 1), 391–399. doi:10.1016/j.archger.2007.01.055

Tariq, S. H., Tumosa, N., Chibnall, J. T., Perry, H. M., & Morley, J. E. (2006). The Saint Louis University Mental Status (SLUMS) examination for detecting mild cognitive impairment and dementia is more sensitive than the Mini-Mental Status Examination (MMSE)—A pilot study. *Journal of American Geriatric Psychiatry, 14*, 900–910.

Treiber, K. A., Carlson, M. C., Corcoran, C., Norton, M. C., Breitner, J. C., Piercy, K., . . . Tschanz, J. T. (2011). Cognitive stimulation and cognitive and functional decline in Alzheimer's disease: The Cache County Dementia Progression Study. *The Journals of Gerontology, Series B: Psychological Sciences and Social Sciences, 66*, 416–425. doi:10.1093/geronb/gbr023

Troyer, A. K., Murphy, K. J., Anderson, N. D., Moscovitch, M., & Craik, F. I. (2008). Changing everyday memory behaviour in amnestic mild cognitive impairment: A randomized controlled trial. *Neuropsychological Rehabilitation, 18*, 65–88. doi:10.1080/09602010701409684

Unverzagt, F. W., Guey, L. T., Jones, R. N., Marsiske, M., King, J. W., Wadley, V. G., . . . Tennstedt, S. L. (2012). ACTIVE Cognitive training and rates of incident dementia. *Journal of the International Neuropsychological Society, 18*, 669–677. doi:10.1017/S1355617711001470

Unverzagt, F. W., Kasten, L., Johnson, K., Rebok, G., Marsiske, M., Koepke, K., . . . Tennstedt, S. (2007). Effect of memory impairment on training outcomes in ACTIVE. *Journal of the International Neuropsychological Society, 13*, 953–960. doi:10.1017/S1355617707071512

Valentijn, S. A., van Hooren, S. A., Bosma, H., Touw, D. M., Jolles, J., van Boxtel, M. P., . . . Ponds, R. W. (2005). The effect of two types of memory training on subjective and objective memory performance in healthy individuals aged 55 years and older: A randomized controlled trial. *Patient Education and Counseling, 57*, 106–114. doi:10.1016/j.pec.2004.05.002

Valenzuela, M., & Sachdev, P. (2009). Can cognitive exercise prevent the most onset of dementia? Systematic review of randomized clinical trials with longitudinal follow-up. *American Journal of Geriatric Psychiatry, 17*, 179–187. doi:10.1097/JGP.0b013e3181953b57

Wang, H. X., Karp, A., Winblad, B., & Fratiglioni, L. (2002). Late-life engagement in social and leisure activities is associated with a decreased risk of dementia: A longitudinal study from the Kungsholmen project. *American Journal of Epidemiology, 155*, 1081–1087. doi:10.1093/aje/155.12.1081

Wechsler, D. (1997a). *Wechsler adult intelligence scale—third edition (WAIS–III)*. San Antonio, TX: Psychological Corporation.

Wechsler, D. (1997b). *Wechsler memory scale—third edition (WMS–III)*. San Antonio, TX: Psychological Corporation.

West, R. L., & Hastings, E. C. (2011). Self-regulation and recall: Growth curve modeling of intervention outcomes for older adults. *Psychology and Aging, 26*, 803–812. doi:10.1037/a0023784

Westerberg, H., Jacobaeus, H., Hirvikoski, T., Clevberger, P., Ostensson, M., Bartfai, A., & Klingberg, T. (2007). Computerized working memory training after stroke—a pilot study. *Brain Injury, 21*, 21–29. doi:10.1080/02699050601148726

Willis, S. L., Tennstedt, S. L., Marsiske, M., Ball, K., Elias, J., Koepke, K. M., . . . Wright, E. (2006). Long-term effects of cognitive training on everyday functional outcomes in older Adults. *JAMA, 296*, 2805–2814. doi:10.1001/jama.296.23.2805

Wilson, R. S., Segawa, E., Boyle, P. A., Anagnos, S. E., Hizel, L. P., & Bennett, D. A. (2012). The natural history of cognitive decline in Alzheimer's disease. *Psychology and Aging, 27*, 1008–1017. doi:10.1037/a0029857

Wolinsky, F. D., Mahncke, H., Kosinski, M., Unverzagt, F., Smith, D., Jones, R., . . . Tennstedt, S. (2009). The ACTIVE cognitive training trial and predicted medical expenditures. *BMC Health Services Research, 9*, 109–118. doi:10.1186/1472-6963-9-109

Xu, W. L., Atti, A., Gatz, M., Pedersen, N., Johansson, B., & Fratiglioni, L. (2011). Midlife overweight and obesity increase late-life dementia risk: A population-based twin study. *Neurology, 76*, 1568–1574. doi:10.1212/WNL.0b013e3182190d09

Yesavage, J. A., Friedman, L., Ashford, J. W., Kraemer, H. C., Mumenthaler, M. S., Noda, A., . . . Hoblyn, J. (2008). Acetylcholinesterase inhibitor in combination with cognitive training in older adults. *The Journals of Gerontology, Series B: Psychological Sciences and Social Sciences, 63*, 288–294. doi:10.1093/geronb/63.5.P288

Zarit, S. H., Femia, E. E., Kim, K., & Whitlack, C. J. (2010). The structure of risk factors and outcomes for family caregivers: Implications for assessment and treatment. *Aging and Mental Health, 14*, 220–231. doi:10.1080/13607860903167861

Zeidan, F., Johnson, S. K., Diamond, B. J., David, Z., & Goolkasian, P. (2010). Mindfulness meditation improves cognition: Evidence of brief mental training. *Consciousness and Cognition, 19*, 597–605. doi:10.1016/j.concog.2010.03.014

CHAPTER 14

LATE-LIFE SLEEP AND SLEEP DISORDERS

Christina S. McCrae, Alicia J. Roth, Roberto Zamora, Natalie D. Dautovich, and Kenneth L. Lichstein

Sleep problems often have complex etiology and progression in older adults, causing some to suggest that they be viewed as a multifactorial geriatric syndrome (Vaz Fragoso & Gill, 2007). Often, other age-related factors, such as increased medical, physical, cognitive, and psychological complaints, are implicated in sleep disorders in this age-group. Depending on the classification system used, the number of diagnosable sleep disorders ranges from 10 (American Psychiatric Association, 2013) to a staggering 78 (American Academy of Sleep Medicine [AASM], 2005). This chapter focuses on three sleep disorders that are experienced *commonly* by older adults, that geropsychologists are *likely* to encounter, and for which there are *evidence-based psychological treatment* approaches: advanced-sleep phase disorder (ASPD), insomnia, and sleep-disordered breathing (SDB).[1] Normal late-life sleep also is discussed.

SLEEP DISORDERS IN OLDER ADULTS

Older adults experience numerous sleep disorders that are prevalent in the general population. Three diagnoses are especially common in older adults: advanced sleep phase disorder, insomnia, and sleep-disordered breathing.

Advanced Sleep Phase Disorder

ASPD is a subtype of circadian rhythm sleep disorders. These disorders are defined by a misalignment of the sleep pattern with societal norms for sleep–wake times (Thorpy, 2011). Characteristics of ASPD include sleep and wake times that are typically more than 3 hr earlier compared with societal norms (Reid & Zee, 2011). Earlier bedtimes are accompanied by afternoon or evening sleepiness (often interfering with activities) and early morning awakening (e.g., 2 to 5 A.M.; Reid & Zee, 2011). Other than the shift of the timing of sleep, the sleep experience itself is typically normal (Reid & Zee, 2011). Both the *Diagnostic and Statistical Manual of Mental Disorders, Fifth Edition* (*DSM–5*; American Psychiatric Association, 2013) and the *International Classification of Sleep Disorders, Second Edition* (*ICSD–2*; AASM, 2005) suggest that there is a complaint of an inability to stay awake in the evening and an inability to remain asleep until the desired awakening time. This complaint results in functional impairment. The *ICSD–2* criteria further specify that the sleep quality and duration are normal for age and that sleep logs or actigraphy used for at least 7 days validate the phase advance (AASM, 2005). Figure 14.1 illustrates the typical timing of the sleep period in comparison to ASPD and its "opposite," delayed sleep phase

---

[1]This chapter's focus on advanced sleep phase disorder, insomnia, and sleep disordered breathing is intended to enhance its practical utility for geropsychologists. Readers interested in more depth coverage are referred to Pandi-Perumal, Monti, & Monjan *Principles and Practice of Geriatric Sleep Medicine*.

http://dx.doi.org/10.1037/14459-014
APA Handbook of Clinical Geropsychology: Vol. 2. Assessment, Treatment, and Issues of Later Life,
P. A. Lichtenberg and B. T. Mast (Editors-in-Chief)

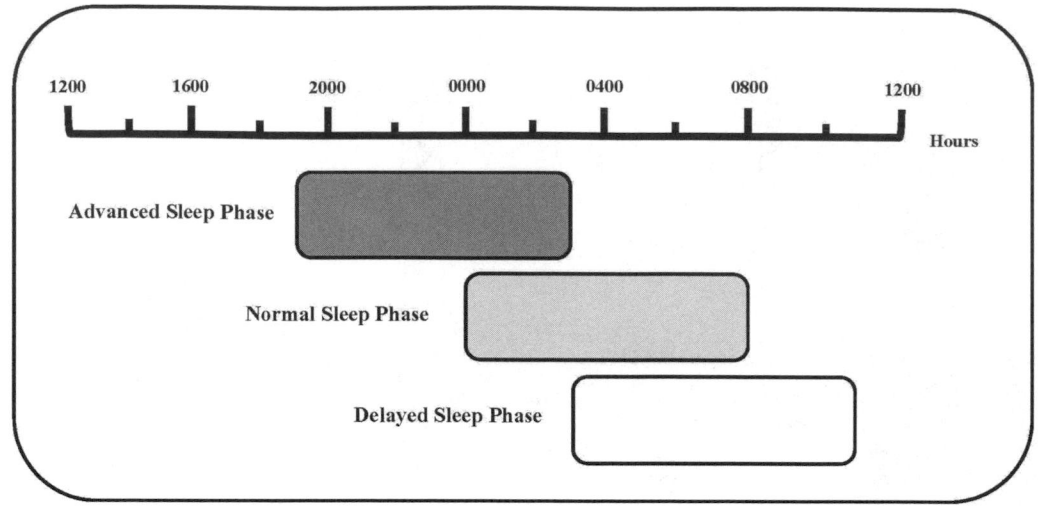

FIGURE 14.1.   Typical timing of the sleep period in comparison with the phase shifting that occurs in advanced and delayed sleep phase disorders.

disorder (DSPD),[2] respectively. Whereas little is known about the prevalence of these disorders (Schrader, Bovim, & Sand, 1993), ASPD generally is considered more common in older adults, perhaps because of reports of earlier bedtimes and wake times among older adults (Czeisler et al., 1992), and 20% of older adults complain of early morning awakening (Foley et al., 1995).

Insomnia

Generally, insomnia is defined as complaint of disturbed sleep that may manifest in difficulty initiating sleep, maintaining sleep, waking up too early, or nonrestorative sleep (Bloom et al., 2009). This complaint occurs despite adequate opportunity for sleep and results in impairment in daytime functioning. As summarized by Lichstein, Taylor, McCrae, and Ruiter (2011), prevalence of insomnia in older adults has been found to range from 12% to 41% depending on the assessment criteria used (Blazer, Hays, & Foley, 1995; Foley et al., 1995; Ford & Kamerow, 1989; Liu & Liu, 2005; Roberts, Shema, & Kaplan, 1999; Schubert et al., 2002). Not surprisingly, more stringent criteria that take into account both the frequency and chronicity of the

insomnia complaints, as well as requiring a complaint of daytime functioning impairment because of poor sleep, produce lower estimates than do criteria involving more general inquiries about whether an individual experienced insomnia over the past year or past month.

Most clinicians rely on the *DSM* and the *ICSD–2* for diagnosing insomnia (Edinger & Wyatt, 2011). Although the exact wording of the criteria differs, both classification systems' definitions of insomnia are similar and are consistent with the general definition previously provided. Where these systems differ is in the level of detail and differentiation. Specifically, the *ICSD–2* is intended for use by specialists and parses insomnia into 12 specific disorders. In contrast, the *Diagnostic and Statistical Manual of Mental Disorders, Fourth Edition, Text Revision* (*DSM–IV–TR*; American Psychiatric Association, 2000) and the *DSM–5* are intended for use by general clinicians and employ broader classifications of sleep disorders, parsing insomnia into three distinct disorders (and a subtype of another) and a single disorder, respectively. A recent study compared each approach in the diagnosis of sleep disorders in adults and found that the simpler, broader categories of the

---

[2]Delayed sleep phase disorder is characterized by later bedtimes and wake times compared with society norms and often is accompanied by reports of sleep-onset difficulties, difficulty waking, and excessive sleepiness early in the day.

DSM–IV–TR more reliably diagnosed sleep–wake disorders compared with the *ICSD–2* approach (Edinger & Wyatt, 2011). The *DSM–5* includes cross-referencing to *ICSD–2* diagnoses.

An important diagnostic consideration is that insomnia that presents with another condition previously was considered "secondary" to that condition. In 2005, the National Institutes of Health (NIH, 2005) released a State-of-the-Science Conference Statement recommending the treatment of insomnia that occurs with other disorders and the adoption of the term *comorbid* to describe such cases. This recommendation is at least partially attributable to the fact that insomnia that begins in response to another condition often takes on a life of its own as patients adopt behaviors and strategies to cope with poor sleep that have the unintended effect of reinforcing and perpetuating the insomnia (i.e., increased caffeine use, napping, snoozing in the morning). Furthermore, accumulating evidence suggests that insomnia can increase risk for developing an Axis I condition, such as depression (Pigeon et al., 2008).

Sleep-Disordered Breathing

SDB typically consists of moments when individuals cease breathing (complete cessation of breathing known as apneas and partial cessation of breathing known as hypopneas; Bloom et al., 2009). Two primary types of SDB are central sleep apnea (CSA) and obstructive sleep apnea (OSA). CSA consists of recurrent episodes of apnea resulting from central nervous system or cardiac dysfunction (Bloom et al., 2009). In OSA, the apneas result form an obstruction of the upper airway (Bloom et al., 2009). As OSA is more prevalent than CSA, it will be the focus of this section.

The first large-scale polysomnographic study of sleep apnea in middle-age adults found that 2% of women and 4% of men met the diagnostic criteria for sleep apnea syndrome (defined as an apnea-hypopnea index [AHI] of five, indicating the cessation or reduction of breathing at least five times per hour, and daytime hypersomnolence; Young et al., 1993). In contrast, in population-based laboratory studies of older adults (minimum age 60–65 years), 15%–24% had an AHI greater than five (Ancoli-Israel

et al., 1996; Phillips et al., 1992). It appears that the laboratory prevalence of sleep apnea increases with age. It is important, however, to consider clinical correlates of the disorder (e.g., unintentional sleep episodes during wakefulness, daytime sleepiness, refreshing sleep, fatigue, or insomnia; Vaz Fragoso & Gill, 2007). When OSA is defined using the AHI combined with clinical complaints, prevalence declines with age (Bixler, Vgontzas, Ten, Tyson, & Kales, 1998).

The *DSM–IV–TR* (American Psychiatric Association, 2000) provides a general diagnosis for a breathing-related sleep disorder based on a sleep disruption leading to excessive sleepiness or insomnia that is the result of a sleep-related breathing condition (OSA, CSA, or central alveolar hypoventilation syndrome). Excessive daytime sleepiness is the most common presenting complaint, with insomnia seen less frequently (American Psychiatric Association, 2000). In contrast to the *DSM–IV–TR* approach, the variants of breathing-related sleep disorder are recognized as three distinct disorders in the *DSM–5*. The *ICSD–2* includes five different types of sleep-related breathing disorders. CSA syndromes (further specified into six subtypes) and OSA (further specified into adult and pediatric types) are two of these five types. The *ICSD–2* diagnostic criteria for OSA–adult type include one complaint from the following list: unintentional sleep episodes during wakefulness, daytime sleepiness, nonrefreshing sleep, fatigue, or insomnia. This criteria is combined with a polysomnographic recording of five or more scoreable respiratory events per hour of sleep and respiratory effort (indicating increased attempts to breathe that are reflected in increased oseophageal pressure) during all or a portion of each respiratory event (i.e., apnea, hypopnea, or respiratory effort-related arousals; AASM, 2005). Respiratory events are deemed scoreable based on established guidelines (e.g., Berry et al., 2012). Alternatively, in place of the previously discussed criteria, a polysomnographic recording showing 15 or more scoreable respiratory events per hour of sleep and respiratory effort during all or a portion of each respiratory event is sufficient (AASM, 2005). Both diagnostic systems require that the disorder is not better explained by another disorder.

MAJOR THEORIES

There are several principal theories regarding the development of normal sleep in older adults as well as the etiology of pathological sleep disorders in older adults.

Normal Late-Life Sleep

The sleep of older individuals has been characterized as shorter (less total sleep time; Espiritu, 2008), lighter (more time spent in light sleep-stages N1 and N2; less time spent in deep sleep-stage N3[3]), and more fragmented (more awakenings, longer sleep latencies, more time spent awake during the night; Bliwise, 2011) compared with that of younger individuals. Meta-analyses of cross-sectional data (Floyd et al., 2007; Ohayon, Carskadon, Guilleminault, & Vitiello, 2004) indicate that many age-dependent sleep architecture changes actually occur before old age (60 years of age) with the notable exception of sleep efficiency (SE), which declines until late-late life (more than 90 years of age). Methodological differences across the studies included in these analyses, however, may cast some doubt on the utility of their findings (Bliwise, 2011). The Sleep Heart Healthy Study collected a single night of polysomnography (PSG) from more than 2,500 individuals ages 37 to 92 years old. Sleep architecture findings from that study may be more representative of age differences, as individuals with common age-related health conditions were included (i.e., hypertension, cardiovascular disease, pulmonary disease). Although there were differences across age-groups for some aspects of sleep, gender differences were more pronounced (see Figure 14.2).

Rates of sleep disorders and sleep complaints tend to increase with age, and older adults use more sleep medications on average than young adults (e.g., Espiritu, 2008). This relationship between complaints and age, however, actually may be attributable to medical, psychiatric, and other health burdens, as the higher rates of complaints in older individuals drop considerably when these factors are taken into account (Vitiello, Moe, & Prinz,

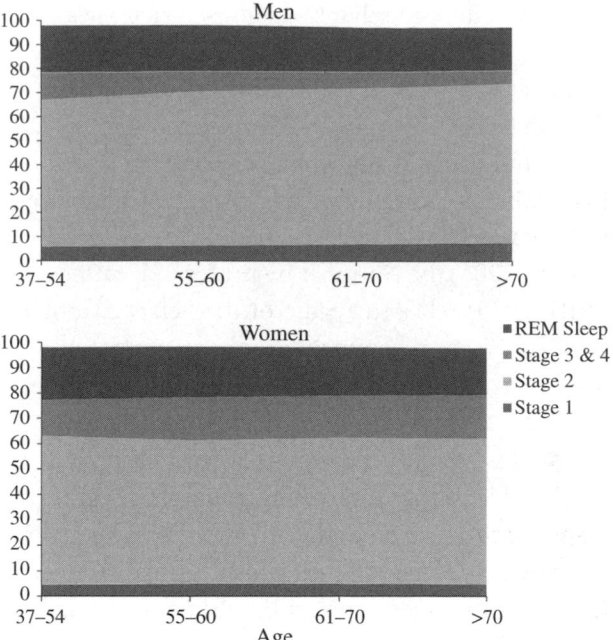

FIGURE 14.2. Mean (confidence interval = 95%) percentage of time spent in each sleep stage as a function of age for men and women. Data from Redline et al. (2004).

2002). Although declining health clearly plays a role, the reasons for the age-dependence of some aspects of sleep architecture and declines in sleep quality are not fully understood. Age-related changes in the somatotropic (i.e., growth hormone), gonadotropic, and hypothalamic-pituitary-adrenal (i.e., cortisol, proinflammatory cytokines) axes as well as other neurobiologic substrates (i.e., hyopcretin/orexin, serotonin, adenosine) may be involved.

Advanced Sleep Phase Disorder

Although the exact etiology of ASPD is unknown, abnormal interaction between the two processes that govern sleep (circadian rhythm, sleep homeostat) is believed to underlie persistent phase advance. The circadian process involved in sleep is closely related to other circadian rhythms, such as core body temperature rhythm, whereas the sleep homeostat refers to the body's tendency to balance sleep and wake, such that the "drive" for sleep increases the longer one is awake and vice versa.

---

[3]In 2007, the AASM published a new manual for scoring sleep and associated events, replacing the previous manual published by Reschaffen and Kales in 1968. Stage N3 in this new system refers to slow wave or deep sleep, which previously was split into stages 3 and stages 4 under the Reschaffen and Kales approach. The "N" was added to indicate that the stage falls within the broader category of non-rapid-eye-movement sleep.

Interaction between these processes influences sleepiness, sleep drive, and how long individuals sleep. Potential mechanisms behind abnormal interaction between these processes include alterations in response to light and other factors affecting the circadian sleep rhythm, shortening of the endogenous length of the sleep period, and gene polymorphisms (i.e., the circadian clock gene *hPer2*, Toh et al., 2001; CKI-delta mutation, Xu et al., 2005; Reid & Zee, 2011).

Age-related changes in the visual system (i.e., cataracts, macular degeneration) may contribute to alterations in older individuals' responses to light. Because the circadian process governing sleep runs slightly longer than 24 hr, it is regularly reset by exposure to the alternating day–night (i.e., light) pattern of the earth. Thus, although other factors also can affect the sleep circadian rhythm (i.e., exercise, social activities), light is the major influence or *zeitgeber* (German for "time giver"). Typically, exposure to bright light starting about 2 hr before bedtime will delay sleep onset and wake-up time, whereas exposure approximately 5 hr after bedtime (when core body temperature is lowest) has the opposite effect–advancing sleep onset and wake-up time. Exactly how age-related visual changes interact with this pattern, however, is unclear.

The suggestion that older individuals have an intrinsic age-related tendency toward phase advance often is made, but the evidence is mixed. Although the amplitude of the sleep–wake rhythm, body temperature, and some hormones decrease with age and can affect the circadian rhythm, the nature of that impact is not consistently in the direction of phase advance.

For example, research has shown older adults to be phase delayed, not advanced, in their melatonin peaks and has failed to find age-related differences in the length of core body temperature rhythm (Reid & Zee, 2011). On the basis of contradictory findings such as these, it has been suggested that homeostatic factors (e.g., napping, insufficient daytime activity) may play a larger role in the phase advances often seen in older adults than do circadian ones.

Insomnia

Multiple theories of chronic insomnia have been proposed and generally agree that insomnia is a disorder of hyperarousal (Perlis, Smith, & Pigeon, 2005). They differ, however, in their explanations of the factors associated with hyperarousal (Table 14.1). How well these theories apply to older individuals is unclear. Evidence supports the role of hyperarousal in primary insomnia in younger individuals, but is sparse and much weaker in older adults (Dzierzewski, O'Brien, Kay, & McCrae, 2010). One potential explanation is the tendency for late-life insomnia to co-occur with other conditions. Hyperarousal plays a major etiological role in primary insomnia, but is likely one of several interacting mechanisms in comorbid insomnia. Thus, a comprehensive model of late-life insomnia needs to include mechanisms related to insomnia more broadly (i.e., hyperarousal, sleep processes, cognition) as well as the impact of comorbid illnesses and age-related changes (sleep architecture, cognition, lifestyle) on those mechanisms.

Hyperarousal. Age-related changes in brain regions associated with the ascending arousal systems

---

TABLE 14.1

Theoretical Models of Insomnia and the Factors They Associate With Hyperarousal

Model	Factors
Physiologic	Trait anxiety and arousal
Behavioral	Behaviors (e.g., caffeine, nicotine), conditioned arousal
Cognitive	Cognitive arousal (rumination, worry)
Neurocognitive	Behaviors, cognitions, and conditioned cortical arousal

Note. From *Principles and Practice of Sleep Medicine* (4th ed., p. 714–725), by M. H. Kryger, T. Roth, and W. C. Dement (Eds.), 2005, Philadelphia, PA: Saunders. Copyright 2011 by Elsevier, Inc. Adapted with permission.

(e.g., increased orexin-A concentrations, decreased serotonergic innervation and noradrenergic cell volume) may help delineate the role of arousal in late-life insomnia (Dzierzewski et al., 2010).

Sleep processes.   The *circadian sleep drive* is influenced by both external (light, exercise, social activities) and internal (melatonin, core body temperature) factors that often are altered with age. For example, age-related visual changes may alter older adults' exposure to light, which in turn may alter the circadian sleep rhythm and other sleep-related circadian processes (i.e., core body temperature regulation). The *sleep homeostat* can be affected negatively by lifestyle-related changes associated with age (often due to retirement or illness). For example, increased napping can reduce sleep drive, whereas reduced exercise can disrupt both the sleep homeostat and core body temperature regulation.

Cognition.   Cognitive factors are relevant to the "subjectivity" of insomnia complaints and the arousal-inducing cognitive patterns that foster the transition from acute to chronic in individuals of all ages. Late-life insomnia may be particularly affected by the cognitive changes associated with normal aging (e.g., reduced working memory, controlled attention). For example, decreased controlled attention may affect the perception of sleep onset by interfering with the deactivation of sensory processing and consciousness centers (Dzierzewski et al., 2010).

Other factors that contribute to older adults' vulnerability to insomnia include age-related changes that slow drug absorption and metabolism and polypharmacy. Additionally, certain neurological diseases, which are more prevalent in the elderly (i.e., Alzheimer's disease, Parkinson's disease), interfere with the sleep of patients and their caregivers alike. Often, these caregivers are older themselves and thus may experience "triple jeopardy" when it comes to sleep: disruptive nighttime behaviors in their patients (i.e., sundowning in Alzheimer's), caregiving-related stress, and age-related comorbidities that increase sleep vulnerability.

Sleep-Disordered Breathing

In patients of all ages, CSA involves a loss of ventilatory drive because of instability in the respiratory control system. Breathing during sleep is heavily dependent on the metabolic control system, particularly arterial carbon dioxide ($PaCO_2$). Central apneic events tend to occur during transitions from wake to sleep as the $PaCO_2$ level that was adequate to stimulate breathing during wake may not be sufficient during sleep. Reasons for this include greater sensitivity or tendency toward instability in the respiratory control system or response to $PaCO_2$, longer circulation times, and improper functioning of the $PaCO_2$ control mechanisms. Insomnia (because it contributes to increased number and frequency of sleep–wake transitions) and some neurological disorders (multiple systems atrophy, Parkinson's disease), which are more common in older individuals, are predisposing factors for CSA.

OSA occurs because of a reduction in the area of the upper airway due to excessive bulk of tissues or abnormality in craniofacial structures (i.e., maxillomandibular malformation, enlarged adenoids or tonsils). Contributory factors include excess body weight, menopause, smoking, endocrine disorder (i.e., hypothyroidism), and Down's syndrome. A family history increases one's risk, and alcohol and nasal congestion can worsen OSA (AASM, 2005).

At one time, it was believed that SDB in older individuals was primarily central in nature, whereas in middle-age adults it was primarily obstructive in nature. Evidence, however, has failed to support this view. Instead, research has shown an increased tendency for upper-airway collapse with aging (AASM, 2005). Age-related loss of muscle and muscle tone in the upper airway increases older individuals' vulnerability. Other factors contributing to decreased muscle tone include medications and other substances with sedative properties (e.g., sleep medications, anxiolytics, alcohol). Sleep medication usage is a particularly important consideration for older individuals as their rate of usage is disproportionately high compared with younger individuals (e.g., Espiritu, 2008). There are also gender-related risk factors. For example, greater mass in the torso and neck is seen more often in men and increases their risk, particularly in middle and old age. Menopause is a factor for women, with postmenopausal rates approaching those of similarly aged men (AASM, 2005).

ASSESSMENT OF SLEEP IN OLDER ADULTS

Sleep can be measured subjectively (i.e., sleep diaries), behaviorally (i.e., actigraphy), or physiologically (i.e., PSG; see Table 14.2).[4] Of these approaches, sleep diaries are the most cost and time efficient (Lichstein, Durrence, Riedel, Taylor, & Bush, 2004). Sleep diaries recently have been standardized to facilitate comparisons across studies (Carney et al., 2012). PSG often is considered the gold standard in the objective assessment of sleep and traditionally has required an overnight stay in a sleep laboratory (Chesson et al., 1997), making it a costly, time involved, and inconvenient endeavor. PSG is recommended only if SDB or other organic sleep disorders (e.g., narcolepsy) are suspected (Schutte-Rodin, Broch, Buysse, Dorsey, & Sateia, 2008). For PSGs conducted in the laboratory, two or three nights may be needed as lack of familiarity with the laboratory setting may affect sleep, especially for older adults (Kales & Kales, 1984). Actigraphy offers another objective sleep measure, but its one-dimensional nature is limiting, particularly in comparison to PSG's multiple physiological measures. Whereas correspondence between actigraphy and PSG can vary widely depending on the variable and population in question, actigraphy is less intrusive; less expensive; and as a result, more feasible for longitudinal objective recording of circadian rhythms (Ancoli-Israel et al., 2005). See Table 14.2 for an overview of these and other sleep-related measures as well as their indications for use in the three disorders focused on in this chapter.

Although not a focus in this chapter, periodic limb movements warrant mention because they are common in older individuals and are an important symptom for differential diagnosis. When limb movements occur frequently and are associated with arousals, the patient may be diagnosed with periodic limb movement disorder (PLMD). The sleep history interview may provide indications of PLMD. For example, the patient (or bed partner) may report kicking during the night or waking up with disheveled sheets. In these cases, distinguishing between the typical leg jerks that are normative when falling asleep (often occurring in the transition from wake to sleep) and leg movements that occur throughout the sleep period is important. When geropsychologists suspect periodic limb movements based on patient (or bed partner) report, PSG is required for diagnosis. PLMD generally is treated with medications or iron supplementation.

Approaches

Sleep assessment as conducted by a geropsychologist typically involves a clinical interview covering the individual's sleep, medical, substance, and psychiatric history (Cuellar, Rogers, Hisghman, & Volpe, 2007; Schutte-Rodin et al., 2008). The AASM has published detailed guidelines for a number of specific sleep-related disorders. The most relevant for geropsychologists are those published by Schutte-Rodin et al. (2008) because they provide two sets of recommendations: minimal guidelines for general clinicians and more detailed guidelines for sleep specialists. At a minimum, they recommend the following: a general medical questionnaire (comorbid disorders, medication), a daytime sleepiness questionnaire (i.e., Epworth Sleepiness Scale; Johns, 1991), and 2 weeks of sleep diaries. Laboratory testing, PSG, and actigraphy are not administered routinely and should be used only when specific symptoms (i.e., apnea, limb movements) are present (Schutte-Rodin et al., 2008). Table 14.3 outlines the six-step sleep evaluation recommended for sleep specialists.

Special Considerations

Older adults with ASPD who resist their new natural sleep architecture by staying up later in the evening tend to experience less sleep time and daytime sleepiness. Thus, assessment should examine whether older adults' sleep complaints are the result of this resistance, ASPD, SDB, or some other organic sleep disorder (Neikrug & Ancoli-Israel, 2010a). For those with suspected insomnia, special consideration

---

[4]Although the administration of sleep diaries and actigraphy falls within psychologists' scope of practice, PSG requires physician referral. Also, as indicated in the text, PSG is not recommended for the evaluation of insomnia. Instead, it is used to evaluate SDB and other organic sleep issues (i.e., narcolepsy, periodic limb movements).

TABLE 14.2

Assessments Recommended for the Clinical Evaluation and Diagnosis of Sleep Disorders

Assessment	Description	Indicated use		
		CPD	I	SDB
	Objective measures			
Polysomnography (PSG)	Multiparametric monitoring system used to record psychophysiological changes and phenomena during sleep, including cortical electrical activity, eye movements, muscle activation, heart rhythm, and respiration; sensitive enough to detect stages of sleep–wake, cardiac events, and respiratory disturbance	O	R	R
Actigraphy	Worn on wrist or ankle to detect changes in movement indicating activity or inactivity and sleep–wake parameters	R	O	O
Portable monitor (PM)	Portable device to detect sleep-related apnea or hypopnea and respiratory disturbance	O	O	G
	Subjective measures			
Sleep log or diary	Allows user to prospectively record their sleep and wake patterns on a night-to-night basis for brief (1–2 days) or longer (7–14 days) periods; typically includes subjective recording of bedtime or arisetime, sleep latency, nighttime awakenings, sleep quality, and presleep behaviors or medications	R	R	O
Sleep history interview/ questionnaire	Structured clinical interview or comprehensive self-report questionnaire used to assess sleep complaints, presleep conditions, average and variable sleep–wake schedule, nocturnal symptoms, and daytime activities and functioning	R	R	R
Pittsburgh Sleep Quality Index (PSQI)	24-item, self-report questionnaire; assesses subjective sleep quality across 7 constructs (e.g., subjective sleep quality, sleep efficiency)	O	R	O
Epworth Sleepiness Scale (ESS)	8-item, self-report questionnaire; briefly assesses subjective sleepiness	O	R	R
Fatigue Severity Scale (FSS)	9-item, self-report questionnaire; briefly assesses daytime fatigue	O	R	O
Insomnia Severity Index (ISI)	7-item, self-report questionnaire; briefly assesses patient perception of insomnia	O	R	O
Dysfunctional Beliefs and Attitudes About Sleep Questionnaire (DBAS)	28-item, self-report questionnaire; assesses negative cognitions about sleep	O	R	O
Morningness–Eveningness Questionnaire (MEQ)	19-item, self-report questionnaire; assesses patterns of activity and rest and preferences for the timing of these activities to determine circadian preference	O	O	O

Note. ASPD = advanced sleep phase disorder (applies to delayed sleep phase disorder as well); I = insomnia; SDB = sleep-disordered breathing; R = recommended use for diagnosis; O = optional use (including use to establish baseline functioning for posttreatment comparisons, identifying comorbid sleep disorders, or differential diagnosis). Data from Epstein et al. (2009), Morgenthaler et al. (2007), and Schutte-Rodin et al. (2008).

TABLE 14.3

Recommended Steps in the Evaluation of Sleep Disturbance

Step	Evaluation	Information collected
1	The primary complaint	Factors leading to sleep disturbance; includes identifying the duration, frequency, severity, course, and factors that increase or decrease symptoms
2	Presleep conditions	The activities and the environment individuals engage in, before and as they attempt to sleep
3	Sleep–wake schedule	Sleep latency, number of awakenings, sleep duration, naps, night-to-night variability in symptoms
4	Nocturnal symptoms	Snoring or cessation of breathing, sleep-related movements, physical sensations and emotions associated with wakefulness[a]
5	Daytime activities and daytime function	Frequency of napping, type of work and work hours, activity lifestyle, cross time zone travel, functional disability, other factors that may be related to sleep disturbances and daytime activities and function
6	Other history	Medical, psychiatric, medication,[b] occupational histories

Note. Data from Schutte-Rodin, Broch, Buysse, Dorsey, and Sateia (2008).

[a]Bed partner interviews can be an asset in the assessment of breathing-related sleep disorders and sleep movement disorders. [b]Polypharmacy and its interaction with sleep disturbances are particularly important because of the increased prevalence of prescriptions in the older adult population.

should be given to other conditions that are particularly common among older individuals, as insomnia is frequently comorbid with other chronic medical and psychiatric conditions (Foley, Ancoli-Israel, Britz, & Walsh, 2004), including (but not limited to) pain, functional disability, and depression. For those with suspected SDB, portable PSG monitors can be used for diagnosis (with a comprehensive sleep evaluation), but they are not recommended for patients with major comorbid conditions (Collop et al., 2007). Portable monitors, however, may be particularly useful for older adults who are unable to undergo in-laboratory PSG because of immobility, safety concerns, or critical illness.

Assessment Controversies and Dilemmas

Subjective versus objective measurement. Sleep assessments can be broadly categorized as either objective or subjective. Although there is a general preferential bias toward objective methods (i.e., PSG, actigraphy), there are also good arguments that subjective methods are equally valid (Lichstein et al., 2004). Lichstein et al. (2004) have argued that the relationship between sleep and measurement of sleep is uncertain. As Heisenberg's

Uncertainty Principle states, the act of measurement alters the object that is being measured, rendering the measurement uncertain (Lichstein et al., 2004). PSG removes individuals from their familiar surroundings and places them in uncomfortable hospital beds with electrodes pasted throughout their body. Thus, it is not surprising that PSG often alters sleep during the first night of recording (Kales & Kales, 1984). Portable PSG monitoring may be an attractive alternative for some older patients. Actigraphy may be as well for examining sleep patterns and circadian issues, but not for assessing SDB. Importantly, when using actigraphy, concurrent sleep diaries also should be collected to help with the determination of sleep versus wake, as actigraphy alone may overrecord actual sleep for older adults who have a sedentary lifestyle (Ancoli-Israel et al., 2005). Sleep diaries, the best measure of subjective sleep (Lichstein et al., 2004), have the advantage of not altering the normal sleep setting or routines, but they do not come without flaws. They do not provide information about sleep stages or the presence of certain sleep disorders (e.g., sleep apnea) and are vulnerable to measurement error because they rely on individuals' ability to record estimated sleep patterns. Despite these limitations, most studies have found diaries to be relatively accurate (Lichstein et al., 2004).

Retrospective versus prospective reports. Retrospective and prospective accounts are distinguished by the duration of time over which respondents are asked to describe their sleep. Retrospective approaches encompass a longer period of time—for example, "Have you had sleep disturbances in the *past month*?" Prospective typically is used to refer to the future when measuring other types of phenomena. When used to measure sleep *subjectively*, however, it generally refers to the period immediately following the sleep period. For example, "Did you have any sleep disturbances *last night*?" In objective methodologies (e.g., actigraphy and PSG), prospective accounts are the in vivo moments of collection. Retrospective accounts are believed to have recall biases that tend to favor exaggerated disturbances (Gorin & Stone, 2001; Korotitsch & Nelson-Gray, 1999). Prospective accounts are likely more accurate and have less prejudice compared with retrospective accounts (Lichstein et al., 2004). Individuals who report last night's behavior have had less time for memory error and cognitive biases to develop compared with those who report sleep disturbances in the past month. Prospective accounts also allow for the collection of multiple sampling points that can be averaged to obtain a more representative sleep estimate than a single retrospective point can provide (Lichstein et al., 2004).

Nursing homes. Older adults living in nursing homes have been shown to have disturbed, highly fragmented (rarely experiencing a single consolidated hour) sleep via actigraphy (Ancoli-Israel et al., 2005; Jacobs, Ancoli-Israel, Parker, & Kripke, 1989; Neikrug & Ancoli-Israel, 2010b). Although sleep compensation, increased time in bed, decreased social constraints, and deterioration of the circadian sleep–wake rhythm (Jacobs et al., 1989; Neikrug & Ancoli-Israel, 2010b) may contribute to this fragmentation, environmental factors also may contribute (i.e., noise, roommate situation, light; Neikrug & Ancoli-Israel, 2010b). Low light levels, a concern for all older individuals given the impact of light on circadian rhythms (Lewy,

1983), represent a particular concern for nursing home residents who may spend a considerable amount of time in dark or poorly lit rooms (Sinoo, van Hoof, & Kort, 2011). Research suggests light therapy may improve sleep consolidation (Shochat, Martin, Marler, & Ancoli-Israel, 2000).

Dementia. Approximately one quarter of persons with dementia (PWD) have sleep disturbances (Rose & Lorenz, 2010). Dementia impairs sufferers' ability to stay asleep as well as awake, and thus results in sleep–wake fragmentation throughout the day and night (Pat-Horenczyk, Klauber, Shochat, & Ancoli-Israel, 1998). SDB, circadian disturbance, and other factors (medications, other conditions), however, also can contribute to the daytime sleepiness often seen in these patients. Actigraphy represents an attractive assessment option for PWDs and others who have difficulty recalling their sleep patterns. For PWDs capable of self-report, the Epworth Sleepiness Scale or similar measure can be used to rule out SDB as the cause for the excessive daytime sleepiness often seen in these patients. For those incapable of self-report, caregivers can provide proxy information to aid with appropriate diagnosis.

CLIENT-PROVIDER ISSUES RELATED TO INTERVENTION

No sleep assessments are specific to an older population. As previously discussed, however, some considerations regarding the assessment and diagnostic process may be unique to older adults. As with patients of all ages, discussion of the rationale for the various measures used and their indication is helpful. Some older patients and their families may be unfamiliar with or concerned about PSG assessment. The geropsychologist can alleviate such concerns by providing education about PSG.

Older patients and their families sometimes assume that poor sleep is simply a part of normal aging and thus downplay the need for (and likelihood of success of) intervention. Education about normative age-related changes (see the following section) is helpful for identifying when sleep issues

TABLE 14.4

Average Effect Sizes Across CBT-I Trials in Middle-Age and Older Adults

Outcome	Effect size
Sleep onset latency	0.51**
Wake after sleep onset	0.73**
Sleep efficiency	1.47***
Mood (depression, anxiety)	1.45***

Note. Data from Bliwise, Friedman, Nekich, and Yesavage (1995), and Irwin, Cole, and Nicassio (2006). * small, ** medium, *** large (Cohen's standards).

represent a problem requiring diagnosis and treatment. Likewise, such education also can alleviate the concerns of older patients who sleep well but are concerned about their sleep because they no longer sleep as well as they did when they were younger. In terms of intervention outcomes, a variety of evidence now exists to indicate that effective treatments exist for late-life sleep disorders. For the most part, interventions that work well for younger individuals also work well for older individuals (see Table 14.4).

Treatment Approaches

ASPD. ASPD can be treated with either chronotherapy or phototherapy. Chronotherapy involves adjusting the sleep–wake schedule by drastically delaying bedtime to shift the circadian rhythm to the desired sleep schedule. For example, if the patient currently sleeps from 3 a.m. to 11 a.m. but wants to sleep from 11 p.m. to 7 a.m., initially their bedtime should be delayed 3 hr (6 a.m. to 2 p.m.). Each successive daily adjustment results in a 3 hr delay (e.g., 9 a.m. to 5 p.m.; 12 p.m. to 8 p.m.; 3 p.m. to 11 p.m., and so on) until the desired schedule is obtained. Because this treatment does not involve entrainment with light or other environmental adjustments, the mechanism by which circadian rhythms are affected is unknown. There is some evidence that short, daily advances of the sleep–wake schedule works (Cvengros & Wyatt, 2009). Phototherapy also may be beneficial for ASPD, including introducing artificial bright light

in presleep hours and avoiding bright light 2 hours following awakening, while implementing adjuvant small delays in bedtime (e.g., 30-minute delay). In addition to these approaches, the AASM practice parameters for the treatment of circadian rhythm disorders indicates timed melatonin administration for treating ASPD (Morgenthaler et al., 2007). DSPD necessitates similar interventions as ASPD; however, light exposure (e.g., optimal time and quantity of light) still is under investigation. The AASM practice parameters do not recommend the use of hypnotics for either APSD or DPSD (Morgenthaler et al., 2007).

Insomnia. Cognitive and behavioral treatments for insomnia include several well-established therapeutic strategies that target a broad range of etiologic factors and symptoms of insomnia, including sleep education, sleep hygiene, stimulus control, sleep restriction or compression, relaxation, and cognitive therapy (Carney & Edinger, 2010). The combination of these stand-alone techniques into one package treatment approach commonly is referred to as cognitive–behavioral therapy (CBT-I). The efficacy of CBT-I is well-documented; effect sizes across numerous trials investigating CBT-I have shown moderate to large effect sizes on a range of sleep and mood-related treatment outcomes (see Table 14.4). Researchers and clinicians (including the NIH) consider CBT-I to be the first-line treatment for chronic insomnia given its numerous advantages over pharmcacological interventions.

Late-life insomnia can develop as the result of various etiologies; therefore, implementing a multicomponent behavioral approach to treatment increases the probability that one or more of these techniques will target factors resulting in a patient's sleep disturbance. Only one technique listed—sleep restriction—has been indicated as a stand-alone behavioral treatment for insomnia. To be considered CBT-I, two of the aforementioned techniques must be included in treatment. The typical CBT-I package, however, includes sleep education, sleep hygiene, relaxation training, stimulus control, sleep restriction, and cognitive therapy (see Exhibit 14.1). Compared with utilizing these techniques as stand-alone treatments, using CBT-I as a package treatment demonstrated greater efficacy (Edinger & Sampson, 2003) and has provided longer maintenance of treatment gains (Morin, Colecchi, Stone, Sood, & Brink, 1999). This combination treatment has resulted in both statistical and clinical improvements in sleep (e.g., sleep onset latency [SOL], wake after sleep onset [WASO], subjective sleep quality ratings) in older adults across several studies (Edinger & Sampson, 2003; Germain et al., 2006; Pallesen et al., 2003). Moreover, a recent meta-analysis evaluating 23 randomized controlled trials (RCTs) that employed behavioral interventions for both middle-age and older adults found that a range of behavioral interventions (e.g., behavioral strategies only, relaxation, and variants of CBT-I) improved SOL, WASO, SE, and subjective sleep quality (Irwin, Cole, & Nicassio, 2006).

Hypnotic medications are the most common treatment prescribed for older adults with insomnia (Dzierzewski et al., 2010). Although a range of medications are indicated for the treatment of insomnia (e.g., benzodiazepine receptor agonists, sedating antidepressants, and melatonin), no single pharmacological method is indicated to treat insomnia. Although the newer benzodiazepine receptor agonist drugs (e.g., zolpidem, zaleplon, zopiclone, eszopiclone) were designed to reduce negative side effects, impaired cognitive functioning, daytime sleepiness, and an increased risk of falls are observed with their use. Additionally, sleep-walking and sleep-eating behaviors that have been observed with these drugs could be especially risky for older adults. Although hypnotics are effective for short-term use, many lose effectiveness over time while retaining the potential for dependence and rebound insomnia (McCrae, Nau, Taylor, & Lichstein, 2006). Nevertheless, hypnotics should be considered for acute insomnia or when behavioral treatments have been unsuccessful.

Double-blind, placebo-controlled studies have provided evidence for 3–6 month use of eszopiclone (Krystal et al., 2003), ramelteon (Mayer et al., 2009), zolpidem (Perlis, McCall, Krystal, & Walsh, 2004), and zaleplon (Ancoli-Israel et al., 2005); however, only zaleplon was investigated utilizing an

---

Exhibit 14.1 Multicomponent Cognitive–Behavioral Therapy for Insomnia (CBT-I)

Sleep hygiene
- Eliminate or reduce caffeine use after 12 P.M.
- Do not drink alcohol within 2 hr of bedtime
- Do not use tobacco within 2 hr of bedtime
- Do not eat heavy meals within 2 hr of bedtime
- Do not exercise within 2 hr of bedtime (though routine exercise is encouraged)

Stimulus control
- Lie down to go to sleep only when you are sleepy
- Do not use the bed for anything except sleep and sex. Do not eat, read, watch television, or worry in bed
- If you cannot fall asleep within 10 min, get up and go to another room. Only return to bed when you feel sleepy again
- If you return to bed and still cannot fall asleep, repeat Step 3. Do this as often as necessary throughout the night
- Set your alarm and get up at the same time every morning regardless of how much you slept during the night. This will help your body acquire a constant sleep rhythm
- Do not nap during the day

Sleep restriction/sleep compression
- Aims to match the patient's time spent in bed to their actual time spent sleeping
- Prescribe bed and wake times that more closely reflect time spent asleep
- Sleep restriction abruptly tailors the time in bed to reflect sleep needs
- Sleep compression gradually reduces time spent in bed to match sleep time

Relaxation
- Diaphragmatic breathing, biofeedback, imagery, and meditation are all appropriate relaxation approaches for insomnia treatment
- Progressive muscle relaxation (PMR) is an empirically supported treatment by the AASM
- Leading patients through a deep breathing exercise, followed by alternatively tensing and relaxing muscle groups (e.g., arms, neck, back, legs) while attending to feelings of relaxation during and after the process

Cognitive therapy
- Identifying maladaptive beliefs about sleep and replacing them with more adaptive thoughts and attitudes
- Integrates basic education about sleep; understanding normative sleep patterns and experiences can be helpful in addressing mistaken beliefs about sleep

older adult population. Glass et al. (2005) conducted a meta-analysis of 24 RCTs of any pharmacological treatment in adults over 60 years old. They found that across different types of hypnotics, subjective sleep quality improved and there were small but significant improvement in nighttime awakenings. The risk of adverse events, however, with sedative use was higher than with placebo; the most prominent side effects being falls, motor vehicle accidents, cognitive events, and daytime fatigue. Glass et al. concluded that benefits associated with the use of hypnotic sleep aids in older adults are minimal and are outweighed by risks, which are exacerbated by other age-related factors, such as polypharmacy and cognitive impairment.

Antidepressant medication, which is not indicated for directly managing sleep disturbances, can have sedating effects that make them appealing choices to prescribe for insomnia. Evidence demonstrates, however, that sedating antidepressants like trazodone can be associated with side effects, such as impairments in short-term memory, verbal learning, equilibrium, and arm muscle endurance, with only minimal benefit to sleep (Roth, McCall, & Liguori, 2011). Older adults may use alcohol or over-the-counter sleep aids to manage their symptoms: 6% of older adults use over-the-counter medication several nights a week and 6% use alcohol several nights a week (Pallesen et al., 2003). Given the risk for polypharmacy, side effects, and lack of research supporting long-term use in older adults, close supervision of use of pharmacological use in older adults is warranted (Dzierzewski et al., 2010), although the AASM suggests that these medications can be prescribed to them with these caveats in mind (Schutte-Rodin et al., 2008).

The combination of CBT-I with pharmacological treatments also may be advantageous in treating insomnia in older adults. Morin et al. (2009) found that CBT-I alone and CBT-I in combination with zolpidem had significant improvements in sleep latency and WASO and SE and also produced equivalent amounts of treatment responders and remission within responders. Despite producing larger initial gains than behavioral or pharmacological

therapy alone, combined therapy had variable long-term effects at 3-, 6-, and 12-month follow-up. Morin et al. postulated this effect was due to poor timing of presentation of the hypnotic and behavioral treatment and suggested that behavioral treatment *follow* hypnotic administration. Another study examining CBT-I, combined CBT-I and temazepam, temazepam, and placebo revealed that active conditions produced equivalent improvements; however, CBT-I was rated as most favorable by patients and had the longest lasting long-term changes at 24-month follow up (Morin et al., 1999). The AASM practice parameters for the treatment of insomnia suggest that this combined therapy does not show a consistent advantage over CBT-I alone and that whenever possible, CBT-I should be the treatment of choice (Schutte-Rodin et al., 2008). Specific recommendation for older adults include consideration of lower doses for all medications especially because of the potential for drug interactions and unwarranted side effects. Other combined pharmacological treatments that should be considered include timing of medications for comorbid medical conditions—for example, timing of administration of diuretics could significantly affect nocturia and subsequent fragmented sleep.

SDP–Continuous Positive Airway Pressure Adherence Issues

The gold standard treatment for OSA in older adults is continuous positive airway pressure (CPAP) devices. By introducing constant airflow through the normally obstructed airway, CPAP masks can reduce the AHI, normalize blood oxygen saturation, and reduce nighttime arousals associated with apnea or hypopnea events (Sawyer et al., 2011). Overnight PSG determines adequate titration levels for the CPAP device to maintain airway patency. Physiological differences may result in older adults requiring lower levels of CPAP than younger adults despite equivalent disease severity (Weaver & Chasens, 2007).

Many issues are associated with CPAP use that serve as barriers to consistent adherence to use of the device. Although the parameters that constitute optimal CPAP adherence are inconsistent, empirical evidence suggests that 4 hr per night on 70% of nights is the generally established dose needed to be considered adherent (Sawyer et al., 2011). The literature on the adequate dose response of CPAPs, however, reveal that 4 hr should not be a standard time, as increased time spent sleeping with the device has demonstrated more improvement on sleep and health-related outcomes. Factors that influence adherence include patient characteristics, titration of the device and device-related side effects, psychological factors, and social influences (Sawyer et al., 2011). Airway anatomy and physiology within individual patients can affect the severity of OSA and thereby adherence. Psychological factors, such as depression and negative mood, low self-efficacy, and coping style also have been found to affect CPAP adherence as well as device factors, such as mask comfort, humidity applied to combat nasal dryness, and claustrophobia. Finally, education about sleep apnea and adapting to a CPAP as well as a patient's living arrangements (i.e., having a bed partner) can influence adherence.

Low adherence in older adults is associated with depression, claustrophobia or mask intolerance, nasal irritation, and increased nocturia; high adherence in older adults is associated with education about risks of untreated OSA and benefits of CPAP treatment, early evaluation of CPAP adherence and barriers to adherence, and individualized treatment plans for adherence (Weaver & Chasens, 2007; Weaver & Sawyer, 2010). Evidence is mixed for the effect of age on adherence, suggesting both lower CPAP adherence with age and higher CPAP adherence with age. Lower rates of adherence in older adults have been associated with poor symptom remission (e.g., daytime sleepiness, snoring, other sleep disturbances), nocturia, CPAP initiation at older age, cigarette use, and lack of participation in CPAP psychoeducation groups (Sawyer et al., 2011). Given the demands of use of the CPAP device, older adults with comorbid medical conditions (including Alzheimer's disease and other dementias) may have difficulty with adherence to treatment.

The efficacy of CPAP treatment has mostly been studied in middle-age adults. Although a few studies are examining solely older adults, many studies do not exclude them. CPAP has been shown to be effective in lowering AHI levels, increasing deep sleep, and decreasing self-reported symptoms (e.g., gasping for air while sleeping, snoring, and witnessed apnea events). Moreover, in older adults, CPAP has been shown to reduce subjective reports, but not objective measures, of daytime sleepiness and to have a positive effect on cardiac functioning. Some evidence also suggests that that nocturia, commonly present in patients with OSA, is reduced with CPAP use (Weaver & Chasens, 2007). Sawyer et al. (2011) suggested several interventions aimed at adherence to CPAP therapy. Patient education regarding the health risks associated with sleep apnea and how to use and adapt to the device is helpful, but it does not produce significant changes alone. CBT that includes education about OSA and CPAP, goal development, managing treatment expectations, and addressing negative cognitions associated with CPAP use also has been implemented. In a study of middle-age adults using CPAP for OSA, implementing CBT resulted in increased CPAP adherence at 1 week and 1 month after treatment compared with those who received treatment as usual. Self-efficacy and social support was also higher in the CBT group (Richards, Bartlett, Wong, Malouff, & Grunstein, 2007). Therefore, targeting the psychosocial factors that CBT affects (e.g., support of bed partner, normalizing CPAP use, self-efficacy for implementing treatment) is an effective approach for increasing adherence of device usage.

CONTROVERSIES AND DILEMMAS IN TREATMENT

There are several controversies and dilemmas in approaching treatment of the various sleep disorders that occur in older adults. These include questioning the efficacy of CBT-I in older adults, treating older adults with comorbid conditions (including apnea), the use of medication versus psychological treatments, implementation issues with special populations, and hypnotic dependence.

Evidence-Based Treatments

Does CBT-I work for older adults? Although initially there was some concern that CBT-I may be inappropriate for use with older adults with insomnia, research on this approach clearly refutes this position. Although investigations of the use of CBT-I in older adults has varied systematically in terms of the age range of participants included in studies (e.g., "older adult" can mean more than 55, 60, or 65 years), the preponderance of evidence of these trials suggests that CBT-I can be just as effective in older adults as in younger or middle-age adults. For example, the recent meta-analysis by Irwin et al. (2006) demonstrated moderate to high effects of CBT for insomnia in older adults age 55 years or more.

Treatment for comorbid insomnia in older adults.

Insomnia comorbid with medical and psychological conditions is common in older adults. The outdated approach was to treat the *primary* medical condition as the primary aim of treatment with the assumption that insomnia would resolve with the resolution of the medical condition (McCrae, Dzierzewski, & Kay, 2009). Insomnia, however, can persist even after the comorbid medical condition has subsided via perpetuating cognitions regarding sleep disturbances (Harvey, 2005). Older adults have increased risk for having numerous health problems; as such, a sole diagnosis of insomnia in older adults in unlikely, and CBT-I does not need to be delayed until medical comorbidities are resolved. Attenuating insomnia symptoms has the potential to improve the concurrent medical conditions.

Utilizing CBT-I has been shown to resolve comorbid insomnia across a range of medical (e.g., breast cancer, fibromyalgia, and other medical conditions; Currie, Wilson, Pontefract, & deLaplante, 2000; Edinger, Wohlgemuth, Krystal, & Rice, 2005; Quesnel, Savard, Simard, Ivers, & Morin, 2003) and psychological (e.g., bereavement, depression, adjustment disorders) conditions. An important advantage of CBT-I for these medical populations is that unlike hypnotics indicated for insomnia, behavioral treatments do not contribute to the risk of polypharmacy and are unlikely to cause side effects that will be dangerous for the comorbid diagnosis. For each distinctive medical diagnosis comorbid with insomnia, specific concerns may interfere with the implementation of these behavioral techniques. Moreover,

specific medical conditions may have distinct sleep-related or illness-related concerns that disrupt sleep.

Hypnotics versus behavioral or CBT approaches to treatment.

The evaluation of hypnotic medications versus behavioral or CBT-I approaches to insomnia reveal several mixed outcomes. Patients have rated CBT-I as more favorable than hypnotic medication, despite both treatments producing similar treatment outcomes (Morin et al., 1999). A trial comparing CBT-I, zopiclone, and placebo revealed that CBT-I yielded significant improvements in total wake time, SE, and time spent in slow-wave sleep. The zopiclone and placebo groups, however, did not differ from one another (Sivertsen, Omvik, & Pallesen, 2006). Psychological approaches to insomnia have demonstrated moderate to large effect sizes (0.65–0.94), with approximately 70%–80% of patients exhibiting improvements posttreatment (Morin, Culbert, & Schwartz, 1994). Therefore, it appears that psychological approaches to insomnia treatment may be preferable, in terms of both improvements in symptoms as well as patient self-reports of treatment satisfaction. Moreover, for older adults, CBT-I has been shown to be more effective in the long-term treatment of insomnia without the association of the mainly short-term benefit and negative side effects ascribed to pharmacological treatments. Despite the empirical evidence to support the use of behavioral approaches, these techniques are still underutilized in favor of pharmacological approaches.

Treatment of comorbid apnea and insomnia.

Research is limited on treatment of concurrent apnea and insomnia. In patients with SDB and comorbid insomnia, cognitive behavioral methods and lifestyle changes (e.g., weight loss) should be attempted before beginning a CPAP regimen (Lavie, 2007). Improvements in insomnia severity and daytime impairments were observed in patients with SDB in addition to chronic insomnia after receiving both CBT and treatment for their SDB (e.g., CPAP, oral appliance, or surgery); however, only moderate improvements in daytime impairments were seen with CBT alone (Krakow et al., 2004). Another study examining SDB in chronic insomnia found surgical intervention for SDB improved sleep quality and respiratory measures for one third of patients, whereas those who received only CBT did not report that their insomnia improved (although CBT increased sleep time and decreased sleep latency; Guilleminault, Davis, & Huynh, 2008).

The use of benzodiazepines in patients with insomnia and apnea is limited because these drugs can reduce upper-airway muscle tone and decrease ventilatory response to hypoxia and can increase and prolong apnea events during the night (Lavie, 2007; Luyster, Buysse, & Strollo, 2010). However, GABAergic non-benzodiazepine drugs, such as zaleplon, zolpidem, and eszopiclone, have fewer effects on muscle tone and may be better suited for insomnia comorbid with OSA. An investigation of eszopiclone, however, found no difference between drug and placebo on AHI scores, arousals, duration of respiratory events, or oxygen saturation, although participants experienced improved SE and WASO (Rosenberg, Roach, Scharf, & Amato, 2007). Similar effects on respiratory events were found with zolpidem; however, sleep latency and number of arousals was reduced (Berry & Patel, 2006). Therefore, hypnotic use for comorbid apnea and insomnia appears to help attenuate insomnia symptoms without disrupting respiratory function, but caution must be exercised in the type and dosage of hypnotic prescribed, and patients must be monitored closely by the prescribing physician. The potential for habituation, dependency, and rebound insomnia also must be taken into consideration. Sequenced studies that evaluate the effect of CBT, CPAP, and hypnotics are warranted to fully understand the optimal treatments and treatment sequences for these highly comorbid conditions (Luyster et al., 2010).

Implementation Issues Surrounding Evidence-Based Treatments

Dementia patients and caregivers. Patients with dementia have an increased risk for developing insomnia; however, the approach to treatment in this special population can be quite complicated. Typically, these patients are treated with hypnotic medications (McCrae et al., 2009). There are some reservations, however, about the efficacy of hypnotics for this population and the potential for

exacerbation of their medical conditions, with the use of hypnotic medication, including the potential for the exacerbation of cognitive decline. Although employing a multicomponent CBT-I protocol with dementia patients may not be appropriate, there have been attempts to train caregivers of these patients to implement these techniques with their care recipient (McCurry, Gibbons, Logsdon, Vitiello, & Teri, 2005). In a study examining dementia patients in a nursing home with nighttime sleep fragmentation, daytime treatment with bright-light therapy did not produce overall improvements in sleep or daytime alertness. Circadian rhythms, however, were delayed and quality of the circadian rhythm was improved with bright-light therapy.

Much attention also has focused on the sleep of caregivers of dementia patients. Caregivers consistently report poorer sleep quality than noncaregivers (McCurry, Vitiello, Gibbons, Logsdon, & Teri, 2006). Sleep difficulties among caregivers has been shown to be predictive of the decision to place dementia patients in full-time care facilities, and caregivers also have reported high levels of vigilance and anxiety during the night regarding the well-being of their care recipient. A brief CBT-I protocol showed improvements in sleep quality and SE in caregivers (McCurry, Logsdon, Vitiello, & Teri, 1998). Additional research is warranted to fully understand the efficacy of particular techniques of CBT-I in caregivers and to evaluate whether caregivers with insomnia can achieve sleep-related improvements similar to noncaregivers with insomnia.

Hypnotic dependence. Because older adults seeking treatment for insomnia are likely to receive hypnotic medications as the first-line treatment, their risk of developing hypnotic-dependent insomnia is high. This condition occurs when insomnia symptoms persist with the use of hypnotics; however, discontinuing the hypnotic would result in worsening sleep (Dzierzewski et al., 2010). Therefore, patients will continue to use medication to avoid worsening sleep, even though the medication is no longer efficacious. CBT-I has been demonstrated to be an effective approach to improving sleep disturbances without necessitating discontinuation of hypnotic medications (Soeffing, Lichstein, & Nau, 2008). In comparison to medication tapering alone, utilizing CBT-I to assist in tapering hypnotic medication also has been shown to be effective in attaining hypnotic abstinence at 12-month follow-up as well as improvement in sleep (Baillargeon et al., 2003). Hence, utilization of CBT-I can be expected to improve sleep even in individuals who continue to use hypnotic medication and effectively make sleep-related improvements during the process of medication tapering and hypnotic abstinence posttreatment.

DISTINGUISHING DEMOGRAPHIC CHARACTERISTICS

Although long neglected, in the past 15 years, data on race and sleep has begun to accumulate. By now it is well established that there are racial differences. Data specifically focusing on older adults is less plentiful. A review comparing the sleep of African Americans (AA) and Caucasians (CA; Durrence & Lichstein, 2006), found that the weight of evidence supports the view that AA experience worse sleep than CA with respect to SOL, rated sleep quality, percent light sleep, and amount of napping. Recent data from a large sample of community-dwelling older men (Song et al., 2012) are consistent with these findings. AA had longer SOL, shorter total sleep time, lower SE, and less slow-wave sleep than CA. Furthermore, Hispanic men slept longer than AA and Asian Americans. But there are contradictions in the literature. For example, AA elders had fewer insomnia complaints than CA (Foley et al., 1995). Furthermore, perceived racial discrimination as a unique source of psychosocial stress, may be an important incremental factor in developing sleep complaints (Grandner, Hale, et al., 2012).

Other sleep disorders show varying patterns. Sleep apnea prevalence is higher in AA compared with CA in middle-age samples (Durrence & Lichstein, 2006), but there are less data, and the differences are less clear among older adults. In older samples, one study found a higher rate among AA (Kripke et al., 1997; unadjusted for body mass index [BMI] and gender risk factors), and another found a higher rate among CA (Redline et al., 1997; adjusted for BMI and gender). One study found no difference in sleep apnea prevalence among older adults

(unadjusted for BMI and gender), but the severity of sleep apnea was worse among AA (Ancoli-Israel et al., 1995). A recent meta-analysis identified a health disparity for sleep apnea (Ruiter et al., 2010). Although it did not focus on older adults, it did find higher prevalence and severity were associated with being AA, and age was not a significant moderator, implying that these differences held at all ages.

The rate of PLMs in AA are less than CA at all ages (Scofield, Roth, & Drake, 2008). Inconsistent results leave unclear whether restless leg syndrome prevalence varies significantly by race or ethnicity (Innes, Selfe, & Agarwal, 2011).

As measured by either income or level of education, socioeconomic status (SES) often is related inversely to insomnia, although not all studies are in accord with this conclusion (Ohayon, 2002). More recently, the association of low SES with higher prevalence of insomnia was replicated after controlling for depression, anxiety, and race (Gellis et al., 2005), suggesting SES effects are independent of race and mood. Mechanisms through which SES contributes to sleep complaints have not been isolated, but social isolation (McHugh, Casey, & Lawlor, 2011) and unhealthy lifestyle (Gerber, Brand, Holsboer-Trachsler, & Puhse, 2010) are possibilities.

Gender also plays a role in the development of sleep disorders in older adults. In some cases, women experience greater frequency or severity, but there are many exceptions to this trend. A higher rate of insomnia among women than men in all age-groups is well established, and this discrepancy widens with increasing age (Ohayon, 2002). Recent data from a large epidemiology study confirm that self-reported sleep disturbance and tiredness are greater in women than men in all age-groups (Grandner, Martin, et al., 2012). In a study of older adult men, decreased slow-wave sleep (N3) was associated with elevated blood pressure (Fung et al., 2011). Similar data are not available for older adult women, but research showing N3 is more depressed in older men than women (Redline et al., 2004) suggests that hypertension derived from this mechanism may be more pronounced in men. Several other sleep disorders exhibit gender-specific trends. Sleep apnea is more common in men at all ages. But with menopause, incident sleep apnea accelerates in women, and in later years, the sleep apnea gap between the sexes shrinks substantially (Bixler et al., 2001). One study (Ancoli-Israel et al., 1991) reported an evolving pattern in periodic PLM among older adults. In the young-old (ages 65–69 years), severe PLM is more common in men, but in the old-old (age greater than 80 years), it is more common in women.

Case Example 1: Comorbid Insomnia With ASPD

MB, an 82-year old woman living in the community with her husband of 60 years, presented to her primary care physician complaining of excessive daytime sleepiness in the late afternoon and early evening. She also reported having "insomnia" which upon further questioning she identified as waking up in the morning at 4 a.m. and being unable to fall back asleep. She endorsed feelings of depression and anxiety related to her relationship with her husband. She noted that she was unable to engage in evening activities with him due to extreme sleepiness and as a result, she feels they are "fighting more." Her medical history includes hypertension, diabetes mellitus, and gastroesophageal reflux disease. She reported spending most of her days indoors with limited physical activity. Given her inability to maintain sleep in the early morning, she was requesting medication to "help her sleep."
On the basis of a week of concurrent sleep diaries and actigraphic assessment, MB's sleep phase was advanced (average sleep onset of 7 p.m. and average wake time of 3:30 a.m.). An assessment of mood and anxiety disorders revealed mild symptoms of depression (which she related to interpersonal conflict). PSG (which accommodated her typical advanced schedule) was negative for other sleep disorders. Given the absence of a major affective disorder or other sleep disorders and the validation of an advanced phase with a clinical history, sleep diaries, and actigraphy, MB was diagnosed with ASPD. Given her limited light exposure, the initial treatment approach consisted of the administration of bright-light therapy in the early evening (e.g., 7 to 9 p.m.) for 7 consecutive days. After completing the treatment, MB reported a bedtime and wake time delay of 1 hr. Second, chronotherapy was implemented in which her bedtime delayed by 1 hr

every 2 days until her desired bedtime was reached. As a result of these approaches, MB achieved her desired bedtime of 11 p.m. and wake time of 7 a.m.

Case Example 2: Hypnotic Dependence

This case on the treatment of a challenging case of an older adult with a history of addictive behavior now dependent on hypnotics previously has been reported (Cooper, Lichstein, & Aguillard, 2003). AB, a retired 70-year-old Caucasian male who lived with his wife of 48 years, presented at an accredited sleep disorders center with an insomnia complaint compounded with hypnotic dependence and was assigned to the behavioral sleep medicine program. His history included past and present multiple serious medical problems, prescription narcotic addiction, and frequent alcohol use. AB was prescribed temazepam 15 mg 3 years earlier by anther provider when difficulty initiating and maintaining sleep first appeared. AB reported that this medication was effective at first, but tolerance and dose escalation shortly followed. In addition, AB reported nightly use of melatonin. Two weeks of sleep diaries confirmed mild insomnia with respect to SOL, WASO, and sleep efficiency (Table 14.5), and average nightly 35 mg of temazepam and 6 mg of melatonin (Figure 14.3). CBT (passive relaxation, stimulus control, cognitive therapy, and sleep hygiene) was implemented simultaneous with gradual drug weaning (approximate 15% weekly reduction of the two medications over 10 weeks). AB was cooperative and mostly adherent throughout the 10-week treatment period. After four weekly treatment sessions, AB requested brief phone contact for subsequent sessions unless any difficulties arose. Four weeks later, AB did request an in-person session to discuss minor side effects and aid in continuing his adherence to the treatment plan. By the end of treatment, AB reported hypnotic abstinence (Figure 14.3, week 12), with no change in sleep. Two follow-up occasions occurred. First, 1 month posttreatment, AB was contacted by phone (designated follow-up week 1, Figure 14.3). He reported no hypnotic use or difficulties with sleep. Second, 1-year posttreatment (designated follow-up week 2, Figure 14.3 and follow-up, Table 14.5), AB was contacted by phone, and he again reported no resumption of medication or difficulties with sleep.

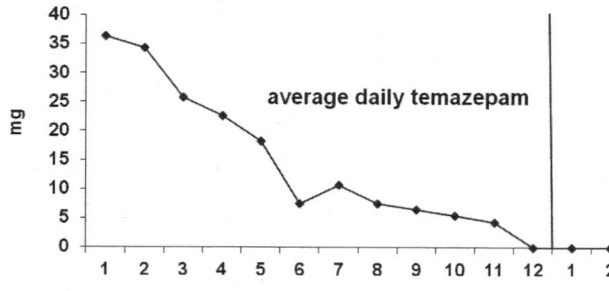

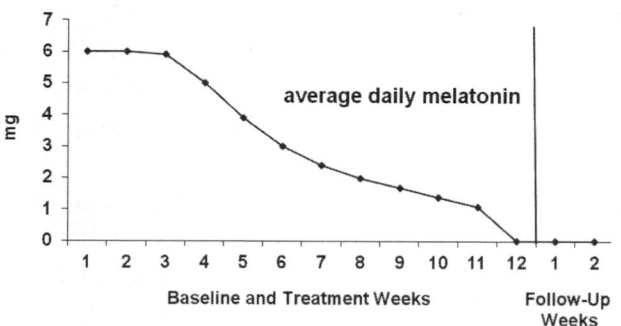

FIGURE 14.3. Average daily medication at baseline (weeks 1–2), treatment (weeks 3–12), and 1-year follow-up.

At that time, he was asked to complete another 2 weeks of sleep diaries to more carefully assess his progress. Sleep diaries confirmed no medication use (Figure 14.3) and not only had sleep not deteriorated, but clinically significant improvement had occurred on several sleep variables (SOL, WASO, and SE; Table 14.5). This case demonstrated long-term sleep improvement in the presence of gradual hypnotic elimination with an older adult. The complicating

factor of a history of addiction required careful monitoring but did not undermine therapeutic progress.

Case Example 3: OSA–CPAP Treatment Adherence

JF, an 83-year-old Caucasian man, was referred to an accredited sleep disorder center for evaluation of insomnia and excessive daytime sleepiness. His wife of 57 years accompanied him and provided collateral information. Mr. F's history was significant for degenerative joint disease, hypertension, gastroesophageal reflux disease, polyneuropathy, sleep apnea, and adjustment disorder. He had been diagnosed with mild cognitive impairment within the past year and was being treated pharmacologically for daytime sleepiness as well as suspected neurodegenerative disease, high blood pressure, and enlarged prostate. Upon interview, he denied difficulties falling asleep, staying asleep, and waking up too early. He reported difficulties with memory and concentration. which he attributed to his tendency to work on his computer late into the early hours of the morning and often falling asleep at his computer. As a result of this, his sleep–wake schedule was highly variable with bedtimes ranging from 10 p.m. to 4 a.m. and total sleep times ranging from 3 to 5 hr. Although he had been prescribed CPAP and had one, he reported he had not used it for the past 5 years. He stated that he had used it for 6 months upon initial prescription, but he discontinued use because he did not notice any improvement, the

TABLE 14.5

Means and Standard Deviations for Sleep Variables at Baseline and Follow-Up

Sleep variable	Baseline		1-year follow-up	
	Mean	*SD*	**Mean**	*SD*
Nap time (min)	4.6	9.7	5.0	12.4
Sleep onset latency (min)	37.0	16.7	2.3	2.5
Number of awakenings	2.1	1.0	2.0	0.9
Wake after sleep onset (min)	21.2	19.3	9.7	5.5
Morning awake time before rising (min)	30.4	19.8	3.9	4.5
Total sleep time (min)	426	53	417	60
Sleep efficiency	82.7	5.5	96.2	2.2
Sleep quality rating (low 1; high 5)	4.0	0.9	4.7	0.6

Note. SD = standard deviation.

airflow was uncomfortable, and maintenance of the device (i.e., cleaning) was too burdensome. His score on the Epworth Sleepiness Scale was 14 (indicative of excessive daytime sleepiness; see Table 14.2 for a review of sleep assessment instruments), and his denial of any current symptoms of depression or anxiety was consistent with his scores on standardized measures of depression and anxiety. Treatment recommendations included therapy aimed at addressing his irregular sleep–wake schedule, behaviorally induced insufficient sleep, and modified motivational enhancement to increase CPAP adherence. JF expressed no desire to work on his CPAP adherence and he had little insight regarding the relationship between (untreated) apnea and cognitive functioning. JF was interested in behavioral treatment to help him adopt and maintain a more stable sleep–wake schedule, and despite his reservations regarding CPAP adherence, he agreed to bring his CPAP device to his first session. He also was asked to complete sleep diaries. At his first therapy appointment, JF reported continuing his pattern of computer usage and expressed a desire for therapy to find him "more hours in the day" to work on his computer. Treatment focused on the establishment of a regular sleep schedule and education regarding the relationship between apnea and cognition. He agreed to begin sleeping in his bed rather than at his computer, but continued to lack insight into the relationship between apnea and cognitive performance and expressed continued lack of interest in using his CPAP (although he did bring his device to the appointment). At his second appointment, he reported he continued to fall asleep at his computer rather than his bed and as a result, to have a very irregular schedule. During this appointment, it also became apparent that JF had forgotten how to use his CPAP device, so instruction was provided. Treatment again focused on adopting a regular schedule and the relationship between daytime performance and apnea, and by the end of the session, JF agreed to wear his CPAP during the upcoming week. At his third session, he reported sleeping in his own bed and using his CPAP on three out of seven nights the previous week. He also reported, however, experiencing mild anxiety due to the airflow pressure. Treatment during this session focused on "in vivo

desensitization" involving the pairing of the mask (device on at therapeutic pressure) with diaphragmatic breathing as well as continued discussion about the relationship between apnea and cognition (as well as health in general). JF was asked to practice diaphragmatic breathing with his mask one time during the day and at nighttime when he got in to bed. At sessions four through six, he reported being able to sleep in his own bed at least five nights a week and experiencing little to no anxiety when doing so. He reported some improvements in his daytime memory and concentration difficulties, and his Epworth Sleepiness Scale score was 6 at his seventh and last treatment session. JF expressed satisfaction with his progress in treatment, and upon follow-up 3 months later, reported continued CPAP adherence, a fairly regular sleep–wake schedule (10 P.M. to 4 A.M. most nights), sleeping in his own bed most nights, and satisfactory daytime functioning.

THE FUTURE ROLE OF THE GEROPSYCHOLOGIST

Geropsychologists can play a very important role in the recognition and treatment of sleep disorders in older individuals. Given the prevalence of late-life sleep disorders, many of the patients seen by geropsychologists are likely to be experiencing some type of sleep difficulty. The information presented in this chapter provides geropsychologists with information relevant to the assessment of sleep problems (from screening to in-depth sleep history interviewing to overnight sleep studies) as well as the utility of various assessment methods for differential diagnosis. By assessing for sleep disorders as part of their routine evaluation of older individuals, geropsychologists can help to ensure that significant sleep comorbidities do not go underrecognized and undertreated. There are many established psychological treatment approaches for sleep disorders, and evidence demonstrates they are generally as effective in older individuals as in younger ones. Some geropsychologists already may have training in the techniques, whereas others may wish to seek additional specialized training in either specific techniques or in the newly recognized specialty, sleep psychology.

Additionally, geropsychologists should maintain a referral list of local sleep disorders centers[5] and potentially a sleep psychologist[6] for consultation and referral for cases for which greater specialization in sleep is warranted. Geropsychologists also play an important role in educating older patients and their families regarding the importance of sleep and the fact that poor sleep is not an inevitable consequence of old age, but rather it is often the sign of a diagnosable and treatable sleep condition. Also, many patients and their families may not recognize the role that geropsychologists can play in addressing compliance-related behaviors, such as CPAP adherence. More broadly, geropsychologists can help to educate the other health care providers with whom they interact regarding the significant sleep issues (and their assessment and treatment) for which older individuals may be at particular risk.

NEXT STEPS IN RESEARCH AND CLINICAL APPLICATION

Although a variety of evidence-based techniques for the treatment of sleep disorders in older adults exist, dissemination of such techniques has lagged far behind their development and testing. For example, the number of older individuals with chronic insomnia who might benefit from CBT for insomnia (and might particularly appreciate a nonpharmacological option) far outweigh those who receive such treatment. Once reason for this disparity is the lack of psychologists who are trained to provide the sleep techniques discussed herein. The American Board of Sleep Medicine offers certification in behavioral sleep medicine, and although the majority of certified providers are psychologists, there are still fewer than 200 (http://www.absm.net). Recognition of sleep psychology is an important step in enhancing the role that geropsychologists can play in the diagnosis and treatment of sleep disorders in older adults. As the specialty of sleep psychology continues to grow and develop, training in the assessment and treatment of sleep disorders will become more

readily available to geropsychologists. In the meantime, researchers are exploring ways to enhance the disseminability of psychological treatments for sleep disorders. Such methods include developing and testing briefer, more primary care friendly versions of CBT for insomnia (CBT-I; traditionally 8–10 sessions) and motivational interviewing for CPAP adherence (i.e., two-session motivational enhancement). In addition to exploring shorter delivery formats, research exploring alternate delivery methods (i.e., telephone, video-conferencing, Internet) is needed. Better integration of geropsychologists in primary care settings also is needed to enhance older patients' access to effective psychological treatments for sleep disorders. More research is needed to explore the negative impact of institutionalization on the sleep of older individuals. In particular, treatment options that take into account the impact of the institutional environment are desperately needed. In general, more research is needed to explore ways to improve the sleep of those older individuals who are most vulnerable. Another important area for research involves hybrid treatments that combine strategies. For example, researchers are exploring the impact of combining a night-watch device to inform caregivers of dementia patients about the patients' nighttime activities with cognitive–behavioral techniques to target poor sleep in the caregiver.

References

American Academy of Sleep Medicine. (2005). *International classification of sleep disorders* (2nd ed.). Darien, IL: Author.

American Psychiatric Association. (2000). *Diagnostic and statistical manual of mental disorders* (4th ed., text rev.). Washington, DC: Author.

American Psychiatric Association. (2013). *Diagnostic and statistical manual of mental disorders* (5th ed.). Arlington, VA: Author.

Ancoli-Israel, S., Klauber, M. R., Stepnowsky, C., Estline, E., Chinn, A., & Fell, R. (1995). Sleep-disordered breathing in African-American elderly. *American Journal of Respiratory and Critical Care Medicine, 152*, 1946–1949. doi:10.1164/ajrccm.152.6.8520760

---

[5]Geropsychologists interested in identifying an accredited sleep disorders center in their area can do so at http://www.aasmnet.org.

[6]Geropsychologists interested in learning more about sleep psychology or locating a sleep psychologist in their area for consultation and/or referral can do so at http://www.behavioralsleep.org or http://www.absm.org.

Ancoli-Israel, S., Kripke, D. F., Klauber, M. R., Mason, W. J., Fell, R., & Kaplan, O. (1991). Periodic limb movements in sleep in community-dwelling elderly. *Sleep, 14*, 496–500.

Ancoli-Israel, S., Kripke, D. F., Klauber, M. R., Mason, W. J., Fell, R., & Kaplan, O. (1996). Sleep-disordered breathing in community-dwelling elderly. *Sleep, 14*, 486–495.

Ancoli-Israel, S., Richardson, G., Mangano, R., Jenkins, L., Hall, P., & Jones, W. (2005). Long-term use of sedative hypnotics in older patients with insomnia. *Sleep Medicine, 6*, 107–113. doi:10.1016/j.sleep.2004.10.015

Baillargeon, L., Landreville, P., Verreault, R., Beauchemin, J., Gregoire, J., & Morin, C. M. (2003). Discontinuation of benzodiazepines among older insomniac adults treated with cognitive behavioural therapy combined with gradual tapering: A randomized trial. *Canadian Medical Association Journal, 169*, 1015–1020.

Berry, R. B., Budhiraja, R., Gottlieb, D. J., Gozal, D., Iber, C., Kapur, V. K., & American Academy of Sleep Medicine. (2012). Rules for scoring respiratory events in sleep: Update of the 2007 AASM Manual for the Scoring of Sleep and Associated Events. Deliberations of the Sleep Apnea Definitions Task Force of the American Academy of Sleep Medicine. *Journal of Clinical Sleep Medicine: JCSM: Official Publication of the American Academy of Sleep Medicine, 8*, 597.

Berry, R. B., & Patel, P. B. (2006). Effect of zolpidem on the efficacy of continuous positive airway pressure as treatment for obstructive sleep apnea. *Sleep, 29*, 1052–1056.

Bixler, E. O., Vgontzas, A. N., Lin, H. M., Ten Have, T., Rein, J., Vela-Bueno, A., & Kales, A. (2001). Prevalence of sleep-disordered breathing in women: Effects of gender. *American Journal of Respiratory and Critical Care Medicine, 163*, 608–613. doi:10.1164/ajrccm.163.3.9911064

Bixler, E. O., Vgontzas, A. N., Ten, T. H., Tyson, K., & Kales, A. (1998). Effects of age on sleep apnea in men: Prevalence and severity. *American Journal of Respiratory and Critical Care Medicine, 157*, 144–148. doi:10.1164/ajrccm.157.1.9706079

Blazer, D. G., Hays, J. C., & Foley, D. J. (1995). Sleep complaints in older adults: A racial comparison. *The Journals of Gerontology, Series A: Biological Sciences and Medical Sciences, 50*, 280–284. doi:10.1093/gerona/50A.5.M280

Bliwise, D., Friedman, L., Nekich, J., & Yesavage, J. (1995). Prediction of outcome in behaviorally based insomnia treatments. *Journal of Behavior Therapy and Experimental Psychiatry, 26*, 17–23. doi:10.1016/0005-7916(94)00073-U

Bliwise, D. L. (2011). Normal aging. In M. H. Kryger, T. Roth, & W. C. Dement (Eds.), *Principles and practice of sleep medicine* (5th ed., pp. 27–41). St. Louis, MO: Saunders. doi:10.1016/B978-1-4160-6645-3.00003-7

Bloom, H. G., Ahmed, I., Alessi, C. A., Ancoli-Israel, S., Buysse, D. J., Kryger, M. H., . . . Zee, P. C. (2009). Evidence-based recommendations for the assessment and management of sleep disorders in older persons. *Journal of the American Geriatrics Society, 57*, 761–789. doi:10.1111/j.1532-5415.2009.02220.x

Carney, C., & Edinger, J. D. (2010). Multimodal cognitive behavior therapy. In M. Sateia & D. Buysse (Eds.), *Insomnia: Diagnosis and treatment* (pp. 342–351). London, England: Informa Healthcare. doi:10.3109/9781420080803.029

Carney, C. E., Buysse, D. J., Ancoli-Israel, S., Edinger, J. D., Krystal, A. D., Lichstein, K. L., & Morin, C. M. (2012). The Consensus Sleep Diary: Standardizing prospective sleep self-monitoring. *Sleep, 35*, 287–302.

Chesson, A. L., Ferber, R. A., Fry, J. M., Grigg-Damberger, M., Hartse, K. M., Hurwitz, T. D., & Rosen, G. (1997). Practice parameters for the indications for polysomnography and related procedures. *Sleep, 20*, 406–422.

Collop, N. A., Anderson, W. M., Boehlecke, B., Claman, D., Goldberg, R., Gottlieb, D. J., & Schwab, R. (2007). Clinical guidelines for the use of unattended portable monitors in the diagnosis of obstructive sleep apnea in adult patients. Portable Monitoring Task Force of the AASM. *Journal of Clinical Sleep Medicine, 3*, 737–747.

Cooper, T. V., Lichstein, K. L., & Aguillard, R. N. (2003). Hypnotic dependent insomnia in an older adult with addiction-prone personality. *Clinical Case Studies, 2*, 247–258. doi:10.1177/1534650103256300

Cuellar, N. G., Rogers, A. E., Hisghman, V., & Volpe, S. L. (2007). Feature article: Assessment and treatment of sleep disorders in the older adult. *Geriatric Nursing, 28*, 254–264. doi:10.1016/j.gerinurse.2007.01.017

Currie, S. R., Wilson, K., Pontefract, A., & deLaplante, L. (2000). Cognitive-behavioral treatment of insomnia secondary to chronic pain. *Journal of Consulting and Clinical Psychology, 68*, 407–416. doi:10.1037/0022-006X.68.3.407

Cvengros, J. A., & Wyatt, J. K. (2009). Circadian rhythm disorders. *Sleep Medicine Clinics, 4*, 495–505. doi:10.1016/j.jsmc.2009.07.001

Czeisler, C. A., Dumont, M., Duffy, J. F., Steinberg, J. D., Richardson, G. S., Brown, E. N., . . . Ronda, J. M. (1992). Association of sleep-wake habits in older people with changes in output of circadian pacemaker. *Lancet, 340*, 933–936. doi:10.1016/0140-6736(92)92817-Y

Durrence, H. H., & Lichstein, K. L. (2006). The sleep of African Americans: A comparative review. *Behavioral Sleep Medicine, 4*, 29–44. doi:10.1207/s15402010bsm0401_3

Dzierzewski, J. M., O'Brien, E. M., Kay, D., & McCrae, C. S. (2010). Tackling sleeplessness: Psychological treatment options for insomnia in older adults. *Nature and Science of Sleep, 2,* 47–61. doi:10.2147/NSS.S7064

Edinger, J. D., & Sampson, W. (2003). A primary care "friendly" cognitive behavioral insomnia therapy. *Sleep, 26,* 177–182.

Edinger, J. D., Wohlgemuth, W., Krystal, A. D., & Rice, J. (2005). Behavioral insomnia therapy for fibromyalgia patients: A randomized clinical trial. *Archives of Internal Medicine, 165,* 2527–2535. doi:10.1001/archinte.165.21.2527

Edinger, J. D., & Wyatt, J. K. (2011). Testing the reliability and validity of *DSM–IV–TR* and *ICSD–2* insomnia diagnoses: Results of a multitrait-multimethod analysis. *Archives of General Psychiatry, 68,* 992–1002. doi:10.1001/archgenpsychiatry.2011.64

Epstein, L. J., Kristo, D., Strollo, P. J., Jr., Friedman, N., Malhotra, A., Patil, S. P., . . . Weinstein, M. D. (2009). Clinical guideline for the evaluation, management and long-term care of obstructive sleep apnea in adults. *Journal of Clinical Sleep Medicine, 5,* 263–276.

Espiritu, J. R. (2008). Aging-related sleep changes. *Clinics in Geriatric Medicine, 24,* 1–14. doi:10.1016/j.cger.2007.08.007

Floyd, J. A., Janisse, J. J., Jenuwine, E. S., & Ager, J. W. (2007). Changes in REM-sleep percentage over the adult lifespan. *Sleep, 30,* 829–836.

Foley, D. J., Ancoli-Israel, S., Britz, P., & Walsh, J. K. (2004). Sleep disturbances and chronic disease in older adults. Results of the 2003 National Sleep Foundation Sleep in America Survey. *Journal of Psychosomatic Research, 56,* 497–502. doi:10.1016/j.jpsychores.2004.02.010

Foley, D. J., Monjan, A. A., Brown, S. L., Simonsick, E. M., Wallace, R. B., & Blazer, D. G. (1995). Sleep complaints among elderly persons: An epidemiologic study of three communities. *Sleep, 18,* 425–432.

Ford, D. E., & Kamerow, D. B. (1989). Epidemiologic study of sleep disturbances and psychiatric disorders. An opportunity for prevention? *JAMA, 262,* 1479–1484. doi:10.1001/jama.1989.03430110069030

Fung, M. M., Peters, K., Redline, S., Ziegler, M. G., Ancoli-Israel, S., Barrett-Connor, E., . . . Osteoporotic Fractures in Men Research. (2011). Decreased slow wave sleep increases risk of developing hypertension in elderly men. *Hypertension, 58,* 596–603. doi:10.1161/HYPERTENSIONAHA.111.174409

Gellis, L. A., Lichstein, K. L., Scarinci, I. C., Durrence, H. H., Taylor, D. J., Bush, A. J., & Riedel, B. W. (2005). Socioeconomic status and insomnia. *Journal of Abnormal Psychology, 114,* 111–118. doi:10.1037/0021-843X.114.1.111

Gerber, M., Brand, S., Holsboer-Trachsler, E., & Puhse, U. (2010). Fitness and exercise as correlates of sleep complaints: Is it all in our minds? *Medicine and Science in Sports and Exercise, 42,* 893–901. doi:10.1249/MSS.0b013e3181c0ea8c

Germain, A., Moul, D., Franzen, P., Miewald, J. M., Reynolds, C., Monk, T. H., & Buysse, D. (2006). Effects of a brief behavioral treatment for late-life insomnia: Preliminary findings. *Journal of Clinical Sleep Medicine, 2,* 403–406.

Glass, J., Lanctot, K. L., Herrmann, N., Sproule, B. A., & Busto, U. E. (2005). Sedative hypnotics in older people with insomnia: Meta-analysis of risks and benefits. *British Medical Journal (Clinical Research Ed.), 331,* 1169. doi:10.1136/bmj.38623.768588.47

Gorin, A. A., & Stone, A. A. (2001). Recall biases and cognitive errors in retrospective self-reports: A call for momentary assessments. *Handbook of Health Psychology, 23,* 405–413.

Grandner, M. A., Hale, L., Jackson, N., Patel, N. P., Gooneratne, N. S., & Troxel, W. M. (2012). Perceived racial discrimination as an independent predictor of sleep disturbance and daytime fatigue. *Behavioral Sleep Medicine, 10,* 235–249. doi:10.1080/15402002.2012.654548

Grandner, M. A., Martin, J. L., Patel, N. P., Jackson, N. J., Gehrman, P. R., Pien, G., . . . Gooneratne, N. S. (2012). Age and sleep disturbances among American men and women: Data from the U.S. Behavioral Risk Factor Surveillance System. *Sleep, 35,* 395–406. doi:10.5665/sleep.1704

Guilleminault, C., Davis, K., & Huynh, N. T. (2008). Prospective randomized study of patients with insomnia and mild sleep disordered breathing. *Sleep, 31,* 1527–1533.

Harvey, A. (2005). A cognitive theory and therapy for chronic insomnia. *Journal of Cognitive Psychotherapy, 19,* 41–59. doi:10.1891/jcop.19.1.41.66332

Innes, K. E., Selfe, T. K., & Agarwal, P. (2011). Prevalence of restless legs syndrome in North American and Western European populations: A systematic review. *Sleep Medicine, 12,* 623–634. doi:10.1016/j.sleep.2010.12.018

Irwin, M. R., Cole, J. C., & Nicassio, P. M. (2006). Comparative meta-analysis of behavioral interventions for insomnia and their efficacy in middle-aged adults and in older adults 55+years of age. *Health Psychology, 25,* 3–14. doi:10.1037/0278-6133.25.1.3

Jacobs, D., Ancoli-Israel, S., Parker, L., & Kripke, D. F. (1989). Twenty-four-hour sleep-wake patterns in a nursing home population. *Psychology and Aging, 4,* 352–356. doi:10.1037/0882-7974.4.3.352

Johns, M. W. (1991). A new method for measuring daytime sleepiness: The Epworth sleepiness scale. *Sleep, 14,* 540–545.

Kales, A., & Kales, J. D. (1984). *Evaluation and treatment of insomnia.* New York, NY: Oxford University Press.

Korotitsch, W. J., & Nelson-Gray, R. O. (1999). An overview of self-monitoring research in assessment and treatment. *Psychological Assessment, 11,* 415–425. doi:10.1037/1040-3590.11.4.415

Krakow, B., Melendrez, D., Lee, S. A., Warner, T. D., Clark, J. O., & Sklar, D. (2004). Refractory insomnia and sleep-disordered breathing: A pilot study. *Sleep and Breathing, 8,* 15–29. doi:10.1007/s11325-004-0015-5

Kripke, D. F., Ancoli-Israel, S., Klauber, M. R., Wingard, D. L., Mason, W. J., & Mullaney, D. J. (1997). Prevalence of sleep-disordered breathing in ages 40-64 years: A population-based survey. *Sleep, 20,* 65–76.

Krystal, A. D., Walsh, J., Laska, E., Caron, J., Amato, D., Wessel, T., & Roth, T. (2003). Sustained efficacy of eszopiclone over 6 months of nightly treatment: Results of a randomized, double-blind, placebo-controlled study in adults with chronic insomnia. *Sleep, 26,* 793–799.

Lavie, P. (2007). Insomnia and sleep-disordered breathing. *Sleep Medicine,* 8(Suppl. 4), S21–S25. doi:10.1016/S1389-9457(08)70005-4

Lewy, A. J. (1983). Effects of light on human melatonin production and the human circadian system. *Progress in Neuro-Psychopharmacology and Biological Psychiatry, 7,* 551–556. doi:10.1016/0278-5846(83)90024-6

Lichstein, K. L., Durrence, H. H., Riedel, B. W., Taylor, D. J., & Bush, A. J. (2004). *Epidemiology of sleep: Age, gender, and ethnicity.* Mahwah, NJ: Erlbaum.

Lichstein, K. L., Taylor, D. J., McCrae, C. S., & Ruiter, M. E. (2011). Insomnia: Epidemiology and risk factors. In M. H. Kryger, T. Roth, & W. C. Dement (Eds.), *Principles and practice of sleep medicine* (5th ed., pp. 827–837). St. Louis, MO: Saunders. doi:10.1016/B978-1-4160-6645-3.00076-1

Liu, X., & Liu, L. (2005). Sleep habits and insomnia in a sample of elderly persons in China. *Sleep, 28,* 1579–1587.

Luyster, F. S., Buysse, D., & Strollo, P. (2010). Comorbid insomnia and obstructive sleep apnea: Challenges for clinical practice and research. *Journal of Clinical Sleep Medicine, 6,* 196–204.

Mayer, G., Wang-Weigand, S., Roth-Schechter, B., Lehmann, R., Staner, C., & Partinen, M. (2009). Efficacy and safety of 6-month nightly ramelteon administration in adults with chronic primary insomnia. *Sleep, 32,* 351–360.

McCrae, C., Dzierzewski, J., & Kay, D. (2009). Treatment of late-life insomnia. *Sleep Medicine Clinics, 4,* 593–604. doi:10.1016/j.jsmc.2009.07.006

McCrae, C., Nau, S., Taylor, D., & Lichstein, K. (2006). Insomnia. In J. Fisher & W. O'Donohue (Eds.), *Practitioner's guide to evidence-based psychotherapy* (pp. 324–334). New York, NY: Springer. doi:10.1007/978-0-387-28370-8_32

McCurry, S. M., Gibbons, L., Logsdon, R., Vitiello, M., & Teri, L. (2005). Night-time insomnia treatment and education for Alzheimer's disease: A randomized, controlled trial. *Journal of the American Geriatrics Society, 53,* 793–802. doi:10.1111/j.1532-5415.2005.53252.x

McCurry, S. M., Logsdon, R., Vitiello, M., & Teri, L. (1998). Successful behavioral treatment for reported sleep problems in elderly caregivers of dementia patients: A controlled study. *The Journals of Gerontology, Series B: Psychological Sciences and Social Sciences, 53,* 122–129. doi:10.1093/geronb/53B.2.P122

McCurry, S. M., Vitiello, M., Gibbons, L., Logsdon, R., & Teri, L. (2006). Factors associated with caregiver reports of sleep disturbances in persons with dementia. *American Journal of Geriatric Psychiatry, 14,* 112–120. doi:10.1097/01.JGP.0000192499.25940.da

McHugh, J. E., Casey, A. M., & Lawlor, B. A. (2011). Psychosocial correlates of aspects of sleep quality in community-dwelling Irish older adults. *Aging and Mental Health, 15,* 749–755. doi:10.1080/13607863.2011.562180

Morgenthaler, T. I., Lee-Chiong, T., Alessi, C., Friedman, L., Aurora, R. N., Boehlecke, B., . . . Standards of Practice Committee of the American Academy of Sleep. (2007). Practice parameters for the clinical evaluation and treatment of circadian rhythm sleep disorders. An AASM report. *Sleep, 30,* 1445–1459.

Morin, C. M., Colecchi, C., Stone, J., Sood, R., & Brink, D. (1999). Behavioral and pharmacological therapies for late-life insomnia: A randomized controlled trial. *JAMA, 281,* 991–999. doi:10.1001/jama.281.11.991

Morin, C. M., Culbert, J., & Schwartz, S. (1994). Nonpharmacological interventions for insomnia: A metaanalysis of treatment efficacy. *American Journal of Psychiatry, 151,* 1172–1180.

Morin, C. M., Vallieres, A., Guay, B., Ivers, H., Savard, J., Merette, C., . . . Baillargeon, L. (2009). Cognitive behavioral therapy, singly and combined with medication, for persistent insomnia: A randomized controlled trial. *JAMA, 301,* 2005–2015. doi:10.1001/jama.2009.682

National Institutes of Health. (2005). National Institutes of Health state of the science conference statement—manifestations and management of chronic insomnia in adults. *Sleep, 28,* 1049–1057.

Neikrug, A. B., & Ancoli-Israel, S. (2010a). Sleep disorders in the older adult–a mini-review. *Gerontology, 56,* 181–189. doi:10.1159/000236900

Neikrug, A. B., & Ancoli-Israel, S. (2010b). Sleep disturbances in nursing homes. *Journal of Nutrition, Health and Aging, 14*, 207–211. doi:10.1007/s12603-010-0051-8

Ohayon, M. M. (2002). Epidemiology of insomnia: What we know and what we still need to learn. *Sleep Medicine Reviews, 6*, 97–111. doi:10.1053/smrv.2002.0186

Ohayon, M. M., Carskadon, M. A., Guilleminault, C., & Vitiello, M. V. (2004). Meta-analysis of quantitative sleep parameters from childhood to old age in healthy individuals: Developing normative sleep values across the human lifespan. *Sleep, 27*, 1255–1274.

Pallesen, S., Nordhus, I. H., Kvale, G., Nielsen, G. H., Havik, O. E., Johnsen, B. H., & Skjotskift, S. (2003). Behavioral treatment of insomnia in older adults: An open clinical trial comparing two interventions. *Behaviour Research and Therapy, 41*, 31–48. doi:10.1016/S0005-7967(01)00122-X

Pat-Horenczyk, R., Klauber, M. R., Shochat, T., & Ancoli-Israel, S. (1998). Hourly profiles of sleep and wakefulness in severely versus mild-moderately demented nursing home patients. *Aging, 10*, 308–315.

Perlis, M., McCall, W., Krystal, A., & Walsh, J. (2004). Long-term, non-nightly administration of zolpidem in the treatment of patients with primary insomnia. *Journal of Clinical Psychiatry, 65*, 1128–1137. doi:10.4088/JCP.v65n0816

Perlis, M., Smith, M., & Pigeon, W. (2005). Etiology and pathophysiology of insomnia. In M. H. Kryger, T. Roth, & W. C. Dement (Eds.), *Principles and Practices of Sleep Medicine* (5th ed., pp. 714–725). St. Louis, MO: Saunders. doi:10.1016/B0-72-160797-7/50067-7

Phillips, B. A., Berry, D. T., Schmitt, F. A., Magan, L. K., Gerhardstein, D. C., & Cook, Y. R. (1992). Sleep-disordered breathing in the healthy elderly. Clinically significant? *Chest, 101*, 345–349. doi:10.1378/chest.101.2.345

Pigeon, W., Hegel, M., Ungeon, J., Fan, M., Sateia, M., Lyness, J., & Perlis, M. (2008). Is insomnia a perpetuating factor for late-life depression in the IMPACT cohort? *Sleep, 31*, 481.

Quesnel, C., Savard, J., Simard, S., Ivers, H., & Morin, C. (2003). Efficacy of cognitive-behavioral therapy for insomnia in women treated for nonmetastatic breast cancer. *Journal of Consulting and Clinical Psychology, 71*, 189–200.

Redline, S., Kirchner, H. L., Quan, S. F., Gottlieb, D. J., Kapur, V., & Newman, A. (2004). The effects of age, sex, ethnicity, and sleep-disordered breathing on sleep architecture. *Archives of Internal Medicine, 164*, 406–418. doi:10.1001/archinte.164.4.406

Redline, S., Tishler, P. V., Hans, M. G., Tosteson, T. D., Strohl, K. P., & Spry, K. (1997). Racial differences in sleep-disordered breathing in African-Americans and Caucasians. *American Journal of Respiratory and Critical Care Medicine, 155*, 186–192. doi:10.1164/ajrccm.155.1.9001310

Reid, K. J., & Zee, P. C. (2011). Circadian disorders of the sleep-wake cycle. In M. H. Kryger, T. Roth, & W. C. Dement (Eds.), *Principles and practice of sleep medicine* (5th ed., pp. 470–482). St. Louis, MO: Elsevier Saunders. doi:10.1016/B978-1-4160-6645-3.00041-4

Richards, D., Bartlett, D., Wong, K., Malouff, J., & Grunstein, R. (2007). Increased adherence to CPAP with a group cognitive behavioral treatment intervention: A randomized trial. *Sleep, 30*, 635–640.

Roberts, R. E., Shema, S. J., & Kaplan, G. A. (1999). Prospective data on sleep complaints and associated risk factors in an older cohort. *Psychosomatic Medicine, 61*, 188–196.

Rose, K. M., & Lorenz, R. (2010). Sleep disturbances in dementia: What they are and what to do. *Journal of Gerontological Nursing, 36*, 9–14. doi:10.3928/00989134-20100330-05

Rosenberg, R., Roach, J. M., Scharf, M., & Amato, D. A. (2007). A pilot study evaluating acute use of eszopiclone in patients with mild to moderate obstructive sleep apnea syndrome. *Sleep Medicine, 8*, 464–470. doi:10.1016/j.sleep.2006.10.007

Roth, A. J., McCall, W. V., & Liguori, A. (2011). Cognitive, psychomotor and polysomnographic effects of trazodone in primary insomniacs. *Journal of Sleep Research, 20*, 552–558. doi:10.1111/j.1365-2869.2011.00928.x

Ruiter, M. E., DeCoster, J., Jacobs, L., & Lichstein, K. L. (2010). Sleep disorders in African Americans and Caucasian Americans: A meta-analysis. *Behavioral Sleep Medicine, 8*, 246–259. doi:10.1080/15402002.2010.509251

Sawyer, A. M., Gooneratne, N. S., Marcus, C. L., Ofer, D., Richards, K. C., & Weaver, T. E. (2011). A systematic review of CPAP adherence across age groups: Clinical and empiric insights for developing CPAP adherence interventions. *Sleep Medicine Reviews, 15*, 343–356. doi:10.1016/j.smrv.2011.01.003

Schrader, H., Bovim, G., & Sand, T. (1993). The prevalence of delayed and advanced sleep phase syndromes. *Journal of Sleep Research, 2*, 51–55. doi:10.1111/j.1365-2869.1993.tb00061.x

Schubert, C. R., Cruickshanks, K. J., Dalton, D. S., Klein, B. E. K., Klein, R., & Nondahl, D. M. (2002). Prevalence of sleep problems and quality of life in an older population. *Sleep, 25*, 889–893.

Schutte-Rodin, S., Broch, L., Buysse, D., Dorsey, C., & Sateia, M. (2008). Clinical guideline for the evaluation and management of chronic insomnia in adults. *Journal of Clinical Sleep Medicine, 4*, 487–504.

Scofield, H., Roth, T., & Drake, C. (2008). Periodic limb movements during sleep: Population prevalence, clinical correlates, and racial differences. *Sleep, 31*, 1221–1227.

Shochat, T., Martin, J., Marler, M., & Ancoli-Israel, S. (2000). Illumination levels in nursing home patients: Effects on sleep and activity rhythms. *Journal of Sleep Research, 9*, 373–379. doi:10.1046/j.1365-2869.2000.00221.x

Sinoo, M. M., van Hoof, J., & Kort, H. S. M. (2011). Light conditions for older adults in the nursing home: Assessment of environmental illuminances and colour temperature. *Building and Environment, 46*, 1917–1927. doi:10.1016/j.buildenv.2011.03.013

Sivertsen, B., Omvik, S., & Pallesen, S. (2006). Cognitive behavioral therapy vs zopiclone for treatment of chronic primary insomnia in older adults: A randomized controlled trial. *JAMA, 295*, 2851–2858. doi:10.1001/jama.295.24.2851

Soeffing, J. P., Lichstein, K., & Nau, S. (2008). Psychological treatment of insomnia in hypnotic dependent older adults. *Sleep Medicine, 9*, 165–171. doi:10.1016/j.sleep.2007.02.009

Song, Y., Ancoli-Israel, S., Lewis, C. E., Redline, S., Harrison, S. L., & Stone, K. L. (2012). The association of race/ethnicity with objectively measured sleep characteristics in older men. *Behavioral Sleep Medicine, 10*, 54–69. doi:10.1080/15402002.2012.636276

Thorpy, M. J. (2011). Classification of sleep disorders. In M. Kryer, T. Roth & W. C. Dement (Eds.), *Principles and practice of sleep medicine* (5th ed., pp. 470–482). St. Louis, MO: Elsevier Saunders.

Toh, K. L., Jones, C. R., He, Y., Eide, E. J., Hinz, W. A., Virshup, D. M., . . . Fu, Y. H. (2001). An hPer2 phosphorylation site mutation in familial advanced sleep phase syndrome. *Science, 291*, 1040–1043. doi:10.1126/science.1057499

Vaz Fragoso, C. A., & Gill, T. (2007). Sleep complaints in community-living older persons: A multifactorial geriatric syndrome. *Journal of the American Geriatrics Society, 55*, 1853–1866. doi:10.1111/j.1532-5415.2007.01399.x

Vitiello, M. V., Moe, K. E., & Prinz, P. N. (2002). Sleep complaints cosegregate with illness in older adults: Clinical research informed by and informing epidemiological studies of sleep. *Journal of Psychosomatic Research, 53*, 555–559. doi:10.1016/S0022-3999(02)00435-X

Weaver, T. E., & Chasens, E. R. (2007). Continuous positive airway pressure treatment for sleep apnea in older adults. *Sleep Medicine Reviews, 11*, 99–111. doi:10.1016/j.smrv.2006.08.001

Weaver, T. E., & Sawyer, A. M. (2010). Adherence to continuous positive airway pressure treatment for obstructive sleep apnoea: Implications for future interventions. *Indian Journal of Medical Research, 131*, 245–258.

Xu, Y., Padiath, Q. S., Shapiro, R. E., Jones, C. R., Wu, S. C., Saigoh, N., . . . Fu, Y. H. (2005). Functional consequences of a CKI-delta mutation causing familial advanced sleep phase syndrome. *Nature, 434*, 640–644. doi:10.1038/nature03453

Young, T., Palta, M., Dempsey, J., Skatrud, J., Weber, S., & Badr, S. (1993). The occurrence of sleep-disordered breathing among middle-aged adults. *New England Journal of Medicine, 328*, 1230–1235. doi:10.1056/NEJM199304293281704

CHAPTER 15

SEXUAL HEALTH AND WELL-BEING IN THE CONTEXT OF AGING

Maggie L. Syme, Colleen C. Cordes, Rebecca P. Cameron, and Linda R. Mona

Sexual expression into older age is an essential health care focus, as older adults are living healthier and longer. This expression encompasses emotional, social, intellectual, and somatic experiences related to sexual and intimate situations. Many older adults identify sexual expression as a key component of well-being and successful aging, and this is linked to several physical and mental health benefits (American Association of Retired Persons [AARP], 2010; Jannini, Fischer, Bitzer, & McMahon, 2009; Thompson et al., 2011). Despite the importance of sexuality as we age, research on strategies to promote sexual well-being among older adults remains insufficient (DeLamater, 2012; Taylor & Gosney, 2011).

Clinical geropsychology providers across treatment settings are called to increase their awareness of older adults as sexual beings who continue to be interested and engage in a spectrum of sexual activities. According to the National Social Life, Health, and Aging Project (Waite, Laumann, Das, & Schumm, 2009), a significant number of adults continue to participate in sexual behaviors through the age of 74 years ("any sex": 39.5% of women and 67% of men), with a decline in sexual behaviors occurring between the ages of 75 and 84 years ("any sex": 16.7% of women and 38.5% of men). Sexual expression, even into the oldest age-groups (70 years or older), continues to include a variety of behaviors, including oral, anal, and vaginal sex, with solo masturbation, vaginal intercourse, and foreplay (e.g., kissing, caressing) as the most frequently reported activities among predominantly heterosexual samples (Schick et al., 2010; Waite et al., 2009).

However, approximately half of older adult men and women who are sexually active indicate they experience at least one sexual problem (Lindau et al., 2007). Losing one's partner and chronic health problems are among the top biopsychosocial factors that precipitate and maintain sexual concerns, yet the topic of sexual health rarely is broached by either older adults or their health care providers because of several psychological and social barriers (e.g., stigma, embarrassment; Hinchliff & Gott, 2011; Laumann, Glasser, Neves, Moreira, & the Global Study of Sexual Attitudes and Behaviors Investigators' Group, 2009). Clinical geropsychologists can improve sexual health care for older adults by routinely screening for sexual health concerns and providing assessment and intervention as needed, in collaboration with both the older adult and the medical team.

This chapter introduces geropsychologists working in integrated care and traditional mental health settings to conceptualization, assessment, and treatment of sexual well-being among older adults. It begins by providing an overview of the biopsychosocial factors that affect sexual well-being in older adults—with a focus on gender, culture, and health care context. To assist with conceptualization and diagnosis, a review of current diagnostic categories for sexual concerns will be provided along with a broadened conceptualization of sexual health and well-being that informs sex- and aging-positive assessment and treatment. Finally, it reviews assessment and treatment strategies for evaluating and enhancing sexual well-being among older adult clients. The chapter concludes with a case example

http://dx.doi.org/10.1037/14459-015
APA Handbook of Clinical Geropsychology: Vol. 2. Assessment, Treatment, and Issues of Later Life,
P. A. Lichtenberg and B. T. Mast (Editors-in-Chief)

illustrating these concepts in an integrated primary care setting.

SEXUAL EXPRESSION AND AGING

Sexual expression among older adults is a multidimensional concept, requiring clinical geropsychologists to attend to several factors. These include the biopsychosocial factors associated with sexual expression, the cultural context within which the behaviors are being expressed, and the health care context within which the clinician is working.

Biopsychosocial Factors

A biopsychosocial approach is essential for a comprehensive examination of the factors that contribute to sexual expression in older adults (Bitzer, Platano, Tschudin, & Alder, 2008). It is important to consider how physiological, psychological, social, and cultural factors may predispose individuals to sexual concerns, trigger or precipitate the onset of sexual concerns, or maintain sexual symptoms (Basson, Wierman, van Lankveld, & Brotto, 2010; Meana & Jones, 2011). This approach to conceptualization can then guide the development of a multifaceted treatment plan.

Physiological factors. Normative physiological aspects of aging can influence sexual expression. Hormonal changes that occur in older adult women as a result of menopause, particularly the cessation of principal estrogen, contribute to changes in blood flow, atrophy of the vaginal wall, vaginal narrowing, and decreases in lubrication (Bitzer et al., 2008; DeLamater, 2012; Hillman, 2011). A review of the research shows that among postmenopausal women the prevalence of sexual concerns ranges from 68% to 86.5%, with elderly women most commonly reporting low libido, problems with arousal, decreased intensity or presence of orgasm, painful intercourse, and attractiveness and body image concerns (Ambler, Bieber, & Diamond, 2012). Men also experience physiological changes that may influence sexual expression, often affecting erectile functioning. The prevalence and severity of erectile dysfunction (ED) increases with advancing age, with one study in a large, national probability

sample showing that up to 77.5% of men over the age of 75 report concerns related to ED (Saigal, Wessells, Pace, Schonlau, & Wilt, 2006, as cited in Albersen, Orabi, & Lue, 2012). Since the introduction of oral phosphodiesterase-5 (PDE5) inhibitors (e.g., Viagra) to treat erectile functioning through pharmacotherapy, increased attention has been placed on male sexual dysfunction in midlife and later life (Hillman, 2011). Other common concerns among older men include reductions in libido, penile sensitivity, arousal, and frequency of morning erections. Additionally, older men often experience prolonged plateau and refractory periods, which may be related to changes in testosterone levels (Albersen et al., 2012).

For men and women, both the increased prevalence of chronic illnesses and their accompanying treatments can influence sexual functioning. Among men, cardiovascular disease and diabetes frequently have been linked to ED (Rheaume & Mitty, 2008). Other conditions common in older adults, including degenerative and rheumatoid arthritis, stroke, cancer, kidney disease, and spinal cord injury, are linked to changes in sexual functioning for men and women. In addition, many medications used to treat chronic illnesses can affect sexual functioning, including antihypertensives, antiandrogens, steroids, and mood stabilizers (DeLamater, 2012).

Psychological factors. Attitudes and beliefs regarding sexual activity influence sexual expression and sexual risk in older adulthood. For example, older adults may have been raised to view sexual expression as serving a reproductive function and sexual behavior other than penile–vaginal intercourse within a monogamous relationship as inappropriate or immoral (Waite et al., 2009). Also, older adults who are sexually active may lack adequate sex education and can be unaware of the need for safe sex practices in the absence of pregnancy risk. These beliefs and attitudes may compromise safer sex practices and result in higher risk for contracting sexually transmitted infections (STIs; Lindau, Leitsch, Lundberg, & Jerome, 2006).

General psychological well-being is also relevant to sexual expression. Changes in one's body as a result of aging (e.g., wrinkles, graying of hair, decline in physical strength, etc.) can influence body and sexual self-esteem, which are linked to sexual interest (Hillman, 2011; Montemurro & Gillen, 2013). Psychological concerns such as depression and anxiety, as well as some pharmacotherapies for these concerns, can significantly affect sexual functioning for older adult men and women (McCall-Hosenfeld et al., 2008; Pesce, Seidman, & Roose, 2002).

Cognitive capacity can significantly affect sexual expression, and providers working with older adults—particularly in dementia care settings—should consider the cognitive status of the client, given the influence it may have on sexual consent capacity (i.e., sexual decision making). At this time, uniform clinical and legal standards for assessing sexual consent capacity in older adults are lacking; however, providers are encouraged to become familiar with the legal and ethical considerations involved in sexual consent for older adults and to consult with colleagues, professional organizations, and legal professionals as needed.

The legal criterion for sexual consent among adults varies from state to state, but generally involves three elements (American Bar Association [ABA]/American Psychological Association [APA], 2008; Lyden, 2007). The first element is *knowledge* of the relevant facts needed to make the decision (e.g., basic knowledge of sexual activities, potential risks and benefits involved). The second element is a *reasoned understanding* of the sexual situation while demonstrating an ability to take into account relevant knowledge when making a sexual decision (e.g., risks to self and other, potential consequences). The third element is *voluntariness*, or the ability to take self-protective measures against coercion when making a sexual decision. Along with legal considerations, the geropsychologist is balancing ethical concerns that include promoting autonomy (e.g., the sexual rights of the older adult) while protecting them from potential harm or coercion (for further details about sexual consent capacity, see ABA/APA, 2008; Hillman, 2011). In team settings, geropsychologists are well situated to be able to educate other health care providers about this issue and provide consultation about the impact of cognitive status on sexual expression.

Social factors. The presence of a partner is predictive of continued sexual expression and satisfaction for both men and women, as shown in predominantly heterosexual samples of older adults (Lindau et al., 2007). Furthermore, because men are more likely than women to be partnered in older age, with 38% of women over the age of 75 years being partnered compared with the 72% of their male counterparts, they often report more frequent sexual activity than their female counterparts (Kontula & Haavio-Mannila, 2009; Lindau et al., 2007). This effect may be compounded in a long-term care setting where the ratio of single women to men is estimated to be 4:1 (Hajjar & Kamel, 2003). Within couples, a partner's poor physical and sexual health can result in lowered frequency of and satisfaction with sexual expression (Bitzer et al., 2008). Additionally, satisfaction with one's intimate partner is related to lower levels of sexual dysfunction, although this relationship is likely bidirectional in nature (Laumann et al., 2009).

Cultural Context of Aging

Providers need to consider the sociocultural context of the older adult and her or his multiple, intersecting identities. Older adults make up unique cultural groups that have been shaped by a myriad of historical and social events (e.g., Korean and Vietnam wars, sexual revolution, gay rights movement, birth control pill and antiretroviral medications), both as a larger group and within separate cohorts—such as the silent generation and baby boomers. Collectively, these experiences and group memberships help to shape the older adult's worldview and affect sexual beliefs, values, and intimate relationships.

As the population ages, older adults are becoming more culturally diverse. It is estimated that 19.3% of older adults identify as a racial or ethnic minority (Administration on Aging, 2008), and rates of growth of racially and ethnically diverse elders are projected to far outpace their White counterparts. Additionally, many older adults are first-generation Americans whose bicultural identities affect their view of sexuality and intimate relationships.

Providers should consider the distinct experiences and needs of lesbian, gay, bisexual, and transgendered (LGBT) older adult clients. LGBT older adults are less likely to be out than their younger counterparts and may not have disclosed their sexual identity to friends, family, or coworkers because of such factors as shame, stigma, and fear of discrimination (Knauer, 2011). As LGBT individuals age, they may face additional barriers related to heterosexist health care settings and prejudices held by health care providers (Hinchliff & Gott, 2011).

As a group, older adults are often perceived as homogenous, with many providers espousing stereotypic views of the elderly (e.g., lonely, frail, dependent, depressed; Hinrichsen, 2006). When considering perceptions of sexuality among older adults, views commonly held by laypeople, providers, and older adults themselves include the following: (a) older adults are and should be asexual, (b) it is shameful to talk about sex as an older adult, (c) older adults are too frail to have sex, and (d) older adult sexuality is disgusting (Bitzer et al., 2008; Hillman, 2011). Societal messages emphasize that sex is for the young and beautiful, which may negatively affect sexual self-esteem and overall adjustment among older adults. These stereotypic beliefs also contribute to ignorance about older adult sexuality and to sexual concerns being under-reported and overlooked. Awareness of multiple facets of diversity among older adult clients, a willingness to examine stereotypes, and the ability to integrate this information into the assessment and conceptualization of sexual health and well-being will aid treatment effectiveness.

Health Care Context

Since the passage of the Patient Protection and Affordable Care Act, increased attention has been placed on the integration of mental, behavioral, and physical health, most commonly in the primary care setting (Collins, Hewson, Munger, & Wade, 2010). In a fully integrated setting, behavioral health providers are working side by side with medical professionals to provide whole-person health care (i.e., *patient-centered* care). Behavioral health providers working in integrated settings must adapt to the fast pace of primary care, often engaging patients in 15 to 30 min encounters with a focus on the *International Classification of Diseases, 10th Edition* (ICD–10; World Health Organization, 1992) medical

diagnoses (e.g., ED). Integrated care affords the opportunity to more readily address the multidimensional nature of sexuality and promotes the development of combination therapies (i.e., medical and psychosocial) that improve on single-modality, medical treatments (Althof, 2010).

Although many health care facilities are moving toward integration, many providers continue to practice in mental health settings that utilize a traditional 50 min clinical hour. This difference in allotted time between providers working in integrated care versus mental health care affects the structure and nature of the clinical assessment and intervention, as will be elaborated. Regardless of setting, patient-centered sexual health care necessitates that behavioral health providers coordinate their services with the medical care older adults are receiving.

CONCEPTUALIZATION AND DIAGNOSIS

Sexuality historically has been perceived through the lens of the biomedical model (Masters & Johnson, 1970), which defines healthy sexual functioning in terms of penile–vaginal intercourse with orgasm as the ultimate goal. The emphasis is on the sexual response cycle (desire, arousal, orgasm, resolution), physiological explanations for problems, and medical solutions to symptoms of sexual dysfunction. For many clients, this approach can lead to increased access to sexual pleasure; however, emphasizing restoration of the mechanical aspects of sexual functioning is limiting, especially for an aging population for whom the form but not the purpose of sexual and intimate encounters may change as a result of normal aging. A sociocultural view of sexuality also can present a biased perspective on older adult sexual expression because of its historical emphasis on heterosexism, partnered behaviors (e.g., penile–vaginal intercourse), and a failure to include those who are stigmatized and have less social power (e.g., sexual minorities, older adults in long-term care settings).

Alternatively, newer models of conceptualization aim to broaden the definition of sexual fulfillment and acknowledge the diversity of sexual experiences (Basson et al., 2010; Metz & McCarthy, 2007, as cited in Meana & Jones, 2011). For example, the

Complete State of Sexual Health (Mona et al., 2011) utilizes a two-dimensional approach to conceptualizing sexuality, focusing on both sexual well-being and dysfunction. Within this framework, providers are encouraged to consider clients' sexual wellness (e.g., satisfaction, pleasure, emotional intimacy) in addition to sexual dysfunction (e.g., sexual pain), with the assumption that an individual can have the presence or absence of sexual well-being regardless of dysfunctional symptoms. For example, a 68 year-old man with a history of prostate cancer and current ED (high in sexual dysfunction) may consider himself sexually well (high in sexual well-being) because of his ability to find pleasure in non-intercourse-related sexual behaviors and the emotional intimacy he has built with his partner. Alternatively, an individual can be low in sexual dysfunction and sexual well-being, having no diagnosable disorders yet reporting an absence of sexually fulfilling experiences. Attending to both wellness and dysfunction provides a sex-positive and broader conceptualization of sexuality for older adults.

With regard to sexual dysfunction, the *Diagnostic and Statistical Manual, Fourth Edition, Text Revision* (*DSM–IV–TR*; American Psychiatric Association, 2000) outlines the criteria for sexual disorders based on the sexual response cycle and intercourse-related pain. For older adult women, the most commonly reported sexual symptoms are low desire, vaginal dryness, and sexual pain; for older adult men, ED is the most common dysfunction (Hillman, 2011; Taylor & Gosney, 2011). Desire disorders—characterized by lack of interest in sex and related distress—are consistent with a cultural expectation that low sexual desire is inherently pathological, rather than reflective of existing variability. For the provider, it is important to distinguish among drive, the biological component of spontaneous desire, and cognitive and motivational factors (e.g., expectations about sex, quality of relationship, depression), as desire happens within a context (Kingsberg & Althof, 2009). Notably, women infrequently report spontaneous desire across age-groups, and an emphasis on responsive desire has been proposed in newer conceptualizations of sexual desire (Brotto, 2010), including in the *Diagnostic and Statistical Manual of Mental Disorders, Fifth Edition* (*DSM–5*; American

Psychiatric Association, 2013). As diagnosed in the *DSM–IV–TR* (American Psychiatric Association, 2000), female sexual arousal disorder includes the inability to achieve vaginal lubrication and swelling, common problems for older adult women. Considerations for diagnosis include differentiating between subjective and genital arousal (Basson et al., 2010), which is especially important for older adult women who may have difficulties with lubrication but continue to be subjectively aroused or experience genital arousal without lubrication (Galinsky, 2012). Arousal problems in older adult men are characterized by the inability to have and sustain an erection during sexual activity (i.e., ED), and considerations for diagnosis should include motivational issues that may precipitate ED as well as concomitant desire disorder. Emerging conceptualizations based on clinical data have viewed sexual interest and arousal symptoms as intertwined for women (Brotto, 2010), which is reflected in the *DSM–5* (American Psychiatric Association, 2013) with the diagnostic category female sexual interest or arousal disorder.

Orgasmic disorders are based on the assumption that healthy sexual activity necessarily includes orgasm, which is in contrast to a broader conceptualization of pleasure and fulfillment that does not rely exclusively on orgasm. When diagnosing orgasmic disorder in women (female orgasmic disorder) and men (male orgasmic disorder and premature ejaculation), it is important to consider situational factors that precipitate and maintain orgasm concerns, such as types of sexual activities and sexual satisfaction with partner. Problems with orgasm are reported more often in older women (33–38%) than in older men (16–33%), in a predominantly heterosexual sample (Waite et al., 2009). For many women, expanding sexual activities beyond penile–vaginal intercourse to include oral, manual, and self-stimulation may increase the frequency of orgasm (Kingsberg & Althof, 2009).

Sexual pain disorders experienced by women include vaginismus and dyspareunia; less frequently, men may experience dyspareunia as well. *Vaginismus* is characterized by discomfort and inability to achieve vaginal penetration due to physical and psychological issues, such as spasms in the vaginal musculature and fear or avoidance of pain

(Kingsberg & Althof, 2009). *Dyspareunia* is persistent pain before, during, or after sexual intercourse that is not caused by vaginismus or problems with lubrication. There is some debate whether or not to combine these two disorders into a single pain and penetration disorder as the clinical distinction between the two cannot be made reliably, or whether they should be considered genital pain disorders instead of sexual disorders (Althof, 2010). In fact, in the *DSM–5* (American Psychiatric Association, 2013), there is a single diagnostic category, genito-pelvic pain and penetration disorder, which includes criteria for vaginal and pelvic pain along with tensing and tightening of pelvic floor muscles. In a sample of older adults, sexual pain—regardless of etiology—was reported by 12–19% of women, and fewer than 4% of men (Laumann, Das, & Waite, 2008, as cited in DeLamater, 2012).

ASSESSMENT OF SEXUAL HEALTH CONCERNS

Across clinical settings, it is critically important to establish rapport and provide a nonthreatening environment so that the older adult can feel comfortable discussing this personal topic. Providers should be attuned and sensitive to intergenerational dynamics that often exist between older adults and their providers, especially in training settings. Attention to these issues, along with awareness of one's own beliefs and values with regards to sexuality and aging, will facilitate a positive therapeutic encounter. When considering treatment setting, providers in a traditional mental health setting may have more flexibility to conduct an in-depth assessment using a clinical interview, supplemented with standardized measures. Providers in integrated care settings, by contrast, may need to adapt their assessment strategies to be brief and focused, gathering sufficient information to determine when a referral to specialized care is warranted.

Assessment in Traditional Mental Health Settings

The recommended approach is one that utilizes both self-report questionnaires and structured interviews to maximize the collection of accurate information

and build client–provider rapport (Mona et al., 2010; O'Connor et al., 2008). The structured clinical interview provides a foundation for conceptualization. Providers working in a traditional mental health setting can explore in more detail their clients' sexual functioning and current symptoms, sexual well-being status, sexual history, beliefs, attitudes, and behaviors as well as medical and mental health histories, as these are possible contributors to the client's presenting concern. An outline for a comprehensive, sex-positive clinical interview is provided (see Appendix 15.1), building on seminal work by Zeiss et al. (1999, as cited in Mona et al., 2010). Providers are advised to engage the older adult client's partner, as available, to collect collateral information about concerns and strengths. It also is suggested that providers assess patient-reported sexual outcomes over time in coordination with the older adult's medical provider.

Standardized measures, such as the European Male Ageing Study Sexual Function Questionnaire (O'Connor et al., 2008), the McCoy Female Sexuality Questionnaire (McCoy, 2000) for postmenopausal women, the Sexual Beliefs and Information Questionnaire (Adams et al., 1996), and the Aging Sexual Knowledge and Attitudes Scale (White, 1982), have specifically been validated with older adults and can be readily integrated into the assessment process. Additionally, several standardized self-report measures for sexual function in the general population have been used in older adult populations, including the International Index of Erectile Function (Rosen et al., 1997) and the Female Sexual Functioning Inventory (Rosen et al., 2000). In contrast, standard assessments for sexual well-being are limited in number and in scope and often are focused on satisfaction. The Female Sexual Well-Being Scale (Rosen et al., 2010), however, recently has been developed and validated to assess four domains of sexual well-being in women: (a) interpersonal, (b) cognitive–emotional, (c) physical arousal, and (d) orgasm satisfaction.

Assessment Considerations for Integrated Care

Although older adults typically view their medical providers as the primary resource to address sexual health concerns, they frequently report discomfort in initiating conversations about sexual health (Hinchliff & Gott, 2011). In one study, 82% of patients with ED reported a desire for their doctors to initiate a conversation regarding their sexual health (Baldwin, Ginsberg, & Harkaway, 2003). Health care providers historically have avoided these conversations because of lack of knowledge, embarrassment, and feeling ill-equipped to address sexual concerns (Hinchliff & Gott, 2011; Taylor & Gosney, 2011). Geropsychology providers working in an integrated care setting may find themselves uniquely positioned to advocate for the sexual health care needs of the older adult. This is particularly true in long-term care facilities and other institutionalized settings where barriers may include both staff attitudes and structural or environmental barriers (e.g., lack of privacy) hindering opportunities for sexual expression. Geropsychology providers in these settings may need to educate medical staff about older adult sexuality to promote universal screening for sexual health concerns and policy changes that may facilitate sexual well-being.

For the provider working in integrated primary care or other medical settings, the clinical assessment will likely be limited to a 15–20 min encounter that aims to simultaneously initiate an intervention. The five As (assess, advise, agree, assist, and arrange) is a leading assessment and intervention approach to chronic health conditions in primary care (Hunter, Goodie, Oordt, & Dobmeyer, 2009). It allows providers to address sexual health needs in a focused manner, as they *assess* beliefs, behaviors, and knowledge regarding sexual expression; *advise* patients by providing specific information and suggestions; *agree* on collaboratively set clinical goals; *assist* patients in identifying strategies to address their concerns; and *arrange* necessary follow-up with specialty services as indicated (Hunter et al., 2009).

TREATMENT APPROACHES

Enhancement of sexual expression among older adults is a collaborative practice, potentially involving the provider, the client, a partner, family members or a caregiver, and other health professionals involved in the elder's health care. Treatment plans should affirm older adult sexuality, attend to dysfunction and well-being, and focus on adaptation and psychological flexibility. A positive therapeutic relationship is key to successful utilization of the therapeutic approaches reviewed in the following sections. These focused, often short-term strategies can be adapted for use across a range of care settings.

Client–Provider Considerations

General recommendations for effective therapeutic encounters with older adults include the following: providing a straightforward rationale for treatment, providing brief education about the treatment process (including clarifying plans for collaboration with other providers and discussing confidentiality), explicitly outlining expectations and potential outcomes for therapy, and normalizing the client's presenting problem to reduce stigma or shame (APA, 2013). Building trust, normalizing concerns and issues, and expressing openness about sexuality are critical factors for treating sexual concerns. Providers also should reflect on their personal beliefs and stereotypes related to older adult sexuality that may interfere with the treatment process, and seek consultation with a colleague if this becomes a barrier to treatment (Mona et al., 2011).

A patient-centered approach to care is central to facilitating treatment to enhance sexual health and well-being. This includes a collaborative therapeutic relationship that emphasizes a partnership rather than a provider–patient hierarchy. Patient-centered therapy considers the goals, objectives, and choice of treatment strategies from the perspective of the older adult client (and partner, when applicable) and expands on traditional symptom-related outcomes (e.g., ED, low desire, pain) to include patient-reported outcomes, such as satisfaction with treatment and overall sexual well-being (Bitzer et al., 2008; Hatzichristou et al., 2010).

Therapeutic Approaches to Address Sexual Health and Well-Being

Sexual health interventions continue to develop beyond the biomedical model toward a biopsychosocial approach that increasingly utilizes combinations of medical—usually pharmaceutical—and psychological treatment components to enhance efficacy (Berner & Günzler, 2012; Bitzer et al., 2008; Meana & Jones, 2011). A combined approach to treatment has continued to evolve in the context of the integrated care movement, which has proven to be beneficial for older adults across diagnostic categories (Gatz, 2007). Thus, the provider is likely to work in collaboration with medical professionals, and it is good clinical practice to refer older adults with sexual concerns to a medical professional to assist with diagnosis and treatment.

Biomedical approaches. Biomedical treatments that address symptoms related to the sexual response cycle have dominated sexual health care since the arrival of PDE5 inhibitors to treat ED. Effective biomedical treatments for ED include administration of PDE5 inhibitors, penile vacuum devices, injectable vasoactive drugs, and penile implants. Effectiveness among older adult males depends on various health status considerations and treatment adherence, which is reportedly low for PDE5 inhibitor use in men (Hillman, 2011; Melnik, Soares, & Nasello, 2008). Contraindications for PDE5 inhibitor use include common conditions in older adult males, such as heart disease, recent stroke or heart attack, high or low blood pressure, and use of nitrate-based medications (Wespes et al., 2012). For premature ejaculation, treatments include administration of topical anesthetic agents and the use of selective serotonin reuptake inhibitors and PDE5 inhibitors, although these uses are off-label (Wespes et al., 2012). At this time, there are no approved pharmaceutical treatments for female sexual dysfunction (FSD). Estrogen therapy has been used successfully to treat vaginal atrophy and arousal problems in postmenopausal women, and nonprescription topical lubricants commonly are used for vaginal dryness (Ambler et al., 2012; Kingsberg & Althof, 2009).

Biopsychosocial approaches. Sex therapy is a specialized psychotherapeutic treatment that addresses sexual functioning and integrates many techniques across therapeutic schools of thought (Althof, 2010; Wincze & Carey, 2001). This can be a complex therapeutic endeavor and providers may be uncertain about conducting sex therapy with older adults, especially if not trained in specific

sex therapy techniques. Several well-known clinical strategies, however, are useful and effective for addressing sexual concerns in older adults. These include psychoeducation, cognitive and behavioral treatments, and acceptance-based and mindfulness interventions. Because of their brevity, these interventions can be readily incorporated into any clinical setting.

In treatment planning, the provider must attend to the level of intervention required as well as the resources available in the current setting. For some older adults, treatment may be less intensive, utilizing basic clinical skills that are effective for many presenting problems, such as building a therapeutic bond, employing empathic understanding, collaborating on goals and objectives for treatment, validating sexual concerns, and providing psychoeducation or self-help materials (Bitzer et al., 2008; Mona et al., 2011; van Lankveld, 2009). Psychoeducation has been found to be an effective component of treatment for ED, premature ejaculation, and arousal and desire disorders in men and women (Basson et al., 2010; Berner & Günzler, 2012; Hatzichristou et al., 2010). Helpful information for the older adult client may include clarifying misconceptions about sexuality, debunking myths, discussing normal age-related changes for men and women, reviewing biopsychosocial determinants of aging sexuality, clarifying safe sex practices and subsequent resources, highlighting the spectrum of potential self and partnered sexual or intimate activities, and providing a description of skills and techniques that may be further developed in therapy (Bitzer et al., 2008). The APA's Office on Aging (2007) provides an online guide for providers wanting more resources and information for aging sexuality.

In contrast, an older adult may have very involved sexual concerns that require either a higher level of provider expertise or more resources than are available in the current treatment setting (e.g., integrated care setting in which duration and number sessions is limited). In these cases, a referral to a sex therapist or another specialty provider may be warranted. If an expert referral is needed, professional organizations may be consulted, such as the American Association of Sex Educators, Counselors, and Therapists, which maintains a national list of providers certified in sex therapy (see http://www.aasect.org/referral-directory).

Established sex therapy approaches. Although the evidence base for biopsychosocial treatments for sexual concerns continues to grow, few treatment studies either include or focus on the older adult population. Empirical studies on sex therapy primarily have addressed ED or premature ejaculation in men and orgasm, sexual pain, or arousal disorders in women—often combining a pharmaceutical or hormonal treatment with a psychosocial approach (Meana & Jones, 2011). Cognitive–behavioral techniques—well-established as effective in older adults with various presenting problems—are the foundation of sex therapy and are consistent with a sex-positive framework that balances the well-being and dysfunction of the older adult client. Specific strategies include decreasing performance anxiety using relaxation techniques (e.g., sensate focus), decreasing maladaptive cognitions and negative sexual self-schemas using cognitive restructuring, increasing stimulus control, and improving communication skills (Heiman, 2002; Wincze & Carey, 2001). Additionally, several specific behavioral techniques have been found to be effective in addressing sexual concerns that can be common for older adults. These include start–stop techniques for premature ejaculation, systematic desensitization for sexual anxiety or pain, use of vaginal dilators for vaginismus, directed masturbation for anorgasmia, behavioral or contingency strategies to improve adherence to medications, and use of erotic materials for lack of desire (for further description of these behavioral techniques, see ter Kuile, Both, & van Lankveld, 2010; Wincze & Carey, 2001).

The goal of sensate focus is for the older adult (or partner) to reach a heightened awareness of sensations related to the sexual experience and to deemphasize performance, which decreases anxiety related to focusing solely on intercourse and orgasm. This approach may be particularly well-suited to older adults for whom health complications present challenges to certain sexual behaviors. In sensate focus, the client is becoming desensitized to the experience of anxiety about her or his

performance as she or he gradually is exposed to a hierarchy of sexual behaviors. Although this often ends with intercourse, the ultimate goal of the sexual encounter depends on the goals of the older adult (Wincze & Carey, 2001).

Sex therapy commonly incorporates cognitive restructuring with the goal to increase flexible thinking and behaving. This can increase sexual self-esteem, lead to more creativity and experimentation, and help the older adult client to focus on pleasure and intimacy goals rather than solely performance-oriented goals. For example, an older adult man with significant ED who is not able to engage in penile–vaginal intercourse regularly may feel inadequate because he cannot please his partner the "way it should be done." He may need to increase cognitive flexibility around what types of behaviors he considers sexual and pleasurable by challenging those rigidly held beliefs (i.e., sexual schemas) about intercourse as the only way to perform sexually. This can be facilitated through reflective questioning and behavioral assignments that include experimenting with a broader spectrum of intimate behaviors. Cognitive restructuring can be useful in treating sexual self-esteem concerns that are common for aging clients (Bitzer et al., 2008) by addressing such maladaptive thoughts as, "I am not sexually attractive anymore" or "I will never be able to please him/her." This approach can be used in conjunction with psychoeducation to address misconceptions (e.g., "I should be able to perform every time"), stigma-related issues (e.g., "Older adults like me shouldn't be having sex/masturbating"), and adherence (e.g., "I tried it already and it doesn't work for me").

Stimulus control is a behavioral technique that aims to optimize the sexual environment—by increasing pleasant and relaxing factors and decreasing interfering factors—to support satisfying sexual experiences. Attending to environmental (e.g., temperature, lighting, noise), temporal (e.g., time of day), biological (e.g., fatigue, painful positioning), psychological (e.g., mood, anxiety), and interpersonal (e.g., personal hygiene, attractiveness, partner's preferences) factors can enhance the intimate experience (Winze & Carey, 2001). Some older adult clients may benefit from reframing the idea of planning their sexual encounters as "planned spontaneity," which may promote buy-in for this intervention.

Cognitive–behavioral therapy (CBT) for the couple is an effective strategy for treatment with older adults and has been shown to improve both male and female sexual dysfunction in an individual-couple and group-couples format (Berner & Günzler, 2012; Bitzer et al., 2008; ter Kuile et al., 2010). Couples therapy often incorporates psycho-education about sexuality and aging; addresses communication problems; and involves behavioral homework assignments, such as initiating a special date night or practicing sensate focus exercises (Banner & Anderson, 2007). When sexual concerns happen in the context of an established relationship, it is recommended that partners be included, as this can harness support for the client, reveal communication issues, verify information, and increase treatment effectiveness for both client and partner sexual concerns (Dean et al., 2008). In addition, it is ethically responsible to attempt to involve the partner in a treatment process that will affect her or him.

Emerging sex therapy approaches. Sex therapy often utilizes nontraditional approaches (e.g., mindfulness) that are common in third-wave CBTs (TWCBTs), such as acceptance and commitment therapy (ACT; Althof, 2010; Meana & Jones, 2011). There are no studies to establish whether TWCBTs are effective in treating sexuality issues in older adults; however, many components are well suited to address sexual concerns in an aging population. For instance, TWCBTs often combine cognitive and behavioral techniques aimed at increasing psychological flexibility with a unique emphases on value-driven behavior, nonjudgmental awareness, and acceptance—concepts that can be integrated easily into a treatment plan. This is true regardless of clinical setting, as emerging research on focused ACT increasingly has applied these principles within the integrated health care setting (Strosahl, Robinson, & Gustavsson, 2012).

Sensual mindfulness. Sensual mindfulness combines a purposeful and nonjudgmental attention to the present moment with the traditional sex therapy technique of sensate focus (Mona et al., 2011). The goal is accepting uncomfortable feelings or thoughts that might arise during intimacy and intentionally attending to present-moment sensations as the older adult (and partner) engages in the sensual behavior hierarchy (e.g., caressing, fondling, kissing, genital stimulation, intercourse). As the level of intimate behavior increases, the older adult client may experience heightened distress or anxiety. The application of mindfulness exercises during intimacy can aid in accepting anxious thoughts as they come, remaining in the present moment, and reducing subsequent distress and avoidance behaviors. The goal is to accept the anxious thoughts (e.g., "My partner isn't turned on by me"), remain present in the experience, and be able to continue to engage in valued sexual or intimate behavior. As a provider, mindfulness techniques and meditations to use with older adults can be found throughout the ACT literature, and specific resources are available online through the Association for Contextual Behavioral Science (ACBS; http://www.contextualscience.org).

Values clarification. Older adults wishing to address sexual concerns or wanting to enhance sexual experiences may benefit from values clarification, which is a process of articulating and exploring personal beliefs and core values about sexuality (Mona et al., 2011). Clarifying sexual and intimate values can help to address misconceptions about sexuality, further explicate the importance of sexuality in the client's life, and promote value-driven behavior. For example, an older adult client may be avoiding sexual expression because of feelings of inadequacy or low sexual self-esteem. Through values clarification exercises, it becomes apparent that a flourishing sexual life is a strongly valued experience for that older adult. The provider and client then work on becoming aware of this discrepancy, setting goals, and strengthening resolve to live according to that value, which includes addressing avoidance of the desired behavior through CBT, mindfulness, or other techniques.

The values clarification process involves having the older adult client and partner answer questions that reveal their values related to sexual and intimate experiences. Questions may include the following: "How important is sex in my life?" "What is a good sexual relationship?" "What role do trust and safety play?" and "What is important in a sexual experience?" Examples of intimate and sexual values held by older adult clients can include (but are not limited to) being adventurous in my sex life, being open in my sexual communication, being able to satisfy my partner, and being willing to think broadly about sex and intimacy. The ACT literature has values-clarification tools available that can assist with exploring sexual and intimate values, which also are available online through the ACBS.

Practical approaches. When treating older adults for sexual concerns, there are relevant practical issues to consider, including the use of sexual enhancement products, strategies for seeking new relationships, and preventative sexual health care practices. In discussing sexual enhancement products, the provider may want to consider such factors as functional limitations, clients' comfort level and interest in trying certain products, and the level of privacy in the older adult's current living situation (e.g., living with roommates or adult children). For this population, sexual products that provide for privacy (e.g., privacy pillows that come with storage pockets for products and erotic material), optimal positioning (e.g., sex cushions), increased lubrication for women (e.g., lubricating gels), or increased genital stimulation (e.g., ergonomically designed vibrators) may be useful. Also, the client may benefit from brief education about use and safety if they are unfamiliar with sexual enhancement products.

Older adult clients—particularly older adult women—may present with sexual concerns that revolve mainly around limited availability of intimate partners. If congruent with the client's beliefs and values, self-stimulation may be an appropriate behavioral intervention for those without available intimate partners. Older adults may be seeking a new romantic relationship and want to discuss opportunities for meeting people (e.g., online dating communities for older adults), get information about the dating scene and current dating practices, or practice talking to potential partners in role-play situations. They also may need cognitive restructuring around low sexual self-esteem issues and may need to address anxiety about meeting new people

or initiating a new sexual relationship. Online dating sites can give the older adult access to potential partners and a place to practice flirting and conversation; however, providers should be sure to educate clients about safety issues, such as confidentiality, physical and psychological safety, and other safety precautions when meeting prospective partners. Initiating a new relationship may necessitate a review of preventative sexual health care practices. Providing information about the protection against STIs, safe sex practices, and resources for the older adult client to receive testing or get condoms is integral to promoting sexual health. A recommended source for sex education and preventative sexual health care practices for older adults is the book *Older, Wiser, Sexually Smarter: 30 Sex Ed Lessons for Adults Only* (Brick, Lunquist, Sandak, & Taverner, 2009).

Case Example: Late-Life Sexuality in Integrated Care

Catherine is 70-year-old African American woman presenting for a visit with her primary care provider (PCP), whom she has seen regularly for the past four years for Type II diabetes and cardiovascular disease. Her physician began their visit by reviewing her most recent lab results and praising her for sustained attention to her complicated health needs. During their meeting, Catherine disclosed to her physician that her husband had passed away 10 months ago from a stroke and she was making attempts to "go forward" with her life. The PCP inquired briefly about her mood and coping abilities and informed her that a behavioral health provider on their interdisciplinary team would be available to talk with her, if desired. Catherine stated that while she missed her husband, she was not feeling depressed, but was searching for answers and information about a new romantic relationship she had begun. After obtaining Catherine's consent, the PCP introduced Catherine to the behavioral health provider, gave a brief overview of the consultation concern, and left them to explore Catherine's concerns.

Catherine previously had worked with the behavioral health provider for motivational enhancement services related to managing her chronic diseases, and a positive rapport had been established. Also, the physician had already identified Catherine's concerns, so the provider was able to begin conducting a focused clinical assessment using a 5As approach. Catherine reiterated that she had begun a new romantic relationship with an African American man that she knows from her church, where they both are active in their Christian faith. She further expressed that her body was not "cooperating" during sexual activity and that she has been dealing with how her new relationship fits with her religious beliefs. The provider validated Catherine's concerns and normalized her experiences by noting the commonalities shared by many women who have lost partners and begin new relationships. They agreed on two main goals: (a) exploring romantic relationship and sexual function issues and (b) addressing her relationship in the context of her religious beliefs. They scheduled three 30 min sessions over the next 2 months to focus on these goals and specifically discussed strategies to involve Catherine's partner between sessions (e.g., active discussion of goals, soliciting preferences), as he was unable to attend therapy.

Session 1.   The initial session focused on gathering specific information about Catherine's sexual function concerns. She described difficulties with vaginal dryness during sexual activity and positioning for both penile–vaginal intercourse and oral sexual activity. She noted that although these difficulties were present on occasion with her husband, they seemed more consistently difficult

with her current partner. Given that Catherine had received limited information on sexuality throughout her life, the provider briefly reviewed basic education on sexuality for the aging female (e.g., sexual anatomy, safe sex practices) and outlined the ways in which age-related changes, chronic health issues, and decreased functional ability might be affecting sexual activity. Specifically, they discussed how diabetes complications (e.g., neuropathy), cardiovascular difficulties (e.g., vascular constriction), and the medications used to treat these conditions could influence sexual arousal. Also, after Catherine briefly described her sexual script, it became clear that she was having difficulties with becoming aroused before engaging in intercourse. Suggestions were given to Catherine that included increasing foreplay time from 10 min to 20–30 min, becoming mindfully aware of her state of arousal to better identify when she is "ready" for sex, and using a topical lubricant to address vaginal dryness and discomfort. Throughout this process, the provider assessed Catherine's comfort with the suggestions to make sure the information was consistent with her belief system.

Session 2.   After a quick check-in, Catherine stated that her partner was open to the ideas previously discussed. She further indicated that the main stressor in their relationship was a "struggle with how it fits with our beliefs." Catherine stated that according to their Christian faith, it was not appropriate to engage in sexual activity outside of marriage. This discussion led the provider to suggest a values clarification exercise to explore her sexual values and clarify how those may or may not "fit" with her religious beliefs. Initially, the provider explained core values, differentiating them from goals or beliefs, and emphasized the importance of living in accordance with your values to enhance well-being. Catherine was assisted with identifying and clarifying intimate relationship and sexual expression values through reflective questioning (e.g., How important is my sex life to me? Can I be sexual without intercourse? Without marriage?). The exercise also included a series of questions to be addressed for each identified value, including "I value this because someone else wants me to"; "I value this because I would be ashamed or guilty, or anxious if I didn't"; and "I value this because it makes my life better, more meaningful, and/or more vital" (Zettle, 2007). The provider then prompted her to explore these values further—both personally and as a couple—before the next session.

Session 3. At the final session, Catherine and her provider discussed her responses to the values clarification exercise and the subsequent conversation with her partner. Catherine indicated that they felt more confident in their decision to engage in sexual expression, but they would like to seek further spiritual guidance about how this could be reconciled with their faith. The provider and Catherine talked about possible resources for referral, including her pastor, a trusted spiritual guide, and an outpatient therapist. At her request, the provider gave Catherine a few additional resources on safe sexual practices and building physical intimacy. At the end of the final session, the behavioral health provider invited Catherine's PCP into the room for a brief summary on their progress before concluding treatment, and they affirmed Catherine for seeking support around an important life experience. The session ended with the providers reminding Catherine of the availability of services within their clinic and to revisit if needed.

CONCLUSION

Providers can empower older adults to be sexually well at any age and any level of physical and sexual functioning. Of central importance is embracing a sex-positive conceptualization by emphasizing pleasure and satisfying sexual experiences along with sexual functioning problems and diagnosable sexual disorders. To do so, providers must be able to think flexibly about sexuality in an aging context, understanding the biopsychosocial contributions to late-life sexuality. It also requires providers to be creative with the available assessment and treatment resources, integrating the evidence-base with preferences of the older adult and adapting the treatment plan as needed based on the patient-reported outcomes.

Recognition of older adult sexuality has just begun, and as the baby boomers move into older adulthood, it is likely to be increasingly salient. This has implications for providers across clinical settings. As health care shifts toward an integrated care model, providers will need to establish procedures for sexual health interventions that include brief assessments and effective, short-term interventions for the older adult client that are part of an overall treatment plan executed by an integrated medical team. This includes providers in long-term care settings where sexuality often is ignored or discouraged and established procedures for addressing sexual expression among residents are rare (Hajjar & Kamel, 2003).

Additionally, older adults represent an increasingly diverse population, and providers must have the tools to address the unique needs of subgroups such as LGBT and racial and ethnic minority elders. To do so, clinicians and researchers first need to advance the knowledge base on late-life sexuality and diversity, which is lacking both in quantity and quality of studies. An increased understanding will lead to more effective sexual health interventions and support sexual wellness across diverse groups of older adults.

APPENDIX 15.1
CLINICAL INTERVIEW OUTLINE

The following outline provides an initial clinical interview to assess sexual health and well-being among older adults. Key areas of assessment are highlighted along with several potential topics for follow-up.

I. Introduction and Presenting Issues and Goals
   A. Nature of the sexual issue and basic goals and hopes for treatment
      i. Client-identified goals; extent of match to or discrepancy with current situation

II. Sexual Functioning and Current Symptoms
These are specific symptoms according to the sexual response cycle. For each symptom, ask about the percentage of time this is occurring or is problematic; when during sexual encounter it occurs (e.g., foreplay, intromission); during what type of activities is this occurring (e.g., masturbation, oral sex, intercourse); with whom it occurs; onset, duration, and frequency of the symptom(s); and what is happening when it is absent or when things go well.
   A. Desire
      i. Difficulties with sexual thoughts, fantasies, interest, urges
   B. Excitement and arousal
      i. Erection problems
         a. Percent of erections obtained typically and maximally; nocturnal or morning erections or emissions; concomitant desire problems
      ii. Lubrication and vasocongestion problems
         a. Typical and maximal labia engorgement obtained; concomitant pain
   C. Orgasm
      i. Lack of orgasm
         a. Typical timing if and when orgasmic; concomitant arousal issues; impact of quality of relationship with partner
      ii. Rapid ejaculation
         a. Duration of erection until ejaculation; postejaculation behavior (self and partner)
   D. Sexual penetration and pain
      i. Unable to have vaginal penetration (digital, penile, etc.); involuntary or voluntary tensing or tightening of pelvic floor

muscles; pain or fear of pain during intercourse, masturbation, etc.

III. Sexual Well-Being Status
   A. Biopsychosocial aspects of sexual wellness
      i. Biological—pleasure; satisfaction (for both individual and partner)
      ii. Psychological—joy; able to adapt sexual behaviors to situation/status; body image; feeling desirable; sexual self-esteem
      iii. Social and relational—ability to pleasure a partner; sexual choices; trusting partnerships; emotional intimacy; available partners
      iv. Cultural —sexual values; sex roles; sexual and reproductive rights

IV. Sexual History
This information tracks sexual health and well-being across time. A collateral source of information is key, if available.
   A. Baseline sexual functioning—when was it going well and what sexual behaviors were occurring
   B. Onset of sexual concerns
      i. Gradual versus abrupt; initial and subsequent sexual symptoms; precipitating factors (e.g., relationship challenges, physical or mental health concerns, partner availability)
   C. Coping strategies
      i. Individual and couple coping strategies; attempts to resolve problem and successes; any upsetting consequences (e.g., doubt, depression, failed relationships)
      ii. Causal beliefs
         a. Client's and partner's beliefs about causes of the sexual problem; openness to alternative explanations

V. Current Sexuality: Behaviors, Relationships, Attitudes, and Beliefs
This information provides a snapshot of the client's current sexuality. Collateral information is also key here, if available. Pursue topic areas as needed for specific client's situation.
   A. Sexual scripts (typical sexual encounter)
      i. Description of the *typical* sexual encounter(s) with prompt to describe in terms of beginning, middle, and end.

Include details of when, where, and with whom sexual expression typically happens. Attend to influences on the sexual script such as living situation, privacy, consent, physical assistance, and sexual initiation.

    a. May include sexual activity with partners of other gender, same gender, or partners outside primary partnership. If so, follow-up topics include experiences, fantasies, and beliefs about sex within these partnership types; ground rules for multiple partner relationships; any differences among those sexual scripts.

  ii. Safe sex practices

    a. Beliefs or values about safe sex and sexual health; current practices; current and past sexual health history; knowledge of sexually transmitted infections and sexual risk; resources available

B. Relationship with primary partner

  i. Perceived quality; expression of affection; emotional intimacy; impact of sexual problems; partner physical and mental health status; communication

C. Sexual orientation and gender identity

  i. Client's self-identification of sexual orientation and gender identity

  ii. Value systems around same gender or opposite gender sexual behavior or activity; stigma or discrimination; impact on family, social, and sexual relationships over time

D. Beliefs, attitudes, and values

  i. General attitudes toward sex including acceptable sexual behaviors and inappropriate or appropriate situations for expression (e.g., outside of marriage, sex as solely reproductive)

  ii. Attitudes and beliefs about aging and sexuality (e.g., impact of disability or functional status, older adults as asexual); ageism (perception of other's beliefs as well as internalized ageism)

  iii. Values about sexual expression and relationships or intimacy

VI. Medical and Mental Health Contributions and History

This information is often part of a general clinical interview and is collected from various resources (e.g., prior treatment, chart review shared information with treatment team).

A. Background information

  i. Life situation (e.g., age, education, work, cultural background, etc.)

  ii. Physical health history and status and health behaviors

  iii. Mental health history and status

  iv. Cognitive health history and status (including any decisional capacity issues)

References

Adams, S. G., Jr., Dubbert, P. M., Chupurdia, K. M., Jones, A., Jr., Lofland, K. R., & Leermakers, E. (1996). Assessment of sexual beliefs and information in aging. Couples with sexual dysfunction. *Archives of Sexual Behavior, 25,* 249–260. doi:10.1007/BF02438164

Administration on Aging. (2008). *Older Americans 2008: Key indicators of well-being.* Retrieved from http://www.agingstats.gov/agingstatsdotnet/Main_Site/Data/Data_2008.aspx

Albersen, M., Orabi, H., & Lue, T. F. (2012). Evaluation and treatment of erectile dysfunction in the aging male: A mini-review. *Gerontology, 58,* 3–4. doi: 10.1159/000329598.

Althof, S. E. (2010). What's new in sex therapy? *Journal of Sexual Medicine, 7,* 5–13. doi:10.1111/j.1743-6109.2009.01433.x

Ambler, D. R., Bieber, E. J., & Diamond, M. P. (2012). Sexual function in elderly women: A review of current literature. *Reviews in Obstetrics and Gynecology, 5,* 16–27.

American Association of Retired Persons. (2010). *Sex, romance, and relationships: AARP survey of midlife and older adults* (Pub. No. D19234). Washington, DC: Author.

American Bar Association/American Psychological Association. (2008). *Assessment of older adults with diminished capacity: A handbook for psychologists.* Washington, DC: Author.

American Psychiatric Association. (2000). *Diagnostic and statistical manual of mental disorders* (4th ed., text revision). Washington, DC: Author.

American Psychiatric Association. (2013). *Diagnostic and statistical manual of mental disorders* (5th ed.). Washington, DC: Author.

American Psychological Association. (2013). *Guidelines for psychological practice with older adults.* Retrieved from http://www.apa.org/practice/guidelines/older-adults.aspx

American Psychological Association Office on Aging. (2007). *Aging and human sexuality resource guide.* Retrieved from http://www.apa.org/pi/aging/resources/guides/sexuality.aspx

Baldwin, K., Ginsberg, P., & Harkaway, R. C. (2003). Under-reporting of erectile dysfunction among men with unrelated urologic conditions. *International Journal of Impotence Research, 15,* 87–89. doi:10.1038/sj.ijir.3900948

Banner, L. L., & Anderson, R. U. (2007). Integrated sildenafil and cognitive-behavior sex therapy for psychogenic erectile dysfunction: A pilot study. *Journal of Sexual Medicine, 4,* 1117–1125. doi:10.1111/j.1743-6109.2007.00535.x

Basson, R., Wierman, M. E., van Lankveld, J., & Brotto, L. (2010). Summary of the recommendations on sexual dysfunctions in women. *Journal of Sexual Medicine, 7,* 314–326. doi:10.1111/j.1743-6109.2009.01617.x

Berner, M., & Günzler, C. (2012). Efficacy of psychosocial interventions in men and women with sexual dysfunctions--a systematic review of controlled clinical trials: Part 1. The efficacy of psychosocial interventions for male sexual dysfunction. *Journal of Sexual Medicine, 9,* 3089–3107. doi:10.1111/j.1743-6109.2012.02970.x

Bitzer, J., Platano, G., Tschudin, S., & Alder, J. (2008). Sexual counseling for elderly couples. *Journal of Sexual Medicine, 5,* 2027–2043. doi:10.1111/j.1743-6109.2008.00926.x

Brick, P., Lunquist, J., Sandak, A., & Taverner, B. (2009). *Older, wiser, and sexually smarter: 30 sex ed lessons for adults only.* Morristown, NJ: Planned Parenthood of Greater Northern New Jersey.

Brotto, L. A. (2010). The *DSM* diagnostic criteria for hypoactive sexual desire disorder in women. *Archives of Sexual Behavior, 39,* 221–239. doi:10.1007/s10508-009-9543-1

Collins, C., Hewson, D. L., Munger, R., & Wade, T. (2010). *Evolving models of behavioral health integration in primary care.* New York, NY: Milbank Memorial Fund. doi:10.1599/EvolvingCare2010

Dean, J., Rubio-Aurioles, E., McCabe, M., Eardley, I., Speakman, M., Buvat, J., . . . Fisher, W. (2008). Integrating partners into erectile dysfunction treatment: Improving the sexual experience for the couple. *International Journal of Clinical Practice, 62,* 127–133. doi:10.1111/j.1742-1241.2007.01636.x

DeLamater, J. (2012). Sexual expression in later life: A review and synthesis. *Journal of Sex Research, 49,* 125–141. doi:10.1080/00224499.2011.603168

Galinsky, A. M. (2012). Sexual touching and difficulties with sexual arousal and orgasm among U.S. older adults. *Archives of Sexual Behavior, 41,* 875–890. doi:10.1007/s10508-011-9873-7

Gatz, M. (2007). Commentary on evidence-based psychological treatments for older adults. *Psychology and Aging, 22,* 52–55. doi:10.1037/0882-7974.22.1.52

Hajjar, R. R., & Kamel, H. (2003). Sex and the nursing home. *Clinics in Geriatric Medicine, 19,* 575–586. doi:10.1016/S0749-0690(02)00099-X

Hatzichristou, D., Rosen, R. C., Derogatis, L. R., Low, W. Y., Meuleman, E. J. H., Sadovsky, R., & Symonds, T. (2010). Recommendations for the clinical evaluation of men and women with sexual dysfunction. *Journal of Sexual Medicine, 7,* 337–348. doi:10.1111/j.1743-6109.2009.01619.x

Heiman, J. R. (2002). Psychologic treatments for female sexual dysfunction: Are they effective and do we need them? *Archives of Sexual Behavior, 31,* 445–450. doi:10.1023/A:1019848310142

Hillman, J. (2011). *Sexuality and aging: Clinical perspectives.* New York, NY: Springer.

Hinchliff, S., & Gott, M. (2011). Seeking medical help for sexual concerns in mid- and later life: A review of the literature. *Journal of Sex Research, 48,* 106–117. doi:10.1080/00224499.2010.548610

Hinrichsen, G. A. (2006). Why multicultural issues matter for practitioners working with older adults. *Professional Psychology: Research and Practice, 37,* 29–35.

Hunter, C. L., Goodie, J. L., Oordt, M. S., & Dobmeyer, A. C. (2009). *Integrated behavioral health in primary care: Step-by-step guidance for assessment and intervention.* Washington, DC: American Psychological Association. doi:10.1037/11871-000

Jannini, E. A., Fischer, W. A., Bitzer, J., & McMahon, C. G. (2009). Is sex just fun? How sexual activity improves health. *Journal of Sexual Medicine, 6,* 2640–2648. doi:10.1111/j.1743-6109.2009.01477.x

Kingsberg, S., & Althof, S. (2009). Evaluation and treatment of female sexual disorders. *International Urogynecology Journal, 20*(Suppl. 1), 33–43. doi:10.1007/s00192-009-0833-x

Knauer, N. (2011). "Gen Silent": Advocating for LGBT elders. *Elder Law Journal, 19,* 101–161.

Kontula, O., & Haavio-Mannila, E. (2009). The impact of aging on human sexual activity and sexual desire. *Journal of Sex Research, 46,* 46–56. doi:10.1080/00224490802624414

Laumann, E. O., Glasser, D., Neves, R., Moreira, E., Jr., & the Global Study of Sexual Attitudes and Behaviors Investigators' Group. (2009). A population-based survey of sexual activity, sexual problems and associated help-seeking behavior patterns in mature adults in the United States of America. *International Journal of Impotence Research, 21,* 171–178. doi:10.1038/ijir.2009.7

Lindau, S. T., Leitsch, S. A., Lundberg, K. L., & Jerome, J. (2006). Older women's attitudes, behavior, and communication about sex and HIV: A community-based study. *Journal of Women's Health, 15,* 747–753. doi:10.1089/jwh.2006.15.747

Lindau, S. T., Schumm, P., Laumann, E. O., Levinson, W., O'Muircheartaigh, C. A., & Waite, L. J. (2007). A study of sexuality and health among older adults in the United Stated. *New England Journal of Medicine, 357,* 762–774. doi:10.1056/NEJMoa067423

Lyden, M. (2007). Assessment of consent capacity. *Sexuality and Disability, 25,* 3–20. doi:10.1007/s11195-006-9028-2

Masters, W., & Johnson, V. (1970). *Human sexual inadequacy.* Boston, MA: Little, Brown.

McCall-Hosenfeld, J. S., Jaramillo, S., Legault, C., Freund, K., Cochrane, B., Manson, J., . . . Bonds, D. (2008). Correlates of sexual satisfaction among sexually active postmenopausal women in the Women's Health Initiative-Observational Study. *Journal of General Internal Medicine, 23,* 2000–2009. doi:10.1007/s11606-008-0820-9

McCoy, N. (2000). The McCoy Female Sexuality Questionnaire. *Quality of Life Research, 9,* 739–745.

Meana, M., & Jones, S. (2011). Developments and trends in sex therapy. *Advances in Psychosomatic Medicine, 31,* 57–71.

Melnik, T., Soares, B., & Nasello, A. G. (2008). The effectiveness of psychological interventions for the treatment of erectile dysfunction: Systematic review and meta-analysis, including comparisons to sildenafil treatment, intracavernosal injection, and vacuum devices. *Journal of Sexual Medicine, 5,* 2562–2574. doi:10.1111/j.1743-6109.2008.00872.x

Mona, L. R., Goldwaser, G., Syme, M., Cameron, R. P., Clemency, C., & Miller, A., . . . Ballan, M. (2010). Assessment and conceptualization of sexuality among older adults. In P. A. Lichtenberg (Ed.), *Handbook of assessment in clinical gerontology* (2nd ed., pp. 331–356). London, England: Elsevier.

Mona, L. R., Syme, M. L., Goldwaser, G., Cameron, R. P., Chen, S., & Clemency, C., . . . Lemos, L. (2011). Sexual health in older adults: Conceptualization and treatment. In K. Sorocco & S. Lauderdale (Eds.), *Cognitive behavioral therapy with older adults: Innovations across care settings* (pp. 261–285). New York, NY: Springer.

Montemurro, B., & Gillen, M. M. (2013). Wrinkles and sagging flesh: Exploring transformations in women's sexual body image. *Journal of Women and Aging, 25,* 3–23. doi:10.1080/08952841.2012.720179

O'Connor, D. B., Corona, G., Forti, G., Tajar, A., Lee, D. M., Finn, J. D., . . . Wu, F. C. (2008). Assessment of sexual health in aging men in Europe: Development and validation of the European Male Ageing Study Sexual Function Questionnaire. *Journal of Sexual Medicine, 5,* 1374–1385. doi:10.1111/j.1743-6109.2008.00781.x

Pesce, V., Seidman, S. N., & Roose, S. P. (2002). Depression, antidepressants and sexual functioning in men. *Sexual and Relationship Therapy, 17,* 281–287. doi:10.1080/14681990220149086

Rheaume, C., & Mitty, E. (2008). Sexuality and intimacy in older adults. *Geriatric Nursing, 29,* 342–349. doi:10.1016/j.gerinurse.2008.08.004

Rosen, R. C., Althof, S., Barbach, L., Dietrich, J., Wanser, R., & Zhang, P. (2010). Female Sexual Well-Being Scale: Responsiveness to interventional product use by sexually functional women. *Journal of Sexual Medicine, 7,* 2479–2486.

Rosen, R. C., Brown, C., Heiman, J., Leiblum, S., Meston, C., Shabsigh, R., . . . D'Agostino, Jr., R. (2000). The Female Sexual Functioning Index (FSFI): A multidimensional self-report instrument for the assessment of female sexual functioning. *Journal of Sex and Marital Therapy, 26,* 191–208.

Rosen, R. C., Riley, A., Wagner, G., Osterloh, I. H., Kirkpatrick, J., & Mishra, A. (1997). The International Index of Erectile Function (IIEF): A multidimensional scale for assessment of erectile dysfunction. *Urology, 49,* 822–830.

Schick, V., Herbenick, D., Reece, M., Sanders, S. A., Dodge, B., Middlestadt, S. E., & Fortenberry, J. D. (2010). Sexual behaviors, condom use, and sexual health of Americans over 50: Implications for sexual health promotion for older adults. *Journal of Sexual Medicine, 7,* 315–329. doi:10.1111/j.1743-6109.2010.02013.x

Strosahl, R., Robinson, P., & Gustavsson, T. (2012). *Brief interventions for radical change: Principles and practice of focused acceptance and commitment therapy.* Oakland, CA: New Harbinger.

Taylor, A., & Gosney, M. A. (2011). Sexuality in older age: Essential considerations for healthcare professionals. *Age and Ageing, 40,* 538–543. doi:10.1093/ageing/afr049

ter Kuile, M. M., Both, S., & van Lankveld, J. J. D. M. (2010). Cognitive behavioral therapy for sexual dysfunctions in women. *Psychiatric Clinics of North America, 33,* 595–610. doi:10.1016/j.psc.2010.04.010

Thompson, W. K., Charoa, L., Vahia, I., Depp, C., Allison, M., & Jeste, D. (2011). Association between higher levels of sexual function, activity, and satisfaction and self-rated successful aging in older postmenopausal women. *Journal of the American*

Geriatrics Society, 59, 1503–1508. doi:10.1111/j.1532-5415.2011.03495.x

van Lankveld, J. (2009). Self-help therapies for sexual dysfunction. *Journal of Sex Research, 46*, 143–155. doi:10.1080/00224490902747776

Waite, L. J., Laumann, E. O., Das, A., & Schumm, L. P. (2009). Sexuality: Measures of partnerships, practices, attitudes, and problems in the National Social Life, Health, and Aging Study. *The Journals of Gerontology, Series B: Psychological Sciences and Social Sciences, 64*(Suppl. 1), 56–66. doi:10.1093/geronb/gbp038

Wespes, E., Amar, E., Eardley, I., Guiliano, F., Hatzichristou, D., Hatzimouratidis, K., . . . Vardi, Y. (2012). Guidelines on male sexual dysfunction: Erectile dysfunction and premature ejaculation.

Retrieved from http://www.uroweb.org/gls/pdf/14%20Male%20Sexual%20Dysfunction_LR.pdf

White, C. B. (1982). A scale for the assessment of attitudes and knowledge regarding sexuality in the aged. *Archives of Sexual Behavior, 11*, 491–502. doi:10.1007/BF01542474

Wincze, J., & Carey, M. (2001). *Sexual dysfunction: A guide for assessment and treatment.* New York, NY: Guilford Press.

World Health Organization. (1992). *The ICD–10 classification of mental and behavioural disorders: Clinical descriptions and diagnostic guidelines.* Geneva, Switzerland: Author.

Zettle, R. (2007). *ACT for depression: A clinician's guide to using acceptance and commitment therapy in treating depression.* Oakland, CA: New Harbinger.

CHAPTER 16

PAIN ASSESSMENT AND MANAGEMENT IN OLDER ADULTS

Thomas Hadjistavropoulos

The International Association for the Study of Pain (IASP), which is the most influential group of pain researchers and clinicians worldwide, has defined pain as "an unpleasant sensory and emotional experience associated with actual or potential tissue damage, or described in terms of such damage" (Merskey & Bogduk, 1994, p. 209). An important element in the definition of pain is the recognition that pain is not only a sensory experience but also has strong emotional components. People in pain often experience considerable psychological distress (e.g., depression) and respond with variety of emotions (e.g., fear, anger, disgust), thoughts, and behaviors (e.g., Hale & Hadjistavropoulos, 1997; Romano & Turner, 1985). These emotional, psychological and cognitive components of the pain experience are a frequent focus of psychological intervention.

CLINICAL CRITERIA

Pain must be contrasted from nociception, which refers to the processing of signals associated with the stimulation of specific receptors (i.e., nociceptors) and has the potential of being experienced as pain (Turk & Melzack, 2011). In contrast to nociception (i.e., a sensation), pain represents a perception and is associated with conscious awareness, learning, appraisal, emotion, and ascribed meaning (Hadjistavropoulos & Craig, 2004; Melzack & Casey, 1968). It is important to note that IASP's definition of pain includes a footnote that indicates "the inability to communicate verbally does not negate the possibility that an individual is experiencing pain and is in need of appropriate pain-relieving treatment (IASP, 2012). This note is especially important for geropsychologists working with seniors who present with severe dementia that is associated with limitations in ability to communicate verbally. That is, IASP recognizes that pain can be suffered in silence or may not be clearly expressed despite its presence.

Persistent pain is a widespread problem among older people, with prevalence estimates ranging from 25% to 65% of seniors living in the community and as high as 80% of those who live in long-term care facilities (Charlton, 2005). Pain that is of relatively short duration is considered to be acute, whereas pain that extends beyond the expected period of healing is considered chronic (Turk & Okijufi, 2001). Chronic pain often is operationalized as pain that persists for more than 3 months (Turk & Okijufi, 2001).

The most common clinical pain problems involve nociceptor activity associated with the muscle, bone, joints, skin, and other connective tissue, whereas problems associated with neuropathic pain are caused by damage in any part of the nervous system (i.e., nociceptive pain results from activation of nociceptors, whereas neuropathic pain occurs because of central nervous system problems due to illness or injury). Common pain conditions in older people fall under both the nociceptive (e.g., osteoarthritis of the spine and joints, other musculoskeletal concerns) and neuropathic categories (e.g., postherpetic neuralgia, herpetic neuralgia, central post-stroke pain, trigeminal neuralgia, radicular; and

http://dx.doi.org/10.1037/14459-016
APA Handbook of Clinical Geropsychology: Vol. 2. Assessment, Treatment, and Issues of Later Life,
P. A. Lichtenberg and B. T. Mast (Editors-in-Chief)

referred pain secondary to degenerative disease of the spine and painful peripheral neuropathy; Hadjistavropoulos et al., 2007). In addition to these problems, some conditions seen in older persons (e.g., fibromyalgia and myofascial pain) have both nociceptive and neuropathic elements (Hadjistavropoulos et al., 2007). Cancer pain can be nociceptive or neuropathic depending on the type of cancer.

Patients with chronic pain conditions sometimes have been classified using the *Diagnostic and Statistical Manual of Mental Disorders, Fourth Edition, Text Revision* (*DSM–IV–TR*; American Psychiatric Association, 2000), wherein a pain condition could be coded under Axis III as a pain disorder associated with a medical condition. In Axis I, relevant categories for certain people with chronic pain included somatization disorder (a polysymptom disorder that cannot be explained by physical factors), pain disorder associated with psychological factors, and pain disorder associated with both psychological factors and a medical condition. In general, pain disorder is a condition in which psychological factors are thought to play a major role in its causation and maintenance and nonpsychological factors are believed to play a minimal role. In *Diagnostic and Statistical Manual of Mental Disorders, Fifth Edition* (*DSM–5*; American Psychiatric Association, 2013), however, somatic symptom disorder was replaced by somatization disorder, undifferentiated somatoform disorder, and pain disorder, although some people with pain can still be diagnosed with psychological factors affecting other medical conditions. The *DSM–5* somatic symptom disorder is characterized by somatic symptoms that cause significant disruption, excessive thoughts, feelings, and behaviors associated with such symptoms and chronicity. This change in the *DSM–5* represents better recognition that the physical and psychological elements of the pain experience are well integrated. In other words, the *DSM–5* appropriately does not encourage separate estimation of the contribution of physical versus psychological factors in pain.

Psychological comorbidities commonly are seen in pain patients. Chronic pain in older adults, for example, often is comorbid with depression (Bonnewyn et al., 2009) and higher levels of anxiety have been associated with more postoperative disability

days for surgical patients (Taenzer, Melzack, & Jeans, 1986). Higher rates of anxiety also have been observed in long-term care residents experiencing pain (Casten, Parmelee, Kleban, Lawton, & Katz, 1995). Moreover, sleep difficulties are common in older chronic pain samples (Chen, Hayman, Shmerling, Bean, & Leveille, 2011) and often are due, at least in part, to physical discomfort. Given such comorbidities, it is not surprising that older people with chronic pain have an increased likelihood of seeking mental health services (Bonnewyn et al., 2009). Pain also can prevent older people from engaging in beneficial physical activity, which may lead to increased rates of obesity and associated cardiovascular risk in chronic pain patients (e.g., McVinnie, 2013).

MAJOR THEORIES OF PAIN

Starting in the 17th century with Descartes' work, *specificity theories of pain* developed. Such theories assumed a direct pain pathway from the location of tissue damage to the brain as well as a one-to-one correspondence between pain and tissue damage. In other words, the implication of these theories is that the greater the tissue damage, the greater the pain and that tissue damage is necessary for pain to be experienced. Over the years, the field evolved and new theories emerged but no theory proved to be satisfactory and capable of accounting for a wide range of phenomena, including observations that the degree of tissue damage experienced and the degree of pain do not always correspond, until Melzack and Wall (1965) proposed the gate control theory of pain. According to the theory, which has received considerable support from basic science, clinical, and psychological research perspectives, the spinal cord has a gating mechanism at the level of substantial gelatinosa. As Melzack and Katz (2004) explained, nerve impulses are transmitted from afferent fibers to spinal cord transmission cells and are modulated by the gating mechanism in the dorsal horn of the spinal cord. This gating mechanism is affected by activity of large diameter fibers (representing sensory neuronal pathways) and small diameter fibers (i.e., pain pathway fibers). Specifically activity of the large diameter fibers tends to close the gate by inhibiting competing transmission of small-diameter fibers. As a practical example, rubbing a painful area often helps improve the pain because rubbing results in activation of the large-diameter fibers thought to inhibit nociceptive transmission. The large- and small-diameter fibers synapse on projection cells, which reach the brain through the spinothalamic tract. When output of the transmission cells reaches a critical threshold, it activates the neural areas that affect the complex patterns of pain experience and expression. Critical to the gate control theory is an understanding that descending cortical input (e.g., cognitive processes such as attention) can facilitate or inhibit the transmission of nociceptive messages. Melzack and Wall's description of the process through which cortical input affects the gating mechanism provides a physiological explanation for the importance of psychological processes in the experience of pain and reinforces arguments for the use of psychological intervention in pain management. The gate control theory has been supplemented by the more recent, Neuromatrix model of pain that was developed to explain phenomena, such as phantom limb pain. This model (Melzack, 2001, 2005) explains how pain can be generated by neural activity through a network of brain structures and that the network can produce pain even in the absence of external sensory stimulation.

Based on the fundamental assertion of the gate control theory that pain can be affected by psychological and cognitive processes, a variety of biopsychosocial models of pain have been developed. These models are consistent with the gate control theory but provide more detail on the role of psychological factors. Although various models exist, a few key models are emphasized in the following sections.

The Operant Model

The *operant model* (e.g., Fordyce, 1976; Fordyce, Shelton, & Dundore, 1982) focuses on the consequences of pain behavior and the role of such consequences in its maintenance and further development. According to this viewpoint, if maladaptive pain behavior (e.g., excessive complaining) is reinforced (e.g., with attention), it would become more likely to be maintained or increased in frequency. By the same token, if avoidance of work or activity are reinforced (e.g., by temporarily reducing pain or by reduced stressful responsibilities), they may persist and

become maladaptive. In the case of an older person who is widowed and has pain, for example, it is possible that frequent pain complaints will be reinforced by increased family visitation. That is not to imply in any way that social support from family is not desirable. On the contrary: Social support is desirable. In situations in which complaining becomes excessive, however, it can create relationship tension. Moreover, where social support becomes excessive, to the point that it is solicitous, it can have negative consequences (Boothby, Thorn, Overduin, & Ward, 2004; McCracken, 2005; Paulsen & Altmaier, 1995) and encourage inactivity and avoidance of beneficial activity. As an example of solicitous support, consider a person who is actively discouraged from completing even very basic and safe physical tasks while relatives offer an excessive amount of assistance (e.g., "Don't get up! I will do this for you"). In such an instance, solicitous support may be contributing to deconditioning, which could interfere with recovery from injury. Although some laboratory support for the operant model exists, a criticism is that it does not account for the important role of appraisals in the pain experience (Sharp, 2001).

Fear Avoidance Model

The *fear avoidance model* (Vlaeyen & Linton, 2000) of pain incorporates elements of both classical and operant conditioning. The assumption is that anxiety is often a component of pain. As such, movement or activity that is associated with pain can become a conditioned stimulus for fear and anxiety. In turn, if avoidance of that activity results in reduced pain, avoidance is reinforced and may become frequent and, sometimes, excessive. According to the model, this process can be further strengthened with catastrophic thoughts about pain and its consequences. The model would predict that an older person, who excessively avoids activity as a means of preventing pain, may become stiff and deconditioned. Such deconditioning could interfere with the ability to overcome certain types of pain problems; it also can worsen them and sometimes can increase the risk of injurious falls. Generally, clinical research investigating aspects of the fear avoidance model has yielded support for many aspects of the model, but the identified effects are generally small (Moseley,

2011). As such, excessive avoidance may be best construed as one of many factors contributing to pain and disability (Moseley, 2011). Treatments designed to overcome excessive avoidance of activity have been developed with some success reported (e.g., George, Wittmer, Fillingim, & Robinson, 2010). Such treatments tend to involve in vivo exposure to various physical tasks with the aim of overcoming pain-related anxiety about performing these tasks (e.g., Boersma et al., 2004).

Cognitive–Behavioral Theory of Pain

According to Skinner, Wilson, and Turk (2012) the five key assumptions of *the cognitive–behavioral theory of pain* (e.g., Sharp, 2001; Turk, Meichenbaum, & Genest, 1987) are as follows:

1. People are active processors of information rather than passive recipients of environmental influence. That is, they interpret their experiences and make sense of them.
2. Beliefs, appraisals, attributions, and expectations can elicit and influence both affect and physiological arousal, which in turn can influence behavior.
3. Behavior is determined reciprocally by both the environment and the person.
4. People may have learned maladaptive ways of feeling, thinking, and responding.
5. People are instrumental in the development and maintenance of maladaptive thoughts and, as such, they should be considered active agents of change for the purposes of clinical intervention.

Examples of maladaptive views in the context of the older adult may include beliefs that pain is a natural part of old age and simply should be endured. Such a belief may make the older person less likely to seek appropriate treatment and pain management solutions. Although pain may be common in old age, it is thought to be related to pathology and not simply aging. Pathology should be treated and pain should be managed irrespective of a person's age. Other counterproductive beliefs may relate to inaccurate assumptions that pain levels in an older person usually cannot be improved with intervention. Cognitive–behavioral approaches to pain often adopt broad perspectives that incorporate

operant and fear avoidance models of pain. For example, operant views are incorporated through the recognition of environmental influences on behavior (see the second key assumption).

A considerable body of research has led to support for the cognitive–behavioral formulation of the pain experience (e.g., Hadjistavropoulos, Craig, et al., 2011). For example, catastrophic thinking about pain is a well-established risk factor in the development of disability and chronicity (Haythornthwaite, Clark, Pappagallo, & Raja, 2003; Linton, 2005; Picavet, Vlaeyen, & Schouten, 2002; Sullivan, Feuerstein, Gatchel, Linton, & Pransky, 2005) and catastrophizing goes hand in hand with pain intensity in older people (Ruscheweyh et al., 2011). Moreover, a variety of effective interventions based on this model have been developed (Day, Thorn, & Burns, 2012).

ASSESSMENT AND INTERVENTION

Pain is a multidimensional experience that is most likely to be assessed and treated effectively using an interdisciplinary (i.e., combinations of approaches, such as physical therapy, psychological intervention, medication) rather than a single-modality approach (e.g., only medication or only cognitive–behavioral therapy [CBT]). With most types of persistent pain, medical, nursing, physical therapy, occupational therapy, psychological, and other expertise may be needed. Although a psychologist may be well equipped to assess the intensity and psychological sequelae of pain, physiological, medical, and physical processes related to pain must be assessed by other professionals. With respect to treatment, a combination of physical therapy, pharmacological, occupational therapy, and psychological regiments may work best. As such, the functioning of an effective interdisciplinary team, for both treatment and assessment, is of critical importance. In instances in which psychologists who work in the community are not part of a formal team, it would be critical to establish open pathways of communication with the treating physician and other health professionals to optimize coordinated care.

Psychologists have been involved in the assessment and treatment of older pain patients at a variety of settings. For example, they provide treatment and assessment services at rehabilitation units, pain clinics, and private practice (e.g., seeing an older adult who is receiving insurance compensation following a motor vehicle accident). Although older adults traditionally have been underrepresented in pain clinics, specialized units for treating pain in older people have begun to develop. For instance, in Montreal, the McGill University Health Centre operates a geriatric pain clinic that includes a psychologist (http://www.mcgill.ca/paincentre/treatments). In long-term care, geropsychologists have been involved as consultants in the assessment of pain (e.g., Ghandehari et al., 2013) as well as in the management of psychological states (e.g., depression; Teri, Logsdon, Uomoto, & McCurry, 1997) that can sometimes result from pain. Although information about the role of psychologists in the pain assessment and management of older adults in primary care, home care, and acute care is extremely limited, psychologists have a key role to play as consultants in the facilitation of the assessment and treatment of older pain patients in such settings.

Assessment

A detailed international interdisciplinary statement on pain assessment in older people (Hadjistavropoulos et al., 2007) outlines the benefits of intedisciplinarity and discusses the importance of considering the effects of biological factors, disease, disuse, and environmental factors affecting functional outcomes. A physical evaluation by a qualified health professional (e.g., a physician) is of utmost importance. Under ideal circumstances, a functional evaluation also will be conducted (usually by a physiotherapist), as will an assessment of emotional functioning (e.g., by a psychologist). Moreover, a comprehensive pain assessment will include a detailed history, which can be the most important initial source of information about the pain and its causes. The history will establish a time frame for the pain, antecedents and consequences, reactions of others, comorbidities, treatments, expectations about outcomes, lifestyle factors, social history, coping efforts, psychological concerns, substance use, and other related areas (see Exhibit 16.1). Interviews with family members are helpful (e.g., family

---

Exhibit 16.1
Central Pain Assessment Domains

- Description of the pain and any related presenting issues (e.g., nature and intensity of pain, inability to perform the duties of one's occupation due to pain)
- Establishment of a timeframe for the pain and its course (e.g., onset, precipitants, fluctuation over time, possible contributors to fluctuations)
- Antecedents of pain flare-ups
  - Examples of physical antecedents: excessive physical activity, specific movements
  - Examples of psychological or situational antecedents: general stress, insomnia
- Consequences of pain flare-ups
  - Example of physical consequences: inability to engage in certain movements
  - Behavioural, psychological, and social: going for massage therapy, irritability, others offering to help, changes in routines, changes in mood
- Comorbidities
  - Example of physical comorbidities: coronary heart disease
  - Examples of psychological comorbidities: major depression, posttraumatic stress disorder
- Litigation and compensation issues
- Coping and pain management efforts
  - Examples of physical coping strategies: using over-the counter medication, application of heat or cold
  - Examples of psychosocial coping strategies: distraction, trying to stay busy with friends, coping self-statements
- History and lifestyle factors
  - Personal history
  - Current stressors
  - Educational and occupational history
  - Brief health history
  - Current social supports
  - Hobbies, exercise habits, health-promoting behaviors
  - Substance use
  - Goals and plans for the future
- Past and current treatment history
- Past history of psychological problems
- Client goals, concerns, and expectations about therapy

Note. This list of clinical interview domains is not meant to be exhaustive but rather is intended to highlight key domains that typically are covered during an interview with a pain patient.

---

members often can serve as collaborators in the treatment) but become critical in cases of seniors who have limited ability to communicate because of dementia.

Pain assessment with people without severe limitations in ability to communicate. Pain cannot be directly observed and typically is assessed using self-report procedures, although the observation of pain-related behavior is also important. In addition to a thorough clinical interview, psychologists typically will use a variety of assessment tools to evaluate an older person with chronic pain. Many assessment tools that have been used by psychologists, however, have psychometric properties that have not been investigated adequately in the context of the older adult. As such, psychologists must be cognizant of the potential limitations of this and aim to use tools that have been validated specifically for older people. Functional analysis of pain and behavior would also be important to conduct with a focus on identifying important antecedents (e.g., stress) and consequences (e.g., anger or irritability, reactions of others) of pain exacerbations. Such antecedents and consequences can become the focus of treatment.

For patients who are able to participate in an assessment that involves self-report (as opposed to patients with severe cognitive impairments) a variety of procedures can be used. Simple self-reports of pain can be obtained using numeric rating scales (0–10; Gagliese, Weizbliz, Ellis, & Chan, 2005; Weiner, Peterson, Logue, & Keefe, 1998) or verbal rating scales in which verbal descriptors to describe pain intensity are used (e.g., using words such as *mild, severe, very severe*; Gagliese & Katz, 2003; Herr, Spratt, Mobily, & Richardson, 2004). The use of horizontal analogue scales (i.e., a 10 cm line anchored by the polar opposites *pain* and *no pain*, which involve the older person marking an $\times$ on the part of the line that represents his or her pain intensity) is not recommended because some researchers have identified unusually high numbers of unscorable responses among older adults (Gauthier & Gagliese, 2011). On the other hand, there are reports that horizontal visual analogue scales have been used with reasonable success in some samples of seniors (e.g., Scherder & Bouma, 2000). Nonetheless, numeric and verbal rating scales may be the simplest and probably most recommended basic pain self-report procedure.

When using self-report procedures, including reports with accommodations for patients' sensory deficits (e.g., use of large fonts), questions can focus on current pain, average pain over the past day, and average pain over the past week. Information concerning fluctuations of the pain problem also can be collected. Specialized tools to assess neuropathic pain, such as the Neuropathic Pain Symptom Inventory (Bouhassira et al., 2004), are available These tools can help clinicians and interdisciplinary teams differentiate a neuropathic from a nociceptive pain problem as the two have distinct qualities. For example, neuropathic pain is more likely to be described as burning or as having electric-like qualities.

Some tools for evaluating coping strategies, such as the Coping Strategies Questionnaire (CSQ; Rosenstiel & Keefe, 1983), have been validated with older adults (e.g., Felton & Revenson, 1984; Keefe et al., 1987). Moreover, a variety of general psychological tools, such as the Satisfaction With Life Scale (Pavot & Diener, 1993), the NEO Personality Inventory (Costa & McCrae, 1992; Costa et al., 1986), and the Hospital Anxiety and Depression Scale (Spinhoven et al., 1997; Zigmond & Snaith, 1983) also have been validated with seniors and may be useful for the assessment of psychological functioning in chronic pain patients (e.g., Costa & McCrae, 1992).

The Multidimensional Pain Inventory (MPI; Kerns, Turk, & Rudy, 1985), a 61-item tool, allows for assessment of several dimensions beyond pain intensity and interference as it incorporates appraisals, such as perceived life control as well as indexes of perceived social support and affective distress. The tool, which has good psychometric properties with younger persons, has been used with success with older adults but more study with older individuals is needed before one can be confident about its properties with this population (Hadjistavropoulos et al., 2007; Kerns et al., 1985).

In cases in which a brief battery (10–15 min) is needed for pain assessment in older adults, Hadjistavropoulos et al. (2007) recommended use of the Brief Pain Inventory (BPI; Cleeland & Ryan, 1994) combined with the Short-Form of the McGill Pain Questionnaire (MPQ-SF; Melzack, 1975). The former tool consists of 11 items and assesses self-reported pain intensity and self-reported interference with function in a variety of domains (e.g., physical, psychological, and recreational). Because the BPI includes questions about mood and enjoyment of life, to some extent, it screens for the psychological impact of pain. Initial evidence suggests that the BPI is valid, sensitive, and reliable when used with older people (see Gauthier & Gagliese, 2011). The MPQ-SF, which consists of 15 pain quality words scored on a Likert severity scale in addition to two general items about current pain intensity and sensation, evaluates specific qualities of the pain (e.g., affective and sensory). The tool has been shown to have satisfactory test–retest reliability as well as high concurrent validity and sensitivity when used with older people (see Gauthier & Gagliese, 2011). A thorough discussion of pain assessment is included in Hadjistavropoulos et al. (2007).

Pain assessment in people with dementia.
A special challenge facing the clinical geropsychologist relates to the assessment of pain in older people who have serious limitations in ability to communicate because of dementia. Pain problems in these populations often are missed by health care staff (because of limited ability to self-report) and can lead to behavioral disturbance, which often is misattributed to possible psychiatric conditions. As a result, patients with severe dementia and pain often are treated with psychotropic rather than analgesic medications (e.g., Balfour & O'Rourke, 2003). This is an important concern not only because the pain is not treated adequately but also because many psychotropic medications have been show to hasten death in seniors (Ballard et al., 2009) often through increased risk of stroke and of falls (Laredo et al., 2011; Lindsey, 2009).

Given the widespread undertreatment of pain among patients with dementia (Ferrell et al., 2001; Horgas, Nichols, Schapson, & Vietes, 2007; Jakobsson, Rahm Hallberg, & Westergren, 2004; Kaasalainen et al., 1998; Martin, Williams, Hadjistavropoulos, Hadjistavropoulos, & MacLean, 2005; Morrison & Sui, 2000; Reynolds, Hanson, DeVellis, Henderson, & Steinhauser, 2008; Robinson, 2007; Won et al., 2004), effective pain assessment becomes extremely important. Research has demonstrated that people with mild to moderate dementia often are able to self-report pain in a reliable and valid fashion (Hadjistavropoulos,

Breau, & Craig, 2011) and that simple self-report tools such as numeric (0–10) and verbal rating scales can be used effectively. One horizontal visual analogue scale that has been used with success in people with mild to moderate dementia (Hadjistavropoulos et al., 1997) is the colored visual analogue scale (CAS; McGrath et al., 1996). The CAS typically is made of plastic and has rectangular shape (like ruler). The front of the scale shows the words *most pain* at the top and *no pain* at the bottom. Moreover, the color of the scale starts as a white to light pink at the bottom and becomes progressively more red as it approaches the top of the scale. The patient uses a plastic glide, that moves along the scale, to indicate his or her level of pain. The back of the scale includes numbers (0–10) that can be recorded by the clinician and signify pain intensity (10 = glide at the top of the scale; 0 = glide at the very top of the scale). Scherder and Bouma (2000) developed a quick protocol that allows clinicians to evaluate the patient's ability to comprehend and use the CAS before the pain assessment (e.g., the patient is asked to point to the scale, the plastic glide, where the glide should be placed if there is no pain).

Some clinicians have used the Faces Pain Scale (FPS; Bieri, Reeve, Champion, Addicoat, & Ziegler, 1990) to evaluate pain intensity in seniors with dementia. The FPS consists of a series of drawings of faces expressing increasing distress and the patient is asked to select the face that best corresponds to his or her pain. Compared with other pain intensity tools, however, this scale sometimes correlates less positively with other pain intensity scales and requires abstract reasoning, which makes its use difficult for many older people with cognitive impairment (Hadjistavropoulos et al., 2007). Scherder and Van Manen (2005), for example, demonstrated that the majority of seniors with dementia who were able to understand the CAS also were unable to understand the FPS. From a clinical standpoint, it is also noted that some seniors may select a face that corresponds to negative (or positive) affect that they may be experiencing rather than a face corresponding to their level of pain. Such a selection would confound interpretation of the scale.

As a rule of thumb, based on the research literature (Weiner, Peterson, Lad, McConnell, & Keefe, 1999;

Chibnall & Tait, 2001), it has been suggested that older adults with Mini-Mental Status Examination (MMSE; Folstein, Folstein, & McHugh, 1975) scores of more than 18 typically can self-report pain whereas those with MMSE scores of 13 or lower tend to have considerable difficulty (Hadjistavropoulos, 2005). No cognitive test, however, can determine with certainty whether a senior with dementia can self-report pain. As such, it is recommended that self-report of pain be attempted in all instances.

As the dementia progresses and language abilities deteriorate, clinicians are faced with the challenge of evaluating pain among patients who cannot self-report their experience. In recent years, a considerable amount of research has been conducted on the development and evaluation of observational tools designed to assess pain in people with dementia (e.g., Fuchs-Lacelle & Hadjistavropoulos, 2004; Villanueva, Smith, Erickson, Lee, & Singer, 2003; Warden, Hurley, & Volicer, 2003).

One of the most researched approaches to the evaluation of pain in people with severe dementia who reside in long-term care facilities is the Pain Assessment Checklist for Seniors With Limited Ability to Communicate (PACSLAC; Fuchs-Lacelle & Hadjistavropoulos, 2004). The PACSLAC consists of 60 pain-related behaviors (e.g., wincing, pulling away, grimacing, guarding sore area) that can be observed by health care personnel. Research has demonstrated that the PACSLAC has strong psychometric properties (Lints-Martindale, Hadjistavropoulos, Lix, & Thorpe, 2012), can improve clinical outcomes in long-term care facilities (Fuchs-Lacelle, Hadjistavropoulos, & Lix, 2008) and is considered to be clinically useful by front-line health care staff (Zwakhalen, Hamers, & Berger, 2006). Moreover, it comprehensively covers all of the pain assessment domains (i.e., facial expressions, verbalizations and vocalizations, body movements, changes in activity patterns and routines, interpersonal interactions, and mental status changes) deemed to be important by the American Geriatrics Society (AGS Panel on Persistent Pain in Older Persons, 2002). More recently, a revised shorter (31 item) version of the PACSLAC, the PACSLAC-II, was developed with initial validation research demonstrating better ability to discriminate pain from nonpain states than the PACSLAC and other

commonly used tools (Chan, Hadjistavropoulos, Lints, & Martindale, 2014). The PACSLAC-II retained coverage of all observational pain assessment domains deemed to be important by the AGS.

Examples of briefer pain assessment tools that have been developed for seniors with dementia and have satisfactory psychometric properties, include, but are not limited to, the Pain Assessment in Advanced Dementia (PAINAD), which consists of five items (Warden et al., 2003), and the Doloplus-2, which consists of 10 items (Wary, 1999). In a study that involved, a clinical comparison of the PACSLAC, the PAINAD, and the Doloplus-2, nursing staff rated the PACSLAC as the most clinically useful of the three tools (Zwakhalen et al., 2006). Although this issue has not been investigated systematically, all of the observational pain tools reviewed here are easy to administer and usually are completed by nursing and special care aide personnel. It is important to note that there is no definitive consensus as to which pain assessment tool is best for seniors with severe dementia. Clinicians should review the literature and select the tool that they consider most appropriate for their clients.

Selecting an appropriate assessment tool is only the beginning of a successful pain assessment. Hadjistavropoulos et al. (2007), Herr et al. (2006), and others have proposed several steps for effective pain assessment. Rather than using cutoff scores to signify pain or its absence, it has been argued that an individualized approach to assessment be used because dementia represents a diverse set of conditions and types of damage to the brain. As a result of the varied pathology, responses to pain differ from person to person. Given this type of diversity, using a single cutoff score may not be indicated. Instead, an individualized approach to assessment can be used wherein pain is assessed on a regular basis and the clinician considers unusual fluctuations from the patient's normal score as possibly signifying changes in pain levels. Such fluctuations then would need to be followed up with physical examinations and appropriate treatment. Exhibit 16.2 shows a general approach to pain assessment in dementia. Figure 16.1 shows a diary (Misson, Savoie, Aubin, Hadjistavropoulos, & Verreault, 2011) involving use of the PACSLAC and how the information gathered can be used.

EXHIBIT 16.2
Guidelines for Assessing Pain With Seniors Who Have
Cognitive Impairments

General guidelines

1. Determine whether Mini-Mental Status Examination scores are available or can be obtained. This would facilitate determination of patient ability to provide valid self-report.
2. Always attempt self-report regardless of level of cognitive functioning.
3. Baseline scores should be collected for each individual (ideally on a regular basis, which would allow for the examination of unusual changes from the person's typical pattern of scores).
4. Patient history and physical examination results should be taken into consideration.
5. If assessments are to be repeated over time, assessment conditions should be kept constant (e.g., use the same assessment tool, use the same assessor where possible and conduct pain assessment during similar situations).
6. Pain assessment results should be used to evaluate the efficacy of pain management interventions.
7. Knowledgeable informants (e.g., caregivers) should be asked about typical pain behaviors of the individual.
8. Other aspects of the pain experience should also be evaluated including environmental factors, psychological functioning and social environment.

Recommendations specific to self-report measures

1. Use of synonyms when asking about the pain experience (e.g., hurt, aching) will facilitate the self-report of some patients who have limitations in ability to communicate verbally.
2. Self-report scales should be modified to account for any sensory deficits that occur with aging (e.g., poor vision, hearing difficulties).
3. Use self-report tools that have been found to be most valid among seniors (e.g., the Numeric Rating Scales, Verbal Rating Scales).
4. Use of horizontal visual analogue scales should be avoided as some investigators have found unusually high numbers of unscorable responses among seniors.

Recommendations specific to observational measures

1. Examples of observational tools that have been shown to be reliable and valid for use in this population include the Pain Assessment Checklist for Seniors With Limited Ability to Communicate (PACSLAC) and Doloplus-2. Nonetheless, clinicians should always exercise caution when using these measures because they are relatively new and research is continuing.
2. When assessing pain in acute-care settings tools that primarily focus on evaluation of change over time should be avoided.
3. Observational assessments during movement-based tasks would be more likely to lead to the identification of underlying pain problems than assessments during rest.
4. Some pain assessment tools, such as the PACSLAC, do not have specific cutoff scores because of recognition of tremendous individual differences among people with severe dementia. Instead, it is recommended that pain be assessed on a regular basis (establishing baseline scores for each patient) with the clinician observing score changes over time.
5. Examination of pain assessment scores before and after the administration of analgesics is likely to facilitate pain assessment.
6. Some of the symptoms of delirium (which is seen frequently in long-term care) overlap with certain behavioral manifestations of uncontrolled pain (e.g., behavioral disturbance). Clinicians assessing patients with delirium should be aware of this. On the positive side, delirium tends to be a transient state, and pain assessment, which can be repeated or conducted when the patient is not delirious, is more likely to lead to valid results. Note also that pain can cause delirium, and clinicians should be astute to avoid missing pain problems among patients with delirium.
7. Observational pain assessment tools are screening instruments only and cannot be taken to represent definitive indicators of pain. Sometimes, they may suggest the presence of pain when pain is not present, and other times they may fail to identify pain.

Outcomes of interest
In addition to improved scores on various assessment tools, evidence of more effective pain management can be observed in such areas as greater participation in activities, improved sleep, reduced behavioral disturbance, improved ability to ambulate, and improved social interactions.

Note. Many of these recommendations are from Hadjistavropoulos et al. (2007) and Herr et al. (2006). Copyright by Thomas Hadjistavropoulos. Reprinted with permission.

Although this section focused primarily on assessment of pain intensity, psychosocial aspects of the pain experience also should be considered (e.g., Does the patient have visitors who would distract him or her from the pain experience? Is he or she engaging in a sufficient number of pleasurable activities such as accompanied walks or visits to the courtyard?). In patients with severe dementia, it is often difficult to separate depression and other conditions that may be caused or exacerbated by chronic pain from direct manifestations of pain. Although a limited number of tools to assess emotional states and quality of life, often based largely on caregiver reports, are available (e.g., the Cornell Scale for Depression in Dementia; Alexopoulos, Abrams, Young, & Shamoian, 1998), such tools tend to assess for the presence or absence of symptoms, such as sleep disturbance and irritability. The difficulty with use of such tools with patients suffering from pain relates to the challenges associated with distinguishing symptoms that are the direct consequence of pain (e.g., pain-related sleep interference) from symptoms that are the result of an emotional disturbance (e.g., insomnia due to an emotional cause). Given this difficulty, the treatment team may try to address the suspected pain problem and determine whether the pain treatment leads to an improvement in the symptoms that overlap with emotional disturbance. If emotional disturbance persists, despite appropriate and thorough pain treatment, it would be necessary to investigate further possible contributors to such disturbance besides pain.

Controversies regarding assessment. Despite the clear identification of the psychological factors in pain, one frequently encounters disagreements about the nature of the experience with contested issues including willingness to dismiss the importance of patient thoughts, feelings, the social environment and the extent to which psychological factors are relevant to the assessment and treatment of pain and injury (for a discussion, see Craig & Hadjistavropoulos, 2004). The biocentric training of many health professionals can make appreciation of psychological elements of the pain experience difficult. As such, it is not uncommon for patients to receive the message that because nothing wrong is physically apparent,

their pain must be caused by psychological factors. Pain, however, has physical, emotional, and cognitive components that tend to be intertwined, difficult to separate, and affect outcomes. As such, it is critical for psychologists to educate other professionals about the psychological components of pain through in-service continuing education, case conferences, and related discussion.

A second point of controversy is the consideration of self-report as the gold standard in pain assessment. In fact, it has been demonstrated that both self-reports and nonverbal pain expressions are critical in understanding pain as they tap different aspects of the pain experience (Hadjistavropoulos, Craig, et al., 2011; Labus, Keefe, & Jensen, 2003). Self-report can be influenced by both situational demand characteristics and relies on cognitive executive mediation, whereas nonverbal pain expressions usually tap more immediate, reflexive aspects of the pain experience. An added related concern from a geropsychologist's standpoint is that although self-report is a critical component of the assessment of pain, it is not particularly useful when assessing individuals with severe cognitive impairments and limitations in ability to communicate. The suggestion that pain is "whatever the patient says it is" (e.g., McCaffery, 1968), although it has a well-intentioned person-centered focus, can result in an underemphasis of adequate assessment within the population of people with severe dementia.

Equally controversial within various organizations caring for older people (e.g., long-term care facilities that often are referred to as "nursing homes") are questions related to how much of their limited funding and resources should be dedicated to adequate pain assessment. Systematic observational and psychological assessment of the pain patient often is viewed as a luxury. As a result, assessment practices, related to pain in older adults, often leave a lot to be desired (Hadjistavropoulos, Marchildon, et al., 2009). Perhaps because of the costs of continuing pain education and time constraints, for example, observational pain tools often are not used for seniors with severe limitations in ability to communicate due to dementia, and research has identified significant education gaps related to pain assessment and management among

PACSLAC PAIN DIARY   Patient NAME: <u>Mr. Case Example</u>

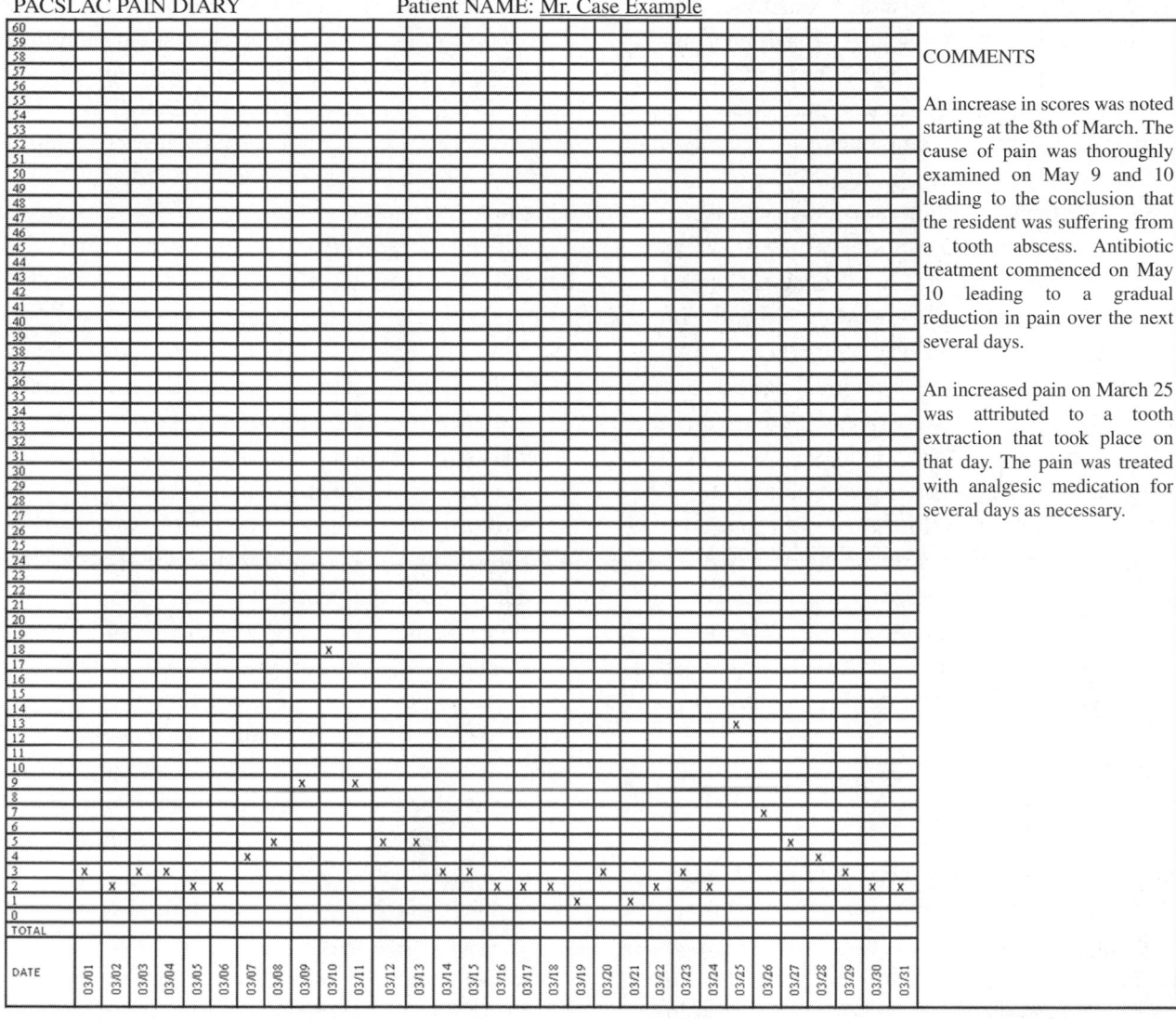

FIGURE 16.1.   Use of a pain diary for the Pain Assessment Checklist for Seniors With Limited Ability to Communicate (PACSLAC). The vertical axis represents scores on the PACLAC (range 0–60). See Misson et al., 2011.

long-term care staff and other health care providers (Martin et al., 2005; Zwakhalen, Hamers, Peijnenburg, & Berger, 2007). Specific cost-effective pain assessment models suitable for long-term care facilities (Hadjistavropoulos, Marchildon, et al., 2009) as well as for community settings (Hadjistavropoulos et al., 2007) have been proposed but have not been implemented on a large-scale basis probably because (although often financially feasible) they still have resource implications. For example, it has been suggested that for effective and systematic pain assessment to occur, long-term care facilities would need to dedicate a nursing position to pain assessment and management (e.g., Hadjistavropoulos, Marchildon, et al. 2009).

Insufficient pain education for health care staff (e.g., Watt-Watson et al., 2009) is a problem that extends outside long-term care (e.g., acute care, home care, and rehabilitation settings). The lack of familiarity with specialized assessment tools for seniors, and especially seniors with dementia, also is observed in primary care, home care, acute care, and rehabilitation facilities.

Finally, although much research has been conducted on pain assessment, there are no perfect tools. Responses to both self-report tools and observational procedures (which sometimes rely on the interpretation of ambiguous behavioral signals) are far from perfect. The limitations of assessment tools also result in professionals (and often insurance organizations) to sometimes question the veracity of patient complaints and to attribute such complaints to factors such as secondary gain or psychiatric disturbance. De Ruderre, Goubert, Vervoort, Kappesser, and Crombez (2013) demonstrated that even raising the possibility of deception within a compensation system in very general terms can have a negative impact on how individual patients are perceived. This unfortunate situation can have implications for the nature of the relationship between patient and clinician (Hadjistavropoulos, 2013). Although older adults often are retired and returning to work may not be an issue for them, they still may be dealing with insurance organizations following various accidents (e.g., motor vehicle). Consequently, many questions about insurance compensation and funding of treatment can be raised.

Client–Provider Issues Related to Intervention

Expectancies regarding intervention and outcome.

Psychological interventions with seniors who reside in the community. The absence of familiarity with both the role of psychological processes in the pain experience and the potential impact of psychological interventions may lead an older person to not have positive expectations about the outcome of psychological therapy. One of the most frequent issues encountered when a person with pain is referred to a psychologist involves questioning the reason for the referral. Clients often will say something like, "I am not sure why I have been referred to you. I'm not crazy." Although the goal of a pain management psychologist may be twofold (i.e., to improve the pain experienced, and to enhance one's quality of life despite the pain), it often is advisable to emphasize the second goal when providing an initial rationale for treatment (i.e., that a person's quality of life can be improved despite the pain) with skeptical clients. Client skepticism tends to be based on widely accepted beliefs, consistent with early biomedical conceptualizations, that pain is purely a

physical experience and that psychological factors are relevant only for individuals who suffer pain as a result of a mental disorder. Once a rapport is established, the pain intensity reduction goal can be introduced in more detail, especially after the client understands the role of psychological influences in the pain experience.

Evidence suggests that prevalent myths about pain in old age also can affect expectations and treatment or referral seeking of both older people and health professionals (Martin et al., 2005). One of the most prevalent myths is that pain is a natural consequence of old age and needs to be endured. As indicated, although pain is frequent in old age, it is not natural and is the result of pathology. If we think of pain as natural, we would be less inclined to treat it. Educating both seniors and those who provide care to older people that pain can and should be managed (and improve quality of life), despite a person's age, is important. Older adults often tend to be stoic about their pain experience (Yong, Gibson, Horne, & Helme, 2001). Some older people may believe that discussing their pain might lead them to be perceived as complainers or to fear that family and others might pressure them to reduce independence, possibly by moving into an assisted living arrangement. It would be important for the clinical geropsychologist to address such concerns through effective client education.

Long-term care. Long-term care staff are often the agents of change in interventions with patients who have dementia. As such, they benefit by education in the administration of appropriate assessment strategies and monitoring of pain levels over time.

Inadequate knowledge of the nature of pain (e.g., discounting the importance of psychological components of pain) could lead long-term care staff to not appreciate (and consequently not adequately support) integrated pharmacological and psychosocial interventions designed to distract patients from their pain experience and to improve quality of life. Knowledge gaps in pain knowledge and education have been well documented among long-term care staff (Martin et al., 2005; Zwakhalen et al., 2007) and nursing curricula do not tend to offer sufficient geriatric pain education (Watt-Watson et al., 2009). Certainly, geropsychologists could provide informal one-on-one pain education. Practitioner-oriented articles (e.g., Hadjistavropoulos, Dever Fitzgerald, & Marchildon, 2010) and other training resources (e.g., Gagnon & Hadjistavropoulos, 2011) exist for this purpose. Geropsychologists also can conduct workshops to educate long-term care staff. When these workshops are conducted in an interactive fashion, they are effective in imparting pain assessment knowledge (Ghandehari et al., 2013) but central management support (e.g., the establishment of improved standards for pain assessment and the provision of protected staff time to conduct adequate pain assessments) typically is needed for long-lasting change in clinical practices (Gagnon, Hadjistavropoulos, & Williams, 2013).

Education of client (and family) about geropsychological assessment and treatment.

Interventions with seniors who live independently in the community. It is of critical importance for the clinical geropsychologist to educate clients about the nature of pain, the critical role of psychological factors, and the outcomes of psychological interventions. Most clients will easily accept that psychological consequences of chronic pain are frequent and that these can be managed. Moreover, educating clients about the interconnections of feelings, thoughts, and behaviors also is important. Like in all types of psychological talk therapy, adopting a dialectic approach (as opposed to lecturing to the client) tends to work best. Using the typical "behavioral experiments" advocated by Beck (1979) and others is very helpful in that the client is most likely to be convinced of something experientially rather than because the therapist said so.

Similarly, education about a wide variety of treatment options for pain (e.g., physical therapy, alternative modalities such as acupuncture) is also important to provide because older adults often believe that medication is their only option. Myths about the relationship of pain and aging (discussed previously) should be addressed, as should the impact of physiological changes that accompany aging (e.g., changes in the body's ability to metabolize medications may result in different prescribed dosages for older people; age-related changes in sleep patterns). Finally, encouraging appropriate communication of pain complaints with others who can provide care is also important as older people sometimes avoid communication of their pain out of concern that they may be pressured to reduce their independence.

Some literature that would facilitate client and family education, regarding pain management in older persons, is available (see Hadjistavropoulos & Hadjistavropoulos, 2008). Multidisciplinary approaches to pain education, where feasible, would be ideal because they could incorporate input from physicians, exercise therapists, and other professionals all of whom would be working together toward common pain management goals.

Long-term care. Including families and long-term care residents as much as possible in pain education and discussion of options for pain management is more than desirable not only because understanding the nature of pain is important but also because it opens pathways of communication that could produce insights about the patients' experiences. Understanding, for example, that uncontrolled pain could lead to behavioral disturbance in residents with dementia could facilitate an understanding of the residents' behavior and even reduce caregiver stress that could be the result of caregiver misattribution of aggressive patient behavior. Family members can become collaborators in treatment (e.g., by assisting with pleasant activity scheduling that could distract the patient from the pain experience).

Geropsychologist–client relationship issues. Like any other client, older people ought to be treated with respect. Advanced empathy skills can facilitate the building of rapport that would allow for effective intervention. Allowing stereotypic beliefs about older people to enter the assessment–therapeutic relationship could result in a lack of openness that would hinder a thorough understanding of the older person's experience. In long-term care in particular, it has been suggested that as dementia progresses, patients are viewed as having reduced personhood (Malloy & Hadjistavropoulos, 2012). As a result, references such as "the broken hip in Room 4" suggest that a patient can sometimes be viewed as an object of care rather than as a unique individual. As such, it has been recommended

(Hicks, 2000) that a self-examination of the health professional may facilitate more authentic relationships between patients and care providers (e.g., asking oneself whether or how one reacts differently when one believes that a patient with dementia has pain as compared with a patient without dementia).

Technical Aspects of Intervention

The most effective treatment approaches for people with chronic pain tend to be interdisciplinary and to incorporate a variety of modalities, such as medical, psychological, and physical (Flor, Fydrich, & Turk, 1992; Nicholas, Wilson, & Goyen, 1992; Peters, Large, & Elkind, 1992). Working with other professionals, psychologists can utilize a variety of approaches focusing on the improved pain management of the older person. Such approaches include CBT (reviewed in more detail later in the next section), psychoeducation, recommendations for self-management programs, support groups, and others. More recently, some support has begun to emerge for the efficacy of mindfulness-based approaches for older people with pain (e.g., Morone, Greco, & Weiner, 2008). Although a variety of more specific strategies have been used with success in younger people (e.g., relaxation therapy, biofeedback), efficacy evidence with older people is limited (Hadjistavropoulos, Hunter, & Dever Fitzgerald, 2009). As is the case with most psychological therapies, a dialectic Socratic style with strong empathy skills is often necessary for therapeutic success.

Controversies. Numerous controversies are related to the management of pain (e.g., optimal pharmacological approaches, alternative treatments), but the focus here is on psychological therapies. The role of the psychologist as a pain management treatment provider often is dismissed by health professionals who ascribe to biocentric approaches to pain. And yet such biocentric perspectives fail to address major challenges of pain control that arise from poorly understood psychosocial determinants of the pain experience, disability, and rehabilitation outcomes, including access to necessary care (Craig & Hadjistavropoulos, 2004). Usually, health professionals are accepting, however, that a chronic

pain patients' quality of life can improve despite the pain with psychological assistance. This represents a common ground upon which psychologists can work with most health professionals.

As indicated elsewhere in the chapter, considering pain as a "normal" part of aging, which represents a commonly held belief, is not helpful when it comes to ensuring that older adults have adequate access to treatment resources. Such beliefs contribute to the undertreatment of pain in this population (Ferrell et al., 2001; Horgas et al., 2007; Martin et al., 2005; Morrison & Sui, 2000; Robinson, 2007; Won et al., 2004).

As is the case with the psychological assessment of pain, scarce resources and limited funding often result in psychological services for older adults with pain taking the back seat to physical interventions. More research on the medical cost offset of psychological interventions for older people with pain potentially could play a key role in persuading policy makers to allocate increased resources to psychological treatment services.

Evidence-based treatments.

Cognitive–behavioral therapy. CBT for chronic pain is typically a time-limited intervention with two primary goals: better management of the patient's pain and improved quality of life despite pain. Recognizing the interconnections among thoughts, feelings, and behaviors, CBT involves largely four broad categories of therapeutic techniques (Skinner et al., 2012): (a) cognitive techniques (e.g., cognitive restructuring and problem solving); (b) behavioral techniques (e.g., relaxation training, pacing, and behavioral activation); (c) supportive techniques (e.g., psychoeducation and supportive therapy); and (d) a diverse set of complementary approaches, including but not limited to biofeedback, relapse, prevention, and hypnosis. A therapist will use some or all of these techniques within the context of CBT. Because an introduction to CBT is beyond the scope of this chapter, brief discussion of the various categories of techniques will consist of examples contextualized in the context of the older adult.

The first category includes *cognitive techniques*. Examples of the types of maladaptive beliefs encountered in therapy (along with thoughts that can substitute these through cognitive restructuring) with older adults include the following:

- "Pain is a normal part of aging that must be endured" potentially could be substituted with "Pain is the result of pathology and can be managed regardless of a person's age."
- "I cannot accomplish anything because I am in pain" potentially could be substituted with "Although I am no longer able to do some of the things that I could do before my chronic pain problem developed, I still can engage in many meaningful activities."

Maladaptive thoughts are tackled using cognitive restructuring and behavioral experiments (see Case Examples). For a discussion of cognitive–behavioral procedures in general, the reader is referred to a wide variety of specialized texts, such as *Managing Chronic Pain: A Cognitive Behavioral Therapy Approach* (Otis, 2007).

Problem solving, as a cognitive technique, is aimed to assist client to address problems of daily living. The problem is defined, often broken down into smaller pieces and then a plan is developed by the client and therapist working together. For example, an older person who has difficulty communicating with his or her physician may problem solve with a therapist about finding potential solutions (e.g., preparing in advance a list of questions for the physician).

The second category of CBT techniques includes *behavioral* procedures. A behavioral technique frequently used with older adults with chronic pain is pacing. Sometimes tasks (e.g., cleaning the house) may seem difficult to accomplish, as a result of pain, leading to procrastination. Other times, clients attempt to do too much at once leading them to associate a given activity (e.g., house cleaning) with pain. This results in anxiety and distress in anticipation of such activity. With pacing, the older person will be encouraged to break down the chore into small, manageable components. Moreover, he or she may be instructed to only engage in the housecleaning activity before significant pain elevations are experienced (e.g., a person who starts to experience pain after 10 min of vacuuming may be encouraged to vacuum for 5 min at a time). This would lead the pain and the activity to become dissociated from each other. As such, decreased distress and anxiety surrounding that activity may result. Other behavioral strategies include relaxation training (which would be especially indicated for pain that can be exacerbated by muscle tension) as well as graded behavioral activation procedures.

The third category of CBT techniques incorporates *adjunctive* and *supportive* approaches. Psychoeducation of the older pain patient, for instance, is critical not only to dispel myths about pain and aging but also to facilitate an understanding of the wide variety of treatment options that are available. Older people frequently are given medication as the sole treatment, whereas approaches such as physical therapy, occupational therapy, and massage also can be helpful. When working within multidisciplinary teams, all health professionals can contribute to patient education. Moreover, support is beneficial for crisis management, pain flare-ups, and other difficult situations that clients may encounter.

Finally, various *complementary approaches* are used in CBT. Relapse prevention (e.g., Ludgate, 2009), for instance, is a key component of therapy. By the end of treatment, the patient should be equipped with a variety of tools that can be used to manage and cope with pain as well as other difficult situations that may be encountered in the future. As part of relapse prevention and management, clients should be prepared to expect setbacks and symptom fluctuations that are common in people with chronic health problems. Relapse prevention also helps clients conceptualize such setbacks as a normal part of the course as opposed to adopting the black-and-white view that a flare-up means that the time they spent learning better ways of managing their pain has gone for waste. Moreover, developing prevention-related coping skills for high-risk (relapse) situations is also an important component of therapy. As indicated, complementary techniques such as biofeedback have been used with success in younger people, but more research is needed to draw firmer conclusions about efficacy in an older sample.

The efficacy of CBT for chronic pain has been well documented (Day et al., 2012) with moderate effect sizes being identified (Butler, Chapman, Forman, & Beck, 2006). Research on the effectiveness of CBT with older adults also has been conducted (e.g., Green, Hadjistavropoulos, Hadjistavropoulos, Martin, & Sharpe, 2009; Waters, Woodward, & Keefe, 2005), but some benefits seem limited to specific areas of functioning, such as beliefs about the nature of pain or pain intensity, rather than in global areas of improvement. Lunde, Nordhus, and Pallesen (2009) conducted a meta-analytic investigation of CBT for chronic pain that specifically focused on older adults. They concluded that the overall effect size (.47) was moderate and that there was a demonstrated benefit on self-reported pain but not on physical function, depression, and medication use. Note, however, that the long-term efficacy of CBT for chronic pain is unknown. More work is needed on the refinement of CBT interventions for older adults with pain.

Mindfulness-based approaches. In addition to CBT, mindfulness approaches (based on principles related to meditation, focus on breathing, body scan, and placing attention nonjudgementally to the body) are gaining in popularity. Some limited data on the effectiveness of such approaches is beginning to emerge. For example, Morone et al. (2008) demonstrated that compared with a control group, older adults who took part in a mindfulness-based intervention program showed improvements with respect to self-reported pain acceptance and self-reported activities engagement. Qualitative research (Morone, Lynch, Greco, Tindle, & Weiner, 2008) also suggested benefits of mindfulness meditation in domains such as pain reduction, improved attention, and improved well-being.

Acceptance and commitment therapy (ACT), which involves people learning to stay in contact with emotions and thoughts, also has been gaining popularity in pain management (e.g., Dahl, Wilson, & Nilsson, 2004; Thorsell et al., 2011; Wetherell et al., 2011). Rather than changing the irrational focus of negative thoughts, such thoughts are viewed as targets for exposure. Mindfulness techniques also are incorporated in ACT. ACT research with older adults is very limited, but McCracken and Jones (2012) have provided initial preliminary evidence in support of the approach for people over 60 years old.

The self-management of pain in older people. Self-management is a term that has been used loosely to describe a variety of programs designed to help patients manage their own symptoms. Approaches that have been described as self-management differ with respect to the extent they rely on support from a facilitator who is sometimes a health professional. Some approaches, for example, involve group meetings led by a health professional or a volunteer (Ersek, Turner, Cain, & Kemp, 2004; Lefort, Gray-Donald, Rowat, & Jeans, 1998). Other self-management approaches (e.g., bibliotherapy) do not rely on a facilitator and involve the use of self-help manuals or other literature (e.g., Hadjistavropoulos & Hadjistavropoulos, 2008). Pain management programs also can be offered through the Internet (e.g., Rini, Williams, Broderick, & Keefe, 2012) with or without therapist support.

Self-management approaches to a variety of health conditions, including pain, are gaining in popularity because demands on the health care system have been increasing and self-management has the potential to result in cost savings (Wheeler, 2003). Moreover, self-management could reach individuals who have limited access to health care services (e.g., residing in remote locations, having limited mobility).

Goals of pain self-management involve creating or maintaining meaningful life roles despite a person's pain, dealing with the emotional consequences of pain conditions, and improving medical management through enhanced adherence with prescribed therapies (Corbin & Strauss, 1988; Hadjistavropoulos, 2012; Lorig & Holman, 2003). Self-management success relies on a variety of core skills, including problem solving, taking action, and creating partnerships with health care providers (Lorig & Holman, 2003). Moreover, patients learn information, techniques, and skills, such as mood management approaches and coping strategies, and they become familiar with a broader set of treatment options (Lorig & Holman, 2003). At the same time, self-management involves certain risks (Hadjistavropoulos, 2011), including the potential of misuse of specific procedures (e.g., in the absence of health professional supervision, a patient may perform a physical exercise incorrectly risking injury). Moreover, compliance with pain management activities may be lower in self-management because of the absence of accountability associated with seeing a health professional on a regular basis, but this is addressed in programs in which health professional support is available. Results of self-management of pain in older adults have been mixed (e.g., Coster & Norman, 2009; Ersek et al., 2004), although older adults report that they enjoy learning about pain management strategies (Barefoot, Hadjistavropoulos, Carleton, & Henry, 2012). Nonetheless, self-management programs specifically focusing on people with arthritis show promise especially in improving pain (within 1 year) and disability in the longer term (more than 26 weeks; Du et al., 2011).

Part of the concern with research on self-management programs is that these programs usually are not standardized and vary across studies. That is, some self-management programs may be better than others and, depending on the program used, research results may vary. As such, it would be important for the field to aim for an across-studies standardization of promising self-management programs. Another consideration is that based on research with conditions other than chronic pain (Newman, Erickson, Przeworsi, & Dzus, 2009), it is likely that the addition of a health professional facilitator may improve outcomes (Hadjistavropoulos, 2012).

CLINICAL APPLICATIONS

This section considers contextual influences on pain. Two case studies also are presented. The first case study focuses on an older adult long-term care resident who suffers from dementia. The second case study describes an independent, community-dwelling senior with chronic pain.

Examination of Socioeconomic Influences and Other Contextual Issues on Clinical Application

Cognitive–behavioral pain assessment and management approaches focusing on older people share many common elements with treatments directed to younger persons. There are, however, some unique considerations. In the first instance, the types of stressors that older people face can be quite different from those encountered by younger adults. With younger people, for example, a common focus of CBT for chronic pain is return-to-work or work-related functioning, whereas with retired older adults, the focus tends to be on other stressors (e.g., loneliness due to both pain and factors, such as widowhood).

Moreover, some of the psychoeducational information offered to the older adult may be different from that offered to other people given the physiological and other changes that occur with age (e.g., changes in sleep patterns associated with aging; different rates of metabolizing medication). Finally, CBT for older adults also will focus on myths around pain and aging such as the ones reviewed earlier in this chapter.

In instances in which the chronic pain problem affects mobility, CBT potentially can be offered at the older adults' home (e.g., Green et al., 2009), but this usually is not feasible. Promising CBT treatments also have been offered via the Internet (e.g., Brattberg, 2006), although the suitability of these treatments for older people remains to be studied.

Cross-cultural and gender issues are important. Most patients with certain types of pain (e.g., rheumatoid arthritis, headache, temporamandibular disorder) are female (Rollman, 2004; Unruh, 1996). Both biological sex and psychological gender roles are predictors of pain threshold, tolerance, and pain unpleasantness. Moreover, clients from certain cultural backgrounds and their families have been found to be more expressive of their pain (see Rollman, 2004). As Rollman (2004) observed, however, much of the relevant research has focused on small samples and the sociocultural groups under investigation often differ on dimensions other than ethnicity (e.g., level of education, income). Moreover, it is not productive to make sweeping statements about pain reactivity across cultural groups. Instead, the focus should be on individuals. Nonetheless, it has been shown that adequate pain management sometimes is more likely to be offered to members of the majority culture than to members of other cultural groups, suggesting disparities in health care (e.g., Sheiner, Sheiner, Shoham-Vardi, Mazor, & Katz, 1999; Todd, Samaroo, & Hoffman, 1993). As such, it is important for psychologists to be attuned to the possibility of such disparities so that they can facilitate the client becoming aware of his or her treatment options.

Case Examples Illustrating Assessment and Intervention

Case example 1: A case illustration of pain assessment in long-term care. In an article entitled "Pain

Assessment as Intervention," Fuchs-Lacelle et al. (2008) demonstrated that regular use of pain assessment in long-term care settings has direct clinical benefits from patients. Exhibit 16.2 includes detailed guidelines of how pain assessments should be conducted and interpreted. A specific recommendation is that assessment should be individualized with the clinician looking for unexpected changes in the patient's pattern of scores.

Figure 16.1 shows a diary (based on Misson et al., 2011) used in a clinical setting to regularly record PACSLAC pain assessment scores. The scores were obtained through observations of the nursing staff, and the diary is based on a male 79-year-old patient with a diagnosis of Alzheimer's disease. A recent MMSE score on the patient was unavailable because he had been inaccessible for cognitive assessment as a result of severe cognitive impairment. The geropsychologist's role in this case was to train the nursing staff in the appropriate use of observational pain assessment protocols and to serve as a consultant (e.g., in the event of behavioral disturbance that often is associated with pain) in his capacity as a member of an interdisciplinary team that also included nurses, a physician, and a physical therapist. The team had access to consultation with outside professionals (e.g., a dentist, medical specialists).

As can be observed on the diary in Figure 16.1, following a period of relative stability in PACSLAC scores, there was an elevation around August 8. The elevation was due to an endorsement of pain behaviors, such as grimacing and frowning. Moreover, restlessness and behavioral disturbance (e.g., aggression) were becoming evident, causing an additional elevation in the PACSLAC scores. In response to the change in the pattern of scores and related observation of the patient, the team met and, through appropriate investigations, determined that the patient was suffering from an abscessed tooth. Following administration of antibiotic medication, the pain scores and associated behavioral disturbance subsided as the tooth infection had been treated. The next time that an elevation of scores was observed was around August 25 at which time the patient had undergone extraction of the tooth that had abscessed. Following recovery from the tooth extraction, the pain scores were reduced again.

Case example 2: A case illustration of CBT—Martha.

Referral. Martha was referred to a psychologist by her primary care physician who recently received a brochure announcing psychological services for people with chronic pain. The referral read: "I am referring this 72-year-old lady to you because she feels depressed. She presents with sciatica and her social network is limited. Please offer her support."

Brief history. Martha is a 72-year-old retired teacher who suffered from back pain associated with sciatica. When Martha was younger, she and her husband were very active both socially and physically. One of her greatest pleasures was her bridge club that got together at least once a week for merriment and bridge. This changed over the past decade, Martha has been unable to organize the gatherings due to increased pain and her husband's passing. Over time, the group stopped meeting.

Martha's 40-year-old son is a computer company executive and moved to Vancouver where he lives with his young family. Martha's 42-year-old daughter works for a publishing house in Winnipeg, Manitoba. With her family away, Martha has been feeling increasingly isolated. Because of her pain condition, she became reluctant to attend social activities and, gradually, as a result of increased social isolation, she begun to feel lonely and depressed.

On the advice on her health professional, she had been attempting to manage her pain with over-the-counter medication and had not been very successful. Martha, had a limited understanding of her condition and was not aware of all treatment options. She felt that she had limited time with her physician and, as a result, was not able to get her questions answered. She had been encouraged to endure her pain "because it is normal for an older person to have aches and pain." Finally, she felt frustrated for not being able to complete many chores (e.g., house cleaning) because of pain. In fact, she would sometimes let chores pile up (because she avoided them since they had become associated with pain) and then, when they absolutely had to be done, she would do too much at once, exacerbating her pain and suffering for several days after. As Martha put it, she "felt like a failure."

Initial assessment. Initial assessment consisted of a clinical interview, the BPI (Cleeland & Ryan,

1994), the GDS (Yesavage et al., 1982), and the CSQ (Rosenstiel & Keefe, 1983). Martha's BPI responses were consistent with moderate pain and with moderate to severe pain-related interference with daily activities as well as mood deflation. Scores on the CSQ revealed elevations in the catastrophizing subscale, indicating the presence of catastrophic thinking about pain (which often is seen among patients with mood deflation), and an unusually low score on the active behavioral coping subscale. Her score on the GDS fell within the depressed range. The clinical interview confirmed the presence of depression, including hopelessness as well as social isolation. Martha also expressed inability to complete her daily chores because of her pain and noted that her not completing such chores tended to exacerbate her mood deflation. The need for pain education also became evident as Martha was unaware of the potential impact of psychological and social factors on the pain experience.

Psychoeducation. Psychoeducation focused on variety of topics, including the interplay of psychological and physical factors in the pain experience; myths related to pain and aging; and the relationship among thinking, behavior, and emotion.

Treatment plan. To provide Martha with improved pain management and quality of life, cognitive–behavioral procedures were planned. Specifically, catastrophic thinking and other maladaptive beliefs about pain would be tackled through cognitive restructuring, while careful pacing and behavioral activation would aim to allow Martha to gradually resume a more productive day-to-day life. Through improved social engagement and ability to examine her thinking, it was anticipated that her mood would improve. Adjunctive strategies, such as relaxation training, also were planned. A brief description of this plan, with Martha's consent, was sent to her physician who was encouraged to contact the psychologist with any questions or concerns.

Process and outcomes. Martha felt quite confused and, perhaps somewhat defensive, about having been referred for psychological therapy. Early during the first session she said, "I don't know why my doctor referred me to you. I'm not crazy!" The psychologist, Dr. Better, well aware that CBT for chronic pain has two primary goals (i.e., to reduce pain intensity and to improve one's quality of life despite the pain) chose to focus his explanation on the second primary goal. He asked Martha how her pain made her feel. Through discussion, it became clear that Martha felt frustrated, upset, and angry during pain exacerbations. As a result of these emotions, she tended to become more pain focused and, consequently, found the pain more difficult to handle. She was able to accept this conceptualization (i.e., the vicious cycle of pain → negative emotion → increased focus on pain → pain feeling increasingly of overwhelming) and agreed to try and see whether the sessions would help her feel better, from a psychological standpoint, despite the pain. A therapeutic alliance had begun to develop and Martha agreed to 10 sessions of therapy with the understanding that the therapeutic contract was subject to alteration and that progress would be reviewed after the fifth session.

In the weeks that followed, several issues were addressed. Through cognitive-restructuring procedures, Martha begun to recognize that pain is not a natural part of growing old and that it is important to manage it regardless of a person's age. She also learned about treatment options and problem-solved about her concern that her physician did not have enough time to answer her questions. Role-plays took place in the session to give Martha the opportunity to practice appropriate assertiveness skills that she used successfully in interactions with health professionals. As a result of better understanding of her treatment options and her assertiveness, her physician referred her for physical therapy, which she found to be helpful in the management of her condition. She also practiced various relaxation procedures.

A primary concern and source of stress for Martha was the association of household chores and pain (and related procrastination). Martha was encouraged to break each challenging chore into smaller components that could be completed in a gradual fashion. Through exploration, Martha acknowledged that vacuuming was one of the most discomforting routine chores, although she could vacuum for 10 min before experiencing pain. In an effort to break the association between pain and vacuuming, she was encouraged to initially vacuum for 5 min at a time while monitoring her pain levels in a diary. Gradually vacuuming became less anxiety provoking (and thus less likely to be avoided) because it was no longer associated with pain. Through such pacing approaches, Martha learned to complete her chores gradually and comfortably.

When her social isolation was tackled, Martha pointed out that her husband passed away and her children had moved. She also said that she had few social connections, and it was difficult for her to make new friends "because people have their own lives and would not be interested in talking to her." She agreed to engage in a "behavioral experiment" to check out her belief that people would not want to talk to her. Specifically, she joined a knitting club at a local seniors' center. Initially she was concerned that she would be disruptive because she could not sit for very long but, by testing out her beliefs, she discovered that she developed new social relationships (including with a woman who was an old acquaintance and who happened to be a member of the same club; the two begun to go for coffee together on a regular basis initially before class and then weekly). Her depression-related beliefs (e.g., "I am a failure") were tackled through cognitive restructuring and behavioral assignments. Indeed, Martha had accomplished a lot in her life. She had come from a poor family and put herself through university. She then became a successful and sought-out teacher and raised two great kids. She then took care of her ailing husband during the last 2 years of his life, something for which he had been very grateful.

Around Session 9, the therapeutic contract was renewed for an additional five sessions, as Martha found the treatment beneficial. The last few sessions focused on relapse prevention and on ensuring that Martha was prepared to anticipate the normal ups and downs that people with chronic conditions tend to experience. At the time of discharge from treatment, her self-reported pain levels and pain-related interference had been reduced to a mild–moderate level, her GDS score fell within the normal range, and the CSQ catastrophizing subscale elevation was reduced to a level that was consistent with norms for her age-group. The active behavioral coping CSQ subscale score was somewhat increased, although

there was still room for improvement. With an expanded social network, better pain management, an adaptive approach to pacing, and the ability to examine the evidence for the validity of distressing thoughts, Martha was no longer feeling depressed nor was she isolated. As Martha put it during the last session: "I have so much to look forward to. I'm grateful for what I have and I can't wait to visit my son in Vancouver and to catch a cruise to Alaska this summer."

FUTURE DIRECTIONS

This section considers the role of the clinical geropsychologist in pain assessment and management. Future directions for research and clinical application also are discussed.

Role of the Geropsychologist

The reality remains that despite demonstrated benefits in the role of the geropsychologist in pain management and assessment, the majority of older chronic pain sufferers do not have access to such expertise. Through advocacy and education of both health professionals and policy makers, it is hoped that more older adults will benefit from such care both in the community as well as in health care facilities (i.e., both long-term and acute care).

Next Steps in Research and Clinical Application

Despite advances in the area of pain assessment in older adults, more remains to be done. Translations of existing assessment tools in languages other than English (e.g., Basler et al., 2006; Santos, Castro-Caldas, & Hadjistavropoulos, 2012; Zwakhalen et al., 2006) have begun to emerge, but more foreign language validation is needed. Moreover, appropriate normative information (for seniors within and outside long-term care) on formalized tools used in pain assessment is limited. In the cases of people with dementia, more research is needed to evaluate the specificity of existing assessment methodologies. That is, it would be important to establish that these methods can discriminate pain from other distress states that are not pain related.

In long-term care facilities, both resource limitations and inadequate staff pain education prevent implementation of potentially beneficial protocols for pain patients. Education gaps can be addressed with effective pain education (e.g., Ghandehari et al., 2013), but central management support often is needed for the permanent implementation of effective protocols (Gagnon et al., 2013). Geropsychologists can play a key role in pain education, given the psychological sequelae of pain as well as the psychological components of the experience itself. Proficient in behavioral assessment, psychologists can provide appropriate pain assessment education.

With respect to intervention, much more needs to be done to reach older people who live in remote areas or who have limited mobility. Psychological interventions as well as assessment can be administered effectively via the Internet but not enough evaluations of Internet-administered pain management interventions have been conducted with older people.

References

AGS Panel on Persistent Pain in Older Persons. (2002). Clinical practice guidelines: The management of persistent pain in older persons. *Journal of the American Geriatrics Society*, *50*, 205–224. doi:10.1046/j.1532-5415.50.6s.1.x

Alexopoulos, G. S., Abrams, R. C., Young, R. C., & Shamoian, C. A. (19981) Cornell Scale for Depression in Dementia. *Biological Psychiatry*, *23*, 271–284.

American Psychiatric Association. (2000). *Diagnostic and statistical manual of mental disorders* (4th edition, text revision). Arlington, VA: Author.

American Psychiatric Association. (2013). *Diagnostic and statistical manual of mental disorders* (5th ed.). Washington, DC: Author.

Balfour, J. E., & O'Rourke, N. (2003). Older adults with Alzheimer disease, comorbid arthritis and prescription of psychotropic medications. *Pain Research and Management*, *8*, 198–204.

Ballard, C., Hanney, M. L., Theodoulou, M., Douglas, S., McShane, R., Kossakowski, K., . . . Jacoby, R. (2009). The dementia antipsychotic withdrawal trial (DART-AD): Long-term follow-up of a randomised placebo-controlled trial. *Lancet Neurology*, *8*, 151–157. doi:10.1016/S1474-4422(08)70295-3

Barefoot, C., Hadjistavropoulos, T., Carleton, R. N., & Henry, J. (2012). A brief report on the evaluation of a pain self-management program for older adults.

Journal of Cognitive Psychotherapy, *26*, 157–168. doi:10.1891/0889-8391.26.2.157

Basler, H. D., Huger, D., Kunz, R., Luckman, J., Lukas, A., Nikolaus, T., & Schuler, M. S. (2006). Assessment of pain in advanced dementia: Construct validity of the German PAINAD. *Schmerz*, *20*, 519–526.

Beck, A. T., Rush, A. J., Shaw, B. F., & Emery, G. (1979). *Cognitive therapy of depression*. New York, NY: Guilford Press.

Bieri, D., Reeve, R. A., Champion, G. D., Addicoat, L., & Ziegler, J. B. (1990). The Faces Pain Scale for the self-assessment of the severity of pain experienced by children: Development, initial validation, and preliminary investigation for ratio scale properties. *Pain*, *41*, 139–150. doi:10.1016/0304-3959(90)90018-9

Boersma, K., Linton, S., Overmeer, T., Jansson, M., Vlaeyen, J., & de Jong, J. (2004). Lowering fear-avoidance and enhancing function through exposure in vivo: A multiple baseline study across six patients with back pain. *Pain*, *108*, 8–16. doi:10.1016/j.pain.2003.03.001

Bonnewyn, A., Katona, C., Bruffaerts, R., Haro, J. M., de Graaf, R., Alonso, J., & Demyttenaere, K. (2009). Pain and depression in older people: Comorbidity and patterns of help seeking. *Journal of Affective Disorders*, *117*, 193–196. doi:10.1016/j.jad.2009.01.012

Boothby, J. L., Thorn, B. E., Overduin, L. Y., & Ward, L. C. (2004). Catastrophizing and perceived partner responses to pain. *Pain*, *109*, 500–506. doi:10.1016/j.pain.2004.02.030

Bouhassira, D., Attal, N., Fermanian, J., Alchaar, H., Gautron, M., Masquelier, E., . . . Boureau, F. (2004). Development and validation of the neuropathic pain symptom inventory. *Pain*, *108*, 248–257. doi:10.1016/j.pain.2003.12.024

Brattberg, G. (2006). Internet-based rehabilitation for individuals with chronic pain and burnout: A randomized trial. *International Journal of Rehabilitation Research*, *29*, 221–227. doi:10.1097/01.mrr.0000210055.17291.f5

Butler, A. C., Chapman, J. E., Forman, E. M., & Beck, A. T. (2006). The empirical status of cognitive–behavioral therapy: A review of meta-analyses. *Clinical Psychology Review*, *26*, 17–31. doi:10.1016/j.cpr.2005.07.003

Casten, R. J., Parmelee, P. A., Kleban, M. H., Lawton, M. P., & Katz, I. R. (1995). The relationships among anxiety, depression, and pain in a geriatric institutionalized sample. *Pain*, *61*, 271–276. doi:10.1016/0304-3959(94)00185-H

Chan, S., Hadjistavropoulos, T., Williams, J., & Lints-Martindale, A. (2014). Evidence-based development and initial validation of the Pain

Assessment Checklist for Seniors With Limited Ability to Communicate—II (PACSLAC–II). *Clinical Journal of Pain, 30,* 816–824. doi:10.1097/AJP.0000000000000039

Charlton, J. E. (2005). *Core curriculum for professional education in pain* (3rd ed.). Seattle, WA: IASP Press.

Chen, Q., Hayman, L. L., Shmerling, R. H., Bean, J. F., & Leveille, S. G. (2011). Characteristics of chronic pain associated with sleep difficulty in older adults: The Maintenance of Balance, Independent Living, Intellect, and Zest in the Elderly (MOBILIZE) Boston study. *Journal of the American Geriatrics Society, 59,* 1385–1392. doi:10.1111/j.1532-5415.2011.03544. x5415.2011.03544.x

Chibnall, J. T., & Tait, R. (2001). Pain assessment in cognitively impaired and unimpaired older adults: A comparison of four scales. *Pain, 92,* 173–186. doi:10.1016/S0304-3959(00)00485-1

Cleeland, C. S., & Ryan, K. M. (1994). Pain assessment: Global use of the Brief Pain Inventory. *Annals Academy of Medicine Singapore, 23,* 129–138.

Corbin, J., & Strauss, A. (1988). *Unending work and care: Managing chronic illness at home.* San Francisco, CA: Jossey-Bass.

Costa, P., & McCrae, R. (1992). *Revised NEO Personality Inventory (NEW PI-R) and NEO Five-Factor Inventory (NEO-FFI): Professional manual.* Odessa, FL: Psychological Assessment Resources.

Costa, P. T., McCrae, R. R., Zonderman, A. B., Barbano, H. E., Lebowitz, B., & Larson, D. M. (1986). Cross-sectional studies of personality in a national sample: 2. Stability in neuroticism, extraversion, and openness. *Psychology and aging, 1,* 144–149. doi:10.1037/0022-3514.54.5.853

Coster, S., & Norman, I. (2009). Cochrane reviews of educational and self-management interventions to guide nursing practice: A review. *International Journal of Nursing Studies, 46,* 508–28. doi:10.1016/j.ijnurstu.2008.09.009

Craig, K. D., & Hadjistavropoulos, T. (2004). Psychological perspectives on pain: Controversies. In T. Hadjistavropoulos & K. D. Craig (Eds.), *Pain: Psychological perspectives* (pp. 303–326). Mahwah, NJ: Erlbaum.

Dahl, J., Wilson, K. G., & Nilsson, A. (2004). Acceptance and commitment therapy and the treatment of persons at risk for long-term disability resulting from stress and pain symptoms: A preliminary randomized trial. *Behavior Therapy, 35,* 785–801. doi:10.1016/S0005-7894(04)80020-0

Day, M. A., Thorn, B. E., & Burns, J. W. (2012). The continuing evolution of biopsychosocial interventions for chronic. *Journal of Cognitive Psychotherapy, 26,* 114–129.

De Ruderre, L., Goubert, L., Vervoort, T., Kappesser, J., & Crombez, G. (2013). Impact of being primed with social deception upon observer responses to others' pain. *Pain, 154,* 221–226. doi:10.1016/j.pain.2012.10.002

Du, S., Yuan, C., Xiao, X., Chu, J., Qiu, Y., & Qian, H. (2011). Self-management programs for chronic musculoskeletal pain conditions: A systematic review and meta-analysis. *Patient Education and Counseling, 85,* e299–e310.

Ersek, M., Turner, J. A., Cain, K. C., & Kemp, C. A. (2004). Chronic pain self-management for older adults: A randomized controlled trial. *BMC Geriatrics, 4,* 1–11. doi:10.1186/1471-2318-4-7

Felton, B. J., & Revenson, T. A. (1984). Coping with chronic illness: A study of illness controllability and the influence of coping strategies on psychological adjustment. *Journal of Consulting and Clinical Psychology, 52,* 343.

Ferrell, B. R., Novy, D., Sullivan, M. D., Banja, J., Dubois, M. Y., Gitlin, M. C., & Livovich, J. (2001). Ethical dilemmas in pain management. *Journal of Pain, 2,* 171–180.

Flor, H., Fydrich, T., & Turk, D. C. (1992). Efficacy of multidisciplinary pain treatment centers: A meta-analytic review. *Pain, 49,* 221–230. doi:10.1016/0304-3959(92)90145-2

Folstein, M. L., Folstein, S. E., & McHugh, P. R. (1975). Mini-mental state: A practical method for grading the cognitive status of patients for the clinician. *Journal of Psychiatric Research, 12,* 189–198.

Fordyce, W. E. (1976). *Behavioral methods for chronic pain and illness.* Saint Louis, MO: Mosby.

Fordyce, W. E., Shelton, J. L., & Dundore, D. E. (1982). The modification of avoidance learning pain behaviors. *Journal of Behavioral Medicine, 5,* 405–414. doi:10.1007/BF00845370

Fuchs-Lacelle, S., & Hadjistavropoulos, T. (2004). Development and preliminary validation of the Pain Assessment Checklist for Seniors With Limited Ability to Communicate (PACSLAC). *Pain Management Nursing, 5,* 37–49.

Fuchs-Lacelle, S., Hadjistavropoulos, T., & Lix, L. (2008). Pain assessment as intervention: A study of older adults with severe dementia. *Clinical Journal of Pain, 24,* 697–707. doi:10.1097/AJP.0b013e31817625a

Gagliese, L., & Katz, J. (2003). Age differences in postoperative pain are scale dependent: A comparison of measures of pain intensity and quality in younger and older surgical patients. *Pain, 103,* 11–20.

Gagliese, L., Weizblit, N., Ellis, W., & Chan, V. W. S. (2005). The measurement of postoperative pain: A comparison of intensity scales in younger and older surgical patients. *Pain, 117,* 412–420.

Gagnon, M., & Hadjistavropoulos, T. (2011). *Pain assessment in long-term care: A training video for long-term care staff* [DVD]. Regina, Saskatchewan, Canada: University of Regina.

Gagnon, M., Hadjistavropoulos, T., & Williams, J. (2013). Development and mixed methods evaluation of a pain assessment video training program for long-term care staff. *Pain Research and Management, 18,* 307–312.

Gauthier, L. R., & Gagliese, L. (2011). Assessment of pain in older persons. In D. C. Turk & R. Melzack (Eds.), *Handbook of pain assessment* (3rd ed., pp. 242–259). New York, NY: Guilford Press.

Ghandehari, O. O., Hadjistavropoulos, T., Williams, J., Thorpe, L., Alfano, D. P., Dal Bello-Haas, V., . . . Lix, L. (2013). A controlled investigation of continuing pain education for long-term care staff. *Pain Research and Management. 18,* 11–18.

George, S. Z., Wittmer, V. T., Fillingim, R. B., & Robinson, M. E. (2010). Comparison of graded exercise and graded exposure clinical outcomes for patients with chronic low back pain. *Journal of Orthopaedic and Sports Physical Therapy, 40,* 694–704. doi:10.2519/jospt.2010.3396.

Green, S. M., Hadjistavropoulos, T., Hadjistavropoulos, H., Martin, R., & Sharpe, D. (2009). A controlled investigation of a cognitive behavioural pain management program for older adults. *Behavioural and Cognitive Psychotherapy, 37,* 221–226. doi:10.1017/S1352465809005177

Hadjistavropoulos, T. (2005). Assessing pain in older persons with severe limitations in ability to communicate. In S. Gibson and D. Weiner (Eds.), *Pain in older persons* (pp. 135–151). Seattle, WA: IASP Press.

Hadjistavropoulos, T. (2012). Self-management of pain in older persons: Helping people help themselves. *Pain Medicine, 13,* S67–S71. doi:10.1111/j.1526-4637.2011.01272.x

Hadjistavropoulos, T. (2013). "Stop the fraud!": What is the effect of social deception priming on health professionals? *Pain, 154,* 185–186. doi:10.1016/j.pain.2012.11.002

Hadjistavropoulos, T., Breau, L. M., & Craig, K. D. (2011). Assessment of pain in adults and children with limited ability to communicate. In D. C. Turk & R. Melzack, *Handbook of pain assessment* (3rd ed.; pp. 260–282). New York, NY: Guilford Press.

Hadjistavropoulos, T., & Craig, K. D. (Eds.). (2004). *Pain: Psychological perspectives.* Mahwah, NJ: Erlbaum.

Hadjistavropoulos, T., Craig, K. D., Duck, S., Cano, A., Goubert, L., Jackson, P., . . . Dever Fitzgerald, T. (2011). A biopsychosocial formulation of pain

communication. *Psychological Bulletin, 137,* 910–939. doi:10.1037/a0023876

Hadjistavropoulos, T., Craig, K. D., Martin, N., Hadjistavropoulos, H., & McMurtry, B. (1997). Toward a research outcome measure of pain in frail elderly in chronic care. *Pain Clinic, 10,* 71–80.

Hadjistavropoulos, T., Dever Fitzgerald, T., & Marchildon, G. (2010). Practice guidelines for assessing pain in older persons who reside in long-term care facilities. *Physiotherapy Canada, 62,* 104–113.

Hadjistavropoulos, T., & Hadjistavropoulos, H. D. (Eds.). (2008). *Pain management for older adults: A self-help guide.* Seattle: IASP Press.

Hadjistavropoulos, T., Herr, K., Turk, D. C., Fine, P. G., Dworkin, R. H., Helme, R. . . . Williams, J. (2007). An interdisciplinary expert consensus statement on assessment of pain in older persons. *Clinical Journal of Pain, 23,* S1–S43. doi:10.1097/AJP.0b013e31802be869

Hadjistavropoulos, T., Hunter, P., & Dever Fitzgerald, T. (2009). Pain assessment and management in older adults: Conceptual issues and clinical challenges. *Canadian Psychology, 50,* 241–254. doi:10.1037/a0015341

Hadjistavropoulos, T., Marchildon, G., Fine, P., Herr, K., Palley, H., Kaasalainen, S., & Beland, F. (2009). Transforming long-term care pain management in North America: The policy clinical interface. *Pain Medicine, 10,* 506–520. doi:0.1111/j.1526-4637.2009.00566.x

Hale, C., & Hadjistavropoulos, T. (1997). Emotional components of pain. *Pain Research and Management, 2,* 217–225.

Haythornthwaite, J. A., Clark, M. R., Pappagallo, M., & Raja, S. N. (2003). Pain coping strategies play a role in the persistence of pain in post-herpetic neuralgia. *Pain, 106,* 453–460. doi:10.1016/j.pain.2003.09.009

Herr, K., Coyne, P. J., Key, T., Manworren, R., McCaffery, M., Merkel, S., . . . Wild, L. (2006). Pain assessment in the nonverbal patient: Position statement with clinical practice recommendations. *Pain Management Nursing, 7,* 44–52. doi:10.1016/j.pmn.2006.02.003

Herr, K. A., Spratt, K., Mobily, P. R., & Richardson, G. (2004). Pain intensity assessment in older adults: Use of experimental pain to compare psychometric properties and usability of selected pain scales with younger adults. *Clinical Journal of Pain, 20,* 207–219.

Hicks, T. J. (2000). Ethical implications of pain management in a nursing home: A discussion. *Nursing Ethics, 7,* 392–397. doi:10.1177/096973300000700504

Horgas, A. L., Nichols, A. L., Schapson, C. A., & Vietes, K. (2007). Assessing pain in persons with dementia:

Relationships among the non-communicative patient's pain assessment instrument, self-report, and behavioral observations. *Pain Management Nursing, 8,* 77–85.

International Association for the Study of Pain. (2012). *IASP taxonomy.* Retrieved from http://www.iasp-pain.org/Content/NavigationMenu/GeneralResourceLinks/PainDefinitions/default.htm

Jakobsson, U., Rahm Hallberg, I. R., & Westergren, A. (2004). Pain management in elderly persons who require assistance with activities of daily living: A comparison of those living at home with those in special accommodations. *European Journal of Pain, 8,* 335–344.

Kaasalainen, S., Middleton, J., Knezacek, S., Hartley, T., Stewart, N., Ife, C., & Robinson, L. (1998). Pain and cognitive status in the institutionalized elderly: Perceptions and interventions. *Journal of Gerontological Nursing, 24,* 24–31.

Keefe, F. J., Caldwell, D. S., Queen, K. T., Gil, K. M., Martinez, S., Crisson, J. E., . . . Nunley, J. (1987). Pain coping strategies in osteoarthritis patients. *Journal of Consulting and Clinical Psychology, 55,* 208.

Kerns, R. D., Turk, D. C., & Rudy, T. E. (1985). The West Haven-Yale Multidimensional Pain Inventory (WHYMPI). *Pain, 23,* 345–356. doi:10.1016/0304–3959(85)90004-1

Labus, J. S., Keefe, F. J., & Jensen, M. P. (2003). Self-reports of pain intensity and direct observations of pain behavior: When are they correlated? *Pain, 102,* 109–24.

Laredo, L., Vargas, E., Blasco, A. J., Aguilar, M. D., Moreno, A., & Portolés, A. (2011). Risk of cerebrovascular accident associated with use of antipsychotics: Population-based case-control study. *Journal of the American Geriatrics Society, 59,* 1182–7. doi:10.1111/j.1532-5415.2011.03479.x.

Lefort, S. M., Gray-Donald, K., Rowat, K., Jeans, M. E. (1998). Randomised controlled trial of a community-based psychoeducation program for the self-management of chronic pain. *Pain, 74,* 297–306.

Lindsey, P. L. (2009). Psychotropic medication use among older adults: What all nurses need to know. *Journal of Gerontological Nursing, 35,* 28–38. doi:10.3928/00989134-20090731-01

Linton, S. J. (2005). Do psychological factors increase the risk for back pain in the general population in both a cross-sectional and prospective analysis? *European Journal of Pain,* 355–361. doi:10.1016/j.ejpain.2004.08.002

Lints-Martindale, A. C., Hadjistavropoulos, T., Lix, L. M., & Thorpe, L. (2012). A comparative investigation of observational pain assessment tools for older adults with dementia. *Clinical Journal of Pain, 28,* 226–237. doi:10.1097/AJP.0b013e3182290d90

Lorig, K. R., & Holman, H. R. (2003). Self-management education: History, definition, outcomes, and mechanisms. *Annals of Behavioral Medicine, 26,* 1–7. doi:10.1207/S15324796ABM2601_01

Ludgate, J. W. (2009). *Cognitive-behavioral therapy and relapse prevention for depression and anxiety.,* Sarasota, FL: Professional Resource Exchange Incorporated.

Lunde, L., Nordhus, I. H., & Pallesen, S. (2009). The effectiveness of cognitive and behavioural treatment of chronic pain in the elderly: A quantitative review. *Journal of Clinical Psychology in Medical Settings, 16,* 254–262. doi:10.1007/s10880-009-9162-y

Malloy, D. C., & Hadjistavropoulos, T. (2012). Philosophical issues in managing pain among seniors with dementia: An existential approach to personhood. *Directions in Psychiatry, 31,* 265–273. doi:10.1111/j.1466-769X.2004.00174.x

Martin, R., Williams, J., Hadjistavropoulos, T., Hadjistavropoulos, H. D., & MacLean, M. (2005). A qualitative investigation of seniors' and caregivers' views on pain assessment and management. *Canadian Journal of Nursing Research, 37,* 142–164.

McCaffery, M. (1968). *Nursing practice theories related to cognition, bodily pain, and man-environment interactions.* Los Angeles: University of California at LA Student.

McCracken, L. M. (2005). Social context and acceptance of chronic pain: The role of solicitous and punishing responses. *Pain, 113,* 155–159. doi:10.1016/j.pain.2004.10.004

McCracken, L. M., & Jones, R. (2012). Treatment for chronic pain for adults in the seventh and eighth decades of life: A preliminary study of Acceptance and Commitment Therapy (ACT). *Pain Medicine, 13,* 860–7. doi:10.1111/j.1526-4637.2012.01407.x.

McGrath, P. A., Seifert, C., Speechley, K. N., Booth, B., Stitt, L., & Gibson, M. C. (1996). A new analogue scale for assessing children's pain: an initial validation study. *Pain, 64,* 435–443.

McVinnie, D. S. (2013). Obesity and pain. *British Journal of Pain, 7,* 163–170. doi:10.1177/2049463713484296

Melzack, R. (1975). The McGill Pain Questionnaire: Major properties and scoring methods. *Pain, 1,* 277–299. doi:10.1016/0304-3959(75)90044-5

Melzack, R. (2001). Pain and the neuromatrix in the brain. *Journal of Dental Education, 65,* 1378–1382.

Melzack, R. (2005). Evolution of the neuromatrix theory of pain. The Prithvi Raj lecture: Presented at The Third World Congress of World Institute of Pain, Barcelona 2004. *Pain Practice, 5,* 85–94. doi:10.1111/j.1533-2500.2005.05203.x

Melzack, R., & Casey, K. L. (1968). Sensory, motivational and central control determinants of pain.

In D. R. Kenshalo (Ed)., *The skin senses* (pp. 423–439). Springfield, IL: Charles C Thomas.

Melzack, R., & Katz, J. (2004). The gate control theory: Reaching for the brain. In T. Hadjistavropoulos & K. D. Craig (Eds.), *Pain: Psychological perspectives* (pp. 13–34). Mahwah, NJ: Erlbaum.

Melzack, R., & Wall, P. D. (1965). Pain mechanisms: A new theory. *Science, 150,* 971–979. doi:10.1126/science.150.3699.971

Merskey, H., & Bogduk, N. (Eds.). (1994). *Classification of chronic pain: Descriptions of chronic pain syndromes and definitions of pain terms.* Seattle, WA: IASP Press.

Misson, L., Savoie, M., Aubin, M., Hadjistavropoulos, T., & Verreault, R. (2011). Challenges to the evaluation of pain in aged individuals with reduced capacity to communicate due to advanced dementia. *Pain: Evaluation, Diagnosis, and Treatment, 12,* 55–64. doi:10.1016/j.douler.2010.09.012

Morone, N. E., Greco, C. M., & Weiner, D. K. (2008). Mindfulness meditation for the treatment of chronic low back pain in older adults: A randomized controlled pilot study. *Pain, 134,* 310–319. doi:10.1016/j.pain.2007.04.038

Morone, N. E., Lynch, C. S., Greco, C. M., Tindle, H. A., & Weiner, D. K. (2008). "I felt like a new person." The effects of mindfulness meditation on older adults with chronic pain: Qualitative narrative analysis of diary entries. *Journal of Pain, 9,* 841–848.

Morrison, R. S., & Siu, A. L. (2000). A comparison of pain and its treatment in advanced dementia and cognitively intact patients with hip fracture. *Journal of Pain and Symptom Management, 19,* 240–248.

Moseley, G. L. (2011). New direction for the fear avoidance model? *Pain, 152,* 2447–2448.

Newman, M. G., Erickson, T., Przeworsi, A., & Dzus, E. (2009). Self-help and minimal contact therapies for anxiety disorders: Is human contact necessary for therapeutic efficacy? *Journal of Clinical Psychology, 59,* 251–274.

Nicholas, M. K., Wilson, P. H., & Goyen, J. (1992). Comparison of cognitive–behavioral group treatment and an alternative nonpsychological treatment for chronic low back pain. *Pain, 48,* 339–347. doi:10.1016/0304-3959(92)90082-M

Otis, J. D. (2007). *Managing chronic pain: A cognitive–behavioral therapy approach.* New York, NY: Oxford University Press.

Paulsen, J. S., & Altmaier, E. M. (1995). The effects of perceived versus enacted social support on the discriminative cue function of spouses for pain behaviors. *Pain, 60,* 103–110. doi:10.1016/0304-3959(94)00096-W

Pavot, W., & Diener, E. (1993). Review of the satisfaction with life scale. *Psychological Assessment, 5,* 164–172. doi:10.1037/1040-3590.5.2.164

Peters, J., Large, R. G., & Elkind, G. (1992). Follow-up results from a randomised controlled trial evaluating in-and outpatient pain management programmes. *Pain, 50,* 41–50. doi:10.1016/0304-3959(92)90110-W

Picavet, H. S. J., Vlaeyen, J. W. S., & Schouten, J. S. A. G. (2002). Pain catastrophizing and kinesiophobia: Predictors of chronic low back pain. *American Journal of Epidemiology, 156,* 1028–1034. doi:10.1093/aje/kwf136

Reynolds, K. S., Hanson, L. C., DeVellis, R. F., Henderson, M., & Steinhauser, K. E. (2008). Disparities in pain management between cognitively intact and cognitively impaired nursing home residents. *Journal of Pain and Symptom Management, 35,* 388–396. doi:10.1016/j.jpainsymman.2008.01.001

Rini, C., Williams, D. A., Broderick, J. E., & Keefe, F. J. (2012) Meeting them where they are: Using the internet to deliver behavioral medicine interventions for pain. *Translational Behavioral Medicine, 2,* 82–92.

Robinson, C. L. (2007). Relieving pain in the elderly. *Health Progress, 88,* 48–53.

Rollman, G. B. (2004). Ethnocultural variations in the experience of pain. In T. Hadjistavropoulos & K. D. Craig (Eds.), *Pain: Psychological perspectives* (pp. 155–178). Mahwah, NJ: Erlbaum.

Romano, J. M., & Turner, J. A. (1985). Chronic pain and depression: Does the evidence support a relationship? *Psychological Bulletin, 97,* 18–34. doi:10.1037/0033-2909.97.1.18

Rosenstiel, A. K., & Keefe, F. J. (1983). The use of coping strategies in chronic low back pain patients: Relationship to patient characteristics and current adjustment. *Pain, 17,* 33–44. doi:10.1016/0304-3959(83)90125-2

Ruscheweyh, R., Nees, F., Marziniak, M., Evers, S., Flor, H., & Knecht, S. (2011). Pain catastrophizing and pain-related emotions: Influence of age and type of pain. *Clinical Journal of Pain, 27,* 578–586.

Santos, R., Castro-Caldas, A., & Hadjistavropoulos, T. (2012). Adaptação Cultural e Validação da Pain Assessment Checklist for Seniors With Limited Ability to Communicate (PACSLAC) para a População Portuguesa. *Dor, 20,* 5–10.

Scherder, E., & Van Manen, F. (2005). Pain in Alzheimer's disease: Nursing assistants' and patients' evaluations. *Journal of Advanced Nursing, 52,* 151–158. doi:10.1111/j.1365-2648.2005.03577.x

Scherder, E. J. A., & Bouma, A. (2000). Visual analogue scales for pain assessment in Alzheimer's disease. *Gerontology, 46,* 47–53. doi:10.1159/000022133

Sharp, T. J. (2001). Chronic pain: A reformulation of the cognitive–behavioural model. *Behaviour Research and Therapy, 39,* 787–800. doi:10.1016/S0005-7967(00)00061-9

Sheiner, E. K., Sheiner, E., Shoham-Vardi, I., Mazor, M., & Katz, M. (1999). Ethnic differences influence caregiver's estimates of pain during labour. *Pain, 81*, 299–305. doi:10.1016/S0304-3959(99)00019-6

Skinner, M., Wilson, H. D., & Turk, D. C. (2012). Cognitive-behavioral perspective and cognitive–behavioral therapy for people with chronic pain: Distinctions, outcomes, and innovations. *Journal of Cognitive Psychotherapy, 26*, 93–113.

Spinhoven, P. H., Ormel, J., Sloekers, P. P. A., Kempen, G. I. J. M., Speckens, A. E. M., & Hemert, A. V. (1997). A validation study of the Hospital Anxiety and Depression Scale (HADS) in different groups of Dutch subjects. *Psychological Medicine, 27*, 363–370.

Sullivan, M. J., Feuerstein, M., Gatchel, R., Linton, S. J., & Pransky, G. (2005). Integrating psychosocial and behavioral interventions to achieve optimal rehabilitation outcomes. *Journal of Occupational Rehabilitation, 15*, 475–489. doi:10.1007/s10926-005-8029-9

Taenzer, P., Melzack, R., & Jeans, M. E. (1986). Influence of psychological factors on postoperative pain, mood and analgesic requirements. *Pain, 24*, 331–342. doi:10.1016/0304-3959(86)90119-3

Teri, L., Logsdon, R. G., Uomoto, J., & McCurry, S. M. (1997). Behavioral treatment of depression in dementia patients: A controlled clinical trial. *The Journals of Gerontology, Series B: Psychological Sciences and Social Sciences, 52*, 159–166.

Thorsell, J., Finnes, A., Dahl, J., Lundgren, T., Gybrant, M., Gordh, T., & Buhrman, M. (2011). A comparative study of 2 manual-based self-help interventions, acceptance and commitment therapy and applied relaxation, for persons with chronic pain. *Clinical Journal of Pain, 27*, 716–723. doi:10.1097/AJP.0b013e318219a933

Todd, K. H., Samaroo, N., & Hoffman, J. R. (1993). Ethnicity as a risk factor for inadequate emergency department analgesia. *JAMA, 269*, 1537–1539. doi:10.1001/jama.269.12.1537

Turk, D. C., Meichenbaum, D., & Genest, M. (1987). *Pain and behavioral medicine: A cognitive–behavioral perspective.* New York, NY: Guilford Press.

Turk, D. C., & Melzack, R. (2011). The measurement of pain and the assessment of people experiencing pain. In D. C. Turk & R. Melzack (Ed.), *Handbook of pain assessment* (3rd ed., pp. 242–259). New York, NY: Guilford Press.

Turk, D. C., & Okifuji, A. (2001). Pain terms and taxonomies. In D. Loeser, S. H. Butler, J. J. Chapman, & D. C. Turk. *Bonica's management of pain* (3rd ed., pp. 18–25). Philadelphia, PA: Lippincott Williams & Wilkins.

Unruh, A. M. (1996). Gender variations in clinical pain experience. *Pain, 65*, 123–167. doi:10.1016/0304-3959(95)00214-6

Villanueva, M. R., Smith, T. L., Erickson, J. S., Lee, A. C., & Singer, C. M. (2003). Pain assessment for the dementing elderly (PADE): Reliability and validity of a new measure. *Journal of the American Medical Directors Association, 4*, 1–8.

Vlaeyen, J. W. S., & Linton, S. J. (2000). Fear-avoidance and its consequences in chronic musculoskeletal pain: A state of the art. *Pain, 85*, 317–332. doi:10.1016/S0304-3959(99)00242-0

Warden, V., Hurley, A. C., & Volicer, L. (2003). Development and psychometric evaluation of the Pain Assessment in Advanced Dementia (PAINAD) scale. *Journal of the American Medical Directors Association, 4*, 9–15.

Wary, B. (1999). Une échelle pour évaluer la douleur [A scale to assess pain]. *Soins Gerontologie, 19*, 25–27.

Waters, S. J., Woodward, J. T., & Keefe, F. J. (2005). Cognitive-behavioural therapy for pain in older adults. In S. J. Gibson & D. K. Weiner (Eds.), *Pain in older persons* (pp. 239–262). Seattle, WA: IASP Press.

Watt-Watson, J., McGillion, M., Hunter, J., Choiniere, M., Clark, A. J., Dewar, A., . . . Webber, K. (2009). A survey of prelicensure pain curricula in health science faculties in Canadian universities. *Pain Research and Management, 14*, 439–444.

Weiner, D., Peterson, B., Ladd, K., McConnell, E., & Keefe, F. (1999). Pain in nursing home residents: An exploration of prevalence, staff perspectives and practical aspects of measurement. *Clinical Journal of Pain, 15*, 92–101. doi:10.1097/00002508-199906000-00005

Weiner, D. K., Peterson, B. L., Logue, P., & Keefe, F. J. (1998). Predictors of pain self-report in nursing home residents. *Aging, 10*, 411–420.

Wetherell, J. L., Afari, N., Rutledge, T., Sorrell, J. T., Stoddard, J. A., Petkus, A. J., . . . Hampton Atkinson, J. (2011). A randomized, controlled trial of acceptance and commitment therapy and cognitive–behavioral therapy for chronic pain. *Pain, 152*, 2098–2107. doi:10.1016/j.pain.2011.05.016

Wheeler, J. R. C. (2003). Can a disease self-management program reduce health care costs? The case of older women with heart disease. *Medical Care, 41*, 706–715.

Won, A. B., Lapane, K. L., Vallow, S., Schein, J., Morris, J. N., & Lipsitz, L. A. (2004). Persistent nonmalignant pain and analgesic prescribing patterns in elderly nursing home residents. *Journal of the American Geriatrics Society, 52*, 867–874.

Yesavage, J. A., Brink, T. L., Rose, T. L., Lum, O., Huang, . . . Leirer, V. O. (1982). Development and validation of a geriatric depression screening scale: A preliminary report. *Journal Psychiatric Research, 17*, 37–49

Yong, H. H., Gibson, S. J., David, J. D. L., & Helme, R. D. (2001). Development of a pain attitudes questionnaire to assess stoicism and cautiousness for possible age differences. *The Journals of Gerontology, Series B: Psychological Sciences and Social Sciences, 56*, 279–284.

Zigmond, A. S., & Snaith, R. P. (1983). The hospital anxiety and depression scale. *Acta Psychiatrica Scandinavica, 67*, 361–370. doi:10.1111/j.1600-0447.1983.tb09716.x

Zwakhalen, S. M. G., Hamers, J. P. H., & Berger, M. P. F. (2006). The psychometric quality and clinical usefulness of three pain assessment tools for elderly people with dementia. *Pain, 126*, 210–220. doi:10.1016/j.pain.2006.06.029

Zwakhalen, S. M. G., Hamers, J. P. H., Peijnenburg, R. H. A., & Berger, M. P. F. (2007). Nursing staff knowledge and beliefs about pain in elderly nursing home residents with dementia. *Pain Research and Management, 12*, 177–184.

CHAPTER 17

DIABETES AND OBESITY
IN LATER LIFE

Erin E. Emery-Tiburcio, Lisa M. Nackers, Steven Bernfeld, and Rebecca Lahey

The prevalence of obesity has been increasing at an alarming rate across all age-groups within the United States. Specifically within the older adult population, the seriousness of this trend is underscored by resulting medical complications, decreased physical function, and impaired quality of life. Diabetes is associated with obesity and further negatively affects functioning and quality of life. Both obesity and diabetes are associated significantly with health behavior and multiple mental health problems, some of which independently increase the risk for obesity and diabetes. This chapter summarizes research on obesity and diabetes among older adults, including the scope of the problem, assessment, and intervention.

OBESITY EPIDEMIC

Obesity, defined as an excess in total body fat, serves as a risk factor for increased morbidity and mortality, making it one of the most important public health epidemics. More specifically, the American College of Cardiology/American Heart Association Task Force on Practice Guidelines (M. D. Jensen et al., 2014) has defined obesity as a body mass index (BMI) of 30–39, and extreme obesity as BMI of greater than 40 for adults (for a discussion of BMI, see discussion in the section Assessment; Kuczmarski, Carroll, Flegal, & Troiano, 1997).

Increasing in prevalence over the past three decades, obesity affects more than 35% of people within the United States (Flegal, Carroll, Kit, & Ogden, 2012). According to data from the National Health and Nutrition Examination

Survey, 35% of adults over the age of 65 years (i.e., approximately 13 million older adults) were obese in 2007–2010 (Fakhouri, Ogden, Carroll, Kit, & Flegal, 2012). Specifically, 41% of adults between the ages of 65 and 74 years and 28% of adults 75 years and older were considered obese.

DIABETES EPIDEMIC

Diabetes mellitus is an impairment of the body's ability to convert glucose to energy, thus resulting in hyperglycemia (excess glucose in the blood). For glucose to be transferred from blood to cells, the hormone insulin is needed. Type 2 diabetes, alternatively referred to as non-insulin-dependent diabetes mellitus (NIDDM) or adult-onset diabetes, typically begins as insulin resistance, in which cells do not properly utilize insulin. Over time, as the need for insulin increases, the pancreas slowly loses its ability to produce insulin. Type 2 diabetes is by far the most common type of diabetes for older adults and the general population, accounting for 90% of all cases (Shaw & Sicree, 2008).

Type 1 diabetes accounts for approximately 5%–10% of diabetes cases. Pathogenesis of type 1 diabetes involves the destruction of pancreatic beta cells, the only cells in the body that make the hormone insulin, leading to complete insulin deficiency. Also known as insulin-dependent diabetes mellitus (IDDM) or juvenile-onset diabetes, type 1 diabetes most often starts during childhood or early adulthood but may develop at any age and may be due to environmental, genetic, or autoimmune factors. At this

http://dx.doi.org/10.1037/14459-017
APA Handbook of Clinical Geropsychology: Vol. 2. Assessment, Treatment, and Issues of Later Life,
P. A. Lichtenberg and B. T. Mast (Editors-in-Chief)

time, there is no known cure or prevention for type 1 diabetes. Survival requires insulin in the form of an injection or pump, blood glucose monitoring, nutritional planning, and ongoing screening for comorbid conditions and other related complications (Daneman, 2006). Less common types of the disease include diabetes related to genetic conditions, medical conditions, medications, and pregnancy (gestational diabetes). Symptoms associated with all of these types of diabetes include frequent need to urinate, excess thirst, blurred vision, and fatigue.

Older adults are at higher risk for diabetes than younger adults, with 10.9 million individuals age 65 years or older (26.9%) diagnosed with the disease, in comparison with 25.6 million American adults age 20 years and older (11.3%) who have diabetes (Centers for Disease Control and Prevention, 2011). Although diabetes prevalence is comparable between genders, men have a significantly higher rate of undiagnosed diabetes (Cowie et al., 2006).

CONCEPTUAL ISSUES

National Health and Nutrition Examination Survey data indicate that men and women do not differ in obesity prevalence; however, among women, a greater percentage of non-Hispanic Black women were obese when compared with non-Hispanic White and Hispanic women (Fakhouri, Ogden, Carroll, Kit, & Flegal, 2012). Within the 65–74 age range, 54% of non-Hispanic Black women were classified as obese compared with 39% and 47% of non-Hispanic White and Hispanic women, respectively. Similarly, 50% of non-Hispanic Black women age 75 years and older were obese compared with 30% of Hispanic women and 28% of non-Hispanic White women (Fakhouri et al., 2012).

Educational trends in obesity also are observed among older adults. Men ages 65–74 years old who obtained a college degree demonstrate lower prevalence of obesity compared with those who had attended some college. In women ages 65–74 years old, a linear trend exists with obesity prevalence decreasing as educational attainment increases. Older adults demonstrate slightly higher rates in obesity compared with their younger counterparts (Ogden, Carroll, Kit, & Flegal, 2012). Whereas men

did not demonstrate a significant difference across age-groups, significantly more older women, compared with women ages 20–39 years old, were classified as obese (Ogden et al., 2012).

Behavioral risk factors, such as sedentary behaviors and maladaptive eating patterns, also place older adults at risk for obesity. Regardless of time spent in moderate-vigorous physical activity, time spent in sedentary behaviors, or on such activities as sleeping, sitting, watching television, and playing on the computer, is associated with increased risk of metabolic syndrome and obesity in older adults (Bankoski et al., 2011; Inoue et al., 2012; Swartz et al., 2012).

Although older adults tend to have better quality diets than their younger and middle-age counterparts (Hiza, Casavale, Guenther, & Davis, 2013), they also have lower energy requirements (Institute of Medicine, 2002). Increased eating frequency and high total energy intake have been associated with greater BMI levels in older adults (Howarth, Huang, Roberts, Lin, & McCrory, 2007), whereas variability in food intake patterns, such as meal skipping, show no clear association with increased weight in older adults (Howarth et al., 2007; Hsiao et al., 2011). Compared with younger adults, however, older adults do demonstrate more regular meal scheduling with slightly less snacking frequency, perhaps because of habit or health concerns (Howarth et al., 2007).

Obesity itself is a significant risk factor for diabetes. Relative to those with normal weight, adults who are obese (BMI = 30–39) are 3.44 times more likely to be diagnosed with diabetes, whereas risk with extreme obesity (BMI = 40+) is 7.37 times that of normal-weight adults (Mokdad et al., 2003). The relationship between obesity and diabetes decreases later in life. In the longitudinal Cardiovascular Health Study of 4,193 older adults, risk of diabetes for those ages 65–74 years with extreme obesity was two to six times that of normal weight, whereas those age 75 years or older had half the risk of those ages 65–74 years (Biggs et al., 2010).

There is a significant disparity in diabetes risk based on ethnicity. When compared with non-Hispanic Whites and maintaining age or sex standardized rates, Native Americans (odds ratio [*OR*] = 2.2), African Americans (*OR* = 1.8), and Mexican

Americans ($OR = 1.7$) are more likely to develop diabetes (Schoenberg, Traywick, Jacobs-Lawson, & Kart, 2008). Of the largest population groups in the United States, African American older adults have the highest prevalence of diabetes (28.5%), followed by older adults of Mexican origin (24.9%), and non-Hispanic Whites (14.3%; Cowie et al., 2006).

Individuals of low socioeconomic status (SES) are likely to have limited access to health care and use fewer outpatient services (Smedley, Stith, & Nelson, 2002). Low SES also is related to low health literacy regarding self-care, poor treatment of pain, suboptimal patient counseling, and a lack of specialist care (Schoenberg et al., 2008). Low income and lack of health insurance are associated with lower health care service utilization (Hargraves & Hadley, 2003). Perhaps as a result, older adults who have had inadequate access to medical care throughout the course of a lifetime are more likely to use unconventional health resources. For example, rural African American and Native American older adults were more than twice as likely ($OR = 2.32, 2.30$, respectively) to use alternative remedies to manage their diabetes as Whites (Arcury et al., 2006).

The environment, including access to quality food and a safe community, is a significant factor in adherence to lifestyle recommendations for obesity and diabetes. Older adults shop for groceries almost exclusively in their immediate neighborhood (Smith, 1991; Smith & Gauthier, 1995), which may be associated with limited transportation and low income (Clifton, 2004; Sharkey & Horel, 2008). Thus, in areas with "food deserts," older adults are severely restricted in their food choices (Zenk et al., 2005). Furthermore, older adults reject outdoor exercise when the threat of crime is perceived as a barrier, particularly among urban African Americans (Lavizzo-Mourey et al., 2001).

Family factors can be both risk and protective factors in diabetes outcomes. As reflected in Exhibit 17.1, family coping, communication patterns, level of stress, and psychopathology all influence diabetes outcomes (Fisher & Weihs, 2000).

Progression and Negative Outcomes

Obesity. There is strong evidence linking obesity with increased disease morbidity within the older adult population. Risk of diabetes, cardiovascular disease, hypertension, hyperlipidemia, asthma, osteoarthritis, and certain cancers increases substantially with excess weight throughout the aging process (Houston, Nicklas, & Zizza, 2009; McTigue, Hess, & Ziouras, 2006; Villareal, Apovian, Kushner, & Klein, 2005). Older adults are also at risk for sarcopenia, which is the loss of skeletal muscle mass and subsequent decrease in muscle strength (Houston et al., 2009). Those who experience sarcopenia in conjunction with obesity are at increased risk for disability and decreased physical functioning (Houston et al., 2009).

Perhaps surprisingly, obesity has been linked to benefits among older adults, including preserved or higher bone mineral density, decreased risk of

---

Exhibit 17.1
Family Risk and Protective Factors for Diabetes Outcomes

Protective factors

- Family closeness and connectedness
- Problem-focused family coping skills
- Clear family organization and decision making
- Direct communication among family members regarding the chronic disease

Risk factors

- Interfamilial hostility, criticism, and blame
- Psychological trauma related to the initial diagnosis and treatment of the disease
- Extrafamilial stress
- Lack of an extrafamilial support system
- Family perfectionism and rigidity
- Presence of psychopathology with onset before the chronic disease

osteoporosis, and protection against hip fractures (Mathus-Vliegen, 2012) as well as decreased mortality. In addition, although obesity is associated with increased mortality in the general population, older adults tend to experience lower risk of death from obesity (Houston et al., 2009; Snih et al., 2007; Stevens, 1998; Villareal et al., 2005). Potential reasons for decreased mortality in older adults include selective survival (i.e., individuals susceptible to effects of excess weight have already died), confounding variables (e.g., smoking, race, etc.), different cohorts, and limited remaining life span. All of these variables may complicate the conclusions researchers are able to draw based on the association between obesity and mortality in older adults (Elia, 2001; Zamboni et al., 2005).

When considering health-related quality of life (HRQOL) and psychosocial effects, however, obesity exacts a toll on older adults. Excess weight contributes to greater frailty and physical disability in addition to earlier decline and poorer physical function. These declines result in limited ability to complete activities of daily living, such as eating, bathing and grooming, shopping, and overall mobility. Indeed, older adults with excess weight experience earlier onset of physical disability (Houston et al., 2009).

Diabetes.   Diabetes creates abnormalities in metabolic functioning (insulin resistance, hyperglycemia, free fatty acids) that lead to atherosclerosis and medial calcification in the vasculature (Creager, Lüscher, Cosentino, & Beckman, 2003). These vascular changes impair blood flow, leading to poor wound healing, neuropathy, diabetic retinopathy, vasculitis, amputation, and stroke (Leslie, 1999). Diabetes also is associated with proteinuria, an abnormally high level of protein in the urine. Proteinuria and hypertension are associated with progressive diabetic nephropathy, which, if untreated, can lead to end-stage renal disease and death (Atkins et al., 2005).

Each of these complications of diabetes is exacerbated in older adults. Loss of sensory function in the context of diabetes is a particular risk for disability among older adults. Diabetic retinopathy is generally higher among older than younger adults and higher among women than men (Eye Diseases

Prevalence Research Group, 2004). Other eye diseases, including glaucoma and cataracts, are more common among older adults with diabetes (Saaddine et al., 2008). Similarly, hearing impairment is approximately twice as common in people with diabetes when controlling for age (Bainbridge et al., 2011). Vision (Sinclair, Bayer, Girling, & Woodhouse, 2000) and hearing losses (Dalton et al., 2003) not only threaten independence but also are associated with significant declines in mobility and quality of life among older adults.

Cognitive dysfunction.   Diabetes may lead to cognitive decline, which then may negatively affect an older individual's ability to prevent or control symptoms of diabetes (Munshi et al., 2006). Those with diabetes are at 1.2 times increased risk of cognitive decline and at 1.6 times greater risk of developing dementia (Cukierman et al., 2005; Evans & Sherwin, 2002). A number of factors may contribute to this relationship. Diabetes is a risk factor for cerebrovascular disease, which may be a mediator between diabetes and cognitive change. In addition, hypoglycemia may negatively affect cognition; however, little evidence exists to support a relationship between chronic cognitive impairment and hypoglycemia. A third factor is hyperglycemia, which may play a role in chronic cognitive impairment, as suggested by postmortem studies of brains of people with Alzheimer's dementia (Cukierman et al., 2005). Utilization of cognitive screening is particularly important in a diabetic population to identify impairment and potential risk for difficulty adhering to diabetes treatments (for further details on cognitive screening instruments, see Volume 1, Chapter 21).

There is also a hypothesis that Alzheimer's disease (AD) is a third variant of diabetes. A critical review of published research on type 3 diabetes suggests that changes in brain insulin levels and insulin-like growth factor (IGF) may represent the beginning of a chain of abnormalities that leads to lesions seen in AD (de la Monte & Wands, 2008). This review also includes experimental research suggesting that medications currently used to treat Type 2 diabetes can be effective in treating experimentally induced type 3 diabetes and in potentially preventing AD. Furthermore, preliminary data suggest that genes associated with diabetes (INPPL1 SNPs) also may be implicated in AD (Accardi et al., 2012).

Ethnicity. Minorities are significantly more likely to have diabetic complications. Rates of kidney disease, blindness, limb amputation, and mortality resulting from amputation among African Americans is more than double that of non-Hispanic Whites (Carter, Pugh, & Monterrosa, 1996; Lanting, Joung, Mackenbach, Lamberts, & Bootsma, 2005; Lustman et al., 2000). Similarly, kidney disease and retinopathy are higher among Latinos (Carter, Pugh, & Monterrosa, 1996; Emanuele et al., 2005; M. I. Harris, Klein, Cowie, Rowland, & Byrd-Holt, 1998; Lanting et al., 2005).

Mortality. Diabetes is the sixth leading cause of death in the United States and is a contributing factor to approximately 225,000 deaths per year (Centers for Disease Control and Prevention, 2011). Because of diabetes and its complications, the life expectancy of men who are diagnosed at age 60 years is reduced by 7.3 years, whereas their quality-of-life years are reduced by 11.1 years. For women diagnosed at 60 years, life expectancy is reduced by 9.5 years, whereas quality-of-life years are reduced by 13.8 years (Narayan, Boyle, & Thompson, 2003).

Pathways to Psychopathology

Obesity. The social and psychological effects of obesity on older adults are profound. Obesity also has been linked with declines in cognitive functioning; specifically, obese older adults and those who experience weight gain have an increased risk of developing dementia (Gustafson, Rothenberg, Blennow, Steen, & Skoog, 2003; Luchsinger, Patel, Tang, Schupf, & Mayeux, 2007). HRQOL worsens in both men and women during old age, especially with respect to physical dimensions like physical functioning, vitality, and bodily pain (Fine et al., 1999; López-García et al., 2003; Strandberg, Strandberg, Salomaa, Pitkala, & Miettinen, 2003; Yan et al., 2004). Specifically in obese older women who gain weight, significant decreases in social functioning and emotional role functioning are found, suggesting the importance of preventing additional weight gain in older adults (León-Muñoz et al., 2005). Finally, nursing home admissions

(Valiyeva, Russell, Miller, & Safford, 2006) and homebound status (G. L. Jensen et al., 2006) are associated with excess weight in older adults.

Diabetes. Psychosocial issues associated with diabetes also can be severe among older adults, including depression and anxiety as well as stress and HRQOL.

Depression. A relationship between diabetes and depression has been clearly established (Anderson, Freedland, Clouse, & Lustman, 2001; Engum, Mykletun, Midthjell, Holen, & Dahl, 2005; Katon et al., 2004). A meta-analysis conducted by Ali and colleagues (2006) indicated that people with Type 2 diabetes are at a significantly higher risk for depression (17.6%) compared with people without diabetes (9.8%). Not only are people with diabetes more likely to develop depression but people with depression also are more likely to develop diabetes. Critical reviews of clinical and community studies point to the bidirectional relationship between diabetes and depression (Campayo, Gómez-Biel, & Lobo, 2011; Golden et al., 2008; Thomas, Ferrier, Kalaria, Brown, & O'Brien, 2001). Although the exact nature of the relationship has yet to be delineated, it can be considered from both physiological and behavioral perspectives.

Diabetes-related vascular changes in the brain, specifically white-matter lesions (Alexopoulos et al., 1997; Thomas et al., 2001), can lead to increased risk for depressive symptoms and, more specifically, "vascular depression" (Mast, Yochim, Mac-Neill, & Lichtenberg, 2004; Thomas et al., 2001). This relationship may be an important factor in potential treatment resistance. Depression-related changes in physiology can influence the development and regulation of diabetes, including impaired glycemic control (see Paschalides et al., 2004) and insulin resistance (Campayo et al., 2011).

Life and health stressors, including the diagnosis of diabetes itself or the complications and stress that accompany its management, also can lead to depression (Katon et al., 2004). Symptoms of depression, such as anhedonia and lethargy, may lead to nonadherence to diabetes treatment plans, including checking blood glucose levels, diet, medications, and physical activity (Paschalides et al., 2004; Van Tilburg et al., 2001). Learned helplessness also may play a role in depression when efforts to manage diabetes do not yield results. Among individuals with comorbid diabetes and depression, the perception of helplessness has been found to diminish engagement in recommended self-care behaviors (Van Tilburg et al., 2001). Conversely, better adherence to treatment recommendations, metabolic control, and quality of life can stem from a heightened sense of one's control over diabetes management (Hampson et al., 2000; Paschalides et al., 2004).

Anxiety. A meta-analysis conducted by Grigsby and colleagues (2002), showed that 14% of adults with diabetes had symptoms consistent with generalized anxiety disorder, 27% had anxiety disorder not otherwise specified, and 40% had elevated symptoms of anxiety. In this analysis, women experienced symptoms of anxiety at a much higher rate than men (55.3% vs. 32.9%, respectively). In contrast, lifetime prevalence of generalized anxiety disorder is approximately 5% in the general population (Wittchen & Hoyer, 2001). Although a causal link between diabetes and anxiety disorders has not been established, Rubin and Peyrot (2001) proposed that people with diabetes are at heightened risk of anxiety disorders because of daily fears associated with the disease, which may include hypoglycemia, medical complications from diabetes, and interference with daily activities related to the disease.

Stress and social support. D. W. Brown and colleagues (2004) reviewed ways in which stress and level of social support relate to hemoglobin A1c (HbA1c) levels (a measure of blood glucose over time; specifically, the percent of hemoglobin that is coated in sugar over 2–3 months) and found that diabetics who also experienced high levels of stress and identified low levels of social support had higher levels of HbA1c than their counterparts with social support. The association between HbA1c and social support was not significant among individuals with lower levels of overall stress.

Health-related quality of life. D. W. Brown and colleagues (2004) found that independent of other factors, diabetes is associated with lower levels of HRQOL for older adults. Furthermore, older adults with diabetes report experiencing nearly two times as many physically or mentally unhealthy days (10.1) as those without diabetes (5.7). Of the older adults in their sample, those who were treated with insulin were 1.71 times more likely to experience 14 or more unhealthy days compared with those who were not.

ASSESSMENT

Physical Measures

Obesity assessment. Although obesity is defined as excess body fat, body fat is often difficult to measure within clinical settings and requires sophisticated technology. Therefore, BMI is the most common metric utilized to classify weight status. BMI of 30 or greater, calculated by body weight in kilograms divided by the square of height in meters, denotes an obesity classification (M. D. Jensen et al., 2014). Measuring obesity in older adults presents challenges. Within the older adult population, changes in body composition result in reduced fat-free mass, greater fat mass, and decreased height, which lead to a discrepancy between BMI and percent total body fat (Sorkin, Muller, & Andres, 1999). Specifically, changes in body composition underestimate fatness and reductions in height overestimate fatness at any given BMI value (Villareal et al., 2005). Although the correlation between BMI and fat mass decreases within the older adult population, only minimal differences exist when compared with the general adult population (McTigue et al., 2006). The effects of increased BMI on mortality risk typically are less pronounced among older adults than their younger counterparts (Janssen & Mark, 2007). Unlike BMI, however, more sophisticated measures of body fatness have few reference standards and no established risk categories linked with various health-related outcomes; therefore, using BMI may hold the strongest clinical utility. In addition, assessing abdominal obesity through a measure of waist circumference may provide further evidence of diseased risk (M. D. Jensen et al., 2014). A waist circumference of 102 cm or more in men and 88 cm or greater in women designates abdominal obesity (M. D. Jensen et al., 2014).

Diabetes assessment. The American Diabetes Association (ADA, 2012) provides guidelines for the assessment of diabetes in adults of all ages. For those who are overweight and have other risk factors, in addition to adults age 45 years and older, it is recommended that screening take place once every 1–3 years using the fasting plasma glucose (FPG), HbA1c, or oral glucose tolerance test. Individuals who are at risk of developing diabetes are alternatively referred to as prediabetic (see Table 17.1). These recommendations are based on evidence that early treatment of Type 2 diabetes is beneficial and that diagnosis often occurs several years after the presence of the disease.

A cluster of cardiometabolic risk factors, known as the metabolic syndrome, plays a strong role in the development of diabetes. Characterized by the presence of at least three of the following: reduced high-density lipoprotein cholesterol, elevated blood pressure, high triglycerides, elevated fasting glucose, and increased waist circumference (see Alberti et al., 2009 for specific cut-point criteria), prevalence of the metabolic syndrome in U.S. adults ranges between 34.3% and 38.5% (Ford, Li, & Zhao, 2010). These ranges increase with age, with adults ages 60–69 years demonstrating the highest rates of metabolic syndrome (i.e., 59.3%–67.3% in men and 55.4%–57.6% in women depending on criteria used for waist circumference; Ford et al., 2010). The risk for developing diabetes is three to four times higher in men and five to six times higher in women with metabolic syndrome when compared with those without metabolic syndrome (Ford, Li, & Sattar, 2008).

Assessment Relevant to Both Obesity and Diabetes

Physical activity.   For older adults, regular physical activity has been shown to correlate with lower weight, prolonged independence, reduced risk of medical disorders such as diabetes, preservation of

energy balance, and possibly increased longevity (Shephard, 1991). Physical activity is also thought to positively influence physical and psychological well-being for older adults (Berger, 1988). Several measures have been designed and validated for use exclusively with older adults. The Community Healthy Activities Model Program for Seniors (CHAMPS; Stewart et al., 2001) assesses weekly frequency and duration of physical activities for older adults. The Modified Baecke Questionnaire measures physical activities, modified from its original for older adults (Voorrips et al., 1991). The Physical Activity Scale for the Elderly was designed for epidemiological studies examining physical activity, health, and physical function in older adults (Washburn, McAuley, Katula, Mihalko, & Boileau, 1999). The Rapid Assessment of Physical Activity is designed for use in clinical settings to assess physical activity level for adults age 50 years and older (Topolski et al., 2006). The Regenstrief Physical Activity and Health Survey assesses physical activity knowledge, perceived barriers to physical activity, self-efficacy, and behavior (Clark, 1999). This measure is unique in that normative data were gathered from urban-dwelling, primarily low-income adults ages 55 years and older, taking into account the unique challenges of that population, and has a lower floor of activity than other measures for more sedentary adults. The Yale Physical Activity Survey (Dipietro et al., 1993) measures the type, amount, and patterning of physical activity and exercise in older adults, age 60 years and older. This interviewer-administered questionnaire includes two sections encompassing eight indexes and provides information related to both frequency and duration of various physical activities. See Table 17.2 for additional

---

TABLE 17.1

Diabetes Assessment Measures

Test	At risk/prediabetes ranges	Diabetes diagnostic criteria
Fasting plasma glucose (FPG)	100 mg/dl (5.6 mmol/l) to 125 mg/dl (6.9 mmol/l)	126 mg/dl (7.0 mmol/l) or greater
Hemoglobin A1c	5.7%–6.4%	6.5% or greater
2 hr oral glucose tolerance test	140 mg/dl (7.8 mmol/l) to 199 mg/dl (11.0 mmol/l)	200 mg/dl (11.1 mmol/l) or greater

TABLE 17.2

Physical Activity Measures

Measure	Construct	Response format	Reliability	Validity
Community Healthy Activities Model Program for Seniors (CHAMPS)	Weekly frequency and duration of physical activities for older adults.	Self-report; 41 items. Response options: yes–no, number of times participated/ week, and total hours/ week, per activity.	6-month intraclass correlation coefficients ranged from 0.58– 0.67	Total activity scores ($\rho = 0.34$) and higher levels of activity (range $\rho = .27-.37$) were associated with accelerometer data, but relationships were weaker with lower levels.
Modified Baecke Questionnaire	Household activities, sporting activities, and other physically active leisure activities.	Interviewer administered; 19 items. Household activities: Likert scales. Sports and other activities measured by type of activity and time.	20-day test–retest reliability $r = 0.89$	Scores correlated with 24 hr activity logs ($r = 0.78$) and with pedometer ($r = 0.72$).
Physical Activity Scale for the Elderly (PASE)	Physical activity of people age 65 years and older for epidemiologic studies.	Self-report; 12 items. Weekly frequency and duration of physical activities on Likert scales. Minimum measurement of at least 1 hr of activity daily, so may be less useful for more sedentary seniors.	Test–retest reliability, assessed over a 3–7 week interval = 0.75	Scores correlated with grip strength ($r = 0.37$), static balance ($r = 0.33$), leg strength ($r = 0.25$), and resting heart rate ($r = -0.13$).
Rapid Assessment of Physical Activity (RAPA)	Participation in light, moderate, and vigorous physical activity for adults over age 50 years.	Self-report; 9 items. Response format: yes–no.	Sensitivity = 81%; specificity = 69%; positive predictive value = 77%; negative predictive value = 75%	Spearman rank order correlation coefficient, $r = 0.59$ ($p < .001$).
Regenstrief Physical Activity and Health Survey	Physical activity knowledge, perceived barriers, self-efficacy, and behavior among adults ages 55 years and older; includes very low level activity.	Interviewer-administered. 21 items with Likert scales and reporting of frequency and duration of physical activities.	Cronbach's alpha coefficients = 0.71 for self-efficacy items and 0.81 for outcome expectations items	Exploratory factor analysis revealed two dimensions (self-efficacy and outcome expectations) that explained 70% of variance in item response. Factor loadings were all over 0.50 and the expected items loaded together.
Yale Physical Activity Survey (YPAS)	Type, amount, and pattern of physical activity/exercise across eight domains in adults age 60 years and older. A seasonal adjustment score can also be calculated.	Self-, telephone-, or interviewer-administered. Assesses participation and time spent on 25 physical activities across 5 activity dimensions.	Test–retest coefficients ranged from $r = 0.42$ ($p < .01$) to 0.65 ($p < 0.01$) for the eight summary indexes	Weekly energy expenditure ($r = -0.47, p = 0.01$) and daily hours sitting ($r = 0.53, p = 0.01$) correlated with resting diastolic blood pressure. Activity index correlated with estimated VO_{2max} ($r = 0.58, p = 0.004$) and inversely with body fat ($r = -0.43, p = 0.03$). Index of vigorous activity correlated with estimated VO2max ($r = 0.60, p = 0.003$). Moving index correlated with BMI ($r = -0.37, p = 0.06$).

information on these measures, noting that reliability and validity data available varied.

Accelerometry. Whereas self-report measures often are utilized to assess type, duration, amount, and frequency of physical activity, recall bias and variations in health, mental, and emotional states may affect the accuracy of self-report in older adults (Rikli, 2000). Accelerometry, or wearable motion-sensing technology, provides an objective measure of daytime and nighttime movement volume and intensity and serves as an alternative method to recording not only structured exercise but also free-living activities (Murphy, 2009). Use of accelerometers significantly improves accuracy in the characterization of physical activity when compared with self-report (T. J. Harris, Owen, Victor, Adams, & Cook, 2009). In older adults, high levels of compliance suggest that accelerometry is a feasible method for assessing activity (Davis & Fox, 2007).

Diet. Typical methods of dietary assessment range from 24 hr recalls to self-monitoring dietary records spanning 1 or more days to food frequency questionnaires that inquire about foods consumed within the previous year. A 24 hr dietary recall consists of self-reported foods and beverages consumed within the previous day. Given the immediate recall period and ability for interviewer probing, this method typically provides reliable information on eating behaviors and dietary intake while lessening bias and burden of respondents (Thompson & Subar, 2013). In addition, given that interviewers typically record responses, assessment is not biased by level of physical functioning or literacy of older adult respondents (Thompson & Subar, 2013). Mainly utilized in large epidemiological studies to provide information on usual dietary intake, food frequency questionnaires, such as the National Cancer Institute's Diet History Questionnaire or the Block Food Frequency Questionnaire, assess frequency of consumption and portion size over the previous year using a large data set of food items (Subar et al., 2001). Food frequency questionnaires are self-administered, relatively inexpensive, and provide useful approximations of typical long-term dietary intake when compared with short-term records.

In general, lower cognitive scores and barriers associated with comprehension, item order, and format have been associated with errors in reports of total energy intake by older adults (Subar et al., 1995), suggesting the importance of assessing cognitive functioning to promote accurate dietary (Pope et al., 2007). Adaptations for dietary assessment, including checklists, pictures, and technology have increased reliability and validity of these reports (Thompson & Subar, 2013). Changes in question structuring also have been made to more recent versions of food frequency questionnaires to improve validity for older adults (Thompson et al., 2002). In addition, direct observation or shelf inventories may be appropriate to best characterize dietary intake in older adults who are unable to provide self-report because of cognitive or physical limitations (de Vries, De Groot, & van Staveren, 2009; Thompson & Subar, 2013). Proxy reports made by a caregiver also may be an alternative for older adults with cognitive impairment. A study of White, community-dwelling women age 65 years and older and their self-designated proxies found consistency in proxy report of easily observable behaviors, such as dressing and walking (Magaziner et al., 1996), suggesting that eating behavior may be as easily observed effectively. Toward that end, spousal proxy reports of diet and health behaviors have been found to be reliable (mean kappa = 0.73) among older Chinese adults (Liang, Binns, Lee, Huang, & Hu, 2008). Further research with older adults is warranted to support this relationship, although research with parents as proxies of children's eating suggest that direct observation of eating behavior is crucial for reliable reporting.

Health-related quality of life. Measures of HRQOL include generic and diabetes-specific measurement tools. For diabetes research, the most common measures of quality of life are the various versions of the Short-Form General Health Survey (McHorney, Ware, Rogers, Raczek, & Lu, 1992) including the SF-12, SF-20, and SF-36 (Rubin & Peyrot, 1999). The Illness Perception Questionnaire-Revised (IPQ-R) measures perceptions of illness via 14 yes–no items, 50 Likert-scale items, and three open-ended items that make up nine dimensions: identity, timeline acute or chronic, consequences, personal control, treatment control, illness coherences, timeline cyclical, emotional representations, and causes (Moss-Morris et al., 2002). The IPQ-R has been translated into more than 15 languages, and it has been adapted for more than 10 different illnesses including diabetes.

Assessment Controversy

As with all self-report measures, recall and social desirability are barriers to accurate reporting. One potential solution to recall deficits is ecological momentary assessment (EMA), which can be utilized in the form of daily diaries, experience sampling in which participants receive signals randomly throughout the day to make reports, and event-based sampling in which records are made when a specific activity (e.g., physical activity, meal) occurs (Cain, Depp, & Jeste, 2009). Given that cognitive impairments in older adults, as well as mood and recall bias, may influence self-report data, this method of monitoring within the moment proves useful for ecological validity in aging research. EMA has used been effectively with older adults in a number of studies, including those examining the relationship between exercise and pain (Focht, Ewing, Gauvin, & Rajeski, 2002), positive affect (Steptoe & Wardle, 2011), perception of discrimination (Taylor, Kamarck, & Shiffman, 2004), and cortisol variation (Ice, Katz-Stein, Himes, & Kane, 2004).

Among older adults with chronic illness, sensory or fine motor deficits and fatigue associated with physical comorbidities may create challenges for self-report measure administration. Although an interview format can be time intensive for administrators, it is effective and often preferable for older adults, given that it is the least burdensome mode (Bowling, 2005) and can help to build rapport with respondents in clinical or research settings.

INTERVENTION

There are multiple levels of intervention, all of which can be affected by provider, client, and family factors as well as by the intervention itself. Choosing the right intervention for the older adult frequently requires the involvement of all of these individuals as well as members of the medical team.

Client–Provider Issues Related to Intervention

Expectancies regarding intervention and outcome. Stigma around mental health issues remains a significant barrier to treatment for many older adults, particularly among older African Americans (Connor et al., 2010). Thus, treatment engagement may be maximized by focusing on health behavior change in a more "coaching" or educational format, perhaps including non-mental-health professionals, such as dietitians or physical therapists. In this context, behavioral activation and improved diet related to obesity or diabetes may improve mental health symptoms. Discussing the potential improvement in "motivation" and energy that may come with increased activity also may be less stigmatizing than discussing behavioral activation in the context of depression. In turn, improving even subsyndromal depressive symptoms helps to improve diabetic symptoms through increased engagement in treatment adherence (Katon et al., 2004; Van Tilburg et al., 2001).

Individual and family perception of disease is a key component of treatment expectancy (Petrie, Jago, & Devcich, 2007). In an ethnographic study of Mexican Americans with diabetes, common themes of diabetes attributions among participant responses involved being "punished" for self-indulgent acts in earlier life (76%) or relating to a life event that happened to them (45%; Hunt et al., 1998). This finding highlights the importance of assessing an individual's understanding of his or her diabetes diagnosis across cultures, as disease conceptualizations can influence self-efficacy, and thus level and manner of diabetes self-management behaviors (Abubakari et al., 2011). Hunt et al. (1998) reinforced that traditional medical explanations of diagnosis and treatment of diabetes should be accompanied by explanations that have contextual relevance to the individual with diabetes to maximize understanding of the disease and its management.

Education of the older adult and family about geropsychological assessment and treatment. Physical health and mental health are related to higher levels of social support, which often includes familial support (D. W. Brown et al., 2004). Fisher and Weihs

(2000) reviewed research that demonstrated the overall effectiveness of educating the diabetic individual's family on chronic disease management. Rather than viewing the family's role as one limited to support, they viewed disease management within the context of the individual's everyday environment. Both the home environment and the family's knowledge of the disease and disease management had an effect on the diabetic individual's level of engagement in self-care and diabetes outcomes. Providing education about the disorder itself, along with communication skills and problem solving related to disease management, is key (Miklowitz, 2004).

Geropsychologist–client relationship

issues. Dealing with chronic conditions, such as obesity and diabetes, is a common theme in work with older adults. Particularly in obesity, diabetes, and comorbid mood disorders, it can be difficult to determine whether symptoms have a psychological or physical etiology. Knight (2004) acknowledged the tendency of older adults to have less ability than younger adults to determine that a problem is psychological and not physical (i.e., racing heart associated with anxiety). Thus, Knight highlighted the importance of educating older adult patients in the therapeutic setting, including explicit discussion of diagnosis and treatment plan. Geropsychologists are encouraged to learn about the medical conditions of their clients and to work closely with medical professionals in treatment. This cotreatment allows for more extensive coverage of symptoms but may create challenges in confidentiality; thus, sensitivity to what other providers need to know is important.

Confidentiality also may be an issue in working with the families of older adults. Involving families in treatment can improve treatment outcome, related both to treatment adherence for older adults with obesity and diabetes (Wen, Shepherd, & Parchman, 2004) and to maximizing coping with disease management (D. W. Brown et al., 2004). The older adult may not want family to be privy to all elements of treatment, however; thus, discussion of confidentiality limits before family involvement is recommended. Family dynamics may complicate the picture (Fisher & Weihs, 2000), particularly if the

family is not supportive of the older adult's health behavior change being addressed in treatment. Families may even attempt to sabotage efforts toward diabetes treatment adherence (Mayberry & Obsorne, 2012).

Geropsychologists must be sensitive to real and perceived barriers to treatment adherence for older adults with obesity and diabetes. For example, obesity can impair mobility and pose barriers to engaging in behavioral activation goals, like physical or social activity (Houston et al., 2009). Diabetes can affect the psychotherapy process. Chronically uncontrolled blood sugar levels, for example, may reinforce negative thought processes that the patient may be trying to manage and potentially could lead to learned helplessness (Van Tilburg et al., 2001).

Obesity Treatment Approaches

In 2014, the American College of Cardiology/American Heart Association Task Force on Practice Guidelines issued treatment guidelines recommending weight loss in older adults when BMI is more than 30 kg/m^2 (M. D. Jensen et al., 2014). Given the lack of consistent data demonstrating beneficial effects of weight loss in older adults and potential adverse effects on muscle and bone loss, the American Society of Nutrition and the North American Association for the Study of Obesity provided an updated position statement supporting weight loss in obese older adults only if functional limitations or medical comorbidities are present (Villareal et al., 2005). Treatment options available for weight loss in older adults are similar to those recommended for the general adult population and include lifestyle intervention with diet, physical activity, and behavioral modification, pharmacotherapy, and surgery (Villareal et al., 2005).

Medical Obesity Interventions

Pharmacotherapy. Older adults are mainly excluded from clinical trials assessing efficacy and safety of pharmacologic agents; therefore, evidence is insufficient to support use of medication for weight loss in older adults (Mathus-Vliegen, 2012; Villareal et al., 2005). Currently, two prescription drugs have been approved by the U.S. Food and Drug Administration for long-term use in the treatment of patients with a BMI more than 30 kg/m² and patients with a BMI of 27–29.9 kg/m² with comorbid obesity-related medical complications. Orlistat (Xenical), a lipase inhibitor, blocks digestion and absorption of up to 30% of dietary fat. Clinical trials have demonstrated a 2%–3% increased weight loss compared with placebo (Mathus-Vliegen, 2012), and an analysis of an older adult subpopulation demonstrated similar effectiveness as in younger adults (Hauptman, Lucas, Boldrin, Collins, & Segal, 2000); however, common side effects include gastrointestinal difficulties, such as flatulence, fecal incontinence, oily spotting, and abdominal cramping (Mathus-Vliegen, 2012; Villareal et al., 2005). Specifically, an older adult population may be at greater risk for fecal incontinence but also may experience benefit with problems of constipation (Mathus-Vliegen, 2012; Villareal et al., 2005). Vitamin supplements also are recommended, as Orlistat reduces absorption of fat-soluble vitamins, such as vitamin D (Mathus-Vliegen, 2012).

In July 2012, the U.S. Food and Drug Administration approved Qsymia, a combination of phentermine (appetite suppressant) and topiramate (antiepileptic) for long-term obesity management. Taken once daily in conjunction with a reduced-calorie diet and increased physical activity, Qsymia works to decrease appetite and increase satiety and has resulted in weight losses of 7%–9% after 1 year of treatment (Cameron, Whiteside, & McKeage, 2012). Although effects in older adults have yet to be demonstrated, side effects that may cause difficulties within an older adult population include elevated heart rate, acute-angle closure glaucoma, cognitive impairment, suicidal ideation and behavior, and metabolic acidosis (Goldenberg, 2012).

Bariatric surgery. Typically reserved for individuals with BMIs greater than 40 kg/m² and those with BMIs between 35 and 39.9 kg/m² with at least one severe chronic medical comorbidity (e.g., hypertension or Type 2 diabetes; NIH Conference, 1991; Yermilov, McGory, Shekelle, Ko, & Maggard, 2009), bariatric surgery serves as the most effective treatment for obesity (Villareal et al., 2005). Roux-en-Y gastric bypass and laparoscopic adjustable gastric band procedures are the most common bariatric surgeries performed (Villareal et al., 2005). Bariatric surgery in older adults remains somewhat uncommon even after the Medicare Coverage Advisory Committee provided evidence supporting the effectiveness and safety of these surgeries in older adults. From 1999 to 2005, only 2.7% of all bariatric surgeries within academic medical centers were performed on older adults (Varela, Wilson, & Nguyen, 2006).

Results from mainly laparoscopic surgery suggest that older adults can achieve significant weight loss, reductions in medical comorbidities, and decreases in medication requirements (Mathus-Vliegen, 2012); however, scientific evidence of effectiveness of bariatric surgery within an older adult population remains limited. Weight loss outcomes appear equivalent between older and midlife and young adult surgical populations (Heinberg, Ashton, Windover, & Merrell, 2012), but older adults may be susceptible to more perioperative morbidity and mortality, longer hospital stays, and fewer improvements in obesity-related medical comorbidities (Varela et al., 2006; Villareal et al., 2005). Older adults who undergo bariatric surgery do not demonstrate increased psychological risk when compared with their younger counterparts (Heinberg et al., 2012); however, preoperative evaluation should include assessment of cognitive capability, social support, stressors, coping ability, outcome expectancies, adherence factors, and mental health issues that may affect postoperative outcomes (Henrickson, Ashton, Windover, & Heinberg, 2009; Villareal et al., 2005). Henrickson et al. (2009) have provided more detailed suggestions for conducting psychological evaluations in older adults interested in bariatric surgery. In addition, given inadequate nutrient intake is common postsurgery, it is recommended that patients take multivitamin supplements to maintain proper nutritional health (Malinowski, 2006).

Medical Diabetes Interventions

A wide variety of antihyperglycemic agents exist to treat diabetes, with the goal of reducing HbA1c. Metformin is a medication that decreases glucose absorption from food, and glucose production by the liver, along with increasing responsiveness to insulin. Metformin often serves as the first-line medication given its low risk of hypoglycemia (Kim et al., 2012; Sue Kirkman et al., 2012); however, older adults with chronic renal insufficiency and heart failure may be at risk of lactic acidosis when taking metformin (Kirkman et al., 2012). Sulfonylureas are a class of medications that increase pancreatic production of insulin and often are used in conjunction with metformin. They may increase the risk of hypoglycemia and subsequent loss of consciousness, falls, fractures, and decreased independence (Kim et al., 2012). Additional medications include meglitinides, incretins, glucagon-like peptide-1 (GLP-1) receptor agonists, dipeptidyl peptidase-4 (DPP-4) inhibitors, thiazolidinediones, and alpha-glucose inhibitors (Kim et al., 2012). Similar to the previously mentioned adverse effects, these agents must be monitored closely for adverse events in older adults. Insulin therapy has been shown to effectively reduce HbA1c levels by 1.5%–3.5% (Kim et al., 2012) and often is required for older adults with chronic diabetes. Among older adults, concerns of manual dexterity, vision problems, and cognitive impairment may lead to difficulties with self-injections and glucose self-monitoring (Kim et al., 2012).

Utilizing intensive treatment to achieve HbA1c less than 6% typically is not recommended for older adults because of potential complications, little benefit, and possible increased mortality (Kim et al., 2012). Given the duration of diabetes and comorbid conditions, the California Healthcare Foundation/American Geriatric Society Panel on Improving Care for Elders With Diabetes (2003) advised that treatment in relatively healthy older adults in good functional status should target HbA1c levels of 7% or lower. For those experiencing greater frailty, having a life expectancy of less than 5 years, and being at risk for negative outcomes with intensive glycemic control, the panel recommended a more flexible HbA1c level of 8%.

Lifestyle Interventions for Obesity and Diabetes

Lifestyle interventions for both obesity and diabetes target diet and physical activity. Interventions for those with obesity are associated with clinically beneficial reductions of 7%–10% total body weight (Diabetes Prevention Program Research Group, 2002; Look AHEAD Research Group & Wing, 2010; Jensen et al., 2014). These types of interventions are just as effective in late middle-age and older adults as in younger participants (Villareal et al., 2005). Typically, an energy deficit of 500–1,000 kcal/day to promote a 0.4–0.9 kg loss per week (Jensen et al., 2014; Villareal et al., 2005) and regular aerobic activity to improve aerobic function and endurance are recommended (Houston et al., 2009). Although a balanced diet of 15–30% energy from protein, 25–30% from fats, and 40–60% from carbohydrates is recommended, older adults also benefit from adequate supplementation of calcium, vitamin D, vitamin B-12, fiber, and multivitamins and minerals to promote bone health and adequate nutrient absorption (Houston et al., 2009). Given the risk of sarcopenia during weight loss, older adults may benefit from increased protein intake of 1.0–1.2 g/kg (Houston et al., 2009; Mathus-Vliegen, 2012).

The American College of Sports Medicine, the American Heart Association, and the U.S. Department of Health and Human Services (USDHHS, 2008) specifically state that regular physical activity that includes aerobic and muscle-strengthening activities is essential for healthy aging of adults 65 years of age and older (Nelson et al., 2007). Specifically, older adults need a minimum of 30 min of moderate-intensity aerobic physical activity on 5 days each week, or 20 min of vigorous-intensity aerobic activity on 3 days per week. In addition, 2 or more days of muscle-strengthening activities and flexibility-promoting activities as well as balance exercises are recommended to promote health and reduce disease risk in older adults (Nelson et al., 2007; USDHHS, 2008). Even 3 days of progressive resistance training has been shown to be effective in improving glycemic control, as a randomized control trial of Latino elders demonstrated (Castaneda et al., 2002). Recommendations also note that older adults should determine intensity level relative to their fitness level and should be cognizant of their abilities and any chronic conditions that may influence their ability to participate in regular physical activity (USDHHS, 2008).

In addition to diet and physical activity, lifestyle interventions typically include behavioral components to facilitate behavioral change. These include self-monitoring, problem solving, goal setting, stimulus control, social support, cognitive restructuring, and contingency management (Jensen et al., 2014). For those with diabetes, interventions also include self-monitoring of blood glucose and blood pressure, medication and insulin self-administration, identification of potential barriers to learning (cultural, social, cognitive, and literacy), smoking cessation, and improving coping skills (Glasgow et al., 1992; Rizvi, 2007). Self-management programs are most effective using the combination of group and individual intervention with educators from various disciplines (California Healthcare Foundation/American Geriatrics Society Panel on Improving Care for Elders With Diabetes, 2003).

Research supports the effectiveness of lifestyle interventions in older adults. For example, the Diabetes Prevention Program Research Group (Knowler et al., 2002) demonstrated that lifestyle intervention resulted in lower onset of diabetes in people at risk when compared with metformin or placebo. Specifically, when comparing across age-groups, results demonstrated that older adults participating in the lifestyle intervention experienced the lowest diabetes incidence rates and had the greatest weight loss, physical activity, and adherence. At 6 months of the lifestyle intervention, 60% of participants 65 years of age and older achieved the 7% weight loss goal, compared with 43% of those participants under age 45 years. At the end of 3 years, 63% of the older adults met and maintained this weight loss goal, compared with 27% of those under age 45 years (Wing et al., 2004). Similarly, the Trial of Nonpharmacologic Interventions in the Elderly demonstrated that older adults with hypertension were able to modify dietary and physical activity through a lifestyle intervention to lose weight and reduce sodium levels to maintain blood pressure levels without the use of medication (Whelton et al., 1998). Lifestyle intervention in conjunction with a comprehensive exercise intervention has been studied in obese older adults at particular risk of sarcopenia and functional decline (Anton et al., 2011). Results demonstrated a clinically significant weight loss, increased walking speed, maintenance of knee extension strength, and improvements in a 4-meter walk test, repeated chair stands, and balance tests. In a meta-analysis of chronic disease self-management programs for older adults, 20 diabetes studies reported HbA1c outcomes, with a pooled effect size of -0.36 (95% confidence interval [CI] $= -0.51$ to -0.21), a reduction of HbA1c of approximately 0.81% (moving from an HbA1c of 8.0%–7.19%; Chodosh et al., 2005). Three specific interventions, which focused mainly on diet and education (Falkenberg et al., 1986; Glasgow et al., 1992; Jaber et al., 1996), demonstrated a pooled effect size for HbA1c of -0.62 (95% CI $= -0.99$ to -0.25), supporting the effectiveness and use of diet and education-focused self-management interventions. Guidelines for adapting such approaches to an older population are provided later in this chapter. Taken together, these studies demonstrate the effectiveness of lifestyle interventions in promoting weight loss, reducing disease risk, and maintaining physical functioning in older adults.

For those with great difficulty in creating behavior change, particularly those with depression, anxiety, or other comorbid mental health issues, psychotherapy may be indicated. Motivational interviewing (MI) and cognitive–behavioral therapy (CBT) have growing bodies of evidence for their effectiveness in health behavior change as well as treating depression in older adults with diabetes and obesity.

MI is designed to explore ambivalence about behavior change, formulate individual goals in behavioral terms, problem solve around barriers to change, explore differences between goals and current behaviors, and support self-efficacy to change behaviors. MI has been shown to effectively improve health behaviors related to physical activity, diet, cholesterol, blood pressure and glycemic control among older adults (for a review, see Cummings, Cooper, & Cassie, 2009).

For older adults experiencing emotional distress in the context of diabetes, CBT may be employed to understand the links between the physical experience of disease symptoms and both cognitions and emotions, to identify and modify negative or unrealistic thoughts about illness or ability to manage it, to increase motivation, to increase self-care activities, and to reduce distress. Some studies of CBT for depression and diabetes have included older adults and reported significant decreases depressive symptoms, although no changes were found in glycemic control (Gonzalez et al., 2010; Katon et al., 2004).

A number of studies have found that treating anxiety with interventions that include biofeedback-assisted relaxation training (BART) improved glucose tolerance and reduced long-term hyperglycemia among adults with Type 2 diabetes (Surwit et al., 2002). Traditional relaxation training also demonstrated improved hemoglobin levels but not glucose tolerance and may be most useful for individuals who are most responsive to stress (Lane, McCaskill, Ross, Feinglos, & Surwit, 1993). From a pharmacological standpoint, benzodiazepines have shown improvements in anxiety among Type 2 diabetics (Okada et al., 1994), and alprazolam use specifically has led to improved glycemic control (Lustman et al., 1995). Benzodiazepines have significant risks for older adults, however (for more information, see Volume 1, Chapter 24, this handbook).

CLINICAL APPLICATIONS OF INTERVENTIONS

Factors including socioeconomic status, education, literacy, stigma, acculturation, and language all affect the manner in which older adults experience and benefit from intervention for diabetes and obesity. Similarly, the composition and protocols of the intervention team have a significant impact.

Contextual Issues

Socioeconomic influences on clinical application. Risk factors for the combination of diabetes and depression include low SES (Katon, 2008), less education (Blazer et al., 2002; Katon, 2008), being unmarried (Katon, 2008), poor social support (Katon, 2008), female gender (Blazer et al., 2002; Katon, 2008), African American race (Blazer et al., 2002; Katon, 2008), Hispanic, Asian–Pacific Islander, and Native American race (Katon, 2008), younger adult (Katon, 2008), higher BMI (Blazer et al., 2002), and both functional and cognitive impairment (Blazer et al., 2002). Similarly, risk factors for obesity and depression include younger age,

female gender, lower education, functional impairment, and diabetes (Blazer et al., 2002).

A. F. Brown and colleagues' (2004) review found that low-resourced adults with a diagnosis of diabetes are affected by "access to and quality of care; social support; community resources; diabetes-related knowledge; communication with providers; ability to adhere to recommended medication; exercise and dietary regimens; and treatment choices" (p. 63). This often relates to the role of community characteristics in the health of its members, taking into consideration the accessibility of health care facilities, places to engage in physical activity, and healthy food options as well as the outlook of the neighborhood toward overall health and health behaviors.

Lower education and lower health literacy are associated with more frequent hospital admissions and poorer overall health. Furthermore, despite traditional education about diabetes, those with lower health literacy are at risk for higher levels of HbA1c and higher rates of retinopathy (A. F. Brown et al., 2004). Language barriers also play a role in diabetes outcomes and self-management behaviors. Adults in the United States with Type 2 diabetes who reported difficulty with English language checked their blood glucose levels less often (A. F. Brown et al., 2004). Furthermore, non-English speakers are less likely to get regular health care, screening, and preventative services than English speakers, and are less satisfied with the health care that they do receive. This may be exacerbated for older individuals whose cultural representations of illness may be more ingrained and less consistent with evidence-based interventions.

Team intervention. Although stigma surrounding working with mental health professionals—even related to diabetes or obesity—is significant for older adults, particularly minority older adults, providing care within an interdisciplinary team can help to reduce this stigma. Evidence-based team interventions based in primary care have been increasing for older adults, including IMPACT (Improving Mood-Promoting Access to Collaborative Treatment; Unützer et al., 2002), PROSPECT (Gallo et al., 2007), PRISM-E (Krahn et al., 2006), and BRIGHTEN (Emery, Lapidos,

Eisenstein, Ivan, & Golden, 2012) as well as the Veterans Administration primary care and home-based primary care programs (Felker et al., 2004; Zeiss & Karlin, 2008). These models may be ideal for holistic care that can involve multiple team members, including the older adult's primary care physician. Research also shows that older adults of all ethnic and SES backgrounds benefit from these programs equally (Areán et al., 2005; Rodríguez-Morales, Ivan, Woodhead, Golden, & Emery, 2010).

Case Examples

Case example 1. Mr. Martinez is an 82-year-old Mexican American man who initially presented in primary care with obesity, hypertension, and an HbA1c of 8.5. He was screened for depression using the Patient Health Questionnaire-9 and was found to have moderate symptoms (15/27). After a complete psychosocial diagnostic interview with the geropsychologist, in which he was found to meet criteria for a moderate major depressive disorder, he was referred for and engaged in CBT. Given his mild reticence to engage in insight-oriented work, along with his moderate symptom level, the geropsychologist initially engaged Mr. Martinez in behavioral activation for both his depression and his diabetes. He was successful in involving his family to increase his physical activity, make dietary adjustments, and regularly check his blood sugar, which initially led to a 5% total weight loss and decrease in depressive symptoms. Over several weeks, however, these efforts failed to make a significant difference in his blood glucose or blood pressure, which led to an increase in depressive symptoms. The geropsychologist challenged thoughts that his behavior had been useless by highlighting improved energy, mood, weight loss, and decreased arthritis pain in his knees to minimize learned helplessness. Mr. Martinez was encouraged to speak with his physician and dietitian about his concerns. In reviewing Mr. Martinez's case more closely, his physician noted that permissive hypertension and slightly elevated HbA1c were preferable to risking hypotension and hypoglycemia, which could exacerbate Mr. Martinez's fall risk (Durso, 2006). The dietitian also reviewed his diet and discovered that Mr. Martinez continued to

drink a quart of orange juice per day, believing that it would help him stay healthy. In psychotherapy, Mr. Martinez was able to recognize the shift in perspective that this permission offered and the strong positive effect it had on his mood as well as to problem solve for other drink options to maximize his health that would not increase blood sugar. Psychotherapy was terminated when Mr. Martinez had demonstrated an ability to maintain his behavioral activation and health behaviors, along with challenging his own negative thoughts about his diabetes management.

Case example 2. Ms. Jackson, a 72-year-old White woman, was referred to the geropsychologist by her endocrinologist, who was concerned about Ms. Jackson's increasingly poor treatment adherence and control of her diabetes, weight gain, and new onset symptoms of anxiety. Ms. Jackson was hesitant to engage in psychotherapy and required multiple conversations over time with the endocrinologist to understand the reason for referral and potential benefits of psychotherapy. When Ms. Jackson finally presented for therapy, she was guarded and was sure that the geropsychologist could not understand her very low income, low education, and highly religious life experience. The geropsychologist gently explored Ms. Jackson's background, openly acknowledging the differences between them. Ms. Jackson revealed that although she had a small pension and Medicare coverage, she quickly fell into the "donut hole" and was not able to afford her diabetes medications. She recently had become dependent on a cane for walking due to her arthritis, which she feared would make her a target for violence in her neighborhood, so she had stopped her regular walking routine. Both of these issues significantly increased anxiety (initial Geriatric Anxiety Inventory score 12/20), as Ms. Jackson knew that her medications and exercise were key to her health, but she felt powerless to make changes. Ms. Jackson also noted that she had fallen a few times recently and wondered whether the new medication she was given for anxiety may have something to do with it. The geropsychologist provided Ms. Jackson with resources to apply for medication coverage assistance through her local senior center. While at the senior center, Ms. Jackson discovered that there were yoga and tai chi classes offered at very low cost. She began taking classes, which not only helped to increase physical activity and manage her weight but also resulted in improvements in her arthritis. The geropsychologist discussed medications with the endocrinologist and provided information about risks of benzodiazepines with older adults (e.g., Cumming & Le Couteur, 2003). The geropsychologist worked with Ms. Jackson to examine the similarity in sensations of hypoglycemia and anxiety, recognizing when she needed to check her blood sugar and when she needed to engage in relaxation. Ms. Jackson was also open to exploring the use of her religious faith through meditative prayer to manage anxiety. Although the therapist believed that Ms. Jackson could benefit from further anxiety relapse prevention, Ms. Jackson decided to terminate therapy once her symptoms had reduced to a mild level (Geriatric Anxiety Inventory score 5/20) and her medication issues were resolved.

Case discussion. These cases both highlight a number of factors. First, working closely with physicians and other providers is important in managing diabetes and obesity. Awareness of and ability to communicate about potential medication interactions, appropriate lab values for older adults, dietary factors, and community resources for maximizing treatment adherence are key for geropsychologists working with this population. Second, the importance of physicians having some understanding of the role of psychotherapy in managing obesity and diabetes cannot be overestimated. Thus, education of potential referral sources is highly valuable. Third, being creative in the use of a client's own strengths (e.g., religion, family) can be highly effective in minimizing both physical and emotional symptoms.

FUTURE DIRECTIONS

The Role of the Geropsychologist
The face of health care is changing rapidly and becoming much more focused on effective management of chronic conditions, including diabetes and obesity. This partly is due to the quickly growing population of older adults with multiple chronic conditions in the context of diminishing resources for treating them. Geropsychologists' expertise in health behavior change and understanding of the interplay between physical and mental health is perfectly suited for the advent of patient-centered medical homes and accountable care organizations, but we will need to magnify our voice to ensure that we are included in the teams.

Next Steps in Research and Clinical Application
The Diabetes Mellitus Interagency Coordinating Committee highlighted research with older adults as a priority area for diabetes translational research (Garfield et al., 2003). This research should include a broader spectrum of sociodemographic factors, to best understand modes of overcoming barriers to effective obesity and diabetes management (Katon et al., 2004). Adapting obesity and diabetes interventions for challenges common to older adults, such as sensory loss, ambulatory challenges, and cognitive decline also are warranted. This may require creativity in interventions reaching older adults where they are, and by people they trust, such as faith-based interventions that may work to modify food culture more broadly (see Boltri et al., 2006); expanding the existing primary care (e.g., Emery et al., 2012) and home-based primary care models (see Leff, Edes, & Kinosian, 2011); and examining the new challenges and strengths that the baby boom generation will bring to later life, including increased web-based programming for older adults (e.g., Bond et al., 2007).

References

Abubakari, A., Jones, M. C., Lauder, W., Kirk, A., Anderson, J., & Devendra, D. (2011). Associations between knowledge, illness perceptions, self-management and metabolic control of type 2 diabetes among African and European-origin patients. *Journal of Nursing and Healthcare of Chronic Illness, 3,* 245–256. doi:10.1111/j.1752-9824.2011.01098.x

Accardi, G., Caruso, C., Colonna-Romano, G., Camarda, C., Monastero, R., & Candore, G. (2012). Can Alzheimer's disease be a form of type 3 diabetes? *Rejuvenation Research, 15,* 217–221. doi:10.1089/rej.2011.1289

Alberti, K. G., Eckel, R. H., Grundy, S. M., Zimmet, P. Z., Cleeman, J. I., Donaton, K. A., . . . International Association for the Study of Obesity. (2009). Harmonizing the metabolic syndrome: A joint interim statement of the International Diabetes Federation Task Force on Epidemiology and Prevention; National Heart, Lung, and Blood Institute; American Heart Association; World Heart Federation; International Atherosclerosis Society; and International Association for the Study of Obesity. *Circulation, 120,* 1640–1645. doi:10.1161/ CIRCULATIONAHA.109.192644

Alexopoulos, G., Meyers, B. S., Young, R. C., Kakuma, T., Silbersweig, D., & Charlson, M. (1997). Clinically defined vascular depression. *American Journal of Psychiatry, 154,* 562–565.

Ali, S., Stone, M. A., Peters, J. L., Davies, M. J., & Khunti, K. (2006). The prevalence of comorbid depression in adults with type 2 diabetes: A systematic review and meta-analysis. *Diabetic Medicine, 23,* 1165–1173. doi:10.1111/j.1464-5491.2006.01943.x

American Diabetes Association. (2012). Standards of medical care in diabetes, 2012 (position statement). *Diabetes Care, 35*(Suppl. 1), S11–S63. doi:10.2337/ dc12-s011

Anderson, R. J., Freedland, K. E., Clouse, R. E., & Lustman, P. J. (2001). The prevalence of comorbid depression in adults with diabetes: A meta-analysis. *Diabetes Care, 24,* 1069–1078. doi:10.2337/diacare. 24.6.1069

Anton, S. D., Manini, T. M., Milsom, V. A., Dubyak, P., Cesari, M., Cheng, J., . . . Perri, M. G. (2011). Effects of a weight loss plus exercise program on physical function in overweight, older women: A randomized controlled trial. *Clinical Interventions in Aging, 6,* 141–149. doi:10.2147/CIA.S17001

Arcury, T. A., Bell, R. A., Snively, B. M., Smith, S. L., Skelly, A. H., Wetmore, L. K., & Quandt, S. A. (2006). Complementary and alternative medicine use as health self-management: Rural older adults with diabetes. *The Journals of Gerontology, Series B: Psychological Sciences and Social Sciences, 61,* 62–70. doi:10.1093/geronb/61.2.S62

Areán, P. A., Ayalon, L., Hunkeler, E., Lin, E., Tang, L., Harpole, L., . . . Unützer, J. (2005). Improving depression care for older, minority patients in primary care. *Medical Care, 43,* 381–390. doi:10.1097/01.mlr.0000156852.09920.b1

Atkins, R. C., Briganti, E. M., Lewis, J. B., Hunsicker, L. G., Braden, G., Champion de Crespigny, P. J., . . . Lewis, E. J. (2005). Proteinuria reduction and progression to renal failure in patients with type 2 diabetes mellitus and overt nephropathy. *American Journal of Kidney Diseases, 45,* 281–287. doi:10.1053/j. ajkd.2004.10.019

Bainbridge, K. E., Hoffman, H. J., & Cowie, C. C. (2011). Risk factors for hearing impairment among U.S. adults with diabetes: National Health and Nutrition Examination Survey 1999–2004. *Diabetes Care, 34,* 1540–1545. doi:10.2337/dc10-2161

Bankoski, A., Harris, T. B., McClain, J. J., Brychta, R. J., Caserotti, P., Chen, K. Y., . . . Koster, A. (2011). Sedentary activity associated with metabolic syndrome independent of physical activity. *Diabetes Care, 34,* 497–503. doi:10.2337/dc10-0987

Berger, B. G. (1988). The role of physical activity in the life quality of older adults. In W. Spirdusko & H. M. Eckert (Eds.), *Physical activity and aging* (pp. 42–58). Champaign, IL: Human Kinetics.

Biggs, M. L., Mukamal, K. J., Lucksinger, J. A., Ix, J. H., Carnethon, M. R., Newman, A. B., . . . Siscovick, D. S. (2010). Association between adiposity in midlife and older age and risk of diabetes in older adults. *JAMA, 303,* 2504–2512. doi:10.1001/jama.2010.843

Blazer, D. G., Moody-Ayers, S., Craft-Morgan, J., & Burchett, B. (2002). Depression in diabetes and obesity: Racial/ethnic/gender issues in older adults. *Journal of Psychosomatic Research, 53,* 913–916. doi:10.1016/S0022-3999(02)00314-8

Boltri, J. M., Davis-Smith, M., Zayas, L. E., Shellenberger, S., Seale, J. P., Blalock, T. W., & Mbadinuju, A. (2006). Developing a church-based diabetes prevention program with African Americans. Focus group findings. *Diabetes Educator, 32,* 901–909. doi:10.1177/0145721706295010

Bond, G. E., Burr, R., Wolf, F. M., Price, M., McCurry, S. M., & Teri, L. (2007). The effects of a web-based intervention on the physical outcomes associated with diabetes among adults age 60 and older: A randomized trial. *Diabetes Technology and Therapeutics, 9,* 52–59. doi:10.1089/dia.2006.0057

Bowling, A. (2005). Mode of questionnaire administration can have serious effects on data quality. *Journal of Public Health, 27,* 281–291. doi:10.1093/pubmed/ fdi031

Brown, A. F., Ettner, S. L., Piette, J., Weinberger, M., Gregg, E., Shapiro, M. F., . . . Beckles, G. L. (2004). Socioeconomic position and health among persons with diabetes mellitus: A conceptual framework and review of the literature. *Epidemiologic Reviews, 26,* 63–77. doi:10.1093/epirev/mxh002

Brown, D. W., Balluz, L. S., Giles, W. H., Beckles, G. L., Moriarty, D. G., Ford, E. S., & Mokdad, A. H. (2004). Diabetes mellitus and health-related quality of life among older adults. Findings from the behavioral risk factor surveillance system (BRFSS). *Diabetes Research and Clinical Practice, 65,* 105–115. doi:10.1016/j.diabres.2003.11.014

Cain, A. E., Depp, C. A., & Jeste, D. V. (2009). Ecological momentary assessment in aging research: A critical review. *Journal of Psychiatric Research, 43,* 987–996. doi:10.1016/j.jpsychires.2009.01.014

California Healthcare Foundation/American Geriatrics Society Panel on Improving Care for Elders With Diabetes. (2003). Guidelines for improving the care of the older person with diabetes mellitus. *Journal of the American Geriatric Society, 51,* 265–280.

Cameron, F., Whiteside, G., & McKeage, K. (2012). Phentermine and topiramate extended release (Qsymia™): First global approval. *Drugs, 72,* 2033–2042. doi:10.2165/11640860-000000000-00000

Campayo, A., Gómez-Biel, C. H., & Lobo, A. (2011). Diabetes and depression. *Current Psychiatry Reports, 13,* 26–30. doi:10.1007/s11920-010-0165-z

Carter, J. S., Pugh, J. A., & Monterrosa, A. (1996). Non-insulin dependent diabetes mellitus in minorities in the United States. *Annals of Internal Medicine, 125,* 221–232. doi:10.7326/0003-4819-125-3-199608010-00011

Castaneda, C., Layne, J. E., Munoz-Orians, L., Gordon, P. L., Walsmith, J., Foldvari, M., . . . Nelson, M. E. (2002). A randomized controlled trial of resistance exercise training to improve glycemic control in older adults with type 2 diabetes. *Diabetes Care, 25,* 2335–2341. doi:10.2337/diacare.25.12.2335

Centers for Disease Control and Prevention. (2011). *National diabetes fact sheet: national estimates and general information on diabetes and prediabetes in the United States.* Atlanta, GA: U.S. Department of Health and Human Services, Centers for Disease Control and Prevention.

Chodosh, J., Morton, S. C., Mojica, W., Maglione, M., Suttorp, M. J., Hilton, L., . . . Shekelle, P. (2005). Meta-analysis: Chronic disease self-management programs for older adults. *Annals of Internal Medicine, 143,* 427–438. doi:10.7326/0003-4819-143-6-200509200-00007

Clark, D. O. (1999). Physical activity and its correlates among urban primary care patients aged 55 years or older. *The Journals of Gerontology, Series B: Psychological Sciences and Social Sciences, 54,* 41–48. doi:10.1093/geronb/54B.1.S41

Clifton, K. J. (2004). Mobility strategies and food shopping for low-income families. *Journal of Planning Education and Research, 23,* 402–413. doi:10.1177/0739456X04264919

Connor, K. O., Copeland, V. C., Grote, N. K., Koeske, G., Rosen, D., Reynolds, C. F., & Brown, C. (2010). Mental health treatment seeking among older adults with depression: The impact of stigma and race. *American Journal of Geriatric Psychiatry, 18,* 531–543. doi:10.109F7/JGP.0b013e3181cc0366

Cowie, C. C., Rust, K. F., Byrd-Holt, D. D., Eberhardt, M. S., Flegal, K. M., Engelgau, M. M., . . . Gregg, E. W. (2006). Prevalence of diabetes and impaired fasting glucose in adults in the U.S. population: National health and nutrition examination survey 1999–2002. *Diabetes Care, 29,* 1263–1268. doi:10.2337/dc06-0062

Creager, M. A., Lüscher, T. F., Cosentino, F., & Beckman, J. A. (2003). Diabetes and vascular disease: Pathophysiology, clinical consequences, and medical therapy: Part I. *Circulation, 108,* 1527–1532. doi:10.1161/01.CIR.0000091257.27563.32

Cukierman, T., Gerstein, H. C., & Williamson, J. D. (2005). Cognitive decline and dementia in diabetes—Systematic overview of prospective observational studies. *Diabetologia, 48,* 2460–2469. doi:10.1007/s00125-005-0023-4

Cumming, R. G., & Le Couteur, D. G. (2003). Benzodiazepines and risk of hip fractures in older people: A review of the evidence. *CNS Drugs, 17,* 825–837. doi:10.2165/00023210-200317110-00004

Cummings, S. M., Cooper, R. L., & Cassie, K. M. (2009). Motivational interviewing to affect behavioral change in older adults. *Research on Social Work Practice, 19,* 195–204

Dalton, D. S., Cruickshanks, K. J., Klein, B. E., Klein, R., Wiley, T. L., & Nondahl, D. M. (2003). The impact of hearing loss on quality of life in older adults. *Gerontologist, 43,* 661–668. doi:10.1093/geront/43.5.661

Daneman, D. (2006). Type 1 diabetes. *Lancet, 367,* 847–858. doi:10.1016/S0140-6736(06)68341-4

Davis, M. G., & Fox, K. R. (2007). Physical activity patterns assessed by accelerometry in older people. *European Journal of Applied Physiology, 100,* 581–589. doi:10.1007/s00421-006-0320-8

de la Monte, S. M., & Wands, J. R. (2008). Alzheimer's disease is type 3 diabetes—Evidence reviewed. *Journal of Diabetes Science and Technology, 2,* 1101–1113. doi:10.1177/193229680800200619

de Vries, J. H., De Groot, L. C., & van Staveren, W. A. (2009). Dietary assessment in elderly people: Experiences gained from studies in The Netherlands. *European Journal of Clinical Nutrition, 63,* S69–S74. doi:10.1038/ejcn.2008.68

Diabetes Prevention Program Research Group. (2002). The diabetes prevention program (DPP): Description of lifestyle intervention. *Diabetes Care, 25,* 2165–2171. doi:10.2337/diacare.25.12.2165

Dipietro, L., Caspersen, C. J., Ostfeld, A. M., & Nadel, E. R. (1993). A survey for assessing physical activity among older adults. *Medicine and Science in Sports and Exercise, 25,* 628–642. doi:10.1249/00005768-199305000-00016

Durso, S. C. (2006). Using clinical guidelines designed for older adults with diabetes mellitus and complex health status. *JAMA, 295,* 1935–1940. doi:10.1001/jama.295.16.1935

Elia, M. (2001). Obesity in the elderly. *Obesity Research, 9,* 244S–248S. doi:10.1038/oby.2001.126

Emanuele, N., Sacks, J., Klein, R., Reda, D., Anderson, R., Duckworth, W., & Abraira, C. (2005). Ethnicity, race, and baseline retinopathy correlates in the veteran's affairs diabetes trial. *Diabetes Care, 28,* 1954–1958. doi:10.2337/diacare.28.8.1954

Emery, E. E., Lapidos, S., Eisenstein, A., Ivan, I., & Golden, R. (2012). The BRIGHTEN Program: Implementation and evaluation of a program to Bridge Resources of an Interdisciplinary Geriatric Health Team via Electronic Networking. *Gerontologist, 52,* 857–865. doi:10.1093/geront/gns034

Engum, A., Mykletun, A., Midthjell, K., Holen, A., & Dahl, A. A. (2005). Depression and Diabetes: A large population-based study of sociodemographic, lifestyle, and clinical factors associated with depression in type 1 and type 2 diabetes. *Diabetes Care, 28,* 1904–1909. doi:10.2337/diacare.28.8.1904

Evans, M. L., & Sherwin, R. S. (2002). Blood glucose and the brain in diabetes: Between a rock and a hard place? *Current Diabetes Reports, 2,* 101–102. doi:10.1007/s11892-002-0065-7

Eye Diseases Prevalence Research Group. (2004). The prevalence of diabetic retinopathy among adults in the United States. *Archives of Ophthalmology, 122,* 552–563.

Fakhouri, T. H. I., Ogden, C. L., Carroll, M. D., Kit, B. K., & Flegal, K. M. (2012). *Prevalence of obesity among older adults in the United States, 2007–2010.* (NCHS Data Brief, No. 106). Hyattsville, MD: National Center for Health Statistics.

Falkenberg, M. G., Elwing, B. E., Goransson, A. M., Hellstrand, B. E., & Riis, U. M. (1986). Problem-oriented participatory education in the guidance of adults with non-insulin-treated type-II diabetes mellitus. *Scandinavian Journal of Primary Health Care, 4,* 157–164. doi:10.3109/02813438609014823

Felker, B. L., Barnes, R. F., Greenberg, D. M., Chaney, E. F., Shores, M. M., Gillespie-Gateley, L., . . . Mornton, C. E. (2004). Preliminary outcomes from an integrated mental health primary care team. *Psychiatric Services, 55,* 442–444. doi:10.1176/appi.ps.55.4.442

Fine, J. T., Colditz, G. A., Coakley, E. H., Moseley, G., Manson, J. E., & Willett, W. C. (1999). A prospective study of weight change and health-related quality of life in women. *JAMA, 282,* 2136–2142. doi:10.1001/jama.282.22.2136

Fisher, L., & Weihs, K. L. (2000). Can addressing family relationships improve outcomes in chronic diseases? *Journal of Family Practice, 49,* 561–566.

Flegal, K. M., Carroll, M. D., Kit, B. K., & Ogden, C. L. (2012). Prevalence of obesity and trends in the distribution of body mass index among US adults, 1999–2010. *JAMA, 307,* 491–497. doi:10.1001/jama.2012.39

Focht, B. C., Ewing, L., Gauvin, L., & Rajeski, W. J. (2002). The unique and transient impact of acute exercise on pain perception in older, overweight, or obese adults with knee osteoarthritis. *Annals of Behavioral Medicine, 24,* 201–210. doi:10.1207/S15324796ABM2403_05

Ford, E. S., Li, C., & Sattar, N. (2008). Metabolic syndrome and incident diabetes: Current state of the evidence. *Diabetes Care, 31,* 1898–1904. doi:10.2337/dc08-0423

Ford, E. S., Li, C., & Zhao, G. (2010). Prevalence and correlates of metabolic syndrome based on a harmonious definition among adults in the US. *Journal of Diabetes, 2,* 180–193. doi:10.1111/j.1753-0407.2010.00078.x

Gallo, J. J., Bogner, H. R., Morales, K., Post, E. P., Lin, J. Y., & Bruce, M. P. (2007). The effect of primary care practice-based depression intervention on mortality in older adults. *Annals of Internal Medicine, 146,* 689–698. doi:10.7326/0003-4819-146-10-200705150-00002

Garfield, S. A., Malozowski, S., Chin, M. H., Venkat Narayan, K. M., Glasgow, R. E., Green, L. W., . . . Krumholz, H. M., & the Diabetes Mellitus Interagency Coordinating Committee (DMICC) Translation Conference Working Group. (2003). Considerations for diabetes translational research in real-world settings. *Diabetes Care, 26,* 2670–2674. doi:10.2337/diacare.26.9.2670

Glasgow, R. E., Toobert, D. J., Hampson, S. E., Brown, J. E., Lewinsohn, P. M., & Donnelly, J. (1992). Improving self-care among older patients with type II diabetes: The "Sixty Something . . ." study. *Patient Education and Counseling, 19,* 61–74. doi:10.1016/0738-3991(92)90102-O

Golden, S. H., Lazo, M., Carnethon, M., Bertoni, A. G., Schreiner, P. J., Diez Roux, A. V., . . . Lyketsos, C. (2008). Examining a bidirectional association between depressive symptoms and diabetes. *JAMA, 299,* 2751–2759. doi:10.1001/jama.299.23.2751

Goldenberg, M. M. (2012). Pharmaceutical approval update. *Pharmacy and Therapeutics, 37,* 668–708.

Gonzalez, J. S., McCarl, L. A., Wexler, D. J., Cagliero, E., Delahanty, L., Soper, T. D., . . . Safren, S. A. (2010). Cognitive behavioral therapy for adherence and depression (CBT-AD) in type 2 diabetes. *Journal of Cognitive Psychotherapy, 24,* 329–343. doi:10.1891/0889-8391.24.4.329

Grigsby, A. B., Anderson, R. J., Freedland, K. E., Clouse, R. E., & Lustman, P. J. (2002). Prevalence of anxiety in adults with diabetes: A systematic review. *Journal of Psychosomatic Research, 53,* 1053–1060. doi:10.1016/S0022-3999(02)00417-8

Gustafson, D., Rothenberg, E., Blennow, K., Steen, B., & Skoog, I. (2003). An 18-year follow-up of overweight and risk of Alzheimer's disease. *Archives of Internal Medicine, 163,* 1524–1528. doi:10.1001/archinte. 163.13.1524

Hampson, S. E., Glassglow, R. E., & Strycker, L. A. (2000). Beliefs versus feelings: A comparison of personal models and depression for predicting multiple outcomes in diabetes. *British Journal of Health Psychology, 5,* 27–40. doi:10.1348/135910700168748

Hargraves, J. H., & Hadley, J. (2003). The contribution of insurance coverage and community resources to reducing racial/ethnic disparities in access to health care. *Health Services Research, 38,* 809–829. doi:10.1111/1475-6773.00148

Harris, M. I., Klein, R., Cowie, C. C., Rowland, M., & Byrd-Holt, D. D. (1998). Is the risk of diabetic retinopathy greater in non-Hispanic Blacks and Mexican Americans than in non-Hispanic whites with type 2 diabetes? *Diabetes Care, 21,* 1230–1235. doi:10.2337/diacare.21.8.1230

Harris, T. J., Owen, C. G., Victor, C. R., Adams, R., & Cook, D. G. (2009). What factors are associated with physical activity in older people, assessed objectively by accelerometry? *British Journal of Sports Medicine, 43,* 442–450. doi:10.1136/bjsm.2008.048033

Hauptman, J., Lucas, C., Boldrin, M. N., Collins, H., & Segal, K. R. (2000). Orlistat in the long-term treatment of obesity in primary care settings. *Archives of Family Medicine, 9,* 160–167. doi:10.1001/archfami.9.2.160

Heinberg, L. J., Ashton, K., Windover, A., & Merrell, J. (2012). Older bariatric surgery candidates: Is there greater psychological risk than for young and midlife candidates? *Surgery for Obesity and Related Diseases, 8,* 616–622. doi:10.1016/j.soard.2011.11.005

Henrickson, H. C., Ashton, K. R., Windover, A. K., & Heinberg, L. J. (2009). Psychological considerations for bariatric surgery among older adults. *Obesity Surgery, 19,* 211–216. doi:10.1007/s11695-008-9768-4

Hiza, H. A. B., Casavale, K. O., Guenther, P. M., & Davis, C. A. (2013). Diet quality of Americans differs by age, sex, race/ethnicity, income, and education level. *Journal of the Academy of Nutrition and Dietetics, 113,* 297–306. doi:10.1016/j.jand.2012.08.011

Houston, D. K., Nicklas, B. J., & Zizza, C. A. (2009). Weighty concerns: The growing prevalence of obesity among older adults. *Journal of the American Dietetic Association, 109,* 1886–1895. doi:10.1016/j.jada.2009.08.014

Howarth, N. C., Huang, T. T., Roberts, S. B., Lin, B. H., & McCrory, M. A. (2007). Eating patterns and dietary composition in relation to BMI in younger and older adults. *International Journal of Obesity, 31,* 675–684.

Hsiao, P. Y., Jensen, G. L., Hartman, T. J., Mitchell, D. C., Nickols-Richardson, S. M., & Coffman, D. L. (2011). Food intake patterns and body mass index in older adults: A review of the epidemiological evidence. *Journal of Nutrition in Gerontology and Geriatrics, 30,* 204–224. doi:10.1080/21551197.2011.591266

Hunt, L. M., Valenzuela, M. A., & Pugh, J. A. (1998). Porque me tocó a mi? Mexican American diabetes patients' causal stories and their relationship to treatment behaviors. *Social Science and Medicine, 46,* 959–969. doi:10.1016/S0277-9536(97)10014-4

Ice, G. H., Katz-Stein, A., Himes, J., & Kane, R. L. (2004). Diurnal cycles of salivary cortisol in older adults. *Psychoneuroendocrinology, 29,* 355–370. doi:10.1016/S0306-4530(03)00034-9

Inoue, S., Sugiyama, T., Takamiya, T., Oka, K., Owen, N., & Shimomitsu, T. (2012). Television viewing time is associated with overweight/obesity among older adults, independent of meeting physical activity and health guidelines. *Journal of Epidemiology, 22,* 50–56. doi:10.2188/jea.JE20110054

Institute of Medicine. (2002). *Dietary reference intakes energy, carbohydrate, fiber, fat, fatty acids, cholesterol, protein, and amino acids (macronutrients).* Washington, DC: Author.

Jaber, L. A., Halapy, H., Fernet, M., Tummalapalli, S., & Diwakaran, H. (1996). Evaluation of a pharmaceutical care model on diabetes management. *Annals of Pharmacotherapy, 30,* 238–243.

Janssen, I., & Mark, A. E. (2007). Elevated body mass index and mortality risk in the elderly. *Obesity Reviews, 8,* 41–59. doi:10.1111/j.1467-789X.2006.00248.x

Jensen, G. L., Silver, H. J., Roy, M. A., Callahan, E., Still, C., & Dupont, W. (2006). Obesity is a risk factor for reporting homebound status among community-dwelling older persons. *Obesity, 14,* 509–517. doi:10.1038/oby.2006.66

Jensen, M. D., Ryan, D. H., Donato, K. A., Apovian, C. M., Ard, J. D., Comuzzie, A. G., . . . Yanovski, S. Z. (2014). 2013 AHA/ACC/TOS guideline for the management of overweight and obesity in adults: A report of the American College of Cardiology/American Heart Association Task Force on Practice Guidelines and The Obesity Society. *Obesity, 22,* 1–410.

Katon, W. J. (2008). The comorbidity of diabetes mellitus and depression. *American Journal of Medicine, 121,* 8–15. doi:10.1016/j.amjmed.2008.09.008

Katon, W. J., Von Korff, M., Lin, E. H., Simon, G., Ludman, E., Russo, J., . . . Bush, T. (2004). The Pathways study: A randomized trial of collaborative care in patients with diabetes and depression. *Archives of General Psychiatry, 61,* 1042–1049. doi:10.1001/archpsyc.61.10.1042

Kim, K. S., Kim, S. K., Sung, K. M., Cho, Y. W., & Park, S. W. (2012). Management of type 2 diabetes mellitus in older adults. *Diabetes and Metabolism, 36,* 336–344. doi:10.4093/dmj.2012.36.5.336

Knight, B. G. (2004). *Psychotherapy with older adults* (3rd ed.). Thousand Oaks, CA: Sage.

Knowler, W. C., Barrett-Connor, E., Fowler, S. E., Hamman, R. F., Lachin, J. M., Walker, E. A., & Nathan, D. M.; Diabetes Prevention Program Research Group. (2002). Reduction in the incidence of type 2 diabetes with lifestyle intervention or metformin. *New England Journal of Medicine, 346,* 393–403.

Krahn, D. D., Bartels, S. J., Coakley, E., Oslin, D. W., Chen, H., McIntyre, J., . . . Levkoff, S. (2006). PRISM-E: Comparison of integrated care and enhanced specialty referral models in depression outcomes. *Psychiatric Services, 57,* 946–953. doi:10.1176/appi.ps.57.7.946

Kuczmarski, R. J., Carroll, M. D., Flegal, K. M., & Troiano, R. P. (1997). Varying body mass index cutoff points to describe overweight prevalence among U.S. adults: NHANES III (1988 to 1994). *Obesity Research, 5,* 542–548. doi:10.1002/j.1550-8528.1997.tb00575.x

Lane, J. D., McCaskill, C. C., Ross, S. L., Feinglos, M. N., & Surwit, R. S. (1993). Relaxation training for NIDDM: Predicting who may benefit. *Diabetes Care, 16,* 1087–1094. doi:10.2337/diacare.16.8.1087

Lanting, L. C., Joung, I. M., Mackenbach, J. P., Lamberts, S. W., & Bootsma, A. H. (2005). Ethnic differences in mortality, end-stage complications, and quality of care among diabetic patients: A review. *Diabetes Care, 28,* 2280–2288. doi:10.2337/diacare.28.9.2280

Lavizzo-Mourey, R., Cox, C., Strumpf, N., Edwards, W. F., Lavisso-Mourey, R., Stineman, M., & Grisso, J. A. (2001). Attitudes and beliefs about exercise among elderly African Americans in an urban community. *Journal of the National Medical Association, 93,* 475–480.

Leff, B. A., Edes, T., & Kinosian, B. (2011). *Medical care for the elderly living at home: Home-based primary care (HBPC) and hospital-at-home programs.* Washington, DC: George Washington University. Retrieved from http://www.nhpf.org/library/forum-sessions/FS_07-22-11_HomeCareElderly.pdf

León-Muñoz, L. M., Guallar-Castillon, P., Banegas, J. R., Gutierrez-Fisac, J. L., Lopez-Garcia, E., Jimenez, F. J., . . . Rodriguez-Artalego, F. (2005). Changes in body weight and health-related quality-of-life in the older adult population. *International Journal of Obesity, 29,* 1385–1391. doi:10.1038/sj.ijo.0803049

Leslie, R. D. G. (1999). United Kingdom prospective diabetes study (UKPDS): What now or so what? *Diabetes/Metabolism Research and Reviews, 15,* 65–71. doi:10.1002/(SICI)1520-7560(199901/02)15:1<65::AID-DMRR3>3.0.CO;2-X

Liang, W., Binns, C., Lee, A. H., Huang, R., & Hu, D. (2008). The reliability of dietary and lifestyle information obtained from spouses in an elderly Chinese population. *Asia-Pacific Journal of Public Health, 20,* 87–93. doi:10.1177/1010539507311183

Look AHEAD Research Group, & Wing, R. R. (2010). Long-term effects of a lifestyle intervention on weight and cardiovascular risk factors in individuals with type 2 diabetes mellitus. *Archives of Internal Medicine, 170,* 1566–1575.

López-García, E., Banegas Banegas, J. R., Gutierrez-Fisac, J. L., Graciani Perez-Regadera, A., Diez-Ganan, L., & Rodriguez-Artalego, F. (2003). Relation between body weight and health-related quality of life among the elderly in Spain. *International Journal of Obesity and Related Metabolic Disorders, 27,* 701–709. doi:10.1038/sj.ijo.0802275

Luchsinger, J. A., Patel, B., Tang, M. X., Schupf, N., & Mayeux, R. (2007). Measures of adiposity and dementia risk in elderly persons. *Archives of Neurology, 64,* 392–398. doi:10.1001/archneur.64.3.392

Lustman, P. J., Anderson, R. J., Freedland, K. E., de Groot, M., Carney, R. M., & Clouse, R. E. (2000). Depression and poor glycemic control: A meta-analytic review of the literature. *Diabetes Care, 23,* 934–942. doi:10.2337/diacare.23.7.934

Lustman, P. J., Griffith, L. S., Clouse, R. E., Freedland, K. E., Eisen, S. A., Rubin, E. H., . . . McGill, J. B. (1995). Effects of alprazolam on glucose regulation in adult diabetic patients: Results of a double-blind, placebo-controlled trial. *Diabetes Care, 18,* 1133–1139. doi:10.2337/diacare.18.8.1133

Magaziner, J., Bassett, S. S., Hebel, J. R., & Gruber-Baldini, A. (1996). Use of proxies to measure health and functional status in epidemiologic studies of community-dwelling women aged 65 years and older. *American Journal of Epidemiology, 143,* 283–292. doi:10.1093/oxfordjournals.aje.a008740

Malinowski, S. S. (2006). Nutritional and metabolic complications of bariatric surgery. *American Journal of the Medical Sciences, 331,* 219–225. doi:10.1097/00000441-200604000-00009

Mast, B. T., Yochim, B., MacNeill, S. E., & Lichtenberg, P. A. (2004). Risk factors for geriatric depression: The importance of executive functioning within the vascular depression hypothesis. *The Journals of Gerontology, Series A: Biological Sciences and Medical Sciences, 59,* 1290–1294. doi:10.1093/gerona/59.12.1290

Mathus-Vliegen, E. M. H. (2012). Obesity and the elderly. *Journal of Clinical Gastroenterology, 46*, 533–544. doi:10.1097/MCG.0b013e31825692ce

Mayberry, L. S., & Osborn, C. Y. (2012). Family support, medication adherence, and glycemic control among adults with type 2 diabetes. *Diabetes Care, 35*, 1239–1245. doi:10.2337/dc11-2103

McHorney, C. A., Ware, J. E., Rogers, W. R., Raczek, A. E., & Lu, J. F. (1992). The validity and relative precision of MOS short- and long-form health status scales and Darmouth COOP Charts: Results from the Medical Outcomes Study. *Medical Care, 30*, 253–265.

McTigue, K. M., Hess, R., & Ziouras, J. (2006). Obesity in older adults: A systematic review of the evidence for diagnosis and treatment. *Obesity, 14*, 1485–1497. doi:10.1038/oby.2006.171

Miklowitz, D. J. (2004). Family-focused treatment for bipolar disorder. In S. G. Hofmann & M. C. Tompson (Eds.), *Treating chronic and severe mental disorders: A handbook of empirically supported interventions* (pp. 159–174). New York, NY: Guilford Press.

Mokdad, A. H., Ford, E. S., Bowman, B. A., Dietz, W. H., Vinicor, F., Bales, V. S., & Marks, J. S. (2003). Prevalence of obesity, diabetes, and obesity-related health risk factors. *JAMA, 289*, 76–79. doi:10.1001/jama.289.1.76

Moss-Morris, R., Weinman, J., Petrie, K., Horne, R., Cameron, L., & Buick, D. (2002). The revised Illness Perception Questionnaire (IPQ-R). *Psychology and Health, 17*, 1–16. doi:10.1080/08870440290001494

Munshi, M., Grande, L., Hayes, M., Ayres, D., Suhl, E., Capelson, R., . . . Weinger, K. (2006). Cognitive dysfunction is associated with poor diabetes control in older adults. *Diabetes Care, 29*, 1794–1799. doi:10.2337/dc06-0506

Murphy, S. L. (2009). Review of physical activity measurement using accelerometers in older adults: Considerations for research design and conduct. *Preventive Medicine, 48*, 108–114. doi:10.1016/j.ypmed.2008.12.001

Narayan, K. M., Boyle, J. P., & Thompson, J. (2003). Lifetime risk for diabetes mellitus in the United States. *JAMA, 290*, 1884–1890. doi:10.1001/jama.290.14.1884

Nelson, M. E., Rejeski, W. J., Blaire, S. N., Duncan, P. W., Judge, J. O., King, A. C., . . . Castaneda-Sceppa, C. (2007). Physical activity and public health in older adults: Recommendations from the American College of Sports Medicine and the American Heart Association. *Medicine and Science in Sports and Exercise, 39*, 1435–1445. doi:10.1249/mss.0b013e3180616aa2

NIH Conference. (1991). Gastrointestinal surgery for severe obesity: Consensus development conference panel. *Annals of Internal Medicine, 115*, 956–961.

Ogden, C. L., Carroll, M. D., Kit, B. K., & Flegal, K. M. (2012). *Prevalence of obesity in the United States, 2009–2010.* (NCHS Data Brief, No. 82). Hyattsville, MD: National Center for Health Statistics.

Okada, S., Ichiki, K., Tanokuchi, S., Ishii, K., Hamada, H., & Ota, Z. (1994). Effects of an anxiolytic on lipid profile in non-insulin-dependent diabetes mellitus. *Journal of Internal Medicine Research, 22*, 338–342.

Paschalides, C., Wearden, A. J., Dunkerley, R., Bundy, C., Davies, R., & Dickens, C. M. (2004). The associations of anxiety, depression and personal illness representations with glycaemic control and health-related quality of life in patients with type 2 diabetes mellitus. *Journal of Psychosomatic Research, 57*, 557–564. doi:10.1016/j.jpsychores.2004.03.006

Petrie, K. J., Jago, L. A., & Devcich, D. A. (2007). The role of illness perceptions in patients with medical conditions. *Current Opinions in Psychiatry, 20*, 163–167.

Pope, S. K., Kritchevsky, S. B., Morris, M. C., Block, G., Tylavsky, F. A., Lee, J. S., . . . & Simonsick, E. M. (2007). Cognitive ability is associated with suspected reporting errors in food frequency questionnaires. *Journal of Nutrition, Health, and Aging, 11*, 55–58.

Rikli, R. E. (2000). Reliability, validity, and methodological issues in assessing physical activity in older adults. *Research Quarterly for Exercise and Sport, 71*(2, Suppl.), 89–96.

Rizvi, A. A. (2007). Management of diabetes in older adults. *American Journal of the Medical Sciences, 333*, 35–47.

Rodríguez-Morales, G., Ivan, I., Woodhead, E., Golden, R., & Emery, E. E. (2010, November). *Effectiveness of an interdisciplinary approach in management of depression in diverse socioeconomic populations.* Paper presented at the meeting of the Gerontological Society of America, New Orleans, LA.

Rubin, R. R., & Peyrot, M. (1999). Quality of life and diabetes. *Diabetes/Metabolism Research and Reviews, 15*, 205–218.

Rubin, R. R., & Peyrot, M. (2001). Psychological issues and treatments for people with diabetes. *Journal of Clinical Psychiatry, 57*, 457–478.

Saaddine, J. B., Honeycutt, A. A., Narayan, K., Zhang, X., Klein, R., & Boyle, J. P. (2008). Projection of diabetic retinopathy and other major eye diseases among people with diabetes mellitus: United States, 2005–2050. *Archives of Ophthalmology, 126*, 1740–1747. doi:10.1001/archopht.126.12.1740

Schoenberg, N. E., Traywick, L. S., Jacobs-Lawson, J., & Kart, C. S. (2008). Diabetes self-care among a multiethnic sample of older adults. *Journal of Cross-Cultural Gerontology, 23,* 361–376.

Shaw, J. E., & Sicree, R. (2008). Epidemiology of type 2 diabetes. In M. N. Feinglos, & M. A. Bethel (Eds.), *Type 2 diabetes mellitus: an evidence-based approach to practical management* (pp. 1–16). New York, NY: SpringerLink eBooks.

Sharkey, J., & Horel, S. (2008). Neighborhood socio-economic deprivation and minority composition are associated with better potential spatial access to the food environment in a large rural area. *Journal of Nutrition, 138,* 620–627.

Shephard, R. J. (1991). Physical fitness: Exercise and ageing. In M. S. Pathy (Ed.), *Principle and practice of geriatric medicine* (pp. 279–294). New York, NY: Wiley.

Sinclair, A. J., Bayer, A. J., Girling, A. J., & Woodhouse, K. W. (2000). Older adults, diabetes mellitus and visual acuity: A community-based case-control study. *Age and Ageing, 29,* 335–339.

Smedley, B. D., Stith, S. Y., & Nelson, A. R. (Eds.). (2002). *Unequal treatment: Confronting racial and ethnic disparities in health care.* Washington, DC: National Academies Press.

Smith, G. C. (1991). Grocery shopping patterns of the ambulatory urban elderly. *Environmental Behavior, 23,* 86–114.

Smith, G. C., & Gauthier, J. J. (1995). Evaluation and utilization of local service environments by residents of low rent senior citizen apartments. *Canadian Journal of Urban Research, 4,* 305–323.

Snih, S. A., Ottenbacher, K. J., Markides, K. S., Kuo, Y. F., Eschbach, K., & Goodwin, J. S. (2007). The effect of obesity on disability vs mortality in older Americans. *Archives of Internal Medicine, 167,* 774–780.

Sorkin, J. D., Muller, D. C., & Andres, R. (1999). Longitudinal change in height of men and women: Implications for interpretation of the body mass index: The Baltimore Longitudinal Study of Aging. *American Journal of Epidemiology, 150,* 969–977.

Steptoe, A., & Wardle, J. (2011). Positive affect measured using ecological momentary assessment and survival in older men and women. *Proceedings of the National Academy of Sciences of the United States of America, 108,* 18244–18248.

Stevens, J., Cai, J., Pamuk, E. R., Williamson, D. F., Thun, M. J., & Wood, J. L. (1998). The effect of age on the association between body-mass index and mortality. *New England Journal of Medicine, 338,* 1–7.

Stewart, A. L., Mills, K. M., King, A. C., Haskell, W. L., Gillis, D., & Ritter, P. L. (2001). CHAMPS physical activity questionnaire for older adults: Outcomes for interventions. *Medicine and Science in Sports and Exercise, 33,* 1126–1141.

Strandberg, T. E., Strandberg, A., Salomaa, V. V., Pitkala, K., & Miettinen, T. A. (2003). Impact of midlife weight change on mortality and quality of life in old age. Prospective cohort study. *International Journal of Obesity and Related Metabolic Disorders, 27,* 950–954.

Subar, A. F., Thompson, F. E., Kipnis, V., Midthune, D., Hurwitz, P., McNutt, S., . . . Rosenfeld, S. (2001). Comparative validation of the Block, Willett, and National Cancer Institute food frequency questionnaires: The eating at America's table study. *American Journal of Epidemiology, 15,* 1089–1099.

Subar, A. F., Thompson, F. E., Smith, A. F., Jobe, J. B., Ziegler, R. G., Potischman, N., . . . Kruse, L. (1995). Improving food frequency questionnaires: A qualitative approach using cognitive interviewing. *Journal of the American Dietetic Association, 95,* 781–788.

Sue Kirkman, M., Broscoe, V. J., Clark, N., Florez, H., Haas, L. B., Halter, J. B., . . . Swift, C. S. (2012). Diabetes in older adults: A consensus report. *Journal of the American Geriatrics Society, 60,* 2342–2356. doi:10.1111/jgs.12035

Surwit, R. S., van Tiburg, M. A. L., Zucker, N., McCaskill, C. C., Parekh, P., Feingloss, M. N., . . . Lane, J. D. (2002). Stress management improves long-term glycemic control in type 2 diabetes. *Diabetes Care, 25,* 30–34.

Swartz, A. M., Tarima, S., Miller, N. E., Hart, T. L., Grimm, E. K., Rote, A. E., . . . Strath, S. J. (2012). Prediction of body fat in older adults by time spent in sedentary behavior. *Journal of Aging and Physical Activity, 20,* 332–344.

Taylor, T. R., Kamarck, T. W., & Shiffman, S. (2004). Validation of the Detroit Area Study Discrimination Scale in a community sample of older African American adults: the Pittsburgh healthy heart project. *International Journal of Behavioral Medicine, 11,* 88–94.

Thomas, A. J., Ferrier, I. N., Kalaria, R. N., Brown, A., & O'Brien, J. T. (2001). A neuropathological study of vascular factors in late-life depression. *Journal of Neurology, Neurosurgery, and Psychiatry, 70,* 83–87. doi:10.1136/jnnp.70.1.83

Thompson, F. E., & Subar, A. F. (2013). Dietary assessment methodology. In A. M. Coulston, C. J. Boushey, & M. G. Ferruzzi (Eds.), *Nutrition in the prevention and treatment of disease* (3rd ed., pp. 5–46). San Diego, CA: Academic Press.

Thompson, F. E., Subar, A. F., Brown, C. C., Smith, A. F., Sharbaugh, C. O., Jobe, J. B., . . . Ziegler, R. G. (2002). Cognitive research enhances accuracy of food frequency questionnaire reports: results of an experimental validation study. *Journal of the American Dietetic Association, 102,* 212–225.

Topolski, T. D., LoGerfo, J., Patrick, D. L., Williams, B., Walwick, J., & Patrick, M. M. B. (2006). The Rapid

Assessment of Physical Activity (RAPA) among older adults. *Preventing Chronic Disease, 3,* 1–8.

Unützer, J., Katon, W., Callahan, C. M., Williams, J. W., Hunkeler, E., Harpole, L., . . . Langston, C. (2002). Collaborative care management of late-life depression in the primary care setting: A randomized controlled trial. *JAMA, 288,* 2836–2845. doi:10.1001/jama.288.22.2836

U.S. Department of Health and Human Services. (2008). *Physical activity guidelines advisory committee report, 2008.* Retrieved from http://www.health.gov/paguidelines/Report

Valiyeva, E., Russell, L. B., Miller, J. E., & Safford, M. M. (2006). Lifestyle-related risk factors and risk of future nursing home admission. *Archives of Internal Medicine, 166,* 985–990.

Van Tilburg, M. A. L., McCaskill, C. C., Lane, J. D., Edwards, C. L., Bethel, A., Feinglos, M. N., & Surwit, R. S. (2001). Depressed mood is a factor in glycemic control in type 1 diabetes. *Psychosomatic Medicine: Journal of Biobehavioral Medicine, 63,* 551–555.

Varela, J. E., Wilson, E. E., & Nguyen, N. T. (2006). Outcomes of bariatric surgery in the elderly. *American Surgeon, 72,* 865–869.

Villareal, D. T., Apovian, C. M., Kushner, R. F., & Klein, S. (2005). Obesity in older adults: Technical review and position statement of the American Society for Nutrition and NAASO, The Obesity Society. *American Journal of Clinical Nutrition, 82,* 923–934.

Voorrips, L. E., Ravelli, A. C., Dongelmans, P. C. A., Deurenberg, P., & Staveren, W. V. (1991). A physical activity questionnaire for the elderly. *Medicine and Science in Sports and Exercise, 23,* 974–979.

Washburn, R. A., McAuley, E., Katula, J., Mihalko, S. L., & Boileau, R. A. (1999). The physical activity scale for the elderly (PASE): Evidence for validity. *Journal of Clinical Epidemiology, 52,* 643–651.

Wen, L. K., Shepherd, M. D., & Parchman, M. L. (2004). Family support, diet, and exercise among older Mexican Americans with type 2 diabetes. *Diabetes Educator, 30,* 980–993.

Whelton, P. K., Appel, L. J., Espeland, M. A., Applegate, W. B., Ettinger, W. H., Jr., Kostis, J. B., . . . Cutler, J. A. (1998). Sodium reduction and weight loss in the treatment of hypertension in older persons: A randomized controlled trial of nonpharmacologic interventions in the elderly (TONE). *JAMA, 279,* 839–846.

Wing, R. R., Hamman, R. F., Bray, G. A., Delahanty, L., Edelstein, S. L., Hill, J. O., . . . Wylie-Rosett, J.; Diabetes Prevention Program Research Group. (2004). Achieving weight and activity goals among diabetes prevention program lifestyle participants. *Obesity Research, 12,* 1426–1434.

Wittchen, H. U., & Hoyer, J. (2001). Generalized anxiety disorder: Nature and course. *Journal of Clinical Psychiatry, 62*(Suppl. 11), 15–19.

Yan, L. L., Daviglus, M. L., Liu, K., Pirzada, A., Garside, D. B., Schiffer, L., . . . Greenland, P. (2004). BMI and health-related quality of life in adults 65 years and older. *Obesity Research, 12,* 69–76.

Yermilov, I., McGory, M. L., Shekelle, P. W., Ko, C. Y., & Maggard, M. A. (2009). Appropriateness criteria for bariatric surgery: Beyond the NIH guidelines. *Obesity, 17,* 1521–1527.

Zamboni, M., Mazzali, G., Zoico, E., Harris, T. B., Meigs, J. B., Di Francesco, V., . . . Bosello, O. (2005). Health consequences of obesity in the elderly: A review of four unresolved questions. *International Journal of Obesity, 29,* 1011–1029.

Zeiss, A. M., & Karlin, B. E. (2008). Integrating mental health and primary care services in the Department of Veterans Affairs Health Care System. *Journal of Clinical Psychology in Medical Settings, 15,* 73–78.

Zenk, S. N., Schulz, A. J., Hollis-Neely, T., Campbell, R. T., Holmes, N., Watkins, G., . . . Odoms-Young, A. (2005). Fruit and vegetable intake in African Americans: Income and store characteristics. *American Journal of Preventive Medicine, 29,* 1–9.

CHAPTER 18

MOBILITY IN LATER LIFE

Dawn A. Skelton and Jennifer Muhaidat

It takes a child 1 year to acquire independent movement and 10 years to acquire independent mobility. An old person can lose both in a day. (Isaacs, 1992, p. 1)

Mobility is a complex function that includes multiple domains of activity and is a critically important functional ability required to maintain social roles and pursuits among older adults. Aging can have negative effects on the safety and independence of mobility due to age-related diseases and declines in motor functioning (W. Zijlstra & Aminian, 2007). Impaired mobility is one of the risk factors for disability in older adults (Topinková, 2008). Comorbidity, low levels of physical activity, and lower limb functional limitations are additional risk factors for decreased functional ability (Stuck et al., 1999). In addition to these physical factors, cognitive impairment and depression also increase the risk of functional decline (Stuck et al., 1999). Indeed, psychological factors have been found to be strong predictors of catastrophic decline in mobility in older adults (Ayis, Gooberman-Hill, Bowling, & Ebrahim, 2006).

More than 30% of adults age 65 years and older express difficulty in walking three city blocks (Centers for Disease Control and Prevention [CDC], 2009). Satariano et al. (2012) identified four public health burdens for mobility disability in older adults: restricted access to services and goods due to walking and driving limitations, the negative effect of sedentary behavior on health, restrictions in social contact, and restricted ability to participate in civic life. All of these factors can lead to poor health outcomes, mortality, and reduced contribution to society by this age-group (Satariano et al., 2012).

DEFINITION

Mobility is classified under activities and participation in the International Classification of Functioning, Disability, and Health (ICF). According to the ICF, mobility is defined as "moving by changing body position or location or by transferring from one place to another, by carrying, moving or manipulating objects, by walking, running or climbing, and by using various forms of transportation" (World Health Organization [WHO], 2001, p. 138). Mobility in this context is changing and maintaining body position (ICF d410–d429) or walking and moving (ICF d450–d469). According to this definition, mobility comprises (WHO, 2001) the following:

- Transferring to, maintaining, and changing into the following positions: lying down, squatting, kneeling, sitting, standing, and bending
- Carrying, moving, and handling objects with the upper and lower extremities
- Walking for short and long distances, on different surfaces, and avoiding obstacles
- Crawling, jumping, climbing, running, and swimming
- Moving indoors and outdoors
- Moving using equipment such as walking aids
- Using transportation to move around

One of the main outcomes of reduced mobility is the avoidance or inability to take part in activity.

http://dx.doi.org/10.1037/14459-018
APA Handbook of Clinical Geropsychology: Vol. 2. Assessment, Treatment, and Issues of Later Life,
P. A. Lichtenberg and B. T. Mast (Editors-in-Chief)

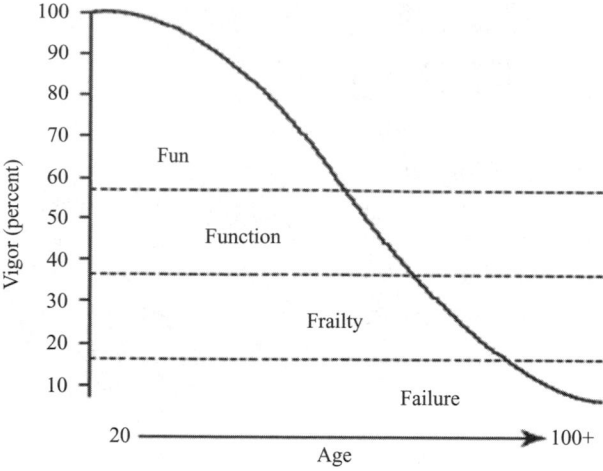

FIGURE 18.1. Physical ability and vigor. From "Sarcopenia and Physical Performance in Old Age: Introduction," by R. S. Schwartz, 1997, *Muscle and Nerve,* 5, p. 11. Copyright 1997 by Muscle and Nerve. Reprinted with permission.

The ICF has defined activity as "the execution of a task or action by an individual" and activity limitations as "difficulties an individual may have in executing activities" (WHO, 2001, p. 123).

Schwartz (1997) described the loss in physical ability as the slippery slope of aging (Figure 18.1). Physical ability was categorized into fun, function, frailty, and failure. Fun is the ability to do whatever one wants for as long as one wants and whenever one wants. Function describes the category of those who consciously make decisions about their activities based on their physical abilities. Frailty includes those who need assistance with basic activities and failure describes those who are entirely dependent in their activities (Schwartz, 1997)

MOBILITY AND PHYSICAL AND PSYCHOLOGICAL HEALTH

For older adults to live an active and independent life, mobility needs to be maintained (WHO, 2007). Forty-four percent of community-dwelling older adults report some type of impairment in mobility, with the majority reporting this complaint for more than 1 year (Iezzoni, McCarthy, Davis, & Siebens, 2000). Mobility is dynamic, and older people often transition through the functional stages of independence and dependence during their lifetime

(Hardy, Dubin, Holford, & Gill, 2005), suggesting that impaired mobility is modifiable.

Webber, Porter, and Menec (2010) identified five key determinants of mobility in their mobility framework: cognitive, psychological, physical, environmental, and financial influences. According to this framework, the determinants are interconnected (Webber et al., 2010). An example of that might be having a balance problem (physical), slow reaction time (cognitive), and fear of falling (psychological), which can enhance the effect of environmental factors, such as crossing a wide busy street, on mobility. Indeed, mobility is a complex interplay between the person and the environment, reflecting the effects of sociodemographic and community-level characteristics, diseases, geriatric syndromes, and neuropsychological conditions on adverse health outcomes (Baker, Bodner, & Allman, 2003; see Figure 18.2).

Mobility impairment can predict mortality (Feeny et al., 2012; Hirvensalo, Rantanen, & Heikkinen, 2000). Decreased mobility and decline in cognitive function increase the risk of nursing home admission (von Bonsdorff, Rantanen, Laukkanen, Suutama, & Heikkinen, 2006). Older adults who experience mobility problems and need help in daily activities are at higher risk of being depressed and of having lower overall and health-related quality of life (HRQOL; Jakobsson, Hallberg, & Westergren, 2007). The perception of a reduced quality of life in

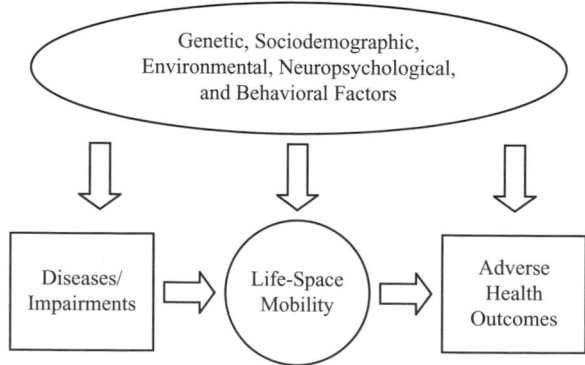

FIGURE 18.2. The conceptual model of the causes of adverse health outcomes. From "Racial Similarities and Differences in Predictors of Mobility Change Over Eighteen Months," by R. M. Allman, P. S. Baker, R. M. Maisiak, R. V. Sims, and J. M. Roseman, 2004, *Journal of General Internal Medicine,* 19, p. 1119. Copyright 2004 by JGIM. Reprinted with permission.

this setting is exemplified by 80% of women age 75 years and older admitting they would rather die than be admitted to a nursing home after a hip fracture (Salkeld et al., 2000).

Nutrition also has an effect on mobility, and in a review of the nutritional determinants of mobility, it was found that a diet rich in fruits and vegetables such as the Mediterranean diet has a positive effect on mobility and healthy aging (Milaneschi, Tanaka, & Ferrucci, 2010). Having adequate levels of calcitriol (D-hormone) and calcium intake also have a beneficial effect on functional mobility as assessed by the timed up and go (TUG) test (Dukas, Staehelin, Schacht, & Bischoff, 2005).

Finally, mobility and mobility decline appear to differ between races and cultures. For example, studies have identified disparities between older African Americans and Whites in functional ability and physical performance. Higher rates of disabling conditions, economic disadvantage, inadequate access to health care, and social factors potentially contribute to this disparity (Allman, Baker, Maisiak, Sims, & Roseman, 2004). In one study (Allman et al., 2004), older African Americans had lower baseline life-space (mobility) than Whites, and this disparity in mobility was accompanied by significant racial differences in socioeconomic and health status. At 18-month follow-up, however, African Americans were less likely to show declines in mobility than Whites. These results might have been due to the lower baseline scores in African Americans, which could have led to a floor effect. Another explanation for such findings might be cultural differences in responding to disease (Allman et al., 2004). Multivariate analyses showed racial differences in the relative importance and strength of the associations between predictors and mobility change. Age and diabetes were significant predictors of mobility decline for both African Americans and Whites. Transportation difficulty, kidney disease, dementia, and Parkinson's disease were significant for African Americans, whereas low education, arthritis or gout, stroke, neuropathy, depression, and poor appetite were significant for Whites (Allman et al., 2004). This finding suggests we need to be cognizant to ethnic differences in predictors of mobility change in our strategies to increase mobility in older people.

Mobility and Health

Although mobility declines are found with normal aging, some health conditions commonly found in older adults, such as stroke, Parkinson's disease, cognitive impairment, and falls, can have a deteriorating effect on mobility. Patients with stroke who suffered from deterioration in somatosensory and perceptual functions and depression demonstrated poorer mobility and self-care when compared with other patients with stroke (Welmer, von Arbin, Murray, Holmqvist, & Sommerfeld, 2007). Back pain associated with osteoporosis was found to explain declines in functional mobility and balance in women age 65–75 years old (Liu-Ambrose et al., 2002). Patients suffering from Parkinson's disease display movement disorders, such as bradykinesia, freezing while walking, and balance problems and falls (Axer, Axer, Sauer, Witte, & Hagemann, 2010; Morris, 2000).

For older adults to lead an independent life in the community, they require aerobic fitness (Higginbotham, Morris, Williams, Coleman, & Cobb, 1986). Higher ventilator threshold (an effort-independent physiological marker of the ability to perform submaximal, prolonged activity) is required to walk at preferred speed with increased aging, which helps explain why older adults walk at slower speeds (Malatesta et al., 2004). Sarcopenia, which is characterized by loss in muscle mass and strength with increased age, also can have a negative effect on mobility and can increase the risk of falling (Montero-Fernández & Serra-Rexach, 2013). The Allied Dunbar National Fitness Survey in the United Kingdom assessed the physical fitness of 1318 men and women ages 50–96 years old (Skelton, Young, Walker, & Hoinville, 1999). Within this survey, leg extensor power, knee extension strength, and cardiorespiratory fitness were assessed and compared to the ability to perform everyday tasks. Across the five half-decades from 50–74 years, men and women both showed a 33% reduction in power-to-weight ratio. In general, women had mean power-to-weight ratios about two thirds of the mean values for men of the same age. Thus, men had the equivalent of a 20-year advantage over the women with respect to this functionally important characteristic (Skelton et al., 1999).

Across the age range, 3% of men and 13% of women age 50–54 years compared with 14% of men and 47% of women age 70–74 years were at risk of being unable to step nearly 1 foot without difficulty. In terms of knee extension strength, in the youngest age-group only 1% of men and 5% of women were at risk of being unable to rise from a low chair, compared with 7% of men and 25% of women in the 70- to 74-year-old age range (Skelton et al., 1999). Most surprising, however, considering that only those healthy enough to undergo these physical appraisal tests were examined, even in the 50- to 54-year-old age range, 23% of women (but only 1% of men) had sufficiently low aerobic capacity that they would find it uncomfortable to walk at only 3 miles per hour (Figure 18.3). This rose to 80% of women and 35% of men age 70–74 years (Skelton et al., 1999).

The use of medication also has an effect on mobility in older adults. Polypharmacy can result in a decline in functional status in older adults (Peron, Gray, & Hanlon, 2011). Moreover, benzodiazepines and anticholinergic drugs in particular also have a negative effect on function (mobility and activities of daily living [ADLs]) in older adults (Peron et al., 2011). Although these health conditions can have an impact on mobility and function in older adults, it often is the impairment and consequent avoidance of activity, not the disease itself, that cause these deteriorations in mobility (Bootsma-van der Wiel et al., 2002).

Mobility and Cognitive Function

Walking used to be considered an automatic task. More recent research, however, has found that gait requires the allocation of attention. This is logical when we think about everyday situations. Walking is seldom performed as a single task. We usually engage in other activities while walking, such as talking, thinking, or carrying objects (Muhaidat, Skelton, Kerr, Evans, & Ballinger, 2010). Walking also requires the ability to plan and execute

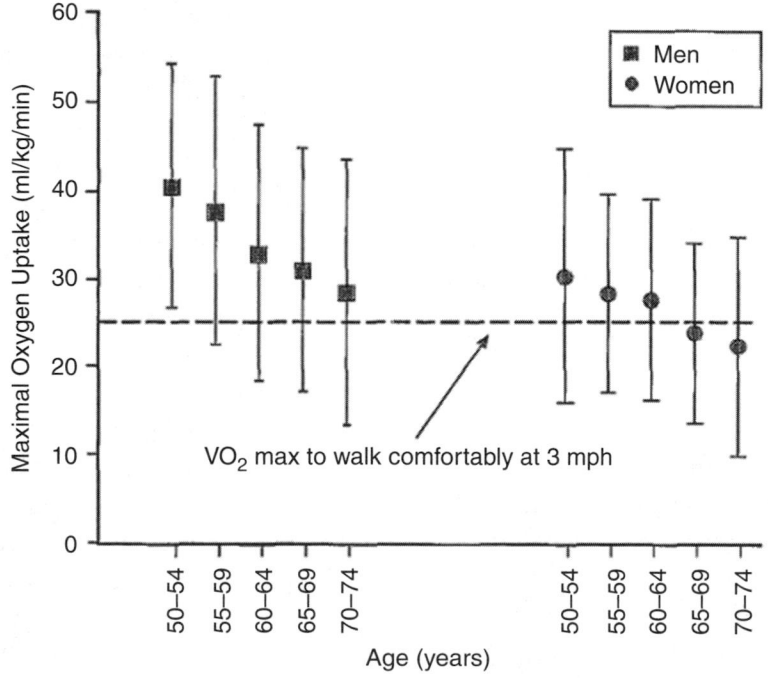

FIGURE 18.3.   Maximal oxygen consumption (VO$_2$ max) in men and women aged 50–74 (M ± 2SD). From *Physical Activity in Later Life: Further Analysis of the Allied Dunbar National Fitness Survey and the HEASAH* (p. 46), by D. A. Skelton, A. Young, A. Walker, and E. Hoinville, 1999, London, England: Health Education Authority. Copyright 1999 by the Health Education Authority. Reprinted with permission.

goal-directed behavior. This means that cognitive domains, such as attention and executive function, need to be intact for us to be able to walk safely and independently (Yogev-Seligmann, Hausdorff, & Giladi, 2008).

Declines in global cognitive function and executive function also are associated with increased risk of falling (Muir, Gopaul, & Montero-Odasso, 2012). These changes might be present in cognitively normal older adults. When cognitive impairment is added to the normal age-related decline in cognitive function, however, the impact on function is exacerbated and the risk of falls is almost doubled (Montero-Odasso, Verghese, Beauchet, & Hausdorff, 2012). Older adults with cognitive impairment have a higher rate of falls (60%–80% annually; Tinetti, Speechley, & Ginter, 1988) than cognitively normal older adults (30% annually; O'Loughlin, Robitaille, Boivin, & Suissa, 1993). Moreover, cognitively impaired fallers have a higher risk of institutionalization and fall-related fractures after a fall (Montero-Odasso et al., 2012).

Gait disturbances are present in older adults suffering from dementia, whether mild cognitive impairment (MCI) or other forms of dementia, such as Alzheimer's disease, vascular dementia, or dementia with Lewy bodies (Axer et al., 2010). These disturbances can be summarized as slow gait speed, greater gait variability, shorter step length, balance disturbance, increased risk of falling, and neurological gait signs resembling Parkinson's disease (Axer et al., 2010). Moreover, patients with

MCI were found to have poorer performance on the TUG test (Onen, Henry-Feugeas, Roy, Baron, & Ravaud, 2008). Older adults with Alzheimer's disease were found to have an increased risk of falling and a decline in mobility when compared with healthy age-matched older adults (Suttanon, Hill, Said, & Dodd, 2013). These mobility problems can affect the ability of the older person to perform daily activities and also can cause an increased burden on the caregiver (Pitkälä, Savikko, Poysti, Strandberg, & Laakkonen, 2013).

One of the common age-related changes in gait is reduced velocity, which was found to be an indicator of increased fall risk (Montero-Odasso et al., 2005). Changes in gait velocity can occur up to 12 years before signs of cognitive impairment become evident (Montero-Odasso et al., 2012). This indicates that mobility assessment can be beneficial in the early detection of cognitive impairment. Slow gait speed actually was found to predict declines in Mini-Mental State Examination (MMSE) scores over a 7-year follow-up period (Alfaro-Acha, Al Snih, Raji, Markides, & Ottenbacher, 2007). These relationships show that falls and cognitive impairment are interrelated (Figure 18.4).

The interplay between cognitive function and mobility has been assessed using the dual-task paradigm. Dual tasking is the performance of two tasks at the same time. This requires the successful allocation and shift of attention between the tasks. The dual-task paradigm originally was developed in the field of cognitive psychology (Kahneman, 1973).

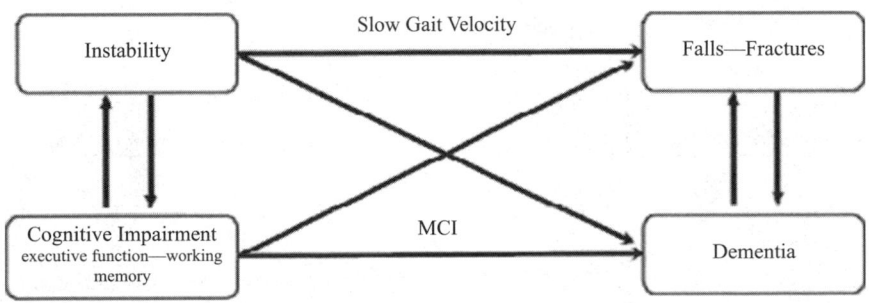

FIGURE 18.4.   The interplay between mobility, cognitive impairment, and falls. MCI = mild cognitive impairment. From "Gait and Cognition: A Complementary Approach to Understanding Brain Function and the Risk of Falling," by M. Montero-Odasso, J. Verghese, O. Beauchet, and J. M. Hausdorff, 2012, *Journal of the American Geriatrics Society, 60,* p. 13. Copyright 2012 by the American Geriatrics Society. Reprinted with permission.

In mobility-related research, the mobility task usually is termed the primary task and the cognitive task is the secondary task (Abernethy, 1988). When two tasks are performed simultaneously, interference might occur (Kahneman, 1973). This interference can cause deterioration in the performance of one or both tasks, or the improvement of one task and the deterioration of the other (Navon & Miller, 1987). Deterioration in the performance of the mobility task in the dual-task condition might be associated with an increased risk of falling. Many of the dual-task studies, however, used complex methods to measure gait or balance performance, such as force platforms and electronic walkways (Nordin, Moe-Nilssen, Ramnemark, & Lundin-Olsson, 2010; Swanenburg, de Bruin, Uebelhart, & Mulder, 2010). These methods might not be available in clinical settings.

In a recent attempt to investigate which dual task test might be best at predicting falls in community-dwelling older adults, Muhaidat, Kerr, Evans, Pilling, and Skelton (2014) found that simple tests that required only the use of a stopwatch, such as carrying a cup of water while performing the TUG or while avoiding a moving obstacle, might be the best predictors of future falls. One interesting assessment question is whether we actually need a dual-task test to predict falls, or is it sufficient to use a challenging single task? There were some indications from this study that a single task, such as avoiding a

ball while walking, might be as good as a dual-task test. This, however, warrants further investigation (Muhaidat et al., 2014).

Mobility and Falls

> Walking is a state of controlled falling in which we always are only one step away from disaster. (Frank & Patla, 2003, p. 157)

Poor mobility and functional independence lead to falls (Daley & Spinks, 2000). Falls are a major problem in the aging population, with 30% of community-dwelling adults over the age of 65 years falling annually (O'Loughlin et al., 1993). As older adults get older or frailer, this rate increases (Skelton & Todd, 2004). Although there are many definitions for falls, the Prevention of Falls Network Europe (ProFaNE) has defined falls as "an unexpected event in which the participants come to rest on the ground or lower level" (Lamb, Jørstad-Stein, Hauer, & Becker, 2005, p. 1619).

More than 400 risk factors for falls have been identified (Masud & Morris, 2001). The most frequently reported factors are age, female gender, a previous history of falls, gait and balance problems, decreased muscle power and strength, visual impairment, polypharmacy, psychological factors (such as fear of falling), anxiety and depression, and cognitive impairment (Skelton & Todd, 2004).

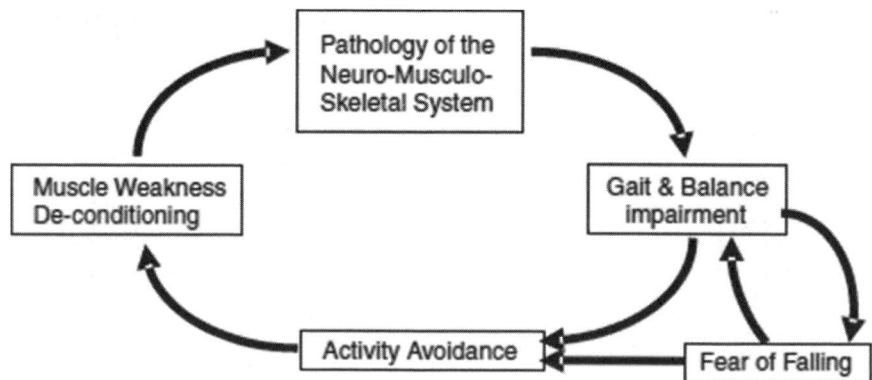

FIGURE 18.5.   The relationship between mobility impairment, physical function, and fear of falling. From "Mobility Assessment in Older People: New Possibilities and Challenges," by W. Zijlstra and K. Aminian, 2007, *European Journal of Ageing, 4,* p. 4. Copyright 2007 by Springer-Verlag. Reprinted with permission.

Psychological factors not only are factors that could contribute to falls but also are the consequence of falls (Figure 18.5). Poor psychological health that follows a fall is termed the *postfall syndrome* (Tinetti et al., 1988). Forty-four percent of older adults who report a fear of falling also report reduced physical activity levels (Bertera & Bertera, 2008). This fear-related avoidance can increase the risk of future falls because of its impact on reducing muscle strength and balance and inappropriate gait alterations (Rubenstein & Josephson, 2002; Skelton & Beyer, 2003; Zijlstra & Aminian, 2007). Fear of falling does not always result in restriction of physical activity. Tinetti, Mendes de Leon, Doucette, and Baker (1994) found that 24% of older adults reporting a fear of falling did not restrict their activity. A previous history of falls is not a prerequisite for developing a fear of falling, however; 40% of older adults who did not report a recent history of falls, did report fear of falling (Skelton & Todd, 2004).

In addition to the psychological consequences, falls also can lead to injury such as fractures (W. P. Berg, Alessio, Mills, & Tong, 1997). Twenty-five percent of fall-related fractures affect the hip (Nevitt, Cummings, Kidd, & Black, 1989). The national fall-related costs in many countries range from 0.85% to 1.5% of the total health care expenditure (Heinrich, Rapp, Rissmann, Becker, & Konig, 2010). This indicates that falls are a major financial burden. Considering the activity avoidance that follows a fall, the ongoing reduced mobility of fallers is an area of continued clinical and research focus. Most successful interventions to reduce future falls have strength and balance exercise at the core of their effectiveness (Gillespie et al., 2012).

Mobility and Vision Impairment

Older adults with visual impairment are more likely to be physically dependent, to have poorer quality of life, and to move into residential settings than their sighted peers (Ivers, Cumming, Mitchell, & Attebo, 1998; Klein, Moss, Klein, Lee, & Cruickshanks, 2003; Tinetti & Williams, 1998). Impairment of vision is associated with a loss of function in ADLs (Brouwer & Sadlo, 2008; Salive, et al., 1994). A U.K. report by Visibility (Campbell, 2005) found that older people with visual impairment are more likely

to avoid activity because of their visual impairment. Anxiety and depression, leading to reduced activity, is common in those with visual impairment (Evans, Fletcher, & Wormald, 2007). There is an association between vision and various health conditions and activity limitations among older people. These include decreases in leisure activities, instrumental activities of daily living (IADL) performance and social function, ADLs, and compromised mobility.

The problems older adults with low vision have in seeking leisure activities may have implications for other health issues. Many older adults do not engage in activities for which they may have sufficient vision because of other factors, such as inactivity and a lack of social connections (Berger, 2012). Challenging environments, struggling to obtain transportation, feelings of vulnerability, having decreased energy, and lacking assertiveness all were identified in interviews with older visually impaired adults as reasons for not being physically active and not feeling competent in such activities (Berger, 2012).

Visual impairment also is associated with increases in the incidence of hip fractures, depression, and falls (Crews & Campbell, 2004). One study reported that activity restriction was present in 45% of those with visual impairment, compared with only 24% in those without visual impairment who had experienced an injurious fall (S. L. Murphy, Williams, & Gill, 2002). Those with visual impairment were more likely to admit to fear of falling (44%) even without a fall history. One study has shown that perceived interference of vision loss on goal-directed behavior and expected activities has a greater influence on distress and is subsequently predictive of disability in comparison with objective symptoms (i.e., visual acuity; Dreer et al., 2008).

Mobility and Foot Health

Foot health problems, such as pain or deformity, often will lead to an older person avoiding activity. The avoidance of physical activity and exercise over the long term causes a reduction in strength and balance, which in turn leads to an increased risk of mobility decline. Foot problems in older people may result from age-related decreases in joint range of motion; dermatological conditions; detrimental effects of footwear; and systemic conditions, such as peripheral vascular disease, diabetes mellitus, and arthritis (Menz & Lord, 1999).

Foot and leg problems are reported by one in three community-dwelling people age 65 years and older. Independent of the influence of age, gender, common medical conditions, and other sociodemographic factors, foot and leg problems have a significant impact on the ability to perform functional tasks integral to independent living (Barr, Browning, Lord, Menz, & Kendig, 2005). In a random sample of 1000 people age 65–94 years old, after adjusting for sociodemographic, physical, and medical factors, foot and leg problems remained significantly associated with impaired TUG performance (odds ratio [OR] = 2.15), difficulty climbing stairs (OR = 3.33), difficulty walking 0.62 miles (OR = 3.13), and history of falling (OR = 1.73).

In one Australian study, 305 people older than 65 years took part in a battery of (a) tests examining clinical measures of foot and ankle strength, range of motion, posture, and deformity; (b) balance tests, including postural sway, maximum balance range, lateral stability, and coordinated stability; and (c) functional ability tests, including alternate step test, sit-to-stand, and a timed 20-foot walk (Spink, Fotoohabadi, et al., 2011). Hallux (big toe) plantar flexion (pushing toes downward) strength and ankle inversion–eversion (sole of foot in toward or away from other foot) range of motion were the most consistent significant and independent predictors of balance and functional test performance, explaining up to 25% of the variance in the test scores. Foot and ankle characteristics, particularly plantar flexor strength of the hallux and ankle inversion–eversion range of motion, are important determinants of balance and functional ability in older people (Spink, Fotoohabadi, et al., 2011).

Disabling foot pain is associated with foot function characteristics, functional ability, and HRQOL in older adults (Mickle, Munro, Lord, Menz, & Steele, 2011). Ankle dorsiflexion strength, hallux strength, stride length, step length, walking speed, and HRQOL were significantly reduced in those with foot pain (Mickle et al., 2011). Sore feet also contribute to concerns about outdoor mobility, as evidenced by a U.K. study of the effects of tactile paving (pavements used to differentiate curb edges and crossings for visually impaired people; Ormerod, 2012). Ormerod (2012) surveyed older participants and found that they were more likely to be concerned for their safety walking across tactile paving if they had balance problems, sore feet, arthritis in their lower limbs, reduced mobility, a fear of falling or crowds, or an injury that interferes with walking. Many people felt that there was an increased risk of slipping on tactile paving if it was wet, icy, or laid on a slope, and concerns were raised about the trip hazards posed by paving blisters.

Mobility and Assistive Devices

More than 4 million people use canes, and more than 1.5 million use walkers in the United States alone (Laplante, Hendershot, & Moss, 1992). Such mobility aids often are required by older adults or by people with various clinical conditions so that they can move about independently and maintain their balance. In addition, these aids can help reduce lower-limb loading and thereby alleviate joint pain or compensate for weakness or injury. Mobility aids can improve balance control by providing mechanical advantages as well as somatosensory feedback. Conversely, some research indicates that mobility aids are significantly associated with falls and injuries. Several attentional, neuromotor, musculoskeletal, physiologic, and metabolic demands are associated with using these devices, and several potential mechanisms may adversely affect balance control. Clinical and biomechanic evaluations of canes and walkers confirm that these devices can improve balance and mobility (Bateni & Maki, 2005). They, however, also can interfere with one's ability to maintain balance in certain situations, and the strength and metabolic demands can be excessive. More research is needed to identify and solve specific problems. Older adults might perceive the use of walking aids as a sign of aging, which in turn is barrier to the use of such devices (Gooberman-Hill & Ebrahim, 2007).

ASSESSMENT OF MOBILITY

Mobility assessment involves the evaluation of the components of mobility such as transfer and gait. Many tests have been developed to assess functional mobility in older adults. Functional mobility tests also are used to assess the risk of falling in older adults (Scott, Votova, Scanlan, & Close, 2007). Objective, performance-based measures of physical function have the disadvantage that performance at the time of assessment may not represent the usual performance of the tested individual. Recent wearable motion-sensing technology, however, means that we now also can objectively assess mobility and physical activity out of the laboratory or clinical environment (de Bruin, Hartmann, Uebelhart, Murer, & Zijlstra, 2008).

Mobility Questionnaires: Self–Report and Subjective

Self-report or subjective reporting of mobility is potentially unreliable and subject to cognition and memory problems (see Exhibit 18.1). It does, however, allow for a quick assessment of mobility and often is used in large surveys and in residential settings where it is not viable to perform an objective assessment of mobility.

Barthel index. The Barthel index was developed to assess functional abilities (Mahoney & Barthel, 1965). This index consists of 10 items evaluating such daily activities as feeding, bathing, and toileting. The level of independence for each item is assessed. The total score is out of 100 with a higher score indicating independence (Mahoney & Barthel, 1965). A review of the reliability of the Barthel index in older adults found that this index is less reliable in older adults with cognitive impairment, and in general, it only had fair to moderate interrater reliability in older adults (Sainsbury, Seebass, Bansal, & Young, 2005).

IADL scale of Lawton and Brody. This scale assesses independence on IADLs, such as housekeeping, medication consumption, and shopping (Lawton & Brody, 1969). The score ranges from 0 to 8 with a higher score indicating less dependency.

Functional independence measure. The functional independence measure (FIM) is an 18-item scale, including motor and cognitive tasks of daily living. The scores range from 18 to 126 with lower scores indicating greater dependence (Keith, Granger,

---

Exhibit 18.1
Potential Instruments to Assess Mobility

Subjective and self-report	Barthel index
	Instrumental activities of daily living (IADL) scale
	Functional independence measure (FIM)
	Life-space mobility (LS)
Objective (gait)	Gait speed
	6-min walk test (6MWT)
	Dynamic gait index (DGI)
	Functional gait assessment (FGA)
Objective (overall mobility)	Performance-oriented mobility assessment (POMA)
	Elderly mobility scale (EMS)
	Short physical performance battery (SPPB)
	Physical performance test (PPT)
	Berg balance scale (BBS)
	Timed up and go (TUG) test
Objective (transfers)	Sit-to-stand test
	Stair negotiation
Fear of falling	Single-item questions
	Falls efficacy scale (FES)
	Falls efficacy scale—international (FES–I)
	Activities-specific balance and confidence (ABC) scale
	Survey of activities and fear of falling in the elderly (SAFFE)
	University of Illinois at Chicago fear of falling measure (UIC–FFM)
	Geriatric fear of falling measure (GFFM)

Hamilton, & Sherwin, 1987; Linacre, Heinemann, Wright, Granger, & Hamilton, 1994). Hobart et al. (2001) found that FIM has excellent test–retest reliability in older adults. Low scores on the FIM were found to predict falls in older adults in inpatient settings (Forrest, Chen, Huss, & Giesler, 2013).

Life-space mobility. Life-space (LS) reflects the person–environment relationship, permitting assessment of the effect of sociodemographic and community-level characteristics on mobility (Baker et al., 2003). LS can be defined as "the area through which a person traveled over a specified time period. Life-space defines movement extending from within one's home to movement beyond one's town or geographic region" (Baker et al., 2003, p. 51). Diseases, geriatric syndromes, and neuropsychological conditions occur in the context of sociodemographic factors and may lead to declines in physical performance and thereby reduce LS. Health behaviors, however, may modify the impact of these factors on LS. LS has been shown to correlate with measures of physical and mental health, including physical performance, ADLs, IADLs, depression, self-reported health, and a number of comorbid conditions (Baker et al., 2003). LS can be measured using the University of Alabama at Birmingham Study of Aging Life-Space Assessment, which measures mobility based on the distance through which a person reports moving during the 4 weeks preceding the assessment. This includes assessing levels of movements, frequency, and use of assistance (Baker et al., 2003).

Mobility Functional Assessments

Mobility functional assessments (objective) can be broadly split into gait assessment (walking), overall mobility functional assessments, and transfers (e.g., sit-to-stand and stair climbing). Newer body-worn sensors also are being used to study human movement.

Walking and gait assessment.

Gait speed. The measurement of gait speed is important in the assessment of older adults (Peel, Kuys, & Klein, 2013). Gait speed is a simple and reliable measure of gait performance (Guralnik et al., 2000). Higher gait speed is associated with a lower risk of disability in older adults (den Ouden, Schuurmans, Arts, & van der Schouw, 2011). A gait speed of less than 1.2 meter/sec was predictive of future mobility disability in community-dwelling middle-age and older adults (Deshpande, Metter, Guralnik, Bandinelli, & Ferrucci, 2013). Moreover, inability to complete a simple gait task or a usual speed of less than 0.5 meter/sec was found to be associated with a higher mortality risk in those age 85 years or older (Toots et al., 2013).

Usual gait speed can be used as a single measure of adverse outcomes such as falls in community-dwelling older adults (Abellan van Kan et al., 2009).

Slower speed also was found to be associated with the risk of falling (Montero-Odasso et al., 2005).

As mentioned earlier, gait and cognitive function are interlinked. Decline in gait speed can be predicted by a decline in global cognitive function and executive function (Atkinson et al., 2007). Moreover, usual gait speed predicted a decline in psychomotor speed and attention in older adults (Inzitari et al., 2008). Other studies found a borderline relationship between usual gait speed and cognitive decline but a strong relationship between fast gait speed and cognitive decline in older adults, with those experiencing cognitive decline walking more slowly (Deshpande, Metter, Bandinelli, Guralnik, & Ferrucci, 2009; Fitzpatrick et al., 2007). The more complex and challenging the gait task is, the greater the reliance on executive function (Yogev-Seligmann et al., 2008).

6-min walk test. The 6-min walk test (6MWT) measures the distance walked in 6 min and gives an indication of endurance. This test is a modified version of the 12-min walk test (American Thoracic Society, 2002) and originally was used with patients with cardiac and pulmonary problems (Southard & Gallagher, 2013). The 6MWT is used to assess submaximal functional exercise capacity (American Thoracic Society, 2002). A walking distance of less than 984 feet in 6 min was found to be a predictor of mortality in patients with mild to moderate congestive heart failure (Rostagno et al., 2003). This test also has been recommended as a reliable and valid tool for assessing mobility in older adults (Harada, Chiu, & Stewart, 1999). With regards to the ability of the 6MWT to predict falls, results are conflicting. Cho, Scarpace, and Alexander (2004) found that this test predicted frequent falls in older adults with mild balance impairment. Desai, Goodman, Kapadia, Shay, and Szturm (2010), however, found that this test did not differentiate between a group of community-dwelling fallers and nonfallers. The distance walked on the 6MWT was associated with cognitive function (MMSE score) in older adults with chronic heart failure (Baldasseroni et al., 2010).

Dynamic gait index. The dynamic gait index (DGI) consists of eight items that assess walking ability at different speeds, with head movements, turns, obstacles, and stair negotiation. The score is out of 24 and a lower score indicates poorer performance, with a score of 19 or less indicating risk of falling (Shumway-Cook & Woollacott, 1995). This measure has been used to evaluate the ability to modify gait and the risk of falling in many populations, such as patients with stroke (Jonsdottir & Cattaneo, 2007), Parkinson's disease (Dibble & Lange, 2006), and multiple sclerosis (McConvey & Bennett, 2005).

Functional gait assessment. The functional gait assessment (FGA) is a 10-item gait assessment that is a modification of the DGI that was developed to enhance reliability and address the ceiling effect of the DGI (Wrisley, Marchetti, Kuharsky, & Whitney, 2004). It eliminated the ambulation around obstacles item from the DGI, and it added three items concerned with gait with narrow base of support, ambulating backward, and gait with eyes closed (Wrisley et al., 2004). The score ranges from 0 to 30, with lower scores indicating poorer performance (Wrisley et al., 2004). A cutoff score of 22 or less on the FGA was proposed to identify those at risk of falling (Wrisley & Kumar, 2010).

Overall mobility functional assessments.

Performance-oriented mobility assessment. Performance-oriented mobility assessment (POMA) was developed by Tinetti (1986). This tool is used to assess mobility and fall risk in older adults. It has 28 items, including 16 for balance (sitting, rising, immediate standing, standing, turning, and sitting down balance) and 12 for gait (initiation of gait, step length and height, step symmetry and continuity, path, trunk sway, and walking stance). A higher score means better mobility and a lower indicates risk of falling. Shumway-Cook and Woollacott (2007) proposed the following categories to classify risk of falling: score 25–28 low risk, 19–24 medium risk, and 19 or less high risk of falling. Scores on the POMA were associated with cognitive flexibility in Korean older adults, indicating that a decline in physical performance is related to a decline in executive function (Huh et al., 2011). Older adults with lower scores on the MMSE had poorer performance on the POMA (Teixeira-Leite & Manhães, 2012). This test also has been recommended by the American and British Geriatric Societies as a tool to assess fall risk (American Geriatrics Society/British Geriatrics Society, 2011).

The elderly mobility scale. The elderly mobility scale (EMS) originally was developed to provide a simple tool to decide whether a person could be discharged from the hospital to their own home or to a care environment. The scale assesses dependency in mobility on seven daily tasks: lying to sitting, sitting to lying, sitting to standing, standing, gait, 20-foot walk, and functional reach (Smith, 1994). This scale is scored out of 20 with a higher score indicating better mobility (Smith, 1994). The EMS detected improvements in mobility in older adults who had completed a course of physiotherapy at a geriatric day hospital (Spilg, Martin, Mitchell, & Aitchison, 2001). This scale, however, was not predictive of discharge or fall risk in inpatient settings (Prosser & Canby, 1997). Moreover, the EMS was not able to discriminate between community-dwelling one-time and multiple fallers (Chiu, Au-Yeung, & Lo, 2003). This was attributed to the simple activities assessed on the scale and the ceiling effect of this scale, as most one-time fallers' scores were between 19 and 20 (Chiu et al., 2003).

Short physical performance battery. The short physical performance battery (SPPB) was developed by Guralnik et al. (1994). It originally was developed to assess lower extremity function (Guralnik et al., 1994). The SPPB consists of three main sections assessing chair stands, balance, and walking. The balance section assesses side-by-side, semitandem, and tandem stances for 10 sec, and these items are scored on an ordinal scale (0–4) with 4 indicating the maximum score. Subjects are asked to rise from a chair five times and to walk 13 feet as fast as they can. The scoring for the walking and chair rise sections is also 0–4 based on the time required to perform the task, with a higher score indicating faster performance (Guralnik et al., 1994).

The SPPB was found to predict loss in the ability to walk 1,312 feet in adults age 65 years and older (Vasunilashorn et al., 2009). Moreover, this measure can predict poor outcomes, including death, after hospital discharge in acutely ill older adults (Volpato et al., 2011). Poorer performance on the SPPB was associated with a higher risk of falling (Mangani et al., 2008).

The physical performance test. The physical performance test (PPT) was developed by Reuben and Siu (1990). This test assesses a variety of daily life tasks. Two versions were developed: a seven-task (scored out of 28) and a nine-task (scored out of 36) test. Tasks assessed include simulated eating, turning 360 degrees, putting on and removing a jacket, lifting a book and putting it on a shelf, picking up a penny from the floor, a 50-foot walk test, and climbing stairs (Reuben & Siu, 1990). This test was found to be an independent predictor of mortality and nursing home admission in older adults (Reuben, Siu, & Kimpau, 1992). This test also was used to classify frailty in older adults (Brown, Sinacore, Binder, & Kohrt, 2000). Moreover, the PPT is a predictor of recurrent falls (score 15 or less) in community-dwelling older adults (VanSwearingen, Paschal, Bonino, & Chen, 1998).

Berg balance scale. The Berg balance scale (BBS) was developed to assess functional balance (K. Berg., 1989). This test has been used widely to assess balance in older adults (Langley & Mackintosh, 2007). The BBS is a 14-item scale that assesses balance in sitting, in standing, and while performing functional tasks, such as reaching forward (K. Berg, 1989). The score is out of 56 with a higher score indicating better balance (K. Berg, 1989). This scale also has been used to assess the risk of falling, and a cutoff score of 45 or lower was proposed to identify those at risk of falling (Bogle Thorbahn & Newton, 1996). However, the results based on this cutoff score to predict falls are inconsistent (Muir, Berg, Chesworth, & Speechley, 2008). Muir et al. (2008) recommended the use of the BBS as a multilevel scale and not as a dichotomous scale to predict multiple falls. Older adults with better performance on executive function tests were found to have better performance on the BBS (Voos, Custódio, & Malaquias, 2011).

TUG test. The TUG test is a reliable and valid test for functional mobility in older adults (Podsiadlo & Richardson, 1991). The American and British Geriatric Societies also have recommended this test as a tool for falls risk assessment (American Geriatrics Society/British Geriatrics Society, 2011). This test involves standing up from a chair, walking 10 feet, turning, and walking back and sitting down again. Instructions can call for preferred speed or walking as fast as possible (Schoene et al., 2013). The TUG was found to be predictive of performance on ADLs, indicating that it is a measure of function (Viccaro, Perera, & Studenski, 2011). Despite fallers requiring a longer time to complete the test than nonfallers (a difference of 0.4 sec), the differences are not considered clinically meaningful in healthy community-dwelling older adults. The difference increased to 4 sec, however, when comparing frailer fallers and nonfallers in institutionalized settings (Schoene et al., 2013). Cutoff scores in independently living older adults varied from 8.1 to 16 sec and in institutionalized older adults from 13 to 32.5 sec when walking at preferred speed. Because of the variation in cutoff scores, no recommendations can be made regarding the most predictive score (Schoene et al., 2013). The time required to perform the TUG test was associated with global cognitive function, executive function, and memory (Donoghue et al., 2012).

Transfers: sit-to-stand and stair use.

Sit-to-stand test. The ability to perform the sit-to-stand movement is an important determinant of functional independence (Kerr, White, Barr, & Mollan, 1994). The general population performs around 60 ± 22 sit-to-stand movements per day (Dall & Kerr, 2010). The sit-to-stand test was developed to assess the strength of the lower extremities (Csuka & McCarty, 1985). The original test consisted of 10 sit-to-stand movements, and the time required to perform these stands was measured (Csuka & McCarty, 1985). Other versions of this test have been used, such as the five-time sit-to-stand test. Time required to perform the five-time sit-to-stand test was found to be a strong predictor of disability in older adults (Guralnik, Ferrucci, Simonsick, Salive, & Wallace, 1995). Requiring more than 13.6 sec to complete five sit-to-stand transfers was predictive of future mobility disability in community-dwelling middle-age and older adults (Deshpande et al., 2013). In addition to measuring lower extremity strength, the five-time sit-to-stand test predicted the occurrence of disability related to ADLs and IADLs in older adults (Zhang et al., 2013). This test was valid for prospectively identifying multiple fallers (12 sec or more; Tiedemann, Shimada,

Sherrington, Murray, & Lord, 2008). Community-dwelling older women with cognitive impairment, determined by the Short Portable Mental State Questionnaire, required longer time to perform the five-time sit-to-stand test (Annweiler et al., 2011). In this study, a cutoff score of 15 sec was suggested for the detection of moderate cognitive impairment.

Because of difficulty of achieving these repetitions, and to avoid the floor effect for this test, the 30-sec chair-stand test was developed. This test was found to be a reliable and valid measure of lower extremity strength in community-dwelling older adults (Jones, Rikli, & Beam, 1999).

Stair negotiation. Stair negotiation is one of the most challenging tasks for older adults, with about 10% of fatal falls occurring while descending stairs (Startzell, Owens, Mulfinger, & Cavanagh, 2000). This task is assessed by clinical observation. The ability to negotiate stairs is a key functional requirement to be discharged from the hospital, and inability to do so is often an indication for nursing home admission (Lin, Hung, Liao, Sheen, & Jong, 2006). Longer time to negotiate three steps was found to be a predictor of functional decline in community-dwelling older adults (Oh-Park, Wang, & Verghese, 2011). The estimate for meaningful improvement in stair negotiation in this population is about 0.2 sec and for decline about 0.5 sec (Oh-Park, Perera, & Verghese, 2012).

Wearable motion-sensing technology. A recent development is the use of wearable motion-sensing technology to study human movement. Based on the use of miniaturized motion sensors, methods are available for long-term monitoring of daily physical activity and the assessment of motor functioning under real-life conditions (de Bruin et al., 2008). A review showed that the number of studies that use pedometers (step counters) or accelerometry to obtain overall measures of physical activity level, or estimations of energy expenditure, form the majority of studies. In contrast, the number of studies that use movement sensors for long-term monitoring of activity patterns, such as postural transitions or time spent in certain activities, is still rather small. Existing literature on movement classification using accelerometry data has been widely varied

in approach, intention, and outcome. At present, therefore, the use of wearable systems for monitoring movement activities in people older than 65 years has not yet reached its full potential (de Bruin et al., 2008).

Assessment of fear of falling. Fear of falling was first described in the literature in 1982 as *ptophobia* (Bhala, O'Donnell, & Thoppil, 1982). This term designates fear of standing or walking due to fear of falling. Fear of falling has been described as part of postfall syndrome (J. Murphy & Isaacs, 1982), which indicates fear of falling and restriction of physical activity after a fall. Recently, the term fear has been substituted by concern to include a wider range and to improve sensitivity (Yardley et al., 2005).

Recent reviews have identified measures of fear of falling in older adults (Greenberg, 2012; Jørstad, Hauer, Becker, & Lamb, 2005; Moore & Ellis, 2008). Some of the measures are described in the following sections (see Exhibit 18.1).

Single-item questions. Single-item questions, such as "are you afraid of falling?" or "Do you have fear of falling?" have been used. Although these questions are direct and specific, they do not capture the scope of fear in terms of various situations in which one might experience fear of falling and the extent of this fear (Howland et al., 1993; Lachman et al., 1998).

Falls efficacy scale. Tinetti, Richman, and Powell (1990) developed the falls efficacy scale (FES). This 10-item scale assesses confidence while performing indoor activities, such as getting on and off the toilet, reaching into cabinets, and getting in and out of bed. Each item can be scored from 1 to 10 with 1 meaning very confident and 10 meaning not confident at all. This scale has been criticized for the narrow scope of activities it includes and for its scoring system (Moore & Ellis, 2008).

Falls efficacy scale–international. The falls efficacy scale—international (FES–I) was developed by ProFaNE (Yardley et al., 2005). This scale consists of 16 items that assess the level of concern about falling. The score for each item is measured by a four-point scale (1 = not at all concerned, 4 = very concerned). The total score ranges from 16 (no concern about falling) to 64 (severe concern about falling). This scale has the additive value over the FES that it assesses outdoor activities and elements of dual tasking.

Activities-specific balance and confidence scale. The activities-specific balance and confidence (ABC) scale measures balance confidence using 16 items ranging from walking inside the house to walking in a mall. This measure was developed by Powell and Myers (1995). Level of confidence can be indicated as a percentage, ranging from 0% indicating no confidence to 100% indicating complete confidence. Despite the wide range of activities covered in this scale, the scoring system might be difficult for older adults especially those with cognitive impairment (Greenberg, 2012).

Survey of activities and fear of falling in the elderly. The survey of activities and fear of falling in the elderly (SAFFE) was developed by Lachman et al. (1998). This survey is administered in an interview format. SAFFE assesses activity, activity restriction, reasons for restriction, and fear of falling. It assesses fear of falling as being worried about falling on a four-point scale while performing 22 ADLs and IADLs. A modified version of the SAFFE includes a 17-item self-administered survey. SAFFE can be used to differentiate between fear of falling that can lead to activity restriction and fear of falling while performing activities (Greenberg, 2012).

University of Illinois at Chicago fear of falling measure. The University of Illinois at Chicago fear of falling measure (UIC–FFM) assesses fear of falling using an interview format (Velozo & Peterson, 2001). The UIC–FFM assesses worrying about falling in 19 activities on a four-point scale (1 = very worried, 4 = not at all worried).

Geriatric fear of falling measure. The geriatric fear of falling measure was developed to assess fear of falling in older adults in Taiwan (Huang, 2006). The advantage of this measure is that it expands over other scales by not assessing only fear experienced while performing activities (Greenberg, 2012). It has 41 items in three subscales: psychometric symptoms, such as inability to sleep due to fear of falling; adopting risk prevention behaviors, such as using a chair while taking a bath; and modifying behavior, such as going out less on rainy days.

INTERVENTIONS TO IMPROVE MOBILITY

A review of interventions to improve mobility in older people showed that effective interventions for enhancing mobility in older adults include walking; aerobic exercise; and resistance training focusing on strength, balance, and flexibility (Yeom, Keller, & Fleury, 2009). Group-based interventions also show significant beneficial effects in increasing mobility. To obtain significant effects of physical activity interventions, patients should participate in the exercise programs for at least 12 weeks, and the typical dose of the physical activity prescription is 20–60 min three times weekly (Yeom et al., 2009). Yeom et al. (2009) concluded that the major challenges of creating mobility enhancement recommendations for older adults include detailing a mobility enhancement program that will delay disability, creating a specific program dose for different populations by gender and ethnicity, and developing culturally appropriate mobility enhancement programs to improve adherence over time. Interventions directed at improving mobility in older adults, however, usually focus on one form of mobility at a time (e.g., walking) without considering the effect of environmental factors (Satariano et al., 2012).

There are many published interventions for reducing mobility problems in older people living in the community. Interventions are aimed at different levels of mobility or ability and have been developed and evaluated in many different settings. A current Cochrane review protocol aims to summarize the evidence for the benefits and safety of mobility training on overall functioning and mobility in frail older people living in the community (Fairhall, Sherrington, & Cameron, 2013).

In a meta-analysis conducted to assess the effect of physical therapy exercises on mobility in community-dwelling older adults, de Vries et al. (2012) found that exercise has a positive effect on improving mobility and physical function in older adults. Moreover, in this review, high-intensity exercise programs, such as weighted vest training, performed three times per week for 12 weeks were found to have better outcomes on mobility than low-intensity training. Older adults with impaired mobility and function seem to benefit more from these exercise programs (de Vries et al., 2012).

It is less clear, however, how mobility can be improved in obese older people. Older adults at risk for disability ($N = 424$, age range: 70–88 years) were randomized to a 12-month physical activity (PA) intervention involving moderate-intensity aerobic, strength, balance, and flexibility exercise (150 min/week) or a successful aging (SA) intervention involving weekly educational workshops (Manini et al., 2010). Individuals were stratified by obesity using a cutoff of body mass index (BMI) of 30 or higher ($n = 179$). Mobility function was assessed as usual walking speed over 1,312 feet and scores on the SPPB. Over 12 months of supervised training, the attendance and total amount of walking time was similar between obese and nonobese subjects, but no weight change was observed. Nonobese participants in the PA group had significant increases in 1,312-foot walking speed ($+1.5\%$), whereas their counterparts in the SA group declined (-4.3%). In contrast, obese individuals declined regardless of their assigned intervention group (PA: -3.1%; SA: -4.9%). SPPB scores, however, increased following PA in both obese (PA: $+13.5\%$; SA: $+2.5\%$) and nonobese older adults (PA: $+18.6\%$; SA: $+6.1\%$; Manini et al., 2010).

In a Cochrane review including 121 trials and 6,700 participants, progressive resistance training was found to improve muscle strength; performance of simple tasks, such as walking; and daily activities, such as bathing, in addition to decreasing pain in older adults with osteoarthritis (Liu & Latham, 2009). Muscle power was found to be a better predictor of function than muscle strength for such tasks as rising from a chair or stair negotiation (Reid & Fielding, 2012). Indeed, interventions that improve strength and power as well as aerobic function (endurance), flexibility, and coordination are the main recommendations from the American College of Sports Medicine for maintaining mobility in older people (Nelson et al., 2007).

Yoga as a physical activity option for older adults is not well studied. A recent pilot randomized controlled trial (RCT) in older adults ($n = 54$) investigated the effects of 12 weeks (twice a week) of the Iyengar yoga program on balance and mobility in older people (Tiedemann, O'Rourke, Sesto, & Sherrington, 2013). The intervention group significantly improved compared with control participants on standing balance, sit-to-stand test, 13-foot walk, and one-legged stand with eyes closed.

Rehabilitation aimed at improving mobility for older people living in long-term care settings gives variable results but mostly positive outcomes on physical health and fitness. A summary of studies concluded that individual studies were often successful in demonstrating benefits to physical health from participating in different types of physical rehabilitation (Crocker et al., 2013). This review included 67 trials of 6,300 participants, with an average age of 83 years.

Interventions Aimed at Older People at Risk of Falls

A recent review showed that group and home exercise programs and programs that reduce environmental hazards at home reduce the rate and risk of falling in community-dwelling older adults (Gillespie et al., 2012). Vitamin D seems to be effective in reducing falls and fall risk only in older adults who have lower vitamin D levels to begin with (Gillespie et al., 2012). Multifactorial interventions, in which participants receive different components of intervention categories, are effective in reducing the rate of falling (e.g., falls per person-year) but not the risk of falling (used a risk ratio [RR] and 95% confidence interval [CI] based on the number of people falling [fallers] in each group; Gillespie et al., 2012).

Exercise to Reduce Rate and Risk of Falls

Exercise programs have been found to be effective in reducing falls in older adults (Chang et al., 2004; Sherrington et al., 2008). Exercises for fall prevention are usually delivered in group settings or prescribed as home exercises and can be categorized according to the ProFaNE taxonomy into gait, balance, and functional training; strength and resistance training; flexibility; three-dimensional training, such as Tai Chi, dance, and other movements in all planes of motion; general physical activity; endurance; and other (Lamb et al., 2011). Gillespie et al. (2012) found that when compared to control conditions, group and home exercises containing multiple exercise components were effective in reducing the risk and rate of falls. Group or home exercises that included only the balance, gait, and functional training component were effective in reducing the rate but not the risk of falling when compared with a control group. Strength and resistance training, on the other hand, failed to reduce the rate of falling or the number of those who fell when delivered in group or home settings. Only a small number of studies were conducted to assess the effect of general physical activity on falls, and the results showed no effect on risk of falling. Only Tai Chi, when used a single exercise, was found to be effective in reducing the rate and risk of falling, but this type of exercise was less effective in groups of high-risk older adults (Gillespie et al., 2012). Martin et al. (2013) found that group exercises administered by a physiotherapist are effective in preventing falls and improving balance. The Otago Exercise Program, which is a home-based program including balance and strength training, was found to be effective in reducing mortality and falls in community-dwelling older adults (Thomas, Mackintosh, & Halbert, 2010).

Integrated cognitive training and mobility interventions seem to be effective in improving cognitive function and physical factors, such as gait performance, as well as reducing the risk of falling (Segev-Jacubovski et al., 2011). The available studies, however, are weak. Dual-task cognitive gait interventions can improve gait performance under dual-task conditions and therefore might reduce the risk of falling (Segev-Jacubovski et al., 2011). Dual-task training also improves gait under challenging conditions in older adults with mild to moderate cognitive impairment (Segev-Jacubovski et al., 2011).

Interventions Aimed at Older People Following Hip Fracture

There are various strategies to improve mobility, including gait retraining and exercise programs, used during a hospital stay and often after discharge from hospital following a hip fracture. A recent Cochrane review included evidence from 19 trials involving 1,589 participants, generally older than 65 years (Handoll, Sherrington, & Mak, 2011). Many of the trials had weak methods, including inadequate follow-up. There was no pooling of data

because no two trials were sufficiently alike. Twelve trials evaluated interventions that started soon after hip fracture surgery. Successful interventions that found improved mobility included a 2-week weight-bearing program, a quadriceps muscle-strengthening exercise program, and electrical stimulation aimed at alleviating pain. Other single trials, however, found no significant improvement in mobility from a treadmill gait retraining program, 12 weeks of resistance training, and 16 weeks of weight-bearing exercise. Of two trials evaluating more intensive physiotherapy regimens, one found no difference in recovery rates, and the other reported a higher level of dropout in the more intensive group. Two trials tested electrical stimulation of the quadriceps: one found no benefit and poor tolerance of the intervention; the other found improved mobility and good tolerance (Handoll et al., 2011).

Seven trials evaluated interventions that started after hospital discharge (Handoll et al., 2011). Two trials, one testing 12 weeks of intensive physical training and another testing a home-based physical therapy program, found improved outcome on mobility. Begun after completion of standard physical therapy, one trial found improved outcome after 6 months of intensive physical training, one trial found increased activity levels from a 1-year exercise program, and one trial found no significant effects of home-based resistance or aerobic training. One trial found improved outcome after home-based exercises started around 22 weeks from injury. Another trial, however, found home-based weight-bearing exercises starting at 7 months produced no significant improvement in mobility (Handoll et al., 2011). In summary, the review found that evidence was insufficient to determine which are the best strategies, whether started in the hospital or after discharge from the hospital, for helping people walk and continue walking after hip fracture surgery (Handoll et al., 2011).

Crotty et al. (2010) conducted a Cochrane review on the effect of rehabilitation interventions on physical and psychosocial functioning following hip fracture in older adults. This review included nine studies with 1,400 participants generally age 65 years or older. The studies involved were heterogeneous and the interventions ranged from inpatient to outpatient interventions. The interventions studied included cognitive–behavioral therapy, motivation, education, and physical therapy. Interventions delivered in the inpatient setting involved reorientation, cognitive–behavioral therapy, and occupational therapy, and these interventions showed no change in physical function, emotional health, length of hospital stay, and death.

In this review, community-based nurse-led interventions (discharge planning) showed conflicting results. One trial showed some beneficial effect of the intervention on outcomes such as death and readmission to hospital. The other trial failed to show any significant changes. Interventions delivered in the outpatient and home setting did not have a significant effect on outcomes (Crotty et al., 2010). Because the trials included in this review were heterogeneous and the sample sizes were small, the authors made no recommendations (Crotty et al., 2010).

Intervention Aimed at Older People With Specific Comorbidities

The effect of physiotherapy interventions on functional abilities of patients with Parkinson's disease was investigated in a Cochrane review, including 33 trials with 1,518 participants (Tomlinson et al., 2012). Physiotherapy interventions, when compared with no or placebo interventions, showed a significant improvement in walking speed, endurance, and step length. Moreover, performance on the TUG test, functional reach, the BBS, and the Unified Parkinson's Disease Rating Scale also improved with physiotherapy interventions (Tomlinson et al., 2012), indicating that physiotherapy has a positive effect on both functional mobility and balance. Despite these beneficial effects, physiotherapy interventions did not have a significant effect on falls and quality of life in this population (Tomlinson et al., 2012).

Treadmill training showed beneficial effects in improving gait hypokinesia (shuffling gait and slowness) by improving gait speed, stride length, and walking distance (Mehrholz et al., 2010). This Cochrane review included eight trials with 203 participants. Despite these beneficial effects, the heterogeneity of the studies does not allow for conclusions

to be drawn on the duration, intensity, and lasting effects of training (Mehrholz et al., 2010).

The effect of physical fitness training on disability and death was investigated in a review by Brazzelli, Saunders, Greig, and Mead (2011). This review consisted of 32 trials with 1,414 participants. The interventions included aerobic, resistance, and mixed interventions. Aerobic training that included walking improved gait speed and capacity. Mixed training that included walking had similar but smaller effects. The effect of resistance training could not be determined because of the lack of adequate data. Despite some beneficial effects identified in this review, the results should be viewed with caution because of the variability in the quality of the studies (Brazzelli et al., 2011). Group circuit class therapy, which is "a model of therapy delivery that utilizes active exercises and activities which are task specific (practicing the functional task itself or part thereof) and provided in an intensive manner," was found to improve mobility after stroke (English & Hillier, 2010, p. 2). English and Hillier's (2010) review included six trials with 292 participants. Circuit training was found to improve walking speed, performance on 6MWT, balance, and balance confidence and earlier discharge from inpatient settings (English & Hillier, 2010). It is still not clear, however, which patients would benefit the most and whether outcomes vary based on the specific task tested (English & Hillier, 2010).

Overground gait training improved gait speed, TUG performance, and the 6MWT in patients with chronic stroke (States, Pappas, & Salem, 2009). Nine studies with 499 participants were included in this review. Although some beneficial effects were found, this type of training had no significant effect on death and disability. Insufficient evidence to support the recommendation of overground training was found in this review because of the wide range of disabilities and the small number of high-quality studies (States et al., 2009). Moseley, Stark, Cameron, and Pollock (2005) conducted a review to assess the effect of treadmill training and body support on walking after stroke. This review included 15 trials with 622 participants. The results of the review showed that treadmill training with and without body support had no significant effect on gait speed and dependence, despite some individual studies indicating a superior effect of treadmill training with body support on gait speed (Moseley et al., 2005).

Studies have been published on the effect of interventions for improving community ambulation in patients with stroke. Recently, a protocol for a Cochrane review aiming to assess this effect was published (Barclay-Goddard, Stevenson, Poluha, Ripat, & Nett, 2012).

Interventions Aimed at Older People With Cognitive Impairment

Littbrand, Stenvall, and Rosendahl (2011) conducted a systematic review to assess the applicability and effect of physical exercise on physical and cognitive function. Ten studies were included in this review. Institutionalized older adults with Alzheimer's disease showed improvement in walking speed and daily activities after exercise. The most feasible exercise in this population was combined functional weight-bearing exercises. Hospitalized older adults with dementia did not benefit from a 2-week exercise program (Littbrand et al., 2011). The effect of physical exercise on cognitive function could not be determined because of the low quality of the studies (Littbrand et al., 2011). In a meta-analysis, including 30 trials with 2,020 participants, exercise was found to improve physical and cognitive function in patients with dementia and cognitive impairment (Heyn, Abreu, & Ottenbacher, 2004).

When the effects of strength and endurance exercise were compared between cognitively impaired and cognitively intact older adults, similar improvements were found in both groups on endurance and strength measures, such as TUG and grip strength (Heyn, Johnson, & Kramer, 2008). In this meta-analysis, 41 studies with 2,921 participants were included. Hauer, Becker, Lindemann, and Beyer (2006) conducted a systematic review including 11 trials to assess the effect of physical training on function and falls in older adults with cognitive impairment. Conflicting evidence was found and the trials included were not of adequate quality, which highlights the need for further research in this area.

Interventions Aimed at Older People With Severe Visual Impairment

An intervention to improve mobility in older people with visual impairment aims to enhance the individual's ability to perform daily living tasks safely and independently, facilitating their safe mobility and improving confidence. There is little research on environmental or behavioral interventions to increase activity in older people with visual impairment (Skelton et al., 2013). Examples of environmental interventions for an individual with visual impairment include the removal of a rug, increased lighting in hallways, and contrasting stripes on stairs. Behavioral interventions include the systematic implementation of procedures that result in lasting positive changes in an individual's behavior (S. N. Markowitz, 2006). These interventions for people with visual impairment might include, but are not restricted to, the teaching of adaptive strategies to enhance changes in an individual's behavior when negotiating and interacting with their environment (M. Markowitz, 2006) and orientation and mobility (O&M) training (Virgili & Rubin, 2003). O&M training aims to teach the visually impaired person how to ambulate and negotiate the environment safely and independently and may contribute to reduced activity limitations and societal participation (G. A. R. Zijlstra et al., 2009). Only two small studies, however, with a total of 63 people comparing O&M training delivered by a trained volunteer to physical exercise were identified in a Cochrane review (Virgili & Rubin, 2003). These studies did not show a difference between the two interventions, but they had little power to do so because of the small sample size and poor methodological quality. Therefore, more work is needed to implement effective interventions to increase mobility in older people with significant visual impairment.

Interventions Aimed at Older People With Foot Problems

Interventions aimed at improving mobility in older people with foot problems mostly focus on orthotics and exercise to improve range of motion and strength of the foot and ankle muscles. One Brazilian study randomly assigned 94 women (more than 60 years old) with osteoporosis to an intervention group with foot orthoses or to a control group without orthoses. Minor adverse effects were noted, as often is the case with orthotic interventions (pain, discomfort, foot heat, or tightness of footwear because of their orthotics). Only subjects from the intervention group displayed improvements in balance (TUG), foot pain, and disability (de Morais Barbosa et al., 2013).

A Japanese study investigated the effects of seated toe and ankle training (8 weeks) for older people (Nagai et al., 2011). A significant improvement was found in quadriceps strength, functional reach, stepping in sitting (alternate stepping with the right and left legs on a board as quickly as possible for 5 sec while seated), and quality of life, together with a possible improvement in toe flexor strength. These results suggest that a training program carried out with the subject in a sitting position and focused mainly on ankle, foot, and toe functions is effective in improving some aspects of motor function. A Portuguese study within nursing homes showed a significant improvement in plantar and dorsiflexion strength after a 6-week (three times per week) seated exercise program using ankle dorsi- and plantar flexion exercises with elastic bands (Ribeiro, Teixeira, Brochado, & Oliveira, 2009). Not only did strength improve but also balance and functional mobility. This approach may help elderly individuals maintain their activity level without increasing risks.

Finally, to determine the effectiveness of a multifaceted podiatry intervention in preventing falls in community-dwelling older people with disabling foot pain, Spink, Menz, et al. (2011) performed a parallel-group RCT in Australia. Some 305 community-dwelling men and women (mean age 74 years) with disabling foot pain and an increased risk of falling were allocated randomly to a multifaceted podiatry intervention or to routine podiatry care, with 12 months' follow-up. The multifaceted podiatry intervention consisted of foot orthotics, advice on footwear, subsidy for footwear (US$93), a home-based program of foot and ankle exercises, a falls prevention education booklet, and routine podiatry care for 12 months. The control group received routine podiatry care for 12 months. Participants in the intervention group experienced 36% fewer falls than participants in the control group. There were also

significant improvements in strength (ankle eversion), range of motion (ankle dorsiflexion and inversion–eversion), and balance (postural sway on the floor when barefoot and maximum balance range wearing shoes).

Interventions to Reduce Fear of Falling

G. A. R. Zijlstra et al. (2007) conducted a systematic review to investigate the effectiveness of interventions aimed to reduce fear of falling in community-dwelling older adults. This review included 19 studies, 3 of which were aimed at reducing the risk of falling, whereas the other studies included fear of falling as one of their outcome measures. The interventions investigated were Tai Chi, multifactorial falls prevention programs, exercise interventions, balance interventions, hip protection interventions, and one intervention to reduce fall risk factors. Evidence is limited evidence that Tai Chi, multifactorial fall risk prevention programs, exercise interventions, and hip protection interventions are effective in reducing the fear of falling. Fear of falling was measured using different versions of the FES or one-item questions (G. A. R. Zijlstra et al., 2007).

A Cochrane review conducted to investigate rehabilitation intervention for improving psychological outcomes after hip fracture included nine studies and 1,400 subjects (Crotty et al., 2010). The results of the review indicated that there is insufficient evidence indicating improvements in psychological outcomes following interventions, such as reorientation measures, intensive occupational therapy, cognitive–behavioral therapy, nurse-led care, and educational and motivational interventions (Crotty et al., 2010).

A multifactorial falls prevention program seems to be effective in reducing fear of falling and depression in older adults (Sjösten, Vaapio, & Kivela, 2008). Tai Chi also has some beneficial effects on reducing the fear of falling (Blake & Hawley, 2012; Sjösten et al., 2008).

CONCLUSION

Functional mobility is necessary for social engagement, physical and mental health, and quality of life. Poor mobility is a marker for both physical and mental health decline and an independent predictor for mortality. A variety of assessment measures have been developed to assess mobility and mobility-associated problems in older adults. Despite mobility disability being a serious problem that affects independence and ADLs, interventions with a range of older adults aimed at improving mobility often are successful at maintaining or improving both mobility and quality of life as well as at reducing falls. The scarcity of high-quality research in this area, suggested by many of the reviews, means that patient-centered mobility interventions still are not delivered routinely following a specific evidence base. Ideally, there is a need for high-quality RCTs that focus on objective measurement of mobility following intervention in a range of older people with comorbidities (not disease specific) in different settings.

References

Abellan Van Kan, G., Rolland, Y., Andrieu, S., Bauer, J., Beauchet, O., Bonnefoy, M., . . . Vellas, B. (2009). Gait speed at usual pace as a predictor of adverse outcomes in community-dwelling older people an International Academy on Nutrition and Aging (IANA) Task Force. *Journal of Nutrition, Health, and Aging, 13,* 881–889. doi:10.1007/s12603-009-0246-z

Abernethy, B. (1988). Dual-task methodology and motor skills research: Some applications and methodological constraints. *Journal of Human Movement Studies, 14,* 101–132.

Alfaro-Acha, A., Al Snih, S., Raji, M. A., Markides, K. S., & Ottenbacher, K. J. (2007). Does 8-foot walk time predict cognitive decline in older Mexicans Americans? *Journal of the American Geriatrics Society, 55,* 245–251. doi:10.1111/j.1532-5415.2007.01039.x

Allman, R. M., Baker, P. S., Maisiak, R. M., Sims, R. V., & Roseman, J. M. (2004). Racial similarities and differences in predictors of mobility change over eighteen months. *Journal of General Internal Medicine, 19,* 1118–1126. doi:10.1111/j.1525-1497.2004.30239.x

American Geriatrics Society/British Geriatrics Society. (2011). Summary of the Updated American Geriatrics Society/British Geriatrics Society clinical practice guideline for prevention of falls in older persons. *Journal of the American Geriatrics Society, 59,* 148–157. doi:10.1111/j.1532-5415.2010.03234.x

American Thoracic Society. (2002). ATS statement: Guidelines for the six-minute walk test. *American Journal of Respiratory and Critical Care Medicine, 166,* 111–117. doi:10.1164/ajrccm.166.1.at1102

Annweiler, C., Schott, A. M., Abellan van Kan, G., Rolland, Y., Blain, H., Fantino, B., . . . Beauchet, O. (2011). The five-times-sit-to-stand test, a marker of global cognitive functioning among community-dwelling older women. *Journal of Nutrition, Health, and Aging, 15,* 271–276. doi:10.1007/s12603-011-0037-1

Atkinson, H. H., Rosano, C., Simonsick, E. M., Williamson, J. D., Davis, C., Ambrosius, W. T., . . . Kritchevsky, S. B. (2007). Cognitive function, gait speed decline, and comorbidities: The health, aging and body composition study. *The Journals of Gerontology, Series A: Biological Sciences and Medical Sciences, 62,* 844–850. doi:10.1093/gerona/62.8.844

Axer, H., Axer, M., Sauer, H., Witte, O. W., & Hagemann, G. (2010). Falls and gait disorders in geriatric neurology. *Clinical Neurology and Neurosurgery, 112,* 265–274. doi:10.1016/j.clineuro.2009.12.015

Ayis, S., Gooberman-Hill, R., Bowling, A., & Ebrahim, S. (2006). Predicting catastrophic decline in mobility among older people. *Age and Ageing, 35,* 382–387. doi:10.1093/ageing/afl004

Baker, P. S., Bodner, E. V., & Allman, R. M. (2003). Measuring life-space mobility in community-dwelling older adults. *Journal of the American Geriatrics Society, 51,* 1610–1614. doi:10.1046/j.1532-5415.2003.51512.x

Baldasseroni, S., Mossello, E., Romboli, B., Orso, F., Colombi, C., Fumagalli, S., . . . Marchionni, N. (2010). Relationship between cognitive function and 6-minute walking test in older outpatients with chronic heart failure. *Aging Clinical and Experimental Research, 22,* 308–313. doi:10.1007/BF03324936

Barclay-Goddard, R. E., Stevenson, T. J., Poluha, W., Ripat, J., & Nett, C. (2012). Interventions for improving community ambulation in individuals with stroke. *Cochrane Database of Systematic Reviews, 11,* CD010200. doi:10.1002/14651858.CD010200

Barr, E. L., Browning, C., Lord, S. R., Menz, H. B., & Kendig, H. (2005). Foot and leg problems are important determinants of functional status in community dwelling older people. *Disability and Rehabilitation: An International, Multidisciplinary Journal, 27,* 917–923. doi:10.1080/09638280500030506

Bateni, H., & Maki, B. E. (2005). Assistive devices for balance and mobility: Benefits, demands, and adverse consequences. *Archives of Physical Medicine and Rehabilitation, 86,* 134–145. doi:10.1016/j.apmr.2004.04.023

Berg, K. (1989). Measuring balance in the elderly: Preliminary development of an instrument. *Physiotherapy Canada, 41,* 304–311. doi:10.3138/ptc.41.6.304

Berg, W. P., Alessio, H. M., Mills, E. M., & Tong, C. (1997). Circumstances and consequences of falls in independent community-dwelling older adults. *Age and Ageing, 26,* 261–268. doi:10.1093/ageing/26.4.261

Berger, S. (2012). Is my world getting smaller? The challenges of living with vision loss. *Journal of Visual Impairment and Blindness, 106*, 5–16.

Bertera, E. M., & Bertera, R. L. (2008). Fear of falling and activity avoidance in a national sample of older adults in the United States. *Health and Social Work, 33*, 54–62. doi:10.1093/hsw/33.1.54

Bhala, R. P., O'Donnell, J., & Thoppil, E. (1982). Ptophobia: Phobic fear of falling and its clinical management. *Physical Therapy, 62*, 187–190.

Blake, H., & Hawley, H. (2012). Effects of Tai Chi exercise on physical and psychological health of older people. *Current Aging Science, 5*, 19–27. doi:10.2174/1874609811205010019

Bogle Thorbahn, L. D., & Newton, R. A. (1996). Use of the Berg balance test to predict falls in elderly persons. *Physical Therapy, 76*, 576–583.

Bootsma-van der Wiel, A., Gussekloo, J., De Craen, A. J., Van Exel, E., Bloem, B. R., & Westendorp, R. G. (2002). Common chronic diseases and general impairments as determinants of walking disability in the oldest-old population. *Journal of the American Geriatrics Society, 50*, 1405–1410. doi:10.1046/j.1532-5415.2002.50363.x

Brazzelli, M., Saunders, D. H., Greig, C. A., & Mead, G. E. (2011). Physical fitness training for stroke patients. *Cochrane Database of Systematic Reviews, 11*, CD003316. doi:10.1002/14651858.CD003316.pub4

Brouwer, D., & Sadlo, G. (2008). Limitations in mobility: Experiences of visually impaired older people. *British Journal of Occupational Therapy, 71*, 414–421.

Brown, M., Sinacore, D. R., Binder, E. F., & Kohrt, W. M. (2000). Physical and performance measures for the identification of mild to moderate frailty. *The Journals of Gerontology, Series A: Biological Sciences and Medical Sciences, 55*, 350–355. doi:10.1093/gerona/55.6.M350

Campbell, S. (2005). *Deteriorating vision, falls and older people: The links.* Retrieved from http://www.visibility.org.uk/what-we-do/research/#Falls

Centers for Disease Control and Prevention. (2009). Prevalence and most common causes of disability among adults—United States, 2005. *Morbidity and Mortality Weekly Report, 58*, 421–426.

Chang, J. T., Morton, S. C., Rubenstein, L. Z., Mojica, W. A., Maglione, M., Suttorp, M. J., . . . Shekelle, P. G. (2004). Interventions for the prevention of falls in older adults: Systematic review and meta-analysis of randomized clinical trials. *British Medical Journal, 328*, 680. doi:10.1136/bmj.328.7441.680

Chiu, A. Y., Au-Yeung, S. S., & Lo, S. K. (2003). A comparison of four functional tests in discriminating fallers from non-fallers in older people. *Disability and Rehabilitation, 25*, 45–50. doi:10.1080/713813432

Cho, B. L., Scarpace, D., & Alexander, N. B. (2004). Tests of stepping as indicators of mobility, balance, and fall risk in balance-impaired older adults. *Journal of the American Geriatrics Society, 52*, 1168–1173. doi:10.1111/j.1532-5415.2004.52317.x

Crews, J. E., & Campbell, V. A. (2004). Vision impairment and hearing loss among community-dwelling older Americans: Implications for health and functioning. *American Journal of Public Health, 94*, 823–829. doi:10.2105/AJPH.94.5.823

Crocker, T., Forster, A., Young, J., Brown, L., Ozer, S., Smith, J., . . . Greenwood, D. C. (2013). Physical rehabilitation for older people in long-term care. *Cochrane Database of Systematic Reviews, 2*, CD004294. doi:10.1002/14651858.CD004294.pub3

Crotty, M., Unroe, K., Cameron, I. D., Miller, M., Ramirez, G., & Couzner, L. (2010). Rehabilitation interventions for improving physical and psychosocial functioning after hip fracture in older people. *Cochrane Database of Systematic Reviews, 1*, CD007624. doi:10.1002/14651858.CD007624.pub3

Csuka, M., & McCarty, D. J. (1985). Simple method for measurement of lower extremity muscle strength. *American Journal of Medicine, 78*, 77–81. doi:10.1016/0002-9343(85)90465-6

Daley, M. J., & Spinks, W. L. (2000). Exercise, mobility and aging. *Sports Medicine, 29*, 1–12. doi:10.2165/00007256-200029010-00001

Dall, P. M., & Kerr, A. (2010). Frequency of the sit to stand task: An observational study of free-living adults. *Applied Ergonomics, 41*, 58–61. doi:10.1016/j.apergo.2009.04.005

de Bruin, E., Hartmann, A., Uebelhart, D., Murer, K., & Zijlstra, W. (2008). Wearable systems for monitoring mobility-related activities in older people: A systematic review. *Clinical Rehabilitation, 22*, 878–895. doi:10.1177/0269215508090675

de Morais Barbosa, C., Barros Bértolo, M., Marques Neto, J. F., Bellini Coimbra, I., Davitt, M., & de Paiva Magalhães, E. (2013). The effect of foot orthoses on balance, foot pain and disability in elderly women with osteoporosis: A randomized clinical trial. *Rheumatology, 52*, 515–522. doi:10.1093/rheumatology/kes300

den Ouden, M. E., Schuurmans, M. J., Arts, I. E., & van der Schouw, Y. T. (2011). Physical performance characteristics related to disability in older persons: A systematic review. *Maturitas, 69*, 208–219. doi:10.1016/j.maturitas.2011.04.008

Desai, A., Goodman, V., Kapadia, N., Shay, B. L., & Szturm, T. (2010). Relationship between dynamic balance measures and functional performance in community-dwelling elderly people. *Physical Therapy, 90*, 748–760. doi:10.2522/ptj.20090100

Deshpande, N., Metter, E. J., Bandinelli, S., Guralnik, J., & Ferrucci, L. (2009). Gait speed under varied challenges and cognitive decline in older persons: A prospective study. *Age and Ageing, 38,* 509–514. doi:10.1093/ageing/afp093

Deshpande, N., Metter, E. J., Guralnik, J., Bandinelli, S., & Ferrucci, L. (2013). Predicting 3-year incident mobility disability in middle-aged and older adults using physical performance tests. *Archives of Physical Medicine and Rehabilitation, 94,* 994–997. doi:10.1016/j.apmr.2012.10.032

de Vries, N. M., van Ravensberg, C. D., Hobbelen, J. S., Olde Rikkert, M. G., Staal, J. B., & Nijhuis-van der Sanden, M. W. (2012). Effects of physical exercise therapy on mobility, physical functioning, physical activity and quality of life in community-dwelling older adults with impaired mobility, physical disability and/or multi-morbidity: A meta-analysis. *Ageing Research Reviews, 11,* 136–149. doi:10.1016/j.arr.2011.11.002

Dibble, L. E., & Lange, M. (2006). Predicting falls in individuals with Parkinson disease: A reconsideration of clinical balance measures. *Journal of Neurologic Physical Therapy, 30,* 60–67. doi:10.1097/01.NPT.0000282569.70920.dc

Donoghue, O. A., Horgan, N. F., Savva, G. M., Cronin, H., O'Regan, C., & Kenny, R. A. (2012). Association between timed up-and-go and memory, executive function, and processing speed. *Journal of the American Geriatrics Society, 60,* 1681–1686. doi:10.1111/j.1532-5415.2012.04120.x

Dreer, L. E., Elliott, T. R., Berry, J., Fletcher, D. C., Swanson, M., & Christopher McNeal, J. (2008). Cognitive appraisals, distress and disability among persons in low vision rehabilitation. *British Journal of Health Psychology, 13,* 449–461. doi:10.1348/135910707X209835

Dukas, L., Staehelin, H. B., Schacht, E., & Bischoff, H. A. (2005). Better functional mobility in community-dwelling elderly is related to D-hormone serum levels and to daily calcium intake. *Journal of Nutrition, Health, and Aging, 9,* 347–351.

English, C., & Hillier, S. L. (2010). Circuit class therapy for improving mobility after stroke. *Cochrane Database of Systematic Reviews, 7,* CD007513. doi:10.1002/14651858.CD007513.pub2

Evans, J. R., Fletcher, A. E., & Wormald, R. P. (2007). Depression and anxiety in visually impaired older people. *Ophthalmology, 114,* 283–288. doi:10.1016/j.ophtha.2006.10.006

Fairhall, N. J., Sherrington, C., & Cameron, I. D. (2013). Mobility training for increasing mobility and functioning in older people with frailty. *Cochrane Database of Systematic Reviews, 5,* CD010494. doi:10.1002/14651858.CD010494

Feeny, D., Huguet, N., McFarland, B. H., Kaplan, M. S., Orpana, H., & Eckstrom, E. (2012). Hearing, mobility, and pain predict mortality: A longitudinal population-based study. *Journal of Clinical Epidemiology, 65,* 764–777. doi:10.1016/j.jclinepi.2012.01.003

Fitzpatrick, A. L., Buchanan, C. K., Nahin, R. L., Dekosky, S. T., Atkinson, H. H., Carlson, M. C., & Williamson, J. D., & the Ginkgo Evaluation of Memory (GEM) Study Investigators. (2007). Associations of gait speed and other measures of physical function with cognition in a healthy cohort of elderly persons. *The Journals of Gerontology, Series A: Biological Sciences and Medical Sciences, 62,* 1244–1251. doi:10.1093/gerona/62.11.1244

Forrest, G. P., Chen, E., Huss, S., & Giesler, A. (2013). A comparison of the functional independence measure and Morse fall scale as tools to assess risk of fall on an inpatient rehabilitation. *Rehabilitation Nursing, 38,* 186–192. doi:10.1002/rnj.86

Frank, J. S., & Patla, A. E. (2003). Balance and mobility challenges in older adults: Implications for preserving community mobility. *American Journal of Preventive Medicine, 25,* 157–163. doi:10.1016/S0749-3797(03)00179-X

Gillespie, L. D., Robertson, M. C., Gillespie, W. J., Sherrington, C., Gates, S., Clemson, L. M., & Lamb, S. E. (2012). Interventions for preventing falls in older people living in the community. *Cochrane Database of Systematic Reviews, 9,* CD007146. doi:10.1002/14651858.CD007146.pub3

Gooberman-Hill, R., & Ebrahim, S. (2007). Making decisions about simple interventions: Older people's use of walking aids. *Age and Ageing, 36,* 569–573. doi:10.1093/ageing/afm095

Greenberg, S. A. (2012). Analysis of measurement tools of fear of falling for high-risk, community-dwelling older adults. *Clinical Nursing Research, 21,* 113–130. doi:10.1177/1054773811433824

Guralnik, J. M., Ferrucci, L., Pieper, C. F., Leveille, S. G., Markides, K. S., Ostir, G. V., . . . Wallace, R. B. (2000). Lower extremity function and subsequent disability: Consistency across studies, predictive models, and value of gait speed alone compared with the short physical performance battery. *The Journals of Gerontology, Series A: Biological Sciences and Medical Sciences, 55,* 221–231. doi:10.1093/gerona/55.4.M221

Guralnik, J. M., Ferrucci, L., Simonsick, E. M., Salive, M. E., & Wallace, R. B. (1995). Lower-extremity function in persons over the age of 70 years as a predictor of subsequent disability. *New England Journal of Medicine, 332,* 556–561. doi:10.1056/NEJM199503023320902

Guralnik, J. M., Simonsick, E. M., Ferrucci, L., Glynn, R. J., Berkman, L. F., Blazer, D. G., . . . Wallace, R. B.

(1994). A short physical performance battery assessing lower extremity function: Association with self-reported disability and prediction of mortality and nursing home admission. *Journal of Gerontology, 49,* M85–M94. doi:10.1093/geronj/49.2.M85

Handoll, H. H. G., Sherrington, C., & Mak, J. C. S. (2011). Interventions for improving mobility after hip fracture surgery in adults. *Cochrane Database of Systematic Reviews, 3,* CD001704. doi:10.1002/14651858.CD001704.pub4

Harada, N. D., Chiu, V., & Stewart, A. L. (1999). Mobility-related function in older adults: Assessment with a 6-minute walk test. *Archives of Physical Medicine and Rehabilitation, 80,* 837–841. doi:10.1016/S0003-9993(99)90236-8

Hardy, S. E., Dubin, J. A., Holford, T. R., & Gill, T. M. (2005). Transitions between states of disability and independence among older persons. *American Journal of Epidemiology, 161,* 575–584. doi:10.1093/aje/kwi083

Hauer, K., Becker, C., Lindemann, U., & Beyer, N. (2006). Effectiveness of physical training on motor performance and fall prevention in cognitively impaired older persons: A systematic review. *American Journal of Physical Medicine and Rehabilitation, 85,* 847–857. doi:10.1097/01.phm.0000228539.99682.32

Heinrich, S., Rapp, K., Rissmann, U., Becker, C., & Konig, H. H. (2010). Cost of falls in old age: A systematic review. *Osteoporosis International, 21,* 891–902. doi:10.1007/s00198-009-1100-1

Heyn, P., Abreu, B. C., & Ottenbacher, K. J. (2004). The effects of exercise training on elderly persons with cognitive impairment and dementia: A meta-analysis. *Archives of Physical Medicine and Rehabilitation, 85,* 1694–1704. doi:10.1016/j.apmr.2004.03.019

Heyn, P. C., Johnson, K. E., & Kramer, A. F. (2008). Endurance and strength training outcomes on cognitively impaired and cognitively intact older adults: A meta-analysis. *Journal of Nutrition, Health, and Aging, 12,* 401–409. doi:10.1007/BF02982674

Higginbotham, M. B., Morris, K. G., Williams, R. S., Coleman, R. E., & Cobb, F. R. (1986). Physiologic basis for the age-related decline in aerobic work capacity. *American Journal of Cardiology, 57,* 1374–1379. doi:10.1016/0002-9149(86)90221-3

Hirvensalo, M., Rantanen, T., & Heikkinen, E. (2000). Mobility difficulties and physical activity as predictors of mortality and loss of independence in the community-living older population. *Journal of the American Geriatrics Society, 48,* 493–498.

Hobart, J. C., Lamping, D. L., Freeman, J. A., Langdon, D. W., McLellan, D. L., Greenwood, R. J., & Thompson, A. J. (2001). Evidence-based measurement: Which disability scale for neurologic

rehabilitation? *Neurology, 57,* 639–644. doi:10.1212/WNL.57.4.639

Howland, J., Peterson, E. W., Levin, W. C., Fried, L., Pordon, D., & Bak, S. (1993). Fear of falling among the community-dwelling elderly. *Journal of Aging and Health, 5,* 229–243. doi:10.1177/089826439300500205

Huang, T. T. (2006). Geriatric fear of falling measure: Development and psychometric testing. *International Journal of Nursing Studies, 43,* 357–365. doi:10.1016/j.ijnurstu.2005.04.006

Huh, Y., Yang, E. J., Lee, S. A., Lim, J. Y., Kim, K. W., & Paik, N. J. (2011). Association between executive function and physical performance in older Korean adults: Findings from the Korean Longitudinal Study on Health and Aging (KLoSHA). *Archives of Gerontology and Geriatrics, 52,* e156–e161. doi:10.1016/j.archger.2010.10.018

Iezzoni, L. I., McCarthy, E. P., Davis, R. B., & Siebens, H. (2000). Mobility problems and perceptions of disability by self-respondents and proxy respondents. *Medical Care, 38,* 1051–1057. doi:10.1097/00005650-200010000-00009

Inzitari, M., Newman, A. B., Yaffe, K., Boudreau, R., de Rekeneire, N., Shorr, R., . . . Rosano, C. (2008). Gait speed predicts decline in attention and psychomotor speed in older adults: The health aging and body composition study. *Neuroepidemiology, 29,* 156–162. doi:10.1159/000111577

Isaacs, B. (1992). *The giants of geriatrics: The challenge of geriatric medicine* (pp. 1–7). New York, NY: Oxford University Press.

Ivers, R. Q., Cumming, R. G., Mitchell, P., & Attebo, K. (1998). Visual impairment and falls in older adults: The Blue Mountains Eye Study. *Journal of the American Geriatrics Society, 46,* 58–64.

Jakobsson, U., Hallberg, I. R., & Westergren, A. (2007). Exploring determinants for quality of life among older people in pain and in need of help for daily living. *Journal of Clinical Nursing, 16,* 95–104. doi:10.1111/j.1365-2702.2006.01584.x

Jones, C. J., Rikli, R. E., & Beam, W. C. (1999). A 30-s chair-stand test as a measure of lower body strength in community-residing older adults. *Research Quarterly for Exercise and Sport, 70,* 113–119. doi:10.1080/02701367.1999.10608028

Jonsdottir, J., & Cattaneo, D. (2007). Reliability and validity of the dynamic gait index in persons with chronic stroke. *Archives of Physical Medicine and Rehabilitation, 88,* 1410–1415. doi:10.1016/j.apmr.2007.08.109

Jørstad, E. C., Hauer, K., Becker, C., & Lamb, S. E. (2005). Measuring the psychological outcomes of falling: A systematic review. *Journal of the American Geriatrics Society, 53,* 501–510. doi:10.1111/j.1532-5415.2005.53172.x

Kahneman, D. (1973). *Attention and effort*. Englewood Cliffs, NJ: Prentice-Hall.

Keith, R. A., Granger, C. V., Hamilton, B. B., & Sherwin, F. S. (1987). The functional independence measure: A new tool for rehabilitation. *Advances in Clinical Rehabilitation, 1,* 6–18.

Kerr, K. M., White, J. A., Barr, D. A., & Mollan, R. A. B. (1994). Standardization and definitions of the sit-stand-sit movement cycle. *Gait and Posture, 2,* 182–190. doi:10.1016/0966-6362(94)90006-X

Klein, B. E., Moss, S., Klein, R., Lee, K., & Cruickshanks, K. (2003). Associations of visual function with physical outcomes and limitations 5 years later in an older population: The Beaver Dam Eye Study. *Ophthalmology, 110,* 644–650. doi:10.1016/S0161-6420(02)01935-8

Lachman, M. E., Howland, J., Tennstedt, S., Jette, A., Assmann, S., & Peterson, E. W. (1998). Fear of falling and activity restriction: The Survey of Activities and Fear of Falling in the Elderly (SAFE). *The Journals of Gerontology, Series B: Psychological Sciences and Social Sciences, 53,* 43–50. doi:10.1093/geronb/53B.1.P43

Lamb, S. E., Becker, C., Gillespie, L. D., Smith, J. L., Finnegan, S., Potter, R., & Pfeiffer, K. (2011). Reporting of complex interventions in clinical trials: Development of a taxonomy to classify and describe fall-prevention interventions. *Trials, 12,* 125–128. doi:10.1186/1745-6215-12-125

Lamb, S. E., Jørstad-Stein, E. C., Hauer, K., & Becker, C. (2005). Development of a common outcome data set for fall injury prevention trials: The Prevention of Falls Network Europe consensus. *Journal of the American Geriatrics Society, 53,* 1618–1622. doi:10.1111/j.1532-5415.2005.53455.x

Langley, F. A., & Mackintosh, S. F. H. (2007). Functional balance assessment of older community-dwelling adults: A systematic review of the literature. *Internet Journal of Allied Health Sciences and Practice, 5,* 317–343.

Laplante, M. P., Hendershot, G. E., & Moss, A. J. (1992). *Assistive technology devices and home accessibility features (prevalence, payment, needs and trends). Advance data from vital and health statistics.* Hyattsville, MD: National Center for Health Statistics.

Lawton, M. P., & Brody, E. M. (1969). Assessment of older people: Self-maintaining and instrumental activities of daily living. *Gerontologist, 9,* 179–186. doi:10.1093/geront/9.3_Part_1.179

Lin, P. C., Hung, S. H., Liao, M. H., Sheen, S. Y., & Jong, S. Y. (2006). Care needs and level of care difficulty related to hip fractures in geriatric populations during the post-discharge transition period. *Journal of Nursing Research, 14,* 251–260. doi:10.1097/01.JNR.0000387584.89468.30

Linacre, J. M., Heinemann, A. W., Wright, B. D., Granger, C. V., & Hamilton, B. B. (1994). The structure and stability of the Functional Independence Measure. *Archives of Physical Medicine and Rehabilitation, 75,* 127–132.

Littbrand, H., Stenvall, M., & Rosendahl, E. (2011). Applicability and effects of physical exercise on physical and cognitive functions and activities of daily living among people with dementia: A systematic review. *American Journal of Physical Medicine and Rehabilitation, 90,* 495–518. doi:10.1097/PHM.0b013e318214de26

Liu, C. J., & Latham, N.K. (2009). Progressive resistance strength training for improving physical function in older adults. *Cochrane Database of Systematic Reviews, 3,* CD002759. doi:10.1002/14651858.CD002759.pub2

Liu-Ambrose, T., Eng, J. J., Khan, K. M., Mallinson, A., Carter, N. D., & McKay, H. A. (2002). The influence of back pain on balance and functional mobility in 65- to 75-year-old women with osteoporosis. *Osteoporosis International, 13,* 868–873. doi:10.1007/s001980200119

Mahoney, F. I., & Barthel, D. W. (1965). Functional evaluation: The Barthel index. *Maryland State Medical Journal, 14,* 61–65.

Malatesta, D., Simar, D., Dauvilliers, Y., Candau, R., Ben Saad, H., Préfaut, C., & Caillaud, C. (2004). Aerobic determinants of the decline in preferred walking speed in healthy, active 65- and 80-year-olds. *Pflügers Archiv: European Journal of Physiology, 447,* 915–921.

Mangani, I., Cesari, M., Russo, A., Onder, G., Maraldi, C., Zamboni, V., . . . Landi, F. (2008). Physical function, physical activity and recent falls. Results from the "Invecchiamento e Longevità nel Sirente (ilSIRENTE)" Study. *Aging Clinical and Experimental Research, 20,* 234–241. doi:10.1007/BF03324778

Manini, T. M., Newman, A. B., Fielding, R., Blair, S. N., Perri, M. G., Anton, S. D., . . . King, A. C., & the LIFE Research Group. (2010). Effects of exercise on mobility in obese and nonobese older adults. *Obesity, 18,* 1168–1175. doi:10.1038/oby.2009.317

Markowitz, M. (2006). Occupational therapy interventions in low vision rehabilitation. *Canadian Journal of Ophthalmology, 41,* 340–347. doi:10.1139/I06-020

Markowitz, S. N. (2006). Principles of modern low vision rehabilitation. *Canadian Journal of Ophthalmology, 41,* 289–312. doi:10.1139/I06-027

Martin, J. T., Wolf, A., Moore, J. L., Rolenz, E., Dininno, A., & Reneker, J. C. (2013). The effectiveness of physical therapist-administered group-based exercise on fall prevention: A systematic review of randomized controlled trials. *Journal of Geriatric Physical Therapy, 36,* 182–193. doi:10.1519/JPT.0b013e3182816045

Masud, T., & Morris, R. O. (2001). Epidemiology of falls. *Age and Ageing, 30*, 3–7. doi:10.1093/ageing/30.suppl_4.3

McConvey, J., & Bennett, S. E. (2005). Reliability of the Dynamic Gait Index in individuals with multiple sclerosis. *Archives of Physical Medicine and Rehabilitation, 86*, 130–133. doi:10.1016/j.apmr.2003.11.033

Mehrholz, J., Friis, R., Kugler, J., Twork, S., Storch, A., & Pohl, M. (2010). Treadmill training for patients with Parkinson's disease. *Cochrane Database of Systematic Reviews, 1*, CD007830. doi:10.1002/14651858.CD007830.pub2

Menz, H. B., & Lord, S. R. (1999). Foot problems, functional impairment, and falls in older people. *Journal of the American Podiatric Medical Association, 89*, 458–467. doi:10.7547/87507315-89-9-458

Mickle, K. J., Munro, B. J., Lord, S. R., Menz, H. B., & Steele, J. R. (2011). Cross-sectional analysis of foot function, functional ability, and health-related quality of life in older people with disabling foot pain. *Arthritis Care and Research, 63*, 1592–1598. doi:10.1002/acr.20578

Milaneschi, Y., Tanaka, T., & Ferrucci, L. (2010). Nutritional determinants of mobility. *Current Opinion in Clinical Nutrition and Metabolic Care, 13*, 625–629. doi:10.1097/MCO.0b013e32833e337d

Montero-Fernández, N., & Serra-Rexach, J. A. (2013). Role of exercise on sarcopenia in the elderly. *European Journal of Physical and Rehabilitation Medicine, 49*, 131–143.

Montero-Odasso, M., Schapira, M., Soriano, E. R., Varela, M., Kaplan, R., Camera, L. A., & Mayorga, L. M. (2005). Gait velocity as a single predictor of adverse events in healthy seniors aged 75 years and older. *The Journals of Gerontology, Series A: Biological Sciences and Medical Sciences, 60*, 1304–1309. doi:10.1093/gerona/60.10.1304

Montero-Odasso, M., Verghese, J., Beauchet, O., & Hausdorff, J. M. (2012). Gait and cognition: A complementary approach to understanding brain function and the risk of falling. *Journal of the American Geriatrics Society, 60*, 2127–2136.

Moore, D. S., & Ellis, R. (2008). Measurement of fall-related psychological constructs among independent-living older adults: A review of the research literature. *Aging & Mental Health, 12*, 684–699. doi:10.1080/13607860802148855

Morris, M. E. (2000). Movement disorders in people with Parkinson disease: A model for physical therapy. *Physical Therapy, 80*, 578–597.

Moseley, A. M., Stark, A., Cameron, I. D., & Pollock, A. (2005). Treadmill training and body weight support for walking after stroke. *Cochrane Database of Systematic Reviews, 4*, CD002840. doi:10.1002/14651858.CD002840.pub2

Muhaidat, J., Kerr, A., Evans, J. J., Pilling, M., & Skelton, D. A. (2014). Validity of simple gait-related dual-task tests in predicting falls in community-dwelling older adults. *Archives of Physical Medicine and Rehabilitation, 95*, 58–64.

Muhaidat, J., Skelton, D. A., Kerr, A., Evans, J. J., & Ballinger, C. (2010). Older adults' experiences and perceptions of dual tasking. *British Journal of Occupational Therapy, 73*, 405–412. doi:10.4276/030802210X12839367526057

Muir, S. W., Berg, K., Chesworth, B., & Speechley, M. (2008). Use of the Berg Balance Scale for predicting multiple falls in community-dwelling elderly people: A prospective study. *Physical Therapy, 88*, 449–459. doi:10.2522/ptj.20070251

Muir, S. W., Gopaul, K., & Montero-Odasso, M. M. (2012). The role of cognitive impairment in fall risk among older adults: A systematic review and meta-analysis. *Age and Ageing, 41*, 299–308. doi:10.1093/ageing/afs012

Murphy, J., & Isaacs, B. (1982). The post-fall syndrome: A study of 36 patients. *Gerontology, 28*, 265–270. doi:10.1159/000212543

Murphy, S. L., Williams, C. S., & Gill, T. M. (2002). Characteristics associated with fear of falling and activity restriction in community-living older persons. *Journal of the American Geriatrics Society, 50*, 516–520. doi:10.1046/j.1532-5415.2002.50119.x

Nagai, K., Inoue, T., Yamada, Y., Tateuchi, H., Ikezoe, T., Ichihashi, N., & Tsuboyama, T. (2011). Effects of toe and ankle training in older people: A cross-over study. *Geriatrics and Gerontology International, 11*, 246–255. doi:10.1111/j.1447-0594.2010.00673.x

Navon, D., & Miller, J. (1987). The role of outcome conflict in dual-task interference. *Journal of Experimental Psychology: Human Perception and Performance, 13*, 435–448. doi:10.1037/0096-1523.13.3.435

Nelson, M. E., Rejeski, W. J., Blair, S. N., Duncan, P. W., Judge, J. O., King, A. C., . . . Castaneda-Sceppa, C. (2007). Physical activity and public health in older adults: Recommendation from the American College of Sports Medicine and the American Heart Association. *Medicine and Science in Sports and Exercise, 39*, 1435–1445. doi:10.1249/mss.0b013e3180616aa2

Nevitt, M. C., Cummings, S. R., Kidd, S., & Black, D. (1989). Risk factors for recurrent nonsyncopal falls: A prospective study. *JAMA, 261*, 2663–2668. doi:10.1001/jama.1989.03420180087036

Nordin, E., Moe-Nilssen, R., Ramnemark, A., & Lundin-Olsson, L. (2010). Changes in step-width during dual-task walking predicts falls. *Gait and Posture, 32*, 92–97. doi:10.1016/j.gaitpost.2010.03.012

Oh-Park, M., Perera, S., & Verghese, J. (2012). Clinically meaningful change in stair negotiation performance in older adults. *Gait and Posture, 36,* 532–536. doi:10.1016/j.gaitpost.2012.05.015

Oh-Park, M., Wang, C., & Verghese, J. (2011). Stair negotiation time in community-dwelling older adults: Normative values and association with functional decline. *Archives of Physical Medicine and Rehabilitation, 92,* 2006–2011. doi:10.1016/j.apmr.2011.07.193

O'Loughlin, J. L., Robitaille, Y., Boivin, J. F., & Suissa, S. (1993). Incidence of and risk factors for falls and injurious falls among the community-dwelling elderly. *American Journal of Epidemiology, 137,* 342–354.

Onen, F., Henry-Feugeas, M. C., Roy, C., Baron, G., & Ravaud, P. (2008). Mobility decline of unknown origin in mild cognitive impairment: An MRI-based clinical study of the pathogenesis. *Brain Research, 1222,* 79–86. doi:10.1016/j.brainres.2008.05.027

Ormerod, M. (2012). *Design guide 003: The design of streets with older people in mind–tactile paving.* Retrieved from http://www.idgo.ac.uk/design_guidance/pdf/DSOPM-Tactile Paving-120904.pdf

Peel, N. M., Kuys, S. S., & Klein, K. (2013). Gait speed as a measure in geriatric assessment in clinical settings: A systematic review. *The Journals of Gerontology, Series A: Biological Sciences and Medical Sciences, 68,* 39–46. doi:10.1093/gerona/gls174

Peron, E. P., Gray, S. L., & Hanlon, J. T. (2011). Medication use and functional status decline in older adults: A narrative review. *American Journal of Geriatric Pharmacotherapy, 9,* 378–391. doi:10.1016/j.amjopharm.2011.10.002

Pitkälä, K., Savikko, N., Poysti, M., Strandberg, T., & Laakkonen, M. L. (2013). Efficacy of physical exercise intervention on mobility and physical functioning in older people with dementia: A systematic review. *Experimental Gerontology, 48,* 85–93. doi:10.1016/j.exger.2012.08.008

Podsiadlo, D., & Richardson, S. (1991). The timed "Up & Go": A test of basic functional mobility for frail elderly persons. *Journal of the American Geriatrics Society, 39,* 142–148.

Powell, L. E., & Myers, A. M. (1995). The Activities-Specific Balance Confidence (ABC) Scale. *The Journals of Gerontology, Series A: Biological Sciences and Medical Sciences, 50,* 28–34. doi:10.1093/gerona/50A.1.M28

Prosser, L., & Canby, A. (1997). Further validation of the Elderly Mobility Scale for measurement of mobility of hospitalized elderly people. *Clinical Rehabilitation, 11,* 338–343. doi:10.1177/026921559701100412

Reid, K. F., & Fielding, R. A. (2012). Skeletal muscle power: A critical determinant of physical functioning in older adults. *Exercise and Sport Sciences Reviews, 40,* 4–12. doi:10.1097/JES.0b013e31823b5f13

Reuben, D. B., & Siu, A. L. (1990). An objective measure of physical function of elderly outpatients. The physical performance test. *Journal of the American Geriatrics Society, 38,* 1105–1112.

Reuben, D. B., Siu, A. L., & Kimpau, S. (1992). The predictive validity of self-report and performance-based measures of function and health. *Journal of Gerontology, 47,* M106–M110. doi:10.1093/geronj/47.4.M106

Ribeiro, F., Teixeira, F., Brochado, G., & Oliveira, J. (2009). Impact of low cost strength training of dorsi- and plantar flexors on balance and functional mobility in institutionalized elderly people. *Geriatrics and Gerontology International, 9,* 75–80. doi:10.1111/j.1447-0594.2008.00500.x

Rostagno, C., Olivo, G., Comeglio, M., Boddi, V., Banchelli, M., Galanti, G., & Gensini, G. F. (2003). Prognostic value of 6-minute walk corridor test in patients with mild to moderate heart failure: Comparison with other methods of functional evaluation. *European Journal of Heart Failure, 5,* 247–252. doi:10.1016/S1388-9842(02)00244-1

Rubenstein, L. Z., & Josephson, K. R. (2002). The epidemiology of falls and syncope. *Clinics in Geriatric Medicine, 18,* 141–158. doi:10.1016/S0749-0690(02)00002-2

Sainsbury, A., Seebass, G., Bansal, A., & Young, J. B. (2005). Reliability of the Barthel index when used with older people. *Age and Ageing, 34,* 228–232. doi:10.1093/ageing/afi063

Salive, M. E., Guralnik, J., Glynn, R. J., Christen, W., Wallace, R. B., & Ostfeld, A. M. (1994). Association of visual impairment with mobility and physical function. *Journal of the American Geriatrics Society, 42,* 287–292.

Salkeld, G., Cameron, I. D., Cumming, R. G., Easter, S., Seymour, J., Kurrle, S. E., & Quine, S. (2000). Quality of life related to fear of falling and hip fracture in older women: A time trade off study. *British Medical Journal, 320,* 341–346. doi:10.1136/bmj.320.7231.341

Satariano, W. A., Guralnik, J. M., Jackson, R. J., Marottoli, R. A., Phelan, E. A., & Prohaska, T. R. (2012). Mobility and aging: New directions for public health action. *American Journal of Public Health, 102,* 1508–1515. doi:10.2105/AJPH.2011.300631

Schoene, D., Wu, S. M., Mikolaizak, A. S., Menant, J. C., Smith, S. T., Delbaere, K., & Lord, S. R. (2013). Discriminative ability and predictive validity of the timed up and go test in identifying older people who fall: Systematic review and meta-analysis. *Journal of the American Geriatrics Society, 61,* 202–208. doi:10.1111/jgs.12106

Schwartz, R. S. (1997). Sarcopenia and physical performance in old age: Introduction. *Muscle and Nerve, 5,* 10–12.

Scott, V., Votova, K., Scanlan, A., & Close, J. (2007). Multifactorial and functional mobility assessment tools for fall risk among older adults in community, home-support, long-term and acute care settings. *Age and Ageing, 36*, 130–139. doi:10.1093/ageing/afl165

Segev-Jacubovski, O., Herman, T., Yogev-Seligmann, G., Mirelman, A., Giladi, N., & Hausdorff, J. M. (2011). The interplay between gait, falls and cognition: Can cognitive therapy reduce fall risk? *Expert Review of Neurotherapeutics, 11*, 1057–1075. doi:10.1586/ern.11.69

Sherrington, C., Whitney, J. C., Lord, S. R., Herbert, R. D., Cumming, R. G., & Close, J. C. (2008). Effective exercise for the prevention of falls: A systematic review and meta-analysis. *Journal of the American Geriatrics Society, 56*, 2234–2243. doi:10.1111/j.1532-5415.2008.02014.x

Shumway-Cook, A., & Woollacott, M. H. (1995). *Motor control: Theory and practical application*. Baltimore, MD: Lippincott Williams & Wilkins.

Shumway-Cook, A., & Woollacott, M. H. (2007). *Motor control: Translating research into clinical practice* (3rd ed.). Philadelphia, PA: Lippincott Williams & Wilkins.

Sjösten, N., Vaapio, S., & Kivelä, S. L. (2008). The effects of fall prevention trials on depressive symptoms and fear of falling among the aged: A systematic review. *Aging and Mental Health, 12*, 30–46. doi:10.1080/13607860701366079

Skelton, D. A., & Beyer, N. (2003). Exercise and injury prevention in older people. *Scandinavian Journal of Medicine and Science in Sports, 13*, 77–85. doi:10.1034/j.1600-0838.2003.00300.x

Skelton, D. A., Howe, T. E., Ballinger, C., Neil, F., Palmer, S., & Gray, L. (2013). Environmental and behavioural interventions for reducing physical activity limitation in community-dwelling visually impaired older people. *Cochrane Database of Systematic Reviews, 6*, CD009233. doi:10.1002/14651858.CD009233

Skelton, D. A., & Todd, C. (2004). *What are the main risk factors for falls among older people and what are the most effective interventions to prevent these falls?* Copenhagen, Denmark: World Health Organization Regional Office for Europe. Retrieved from http://www.euro.who.int/document/E82552.pdf

Skelton, D. A., Young, A., Walker, A., & Hoinville, E. (1999). *Physical activity in later life: Further analysis of the Allied Dunbar National Fitness Survey and the HEASAH*. London, England: Health Education Authority.

Smith, R. (1994). Validation and reliability of the elderly mobility scale. *Physiotherapy, 80*, 744–747. doi:10.1016/S0031-9406(10)60612-8

Southard, V., & Gallagher, R. (2013). The 6MWT: Will different methods of instruction and measurement affect performance of healthy aging and older adults? *Journal of Geriatric Physical Therapy, 36*, 68–73. doi:10.1519/JPT.0b013e318264b5e8

Spilg, E. G., Martin, B. J., Mitchell, S. L., & Aitchison, T. C. (2001). A comparison of mobility assessments in a geriatric day hospital. *Clinical Rehabilitation, 15*, 296–300. doi:10.1191/026921501675281708

Spink, M. J., Fotoohabadi, M. R., Wee, E., Hill, K. D., Lord, S. R., & Menz, H. B. (2011). Foot and ankle strength, range of motion, posture, and deformity are associated with balance and functional ability in older adults. *Archives of Physical Medicine and Rehabilitation, 92*, 68–75. doi:10.1016/j.apmr.2010.09.024

Spink, M. J., Menz, H. B., Fotoohabadi, M. R., Wee, E., Landorf, K. B., Hill, K. D., & Lord, S. R. (2011). Effectiveness of a multifaceted podiatry intervention to prevent falls in community dwelling older people with disabling foot pain: Randomised controlled trial. *British Medical Journal, 342*, 1–8. doi:10.1136/bmj.d3411

Startzell, J. K., Owens, D. A., Mulfinger, L. M., & Cavanagh, P. R. (2000). Stair negotiation in older people: A review. *Journal of the American Geriatrics Society, 48*, 567–580.

States, R. A., Pappas, E., & Salem, Y. (2009). Overground physical therapy gait training for chronic stroke patients with mobility deficits. *Cochrane Database of Systematic Reviews, 3*, CD006075. doi:10.1002/14651858.CD006075.pub2

Stuck, A. E., Walthert, J. M., Nikolaus, T., Bula, C. J., Hohmann, C., & Beck, J. C. (1999). Risk factors for functional status decline in community-living elderly people: A systematic review. *Social Science and Medicine, 48*, 445–469. doi:10.1016/S0277-9536(98)00370-0

Suttanon, P., Hill, K. D., Said, C. M., & Dodd, K. J. (2013). A longitudinal study of change in falls risk and balance and mobility in healthy older people and people with Alzheimer disease. *American Journal of Physical Medicine and Rehabilitation, 92*, 676–685. doi:10.1097/PHM.0b013e318278dcb3

Swanenburg, J., de Bruin, E. D., Uebelhart, D., & Mulder, T. (2010). Falls prediction in elderly people: A 1-year prospective study. *Gait and Posture, 31*, 317–321. doi:10.1016/j.gaitpost.2009.11.013

Teixeira-Leite, H., & Manhães, A. C. (2012). Association between functional alterations of senescence and senility and disorders of gait and balance. *Clinics, 67*, 719–729. doi:10.6061/clinics/2012(07)04

Thomas, S., Mackintosh, S., & Halbert, J. (2010). Does the Otago exercise programme reduce mortality and falls in older adults? A systematic review and meta-analysis. *Age and Ageing, 39*, 681–687. doi:10.1093/ageing/afq102

Tiedemann, A., O'Rourke, S., Sesto, R., & Sherrington, C. (2013). A 12-Week Iyengar yoga program improved balance and mobility in older community-dwelling people: A pilot randomized controlled trial. *The Journals of Gerontology, Series A: Biological Sciences and Medical Sciences, 68,* 1068–1075.

Tiedemann, A., Shimada, H., Sherrington, C., Murray, S., & Lord, S. (2008). The comparative ability of eight functional mobility tests for predicting falls in community-dwelling older people. *Age and Ageing, 37,* 430–435. doi:10.1093/ageing/afn100

Tinetti, M. E. (1986). Performance-oriented assessment of mobility problems in elderly patients. *Journal of the American Geriatrics Society, 34,* 119–126.

Tinetti, M. E., Mendes de Leon, C. F., Doucette, J. T., & Baker, D. I. (1994). Fear of falling and fall-related efficacy in relationship to functioning among community-living elders. *Journal of Gerontology, 49,* M140–M147. doi:10.1093/geronj/49.3.M140

Tinetti, M. E., Richman, D., & Powell, L. (1990). Falls efficacy as a measure of fear of falling. *Journal of Gerontology, 45,* 239–243. doi:10.1093/geronj/45.6.P239

Tinetti, M. E., Speechley, M., & Ginter, S. F. (1988). Risk factors for falls among elderly persons living in the community. *New England Journal of Medicine, 319,* 1701–1707. doi:10.1056/NEJM198812293192604

Tinetti, M. E., & Williams, C. S. (1998). The effect of falls and fall injuries on functioning in community-dwelling older persons. *The Journals of Gerontology, Series A: Biological Sciences and Medical Sciences, 53,* 112–119. doi:10.1093/gerona/53A.2.M112

Tomlinson, C. L., Patel, S., Meek, C., Clarke, C.E., Stowe, R., Shah, L., Sackley, C. M., Deane, K. H. O., Herd, C. P., Wheatley, K., & Ives, N. (2012). Physiotherapy versus placebo or no intervention in Parkinson's disease. *Cochrane Database of Systematic Reviews, 8,* CD002817. doi:10.1002/14651858.CD002817.pub3

Toots, A., Rosendahl, E., Lundin-Olsson, L., Nordström, P., Gustafson, Y., & Littbrand, H. (2013). Usual gait speed independently predicts mortality in very old people: A population-based study. *Journal of the American Medical Directors Association, 14,* 1–6. doi:10.1016/j.jamda.2013.04.006

Topinková, E. (2008). Aging, disability and frailty. *Annals of Nutrition and Metabolism, 52,* 6–11. doi:10.1159/000115340

VanSwearingen, J. M., Paschal, K. A., Bonino, P., & Chen, T. W. (1998). Assessing recurrent fall risk of community-dwelling, frail older veterans using specific tests of mobility and the physical performance test of function. *The Journals of Gerontology, Series A: Biological Sciences and Medical Sciences, 53,* 457–464. doi:10.1093/gerona/53A.6.M457

Vasunilashorn, S., Coppin, A. K., Patel, K. V., Lauretani, F., Ferrucci, L., Bandinelli, S., & Guralnik, J. M. (2009). Use of the Short Physical Performance Battery Score to predict loss of ability to walk 400 meters: Analysis from the InCHIANTI study. *The Journals of Gerontology, Series A: Biological Sciences and Medical Sciences, 64,* 223–229. doi:10.1093/gerona/gln022

Velozo, C. A., & Peterson, E. W. (2001). Developing meaningful fear of falling measures for community dwelling elderly. *American Journal of Physical Medicine and Rehabilitation, 80,* 662–673. doi:10.1097/00002060-200109000-00006

Viccaro, L. J., Perera, S., & Studenski, S. A. (2011). Is timed up and go better than gait speed in predicting health, function, and falls in older adults? *Journal of the American Geriatrics Society, 59,* 887–892. doi:10.1111/j.1532-5415.2011.03336.x

Virgili, G., & Rubin, G. (2003). Orientation and mobility training for adults with low vision. *Cochrane Database of Systematic Reviews, 1,* CD003925. doi:10.1002/14651858.CD003925

Volpato, S., Cavalieri, M., Sioulis, F., Guerra, G., Maraldi, C., Zuliani, G., . . . Guralnik, J. M. (2011). Predictive value of the Short Physical Performance Battery following hospitalization in older patients. *The Journals of Gerontology, Series A: Biological Sciences and Medical Sciences, 66,* 89–96. doi:10.1093/gerona/glq167

von Bonsdorff, M., Rantanen, T., Laukkanen, P., Suutama, T., & Heikkinen, E. (2006). Mobility limitations and cognitive deficits as predictors of institutionalization among community-dwelling older people. *Gerontology, 52,* 359–365. doi:10.1159/000094985

Voos, M. C., Custódio, E. B., & Malaquias, J., Jr. (2011). Relationship of executive function and educational status with functional balance in older adults. *Journal of Geriatric Physical Therapy, 34,* 11–18.

Webber, S. C., Porter, M. M., & Menec, H. M. (2010). Mobility in older adults: A comprehensive framework. *Gerontologist, 50,* 443–450. doi:10.1093/geront/gnq013

Welmer, A. K., von Arbin, M., Murray, V., Holmqvist, L. W., & Sommerfeld, D. K. (2007). Determinants of mobility and self-care in older people with stroke: Importance of somatosensory and perceptual functions. *Physical Therapy, 87,* 1633–1641. doi:10.2522/ptj.20060349

World Health Organization. (2001). *International classification of functioning, disability and health.* Geneva, Switzerland: Author.

World Health Organization. (2007). *Global age-friendly cities: A guide.* Geneva, Switzerland: Author.

Wrisley, D. M., & Kumar, N. A. (2010). Functional gait assessment: Concurrent, discriminative, and predictive validity in community-dwelling older adults. *Physical Therapy*, *90*, 761–773. doi:10.2522/ptj.20090069

Wrisley, D. M., Marchetti, G. F., Kuharsky, D. K., & Whitney, S. L. (2004). Reliability, internal consistency, and validity of data obtained with the functional gait assessment. *Physical Therapy*, *84*, 906–918.

Yardley, L., Beyer, N., Hauer, K., Kempen, G., Piot-Ziegler, C., & Todd, C. (2005). Development and initial validation of the falls efficacy scale—international (FES–I). *Age and Ageing*, *34*, 614–619. doi:10.1093/ageing/afi196

Yeom, H. A., Keller, C., & Fleury, J. (2009). Interventions for promoting mobility in community-dwelling older adults. *Journal of the American Academy of Nurse Practitioners*, *21*, 95–100. doi:10.1111/j.1745-7599.2008.00390.x

Yogev-Seligmann, G., Hausdorff, J. M., & Giladi, N. (2008). The role of executive function and attention in gait. *Movement Disorders*, *23*, 329–342. doi:10.1002/mds.21720

Zhang, F., Ferrucci, L., Culham, E., Metter, E. J., Guralnik, J., & Deshpande, N. (2013). Performance on five times sit-to-stand task as a predictor of subsequent falls and disability in older persons. *Journal of Aging and Health*, *25*, 478–492. doi:10.1177/0898264313475813

Zijlstra, G. A. R., van Haastregt, J. C. M., van Rossum, E., van Eijk, J. T. M., Lucy Yardley, L., & Kempen, G. I. J. M. (2007). Interventions to reduce fear of falling in community-living older people: A systematic review. *Journal of the American Geriatrics Society*, *55*, 603–615. doi:10.1111/j.1532-5415.2007.01148.x

Zijlstra, G. A. R., van Rens, G. H., Scherder, E. J., Brouwer, D. M., van der Velde, J., Verstraten, P. F., & Kempen, G. I. (2009). Effects and feasibility of a standardised orientation and mobility training in using an identification cane for older adults with low vision: Design of a randomised controlled trial. *Biomedcentral: Health Services Research*, *9*. doi:10.1186/1472-6963-9-153

Zijlstra, W., & Aminian, K. (2007). Mobility assessment in older people: New possibilities and challenges. *European Journal of Ageing*, *4*, 3–12. doi:10.1007/s10433-007-0041-9

PART II

INDEPENDENCE, LIFE TRANSITIONS, AND SOCIAL ADJUSTMENTS

DRIVING AND THE TRANSITION TO NONDRIVING MOBILITY: CHANGE PROCESS AND OPPORTUNITIES FOR INTERVENTION

Thomas M. Meuser

Aging-related changes in preference, confidence, health, or functional capacity often necessitate restriction and eventual retirement from driving a motor vehicle. Today, it is almost normative for people living into their seventh decade and beyond to face the driving to nondriving transition for reasons of safety and quality of life. Most individuals make this transition on their own terms—usually with support from family members and friends—but few plan for it explicitly. Geropsychologists, as well as other health and social service professionals, become involved when warning signs appear and may assist by raising the issue of driving-related compromise and assessing for evidence of modifiable or permanent problems. Geropsychologists also play assessment and counseling roles later on in the experience, sometimes after initial efforts to dissuade an unsafe driver have failed. The driving transition, like most experiences in advancing age, involves a progression of life events and a process of adaptation. Professionals may apply their clinical skills at various times. Geropsychologists, especially, are looked to for their expertise in assessing cognitive, attitudinal, and emotional factors; but their involvement is not limited to these areas. Based on an understanding of driving as an instrumental activity of daily living (IADL), this chapter examines the driving to nondriving transition from the perspective of the individual older adult: his environment, her support network, and the interprofessional context for psychological, physical health, and social care. Evidence-based approaches and tools are suggested for community-based practice with emphases on person-centered intervention and the promotion of *positive mobility* (if not optimal mobility) in advancing age.

DRIVING AND THE TRANSITION TO NONDRIVING MOBILITY

Much is known about the aging process—normal and pathological (i.e., disease-related)—and its impacts on individual function and well-being. Changes in vision, attention, memory, physical strength and stamina, range of motion, reaction time, and a host of other capabilities, challenge people to adapt and remain engaged in both necessary and valued activities and relationships. IADLs necessary for independent living in the community, such a managing finances and shopping, often are compromised sooner than basic care skills, especially when cognitive deficits are present (Njegovan, Man-Son-Hing, Mitchell, & Molnar, 2001). Personal mobility—whether through walking, driving a motor vehicle, or another means of transit—is another important IADL that can be affected by mild changes in cognition or physical functioning in advancing age (Dickerson, Reistetter, Davis, & Monahan, 2011; Wadley et al., 2009). This chapter focuses on the community-based clinician and opportunities for professional intervention in the driving to nondriving transition process.

This chapter reflects the clinical, research and training perspectives of Thomas M. Meuser, Gerontology Program, University of Missouri—St. Louis. The author is part of an extended, interdisciplinary team of colleagues from the health and social service professions in the St. Louis area. He has also served as a trainer and program evaluator for the Older Drivers Project of the American Medical Association. Approaches, strategies, and tools from these collaborations informed the structure, themes, and recommendations of this chapter.

http://dx.doi.org/10.1037/14459-019
APA Handbook of Clinical Geropsychology: Vol. 2. Assessment, Treatment, and Issues of Later Life,
P. A. Lichtenberg and B. T. Mast (Editors-in-Chief)

Losses in personal mobility are especially worrisome to older adults, as they can have broad implications for independence and quality of life (Gabriel & Bowling, 2004). An unexpected fall, for example, can lead to a generalized a fear of falling, avoidance behaviors that restrict valued and necessary activities, and excess disability (i.e., function below one's actual level of ability) in some individuals (Lach, 2005; Scheffer, Schuurmans, van Dijk, van der Hooft, & de Rooij, 2008). Physical frailty and associated mobility loss can challenge individual self-worth and identity (Fillit & Butler, 2009). Retirement from driving has been linked to a host of negative outcomes, including depression (Ragland, Satariano, & MacLeod, 2005), social isolation (Adler & Rottunda, 2006), and worsening physical health (Edwards, Lunsman, Perkins, Rebok, & Roth, 2009).

Although driving retirement can have negative consequences for some, such outcomes can be addressed and their effects mitigated with thoughtful, individualized support (Berg-Weger, Meuser, & Stowe, 2013). Regardless of how people get from point A to B in their daily lives, the key is that they continue to do so and enjoy the benefits to health, productive engagement, and general well-being that prolonged mobility can bring (Oxley & Whelan, 2008). Mobility loss is a "big deal" for older adults, and thus it constitutes a worthy target for individualized discussion, assessment, and intervention by psychologists and other professionals.

From Crisis Response to Proactive Planning

Few older adults plan ahead for eventual mobility loss, but rather wait to deal with it until life events or warning signs can no longer be ignored (King et al., 2011; Liddle, McKenna, & Broome, 2003). Proactive intervention is desirable in most cases but often is possible only if family members and professional stakeholders communicate and work together (Berg-Weger et al., 2013; Perkinson et al., 2005). Although initiating a safe-driving dialogue can be challenging, older adults and their adult children can and do find common ground for mutual understanding and shared goals concerning future mobility (Connell, Harmon, Janevic, & Kostyniuk, 2012). One of the best resources for raising the issue is a free booklet produced by the Massachusetts Institute of Technology AgeLab and the Hartford for Mature Market Excellence entitled *We Need to Talk: Family Conversations With Older Drivers* (The Hartford, n.d.).

As noted in *We Need to Talk* (The Hartford, n.d.), it is desirable to start the conversation before a crisis situation, such as a moving violation or crash. A popular media example gives context to this recommendation. In the classic movie, *Driving Miss Daisy*, the lead character, played by Jessica Tandy, leaves her suburban home to run an errand, only to end up backing her large, four-door sedan over an embankment and into her neighbor's back yard. Her son, played by Dan Aykroyd, sounds the alarm and, over his mother's vehement protestations, hires a driver, Hoke, played by Morgan Freeman, to facilitate her transition to nondriving mobility. Still nimble on her feet and feeling resentful, Miss Daisy turns to walking as her chosen means of getting around, and only later does she grudgingly accept Hoke's role as her driver. If you have seen the movie, you know that Miss Daisy and Hoke develop a strong bond of care and mutual reliance, and that's the real story: Her acceptance of Hoke's assistance allows her to remain reasonably mobile and independent in activities that matter to her. The intervention worked in the end.

By introduction, this story raises a number of important issues for the remainder of this chapter and the roles of the psychologist and other health and social service professionals:

1. Although the outcome of continued mobility for Miss Daisy was positive, the process was not. Car crashes rarely motivate careful, inclusive, proactive planning, and that certainly did not occur in this case. Her son stepped in and forced a solution upon her. She had no direct say in the matter, except to refuse Hoke's assistance in subsequent weeks. How might this have developed had she been engaged in the planning process from the start?

2. Unless there is an acute medical issue, such as a stroke or other sudden debilitating condition, driving ability does not change overnight. Driving is an overlearned activity and so subject to compensation in the face of mild deficits (Brouwer & Ponds, 1994; Craik & Anderson, 1999). The impacts of normal aging and

---

Exhibit 19.1
General Warning Signs for Risk Stratification

AARP[a]

Car crash caused in whole or part by driver

Almost crashing, with frequent "close calls"

Dents or scrapes on the car from hitting curbs and objects along roadway

Getting lost, especially in familiar locations

Trouble seeing or following traffic signs, road signs, and pavement markings

Responding more slowly to unexpected situations or having trouble moving foot from gas to brake pedals (or pedal confusion)

Misjudging gaps in traffic at intersections and on highway ramps

Causing other drivers to honk or complain

Easily distracted or irritated while driving

Failure (or difficulty) to turn and check mirrors when backing up or changing lanes

Multiple tickets or warnings from law enforcement personnel

The Hartford[b]

Decrease in confidence while driving

Regular use and desire for a "copilot"

Parking inappropriately

Driving at in appropriate speeds

Not anticipating potentially dangerous situations

Stopping in traffic for no reason

Failure to notice important activity on the side of the roadway

Poor judgment on making left hand turns

Difficulty maintaining lane position or moving into the wrong lane without recognition

Note. [a]Data from AARP (2010); [b]Data from The Hartford (n.d.)

---

age-associated diseases are usually gradual, and warning signs (see Exhibit 19.1) typically appear months before something as serious as a moving violation or crash (Meuser et al., 2008). The key is for family members and the professionals who serve older adults to recognize such signs, quantify them, and bring them into the care dialogue earlier rather than later (Odenheimer, 2006).

3. Miss Daisy's gender is relevant, here, too. Older women tend to drive less than older men (Bauer, Rottunda, & Adler, 2003), and evidence suggests that they are more likely to retire from driving when still objectively fit to drive (Siren, Hakamies-Blomqvist, & Lindeman, 2004). According to Siren et al. (2004) their decision to retire often is based more on general health changes and quality-of-life issues. Some later regret the decision to restrict or stop driving and might welcome an opportunity to return to this role if supported to do so (Wilkins, Stutts, & Schatz, 1999). On the flip side, men generally are less likely than women to restrict driving as they age—in some cases, they may be forced to

continue if their spouse retires prematurely—and they may drive past the point of objective deficit (Adler & Rottunda, 2006). Older men are more likely to be reported as unfit to drive to a state licensing authority, for example (Meuser, Carr, & Ulfarsson, 2009). Although gender is not a predictor of driver fitness, it is reasonable to consider gender in the context of the decision to retire from driving and support needs to maintain driving mobility.

4. For the psychologist, there are two primary targets for professional practice with respect to the driving transition in the opinion of this author: (a) assessment of the individual's cognitive–functional fitness to drive, and (b) assessment and counseling with respect to the individual's psychological response (including relevant attitudes and beliefs about aging and independence, identification of valued activities and destinations, and planning for present and future mobility needs). The crash was evidence enough for Miss Daisy's son to frame Target A in the negative from the start, although her functional

presentation in the film is not necessarily damning. Her demonstrated ability to walk successfully, for example, suggests that she might still have driven successfully with other compensatory support (Stav, Justiss, McCarthy, Mann, & Lanford, 2008). Target B was subject to a form of professional intervention, if you will, in the character of Hoke. He played a dual role of driver and counselor for Miss Daisy and so facilitated processing and eventual acceptance of her nondriving status.

Understanding Mobility Transitions in Aging

Aging can be thought of as a series of transitions toward the universal endpoint we all share, death (Settersten, 2003). The transition from driving to nondriving mobility is a common experience along this journey. The transition from independent ambulation (i.e., walking unaided) to dependent ambulation (i.e., with a cane or walker) is another. These transitions do not necessarily co-occur, and often positive mobility in one domain can be maintained even in the face of significant impairment in the other. How many people can hardly walk and yet still drive? Those who navigate these transitions do so successfully because of who they are (i.e., their attitudes, self-understanding, ways of coping), their support networks and available resources, and where they live or choose to live if moving is an option (among other factors). Miss Daisy's good physical health, supportive family and servants, suitable home for aging in place, and financial resources allowed for the purchase of in-home services to keep her mobile and productive. Hers is just one "context" for mobility transition in aging, however; each person is different and there are no one-size-fit-all solutions in this field. Each person-specific context requires evaluation and tailored intervention.

The complexities of personal mobility and aging have fostered significant fragmentation in research and clinical applications over the years, and a number of relatively separate literatures have developed (Dickerson et al., 2007). On the ambulation side, older adults who experience health or functional changes that significantly affect walking distances and climbing stairs may be labeled *mobility disabled* (Gill, Allore, Hardy, & Guo, 2006). Various

approaches to assess this form of personal mobility (e.g., Rivermead Mobility Index: Collen, Wade, Robb, & Bradshaw, 1991; Short Physical Performance Battery: Guralnik et al., 1994) and intervene to enhance physical capacity and endurance for independence in daily life tasks have been developed (e.g., the Lifestyle Interventions and Independence for Elders Pilot: Espeland et al., 2007; LIFE Study Investigators, 2006). Concerns associated with gait, balance, and fall risk encompass yet another domain of assessment (e.g., Fall Risk Index: Tinetti, Franklin Williams, & Mayewski, 1986; Timed Get Up and Go Test: Whitney, Lord, & Close, 2005) and intervention approaches (e.g., Home Intervention Team Approach: Nikolaus & Bach, 2003).

On the driving mobility side, further divisions of research and practice exist. Extensive literatures examine functional systems and age-associated diseases with respect to driver fitness, including vision (e.g., Owsley & Ball, 1993), attention (e.g., Ball, Owsley, Sloane, Roenker, & Bruni, 1993; Caird, Edwards, Creaser, & Horrey, 2005), divided attention and mental status (e.g., Kantor, Mauger, Richardson, & Unroe, 2004), Alzheimer's disease (e.g., Brown et al., 2005; Dubinsky, Williamson, Gray, & Glatt, 1992), Parkinson's disease (e.g., Heikkilä, Turkka, Korpelainen, Kallanranta, & Summala, 1998), and a host of other conditions. Others examine the issue from the perspective of on-road events, such as crashes (e.g., Lyman, Ferguson, Braver, & Williams, 2002), roadway design (e.g., Staplin, Lococo, & Byington, 1998), and transportation infrastructure and community planning (e.g., Cunningham & Michael, 2004). Although studies in these areas all help to guide our understanding of mobility concerns in aging, efforts at integration are lacking and represent a priority for present and future research (Dickerson et al., 2007).

This lack of integration is particularly apparent, according to Dickerson et al. (2007), with respect to linkages between evaluation of fitness to drive (Target A), the psychology of driving restriction and retirement (Target B), and the adoption or utilization of alternative transportation options. Psychologists are well suited to engage in research and clinical practice to bridge these areas for the benefit of older clients and their families.

One approach to this bridging may be letting go of disciplinary definitions of mobility for a more unified framework; something that places the person in a daily life context in which activities and mobility are considered together. A driving trip to a doctor's appointment or to have lunch out with friends, for example, are more than discrete events in a person's life, they also are reflections of personal choice and independence. We each operate in a preferred "life-space" that revolves around our home and immediate community (Stalvey, Owsley, Sloane, & Ball, 1999). We are mobile within this life-space to meet necessary and desired objectives. How we get around in this space, whether walking out to pick up the morning newspaper or driving to a distant city, is one element in a larger mobility context. It is possible to have a good quality of life even if quite mobility disabled; it comes down to the individual and what makes life meaningful for him or her (King et al., 2011).

A recent paper provided a helpful definition of this context for research and practice (Webber, Porter, & Menec, 2010). Webber et al. (2010) applied established models of environmental press and personal competence (Lawton & Nahemow, 1973) and life-space (Stalvey et al., 1999) to daily life activities. The authors pointed out that individuals are mobile in different ways (walking, riding, driving) and for different purposes across the places that define their lives, from within one's home, to outdoors in one's neighborhood, to accessing community services (e.g., grocery store), and to the larger world around. For some, this larger world may include locations in a relatively tight radius of home, whereas for others it might mean travel across state and national boundaries. On an individual level, life-space is defined by these oft-visited places and, by extension, how the person moves about and functions to achieve their desires. Traveling distances by car may be essential for quality of life in one person, but immaterial for another who finds value close to home (King et al., 2011). According to Webber et al. (2010),

> Also intrinsic to the model is the concept that deficits affecting mobility at a particular life-space may be compensated for by altering other determinants affecting mobility at that level . . . people

compensate for real or perceived mismatches in skills and environmental demands by investing more time or effort to improve abilities, by drawing on latent skills, and/or by acquiring new skills. . . . This new theoretical framework recognizes that all forms of movement are important and that many interrelated determinants influence mobility. . . . From a clinical perspective, it provides a more holistic view of mobility and may, thus, promote more effective assessment and treatment practices. (pp. 447–448)

An ideal for many older adults, today, is to "age in place," that is, to remain in their current homes with modifications and supportive services to allow for an acceptable level function and independence (Farber, Shinkle, Lynott, Fox-Grage, & Harrell, 2011). Per Webber et al.'s (2010) mobility framework, an important aspect of aging in place is learning to compensate for age-related challenges and limitations. An individual may not be as mobile at 80 years old as she was at 60 years old, but some adjustments in her mobility context (e.g., changed expectations, revised activity plans, addition of a new service) can allow her to remain positively mobile, if not optimally so. The Subcommittee on Elder Mobility & Safety of the Missouri Coalition for Roadway Safety (SEMS; 2009) provided the following aspirational definition for positive mobility in advancing age:

- Freedom to travel to valued destinations
- Independence and choice in transportation
- Roadways and systems designed for their needs
- Knowledge of available options for mobility
- Support to make choices for access and safety

These components emphasize aspects of the person and their context, notably the transportation infrastructure and the importance of safe access. Ensuring that older adults have access to desired places fits well in Webber et al.'s framework and is a top priority of the National Center for Senior Transportation (Leary & Bernardy, 2010).

Figure 19.1 combines aspects of life-space and associated elements from Webber et al. (2010),

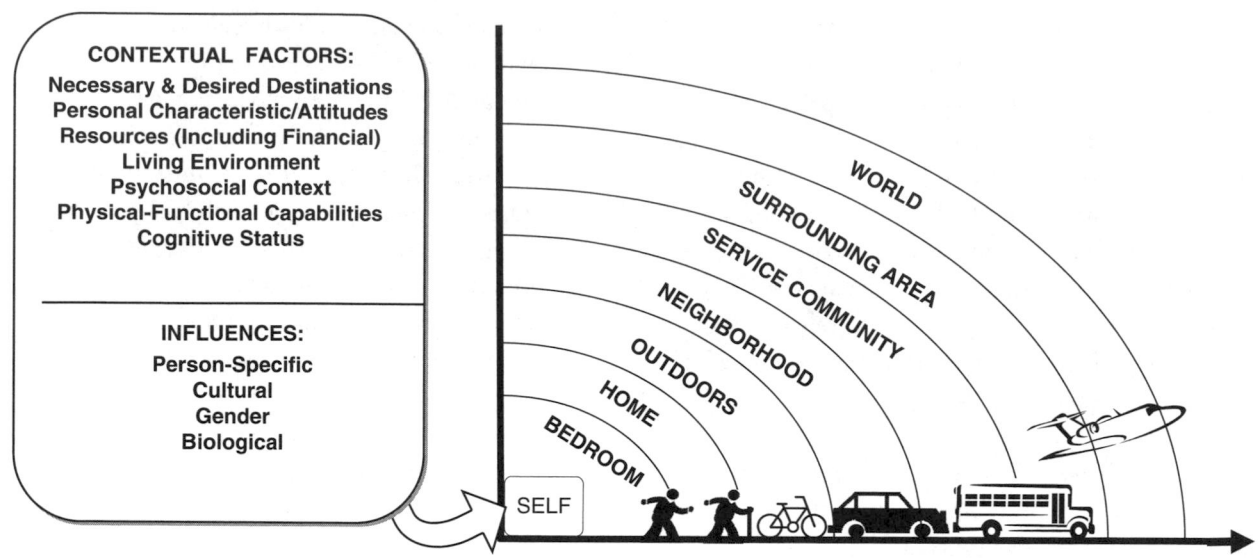

FIGURE 19.1. Life-space and contextual factors in personal mobility.

Stalvey et al. (1999), and Meuser, Berg-Weger, Chibnall, Harmon, and Stowe (2013) to show the larger mobility context. A given individual's mobility status is multiply determined and defies ready reduction. Although it may be necessary to adopt a narrow view when assessing vision or attention, for example, such findings only make sense when framed in the larger context. A warning sign concerning driver fitness, such as difficulty reading street signs, will have differential relevance and impact depending on the mix of person-specific and other factors involved. Perhaps the vision issue can be corrected with a new eyeglass prescription? Or, maybe the vision issue has little personal relevance because driving is not a primary means of transport for the individual in question? Maybe a local resource, such as a volunteer driver program, could take the place of driving mobility if the vision issue cannot be corrected? New meanings and options appear as the context is considered and analyzed.

THE TRANSITION PROCESS AND PROFESSIONAL INTERVENTION

The driving to nondriving transition is one of many aging-related transitions that adults may experience during the second half of life. Much has been written, for example, about the transition from working to retirement (e.g., Reitzes & Mutran, 2004;

M. Wang, 2007) and the transition to single status brought by the death of a spouse (e.g., Carr et al., 2000; Thomas, Digiulio, & Sheehan, 1988). These common transitions involve significant psychological and instrumental adjustment processes that can last for months or years, depending on the person. The driving transition involves a similar adjustment process, yet less is known about how this process unfolds and best practices for intervention. Although common, the driving to nondriving transition is not as accepted and normalized in our society as other common transitions (Alsnih & Hensher, 2003). A real or perceived lack of alternative nondriving mobility options complicates acceptance of and planning for this transition (Kostyniuk & Shope, 2003).

The transtheoretical model (TTM; Prochaska, DiClemente, Velicer, Ginpil, & Norcross, 1985; Prochaska, Redding, & Evers, 2002) is helpful for understanding the driving mobility transition, notably individual differences in adjustment and targets for intervention (Berg-Weger et al., 2013; King et al., 2011). The TTM originally was developed to address addiction-related behaviors and change processes, but it has since been applied to range of health-related behaviors in aging, such as physical exercise and nutrition (Burbank & Riebe, 2002; Nigg et al., 1999). The TTM is depicted with an emphasis on the driving transition in Figure 19.2.

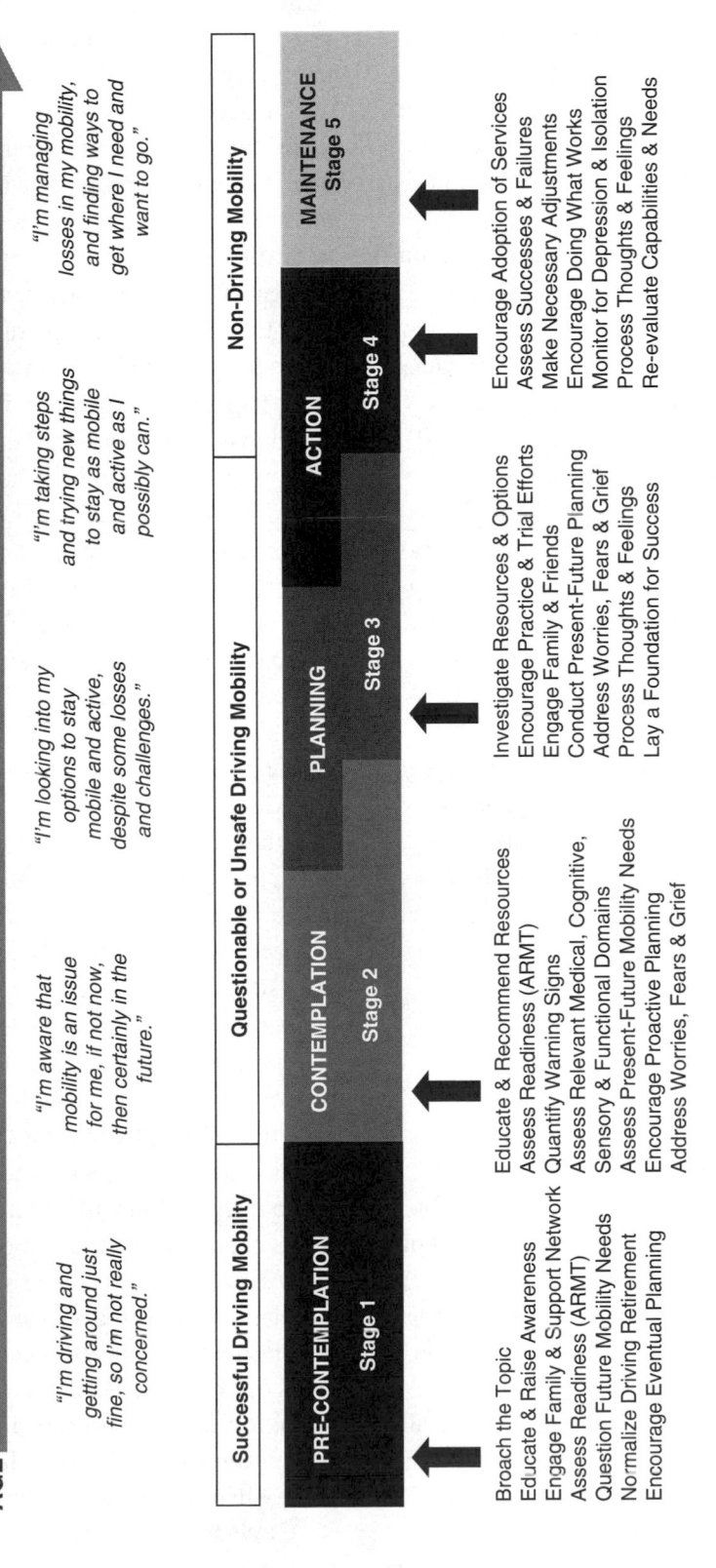

FIGURE 19.2. Stages in the driving to nondriving mobility transition.

Age is represented by the arrow across the top of the figure, both to denote advancing chronological age and the passage of time in a change process. Numbers were omitted intentionally, as the driving transition unfolds on different timetables depending on the person involved. It generally is accepted that people who live into their seventh decade and beyond are at higher risk for health and functional problems, which can impair driver safety (C. C. Wang & Carr, 2004). It has been estimated that, on average, U.S. men will outlive their driving life expectancy by 6–7 years and women by 8–10 years (Foley, Heimovitz, Guralnik, & Brock, 2002). Crash rates for older drivers involving fatalities increase significantly after age 70 years (Lyman et al., 2002), in part because of the increased physical fragility that comes with aging (Li, Braver, & Chen, 2003). These and other findings suggest that it may be reasonable to consider the 70- to 80-year-old age range as a target period for driving-related evaluation and possible reduction or cessation. Some states have adopted this approach in their driver licensing systems. In Illinois, for example, drivers renewing a license after turning 75 years old must participate in on-road testing to ensure ongoing fitness and safety (http://seniordriving.aaa.com/states/illinois). Age can serve as a general guide, only, as individual trajectories often vary. A physically healthy, cognitively intact 90-year-old may be safer behind the wheel than a less healthy 65-year-old. Quantification of individual performance is critical, as shall be discussed later in this chapter (Wood, Anstey, Kerr, Lacherez, & Lord, 2008).

Most drivers experience a long period of successful driving mobility before age-related changes in health or function appear. Crash risk is quite stable at about 4% per year for drivers between the ages of approximately 20 and 74 years (Massie, Campbell, & Williams, 1995). This period of safe driving is depicted along with the initial precontemplation stage of the TTM in Figure 19.2. The quote "I'm driving and getting around just fine, so I'm not really concerned" captures a common attitude at this stage. As noted earlier, few drivers plan for the impact of aging on driving; most people deal with it when forced to do so by changing health or an acute event, such as a crash. The bottom row of Figure 19.2

suggests tasks and targets for intervention at each stage of awareness and change. These stages are discussed further in the following paragraphs with respect to professional roles and opportunities for intervention.

The second stage of the TTM, contemplation, is linked with a period of questionable or objectively unsafe driving mobility. The quote "I'm aware that mobility is an issue for me, if not now, then certainly in the future" demonstrates the importance of awareness of deficit as a precursor to later action. Although the precontemplation and maintenance stages are separated by a vertical line, the middle three stages (contemplation, planning, and action) are shown as overlapping. Thinking about one's options, planning for the future, and taking relevant actions are likely to co-occur as the individual comes to terms with the reality of driving cessation and experiments with nondriving mobility options. The final maintenance stage, like precontemplation, is depicted as a discrete period of long-term, if not permanent, nondriving mobility.

Older drivers work through these stages with family members, friends, and other stakeholders, including health and social service professionals (Perkinson et al., 2005). Family members are often in the best position to recognize a problem with driving and offer both emotional and instrumental support in the retirement process (Connell et al., 2012; D'Ambrosio, Coughlin, Mohyde, Gilbert, & Reimer, 2007; Johnson, 1998). A recent intervention study highlighted the value of education and peer support for working through these stages and trying nondriving mobility options (Liddle et al., 2013). Liddle et al. (2013) tested a six-session, peer-led group intervention with community-dwelling older adults coping with the driving to nondriving transition. Despite some problems with attrition in their sample, they observed a clear difference in adoption of nondriving options between intervention participants (more) versus controls (less).

Input from primary care and specialist physicians is often critical to the change process, especially when authoritative confirmation is needed (C. C. Wang & Carr, 2004). *Medical fitness to drive* encapsulates the physician's primary target for evaluation and intervention (Molnar, Byszewski,

Marshall, & Man-Son-Hing, 2005). The "medically fit" driver has sufficient vision (e.g., acuity, depth perception, peripheral vision), cognition (e.g., attention, executive skills, memory) and physical–functional capacity (e.g., stamina, neck range of motion, speed of reaction) to manage the operational, tactical, and strategic aspects of the driving task (Eby, Molnar, & Kartje, 2009; Meuser, Carr, Berg-Weger, Niewoehner, & Morris, 2006). The role of the physician (clinician) is best summarized as follows:

> Functional assessment, which can include driving ability, is a key component for clinicians involved in providing geriatric care. Clinicians should determine whether their patients are currently driving, provide information on healthy driving behaviors, assess medical conditions or physiologic variables that place their patients at increased risk for motor vehicle injury or driving cessation, and intervene and treat medical illnesses that can impair driving skills. (Carr & Rebok, 2006, p. 46)

The physician has roles to play across all TTM stages in Figure 19.2, but with special emphasis on stages 2 and 5, where comprehensive evaluation and reevaluation are critical for individualized planning.

Other professionals involved in the driving to nondriving mobility transition are presented in Exhibit 19.2. Whereas physicians bring important medical expertise and team leadership, other professionals have relevant contributions to make. The on-road driving test is considered by many to be the "gold standard" for determining fitness to drive (Carr & Ott, 2010). Three professionals—driver examiners, driving instructors, and occupational therapists—offer expertise in this area. Driver examiners apply standards set by a government licensing authority in the context of a fitness-related report or mandated testing at license renewal (Meuser, 2008). Testing by a driver examiner usually is binding on the older driver and could result in license restriction or revocation. Private driving instructors and certain occupational therapists (e.g., those credentialed as certified driver rehabilitation specialists

[CDRS]) can similarly assess driving skills, but they also can offer advice and training to enhance performance of those on the margin of safety. Driver rehabilitation is a growing field of research and practice, of which occupational therapists are at the forefront (Classen et al., 2006; Kua, Korner-Bitensky, Desrosiers, Man-Son-Hing, & Marshall, 2007). Specialized assessment, such as on-road testing, is relevant at both TTM stages 2 and 5.

Social workers are another important professional stakeholder in the driving to nondriving mobility transition (Bauer, Adler, Kuskowski, & Rottunda, 2003; Berg-Weger et al., 2013). They are trained to consider the whole person and individual functioning in daily life context, especially with respect to valued activities, social supports, and service needs. Social workers are well suited to help older adults identify mobility-related resources, develop and implement plans to try nondriving options, and evaluate success over time. TTM stages 2–5 are especially ripe for social work involvement.

Like social workers, geropsychologists, too, are trained to evaluate people in a holistic fashion and integrate findings from a variety of person-specific and contextual sources. The psychologist brings particular expertise with respect to understanding individual differences in attitude, personality, coping, and function. Like physicians, geropsychologists can contribute to all five TTM stages, but they may have the greatest professional impact in stages 1 and 2 where awareness of deficit and psychological adjustment take center stage.

WARNING SIGNS, PRACTICE GUIDELINES, AND INDIVIDUAL RISK STRATIFICATION

Warning signs of driver fitness concerns are shown in Exhibit 19.1. Common and descriptive signs emphasized by the American Association of Retired Persons (AARP) and The Hartford's (n.d.) *We Need to Talk* guide are shown. Many involve likely deficits in vision, visual processing, attention or general orientation, and mental status. For example, failure to notice important activity on the side of the roadway (e.g., a pedestrian wishing to cross) could be due to a failure of peripheral vision, visual scanning, and attention or initiation processes. Most of these signs

Exhibit 19.2
The Interprofessional Context of the Driver Fitness Intervention

Profession	Expertise	Contributions	Opportunities
Driver examiner (government)	Proper operation of a motor vehicle on public roadways and associated rules and regulations	On-road testing of driving skills based on established minimum competency standards Contributor to official driver licensing, restriction, suspension and revocation decisions	Specialized training concerning the aging process and potential impacts on driving Early intervention and prevention activities
Driving instructor (private)	Proper operation of a motor vehicle on public roadways and associated rules and regulations	On-road testing of driving skills Driver training to meet and exceed minimum driver competency standards for full or restricted licensure	Specialized training concerning the aging process and potential impacts on driving Early intervention and prevention activities
Occupational therapist (OT)	Integration of cognitive, sensory, and physical functioning in ADL and IADL tasks	Evaluation of driving-related functional skills in context of general capacity Rehabilitation to enhance functioning in those found to be at lower risk and still fit to drive with specific supports On-road or simulator-based driving skills assessment (some providers)	Specialization as a certified driver rehab specialist (CDRS)
Psychologist	Integration and application of cognitive, emotional, attitudinal, and related factors to behavioral integrity and quality of life	Counseling to facilitate recognition, comprehension, discussion, and planning associated with warning signs of a driver fitness concern Assessment of relevant cognitive, neuropsychological, affective, and other individual difference factors Simulator-based driving skills assessment (some providers)	Early intervention and prevention activities Mobility transition counseling (MTC) to promote adjustment to nondriving status
Physician	Evaluation, treatment, and management of physical and functional health problems	Comprehensive evaluation of physical and related functional health problems associated with the driving task Treatment and management of health problems to maintain driving ability or to promote successful nondriving mobility Leader of interprofessional teams responsible for integrating information from various sources and directing care	Engagement with other professionals through referral and collaborative care approaches Provision of expert medical input to government licensing bodies to encourage prudent driver restriction (when possible) ahead of outright license revocation
Social worker	Comprehensive assessment of the "whole" person and associated wants and needs in home and community contexts	Counseling to facilitate recognition, comprehension, discussion, and planning associated with warning signs of a driver fitness concern Mobility management planning to link identified client wants and needs with available resources and services MTC to promote adjustment to nondriving status	Specialization in mobility counseling and management Service as a "physician extender" with respect to the overall process of mobility transition in aging
Other senior care or service profession	Firsthand knowledge of individual capabilities and needs in home and community contexts	Depending on context (home, community, church, etc.), this professional may serve important recognition, discussion, planning, or referral functions	Engagement of specific professionals (e.g., parish nurses, geriatric care managers) to focus on the driving to nondriving transition

can be quantified readily by family members and others who may ride with the driver in question. As a general rule of thumb, the more warning signs that are identified, the more an older driver may be at risk and should be assessed for compensatory support or driving retirement. Common compensatory activities include the AARP Driver Safety Course (http://www.aarp.org/home-garden/transportation/driver_safety), updated recently for in-person and online training, and the CarFit Program sponsored by a number of national organizations (http://www.car-fit.org).

Formal guidelines are also available. Years ago, the American Academy of Neurology (AAN) recommended that dementia-related cognitive impairment consistent with a rating of 1.0 (mild impairment) on the Clinical Dementia Rating (CDR; Morris, 1993) warranted professional intervention in support of driving cessation (Dubinsky, Stein, & Lyons, 2000). Because primary care physicians have difficulty diagnosing dementia up to the mild-moderate stage (Valcour, Masaki, Curb, & Blanchette, 2000), some question whether the CDR 1.0 cessation guideline is workable in the real world (Carr & Ott, 2010). In 2010, the AAN added additional behavioral and contextual elements to their driving and dementia guideline (Iverson et al., 2010).

Practitioners may consider all of the following when weighing individual risk; the more that are positive, the higher the risk and the greater the justification for driving restriction or retirement:

- CDR score of 0.5 (very mild) or higher
- Driver rated as marginal or unsafe by a family informant
- A history of traffic citations
- A history of crashes
- Reduced driving mileage (less than 60 miles per week)
- Self-reported avoidance of certain driving situations (e.g., left turns)
- A Mini-Mental State Examination (MMSE) score less than 25
- A history of aggressive or impulsive behaviors

The older driver with cognitive impairment at the CDR 0.5 or 1.0 level, but none of the other risk factors, would be considered at relatively low risk.

A recommendation of driving retirement at this level would be premature and also likely to be resisted by the patient-client. Conversely, a CDR 1.0 individual who displays aggressive behaviors when driving, was recently pulled over by police and cited, and with whom family members will not ride is at high risk. The original guideline for immediate driving cessation for someone at the CDR 2.0 level still holds, regardless of other indicators.

Although many look to the AAN for definitive guidance on driver fitness, other medical associations offer differing advice. The American Psychological Association is quiet on the matter, but the American Association of Geriatric Psychiatry recommends that anyone diagnosed with Alzheimer's disease, the most common form of dementia, retire from driving regardless of impairment level. The American Psychiatric Association, in contrast, agrees with the combined AAN recommendations reviewed previously. The Alzheimer's Association recommends cessation only when a serious risk for harm is apparent. See a detailed review of these and other recommendations in Carr and Ott (2010).

Quantification of warning signs and application of practice guidelines provide a starting point for addressing Target A, the assessment of fitness to drive. Determining whether an older driver is truly unfit to drive involves quantification (testing) along with a healthy dose of clinical judgment. Input from family members that a driver is unsafe is an important red flag for action, even if other warning signs are not immediately evident (D'Ambrosio et al., 2007). A practical question that often gets to the heart of the matter is this: "Would you allow [Name] to drive alone and pick up the grandchildren after school on a busy Friday afternoon?" An answer of "no" is often diagnostic.

Task A: Formal Screening for Cognitive–Functional Indicators of Risk

In addition to quantifying warning signs and asking pointed questions about driving and on-road safety, the psychologist or other professional can evaluate driver fitness through the use neuropsychological measures. Although a number of

---

Exhibit 19.3
Cognitive Screening Batteries

Tool	Link	References
Physician's Guide to Assessing and Counseling Older Drivers Assessment of Driving Related Skills (ADReS)	http://www.ama-assn.org//ama/pub/ physician-resources/public-health/ promoting-healthy-lifestyles/ geriatric-health/older-driver-safety/ assessing-counseling-older-drivers. page	Meuser et al., 2010; Wang and Carr, 2004
The Driving and Dementia Toolkit for Health Professionals	http://www.candrive.ca/en/resources/ physician-resources/19-driving-toolkit.html	Byszewski et al., 2003; Molnar et al., 2007
DriveABLE Cognitive Assessment Tool	http://www.driveable.com/index.php/ products/in-office	Dobbs, 2013; Korner-Bitensky and Sofer, 2009; McCracken, 2007
Driving Health Inventory (DHI)	http://drivinghealth.com/ screeningassessment.html	Myers, Blanchard, MacDonald, and Porter, 2008; Staplin, Lococo, Gish, and Decina, 2003
UMTRI Assessment Battery for Older Drivers	http://www.umtri.umich.edu/content. php?id=1020&i=&t=6KrBysqJyE DIdeepblue.lib.umich.edu/bitstream/ handle/2027.42/57294/100251.pdf	Eby, Molnar, Nation, Shope, and Kostyniuk, 2006; Eby, Molnar, Shope, and Dellinger, 2007
OT Driver Off Road Assessment Battery	http://www.aota.org/Driving/ Professionals/Get-Started/Screening-Self-Assessment/OT-DORA.aspx	Unsworth, Pallant, Russell, Germano, and Odell, 2010
Fitness-to-Drive Screening Measure Online	http://fitnesstodrive.phhp.ufl.edu	Classen (n.d.)

---

screening measures and approaches are available for brief, in-office practice (see Exhibit 19.3), definitive evidence of predictive validity often is lacking because of the multifactorial nature of the driving task (Bédard, Weaver, Dārzin, & Porter, 2008). Although some specialized tests, such as the useful field of view (Ball & Owsley, 1993), have shown efficacy for predicting crash risk (Langford, 2008), other screening measures appropriate for in-office use are necessarily imperfect. Researchers have addressed this problem by grouping tests together (i.e., battery approach) and emphasizing the weight of evidence in making determinations of individual fitness and risk. At a minimum, a test battery should include tests of visuospatial functioning and executive skills (Brown & Ott, 2004) and an accepted measure of mental status (Meuser et al., 2006). The American Psychological Association teamed with the American Bar Association to publish a helpful booklet on capacity assessment for psychologists in 2008. The

chapter on driving is an excellent resource on assessment approaches for those wishing to learn more (American Bar Association & American Psychological Association, 2008).

One of the most recognized battery approaches to screening for driver fitness concerns comes from the Older Drivers Project (ODP) of the American Medical Association (Odenheimer, 2006; C. C. Wang & Carr, 2004). The *Physician's Guide to Assessing and Counseling Older Drivers* (Carr, Schwartzberg, Manning, & Sempek, 2010) and its companion online training system (http://medical-fitnesstodrive.nogginlabs.com/php) encourage physicians and others to consider driving fitness in context with various health and functional problems in aging. On the basis of input from more than 60 experts in geriatric care and driver safety, the ODP developed the Assessing Driving-Related Skills (ADReS) battery for general practice. The ADReS includes simple tests of visual acuity (Snellen Chart), visual fields (by confrontation), rapid pace walk (10 feet there and back in less than 9 sec with normal gait), neck and extremity range of motion, extremity motor strength, the Trail Making Test—Part B (a test of scanning and divided attention completed correctly in less than 180 sec; Reitan, 1958), and the Clock Drawing Test (Freund, Gravenstein, Ferris, Burke, & Shaheen, 2005). This battery, along with a driving and mobility history and thorough medical and medications review, provides a basis for reasoned clinical judgment concerning driver safety. The ODP training materials have been shown to be applicable to community-based practice with older adults, and this approach is something that physicians and other professionals can readily learn and adopt (Meuser, Carr, Irmiter, Schwartzberg, & Ulfarsson, 2010; Meuser et al., 2006).

Because level of dementia-related impairment is an important factor to consider with respect to risk stratification, the use of a mental status measure also is suggested. The most researched measure of this type with respect to driving is the MMSE (Folstein, Robins, & Helzer, 1983). People who score below the cutoff based on age and education norms are considered to be at risk for dementia and in need of further evaluation (Tangalos et al., 1996). The MMSE, alone, is neither sensitive nor specific enough to predict driving performance in older adults, especially when the patient or client scores in the low 20s (Crizzle, Classen, Bédard, Lanford, & Winter, 2012). On the other hand, scores in the teens and below, along with other indicators of impairment from the ADReS and warning signs list, would support a clinical judgment of "unsafe to drive." The clinician must weigh all the available evidence and make a best judgment. Other mental status measures, such as the Short Portable Mental Status Questionnaire (Pfeiffer, 1975), the Short Blessed Test (Katzman et al., 1983), and the Saint Louis University Mental Status questionnaire (Tariq, Tumosa, Chibnall, Perry, & Morley, 2006), can provide similar data.

A conclusion of "safe to drive" or "unsafe to drive" is often easier to make than a decision on mixed findings that point in both directions. An important aspect of risk stratification is applying findings from various sources to the driving task

(e.g., operation of the controls, tactical decisions about lane usage and speed, strategic planning of a route) and weighing the likely impact of known deficits (Meuser et al., 2012). Significant memory loss may affect tactical and strategic decisions more than overlearned operational tasks, for example. Peripheral neuropathy of the feet (often resulting from diabetes) might impair operation of the gas pedal and brake but otherwise have no impact. If such weighing does not lead to a reasoned judgment, then additional specialist input will be important. Referral for on-road testing from an occupational therapist is preferable (Carr et al., 2010), but this service may not be available in every community. Another specialist, such as a geriatrician, neurologist, geriatric psychiatrist, or neuropsychologist, may be a good secondary option for referral to obtain clarifying data and recommendations on safety.

Few geropsychologists, physicians, or other professionals—unless employed by the state—have the authority to make a definitive and binding decision concerning driver fitness. Although state departments of motor vehicles usually value the expert opinion of physicians and other professionals, only the state has the authority to restrict or revoke a driver license. If you are screening an older adult concerning fitness to drive, it is important that you utilize an accepted approach, such as the ADReS or like battery (see Appendix 19.1), and that you communicate your findings clearly and document them in the patient's record. It is up to the patient-client and family to act on your recommendation. What if your recommendation is rejected? Most states have mechanisms whereby a professional can report a driver as unfit to the licensing authority for reevaluation. This is a prudent step when you know that a client is unfit and yet continues to drive despite the best efforts of immediate stakeholders to stop this behavior (Carr et al., 2010; Meuser et al., 2008).

Task B: Assessing Psychological Adjustment

Although the assessment of fitness is an important step in the change process, it is not a reasonable endpoint in most instances. As discussed earlier, loss of the driving privilege can challenge and even threaten an individual's sense of worth, purpose, and quality of life. The personal implications of this aging-related loss are worthy of discussion and counseling support (Carr et al., 2010). Coping theory suggests that how an individual appraises (understands) a significant life event, such as the driving to nondriving mobility transition, will influence later coping behaviors and adjustment (Lazarus & DeLongis, 1983). Coping behaviors are also influenced by antecedent factors, such as personality traits and similar stable aspects of the individual (McCrae & Costa, 1986). How flexible and open a person is to modifying life goals and compensating for challenges is also relevant (i.e., as in the selection-optimization-compensation [SOC] model; Lang & Carstensen, 1994).

My own work on the psychology of the driving to nondriving transition suggests another antecedent construct, namely, *emotional and attitudinal readiness*. A series of focus groups with community-dwelling elders examined this construct (King et al., 2011). Four groups were formed based on responses to a presurvey focused on functional level (fully functional vs. somewhat impaired) and life-space (daily life involving little community travel vs. broad life space). Participants (*n* = 30) answered the same set of questions about expectations concerning mobility change in aging and sense of personal readiness to manage what was to come. Those in the fully functional and broad life-space group found the concept of mobility loss foreign and difficult to grasp. In contrast, anyone who reported some physical limitation in the presurvey was eager to share detailed perspectives on how they still managed to be mobile. These discussions made clear that lived, personal experience of aging-related mobility change is an important aspect of readiness. Regardless of functional level, those participants who evidenced flexible and accepting ideas of aging also seemed more prepared with respect to future mobility loss.

Meuser et al. (2013) tested a list of statements reflecting a range of views from these focus groups on a new sample of community-dwelling elders (*n* = 297) with the goal of developing a measure of

the readiness construct. This effort resulted in the formation of the Assessment of Readiness for Mobility Transition (ARMT) scale; the new Short Form (ARMT–SF) is published for the first time in Appendix 19.1. The ARMT is a 24-item, disagree–agree, self-report measure (five-point Likert scale) composed of four factors (subscales): (a) anticipatory anxiety (i.e., anxiety and felt concern about loss of personal integrity and independence in the face of significant mobility loss); (b) perceived burden (i.e., worry associated with becoming overly dependent and a burden on others); (c) avoidance (i.e., a general resistance to address the topic of mobility loss); and (d) adverse situation (i.e., a global perception of significant mobility loss as very harmful to individual well-being and quality of life). A total mean item score (range 1–5) summarizes these four components and is recommended for clinical and research use pending further validations studies (Meuser et al., 2013).

High scorers on the ARMT are conceptualized as strongly independent and self-reliant individuals who worry about aging and wish to avoid burdening others if at all possible. They also may harbor rigid, pessimistic views about aging and their own ability to adapt. Low scorers, in contrast, are conceptualized as more open to what aging has to bring, flexible in their views of personal independence–dependence, and willing to lean on others and try out new alternatives in response to age-related changes. The ARMT total score was shown to correlate with openness to experience from the Five Factor Model of Personality, such that low scorers were more open, and with a number of other construct validity measures (Meuser et al., 2013). A subsequent validation study with 135 community-dwelling elders (Berg-Weger et al., 2013) found associations between the total score and a number of adaptive and maladaptive coping behaviors. Our team is now in the midst of a prospective validation study to confirm our contention that high scorers are at greater risk for negative outcomes when confronted with a mobility transition. We are partnering with ITNAmerica, a grassroots, door-through-door transportation service for seniors in 20 U.S. cities, to confirm the predictive validity of the

---

Exhibit 19.4
Psychological, Functional, and Other Mobility Measures

Tool	Link	Reference
The Safe Driving Behavior Measure	http://www.dot.state.fl.us/research-center/Completed_Proj/Summary_TE/FDOT_BDK77_977-17_rpt.pdf	Classen et al., 2010
Falls Efficacy Scale—International Version	http://www.profane.eu.org/documents/FES-I/FES-I_English.pdf	Yardley et al., 2005
Life-Space Questionnaire	Form unavailable online; contact author	Stavley et al., 1999
The Community Mobility Self-Efficacy Scale	Form unavailable online; contact author	Fortinsky, Vine, Hennig, and Freund, 2009
The Driving Decisions Workbook	http://www.aota.org/DocumentVault/Driving/Workbook.aspx	Eby, Molnar, Shope, Vivoda, and Fordyce, 2003

ARMT.[1] Our work on the ARMT, including video case and text-based training materials, is freely available on our website (http://www.umsl.edu/mtci/index.html).

In future work, we hope to examine the ARMT in the context of the SOC model and other conceptualizations of coping and adaptation in advancing age. The ARMT–SF is presented for the reader to use and distribute for clinical care and educational purposes. Unlike the ARMT, the ARMT–SF utilizes a single, summed total score. Those scoring 29 points or higher are considered to have low emotional and attitudinal readiness, and thus at risk in the face of a mobility transition, such as retirement from driving. The purpose of the ARMT is not to label but rather to raise awareness and initiate a dialogue. Although they may not like the results, low scorers will readily accept news of an age-related challenge and seek to manage the problem directly. High scorers, in contrast, likely will struggle to hear and integrate such news and will need time to process and work toward acceptance. The obtained score is mainly to help the professional understand where the client is coming from and be able to tailor a counseling approach that can meet the client at the appropriate place for productive discussion and eventual planning.

Returning to Target A for a moment, a clear finding that a person is unfit to drive because of advancing dementia, on-road incidents, and other warning signs needs to be communicated in a way that it will be heard and acted on. The ARMT provides a window into the attitudes and feelings of the individual that can help frame this discussion for maximal benefit. Psychologists have the training and sensitivity to individual differences, such as represented by the ARMT, to manage potentially difficult conversations. High scorers need understanding, patience, and space to work through their feelings and address strong negative beliefs before moving into active planning. A number of other scales for assessing psychological, functional, and other factors in the driving to nondriving mobility transition are listed in Exhibit 19.4.

CONCLUSION

The provision of assessment and counseling support for those in the driving to nondriving mobility transition will become increasingly important as the baby boom population grows in the coming decades. Psychologists bring important integrative perspective and therapeutic skills to this transition, both as

---

[1]ITNAmerica represents one of a growing number of nondriving mobility options to allow older adults to remain positively mobile and have access to the places and activities they value (see http://itnamerica.org/). Two other excellent resources for nondriving mobility are the National Center on Senior Transportation (http://seniortransportation.easterseals.com) and the Beverly Foundation (http://beverlyfoundation.org).

primary providers at each stage of transition (see Figure 19.2) and as consultants to other professionals at specific points. A psychologist could partner with a physician to provide follow-up counseling for those struggling to come to terms with lost function and independence. This same psychologist could refer clients to a social worker to quantify future mobility needs and develop a person-centered mobility and transportation plans.

The emotional and identity impacts of driving retirement are many but not necessarily well understood with respect to clinical intervention. Little is written, for example, about grief reactions in this unique loss experience. Work concerning the construct of readiness suggests that tangible opportunities for psychotherapeutic support exist in this life transition. Psychologists can and should be at the forefront of efforts to assist older adults with the personal implications of the driving to nondriving transition.

Case Example 1

Background. John Smith, age 82, a retired attorney, was referred by his primary care physician (PCP) to see a geropsychologist pursuant to a recent diagnosis of mild Alzheimer's dementia and concern about fitness to drive. Mr. Smith was found by police to be "at fault" in a recent crash in which he turned left into the path of an oncoming vehicle. No one was hurt, but the crash was a wakeup call to Mr. Smith and his wife, Helen, age 68 years. Mrs. Smith took over most of the driving, but Mr. Smith continued to drive himself to his midmorning swim at the YMCA and to evening church committee meetings. His PCP believed that Mr. Smith should retire from driving immediately and requested a second opinion on this issue from the geropsychologist. Apart from his dementia diagnosis, Mr. Smith's physical health was excellent for his age, including 20–20 corrected vision and above-average agility and stamina. His only prescription medication was a cholinesterase inhibitor medication for dementia.

Geropsychologist evaluation. Mr. and Mrs. Smith were seen together. A driving history revealed that the recent crash was Mr. Smith's first on-road incident in more than 40 years. No other red flags were

reported. Mr. Smith expressed a willingness to ride with his wife for most trips, but emphasized the quality of life aspects of his continued driving on a limited basis. "I really need to still do some things for myself, and these small trips are important to me," he commented. His wife reported that the crash occurred on a rainy night and that she disagreed with the police about her husband's level of responsibility: "The other driver was speeding, too, but was just so adamant about my husband's guilt, that I think officer gave up. Plus, she was 40 something and my husband is in his 80s," she stated. Mr. Smith scored 25 of 30 (just below the cutoff for cognitive impairment) on the MMSE and 19 on the ARMT–SF.

Recommendations. The MMSE score was consistent with the PCP's diagnosis of mild dementia. The ARMT–SF score of 19 suggested that Mr. Smith had flexible attitudes about aging and mobility loss and would be open to reasoned discussion and planning for future mobility needs. The extenuating circumstances about the crash and the lack of other red flags appeared to place him in lower risk range based on current AAN criteria (see Exhibit 19.1). Glare from oncoming traffic at night is challenging for many older adults, even those with good visual acuity. Weighing these factors and the shared opinion of both Mr. and Mrs. Smith that his quality of life would benefit from some continued driving, the geropsychologist recommended that Mr. Smith continue to drive to his midmorning swim but should rely on his wife for all night driving in future. The geropsychologist further recommended that Mr. Smith's cognitive status be monitored closely for signs of dementia progression and that his driving fitness be reevaluated in 6–12 months, unless a serious change or incident warranted a more immediate response. With Alzheimer's dementia, it is not a matter of if driving retirement will become necessary but when. Each person is somewhat different, but all eventually will need to retire from driving for reasons of personal and public safety. The geropsychologist's final recommendation was that an on-road evaluation with an occupational therapist be pursued should Mr. Smith wish to continue driving past the next year.

APPENDIX 19.1 ASSESSMENT OF READINESS FOR MOBILITY TRANSITION—SHORT FORM (ARMT–SF)

About the ARMT–SF

The Assessment of Readiness for Mobility Transition—Short Form (ARMT–SF) is a clinical tool to assess emotional and attitudinal readiness to cope effectively with a significant mobility-related transition, such as retirement from driving. It is intended for face-to-face administration in the context of a mobility planning or counseling intervention. Additional information and case applications may be viewed online at http://www.umsl.edu/mtci/. Questions about this abbreviated version and the full 24-Item ARMT may be addressed to the first author, Tom Meuser, PhD, University of Missouri—St. Louis (meusert@umsl.edu; 314-516-5421).

Instructions for Administration (read aloud to the respondent)

Consider what would happen if you could not get yourself to valued destinations and activities independently. Maybe this is occurring already in your life; maybe it could happen in the future. I will read a series of statements to you. Consider if you agree or disagree and how strongly. You will respond on a five point scale: 5 = Strongly Agree, 1 = Strongly Disagree. You would respond 4 if you generally agree, but not strongly so. Likewise, you would respond 2 if you generally disagree, but not strongly so. You would respond 3 if you agree and disagree with the statement. Do you have any questions? Then let's get started.

ARMT–SF Items	Strongly Disagree				Strongly Agree	Selected Score
I am a burden if I ask others for help with transportation.	1	2	3	4	5	
It is devastating for older people to have someone take away their car keys.	1	2	3	4	5	
I feel depressed at the thought of being limited in my mobility.	1	2	3	4	5	
There is no way to plan for loss of mobility in aging.	1	2	3	4	5	
My future independence hinges on my ability to get myself around.	1	2	3	4	5	
I have not thought much about my future mobility before today.	1	2	3	4	5	
I've seen others become frail and immobile in older age, and I am determined to avoid this fate at whatever cost.	1	2	3	4	5	
It is not easy for me to ask for help with transportation when I need it.	1	2	3	4	5	
					Sum of Selected Scores =	

Interpretation (for more information, see http://www.umsl.edu/mtci)

A total score of 29 indicates low readiness and suggests high risk for difficulty when adjusting to a significant mobility limitation. Scores in the 29+ range are characterized by significant felt anxiety, worry about a loss of personal independence, and concern about becoming a burden on others. Pessimistic, inflexible thinking also may be part of this profile. High scorers may resist depending on others for transportation and so delay making mobility-related plans until a crisis ensues. In these ways, a high total score suggests that the respondent may not be fully ready (i.e., from an emotional and attitudinal perspective) to adapt successfully to a new mobility loss/change.

High scorers can still plan for their present and future mobility needs, but they likely will need extra one-on-one guidance and support. High scorers may benefit from counseling to discuss their beliefs in light of their present functional status, available resources, and future mobility needs and goals. Often, strong negative views about nondriving mobility will need to be challenged in this process. Whereas low scorers may come to the mobility-planning encounter with attitudes consistent with learning new options, high scorers will need to be eased into a planning process of their own choosing. An immediate presentation of local bus and taxi options, for example, likely will be met with resistance from a high scorer. Their "readiness" must first be understood and cultivated.

References

AARP. (2010). *10 signs that it's time to limit or stop driving.* Retrieved from http://www.aarp.org/home-garden/transportation/info-05-2010/Warning_Signs_Stopping.html

Adler, G., & Rottunda, S. (2006). Older adults' perspectives on driving cessation. *Journal of Aging Studies, 20,* 227–235. doi:10.1016/j.jaging.2005.09.003

Alsnih, R., & Hensher, D. A. (2003). The mobility and accessibility expectations of seniors in an aging population. *Transportation Research Part A, Policy and Practice, 37,* 903–916. doi:10.1016/S0965-8564(03)00073-9

American Bar Association & American Psychological Association. (2008). *Assessment of older adults with diminished capacity: A handbook for psychologists.* Washington, DC: American Psychological Association. Retrieved from http://www.apa.org/pi/aging/programs/assessment/capacity-psychologist-handbook.pdf

Ball, K., & Owsley, C. (1993). The useful field of view test: A new technique for evaluating age-related declines in visual function. *Journal of the American Optometric Association, 64,* 71–79.

Ball, K., Owsley, C., Sloane, M. E., Roenker, D. L., & Bruni, J. R. (1993). Visual attention problems as a predictor of vehicle crashes in older drivers. *Investigative Ophthalmology and Visual Science, 34,* 3110–3123.

Bauer, M. J., Adler, G., Kuskowski, M. A., & Rottunda, S. (2003). The influence of age and gender on the driving patterns of older adults. *Journal of Women and Aging, 15,* 3–16. doi:10.1300/J074v15n04_02

Bauer, M. J., Rottunda, S., & Adler, G. (2003). Older women and driving cessation. *Qualitative Social Work, 2,* 309–325. doi:10.1177/14733250030023006

Bédard, M., Weaver, B., Dārzin, P., & Porter, M. M. (2008). Predicting driving performance in older adults: We are not there yet! *Traffic Injury Prevention, 9,* 336–341. doi:10.1080/15389580802117184

Berg-Weger, M., Meuser, T. M., & Stowe, J. (2013). Addressing individual differences in mobility transition counseling with older adults. *Journal of Gerontological Social Work, 56,* 201–218. doi:10.1080/01634372.2013.764374

Brouwer, W. H., & Ponds, R. W. H. M. (1994). Driving competence in older persons. *Disability and Rehabilitation, 16,* 149–161. doi:10.3109/09638289409166291

Brown, L. B., & Ott, B. R. (2004). Driving and dementia: A review of the literature. *Journal of Geriatric Psychiatry and Neurology, 17,* 232–240. doi:10.1177/0891988704269825

Brown, L. B., Ott, B. R., Papandonatos, G. D., Sui, Y., Ready, R. E., & Morris, J. C. (2005). Prediction of on-road driving performance in patients with early Alzheimer's disease. *Journal of the American Geriatrics Society, 53,* 94–98. doi:10.1111/j.1532-5415.2005.53017.x

Burbank, P. M., & Riebe, D. (Eds.). (2002). *Promoting exercise and behavior change in older adults: Interventions with the transtheoretical model.* New York, NY: Springer.

Byszewski, A. M., Graham, I. D., Amos, S., Man-Son-Hing, M., Dalziel, W. B., Marshall, S., . . . Guzman, D. (2003). A continuing medical education initiative for Canadian primary care physicians: The Driving and Dementia Toolkit: A pre- and postevaluation of knowledge, confidence gained, and satisfaction. *Journal of the American Geriatrics Society, 51,* 1484–1489. doi:10.1046/j.1532-5415.2003.51483.x

Caird, J. K., Edwards, C. J., Creaser, J. I., & Horrey, W. J. (2005). Older driver failures of attention at intersections: Using change blindness methods to assess turn decision accuracy. *Human Factors, 47,* 235–249. doi:10.1518/0018720054679542

Carr, D. B., House, J. S., Kessler, R. C., Nesse, R. M., Sonnega, J., & Wortman, C. (2000). Marital quality and psychological adjustment to widowhood among older adults: A longitudinal analysis. *The Journals of Gerontology, Series B: Psychological Sciences and Social Sciences, 55,* S197–S207. doi:10.1093/geronb/55.4.S197

Carr, D. B., & Ott, B. R. (2010). The older adult driver with cognitive impairment. *JAMA, 303,* 1632–1641. doi:10.1001/jama.2010.481

Carr, D. B., & Rebok, G. W. (2006). The older adult driver. In J. J. Gallo, H. R. Bogner, T. Fulmer, & G. J. Paveza (Eds.), *Handbook of geriatric assessment* (4th ed., pp. 45–54). Sudbury, MA: Jones & Bartlett.

Carr, D. B., Schwartzberg, J. G., Manning, L., & Sempek, J. (2010). *Physician's guide to assessing and counseling older drivers* (2nd ed.). Washington, DC: NHTSA.

Classen, S. (n.d.). *Fitness to drive screening measure (FTDS) user manual.* Gainesville: University of Florida Institute for Mobility, Activity, and Participation. Retrieved from http://fitnesstodrive.phhp.ufl.edu/pdf/user_manual.pdf

Classen, S., Garvan, C. W., Awadzi, K., Sundaram, S., Winter, S., Lopez, E. D., & Ferree, N. (2006). Systematic literature review and model for older driver safety. *Topics in Geriatric Rehabilitation, 22,* 87–98. doi:10.1097/00013614-200604000-00001

Classen, S., Winter, S. M., Velozo, C. A., Bédard, M., Lanford, D. N., Brumback, B., & Lutz, B. J. (2010). Item development and validity testing for a self-and proxy report: The Safe Driving Behavior Measure. *American Journal of Occupational Therapy, 64,* 296–305. doi:10.5014/ajot.64.2.296

Collen, F. M., Wade, D. T., Robb, G. F., & Bradshaw, C. M. (1991). The Rivermead Mobility Index: A further development of the Rivermead Motor Assessment. *Disability and Rehabilitation, 13,* 50–54. doi:10.3109/03790799109166684

Connell, C. M., Harmon, A., Janevic, M. R., & Kostyniuk, L. P. (2012). Older adults' driving reduction and cessation: Perspectives of adult children. *Journal of Applied Gerontology*, [Advance online publication]. doi:10.1177/0733464812448962

Craik, F. I. M., & Anderson, N. D. (1999). Applying cognitive research to problems in aging. In D. Gopher & A. Koriat (Eds.), *Attention and performance* (pp. 583–616). New York, NY: Academic Press.

Crizzle, A. M., Classen, S., Bédard, M., Lanford, D., & Winter, S. (2012). MMSE as a predictor of on-road driving performance in community dwelling older drivers. *Accident Analysis and Prevention, 49,* 287–292. doi:10.1016/j.aap.2012.02.003

Cunningham, G. O., & Michael, Y. L. (2004). Concepts guiding the study of the impact of the built environment on physical activity for older adults: A review of the literature. *American Journal of Health Promotion, 18,* 435–443. doi:10.4278/0890-1171-18.6.435

D'Ambrosio, L. A., Coughlin, J. F., Mohyde, M., Gilbert, J., & Reimer, B. (2007). Family matter: Older drivers and the driving decision. *Transportation Research Record: Journal of the Transportation Research Board, 2009,* 23–39. doi:10.3141/2009-04

Dickerson, A. E., Molnar, L. J., Eby, D. W., Adler, G., Bédard, M., Berg-Weger, M., . . . Trujillo, L. (2007). Transportation and aging: A research agenda for advancing safe mobility. *Gerontologist, 47,* 578–590. doi:10.1093/geront/47.5.578

Dickerson, A. E., Reistetter, T., Davis, E. S., & Monahan, M. (2011). Evaluating driving as a valued instrumental activity of daily living. *American Journal of Occupational Therapy, 65,* 64–75. doi:10.5014/ajot.2011.09052

Dobbs, A. R. (2013). Accuracy of the DriveABLE cognitive assessment to determine cognitive fitness to drive. *Canadian Family Physician, 59,* e156–e161.

Dubinsky, R. M., Stein, A. C., & Lyons, K. (2000). Practice parameter: Risk of driving and Alzheimer's disease (an evidence-based review) Report of the Quality Standards Subcommittee of the American Academy of Neurology. *Neurology, 54,* 2205–2211. doi:10.1212/WNL.54.12.2205

Dubinsky, R. M., Williamson, A., Gray, C. S., & Glatt, S. L. (1992). Driving in Alzheimer's disease. *Journal of the American Geriatrics Society, 40,* 1112–1116.

Eby, D. W., Molnar, L. J., & Kartje, P. S. (2009). *Maintaining safe mobility in an aging society.* New York, NY: CRC Press.

Eby, D. W., Molnar, L. J., Nation, A., Shope, J. T., & Kostyniuk, L. P. (2006). *Development and testing of an assessment battery for older drivers.* (UMTRI-2006-04.) Ann Arbor: University of Michigan Transportation Research Institute.

Eby, D. W., Molnar, L. J., Shope, J. T., & Dellinger, A. M. (2007). Development and pilot testing of an assessment battery for older drivers. *Journal of Safety Research, 38,* 535–543. doi:10.1016/j.jsr.2007.07.004

Eby, D. W., Molnar, L. J., Shope, J. T., Vivoda, J. M., & Fordyce, T. A. (2003). Improving older driver knowledge and self-awareness through self-assessment: The driving decisions workbook. *Journal of Safety Research, 34,* 371–381. doi:10.1016/j.jsr.2003.09.006

Edwards, J. D., Lunsman, M., Perkins, M., Rebok, G. W., & Roth, D. L. (2009). Driving cessation and health trajectories in older adults. *The Journals of Gerontology, Series A: Biological Sciences and Medical Sciences, 64,* 1290–1295. doi:10.1093/gerona/glp114

Espeland, M. A., Gill, T. M., Guralnik, J., Miller, M. E., Fielding, R., Newman, A. B., & Pahor, M. (2007). Designing clinical trials of interventions for mobility disability: Results from the lifestyle interventions and independence for elders pilot (LIFE-P) trial. *The Journals of Gerontology, Series A: Biological Sciences and Medical Sciences, 62,* 1237–1243. doi:10.1093/gerona/62.11.1237

Farber, N., Shinkle, D., Lynott, J., Fox-Grage, W., & Harrell, R. (2011). *Aging in place: A state survey of livability policies and practices.* Retrieved from http://assets.aarp.org/rgcenter/ppi/liv-com/aging-in-place-2011-full.pdf

Fillit, H., & Butler, R. N. (2009). The frailty identity crisis. *Journal of the American Geriatrics Society, 57,* 348–352. doi:10.1111/j.1532-5415.2008.02104.x

Foley, D. J., Heimovitz, H. K., Guralnik, J. M., & Brock, D. B. (2002). Driving life expectancy of persons aged 70 years and older in the United States. *American Journal of Public Health, 92,* 1284–1289. doi:10.2105/AJPH.92.8.1284

Folstein, M. F., Robins, L. N., & Helzer, J. E. (1983). The mini-mental state examination. *Archives of General Psychiatry, 40,* 812. doi:10.1001/archpsyc.1983.01790060110016

Fortinsky, R., Vine, J., Hennig, L., & Freund, K. (2009). Can you get a ride when you need one? Measurement of community mobility self-efficacy. *Gerontologist, 49*(Suppl. 2), 62.

Freund, B., Gravenstein, S., Ferris, R., Burke, B. L., & Shaheen, E. (2005). Drawing clocks and driving cars. *Journal of General Internal Medicine, 20,* 240–244. doi:10.1111/j.1525-1497.2005.40069.x

Gabriel, Z., & Bowling, A. (2004). Quality of life from the perspectives of older people. *Ageing and Society, 24,* 675–691. doi:10.1017/S0144686X03001582

Gill, T. M., Allore, H. G., Hardy, S. E., & Guo, Z. (2006). The dynamic nature of mobility disability in older persons. *Journal of the American Geriatrics Society, 54,* 248–254. doi:10.1111/j.1532-5415.2005.00586.x

Guralnik, J. M., Simonsick, E. M., Ferrucci, L., Glynn, R. J., Berkman, L. F., Blazer, D. G., . . . Wallace, R. B. (1994). A short physical performance battery assessing lower extremity function: Association with self-reported disability and prediction of mortality and nursing home admission. *Journal of Gerontology, 49,* M85–M94. doi:10.1093/geronj/49.2.M85

The Hartford. (n.d.). *We need to talk: Family conversations with older drivers.* Hartford, CT: The Hartford Financial Services Group. Retrieved from http://hartfordauto. thehartford.com/UI/Downloads/FamConHtd.pdf

Heikkilä, V. M., Turkka, J., Korpelainen, J., Kallanranta, T., & Summala, H. (1998). Decreased driving ability in people with Parkinson's disease. *Journal of Neurology, Neurosurgery, and Psychiatry, 64,* 325–330. doi:10.1136/jnnp.64.3.325

Iverson, D. J., Gronseth, G. S., Reger, M. A., Classen, S., Dubinsky, R. M., & Rizzo, M. (2010). Practice Parameter update: Evaluation and management of driving risk in dementia report of the Quality Standards Subcommittee of the American Academy of Neurology. *Neurology, 74,* 1316–1324. doi:10.1212/WNL.0b013e3181da3b0f

Johnson, J. E. (1998). Older rural adults and the decision to stop driving: The influence of family and friends. *Journal of Community Health Nursing, 15,* 205–216. doi:10.1207/s15327655jchn1504_2

Kantor, B., Mauger, L., Richardson, V. E., & Unroe, K. T. (2004). An analysis of an older driver evaluation program. *Journal of the American Geriatrics Society, 52,* 1326–1330. doi:10.1111/j.1532-5415.2004.52363.x

Katzman, R., Brown, T., Fuld, P., Peck, A., Schecter, R., & Schimmel, H. (1983). Validation of a short orientation-memory-concentration test of cognitive impairment. *American Journal of Psychiatry, 140,* 734–739.

King, M. D., Meuser, T. M., Berg-Weger, M., Chibnall, J. T., Harmon, A. C., & Yakimo, R. (2011). Decoding the Miss Daisy syndrome: An examination of subjective responses to mobility change. *Journal of Gerontological Social Work, 54,* 29–52. doi:10.1080/01634372.2010.522231

Korner-Bitensky, N., & Sofer, S. (2009). The DriveABLE Competence Screen as a predictor of on-road driving in a clinical sample. *Australian Occupational Therapy Journal, 56,* 200–205. doi:10.1111/j.1440-1630.2008.00749.x

Kostyniuk, L. P., & Shope, J. T. (2003). Driving and alternatives: Older drivers in Michigan. *Journal of Safety Research, 34,* 407–414. doi:10.1016/j.jsr.2003.09.001

Kua, A., Korner-Bitensky, N., Desrosiers, J., Man-Son-Hing, M., & Marshall, S. (2007). Older driver retraining: A systematic review of evidence of effectiveness. *Journal of Safety Research, 38,* 81–90. doi:10.1016/j.jsr.2007.01.002

Lach, H. W. (2005). Incidence and risk factors for developing fear of falling in older adults. *Public Health Nursing, 22,* 45–52. doi:10.1111/j.0737-1209.2005.22107.x

Lang, F. R., & Carstensen, L. L. (1994). Close emotional relationships in late life: Further support for proactive aging in the social domain. *Psychology and Aging, 9,* 315–324. doi:10.1037/0882-7974.9.2.315

Langford, J. (2008). Usefulness of off-road screening tests to licensing authorities when assessing older driver fitness to drive. *Traffic Injury Prevention, 9,* 328–335. doi:10.1080/15389580801895178

Lawton, M. P., & Nahemow, L. (1973). Ecology and the aging process. In C. Eisdorfer & M. P. Lawton (Eds.), *The psychology of adult development and aging* (pp. 619–674). Washington, DC: American Psychological Association.

Lazarus, R. S., & DeLongis, A. (1983). Psychological stress and coping in aging. *American Psychologist, 38,* 245–254. doi:10.1037/0003-066X.38.3.245

Leary, M., & Bernardy, R. (2010). Evaluating access: An instrument to measure accessible transportation. Proceedings from *TRANSED 2010: 12th International Conference on Mobility and Transport for Elderly and Disabled Persons.* Hong Kong, China: Hong Kong Society for Rehabilitation.

Li, G., Braver, E. R., & Chen, L. H. (2003). Fragility versus excessive crash involvement as determinants of high death rates per vehicle-mile of travel among older drivers. *Accident Analysis and Prevention, 35,* 227–235. doi:10.1016/S0001-4575(01)00107-5

Liddle, J., Haynes, M., Pachana, N. A., Mitchell, G., McKenna, K., & Gustafsson, L. (2013). Effect of a group intervention to promote older adults' adjustment to driving cessation on community mobility: A randomized controlled trial. *Gerontologist* [Advance online publication]. doi:10.1093/geront/gnt019.

Liddle, J., McKenna, K., & Broome, K. (2003). *Older road users: From driving cessation to safe transportation,* University of Queensland, Brisbane, Australia.

LIFE Study Investigators. (2006). Effects of a physical activity intervention on measures of physical performance: Results of the lifestyle interventions and independence for Elders Pilot (LIFE-P) study. The *Journals of Gerontology, Series A: Biological Sciences and Medical Sciences, 61,* 1157. doi:10.1093/gerona/61.11.1157

Lyman, S., Ferguson, S. A., Braver, E. R., & Williams, A. F. (2002). Older driver involvements in police reported crashes and fatal crashes: Trends and projections. *Injury Prevention, 8,* 116–120. doi:10.1136/ip.8.2.116

Massie, D. L., Campbell, K. L., & Williams, A. F. (1995). Traffic accident involvement rates by driver age and gender. *Accident Analysis and Prevention, 27,* 73–87. doi:10.1016/0001-4575(94)00050-V

McCracken, P. N. (2007). The DriveABLE assessment: A review. *Canadian Review of Alzheimer's disease and Other Dementias, 10,* 4–7.

McCrae, R. R., & Costa, P. T. (1986). Personality, coping, and coping effectiveness in an adult sample. *Journal of Personality, 54*, 385–404. doi:10.1111/j.1467-6494.1986.tb00401.x

Meuser, T. M. (2008). License renewal policy & reporting of medically unfit drivers: Descriptive review & policy recommendations. In E. Eby, & L. Molnar. (Eds.), *2008 North American License Policies Workshop Proceedings* (pp. 105–122). Washington, DC: AAA Foundation for Traffic Safety. Retrieved from http://www.aaafoundation.org/pdf/LPWorkshopProceedings.pdf

Meuser, T. M., Berg-Weger, M., Chibnall, J. T., Harmon, A. C., & Stowe, J. N. (2013). Assessment of readiness for mobility transition (ARMT): A tool for mobility transition counseling with older adults. *Journal of Applied Gerontology, 32*, 484–507. doi:10.1177/0733464811425914

Meuser, T. M., Berg-Weger, M., Niewoehner, P. M., Harmon, A. C., Kuenzie, J. C., Carr, D. B., & Barco, P. P. (2012). Physician input and licensing of at-risk drivers: A review of all-inclusive medical evaluation forms in the U.S. and Canada. *Accident Analysis and Prevention, 46*, 8–17. doi:10.1016/j.aap.2011.12.009

Meuser, T. M., Carr, D. B., Berg-Weger, M., Niewoehner, P., & Morris, J. C. (2006). Driving and dementia in older adults: Implementation and evaluation of a continuing education project. *Gerontologist, 46*, 680–687. doi:10.1093/geront/46.5.680

Meuser, T. M., Carr, D. B., Irmiter, C., Schwartzberg, J. G., & Ulfarsson, G. F. (2010). The American Medical Association Older Driver Curriculum for Health Professionals: Changes in trainee confidence, attitudes, and practice behavior. *Gerontology and Geriatrics Education, 31*, 290–309. doi:10.1080/02701960.2010.528273

Meuser, T. M., Carr, D. B., & Ulfarsson, G. F. (2009). Motor vehicle crash history and licensing outcomes for older drivers reported as medically impaired in Missouri. *Accident Analysis and Prevention, 41*, 246–252. doi:10.1016/j.aap.2008.11.003

Meuser, T. M., Carr, D. B., Ulfarsson, G. F., Berg-Weger, M., Niewoehner, P., Kim, J. K., . . . Osberg, S. (2008). *Medical fitness to drive and a state voluntary reporting law: Characteristics of reported older drivers and safety outcomes.* Washington, DC: AAA Foundation for Traffic Safety. Retrieved from http://www.aaafoundation.org/pdf/MedicalFitnesstoDriveReport.pdf

Molnar, F. J., Byszewski, A. M., Marshall, S. C., & Man-Son-Hing, M. (2005). In-office evaluation of medical fitness to drive: Practical approaches for assessing older people. *Canadian Family Physician, 51*, 372–379.

Molnar, F. J., Marshall, S. C., Man-Son-Hing, M., Wilson, K. G., Byszewski, A. M., & Stiell, I. (2007). Acceptability and concurrent validity of measures to predict older driver involvement in motor vehicle crashes: An emergency department pilot case–control study. *Accident Analysis and Prevention, 39*, 1056–1063. doi:10.1016/j.aap.2007.02.003

Morris, J. C. (1993). The Clinical Dementia Rating (CDR): Current version and scoring rules. *Neurology, 43*, 2412–2414. doi:10.1212/WNL.43.11.2412-a

Myers, A. M., Blanchard, R. A., MacDonald, L., & Porter, M. M. (2008). Process evaluation of the American Automobile Association Roadwise Review CD-ROM: Observed and reported experiences of older drivers. *Topics in Geriatric Rehabilitation, 24*, 224–238. doi:10.1097/01.TGR.0000333755.67679.3a

Nigg, C. R., Burbank, P. M., Padula, C., Dufresne, R., Rossi, J. S., Velicer, W. F., . . . Prochaska, J. O. (1999). Stages of change across ten health risk behaviors for older adults. *Gerontologist, 39*, 473–482. doi:10.1093/geront/39.4.473

Nikolaus, T., & Bach, M. (2003). Preventing falls in community-dwelling frail older people using a home intervention team (HIT): Results from the randomized Falls-HIT trial. *Journal of the American Geriatrics Society, 51*, 300–305. doi:10.1046/j.1532-5415.2003.51102.x

Njegovan, V., Man-Son-Hing, M., Mitchell, S. L., & Molnar, F. J. (2001). The hierarchy of functional loss associated with cognitive decline in older persons. The *Journals of Gerontology, Series A: Biological Sciences and Medical Sciences, 56*, M638–M643. doi:10.1093/gerona/56.10.M638

Odenheimer, G. L. (2006). Driver safety in older adults. *Geriatrics, 61*, 14–21.

Owsley, C., & Ball, K. (1993). Assessing visual function in the older driver. *Clinics in Geriatric Medicine, 9*, 389–401.

Oxley, J., & Whelan, M. (2008). It cannot be all about safety: The benefits of prolonged mobility. *Traffic Injury Prevention, 9*, 367–378. doi:10.1080/15389580801895285

Perkinson, M. A., Berg-Weger, M. L., Carr, D. B., Meuser, T. M., Palmer, J. L., Buckles, V. D., . . . Morris, J. C. (2005). Driving and dementia of the Alzheimer type: Beliefs and cessation strategies among stakeholders. *Gerontologist, 45*, 676–685. doi:10.1093/geront/45.5.676

Pfeiffer, E. (1975). A short portable mental status questionnaire for the assessment of organic brain deficit in elderly patients. *Journal of the American Geriatrics Society, 23*, 433–441.

Prochaska, J. O., DiClemente, C. C., Velicer, W. F., Ginpil, S., & Norcross, J. C. (1985). Predicting change in smoking status for self-changers. *Addictive Behaviors, 10*, 395–406. doi:10.1016/0306-4603(85)90036-X

Prochaska, J. O., Redding, C. A., & Evers, K. E. (2002). The transtheoretical model and stages of change. In K. Glanz, B. K. Rimer, & F. M. Lewis (Eds.), *Health behavior and health education: Theory, research, and practice* (3rd ed., pp. 99–120). San Francisco, CA: Jossey-Bass.

Ragland, D. R., Satariano, W. A., & MacLeod, K. E. (2005). Driving cessation and increased depressive symptoms. The *Journals of Gerontology, Series A: Biological Sciences and Medical Sciences, 60*, 399–403. doi:10.1093/gerona/60.3.399

Reitan, R. M. (1958). Validity of the trail making test as an indicator of organic brain damage. *Perceptual and Motor Skills, 8,* 271–276. doi:10.2466/pms.1958.8.3.271

Reitzes, D. C., & Mutran, E. J. (2004). The transition to retirement: Stages and factors that influence retirement adjustment. *International Journal of Aging and Human Development, 59,* 63–84. doi:10.2190/NYPP-RFFP-5RFK-8EB8

Scheffer, A. C., Schuurmans, M. J., van Dijk, N., van der Hooft, T., & de Rooij, S. E. (2008). Fear of falling: Measurement strategy, prevalence, risk factors and consequences among older persons. *Age and Ageing, 37,* 19–24. doi:10.1093/ageing/afm169

Settersten, R. A., Jr. (2003). Age structuring and the rhythm of the life course. In J. T. Mortimer & M. J. Shanahan (Eds.), *Handbook of the life course* (pp. 81–98). New York, NY: Kluwer. doi:10.1007/978-0-306-48247-2_4

Siren, A., Hakamies-Blomqvist, L., & Lindeman, M. (2004). Driving cessation and health in older women. *Journal of Applied Gerontology, 23,* 58–69. doi:10.1177/0733464804263129

Stalvey, B. T., Owsley, C., Sloane, M. E., & Ball, K. (1999). The Life Space Questionnaire: A measure of the extent of mobility of older adults. *Journal of Applied Gerontology, 18,* 460–478. doi:10.1177/073346489901800404

Staplin, L., Lococo, K., & Byington, S. (1998). *Older driver highway design handbook.* Washington, DC: Federal Highway Administration. Retrieved from http://www.fhwa.dot.gov/publications/research/safety/97135/index.cfm

Staplin, L., Lococo, K., Gish, K., & Decina, L. (2003). *Model driver screening and evaluation program final technical report.* Washington, DC: National Highway Traffic Safety Administration. Retrieved from http://www.nhtsa.gov/people/injury/olddrive/modeldriver/volume_i.htm

Stav, W. B., Justiss, M. D., McCarthy, D. P., Mann, W. C., & Lanford, D. N. (2008). Predictability of clinical assessments for driving performance. *Journal of Safety Research, 39,* 1–7. doi:10.1016/j.jsr.2007.10.004

Subcommittee on Elder Mobility & Safety (SEMS). (2009). *Print information card.* Jefferson City: Missouri Coalition for Roadway Safety.

Tangalos, E. G., Smith, G. E., Ivnik, R. J., Petersen, R. C., Kokmen, E., Kurland, L. T., . . . Parisi, J. E. (1996). The Mini-Mental State Examination in general medical practice: Clinical utility and acceptance. *Mayo Clinic Proceedings, 71,* 829–837. doi:10.4065/71.9.829

Tariq, S. H., Tumosa, N., Chibnall, J. T., Perry, M. H., III, & Morley, J. E. (2006). Comparison of the Saint Louis University Mental Status examination and the Mini-Mental State Examination for detecting dementia and mild neurocognitive disorder—A pilot study. *American Journal of Geriatric Psychiatry, 14,* 900–910. doi:10.1097/01.JGP.0000221510.33817.86

Thomas, L. E., Digiulio, R. C., & Sheehan, N. W. (1988). Identity loss and psychological crisis in widowhood: A re-evaluation. *International Journal of Aging and Human Development, 26,* 225–239. doi:10.2190/HJ85-CPV9-0WRU-A8PX

Tinetti, M. E., Franklin Williams, T., & Mayewski, R. (1986). Fall risk index for elderly patients based on number of chronic disabilities. *American Journal of Medicine, 80,* 429–434. doi:10.1016/0002-9343(86)90717-5

Unsworth, C. A., Pallant, J. F., Russell, K. J., Germano, C., & Odell, M. (2010). Validation of a test of road law and road craft knowledge with older or functionally impaired drivers. *American Journal of Occupational Therapy, 64,* 306–315. doi:10.5014/ajot.64.2.306

Valcour, V. G., Masaki, K. H., Curb, J. D., & Blanchette, P. L. (2000). The detection of dementia in the primary care setting. *Archives of Internal Medicine, 160,* 2964–2968. doi:10.1001/archinte.160.19.2964

Wadley, V. G., Okonkwo, O., Crowe, M., Vance, D. E., Elgin, J. M., Ball, K. K., & Owsley, C. (2009). Mild cognitive impairment and everyday function: An investigation of driving performance. *Journal of Geriatric Psychiatry and Neurology, 22,* 87–94. doi:10.1177/0891988708328215

Wang, C. C., & Carr, D. B. (2004). Older driver safety: A report from the Older Drivers Project. *Journal of the American Geriatrics Society, 52,* 143–149. doi:10.1111/j.1532-5415.2004.52025.x

Wang, M. (2007). Profiling retirees in the retirement transition and adjustment process: Examining the longitudinal change patterns of retirees' psychological well-being. *Journal of Applied Psychology, 92,* 455–474. doi:10.1037/0021-9010.92.2.455

Webber, S. C., Porter, M. M., & Menec, V. H. (2010). Mobility in older adults: A comprehensive framework. *Gerontologist, 50,* 443–450. doi:10.1093/geront/gnq013

Whitney, J. C., Lord, S. R., & Close, J. C. (2005). Streamlining assessment and intervention in a falls clinic using the Timed Up and Go Test and Physiological Profile Assessment. *Age and Ageing, 34,* 567–571. doi:10.1093/ageing/afi178

Wilkins, J. W., Stutts, J. C., & Schatz, S. J. (1999). Premature reduction and cessation of driving: Preliminary study of women who choose not to drive or to drive infrequently. *Transportation Research Record, 1693,* 86–90. doi:10.3141/1693-13

Wood, J. M., Anstey, K. J., Kerr, G. K., Lacherez, P. F., & Lord, S. (2008). A multi domain approach for predicting older driver safety under in-traffic road conditions. *Journal of the American Geriatrics Society, 56,* 986–993. doi:10.1111/j.1532-5415.2008.01709.x

Yardley, L., Beyer, N., Hauer, K., Kempen, G., Piot-Ziegler, C., & Todd, C. (2005). Development and initial validation of the Falls Efficacy Scale—International (FES–I). *Age and Ageing, 34,* 614–619. doi:10.1093/ageing/afi196

CHAPTER 20

ASSESSMENT AND TREATMENT OF FAMILY CAREGIVERS

Steven H. Zarit and Allison R. Heid

Over the past 40 years, care of older people has emerged as a major social and clinical issue. Becoming a family caregiver is now a normative experience that affects most people's lives. One national survey estimated that 48.9 million people in the United States, or just over one in five adults, were providing ongoing care to another adult with disabilities, with 92% of them assisting someone over the age of 50 years (National Alliance for Caregiving, 2009). Moreover, caregiving frequently is associated with high levels of stress that have adverse consequences on caregiver's health and well-being. The rate of major depression has been estimated to be between 22% and 33% among caregivers (Cuijpers, 2005; Pinquart & Sorensen, 2003), with many more reporting significant levels of symptoms that do not reach the threshold for diagnosis. Caregiving stress also may lead to an increased risk of illness (e.g., Haley, Roth, Howard, & Safford, 2010; Martire & Schulz, 2012) and death (Perkins et al., 2013; Schulz & Beach, 1999).

Given the high prevalence of caregiving in the population, clinicians who treat a general adult population will have clients who are caregivers, who are becoming caregivers, who assist parents or siblings who are caregivers, or who are dealing with emotional consequences of having been a caregiver. Clinicians can make meaningful differences by implementing treatment that is informed by an understanding of the disabilities experienced by the care recipient, by recognizing the opportunities for intervention to improve caregivers' behavioral and emotional responses to stressors and other challenges in the care situation,

and by considering the unique family processes that shape each particular caregiving career. This chapter examines clinical interventions that help family caregivers address the multiple challenges they face. The chapter is divided into three sections: (a) understanding caregivers and caregiving, including a brief introduction to evolving societal trends that influence caregiving and a discussion of the diversity in who becomes a caregiver; (b) setting up treatment, including examining the sources of caregiver stress or burden and strategies for assessment and goal setting; and (c) implementing treatment and other interventions, including evidence for their efficacy and effectiveness.

Throughout the chapter, we emphasize what we call "ethical" approaches to treatment, in which we consider the values, preferences, and implications of treatment decisions for each person—caregiver and care receiver. We view the care receiver from a person-centered perspective—that is, as an individual who is more than a collection of symptoms and problems but who also has emotions and needs (Baldwin, 2008; Kitwood, 1997). A person-centered perspective is especially important when the care recipient has dementia, chronic mental illness, or other conditions that substantially affect cognition, behavior, and emotion and that may cause other people to disregard the care recipient's values and choices. At times, the caregiver's and care receiver's welfare may differ, but we believe that treatment sometimes can reconcile these differences. Even when that is not possible, clinicians can be more effective and more responsible in their actions when they are fully informed about each person's needs.

http://dx.doi.org/10.1037/14459-020
APA Handbook of Clinical Geropsychology: Vol. 2. Assessment, Treatment, and Issues of Later Life,
P. A. Lichtenberg and B. T. Mast (Editors-in-Chief)

UNDERSTANDING CAREGIVERS AND CAREGIVING

Caregiving has emerged as a prominent social and clinical issue because of the convergence of several social trends. First, the number of older people needing care has increased. As a result of the dramatic increases in life expectancy during the 20th century, more people are living to old age than ever before and most will likely need care for a period of time before their deaths. Furthermore, there is growing evidence that people are living longer after the onset of chronic disease and disability (Murray et al., 2012). As an example, median life expectancy after onset of Alzheimer's disease is estimated at 11 years, and it is not uncommon for some individuals to live 20 years or more (Aneshensel, Pearlin, Mullan, Zarit, & Whitlatch, 1995). Similar extensions of life expectancies are found following the onset of other diseases of later life as well (Murray et al., 2012). The result of these trends is that more older people need care than ever before, and they often need care for more severe disabilities and for longer periods of time than in the past.

A parallel trend is that the resources available for families to provide care to an elder have diminished. Family size has decreased steadily, so there are fewer potential caregivers among offspring to assist aging parents. Women's increased participation in the workforce means that many women who traditionally served as caregivers do not have the time to give full-time care to a parent. Finally, trends such as increased divorce rates and decline of economic well-being of the average family have resulted in fewer resources available to help an elder.

Given the convergence of increasing need and decreasing resources, caregiving—not surprisingly—is exhausting and overwhelming. And unlike many other economically advanced countries, the United States does not have an organized system of long-term care that can support the efforts of family caregivers and relieve some of the burdens of care. Despite the often-overwhelming challenges, many caregivers report positive experiences (Bertrand et al., 2012). These experiences may be intrinsic to the care they are providing—that is, they gain satisfaction from being able to help their relative with tasks of daily living. They also may gain a sense of reward from being in the role of caregiver. They feel they are fulfilling an obligation and doing the right thing for a spouse or parent. These positive experiences may help buffer the effects of the stressors in their lives.

Although there are common challenges and experiences at the core of caregiving, it is not a uniform experience, and it does not unfold through a set of common steps, stages, or psychological processes. Caregivers and the people they are caring for are extensively diverse. They differ by type of relationship to the care receiver (e.g., spouse, adult offspring), ethnicity, and other factors (e.g., Aneshensel et al., 1995; Blum & Sherman, 2010; Haley et al., 2009; Haley, LaMonde, Han, Burton, & Schonwetter, 2003; Martire & Schulz, 2012; Roth, Perkins, Wadley, Temple, & Haley, 2009). Some general approaches inform any clinical intervention with caregivers, but knowing the particulars about the relationship between care recipients and caregivers, the care recipient's needs and resources, the challenges that individual caregivers face and the resources they can draw on, and the support available from family, friends, and the broader community are all important to optimize clinical interventions. Just as clinicians would not view a client with major depression as just a diagnosis, we likewise view caregivers as more than their role and help them with the specific concerns they raise in the context of their longstanding relationship with their care recipient.

Diversity in Relationships Between Care Recipients and Caregivers

Caregiving is provided by men and women; by spouses, children, and other relatives; and sometimes by non-kin. Figure 20.1 uses national data to show the relationship of primary caregivers to care recipients (Wolff & Kasper, 2006). The primary caregiver is the individual who has the most responsibility for assisting an elder. When the care recipient is married, the most likely person to take on that role is a spouse. Wives outnumber husbands as caregivers (21.9% vs. 16.4%), but the difference largely is due to women's greater life expectancy and that they tend to marry men who are older than they are. Daughters are the single largest group of caregivers

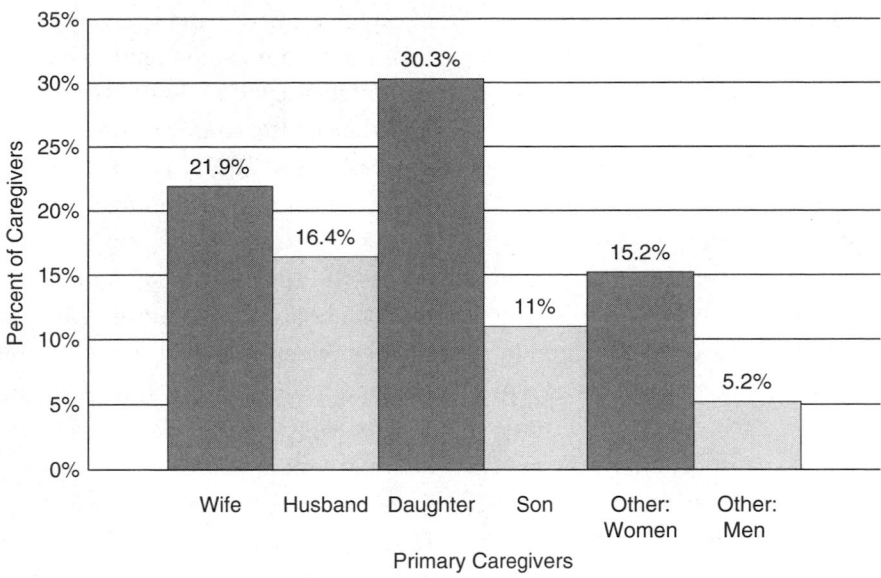

FIGURE 20.1. National data on the relationship of primary caregivers to care recipients.

(30.3%), whereas a smaller group of sons (11%) take on primary care of parents, although this number appears to be increasing (Wolff & Kasper, 2006). Additionally, Figure 20.1 shows two groups of "other" caregivers. These categories not only include daughters-in-law and sons-in-law but also a diverse group of people usually not identified as primary caregivers, including siblings, nieces and nephews, grandchildren, more distant relatives, and non-kin.

The type of relationship between a caregiver and care recipient has implications for the practical and emotional challenges that caregivers face. The clinician may see a client because of caregiving issues, but that person has been a wife, husband, daughter, or son of the care recipient for a much longer period of time, and so past experiences as well as normative expectations about giving care are important to consider when planning treatment. For example, differences have been noted in how wives and husbands approach caregiving (Bookwala & Schulz, 2000; Miller, 1990; Miller & Guo, 2000; Zarit, Todd, & Zarit, 1986). Husbands often view the role as a job, organizing the tasks much as they did their work. They may welcome the commitment because it gives them something to do that replaces work, although they may be challenged by some household tasks and experience increasing emotional distress over time (Ducharme, Lévesque, Zarit, Lachance, & Giroux,

2007; Zarit et al., 1986). Yet they often receive less support from children and other relatives as well, which partly is due to their not being open about the problems they are having. This lack of support is one of the strongest predictors of poor outcomes (Ducharme et al., 2007).

Wives, on the other hand, tend to respond more emotionally to the role, expressing sadness over their husband's condition and the quality of their own life (Miller, 1990; Zarit et al., 1986). Wives may have difficulty addressing practical issues because they believe that their emotional distress will not be affected by making practical changes to the care situation. Many wives also have more difficulty with physically strenuous activities, such as having to lift their husbands. For both husbands and wives, the loss of a confidant, friend, and lover is painful. A husband who was caring for a wife with dementia once described his situation this way: "I am married, and I am alone."

Of course, the quality and duration of the marriage affects caregiving. For couples that have had good marriages regardless of length, care emerges willingly from the traditional marriage vow, "in sickness and in health." The commitment can be profound and open-ended, and these couples can be a delight to work with. One couple participating in a clinical intervention for early stage Alzheimer's disease described how their efforts to come to terms with the diagnosis and its implications brought out more strongly the love they have for one another. Of course, other spouses may see the role as one more imposition in a relationship that has not been satisfying, and they may approach care as just another issue over which they struggle with their spouse. A troubled marital history, however, does not always mean that a spouse will be less committed to providing help. Examples from clinical experience suggest some spouses are surprisingly capable and committed as caregivers, despite long-standing problems in the marriage (Zarit, Orr, & Zarit, 1985). Additionally, couples who married late in life after previous marriages may experience as strong as a commitment to one another as couples who have been married longer, but they may face other challenges, such as being less likely to receive support from children (Ganong & Coleman, 1998).

One other consideration for spouses as caregivers is that they tend to be older themselves. In the Wolff and Kasper study (2006) previously mentioned, spouses had an average age of 73.8 years. Thus, they may be experiencing health problems or other limitations associated with their own aging.

Adult daughters and daughters-in-law often have been described as the "sandwich generation," caught between the competing needs of parents and children (Schwartz, 1978). It has been estimated that one third of women ages 43–54 years old are assisting parents or parents-in-law and children simultaneously (Pierret, 2006). These competing roles may or may not be experienced as stressful depending on the circumstances of care and resources available to help with caregiving. In some instances, children are older and support their mother by helping their grandparents. Among daughters who are married, some will have husbands who resent the help their wives give their parents, whereas others will be supportive and provide help as well. The main competing role outside the family is employment, which limits the time that daughters can spend assisting parents. Not all employed caregivers, however, experience difficulties. Some report little or no strain, and even indicate that the time they spend at work is satisfying because they feel they are able to accomplish something (Aneshensel et al., 1995). Women who experience high levels of strain from competing roles

of caregiver, wife, parent, and employee have fewer financial resources and tend to be caring for parents with higher levels of disability than women who experience little strain (Stephens, Townsend, Martire, & Druley, 2001). Yet experiencing rewards from helping a parent also diminishes the effects of competing roles (Stephens, Franks, & Townsend, 1994).

Beyond spouses and daughters, much less is known about the commitment and challenges faced by other caregivers, including sons, other relatives and non-kin caregivers. Caregivers of lesbian, gay, bisexual, and transgender (LGBT) older adults are an important but commonly overlooked group. These caregivers face unique challenges (Grossman, D'Augelli, & Dragowski, 2005). For example, in states that do not recognize gay marriage, partners can experience difficulties gaining access to medical information or being involved in medical decision making. The relationship of the caregiver with the care recipient's kin also can be problematic if that person has not been open about his or her sexual orientation, or if the family has not been accepting of it.

Another overlooked group is family caregivers of adults who have developmental disabilities or chronic mental health problems. Caregivers may be parents, siblings, adult offspring, or even grandparents in some instances (Hogan, 2012). The help they provide is often critical to the functioning and well-being of the individual with developmental disabilities or chronic mental illness, although the relationship may be characterized by long-standing tensions that complicate how care is given and received, and by high levels of distress and burden among caregivers (e.g., Awad & Voruganti, 2008; Ha, Hong, Seltzer, & Greenberg, 2008; Seltzer, Floyd, Song, Greenberg, & Hong, 2011). Although the specific types of involvement and challenges that each family faces is likely to vary, a common theme is how to ensure that the necessary care is provided if the care recipient outlives the caregiver. Roberto (1993) has provided a comprehensive overview of problems faced by these older caregivers and strategies for meeting these challenges.

Although the responsibilities for care typically falls on one person, the primary caregiver, other family members often provide indispensible help that makes the difference between whether the main caregiver becomes overwhelmed or is able to continue providing care. Thus, their relationship with the care receiver and primary care provider also may prove to be critical in designing treatment.

Diversity in Care Recipients' Needs

Another major source of diversity in caring relationships is the type of illness and associated disabilities of the care recipient. Illness and disabilities have four important implications for caregiving. First, the severity of a care recipient's problems and the amount of help that he or she needs directly affects the caregiver's routines, abilities, and energies (Aneshensel et al., 1995). Second, the emotional scaffolding around giving and receiving care can affect a caregiver's experience. Some care recipients are grateful for the help they receive and may even find ways to continue giving support in one form or another to the caregiver. Other care recipients are upset or angry over their disability and make it difficult for caregivers to assist them. Still other care situations are colored by long-standing emotional conflicts between care recipients and caregivers. Some of the most challenging care situations emerge when a son or daughter is providing assistance to a parent who has a personality disorder or other chronic mental illness (Awad & Voruganti, 2008; Zarit & Zarit, 2007). Even when needs for assistance with daily life are low, caregivers may be confronted with emotional outbursts, manipulations, stubbornness, suspiciousness, and other problematic behaviors that typically have a long history in their relationship with their parent.

The third factor is whether the care recipient suffers from Alzheimer's disease or other types of dementia. The problems associated with dementia, including its downward course, are particularly challenging for caregivers. As dementia progresses, difficulties with memory, comprehension, reasoning and language increase and individuals with dementia (IWDs) have diminished awareness of their problems. As a result, caregivers are less likely to know the IWD's preferences in many situations (Reamy, Kim, Zarit, & Whitlatch, 2011) and are more likely to encounter resistance in trying to provide assistance. Behavioral and emotional problems also can increase. Continuing progression of symptoms can undo strategies that caregivers previously had found effective in managing the situation. As an example, some caregivers find that they can leave notes as reminders for an IWD, but with progression of the disease, the IWD no longer may be able to read the notes or remember to look at them.

The fourth consideration is the degree to which the illness is life threatening. In older people with serious illness, nearness to death is always an issue, but some diseases have a more defined trajectory. When working with caregivers of people with metastasized cancers, for example, clinicians are likely to focus on emotions and concerns about their relative's death, and planning for important end-of-life decisions, such as whether and when to end active treatments and about the use of hospice (Haley, 2003a, 2003b). With care recipients for whom the life trajectory is more uncertain, these issues might be relevant at times, but the clinical focus is more likely to be on other concerns.

Diversity in Living Situations

Many caregivers share the same household or live close by to the care recipient. Some adult offspring, however, may live at considerable distance from parents. They may encounter difficulties trying to determine exactly how serious problems are and in arranging paid help for parents. Parents may not recognize the need for care or stubbornly resist assistance, and the formal service system can be balky and unresponsive at times. Care management services are widely available to help with these tasks, but they vary in quality.

Thus, overall diversity in caregiving circumstances, relationships, and experience forms the foundation for clinical intervention—the importance of meeting each family where they are without preconceived notions of what they "ought" to be experiencing.

PLANNING FOR TREATMENT

Burden is a unifying construct for assessment and treatment of caregivers. In its broadest sense, burden represents the problems that arise as a result of the care situation that are stressful and challenging for caregivers (Brodaty et al., 2002). The goal of treatment is to identify sources of burden for a particular caregiver and the strategies for potentially managing them. Interventions that reduce burden may allow caregivers to keep their relative at home longer and prevent deterioration in caregivers' health and well-being (e.g., Belle et al., 2006; Mittelman, Ferris, Shulman, Steinberg, & Levin, 1996).

Understanding Caregiving Burden and Its Sources

Our view of burden is informed by stress theory (Lazarus & Folkman, 1984; Pearlin, Liberman, Menaghan, & Mullan, 1981). From this perspective, we consider both the specific caregiving events or challenges that are present in a given situation as well as which events caregivers find to be stressful or burdensome. This step of differentiating the occurrence of events from those which are perceived as stressful by caregivers is important. Stress research has long found that it is the subjective dimension of how people appraise events that has the strongest impact on well-being (Almeida, 2005; Bolger, Davis, & Rafaeli, 2003; Lazarus & Folkman, 1984; Sliwinski, Almeida, Smyth, & Stawski, 2009). The same results have been found in caregiving—it is not whether a symptom or problem occurs, but how stressful caregivers perceive these events that determines their subjective feelings of burden and well-being (Aneshensel et al., 1995; Vitaliano, Russo, Young, Becker, & Maiuro, 1991; Zarit, Reever, & Bach-Peterson, 1980).

To illustrate, many people believe that caring for someone who is incontinent is very stressful, yet there is considerable variability in how caregivers react to this problem. One clinician worked with a caregiver over many years who was assisting his wife who had an atypical dementia. Early on in her illness, she began to have trouble managing the family finances. Her husband found it extremely stressful to handle the money. Yet, much later in her illness, she became incontinent, and he managed that without any difficulty. Thus, we need to consider which problems are present and which are stressful for caregivers.

In addition to the challenges posed by specific symptoms and behaviors, caregivers may experience a loss of the relationship with the other person (Adams, McClendon, & Smyth, 2008; Pearlin, Mullan, Semple, & Skaff, 1990). Loss is particularly poignant in cases of dementia, but other disabilities also erode valuable pieces of the relationship. Spouses may experience the loss of a companion, confidant, and sexual partner. They also may have to take on a variety of household tasks that their spouse previously performed. Gendered tasks, such as cleaning and cooking for husbands and car maintenance for wives, can be particularly challenging. Adult offspring caring for a parent may lose the companionship and support as well as tangible help their parent provided. Children sometimes hold the belief that they might be able to resolve long-standing relationship issues with parents, but a serious illness, especially one that involves cognitive decline, can close the door on working through these matters. Feelings of loss of the relationship may be a form of anticipatory grief and are associated with lower depression following the care recipient's death (Aneshensel et al., 1995).

Furthermore, burden consists both of stressors or challenges directly related to the diseases as well as the way in which problems may spill over into other areas of the person's life (Aneshensel et al., 1995). That is, caregivers face the challenge of managing symptoms of their relative's disease as well as the effect that the time, effort, and energy involved in providing care has on other roles and relationships in their life. These challenges may include balancing work and caregiving, carrying out other family responsibilities, and having time for personal or leisure activities (Aneshensel et al., 1995). These challenges also have a subjective component. People who are balancing work and care sometimes feel overwhelmed, but they sometimes also find that work is gratifying or rewarding (Aneshensel et al., 1995; Zarit, Kim, Femia, Almeida, & Klein, 2014). Likewise, family and friends can be a source of emotional and practical support or a source of conflict. Family may be critical of the primary caregiver or withhold giving any assistance. Caregivers also may face financial strains due to the costs of care and lost earnings. Having the financial resources to pay for help thus can relieve caregivers of responsibility for part of the care. At a psychological level, the threat to or erosion of valued activities may leave caregivers feeling trapped or engulfed by the caregiving role (Skaff & Pearlin, 1992). They feel that valued parts of their identity are being stripped away by the overwhelming demands related to caregiving.

The implications for clinicians are to identify those problems that are the most stressful or challenging for caregivers and to identify treatable components of those problems. Although little can be done to alter the course of the care recipient's disease, changes in how caregivers view and respond to the challenges they face and the personal, social, and economic resources they can bring to bear can lead to meaningful clinical change, reducing the burden on the caregiver and improving care for the care recipient.

Assessment Strategies

As with any initial clinical interview, a meeting with a caregiver begins with identifying why he or she is seeking help at the given time. Many caregivers initially seek treatment not for their problems as a caregiver but rather to get the care recipient to change his or her behavior. As you gather information, you will want to consider whether conjoint treatment with the care recipient would be warranted. In some instances, it will not be possible to work with the care recipient. The care recipient may not want treatment or have cognitive deficits or other problems too severe to benefit from including him or her in treatment. The caregiver might also prefer working alone to have more time to focus on his or her concerns. In those cases, the goal of treatment will need to be reframed as helping the caregiver to manage the challenges posed by the care recipient more effectively.

It might be necessary to meet with the care recipient before deciding on the course of treatment. An interview could be used to determine his or her willingness and ability to participate in treatment. If the caregiver brings the care recipient along to the initial appointment, leaving time to meet separately with each person is useful. When dementia is suspected, some brief testing could indicate severity of deficits. As important as a test score is the awareness that the person with dementia has about his or her deficits is (Clare, 2004; Clare, Marková, Verhey, & Kenny,

2005). A person who has an awareness of his or her disease and the problems it causes can be an active partner in treatment. If it appears feasible to involve the care recipient, the situation should be approached clinically in a similar manner to marital therapy (Zarit & Zarit, 2007). Specifically, the clinician cannot ally with the caregiver, and the goal cannot be to "fix" the care recipient. Instead, the focus is on how the couple can mutually respond to the challenges created by the illness. We discuss dyadic approaches in caregiving later.

In addition to joint sessions, separate meetings with a caregiver and care receiver also can allow for the examination of a caregiver's own cognitive impairment or other relationship concerns, such as abuse. It may be that the caregiver is simultaneously struggling with cognitive deficits, which are exacerbating subjective stress reactions. This may be particularly true for spouses, as the likelihood for one spouse to exhibit cognitive decline when their partner has dementia is as high as six times the rate as those who are caring for a spouse without dementia (Norton et al., 2010). In such a case, additional follow-up with cognitive screening may prove useful.

An assessment begins by identifying the care recipient's medical problems and symptoms, behavioral, and emotional problems, and need for assistance with activities of daily living. The clinician also should determine when problems occur (e.g., time of day, in particular situations), how often these problems occur, whether the caregiver or someone else provides assistance for these problems, and which problems are the most stressful for caregivers. It also is helpful to ask about how caregivers respond to specific problems. For example, if a person with dementia asks the same question over and over again, does the caregiver confront the person, thereby worsening the situation, or does the caregiver ignore the problem or try to distract the person. Finding out what the caregiver does that helps is as important as identifying strategies that do not help.

A clinical interview can be supplemented with assessment tools to explore systematically the problems a caregiver may be facing. Examples of widely used assessment measures are shown in Exhibit 20.1. For behavior and emotional problems associated with dementia, the Revised Memory and Behavior

Exhibit 20.1
Examples of Measures for Clinical Assessment of Caregivers

Measure	Citation	Measure description
Behavior problems		
Cohen-Mansfield Agitation Inventory (CMAI)	Cohen-Mansfield et al. (1989); http://www.dementia-assessment.com.au/symptoms/CMAI_Scale.pdf	Ratings of frequency and disruptiveness of 29 agitated behaviors; developed for use in nursing homes, but has been used in other settings; clinician and self-administered
Neuropsychiatric Inventory (NPI)	Cummings et al. (1994); http://www.dementia-assessment.com.au/behavioural/NPI.pdf	10 behavioral domains occurring in dementia; frequency and severity of disturbances are assessed; clinician administered
Neuropsychiatric Inventory—Clinician Rating Scale (NPI–C)	de Medeiros et al. (2010)	An expanded list of domains and items within each category from the NPI; measures frequency, severity and caregiver distress; clinician administered
Revised Behavior and Memory Problems Checklist	Teri et al. (1992); http://www.apa.org/pi/about/publications/caregivers/practice-settings/assessment/tools/memory-behavior.aspx	25 common behavioral and emotional problems of persons with dementia; identifies frequency and subjective feelings of being upset by problems; can be administered by the clinician or filled out by the caregiver
Caregiver burden		
Caregiver Appraisal Scale (revised)	Lawton, Moss, Hoffman, and Perkinson (2000); http://www.polisherresearchinstitute.org/#!assessment-instruments/c16rg	Multidimensional scale, including work disruptions and positive items; clinician or self-administered
Caregiver Burden Inventory (CBI)	Novak and Guest (1989); http://www.quia.com/files/quia/users/katekelly/Caregiver-Burden-Inventory	24 items grouped into five dimensions of perceived burden: time-dependence, developmental, physical, social, and emotional; clinician or self-administered
Zarit Burden Interview—Revised (ZBI)	Zarit, Reever, and Bach-Peterson (1980); http://www.mapi-trust.org/services/questionnairelicensing/catalog-questionnaires/307-zbi	22 items that address the subjective experience of burden; clinician or self-administered
Other measures		
Family Conflict	Aneshensel et al. (1995); Pearlin et al. (1990)	11 items assessing family conflict, including disagreement over the disease, and care or support to the caregiver; clinician or self-administered
Instrumental Activities of Daily Living (IADL) and Personal Activities of Daily Living (PADL)	Lawton and Brody (1969) IADL: https://www.abramsoncenter.org/pri/documents/IADL.pdf; PADL: http://www.polisherresearchinstitute.org/#!assessment-instruments/c16rg	9 items assessing performance of instrumental activities (e.g., food preparation, managing finances) and 6 items assessing personal activities (e.g., using the toilet, bathing); clinician administered to caregivers or to care recipients with good cognitive functioning
Job–Caregiving Conflict	Aneshensel et al. (1995); Pearlin et al. (1990)	5 items indicating interference of caregiving with work activities and 4 items assessing positive work experience; clinician or self-administered

Problems Checklist (Teri et al., 1992) can be self-administered by caregivers and identifies the frequency of occurrence of problems and how stressful caregivers perceive them. The Neuropsychiatric Inventory—Clinician Rating Scale (NPI–C) is another useful tool that identifies occurrence, severity, and caregiver's distress for common behavioral problems in dementia (de Medeiros et al., 2010). The Cohen-Mansfield Agitation Inventory (CMAI; Cohen-Mansfield, Marx, & Rosenthal, 1989) provides more detailed assessment of physical and verbal aggression and other highly disruptive behaviors. Basic activities of daily living (ADLs) and instrumental activities of daily living (IADLs) are still best assessed with the classic scales developed by Lawton and Brody (1969).

The clinician then wants to determine how these problems have affected the caregiver's other roles and relationships. If the caregiver is employed, what are the challenges involved for this caregiver in balancing work and caregiving? Family relationships are another important area. Who in the family is helpful and supportive? Are there some people not helping who the caregiver thinks should? The goal is to gain an initial impression about family functioning, but more information likely will emerge over time as the clinician explores the caregiver's and care recipient's relationships with other family members. Another area is what activities or interests the caregiver has given up as a result of his or her involvement in providing care. These areas are best explored through discussion with caregivers, but this assessment can be supplemented through the use of global burden measures such as those shown in Exhibit 20.1. Specific measures of work-caregiving strain and family conflict also can be found in Exhibit 20.1.

Another area to assess is whether the caregiver is using paid help, such as someone to assist the care recipient in the home or adult day care. Caregivers may report running into problems when they tried to use paid services. Understanding what the caregiver tried and why there were problems is important. Clinicians should not make suggestions about help the caregivers might use without finding out first if they tried something already. Rather, a plan for using services would need to address whatever problems the caregiver encountered in the past.

Clinicians also should assess the legal and financial issues in the situation. Are the caregiver or care recipient experiencing financial problems? Does the caregiver or anyone else have power of attorney for health care and finances?

Additional important areas for assessment are caregivers' overall burden, emotional well-being, and their health. Several scales are available to provide a global measure of subjective burden (see Exhibit 20.1). Emotional well-being should include assessment of depressive feelings, worry, anger, and positive affect. Depression of course can encompass feelings of hopelessness and helplessness and can be a barrier to caregivers taking practical steps that might improve their situation. When caregivers report beliefs typical of depression, treatment can include cognitive approaches that help them examine these beliefs. Additionally, anger often is overlooked but can be an important part of caregivers' responses. Feelings of anger toward the care recipient, and sometimes toward other family members, can be upsetting and can increase the risk of abusive behavior. Anger is responsive to treatment, including increasing caregivers' time away from the care recipient through respite services such as adult day services (Zarit, Stephens, Townsend, & Greene, 1998). A clinical assessment is sufficient, but the clinician can monitor treatment response by repeating administration of standard clinical measures of depression and anger.

Positive affect is not just the opposite of depression. Rather, caregivers may have low levels of positive emotions or enjoyment of life, but may not necessarily report high levels of depression or anger (Robertson, Zarit, Duncan, Rovine, & Femia, 2007). Low positive affect has been linked to a decreased ability to adapt to challenges in one's life (Fredrickson, 2001). When caregivers have low positive emotions, the clinician can consider implementing treatment that specifically will lead to an increase of these emotions, such as engaging in pleasant activities (Teri et al., 1997). The caregiver not only will experience immediate positive emotions but also the gain should lead to improved efforts to address problems.

Regarding caregiver's health, some caregivers may have physical limitations that make it difficult for them to assist their care recipient with some activities. Helping a care recipient out of bed or from a chair to standing is very difficult for many caregivers. Caregivers also may have health conditions, such as cardiovascular disease and hypertension, that are made worse by stress. As mentioned earlier, caregivers may not take the time to care for their own health problems by going to the doctor or maintaining therapeutic regimens. In addition, they may have habits that contribute to poor health and feelings of distress, for example, eating too much or too little, smoking, excessive alcohol use, and lack of exercise. Caregivers may underreport concerns about their own health, but other family members may be concerned and may put pressure on caregivers to place the care recipient in an institution. Improving caregivers' health behaviors and self-care are often important targets for treatment.

Finally, as with any other client, clinicians should be aware of the possibility that caregivers might have suicidal thoughts or thoughts about ending the care recipient's life and their own. The risk of suicide appears low during the period of active caregiving, but there may be an increased risk after the death of the person they were caring for (e.g., Rosengard & Folkman, 1997). Homicide–suicide by family caregivers appears to be relatively infrequent as well (Malphurs & Cohen, 2005). When it does occur, homicide–suicide is almost always perpetrated by a husband caring for a wife. Decline in the caregiver's own health, depression, and an impending move of the care recipient to an institution increase the risk (Bourget, Gagné, & Whitehurst, 2010; Malphurs, Eisdorfer, & Cohen, 2001). A history of prior spousal abuse also is a risk factor.

Increasingly, states are allowing for physician-assisted suicide for people with serious illnesses who are competent to make the decision. In a large survey of a heterogeneous sample of seriously ill patients and their caregivers, more than 60% of patients indicated they had thought about patient-assisted suicide but only 11% had more actively considered seeking assistance (Emanuel, Fairclough, & Emanuel, 2000). It was rare that patients and caregivers had discussed physician-assisted suicide together, and only a small number of patients had asked caregivers to assist them in ending their

lives. Eleven percent of caregivers of people who died during the course of the study, however, indicated that if they had been asked, they would have assisted their relative in suicide or supported physician-assisted suicide. This study is now more than a decade old, and it is likely that interest in the possibility of physician-assisted suicide has increased. The noteworthy finding from this study is that patient and caregiver may both be thinking of euthanasia but are not discussing it with each other. Clinicians will want to follow up on statements by either person that directly or indirectly indicate they may be thinking of euthanasia. That also means that clinicians need to be prepared to find themselves suddenly in the middle of an intense discussion of physician-assisted suicide. As with other issues related to suicide, the clinician needs to treat this issue within the framework of state law and to be able to differentiate his own beliefs about the appropriateness of physician-assisted suicide from the values and beliefs of the caregiver and patient.

The Assessment Process and Intervention Goals
Goals for treatment emerge from the assessment process and are informed by information from three areas: the caregiver's and care recipient's values and preferences, family dynamics, and the caregiver's preferences and resources concerning whether care will be continued at home or the older person will be moved to an institutional setting.

The initial assessment should identify, at least in a preliminary way, the problems that most concern the caregiver. As articulated, potentially treatable aspects of the care situation emerge from examination of stressors and gathering information about the extended family and other resources the caregiver might draw on. Goals can be derived directly from these concerns and resources. In some cases, however, the clinician may have to reframe the caregiver's goals to identify modifiable features of the situation. For example, a caregiver may hope to improve the care receiver's memory. That goal may not be achievable, but treatment can help the caregiver to use better strategies for responding to the care recipient's memory problems. We address this issue further in the treatment section.

The guiding principle behind setting treatment goals is identifying how to reduce the subjective stress or burden associated with care-related problems, and to do so by increasing resources that are brought to bear on modifiable dimensions of the problems. Treatment can help caregivers utilize their existing psychological, social, and economic resources to manage care-related stressors or to identify new resources. The information that the clinician obtains during the initial assessment also will indicate areas where help from other family members can be increased or redirected to better meet the care receiver's and caregiver's needs.

Some caregivers are quite competent in many areas of their lives but feel helpless when dealing with their relative's inability to care for him- or herself. Often a direct clinical approach is helpful. The clinician can discuss with the caregiver the coping skills he or she uses in other situations, and how those skills can work in dealing with care-related problems as well. Caregivers often will be able to make this connection. In other cases, caregivers will need to modify their skills or learn new skills.

Building value-based goals. Treatment goals often address practical steps that caregivers can take but also should be informed by an examination of the values and preferences of caregivers and care recipients. Each person approaches treatment with a core set of personal values that will shape his or her willingness and ability to respond to treatment in particular ways. For example, although all individuals pursue the needs of autonomy, relatedness, and competence (Deci & Ryan, 2000), individuals differ in the degree to which they strive for such needs and value differential ways of achieving such needs. A person who highly values interdependence and relatedness may be more receptive to intervention-based goals that rely on others. That person, however, may lack the skills to initiate such help. Treatment goals can be set up then to work with this individual's preference and personal value to include others in care. Meanwhile, a person whose identity and self-worth is highly entrenched in his or her sense of independence and autonomy may be more reluctant to ask for help from others. In such circumstances, a model such

as selection-optimization-compensation (Freund & Baltes, 1998) may be meaningful, helping caregivers select tasks that they can manage well (optimize) to better focus their energies and then to accept support (i.e., compensate) in other areas. This would allow the individual to remain in control of specific tasks, without trying to maintain control over all aspects of care. In both cases, a clinician can guide caregivers or care recipients into focusing on goals that are also consistent with their core personal values.

Beyond broad personal values, the clinician can build goals based on values held in relation to care tasks. Values and preferences in care can be conceptualized as the psychosocial preferences of an individual in regard to daily care or long-term care decision making, such as self-identity, safety, or relationships (Whitlatch, Piiparinen, & Feinberg, 2009). Whitlatch et al. (2009) have offered a comprehensive form for assessing values and preferences of an elder, which could be utilized with both caregivers and care recipients to understand who values what in care. Specifically, they have developed a 37-item battery of questions to ask the individual about the values and preferences in daily care that are important to him or her. Items ask, "How important is it for you to . . ." do or have, such as to have privacy, live in one's own home, come and go as one pleases, be with family or friends, do things with other people, or make one's own financial decisions (Whitlatch et al., 2009)? This measure shows promise in capturing the multidimensionality of individuals' values and preferences in care. Although this specific measure predominately has been used and evaluated with individuals who have mild to moderate dementia (Clark, Tucke, & Whitlatch, 2008; Feinberg & Whitlatch, 2001; Whitlatch, Feinberg, & Tucke, 2005a, 2005b), it is likely to be effective with other older adults and caregivers. Other measures of personal preferences have been developed to help identify what is important to individuals in care (e.g., Carpenter, Van Haitsma, Ruckdeschel, & Lawton, 2000; Karel, Moye, Bank, & Azar, 2007).

Assessment of the caregiver's and care recipient's values and preference in care can establish a person-centered orientation to treatment. By identifying each person's values, the clinician can facilitate the maintenance of self-direction in the care process, even when care recipients must rely on the support of others. With information about values, clinicians can guide the development of goals based on each person's preferences, and in the case of dyadic intervention, jointly include the care recipient. As described later, such-value based assessments can assist in clarifying which challenges in care are the most important to tackle from each person's perspective.

The values and preferences of caregivers and care receivers may differ in fundamental ways. Accumulating evidence suggests that each party may not fully recognize the importance of values held by the other person. This lack of understanding of the other person's values can occur in any caregiving situation, but it may be especially pronounced when the care recipient suffers from dementia (Carpenter et al., 2000; Fagerlin, Ditto, Hawkins, Schneider, & Smucker, 2002; McCullough, Wilson, Teasdale, Kolpakchi, & Skelly, 1993; Reamy et al., 2011; Uhlmann, Pearlman, & Cain, 1988; Whitlatch & Feinberg, 2003). These differences may prove to be particularly meaningful points for intervention, whereby clinicians can explore differences and find areas of common ground between caregiver and care recipient (Whitlatch, Judge, Zarit, & Femia, 2006). Even when only the caregiver is involved in treatment, it is still helpful to consider the care recipient's goals, as what steps the caregiver is willing to take will be shaped by his or her understanding of what the care recipient will be receptive to. Much of the delicate work of treatment involves balancing the best interests of the two people, while understanding that these interests may not always be reconciled. Goal setting then must be built based on values but balanced within a family context.

Balancing treatment goals within a family context. Treatment goals often are embedded in the four main ethical principles of autonomy, beneficence, nonmaleficence, and justice (Harnett & Greaney, 2008; Hughes & Baldwin, 2006). In this frame, commonly discussed in medical ethics, autonomy is the ability for an individual to decide what he wants to have happen or to be done.

Beneficence is that one should try to do good for the people for whom one cares. Nonmaleficence says one should try to avoid doing people harm. And, lastly, justice denotes that people should be treated fairly and equally. In the scope of family caregiving, autonomy of one individual often is held up against the other principle of doing good (beneficence). Such ideals may emerge in a discussion of what is more important: the autonomy of honoring the elder's wishes, or the caregiver's conceptualization of the best interests of the elder. Furthermore, the value of autonomy often can be set up against the caregiver's perceived need for safety for the care recipient (Kane, 1995). Clinicians then must be prepared to assist families in navigating such discussions and helping both the caregiver and care receiver realize what is important to each individual. If a care recipient feels that maintaining as much independence as possible is a key goal for him or her, but the caregiver feels allowing the individual to live at home fully independent of any in-home help is unsafe because of the risk for falling, then compromises may need to be proposed. In balancing these difficult issues in particular, clinicians need to remember that although safety may preserve life, maintenance of autonomy has been linked to improved quality of life, health, and well-being (Langer, 1983).

Given the central role of other family members as a source of emotional and tangible support, finding ways to encourage collaboration and reduce criticism of the caregiver are an important part of treatment. To achieve those goals, it is valuable to view the caregiver and care recipient within a wider family system (Qualls & Noecker, 2009; Zarit et al., 1985). As everyone who has worked with families knows, each family system has its own norms and expectations, and each person has a different place in that system that affects how other people view him or her. Interventions reverberate through the family system, with people reacting differently from one another and sometimes in quite unexpected ways. These reactions reflect in part long-standing relationships, alliances within the family and the power or influence each person has vis-à-vis others. Consider, for example, how the caregiver's position in the family can affect responses by other people. A caregiver whom other family members see as competent or powerful may get less help because everyone views that person as able to manage on his or her own. By contrast, a caregiver who is viewed by other family members as weak will get advice and criticism but not necessarily the emotional and tangible support that would be useful. Clinicians, thus, must keep these dynamics in mind.

Furthermore, care for a parent often intensifies sibling competition and other long-dormant feelings in those relationships. The sibling who takes over primary responsibility for a parent may be resented and criticized by another sibling. The types of responses are affected by gender. A daughter may take on the caregiving role, knowing her brother would not be capable of doing so but still resent that he does not help her much. Family relationships also are affected by money. The person who is acting as a caregiver may be making financial decisions that siblings view as depleting their inheritance. In most cases, these expenses are necessary for the older person's health and well-being, but caregivers sometimes may misappropriate a parent's funds. How the parent's estate is distributed is also likely to be a source of tension. A caregiving child may expect a larger share, while other children may believe that only an equal distribution of the parent's assets is justified. There may be long-standing emotional reasons that contribute to conflict over the parent's estate, but in the end, clinicians should not lose sight of the fact that money is a potent issue that can spark intense conflict. Of course, some siblings work together quite well in assisting a parent. In fact, some siblings work out clever arrangements that allow the burden of care to be distributed fairly equally and therefore not falling too heavily on one person. Regardless of the outcome, these family dynamics ultimately come into play when balancing the goals of treatment in the context of one's family and often shape which goals are achievable versus not.

Addressing the goal of placement. Where the best interests of caregiver and receiver are likely to diverge is around the question of whether to continue to provide care at home or to move the care receiver to an institution. From the perspective of the older person, remaining at home often has advantages over moving. Most older people prefer to remain at home for as long as it is possible. Home is a familiar and comfortable place, and the older person is surrounded by possessions that convey memories of the life he or she lived. In effect, home is a fundamental support to identity, especially when disability has narrowed the world in which a person lives. Furthermore, living at home means that people do not have to follow institutional rules that regulate their daily routines and habits, such as when to get up, what to eat and even what activities in which to engage. Institutional routines have the effect of stripping away the older person's autonomy and identity (Baltes & Wahl, 1992; Persson & Wästerfors, 2009). Placement also is associated with potential adverse psychological and health effects for the older individual (e.g., Aneshensel, Pearlin, Levy-Storms, & Schuler, 2000). Some older people, however, do not want to become a burden on their families and do prefer to receive care in an institutional setting. There are also situations in which the care provided by the family is abusive and negligent, in which case institutions offer a better alternative.

Many family caregivers are committed to keeping their relative at home. Health care providers, however, can be quick to recommend placing an older person in an institutional setting because of the belief that the burden of ongoing care will be too much for the caregiver. Other family members also may make this argument to the primary caregiver. Placement does not necessarily relieve burden, however, but rather changes the source of burden (Gaugler, Anderson, Zarit, & Pearlin, 2004; Gaugler, Mittelman, Hepburn, & Newcomer, 2010; Zarit & Whitlatch, 1992). The strain of providing hands-on care is reduced, but new stressors associated with institutional life emerge. Older caregivers may have difficulty traveling to visit their spouse in an institution. Rather than being relieved of care responsibilities, many caregivers continue to provide a considerable amount of care in a nursing home or assisted living facility. Interacting with staff and trying to ensure a high-quality of care also can be stressful. Discussions with caregivers about potential placement of the care receiver need to be tempered by several considerations. Just as we do not try to talk caregivers into placement, we also do not want to talk them out of it or discourage them from considering it. We want to convey that placement is an option and to be sure that caregivers are comfortable discussing it. If a clinician does not acknowledge placement as a possible option, caregivers who are ambivalent about it may feel too ashamed or guilty to raise the idea on their own. Conversely, some caregivers will bring up placement because they are not aware of other options for getting help, such as adult day services or in-home care that could improve their situation.

Another consideration is the care receiver's competence to make decisions about where to live. It is not uncommon for older people to insist they want to remain at home, even in circumstances that involve some risk and discomfort. As mentioned when discussing values, families often are concerned that an older person living alone might fall or be unable to get help in a health emergency or become a victim of crime. A care recipient who is competent to make this decision, that is, who understands the potential harmful consequences of staying at home, has the right to decide to remain at home despite those risks. Furthermore, living in a residential facility is not risk-free. Residents can fall, receive incorrect medications, or experience other adverse events. In a fundamental way, an older person who wants to stay at home is choosing to live out his or her life in a particular way, making a trade-off of risks for the comfort and meaning of home. Of course, safeguards such as environmental modifications or someone to help the older person at home can be put in place and those steps should reduce risk and lower concerns of other family members.

In situations in which the caregiver and a capable care receiver differ on where or how the latter should live, the clinician needs to help caregivers shift the focus of the discussion. Older people sometimes stubbornly resist suggestions by caregivers as a way of maintaining control of their life in the face of challenges that are undermining their independence. Telling the older person that he or she must do something may only lead to increased resistance. In these situations, we encourage caregivers to take a more indirect approach. Rather than telling the older person what to do, caregivers could respond with empathy, reflecting the importance of doing things one's own way. Caregivers also could talk

about possible resources that could improve the situation, and offer to look into them, when the care recipient is ready. Overall, this strategy avoids the cycle of advice and resistance, which has not been productive, and instead takes a more indirect approach.

One problem with bringing in home help is that the older person may "fire" the helper. Caregivers should work with the agency to make sure that care staff understand the older person's condition and that they will find ways to make the situation work. Unfortunately, many home care agencies are not sophisticated in handling these situations and caregivers must continue to advocate for the services their relative may need.

The same perspective needs to be applied to the risks that caregivers face. A caregiver who is under considerable stress may insist on continuing to provide care at home, even though it poses a risk to his or her own health. This is a choice that the person has the right to make. The role of the clinician is to help caregivers explore their options, including the importance of making changes in the situation that can reduce the strain on caregivers.

One final consideration is the cost of nursing homes and other residential settings. When an older person needs long-term care in an assisted living facility, nursing home, or other type of residence, he or she must pay privately. Medicare only pays for short-term nursing home stays following hospitalization. Private long-term care insurance can offset some of the costs. Medicaid will pay for nursing home care, but only after people have spent down their assets below an allowable amount. Sometimes, however, they may have to move from a private-pay facility to one that accepts Medicaid. The financial implications are particularly important for a spouse, who must spend a portion of shared assets on nursing home care before the care recipient becomes eligible for Medicaid. We have included links to websites that explain options for paying for long-term care and also encourage clinicians to explore the rules for Medicaid in their own state (see Exhibit 20.2). Local area agencies on aging are able to provide such information.

Lastly, we want to stress that goal setting is an ongoing process. As caregivers make progress in

---

Exhibit 20.2
Resources on Paying for Long-Term Care

Organization	Website link	Description of resource
Medicare	http://www.medicare.gov/nursing/payment.asp	This website summarizes the coverage of long-term care by the federally funded programs of Medicare and Medicaid as well as other forms of payment. It also links you to additional information about Medicare coverage for older adults and to helpful resources such as Nursing Home Compare, a site to search information about the quality of nursing homes in a specified region.
American Association of Retired Persons (AARP)	http://www.aarp.org/health/medicare-insurance/info-09-2010/ask_ms_medicare_question_89.html	This links to a discussion in AARP's Bulletin on paying for nursing home care, which articulates the distinct roles Medicaid and Medicare cover in helping to pay for long-term care for elders.
American Association of Retired Persons (AARP)	http://www.aarp.org/relationships/caregiving-resource-center/LTCC/?intcmp=FTR-LINKS	AARP also provides a long-term care cost calculator. On this site an individual can fill in information about their location of residence and long-term care needs to receive estimates on cost for specified services.
AssistGuide Information Services (AGIS)	http://www.agis.com	An organization founded by caregivers, AGIS also provides user-friendly information for caregivers on paying for long-term care. Their website also links out to other resources for caregivers, including information on financial planning and supportive services.
Department of Health and Human Services, National Clearinghouse for Long Term Care Information	http://www.longtermcare.gov	This website run by the Department of Health and Human Services provides brief information about paying for long-term care, including information on the potential costs, public programs, private financing options, and a link to find services.

treatment or encounter new challenges, their perspectives will change and they will change their goals. Treatment should accommodate such adaptability and continually revisit the goals at hand.

CLINICAL INTERVENTIONS

Clinical interventions with family caregivers are short-term and problem focused, designed to address the most pressing care-related problems with which the person is dealing. These problems may include the direct or primary challenges of giving care or the disruptions that the caregiving role produces in other areas of the person's life. We conceptualize treatment as focusing on the here-and-now of caregivers' experiences. We do not view most caregivers as needing long-term therapy for fundamental emotional or personality issues. Although the

past always makes a contribution to present circumstances, caregivers usually can make progress on practical and emotional concerns without extensive exploration of the past. And, although the main part of treatment is likely short term, caregivers often return for treatment when their circumstances change, such as considering moving their care recipient to a facility or facing end-of-life decisions for their relative. Some caregivers, of course, are experiencing multiple problems in their lives in addition to caregiving or have long-standing social and emotional problems that they want to address, and in those cases, the clinician may want to see them on a more extended basis (e.g., Zarit et al., 1985; Zarit & Zarit, 2007).

This section begins with a presentation of clinical approaches that focus primarily on the caregiver. It starts with a discussion of short-term treatment primarily focused on the caregiver and his or her family, in which the care recipient is not involved, because of dementia or other issues that leave the care recipient unable or unwilling to participate in treatment. It then discusses dyadic interventions that involve both the caregiver and care recipient, including cases in which someone has early mild symptoms of dementia or in which the care recipient is otherwise capable of taking part in treatment.

As a note, no simple assessment or test score can indicate whether a person with dementia can participate in or benefit from treatment. As clinicians gain experience with this population, they will develop a sense about when the person with dementia has the ability to be part of the treatment. As stated, one major consideration is the person's awareness of the diagnosis and its implications (for a thorough discussion of awareness and its assessment in dementia, see Clare, 2004; Clare et al., 2005). With Alzheimer's disease and other dementias being diagnosed earlier in the disease process, clinicians are more likely to encounter individuals with dementia when symptoms are early and mild. It is important, however, not to look just at memory or mental status scores but also to consider the person's ability to reflect on one's ongoing experiences and feelings. The willingness of the individual with dementia to take part in treatment is important. The clinician can explore whether the person with dementia is capable of participating in and benefiting from treatment by working with both people initially, seeing them together and spending some time separately with each person (Zarit & Zarit, 2007). These sessions can be a valuable source of information about problems each person is having. Furthermore, the individual with dementia may get support from the sessions, while the caregiver can work on addressing stressful aspects of the situation.

Interventions With Caregivers

We present several components of treatment with caregivers that have been empirically validated in clinical trials (Belle et al., 2006; Castleman, Gallagher-Thompson, & Naythons, 1999; Mittelman, Epstein, & Pierzchala, 2002; Qualls & Williams, 2013; Teri, Logsdon, Uomoto, & McCurry, 1997; Zarit et al., 1985). The focus of these interventions

is on caregivers of people with dementia, which has been studied more extensively than other care situations, but the principles and many of the techniques can be applied to other types of caregiving. Rather than describe each trial, we present an integrated clinical approach that has utilized these strategies in a private practice and clinic settings (Qualls & Williams, 2013; Zarit & Zarit, 2007). The components are (a) development of a therapeutic relationship, (b) understanding the care recipient's illness and its effects, (c) problem solving for managing the care recipient's behavioral and emotional problems, (d) creating a balance of caregiving with other activities, and (e) identifying and obtaining sources of help from family members, friends, and service agencies that will provide caregivers with continued support over time and relief from some of the demands being placed on them.

The therapeutic relationship in caregiving and treatment process. Working with caregivers encompasses more than giving information or following a script from the treatment manual of a psychoeducational intervention. All too often, these scripted interventions are based on the notion that all caregivers need is some information about the problem and then they will be able to carry on for themselves. Some caregivers certainly are able to do that, but many of them need to interact with an active listener who, by conveying understanding of their perspective, becomes an ally who can guide them through the mix of often-powerful emotions they have about their role and responsibilities and to help them make the changes in their care situations that will lower burden. As they do with other clients, clinicians need to build a relationship characterized by empathy and trust, which will give caregivers confidence to examine the challenges and the choices facing them, and to take the risk of implementing changes in their situation.

Treatment often can proceed quickly, and caregivers may embrace the various practical strategies that can help them manage their situation more effectively. Many caregivers, however, will reach impasses and have difficulty moving forward. These impasses are clinically meaningful, and the clinician will want to engage the caregiver in exploring beliefs that are preventing him or her from moving forward.

We identify four of the more common reasons for impasses. First, the goal-setting process may not have been sufficient. Encountering resistance early on in the treatment process often indicates that the caregiver is not yet ready to let go of hope that somehow the problem will go away or that some miraculous treatment might still be found that makes the care recipient better. Helping these caregivers understand what realistically can be accomplished is necessary before they are willing to focus on how to cope with the current reality.

Second, caregivers may have ambivalence about their role. This ambivalence is expressed in half-hearted efforts to make changes or being unable to decide on a direction for change. There are several sources of ambivalence. A caregiver may resent having been thrust into the role. A spouse may have been hoping for a golden retirement and instead finds him- or herself coping with an unrelentingly distressing and demanding caregiving experience. A daughter may be angry at having been the one among her siblings who had to step forward or harbor resentment toward a parent who was not loving enough or generous enough. Another source of ambivalence is if caregivers believe their commitment is completely open-ended and that they have to do everything themselves that the care situation demands. A starting point in these situations is discussing how much caregivers are willing to do and establishing that they can choose not to continue, if the demands on them become excessive. In this process, the clinician must attend to guilt or other emotions and help caregivers explore the beliefs that underlie these feelings. If they can articulate expectations for the amount of care they are willing to provide and identify choices they have around setting limits on their involvement, they then will be freed to make changes in their current situation without feeling that they will not be able to extract themselves from the caregiving role at a later time. Part of this process involves exploring practical strategies for getting help with care, for example, involving family members or paid help, as discussed later.

A third reason for an impasse is that caregivers may be afraid of making any change because they think it might make the situation worse. This type of impasse is akin to the hopelessness expressed by clinically depressed people. For someone who is stuck for this reason, use of the pros and cons strategy (Beck, Rush, Shaw, & Emery, 1979), in which the clinician guides the caregiver in weighing the advantages and disadvantages of a specific action compared with doing nothing or to taking a different action, can be helpful. This exercise also may uncover beliefs that are holding the caregiver back from making changes.

A fourth reason why clinicians may run into difficulties in implementing treatment is that a caregiver may not have the cognitive, emotional, or economic resources necessary to carry out parts of the intervention. Some caregivers may be too concrete in their thinking and have trouble learning new ways to view the situation or adapting new strategies for managing it. Clinicians may need to simplify their language and approach, so that it is more easily accessible. For some low-income caregivers, the assistance they are giving to a relative may be a small part of the problems they are facing. Finding money to pay the rent each month or other practical concerns may be more pressing than learning about new approaches to care for a parent.

Understanding the care recipient's illness and its effects. Early in treatment, the clinician will want to determine what caregivers know about their relative's illness, its causes, and about treatment options and outcomes of the illness. There is now extensive information in the media about diseases, such as Alzheimer's. Unfortunately this information can be misleading and some of it is outright fiction. Clinicians can discuss with caregivers what they know and answer their questions. It is not sufficient to just point caregivers to websites, but rather one must be able to provide accurate information drawn from reliable sources. As an example, caregivers for a person with Alzheimer's disease may believe that the disease can be cured when it cannot, especially now that patients are routinely prescribed medications for their illness. Thus, they may wonder why you are asking them to make adjustments to how they respond to behavior problems or other aspects of the care situation. Identifying their beliefs about the illness and treatments and helping them form reasonable expectations, given the current state of scientific knowledge, can help caregivers focus on those steps that can make a difference in their situation. It is also important to support the caregiver against the efforts of family members who push to get them to try treatments that are known not to work.

Of course, clinicians need reliable information themselves to be able to help caregivers understand the causes, symptoms, and treatment options for a disease. Clinicians who do a lot of work with older people will acquire an understanding of the most common diseases in later life through experience and from reliable continuing education programs. The Internet offers a wealth of resources, but we strongly advise seeking information only from trustworthy mainstream sources like the National Institutes of Health or disease-related foundations. Although many people may be drawn to natural, holistic approaches to disease, many of these treatments have no valid empirical foundation and have no place in our practice as psychologists. If a caregiver wants to pursue an avenue of treatment for a care receiver that is relatively harmless and inexpensive, however, there is no reason to be discouraging. In cases in which a treatment is expensive and potentially dangerous or has no therapeutic benefits, it is appropriate to have a discussion about those decisions.

We now turn from information about the disease to caregivers' understanding of the care receiver's behaviors and emotions. Caregivers of people with dementia often believe that cognitive and behavioral problems are under the person's control (Zarit & Zarit, 2007). One of the most common and annoying problems for caregivers is for the person with dementia to ask the same question over and over again. Caregivers may attribute this problem to a lack of attention. They assume that the person with dementia just needs to pay more attention, and then they will remember the information. They become more and more frustrated when the person continues repeating the question. They may attribute the person's problem to not trying, to laziness, or to deliberately trying to annoy the caregiver. It is rare to find any caregiver who has not been annoyed or upset by this type of problem, and some get into

tremendous rows with their relative over their inability to control their forgetting or even to acknowledge they are forgetful.

A useful strategy for working with caregivers in these situations is to identify the attribution they are making about their relative's behavior, for example, that he could control the repetitive questions if he tried, or she is just trying to get attention. The clinician then can discuss with the caregiver that these behaviors are part of the disease and not under their relative's control (Hepburn, Tornatore, Center, & Ostwald, 2001; Zarit & Zarit, 2007). Why, for example, does someone with a memory impairing disorder ask the same question over and over again? It is because of memory loss, not volition (although there are instances in which there may be some volition involved). Once caregivers see the role of the disease in these behaviors, clinicians then encourage them to come up with new strategies for responding. Caregivers can learn to patiently answer their relative's questions or change the subject. Often, this type of repetitive behavior reflects boredom, and so getting the person with dementia involved in an activity may be effective.

Another type of problem that can be very upsetting to caregivers is when care receivers make statements that contradict reality. Persons with dementia might say they want to go home, when they are at home, or that they want to visit their mother who is long-deceased, or that they want to go to work, although they retired long ago. Arguing with a person with dementia over factual information does not work. It is not possible to convince them that they are wrong about these beliefs, and there is no evidence to support that "reorienting" them to reality will do any good (Zarit & Zarit, 2007). Instead, the clinician can work with caregivers to understand that these beliefs are due to the disease. A person with dementia believes her mother is alive because of deficiencies in processing and remembering information. Furthermore, these statements are composed of two components: factual and emotional (Zarit & Zarit, 2007). Although caregivers cannot change what a person with dementia believes is factual, they can respond to what he or she might be feeling. For example, what might someone with dementia be feeling when she asks to see her mother? She may be feeling lonely, sad, or want the affection and security her mother gave her. When a caregiver tells this woman her mother is dead, it does not correct the information but instead raises the sadness or anxiety she is feeling. A more effective strategy will be to have the caregiver say, "You must be missing your mother," or "Let's sit down and talk about your mother." They might look at photos of her mother. Or the caregiver might use it as an opportunity to interact with the person with dementia and give her emotional support. For some people, just changing the subject will work, too.

Care recipients who suffer from chronic mental health problems, such as depression or personality disorders, can draw caregivers into similar arguments that have no possible resolution. For example, the care recipient may distort past events or present a completely different view of family history than the caregiver, which often also imply criticism of the caregiver. Reasoning or even factual evidence will not change the care recipient's mind and will only leave caregivers angry and frustrated. In the end, they need to see that it does not matter what the care recipient believes is true about the past. Helping caregivers learn how to avoid these types of arguments can be very useful for lowering stress.

Managing behavioral and emotional problems.
Behavior management approaches are used in most of the empirically validated treatment models (e.g., Belle et al., 2006; Teri et al., 1997; Whitlatch, Zarit, & von Eye, 1991). The basic framework is that behavior problems are triggered by an antecedent event and reinforced by the responses to it. Teri et al. (1997) have introduced the acronym ABC—Antecedent, Behavior, Consequence—to help caregivers apply this approach for behavior problems. Caregivers are taught to monitor when behaviors occurred, what happened right before, and what happened afterward. This information is best gathered by direct observation, rather than by trying to recall events from the past, and thus caregivers can be encouraged to carry a log in which they can write down when problems occur and the possible antecedents and consequences.

Once antecedents and consequences have been identified, caregiver and clinician collaborate in a problem-solving process to identify possible solutions. The solutions may emerge from the observation of the patterns of antecedents and consequences, or from a novel suggestion by the caregiver. For example, when a care receiver has periods of restlessness or agitation, a frequent antecedent is inactivity and a consequence often is receiving attention. By viewing restlessness this way, the caregiver then may be able to identify strategies to head it off, such as introducing an activity at a scheduled time before the restlessness occurs. Some caregivers will readily identify strategies for controlling behavioral and emotional problems of the care receiver, but others will feel stuck and hopeless. The clinician may need to encourage them to brainstorm or not censor any ideas they might have for addressing the problem (Zarit & Zarit, 2007). Getting caregivers to brainstorm can help them start to look at the situation as having potential solutions. Ultimately, if caregivers can generate their own solutions, they are more likely to implement them.

When a strategy is identified, clinician and caregiver then need a plan to implement it. It is not enough to tell the caregiver to try it, but instead, consistent with standard behavioral and cognitive approaches, there needs to be a specific plan for what the caregiver will do and when. This specificity increases the likelihood that the individual will carry out the plan. Failure to carry out a plan occurs mainly when it comes across more like advice than a detailed strategy that emerges collaboratively with the caregiver.

During the process of developing a plan, the clinician and caregiver will discuss whether there are potential obstacles to carrying it out (for a useful discussion of obstacles, see Beck et al., 1979). Some obstacles are practical. To use the previous example, a caregiver may recognize that getting the care receiver to be more active would be useful to decrease restlessness, but she may not have the energy to do so. This information then could lead to discussions of what other ways there may be to increase activities, other than by the primary caregiver. Using paid help, such as in-home care or adult day care, or scheduling visits from friends or relatives are possible alternatives. Identifying these types of obstacles leads to refinement of the plan.

As noted, sometimes caregivers are stuck and need help making a decision to take new actions. Analysis of pros and cons of possible strategies, sometimes compared with each other or to the status quo, will help in this situation (Beck et al., 1979; Zarit & Zarit, 2007).

The final steps are to implement the strategy and evaluate it. Caregivers can be asked to continue recording in a daily log when a problem occurred and how long it lasted. Evidence that a behavior problem is decreasing in frequency will help caregivers gain a sense of control over a situation that seemed entirely out of their control. This type of problem-solving approach has been found to be feasible and associated with improvements in behavior and in the caregiver's own subjective burden and well-being (Logsdon, McCurry, & Teri, 2007; Teri et al., 1997; Whitlatch et al., 1991).

A useful variation on this approach is training caregivers to use behavioral management and sleep hygiene techniques for sleep problems of people with dementia (McCurry, Gibbons, Logsdon, Vitiello, & Teri, 2005; McCurry et al., 2011). Antecedents may include little exposure to sunlight, late afternoon naps, and excessive caffeine ingestion. Caregivers are taught to modify these antecedents, for example, by walking outdoors with the person with dementia during the daytime and implementing a calming bedtime routine. Trials of this approach led to reduced nighttime awakenings and longer times asleep for the person with dementia. This approach could be used with people who have other types of illnesses besides dementia.

Medication is a frequent treatment for behavior problems in dementia. Although medications can be effective in individual cases, the research literature suggests that benefits compared with placebo are minimal (e.g., Sink, Holden, & Yaffe, 2005). There also can be serious side effects of neuroleptics (Schneider, Dagerman, & Insel, 2006), which have led to warnings about their use with older people (National Center for Biotechnology Information, 2010). Nursing home regulations now mandate that behavioral treatment be tried first before medications, and a similar approach should be used in community settings.

Creating a balance of caregiving and other activities. As we have emphasized, caregiving can leave little room for other activities or for caregivers to take care of their own health and emotional needs. A critical part of treatment is to identify ways that caregivers can balance the demands on their lives, which allows them to continue providing care without excessive burden. A first step in the process is identifying what the caregiver needs, whether it is to be able to work, see friends, or engage in leisure activities or just to get regular breaks from caregiving. Use of the problem-solving approach—brainstorming solutions, looking at their pros and cons, and identifying any barriers to implementing them—can be very helpful.

Some solutions involve caregivers learning to set boundaries and limits that free up their time. Other solutions include reaching out to family or friends or using paid help to free up caregivers from time they would be providing care. Clinicians can help caregivers identify potential sources of informal help and also give information about paid services that could meet their needs. Caregivers often are reluctant to ask for help and may have reservations about turning care over to anyone else. Using a cognitive–behavioral approach for examination of these beliefs can help caregivers use help in ways that provide them relief (Beck et al., 1979; Zarit & Zarit, 2007).

Paid help can have its own problems, and clinicians need to be able to work with caregivers to come up with plans for potential difficulties. Caregivers who use in-home help have a quandary about where they should go when the helper comes. Situations in which caregivers stay home with the helper do not work well because the caregiver does not get rest and the care recipient does not form a relationship with the helper. Adult day service is a reliable source of help that has been shown to reduce exposure to stressors for caregivers (Zarit et al., 2011) and that leads to reduced emotional distress (Zarit et al., 1998, 2014). Adult day services, however, are not without their problems. Caregivers sometimes find it difficult to get the care recipient ready to go to adult day care or have trouble letting the person go. They also may be concerned about whether the program would be demeaning to the person or if the person would allow for the separation from the caregiver. Good adult day service programs, however, are able to manage the transfers and engage clients in meaningful and therapeutic activities. Adult day service programs have therapeutic benefits for people with dementia, including reduced behavioral and sleep problems (Femia, Zarit, Stephens, & Greene, 2007).

Beyond tangible help, many caregivers benefit from emotional support from family and friends (Aneshensel et al., 1995). Often, however, they find themselves cut off from normal interactions with family and friends. This lack of support may come from both sides. Caregivers may be reluctant to engage in social activities because they are embarrassed by the care recipient's behavior or the care recipient may have difficulties in social situations. Or caregivers may feel they cannot leave the care recipient alone so that they might go out with friends. On the other side, friends and family may cut down their interactions because they do not know what to say to the caregiver or are uncomfortable around the care receiver.

Clinicians can help caregivers increase help and support by identifying potential barriers, and developing a plan for caregivers to reach out to specific people. The clinician will need to attend to caregivers' hurt feelings and to negative beliefs that may be holding them back from seeking support. Examples of those beliefs are that friends and family should know what help the caregiver needs without being asked or that they would be burdened too much by being asked to help. These approaches can be successful working through the caregiver, but a more powerful intervention is holding a meeting with family and friends that creates the opportunity to address support issues directly.

Obtaining and sustaining help: The family meeting.   Family meetings led by clinicians were developed specifically because the support of family and friends is vitally important for caregivers, and the most direct way of increasing support is to bring the key people in a caregiver's social network together (Zarit et al., 1985; Zarit & Zarit, 1982; 2007). One or more family meetings have been part of several empirically validated treatment protocols that reduce caregiver burden and distress (Marriott, Donaldson, Tarrier, & Burns, 2000; Mittelman,

Roth, Coon, & Haley, 2004; Whitlatch et al., 1991). Family meetings in these studies were part of a multidimensional treatment, so the outcomes cannot be attributed solely to the family intervention, but the results support the idea that meeting directly with family and friends may be an effective way to increase support and lower caregivers' subjective burden. The work by Mittelman et al. (2002) is particularly noteworthy because benefits of the treatment have been found to be sustained for 3 years compared with a control group.

The information that the clinician obtains during the initial assessment will indicate areas in which help from other family members can be increased or redirected to better meet the care receiver's or caregiver's needs. The assessment may reveal that family members or friends are a source of conflict for the caregiver, and so the clinician then would consider whether an intervention with the wider family network might be useful. In some situations, it will be obvious that there is serious dysfunction in the extended family, and so there may be little that could come from reaching out to other family members. More often, caregivers are reluctant to bother or burden their family or are upset because they believe the family should volunteer help without being asked. In these situations, the clinician can help caregivers explore why they are reluctant to reach out to family and help them better understand how additional support can be of value. They then may be more willing to talk with family on their own or meet with them with the clinician present.

The goals of the family meeting are to provide families with information about the care recipient's illness and treatment options, address misunderstandings or sources of conflict related to the illness or caregiver, and increase emotional and tangible support for the caregiver. The family meeting should be differentiated from family therapy. Specifically, the family meeting is not designed for addressing long-standing issues in the family. People do not go to a family meeting for therapy, and although some people might begin to rehash past conflicts, the clinician needs to keep the focus on those concerns related to the care recipient and caregiver. Even families in which there are long-standing differences can respond to a family meeting (for examples, see Zarit et al., 1985).

Before the meeting, the clinician and caregiver need to plan whom to invite and what help the caregiver will ask for. During the planning process, the clinician also will learn about family functioning and dynamics from the caregiver's perspective. It is useful to know the role the caregiver has in the family, who in the family is influential, and what longstanding conflicts or tensions exist. At the same time, the clinician needs to recognize that the family is likely to differ in some ways from the caregiver's description and so be prepared for surprises. Friends and neighbors also may be included when they are key parts of the caregiver's support network.

Out-of-town relatives should be included, if possible, especially when they are important to the caregiver and influential in the family. The clinician leading the meeting, however, should be prepared to deal with the out-of-town relative syndrome. Being away from the situation, the out-of-town offspring or sibling will have a partial and often incorrect understanding of the care recipient's illness or the caregiver's needs. Patience often is needed in helping the out-of-town relative get a more realistic understanding of the care recipient's condition and what can be done. Spending time with the care recipient can be a sobering experience, although sometimes the care recipient can rally and show off his or her best side to out-of-town relatives.

The caregiver and clinician will set a date, and the caregiver will invite people to the meeting. Meetings can be held in the clinician's office, in the caregiver's home, or in another relative's home. Each location has advantages and disadvantages, and the clinician needs to think about how the people attending the meeting are responding to the choice of site (Zarit & Zarit, 2007).

The family meeting typically has two phases. The first phase involves bringing everyone up to date about the care recipient's medical condition and what has been done to treat it. This discussion is often necessary because it can be difficult to focus on the caregiver's needs if family members hold onto the belief that there is a possibility of a cure for the care recipient's illness, or if they do not understand its severity or impact on the caregiver. After a

discussion and everyone's questions are answered, the focus of the meeting shifts to the caregiver's needs. Sometimes the clinician initiates this discussion, and sometimes the caregiver or another family member will do so. Often a family member will take the lead in coming up with a plan to meet the caregiver's needs. The clinician wants to make sure that no major player in the family is left out of the plan and that people do not commit more than they are capable of doing. It is also useful to defuse comparisons of who is doing more by stating that each type of help is important, and if one person is making calls to the caregiver and another is visiting, both are equally important. Examples of family meetings can be found in Qualls and Williams (2013) and Zarit et al. (1985).

Whether to include the care receiver at the family meeting depends on his or her ability and willingness to participate and the caregiver's preferences. From an ethical perspective, these meetings should include a care receiver who is competent to make his or her own decisions. Sometimes a caregiver will want a care recipient with dementia to be at the meeting, even if that person may have trouble following the discussion.

Some family caregiving interventions are structured to include multiple family members from the start (Mittelman et al., 2002). This approach can be followed when the caregiver is comfortable with the approach. The clinician will want to determine whether the caregiver has some concerns or issues he or she does not want to raise in a larger group. It also will be important to make sure more vocal family members do not drown out the caregiver's perspective in the family meeting.

Long-term maintenance and the use of groups.
Many caregivers are able to achieve their goals in short-term treatment, but they may benefit from occasional follow-up appointments, particularly when new problems arise. An advantage of the Mittelman protocol (Mittelman et al., 2004) is that compared with all other treatment trials, there is long-term maintenance provided by support groups and by the availability of therapists in a crisis situation.

Support groups have advantages that are not found in individual treatment (Zarit & Zarit, 2007).

Caregivers can learn about which medical and community services are most helpful. Their reluctance to use these services may decrease as they see other caregivers getting help. They also may learn skills for managing behavior and other problems more effectively by modeling on the efforts of other people in the group.

Support groups are offered in many communities at little or no cost. Some groups are peer led. We recommend a leader with clinical training, however, because that person will be able to identify when a caregiver is having problems that should be addressed outside the group. Someone with training in group treatment also will have a better understanding of how to maximize the therapeutic potential of groups, while minimizing their problems, such as one person who dominates the group, or failing to build cohesion among participants. Support groups also can be effective as an initial service for caregivers (Ducharme et al., 2011; Hepburn et al., 2001).

Given the long-term course of caregiving, many caregivers may prefer seeing the clinician on an occasional basis, either in addition to or instead of attending a group. Individuals also may seek support later around stressful events, such as placement (discussed in the section Addressing the Goal of Placement), when the care recipient is nearing death, or the care recipient's passing. In particular, as the care recipient nears death, the caregiver may benefit from examination of care alternatives (Zarit & Zarit, 2007). People may want to avoid prolonging suffering, yet the medical system often responds reflexively to providing treatment beyond the point that the patient would have wanted. Helping caregivers understand the decisions they are facing and implementing care that the patient would have wanted is very important. Hospice can play a valuable role in these situations, although the family may have to insist that the patient receive it. Following death of the care recipient, many caregivers may have a normal course of grief, but some may have prolonged grief (Haley et al., 2008). Wives appear particularly at risk for prolonged grief. A recent review suggests that mourners who experience complicated grief (i.e., prolonged cognitive, emotional, and behavioral symptoms that interfere with daily functioning) benefit from treatment that addresses the specific stressors, appraisals, coping processes, and social factors associated with symptoms (Wittouck, Van Autreve, De Jaegere, Portzky, & van Heeringen, 2011).

Overall, clinical interventions with the caregiver should build a therapeutic relationship throughout the treatment process, help with understanding the care recipient's illness, provide problem-solving techniques for managing the care recipient's behavioral or emotional problems, help create a balance of caregiving with other activities, and identify ways to maintain support over time. Such efforts are likely to diminish the experience of burden brought on by caregiving and translate into improvements in well-being and health for the caregiver and possibly the care recipient.

Treatment Involving the Care Recipient

A growing literature documents benefits of working with the caregiver and care recipient together (Martire, Lustig, Schulz, Miller, & Helgeson, 2004; Martire, Schulz, Helgeson, Small, & Saghafi, 2010). Treatment that includes both people can focus on maximizing the potential benefits of family involvement, reducing areas of tension or conflict and also alleviating the burden of those family members involved in care. This type of treatment is not without its risks, however, and should not be undertaken by clinicians inexperienced in marital or family therapy. We discuss three treatment approaches for three conditions that involve care recipient, caregiver, and sometimes other family members: (a) early, mild dementia; (b) depression and other mental health problems; and (c) management of physical illness. The overlap of physical and mental health is considerable, and it is usually necessary to address both.

Early stage dementia: Hearing both voices. With trends toward earlier diagnosis, more people are being diagnosed with dementia when they have an awareness of their illness. People with early, mild symptoms of dementia can participate actively in treatment, reliably reporting their preferences for how they would like to be cared for (Reamy et al., 2011; Whitlatch et al., 2005b). Goals of interventions typically focus on providing information to participants and addressing practical and emotional implications of the diagnosis. Group treatments for people with early stage dementia and their caregivers have been found to be acceptable to individuals with dementia and their caregivers. These interventions improve quality of life for people with dementia (Gaugler et al., 2011; Logsdon et al., 2010; Zarit, Femia, Watson, Rice-Oeschger, & Kakos, 2004). Caregivers report increased feelings of being prepared and increased confidence in managing care problems, but the interventions have had more limited benefits for caregivers' quality of life.

A major goal for early stage interventions is to prevent some of the predictable experiences that caregivers have as their relative's illness progresses, particularly, the build-up of stressors and reluctance to utilize paid or informal help that could lower stress. A short-term dyadic treatment has been developed that engages caregivers and care receivers in preparing for changes that occur as the disease progresses (Whitlatch et al., 2006). The intervention uses visual planning tools that reduce the load on memory for both participants. The caregiver and person with dementia independently and then together assign responsibility for who will manage 19 different tasks that someone with dementia may need help with as the disease progresses. Initially, most dyads assign tasks so that the caregiver will be doing almost everything. The counselor then helps the dyad explore how realistic the plan is and whether the caregiver will be able to do everything by him- or herself. In most situations, this discussion prompts the caregiver and person with dementia to identify informal or paid services they will use if the situation becomes more than the caregiver can handle. This care plan is then written down in a treatment workbook so that the dyad can refer to it in the future. Underlying this approach is the assumption that involving the care recipient in planning care and taking into account his or her preferences about who should provide assistance will reduce refusals to accept care later in the disease. It also is hoped that the care recipient's agreement to use help will be empowering for caregivers to obtain help when it becomes necessary. Another part of the intervention is developing plans for each person to take care of his or her own health and well-being. Preliminary findings have been encouraging

(Whitlatch, Judge, Zarit, & Femia, 2006), but long-term outcomes have not yet been obtained.

Dyadic interventions for mental health problems. There has long been recognition that a spouse or other family members can play an important role in the genesis as well as resolution of mental health problems of younger adults, and similar effects have been found for older adults. Pioneering work by Hinrichsen (e.g., Hinrichsen, 1992; Hinrichsen & Hernandez, 1993) on older people suffering from major depression has demonstrated that families have an impact on recovery. Specifically, patients have a poorer response to treatment when family members who are assisting them have more psychiatric symptoms. Higher rates of expressed emotion among adult offspring, who were caregivers, also have been found to increase rates of relapse in their parents, but a similar effect has not been found for spousal caregivers (Hinrichsen & Pollack, 1997). Characteristics of the family caregiver also affect subsequent suicide attempts (Zweig & Hinrichsen, 1993). Attempts are more likely when family caregivers have more psychiatric symptoms and greater subjective difficulty helping their relative. Successful treatment of the patient's depressive symptoms has been found to lower caregivers' burden (Martire et al., 2008). These findings suggest that involving key family members in treatment of depression and other mental health problems might facilitate improvement, enhance maintenance of the gains of the patient, and contribute to lowering burden for the caregiver.

There are other potential benefits of bringing family members into mental health treatment (Zarit & Zarit, 2007). Family members can provide information and observations that help the clinician formulate a diagnosis and treatment plan. Meeting with family members, with the patient's consent of course, always will lead to some surprises, and the new information that the clinician obtains about the family and their interactions with the patient will be useful in planning treatment. For example, it may quickly become apparent that the patient cannot rely on family for much support, whereas in other cases, the clinician may become aware of ways the family could support treatment, for instance, by helping the older person engage in activities.

Dyadic and family interventions for medical problems. For chronic and serious health problems, there has been increasing interest in involving the family in educational or psychological interventions to improve outcomes for both the patient and their family (Martire et al., 2004). A growing literature focuses specifically on married couples or partners, suggesting that good relationship quality is associated with positive health outcomes with a poor relationship having negative effects (Kiecolt-Glaser & Newton, 2001; Martire et al., 2010). A spouse or other key family members may be supportive of the patient's morale and improved health behavior and illness management, or conversely, the family's current behaviors and attitudes may be preventing more adaptive responses by the patient (Martire et al., 2004, 2013).

Dyadic and family treatments have been developed for several health conditions: cardiovascular disease, cancer, osteoarthritis, type 2 diabetes, HIV, chronic pain and frailty (Martire et al., 2004; Martire et al., 2010). Components of treatments are similar to those described earlier for caregivers and include disease-specific education, emotional support, skills training, and health care planning. Treatment protocols vary in terms of which components are included. Furthermore, some protocols just focus on disease management, whereas others consider how the couple's interactions contribute to or get in the way of better management.

Martire et al. (2010) conducted meta-analyses of couple-oriented and family interventions across a variety of health conditions. Treatments typically were compared with usual care or psychosocial interventions with the patient. Couple-oriented treatments had significant benefits for both care receivers and partners across treatments, compared with the control conditions. Care recipients reported lower depression and pain and improved marital functioning. Care partners, in turn, reported improvements across a variety of psychological domains (stress, self-efficacy, mastery, and anxiety) as well as for marital functioning.

In another analysis, Martire et al. (2004) compared treatment outcomes for whether the focus was on a spouse only or a mixed group of family members, and whether or not the patient was included.

Turning first to patient outcomes, inclusion of a spouse was associated with decreased depression, but inclusion of mixed family members had no impact. Turning to outcomes for family members, spouses and mixed family members had lower burden following treatment, and other family members also reported lower depression. Better outcomes also were found when the patient was not included with the family members. Furthermore, the results showed that a focus on relationship issues was related to better outcomes for family members. Taken together, these two meta-analyses (Martire et al., 2004, 2010) suggest that couples and family treatments have advantages over patient-only and usual-care conditions. More information is needed, however, on which components are effective and on the effects of type of disease on outcomes for each person. For references in conducting such forms of treatment see Martire and Schulz (2012).

The inclusion of the care recipient or other family members in the treatment of caregiver burden appears meaningful. As articulated throughout this chapter, such decisions for inclusion must be made on a situation-by-situation basis. The ultimate goal is to match treatment choice to the needs and circumstances of each specific individual or family.

CONCLUSION

The task of working with family caregivers and care recipients may seem daunting given the complexity and diversity of the issues, needs, and intervention strategies presented. Clinicians, however, often are in the best-seated position to make a real, meaningful difference in the lives of these individuals. With care and attention given to what a person is going through, the unique contextual challenges each client is experiencing, and familiarity with clinical intervention options, a clinician can effectively support a caregiver and his or her family and create conditions for a positive outcome in the face of some of life's greatest challenges.

References

Adams, K. B., McClendon, M. J., & Smyth, K. A. (2008). Personal losses and relationship quality in dementia caregiving. *Dementia, 7,* 301–319. doi:10.1177/1471301208093286

Almeida, D. M. (2005). Resilience and vulnerability to daily stressors assessed via diary methods. *Current Directions in Psychological Science, 14,* 64–68. doi:10.1111/j.0963-7214.2005.00336.x

Aneshensel, C., Pearlin, L. I., Mullan, J. T., Zarit, S. H., & Whitlatch, C. J. (1995). *Profiles in caregiving: The unexpected career.* New York, NY: Academic Press.

Aneshensel, C. S., Pearlin, L. I., Levy-Storms, L., & Schuler, R. H. (2000). The transition from home to nursing home: Mortality among people with dementia. *The Journals of Gerontology, Series B: Psychological Sciences and Social Sciences, 55,* 152–162. doi:10.1093/geronb/55.3.S152

Awad, A. G., & Voruganti, L. N. P. (2008). The burden of schizophrenia on caregivers: A review. *PharmacoEconomics, 26,* 149–162. doi:10.2165/00019053-200826020-00005

Baldwin, C. (2008). Toward a person-centered ethic in dementia care: Doing right or being good? In M. Downs & B. Bowers (Ed.), *Excellence in dementia care: Research into practice* (pp. 103–118). New York, NY: McGraw-Hill Open University Press.

Baltes, M. M., & Wahl, H. W. (1992). The dependency-support script in institutions: Generalization to community settings. *Psychology and Aging, 7,* 409–418. doi:10.1037/0882-7974.7.3.409

Beck, A. T., Rush, A. J., Shaw, B. F., & Emery, G. (1979). *Cognitive therapy of depression.* New York, NY: Guilford Press.

Belle, S. H., Burgio, L., Burns, R., Coon, D., Czaja, S. J., Gallagher-Thompson, D., . . . Zhang, S. (2006). Enhancing the quality of life of dementia caregivers from different ethnic or racial groups. *Annals of Internal Medicine, 145,* 727–738. doi:10.7326/0003-4819-145-10-200611210-00005

Bertrand, R. M., Saczynski, J. S., Mezzacappa, C., Hulse, M., Ensrud, K., & Fredman, L. (2012). Caregiving and cognitive function in older women: Evidence for the healthy caregiver hypothesis. *Journal of Aging and Health, 24,* 48–66. doi:10.1177/0898264311421367

Blum, K., & Sherman, D. W. (2010). Understanding the experience of caregivers: A focus on transitions. *Seminars in Oncology Nursing, 26,* 243–258. doi:10.1016/j.soncn.2010.08.005

Bolger, N., Davis, A., & Rafaeli, E. (2003). Diary methods: Capturing life as it is lived. *Annual Review of Psychology, 54,* 579–616. doi:10.1146/annurev.psych.54.101601.145030

Bookwala, J., & Schulz, R. (2000). A comparison of primary stressors, secondary stressors, and depressive symptoms between elderly caregiving husbands and wives: The caregiver health effects study. *Psychology and Aging, 15,* 607–616. doi:10.1037/0882-7974.15.4.607

Bourget, D., Gagné, P., & Whitehurst, L. (2010). Domestic homicide and homicide-suicide: The older offender. *Journal of the American Academy of Psychiatry and the Law, 38,* 305–311.

Brodaty, H., Green, A., Banerjee, S., Mittelman, M., Schulz, R., Whitehouse, P., . . . Zarit, S. (2002). Towards harmonisation of caregiver outcome measures. *Brain Aging, 2,* 3–12.

Carpenter, B. D., Van Haitsma, K., Ruckdeschel, K., & Lawton, P. (2000). The psychosocial preferences of older adults: A pilot examination of content and structure. *Gerontologist, 40,* 335–348. doi:10.1093/geront/40.3.335

Castleman, M., Gallagher-Thompson, D., & Naythons, M. (1999). *There's still a person in there: The complete guide to treating and coping with Alzheimer's.* New York, NY: G. P. Putnam's Sons.

Clare, L. (2004). The construction of awareness in early-stage Alzheimer's disease: A review of concepts and models. *British Journal of Clinical Psychology, 43,* 155–175. doi:10.1348/014466504323088033

Clare, L., Marková, I., Verhey, F., & Kenny, G. (2005). Awareness in dementia: A review of assessment methods and measures. *Aging and Mental Health, 9,* 394–413. doi:10.1080/13607860500142903

Clark, P. A., Tucke, S. S., & Whitlatch, C. J. (2008). Consistency of information from persons with dementia: An analysis of differences by question type. *Dementia, 7,* 341–358. doi:10.1177/1471301208093288

Cohen-Mansfield, J., Marx, M. S., & Rosenthal, A. S. (1989). A description of agitation in a nursing home. *Journal of Gerontology, 44,* M77–M84. doi:10.1093/geronj/44.3.M77

Cuijpers, P. (2005). Depressive disorders in caregivers of dementia patients: A systematic review. *Aging and Mental Health, 9,* 325–330. doi:10.1080/13607860500090078

Cummings, J. L., Mega, M., Gray, K., Rosenberg-Thompson, S., Carusi, D. A., & Gombein, J. (1994). The Neuropsychiatric Inventory: Comprehensive assessment of psychopathology in dementia. *Neurology, 44,* 2308–2314. doi:10.1212/WNL.44.12.2308

Deci, E. L., & Ryan, R. M. (2000). The "what" and "why" of goal pursuits: Human needs and the self-determination of behavior. *Psychological Inquiry, 11,* 227–268. doi:10.1207/S15327965PLI1104_01

de Medeiros, K., Robert, P., Gauthier, S., Stella, F., Politis, A., Leoutsakos, J., . . . Lyketsos, C. (2010). The Neuropsychiatric Inventory—Clinician Rating Scale (NPI–C): Reliability and validity of a revised assessment of neuropsychiatric symptoms in dementia. *International Psychogeriatrics, 22,* 984–994. doi:10.1017/S1041610210000876

Ducharme, F., Lévesque, L., Zarit, S. H., Lachance, L., & Giroux, F. (2007). Changes in health outcomes among older husband caregivers: A one-year longitudinal study. *International Journal of Aging and Human Development, 65*, 73–96. doi:10.2190/9754-21RH-5148-8025

Ducharme, F. C., Lévesque, L. L., Lachance, L. M., Kergoat, M.-J., Legault, A. J., Beaudet, L. M., & Zarit, S. H. (2011). "Learning to become a family caregiver": Efficacy of an intervention program for caregivers following diagnosis of dementia in a relative. *Gerontologist, 51*, 484–494. doi:10.1093/geront/gnr014

Emanuel, E. J., Fairclough, D. L., & Emanuel, L. L. (2000). Attitudes and desires related to euthanasia and physician-assisted suicide among terminally ill patients and their caregivers. *JAMA, 284*, 2460–2468. doi:10.1001/jama.284.19.2460

Fagerlin, A., Ditto, P. H., Hawkins, N. A., Schneider, C. E., & Smucker, W. D. (2002). The use of advance directives in end-of-life decision making: Problems and possibilities. *American Behavioral Scientist, 46*, 268–283. doi:10.1177/000276402236678

Feinberg, L. F., & Whitlatch, C. J. (2001). Are persons with cognitive impairment able to state consistent choices? *Gerontologist, 41*, 374–382. doi:10.1093/geront/41.3.374

Femia, E. E., Zarit, S. H., Stephens, M. A. P., & Greene, R. (2007). Impact of adult day services on behavioral and psychological symptoms of dementia. *Gerontologist, 47*, 775–788. doi:10.1093/geront/47.6.775

Fredrickson, B. L. (2001). The role of positive emotions in positive psychology: The broaden-and-build theory of positive emotions. *American Psychologist, 56*, 218–226. doi:10.1037/0003-066X.56.3.218

Freund, A. M., & Baltes, P. B. (1998). Selection, optimization, and compensation as strategies of life management: Correlations with subjective indicators of successful aging. *Psychology and Aging, 13*, 531–543. doi:10.1037/0882-7974.13.4.531

Ganong, L. H., & Coleman, M. (1998). Attitudes regarding filial responsibilities to help elderly divorced parents and stepparents. *Journal of Aging Studies, 12*, 271–290. doi:10.1016/S0890-4065(98)90004-4

Gaugler, J. E., Anderson, K. A., Zarit, S. H., & Pearlin, L. I. (2004). Family involvement in the nursing home: Effects on stress and well-being. *Aging and Mental Health, 8*, 65–75. doi:10.1080/136078603100 01613356

Gaugler, J. E., Gallagher-Winker, K., Kehrberg, K., Lunde, A. M., Marsolek, C. M., Ringham, K., . . . Barclay, M. (2011). The memory club: Providing support to persons with early-stage dementia and their care partners. *American Journal of Alzheimer's Disease and Other Dementias, 26*, 218–226. doi:10.1177/1533317511399570

Gaugler, J. E., Mittelman, M. S., Hepburn, K., & Newcomer, R. (2010). Clinically significant changes in burden and depression among dementia caregivers following nursing home admission. *BMC Medicine, 8*(85). doi:10.1186/1741-7015-8-85

Grossman, A. H., D'Augelli, A. R., & Dragowski, E. A. (2005). Caregiving and care receiving among older lesbian, gay, and bisexual adults. *Journal of Gay and Lesbian Social Services, 18*, 15–38. doi:10.1300/J041v18n03_02

Ha, J.-H., Hong, J., Seltzer, M. M., & Greenberg, J. S. (2008). Age and gender differences in the well-being of midlife and aging parents with children with mental health or developmental problems: Report of a national study. *Journal of Health and Social Behavior, 49*, 301–316. doi:10.1177/002214650804900305

Haley, W. E. (2003a). The costs of family caregiving: Implications for geriatric oncology. *Critical Reviews in Oncology/Hematology, 48*, 151–158. doi:10.1016/j.critrevonc.2003.04.005

Haley, W. E. (2003b). Family caregivers of elderly patients with cancer: Understanding and minimizing the burdens of care. *Journal of Supportive Oncology, 1*(Suppl. 2), 25–29.

Haley, W. E., Allen, J. Y., Grant, J. S., Clay, O. J., Perkins, M., & Roth, D. L. (2009). Problems and benefits reported by stroke family caregivers: Results from a prospective epidemiological study. *Stroke, 40*, 2129–2133. doi:10.1161/STROKEAHA.108.545269

Haley, W. E., Bergman, E. J., Roth, D. J., McVie, T., Gaugler, J. E., & Mittelman, M. S. (2008). Long-term effects of bereavement and caregiver intervention on dementia caregiver depressive symptoms. *Gerontologist, 48*, 732–740. doi:10.1093/geront/48.6.732

Haley, W. E., LaMonde, L. A., Han, B., Burton, A. M., & Schonwetter, R. (2003). Predictors of depression and life satisfaction among spousal caregivers in hospice: Application of a stress process model. *Journal of Palliative Medicine, 6*, 215–224. doi:10.1089/109662103764978461

Haley, W. E., Roth, D. L., Howard, G., & Safford, M. M. (2010). Caregiving strain and estimated risk for stroke and coronary heart disease among spouse caregivers: Differential effects by race and sex. *Stroke, 41*, 331–336. doi:10.1161/STROKEAHA.109.568279

Harnett, P. J., & Greaney, A.-M. (2008). Operationalizing autonomy: Solutions for mental health nursing practice. *Journal of Psychiatric and Mental Health Nursing, 15*, 2–9. doi:10.1111/j.1365-2850.2007.01183.x

Hepburn, K. W., Tornatore, J., Center, B., & Ostwald, S. W. (2001). Dementia family caregiver training: Affecting beliefs about caregiving and caregiver outcomes. *Journal of the American Geriatrics Society*, *49*, 450–457. doi:10.1046/j.1532-5415.2001.49090.x

Hinrichsen, G. A. (1992). Recovery and relapse from major depressive disorder in the elderly. *American Journal of Psychiatry*, *149*, 1575–1579.

Hinrichsen, G. A., & Hernandez, N. A. (1993). Factors associated with recovery from and relapse into major depressive disorder in the elderly. *American Journal of Psychiatry*, *150*, 1820–1825.

Hinrichsen, G. A., & Pollack, S. (1997). Expressed emotion and the course of late-life depression. *Journal of Abnormal Psychology*, *106*, 336–340. doi:10.1037/0021-843X.106.2.336

Hogan, D. (2012). *Family consequences of children's disabilities*. New York, NY: Russell Sage Foundation.

Hughes, J. C., & Baldwin, C. (2006). *Ethical issues in dementia care: Making difficult decisions*. London, England; Philadelphia, PA: Jessica Kingsley.

Kane, R. A. (1995). Decision making, care plans, and life plans in long-term care: Can case managers take account of clients' values and preferences? In L. B. McCullough & N. L. Wilson (Eds.), *Long-term care decisions: Ethical and conceptual dimensions* (pp. 87–109). Baltimore, MD: The Johns Hopkins University Press.

Karel, M. J., Moye, J., Bank, A., & Azar, A. R. (2007). Three methods of assessing values for advance care planning: Comparing persons with and without dementia. *Journal of Aging and Health*, *19*, 123–151. doi:10.1177/0898264306296394

Kiecolt-Glaser, J. K., & Newton, T. L. (2001). Marriage and health: His and hers. *Psychological Bulletin*, *127*, 472–503. doi:10.1037/0033-2909.127.4.472

Kitwood, T. (1997). *Dementia reconsidered: The person comes first*. Bristol, PA: Open University Press.

Langer, E. J. (1983). *The psychology of control*. Beverly Hills, CA: Sage.

Lawton, M. P., & Brody, E. M. (1969). Assessment of older people: Self-maintaining and instrumental activities of daily living. *Gerontologist*, *9*, 179–186. doi:10.1093/geront/9.3_Part_1.179

Lawton, M. P., Moss, M., Hoffman, C., & Perkinson, M. (2000). Two transitions in daughters' caregiving careers. *Gerontologist*, *40*, 437–448. doi:10.1093/geront/40.4.437

Lazarus, R. S., & Folkman, S. (1984). *Stress, appraisal, and coping*. New York, NY: Springer.

Logsdon, R. G., McCurry, S. M., & Teri, L. (2007). Evidence-based psychological treatments for disruptive behaviors in individuals with dementia. *Psychology and Aging*, *22*, 28–36. doi:10.1037/0882-7974.22.1.28

Logsdon, R. G., Pike, K. C., McCurry, S. M., Hunter, P., Maher, J., Snyder, L., & Teri, L. (2010). Early-stage memory loss support groups: Outcomes from a randomized controlled clinical trial. *The Journals of Gerontology, Series B: Psychological Sciences and Social Sciences*, *65*, 691–697. doi:10.1093/geronb/gbq054

Malphurs, J. E., & Cohen, D. (2005). A statewide case-control study of spousal homicide-suicide in older persons. *American Journal of Geriatric Psychiatry*, *13*, 211–217.

Malphurs, J. E., Eisdorfer, C., & Cohen, D. (2001). A comparison of antecedents of homicide-suicide and suicide in older married men. *American Journal of Geriatric Psychiatry*, *9*, 49–57.

Marriott, A., Donaldson, C., Tarrier, N., & Burns, A. (2000). Effectiveness of cognitive-behavioral family intervention in reducing the burden of care in carers of patients with Alzheimer's disease. *British Journal of Psychiatry*, *176*, 557–562. doi:10.1192/bjp.176.6.557

Martire, L., & Schulz, R. (2012). Caregiving and care receiving in later life. In A. Baum, T. A. Revenson, & J. Singer (Eds.), *Handbook of health psychology* (pp. 293–307). New York, NY: Psychology Press, Taylor & Francis Group.

Martire, L. M., Lustig, A. P., Schulz, R., Miller, G. E., & Helgeson, V. S. (2004). Is it beneficial to involve a family member? A meta-analysis of psychosocial interventions for chronic illness. *Health Psychology*, *23*, 599–611. doi:10.1037/0278-6133.23.6.599

Martire, L. M., Schulz, R., Helgeson, V. S., Small, B. J., & Saghafi, E. M. (2010). Review and meta-analysis of couple-oriented interventions for chronic illness. *Annals of Behavioral Medicine*, *40*, 325–342. doi:10.1007/s12160-010-9216-2

Martire, L. M., Schulz, R., Reynolds, C. F., III, Morse, J. Q., Butters, M. A., & Hinrichsen, G. A. (2008). Impact of close family members on older adults' early response to depression treatment. *Psychology and Aging*, *23*, 447–452. doi:10.1037/0882-7974.23.2.447

Martire, L. M., Stephens, M. A., Mogle, J., Schulz, R., Brach, J., & Keefe, F. J. (2013). Daily spousal influence on physical activity in knee osteoarthritis. *Annals of Behavioral Medicine*. doi:10.1007/s12160-012-9442-x

McCullough, L. B., Wilson, N. L., Teasdale, T. A., Kolpakchi, A. L., & Skelly, J. R. (1993). Mapping personal, familial, and professional values in long-term care decisions. *Gerontologist*, *33*, 324–332. doi:10.1093/geront/33.3.324

McCurry, S. M., Gibbons, L. E., Logsdon, R. G., Vitiello, M. V., & Teri, L. (2005). Nighttime insomnia treatment and education for Alzheimer's disease: A randomized controlled trial. *Journal of the American Geriatrics Society*, *53*, 793–802. doi:10.1111/j.1532-5415.2005.53252.x

McCurry, S. M., Pike, K. C., Vitiello, M. V., Logsdon, R. G., Larson, E. V., & Teri, L. (2011). Increasing walking and bright light exposure to improve sleep in community-dwelling persons with Alzheimer's disease: Results of a randomized, controlled trial. *Journal of the American Geriatrics Society, 59,* 1393–1402. doi:10.1111/j.1532-5415.2011.03519.x

Miller, B. (1990). Gender differences in spouse caregiver strain: Socialization and role expectation. *Journal of Marriage and the Family, 52,* 311–321. doi:10.2307/353028

Miller, B., & Guo, S. (2000). Social support for spouse caregivers of persons with dementia. *The Journals of Gerontology, Series B: Psychological Sciences and Social Sciences, 55,* 163–172. doi:10.1093/geronb/55.3.S163

Mittelman, M. S., Epstein, C., & Pierzchala, A. (2002). *Counseling the Alzheimer's caregiver: A resource for health care professionals.* Chicago, IL: American Medical Association.

Mittelman, M. S., Ferris, S. H., Shulman, E., Steinberg, G., & Levin, B. (1996). A family intervention to delay nursing home placement of patients with Alzheimer disease: A randomized controlled trial. *JAMA, 276,* 1725–1731. doi:10.1001/jama.1996.03540210033030

Mittelman, M. S., Roth, D. L., Coon, D. W., & Haley, W. E. (2004). Sustained benefit of supportive intervention for depressive symptoms in caregivers of patients with Alzheimer's disease. *American Journal of Psychiatry, 161,* 850–856. doi:10.1176/appi.ajp.161.5.850

Murray, C. J., Vos, T., Lozano, R., Naghavi, M., Flaxman, A. D., Michaud, C., . . . Lopez, A. D. (2012). Disability-adjusted life years (DALYs) for 291 diseases and injuries in 21 regions, 1990-2010: A systematic analysis for the Global Burden of Disease study 2010. *Lancet, 380,* 2197–2223.

National Alliance for Caregiving. (2009). *Caregiving in the U.S.* Retrieved from http://www.caregiving.org/pdf/research/CaregivingUSAllAgesExecSum.pdf

National Center for Biotechnology Information. (2010). *Appendix C: Black box warnings for included drugs.* Retrieved from http://www.ncbi.nlm.nih.gov/books/NBK50582

Norton, M. C., Smith, K. R., Østbye, T., Tschanz, J. T., Corcoran, C., Schwartz, S., . . . Welsh-Bohmer, K. A. (2010). Greater risk of dementia when spouse has dementia? The Cache county study. *Journal of the American Geriatrics Society, 58,* 895–900. doi:10.1111/j.1532-5415.2010.02806.x

Novak, M., & Guest, C. (1989). Application of a multi-dimensional caregiver burden inventory. *Gerontologist, 29,* 798–803. doi:10.1093/geront/29.6.798

Pearlin, L. I., Liberman, M. A., Menaghan, E. G., & Mullan, J. T. (1981). The stress process. *Journal of Health and Social Behavior, 22,* 337–356. doi:10.2307/2136676

Pearlin, L. I., Mullan, J. T., Semple, S. J., & Skaff, M. M. (1990). Caregiving and the stress process: An overview of concepts and their measures. *Gerontologist, 30,* 583–594. doi:10.1093/geront/30.5.583

Perkins, M., Howard, V., Wadley, V. G., Crowe, M., Safford, M. M., Haley, W. E., . . . Roth, D. L. (2013). Caregiving strain and all-cause mortality: Evidence from the REGARDS Study. *The Journals of Gerontology, Series B: Psychological Sciences and Social Sciences, 68,* 504–512. doi:10.1093/geronb/gbs084

Persson, T., & Wästerfors, D. (2009). Such trivial matters: How staff accounts for restrictions of residents' influence in nursing homes. *Journal of Aging Studies, 23,* 1–11. doi:10.1016/j.jaging.2007.09.005

Pierret, C. R. (2006, September). The "sandwich generation": Women caring for parents and children. *Monthly Labor Review,* 3–9.

Pinquart, M., & Sorensen, S. (2003). Differences between caregivers and noncaregivers in psychological health and physical health: A meta-analysis. *Psychology and Aging, 18,* 250–267. doi:10.1037/0882-7974.18.2.250

Qualls, S. H., & Noecker, T. R. (2009). Caregiver family therapy for conflicted families. In S. H. Qualls & S. H. Zarit (Eds.), *Aging families and caregiving* (pp. 155–188). New York, NY: Wiley.

Qualls, S. H., & Williams, A. A. (2013). *Caregiver family therapy: Empowering families to meet the challenges of aging.* Washington, DC: American Psychological Association.

Reamy, A. M., Kim, K., Zarit, S. H., & Whitlatch, C. J. (2011). Understanding discrepancy in perceptions of values: Individuals with mild to moderate dementia and their family caregivers. *Gerontologist, 51,* 473–483. doi:10.1093/geront/gnr010

Roberto, K. A. (1993). Family caregivers of aging adults with developmental disabilities: A review of the literature. In K. A. Roberto (Ed.), *The elderly caregiver: Caring for adults with developmental disabilities* (pp. 3–18). Newbury Park, CA: Sage. doi:10.4135/9781483326511.n1

Robertson, S. M., Zarit, S. H., Duncan, L. G., Rovine, M., & Femia, E. E. (2007). Family caregivers' patterns of positive and negative affect. *Family Relations, 56,* 12–23. doi:10.1111/j.1741-3729.2007.00436.x

Rosengard, C., & Folkman, S. (1997). Suicidal ideation, bereavement, HIV serostatus and psychosocial variables in partners of men with AIDS. *AIDS Care, 9,* 373–384. doi:10.1080/713613168

Roth, D. L., Perkins, M., Wadley, V. G., Temple, E. M., & Haley, W. E. (2009). Family caregiving and emotional strain: Associations with quality of life in a large national sample of middle-aged and older adults. *Quality of Life Research, 18,* 679–688. doi:10.1007/s11136-009-9482-2

Schneider, L. S., Dagerman, K., & Insel, P. S. (2006). Efficacy and adverse effects of atypical antipsychotics for dementia: Meta-analysis of randomized, placebo-controlled trials. *American Journal of Geriatric Psychiatry, 14,* 191–210. doi:10.1097/01.JGP.0000200589.01396.6d

Schulz, R., & Beach, S. R. (1999). Caregiving as a risk factor for mortality: The Caregiver Health Effects Study. *JAMA, 282,* 2215–2219. doi:10.1001/jama.282.23.2215

Schwartz, A. N. (1978). Psychological dependency: An emphasis on the later years. In P. K. Ragan (Ed.), *Aging parents* (pp. 116–125). Los Angeles: University of Southern California Press.

Seltzer, M. M., Floyd, F., Song, J., Greenberg, J., & Hong, J. (2011). Midlife and aging parents of adults with intellectual and developmental disabilities: Impacts of lifelong parenting. *American Journal on Intellectual and Developmental Disabilities, 116,* 479–499. doi:10.1352/1944-7558-116.6.479

Sink, K. M., Holden, K. F., & Yaffe, K. (2005). Pharmacological treatment of neuropsychiatric symptoms of dementia: A review of the evidence. *JAMA, 293,* 596–608. doi:10.1001/jama.293.5.596

Skaff, M. M., & Pearlin, L. I. (1992). Caregiving: Role engulfment and the loss of self. *Gerontologist, 32,* 656–664. doi:10.1093/geront/32.5.656

Sliwinski, M. J., Almeida, D. M., Smyth, J., & Stawski, R. S. (2009). Intraindividual change and variability in daily stress processes: Findings from two measurement-burst diary studies. *Psychology and Aging, 24,* 828–840. doi:10.1037/a0017925

Stephens, M. A., Franks, M. M., & Townsend, A. L. (1994). Stress and rewards in women's multiple roles: The case of women in the middle. *Psychology and Aging, 9,* 45–52. doi:10.1037/0882-7974.9.1.45

Stephens, M. A., Townsend, A. L., Martire, L. M., & Druley, J. A. (2001). Balancing parent care with other roles: Interrole conflict of adult daughter caregivers. *The Journals of Gerontology, Series B: Psychological Sciences and Social Sciences, 56,* 24–34. doi:10.1093/geronb/56.1.P24

Teri, L., Logsdon, R. G., Uomoto, J., & McCurry, S. M. (1997). Behavioral treatment of depression in dementia patients: A controlled clinical trial. *The Journals of Gerontology, Series B: Psychological Sciences and Social Sciences, 52,* 159–166. doi:10.1093/geronb/52B.4.P159

Teri, L., Truax, P., Logsdon, R., Uomoto, J., Zarit, S. H., & Vitaliano, P. P. (1992). Assessment of behavioral problems in dementia: The revised memory and behavior problems checklist. *Psychology and Aging, 7,* 622–631. doi:10.1037/0882-7974.7.4.622

Uhlmann, R. F., Pearlman, R. A., & Cain, K. C. (1988). Physicians' and spouses predictions of elderly patients' resuscitation preferences. *The Journals of Gerontology, Series A: Biological Sciences and Medical Sciences, 43,* 115–121.

Vitaliano, P. P., Russo, J., Young, H. M., Becker, J., & Maiuro, R. D. (1991). The screen for caregiver burden. *Gerontologist, 31,* 76–83. doi:10.1093/geront/31.1.76

Whitlatch, C. J., & Feinberg, L. F. (2003). Planning for the future together in culturally diverse families: Making everyday care decisions. *Alzheimer's Care Quarterly, 4,* 50–61.

Whitlatch, C. J., Feinberg, L. F., & Tucke, S. (2005a). Accuracy and consistency of responses from persons with cognitive impairment. *Dementia, 4,* 171–183. doi:10.1177/1471301205051091

Whitlatch, C. J., Feinberg, L. F., & Tucke, S. S. (2005b). Measuring the values and preferences for everyday care of persons with cognitive impairment and their family caregivers. *Gerontologist, 45,* 370–380. doi:10.1093/geront/45.3.370

Whitlatch, C. J., Judge, K., Zarit, S. H., & Femia, E. E. (2006). A dyadic intervention for family caregivers and care receivers in early stage dementia. *Gerontologist, 46,* 688–694. doi:10.1093/geront/46.5.688

Whitlatch, C. J., Piiparinen, R., & Feinberg, L. F. (2009). How well do family caregivers know their relatives' care values and preferences? *Dementia, 8,* 223–243. doi:10.1177/1471301209103259

Whitlatch, C. J., Zarit, S. H., & von Eye, A. (1991). Efficacy of interventions with caregivers: A reanalysis. *Gerontologist, 31,* 9–14. doi:10.1093/geront/31.1.9

Wittouck, C., Van Autreve, S., De Jaegere, E., Portzky, G., & van Heeringen, K. (2011). The prevention and treatment of complicated grief: A meta-analysis. *Clinical Psychology Review, 31,* 69–78. doi:10.1016/j.cpr.2010.09.005

Wolff, J. L., & Kasper, J. D. (2006). Caregivers of frail elders: Updating a national profile. *Gerontologist, 46,* 344–356. doi:10.1093/geront/46.3.344

Zarit, S. H., Femia, E. E., Watson, J., Rice-Oeschger, L., & Kakos, B. (2004). Memory club: A group intervention for people with early-stage dementia and their care partners. *Gerontologist, 44,* 262–269. doi:10.1093/geront/44.2.262

Zarit, S. H., Kim, K., Femia, E. E., Almeida, D. M., & Klein, L. C. (2014). The effects of adult day services on family caregivers' daily stress, affect and health: Outcomes from the DaSH Study. *Gerontologist, 54,* 570–579. doi:10.1093/geront/gnt045

Zarit, S. H., Kim, K., Femia, E. E., Almeida, D. M., Savla, J., & Molenaar, P. C. M. (2011). Effects of adult day care on daily stress of caregivers: A within person approach. *The Journals of Gerontology, Series B: Psychological Sciences and Social Sciences, 66,* 538–546. doi:10.1093/geronb/gbr030

Zarit, S. H., Orr, N. K., & Zarit, J. M. (1985). *The hidden victims of Alzheimer's disease: Families under stress.* New York, NY: NYU Press.

Zarit, S. H., Reever, K. E., & Bach-Peterson, J. (1980). Relatives of the impaired elderly: Correlates of feelings of burden. *Gerontologist, 20,* 649–655. doi:10.1093/geront/20.6.649

Zarit, S. H., Stephens, M. A. P., Townsend, A., & Greene, R. (1998). Stress reduction for family caregivers: Effects of day care use. *The Journals of Gerontology, Series B: Psychological Sciences and Social Sciences, 53,* 267–277. doi:10.1093/geronb/53B.5.S267

Zarit, S. H., Todd, P. A., & Zarit, J. M. (1986). Subjective burden of husbands and wives as caregivers: A longitudinal study. *Gerontologist, 26,* 260–266. doi:10.1093/geront/26.3.260

Zarit, S. H., & Whitlatch, C. (1992). Institutional placement: Phases of the transition. *Gerontologist, 32,* 665–672. doi:10.1093/geront/32.5.665

Zarit, S. H., & Zarit, J. M. (1982). Families under stress: Interventions for caregivers of senile dementia patients. *Psychotherapy: Theory, Research, Practice, Training, 19,* 461–471. doi:10.1037/h0088459

Zarit, S. H., & Zarit, J. M. (2007). *Mental disorders in older adults* (2nd ed.). New York, NY: Guilford Press.

Zweig, R. A., & Hinrichsen, G. A. (1993). Factors associated with suicide attempts by depressed older adults: A prospective study. *American Journal of Psychiatry, 150,* 1687–1692.

CHAPTER 21

COMPETENCY AND DECISION-MAKING CAPACITY: NEGOTIATING HEALTH AND FINANCIAL DECISION MAKING

Peter A. Lichtenberg, Sara Honn Qualls, and Michael A. Smyer

Competency is a legal term determined by the court system (Moye & Braun, 2010). *Capacity* can be viewed both as a clinical term indicating the geropsychologist's assessment of an older adult's ability in a specific area (e.g., decide not to have a surgery; create a will) and a term indicating the judgment of a geropsychologist regarding how the older adult's abilities match with the legal standards for the capacity in question. The focus on this chapter will be the latter; how geropsychologists use appropriate assessment techniques to give an opinion about capacity that is tied to the legal standards in question (Lichtenberg & Luborsky, in press). We review the major conceptual and research work on capacity for medical and financial decisions. We will provide ideas for geropsychologists on how to work as experts on capacity assessments, including standards and strategies for evaluation and reporting, the processes of communicating with the legal system, and the specific ways in which capacity assessments can be different from clinical ones.

The growth in interest about capacity assessment followed the significant changes in laws determining competency. Functional tests and the presence of neurocognitive and mental health diagnoses replaced the mere presence of one or more mental health diagnoses as the legal standards for incompetence across the United States (for a review, see Appelbaum & Grisso, 1988). Geropsychology, with its focus on how older adults' mental health and neurocognitive disorders apply to specific situations, makes its training and skill set well suited for those interested in capacity.

On the basis of practice guidelines (American Bar Association Commission on Law and Aging and American Psychological Association [ABA/APA], 2008; Baker et al., 1998) and clinical experience, capacity evaluations must include assessments that address five criteria involved in determining capacity. The first criterion is to determine whether an older adult suffers from a mental health condition or neurocognitive disorder or decline; in other words, a cause for the diminished capacity must be established. Secondly, the mental health or neurocognitive disorder must affect functional abilities. The term *functional abilities* is used here as legal terminology, which differs from how geropsychologists typically use the term. In legal terms, functional abilities refer to intact decisional abilities. These include evidence of choice, understanding, reasoning, and appreciation (Appelbaum & Grisso, 1988). Geropsychologists, on the other hand, define functional abilities as the ability to perform instrumental activities of daily living (IADLs) and basic activities of daily living (ADLs). Because geropsychologists seek to enhance autonomy wherever possible, a third area of concern is the older adult's awareness and whether compensatory strategies would be useful for him or her; this criterion is especially salient. Fourth, older adults' decisions must be of their own free will and not subject to undue influence. Finally, best practice requires integrating the legal standards for incapacity with the first four criteria.

Consistent with this framework, the methods and procedures used in an evaluation often include

http://dx.doi.org/10.1037/14459-021
APA Handbook of Clinical Geropsychology: Vol. 2. Assessment, Treatment, and Issues of Later Life,
P. A. Lichtenberg and B. T. Mast (Editors-in-Chief)

the following: (a) interview of the individual older adult whose capacity is in question, and interview of key informants; (b) cognitive testing; (c) decisional ability assessment, which often is accomplished with specific assessment of the skills in question (e.g., health decision testing for someone whose capacity to make medical decisions is in question); (d) a process to identify needed adaptations and environmental support; and (e) integration of the findings with the relevant legal standards. Whether all of these procedures and steps are included depends upon the case. For example, Lichtenberg and Luborsky (in press) noted that key informants may have significant motivation to over- or underreport symptoms because of issues of secondary gain, and thus they may not always be interviewed in a capacity assessment.

Geropsychologists must consider several basic issues in assessing capacity. First, and foremost, one always must be aware of the fundamental tension between autonomy (self-determination) and protection (beneficence; Moberg & Kniele, 2006; Moye & Marson, 2007). It can be tempting to use generalized findings, such as the fact that older adults are at risk for financial scams and theft, and apply them to each individual case no matter the circumstances to protect the older adult. In one case, a 94-year-old man without any cognitive impairment was recommended to have a conservator because the assessing psychologist thought the newly widowed man might need protection "as all older adults do." The same problem can be found with health decisions. In another case, an 80-year-old woman was hospitalized with kidney failure and was discovered to have multiple myeloma, a form of cancer. Within the first few months of her chemotherapy, she was extremely weak and her kidneys were not doing well. She was advised that dialysis may be necessary. She collected the information about dialysis and declined under any circumstances to be treated with dialysis. Some family members wondered whether this decision was simply her fear talking and reflected lower capacity and encouraged her to be more open-minded. She was cognitively intact and there was no question that the refusal of dialysis was a capable decision. Her autonomy was promoted. Three years later, after responding exceedingly well to chemotherapy, she has been

functioning at a high level and her kidneys were doing so well that chemotherapy was stopped for an extended time.

Second, capacity must be viewed as decision and domain specific (i.e., capacity to decide on a specific medical procedure or treatment) and not as a global judgment (Moberg & Rick, 2008). Brisk (2012) pointed out, for example, that different levels of capacity affect how one views an older adult's capacity for the specific circumstance. Brisk observed that at one end of the continuum are older adults who need someone to make decisions for them because of their demented or mentally disturbed state, yet other older adults can make many informed decisions about their money even though they have lost the cognitive abilities to balance a checkbook or budgets.

Third, the field still lacks agreement on methodological and procedural guidelines and empirical support for predicting real-world situations despite all of the excellent research progress in the area of capacity reviewed in this chapter (Moore, Palmer, Patterson, & Jeste, 2007). Moore et al. reviewed Pub Med for the past 40 years to determine performance-based, validated financial skill tools. Moore et al. found 16 in all but only recommended 3, and only one of them, Marson's Financial Capacity Instrument (FCI), was related specifically to late-life dementia. Part of the difficulty lies in the dichotomous judgment (yes–no) that geropsychologists sometimes are forced to make in capacity assessments (Moye & Marson, 2007). Another issue relates to the fact that many geriatric syndromes, such as dementia (and Alzheimer's disease), delirium, and frailty are clinical diagnoses vulnerable to misdiagnosis (Lichtenberg, 2012; White et al., 2005). Variability in day-to-day function further complicates assessments of capacity during a period of decline when daily fluctuations literally can shift decision-making capacity from day to day.

Geropsychology, through a unique collaboration between the American Bar Association and the American Psychological Association's Office on Aging, has made significant progress in providing best practices in capacity assessment. Building on past efforts in psychology, including the Department of Veterans Affairs' practice guidelines for psychologists in capacity assessment (Baker, Lichtenberg, & Moye, 1998), the ABA/APA published its *Assessment of Older Adults with Diminished Capacity: A Handbook for Psychologists* in 2008. This handbook had been preceded by volumes for judges and attorneys. More than 100,000 copies of these valuable resources (in paper or downloads) have been obtained by professionals around the world.

This chapter addresses health care decision making and financial decision making separately because each requires different approaches to assessment. Each section will include a review of assessment approaches and instruments as well as the ethical issues, communication issues, and considerations for the written report. We will use case examples to illustrate many of the essential elements.

CAPACITY TO MAKE HEALTH CARE DECISIONS

The following two case examples illustrate the medical, legal, social, and ethical issues embedded in health care decision making.

Case Example 1

Sandy Erikson insists that a new orthotic shoe will eliminate the pain she experiences when walking, despite repeated explanations of the structural damage to her foot from diabetic neuropathy. At each case consultation, she listens patiently to the explanations, and demands that her doctor provide her with a prescription for a new shoe. Sandy faces amputation, sooner or later, as a required strategy for limiting infection. Amputation is an immediate solution to the pain, but hard for her to accept. She seems unable to grasp the information or recall it from meeting to meeting. The physician has begun to question whether she has capacity to make the amputation decision alone.

Case Example 2

Juan Jiminez is still struggling to swallow 2 weeks after his stroke, and refuses food and drink. He claims to be "waiting for my throat to open up again." Juan's three daughters and two sons are with him round the clock, insisting that he eat and drink,

but with little success. The health team is concerned that dehydration is putting him at risk, and have attempted to persuade Juan to ingest more liquids. Although Juan acknowledges that the staff are right to insist that he drink, he refuses to attempt to drink water, either regular or "thickened." The family is growing frantic, and insists that a feeding tube be inserted, against Juan's wishes and the clearly stated preferences in Juan's advanced directives. Juan's oldest son, who is the designated health proxy decision maker, insists that Juan's earlier statements about wishing to avoid a feeding tube are "what he really wanted and still wants." The hospital wants to know if Juan has capacity to make this decision, or whether his son's status as a proxy decision maker be activated or acknowledged.

Overview

This section reviews some of the history and general clinical recommendations related to medical decision-making capacity evaluations, reviews and critiques older adult capacity research, reviews some of the more popular medical decision-making scales, and provides case examples and analysis. Moberg and Rick (2008) outlined some important general steps in the assessment process, including the following:

1. Clarify the referral question and determine whether the person receiving the request is capable of addressing the question.
2. Plan the assessment; attend to informed consent and limits of confidentiality.
3. Conduct the assessment.
4. Communicate the results of the assessment.
5. Recommend any additional evaluations needed.

Moberg and Rick noted that clinicians' most frequent error when performing capacity evaluations is viewing incapacity as global and not decision specific.

Health care researchers agree on the key issues of consent to medical treatments. These include the older adult's ability to communicate choices, understand relevant information, appreciate the situation and consequences, and manipulate information rationally (Appelbaum & Grisso, 1988; Roth, Meisel, & Lidz, 1977). Historically, much of the capacity literature for health care decision making was tied to the mental health field. Gutheil and Bursztajn (1986) provided mental health clinicians with some steps to follow in decision making with mentally impaired individuals: (a) intervene clinically first, and use the court as a last resort; (b) anticipate thorough documentation and develop awareness of the competency requirements; (c) avoid extreme or global judgments, and clearly articulate clinical findings; (d) enlist family and staff support; and (e) obtain consultation. Gutheil and Bursztayn's clinical suggestions expose one of the more difficult dilemmas in capacity work: the tension between the requirements of a clinician to ensure confidentiality and that of an expert to share findings with the court.

Grisso (2003) elaborated on the intellectual factors of choice, understanding, appreciation, and reasoning involved in capacity assessment. The older adult's choice must be clearly communicated. Understanding refers to the nature of the proposed decision and some explanation or awareness of its risks and benefits. Appreciation refers to the situation and its consequences. Often appreciation involves understanding the impact of the decision on the older adults and on others. Grisso pointed out that lack of awareness of deficit and delusions or distortions are the most common causes of impairment in appreciation. Reasoning includes the comparison of different treatment options in the case of health care decision making. It also includes the ability to provide a rationale for the decision, that is, an explanation of the choice communicated.

Although the intellectual factors associated with decisional abilities are well documented, there is debate about how to apply those standards. In particular, there are ethical questions about whether the geropsychologist's judgment about decisional abilities differs according to the context of the decision. In reviewing human subjects research, for example, the more potential harm to a participant, the more scrutiny an institutional review board gives to the quality of the science. Drane (1984), for one, recommended that the standard for competent decision making should vary by the dangerousness of the situation. For medical decisions that are not dangerous, awareness and assent are all that is needed. With chronic illness decisions, or more potentially dangerous treatment that has alternative choices, he argued that the patient must understand

the risks and outcomes and make a choice based on that understanding. Finally, for cases in which the diagnosis is fairly certain, there is effective treatment, and death is likely due to refusal, there must be the highest degree of understanding demonstrated, and rational decision making evidenced. The 1982 Presidential Commission for the Study of Ethical Problems in Medicine recommended that decision-making capacity be assessed at bedside (Jones & Holden, 2004) Jones and Holden also differentiated health care decision-making capacity from legal competence, indicating that the older adult's health care decision-making capacity often is assessed entirely within the clinical arena. Essentially, similar to Drane (1984), Jones and Holden encouraged the assessor to determine the balance of risk and benefit; the higher the risk, the more reasoning and understanding are required. Jones and Holden underscored the importance of patient self-determination in medical care and the relevance of the patient's set of values and goals. They offered an algorithm for clinicians, which included the following:

1. Does the history and physical confirm that the patient can communicate a choice?
2. Does the patient understand elements of the informed consent, including what is the condition, what are the treatment recommendations, what might happen if the patient decides not to have treatment, and what alternative treatments are available and the possible consequences of these? At the core of these is the ability of the patient to weigh risks and benefits.
3. Can the patient assign personal values to the risks and benefits of the potential interventions?
4. Is information processed and described rationally and logically by the patient?
5. Is the patient's decision-making capacity stable over time (i.e., hours, days)?

Descriptive Empirical Research on Physician Judgment in Medical Decision Making

Early empirical research in the area of medical decision making focused on the prevalence of impaired decision making by patients and methods of imparting information to patients. These early investigations left the field with some lasting products: the use of clinical vignettes as an evaluation tool, and the importance of assessing cognitive ability. Fitten and Waite (1990) studied decision making in hospitalized elderly. Three clinical vignettes were developed to assess treatment decision-making capacity. The authors compared 25 medical patients judged to be competent with 25 age- and education-matched normal controls. The authors concluded that 28% of the medical patients had impaired decision making but that this impairment often went unrecognized. Using the same vignettes and control group, Fitten, Lusky, and Hamann (1990) investigated treatment decision making in nursing home patients. Although physicians judged only 33% of the patients to have impaired decision-making capacity, 70% of the patients scored on the impaired range on the vignettes, reflecting a possible problem with the test. Alexander (1988) examined 92 consecutive admissions to a neurobehavioral service to assess the prevalence of mental competence. Three steps of competence were assessed: making decisions, passing minimal cognitive criteria, and compensating for deficits. Forty-seven patients had a single defect in mental competence and 36 had multiple defects. These early studies point toward the inherent difficulty in capacity research. Two main challenges in this work included that (a) clinical judgment is still the gold standard (Moye et al., 2006) and (b) capacity is a specific quality not a general one. This latter point makes it difficult to determine capacity based on hypothetical or neutral stimuli only; at some level, the specific decision needs to be assessed directly.

One area of research, used often in informed consent research, is how the delivery of information affects decision making. Tymchuk, Ouslander, Rahbar, and Fitten (1988) presented alternate methods of consent to nursing home residents. They compared a typical consent process to one that included a simplified or story version among 70 older adults whose average Mini-Mental State Examination (MMSE) score was 24.4. Decision making was better in the simplified or story version, and there was less deterioration of understanding in those versions over a week period than there was in those who received consent in the standard format. Consent documents need to be constructed to elicit true consent, ensuring comprehension among the populations the clinician evaluates.

Geropsychologists need to heed the lesson of informed consent (i.e., providing those older adults with less education a document that is written at an appropriate reading level) when evaluating and making judgments about cognitive functioning. Lichtenberg (1998), for example, demonstrated that some older adults have vastly different reading scores than stated years of education, which is interpreted as reflecting the lower quality of that education for those older adults. Without correcting for education level through reading scores, or other similar measures, cognitive deficits can be inflated artificially, especially among African American elders, causing a significant false-positive problem and a damaging clinical decision, which can have direct effects on capacity judgments (Lichtenberg, 2012).

Empirical Research Into Modifiers of Medical Decision Making

Geropsychologists have led research examining the relationship between cognition and medical decision-making capacity (Marson, Chatterjee, Ingram, & Harrell, 1996; Marson, Ingram, Cody, & Harrell, 1995; Pruchno et al., 1995). This was the first research examining how well cognitive testing related to judgments of capacity. Pruchno et al. (1995) examined performance on competency measures in three nursing home units. All subjects had to exceed 15 on their MMSE to be included in the study. Fifty (39% of those approached) agreed to participate. Performance on the MMSE, the Hopemont Capacity Assessment Inventory (HCAI), and the Understanding Treatment Disclosure instrument (for description of measures, see the section Assessment) was compared with clinical judgments made by psychologists. Capacity scores, as rated by the psychologists, were highly related to MMSE ($r = .70$; $p < .05$) the HCAI ($r = .61$; $p < .05$), and the Understanding Treatment Disclosure recognition task ($r = .60$; $p < .05$), but none of these relationships explained more than half of all variance, reminding us of the difference between clinical and statistical significance.

Marson et al. (1995) created two new specialized vignettes to focus their research on competency to consent to medical treatment. The vignettes and the questioning take 20–25 min to administer. Forty-four subjects participated, 15 normal controls and 29 individuals with probable Alzheimer's disease. Capacity was assessed by expert raters across five legal standards. Significant differences between the normal controls and the patients with Alzheimer's disease were evident in three of the areas: legal standards related to appreciation, reasoning, and understanding. There was significant variability, however, with only half of those in the stage of mild Alzheimer's disease scoring in the impaired range on reasoning, for example. Marson et al. (1996) reported that of 22 neuropsychological tests administered, eight of the neuropsychological measures correlated significantly with competency scores ranging from ($r = .44$ to $r = .60$; $p < .05$). Notably, all of the participants demonstrated similar evidence of capacity for choice.

Although the new vignettes were a major improvement in standardized assessment, Marson, McInturff, Hawkins, Bartolucci, and Harrell (1997) reported on the relatively poor interrater reliability by physicians who viewed videotapes of the administration of the Standardized Consent and Capacity Instrument to 16 controls and 29 participants with either mild or moderate Alzheimer's disease. The five physicians who made the ratings were blinded to diagnosis of the participant. Overall, there was 98% agreement for the controls but only 56% agreement for the patients with Alzheimer's disease. The differences in physician ratings were most pronounced among those patients with mild Alzheimer's disease, with a range of judgments from 90% lacking capacity to 0%.

Enhancing Reliability and Using Modifiers in Medical Decision-Making Research

Daniel Marson's work played a key role in spurring the maturation of medical decision-making research. He realized from his 1997 study that some training is necessary for all health professionals to improve the consistency of their capacity evaluations. His 1997 work demonstrated the significant weakness in the field: a lack of consistent judgment across seasoned physicians. Subsequent work by Marson, Earnst, and Jamil (2000) repeated the 1997 study after training the physicians to use the legal standards of choice, appreciation, reasoning, and understanding. Using the two vignettes from the Capacity to Consent to Treatment Instrument (CCTI), they found an improved interrater agreement—up to an overall mean of 76% for patients with mild Alzheimer's disease, a high of 84% was found for choice, and a low of 67% was found for appreciation. Additionally, 48% of cases of patients with Alzheimer's disease were judged to have medical decision-making capacity.

Kim et al. (2001) used a hypothetical clinical trial and the MacArthur Competence Assessment Tool (MaCat) to assess capacity for consent in 37 older people with Alzheimer's disease and 15 normal controls. Within this relatively highly educated group (more than 13 years on average), people with Alzheimer's disease had significantly lower scores on the MMSE (23 vs. 29) and much higher rates of incapacity (62% vs. 0%) to give informed consent based on expert judgment. When using a cutoff score from the MaCat, 84% scored in the range of lacking capacity. Interscorer reliability was high.

Moye et al. (2004) studied a large sample of people with dementia and normal controls (88 in each group) and compared the groups on three different capacity instruments, including the MaCat, the HCAI, and the CCTI. The MaCat is unique in that it utilizes the actual medical decision in question. Each of the other instruments uses vignettes of hypothetical situations to which respondents are to apply the legal standards of choice, understanding, appreciation, and reasoning. A majority of participants with mild Alzheimer's disease scored within normal limits and in the range of having capacity, leading Moye et al. to conclude that most people with mild dementia can participate in informed decisions. Overall, however, there was some significant variability among results using the various instruments. Although understanding was impaired on all three measures of capacity, appreciation was impaired on only one (CCTI), reasoning was impaired on two (MaCat, CCTI), and yet decisional capacity was largely within normal limits.

Gurrera, Moye, Karel, Azar, and Armesto (2006) used this sample to examine how well neuropsychological performance predicted the legal standards of capacity. Verbal retrieval, knowledge, and problem solving were consistently significant predictors of capacity for each legal standard, with verbal retrieval being the strongest predictor. Although the percent of the variance accounted for varied across domains, there were significant findings relating retrieval to choice, appreciation, reasoning, and understanding.

Sessums, Zembrzuska, and Jackson (2011) reviewed 43 studies of instruments measuring incapacity for medical inpatients making health care decisions. A total of 3,684 participants were included, of whom 1,425 were diagnosed with Alzheimer's disease and 148 with Parkinson's disease. Overall, 2.8% of normal controls were judged to have incapacity, whereas 26% of medical inpatients were judged to have incapacity. Physician judgment often differed from the results of a capacity instrument, such that 58% of the time physicians "failed" to recognize incapacity. The study also examined how MMSE scores related to capacity–incapacity risk. Scores above 24 reduced the likelihood of an older adult being found to lack capacity, whereas scores from 20–24 had no effect. Older adults with scores less than 20, and particularly less than 16, were the most likely to be judged to have incapacity. The authors recommended the use of the Aid to Capacity Evaluation (ACE) instrument for capacity assessments, noting that this semistructured interview is based on the actual decision the patient is facing.

Research Summary

In the past two decades medical decision-making research in older adults has moved from a number of descriptive studies to more careful analysis of measurement reliability and validity of clinical judgments and to the creation of standardized tools to assist in the capacity assessment process (to be more thoroughly reviewed in a later section). Marson's research demonstrating that consistency of physician judgment could be improved dramatically by explicitly using the legal standards helped to improve the reliability of expert judgment. In a recent handbook for psychologists on assessment of diminished capacity, these legal standards were underscored again (ABA/APA, 2008). Convergent validity research across multiple populations of older adults demonstrated that cognition was related to different legal standards overall. The cautionary tale, however, is that every study had considerable variability within the samples and that especially in the mild stage of dementia or other neurocognitive disorder, older adults often possessed capacity for their health decisions. The science of medical decision-making capacity thus has demonstrated improved assessment tools, increased reliability of judgment, and the overall construct validity of cognitive factors in capacity.

Assessment of Medical Decision-Making Capacity

This section shifts from the research literature to clinical applications. Specifically, we focus on how to perform clinical assessments. Baker, Lichtenberg, and Moye (1998), and more recently the ABA/APA (2008) handbook, underscored the need to first understand the nature of the referral. It is critical to obtain informed consent from the individual being evaluated and in particular describe the limits of confidentiality. Moberg and Kniele (2006) recommended five steps for capacity assessments, including (a) interviewing the individual whose capacity is in question and other informants, (b) performing cognitive or neuropsychological testing, (c) assessing decisional abilities (i.e., *functional* in legal terms), (d) reviewing the legal standards, and (e) identifying needed adaptations and environmental support. One way to organize an assessment is to return to the criteria for incapacity that we reviewed initially.

Determine whether an older adult is suffering from a mental health or neurocognitive disorder. Typically, questions of incapacity in older adults are raised when there are concerns about dementia or psychopathological symptoms that accompany dementia such as delusions. One dilemma facing geropsychologists is whether to use cognitive screening tests or more complete neuropsychological test batteries. Many aspects of capacity are heavily reliant on cognitive abilities. In the medical professions, including neurology and psychiatry, and to some extent psychology, cognition is assessed using broad basic screening measures. The value of screening measures is brevity in detection of any degree of cognitive impairment. Their weaknesses that are problematic for capacity work are the large numbers of false negatives; people who appear normal on cognitive screen only to exhibit significant cognitive deficits on extended assessment. Indeed, thorough cognitive assessment assesses five domains of cognition: attention, language, memory, visuospatial, and executive functioning. Cognitive assessment identifies a more complete pattern of strengths and deficits, and differentiates permanent states of cognitive impairment (dementia) versus more transient states of cognitive deficits (delirium) in addition to assisting with dementia diagnosis and staging the severity of a dementia. The research literature cited previously provides an illustration of the importance of accurately staging the severity of the dementia (see chapters on dementia and geriatric neuropsychology). As will be highlighted, older adults in the mild stage of dementia often were found to have retained capacity for medical decision making, whereas incapacity was dramatically more likely in those with moderate stage dementia.

Determine whether the mental health or neurocognitive disorder affects decisional (functional) abilities. The legal standards of choice, understanding, reasoning, and appreciation more recently have been accompanied by an assessment of an individual's values and how the choice is or is not consistent with those values. Thus, the following five areas are standard in the assessment of an individual's decisional abilities:

1. Evidence of choice relative to the capacity in question.
2. Ability to communicate reasoning surrounding choice.
3. Appreciation of the consequences of choice (including risks–benefits, awareness of past problems, and plans to compensate for these problems).
4. Understanding of the choice.
5. Consistency of the choice with the individual's values.

Edelstein (2000) described the challenges involved in assessing decisional abilities. First, the issue of autonomy often arises when the choices of the older adult do not match those of their health provider or family, and when the health provider believes the choice has significant consequences. Decisional abilities then are assessed using hypothetical scenarios, and it is assumed that decision-making skills are used across several different situations and thus are generalizable. This approach also invokes the use of norm referenced tests. Specifically, normative data on the same hypothetical stimuli permit comparisons to be made to the older adult whose capacity is being assessed. Kapp and Mossman (1996), in contrast, have argued that geropsychologists must use decision-specific assessments. The most common instruments to assess decisional abilities for medical choices use either a normative or specific decision-based approach. These are briefly described and reviewed in the following sections. Moye et al. (2006) and Sturman (2005) have provided a more detailed and complete description. A number of other scales are reviewed by Moye and Sturman; we describe the ones most often used by geropsychologists.

Capacity to Consent to Treatment. Marson et al. (1995) created two clinical vignettes; one regards a neoplasm and a second regards a cardiac condition. The vignettes are presented to the older adult orally and in writing. Questions then are presented to the older adult about the vignettes, and from this, an assessment of choice, understanding, reasoning, and appreciation are determined. Since the CCTI's creation, Marson et al. have tied their instrument to the legal standards described previously and have demonstrated excellent interrater reliability and convergent validity.

Hopemont Capacity Assessment Interview. Edelstein (1999) created the HCAI to assess medical decision-making capacity in nursing home residents. Two vignettes were created, one about an eye infection and a second about cardiopulmonary resuscitation. The vignettes are presented to the nursing home residents and simple questions are used to prompt other answers that require the resident to recount factual information and to demonstrate choice, understanding, appreciation, and reasoning. High levels of interrater agreement have been reported.

Aid to Capacity Evaluation. Etchells et al. (1999) developed the ACE for use by physicians as a bedside measure of capacity. It is a semistructured assessment interview that examines seven facets of the actual medical decision in question. Patients must demonstrate the ability to understand (a) the medical problem, (b) the proposed treatment, (c) alternate treatments, and (d) the option to refuse treatment while also needing to perceive the consequences of (e) accepting the treatment and (f) refusing the treatment. The seventh and final component is that the patient's decision must not be based on hallucinations, delusions, or depression. In their review, Sessums et al. (2011) recommended that physicians use the ACE for bedside evaluations.

MacArthur Competence Assessment Tool– Treatment. Through the MacArthur Mental Health Research Network, Grisso and Appelbaum have been leaders in clarifying the legal standards involved in capacity assessments (Grisso, Appelbaum, & Hill-Fotouhi, 1997). The MaCat– Treatment (MaCat-T) initially was developed for adults with psychosis and not older adults. In the past 15 years, they have created several tools, of which the McCat-T may be the most popular. It is a semistructured interview that guides clinicians through the assessment of capacity, and like the ACE, it focuses on the actual decision facing the patient. There are four steps in using the instrument: (a) the patient receives information about his or her disorder, (b) the patient is asked to describe his or her understanding of the disorder, (c) the patient receives information about the treatment and risks and benefits of the treatment and of alternative treatments, and (d) the patient is asked to describe these risks and benefits. Appreciation and ability to express choice also are evaluated. Patient answers are rated for communication of choices, understanding, comprehension of risks and benefits, insight and choice process, and judgment.

None of the instruments have overt questions, however, that investigate the values held by the older adult that might be pertinent to his or her decision. The ABA/APA (2008) handbook for

psychologists noted that exploration of values is an important part of the capacity evaluation. It is important to understand the older adult's long-held and cherished values that might affect the health decision the older adult is making, through review of any legal documents created to guide health decisions, direct discussion with the older adult, and communication with informants.

Determine whether the older adult is aware of any deficits and whether any compensatory strategies can be used to improve capacity. An older adult's awareness of deficit is a key component to capacity assessments (Baker, Lichtenberg, & Moye, 1998; Lichtenberg, 1998) because of its direct influence on an older adult's ability and willingness to use compensatory strategies. Awareness is the cornerstone of appreciation—the ability to understand and communicate potential impacts and consequences. Older adults with insight into their cognitive impairment, for example, might benefit from a simplified version of the information and a brief written summary. Older adults with some awareness of deficit also may be more likely to indicate aspects of the treatment decisions that he or she does not understand.

More broadly, compensatory strategies should be used when illiteracy, lack of education, or native language is an issue. Most written treatment consent documents, although supposed to be written at the fifth- or eighth-grade level, usually are more complex and can leave an older adult with lower literacy skills confused. The importance of simplifying information in these circumstances cannot be overstated. Pérez-Stable, Nápoles-Springer, and Miramontes (1997) have demonstrated the importance of having health providers available who speak the same language (e.g., Spanish) as the older adult facing a health decision.

Integrate the findings from steps 1–3 and make a recommendation. Geropsychologists must integrate their assessments of mental health or cognition, with the assessment of decisional abilities and any compensatory efforts that need to be or were tried, to reach a conclusion about whether or not the older adult has capacity to make the specific medical decision in question. The following case studies demonstrate some of the assessment and family issues that are important for geropsychologists to consider in making their final conclusion.

Case Example 3

A primary care clinic contacted a university-based training clinic serving older adults with a request to assess the ability of Ms. Wood to live independently safely and to make informed decisions about her health. Ms. Wood had reported to her provider repeatedly that someone was stealing from her. A home care worker reported that Ms. Wood's home was dangerously cluttered and she did not appear to be eating regularly because the only food available required food she would not prepare. Ms. Wood was certain that she has "head damage" from being kicked by a horse a few years previously. She hoped the assessment would help providers identify coping strategies she could learn to compensate for memory problems, fatigue, and high-intensity anger reactions. She refused to consider moving into an assisted living facility and denied any difficulties managing her self-care at home. Terms of the assessment were negotiated and medical records provided. The assessment was completed, including an interview with Ms. Wood's ex-husband and a written report that subsequently was shared with the primary care provider (PCP).

Ms. Wood was born (1938) and raised by her parents in a rural community in Alabama along with one older and three younger siblings. She reported several instances of physical abuse by her parents, including being struck in the head. She denied any learning disabilities or difficulties in school. She started but did not complete practical nursing training because of her decision to marry and become a homemaker. She later worked intermittently as a saleswoman in a retail clothing shop. She was married twice. Her first marriage of 7 years ended soon after her husband returned from a military tour in Vietnam because of his "depression and acting crazy." After 10 years of being single, she married again, and reports that she and this husband were compatible and happy until she suffered the head injury in 2003 after which she had no interest in sex. She has no children from either marriage and lives alone in a two-bedroom apartment within a subsidized senior housing complex. She reports having acquaintances in her apartment complex with whom she rarely socializes. She attends one class per month at the senior community center and attends Catholic Church intermittently. Her income consists of a minimal Social Security payment and Supplemental Security Income; Medicaid is her health insurance.

Medical records indicate previous diagnoses of osteoporosis, a skin malignancy, irritable bowel syndrome, osteoarthritis, hypothyroidism, hypertension, and depression. She was diagnosed with fibromyalgia in 1998. She reports suffering from chronic pain due to a back injury at age 16 years. In 1993, she was involved in an automobile accident that resulted in a neck injury that resolved with months of treatment. The 2003 incident in which she was kicked in the head by a horse left her in a coma for 3 months. She does not know whether the coma was naturally occurring or medically induced and records were not available. In 2004, she had a shunt placed in her brain to drain fluid from an infection that resulted from the accident. She denied experiencing seizures, or any other injuries, illnesses, or hospitalizations.

In the 6 months immediately before the evaluation, Ms. Wood reported being increasingly confused and having difficulty with "staying on top of things." She lost 8 pounds, which places her at the low end of the normal weight range for her height and age. At the time of referral, her PCP was concerned that she was not capable of managing her medication regimen, finances, or nutrition. The PCP also expressed concern that Ms. Wood's unwillingness to accept additional home care services or to move into assisted living where structured supports would be available to her was placing her at risk for health decline, social isolation that exacerbates her depression, and malnutrition. Driving was not a concern because she has voluntarily surrendered her driver's license after chronic pain made driving difficult. A brief mental status exam conducted by the PCP yielded results indicating significant cognitive impairment that was growing from baseline levels collected 2 years previously. Ms. Wood was her own legal decision maker and involved no one in health care decisions. She has no will or other advanced directives other than those completed at the hospital at the time of her last hospitalization when she had designated her then-husband as her durable power of attorney for health.

1. *Neurocognitive abilities.* Ms. Wood was fully cooperative with the assessment, approaching the testing with a relaxed attitude she described as "laid back." Moderate pain behaviors were observed and accommodated with frequent breaks to move about in the room. Ms. Wood scored in the severely impaired range on measures of attention and concentration (see Exhibit 21.1). Her reports of physical pain may indicate that pain interfered with her performance on these measures. Attention and concentration impairments are likely to affect deleteriously more complex cognitive functions.

   Information-processing speed was in normal range, but information-processing capacity and working memory were severely impaired. Auditory–verbal memory scores were low on initial trials in a word learning task, but she was able to learn at a normal rate. She performed in the average range on visual memory tasks, visual–spatial construction tasks, and language abilities (both receptive and expressive). Her performance on tasks that rely on executive functions (organizing, initiating, and following through with goals; critically evaluating one's problem-solving efforts; and making adjustments to approaches to problem solving) were generally in the normal range. Although aware of her errors, she was inconsistently able to self-correct. Problems with initiating and following through with goals also are noted. On the basis of Ms. Wood's report and that of her PCP, she has experienced functional decline as a result of her cognitive difficulties. She meets criteria for nonamnestic multiple domain mild cognitive impairment. That is, she has evidence of cognitive decline from a previous level of functioning yet preserved functional ability. Her cognitive difficulties likely result from her traumatic brain injury, possibly exacerbated by effects of previous milder head injuries. Because of her history of hypertension, other factors such as vascular ischemic disease, cannot be ruled out.

2. *Decisional abilities.* On tasks assessing skills and knowledge needed for everyday living (independent living skills, including money management and health and safety decisions), Ms. Wood's performance was in the high functioning range. Specifically, she was able to write two checks and balance a mock checkbook correctly, and she was able to describe appropriate actions for emergency situations.

3. *Awareness of deficit and ability to compensate.* Ms. Wood demonstrated insight into the nature and extent of her cognitive difficulties. She was able to compensate for them to perform well on practical tasks related to financial management, health, and safety. She described her difficulties with food preparation that she believed led to her recent weight loss in a logical way and recognized that she needed to modify her marketing strategies to include more items that would not require significant preparation. It was noted, however, that she is not consistently able to use her awareness in daily life.

Exhibit 21.1
Test Score Summary (Percentile Scores)

Mental Control	5
Digit Span–Forward	1
Digit Span–Backward	<1
Rey AVLT I–1st Recall Score	5
Rey AVLT I–LOT	10
Rey AVLT I–List B	9
Rey AVLT I–Trial 6	50
BVMT–R–Trial 1	61
BVMT–R–Trial 2	10
BVMT–R–Trial 3	32
BVMT–R Total Recall	27
BVMT–R Learning	34
Trails A	25
Trails B	9
Math	Within normal limits
Rey AVLT II–Trial 7	50
Rey AVLT II–Recognition	50
BVMT–R Delay Recall	42
Clock Face	Within normal limits
NAB Picture Naming	73
Behavioral Dyscontrol Scale	25

Note. AVLT = Auditory Verbal Learning Test; BVMT = Benton Visual Memory Test; NAB = Neuropsychological Assessment Battery.

4. *Health and self-care decision capacity*. Ms. Wood is capable of making health and self-care decisions, but she may require assistance to ensure that she attends to relevant important information. Specifically, the level of deficit in attention, concentration, and working memory render her vulnerable to missing and confusing information. She can learn new information needed to make decisions, but the information will need to be presented in small doses and with repetition to ensure that she can encode it effectively. She will benefit from assistance or prompting to compensate for working memory deficits, especially related to medication management, making financial or legal decisions such as entering into a contract, or making financial commitments. She should not engage in activities that involve multitasking, and she needs to continue to refrain from driving. In making health decisions, Ms. Wood needs to be provided information in small quantities, repeatedly, in a distraction-free environment until she can report them accurately. Asking her to repeat what she has heard will ensure that she has understood the relevant information.

Ms. Wood requires minimal reminders to maintain her safety and health. She will benefit from a living situation in which she is given support and assistance to make sure she is taking care of IADLs (e.g., medication compliance, transportation, food preparation). It may be beneficial for Ms. Wood to consider moving to a facility that will be able to accommodate any future cognitive or physical decline she may experience in the future. In her current environment, prompting technologies may be useful to improve consistency in attending to ADLs.

Ms. Wood is at increased risk for further cognitive decline so she should consider putting her legal and financial affairs in order while she still has capacity. This is a good time to establish a legal will and advanced directives. It is also a good time to select and involve a decision-making partner who can collaborate with her to ensure that she thoroughly understands information needed to make effective decisions. Engaging someone now in attending health care appointments would provide an excellent basis for proxy decision making in the future.

5. *Integration with legal standards*. Ms. Wood was deemed capable to make health and safety decisions, yet the conditions to support that legal right also were specified (use of specific strategies to ensure that she gathers and understands relevant information; use of prompting strategies for self-care tasks).

6. *Disposition and commentary*. Ms. Wood received the evaluation feedback with relief that she would not be "forced into one of those old age homes." She also recognized the wisdom of proceeding to engage now someone who could assist her with health decisions. She identified two people and after discussing her needs with them both, selected one to attend medical appointments with her as a helper and future decision-making proxy. This friend attended a caregiver counseling session with Ms. Wood to make a plan for how and when she would be involved in Ms. Wood's care. At her friend's prompting, Ms. Wood worked with the case manager in the primary care office to complete a legally binding form outlining her advanced directives, and later, a will. Within 18 months of this evaluation, Ms. Wood's functioning appeared to be declining again, and she was referred for follow-up testing. Another neuropsychological evaluation documented significant decline in cognitive abilities, self-awareness, and functional safety decision making. Ms. Wood's friend began taking the lead on health decisions, and within a few months, helped Ms. Wood transition to assisted living.

The geropsychologist performed a key role in the slow transition of Ms. Wood from full independent legal decision-making status to the point at which her friend was recognized as the legally binding proxy decision maker.

Summary of Medical Decision-Making Section

Case Example 3 illustrates how to use an assessment approach that integrates finding from research and from best practice guidelines. Neurocognitive abilities and functional abilities are assessed and integrated with issues of awareness and the legal standards for medical decision making. The next section turns attention to financial capacity in older adults.

FINANCIAL CAPACITY

Case Example 4

Helen Swift is thrilled to have met a man as fine as Jack for what she considers her last marriage at age 84 years. After a hard life, he deserves the kind of support her estate can offer them both in the waning years of life. Helen's children are livid and confront Helen with a verbal barrage of reasons why it is clear that Jack is after her money. No persuasion is effective, and Helen proceeds with the marriage, enraged at her children's selfishness. Despite some misgivings, Helen agrees with Jack's desire to buy vacation homes in Hawaii and Greece. The children are shocked because Helen's frugality was a constant source of tension between her and their father while they were married, and they seek consultation about whether something legal should be done.

Case Example 5

Angel Martinez owns very little, despite having scrimped and saved while working hard as a housekeeper. She recently moved into an assisted living facility where the staff care for her so well she remarks, "I feel like a queen." She is particularly fond of a young man who reminds her of her nephew who died in Iraq. She wants to help his struggling family and offers him free rent in the little house she has not yet sold along with use of her car. Angel is very upset with the facility for firing him for receiving these gifts, and calls the Area Agency on Aging ombudsman for help identifying an alternative place where they "treat their staff like people." The ombudsman contacts you with her concerns about Angel's ability to handle her own financial decisions.

Case Example 6

When Jennifer, his only daughter, discovered that Daniel Horn's bank account was near empty, she was shocked and terrified. Her brother, who has Daniel's financial durable power of attorney, just built a new house that seemed extravagant but Jennifer cannot imagine he would actually steal from their father. The social worker at the skilled nursing facility where Daniel lives dreaded telling Jennifer that the facility bill had not been paid for 3 months. Jennifer and her father's attorney contact you for help documenting that Daniel did not have capacity to gift $300,000 to her brother as he claimed.

Overview

This section examines financial capacity and financial exploitation, briefly reviewing the literature and concepts from both of these areas of research and practice. Subsequently, attention will be paid to cases of financial capacity in which the geropsychologist is acting as an expert and providing information to attorneys, the courts, or both. To date, there has been a significant lack of clinical research and assessment tools that assess financial decision making and financial judgment for the specific transaction in question. The final part of this section introduces a newly created scale. In addition, a case example is used to examine process issues and to review communication and written report issues.

Elder mistreatment is defined as intentional actions that cause harm or create serious risk of harm to an older adult by someone who stands in a trust relationship to the elder or is a caregiver (Dong & Simon, 2012). Blancato (2012) reviewed the legislative history regarding elder abuse and elder mistreatment highlighting key legislation:

- 1992 and 2006 Title VII of Older Americans Act—authorized elder abuse prevention activities
- 1970s Authorization for Adult Protective Services under the Social Security Act
- 1987 OBRA for Long-Term Care—defined elder abuse and mandated state investigations
- 1980s first national center on Elder Abuse at Administration on Aging is formed
- 1992 Amendment to Older Americans Act regarding elder mistreatment, which provided a broader definition for what constituted abuse of older adults—but funding remained static for 20 years and counting
- 2011 Elder Justice Act as part of the Affordable Care Act, which recognized in federal law older adults' rights to be free from abuse and exploitation

Financial Autonomy and Elder Justice

Stiegel (2012) vividly described the fact that financial capacity and financial exploitation are "entwined" (p. 73). That is, that older adults' vulnerability is twofold: (a) the potential loss of financial skills and financial judgment and (b) the inability to detect and therefore prevent financial exploitation. Nerenberg, Davies, and Navarro (2012) highlighted the term elder justice, which holds that the right of older adults to live free from abuse, neglect, and exploitation is a fundamental right. As critical as it is to protect older adults from financial exploitation, it is equally critical to protect older adults' financial autonomy. Both under- and overprotection of older adults can lead to damaging consequences. Underprotection for older adults can lead to gross financial exploitation that can affect every aspect of the older adult's life, including the ability to pay for needed services during times of vulnerability. The dilemma is that overprotection can be equally costly. Many older adults have strong needs for autonomy and control and to limit autonomy unnecessarily can lead to increased health problems and shortened longevity. Thus, assessing the integrity of older adults' financial judgment abilities often falls on the shoulders of clinical geropsychologists.

Financial Exploitation

Older adults continue to be financially exploited at disturbing rates (Conrad, Iris, Ridings, Langley, & Wilber, 2010; MetLife Mature Market Institute, 2009, 2011). Compared with their MetLife (2009) study, Teaster et al. (2012) found 389 unduplicated media articles about financial exploitation across 3 months. These accounted for $530 million in losses, including $240 million in losses tied to other family members and, stunningly, 51% of cases involving strangers.

Conrad et al. (2010) suggested six pertinent domains of financial exploitation: (a) theft and scams, (b) abuse of trust, (c) financial entitlement, (d) coercion, (e) signs of possible financial exploitation, and (f) money-management difficulties. Specifically, Conrad et al. defined financial exploitation as illegal or improper use of an older adult's funds or property for another person's profit or advantage.

Conrad et al. rank-ordered their domains by severity of the problem, with thefts and scams being the most severe form of financial exploitation. Thefts and scams represent the taking of an older adult's monies without permission either by outright stealing or committing fraudulent activities (i.e., scam). Terms such as "abuse of trust" or "financial entitlement" are thus categories of financial exploitation that imply an ongoing relationship between the parties.

Four recent random sample studies of community-dwelling older adults have documented the alarming rates of financial exploitation and their correlates, while a fifth provided a new way to classify financial exploitation. For the most part, these studies gathered data on abuse of trust, coercion, and financial entitlement. Acierno et al. (2010) reported that 5.2% of all respondents have experienced financial exploitation by a family member during the previous year. Sixty percent of the mistreatment consisted of family members' misappropriation of money. The authors also examined a number of demographic, psychological, and physical correlates of reported financial exploitation. Only two variables—deficits in the number of ADLs the older adult could perform and nonuse of social services—were related significantly to financial exploitation.

Laumann, Leitsch, and Waite (2008) reported that 3.5% of their sample was a victim of financial exploitation during the previous year. Younger older adults, ages 55–65 years, were the most likely to report financial exploitation. African Americans were more likely than non-Hispanic Caucasians to report financial exploitation, whereas Latinos were less likely than non-Hispanic Caucasians to report having been victimized. Finally, participants with a romantic partner were less likely to report financial exploitation.

Beach, Schulz, Castle, and Rosen (2010) found that 3.5% of their sample reported experiencing financial exploitation during the 6 months before the interview, and almost 10% had at some point since turning 60 years old. The most common experience was signing documents the participant did not fully understand. The authors found that directly related to theft and scams, 2.7% of their sample believed that someone had tampered with their money within the previous 6 months. In their sample, African Americans were more likely to report financial exploitation than were non-Hispanic Caucasians. Depression and ADL deficits were other correlates of financial exploitation.

Lichtenberg, Stickney, and Paulson, (2013) focused on older adults' experience of fraud (defined as someone else inflicting financial losses other than by robbery or theft). This is the first population-based study to gather prospective data to predict financial exploitation of any kind. A Health and Retirement Survey substudy, the 2008 Leave-Behind Questionnaire, including 4,400 older adult participants. The prevalence of fraud across the past 5 years was 4.5%, and among measures collected in 2002, age, education, and depression were significant predictors of fraud. Using depression and social need fulfillment to determine the most psychologically vulnerable older adults, Lichtenberg et al. found that fraud prevalence in those with the highest depression and the lowest social need fulfillment was three times as high (14%) as compared to the rest of the sample's 4.1% prevalence ($\chi^2 = 20.49$; $p < .001$).

Jackson and Hafemeister (2012) compared the experiences of pure financial exploitation with hybrid financial exploitation. Hybrid financial exploitation refers to cases in which psychological abuse, physical abuse, or neglect was found along with the financial exploitation. In cases of hybrid financial exploitation, the older adults were less healthy and more likely to be abused by those who cohabitated with the older adult. This important research underscored the variability and heterogeneity of financial exploitation of older adults.

Several researchers focused on understanding financial exploitation point out the need for more ongoing education in determining capacity and for more resources for evaluations (Nerenberg et al., 2012). They also have stressed that differentiating financial exploitations from legitimate transactions may be difficult because of indications of consent by an older adult (e.g., signed document, apparent gift). The lack of work on assessments of financial decision making or financial judgment hinders research and policy in the area of financial exploitation. Kemp and Mosqueda (2005) discussed the lack

of validated assessment procedures to evaluate elder financial abuse and the importance of a qualified expert to conduct an appropriate assessment. These authors also advocated strongly for a team approach. Chapter 26 in this volume on elder abuse expands on many of these themes and findings. Interestingly, the field of financial capacity assessment has not overlapped greatly with the field of financial exploitation assessment.

Financial Capacity and Neurocognitive Abilities

Although financial exploitation research demonstrates the significant need for protection of older adults in the pursuit of elder justice, financial capacity research highlights the importance of protecting autonomy and autonomous choices of capable older adults. Financial capacity, defined here as the ability to manage "money and financial assets in ways consistent with one's values or self-interest" (Flint, Sudore, & Widera, 2012, p. 59; see also Marson, 2001), is assumed until evidence to the contrary is brought forward. Pinsker et al. (2010) proposed that three abilities underlie financial capacity: (a) declarative knowledge (e.g., the ability to describe financial concepts), (b) procedural knowledge (e.g., writing checks), and (c) judgment to make sound financial decisions. Because dementia is a key part of financial incapacity, Pinsker et al. concluded that a comprehensive cognitive evaluation should form an integral part of the financial capacity assessment of older persons. Mental health conditions, such as depression, anxiety, and psychosis, also can affect capacity.

The impact of age-related dementia (e.g., Alzheimer's disease) on financial capacity (Marson, 2001) also threatens financial autonomy. Marson and his group have examined financial capacity in cognitively intact older persons, to those suffering from mild cognitive impairment to mild and moderate Alzheimer's disease. Marson noted that a disproportionately high number of older adults subject to conservatorship proceedings suffer from dementia. Marson (2001) conceived of financial capacity as relating to three things: (a) specific financial abilities, (b) broad domains of financial activity, and (c) overall financial capacity. In his 2001 study, for example, financial capacity was strongly linked to stage of Alzheimer's disease. Whereas 53%, 47%, and 13% of those in the mild stage of Alzheimer's were rated as fully capable of basic monetary skills, financial concepts, and financial judgment, respectively, only 10%, 5%, and 0% of those in the moderate stage were rated as fully capable in those same domains. When taking into account marginally capable individuals, it is clear that having mild-stage Alzheimer's disease does not equate with incapable financial capacity. Fully 50% of older adults with mild-stage Alzheimer's disease were judged capable or marginally capable of financial judgment, whereas 70% and 60% of Alzheimer's patients in the mild stage were fully or marginally capable of basic monetary skills and financial concepts. In regression analyses, memory functioning and word-finding skills were significant predictors of financial judgment, accounting for 25%–49% of the variance.

In each subsequent study, Marson and colleagues have utilized the eight-domain FCI (Martin et al., 2008) or a semistructured interview to evaluate financial capacity (Marson et al., 2009), including assessments of the following:

- basic monetary skills,
- financial knowledge,
- cash transactions,
- checkbook management,
- bank statement management,
- financial judgment,
- bill payment and,
- knowledge of personal assets and estate arrangements.

Martin et al. (2008) investigated declining financial capacity using the FCI in normal older adults and those with mild Alzheimer's disease across a 12-month time period. At baseline, people suffering from Alzheimer's disease scored below the healthy elders on the eight domains of the FCI and an overall rating of financial capacity. Over the year-long period, Alzheimer's patients showed declines of about 10% in almost every domain. Scores of healthy older adults remained stable. Among the patients, bank statement management, investment decisions, financial judgment, and cash transactions showed the greatest decline over the year period,

whereas knowledge of assets and estate arrangements showed the least change. The MMSE was related strongly to the FCI overall score at baseline ($r = .71; p < .05$).

Sherod et al. (2009) investigated the neurocognitive predictors of FCI domains across 85 healthy normal elders, 113 older adults with MCI, and 43 with mild Alzheimer's disease. Arithmetic was the single best predictor of FCI scores; accounting for 27% of the variance in healthy elders and 46% of the FCI variance in those with mild Alzheimer's disease. When it came to self-assessment, Okonkwo et al. (2009) reported that even those older adults in the earlier stages of cognitive decline, with only mild cognitive impairment (for a definition and discussion of mild cognitive impairment, see Chapter 7 in this volume on dementia and Alzheimer's disease), were more likely to overestimate their cognitive skills compared with normal controls. Financial judgment, however, remained intact among those with mild cognitive impairment, relative to normal controls. Thus, the great variability of the impact of early cognitive decline and early dementia on financial judgment highlights the need for new and more specific instruments to assess specific financial judgments in older adults suffering from cognitive impairment.

Kershaw and Webber (2008) introduced a financial capacity test similar to Marson's, titled the Financial Capacity Assessment Instrument (FCAI). The 38-item measure includes six subscales. Its subscales include everyday financial abilities, financial judgment, estate management, cognitive function related to financial tasks, debt management, and support resources. The FCAI is presented as a scale with broader validation than Marson's FCI, including adult populations suffering from schizophrenia and traumatic brain injury. Its initial reliability and validity data were promising. The authors reported that the FCAI domains were related significantly to the MMSE and the Independent Living Scales Money Management subtest. Finally, unlike the FCI, the FCAI is widely available for clinical and research use.

Although several studies have documented good interrater reliability and construct validity for the FCI, and there is promising work for the FCAI, financial judgment had one of the lowest percent agreements by raters among those with mild cognitive impairment and mild Alzheimer's disease. One significant weakness of the otherwise-excellent current financial domain assessment instruments (e.g., Kershaw & Webber, 2008; Marson et al., 2009) is that they use neutral or hypothetical stimuli (e.g., how could you be sure the price of a car is fair?). Accordingly, it is critical that valid and reliable tools exist to adequately assess specific financial decision-making abilities relevant to the individual at risk, especially regarding *sentinel financial transactions*, defined as transactions that can result in significant losses or harmful consequences. Later in the chapter, we look specifically at a new instrument to assess financial decision making.

The Intersection of Financial Exploitation and Financial Capacity

Shulman, Cohen, and Hull (2005) examined 25 cases in which there were challenges to the testamentary capacity of an older adult. Testamentary capacity, examples of which include making a donation or signing a real estate contract (e.g., reverse mortgage) in addition to changing a will, are weighted heavily toward financial judgment skills as opposed to actual management of finances or even performing cash transactions. In 72% of the challenged cases, radical changes were made to the previous will. Fifty-six percent of the cases had documented issues of undue influence, and 40% of the cases were associated with dementia. Other psychiatric and neurologic conditions were found in 28% of the cases. Flint, Sudore, and Widera (2012) also found that impaired financial judgment was linked not only linked to cognitive impairment but also to behavioral and psychological symptoms of dementia, including lack of awareness and delusional thinking. Thus, financial incapacity assessment must include assessments related to values, undue influence and other contextual variables in addition to assessing neurocognitive functioning and diagnostic issues.

CAPACITY ASSESSMENT AND EXPERT GEROPSYCHOLOGICAL ASSESSMENT

Today, we know that the mere presence of a mental disorder does not create legal incompetence (Grisso, 1994). A diagnosis of a neurologic condition does not automatically render one incapable of self-care determination; rather, a clinical disorder must be linked to specific disabilities. Second, we know that legal incompetence is not an all-or-nothing status (Grisso, 1994). The question should be, incompetent for what? Limited incompetency judgments may become more the norm than global determinations of incompetency. Third, legal incompetence is not to be conceptualized as permanent. For example, delirium (due to treatable a fever, infection, or drug reaction) may produce an incompetency judgment, but when treated and cured, the person regains her or his capacity. Finally, there still is no single legal definition of incompetence, so a causal link must be established between cognitive deficits and the particular capacity in question. One element that is included in the following model but is not technically a capacity issue is undue influence. This element, often present in cases of financial incapacity, is clearly a financial exploitation element. In assessment with older adults, undue influence is an important issue to consider and assess in any financial capacity evaluation.

Assessing Financial Capacity When Working With the Legal System

Issues of whether to appoint a conservator, or whether a will or contract is valid, are often disputed cases of capacity and involve the legal system. This section provides an introduction to the practicalities of working with attorneys and the legal system followed by a case example.

Negotiating referral. A court representative or attorney advocating for one side may approach an expert. The expert must determine (a) what capacity is in question; (b) whether it is a forensic assessment (medical records only as if the older person died), or whether it will require a new assessment; (c) which legal standards (i.e., state court case law) are germane to the specific capacity; (d) the time frame for which the analysis is needed; (e) whether the hiring party understands that the assessment is impartial and that, regardless of who hires the expert, the conclusions are not mutable; and (f) that a fee is agreed upon.

Obtaining records and setting the evaluation. An expert often must persistently push to get both medical and legal records. These allow the expert to create a timeline of relevant events. The medical records serve as a fundamental source of unbiased information, often including notations about cognitive decline or dementia. Being able to view the absence or presence of progressive decline is essential to establish the correct diagnosis. When scheduling the evaluation, the expert must explain who will be involved (e.g., family caregiver or other informants interviewed). The expert must clarify that no one except the examiner and the older person can be present.

Obtaining informed consent. Strikingly, unlike in other evaluations, no protection is provided for patient confidentiality with respect to medical facts. Thus, before the interview and formal assessment, the person must give informed consent or (if not possible) assent. The expert must explain to the older adult that unlike almost all health procedures, results of the capacity assessment are shared with all parties in the legal proceedings. This lack of confidentiality is a glaring, underappreciated contrast between a clinical and a legal capacity assessment. A clinical assessment, with a goal of helping with diagnosis and treatment planning, is completed on behalf of the older adult, and the results are shared with the older adult and, in general and only with the permission of the older adult, a few other close family members (i.e., spouses, adult child). In an inpatient or outpatient clinical setting, where there is an identified team, permission is sought from the older adult to share the assessment results and treatment recommendations with the other team members. An expert assessment case, in contrast, may well be shared with all of the parties involved in the legal dispute, and parts of a report may even end up in the judicial record should the case go to an appellate court. Clinicians who work with older adults who are at risk for having age-related dementia would do well to clearly communicate during the informed consent process the circumstances under which their assessment results in fact would be shared with parties in the legal system.

Preliminary discussion of results with older person and hiring party. After the assessment, it is important to review with the older person the next steps

in the process. Thank the older person for his or her cooperation and explain that the results will be shared with his or her attorney who then can share it with the older adult. If the court is the hiring party, then the judge and two attorneys have agreed to use the results of the assessment and so the formal report is prepared and shared. If the expert was hired by an attorney advocating for one side, then it is crucial that the expert speaks to the hiring attorney first before generating a report. For example, in one of Lichtenberg's cases, an older woman changed her will (testamentary capacity). Evaluation documented that although her cognitive impairments were mild, she changed the will based on a paranoid delusion that her son was trying to get her money. But, in fact, a second son who lived with her was stealing the money while poisoning her relationship with the first son. The attorney accepted the feedback but asked that no report be produced.

Verbal detailed discussion of issues in report with hiring attorney. Once an attorney requests a report, germane facts are determined by the expert and then crystallized for verbal discussion with the attorney (see the section Discovery). An expert's conclusion is only as good as the accuracy of his or her assessment, understanding of the history, and integration with the legal standards. Verbally discussing findings allows the expert and the attorney to double check facts but also ensures that the expert is addressing the legal standards and the capacity issues in question.

Sharing the report with a hiring attorney. The report should be shared only with the hiring attorney. Factual errors can be detected (e.g., incorrect dates on historical documents in the report) and corrected. The expert should realize that any other change, such as rewording the conclusion, is discoverable. That is, any written communications, including e-mail, between attorney and expert can be subpoenaed by the opposing attorney. To find that the opinion changed because of one attorney's comments would undermine the expert's credibility as an independent evaluator. Geropsychologists need to understand that different attorneys work in different ways. For many elder law attorneys working on probate court matters such as financial capacity, little is done by way of discovery (i.e., depositions, subpoena of records), but for others, a detailed discovery always includes a subpoena to see e-mails between the expert and the attorney who hired him or her.

Sharing results verbally during the deposition, hearing, or trial. Findings must be clear and concisely presented so the judge or jurors can understand what took place in the assessment and the expert's conclusions. Often, the expert will meet with the attorney earlier to discuss the questions and answers for the direct examination. The clinical expert must learn how to defend his report upon cross-examination in an effective and responsive way. Questions asked must be answered, but learning to incorporate testimony given on direct examination into the questions during cross-examination is critical.

Case Example 7

A clinician was called by an elder law attorney and asked to assess her client who did not want to lose autonomy with his money. Terms of the assessment were negotiated and medical records provided. An assessment was completed and at the direction of the attorney, a report was written. The contents of the report were shared during the clinician's testimony at a probate court in front of a judge. The following are excerpts from the report.

Historical background. Mr. V, born in 1931, was raised in childhood by his grandparents when he became very ill with the mumps and his parents' house was overly crowded with nine children. His grandparents only spoke Spanish, and as a result, Mr. V did very poorly in school because of his poor skills in the English language. After sixth grade, which he reports he completed but did not pass, he left traditional school and went to trade and art school. For several years he worked for a milkman and then worked in a small tool and die shop keeping track of the parts they made. He reported having excellent math skills, stating, "I am very good with numbers." After serving in the army for 2 years, he worked as a machinery repair man for 21 years at a dairy farm. He met his wife Mary through his job and they were married before his 30th birthday, and remained married (without children) until her death in 2010. During his 40s he followed his wife

to California where she was caring for her elderly parents. He got a job with Company Y and welded precious metals for them for 15 years. He then retired and quickly found himself bored. He began taking a class in stained glass, and it became his central hobby. Indeed, his talents led him to become an instructor to others who were beginning work with stained glass.

Upon his wife's rheumatoid arthritis and osteoporosis leading to her death, Mr. V sought out an attorney to update his trust, created in 1994 and updated a final time on March 22, 2011. At that time, Mr. V appointed his brother James V as a durable power of attorney for health care, and appointed his friend Kim B as his durable power of attorney for finances, with James V being his first alternate agent. James was also named as the executor for Mr. V's will. Mr. V moved back to his hometown in 2011, stating that his brother James told him that he would assist.

Mr. V was a patient at a local hospital several times throughout the early fall of 2012 and "was not following through with recommendations." His diagnoses included chest pain, increased cardiac enzymes, bradycardia, debility, and dementia. On October 17, 2012, Dr. M, a psychiatrist, evaluated Mr. V. Dr. M stated that Mr. V was "unable to rationally manipulate information or understand risks and benefits of his treatment" and concluded that Mr. V had early dementia and lacked capacity. After Mr. V returned home, James applied for conservatorship. Mr. V, outraged, hired an attorney who hired a clinician to perform a capacity assessment.

Neurocognitive abilities. Mr. V was fully cooperative with the assessment. He proved to be an excellent historian. Before testing, Mr. V reported that he suffered from significant memory problems although he thought his language and problem-solving abilities remained intact. Mr. V's percentile scores are presented in Exhibit 21.2. It is always an important issue for the geropsychologist to determine which set of normative data to use. It is a good exercise to apply a variety of norms to these scores and determine how, if at all, the different resulting scaled or percentile scores influence test interpretation.

Mr. V's reading score was in the low average range for his cohort, and he read at the second-grade

Exhibit 21.2
Test Score Summary (Percentile Scores)

WRAT IV Reading	34
Benton BTOT	1
Animal Naming Test	50
MAE Aural comprehension	40
Mattis Dementia Rating Scale–2	
Attention	50
Initiation/Perseveration	30
Construction	25
Conceptualization	40
Memory	3
Total	25
Visual Form Discrimination Test	34
Logical Memory I	1
Logical Memory II	3
Hooper Visual Organization Test	60
Boston Naming Test	25
Stroop Test	
Words	40
Color	65
Color/Word	55
Geriatric Depression Scale	15/30
Fuld Object Memory Evaluation	
Storage	1
Retrieval	1

equivalency level, entirely consistent with his report about his school history. On a cognitive screening test he scored in the impaired range, with some disorientation to date and time noted, and with strengths in verbal fluency for a semantic category. On a basic test of cognitive functioning, his overall score was in the low-average range, with mild deficits noted in recall of sentences and strengths in attention, initiation, and conceptualization. On tests of language comprehension and naming, Mr. V scored in the unimpaired range. Similarly on tests of visual matching and visual integration as well as tests of disinhibition, he scored in the unimpaired range, indicating strengths in visuospatial and executive functioning abilities. On tests of memory, even when objects were felt and seen, Mr. V scored in the moderate to severely impaired range for learning new information.

Mr. V scored in the moderately depressed range. He complained that since he came to Michigan, his mind has not been challenged, and he has not developed any significant social connections. He is bored and lonely, and wants to return to California and take up his stained glass work again.

Mr. V's neuropsychological test results are entirely consistent with the condition of mild cognitive impairment and major depression. Mild cognitive impairment is viewed as a condition that occurs before early dementia. In contrast to Dr. M's findings, Mr. V exhibited excellent awareness of his deficits and possessed good insight and problem-solving skills. Mr. V exhibits significant memory loss and depression but remains functionally capable of basic and advanced self-care.

Decisional abilities. Mr. V is paying his own bills with some assistance from his home aide. He has his checkbook, stamps, and return addresses in a specific box, which he retrieved and showed to me. His checkbook was neat, with recent checks numbered and appropriately labeled.

Mr. V clearly expressed his choice that his friend Kim B assist him with his bills and that he no longer work with his brother James. He described his rationale; his relationship with James has changed dramatically since James began assisting him. He described James as wanting to do things "his way" and that this extended to things like shopping as well as finances. He reported that he learned that James had withdrawn cash a few times ($200 each time) without Mr. V's permission and that Mr. V had no idea what happened to the money. Mr. V stated that James is very likely to use his money without his permission if left unchecked. Mr. V expressed a clear understanding of the choice he wants to make stating that James will be upset with this choice and is likely to be very hurt and angry. Mr. V also demonstrated an appreciation of the consequences of his choice stating that he is currently lonely most of the time and needs to be with people and that he feels downhearted and blue most of the time. He recognizes that the move to Michigan has not worked out and that he is currently isolated and suffering from the isolation. Mr. V's decision is consistent with his lifetime values of autonomy and a sense of personal control. Despite having limited reading abilities, Mr. V achieved significant status and accomplishment through his independence and hard work.

Awareness of deficit and ability to compensate. Mr. V demonstrates an excellent understanding of his memory deficits. As a result, he is working actively to compensate for these. He has hired a home aide who checks that he has taken his medication, who sits with him and helps to pay bills, and who socializes with him by going out to lunch. He uses his calendar to keep track of his appointments. He was called to confirm the assessment appointment 2 days ahead, and he was prepared for the evaluator when he came.

Undue influence. There was no relationship in which Mr. V was being unduly influenced and he had not lost any monies (except possibly to his brother James).

Integration with legal standards. In the state of Michigan, where this case was heard, clear and convincing evidence must be provided on two issues:

1. The individual is unable to manage property and business affairs effectively for reasons of mental illness or mental deficiency, and
2. The individual has property that will be wasted or dissipated unless proper management is provided.

Mr. V is not demonstrating an inability to manage his property or business affairs because of mental deficiency. Although he does demonstrate memory deficits, Mr. V exhibits significant strengths in problem-solving abilities and compensatory strategies, and for the past few weeks, since the petition for conservatorship, has indeed been managing his own finances effectively. This is entirely consistent with having mild cognitive impairment. The memory deficits in mild cognitive impairment are not yet severe enough to disrupt functional abilities. Furthermore, there is absolutely no evidence that Mr. V's property will be wasted or dissipated without a conservator. Approximately 20 months ago, Mr. V named a durable power of attorney for finances and has shown no propensity for unusual or extravagant spending. His estate value plus his property has remained stable.

Disposition and commentary. James' request for the appointment of a conservator was denied. This case demonstrates the fact that an older adult's incapacity at one time (e.g., in the hospital where Mr. V was clearly much more confused and disoriented) does not mean necessarily that there is permanent incapacity. Second, by rushing in without including Mr. V in discussion about the doctor's concerns, James damaged the relationship between the brothers, probably permanently.

A New Approach to Financial Decision-Making Capacity for Specific Sentinel Financial Decisions or Transactions

Framework. None of the available instruments directly assess financial judgment capacity and the underlying decisional abilities of the older adult. As will be described, we carried out an in-depth process to create a new evaluation tool, the Lichtenberg Financial Decision Rating Scale (LFDRS), an instrument that specifically focuses on the financial decision in question. First, a new conceptual model, Financial Decisional Abilities (FDA), was developed. FDA integrates the key contextual factors and intellectual factors influencing the major financial decisions older adults make. The model is illustrated in Figure 21.1.

Figure 21.1 illustrates the conceptual foundation for the LFDRS, which combines key contextual and intellectual factors influencing decision making. As can be seen in Figure 21.1, contextual factors include Financial Situational Awareness (FSA); Psychological Vulnerability (PV), including loneliness and depression; Undue Influence (I); and Financial Exploitation (FE). Contextual factors have a direct

Key Components of the Financial Decisional Abilities Model

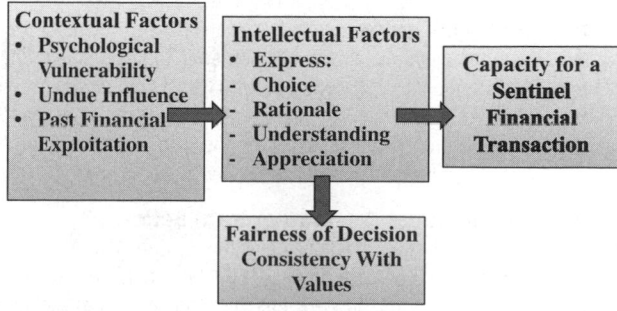

FIGURE 21.1. Key components of the financial decisional abilities model.

influence on the intellectual factors associated with decisional abilities for a sentinel financial transaction or decision (see Figure 21.1).

Intellectual factors refer to functional abilities needed for financial decision-making capacity and include an older adult's ability to (a) express a Choice (C), (b) communicate the Rationale (R) for the choice, (c) demonstrate an Understanding (U) of the choice, (d) demonstrate an Appreciation (A) of the relevant factors involved in that choice, and (e) having the choice be consistent with past cherished Values (V). The intellectual factors, unless they are overwhelmed by the impact of the contextual factors, are the most proximal and central to determining the integrity of financial decisional abilities.

LFDRS construction. Lichtenberg developed an initial conceptual model drawing on decisional abilities work in general and financial exploitation work specifically; this model was used to create a set of questions to generate the LFDRS. Guided by financial exploitation and assessment tool experts Ken Conrad and Madelyn Iris, the group pulled together two groups of experts: those expert in financial capacity work and those who work directly with older adults making sentinel financial decisions and transactions on a daily basis (e.g., law enforcement, bank personnel, adult protective services case workers, financial planners, elder law attorneys). Separate conference calls were held with the group of experts, presenting the model and questions. On the basis of their extensive feedback, the final conceptual model was refined as was a broader set of questions and a multiple choice format. Three months after the first set of conference calls were held, new versions of the LFDRS were distributed and new conference calls were set up to receive a second round of feedback. The feedback given during the second round of calls indicated a need for only minor revisions, and the LFDRS thus was completed soon afterward.

The final scale consists of 65 multiple choice questions with separate sections measuring financial situational awareness, psychological vulnerability, undue influence, past financial exploitation, and intellectual factors. Final instructions for administration and scoring of the LFDRS also were completed at this time. Sample items from the LFDRS are provided in Exhibit 21.3. (A copy of the full

---

Exhibit 21.3
Sample Items From the Lichtenberg Financial Decision-Making Rating Scale

Financial situational awareness
- What are your current sources of income?
- How worried are you about having enough money to pay for things?
- Who manages your money day to day?
- Do you regret or worry about financial decisions you have made recently?
- Are you helping anyone financially on a regular basis?
- Have you gifted or lent money to someone in the past couple of year?

Psychological vulnerability
- How often do you wish you had someone to talk to about financial decisions or plans?
- Have you recently lost someone who was a confidante?
- How often do you feel downhearted or blue about your financial situation or decisions?
- Is your memory, thinking skills, or ability to reason with regard to finances worse than a year ago?
- When it comes to making financial decisions, how often are you treated with less courtesy and respect than other people?

Sentinel financial decision or transaction
- What current major financial decisions or transactions are you intending to make?
- What are your personal (financial) goals with this transaction?
- Now and over time, how will this decision and/or transaction impact you financially?
- How much risk is there that this transaction could result in a loss of funds?
- Who will be adversely affected by the current decision/transaction? How will they react?

- To what extent did you consult with anyone before making the financial decision?
- Who did you discuss this with?
- Would someone who knows you well say this decision was unusual for you?

Financial exploitation
- Have you ever had checks missing from or out of sequence in your checkbook?
- Do you have a credit or debit card that you allow someone else to use?
- Has anyone ever signed your name to a check?
- How often in the past few months has someone asked you for money?

Undue influence
- Have you had any conflicts with anyone about the way you spend money or to whom you give money?
- Has anyone asked you to change your will?
- Has anyone recently told you to stop getting financial advice from someone?
- Was this transaction your idea or did someone else suggest it?
- Did this person drive or accompany you to carry out this financial transaction?

scale along with instructions for administration and scoring is available from Peter A. Lichtenberg.) Ten experts rated the financial integrity of five older adults after watching videotaped administrations of the LFDRS. Very good to excellent interrater agreement was noted.

CONCLUSION

Capacity issues are important to assess and reassess in the management of chronic conditions in later life because decisions made during this period often include both financial and health care decisions. Capacity is influenced by a number of factors causing it to vary in the same person with the same presentation but in different settings. Capacity will vary across individuals, depending on history and values, and capacity will vary across the setting of the legal jurisdiction. Older adults exhibit a diversity of education, culture, and health or functional experiences that also influence capacity. Long-term care decisions often include decisions about placement, financial control, and end-of-life issues for individuals and families. Taking all of these and other complex factors and integrating them into a reliable and informed assessment is the task of a geropsychologist who is asked to perform a capacity assessment. Our goal for this chapter was to describe the research base for capacity assessment work, provide an overview of some of the most-often used tools, identify gaps in knowledge, and review some of the

capacity assessment practices that currently are available.

References

Acierno, R., Hernandez, M. A., Amstadter, A. B., Resnick, H. S., Steve, K., Muzzy, W., & Kilpatrick, D. G. (2010). Prevalence and correlates of emotional, physical, sexual, and financial abuse and potential neglect in the United States: The National Elder Mistreatment Study. *American Journal of Public Health, 100*, 292–297. doi:10.2105/AJPH.2009. 163089

Alexander, M. P. (1988). Clinical determination of mental competence: A theory and a retrospective study. *Archives of Neurology, 45*, 23–26. doi:10.1001/ archneur.1988.00520250029013

American Bar Association Commission on Law and Aging and American Psychological Association. (2008). *Assessment of older adults with diminished capacity: A handbook for psychologists.* Washington, DC: Author.

Appelbaum, P. S., & Grisso, T. (1988). Assessing patients' capacities to consent to treatment. *New England Journal of Medicine, 319*, 1635–1638. doi:10.1056/ NEJM198812223192504

Baker, R. R., Lichtenberg, P. A., & Moye, J. (1998). A practice guideline for assessment of competency and capacity of the older adult. *Professional Psychology: Research and Practice, 29*, 149–154. doi:10.1037/0735-7028.29.2.149

Beach, S. R., Schulz, R., Castle, N. G., & Rosen, J. (2010). Financial exploitation and psychological mistreatment among older adults: Differences between African Americans and non-African Americans in a population-based survey. *Gerontologist, 50*, 744–757. doi:10.1093/geront/gnq053

Blancato, R. B. (2012). Elder abuse and the elder justice movement. *Generations, 36,* 9–11.

Brisk, W. J. (2012). An elder law attorney's view of the financial competence of older adults. *Generations, 36,* 88–93.

Conrad, K. J., Iris, M., Ridings, J. W., Langley, K., & Wilber, K. H. (2010). Self-report measure of financial exploitation of older adults. *Gerontologist, 50,* 758–773. doi:10.1093/geront/gnq054

Dong, X., & Simon, M. A. (2012). Elder abuse: Existing national policies and programs to defend the rights and safety of older adults. *Public Policy and Aging Report, 22,* 1–7.

Drane, J. F. (1984). Competency to give an informed consent: A model for making clinical assessments. *JAMA, 252,* 925–927. doi:10.1001/jama.1984.033 50070043021

Edelstein, B. (1999). *Hopemont Capacity Assessment Interview manual and scoring guide.* Morgantown: West Virginia University.

Edelstein, B. (2000). Challenges in the assessment of decision-making capacity. *Journal of Aging Studies, 14,* 423–437. doi:10.1016/S0890-4065(00)80006-7

Etchells, E., Darzins, P., Silberfeld, M., Singer, P. A., McKenny, J., Naglie, G., . . . Strang, D. (1999). Assessment of patient capacity to consent to treatment. *Journal of General Internal Medicine, 14,* 27–34. doi:10.1046/j.1525-1497.1999.00277.x

Fitten, L. J., Lusky, R., & Hamann, C. (1990). Assessing treatment decision-making capacity in elderly nursing home residents. *Journal of the American Geriatrics Society, 38,* 1097–1104.

Fitten, L. J., & Waite, M. S. (1990). Impact of medical hospitalization on treatment decision-making capacity in the elderly. *Archives of Internal Medicine, 150,* 1717–1721. doi:10.1001/archinte.1990.0004003 1717022

Flint, L. A., Sudore, R. L., & Widera, E. (2012). Assessing Financial Capacity Impairment in Older Adults. *Generations, 36,* 59–65.

Grisso, T. (1994). Clinical assessments for legal competence of older adults. In M. Storandt & G. R. VandenBos (Eds.), *Neuropsychological assessment of dementia and depression in older adults: A clinician's guide* (pp. 119–139). Washington, DC: American Psychological Association. doi:10.1037/10157-006

Grisso, T. (2003). *Evaluating competencies: Forensic assessments and instruments* (2nd ed.). New York, NY: Kluwer Academic/Plenum.

Grisso, T., Appelbaum, P. S., & Hill-Fotouhi, C. (1997). The MacCAT-T: A clinical tool to assess patients' capacities to make treatment decisions. *Psychiatric Services, 48,* 1415–1419.

Gurrera, R. J., Moye, J., Karel, M. J., Azar, A. R., & Armesto, J. C. (2006). Cognitive performance predicts treatment decisional abilities in mild to moderate dementia. *Neurology, 66,* 1367–1372. doi:10.1212/01.wnl.0000210527.13661.d1

Gutheil, T. G., & Bursztajn, H. (1986). Clinicians' guidelines for assessing and presenting subtle forms of patient incompetence in legal settings. *American Journal of Psychiatry, 143,* 1020–1023.

Jackson, S. L., & Hafemeister, T. L. (2012). APS investigation across four types of elder maltreatment. *Journal of Adult Protection, 14,* 82–92. doi:10.1108/14668201211217530

Jones, R. C., & Holden, T. (2004). A guide to assessing decision-making capacity. *Cleveland Clinic Journal of Medicine, 71,* 971–975. doi:10.3949/ccjm.71.12.971

Kapp, M. B., & Mossman, D. (1996). Measuring decisional capacity: Cautions on the construction of a capacimeter. *Psychology, Public Policy, and Law, 2,* 73–95. doi:10.1037/1076-8971.2.1.73

Kemp, B. J., & Mosqueda, L. A. (2005). Elder financial abuse: An evaluation framework and supporting evidence. *Journal of the American Geriatrics Society, 53,* 1123–1127. doi:10.1111/j.1532-5415.2005.53353.x

Kershaw, M. M., & Webber, L. S. (2008). Assessment of financial competence. *Psychiatry, Psychology, and Law, 15,* 40–55. doi:10.1080/13218710701873965

Kim, S. Y., Caine, E. D., Currier, G. W., Leibovici, A., & Ryan, J. M. (2001). Assessing the competence of persons with Alzheimer's disease in providing informed consent for participation in research. *American Journal of Psychiatry, 158,* 712–717. doi:10.1176/appi.ajp.158.5.712

Laumann, E. O., Leitsch, S. A., & Waite, L. J. (2008). Elder mistreatment in the United States: Prevalence estimates from a nationally representative study. *The Journals of Gerontology, Series B: Psychological Sciences and Social Sciences, 63,* 248–254. doi:10.1093/geronb/63.4.S248

Lichtenberg, P. A. (1998). *Mental health practice in geriatric healthcare settings.* New York, NY: Haworth Press.

Lichtenberg, P. A. (2012). Misdiagnosis of Alzheimer's disease: Cases of capacity. *Clinical Gerontologist, 35,* 42–56. doi:10.1080/07317115.2011.626516

Lichtenberg, P. A., & Luborsky, M. L. (in press). Alzheimer's diagnosis on trial: Ethical consequences at the intersection of health and law. *Handbook of communication.* New York, NY: Wiley.

Lichtenberg, P. A., Stickney, L., & Paulson, D. (2013). Is psychological vulnerability related to the experience of fraud in older adults? *Clinical Gerontologist, 36,* 132–146. doi:10.1080/07317115. 2012.749323

Marson, D. C. (2001). Loss of financial competency in dementia: Conceptual and empirical approaches. *Aging, Neuropsychology, and Cognition, 8,* 164–181. doi:10.1076/anec.8.3.164.827

Marson, D. C., Chatterjee, A., Ingram, K. K., & Harrell, L. E. (1996). Toward a neurologic model of competency: Cognitive predictors of capacity to consent in Alzheimer's disease using three different legal standards. *Neurology, 46,* 666–672. doi:10.1212/WNL.46.3.666

Marson, D. C., Earnst, K. S., & Jamil, F. (2000). Consistency of physicians' legal standard and personal judgments of competency in patients with Alzheimer's disease. *Journal of the American Geriatrics Society, 48,* 911–918.

Marson, D. C., Ingram, K. K., Cody, H. A., & Harrell, L. E. (1995). Assessing the competency of patients with Alzheimer's disease under different legal standards: A prototype instrument. *Archives of Neurology, 52,* 949–954. doi:10.1001/archneur.1995.0054034 0029010

Marson, D. C., Martin, R. C., Wadley, V., Griffith, H. R., Snyder, S., Goode, P. S., . . . Harrell, L. E. (2009). Clinical interview assessment of financial capacity in older adults with mild cognitive impairment and Alzheimer's disease. *Journal of the American Geriatrics Society, 57,* 806–814. doi:10.1111/j.1532-5415.2009.02202.x

Marson, D. C., McInturff, B., Hawkins, L., Bartolucci, A., & Harrell, L. E. (1997). Consistency of physician judgments of capacity to consent in mild Alzheimer's disease. *Journal of the American Geriatrics Society, 45,* 453–457.

Martin, R., Griffith, H. R., Belue, K., Harrell, L., Zamrini, E., Anderson, B., . . . Marson, D. (2008). Declining financial capacity in patients with mild Alzheimer disease: A one-year longitudinal study. *American Journal of Geriatric Psychiatry, 16,* 209–219. doi:10.1097/JGP.0b013e318157cb00

MetLife Mature Market Institute. (2009). *Broken trust: Elders, family, and finances.* New York, NY: Metropolitan Life Insurance Company.

MetLife Mature Market Institute. (2011). *The MetLife study of elder financial abuse: Crimes of occasion, desperation, and predation against America's elders.* New York, NY: Metropolitan Life Insurance Company.

Moberg, P. J., & Kniele, K. (2006). Evaluation of competency: Ethical considerations for neuropsychologists. *Applied Neuropsychology, 13,* 101–114. doi:10.1207/s15324826an1302_5

Moberg, P. J., & Rick, J. (2008). Decision-making capacity and competency in the elderly: A clinical and neuropsychological perspective. *NeuroRehabilitation, 23,* 403–413.

Moore, D. J., Palmer, B. W., Patterson, T. L., & Jeste, D. V. (2007). A review of performance-based measures of functional living skills. *Journal of Psychiatric Research, 41,* 97–118. doi:10.1016/j.jpsychires.2005.10.008

Moye, J., & Braun, M. (2010). Assessment of capacity. In P. A. Lichtenberg (Ed.), *Handbook of assessment in clinical gerontology* (2nd ed., pp. 581–618). New York, NY: Elsevier.

Moye, J., Gurrera, R. J., Karel, M. J., Edelstein, B., & O'Connell, C. (2006). Empirical advances in the assessment of the capacity to consent to medical treatment: Clinical implications and research needs. *Clinical Psychology Review, 26,* 1054–1077. doi:10.1016/j.cpr.2005.04.013

Moye, J., Karel, M. J., Azar, A. R., & Gurrera, R. J. (2004). Capacity to consent to treatment: Empirical comparison of three instruments in older adults with and without dementia. *Gerontologist, 44,* 166–175. doi:10.1093/geront/44.2.166

Moye, J., & Marson, D. C. (2007). Assessment of decision-making capacity in older adults: An emerging area of practice and research. *The Journals of Gerontology, Series B: Psychological Sciences and Social Sciences, 62,* 3–11. doi:10.1093/geronb/62.1.P3

Nerenberg, L., Davies, M., & Navarro, A. E. (2012). In pursuit of a useful framework to champion elder justice. *Generations, 36,* 89–96.

Okonkwo, O., Griffith, H. R., Vance, D. E., Marson, D. C., Ball, K. K., & Wadley, V. G. (2009). Awareness of functional difficulties in mild cognitive impairment: A multidomain assessment approach. *Journal of the American Geriatrics Society, 57,* 978–984. doi:10.1111/j.1532-5415.2009.02261.x

Pérez-Stable, E. J., Nápoles-Springer, A., & Miramontes, J. M. (1997). The effects of ethnicity and language on medical outcomes of patients with hypertension or diabetes. *Medical Care, 35,* 1212–1219. doi:10.1097/00005650-199712000-00005

Pinsker, D. M., Pachana, N. A., Wilson, J., Tilse, C., & Byrne, G. J. (2010). Financial capacity in older adults: A review of clinical assessment approaches and considerations. *Clinical Gerontologist, 33,* 332–346. doi:10.1080/07317115.2010.502107

Pruchno, R. A., Smyer, M. A., Rose, M. S., Hartman-Stein, P. E., & Henderson-Laribee, D. L. (1995). Competence of long-term care residents to participate in decisions about their medical care: A brief, objective assessment. *Gerontologist, 35,* 622–629. doi:10.1093/geront/35.5.622

Roth, L. H., Meisel, C. A., & Lidz, C. A. (1977). Tests of competency to consent to treatment. *American Journal of Psychiatry, 134,* 279–284.

Sessums, L. L., Zembrzuska, H., & Jackson, J. L. (2011). Does this patient have medical decision-making capacity? *JAMA, 306,* 420–427. doi:10.1001/jama.2011.1023

Sherod, M. G., Griffith, H. R., Copeland, J., Belue, K., Krzywanski, S., Zamrini, E. Y., . . . Marson, D. C. (2009). Neurocognitive predictors of financial capacity across the dementia spectrum: Normal aging, mild cognitive impairment, and Alzheimer's disease. *Journal of the International Neuropsychological Society, 15,* 258–267. doi:10.1017/S1355617709090365

Shulman, K. I., Cohen, C. A., & Hull, I. (2005). Psychiatric issues in retrospective challenges of testamentary capacity. *International Journal of Geriatric Psychiatry, 20,* 63–69. doi:10.1002/gps.1257

Stiegel, L. A. (2012). An overview of elder financial exploitation. *Generations, 36,* 73–80.

Sturman, E. D. (2005). The capacity to consent to treatment and research: A review of standardized assessment tools. *Clinical Psychology Review, 25,* 954–974. doi:10.1016/j.cpr.2005.04.010

Teaster, P. B., Roberto, K. A., Migliaccio, J. N., Timmerman, S., & Blancato, R. B. (2012). Elder financial abuse in the news. *Public Policy and Aging Report, 22,* 33–36.

Tymchuk, A. J., Ouslander, J. G., Rahbar, B., & Fitten, J. (1988). Medical decision-making among elderly people in long term care. *Gerontologist, 28,* 59–63. doi:10.1093/geront/28.Suppl.59

White, L., Small, B. J., Petrovitch, H., Ross, G. W., Masaki, K., Abbott, R. D., . . . Markesbery, W. (2005). Recent clinical-pathologic research on the causes of dementia in late life: Update from the Honolulu-Asia Aging Study. *Journal of Geriatric Psychiatry and Neurology, 18,* 224–227. doi:10.1177/0891988705281872

CHAPTER 22

GEROPSYCHOLOGICAL PRACTICE WITH PEOPLE NEAR THE END OF LIFE

Brian D. Carpenter

Psychologists who work with older adults near the end of life have an opportunity to help people at one of the most important phases of life. Although it might sound odd to think of it this way, death is a fundamental developmental milestone, along with puberty, completing formal education, finding a life partner, starting a family, and retirement, among other milestones. Obviously it is the last developmental milestone, but it is nonetheless a central event, one that is shaped by the lifelong events that precede it, and one that can be navigated with varying degrees of success. At the risk of burdening people near the end of life (and the clinicians helping them), how individuals navigate dying and death can be a capstone, a bookend to birth that encapsulates, distills, and summarizes all that came before. And so, it is the job and privilege of a clinical geropsychologist to help people end life with as much insight, coherence, and dignity as possible.

It is worthwhile to begin by recognizing that the "end of life" is a vague description of a phase that can happen at many different ages, for many different reasons. We advance toward death from the moment we are born, but of course some people are closer to death than others. Yet because a 60-year-old with Stage IV cancer may have just weeks to live, but an 85-year-old with mild hypertension many years, age, by itself, is of limited help in characterizing when the end of life begins. Instead, the end of life is most often set in motion by less predictable factors, such as an event, some type of medical illness (acute or chronic) or traumatic event (insidious or catastrophic) that triggers a cascade of physiological deterioration and functional impairment leading to death. The end of life can come quickly following a stroke, a heart attack, or a car accident; or slowly, with advancing dementia, worsening chronic pulmonary insufficiency, or gradual but irreversible weight loss. But dying and death are so much more than the biological process. What makes dying and death so clinically complex, so psychologically rich, so socially challenging, and so spiritually demanding is that dying and death are the confluence of multiple processes—a final bio-psycho-social-spiritual nexus.

This chapter summarizes some of the opportunities and challenges of providing psychological services to people near the end of life. As I will discuss shortly, mental health professionals in general, and psychologists in particular, are relative latecomers to end-of-life care, even though clinicians as early as Freud (1918) addressed the topic. But given their disciplinary scope, psychologists are ideally positioned to help people who are dying. They are adept at conducting a holistic assessment of psychological well-being, although the end of life presents some unique challenges to the process of assessment and its accuracy. Psychologists also have a range of tools for psychological treatment to address discrete symptoms as well as more broad concerns people may face as they are dying. Psychotherapy, too, may look somewhat different when undertaken with people who are near death. Despite recent attention on end-of-life care, much more research is needed to substantiate the assessments and treatments that psychologists use, and this is another opportunity.

http://dx.doi.org/10.1037/14459-022
APA Handbook of Clinical Geropsychology: Vol. 2. Assessment, Treatment, and Issues of Later Life,
P. A. Lichtenberg and B. T. Mast (Editors-in-Chief)

So this chapter outlines some of what is known—about psychological assessment and treatment and about research gaps—and can be a starting point for additional professional development.

To begin with a bit of recent history about psychology's role in end-of-life care, in 1997 the U.S. Supreme Court issued a ruling in *Vacco v. Quill* (1997) upholding a New York state ban on physician-assisted suicide. The American Psychological Association (APA) issued two resolutions at that time, the first stating APA's neutral position on physician-assisted suicide, the second encouraging more research and training to promote quality of life and attention to mental health issues at the end of life (Farberman, 1997). APA also established a working group charged with addressing the relative absence of psychologists in end-of-life care, recommending methods to increase psychology's visibility and role in decision making and quality of care. An Ad Hoc Committee on End-of-Life Issues subsequently was created to implement recommendations made by the Working Group (for additional history, see APA Working Group on Assisted Suicide and End-of-Life Decisions, 2000). One outcome was a prescient and still influential paper by Haley, Larson, Kasl-Godley, Neimeyer, and Kwilosz (2003) that outlined roles for psychologists in end-of-life care and the broad set of issues facing clinicians.

Historically, the Veterans Administration (VA) has been at the forefront of many developments in health care and that has been true for end-of-life care as well. As long ago as 1992 the VA begin to implement a policy ensuring access to hospice care to all veterans. Another milestone was the Training and Program Assessment for Palliative Care (TAPC) project conducted in 2001, which led to the creation of postdoctoral Interprofessional Palliative Care Fellowships at six VA medical centers. Positions for psychology trainees were earmarked in that program, and it remains an important training conduit for psychologists. By 2003, the VA mandated that all facilities have a Palliative Care Consultation Team (PCCT) in place, and many of those teams have at least a part-time psychologist, although the precise configuration varies from one medical center to another. Outside the VA system, psychologists have played an important role for many years in other health care arenas in which patients, families, and other providers confront dying and death, including hematology and oncology, organ transplant, pulmonary, and neurology, to name a few, in settings ranging from acute care to long-term care. Many psychologists may have been providing end-of-life care for decades, although that might not have been their exclusive domain of practice and they might not have received formal training in that focus area, much like many psychologists who end up working with older adults may not consider themselves geropsychologists.

At about the same time that psychology was formalizing its presence in end-of-life care, related mental health disciplines were intensifying their work in the area as well. Within psychiatry, the Academy of Psychosomatic Medicine (1998) issued a position statement on psychiatric aspects of end-of-life care, and the American Psychiatric Association (2001) issued a similar document on essential features of end-of-life care. Within social work, 2002 brought a national summit on end-of-life and palliative care. Following the summit, the National Association of Social Workers (2004) issued practice standards for palliative and end-of-life care and a subsequent update for practitioners in hospice and palliative care. Because their presence is mandated in regulations by both the VA and Medicare, among the mental health disciplines, social workers have had the most consistent presence in end-of-life care.

Turning now to psychology's role specifically, it might be worth asking, what is it that people need to be mentally healthy as they near the end of life? And the question that follows, how is it that psychologists can help? One place to start to answer these questions is to consider one broad definition of mental health by the World Health Organization (2001): "A state of well-being in which every individual realizes his or her own abilities, can cope with the normal stresses of life, can work productively and fruitfully, and is able to make a contribution to her or his community" (p. 1). First, it is worth noting that some aspects of this definition may be different for people near the end of life compared with people who are not. "Abilities" may refer to more circumscribed but still important skills (e.g., basic self-care, meaningful communication); "normal stresses" may come to include a unique set of responsibilities (e.g., managing complicated and uncomfortable treatments, devoting substantial time to coordinating medical appointments); being "productive" may not involve paid work but rather other meaningful pursuits (e.g., taking the initiative to get one's affairs in order); and "contributions" may focus closer to home (e.g., helping in the household in ways that are still possible, sharing one's knowledge and experience with others). Second, note that this definition focuses not just on the *absence* of significant psychological distress, but also on the *presence* of life-fulfilling activities that promote flourishing (Keyes, 2002), even as death nears. It is easy for clinicians to be drawn exclusively to the significance of the end, when there is still a need to make the most of *life* up until that end. Psychologists have an obvious role to play in addressing classic mental health syndromes (e.g., depression, anxiety). But, in addition, our treatments can enhance quality of life more broadly by helping patients clarify goals and values, adopt beneficial coping skills, use effective communication strategies, maximize remaining abilities, and grapple with questions about identity and meaning in the face of mortality.

Another distinction worth noting is how end-of-life issues may differ for older adults compared with younger people. Basically this means thinking about the biological, psychological, and social changes that come with aging for all individuals, but with severe illness superimposed on them. For instance, the challenge of a life-limiting medical illness may be compounded by the presence of common, age-related comorbidities such as diabetes, chronic obstructive pulmonary disease, and arthritis that continue to demand attention. Likewise, by virtue of the number of years they have lived and their place in the life span, older adults may have more life experiences to draw on for coping, may have a different time orientation (i.e., death as more expected or "on time"), and may have different emotional regulation skills. From a social perspective, older adults may have gained experience with death by watching their friends and family members die before them but also may be more socially isolated because of those losses. There also may be cohort differences in attitudes about death, such as the degree to which

death is discussed, and in attitudes about psychological distress, such as the appropriateness of talking about one's fears and anxieties. More pragmatically, older adults may have access to age-specific programs (e.g., Medicare and its hospice benefit; Social Security) and resources (e.g., local area agencies on aging). Altogether, an older adult approaching death may have both advantages and disadvantages relative to younger people, but it probably is the case that there is just as much diversity *among* older adults in this regard as there are differences *between* age groups.

ASSESSMENT

Psychological assessment with people near the end of life includes gathering wide-ranging information from patients, family members, other health care providers, and medical records. This can begin with a thorough clinical interview with patients, investigating typical psychological symptoms, such as depression and anxiety, but also medical diagnoses, treatments, social support networks, work status, financial considerations, and spiritual background. In a word, these are all the usual domains reflected in a clinical interview, although obtained from people who may be unusually vulnerable and sometimes quite limited in their ability to provide information. A primary consideration in the process is understanding the patient's capabilities: sensory impairments that could limit their ability to hear questions or read materials, receptive or expressive communication limitations that influence the ability to understand what is being asked and to share information, stamina to sit through a lengthy evaluation, and even level and variability of consciousness in patients who are heavily sedated or very near death. Clinicians can consider ways to maximize a patient's ability to participate in an assessment. For instance, make sure assistive devices and technologies, such as reading glasses, large-print format materials, and hearing aids, are available and operating. Ensure a quiet, distraction-free, comfortable environment. Space assessments over multiple sessions to avoid fatigue. Time assessments to match the time of day when patients have the most energy, when their pain is well controlled, when they have had a recent opportunity to use the bathroom, and when competing appointments are not likely to disrupt the evaluation. Additional suggestions are offered in the classic resource by Knight (2004) on conducting psychotherapy with older adults.

The location of the patient also can present assessment challenges. On the one hand, patients at home have the benefit of being in a comfortable, familiar environment, easing the assessment process, although home is also a place where interruptions might be more likely (e.g., telephones, the doorbell, visiting neighbors). On the other hand, patients in long-term care, rehabilitation, or acute inpatient settings might be easier for a psychologist to locate and schedule for an assessment, captive as patients are in those settings, although the physical milieu may not be ideal (e.g., overhead paging and alarm systems interrupt, roommates complicate confidentiality) and institutional rhythms can be inconvenient (e.g., staff on rounds can appear midevaluation, dinner arrives at a peculiar time, a technician arrives for a portable x-ray during a sensitive discussion). Some of the same challenges are present in inpatient settings, where most end-of-life care is provided or at least initiated. Although it takes extra planning, clinicians can maximize privacy by knowing when roommates will be out for tests or appointments, when family conclude their visits, and when there is a lull in rounds and fewer interruptions likely by other members of the care team. Nursing staff can be invaluable in providing suggestions on when is the best time to meet with a patient (at least from an institutional point of view). In my experience, most colleagues from other disciplines are quite willing to absent themselves from the room when they know a weighty conversation is about to take place. Clinicians also face the challenge of helping patients and family members understand who they are and what role they play when the cast of characters in most inpatient settings is large and often changing from day to day, if not hour to hour. When appropriate, leaving a business card or some identifying information with the patient can be a useful prompt and lets colleagues know you are involved. Location aside, information from family and staff proxies may help fill in the gaps, but those sources are limited to some extent

by their second-person perspective and by the fact that they themselves may be under tremendous stress.

To return to the patient's abilities again, energy level is something to consider for assessment in general. When patients are compromised, it is worth asking what is essential to learn about the patient to promote quality of care. When patients have a limited amount of time and energy, and when that time and energy could be better spent on the activities that enhance psychological well-being, psychologists may accept that they can work with a more circumscribed set of questions and answers. An initial decision, then, is what to target in an assessment. It may be tempting to overlook the need to assess for frank psychopathology in a patient with severe illness when medical problems seem so dominant and pressing. That would be a mistake. Base rates for psychiatric symptoms in medically compromised samples are substantial. For instance, in one review of symptom prevalence in patients with cancer, AIDS, heart disease, and chronic obstructive pulmonary disease, maximal prevalence rates of anxiety ranged from 34% to 79% (mean = 64%) and rates of depression ranged from 36% to 82% (mean = 65%; Solano, Gomes, & Higginson, 2006). In another study with hospice patients, 19.3% qualified for a diagnosis of major depressive disorder and 36.3% met criteria for any depressive syndrome (Rayner et al., 2011). Therefore, when possible, it is important to conduct a thorough evaluation for all potential Axis I and Axis II disorders. A structured diagnostic interview, such as the Structured Clinical Interview for *Diagnostic and Statistical Manual of Mental Disorders, Fourth Edition, Text Revision* (*DSM–IV–TR*; American Psychiatric Association, 2000) Axis I and II Disorders (SCID–I and SCID–II; First, Gibbon, Spitzer, Williams, & Benjamin, 1997; First, Spitzer, Gibbon, & Williams, 1996) may be too detailed and burdensome for debilitated patients to complete. Brief alternatives are the Mini-International Neuropsychiatric Interview (Sheehan et al., 1998) and the Personality Diagnostic Questionnaire (PDQ–4; Hyler et al., 1988), which can be used to screen for Axis I and Axis II disorders, respectively, allowing for follow-up with specific SCID modules when indicated. In circumstances in which patients may not be able to complete an extensive structured interview, a focused clinical interview, reviewing key diagnostic criteria, may be most practical.

A variety of self-report questionnaires also can be used effectively with patients who have more advanced illness. The Hospital Anxiety and Depression Scale (HADS; Snaith, 2003; Zigmond & Snaith, 1983) is a widely used, well-validated, 14-item measure of anxiety and depression suitable for medical patients. The advantages of the HADS include its content coverage for both anxiety and depression, relative brevity, and availability in more than 60 languages. The Patient Health Questionnaire (Kroenke, Spitzer, & Williams, 2001) is a nine-item scale to measure the severity of depressive symptoms. It is well validated in a range of medical populations, it is brief, and its clinical cut-points can be used to make a tentative depression diagnosis (Kroenke & Spitzer, 2002). The Geriatric Depression Scale (GDS; Yesavage et al., 1982–1983) is likely familiar to many geropsychologists, and it, too, has its place in assessment with patients near the end of life. In terms of anxiety, the Geriatric Anxiety Inventory (Pachana et al., 2007) is a 20-item self-report or nurse-administered, multidimensional measure of anxiety that uses a simple dichotomous response scale to ease administration. It has excellent psychometric properties and was developed specifically for older adults. The Beck Anxiety Inventory (Beck & Steer, 1993) contains 21 items rated on a three-point scale, although there has been some concern in the literature about its overlap with depression and the validity of its somatic items as markers of anxiety in medically ill populations (Krasucki, Howard, & Mann, 1998; Wetherell & Gatz, 2005).

One caveat associated with these instruments—true for individual-scale items as well as individual *DSM* diagnostic criteria—is that they may conflate psychiatric and physical symptoms. Low energy, poor appetite, and disrupted sleep may reflect depression or the effects of anemia, thyroid dysfunction, cancer, chemotherapy, and radiation. Muscle tension, heart palpitations, dizziness, and dyspnea may reflect anxiety or the effects of chronic obstructive pulmonary disease, hyperglycemia, hyperthyroidism, drug side effects, or treatments that evoke anxiety through operant conditioning (e.g., anxiety conditioned to occur before radiation treatment). Likewise, some overt behaviors might logically change with advanced illness (e.g., crying, dropping activities). Therefore, the validity of some items and criteria may be questionable, and a focus on cognitive symptoms may turn out to be most informative (i.e., hopelessness, worthlessness, guilt, fear, dread; APA, 2007; Cusin, Yang, Yeung, & Fava, 2009; Simon & Von Korff, 2006).

Clinicians occasionally may find themselves in a circumstance when they would like to obtain a standardized assessment of other constructs beyond psychiatric symptoms alone, either to identify possible clinical targets for treatment, to establish a baseline at the beginning, or to monitor treatment progress. A relatively concise and useful scale to measure several facets of overall functioning is the Outcome Questionnaire (Lambert et al., 1996), which has subscales that address symptom distress (concentrating on depression and anxiety), interpersonal functioning, and social roles. There are 30- and 45-item versions, both available in multiple languages and well validated, and a 10-item screening version. Shorter still is the 12-item General Health Questionnaire (Golderberg & Williams, 1998), which can be used to screen for general psychological distress experienced over the past few weeks.

A more extensive resource is the National Institutes of Health–sponsored Patient Reported Outcomes Measurement Information System (PROMIS; http://www.nihpromis.org). PROMIS is a collection of self-report assessment tools that covers physical health (pain, fatigue, sleep, and physical functioning), mental health (depression, anxiety, anger, applied cognition, alcohol use, and psychosocial illness impact), and social health (satisfaction with roles and activities, support, isolation, and companionship). The advantages of these instruments is that they can be used with patients across a wide variety of diseases; have high reliability and validity; are flexible in terms of method of administration; and are inclusive with respect to literacy, language, physical function, and place in the life course. The utility of the instruments mentioned previously extends beyond psychologists' work with patients who are dying to include assessment and treatment with family members, both before and after death.

Several diagnostic complexities arise in end-of-life care that deserve special note. One is making the distinction in patients between depression and expected preparatory grief. Some depression-like symptoms are common and perhaps natural as death approaches, so to characterize those experiences as pathological overdramatizes what might be a normative process. Kasl-Godley (2011) provided a useful framework for differentiating the two, contrasting their presentation along several facets. On the one hand, depression is unremitting, of constant intensity, with prominent anhedonia and worthlessness, and pessimism about the future. On the other hand, preparatory grief is more intermittent, variable in its intensity, with some ability to experience of pleasure retained, along with preserved self-image and some positive anticipation of future events.

A second conundrum facing psychologists is differentiating a desire for hastened death from suicidal ideation. In both, patients may feel and express a hope that death comes quickly. Symptom burden may be high, and patients may reach a state wherein the conditions of life are perceived as worse than death. When a patient says, "If I went to sleep tonight and didn't wake up in the morning, I'd be fine with that," it could reflect an acceptance of and a genuine readiness for death. Or it could reflect a type of passive suicidal ideation. As Kasl-Godley (2011) noted, key differences include whether the thought is continuous and whether it is associated with a concrete plan to achieve the hastened death (both signs associated with goal-directed suicidal ideation). One of the most widely used scale in this area, the Schedule of Attitudes Toward Hastened Death (Rosenfeld et al., 1999) has excellent psychometric properties, but items intermingle what might be thought of as readiness for death with an active plan to end life. Therefore, the scale might be most useful when followed by careful questioning about responses that were endorsed.

Another important skill in work with family members after a patient's death is differentiating expected grief from complicated grief, a more severe form with a distinct symptom pattern and response to treatment (Prigerson, Vanderwerker, & Maciejewski, 2008). Most definitions of complicated grief include a requirement that at least 6 months

have passed since the loss; so at this point, we cannot predict before the death or even shortly after the death who will develop complicated grief. Certain factors, however, appear to be associated with greater risk, such as features of the death itself (e.g., unexpected or violent) and characteristics of the bereaved (e.g., closeness with the deceased; pessimistic thinking; history of mood, anxiety, or personality disorder; Kristjanson, Lobb, Aoun, & Monterosso, 2006; Prigerson et al., 2009). For an excellent review of available instruments in this area, see Neimeyer, Hogan, and Laurie (2008).

A clinical situation familiar to many geropsychologists involves questions about a patient's capacity to make decisions. Questions may arise about a patient's ability to consent to treatments or refuse treatments recommended by the health care team. Likewise, patients who are called on to designate powers of attorney or complete a will may have fluctuating or focal deficits, as in the case of delirium or a circumscribed stroke, that require evaluation to assess their true capabilities. The APA, in collaboration with the American Bar Association, has an exceptional, comprehensive handbook for psychologists to guide these evaluations (American Bar Association/APA Assessment of Capacity in Older Adults Project Working Group, 2008).

A final assessment issue is a reconsideration of how we usually think about psychometrics and interpretation of standardized scales in the context of end-of-life care. In the case of test–retest reliability, for instance, we typically expect scores on our instruments to be relatively stable, but in the context of end-of-life care, the timeframe between assessments might be particularly important. Among patients with a rapidly changing medical status, we might expect a similar rapidly changing psychological status. Greater intraindividual variability would mean more fluctuation in psychological symptoms and concomitantly lower reliability coefficients, and both might be expected as a person is approaching death. In this situation, score changes reflect not measurement unreliability but real shifts in patient experience. Likewise, in terms of validity, determining what is normal and abnormal is complicated. Are *DSM* criteria necessarily valid when applied to people near the end of life? Few empirical data are available to answer this question. In addition, some of the other psychological constructs we might be most interested in assessing may be elusive to usual methods. Coherence, acceptance, forgiveness, dignity, and peacefulness are important ideas that circulate in end-of-life care, but efforts to measure them are rudimentary. Lastly, some psychological assessments will interface closely with the assessments conducted by other disciplines on the care team, and true interdisciplinary assessment can yield important insights. When a care team learns that a patient believes in an afterlife and an ongoing existence for the soul, that information alone is not helpful unless the entire care team also knows whether that belief is a source of comfort ("I can accept death because I will be reunited with my husband.") or trepidation ("I'm afraid I will be punished for my sins.") for that individual patient. Therefore, triangulation of assessment information among disciplines is critical.

TREATMENT AND INTERVENTION

This section focuses on psychological treatments, such as those designed to address specific mental health syndromes or symptoms, and other interventions that psychologists may use in end-of-life practice, such as offering supportive services to other health care providers. The section begins with an overview of general issues in clinical practice, followed by a discussion of technical aspects of treatment.

When Might Psychological Services Be Appropriate?

Individuals can benefit from psychological interventions near the end of life at several different time points along their journey (see the summary in Exhibit 22.1). Even before people face a life-limiting illness, psychologists can play a role in promoting the pursuit of advanced care planning, encouraging their clients to complete wills and living wills, to

---

Exhibit 22.1
Psychological Interventions Throughout the End-of-Life Timeline

Phase

Healthy populations	Patients before diagnosis	At receipt of diagnosis	Approaching death	After death
		Intervention		
■ Educate the public about advance care planning ■ Promote completion of advance directives, durable power of attorneys, and wills ■ Encourage patients to discuss values and end-of-life care preferences with family and friends	■ Facilitate active consideration of pros and cons of seeking diagnosis ■ Prepare patients for effective communication with health care providers ■ Prepare patients for evaluation results	■ Help patients and family members understand their diagnosis ■ Encourage adaptive emotional and behavioral coping ■ Assist patients and family members in mobilizing supports and services	■ Provide psychotherapy to address psychopathology and subsyndromal symptoms ■ Address quality-of-life issues ■ Implement interventions to promote treatment adherence ■ Facilitate discussions about goals of care ■ Help patients identify and articulate care preferences and values ■ Facilitate preparation for death	■ Provide bereavement support

---

establish durable powers of attorney, and to discuss their values and end-of-life care preferences with friends and family members. Before actual diagnosis, when patients may suspect something is amiss, psychologists can help patients determine whether they want to seek evaluation, how to communicate their expectations and concerns effectively to their health care providers, and how to be prepared for the outcome of their evaluation. When an official diagnosis is received, psychologists can help patients understand their diagnosis, manage their emotional reactions, clarify next steps, mobilize services and social supports, and communicate treatment preferences to medical providers. At this point, psychologists can help family members with some of these same issues. In advanced care, when a patient is dying (a period that could cover months, weeks, or days), psychologists can provide treatments to address psychopathology and subsyndromal symptoms, address other quality-of-life issues, implement interventions to promote treatment adherence, facilitate discussions about goals of care, help clients clarify preferences and values, and help clients undertake the psychological work required to be ready for death. At the same time, psychologists can offer support to family members through this process. Finally, after death, psychologists can provide bereavement support to family members.

Client-Provider Issues

Patients who are nearing death likely have had interactions with many different health care providers over weeks, months, or even years. A psychologist may be a new addition to the care team, and it is essential to provide some orientation to the psychologist's purpose for being involved, what the psychologist can do (e.g., provide emotional support) and cannot do (e.g., make anxiety disappear overnight), and the patient's role in any interventions. Some patients may have experience with a psychotherapist from an earlier time in their life, whereas others may know what a psychologist does only from media presentations, accurate or inaccurate. It is particularly important to be clear about how the psychologist works with other team members, how the psychologist's role complements those of other team members, and with whom the psychologist will communicate.

End-of-life care presents some complexities when it comes to confidentiality, much like those that arise when providing care in any interdisciplinary setting. A clear conversation about the limits of confidentiality should occur at the beginning of any therapeutic relationship. One advantage a psychologist may have over other members of the care team, whose patient load or responsibilities may be too great to give them that same luxury, is the opportunity to spend regular, extended time with a patient. That opportunity increases the likelihood, however, that a psychologist will learn things about the patient that others do not know, and it is vital for all parties—patient, family, and care team—to understand what will and will not be shared by the psychologist, in conversation and documentation. Informed consent should be sought, and even in inpatient settings in which patients often sign a blanket consent form for treatment, it is worth asking whether the patient indeed wants to talk to the psychologist. Psychotherapy is not without risks, and patients have the right to refuse psychotherapy, just as they do other treatments.

General Differences in Clinical Practice

Clinicians who are accustomed to working in other settings may be surprised by some differences, or what may feel like outright unorthodoxies, in providing psychological services with people near the end of life. For example, whereas in other patients the use of tobacco, alcohol, and drugs may be viewed as a maladaptive coping strategy worthy of intervention, a more liberal attitude is sometimes appropriate for patients with little time left to live. For a patient with a longstanding heroin abuse history with only weeks to live, using drugs may be one of life's few remaining pleasures and may provide some relief from intractable distress or discomfort. That attitude is not meant to be an endorsement of excessive substance use that compromises the effectiveness of other treatments or interferes with a patient's ability to prepare for death, but it is a suggestion that treatment priorities may be different when a patient's time is limited and a broadminded consideration of coping strategies is needed. The same could be said of defense mechanisms such as denial, intellectualization, and repression, which in some situations may serve an adaptive function in people near to death (and in the people who care for them).

The immediacy of momentous, abstract questions is another cardinal feature of this work. Why am I still alive? What will happen to my soul after I die? What did my life mean? What impact did I have? Of course these are not uncommon questions that clients address in any therapy, but near the end of life they are questions that are particularly salient and pressing; people no longer have years to figure out the answers. And just as their clients are voicing these questions and grappling with the answers, clinicians who are observing their clients wrestle with them will likely find themselves asking the very same questions. It is challenging clinical work to help anyone plumb these questions, and even more so when you are, at the same time, trying to answer them for yourself (Otis-Green, 2011).

Boundaries regarding administrative procedures, touch, self-disclosure, and other practice features also might be different. Charges for missed appointments, rigid appointment times, and adherence to strict treatment plans may fall by the wayside when patients cannot make it to an appointment because their central line needs to be replaced unexpectedly, because they have to leave early to make it to a radiation appointment, or because this week they discovered cancer has spread to lymph nodes causing a radical shift in their prognosis. The unexpected is the norm; flexibility is fundamental. Casual touch, avoided in most other clinical contexts, can be a powerful intervention in and of itself; a way to establish a literal and figurative connection to clients who may experience very little physical contact in their lives, as family and friends are uncertain whether touch is welcome, and as the touch patients do receive in residential settings is limited to purely functional "bed and body" work. Greater self-disclosure can be another clinical asset, as therapists share their own experiences, what they have observed in their work with other clients (preserving confidentiality, of course), and their own beliefs and opinions when it is in the service of helping clients clarify their own needs. Finally, there may be opportunities to deliver clinical care in settings that are unusual but that respond to the patient's current capabilities and circumstances. Effective, sensitive patient-centered psychotherapeutic interventions can take place at the bedside, in a chemotherapy suite, while pushing a client in a wheelchair, or outside at a favorite park or restaurant. Again, flexibility is important, and meeting the patient where they are (literally) communicates a degree of investment and compassion that some patients appreciate. Here again, these modifications are recommended only when they are undertaken with careful consideration about liability and about their clinical value.

Finally, as is true in other settings, end-of-life care involves frequent and intense collaboration with families and interdisciplinary health care teams. This skill is part and parcel of what any geropsychologist likely experiences, but the work with patients who are dying can bring with it a unique urgency and concentration.

Types of Treatments and Interventions

Selection of a treatment approach depends, in part, on the focus of treatment and the goals of the patient. For treatment of psychopathology or subsyndromal symptoms, well-established treatments may be useful, even though they have not been validated extensively, if at all, when used with patients near the end of life. Cognitive–behavioral, interpersonal, psychodynamic, and client-centered approaches—the historic core psychotherapies—are reasonable approaches, although as is so often the case, more research is needed to determine whether these approaches are effective with seriously ill patients and whether modifications are required in end-of-life care (Kasl-Godley, 2011). Other, perhaps less traditional, psychotherapies may be, based on their theoretical foundations, particularly relevant to care at the end of life. Acceptance and commitment therapy (Angiola & Bowen, 2013; Hayes, Strosahl, & Wilson, 2012), for example, with its emphasis on acknowledging symptoms without the insistence that they disappear, may be helpful for patients whose medical conditions bring physical and psychological experiences that are real, persistent, may not improve, and may even get worse. As another example, existential therapy is an approach with obvious resonance given the proximity of death and the poignantly immediate challenge of coming to terms with a foreshortened future and impending mortality. Here again, the evidence base for these approaches is just beginning to emerge in the context of end-of-life care (e.g., Fegg et al., 2013; Spira, 2000).

In recent years, several new psychotherapies have emerged that have been designed specifically to address the challenges faced by patients near the end of life. Meaning-centered group therapy (MCGT; Breitbart, Gibson, Poppito, & Berg, 2004) has its theoretical foundations in the writings of Victor Frankl and combines existential and cognitive–behavioral techniques to help very ill patients restore meaning to their life. In its current iteration, MCGT involves eight, weekly group sessions, 90 min in length that include didactics, discussion, and experiential exercises to help patients understand their illness and sustain hope and meaning (Greenstein & Breitbart, 2000). Recent evaluations of MCGT have found significant improvement in sense of meaning, faith, and spiritual well-being and significant decline in symptom-related distress and a desire for death (Breitbart et al., 2010, 2012). Of note, no significant changes were seen in optimism, anxiety, or depression.

Another newer treatment option is dignity therapy (DT; Chochinov et al., 2005), an individual psychotherapy that, like MCGT, is not designed to address a specific psychopathology, but rather to promote psychological well-being amid the many physical and psychological challenges of living with a life-limiting illness. DT is based on a guided set of questions posed by the therapist, something like a structured interview to help patients identify and explore past accomplishments, values, and goals. Themes that are addressed include generativity, continuity of self, role preservation, maintenance of pride, hopefulness, and concerns about the aftermath of one's death. Examples of probes used in DT include the following: What parts of your life do you remember the most or think are most important? When did you feel most alive? What specific things do you want your family to know about you or remember? What are your most important roles and accomplishments; what are you most proud of? Are there things that need to be said, or need to be said again? What words of advice would you like to pass on? DT sessions with patients can be recorded, and a transcript can be used to create a "legacy document" that captures the patient's life in a form that can be shared and retained by family members. Although initial studies have found no impact on primary outcomes, such as anxiety and depressive symptoms, symptoms concerns, and quality of life, patients who complete the treatment report that the therapy was helpful to them and their families (Chochinov et al., 2011; Hall, Goddard, Opio, Speck, & Higginson, 2012). As a set, these are impressive and much needed explorations that deserve wider evaluation and implementation.

Any psychotherapy used with people near the end of life, and particularly manualized psychotherapies, may encounter several implementation challenges. First, acute medical crises and swift changes in prognosis may by necessity demand a shift in therapeutic focus; flexibility may take precedence over standardization. Indeed, finding samples with whom to develop and evaluate new evidence-based approaches is a challenge, given the difficulty of recruitment into a therapy trial when patients are dealing with many other stressors. Second, setting treatment goals can be a delicate enterprise, requiring patients and therapists to be mindful of prognosis while at the same time retaining hope for change. Third, finding a predictable time for therapy, in a private, comfortable space, can be difficult when patients have a variable schedule or live in proximity to other people. Fourth, it can be difficult to find mental health professionals who are interested in (a) a dying population and (b) learning innovative treatments. Just as geropsychology tends to draw a certain type of clinician to it, the same may be true for end-of-life care. Self-selection is a passive method for bringing clinicians into the practice, and more active solicitation and training are needed. The VA currently offers interdisciplinary postdoctoral fellowships in palliative care at several medical centers, training that is also available at some non-VA facilities, and these initiatives are important for bringing psychologists into this area of practice.

ADDITIONAL FACETS OF CLINICAL PRACTICE

Several additional considerations span both assessment and treatment. Some of these are unique to practice in this area, whereas others are more universal.

Diversity and Individual Differences

As geropsychologists, we celebrate the diversity of older adults and the divergence of their life paths, and that divergence extends into dying and death as well. To state the obvious, everyone dies, but each person brings a unique developmental history and set of individual characteristics that can shape their experience at the end of life. As in all their work, geropsychologists collaborating with people near the end of life need to consider how individual differences might matter. All of the usual caveats about working with diverse older adults hold true, but being at the end of life presents its own differences. For example, in terms of standardized assessment instruments, appropriate norms are rarely available for older adults based on gender, race or ethnicity, or socioeconomic status, let alone for older adults in these groups who are dying. Consequently, we do not know what is "normal" at the end of life in terms of important psychological constructs within personality (e.g., locus of control, neuroticism), emotion (e.g., breadth and variability), and cognition (e.g., memory changes, attentional resources). Likewise, evidence-based psychotherapeutic treatments for individuals near the end of life are so early in their development that there have been virtually no evaluations to address effectiveness in subgroups of diverse patients or whether modifications would be helpful.

Differences in culture can affect how illness is experienced, how decisions are made, and how relationships are navigated with care providers, and psychologists need to be aware of those differences (Mazanec, Panke, Ferrell, & Coyle, 2010). For example, although a generalization, in some Latino cultures, patients may adopt a more family-centered medical decision-making model that emphasizes the needs of the family and community, above the wishes of the individual (Peterson-Iyer, 2008).

Moreover, recent literature reviews suggest that African Americans use hospice services less frequently than White, Asian, and Latino patients (Cohen, 2008) and that different cultural groups have different attitudes about life-extending interventions (Blackhall et al., 1999; Degenholtz, Thomas, & Miller, 2003). Beyond these specifics, clinicians may find it most beneficial to adopt the kind of cultural sensitivity recommended by A. K. Smith, Sudore, and Perez-Stable (2009), not only paying attention to cultural scripts but also recognizing the variability *within* groups based on such factors as socioeconomic status, acculturation, and spiritual beliefs. In addition, several organizations have issued practice recommendations that guide culturally sensitive practice during terminal care (e.g., Crawley, Marshall, Lo, & Koenig, 2002; Levy et al., 2009; National Consensus Project for Quality Palliative Care, 2013).

Working With the Interdisciplinary Team

As in so many contexts, geropsychologists working with patients near the end of life will interface with colleagues from a variety of other disciplines (Zeiss & Steffen, 1996). Teams in palliative care and hospice typically consist of a physician, nurse, social worker, chaplain, and volunteers (in the case of hospice). But other providers are likely to make significant, if less primary, contributions to a patient's care. Indeed, the Medicare hospice benefit also covers services by physical therapists, occupational therapists, speech-language pathologists, and aides and homemakers. Even beyond those disciplines, others who play an important role include pharmacists, psychiatrists, home care workers, and funeral directors. Lastly, the most essential members of the team—and they should be considered part of the team at every moment—are the patient and the family, who bring their own unique expertise, agenda, and expectations.

Effective interdisciplinary care depends on several factors, including timely and comprehensive communication among team members, a shared philosophy about care, transparent decision making, a clear delineation of roles, respect for the competencies each discipline brings to the care plan,

---

Exhibit 22.2
Expertise of a Clinical Geropsychologist Relevant to End-of-Life Care

General areas of expertise	■ Emotions, their origins, and interrelationships with cognitions and behavior ■ Personality and its influence on behavior ■ Life span developmental theories ■ Family systems theories ■ Bio-psycho-social-spiritual perspective on health ■ Interpersonal dynamics and team functioning ■ Communication skills ■ Social influences on behavior
Clinical assessment	■ Diagnostic criteria for major psychopathologies ■ Knowledge of reliable and valid standardized tools for assessing facets of mental health ■ Clinical interviewing, particularly around sensitive topics
Psychological treatment	■ Administering evidence-based treatments for symptom-specific disorders ■ Teaching and supervising other mental health professionals in the delivery of treatments
Research	■ Extensive training in research design and statistical methods ■ Knowledge regarding assessment and measurement principles (i.e., understanding psychometrics and their impact on data interpretation) ■ Data analysis and interpretation

---

and provision of mutual support. Additional information about some of the specifics of interdisciplinary teams in end-of-life care can be found in several excellent resources (e.g., Hanks et al., 2009; Youngwerth & Twaddle, 2011). Particularly for psychologists working in this arena, it is important to negotiate roles with other team members. Assessment of mood or other symptoms and provision of counseling or therapy could be undertaken within the typical responsibilities of several disciplines (e.g., nursing, physical or occupational therapy, social work, chaplaincy), so it is important to have explicit discussions about who will be responsible for what in the patient's care and to be aware of potential entanglements related to professional "turf." Because psychologists historically have not been at the center of end-of-life care, they may find it necessary to educate other disciplines about what a psychologist can bring to the team. Professionals from other disciplines may have their own ideas—based on actual experience or just stereotype, and therefore more or less accurate—about the boundaries of a psychologist's expertise and may not understand how a psychologist can contribute to a patient's care or to the functioning of the team itself.

Exhibit 22.2 offers a few talking points that can clarify how a psychologist could be helpful.

Importance of Self-Care

Psychotherapy challenges all clinicians, as it immerses them in other people's pain (Strada, 2011); its rewards emerge from that as well. Yet patients near the end of life bring a particular intensity to the work. They often are debilitated or compromised by uncomfortable physical symptoms, they face many practical and financial stresses every day, they have a limited number of days ahead of them, and they have to resolve some of the most important questions and issues in that limited time. Options are often ambiguous, opinions often contradictory; pressure to do things "right" is immense, and emotions run high; a usual routine evaporates, and chaos becomes the norm. Psychologists enter this maelstrom and try to bring some calm and clarity, but death is rarely as quick, painless, and picturesque as everyone wishes. Instead, it is usually messy, painful, and protracted.

It can be draining for a clinician to be exposed to so much debility and distress. Particularly for professionals whose work depends on their own well-oiled cognitive functions, witnessing the decline of mental faculties can be unnerving. It is nearly impossible to work with patients who are dying and not consider one's own mortality, or at least clinicians do their patients a disservice if they have not given some thought to their own death and its implications. Patients who are dying remind us of people we have lost in our own lives, or people we will some day lose, and of our self that will one day be gone. That is a sobering confrontation. Psychologists must have the willingness to confront their own thoughts and feelings about death to ensure that those thoughts and feelings do not impede what could be beneficial for patients. A therapist who has some unacknowledged fears about death may not actively welcome patients to talk about their own fears. A therapist whose family dynamics are unbalanced and is unaware of it may have a hard time helping patients consider what conversations would be important to have in their own family and with whom. A therapist who has not reflected on the nature of their soul and its future after death may overlook the importance of that topic for a patient with deep spiritual faith.

Psychologists working with patients near the end of life often are asked, "Isn't working with dying people depressing?" Certainly, psychologists witness great suffering and loss among people who are at their most vulnerable. What can be accomplished in terms of therapeutic goals may seem more modest because of time constraints and competing concerns. And many, if not most, psychologists will have patients who die. So, yes, the work is challenging, but it is usually more inspiring than depressing. When it starts to feel depressing, and consistently so, this can be a sign that the clinician should evaluate whether they have kept up with their own self-care.

Burnout is characterized by several experiences or symptoms (Maslach, 2001). Emotional exhaustion is perhaps the cardinal feature, as clinicians feel less able to persevere with their hard work and become chronically discouraged and pessimistic. At the same time, clinicians can come to feel disconnected from their patients and maintain distance in their relationship; they may feel angry with them, feel disappointed when patients fail to follow through on treatment recommendations, or become impatient with perceived slights and cynical about

patients' motivations and actions. Clinicians may begin to doubt their skills and competence. Several risk factors for burnout have been identified (e.g., time pressure, self-doubt about competence, frequent exposure to suffering, team conflict) but also protective factors (e.g., ample time to spend with patients and families, adequate training about communication principles, stable personal and professional relationships, positive professional appraisal) (Pereira, Fonseca, & Carvalho, 2011). When a clinician feels burnout creeping in, remedies include obtaining peer consultation and supervision, seeking continuing education, establishing a satisfying work-life balance, and recognizing when down time is needed and taking it (Meier & Beresford, 2006; Seed & Walton, 2012; Vachon, 2006).

Reimbursement Issues

Psychologists who work in a fee-for-service environment face no unusual obstacles in working with patients near the end of life; private pay, standard private insurance, Medicare, and Medicaid offer the usual benefits when significant psychological disorders are present when a patient is dying. Similarly, psychologists who work in clinics, hospitals, residential settings, and other similar settings also are unlikely to have to adjust their billing practices for the sole reason that their patient has a life-limiting illness. It is worth noting, however, that even though the holistic philosophy of palliative care and hospice emphasizes psychological well-being, the Medicare hospice benefit does not directly cover services provided by a psychologist. Hospice care is mandated to provide social work services, and counseling is provided by various professionals, including social workers, chaplains, and skilled nurses and physicians. Here is the description of the counseling that can be provided:

> Counseling services are provided to the terminally ill individual and the family members or other persons caring for the individual at home. Counseling, including dietary counseling, may be provided both for the purpose of training the individual's family or other caregiver to provide care, and for the purpose of

helping the individual and those caring for the individual to adjust to the individual's approaching death. Bereavement counseling is available to the patient and his or her immediate family to provide emotional, psychosocial, and spiritual support and services before and after the death of the patient and to assist with issues related to grief, loss, and adjustment for up to 1 year after the patient's death. (Centers for Medicare and Medicaid Services, 2012, p. 15)

Psychological assessment and treatment are not covered by the hospice benefit. Yet psychologists can continue to see patients and bill Medicare as long as their service is distinct from that provided by other team members. For example, a psychologist with a longstanding relationship with a patient who has a history of depression could continue to treat that patient after the patient has enrolled in hospice. Therefore, psychologists who want to work with hospice or palliative care teams must bill for their services separately or enter into some sort of contractual agreement for payment from the larger care system, yet another obstacle to embedding psychologists into end-of-life care.

Case Example

What follows is an example of a psychologist's role in working with an interdisciplinary care team that provided consult services throughout a major medical center. (Details of this case have been modified to protect the patient's confidentiality.) Other members of the team included a board-certified palliative care physician, a nurse practitioner, social worker, and chaplain. Occasional input was provided by a neurologist with expertise in pain management and a pharmacist.

Mr. Moresby was a 69-year-old, Caucasian gentleman who was 10 years into his second marriage ("This time I feel like I finally got it right."). He had retired 1 year ago, eager to enjoy his leisure pursuits, which included fishing, bowling, playing cards, and spending time with his family. He had one adult child from his previous marriage who was living in a neighboring state, and two adult children

from his second marriage, both of whom lived nearby. The recent arrival of a first grandchild was a significant milestone in the family.

Two months after his retirement, during an office visit to investigate shortness of breath and a persistent cough, Mr. Moresby was diagnosed with Stage IV non-small-cell lung cancer with metastases to his liver. He had smoked several packs of cigarettes per day for most of his teenage years and adult life. Since his diagnosis, he had undergone a course of chemotherapy, but the size of the tumors in both lungs and the extent of the metastases suggested a poor prognosis. He had several other chronic illnesses, including diabetes and osteoarthritis. In fact, he had one knee replaced shortly after diagnosis to improve his ambulation. He could walk slowly with a cane.

His wife had taken early retirement upon learning of her husband's diagnosis so they could "spend as much time together as we can." She provided the bulk of his emotional and practical support. Mr. Moresby was independent in his activities of daily living, although his wife performed most of the cooking and cleaning, as had been the case throughout their marriage. Mr. Moresby was no longer able to complete his typical chores around the house, but his son-in-law helped with lawn care and home maintenance.

The palliative care team originally was consulted to assist with pain management, and the nurse practitioner had instituted an aggressive pain management regimen, collaborating with the neurologist. The social worker had spoken with Mr. Moresby and his wife about advanced care planning, although Mr. Moresby had declined to complete an advance directive. He also had declined a visit by the chaplain. The nurse practitioner asked the psychologist, Dr. Eliot, to visit the patient because of possible depression. Before meeting with Mr. Moresby, Dr. Eliot reviewed Mr. Moresby's medical record and spoke with the nurse practitioner, who revealed that she had not mentioned to Mr. Moresby that a psychologist might be coming to visit him.

Dr. Eliot discovered that Mr. Moresby was receiving weekly outpatient chemotherapy and was due back in the clinic later in the week. The psychologist dropped by the clinic and introduced herself to Mr. Moresby and his wife, who was sitting next to him, working on a word puzzle while Mr. Moresby received his chemotherapy. Dr. Eliot described her role on the palliative care team and explained why the nurse practitioner suggested she visit with Mr. Moresby. Initially, Mr. Moresby said he did not think he needed to speak with a "shrink," but he agreed to allow Dr. Eliot to sit with him and chat while he received his treatment. His wife asked if she should leave, and Mr. Moresby asked her to stay. This first session included a brief, introductory clinical interview, with Dr. Eliot asking about Mr. Moresby's diagnosis and treatment, how he was managing at home, and his plans for an upcoming holiday. As the conversation drew to a close, Dr. Eliot asked if it would be all right if she returned next week during his next chemotherapy appointment, and Mr. Moresby agreed, although he said he did not want to waste Dr. Eliot's time and "somebody else could probably use you more than me."

The following week, Dr. Eliot returned to the chemotherapy suite and again met Mr. Moresby and his wife. This time his wife excused herself to go to the cafeteria, a tacit acknowledgment on her part that Dr. Eliot might want a private meeting with her husband. This gave Dr. Eliot the chance to query Mr. Moresby about his psychological state, and he acknowledged several somatic symptoms that concerned him (initial insomnia and early wakening, poor concentration, fatigue, and low energy) and mentioned in an offhand manner that he was worried about what would happen to his wife after he died. With his permission, Dr. Eliot administered the Geriatric Depression Scale, and Mr. Moresby had a score of 19, suggesting a moderate degree of depressive symptoms. He denied low mood and anhedonia, although when his wife returned and joined the conversation, she said she thought her husband was not as involved as he had been, seemed less interested in social activities, and was "grumpier" than usual. Dr. Eliot considered a possible Major Depressive Disorder diagnosis but wanted to gather additional information. Also during this appointment Dr. Eliot asked about Mr. Moresby's experience with chemotherapy and investigated what Mr. Moresby knew about his cancer, his prognosis, and the team's expectations regarding the impact of chemotherapy. As it turned

out, Mr. Moresby knew little about the severity of his cancer and believed there was an "I'd say 50% chance that the chemotherapy will get rid of the cancer," although notes from the treating oncologist suggested treatment was undertaken for palliative, not curative, reasons. Dr. Eliot asked if Mr. Moresby had any questions that had not been answered about his diagnosis or treatment, and he said he was confused about some details. Explaining she would like to talk with the other team members about Mr. Moresby's questions, and with Mr. Moresby's permission, Dr. Eliot talked with the oncologist and other members of the palliative care team about gaps in Mr. Moresby's knowledge and the potential value of a family meeting in which the oncologist could review his treatment plan. The social worker agreed that another conversation about advance care planning might be more fruitful if Mr. Moresby understood the gravity of his circumstances.

At the third session, Dr. Eliot found Mr. Moresby again in the chemotherapy suite, with another patient sitting nearby who was also receiving treatment, although asleep. His wife had left the room to make a telephone call. Dr. Eliot inquired further about depressive symptoms, and Mr. Moresby acknowledged that he felt guilty about his functional decline and burden on his wife. He was worried about how she would manage after he died and was angry that he had received his diagnosis just when his life was looking so good. Death came to his mind throughout the day, but he denied suicidal ideation. The patient nearby woke up midway through the visit, and he and Mr. Moresby began talking about their respective chemotherapies and about their mutual military service. Mr. Moresby had served for 3 years overseas as part of an elite unit, but he declined to provide details. This session concluded with a plan to undertake behavioral activation, with his wife's assistance, to reengage in social events in the week ahead and make one outing in his boat to fish. In the hallway after Dr. Eliot left the chemotherapy suite, Mrs. Moresby said she thought getting more involved would be helpful for Mr. Moresby. Dr. Eliot also inquired about her own health, and Mrs. Moresby said she had periods of sadness but was uplifted by her children and her desire to make the most of the time remaining. Of note, the wife's knowledge of Mr. Moreby's prognosis seemed more insightful than his own.

In two subsequent sessions Dr. Eliot continued to check in during Mr. Moresby's chemotherapy treatments, monitoring behavioral activation, which prompted a slight improvement in Mr. Moresby's mood. He had made plans for a short vacation several months in the future, and his affect was brighter during conversations with Dr. Eliot, although he continued to see "my shrink" in a lighthearted, begrudging way. With careful probing, Dr. Eliot explored what Mr. Moresby had learned from a family meeting that had taken place with the oncologist, and he acknowledged his prognosis was not good. This was the first moment when Mr. Moresby showed deep emotion, tearful about his foreshortened future and regretful about the milestones he would miss in his children's lives. He commented that he had "seen a lot of death in my career in the military," but he did not want to discuss it. With the possibility of posttraumatic stress disorder complicating the clinical picture, Dr. Eliot wanted to gather more information, particularly to help clarify the differential diagnosis, but Mr. Moresby was unwilling to allow any exploration into his combat experience, saying, "Thinking about that just gets me into trouble. That's all behind me, and I don't want to talk about it." Separately, his wife said that she knew he had killed people, but he had refused to talk about it with her.

Mr. Moresby's chemotherapy cycle concluded, and he said he was not interested in continuing outpatient psychotherapy appointments because of transportation issues. The next time Dr. Eliot saw Mr. Moresby was when he was in for an appointment with his oncologist. In the intervening weeks he said he had been feeling better, after the side effects of the chemotherapy waned a bit. He and his wife had been fishing several times, and he had felt strong enough to help his stepson with a construction task on his property. He said his mood was better, and he scored 12 on the GDS, a slight decrease from his original 19. Poor sleep and low energy remained, but he said he felt more positive about the future, while at the same time acknowledging that his time was likely limited. With the guidance of the social worker, he had completed an advance directive and updated his will.

In this case, Dr. Eliot faced several challenges that are not uncommon when working with patients near the end of life: a complex interplay between physical illness and psychological distress, a patient who may have incomplete knowledge about his medical conditions and treatments, possible psychiatric comorbidities, multiple people involved in the care of the patient, psychotherapy that must be delivered in an unconventional space, an involved but overwhelmed family caregiver with her own needs, and limited time to complete an assessment and course of treatment. Dr. Eliot was an important bridge between other professionals on the treatment team, and between the team and Mr. Moresby and his family. Dr. Eliot was able to provide needed education about Mr. Moresby's medical conditions and treatments and help him formulate and articulate his questions for the treatment team. With her knowledge of depression and anxiety, she was able to relay to the treatment team how those symptoms might be influencing Mr. Moresby's treatment decisions and the quality of his life more broadly. Finally, Dr. Eliot invited Mr. Moresby to explore his feelings about his death, at his own pace and depth. Was this a case in which the psychologist provided a transformative therapy that brought harmony and closure to a sun-dappled death? No. But the psychologist was a vital member of the team who brought attention to the psychological well-being of Mr. Moresby and his wife.

CONCLUSION

Despite their considerable and relevant skill-set, geropsychologists need to advocate for their professional role in end-of-life care. Reimbursement structures position psychologists mostly as independent practitioners or ancillary services in palliative care and hospice, rather than as central team members. In fact, in its detailed recommendations for how to staff a palliative care program, the Center to Advance Palliative Care does not mention psychologists; psychiatrists are mentioned as consultants, presumably to address mental health and capacity issues (http://www.capc.org/building-a-hospital-based-palliative-care-program/implementation/staffing). The VA continues to be the setting where psychologists are most readily integrated into palliative care, and psycho-oncologists in non-VA settings have a long history of providing assessment and treatment to patients with cancer and their families. A more systematic presence in the health care system is lacking. Raising the prominence of geropsychologists in end-of-life care will require individual and group efforts.

As individual practitioners, geropsychologists can pursue additional training in end-of-life care through formal continuing education programs and self-study (see Exhibit 22.3). Joining professional organizations, attending their conferences, and presenting at those conferences can enhance visibility for the contributions psychologists can make. Pursuing clinical opportunities in assisted living, long-term care,

---

Exhibit 22.3
Professional Development Resources for Geropsychologists Interested in End-of-Life Care

Books
- *End-of-Life Issues, Grief, and Bereavement: What Clinicians Need to Know* (Qualls & Kasl-Godley, 2011)
- *Handbook of Psychiatry in Palliative Medicine* (Chochinov & Breitbart, 2009)
- *Life and Death Decisions: Psychological and Ethical Considerations in End-of-Life Care* (Kleespies, 2003)
- *Psychosocial Issues Near the End of Life* (Werth & Blevins, 2006)
- *Psychosocial Issues in Palliative Care* (Lloyd-Williams, 2008)
- *Staring at the Sun: Overcoming the Terror of Death* (Yalom, 2008)

Journals
- *American Journal of Hospice and Palliative Care*
- *Journal of Hospice and Palliative Nursing*
- *Journal of Pain and Symptom Management*
- *Journal of Palliative Care*
- *Journal of Palliative Medicine*
- *Journal of Palliative and Supportive Care*
- *Journal of Psychosocial Oncology*
- *Omega: The Journal of Death and Dying*
- *Pain*
- *Palliative Medicine*
- *Progress in Palliative Care*
- *Psycho-Oncology*
- *Supportive Care in Cancer*

Continuing education opportunities
- APA End-of-Life Issues for Mental Health Providers modules
- Education for Physicians in End-of-Life Care (EPEC)
- End-of-Life Nursing Education Consortium (ELNEC)
- National Association of Social Workers WebEd courses (*Understanding End of Life Care, Achieving Cultural Competence to Reduce Health Disparities in End of Life Care, End of Life Care: The Social Worker's Role*)

Professional organizations
- American Academy of Hospice and Palliative Medicine
- American Cancer Society
- Americans for Better Care of the Dying
- Association for Death Education and Counseling
- Center to Advance Palliative Care
- Death With Dignity
- International Association for Hospice and Palliative Care
- National Academy of Hospice and Palliative Medicine
- National Cancer Institute
- National Hospice Foundation
- National Hospice and Palliative Care Organization
- National Palliative Care Research Center
- Veterans Affairs Office of Geriatrics and Extended Care

and hospice is another option. Even if psychologists are not providing the direct care themselves, they can play a key role in training other members of the care team to administer some types of psychotherapeutic interventions, as when nurses provide cognitive–behavioral therapy (Lee, Lim, Yoo, & Kim, 2011) or chaplains undertake meaning-oriented therapy or mind–body interventions (Puchalski et al., 2009).

Equally substantial are the opportunities to make important research contributions. Broad and deep gaps remain in our knowledge about psychological assessment with patients near the end of life. Age- and other subgroup-appropriate norms are sorely lacking, and psychologists could play an important role in developing and validating assessments instruments. Beyond symptom- or syndrome-specific instruments, missing are well-validated scales that can be used to assess more abstract constructs that are relevant to end-of-life care. As one example, the Ryff Scales of Psychological Well-Being (Ryff & Keyes, 1995), with subscales that address personal growth, purpose in life, and self-acceptance, among other constructs, have been used in research protocols, although their content is germane in some clinical contexts as well. Scale development and validation research may not be the most glamorous type of research, and it comes with its own challenges in terms of generating relevant items and obtaining a sample size sufficient for sophisticated item analysis, but it is essential, and psychologists possess the skills to make this contribution. A secondary benefit of this kind of research is that it raises the visibility of psychologists in end-of-life care and gives other disciplines an example of how psychologists can contribute.

The same can be said for psychotherapeutic treatments. Standard psychotherapies have not been evaluated in any systematic way with patients near the end of life, so the evidence base for their effectiveness is virtually nonexistent. Newly developed therapies, such as dignity therapy, have undergone some clinical trials, but with relatively small samples and without replication from researchers beyond the developers. With expertise in research design and statistical analysis, psychologists could collaborate with other researchers in developing and evaluating a range of psychologically based interventions to

address specific symptoms (e.g., dyspnea, pain) or more broad concerns (e.g., meaning, purpose, regrets). Psychologists could also play a role in evaluating different service delivery models, staff training paradigms, effective interdisciplinary communication and collaboration, and beneficial approaches to self-care. Based on the roots of their discipline, psychologists could share more widely principles regarding information processing, heuristics, decision making, and coping to help patients in practical responsibilities, such as understanding their illness and treatment options, communicating with health care professionals, and preparing for the end of life.

Finally, research and clinical gaps are widest in the psychological needs of traditionally overlooked but important groups. Psychologists could take on a more active role in promoting end-of-life care for people with chronic mental illness, individuals with developmental disorders, people living in prisons, undocumented immigrants, and people without permanent homes. The opportunities are many, as are the potential rewards.

References

Academy of Psychosomatic Medicine. (1998). Psychiatric aspects of excellent end-of-life care: A position statement of the Academy of Psychosomatic Medicine. *Journal of Palliative Medicine, 1,* 113–115.

American Bar Association/American Psychological Association Assessment of Capacity in Older Adults Project Working Group. (2008). *Assessment of older adults with diminished capacity: A handbook for psychologists.* Washington, DC: Author.

American Psychiatric Association. (2000). *Diagnostic and statistical manual of mental disorders* (4th ed., text revision). Washington, DC: Author.

American Psychiatric Association. (2001). *Position statement on the core principles for end-of-life care.* Retrieved from http://www.psychiatry.org/File%20Library/Advocacy%20and%20Newsroom/Position%20Statements/ps2001_EndOfLifeCare.pdf

American Psychological Association. (2007). *End-of-life issues for mental health providers.* Washington, DC: Author.

American Psychological Association Working Group on Assisted Suicide and End-of-Life Decisions. (2000). *Report to the Board of Directors.* Retrieved from http://www.apa.org/pi/aseol/introduction.html

Angiola, J. E., & Bowen, A. M. (2013). Quality of life in advanced cancer: An Acceptance and Commitment

Therapy view. *Counseling Psychologist, 41,* 313–335. doi:10.1177/0011000012461955

Beck, A. T., & Steer, R. A. (1993). *Beck Anxiety Inventory manual.* San Antonio, TX: Harcourt Brace.

Blackhall, L. J., Frank, G., Murphy, S. T., Michel, V., Palmer, J. M., & Azen, S. P. (1999). Ethnicity and attitudes towards life sustaining technology. *Social Science and Medicine, 48,* 1779–1789. doi:10.1016/S0277-9536(99)00077-5

Breitbart, W., Gibson, C., Poppito, S. R., & Berg, A. (2004). Psychotherapeutic interventions at the end of life: A focus on meaning and spirituality. *Canadian Journal of Psychiatry, 49,* 366–372.

Breitbart, W., Poppito, S., Rosenfeld, B., Vickers, A. J., Li, Y., Abbey, J., . . . Cassileth, B. R. (2012). Pilot randomized controlled trial of individual meaning-centered psychotherapy for patients with advanced cancer. *Journal of Clinical Oncology, 30,* 1304–1309. doi:10.1200/JCO.2011.36.2517

Breitbart, W., Rosenfeld, B., Gibson, C., Pessin, H., Poppito, S., Nelson, C., . . . Olden, M. (2010). Meaning-centered group psychotherapy for patients with advanced cancer: A pilot randomized controlled trial. *Psycho-Oncology, 19,* 21–28. doi:10.1002/pon.1556

Centers for Medicare and Medicaid Services. (2012). *Medicare benefit policy manual.* Retrieved from http://www.cms.gov/Regulations-and-Guidance/Guidance/Manuals/downloads/bp102c09.pdf

Chochinov, H. M., & Breitbart, W. (Eds.) (2009). *Handbook of psychiatry in palliative medicine.* New York, NY: Oxford University Press.

Chochinov, H. M., Hack, T., Hassard, T., Kristjanson, L. J., McClement, S., & Harlos, M. (2005). Dignity Therapy: A novel psychotherapeutic intervention for patients near the end of life. *Journal of Clinical Oncology, 23,* 5520–5525. doi:10.1200/JCO.2005.08.391

Chochinov, H. M., Kristjanson, L. J., Breitbart, W., McClement, S., Hack, T., Hassard, T., & Harlos, M. (2011). The effect of dignity therapy on distress and end-of-life experience in terminally ill patients: A randomised controlled trial. *Lancet Oncology, 12,* 753–762. doi:10.1016/S1470-2045(11)70153-X

Cohen, L. L. (2008). Racial/ethnic disparities in hospice care: A systematic review. *Journal of Palliative Medicine, 11,* 763–768. doi:10.1089/jpm.2007.0216

Crawley, L. M., Marshall, P. A., Lo, B., & Koenig, B. A. (2002). End-of-Life Care Consensus Panel. Strategies for culturally effective end-of-life care. *Annals of Internal Medicine, 136,* 673–679. doi:10.7326/0003-4819-136-9-200205070-00010

Cusin, C., Yang, H., Yeung, A., & Fava, M. (2009). Rating scales for depression. In L. Baer & M. A. Blais (Eds.),

Handbook of clinical rating scales and assessment in psychiatry and mental health (pp. 7–35). New York, NY: Humana Press. doi:10.1007/978-1-59745-387-5_2

Degenholtz, H. B., Thomas, S. B., & Miller, M. J. (2003). Race and the intensive care unit: Disparities and preferences for end-of-life care. *Critical Care Medicine, 31,* S373–S378. doi:10.1097/01.CCM.0000065121.62144.0D

Farberman, R. K. (1997). Terminal illness and hastened death requests: The important role of the mental health professional. *Professional Psychology: Research and Practice, 28,* 544–547. doi:10.1037/0735-7028.28.6.544

Fegg, M. J., Brandstatter, M., Kogler, M., Hauke, G., Rechenberg-Winter, P., Fensterer, V., . . . Borasio, G. D. (2013). Existential behavioural therapy for informal caregivers of palliative patients: A randomized controlled trial. *Psycho-Oncology, 22,* 2079–2086. doi:10.1002/pon.3260

First, M. B., Gibbon, M., Spitzer, R. L., Williams, J. B. W., & Benjamin, L. S. (1997). *Structured Clinical Interview for DSM–IV Axis II Personality Disorders (SCID–II).* Washington, DC: American Psychiatric Press.

First, M. B., Spitzer, R. L., Gibbon, M., & Williams, J. B. W. (1996). *Structured Clinical Interview for DSM–IV Axis I Disorders, Clinician Version (SCID–CV).* Washington, DC: American Psychiatric Press.

Freud, S. (1918). *Reflections on war and death* (A. A. Brill & A. B. Kuttner, Trans.). New York, NY: Moffat, Yard.

Golderberg, D., & Williams, P. (1998). *A user's guide to the General Health Questionnaire.* Windsor, England: NFER-Nelson.

Greenstein, M., & Breitbart, W. (2000). Cancer and the experience of meaning: A group psychotherapy program for people with cancer. *American Journal of Psychotherapy, 54,* 486–500.

Haley, W. E., Larson, D. G., Kasl-Godley, J., Neimeyer, R. A., & Kwilosz, D. M. (2003). Roles for psychologists in end-of-life care: Emerging models of practice. *Professional Psychology: Research and Practice, 34,* 626–633. doi:10.1037/0735-7028.34.6.626

Hall, S., Goddard, C., Opio, D., Speck, P., & Higginson, I. J. (2012). Feasibility, acceptability and potential effectiveness of Dignity Therapy for older people in care homes: A phase II randomized controlled trial of a brief palliative care psychotherapy. *Palliative Medicine, 26,* 703–712. doi:10.1177/0269216311418145

Hanks, G., Cherny, N. I., Christakis, N. A., Fallon, M., Kaasa, S., & Portenoy, R. K. (Eds.). (2009). *Oxford textbook of palliative medicine* (4th ed.). Oxford, England: Oxford University Press. doi:10.1093/med/9780198570295.001.0001

Hayes, S. C., Strosahl, K. D., & Wilson, K. G. (2012). *Acceptance and commitment therapy: The process and practice of mindful change* (2nd ed.). New York, NY: Guilford Press.

Hyler, S. E., Rieder, R. O., Williams, J. B. W., Spitzer, R. L., Hendler, J., & Lyons, M. (1988). The Personality Diagnostic Questionnaire: Development and preliminary results. *Journal of Personality Disorders, 2,* 229–237. doi:10.1521/pedi.1988.2.3.229

Kasl-Godley, J. (2011). Serious mental illness. In S. Qualls & J. Kasl-Godley (Eds.), *End-of-life issues, grief, and bereavement: What clinicians need to know* (pp. 85–115). New York, NY: Wiley.

Keyes, C. L. (2002). The mental health continuum: From languishing to flourishing in life. *Journal of Health and Social Behavior, 43,* 207–222.

Kleespies, P. M. (2003). *Life and death decisions: Psychological and ethical considerations in end-of-life care.* Washington, DC: American Psychological Association.

Knight, B. G. (2004). *Psychotherapy with older adults* (3rd ed.). Thousand Oaks, CA: Sage.

Krasucki, C., Howard, R., & Mann, A. (1998). The relationship between anxiety disorders and age. *International Journal of Geriatric Psychiatry, 13,* 79–99. doi:10.1002/(SICI)1099-1166(199802)13:2<79::AID-GPS739>3.0.CO;2-G

Kristjanson, L., Lobb, E., Aoun, S., & Monterosso, L. (2006). *A systematic review of the literature on complicated grief.* Churchlands, Australia: Department of Health and Aging. doi:10.1037/e677472010-001

Kroenke, K., & Spitzer, R. L. (2002). The PHQ-9: A new depression and diagnostic severity measure. *Psychiatric Annals, 32,* 509–521.

Kroenke, K., Spitzer, R. L., & Williams, J. B. (2001). The PHQ-9: Validity of a brief depression severity measure. *Journal of General Internal Medicine, 16,* 606–613. doi:10.1046/j.1525-1497.2001.016009606.x

Lambert, M. J., Burlingame, G. M., Umphress, V., Hansen, N. B., Vermeersch, D. A., Clouse, G. C., & Yanchar, S. C. (1996). The reliability and validity of the Outcome Questionnaire. *Clinical Psychology and Psychotherapy, 3,* 249–258.

Lee, H., Lim, Y., Yoo, M. S., & Kim, Y. (2011). Effects of a nurse-led cognitive-behavior therapy on fatigue and quality of life of patients with breast cancer undergoing radiotherapy: An exploratory study. *Cancer Nursing, 34,* E22–E30. doi:10.1097/NCC.0b013e31820d1734

Levy, M. H., Back, A., Benedetti, C., Billings, J. A., Block, S., Boston, B., . . . Weinstein, S. M. (2009). NCCN clinical practice guidelines in oncology: Palliative care. *Journal of the National Comprehensive Cancer Network, 7,* 436–473.

Lloyd-Williams, M. (2008). *Psychosocial issues in palliative care.* New York, NY: Oxford University Press.

Maslach, C. (2001). What we have learned about burnout and health. *Psychology and Health, 16,* 607–611. doi:10.1080/08870440108405530

Mazanec, P., Panke, J. T., Ferrell, B. R., & Coyle, N. (2010). Cultural considerations in palliative care. In B. Ferrell & N. Coyle (Eds.), *Oxford textbook of palliative nursing* (3rd ed., pp. 701–712). New York, NY: Oxford University Press. doi:10.1093/med/9780195391343.003.0038

Meier, D. E., & Beresford, L. (2006). Preventing burnout. *Journal of Palliative Medicine, 9,* 1045–1048. doi:10.1089/jpm.2006.9.1045

National Association of Social Workers. (2004). *NASW standards for palliative and end of life care.* Retrieved from http://www.socialworkers.org/practice/bereavement/standards/standards0504New.pdf

National Consensus Project for Quality Palliative Care. (2013). *Clinical practice guidelines for quality palliative care* (3rd ed.). Pittsburgh, PA: Author.

Neimeyer, R. A., Hogan, N., & Laurie, A. (2008). The measurement of grief: Psychometric considerations in the assessment of reactions to bereavement. In M. Stroebe, R. O. Hansson, H. Schut, & W. Stroebe (Eds.), *Handbook of bereavement research: 21st-century perspectives* (pp. 133–162). Washington, DC: American Psychological Association.

Otis-Green, S. (2011). Embracing the existential invitation to examine care at the end of life. In S. Qualls & J. Kasl-Godley (Eds.), *End-of-life issues, grief, and bereavement: What clinicians need to know* (pp. 310–324). New York, NY: Wiley.

Pachana, N. A., Byrne, G. J., Siddle, H., Koloski, N., Harley, E., & Arnold, E. (2007). Development and validation of the Geriatric Anxiety Inventory. *International Psychogeriatrics, 19,* 103–114. doi:10.1017/S1041610206003504

Pereira, S. M., Fonseca, A. M., & Carvalho, A. S. (2011). Burnout in palliative care: A systematic review. *Nursing Ethics, 18,* 317–326. doi:10.1177/0969733011398092

Peterson-Iyer, K. (2008). *Culturally-competent care for Latino patients.* Retrieved from http://www.scu.edu/ethics/practicing/focusareas/medical/culturally-competent-care/hispanic.html

Prigerson, H. G., Horowitz, M. J., Jacobs, S. C., Parkes, C. M., Aslan, M., Goodkin, K., . . . Maciejewski, P. K. (2009). Prolonged grief disorder: Psychometric validation of criteria proposed for *DSM–5* and *ICD–11. PLoS Medicine, 6,* e1000121. doi:10.1371/journal.pmed.1000121

Prigerson, H. G., Vanderwerker, L. C., & Maciejewski, P. K. (2008). A case for inclusion of prolonged grief disorder in *DSM–5*. In M. S. Stroebe, R. O. Hansson, H. Schut, W. Stroebe, & E. Van den Blink (Eds.), *Handbook of bereavement research and practice: Advances in theory and intervention* (pp. 165–186). Washington, DC: American Psychological Association.

Puchalski, C., Ferrell, B., Virani, R., Otis-Green, S., Baird, P., Bull, J., . . . Sulmasy, D. (2009). Improving the quality of spiritual care as a dimension of palliative care: The report of the Consensus Conference. *Journal of Palliative Medicine, 12*, 885–904. doi:10.1089/jpm.2009.0142

Qualls, S., & Kasl-Godley, J. (Eds.). (2011). *End-of-life issues, grief, and bereavement: What clinicians need to know* (pp. 85–115). New York, NY: Wiley.

Rayner, L., Lee, W., Price, A., Monroe, B., Sykes, N., Hansford, P., . . . Hotopf, M. (2011). The clinical epidemiology of depression in palliative care and the predictive value of somatic symptoms: Cross-sectional survey with four-week follow-up. *Palliative Medicine, 25*, 229–241. doi:10.1177/0269216310387458

Rosenfeld, B., Breitbart, W., Stein, K., Funesti-Esch, J., Kaim, M., Krivo, S., & Galietta, M. (1999). Measuring desire for death among patients with HIV/AIDS: The Schedule of Attitudes Towards Hastened Death. *American Journal of Psychiatry, 156*, 94–100.

Ryff, C. D., & Keyes, C. (1995). The structure of psychological well-being revisited. *Journal of Personality and Social Psychology, 69*, 719–727. doi:10.1037/0022-3514.69.4.719

Seed, S., & Walton, J. (2012). Caring for self: The challenges of hospice nursing. *Journal of Hospice and Palliative Nursing, 14*, E1–E8. doi:10.1097/NJH.0b013e31825c1485

Sheehan, D. V., Lecrubier, Y., Harnett-Sheehan, K., Amorim, P., Janavs, J., Weiller, E., . . . Dunbar, G. (1998). The Mini International Neuropsychiatric Interview (M.I.N.I.): The development and validation of a structured diagnostic psychiatric interview. *Journal of Clinical Psychiatry, 59*, 22–33.

Simon, G. E., & Von Korff, M. (2006). Medical comorbidity and validity of *DSM–IV* depression criteria. *Psychological Medicine, 36*, 27–36. doi:10.1017/S0033291705006136

Smith, A. K., Sudore, R. L., & Perez-Stable, E. J. (2009). Palliative care for Latino patients and their families. *JAMA, 301*, 1047–1057. doi:10.1001/jama.2009.308

Snaith, R. P. (2003). The Hospital Anxiety and Depression Scale. *Health and Quality of Life Outcomes, 1*(29). doi:10.1186/1477-7525-1-29

Solano, J. P., Gomes, B., & Higginson, I. J. (2006). A comparison of symptom prevalence in far advanced cancer, AIDS, heart disease, chronic obstructive pulmonary disease, and renal disease. *Journal of Pain and Symptom Management, 31*, 58–69. doi:10.1016/j.jpainsymman.2005.06.007

Spira, J. (2000). Existential psychotherapy in palliative care. In H. M. Chochinov & W. Breitbart (Eds.), *Handbook of psychiatry in palliative medicine* (pp. 197–214). New York, NY: Oxford University Press.

Strada, E. A. (2011). Professional self-care. In S. Qualls & J. Kasl-Godley (Eds.), *End-of-life issues, grief, and bereavement: What clinicians need to know* (pp. 294–309). New York, NY: Wiley.

Vacco v. Quill, 117 S.Ct. 2293 (LexisNexis 1997).

Vachon, M. (2006). *Avoiding burnout and compassion fatigue: Feeding one's soul.* Edmonton, Alberta, Canada: Pallium Project Development Office.

Werth, J., & Blevins, D. (2006). *Psychosocial issues near the end of life.* Washington, DC: American Psychological Association.

Wetherell, J. L., & Gatz, M. (2005). The Beck Anxiety Inventory in older adults with generalized anxiety disorder. *Journal of Psychopathology and Behavioral Assessment, 27*, 17–24. doi:10.1007/s10862-005-3261-3

World Health Organization. (2001). *Strengthening mental health promotion* (Fact Sheet No. 220). Geneva, Switzerland: Author.

Yalom, I. D. (2008). *Staring at the sun: Overcoming the terror of death.* San Francisco, CA: Jossey-Bass.

Yesavage, J. A., Brink, T. L., Rose, T. L., Lum, O., Huang, V., Adey, M., & Leier, V. O. (1982–1983). Development and validation of a geriatric depression screening scale: A preliminary report. *Journal of Psychiatric Research, 17*, 37–49. doi:10.1016/0022-3956(82)90033-4

Youngwerth, J., & Twaddle, M. (2011). Cultures of interdisciplinary teams: How to foster good dynamics. *Journal of Palliative Medicine, 14*, 650–654. doi:10.1089/jpm.2010.0395

Zeiss, A. M., & Steffen, A. (1996). Interdisciplinary health care teams: The basic unit of geriatric care. In L. L. Carstensen, B. A. Edelstein, & L. Dornbrand (Eds.), *The handbook of clinical geropsychology* (pp. 423–450). Thousand Oaks, CA: Sage.

Zigmond, A. S., & Snaith, R. P. (1983). The Hospital Anxiety and Depression Scale. *Acta Psychiatrica Scandinavica, 67*, 361–370. doi:10.1111/j.1600-0447.1983.tb09716.x

CHAPTER 23

RETIREMENT REDEFINED

Harvey L. Sterns and Cynthia K. McQuown

Retirement has become more individualized and has evolved from the idea of a total withdrawal from the workforce to a gradual retreat, often accompanied by continued active involvement in the world of work. Whether one refers to this phase of life as a period of "renewment" (Bratter & Dennis, 2008), "revitalizing retirement" (Schlossberg, 2010) or reinvention (Merrill Lynch Wealth Management, 2013), the nature, timing, and appearance of retirement has changed. Dychtwald, Erickson, and Morrison (2004) argue that it is time to retire the concept of retirement.

THE HISTORY AND EVOLUTION OF RETIREMENT

A number of recent books address the complexity and richness of the history and major trends in career, work, and retirement (Blustein, 2013; Hedge & Borman, 2012; Wang, 2013; Wang, Olson, & Shultz, 2013). Several historical changes have significantly influenced the nature of retirement (Quinn, 2010; Zickar, 2013). At one time, companies depended on a large and loyal workforce and, to that end, provided defined benefits plans. The assurance of wealth and continued health care ensured that older workers would be willing to leave the workforce (Wang, 2012). The Age Discrimination and Employment Act (1986) also changed the nature of retirement, by eliminating a mandatory retirement age for all but a few select occupations; under the Act, anyone older than 40 is defined as belonging to a protected class. Furthermore, the

Americans With Disabilities Act (1990) required that a workplace provide "reasonable accommodation" for disabled workers, to enable them to remain in the workplace.

Changes in Social Security's benefit calculation rules now allow workers to delay receiving benefits, with the incentive of receiving more benefits if they wait (Wheaton & Crimmins, 2013). The steady shift from a company's providing defined benefits plans to offering defined contribution plans—and the expectation that retirees will bear the costs of their health care insurance—also have extended the average person's work life and changed how and when that person will retire. The world of work has evolved from one that incentivized early retirement to one that, in many cases, discourages it.

Retirement age is being chosen by the individual, based on his or her preferences and needs, and no longer by a mandated age or company incentives. Warner, Hayward, and Hardy (2010), in their update of age-graded regularities of the U.S. retirement life course, found that at age 50 years, men can expect to spend half of their remaining lives working for pay, whereas women can expect to spend one third. Half of all men had left the workforce by age 63 years and half of all women by age 61 years; the majority of those exits were final. The authors also observed that there is great variability in the retirement process: Nearly one third of men and women who had retired later resume some type of employment.

A 2012 survey by the American Association of Retired Persons and the Society for Human Resource

http://dx.doi.org/10.1037/14459-023
APA Handbook of Clinical Geropsychology: Vol. 2. Assessment, Treatment, and Issues of Later Life,
P. A. Lichtenberg and B. T. Mast (Editors-in-Chief)

Management of 1,004 adults age 50 years and older who were either employed full or part time or looking for work found that 77% of employed workers planned to remain in their current jobs until they stopped working completely, whereas 9% planned to change jobs but stay in the same field (Brown, 2012). Six percent hoped to find work in a different field, and another 6% intended to start their own business (Brown, 2012). For those 50 years and older, working longer may be related to financial circumstances or a desire to remain productive (Brown, 2012; Sterns & Sterns, 1995, 2013). This desire to work longer has been evident throughout the literature on aging, work, and retirement (Cappelli & Novelli, 2010; Czaja & Sharit, 2009; Feldman, 2007; Hedge, Borman, & Lammlein, 2006; Rothwell, Sterns, Spokus, & Reaser, 2008; Shultz & Adams, 2007; Sterns, 1986; Sterns & Alexander, 1987; Sterns & Doverspike, 1989; Sterns & Hyuck, 2001; Sterns & Patchett, 1984; Wang et al., 2013). The workplace is changing to attract and accommodate these aging workers; a 2011 study (Forbes, 2011) found that nearly one of three firms expected to have a significantly higher proportion of older workers (65 years and older) in the next 5 years, and 43% reported that retention and development of talent is a priority. Seventy-two percent offered diversity and inclusion programs focused on age.

Changes in Older Workers

Between 2006 and 2011, the numbers of those 55 years and older in the workforce grew, while millions of younger workers were displaced or left the workforce (Merrill Lynch Wealth Management, 2013). Between 2007 and 2012, the 55-and-older age-group increased from 27.1 million to 33.1 million, and the Bureau of Labor Statistics predicts that by 2020, workers 55 years and older will reach 40 million, representing 25% of the workforce (Toossi, 2012b). Because aging adults now live longer and healthier lives than ever before, the population of adults over 65 years old will double in the United States by 2050; the number of working adults 65 years old and older rose from 14% of the workforce in 2003 to 17.4% in 2010 (Toossi, 2012a). The traditional pattern of exiting the workforce

entirely at a given age has changed, and a long-term plan is now necessary to ensure that the financial, social, and health needs of increased longevity will be met.

Kantarci (2013) examined how number of hours worked affected the physical or mental health conditions of U.S. residents between 50 and 75 years old over eight waves (1994–2008) of the Health and Retirement Study (HRS). Working part or full time was found to deteriorate overall health and memory skills and reduced body weight. On the other hand, part-time white-collar work substantially improved word recall, while both part-time and full-time workers were less prone to depression. In general, the health status of the elderly responds more strongly to working part time than it does to working full time, suggesting that the effect on health outcomes of the number of hours worked is nonlinear.

Retirement Patterns and Options

Retirement used to be perceived as an abrupt life transition—"the final exit from employment" or "the movement from the midlife to old age" (J. Kim & Moen, 2001, p. 487). Because of changes in the workforce, economic and social shifts, and increased longevity, however, retirement has become a more phased, complex, and dynamic process. Individual characteristics, both work- and non-work-related, affect retirement choices (Moen, 2012).

Multiple exit patterns have replaced the traditional, one-time transition (Mutchler, Burr, Pienta, & Massagli, 1997). Identifying 65 years old as the typical retirement age may no longer be appropriate, as many individuals retire, initiate blurred transitions, or receive Social Security and pension income before this age (Cornman & Kingson, 1996; Mutchler et al., 1997). In recognition of these diverse pathways, a now classic study (Mutchler et al., 1997) examined the frequency and antecedents of different exit patterns in a sample of 2,226 White and Black men age 55–74 years old who had reported at least 6 months of continuous work history at some time during their lives. Using data from the 1984 panel of the Survey of Income and Program Participation (SIPP), researchers divided subjects into four categories. Pattern A consisted of subjects who had worked during all waves of the SIPP, including those who had moved between full-time and part-time work and those who reported a single experience of being unemployed during one wave of the SIPP. Pattern B subjects had been unemployed continuously during the survey. Pattern C, the crisp exiters, included those who had a single exit from the workforce. Subjects in pattern D, the blurred exit pattern, reported two or more transitions between labor-force participation and nonparticipation, which could include periods of employment and unemployment and periods of employment and labor-force exit followed by reentry to the workforce. Patterns of continuous work, continuous nonwork, crisp exits, and blurred exits were examined over a period of 28 months, with the following results: crisp transitioners, 10%; blurred transitioners, 15%; continuous work, 34%; and continuous nonwork, 41%.

Crisp and blurred transitioners also were found to differ in terms of age, financial resources, and health status. Crisp transitioners tended to be younger than 65 years old. Although not associated with any particular age-group, blurred transitions were rare past the age of 68 years old. In contrast to crisp exiters, blurred transitioners were more likely to have limited financial resources, such as pensions and nonwage income: Inadequate income seemed to prompt those individuals to continue to work, although somewhat sporadically. Last, individuals with poor health were more likely to be blurred transitioners than continuous workers. Those with the poorest health, however, were more likely to either exit crisply or not work at all during the period studied.

Cahill, Giandrea, and Quinn (2006) examined retirement patterns based on longitudinal data from the HRS during 1992 and 2002, which included 12,600 individuals ages 51–61 years old. They found that a majority of older workers appeared to take a phased approach to retirement, in which those who left full-time career jobs moved first to a bridge job, rather than directly out of the labor force. Older workers without defined-benefit pension plans and those at the lower and upper ends of the wage distribution took bridge jobs more than others. Bridge

employment can be beneficial to older workers, in that they can remain productive and make money (Doeringer & Terkla, 1990); according to Wang and Shultz (2010), however, bridge employment has a positive impact on mental health only if the person remains in the same career field. Zhan, Wang, Lui, and Shultz (2009) found that individuals who engaged in bridge employment reported better physical health than individuals who were fully retired, and individuals pursuing career bridge employment also indicated better mental health.

As retirement evolves into a process rather than an event, it becomes harder to examine why people retire and what factors may influence the process (Sterns & Kaplan, 2003). For example, the economic downturn of 2007 led some individuals to continue to delay retirement, whereas others sought work without success and still others, the so-called discouraged workers, stopped searching and retired by default.

Freedman (2007) described what he refers to as the "encore career": a 10- to 15-year career in which the person follows traditional career success with work of greater significance that may not last as long but is more important or gratifying than the first career. Freedman examined major trends that influenced baby boomers' (born between 1945 and 1965) decision to seek a different type of work in mid- to later life, including (a) insecurity about future retirement income; (b) cost and availability of health coverage; (c) a shift from company-defined benefit plans to defined-contribution plans, which are more subject to the vagaries of a changing economic market; and (d) the opportunity to remain active and involved.

Special Issues for Women and Minorities

Women and minorities may be more vulnerable to economic difficulties upon retirement, which presumably affects decisions regarding when—or even whether—they will retire (Griffin, Loh, & Hesketh, 2013). Women and minority groups are overrepresented in the ranks of low-income workers and therefore are more likely to have fewer financial resources in older age and retirement (Taylor & Geldhauser, 2007). Social Security was never meant to be the sole source of retirement income, but low-income groups may be more dependent on it as their sole source of income. Low-income jobs are also more likely to lack the skills needed to prepare for the cost of retirement; this dearth of formal financial planning and occupational training frequently translates into inadequate financial resources for retirement. Taylor and Geldhauser (2007) have offered suggestions for improving this situation, including programs that would encourage retirement education and planning for all adult and older-adult low-income workers, train low-income workers how to prepare a resume, link them to job support and networking resources, and integrate financial planning into lower wage earners' workplaces.

Women's presence in the workforce has redefined both the workplace and retirement. Their patterns of exiting the workforce and adjusting to retirement are influenced by many factors: the desire for both spouses to retire at the same time, financial resources, health, and the desire to continue in a career that may be reaching its full potential after interruptions while raising children. Bratter and Dennis (2008) explored the concept of women's "renewment," in which retirement becomes an opportunity to fulfill spiritual, relational, or interest goals that may or may not be a source of income. The authors examine women's diverse needs as they enter retirement and the wealth of talent among women who set the standard for careers outside of the home (Griffin et al., 2013). Bratter and Dennis conceived of retirement not as the end of working, but as the process of discerning one's roles and ways to experience meaning in later life. The authors also suggested that for women who pursued careers and have varying needs and interests, retirement may best be characterized by a process of drawing on the resources they developed in their careers rather than by turning away from them.

Many women plan to continue working past 65 years of age (J. Kim & Moen, 2001; Wheaton & Crimmins, 2013). J. Kim and Moen (2001) found that in the United States, women tend to exit their primary career later than men. In a study of men and women who held their masters of business administration, women who planned to remain in their work role past age 65 years had more positive views of their work, spouses who were also continu-

ing to work past 65 years, and more nontraditional attitudes toward gender roles (Frieze, Olson, & Murrell, 2011).

Factors Related to the Decision to Retire

J. Kim and Moen (2001) found that factors related to leaving work before one had planned to include health problems (34%), having enough money for retirement (27%), and job loss (24%). Also, for women, caregiving (14%) and time with family (19%) are also important. The Patient Protection and Affordable Care Act (ACA, 2010) inadvertently may begin to affect retirement patterns: Because employers are required to provide insurance for full-time workers, they may reduce full-time staff hours to avoid this cost. A 2013 study by the University of California, Berkeley Labor Center (Graham-Squire & Jacobson, 2013) found that the ACA will put 2.3 million workers at greater risk for reduction in hours, particularly those in the restaurant, accommodation, building services, nursing home care, and retail service industries. How this will affect aging Americans is yet to be seen. For some, reduced hours may benefit those who wish to continue working, but for fewer hours. For those in need of health care, however, the ACA may make it more difficult to afford adequate care.

Mental health issues may influence decisions to exit the workforce, whether completely or temporarily, or to move to part-time employment. Doshi, Cen, and Polsky (2008) studied six biennial waves (1992–2002) of the HRS and found that the presence of active depression in late middle-age workers significantly increased the likelihood of retirement for both men and women. In addition, depressed workers were more likely to retire completely than nondepressed workers. For women, subthreshold depression was also a predictor of retirement. Doshi et al. (2008) pointed out that a primary concern raised by these findings is the subsequent adverse impact on financial well-being and access to appropriate health care and treatment, as most of these retirees will not qualify for Social Security benefits until age 62 years or Medicare benefits until age 65 years.

Calvo, Sarkisian, and Tamborini (2013) also used data from the HRS and found that early retirement can have a negative impact on both physical and emotional health. For instance, a depressed worker may conclude that retirement is his or her only choice. Mandal and Roe (2008) found that the voluntariness of one's departure from the workforce is a predictor of adjustment: Involuntary job loss worsens mental health, and reemployment can reverse the decline.

Reitzes and Mutran (2004) found that preretirement planning and voluntary retirement improved retirement adjustment, but the effect may be time-limited. In their examination of the transition to retirement, by 24 months the beneficial impact of preretirement planning had become less important to retirement adjustment. Salami (2010) examined the relationship of retirement context and psychological factors to well-being and found that retirement status (whether voluntary or involuntary), job challenges, financial situation, physical health, activity level, and social support each separately predicted psychological well-being in retirement. In addition, preretirement expectations, self-efficacy, perceived stress, and optimism separately predicted psychological well-being. The authors suggested targeting preretirement expectations in preretirement counseling to help people develop more realistic expectations about lifestyle adjustments, importance of building social supports, and managing health care. Postretirement counseling programs could focus on use of leisure time and building and maintaining vocational skills to ease the transition to retirement (Salami, 2010).

Bender and Jivan (2005) examined what contributes to retiree happiness, using the 2000 wave of the HRS, and found that economic well-being increased overall well-being. The effect was small, however, and those who had a defined-benefits plan experienced greater well-being than those with only a defined-contribution plan or no pension. In addition, retirees who were healthier and who said that they had voluntarily retired had greater well-being than those who reported poorer health and involuntary retirement. Finally, the authors reported that about 60% of retirees were very satisfied with their retirement; another 32.4% were moderately satisfied, whereas about 8% were not satisfied.

Model for Conceptualizing Decision Making About and Adjustment to Retirement

Three lenses through which decision making about retirement can be viewed are (a) the life-span perspective of adult development, (b) career self-management, and (c) the role of resilience. Inherent to the first approach, the life-span perspective, is the idea that development is continuous throughout the course of one's life. This seems well suited to the evolving nature of retirement, in which adults continuously are redefining and adapting to what it means to enter retirement without necessarily stepping away from the role that work has played in their lives.

Hall and Mirvis's (1996) and N. Kim and Hall's (2013) discussion of the second approach, the protean or self-managed career, departs from the concept of the *organizational man or woman*, in which one committed to a single organization for life that would repay loyalty with defined retirement benefits. The idea that one's career is shaped more by the individual and less by the organization also fits well with the changing nature of work and the increasing number of options available for retirement. The net effect is a change in how the workplace sees workers and how workers see themselves. For instance, organizations in a contracting economy that have a large pool of older workers are sensitive to the cost of retirement and health care benefits for these workers. This concept of a self-managed career, which offers greater self-control—but also requires one to bear more responsibility—is well suited to a life-span perspective, which considers the employee's multiple contexts and the interactions among them. In *Working Longer: New Strategies for Managing, Training, and Retraining Older Workers*, Rothwell et al. (2008) offered numerous examples of how many factors—one's sense of time, perceived control, personal influences, awareness of current situation and future obligations, ability to self-manage, perceived norms, past and future selves, and self-esteem within the organization—can influence career decisions. Flexibility, which is essential for a self-managed career, is critical for a self-managed retirement.

The third approach considers the role resilience plays in decision making about and adjustment to retirement. Resilience styles are a means by which older workers can adapt more readily to changes and challenges within the current world of work and make optimal use of available resources as they approach retirement (Sterns & Dawson, 2012). Sterns and Dawson (2012) discussed how the resilience patterns described by Polk (1997) can support older workers as they adjust to adversity, learn to maintain their equilibrium, and gain control of their environment. The four patterns of resilience are dispositional, relational, situational, and philosophical (Polk, 1997). The dispositional pattern describes the physical and ego-related psychosocial attributes that contribute to resilience, which include personality traits like optimism, humor, extroversion, and autonomy. The relational pattern refers to those aspects of relationships and roles that can affect a person's resilience, such as social support groups. The situational pattern is how a person approaches his or her circumstances and is demonstrated by problem-solving abilities and cognitive appraisal skills. The philosophical pattern is exhibited through a person's belief system or values, such as how one defines one's purpose in life. Such resilience skills may assist the older worker in preparing for and adjusting to work-life changes, including retirement, moving from full time to part time, or beginning an entirely new work endeavor.

There does still seem to be a lag between the self-managed career and the world of work. The self-managed career is ideally suited for an older worker who may be more interested in a workplace with greater flexibility with hours, scheduling, and benefits. Employers will continue to need workers who are skilled and motivated, yet they also will need to manage costs. Data from the HRS indicate that older workers are more often drawn to part-time work, may be willing to work for less monetary compensation, and prefer jobs that afford them greater flexibility in scheduling. Organizations would do well to manage their bottom line by offering policies and compensation packages that appeal to older workers, such as flexible scheduling, phased retirement programs, and prorated benefits. It may be more difficult to find a job or reenter the workforce for older adults. Workers 55 years and older averaged 35.5 weeks of joblessness compared with 23.3 weeks for the 16- to 24-year-old age-group and 30.3 weeks for the 25- to 54-year-old age-group (U.S. Department of Labor, Bureau of Labor Statistics, 2010) Two thirds of those in the 55–64 age range who took new jobs after retirement earned, on average, 18% less (Raphaelson, 2013). Between ages 55 and 64 years about two thirds of Americans are in the labor force

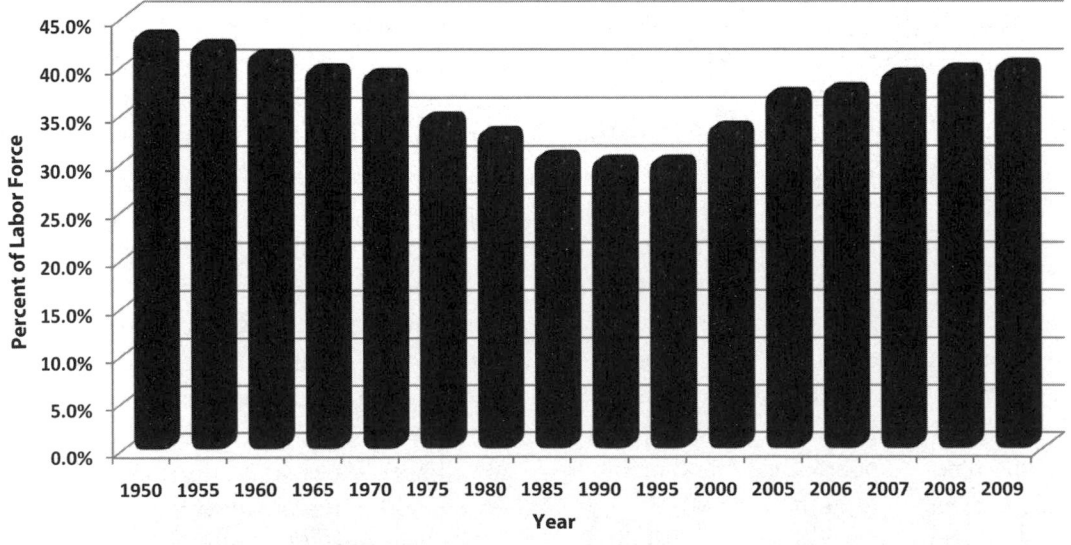

FIGURE 23.1. Labor force participation rates for age 55 years and older. Data from the U.S. Bureau of Labor Statistics (2010).

(Rix, 2013). The reemployment rate for this age-group was 47%, but dropped to only 24% after age 64 years (U.S. Department of Labor, Bureau of Labor Statistics, 2012). According to the AARP Public Policy Institute, between 60% and 80% of workers expect to work in retirement, yet only a little over 18% of people older than 65 years currently were working (Raphaelson, 2013).

Retirement Education

Major shifts in the nature and type of work, as well as demographics of the U.S. population and resulting cohort characteristics, have precipitated a *retirement revolution* in which older workers are extending their work lives, entering new careers, and redefining how to ensure security throughout a longer life span. The psychologist will need to understand these changes, the characteristics of older workers, and the changing context of work, with the aims of helping workers devise successful retirement strategies and remaining aware of factors that can interfere with adjustment to both the workplace and retirement.

Dating to the late 1960s, extensive attention has been paid to retirement preparation (Dennis, 1984, 1988; Dennis & Fike, 2012; Dychtwald & Kadlec, 2009; Hunter, 1976; Nelson & Bolles, 2007; Noone, Stephens, & Alpass, 2009). One of the major goals of retirement education is the focus on key issues, which include adjustment to retirement, the stages of retirement, use of time, health and mental health considerations, financial planning, leisure activities, family and friends, where to live, and legal affairs. Another key issue, given the evolution in the nature of retirement, is continued career development, either through paid employment or volunteer activities. Much of the current emphasis is on clarifying one's values, getting in touch with personal feelings, and becoming aware of significant others' viewpoints (Sterns & Subich, 2002, 2005). Staudinger (1999) and Smith (1996) have presented important work on the development of planning capability, wisdom regarding life events, and fostering an approach to the art of living. Retirement decisions are complex, and a wide range of issues can influence the decision-making process and adjustment to retirement. Retirement planning and voluntary retirement have been found to be related

to positive attitudes toward retirement (Reitzes & Mutran, 2004), as has retiring "on time" versus retiring early (Calvo et al., 2013).

Poor health has been found to decrease positive attitudes toward retirement and well-being over time (Reitzes & Mutran, 2004; Wang, 2012). Calvo et al. (2013) examined six biennial waves of the HRS, and, beginning with workers who had been 53–58 years old in 1994, tracked their subjects' status for every wave through 2002. They found that for women, the prevalence of active depression was 17.2%; for men, it was 11.5%. The presence of depression and depressive symptoms have been found to be significantly related to retirement in late-middle-age adults, resulting in increased risk of early exit from the workforce, likely loss of income, and health issues due to depression.

In his discussion of career development and training, Sterns (1986) viewed the option of full- or part-time retirement as part of the decision to no longer be as actively involved in career development and work activities. Decisions regarding career and updating are based on many dimensions, but individuals still can move in or out of the work role. In their discussion of Sterns' 1986 model, Sterns and Subich (2002) assisted in conceptualizing the multiple domains involved in the question of whether to continue working, decision making about retirement, and adjustment to retirement. The model offers the practitioner a starting point for what otherwise can seem like an overwhelming array of issues. Retirement can be a demanding life transition; research (Bossé, Spiro, & Kressin, 1996) has demonstrated that for about 30% of people, the retirement process or state of retirement is stressful. The psychologist may be called on to intervene, in a counseling setting, with those who are struggling (Sterns & Subich, 2005).

Factors Related to Postretirement Adjustment

It has been suggested that retirement adjustment is related to a complex array of variables in the work–life context. Adjustment to the retirement process has been found to be related to preretirement planning (Doverspike & Taylor, 2003), marital status and quality (Rosenkoetter & Garris, 1998), financial resources, physical health, psychological health, type of retirement exit pattern, and personal control.

Poorer retirement adjustment outcomes have been associated with earlier retirement due to worker displacement (Klehe, Koen, & DePater, 2012), mental health disorders such as depression, marital dissatisfaction, and loss of social connection (Doshi et al., 2008; J. Kim & Moen, 2001). In fact, one of the most powerful predictors of retirement adjustment difficulty is a lack of control over the retirement transition (van Solinge, 2013).

For individuals with adjustment challenges, the development of mastery, locus of control, or self-efficacy may be the cornerstones upon which the counseling psychologist can provide support and develop interventions. Fretz et al. (1989) examined the improvement of self-efficacy through active participation in retirement-planning seminars.

The counseling psychologist can play a valuable role for older adults who are encountering difficulties in adjusting to transitions (Bobek & Robbins, 2005; Duffy, 1999; Hill, Thorn, & Packard, 2000). Shultz and Wang (2011) discussed the important contributions that psychologists have made to our understanding of retirement not just as a decision-making event, but as a major life transition that takes place over time and in uniquely defined contexts. They support the psychologist's role in helping people plan and prepare for retirement, which is associated with prospective retirees' confidence in their ability to retire successfully (Taylor-Carter, Cook, & Weinberg, 1997). To assist a client in adjusting to retirement, the psychologist may help clients identify problem areas. Using inventories and checklists as a springboard, the psychologist can guide discussion of areas that may be presenting problems for the client.

ASSESSMENT RESOURCES

In order to assist older workers most effectively, it is useful to consider the domains of retirement readiness, life stage adjustment, and mental health. Each of these domains may affect and be affected by the others, and assessing each area is instrumental in treatment planning.

Retirement Readiness

Clients may need to evaluate their situation differently, depending on whether they are considering retiring in the future, have retired by choice, or have retired due to circumstances beyond their control. The psychologist can suggest resources for professional guidance to develop a financial plan and address the issues that many workplace preretirement education programs do not. Beginning with Hunter (1976) and expanding in the decades that followed, the use of checklists to aid in self-awareness and self-evaluation in retirement preparation and adjustment has become standard. The use of such checklists can help prospective retirees organize their thoughts and obtain concrete information about what issues are important in retirement planning and adjustment. Hunter (1976) included checklists that remain relevant today for anyone facing retirement preparation and adjustment, including a Retirement Readiness score based on the total of scores for five checklists:

- Preparing to live on my income after retirement
- Preparing for good health in retirement
- Preparing for things to do after I retire
- Preparing for a good family life after I retire
- Preparing for a place to live after I retire

The Retirement Readiness score reflects one's preparedness relative to retirement decision making. The psychologist's role is to provide self-assessment tools that address key issues for retirement planning and adjustment: income, health, use of time, social relationships, and living situation.

Assessment of Adjustment and Mental Health Issues

In working with issues related to adjustment to retirement, the psychologist will need tools that not only enhance the client's awareness but also assist the psychologist in evaluating the client's mental health and status in the context of retirement.

The *Treatment of Depression in Older Adults*, an evidence-based practices kit for practitioners (Substance Abuse and Mental Health Services Administration [SAMHSA], 2011), identifies risk factors for depression, such as changes in an older adult's physical health or functioning, mental health, circumstances, or social support. Screening for depression is considered a best practice for aging adults at any stage of the retirement process (U.S. Department of Human Services, 2011). Depression also may contribute to other health issues, including the pain experience and alcohol use. Many available depression-screening tools are useful in an older adult population. The Geriatric Depression Scale (Brink et al., 1982; Yesavage et al., 1982–1983) is a basic screening tool and is available in either a short (15 items) or long (30 items) version, in multiple languages, and as a free iPhone or Android app that can be administered and scored on those devices. It is also in the public domain.

Screening for alcohol use is also appropriate when adjustment to retirement is in question. Older adults are more vulnerable to the harmful effects of alcohol and may not understand how medications, physiology, and alcohol use can contribute to mood and health problems. Nearly 60% of older people abstain from alcohol—yet drinking problems are the largest category of substance-use disorders in older adults (Blazer & Wu, 2009). The Screening and Brief Intervention and Referral for Elders project has demonstrated that this intervention is an effective means of identifying cases that often are overlooked in traditional service systems, reduces depression and alcohol severity, and enhances proper medication use (Schonfeld et al., 2010). Yet many older adults may lack the knowledge to ask for screening if it is not offered routinely. Efforts to increase older adults' awareness of their unique vulnerability to problems with medications and alcohol may reduce risk.

Useful screening tools include the Alcohol Use Identification Test (Saunders, Aasland, Babor, de la Fuente, & Grant, 1993) and the Michigan Alcoholism Screening Test—Geriatric Version (MAST–G; Blow et al., 1992). The MAST–G (Blow et al., 1992) was the first short-form alcoholism screening instrument tailored to the needs of older adults. Two or more yes responses suggest an alcohol problem. Current SAMHSA guidelines recommend that a screening test like the MAST–G be the first step in Screening Brief Intervention, Referral to Treatment. The Alcohol Use Disorders Intervention Test

(AUDIT) was developed to screen for excessive drinking and, in particular, to help practitioners identify those who would benefit from reducing their use of alcohol or quitting entirely (Saunders et al., 1993). The majority of excessive drinkers are undiagnosed and often present with symptoms or problems that normally would not be linked to alcohol use. The AUDIT can help the practitioner determine whether the person demonstrates signs of hazardous (or risky) drinking, harmful drinking, or alcohol dependence.

For individuals with adjustment challenges, the development of mastery, locus of control, or self-efficacy may be the cornerstones upon which the counseling psychologist can provide support and develop interventions.

THERAPEUTIC ISSUES FOR THE OLDER WORKER

Several issues are unique to counseling older workers and often are neglected or overlooked entirely in employer-based retirement preparation programs. Most such programs cover financial planning, often neglecting other aspects of adjustment to retirement. The psychologist can help address other aspects of retirement adjustment. For example, Earl and Yu (2012) have developed a retirement intervention based on the concept of self-efficacy and created an inventory to identify retirement resources based on Wang and Shultz's (2010) six domains: physical, financial, social, emotional, cognitive, and motivational. Earl and Yu's instrument, the Retirement Resources Inventory, has shown promise in improving postretirement behavior. Training modules, in which subjects model retiree behavior and participate in problem solving, improve mastery; greater mastery is predictive of retirement adjustment. Connolly (1992) found that participants in programs that included problem solving, experienced higher levels of control over the retirement process than those who had attended a program that only used a lecture format.

Useful models for counseling the older worker have been proposed by Richardson (1993) and Anderson, Goodman, and Schlossberg (2012). In Sterns and Subich (2005), a discussion of Richardson's model was examined for use in retirement counseling. It has three phases: listening, assessment, and intervention. It should be noted that from a life span approach, the same counseling techniques would be expected to be effective with all ages. In the listening phase, the psychologist joins with the client by offering openness and acceptance while exploring the client's experiences with or expectations for retirement. Of utmost importance in this phase is discerning the precipitating event that led to the client's decision to seek help.

Richardson's (1993) second phase, assessment, involves understanding the history of the issue the client presents and the client's perception of its severity and emotional impact. The psychologist must identify which phase of retirement the client is in: preretirement, retirement decision making, or adjustment. This aspect of Richardson's model is particularly valuable, as present-day older adults may move in and out of the workforce, either in a crisp retirement (Sterns & Gray, 1999), a more phased retirement or move to bridge employment (Doeringer & Terkla, 1990), or by means of a second or encore career (Freedman, 2007). Each phase poses important decisions for the client that will have implications for future adjustment. Ideally, the assessment phase results in a defined goal for counseling.

In the intervention phase, Richardson (1993) identified three strategies: nondirective, directive, and collaborative. The nondirective approach is best used in cases in which the client has mild concerns, as this approach is supportive, draws on the client's resources, and concentrates on supporting the client in taking action to resolve his or her concerns. The directive approach is appropriate for the client whose functioning is highly compromised by severe mental health issues, such as suicidal thoughts. In this strategy, the psychologist plays a much more active role, geared toward protecting the client and helping him or her function more effectively. The collaborative strategy is most effective when the client presents with serious concerns that likely can benefit from additional support from and guidance by the psychologist. With this approach, the psychologist plays a more active role, in terms identifying resources, brainstorming options, and providing information that will assist the client.

Lowman (1993) offered another way to conceptualize the psychologist's role in *Counseling and Psychotherapy Work Dysfunctions*. Lowman has contended that the clinician's task is to assess the type of work-related problem presented, determine the relation of the problems to other aspects of personality and psychopathology, and develop the initial intervention strategy.

Anderson et al. (2012) proposed a model that applies Schlossberg's (1981, 1984) framework for transitions to transitions that commonly are experienced throughout the adult life span, such as retirement. Anderson et al. offered psychologists a three-part framework for listening to clients' diverse stories: approaching the transition, using the 4S system to inventory the client's circumstance, and strengthening resources. In the first stage, approaching the transition, the psychologist identifies the type of transition (which can be to an event or nonevent) and what change is occurring, about to occur, or did not occur as expected. This model emphasizes the importance of determining where the client is in the transition process—beginning, middle, or end—because this will affect the choice of approach.

In the second stage of Anderson et al.'s (2012) model, the 4S system is used to assess the client's situation, identify sources of support, establish strategies, and take stock of resources. Each situation will vary according to the catalyst for the transition, the timing of the transition, and the person's level of control over the transition. Additional factors include (a) the impact of the transition on role change, (b) whether the transition is permanent or temporary, (c) whether the individual has experienced a similar transition, (d) whether other stressors are occurring simultaneously, (e) and how the person assesses the transition. The individual also will present with unique strengths and weaknesses; personal and demographic characteristics, such as socioeconomic status and ethnicity or culture; and psychological resources, such as optimism and self-efficacy. These also will need to be assessed to offer the client the appropriate assistance. The psychologist and client then can inventory the types and functions of social supports available. Coping strategies are the final aspect of the client's resources to be evaluated; these resources are critical to how the client will handle the transition in question.

In the third stage of the model, the emphasis is on strengthening the client's resources as identified in the 4S system. At this point, the psychologist assists the client in taking control of how he or she will manage the transition.

A model that could be used to counsel workers who are in the midst of a transition and wish to extend their work life would require strategies that could be used by workers from all socioeconomic ranges, employment categories, and ethnicities. Blustein, Kenna, Gill, and De Voy (2008) have constructed such a framework. The *psychology of working* perspective goes beyond viewing work as a choice and contends that many workers, due to social class, race, or minority status, have not had access to work that engages their interests or values. They also have not had opportunities to acquire the skills necessary to advance in the workplace. Blustein et al. (2008) argued that the psychologist should be willing routinely to consider the work context of any person presenting for counseling, which would highlight the importance of work to human lives. Using this approach, the psychologist intentionally includes work in what will be discussed and supports the client in determining the amount of that work material that will be included in the counseling process. Franklin and Medvide (2013) have taken a similar approach, suggesting that the integration of psychotherapy and career counseling, although not developed specifically for work with aging adults, makes sense when working with issues related to retirement.

Blustein et al. (2008) also outlined four core goals for the inclusive psychological practice: fostering empowerment, fostering critical consciousness, promoting clients' skill building for the changing workforce, and providing scaffolding in support of volition. These goals provide the practitioner with guidelines for helping clients address work-related issues regardless of race, skill level, or access to resources. Incorporating the psychology of work framework, the skilled practitioner will be able to better identify the client's specific needs and continuously assess the knowledge, skills, and abilities that could be relevant for greater workplace success.

The framework requires the psychologist to be flexible and adapt to the client's needs by serving as career counselor, coach, case manager, and advocate. By doing so, the psychologist can model the flexibility and adaptability necessary for success in the ever-changing world of work.

Unson and Richardson (2013) further explored the flexibility and adaptability that older workers need to continue participating successfully in the workplace. Applying P. B. Baltes and Baltes's (1990) selection-optimization-compensation (SOC) model for successful aging or adaptive competence, Unson and Richardson identified both barriers to and strategies for success for older workers who continue to work beyond their primary careers. Study participants included both those who had continued to work in their primary occupation and those who had chosen or been compelled to shift to a new occupation. The average age of participants was 67 years old, and reasons for their extending their work lives included retirement, personal choice, and redundancy. This qualitative study of 30 aging adults yielded a number of findings of use to the psychologist. Unson and Richardson found that potential barriers to successful transition from a person's primary work or career to an encore career (Freedman, 2007) were adjusting to the new workplace, coworkers, and job tasks as well as ageism. Other barriers to adjustment included lack of self-confidence and health concerns. Unson and Richardson also found that success in this type of transition is related to the ability to be positive and open to change, to be willing to ask for help and continue learning, and to be prepared to maintain and draw on professional and social networks. The authors also emphasized the importance of the older worker's remaining adaptable to change and being a strong career self-manager. B. B. Baltes, Rudolph, and Bal (2012) discussed the SOC model and its application to the world of work and aging workers who continue in the workplace.

In their examination of older adults' work and retirement patterns, Sterns and Dawson (2012) underscored the benefits of assisting older workers to access the tools and resources that will help them successfully adapt to evolving work demands and age-related changes. The retirement adjustment process is navigated successfully by most, but

611

various studies have indicated that for about 30% of people in this transition, retirement is stressful (Bossé et al., 1996). For that population, the psychologist can draw on an individual's resilience capabilities. To promote development of resilience, for instance, the psychologist could examine the four domains of resilience that the client has available, identify areas of vulnerability and strengths, and assist the client in actions that will enhance their resilience capabilities. Such outcomes can occur by supporting older workers in their ongoing efforts to evaluate their expectations for retirement and become open to greater possibilities. Additionally, the client can be encouraged to update knowledge, skills, and abilities to remain competitive in the workforce or in a volunteer role. A review of plans for retirement and participation in retirement planning can help a client make decisions about his or her available options. These activities will empower the client in negotiating the demands of the retirement process.

CONCLUSION

The decision to retire or continue working reflects a complex array of factors, including economic well-being, personal preferences, subjective health, attitudes regarding leisure, and the desire—or lack of desire—to continue working. Emphasis should be placed on individual differences in the nature of life and work experience: Satisfaction and the ability to work reflect the normative aging, generational differences, and unique life events of the older adult worker. Intervention in the workplace in such areas as wellness promotion, training and retraining, and human resources management may make working longer a more frequent and normative choice. The ultimate responsibility for maintaining professional competence, however, rests with the individual employee. At the same time, an organization can foster competence by providing opportunities to update knowledge and skills, for challenging work assignments, and for interactions with coworkers and management that benefit not only the aging worker but also all workers.

Research on retirement indicates that in the coming years, we need to carefully weigh the importance of voluntary and involuntary decisions to retire and the relevant factors related to job satisfaction, health, sense of purpose and meaning, and financial well-being. For more than 20 years, a major emphasis has been on the positive aspects and normalcy of retirement and approaches to facilitate the transition. At the same time, the United States has been a leader in advocacy for the rights of older adult workers to continue to work if they are capable. A serious question for the future is, How can we make the workplace more attractive to an extended work life? Demand for professional retirement education and retirement counseling will continue to rise as baby boomers age. Psychologists and others must meet the counseling needs of aging adults and the numerous options for work-to-retirement transitions; an up-to-date geropsychological research paradigm will be essential for attaining that goal.

References

Age Discrimination in Employment Act, 29 U.S.C. Sec. 621 et seq. (1976 & Supp V. 1981 & 1986).

Americans With Disabilities Act of 1990, Pub. L. No. 101-336, Sec.1211, 9. (1990).

Anderson, M. L., Goodman, J., & Schlossberg, N. K. (2012). *Counseling adults in transition: Linking Schlossberg's theory with practice in a diverse world.* New York, NY: Springer.

Baltes, B. B., Rudolph, C. W., & Bal, A. C. (2012). A review of aging theories and modern work perspectives. In J. W. Hedge & W. C. Borman (Eds.), *The Oxford handbook of work and aging* (pp. 117–136). New York, NY: Oxford University Press. doi:10.1093/oxfordhb/9780195385052.013.0069

Baltes, P. B., & Baltes, M. M. (Eds.). (1990). *Successful aging: Perspectives from the behavioral sciences.* Cambridge, MA: Cambridge University Press. doi:10.1017/CBO9780511665684

Bender, K. A., & Jivan, N. A. (2005). *What makes retirees happy?* Chestnut Hill, MA: Center for Retirement Research at Boston College. Retrieved from http://crr.bc.edu/briefs/what-makes-retirees-happy

Blazer, D. G., & Wu, L. (2009). The epidemiology of at-risk and binge drinking among middle-aged and elderly community adults: National survey on drug use and health. *American Journal of Psychiatry, 166,* 1162–1169. doi:10.1176/appi.ajp.2009.09010016

Blow, F. C., Brower, K. J., Schulenberg, J. E., Demo-Dananberg, L. M., Young, J. P., & Beresford, T. P. (1992). The Michigan Alcoholism Screening Test—Geriatric Version (MAST–G): A new elderly-specific screening instrument. *Alcoholism, Clinical and Experimental Research, 16,* 372.

Blustein, D. L. (Ed.). (2013). *The Oxford handbook of the psychology of working.* New York, NY: Oxford University Press. doi:10.1093/oxfordhb/97801997 58791.001.0001

Blustein, D. L., Kenna, A. C., Gill, N., & DeVoy, J. E. (2008). The psychology of working: A new framework for counseling practice and public policy. *Career Development Quarterly, 56,* 294–308. doi:10.1002/j.2161-0045.2008.tb00095.x

Bobek, B. L., & Robbins, S. B. (2005). Counseling for career transition: Career pathing, job loss, and reentry. In S. D. Brown & R. W. Lent (Eds.), *Career development and counseling* (pp. 625–650). Hoboken, NJ: Wiley.

Bossé, R., Spiro, A., III, & Kressin, N. R. (1996). The psychology of retirement. In R. T. Woods (Ed.), *Handbook of the clinical psychology of ageing* (pp. 141–157). Chichester, England: Wiley.

Bratter, B., & Dennis, H. (2008). *Project renewment: The first retirement model for career women.* New York, NY: Scribner.

Brink, T. L., Yesavage, J. A., Lum, O., Heersema, P., Adey, M. B., & Rose, T. L. (1982). Screening tests for geriatric depression. *Clinical Gerontologist, 1,* 37–43. doi:10.1300/J018v01n01_06

Brown, S. K. (2012). *What are older workers seeking? An AARP/SHRM survey of 50+ workers.* Washington, DC: AARP.

Cahill, K. E., Giandrea, M. D., & Quinn, J. F. (2006). Retirement patterns from career employment. *Gerontologist, 46,* 514–523. doi:10.1093/geront/46.4.514

Calvo, E., Sarkisian, N., & Tamborini, C. R. (2013). Causal effects of retirement timing on subjective physical and emotional health. *The Journals of Gerontology, Series B: Psychological Sciences and Social Sciences, 68,* 73–84. doi:10.1093/geronb/gbs097

Cappelli, P., & Novelli, W. (2010). *Managing the older worker: How to prepare for the new organizational order.* Boston, MA: Harvard Business Press.

Connolly, J. (1992). Participatory versus lecture/discussion preretirement education: A comparison. *Educational Gerontology, 18,* 365–379. doi:10.1080/0360127920180405

Cornman, J. M., & Kingson, E. R. (1996). Trends, issues, perspectives and values for the aging of the baby boom cohorts. *Gerontologist, 36,* 15–26. doi:10.1093/geront/36.1.15

Czaja, S. J., & Sharit, J. (2009). *Aging and work: Issues and implications in a changing landscape.* Baltimore, MD: Johns Hopkins University Press.

Dennis, H. (1984). *Retirement preparation.* Lexington, MA: DC Heath and Company.

Dennis, H. (1988). *Fourteen steps in managing an aging workforce.* Lexington, MA: DC Heath and Company.

Dennis, H., & Fike, A. T. (2012). Retirement planning: New context, process, language, and players. In J. W. Hedge & W. C. Borman (Eds.), *The Oxford handbook work and aging* (pp. 538–548). New York, NY: Oxford University Press.

Doeringer, P. B., & Terkla, D. G. (1990). Business necessity, bridge jobs, and the nonbureaucratic firm. In P. B. Doeringer (Ed.), *Bridges to retirement: Older workers in a changing labor market* (pp. 146–171). Ithaca, NY: ILR Press.

Doshi, J. A., Cen, L., & Polsky, D. (2008). Depression and retirement in late middle-aged U.S. workers. *Health Services Research, 43,* 693–713. doi:10.1111/j.1475-6773.2007.00782.x

Doverspike, D., & Taylor, M. (2003). Retirement planning and preparation. In T. Beehr & G. Adams (Eds.), *Retirement: Current research and future directions* (pp. 53–82). New York, NY: Springer.

Duffy, M. (1999). *Handbook of counseling and psychotherapy with older adults.* Hoboken, NJ: Wiley.

Dychtwald, K., Erickson, T., & Morrison, B. (2004). It is time to retire. Retirement. *Harvard Business Review, 82,* 48–57.

Dychtwald, K., & Kadlec, D. J. (2009). *A new purpose: Redefining money, family, work, retirement, and success.* New York, NY: Collins Living.

Earl, J. K., & Yu, T. (2012). *Promoting the Australian retirement experience.* Report prepared for National Seniors Australia, based on data collected by the University of New South Wales. Retrieved from http://library.constantcontact.com/download/get/file/1101901198311-1148/Promoting+The+Australian+Retirement+Experience+Report.pdf

Feldman, D. C. (2007). Career mobility and career stability among older workers. In K. S. Shultz & G. A. Adams (Eds.), *Aging and work in the 21st century* (pp. 179–197). Mahwah, NJ: Erlbaum.

Forbes. (2011). *Fostering innovation through a diverse workforce.* New York, NY: Forbes Insight. Retrieved from http://images.forbes.com/forbesinsight/study PDFs/Innovations_Through_Diversity.pdf

Franklin, A. J., & Medvide, M. B. (2013). Psychotherapy and the integration of the psychology of working into therapeutic practice. In D. L. Blustein (Ed.), *The Oxford handbook of the psychology of working* (pp. 252–270). New York, NY: Oxford University Press. doi:10.1093/oxfordhb/9780199758791.013.0015

Freedman, M. (2007). The social-purpose encore career: Baby boomers, civic engagement, and the next stage of work. *Generations, 4,* 43–46.

Fretz, B. R., Kluge, N. A., Ossana, S. M., Jones, S. M., & Merikangas, M. W. (1989). Intervention targets for reducing preretirement anxiety and depression. *Journal of Counseling Psychology, 36*, 301–307. doi:10.1037/0022-0167.36.3.301

Frieze, I. H., Olson, J. E., & Murrell, A. J. (2011). Working beyond 65: Predictors of late retirement for women and men MBAs. *Journal of Women and Aging, 23*, 40–57. doi:10.1080/08952841.2011.540485

Graham-Squire, D., & Jacobson, K. (2013) *Which workers are most at risk of reduced work hours under the Affordable Care Act?* Retrieved from http://www.laborcenter.berkeley.edu/healthcare

Griffin, B., Loh, V., & Hesketh, B. (2013). Age, gender, and the retirement process. In M. Wang (Ed.), *The Oxford handbook of retirement* (pp. 202–214). New York, NY: Oxford University Press.

Hall, D. T., & Mirvis, P. H. (1996). The new protean career: Psychological success and the path with a heart. In D. T. Hall (Ed.), *The career is dead—long live the career: A relational approach to careers* (pp. 15–45). San Francisco, CA: Jossey-Bass.

Hedge, J. W., & Borman, W. C. (2012). *The Oxford handbook of work and aging.* New York, NY: Oxford University Press.

Hedge, J. W., Borman, W. C., & Lammlein, S. E. (2006). *The aging workforce: Realities, myths, and implications for organizations.* Washington, DC: American Psychological Association. doi:10.1037/11325-000

Hill, R. D., Thorn, B. L., & Packard, T. (2000). Counseling older adults: Theoretical and empirical issues in prevention and intervention. In S. D. Brown & R. W. Lent (Eds.), *Handbook of counseling psychology* (3rd ed., pp. 499–531). New York, NY: Wiley.

Hunter, W. W. (1976). *Preparation for retirement* (3rd ed.). Ann Arbor: Institute of Gerontology, University of Michigan-Wayne State University.

Kantarci, T. (2013). *The effects of partial retirement on health.* Netspar Discussion Paper No. 10/2013.037.

Kim, J. E., & Moen, P. (2001). Moving into retirement: Preparation and transitions in late midlife. In M. E. Lachman (Ed.), *Handbook of midlife development* (pp. 487–527). New York, NY: Wiley.

Kim, N., & Hall, D. T. (2013). Protean career model and retirement. In M. Wang (Ed.), *The Oxford handbook of retirement* (pp. 102–116). New York, NY: Oxford University Press.

Klehe, U.-C., Koen, J., & DePater, I. E. (2012). Ending on the scrap heap? The experience of job loss and job search among older workers. In J. W. Hedge & W. C. Borman (Eds.), *The Oxford handbook of work and aging* (pp. 313–340). New York, NY: Oxford University Press.

Lowman, R. (1993). *Counseling and psychotherapy of work dysfunctions.* Washington, DC: American Psychological Association. doi:10.1037/10133-000

Mandal, B., & Roe, B. (2008). Job loss, retirement and the mental health of older Americans. *Journal of Mental Health Policy and Economics, 11*, 167–176.

Merrill Lynch Wealth Management. (2013). *Americans' perspectives on new retirement realities and the longevity bonus: A 2013 Merrill Lynch retirement study, conducted in partnership with Age Wave.* New York, NY: Author.

Moen, P. (2012). Retirement dilemmas and decisions. In J. W. Hedge & W. C. Borman (Eds.), *The Oxford handbook on work and aging* (pp. 549–569). New York, NY: Oxford University Press.

Mutchler, J. E., Burr, J. A., Pienta, A. M., & Massagli, M. P. (1997). Pathways to labor force exit: Work transitions and work instability. *The Journals of Gerontology, Series B: Psychological Sciences and Social Sciences, 52*, 252–261.

Nelson, J. E., & Bolles, R. N. (2007). *What color is your parachute? For retirement.* Berkeley, CA: Ten Speed Press.

Noone, J., Stephens, C., & Alpass, F. (2009). Preretirement planning and well-being in later life. *Research on Aging, 31*, 295–317. doi:10.1177/0164027508330718

Patient Protection and Affordable Care Act. Title IV, x4207, USC HR, 3590, (2010).

Polk, L. V. (1997). Toward a middle-range theory of resilience. *Advances in Nursing Science, 19*(3), 1–13. doi:10.1097/00012272-199703000-00002

Quinn, J. F. (2010). Work, retirement, and the encore career: Elders and the future of the American workforce. *Generations, 34*, 45–55.

Raphaelson, E. (2013, September 30). Working after you retire has its hurdles. *Chicago Tribune.*

Reitzes, D. C., & Mutran, E. J. (2004). The transition to retirement: Stages and factors that influence retirement adjustment. *International Journal of Aging and Human Development, 59*, 63–84. doi:10.2190/NYPP-RFFP-5RFK-8EB8

Richardson, V. E. (1993). *Retirement counseling: A handbook for gerontology practitioners.* New York, NY: Springer.

Rix, S. E. (2013). *The employment situation: May 2013: Some good news for older workers tempered by continuing problems.* Washington, DC: AARP Public Policy Institute.

Rosenkoetter, M. M., & Garris, J. M. (1998). Psychosocial changes following retirement. *Journal of Advanced Nursing, 27*, 966–976. doi:10.1046/j.1365-2648.1998.t01-1-00569.x

Rothwell, W. J., Sterns, H. L., Spokus, D., & Reaser, J. M. (2008). *Working longer: New strategies for managing, training, and retaining older workers*. New York, NY: American Management Association.

Salami, S. O. (2010). Retirement context and psychological factors as predictors of well-being among retired teachers. *Europe's Journal of Psychology, 6*, 47–64. doi:10.5964/ejop.v6i2.184

Saunders, J. B., Aasland, O. G., Babor, T. F., de la Fuente, J. R., & Grant, M. (1993). Development of the Alcohol Use Disorders Identification Test (AUDIT): WHO collaborative project on early detection of persons with harmful alcohol consumption. II. *Addiction, 88*, 791–804. doi:10.1111/j.1360-0443.1993.tb02093.x

Schlossberg, N. K. (1981). A model for analyzing human adaptation to transition. *Counseling Psychologist, 9*, 2–18. doi:10.1177/001100008100900202

Schlossberg, N. K. (1984). *Counseling adults in transition*. New York, NY: Springer.

Schlossberg, N. K. (2010). *Revitalizing retirement: Reshaping your identity, relationships, and purpose*. Washington, DC: American Psychological Association.

Schonfeld, L., King-Kallimanis, B., Duchene, D. M., Etheridge, R. L., Herrera, J. R., Barry, K. L., & Lynn, N. (2010). Screening and brief intervention for substance misuse among older adults: The Florida BRITE project. *American Journal of Public Health, 100*, 108–114. doi:10.2105/AJPH.2008.149534

Shultz, K. S., & Adams, G. A. (2007). *Aging and work in the 21st century*. Mahwah, NJ: Erlbaum.

Shultz, K. S., & Wang, M. (2011). Psychological perspectives on the changing nature of retirement. *American Psychologist, 66*, 170–179. doi:10.1037/a0022411

Smith, J. (1996). Planning about life: A social-interactive and life-span perspective. In P. Baltes & U. M. Staudinger (Eds.), *Interactive minds: Life-span perspectives on the social foundation of cognition* (pp. 242–272). Hillsdale, NJ: Erlbaum.

Staudinger, U. M. (1999). Social cognition and a psychological approach to an art of life. In T. M. Hess & F. Blanchard-Fields (Eds.), *Social cognition and aging* (pp. 343–375). San Diego, CA: Academic Press. doi:10.1016/B978-012345260-3/50016-1

Sterns, H. L. (1986). Training and retraining adult and older worker. In J. E. Birren & J. Livingston (Eds.), *Age, health, and employment* (pp. 93–113). Englewood Cliffs, NJ: Prentice-Hall.

Sterns, H. L., & Alexander, R. A. (1987). Industrial gerontology: The aging individual and work. In K. W. Schaie (Ed.), *Annual review of gerontology and geriatrics* (pp. 93–113). New York, NY: Springer.

Sterns, H. L., & Dawson, N. (2012). Emerging perspectives on resilience in adulthood and later life: Work, retirement and resilience. In B. Hayslip & G. Smith (Eds.), *Annual review of gerontology and geriatrics: Emerging perspectives on resilience in adulthood and later life* (pp. 211–230). New York, NY: Springer.

Sterns, H. L., & Doverspike, D. (1989). Aging and training and learning process. In R. A. Katzell (Ed.), *Training and development in organizations* (pp. 299–332). San Francisco, CA: Jossey-Bass.

Sterns, H. L., & Gray, J. H. (1999). Work, leisure, and retirement. In J. C. Cavanaugh & S. K. Whitbourne (Eds.), *Gerontology: An interdisciplinary perspective* (pp. 355–389). New York, NY: Oxford University Press.

Sterns, H. L., & Hyuck, M. H. (2001). Midlife and work. In M. E. Lachman (Ed.), *Handbook of midlife development* (pp. 447–486). New York, NY: Wiley.

Sterns, H. L., & Kaplan, J. (2003). Self-management of career and retirement. In T. Beehr & G. Adams (Eds.), *Retirement: Current research and future directions* (pp. 188–213). New York, NY: Springer.

Sterns, H. L., & Patchett, M. (1984). Technology and the aging adult: Career development and training. In P. R. Robinson & J. E. Birren (Eds.), *Aging and technology* (pp. 261–277). New York, NY: Plenum Press. doi:10.1007/978-1-4613-2401-0_26

Sterns, H. L., & Sterns, A. A. (1995). Age, health, and employment capability of older Americans. In S. Bass (Ed.), *Older and active* (pp. 10–34). New Haven, CT: Yale University Press.

Sterns, H. L., & Sterns, A. A. (2013). Approaches to aging and working. In D. L. Bluestein (Ed.), *The Oxford handbook of the psychology of working* (pp. 160–184). New York, NY: Oxford University Press.

Sterns, H. L., & Subich, L. M. (2002). Career development in midcareer. In D. C. Feldman (Ed.), *Work careers: A developmental perspective* (pp. 186–213). San Francisco, CA: Jossey-Bass.

Sterns, H. L., & Subich, L. M. (2005). Counseling for retirement. In S. D. Brown & R. W. Lent (Eds.), *Career development and counseling handbook: Putting theory and research to work* (pp. 506–521). New York, NY: Wiley.

Substance Abuse and Mental Health Services Administration. (2011). *The treatment of depression in older adults: Practitioner's guide for working with older adults with depression*. Rockville, MD: Author.

Taylor, M. A., & Geldhauser, H. A. (2007). Low income older workers. In K. S. Shultz & G. A. Adams (Eds.), *Aging and work in the 21st century* (pp. 25–49). Hillsdale, NJ: Erlbaum.

Taylor-Carter, M. A., Cook, K., & Weinberg, C. (1997). Planning and expectations of the retirement experience. *Educational Gerontology, 23*, 273–288. doi:10.1080/0360127970230306

Toossi, M. (2012a). Labor force projections to 2020: A more slowly growing workforce. *Monthly Labor Review, 135*, 43–64.

Toossi, M. (2012b). Projections of the labor force to 2050: A visual essay. *Monthly Labor Review, 135*, 3–16.

Unson, C., & Richardson, M. (2013). Insights into the experience of older workers and change: Through the lens of selection, optimization, and compensation. *Gerontologist, 53*, 484–494. doi:10.1093/geront/gns095

U.S. Department of Human Services. (2011). The treatment of depression in older adults: Key issues. *HHS Publication SMA 11-4631*. Rockville, MD: Author.

U.S. Department of Labor, Bureau of Labor Statistics. (2010). *Record unemployment among older workers does not keep them out of the job market*. Retrieved from http://www.bls.gov/opub/ils/summary_10_04/older_workers.htm

U.S. Department of Labor, Bureau of Labor Statistics. (2012). *Employment status of displaced workers*. Retrieved from http://www.bls.gov/opub/ted/2012/ted_20120828.htm

van Solinge, H. (2013). Adjustment to retirement. In M. Wang (Ed.), *The Oxford handbook of retirement* (pp. 311–324). New York, NY: Oxford University Press.

Wang, M. (2012). Health and fiscal and psychological well-being in retirement. In J. W. Hedge & W. C. Borman (Eds.), *The Oxford handbook of work and aging* (pp. 570–586). New York, NY: Oxford University Press. doi:10.1093/oxfordhb/9780195385052.013.0165

Wang, M. (Ed.). (2013). *The Oxford handbook of retirement*. New York, NY: Oxford University Press.

Wang, M., Olson, D. A., & Shultz, K. S. (2013). *Mid and later career issues: An integrative perspective*. New York, NY: Routledge.

Wang, M., & Shultz, K. S. (2010). Employee retirement: A review and recommendations for future investigation. *Journal of Management, 36*, 172–206. doi:10.1177/0149206309347957

Warner, D. F., Hayward, M. D., & Hardy, M. A. (2010). The retirement life course in America at the dawn of the 21st century. *Population Research and Policy Review, 29*, 893–919. doi:10.1007/s11113-009-9173-2

Wheaton, F., & Crimmins, E. M. (2013). The demography of aging and retirement. In M. Wang (Ed.), *The Oxford handbook of retirement* (pp. 22–41). New York, NY: Oxford University Press.

Yesavage, J. A., Brink, T. L., Rose, T. L., Lum, O., Huang, V., Adey, M., & Leier, V. O. (1982–1983). Development and validation of a geriatric depression screening scale: A preliminary report. *Journal of Psychiatric Research, 17*, 37–49. doi:10.1016/0022-3956(82)90033-4

Zhan, Y., Wang, M., Lui, S., & Shultz, K. S. (2009). Bridge employment and retirees' health: A longitudinal investigation. *Journal of Occupational Health Psychology, 14*, 374–389. doi:10.1037/a0015285

Zickar, M. J. (2013). The evolving history of retirement within the United States. In M. Wang (Ed.), *The Oxford handbook of retirement* (pp. 10–21). New York, NY: Oxford University Press.

CHAPTER 24

MARRIAGE, SECOND COUPLEHOOD, DIVORCE, AND SINGLEHOOD IN OLD AGE

Liat Ayalon and Chaya Koren

This chapter explores marital status in old age. Specifically, we focus on marriage, second couplehood, divorce, and singlehood. It does not discuss widowhood, which is reviewed in a separate chapter in this book. This review discusses both change and continuity in marital status over time, and it adopts the life-course perspective of families over time. This approach argues that to understand continuity and change over time, one has to take into consideration three different *time clocks* of potential influence on the family dynamic. The first is the *ontogenetic time*, which can be equated roughly with one's chronological age. Accordingly, the individual's behavior within the family can be attributed partially to this individual's chronological age as well as to the chronological ages of the other family members. The *generational time* refers to one's generational position within the family and the roles and expectations associated with this particular generation. Finally, *historical time* or cohort effect refers to sociocultural macro influences that affect the family (Bengtson & Allen, 1993).

Following this rationale, when we discuss the various marital statuses, we pay attention to all three time clocks. For instance, we focus on the age at which divorce takes place (i.e., ontogenetic time), following the assumption that the experience of divorce at 40 years old is not the same as divorce at 75 years old. In addition, the roles and expectations associated with divorced fathers versus divorced grandfathers (i.e., generational time) and the specific period in which divorce takes place and how societal norms and expectations affect the

experience of divorce (i.e., historical time) should be taken into consideration to obtain a comprehensive understanding of the etiology and impact of the various marital statuses on the lives of older adults.

As can be seen in Table 24.1, there are marked differences in the prevalence of the four marital statuses discussed in this chapter. Although marriage remains the most common marital status among those between the ages of 65 and 75 years, as it is among the younger age-groups, this is not the case for women over the age of 75 years (mainly because of the increase in the prevalence of widowhood). In addition, although marital trends for men and women remain consistent, some diversions clearly allude to the importance of gender when examining the prevalence, etiology, and consequences of the various marital statuses.

Table 24.1 summarizes statistics concerning the prevalence of married, divorced, and never-married individuals based on the 2010 and 1940 statistics. Although, for the most part, marriage rates are consistent across these two time periods, they reflect a different distribution of marital statuses, as the rate of divorce was nearly zero in 1940, whereas by 2010, divorce has become a normative experience in certain sectors of society (U.S. Census Bureau, 1940).

These various statistics concerning marital status should be reviewed in light of a macro, sociocultural context as they are largely a product of changes in the average life span over the past century. In addition to the increase in life expectancy, the increase in education attainment and the entrance of women

http://dx.doi.org/10.1037/14459-024
APA Handbook of Clinical Geropsychology: Vol. 2. Assessment, Treatment, and Issues of Later Life,
P. A. Lichtenberg and B. T. Mast (Editors-in-Chief)

TABLE 24.1

Marital Status by Age and Gender Based on the 2010 and 1940 Census Reports

Year	Age-group (years)	Men			Women		
		Married	Divorced	Never married (single in the 1940 Census[a])	Married	Divorced	Never married (single in the 1940 Census[a])
U.S. Census Bureau, 2010	65–74	78%	11%	4.5%	55.9%	15%	5.1%
	>75	69.8%	5.6%	3.5%	32.3%	7%	3.9%
U.S. Census Bureau, 1940	65–69	70%	<1%	11.6%	51%	<1%	10.3%
	75–79	62.8%	<1%	10.7%	37.9%	<1%	10.7%

[a]The different terminology employed in the two censuses implies different categories. It is likely that some divorced individuals were classified as single in the 1940 census. Percent widowed is not reported.

into the workforce also should be considered as partially responsible for the tremendous changes in societal norms and expectations concerning marriage and family life.

While informative, it is important to note that the statistics presented in Table 24.1 reflect a static picture of prevalence rates during a single time point. As such, these statistics fail to capture the incidence (i.e., new cases) of divorce or marriage. Whereas the prevalence rate gives an indication about the proportion of the population that is characterized as divorced at a particular point in time, the incidence of divorce relates to the risk of experiencing a new divorce at a particular time point. As a result, the prevalence rates of married older adults, for example, fail to reflect the number of remarriages. Similarly, the prevalence rates of divorced older adults fail to reflect that timing at which the divorce took place.

This review discusses four unique types of marital status in old age: lifelong marriage, second couplehood, divorce, and singlehood. In addition, we discuss relational issues related to lesbian, gay, bisexual, and transgender (LGBT) older adults. Each of these topics is followed by a review of available psychosocial interventions that specifically target the particular population group at hand. We conclude with a review of assessment tools of potential use for addressing relational issues in older adults.

LIFELONG MARRIAGE AMONG OLDER ADULTS

Lifelong marriage is defined as first marriage that began when one or both partners were younger than 40 years old and has continued until one or both partners is older than 65 years old. Lifelong marriages in old age might be considered a common, taken-for-granted phenomenon with no particular interest. Older adults belong to a cohort for whom the general rule is to remain married for better or worse, rather than divorce when things get rough. Most of the very old are widowed and not remarried, however, turning a lifelong marital relationship into the exception. In addition, although there is a general increase in divorce rates among all age-groups, divorce rates are relatively lower among people age 55 years and older (U.S. Census Bureau, 2010). Although the increase in widowhood turns lifelong marriages among the very old into the exception, the decrease in divorce rates within this age-group indicates that these couples tend to stay together. Therefore, a deeper understanding as to what keeps them together is called for.

The literature addressing lifelong marriages from a life-course perspective usually compares middle-age couples and older couples (Smith et al., 2009) whereas some literature also includes younger couples (Hatch & Bulcroft, 2004). Issues addressed in the literature regarding lifelong marriages relate to structure and dynamics, continuity and change (Weishaus & Field, 1988), intimacy and autonomy (Goodman, 1999), togetherness (we-ness) and separateness (Seider, Hirschberger, Nelson, & Levenson, 2009), sexuality (Hinchliff & Gott, 2004), commitment (Swensen & Trahaug, 1985), disagreement, disappointments and conflict (R. G. Henry, Miller, & Giarrusso, 2005), health and relationship dynamics (Walker & Luszcz, 2009), and marital interaction and satisfaction (Schmitt, Kliegel, & Shapiro, 2007).

Structure and Dynamics of Lifelong Marriages: Continuity and Change

Earlier literature on the dynamics of lifelong marriages over the life course reveals controversies. Studies have indicated that perceived quality and satisfaction from lifelong marriages are curvilinear (Orbuch, House, Mero, & Webster, 1996). Other studies question this finding, claiming that this is true only from a retrospective point of view, whereas a prospective view indicates that quality and satisfaction decline with time (Vaillant & Vaillant, 1993). To strengthen this argument, in cross-sectional studies, marriages of poorer quality might not be examined because of divorce. This allows examining only high-quality marriages. As a result, it appears as if marriages' quality improves in later life (Umberson, Williams, Powers, Chen, & Campbell, 2005).

Others (Weishaus & Field, 1988) have suggested a typology that classifies different types of marriages from a 50-year prospective longitudinal perspective; some marriages are characterizes as stable either positive, neutral, or negative; some marriages are categorized as curvilinear; and yet other marriages are characterized as continuous in either decline or increase in satisfaction. The study was based on the longitudinal Berkeley Older Generation Study, which focused on case records of 17 marriages that have lasted between 50 and 69 years. The participants have been interviewed from the time their children were born over a period of 54 years (starting in 1928–1929 up to 1982–1984). Nearly three quarters of the marriages showed either the curvilinear or the stable–positive patterns in terms of quality

and satisfaction with the marriage. An important finding was that the future of a marriage could not be predicted from its quality at any given point (Weishaus & Field, 1988).

A life-course perspective can provide explanations to contrasting findings regarding the relationship between duration of a marriage and a decrease or an increase in marital satisfaction and marital disagreement (Hatch & Bulcroft, 2004; Umberson et al., 2005). For instance, Hatch and Bulcroft (2004) have indicated that factors other than the duration of the marriage, such as family life-course stage, age, or birth cohort could explain the lower frequency of marital disagreements reported by older wives and husbands.

A life-course perspective (an 8-year period in the life course of individuals between the ages of 24 and 96 years) on marital quality found that it tends to decline over time (Umberson et al., 2005). Although negative marital experiences tend to increase, positive marital experiences tend to diminish over time. Some couples, however, start with higher levels of marital quality and others with lower, so the decline has different meanings for different marriages. Regarding marital quality, age was a stronger predictor of the quality of lifelong marriage than marital duration. Therefore, it was suggested that greater emphasis should be placed on developmental changes in marital quality that may occur as people age. Parenting also shapes the marriage over the life course, with more rewards being perceived in later life.

Time as a multidimensional concept also plays a part in marital quality. Time includes the passage of years, the function of one's chronological age, and marital duration. The timing of parenting and parenting transitions in the life course is significant for marital quality change. Although marital quality tends to decline over time, it was found that age is associated positively with marital quality. This probably is due to differences among cohorts that have different norms related to the right age for marriage or for building up a family. Umberson et al. (2005) concluded that it is important to consider the multidimensionality of time, including age and marital duration, and to consider family transitions related to having children and to emptying and refilling the nest in creating the meaning and experiences of marriage over time.

The classification of married couples as happily versus unhappily married is another way to examine the quality of the marriage (Carstensen, Gottman, & Levenson, 1995). As for couples who have stayed together for long periods of time but were not satisfied with their marriages, findings suggest that these couples may have learned to "leave well enough alone" by staying in affectively neutral interactive sequences and avoiding escalation to negative affect (Carstensen et al., 1995). Studies have found evidence that positive marital relations (characterized by support and closeness) may be protective of psychological well-being, whereas negative marital relations (characterized by disagreement, dissatisfaction, and distress) are associated with poor mental health outcomes for one or both members of the couple, irrespective of health status and other sociodemographic variables (Walker & Luszcz, 2009).

Most studies focus merely on disagreements in marital relationships among older couples. It is suggested, however, that collaboration in problem solving among older couples is perhaps more relevant to examine due to the changes couples have to go through together and the more time they are bound to spend together after retirement (Smith et al., 2009). A study that examined differences between middle-age couples (40–50 years old) and older couples (60–70 years old) regarding disagreements and collaborative problem solving found that older couples reported less negative affect and more positive appraisals of spouses during disagreement and displayed friendlier and less hostile behavior and more warmth. These behaviors, however, were not apparent when marital satisfaction was controlled for, suggesting that the results have more to do with marital adjustment than with age (Smith et al., 2009).

In examining predictors of marital satisfaction in old age, a high quality of dyadic interaction (Schmitt et al., 2007) and the use of we-ness language (Seider et al., 2009) were particularly important for women. Women tend to experience higher levels of burnout throughout the marriage, and in late-life this trend continues, whereas husbands report higher levels of satisfaction (Kulik, 2002).

Spousal Conflict and Lifelong Marriage

Studies of marital conflict have concluded that the frequency of disagreement between spouses declines over time in a marital relationship because spouses have accommodated to one another (Condie, 1989). More recent results, however, have refuted this idea by indicating that spousal conflicts depend on life-course stages such as children launching and empty nest or norms related to cohort rather than on the duration of the marriage (Hatch & Bulcroft, 2004).

A study of 105 couples (ages 52–86 years) in lifelong marriages (42 years in average) analyzed responses to an open-ended question about difficulties, disagreements, and disappointments in the marriage (R. G. Henry et al., 2005). The study found 10 themes that inductively emerged from the data and were related to arousing difficulties. These included leisure activities (23%), intimacy (13%), finances (11%), no problems (11%), personality (9%), intergenerational relations (9%), household concerns (9%), personal habits (7%), health issues (6%), and work and retirement (2%). The dyadic data also were examined within the relationship. It was found that 54% of the couples had divergent responses, 30% had somewhat congruent responses, and 16% couples were completely congruent on the types of challenges each partner reported. When wives reported no problems, 46% of their husbands also reported no problems in the relationship, whereas 23% of them complained about intimacy in the relationship. When husbands reported no problems, however, only 19% of their wives also reported no problems, whereas 16% reported issues with intimacy.

Sexual Relationships Within Lifelong Marriages

Having a sexual relationship with one's spouse is part of intimacy within marriages and contributes to one's well-being. The topic, however, scarcely has been studied among older couples in long-term marriages. Perhaps this is because of the assumption that sexuality is not relevant for older people. Findings from a qualitative study on the meaning of sexual relationships within long-term marriages (minimum 20 years; mean length of marriage 43 years), relate to the importance of sex within a marriage also in old age and describe perceptions concerning the benefits of sexual engagement, which allows pleasuring not only oneself but also one's partner, as a way to express and enhances one's love (Hinchliff & Gott, 2004).

The study also addressed changes experienced in married sexual relationships in later life. One such change identified by participants was the inability to have penetrative sex. Instead, kissing, hugging, and cuddling were used to express, preserve, and enhance togetherness. Another form of change was identified by those who still engage in penetrative sex: These participants reported being more patient and trying new ways of arousal that were not necessarily sexual in nature but also were a result of togetherness (Hinchliff & Gott, 2004).

Lifelong Marriages, Health, and Well-Being

In general, marriage is considered to have a beneficial effect on older adults' health and well-being (Schulz et al., 2004), across a range of chronic conditions, functional limitations, and disability and also unrelated to demographic characteristics, such as race or ethnicity (Pienta, Hayward, & Jenkins, 2000). The positive effect of marriage even transcends to mortality, with individuals in lifelong marriages having the lowest mortality risk (Rogers, 1995). Men experience more benefits from marriage than women. This partially is attributed to the fact that women have more extensive social support networks. As a result, unmarried men are at a particular risk for negative health consequences and have the highest risk for mortality (Hu & Goldman, 1990).

Two competing explanations were proposed to account for the more favorable health and mental health status of married older adults relative to single or divorced older adults. The first is the social selection hypothesis, which suggests that individuals of poor physical or mental health are less likely to marry or to remain married (Goldman, 1993). The causation hypothesis, on the other hand, suggests that marriage has beneficial social, financial, and psychological effects on the individual (Williams & Umberson, 2004). Consistently, the life-strains perspective suggests that the strains associated with not being married continue throughout the life course (Pearlin & Johnson, 1977).

Therapy With Older Couples in Lifelong Marriages

Despite the increase in the proportion of older adults in the population, the number of articles on therapy with older adults in leading journals in the field of marital and family therapy (MFT) has not increased over the past few decades and stands at less than 3% (Lambert-Shute & Fruhauf, 2011). Consistent with this finding concerning limited empirical research on the topic, a study found ageist attitudes among experienced marriage and family therapists as well as among therapists in training. Apparently, the relational and mental health concerns and needs experienced by younger adults were viewed with a greater level of seriousness and concern when compared with identical concerns and needs reported by older couples (Ivey, Wieling, & Harris, 2000). These findings coincide with the low availability of gerontological training in graduate-level MFT training programs accredited by the American Association of Marriage and Family Therapy (Barber & Lyness, 2002). Given the limited empirical research on the topic, our review is based primarily on review papers, case studies, and small-scale quasi-experimental designs.

A review of the literature has shown that topics discussed in articles concerning MFT with older couples, roughly concern issues of physical health or mental illness and their impact on the dyadic relationship and sexuality. According to the review, the most common type of family therapy orientation discussed was the family lifecycle (Lambert-Shute & Fruhauf, 2011). A different study of older adults at risk for depression who received MFT found that the majority of referrals for MFT concerned widowed or married older adults. Difficulties in adjusting to loss or change were the main topics discussed, followed by difficulties coping with health problems and psychosomatic issues. Although participants reported high levels of satisfaction from these interventions, these were not evaluated systematically and there was no differentiation between marital therapy and family therapy, which pose two different therapeutic orientations (Carpenter, 1994). Another theoretical study has argued for the benefits of MFT for older adults over medications (Greggo, 2003), whereas a case study described the use of paradoxical interventions with older adults (Gilewski, Kuppinger, & Zarit, 1985).

Caregiving issues. Interventions that by default may address the dyadic relationship of couples can be found in the caregiving literature. In general, research has shown that psychoeducation, skill training, and therapeutic counseling interventions are effective with family caregivers. These various interventions have shown to reduce caregivers' stress, increase self-efficacy, and reduce quality of life (Northouse, Katapodi, Song, Zhang, & Mood, 2010; Sörensen, Pinquart, & Duberstein, 2002). Although reassuring, these interventions did not always target couples, but rather the focused on intergenerational caregiving. Moreover, with few exceptions (e.g., Scherrer, Ingersoll-Dayton, & Spencer, 2014), even when an intervention targeted the couple, interventions usually are delivered separately to the patient and the caregiver, especially if the patient suffers from dementia. A different meta-analysis of couple-oriented interventions for caregivers of partners who suffer from a chronic illness found that these interventions have small effects that can be strengthened by focusing on couples with high levels of distress and conflict (Martire, Schulz, Helgeson, Small, & Saghafi, 2010). This analysis, however, was not limited to older adults.

Sexual issues. An issue that is often highly relevant in couple's therapy is sexual relationship and sexuality. Although sexual problems among older adults are frequent, they are discussed infrequently (Lindau et al., 2007). The topic of older adults' sexuality has been overlooked by both the sexual literature and the gerontological literature (Muzacz & Akinsulure-Smith, 2013). Research has shown that health care professionals rely on stereotypes rather than on true knowledge of the topic (Gott, Hinchliff, & Galena, 2004). Hence, it is not surprising that few patients actually discuss sexual issues with their physicians (Lindau et al., 2007). Nevertheless, research has shown that the more clinicians are comfortable talking about sex with older adults, the more likely are older adults to talk freely about their sexuality (Willert & Semans, 2000).

Because of the reliance on the biomedical model, both health care providers and older adults tend to attribute a decline in sexual desire to age and age-related changes. Nevertheless, psychosocial aspects might prove as highly important in determining the sexual activity level of older adults (DeLamater & Sill, 2005). Awareness of stereotypes among health providers and older adults alike is important (Mayers & McBride, 1998), as these stereotypes likely affect the use of services and the potential interventions offered to older adults.

Taking a sexual history is recommended but can be challenging because of memory problems in some instances and discomfort to discuss challenging issues in other instances. Key issues in taking a sexual history concern sexual orientation and the frequency and variety of sexual activity (Ross, Chanon-Little, & Rosser, 2000). Obtaining such a history provides an opportunity to discuss difficulties and concerns. This also provides older adults with the legitimacy to engage in a variety of sexual behaviors and preferences and an opportunity for psychoeducational training.

Psychoeducational training for older adults seems to be particularly needed in the case of sexually transmitted diseases. For instance, people over the age of 50 years old are at a particular risk for catching HIV/AIDS (Centers for Disease Control and Prevention, 2009). Physiological changes and the deterioration of the immune system put older adults at a greater risk for developing HIV/AIDS (AIDS Community Research Initiative of America, 2008). The tendency of older adults to think that if they are beyond the reproductive age, they are unlikely to contract a sexually transmitted disease poses another risk factor. Finally, health professionals' failure to discuss sexual issues with older adults is probably another risk factor.

SECOND COUPLEHOOD IN OLD AGE

Along with the increase in life expectancy, the number of older people who remain single because of widowhood or divorce also increases (S. L. Brown, Bulanda, & Lee, 2012). One solution to this is to live in a second couplehood relationship, entered in old age (Stevens, 2002). Most studies on the topic focus on the perspective of the older people who live in such relationships (S. L. Brown & Lin, 2012) and indicate that the phenomenon is not always welcomed among offspring (children and grandchildren; S. L. Brown & Lin, 2012) or even at the broader social level in some countries, such as Israel (Koren & Eisikovits, 2011).

Second couplehood in old age does not have a unanimous definition. There are studies that relate to the phenomenon in a broad sense, including people age 50 years and older (S. L. Brown, Lee, & Bulanda, 2006; S. L. Brown & Lin, 2012) or 55 years and older (de Jong Gierveld, 2004), and other studies restrict the phenomenon to when a person is considered socially old, such as the age at which people are required to retire (Moustgaard & Martikainen, 2009). Most studies refer to people who previously have lived in a heterosexual marital relationship, but not all studies emphasize that the previous marital relationship was lifelong and that it included raising a family.

The literature reveals three forms of living in second couplehood in old age defined by the external (physical) dimension of couplehood, including living arrangements and the degree of formality of the relationship (Koren, 2008), formally remarried (Cooney & Dunne, 2001), cohabitation (S. L. Brown et al., 2006, 2012; Chevan, 1996), and living apart together (LAT; Duncan & Phillips, 2010; Levin, 2004). In contrast, four types of second couplehood in old age were identified in an Israeli study (Koren, 2014b) based on the combination between the external (physical) dimension of living arrangement, the formality of the relationship, and the relational (emotional) dimensions of couplehood, which included issues of togetherness versus separateness, I-ness versus we-ness, and autonomy versus intimacy: (a) living together emotionally and physically; (b) living together emotionally, apart physically; (c) living together physically, apart emotionally; and (d) living apart physically and emotionally.

U.S. literature provides prevalence rates and distinguishes between remarriage and cohabitation in later life (S. L. Brown et al., 2006, 2012; Calasanti & Kiecolt, 2007; Cooney & Dunne, 2001), but it fails to acknowledge the option of living apart together. Dutch (de Jong Gierveld, 2004), Scandinavian (Levin, 2004; Levin & Trost, 1999), British

(Haskey & Lewis, 2006), and Israeli (Koren, 2011; Koren & Eisikovits, 2011) literature, on the other hand, refers to living apart together relationships later in life in addition to remarriages and cohabitation. The American, Dutch, some Finish, and Israeli research refers only to older people, whereas research that originated in other countries refers to all age-groups, making no attempt to explore the unique characteristics of remarriage in old age.

In the United States, adults over the age of 65 years represented about 6% of all remarriages in 2010 (Cruz, 2012). In addition, about 4% of the unmarried population age 50 years and older was cohabiting (S. L. Brown et al., 2006, 2012). Drawing on the Netherlands' Living Arrangements and Social Networks survey of men and women age 55 to 89 years old ($N = 4,494$), a total of 21% repartnered. Men repartnered more frequently (41%) than women (10%). Most men were remarried, whereas most women were living apart together (de Jong Gierveld, 2004). In a Scandinavian study, 4% of the respondents of all age-groups answered that they were in a living apart together relationship (Levin & Trost, 1999).

Although married older adults and cohabitants differ regarding legal and financial obligations, they have a lot in common in comparison to those living apart together. They live in the same household and their daily routines coincide (Levin, 2004). Older adults living apart together in Britain, who participated in a qualitative section of a national survey made a sharp distinction between living apart together and coresidence, whether in the form of cohabitation or marriage. Reasons for choosing to live apart together and remaining in such a form of couplehood were related to being cautious financially and emotionally. It also referred to issues of independence and worries that cohabitation or marriage could alter a satisfying relationship and the wish to keep things as is (Haskey & Lewis, 2006). Consistently, research based on a qualitative sample among higher middle-class retired older persons in second couplehood in Israel revealed many similarities between the remarried and the cohabiters in comparison with those not living in the same household (Koren, 2014b).

Cohabitation and remarriage have more in common with each other than with living apart together; however, they differ in some respect. Research conducted in the United States (S. L. Brown et al., 2006) and Finland (Moustgaard & Martikainen, 2009) indicated that the formally remarried differ from those who are cohabitating in informal unions. Consistent with the findings concerning the younger generations, older cohabiters appear to be more disadvantaged and less privileged than remarrieds, especially women who were found to lack health care insurance, had a lower income than marrieds, and did not own a house in comparison with men (S. L. Brown et al., 2006; Moustgaard & Martikainen, 2009). Both men and women cohabitators reported more depressive symptoms in comparison with marrieds, with cohabitating men reporting significantly higher depressive scores (S. L. Brown, Bulanda, & Lee, 2005). Differences also were found regarding the willingness to be a caregiver. Married older persons were more likely to receive caregiving from their spouse in comparison with cohabiters. In addition, cohabiters who did receive caregiving from a partner received more hours of care from their partner and less from other kin in comparison with marrieds (Noël-Miller, 2011).

During later life, cohabitation appears to be a long-term alternative to marriage (S. L. Brown et al., 2012) in comparison with cohabitation at much younger ages in which it operates as a temporary condition before marriage (King & Scott, 2005). Nonetheless, religiosity serves as a reason for marriage in comparison with other forms of couple union at all age-groups (S. L. Brown et al., 2012), including old age (Koren, 2014b).

Choosing one of the forms of second couplehood also requires intergenerational considerations (Cooney & Dunne, 2001), which are related to how the parents' couplehood union could affect the parents' and the offspring's economic resources and caregiving duties (S. L. Brown et al., 2006). Nevertheless, recent research has indicated that there is no clear relationship between levels of closeness to children and the decision to reform a marital union (S. L. Brown et al., 2012).

Type of marital union also is affected by broader social structural reasons related to familial social norms (Davidson & Fennell, 2002) accustomed to by the cohort to which one belongs (Davidson, 2002). It is expected that U.S. society will be more open to cohabitation among older unmarried couples because of the norms of the baby boomer generation who cohabitated as young adults (S. L. Brown et al., 2006; Bumpass & Lu, 2000).

Second couplehood has advantages, such as helping to alleviate loneliness or as an alternative to being dependent on offspring for help (Cooney & Dunne, 2001; Koren, 2014a). Some disadvantages may result from gender differences associated with the reasons for entering second couplehood in old age, which in turn, affect the choice of living arrangements. Women seek someone to go out with (Bulcroft & O'Connor, 1986; Davidson, 2002; van der Pas & van Tilburg, 2010), whereas men tend to seek a partner for emotional intimacy (Bograd & Spilka, 1996; Stevens, 2002). Therefore, women prefer living apart together to preserve their autonomy (Davidson, 2002; Karlsson & Borell, 2002), whereas men prefer cohabitation to enjoy the traditional gender-based division of domestic duties. Contemporary findings show how men and women with contrasting priorities regarding living arrangements construct the meaning of their relationship. Men tend to emphasize the romantic aspects of being constantly reunited when living apart together and women explain how when living under the same roof, they preserved their autonomy by conducting household chores by choice rather than by obligation (Koren, 2011).

Second Couplehood in Old Age, Intergenerational Relationships, and Cultural Diversities

Research on second couplehood in old age from an intergenerational relationship perspective is scarce. Most research is from the individual perspective of one spouse or one generation. Findings from these studies show that older people in second couplehood are less in contact with their social network in comparison with single older people or those in long-term marriages (S. L. Brown et al., 2012; de Jong Gierveld & Peeters, 2003). It is not clear, however, whether second couplehood is the cause or the consequence—that is, whether second couplehood loosens the relationship with the social network or that, to begin with, a loose social network enhances the likelihood of second couplehood.

Findings indicate that second couplehood in old age raises problems and difficulties at the intergenerational level. First, the older people have to feel sure about their decision to be in such a relationship. A study on remarriage in the United States suggested that one of the reasons for offspring to object to older parents' second couplehood relationship is because the parent is uncertain about it (Adamec, 1992). Second, families need time to accept and adjust to past losses in light of new realities and the need to transition to their new family constellation. Third, when the health of one of the spouses deteriorates and he or she needs ongoing caregiving (e.g., in the case of Alzheimer's disease), this could cause arguments between the biological children of the spouse needing care and the healthier spouse who is the actual caregiver (Sherman & Bauer, 2008; Sherman & Boss, 2007). Similar to the findings reported by Noël-Miller (2011), remarried women in the United States, whose partner had Alzheimer's disease and was in need of caregiving, reported receiving support from their own family but noted they did not receive help or assistance from their stepfamily members (Sherman, 2012). Intergenerational normative responsibility and obligation of adult children toward their older parents to assist them financially and otherwise were found to be greater toward biological parents in comparison with stepparents (Ganong & Coleman, 2006; Hans, Ganong, & Coleman, 2009; Pezzin, Pollak, & Schone, 2008). Interestingly, research conducted in the United States examined similarities and differences among Whites, Blacks, Asians, and Hispanics, regarding beliefs about intergenerational assistance to older family members in second couplehood. Results showed that the similarities among the various ethnic groups were greater than the differences (Coleman, Ganong, & Rothrauff, 2006).

Research on second couplehood in old age from a cultural perspective is relatively new (Davidson & Fennell, 2002). Studies have been conducted within Western societies characterized by modern culture (Davidson, 2002; Ghazanfareeon Karlsson, 2004; Stevens, 2002) and more traditional cultures

(Hoonaard, 2002), including Far Eastern cultures (Mehta, 2002). Modern cultures allows for the establishment of new types of relationships, such as second couplehood in old age. Once such a relationship is established, however, its members have to deal with the traditional aspects of society that do not take such relationships for granted. Such a situation leads to a paradox that can be bridged by using accounts (Scott & Lyman, 1968) of excuses, such as finding oneself in a relationship without planning and justifications or finding unexpected happiness (Koren & Eisikovits, 2011). The need to account for a phenomenon that enriches older people's lives indicates that it is not accepted by all sectors in society and, therefore, is not perceived as a normative choice in old age in some countries, such as in Israel (Koren & Eisikovits, 2011). As a consequence, older people who live in such a relationships perceive it as discontinuous to the rest of their life (Koren, 2011).

Therapy With Older People in Second Couplehood and Their Families

Empirical literature on second couplehood in old age is scarce in comparison to second couplehood at other stages of the life course (Koren & Eisikovits, 2011). Empirical literature on therapeutic interventions in second couplehood is almost nonexistent. A July 2013 literature search of databases, including PsycINFO and AgeLine, using various combinations of such keywords as aging, old age, older persons, second couplehood, remarriage, repartnering, cohabitation, living apart together, therapy, marital therapy, and family therapy yielded no results. Thus, the current suggestions are based on the practical implications that emerge from various empirical studies mentioned in the literature reviewed previously and from professional experience working with and researching older couples.

Given the limited research in the field, it is highly expected that even experienced therapists will find it hard to address second couplehood in old age or to identify issues of potential importance to older adults in second couplehood. It is important that the therapist acknowledge his or her potential biases concerning second couplehood in old age and become familiar with the variety of biases currently used to represent old age. Acknowledging the potential distinctions between the various types of second couplehood and the various life choices older adults can make is an important first start. Issues concerning second couplehood may evolve around the personal, dyadic, and intergenerational levels.

At the *personal level*, second couplehood may bring with it a positive change in the lives of some older adults. For instance, older women age 70 years and above who were in a second couplehood reported that for the first time in their lives they discovered their sexuality and the pleasure of being in a sexual relationship: As one woman stated, "when I started dating men, I discovered that it (sex) interests me very much and I didn't realize this could happen in old age" (Koren, 2011, p. 694). This could inform professionals about the potential for positive changes in second couplehood as well as about the important place that sexuality can take in the lives of older adults in second couplehood.

At the *dyadic level* (e.g., the couple), issues related to autonomy and dependency or the degree of intimacy one is willing to share with a partner are likely to arise. It is expected that older adults in second couplehood will have to renegotiate their newly formed relationships in light of their past experiences with their partners. It is highly likely that expectations formed in one's first marriage might prove misleading or inappropriate in second couplehood. Hence, the therapist's role is to assist the older couple in negotiating current expectations and relationships as well as in becoming aware of how their past relationships influence their current ones.

A prominent dyadic issue that counseling could address relates to gender differences in preferences regarding living arrangements. As mentioned, women tend to prefer to live apart together, whereas men prefer cohabitation (Davidson, 2002; Davidson & Fennell, 2002; Karlsson & Borell, 2002). The following example of a man living apart together illustrates how he was able to reconstruct the benefits associated with this living arrangement even though he initially preferred cohabitation. He explained, "when we are apart for two days we miss each other very much; yes, I believe it's never too late to find happiness" (Koren, 2011, p. 693). The man was offended when his girlfriend announced that she preferred living apart together and he ended

up interpreting this as a rejection. When he learned that such situations were normative, however, and considered the benefits of being in a constant state of courting, it became easier for him to accept it.

At the *intergenerational level*, research has found that one of the reasons adult children oppose their parent's second couplehood relationship is because they have difficulties acknowledging their parent's sexuality outside the parental marital relationship with the biological parent (Hoonaard, 2002; Schlesinger & Schlesinger, 2004). For example, one of the men interviewed in a study on the meaning of second couplehood in old age reported that his children encouraged him to enter second couplehood. They did this by introducing him to women they believed could fulfill the tasks that his deceased wife fulfilled, such as babysitting and cooking. He chose a different woman, however, who preferred not to fulfill such duties and whom his children disliked. The reason for his choice was that with the woman partner he chose, his sexual needs were fulfilled in a way he never experienced in his lifelong marriage, but he felt uncomfortable explaining this to his children. Such issues could be addressed in MFT and counseling.

Caregiving issues are unique and different from the ones explored in lifelong marriages. Again, the implications of second couplehood come to play at several different levels. At the dyadic level of the couple, some factors promote caregiving by second couplehood partners and others that hinder it. One of the main reasons women give for preferring to live apart together is to avoid taking over the caregiver's role (Davidson, 2002). Other studies, on the other hand, show that whereas caregiving in lifelong marriage is provided primarily out of obligation, in second couplehood in old age, it is provided out of will rather than obligation. As one participant stated, "my wife, I couldn't leave her because she was sick . . . Sarah, I don't have to care for her, but I want to" (Koren, 2011, p. 694). Such a range of possibilities should be acknowledged when counseling couples in such relationships.

Furthermore, families of partners in second couplehood in old age may need time to adjust to past losses. Families also need to be flexible enough to create relationships within the new extended family because of the lifelong history within the original families of each partner (Connidis, 2010; Kuhn, Morhardt, & Monbrod-Framburg, 1993). Prior research indicates that late life remarried couples' lack of shared time and family history with stepfamily may undermine the development of a shared sense of family (Sherman & Boss, 2007). As such, it constrains the potential of positive support and increases the likelihood of a lack of support when remarried spouses end up providing care for a sick partner (Sherman, 2012). Primary findings from a study presently being conducted on second couplehood reveal that one of the reasons or justifications that make it easier for family members to accept the phenomenon of second couplehood or to accept a specific partner, is by telling themselves that second couplehood provides a way for their parent or grandparent to deal with his or her loneliness, while at least partially, releasing them from the burden of caring. Such findings could provide family therapists with necessary knowledge when treating relevant clients.

The unique characteristics of second couplehood, uniting two individuals with existing families who have expectations regarding financial inheritance, brings up the need for legal financial arrangements to secure the offspring's rights (Koren, 2011). This also may be a hot debate in therapy as financial inheritance symbolizes many things, such as love, support, and allegiances in addition to its monetary value.

DIVORCE AND OLDER ADULTS

Divorce is a common occurrence, with about 45% of all marriages expected to end in divorce. Interestingly, there has been a sharp increase in the rates of divorce specifically for middle-age and older adults. For this group, the rate of divorce has more than doubled over the past two decades, whereas the pattern of divorce for the U.S. population as a whole has remained relatively stable (Amato, 2010).

Researchers have projected that even if the divorce rate were to remain stable, the number of middle-age and older adults who experience divorce will continue to increase (S. L. Brown & Lin, 2012). The increase in older adults in higher order marriages

(i.e., divorce and then remarriage) is one potential explanation for the projected rise in divorce rate, as past research has shown that those who divorced once are more likely to divorce in the future. The fact that social norms are more lenient toward divorce at the present time also may encourage higher rates of divorce. In addition, the entrance of women into the workforce, the increased independence of women, as well as the increase in the average life span, are additional factors of potential impact on the projected rise in divorce rate (Ruggles, 1997; Uhlenberg & Myers, 1981). Researchers have noted several demographic trends associated with divorce. Apparently, divorce disproportionately affects already vulnerable segments of the population. Divorce rate is higher for women, Blacks, and those of lower levels of education. In addition, those who previously had divorced and those who maintained their previous marriage for a shorter period of time are more likely to divorce (S. L. Brown & Lin, 2012).

There has been limited interest in the study of divorce in old age (Uhlenberg, Cooney, & Boyd, 1990). This observation, made in the early 1990s of the past century, still is relevant today. The limited research available tends to provide a gloomy picture on the negative consequences of divorce among older adults. These negative consequences concern health, well-being, financial resources, and familial support. As a result, divorced older adults represent a particularly vulnerable group.

Exiting marriage through divorce results in more negative health consequences than never being married. The negative effects are particularly pronounced for ethnic minorities (Pienta et al., 2000). As for loneliness, research has shown that marriage has a protective effect on older adults. In turn, contacts with friends, siblings, children, and neighbors have shown to be more beneficial for single or divorced older adults than for married older adults. Whereas divorced individuals benefited the most from contact with adult children, never-married individuals benefited from contacts with friends, siblings, and neighbors (Pinquart, 2003). These findings provide support to the hierarchical compensatory model of support, which predicts that the primacy of the relationship determines the use of support (Cantor, 1979).

Research also has shown that divorced men were more likely to experience loneliness than divorced women. The deleterious effects of divorce on men were explained by the fact that they have less contact with their children or friends as they tend to rely on their wives as gatekeepers for social support and family ties (Pinquart, 2003). Support for the relative fragility of divorced men can be found in another study that has shown that for men in particular, divorce is associated with the increased likelihood of depression in old age (Kamiya, Doyle, Henretta, & Timonen, 2013).

Another indicator to the heightened vulnerability of divorced older adults, in general, can be seen in the finding that functional status had no impact on loneliness among married couples, but it was negatively associated with loneliness among divorced or never-married older adults. This was attributed to the fact that unmarried older adults should be mobile to maintain their social network in contrast to married couples, who can rely on one another for support (Pinquart, 2003). This alludes to a double jeopardy of age and disability, which may become particularly pronounced in old age.

The negative financial impact of divorce continues into the preretirement years for those who remarry and for those who do not (Holden & Kuo, 1996). A study that focused solely on women has shown that divorced women are less likely to own a home, are more likely to share a residence with others, exhibit lower levels of financial well-being, and are more likely to be employed compared with married women (Uhlenberg et al., 1990). Consistently, researchers attributed the fact that late divorces are associated with weaker intentions to retire early to the financial strain placed by the divorce (Damman, Henkens, & Kalmijn, 2011).

Divorce and Intergenerational Relations

Much of the literature on the impact of divorce in old age has concentrated on adult children–older parents' relationship. In general, this literature provides a pessimistic look at the impact that divorce has on intergenerational relationships. For instance, a study that compared divorced men with never-divorced married men found that divorce resulted in reduced contact with one's children, a significantly

lower likelihood of sharing a household with children and a lower likelihood of viewing one's children as potential helpers at times of need. The study also found that more educated fathers and those who live in proximity to their children are more likely to maintain contact with their children. In contrast, the longer the time since the divorce, the less likely was the father to maintain contact with his children (Cooney & Uhlenberg, 1990).

A different study that focused on adult children found similar results, demonstrating perceived lower quality of relationship with parents, particularly fathers, among adult children whose parents divorced. Compared with adult children of married parents, adult children of divorced parents were less satisfied with their relationship with their parents. They felt less loved and less listened to by their parents and had significantly less contact with their parents (Webster & Herzog, 1995). Similar findings concerning the decline in intergenerational solidarity were reported more recently by a Norwegian study (Daatland, 2007).

Transfers from parents to their children are also different in families that have experienced a divorce compared with families that have not experienced a divorce. The exact time at which the divorce took place, however, has a differential impact on the transfers. For instance, transition to divorce in midlife has shown to slightly increase the probability of a financial transfer (measured as total dollar value, average value, total number of transfers and total number of children given money to). The authors argued that this points to the strength of intergenerational bonds and provides some support for the altruistic perspective on financial transfers, which suggests that these transfers are given unrelated to the parents' marital status. In contrast, those who were divorced for a longer period of time made fewer financial transfers, to fewer children, at lower amounts, providing support for the contingent approach, which suggests that these transfers from parents to their children are contingent on the exact circumstances (Shapiro & Remle, 2011).

These findings have potentially important ramifications for the well-being of divorced older adults and their adult children. Given the higher risk for divorce and depression among adult children whose parents divorced, it is expected that these children will be less available to support their older parents at times of need. Moreover, given the potential impact of divorce on adult children, these children might be at a great need for emotional and financial support from their older parents.

Indeed, past research has shown that adult children were somewhat less likely to feel financially responsible toward their older parents when the parents experienced a divorce or a remarriage (Hans et al., 2009). Consistently, a recent study has shown that divorce is a risk for reduced levels of assistance from adult children to their older parents (Pezzin et al., 2008). Not surprisingly, a study on the predictors of nursing home admission found that the risk for nursing home is higher among unmarried older adult, net of the effect of health, sociodemographic characteristics, and economic status. This study, however, lumped together single, widowed, and divorced older adults (Freedman, 1996). Nonetheless, a different study found that even though the rate of divorce increased over time, the support available to older adults did not decline. The authors argued that this potentially could imply that the negative effects of marital disruptions on support in early old age may be weakening over time (Glaser, Tomassini, & Stuchbury, 2008).

Therapy With Divorced Older Adults

Given the fact that divorce is on the rise, a key issues would be assisting older adults through their divorce. Capitalizing on the increasing prevalence of this phenomenon, might be beneficial for older adults who go through a divorce. Research indicates that late-life divorce is primarily a result of developmental issues associated with personal growth in old age (Wu & Schimmele, 2007). As such, change through a divorce is anticipated to improve life rather than worsen it. The previous literature review, however, indicates that research focuses mainly on the negative consequences associated with a divorce (Wu & Schimmele, 2007). Hence, the therapist potentially could assist the older adult to view the divorce as a life transition, when continuity in marital relations is no longer desired.

The potentially negative consequences of divorce, such as loneliness (Pinquart, 2003),

especially for older adults, also should be taken into consideration. Although the experiences of loneliness and depression are highly prevalent both among younger and older divorced individuals, in old age, these experiences take a particular toll (Kamiya et al., 2013). Because divorced older adults tend to be in worse health status than married older adults, they are in a particular need for assistance. Therapy might be useful in assisting older adults identifying potential sources of support and assistance, in the absence of an available spouse and in light of the potentially reduced availability of children as caregivers.

One technique specifically recommended for postdivorce counseling consists of group counseling. The advantages of the group might be particularly pronounced when individuals go through experiences that are somewhat nonnormative or stigmatized. The group provides a sense of belonging and an opportunity to explore negative feelings concerning the divorce. The group can provide a more normative perspective concerning divorce (Lee & Hett, 1990). These recommendations concerning the potentially beneficial use of group therapy, however, are not specific for older adults who go through a divorce, but rather target the general postdivorce adult population.

Another potential area of focus might concern the experience of loneliness among divorced older adults. Although not specifically focused on divorced older adults, a recent meta-analysis of interventions to reduce loneliness identified four primary intervention strategies. These include (a) the improvement of social skills, (b) the enhancement of social support, (c) increased opportunities for social interactions, and (d) the challenge of maladaptive social cognitions. The latter strategy was identified as yielding the highest effect sizes (Masi, Chen, Hawkley, & Cacioppo, 2011). Hence, cognitive techniques might prove particularly beneficial when addressing loneliness in this population of divorced older adults.

Our review did not find intervention studies that specifically targeted divorced older adults. Nevertheless, we did find a study that compared antidepressant medication plus clinical management alone versus the addition of dialectic behavioral therapy (DBT) skills training and scheduled telephone coaching sessions for depressed individuals over 60 years old. Although not specifically geared for divorced older adults, about 41% of the sample were divorced or separated. The study found that both treatment arms demonstrated significant and roughly equivalent reductions in clinician's rated depression score. Only the combination of medication–clinical management plus DBT skills training and a scheduled telephone session showed a significant decrease in self-rated depression score. In addition, a higher percentage of individuals in the combined group were in remission. Moreover, only the combined group showed improvement in dependency and adaptive coping (Lynch, Morse, Mendelson, & Robins, 2003).

SINGLEHOOD IN OLD AGE

Many terms can describe singlehood. These terms partially vary by gender and age and to some degree reflect a combination of ageist and sexist views that become most pronounced in the case of older never-married women. In her review, Baumbusch (2004) listed different terms, including "bachelor," "old maid," "spinster," "unclaimed treasures," "unattached," "never-married," "unmarried," "ever-single," and "lifelong singlehood," to describe never-married women versus men, arguing that even the terms used to describe never-married women put them at a particular disadvantage (Baumbusch, 2004). The various terms also may reflect the ambivalence concerning this phenomenon, which has received minimal research attention to date.

In the research literature, never-married older adults often are compared to individuals of other marital statuses. This makes the study of singlehood as a unique marital status in its own right more difficult. Moreover, in some studies, never-married, divorced, and widowed are lumped together under the term "single." There are many reasons against this tendency to do so. Whereas widowhood is an expected part of life, divorce and singlehood represent deviations from expected life scripts. In addition, whereas widowhood and divorce represent discontinuation in marital statuses, being never-married represents a continuation into old age. Never-married individuals also do not have to deal

with the loss of social support, which might be most pronounced in the case of divorced or widowed older adults (Pudrovska, Schieman, & Carr, 2006).

The increase in the prevalence of never-married individuals in the United States is evident primarily in the case of Blacks. In 1986, only 3.5% of the Blacks were never married, but in 2009, as many as 13% were never married. This is quite different from the White population, in which the never-married rate stands at around 5% and the Asian population in which the rate declined from 9.7% to 4.8% over this time period. In addition, men are more likely than women to never marry (Kreider & Ellis, 2011).

As with the other marital statuses, sociocultural factors tend to play an important role in determining the life course of those who never marry. For baby boomers (born between 1946 and 1964), for example, marriages take place at an older age and last for a shorter period of time and cohabitation and nonmarital childbearing have become more common. As a result, singlehood is a more accepted life choice for this cohort than for previous ones (Cherlin, 2010), and baby boomers are more likely than the previous generation to be never married in midlife (Frey, 2010). This is reflected by the fact that the proportion of adults age 45–54 years old who had never married increased by 300% from 1986 to 2009 (Kreider & Ellis, 2011).

Research has shown that never-married older adults represent a heterogeneous group. The etiology of being never married in old age varies dramatically. Some may be homosexuals, others may be devoted to their career or to caregiving, and yet others have lived in a restricted environment in terms of potential partners (Rubinstein, 1987).

The majority of studies addressed the negative consequences associated with singlehood. A qualitative study of eight women between the ages of 65 and 77 years old found that similar to society at large, never-married women viewed their experiences as nonnormative and used married women as a comparison group (Baumbusch, 2004). It has been argued that loneliness and the absence of a social safety net become particularly pronounced in old age (Baumbusch, 2004), with never-married men being particularly likely to live alone (Lin & Brown, 2012). Others have argued that although never-married older adults may experience loneliness, they are not socially isolated (Rubinstein, 1987). In support of this argument, a qualitative study found that for never-married women, the family was still very central, but it was the family of origin, rather than the family of procreation (Allen & Pickett, 1987).

Consistently, a different study found that never-married childless older adults do have available support. Nevertheless, the study also found that although siblings tended to provide support, they often failed to provide adequate emotional support (Wu & Pollard, 1998). Because spouses usually form the natural caregivers, it is not clear who will take care of never-married older adults (Lin & Brown, 2012). Consistent with the hypothesis regarding the inadequate informal support available to never-married older adults, research has shown that once paid arrangements are in place to support never-married older adults who experienced a deterioration in their functioning level, these arrangements are maintained even once their level of functioning improves (Freedman, Aykan, Wolf, & Marcotte, 2004).

Earlier studies claimed that never-married older adults are less happy than married older adults and only slightly happier than widowed or divorced. The lower well-being of never-married older adults was attributed to changes in lifestyle that take place in old age and to reduced social support available in old age (Ward, 1979).

Never-married women are thought to be particularly disadvantaged when it comes to retirement. This is because many have invested much of their adult life in their career. As a result, retirement is perceived as more challenging among these women, who miss the social contact and the sense of meaning associated with one's work (Veroff, Douvan, & Kulka, 1981).

Nevertheless, more recent studies portrayed a somewhat more balanced picture of singlehood in old age. A qualitative study emphasized the perceived benefits associated with singlehood and the independence it provides (Baumbusch, 2004). In addition, relative to never-married older adults, divorced older adults reported higher stress associated with their marital status. This primarily was attributed to the fact that never-married older adults likely have developed skills and resources throughout their lives to help them deal with the stress associated with single life (Pudrovska et al., 2006). Consistently, others have shown that being never married is not associated with increased depression once late-life events are considered (Kamiya et al., 2013).

Others have claimed that never-married women actually embraced retirement and enjoyed a better financial situation than formerly married women. The study found that in old age, never-married women are not at a disadvantage compared with the formerly married. Apparently, when compared with widowed, divorced, and separated women, never-married women were less vulnerable. They were happier with their life and reported more favorable attitudes toward retirement (Keith, 1985).

Given the scarcity of research on this marital status in old age, it is safe to say that, overall, findings concerning this particular group of older adults are inconsistent and are somewhat limited by a tendency to lump the various groups of unmarried individuals together as well as by a tendency to compare never-married older adults with individuals of other marital groups, rather than the establishment of a true understanding of this group and its unique features.

Therapy With Never-Married Older Adults

Research on the topic of therapy with never-married older adults is almost nonexistent. The limited research available suggests that the state of being never married is viewed as deviant and this likely affects the therapist's interpretation of the therapeutic context. When conducting therapy with never-married older adults, the therapist must be aware of his or her assumptions regarding the lifestyle of never-married older adults as well as regarding what constitutes a desired marital status. It is important for the therapist to be able to recognize the advantages and disadvantages of all marital statuses, including that of those who have never-married. The therapist is advised to examine the interpersonal needs as well as the sexual needs of never-married individuals (Johnston & Eklund, 1984). Although potentially applicable to older adults, these recommendations were not specifically made for older adults.

The context of being never married in old age should be taken into consideration in therapy. As noted earlier, haven never married often is considered a nonnormative life situation, especially for the older cohorts. Nevertheless, it does not represent a disruption of one's experiences, but rather a lifelong continuation. Therefore, it is likely that never-married older adults will seek psychotherapy not necessarily for dealing with their marital status per se, but rather for dealing with some of the consequences associated with the lifestyle they have adopted.

For instance, an overreliance on work and work-related achievements might put never-married older adults at a particular risk for depression or loss of self-esteem upon their retirement. Helping never-married older adults find other outlets of confidence and self-esteem in the form of volunteering or social clubs could be beneficial. Identifying potential sources of social stimulation and support also might prove useful. Similarly, if a never-married older adult spent most of his or her adult life caring for older parents, the death of the parents might leave an empty hole in the never-married older adult's life. The therapist will have to assist the older adult in identifying other outlets for social interaction and meaning in life.

Lesbian, Gay, Bisexual, and Transgender Relationships

Despite dramatic changes in the social construction of gender and sexual identity over the past few decades, the academic interest in older LGBT individuals has remained limited, leading some researchers to argue that the experiences of LGBT older adults have been excluded from both queer and gerontological research and theory (M. T. Brown, 2009). LGBT older adults have experienced dramatic shifts in the social construction of their gender or sexual identify over the years. Many of them likely have experienced the social exclusion and medicalization of homosexuality as a psychiatric condition in their youth. They have witnessed the HIV/AIDS epidemic and its devastating impact on the community and currently are witnessing active attempts for the legitimization and mainstreaming of

LGBT issues (Vaid, 1996). These dramatic experiences probably have a major impact not only on their health and well-being but also on their interpersonal relationships with significant others.

Despite these societal changes, a study conducted among older Israeli lesbian women and gay men found that this population suffers both from the stigma associated with homophobia as well as with age-related stigma directed toward them from society at large. Moreover, this population of older lesbian women and gay men also suffers from ageism within the gay-lesbian community and is viewed as an outcast within the community (Meri-Esh & Doron, 2009).

The limited research available suggests that LGBT older adults are more likely to be single, live alone, and have no children compared with heterosexual older adults. This likely affects their social support network as well as their health care choices and practices (Gabrielson, 2011b). Whereas older lesbian women tend to have a more diverse network in terms of age and to reject normative beauty standards, the aging experience of older gay men is portrayed as more challenging, given the emphasis on youth and youthful appearance in the gay community (Hash & Rogers, 2013).

Nevertheless, despite the emphasis on a youthful appearance in the gay community, research has shown that the well-being of older and younger gay men is comparable. Whereas gay men over the age of 60 years are more likely to live alone, they are just as likely to be in a relationship as their younger counterparts and to be open about their relationships (Lyons, Pitts, & Grierson, 2013). In addition, despite cohort effects in the construction of gender and sexual identity, a developmental study has found that both younger and older adults tend to report that they first became aware of their sexual orientation early in life. This suggests limited cohort effects in terms of the development of sexual orientation (Calzo, Antonucci, Mays, & Cochran, 2011).

Similar to the findings regarding singlehood in old age (Kamiya et al., 2013), it would be empirically groundless to claim that lesbian women and gay men are depressed, lonely, desperate, or inactive sexually. On the contrary, old age seems to have some liberating aspects that free older adults from undesired sexual influences and multiple personal and social obligations (Meri-Esh & Doron, 2009).

Therapy With LGBT Older Adults

An important issue to consider when conducting psychotherapy with LGBT older adults is the lack of empirical research on the topic. We found no relationship scales specifically designed for use with LGBT older adults. In addition, with the exception of several case studies (e.g., Hash & Rogers, 2013; Kertzner, Barber, & Schwartz, 2011), there are no empirically validated therapeutic guidelines for use with LGBT older adults who undergo relationship difficulties.

Another important issue to remember when conducting therapy with LGBT is the potential for countertransference, which may consist of homophobic feelings, stigma, or discrimination among heterosexual therapists. This likely is amplified by the lack of training or inadequate training on issues pertaining to LGBT. For instance, a contemporary study has shown that area agencies are undertrained and unprepared to work with older LGBT individuals, and there is a general resistance to providing services to this population (A. K. Hughes, Harold, & Boyer, 2011; Knochel, Croghan, Moone, & Quam, 2012). Discrimination and prejudice toward LGBT is evident even in long-term care institutions, with research showing that nursing home staff view same-sex sexual relationships more negatively than heterosexual sexual relationships (Hinrichs & Vacha-Haase, 2010). Because of the potential exposure to discrimination and seclusion, some LGBT older adults choose to live in LGBT continuous care settings that likely protect them from further discrimination based on their sexual orientation (Gabrielson, 2011a).

Given the fact the LGBT older adults are more likely to live alone and to be childless, important issues in therapy might include social networks and support or even loneliness (Gabrielson, 2011b). When working with LGBT older adults, the clinician should be aware of the fact that many of these individuals rely on nontraditional forms of support. Similar to the situation in the general population, the need for social support might be particularly pronounced with the advancement of age, as one's health deteriorates (Gabrielson, 2011b).

ASSESSMENT OF INTIMATE RELATIONSHIPS

In our review of the literature, we found a very small number of relationship scales directly related to the assessment of older couples. This is unfortunate, given the fact that the experiences of older couples likely differ from the experiences of younger couples in many ways. For instance, whereas younger couples might cope with work–family conflict or the challenges associated with raising young children and forming a family, older couples are more likely to be concerned with their retirement plans, health problems, or caregiving issues.

The review first discusses those scales that were designed specifically for the assessment of intimate relationship in older couples, followed by scales that are not specific to older couples but that have been used previously with this population. Given the interest in the nature of the interaction between partners, some measures of couples' relationships consist of behavioral observations rather than on paper-and-pencil questionnaires. Another distinction between measures stems from the fact that some rely on the partner's ratings, some rely on the person who is the focus of inquiry, and other measures are clinician's ratings. In addition, some scales focus on interpersonal relationships and their quality, whereas other measures focus on sexuality. There is also a differentiation between actual behaviors or experiences and attitudes or knowledge about a certain phenomenon relevant to interpersonal relationships or sexuality. Finally, this review briefly discusses general scales of well-being, social support, loneliness, and meaning in life, which could be highly relevant when assessing older adults' relationship. As with the relationship scales, not all measures were designed specifically for use with older adults, but all measures reviewed were used extensively with this population.

This list is not exhaustive, but rather it represents a broad overview of some of the most frequently used scales of potential relevance for the assessment of intimate or sexual relationship. Many of the following measures have both abbreviated and long forms. In addition, most measures were translated into various languages and their psychometric properties have been evaluated internationally.

Relationship Measures Specifically Developed for Use With Older Adults

Several relationship measures were specifically developed for use with older adults. This was done due to the realization that relationships in old age might have different characteristics from those at younger age groups. This is because relationships in old age often occur over an extended period of time and involve a different level of intimacy from relationships that occur over a shorter time period. In addition, marital relationships in old age might evolve around different concerns and interests from those that take place at earlier periods of life.

Marital Satisfaction Questionnaire for Older Persons. The Marital Satisfaction Questionnaire for Older Persons (Haynes et al., 1992) was constructed based on five studies that evaluated its psychometric properties for use with older adults. This measure consists of 24 items with one major and two minor factors. Factor scores and the total marital satisfaction scale score were found to be homogenous, temporally stable, and significantly correlated with multiple measures of marital adjustment, life satisfaction, perceived spouse behaviors, and observer ratings of marital communication.

Marriage Problem Scale 50+. The Marriage Problem Scale 50+ (Clements & Swensen, 1999) was designed specifically for use with individuals over the age of 50 years. The measure consists of 50 items and has shown good reliability and validity in past research.

Relationship Measures for the General Population

Although relationships of older adults might have their own unique characteristics, they certainly have some resemblance to relationships that occur at earlier age periods. Therefore, some of the relationships measures used with the general population are applicable for use with older adults. The use of general measures has the advantage of allowing easy comparisons across age groups or developmentally, over time.

Areas of Disagreement Scale. The Areas of Disagreement Scale (Fincham, 1985) contains a list of 13 topics on which a couple may disagree. Among the topics addressed are sex, household responsibilities, and finances. Participants rate how long the particular topic had been a topic of disagreement and how much time they spend disagreeing with their spouse on this particular topic.

Dyadic Adjustment Scale. The Dyadic Adjustment Scale (Spanier, 1976) is a self-report measure of relationship adjustment. The 32 scale questions address such issues as marital satisfaction, cohesion and level of affectionate expression. Most items are coded on a frequency scale, two are dichotomous, and the final two items concern the degree of happiness in the relationship and expectations concerning the future of the relationship (Spanier, 1976). Whereas higher scores represent better marital adjustment, very high scores are potentially indicative of psychopathology, as they represent enmeshment or idealization of the relationship (Kazak, Jarmas, & Snitzer, 1988).

Marital Adjustment Test. The Marital Adjustment Test (Locke & Wallace, 1959) is a 15-item measure that assesses the level of marital adjustment. Items address issues such as overall satisfaction with the marriage and areas of agreement or disagreement with one's spouse. The measure provides data on marital satisfaction, with a lower score indicating poorer satisfaction. It has shown to successfully differentiate satisfied from dissatisfied couples (Locke & Wallace, 1959). The measure also has shown adequate concordance with clinician's ratings of marital functioning (Crowther, 1985). Using this measure, older couples were found to report higher levels of satisfaction than middle-age couples (N. J. M. Henry, Berg, Smith, & Florsheim, 2007).

Social Support Questionnaire. The Social Support Questionnaire (Sarason, Levine, Basham, & Sarason, 1983) is a general measure that assesses the number of social support sources and the level of satisfaction with available support. Participants first list all of the people they can count on in a given domain and then rate their satisfaction with the support provided by each person on a six-point scale. Average satisfaction with spousal support is calculated by summing up the satisfaction scores for spouse support divided by the number of times the spouse was mentioned as a source of support.

Observational Measures of the Relationship

Although self-report measures are highly utilized, there is a potential for bias due to explicit attempts for self-presentation in certain ways. Another disadvantage might stem from the fact that self-report measure capitalize on the verbal abilities of the respondents and, thus, might not be applicable for use with less verbal populations or with populations who do not speak the national language. Observational measures have the advantage of overcoming these barriers. However, they tend to be more expensive and cumbersome to administer and often require extensive training of research assistants in observational methods.

Marital Interaction Coding System IV. The Marital Interaction Coding System IV (Heyman, Weiss, & Eddy, 1995) is the most widely used marital behavioral coding system. The coding is focused on problem-solving behaviors during a 30-min marital resolution task. The task resolution is recorded and agreement between judges is obtained. The measure has shown to discriminate well between happy and unhappy couples and is sensitive to detecting changes following marital therapy.

Structural Analysis of Social Behavior. The Structural Analysis of Social Behavior (Benjamin, Rothweiler, & Critchfield, 2006) measure is used to assess interpersonal and intrapsychic interactions in terms of three underlying dimensions: (a) the focus of the behavior can be on others versus self, (b) degree of affiliation versus hostility in the interaction, and (c) the level of enmeshment versus differentiation of the interaction. Ratings are completed by following specific coding schemes. The measure can be completed by self-report, significant other-report, or a clinician-report.

Sexuality Measures Specifically Developed for Use With Older Adults

The same underlying assumptions which stands at the development and use of relationship measures specifically designed for use with older adults, stands at the development and use of sexuality measures for use with older adults. The long-term nature of many of the relationships that occur in old age and the fact that cognitive and physical changes often take place in old age should be taken into account in the assessment of sexual relationships. In addition, cohort effects that are shaped by norms and expectations regarding relationships and sexuality also play a role and likely color the sexual behaviors of older adults. The use of specific measures developed for this population attempts to address these unique characteristics of the population of older adults.

Ageing Sexual Knowledge and Attitudes Scale. The Ageing Sexual Knowledge and Attitudes Scale (White, 1982) consists of 61 items. The first 35 items constitute the knowledge subscale. One point is given for each correct response. The latter items concern attitudes toward sexuality, rated on a seven-point scale. The scale was based on several studies concerning sexual functioning in older adults, families of older adults, and people who work with them. Factor analysis supports the two dimensions of knowledge and attitudes.

National Social, Life, Health, and Aging Project. The National Social, Life, Health, and Aging Project (NSHAP; Waite, Laumann, Das, & Schumm, 2009) is a U.S. national study aimed to better understand the well-being of community-dwelling older Americans by examining a large array of predictors. The survey provides an excellent source for short measures concerning sexuality, partnership, practices, attitudes, and problems in the relationship. The advantages offered by the measures used by NSHAP include their brevity (most domains consist on very few items) and the availability of U.S. national normative data.

Well-Being Measures for the General Population

One of the most studied construct in the psychological field is well-being. The term refers to an overall evaluation of one's life from a positive perspective. This is not a uniform construct, but instead can divided into various aspects, such as emotional well-being, physical well-being, subjective well-being, objective well-being, cognitive well-being, and so on.

SF-36. The SF-36 (Ware & Sherbourne, 1992) is a widely used measure of health and well-being. It consists of 36 items, which form eight scale profiles. The measure has been used with a variety population groups and has been translated to numerous languages.

World Health Organization–5. The World Health Organization–5 (Heun, Bonsignore, Barkow, & Jessen, 2001) is a five-item well-being index. The measure consists of positively worded items. It has shown to be a reliable measure of emotional functioning and may serve as an adequate depression screen for older adults (Ayalon, Goldfracht, & Bech, 2010)

Social Support Measures Specifically Developed for Use With Older Adults

Because older adults face certain challenges that are unique to this age group, certain measures were developed to assess social support specifically among older adults. For instance, in the face of deteriorated cognitive and physical health, social support might take a very different angle and might serve different purposes from social support at times of health. Because many older adults pursue either caregiving or care receiving roles, the assessment of social support among this age group often targets these unique roles.

Measure of Social Support Among Older Adults.

The Measure of Social Support Among Older Adults (Krause & Markides, 1990) assesses four different aspects of social support: informational support, tangible assistance, emotional support, and integration.

Social Support Measures for the General Population

Social support is of great importance for the wellbeing and quality of life of individuals. The use of measures that have been validated in the general population with older adults is valuable for several reasons. First, some aspects of social support likely have a consistent meaning and importance across all age groups and as such, should also be evaluated among older adults. Moreover, the use of general measures of social support might provide an

opportunity to compare social support across different age groups or developmentally, over time.

Duke Social Support Index. The Duke Social Support Index (Landerman, George, Campbell, & Blazer, 1989) measure has two subscales. The first subscale evaluates the size and structure of the social network, whereas the second subscale evaluates perceived satisfaction with the support available. The two subscales often are analyzed separately.

Social Support Questionnaire. The Social Support Questionnaire (Sarason et al., 1983) is a 27-item questionnaire that measures the perception of availability of social support and satisfaction with it. In the first part, participants list all the people who fit in the description of the particular item, whereas the second part asks for the degree of satisfaction with the particular person listed.

Loneliness Measures

de Jong Gierveld Loneliness Scale. The original 11-item de Jong Gierveld Loneliness Scale (de Jong-Gierveld & Kamphuls, 1985) consists of six negatively worded items and five positively worded items. The measure differentiates between emotional (i.e., the perceived absence of intimate relationship) and social (i.e., the perceived absence of a broader social network) loneliness. It also can be used as a single scale, indicative of overall loneliness.

UCLA Loneliness Scale. The UCLA Loneliness Scale (Russell, Peplau, & Ferguson, 1978) is a 20-item measure that evaluates one's subjective feelings of loneliness. The frequency at which each statement is experienced is ranked on a four-point scale. The measure is highly used, with a three-item version currently included as part of the Health and Retirement Study (M. E. Hughes, Waite, Hawkley, & Cacioppo, 2004). Hence, U.S. normative data on individuals over the age of 50 years are available.

Meaning in Life Measures

Assessing one's meaning in life stems from the general notion that the ability to find meaning in life serves an adaptive function of potential growth, flourish and self-actualization. There are several theoretical orientations that favor the assessment of meaning in life, including existential philosophy and psychology and positive psychology.

Purpose in Life Test.   The Purpose in Life Test (Crumbaugh, 1968) tests Victor Frankl's thesis that a lack of meaning in life results in an existential vacuum characterized by cumulative frustration. The measure includes 20 items scored on a seven-point scale, with 1 representing the most negative situation and 7 the most positive. The total score can range from 20 to 140. Scores between 92 and 112 represent indecisiveness; a score above 112 indicates definite purpose and meaning in life, whereas a score below 92 indicates a lack of clear meaning and purpose in life (Crumbaugh & Maholick, 1969).

Meaning in Life Questionnaire.   The Meaning in Life Questionnaire (Steger, Frazier, Oishi, & Kaler, 2006) includes 10 items. Five items examine the existence of meaning in one's life (e.g., "I have discovered a satisfying life purpose"), and the remaining five items assess the search for meaning (e.g., "I am seeking a purpose or mission for my life"). The participant is presented with a scale that ranges between 1 (absolutely untrue) and 7 (absolutely true).

CONCLUSION

This chapter provides an overview of marital status in old age. As is clearly evident from this review, the most research attention has been given to lifelong marriage followed by some attention being given to second couplehood in old age, and only very limited attention being given to divorce and singlehood in old age. Given current demographic trends, the latter two marital statuses certainly deserve greater attention.

The timeframe during which the particular marital transition occurs is one factor that deserves attention in future studies. For example, research should make a distinction between divorce at different periods of the life course; older people who divorce at old age do not necessarily face the same challenges as older people who divorce at younger ages. In addition to ontogenetic time and generational time, historical time should be taken into consideration when examining marital statuses.

The historical time related to changing trends in what is considered a normative behavior also should be taken into account. Changes in the acceptability of a phenomenon, such as being never married, getting divorced, or entering second couplehood in old age, likely will affect intergenerational relationships in the family and the level of formal and informal social support one receives.

This review has suggested that more refined distinctions should be made when studying individuals who are not in a lifelong marriage. For example, being never married does not necessarily equate with not living in a meaningful couplehood relationship. Thus, a distinction should be made between those who never married but have had a meaningful relationship and those who never married and never had a meaningful relationship.

The terminology used to describe the various marital statuses can serve as one indicator of cultural differences between countries. For example, studies on second couplehood conducted outside the United States refer to all three forms of second couplehood: remarriage, cohabitation, and living apart together. In contrast, studies conducted in the United States refer only to remarriage and cohabitation (S. L. Brown et al., 2006, 2012), ignoring the possibility of living apart together. Terminology is important as it determines what is studied and what is ignored. Terminology also determines which statuses are perceived as similar and which are perceived as different. For example, categorizing divorced, never-married, and widowed older adults as single without referring to the uniqueness of each situation, ignores the many differences in life-course trajectories and choices across these different marital statuses. Additionally, there is a great need for research that explores the uniqueness of each marital status as well as for comparative research that offers more innovative comparisons.

Therapy with older people in either marital status has been given limited attention. This could be related to ageist attitudes (Ivey et al., 2000) concerning the ability of older people to change. Despite these dominant beliefs concerning the inability or lack of interest of older adults to pursue change, research has shown that older people do engage in voluntary change in old age and do not necessarily seek continuity (Koren, 2011; Nimrod & Kleiber, 2007). This view is in contrast with the general expectations of old age as a continuation of earlier periods (Atchley, 1989).

The limited attention given to therapeutic interventions geared specifically to address issues concerning the marital status of older adults poses a true challenge for therapists interested in working with this population. Although some techniques and theoretical orientations can be borrowed from the general knowledgebase concerning adults, this review clearly demonstrates the many unique challenges and needs of older adults. As such, more intervention research on this highly diverse population of older adults is needed.

References

Adamec, C. (1992). When parents remarry. *Golden Years*, 14(2), 40–42.

Allen, K. R., & Pickett, R. S. (1987). Forgotten streams in the family life course: Utilization of qualitative retrospective interviews in the analysis of lifelong single women's family careers. *Journal of Marriage and Family, 49*, 517–526. doi:10.2307/352197

Amato, P. R. (2010). Research on divorce: Continuing trends and new developments. *Journal of Marriage and Family, 72*, 650–666. doi:10.1111/j.1741-3737.2010.00723.x

AIDS Community Research Initiative of America. (2008, April). *HIV overview: HIV and older adults*. Presented at the training on HIV and Older Adults co-sponsored by ACRIA and the Council of Senior Centers and Services of NYC (CSCS), New York, NY.

Atchley, R. C. (1989). A continuity theory of normal aging. *Gerontologist, 29*, 183–190. doi:10.1093/geront/29.2.183

Ayalon, L., Goldfracht, M., & Bech, P. (2010). "Do you think you suffer from depression?" Reevaluating the use of a single item question for the screening of depression in older primary care patients. *International Journal of Geriatric Psychiatry, 25*, 497–502. doi:10.1002/gps.2368

Barber, C. E., & Lyness, K. P. (2002). Gerontology training in marriage and family therapy accredited training programs. *Gerontology and Geriatrics Education, 22*, 1–12. doi:10.1300/J021v22n01_01

Baumbusch, J. L. (2004). Unclaimed treasures: Older women's reflections on lifelong singlehood. *Journal of Women and Aging, 16*, 105–121. doi:10.1300/J074v16n01_08

Bengtson, V. L., & Allen, K. R. (1993). The life course perspective applied to families over time. In P. G. Boss, W. J. Doherty, R. LaRossa, W. R. Schumm, & S. K. Steinmetz (Eds.), *Sourcebook of family theories and methods: A contextual approach* (pp. 469–504). New York, NY: Plenum Press. doi:10.1007/978-0-387-85764-0_19

Benjamin, L. S., Rothweiler, J. C., & Critchfield, K. L. (2006). The use of Structural Analysis of Social Behavior (SASB) as an assessment tool. *Annual Review of Clinical Psychology, 2*, 83–109. doi:10.1146/annurev.clinpsy.2.022305.095337

Bograd, R., & Spilka, B. (1996). Self-disclosure and marital satisfaction in mid-life and late-life remarriages. *International Journal of Aging and Human Development, 42*, 161–172. doi:10.2190/W87M-WCK7-MHTT-N34F

Brown, M. T. (2009). LGBT aging and rhetorical silence. *Sexuality Research and Social Policy: A Journal of the National Sexuality Resource Center, 6*, 65–78.

Brown, S. L., Bulanda, J. R., & Lee, G. R. (2005). The significance of nonmarital cohabitation: Marital status and mental health benefits among middle-aged and older adults. *The Journals of Gerontology, Series B: Psychological Sciences and Social Sciences, 60*, 21–29. doi:10.1093/geronb/60.1.S21

Brown, S. L., Bulanda, J. R., & Lee, G. R. (2012). Transitions into and out of cohabitation in later life. *Journal of Marriage and Family, 74*, 774–793.

Brown, S. L., Lee, G. R., & Bulanda, J. R. (2006). Cohabitation among older adults: A national portrait. *The Journals of Gerontology, Series B: Psychological Sciences and Social Sciences, 61*, 71–79. doi:10.1093/geronb/61.2.S71

Brown, S. L., & Lin, I. F. (2012). The gray divorce revolution: Rising divorce among middle-aged and older adults, 1990–2010. *The Journals of Gerontology, Series B: Psychological Sciences and Social Sciences, 67*, 731–741. doi:10.1093/geronb/gbs089

Bulcroft, K., & O'Connor, M. (1986). The importance of dating relationships on quality of life for older persons. *Family Relations, 35*, 397–401. doi:10.2307/584367

Bumpass, L., & Lu, H.-H. (2000). Trends in cohabitation and implications for children's family contexts in the United States. *Population Studies, 54*, 29–41. doi:10.1080/713779060

Calasanti, T., & Kiecolt, K. J. (2007). Diversity among late-life couples. *Generations, 31*, 10–17.

Calzo, J. P., Antonucci, T. C., Mays, V. M., & Cochran, S. D. (2011). Retrospective recall of sexual orientation identity development among gay, lesbian, and bisexual adults. *Developmental Psychology, 47*, 1658–1673. doi:10.1037/a0025508

Cantor, M. H. (1979). Neighbors and friends: An overlooked resource in the informal support system. *Research on Aging, 1,* 434–463. doi:10.1177/016402757914002

Carpenter, J. (1994). Older adults in primary health care in the United Kingdom: An exploration of the relevance of family therapy. *Family Systems Medicine, 12,* 133–148. doi:10.1037/h0089229

Carstensen, L. L., Gottman, J. M., & Levenson, R. W. (1995). Emotional behavior in long-term marriage. *Psychology and Aging, 10,* 140–149. doi:10.1037/0882-7974.10.1.140

Centers for Disease Control and Prevention. (2009). *HIV/AIDS Surveillance Report 2007.* Atlanta, GA: U.S. Department of Health and Human Services, Centers for Disease Control and Prevention.

Cherlin, A. (2010). Demographic trends in the United States: A review of research in the 2000s. *Journal of Marriage and Family, 72,* 403–419. doi:10.1111/j.1741-3737.2010.00710.x

Chevan, A. (1996). As cheaply as one: Cohabitation in the older population. *Journal of Marriage and Family, 58,* 656–667. doi:10.2307/353726

Clements, R., & Swensen, C. H. (1999). Development of a Marriage Problems Scale for use with older couples. *Clinical Gerontologist, 20,* 35–46. doi:10.1300/J018v20n02_04

Coleman, M., Ganong, L. H., & Rothrauff, T. C. (2006). Racial and ethnic similarities and differences in beliefs about intergenerational assistance to older adults after divorce and remarriage. *Family Relations, 55,* 576–587. doi:10.1111/j.1741-3729.2006.00427.x

Condie, S. J. (1989). Older married couples. In S. J. Bahr & E. T. Peterson (Eds.), *Aging and the family* (pp. 143–158). Lexington, MA: Lexington Books.

Connidis, I. A. (2010). *Family ties and aging* (2nd ed.). Thousand Oaks, CA: Sage Publication.

Cooney, T. M., & Dunne, K. (2001). Intimate relationships in later life: Current realities, future prospects. *Journal of Family Issues, 22,* 838–858. doi:10.1177/019251301022007003

Cooney, T. M., & Uhlenberg, P. (1990). The role of divorce in men's relations with their adult children after mid-life. *Journal of Marriage and Family, 52,* 677–688. doi:10.2307/352933

Crowther, J. H. (1985). The relationship between depression and marital maladjustment. A descriptive study. *Journal of Nervous and Mental Disease, 173,* 227–231. doi:10.1097/00005053-198504000-00004

Crumbaugh, J. C. (1968). Cross-validation of Purpose-in-Life test based on Frankl's concepts. *Journal of Individual Psychology, 24,* 74–81.

Crumbaugh, J. C., & Maholick, L. T. (1969). *Manual of instructions for the Purpose in Life Test.* Munster, IN: Psychometric Affiliates.

Cruz, J. (2012). *First marriage vs. remarriage in the U.S., 2010.* Bowling Green, OH: National Center for Family and Marriage Research, Bowling Green State University. Retrieved from http://ncfmr.bgsu.edu/pdf/family_profiles/file119796.pdf

Daatland, S. O. (2007). Marital history and intergenerational solidarity: The impact of divorce and unmarried cohabitation. *Journal of Social Issues, 63,* 809–825. doi:10.1111/j.1540-4560.2007.00538.x

Damman, M., Henkens, K. N., & Kalmijn, M. (2011). The impact of midlife educational, work, health, and family experiences on men's early retirement. *The Journals of Gerontology, Series B: Psychological Sciences and Social Sciences, 66,* 617–627. doi:10.1093/geronb/gbr092

Davidson, K. (2002). Gender differences in new partnership choices and constraints for older widows and widowers. *Ageing International, 27,* 43–60. doi:10.1007/s12126-002-1014-0

Davidson, K., & Fennell, G. (2002). New intimate relationships in later life. *Ageing International, 27,* 3–10. doi:10.1007/s12126-002-1011-3

de Jong Gierveld, J. (2004). Remarriage, unmarried cohabitation, living apart together: Partner relationships following bereavement or divorce. *Journal of Marriage and Family, 66,* 236–243. doi:10.1111/j.0022-2445.2004.00015.x

de Jong-Gierveld, J., & Kamphuls, F. (1985). The development of a Rasch-type loneliness scale. *Applied Psychological Measurement, 9,* 289–299. doi:10.1177/014662168500900307

de Jong Gierveld, J., & Peeters, A. (2003). The interweaving of repartnered older adults' lives with their children and siblings. *Ageing and Society, 23,* 187–205. doi:10.1017/S0144686X02001095

DeLamater, J. D., & Sill, M. (2005). Sexual desire in later life. *Journal of Sex Research, 42,* 138–149. doi:10.1080/00224490509552267

Duncan, S., & Phillips, M. (2010). People who live apart together (LATs)—How different are they? *Sociological Review, 58,* 112–134. doi:10.1111/j.1467-954X.2009.01874.x

Fincham, F. D. (1985). Attribution processes in distressed and nondistressed couples: II. Responsibility for marital problems. *Journal of Abnormal Psychology, 94,* 183–190. doi:10.1037/0021-843X.94.2.183

Freedman, V. A. (1996). Family structure and the risk of nursing home admission. *The Journals of Gerontology, Series B: Psychological Sciences and Social Sciences, 51,* 61–69. doi:10.1093/geronb/51B.2.S61

Freedman, V. A., Aykan, H., Wolf, D. A., & Marcotte, J. E. (2004). Disability and home care dynamics among older unmarried Americans. *The Journals of Gerontology, Series B: Psychological Sciences and Social Sciences, 59,* 25–33. doi:10.1093/geronb/59.1.S25

Frey, W. H. (2010). Baby Boomers and the new demographics of America's seniors. *Generations—Journal of the American Society on Aging, 34,* 28–37.

Gabrielson, M. L. (2011a). "I will not be discriminated against": Older lesbians creating new communities. *Advances in Nursing Science, 34,* 357–373. doi:10.1097/ANS.0b013e3182300db8

Gabrielson, M. L. (2011b). "We have to create family": Aging support issues and needs among older lesbians. *Journal of Gay and Lesbian Social Services, 23,* 322–334. doi:10.1080/10538720.2011.562803

Ganong, L., & Coleman, M. (2006). Patterns of exchange and intergenerational responsibilities after divorce and remarriage. *Journal of Aging Studies, 20,* 265–278. doi:10.1016/j.jaging.2005.09.005

Ghazanfareeon Karlsson, S. B. K. (2004). Intimacy and autonomy, gender and ageing: Living apart together. In K. Davidson & G. Fennell (Eds.), *Intimacy in later life* (pp. 11–26). New Brunswick, NJ: Transaction.

Gilewski, M. J., Kuppinger, J., & Zarit, S. H. (1985). The aging marital system: A case study in life changes and paradoxical intervention. *Clinical Gerontologist, 3,* 3–15. doi:10.1300/J018v03n03_02

Glaser, K., Tomassini, C., & Stuchbury, R. (2008). Differences over time in the relationship between partnership disruptions and support in early old age in Britain. *The Journals of Gerontology, Series B: Psychological Sciences and Social Sciences, 63,* 359–368. doi:10.1093/geronb/63.6.S359

Goldman, N. (1993). Marriage selection and mortality patterns: Inferences and fallacies. *Demography, 30,* 189–208. doi:10.2307/2061837

Goodman, C. (1999). Intimacy and autonomy in long term marriage. *Journal of Gerontological Social Work, 32,* 83–97. doi:10.1300/J083v32n01_06

Gott, M., Hinchliff, S., & Galena, E. (2004). General practitioner attitudes to discussing sexual health issues with older people. *Social Science and Medicine, 58,* 2093–2103. doi:10.1016/j.socscimed.2003.08.025

Greggo, S. P. (2003). The virtues of talk therapy for the aging: A family-focused case example. *Marriage and Family: A Christian Journal, 6,* 471–482.

Hans, J. D., Ganong, L. H., & Coleman, M. (2009). Financial responsibilities toward older parents and stepparents following divorce and remarriage. *Journal of Family and Economic Issues, 30,* 55–66. doi:10.1007/s10834-008-9137-4

Hash, K. M., & Rogers, A. (2013). Clinical practice with older LGBT clients: Overcoming lifelong stigma through strength and resilience. *Clinical Social Work Journal, 41,* 249–257.

Haskey, J., & Lewis, J. (2006). Living-apart-together in Britain: Context and meaning. *International Journal of Law in Context, 2,* 37–48. doi:10.1017/S1744552306001030

Hatch, L. R., & Bulcroft, K. (2004). Does long-term marriage bring less frequent disagreements? Five explanatory frameworks. *Journal of Family Issues, 25,* 465–495. doi:10.1177/0192513X03257766

Haynes, S. N., Floyd, F. J., Lemsky, C., Rogers, E., Winemiller, D., Heilman, N., . . . Cardone, L. (1992). The Marital Satisfaction Questionnaire for Older Persons. *Psychological Assessment, 4,* 473–482. doi:10.1037/1040-3590.4.4.473

Henry, N. J. M., Berg, C. A., Smith, T. W., & Florsheim, P. (2007). Positive and negative characteristics of marital interaction and their association with marital satisfaction in middle-aged and older couples. *Psychology and Aging, 22,* 428–441. doi:10.1037/0882-7974.22.3.428

Henry, R. G., Miller, R. B., & Giarrusso, R. (2005). Difficulties, disagreements, and disappointments in late-life marriages. *International Journal of Aging and Human Development, 61,* 243–264. doi:10.2190/EF1G-PNXF-J1VQ-6M72

Heun, R., Bonsignore, M., Barkow, K., & Jessen, F. (2001). Validity of the five-item WHO Well-Being Index (WHO-5) in an elderly population. *European Archives of Psychiatry and Clinical Neuroscience, 251,* 27–31. doi:10.1007/BF03035123

Heyman, R. E., Weiss, R. L., & Eddy, J. M. (1995). Marital interaction coding system: Revision and empirical evaluation. *Behaviour Research and Therapy, 33,* 737–746. doi:10.1016/0005-7967(95)00003-G

Hinchliff, S., & Gott, M. (2004). Intimacy, commitment, and adaptation: Sexual relationships within long-term marriages. *Journal of Social and Personal Relationships, 21,* 595–609. doi:10.1177/0265407504045889

Hinrichs, K. L. M., & Vacha-Haase, T. (2010). Staff perceptions of same-gender sexual contacts in long-term care facilities. *Journal of Homosexuality, 57,* 776–789. doi:10.1080/00918369.2010.485877

Holden, K. C., & Kuo, H.-H. D. (1996). Complex marital histories and economic well-being: The continuing legacy of divorce and widowhood as the HRS cohort approaches retirement. *Gerontologist, 36,* 383–390. doi:10.1093/geront/36.3.383

Hoonaard, D. (2002). Attitudes of older widows and widowers in New Brunswick, Canada towards new partnerships. *Ageing International, 27,* 79–92. doi:10.1007/s12126-002-1016-y

Hu, Y. R., & Goldman, N. (1990). Mortality differentials by marital status: An international comparison. *Demography, 27*, 233–250. doi:10.2307/2061451

Hughes, A. K., Harold, R. D., & Boyer, J. M. (2011). Awareness of LGBT aging issues among aging services network providers. *Journal of Gerontological Social Work, 54*, 659–677. doi:10.1080/01634372.2011.585392

Hughes, M. E., Waite, L. J., Hawkley, L. C., & Cacioppo, J. T. (2004). A short scale for measuring loneliness in large surveys: Results from two population-based studies. *Research on Aging, 26*, 655–672. doi:10.1177/0164027504268574

Ivey, D. C., Wieling, E., & Harris, S. M. (2000). Save the young—the elderly have lived their lives: Ageism in marriage and family therapy. *Family Process, 39*, 163–175. doi:10.1111/j.1545-5300.2000.39202.x

Johnston, M. W., & Eklund, S. J. (1984). Life-adjustment of the never-married: A review with implications for counseling. *Journal of Counseling and Development, 63*, 230–236. doi:10.1002/j.1556-6676.1984.tb02808.x

Kamiya, Y., Doyle, M., Henretta, J. C., & Timonen, V. (2013). Depressive symptoms among older adults: The impact of early and later life circumstances and marital status. *Aging and Mental Health, 17*, 349–357. doi:10.1080/13607863.2012.747078

Karlsson, S., & Borell, K. (2002). Intimacy and autonomy, gender and ageing: Living apart together. *Ageing International, 27*, 11–26. doi:10.1007/s12126-002-1012-2

Kazak, A. E., Jarmas, A., & Snitzer, L. (1988). The assessment of marital satisfaction: An evaluation of the Dyadic Adjustment Scale. *Journal of Family Psychology, 2*, 82–91. doi:10.1037/h0080475

Keith, P. M. (1985). Work, retirement and well-being among unmarried men and women. *Gerontologist, 25*, 410–416. doi:10.1093/geront/25.4.410

Kertzner, R. M., Barber, M. E., & Schwartz, A. (2011). Mental health issues in LGBT seniors. *Journal of Gay and Lesbian Mental Health, 15*, 335–338. doi:10.1080/19359705.2011.606680

King, V., & Scott, M. E. (2005). A comparison of cohabiting relationships among older and younger adults. *Journal of Marriage and Family, 67*, 271–285. doi:10.1111/j.0022-2445.2005.00115.x

Knochel, K. A., Croghan, C. F., Moone, R. P., & Quam, J. K. (2012). Training, geography, and provision of aging services to lesbian, gay, bisexual, and transgender older adults. *Journal of Gerontological Social Work, 55*, 426–443. doi:10.1080/01634372.2012.665158

Koren, C. (2011). Continuity and discontinuity: The case of second coupledhood in old age. *Gerontologist, 51*, 687–698. doi:10.1093/geront/gnr018

Koren, C. (2014a). The intertwining of second coupledhood and old age, *Ageing and Society*. Advance online publication. doi:10.1017/S0144686X14000294

Koren, C. (2014b). Together and apart: A typology of re-partnering in old age. *International Psychogeriatrics, 26*, 1327–1350.

Koren, C., & Eisikovits, Z. (2011). Life beyond the planned script: Accounts and secrecy of older persons living in second coupledhood in old age in a society in transition. *Journal of Social and Personal Relationships, 28*, 44–63. doi:10.1177/0265407510385430

Krause, N., & Markides, K. (1990). Measuring social support among older adults. *International Journal of Aging and Human Development, 30*, 37–53. doi:10.2190/CY26-XCKW-WY1V-VGK3

Kreider, R. M., & Ellis, R. (2011). *Number, timing, and duration of marriages and divorces: 2009 Household and economic studies*. Washington, DC: U.S. Census Bureau.

Kuhn, D. R., Morhardt, D. J., & Monbrod-Framburg, G. (1993). Late-life marriages, older stepfamilies, and Alzheimer's disease. *Families in Society, 74*, 154–162.

Kulik, L. (2002). Marital equality and the quality of long-term marriage in later life. *Ageing and Society, 22*, 459–481. doi:10.1017/S0144686X02008772

Lambert-Shute, J., & Fruhauf, C. A. (2011). Aging issues: Unanswered questions in marital and family therapy literature. *Journal of Marital and Family Therapy, 37*, 27–36. doi:10.1111/j.1752-0606.2009.00152.x

Landerman, R., George, L. K., Campbell, R. T., & Blazer, D. G. (1989). Alternative models of the stress buffering hypothesis. *American Journal of Community Psychology, 17*, 625–642. doi:10.1007/BF00922639

Lee, J. M., & Hett, G. G. (1990). Post-divorce adjustment: An assessment of a group intervention. *Canadian Journal of Counselling and Psychotherapy, 24*, 199–209.

Levin, I. (2004). Living apart together: A new family form. *Current Sociology, 52*, 223–240. doi:10.1177/0011392104041809

Levin, I., & Trost, J. (1999). Living apart together. *Community, Work and Family, 2*, 279–294. doi:10.1080/13668809908412186

Lin, I. F., & Brown, S. L. (2012). Unmarried Boomers confront old age: A national portrait. *Gerontologist, 52*, 153–165. doi:10.1093/geront/gnr141

Lindau, S. T., Schumm, L. P., Laumann, E. O., Levinson, W., O'Muircheartaigh, C. A., & Waite, L. J. (2007). A study of sexuality and health among older adults in the United States. *New England Journal of Medicine, 357*, 762–774. doi:10.1056/NEJMoa067423

Locke, J. J., & Wallace, K. M. (1959). Short Marital-Adjustment and prediction tests: Their reliability and validity. *Marriage and Family Living, 21,* 251–255. doi:10.2307/348022

Lynch, T. R., Morse, J. Q., Mendelson, T., & Robins, C. J. (2003). Dialectical behavior therapy for depressed older adults: A randomized pilot study. *American Journal of Geriatric Psychiatry, 11,* 33–45. doi:10.1097/00019442-200301000-00006

Lyons, A., Pitts, M., & Grierson, J. (2013). Growing old as a gay man: Psychosocial well-being of a sexual minority. *Research on Aging, 35,* 275–295. doi:10.1177/0164027512445055

Martire, L. M., Schulz, R., Helgeson, V., Small, B., & Saghafi, E. (2010). Review and meta-analysis of couple-oriented interventions for chronic illness. *Annals of Behavioral Medicine, 40,* 325–342. doi:10.1007/s12160-010-9216-2

Masi, C. M., Chen, H.-Y., Hawkley, L. C., & Cacioppo, J. T. (2011). A meta-analysis of interventions to reduce loneliness. *Personality and Social Psychology Review, 15,* 219–266. doi:10.1177/1088868310377394

Mayers, K., & McBride, D. (1998). Sexuality training for caretakers of geriatric residents in long term care facilities. *Sexuality and Disability, 16,* 227–236. doi:10.1023/A:1023003310885

Mehta, K. (2002). Perceptions of remarriage by widowed people in Singapore. *Ageing International, 27,* 93–107. doi:10.1007/s12126-002-1017-x

Meri-Esh, O., & Doron, I. (2009). Aging with pride in Israel: An Israeli perspective on the meaning of homosexuality in old age. *Ageing International, 34,* 42–59. doi:10.1007/s12126-009-9035-6

Moustgaard, H., & Martikainen, P. (2009). Nonmarital cohabitation among older Finnish men and women: Socioeconomic characteristics and forms of union dissolution. *The Journals of Gerontology, Series B: Psychological Sciences and Social Sciences, 64,* 507–516. doi:10.1093/geronb/gbp024

Muzacz, A. K., & Akinsulure-Smith, A. M. (2013). Older adults and sexuality: Implications for counseling ethnic and sexual minority clients. *Journal of Mental Health Counseling, 35,* 1–14.

Nimrod, G., & Kleiber, D. A. (2007). Reconsidering change and continuity in later life: Toward an innovation theory of successful aging. *International Journal of Aging and Human Development, 65,* 1–22. doi:10.2190/Q4G5-7176-51Q2-3754

Noël-Miller, C. M. (2011). Partner caregiving in older cohabiting couples. *The Journals of Gerontology, Series B: Psychological Sciences and Social Sciences, 66,* 341–353. doi:10.1093/geronb/gbr027

Northouse, L. L., Katapodi, M. C., Song, L., Zhang, L., & Mood, D. W. (2010). Interventions with family caregivers of cancer patients: Meta-analysis of randomized trials. *CA: A Cancer Journal for Clinicians, 60,* 317–339.

Orbuch, T. L., House, J. S., Mero, R. P., & Webster, P. S. (1996). Marital quality over the life course. *Social Psychology Quarterly, 59,* 162–171. doi:10.2307/2787050

Pearlin, L. I., & Johnson, J. S. (1977). Marital status, life-strains and depression. *American Sociological Review, 42,* 704–715. doi:10.2307/2094860

Pezzin, L. E., Pollak, R. A., & Schone, B. S. (2008). Parental marital disruption, family type, and transfers to disabled elderly parents. *The Journals of Gerontology, Series B: Psychological Sciences and Social Sciences, 63,* 349–358. doi:10.1093/geronb/63.6.S349

Pienta, A. M., Hayward, M. D., & Jenkins, K. R. (2000). Health consequences of marriage for the retirement years. *Journal of Family Issues, 21,* 559–586. doi:10.1177/019251300021005003

Pinquart, M. (2003). Loneliness in married, widowed, divorced, and never-married older adults. *Journal of Social and Personal Relationships, 20,* 31–53. doi:10.1177/02654075030201002

Pudrovska, T., Schieman, S., & Carr, D. (2006). Strains of singlehood in later life: Do race and gender matter? *The Journals of Gerontology, Series B: Psychological Sciences and Social Sciences, 61,* 315–322. doi:10.1093/geronb/61.6.S315

Rogers, R. G. (1995). Marriage, sex, and mortality. *Journal of Marriage and Family, 57,* 515–526. doi:10.2307/353703

Ross, M. W., Chanon-Little, L. D., & Rosser, B. R. S. (2000). *Sexual health concerns: Interviewing and history taking for health practitioners.* Philadelphia, PA: F.A. Davis Gompan.

Rubinstein, R. L. (1987). Never married elderly as a social type: Re-evaluating some images. *Gerontologist, 27,* 108–113. doi:10.1093/geront/27.1.108

Ruggles, S. (1997). The rise of divorce and separation in the United States, 1980–1990. *Demography, 34,* 455–466. doi:10.2307/3038300

Russell, D., Peplau, L. A., & Ferguson, M. L. (1978). Developing a measure of loneliness. *Journal of Personality Assessment, 42,* 290–294. doi:10.1207/s15327752jpa4203_11

Sarason, I. G., Levine, H. M., Basham, R. B., & Sarason, B. R. (1983). Assessing social support: The Social Support Questionnaire. *Journal of Personality and Social Psychology, 44,* 127–139. doi:10.1037/0022-3514.44.1.127

Scherrer, K., Ingersoll-Dayton, B., & Spencer, B. (2014). Constructing couples' stories: Narrative practice insights from a dyadic dementia intervention. *Clinical Social Work Journal, 42,* 90–100.

Schlesinger, R. A., & Schlesinger, B. (2004). *Canadian–Jewish seniors: Marriage/cohabitation after age 65.*

Paper presented at the 10th Biennial Jerusalem Conference in Canadian Studies.

Schmitt, M., Kliegel, M., & Shapiro, A. (2007). Marital interaction in middle and old age: A predictor of marital satisfaction? *International Journal of Aging and Human Development, 65*, 283–300. doi:10.2190/AG.65.4.a

Schulz, R., Belle, S. H., Czaja, S. J., McGinnis, K. A., Stevens, A., & Zhang, S. (2004). Long-term care placement of dementia patients and caregiver health and well-being. *JAMA, 292*, 961–967. doi:10.1001/jama.292.8.961

Scott, M. B., & Lyman, S. M. (1968). Accounts. *American Sociological Review, 33*, 46–62. doi:10.2307/2092239

Seider, B. H., Hirschberger, G., Nelson, K. L., & Levenson, R. W. (2009). We can work it out: Age differences in relational pronouns, physiology, and behavior in marital conflict. *Psychology and Aging, 24*, 604–613. doi:10.1037/a0016950

Shapiro, A., & Remle, R. C. (2011). Generational jeopardy? Parents' marital transitions and the provision of financial transfers to adult children. *The Journals of Gerontology, Series B: Psychological Sciences and Social Sciences, 66*, 99–108. doi:10.1093/geronb/gbq010

Sherman, C. W. (2012). Remarriage as context for dementia caregiving: Implications of positive support and negative interactions for caregiver well-being. *Research in Human Development, 9*, 165–182. doi:10.1080/15427609.2012.680845

Sherman, C. W., & Bauer, J. W. (2008). Financial conflicts facing late-life remarried Alzheimer's disease caregivers. *Family Relations, 57*, 492–503. doi:10.1111/j.1741-3729.2008.00517.x

Sherman, C. W., & Boss, P. (2007). Spousal dementia caregiving in the context of late-life remarriage. *Dementia (London), 6*, 245–270. doi:10.1177/1471301207080367

Smith, T. W., Berg, C. A., Florsheim, P., Uchino, B. N., Pearce, G., Hawkins, M., . . . Olsen-Cerny, C. (2009). Conflict and collaboration in middle-aged and older couples: I. Age differences in agency and communion during marital interaction. *Psychology and Aging, 24*, 259–273. doi:10.1037/a0015609

Sörensen, S., Pinquart, M., & Duberstein, P. (2002). How effective are interventions with caregivers? An updated meta-analysis. *Gerontologist, 42*, 356–372. doi:10.1093/geront/42.3.356

Spanier, G. B. (1976). Measuring dyadic adjustment: New scales for assessing the quality of marriage and similar dyads. *Journal of Marriage and Family, 38*, 15–28. doi:10.2307/350547

Steger, M. F., Frazier, P., Oishi, S., & Kaler, M. (2006). The meaning in life questionnaire: Assessing the presence of and search for meaning in life. *Journal of Counseling Psychology, 53*, 80–93. doi:10.1037/0022-0167.53.1.80

Stevens, N. (2002). Re-engaging: New partnerships in late-life widowhood. *Ageing International, 27*, 27–42. doi:10.1007/s12126-002-1013-1

Swensen, C. H., & Trahaug, G. (1985). Commitment and the long-term marriage relationship. *Journal of Marriage and Family, 47*, 939–945. doi:10.2307/352337

Uhlenberg, P., Cooney, T., & Boyd, R. (1990). Divorce for women after midlife. *Journal of Gerontology, 45*, S3–S11. doi:10.1093/geronj/45.1.S3

Uhlenberg, P., & Myers, M. A. P. (1981). Divorce and the elderly. *Gerontologist, 21*, 276–282. doi:10.1093/geront/21.3.276

Umberson, D., Williams, K., Powers, D. A., Chen, M. D., & Campbell, A. M. (2005). As good as it gets? A life course perspective on marital quality. *Social Forces, 84*, 493–511. doi:10.1353/sof.2005.0131

U.S. Census Bureau. (1940). *Sixteenth census of the United States—1940 population: Volume IV, characteristics by age, part 1: United States summary.* Washington, DC: Government Printing Office.

U.S. Census Bureau. (2010). *America's families and living arrangements: 2010, table 1A. Marital status of people 15 years and over, by age, sex, personal earnings, race, and Hispanic origin.* Washington, DC: Government Printing Office.

Vaid, U. (1996). *Virtual equality: The mainstreaming of gay and lesbian liberation.* New York, NY: Anchor Books.

Vaillant, C. O., & Vaillant, G. E. (1993). Is the U-curve of marital satisfaction an illusion? A 40-year study of marriage. *Journal of Marriage and Family, 55*, 230–239.

van der Pas, S., & van Tilburg, T. G. (2010). The influence of family structure on the contact between older parents and their adult biological children and stepchildren in the Netherlands. *The Journals of Gerontology, Series B: Psychological Sciences and Social Sciences, 65*, 236–245.

Veroff, J., Douvan, E. A. M., & Kulka, R. A. (1981). *The inner American: A self-portrait from 1957 to 1976.* New York, NY: Basic Books.

Waite, L. J., Laumann, E. O., Das, A., & Schumm, L. P. (2009). Sexuality: Measures of partnerships, practices, attitudes, and problems in the National Social Life, Health, and Aging Study. *The Journals of Gerontology, Series B: Psychological Sciences and Social Sciences, 64*, 56–66.

Walker, R. B., & Luszcz, M. A. (2009). The health and relationship dynamics of late-life couples: A systematic review of the literature. *Ageing and Society, 29*, 455–480.

Ward, R. A. (1979). The never-married in later life. *Journal of Gerontology, 34*, 861–869.

Ware, J. E., Jr., & Sherbourne, C. D. (1992). The MOS 36-item short-form health survey (SF-36). I.

Conceptual framework and item selection. *Medical Care, 30*, 473–483.

Webster, P. S., & Herzog, A. R. (1995). Effects of parental divorce and memories of family problems on relationships between adult children and their parents. *The Journals of Gerontology, Series B: Psychological Sciences and Social Sciences, 50*, 24–34.

Weishaus, S., & Field, D. (1988). A half century of marriage: Continuity or change? *Journal of Marriage and Family, 50*, 763–774.

White, C. (1982). A scale for the assessment of attitudes and knowledge regarding sexuality in the aged. *Archives of Sexual Behavior, 11*, 491–502.

Willert, A., & Semans, M. (2000). Knowledge and attitudes about later life sexuality: What clinicians need to know about helping the elderly. *Contemporary Family Therapy, 22*, 415–435.

Williams, K., & Umberson, D. (2004). Marital status, marital transitions, and health: A gendered life course perspective. *Journal of Health and Social Behavior, 45*, 81–98.

Wu, Z., & Pollard, M. S. (1998). Social support among unmarried childless elderly persons. *The Journals of Gerontology, Series B: Psychological Sciences and Social Sciences, 53*, 324–335.

Wu, Z., & Schimmele, C. (2007). Uncoupling in late life. *Generations, 31*, 41–46.

CHAPTER 25

BEREAVEMENT IN LATER LIFE: THEORY, ASSESSMENT, AND INTERVENTION

Robert A. Neimeyer and Jason M. Holland

In the midst of a protracted caregiving relationship with her husband who had been diagnosed with a terminal cancer, Rosa, a 67-year-old Latina woman, followed her husband in the final weeks of his life to an inpatient hospice unit. As Rosa and her husband were skeptical of the hospital, its staff, and the bureaucratic system that governed it, Rosa preferred to stay in her husband's room at all times, only leaving for brief periods while another family member sat in her place. As the days and weeks wore on in this way, it was clear from her tired eyes and slowed movements that the late nights and round-the-clock caregiving was starting to take its toll. Although hospice staff encouraged her to rest and take better care of herself, Rosa stoically insisted that she was handling things fine and needed to stay close to her husband, as only she could assist with "private matters," such as helping him use the restroom. Only complicating the situation, Rosa found herself feeling alienated from her American-born adult children, who tended to grieve in more emotionally expressive ways and were confused by their mother's lack of outward emotion. Nearly 2 years after her husband's death, however, Rosa continued to exhibit signs of complication in her emotional response to the loss, withdrawing from family and friends, persistently aching for her husband, and finding herself lost without her caregiving role, all of which had once imbued life with a sense of meaning and purpose.

In many ways, Rosa's story exemplifies the kinds of clinical situations that psychologists of the 21st century increasingly are facing as the U.S. population grows older and more diverse. The death of a loved one is arguably one of the most ubiquitous and stressful life events that older adults must contend with, as evidenced by multiple studies on late-life stress (Hardy, Concato, & Gill, 2002; Murrel, Norris, & Hutchins, 1984). Thus, the need is growing for 21st-century psychologists to gain knowledge about the prevalence of loss and different patterns of grieving in older adulthood as well as to build skills in bereavement-related assessments and interventions that are informed empirically and based on current theoretical models. This chapter orients the reader to these topics, including a discussion of (a) the prevalence of resilience and bereavement-related problems in later life, (b) theoretical models of adjustment to loss and the support accruing for them, (c) assessment and intervention with bereaved older adults, (d) special issues in bereavement care for diverse populations, and (e) recommendations for future directions in bereavement research, policy, and training.

http://dx.doi.org/10.1037/14459-025
APA Handbook of Clinical Geropsychology: Vol. 2. Assessment, Treatment, and Issues of Later Life,
P. A. Lichtenberg and B. T. Mast (Editors-in-Chief)

PREVALENCE OF RESILIENCY AND BEREAVEMENT-RELATED PROBLEMS

By the age of 65 years, one half of all women and 10% of all men experience the loss of a spouse, and these figures rise to 80% and 40%, respectively, by age 85 years (Rosenzweig, Prigerson, Miller, & Reynolds, 1997). The cumulative losses experienced by older adults dramatically surpasses these figures, as the loss of siblings and friends exceed spousal bereavement by a factor of three-to-one and nine-to-one, respectively (Hays, Gold, & Peiper, 1997). Despite the difficulty of such losses, however, the best evidence suggests that most older adults are fairly resilient. Specifically, in a recent reanalysis of the Changing Lives of Older Couples (CLOC) study (Bonanno et al., 2002; Bonanno, Wortman, & Nesse, 2004), 66.3% of roughly 300 older bereaved spouses were found to exhibit a resilient trajectory, characterized by minimal depressive symptoms from baseline (before the loss occurred) to 6, 18, and 48 months postloss as illustrated in Figure 25.1.

Although many of these individuals likely experienced some transitory distress following the loss, for the most part, resilient grievers were able to draw on their intra- and interpersonal resources and find ways to reengage in life without dwelling in a persistent state of depression. It is notable that these researchers found no evidence of a delayed grief reaction, indicating that those who were reporting minimal problems 6 months after the loss were genuinely resilient and not necessarily at risk for later problems. In this more recent analysis of the CLOC data, there was also little support for an inverted V-shaped bereavement trajectory, whereby individuals exhibited low levels of preloss depression followed by elevated symptoms at 6 months postloss that then receded by the 18- and 48-month follow-ups, challenging the once widely held belief that this pattern of recovery is most common.

To the surprise of most psychological researchers and clinicians, another 10.1% of the older adults in this study actually exhibited a pattern of *improved* depression after the loss of their spouse. In particular,

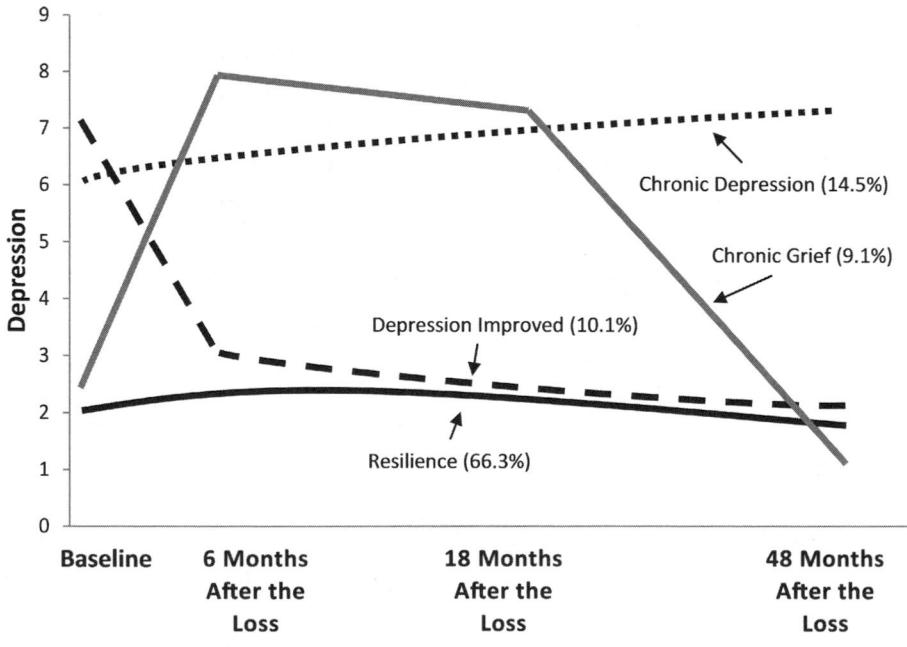

FIGURE 25.1. Trajectories through spousal loss in later life. From "Beyond Normality in the Study of Bereavement: Heterogeneity in Depression Outcomes Following Loss in Older Adults," by I. R. Galatzer-Levy and G. A. Bonanno, 2012, *Social Science and Medicine, 74,* p. 1992. Copyright 2012 by Elsevier. Adapted with permission.

these individuals showed elevated levels of depression before the loss occurred that then abated 6 months after the death and remained relatively low at the 18- and 48-month postloss assessments. Upon further analysis, many of these individuals with improved depression were found to have been in abusive or burdensome caregiving relationships (Bonanno et al., 2002). Thus, for this smaller subset of bereaved spouses, the loss actually seemed to provide a newfound freedom to explore new possibilities and life roles that once had seemed unavailable.

Another 14.5% of the participants in this study showed elevated levels of depression before the death of their spouse, which remained elevated after the loss. Although the loss of their spouse led to a small rise in depression, for the most part, these individuals seemed to carry many of the same problems that they had as married people into the bereavement phase of their lives. Finally, 9.1% of the sample exhibited a chronic grief trajectory characterized by low levels of depression before the loss that then sharply increased 6 months following the death and stayed elevated by 18 months postloss. Interestingly, by 48 months postloss, most of these chronic grievers had returned to their previous low level of depression, perhaps indicating that the natural course of these more complicated reactions is somewhere between 18 and 48 months after the loss has occurred. It is these complicated reactions to which we now shift our attention. It is worth noting, however, that the general pattern of prevalence rates and results described thus far have been replicated in other samples, including bereaved Alzheimer's caregivers (Schulz et al., 2003; Zhang, Mitchell, Bambauer, Jones, & Prigerson, 2008), men who have lost a life partner to AIDS, and bereaved parents (Bonanno, Moskowitz, Papa, & Folkman, 2005).

Although a comparatively smaller subset of the bereaved, studies consistently have shown that around 10%–15% of older adults who have lost a loved one exhibit symptoms consistent with complicated grief—a prolonged form of grieving that persists for 6 months or longer and is characterized by intense separation distress, a sense of meaninglessness and purposelessness, excessive bitterness over the loss, and impairments in day-to-day functioning (e.g., relationship problems, sleep disturbances, or greater difficulty with household tasks; Prigerson, Vanderwerker, & Maciejewski, 2008). The proposed diagnostic criteria for complicated grief (also referred to as prolonged grief disorder) are presented in Exhibit 25.1 and currently are under consideration for inclusion in the *International Classification of Diseases, Eleventh Revision* (Maercker et al., 2013).

Although complicated grief does co-occur with other psychiatric disorders, many older complicated grievers do not show signs of comorbidity, with only 9.7% meeting criteria for major depressive disorder and 17.2% meeting criteria for an anxiety disorder in one recent epidemiological study (Newson, Boelen, Hek, Hofman, & Tiemeier, 2011). Furthermore, complicated grief symptoms have been shown to be unique from the symptoms of other disorders, such as anxiety, depression, and posttraumatic stress (Boelen & van den Bout, 2005; Boelen, van den Bout, & de Keijser, 2003; Prigerson et al., 1996). In particular, complicated grief is conceptualized as an attachment-based disorder, primarily distinguished by its emphasis on separation distress

---

Exhibit 25.1
Diagnostic Features of Complicated Grief

1. Duration of bereavement of at least 6 months
2. Marked and persistent separation distress, reflected in intense feelings of loneliness, yearning for, or preoccupation with the person who has died
3. At least five of the following nine symptoms experienced nearly daily to a disabling degree:
   - Diminished sense of self (e.g., as if a part of oneself has died)
   - Difficultly accepting the loss on emotional as well as intellectual levels
   - Avoidance of reminders of the reality of the loss
   - Inability to trust others or to feel that others understand
   - Bitterness or anger over the death
   - Difficulty "moving on," or embracing new friends and interests
   - Numbness or inability to feel
   - Sensing that life or the future is without purpose or meaning
   - Feeling stunned, dazed, or shocked by the death
4. Significant impairment in social, occupational, or family functioning

Note. Data from Prigerson et al. (2009) and Shear et al. (2011).

(e.g., longing, yearning, pining) following the loss of a significant attachment figure. Studies have found that these symptoms can have profound implications, even after accounting for the effects of other psychiatric disorders, uniquely predicting detrimental outcomes, such as cardiac problems, high blood pressure, incidence of cancer, changes in eating and smoking habits, suicidal ideation, and global psychological functioning (Bonanno et al., 2007; Latham & Prigerson, 2004; Prigerson et al., 1997).

Complicated grief is not the only possible negative outcome for bereaved older adults. In one review of depression and anxiety in the first year of widowhood, roughly 22% met criteria for major depressive disorder and 12% were diagnosed with posttraumatic stress disorder (PTSD; Onrust & Cuijpers, 2006). Similar percentages of generalized anxiety and panic also were noted, and generally speaking, rates of psychopathology were found to be higher among widows compared with married controls. The loss of a loved one can have serious health consequences as well (Stroebe, Schut, & Stroebe, 2007). Studies have documented negative physical health outcomes among bereaved individuals, such as depressed immune functioning (Bartrop, Luckhurst, Lazarus, Kiloh, & Penny, 1994), cardiovascular risk factors (Buckley, McKinley, Tofler, & Bartrop, 2010), physical pain (Bradbeer, Helme, Yong, Kendig, & Gibson, 2003), and increased medication usage (L. W. Thompson, Breckenridge, Gallagher, & Peterson, 1984).

Widowed and other bereaved individuals are also at significantly higher risk for mortality—a trend that often is referred to as the "broken-heart" phenomenon (Moon, Kondo, Glymour, & Subramanian, 2011). This phenomenon appears hold across different age-groups and has been shown to be particularly pronounced for men and those in the first 6 months of loss, who are 1.41 and 1.23 times more likely to die, respectively, compared with nonbereaved controls. The precise mechanisms by which this mortality increase occurs are poorly understood. It is possible that increases in depression, anxiety, and complicated grief may be partly responsible.

Alternate explanations have been proposed, however, such as the possibility that the disruption in routines and circadian rhythms in the aftermath of loss may pose a physiological threat, particularly if the deceased fulfilled important instrumental functions in the relationship (e.g., transportation, monitoring health, cooking; Holland et al., 2014). Indeed, past research suggests that widowhood in late life is associated with poor eating behaviors and nutrient intake (Rosenbloom & Whittington, 1993), disrupted social rhythms (Brown et al., 1996), and sleep impairment (Richardson, Lund, Caserta, Dudley, & Obray, 2003). In support of this view, one study found that compared with nonbereaved controls, older bereaved individuals who experienced a range of losses were more likely to show dysregulated cortisol patterns (a physiological biomarker of stress), but this difference did not appear to be explained by depressive symptoms or complicated grief (Holland et al., 2014). Instead, those who had recently lost a spouse were at the greatest risk for cortisol abnormality, possibly indicating that the abrupt loss of relationships that provide both emotional and instrumental support on a daily basis are the most taxing from a physiological standpoint.

THEORETICAL MODELS OF ADJUSTMENT TO LOSS

As the field of bereavement research has evolved, so too have the conceptual lenses through which adaptation to loss has been viewed. Only a generation ago grief was assumed by both professionals (Downe-Wamboldt & Tamlyn, 1997) and the general public (Kübler-Ross, 1969) to progress largely in stage-like terms, beginning with shock and denial, and moving through phases of anger, protest, and depression before reaching—at least ideally—a stage of acceptance, recovery, or the like. Recent research, however, has called such assumptions into question, as indicators of the magnitude of these various emotional processes fail to correspond to their presumed sequential salience in normative later life bereavement (Maciejewski, Zhang, Block, & Prigerson, 2007), in which acceptance tends to predominate from quite early on, and anger and denial occur at low levels throughout the first 2 years of adjustment. Still less evidence supports the cogency of stage models in cases of sudden, violent death through suicide, homicide, or accident, where little clear separation of emotional phases can be discerned over time (Holland & Neimeyer, 2010). Similarly, accumulating evidence (Stroebe, 1992–1993; Wortman & Silver, 2001) has undermined confidence in the "grief work" hypothesis, the assumption that grieving adaptively primarily entails expressing, exploring, and "working through" the painful emotions associated with the loss to "let go" of the attachment to the deceased and invest in other relationships (Freud, 1917/1957). In the place of these traditional models, a variety of theories have been proposed to account for manifest differences in bereavement outcome as well as to specify adaptive processes by which people cope with loss.

The first of these models, premised on the cardinal role of attachment in human development, has the greatest affinity with early psychodynamic formulations (Parkes & Prigerson, 2009). In this view, humans have evolved as social beings whose sense of felt security depends critically on bonds with caregivers—typically one's parents—in early life, from which children develop "internal working models" that implicitly shape expectations regarding the availability of others as sources of support and regarding one's own resourcefulness and lovability in later relationships (Bowlby, 1980). Under optimal circumstances, people develop secure attachments presuming the availability of others as a "safe haven" to which they can return in times of stress and a "secure base" from which they can venture to explore new relationships. Early experiences of loss, neglect, or abuse by caregivers, however, may render such assumptions tenuous, and one's attachment insecure and anxious. Given the powerful challenge to conservation of an attachment bond posed by the death of a loved one, it is not surprising that older widows and widowers who display an insecure and dependent attachment on their spouse tend to fare poorly across the first 4 years of bereavement (Bonanno, Wortman, & Nesse, 2004). Interestingly, however, avoidant attachment—essentially maximizing one's sense of self-reliance and minimizing one's dependence on others—seems to mitigate grief-related distress, at least until challenged by traumatic and violent losses (Meier, Carr, Currier, & Neimeyer, 2013). In general, however, insecure

attachment seems to be an empirically established risk factor for complicated bereavement (Burke & Neimeyer, 2013).

The related continuing bonds perspective extends attachment theory by focusing on the reformulation of the relationship specifically to the deceased in the aftermath of bereavement. Once considered patently pathological, the retention rather than relinquishment of such attachment to the loved one is now regarded as normative (Klass, Silverman, & Nickman, 1996), although the character of such attachment can determine its adaptiveness. For example, bonds that are characterized by preoccupation and unwelcome sensory hallucination of the deceased person's presence across a considerable period of time or that rely on tangible "proximity-seeking" behaviors, such as frequent trips to the gravesite or only feeling close to the loved one in the presence of his or her possessions, have been linked to greater long-term distress (Field, Gal-Oz, & Bonanno, 2003; Field, Gao, & Paderna, 2005). On the other hand, sensing the presence of the deceased as a source of comfort, being able to have inner conversations with the loved one, and drawing on his or her values and love as a source of inspiration in one's ongoing life appear to be associated with more favorable bereavement outcomes (Datson & Marwit, 1997; Field et al., 2003; Hedtke & Winslade, 2004). There is also some evidence that the character of the continuing bond evolves across the course of grieving, as frequently resorting to "continuing bonds coping" (e.g., consciously reminiscing about the deceased throughout the day) seems to be associated with higher levels of negative emotion in the early months of widowhood, whereas similar processes are linked to reports of more positive emotion after 2 years of bereavement (Field & Friedrichs, 2004). One theory that accommodates such findings is the two-track model of bereavement (TTMB), which posits that grief proceeds along two avenues simultaneously: the first concerned with the mourner's *biopsychosocial functioning*, such as disruptions in mood, social behavior, physical health, and capacity for work; and the second focused on one's *relationship to the deceased*, not only before the death but also in one's ongoing life (Rubin, 1999; Rubin, Malkinson, & Witztum, 2003). In the latter case, for example, the bereaved may access or avoid memories of times spent with the deceased, carry out public or private rituals of remembrance, pursue projects that extend the essential purposes of the loved one, or feel compelled to grieve as a sign of loyalty to him or her. One advantage of the TTMB is its capacity to conceptualize difficulties in adaptation that arise on one or both tracks of the model, serving as a useful guide to clinical assessment and intervention (Rubin, Malkinson, & Witztum, 2011), a topic to which we shall turn in the following paragraphs.

A second theory to posit binary processes in grieving is the dual process model (DPM) of coping with bereavement, which distinguishes between loss-oriented activities and those that are restoration oriented (Stroebe & Schut, 1999, 2010). The *loss orientation*, as conceived by these theorists, encompasses the traditional domain of "grief work," as the mourner contends with painful waves of grief, strives to relocate the deceased in his or her ongoing life, and often avoids engagement with the demands of daily life to spend time reviewing the loss and striving to accommodate it privately or in the presence of intimate others. In contrast, the *restoration orientation* entails reengaging these same family, social, and workplace demands as a means of distracting oneself or "dosing" one's grief and as a means of reviewing and revising those roles and goals that are no longer workable in the physical absence of the deceased. Central to the DPM is its proposal that adaptive grieving entails a normative *oscillation* between these two orientations, whether measured in minutes, hours, days, or weeks of residence in one sphere or the other. Theoretically, the pendulum swing between these processes slows over time, as one gradually consolidates a restored life, albeit one in which the loss is revisited, sometimes poignantly, into the indefinite future. From this perspective, difficulties can arise in grieving when the survivor (a) becomes "stuck" in the loss orientation, unable to embark on restoration; (b) rushes toward restoration, coping avoidantly with grief; or (c) struggles with unpredictable oscillation across a considerable period, unable to engage in necessary emotion regulation. The DPM has helped inspire some of the more promising interventions for bereavement-related problems.

A final model of recent origin posits that grieving entails an attempt to reaffirm or reconstruct a world of meaning that has been challenged by loss (Neimeyer, 2001). From this meaning reconstruction standpoint, the death of a loved one frequently undermines the survivor's *self-narrative*, understood as that cognitive-affective-behavioral structure that organizes the micronarratives of our daily lives into a macronarrative that confers a sense of our evolving identity, establishes our characteristic range of emotions and goals, and guides our performance on the stage of the social world (Neimeyer, 2004). Especially when the deceased played a central role in the story of our lives or when the death itself shatters the core assumptions on which our sense of self and world is built (Janoff-Bulman & Berger, 2000), the mourner can be thrown into an anguished search for meaning in both the death itself and in his or her life in its aftermath. Acute grieving therefore entails two primary narrative dimensions: processing the "event story" of the death and accessing the "back story" of the relationship with the loved one in a way that reaffirms some sense of attachment security (Neimeyer, 2011a). Under favorable circumstances, these processes result in a grief that is not so much "recovered from" as it is integrated into a (subtly or profoundly) changed self-narrative, holding the prospect of both progressive and regressive change in identity.

A good deal of evidence supports key propositions of this model. For example, older widowed persons who struggle to find meaning in the early months following their spouse's death show greater grief and depression across the first few years of loss, whereas those who succeed in making sense of the unwelcome transition in the initial phases of bereavement experience higher levels of pride, joy, and well-being a full 48 months later (Coleman & Neimeyer, 2010). Similarly, the ability to make sense of the loss or find benefit in it—alternately termed *meaning as comprehensibility* and *meaning as significance*, respectively (Park, 2010)—has been associated with lower levels of complicated grief in studies of several populations, including bereaved parents (Keesee, Currier, & Neimeyer, 2008; Lichtenthal, Currier, Neimeyer, & Keesee, 2010) and young adults (Holland,

Currier, & Neimeyer, 2006). There is also evidence that meaning making or its absence mediate the impact of violent death bereavement (Currier, Holland, & Neimeyer, 2006) and spiritual struggle (Lichtenthal, Burke, & Neimeyer, 2011) on consequent bereavement complications. Furthermore, bereaved people who make gradual progress in integrating the meaning of the loss over a period of months show a significant diminution of grief symptomatology (Holland, Currier, Coleman, & Neimeyer, 2010), suggesting that interventions that explicitly encourage meaning making could play a constructive role in treatment. We return to these clinical implications in the following section.

ASSESSMENT AND INTERVENTION

Contemporary clinical assessment and intervention in bereavement are increasingly theoretically grounded and evidence informed. Here we summarize contributions to both areas that have particular relevance to older adults, noting their linkage to the foregoing contemporary models of grief and their clinical utility.

Assessment of Bereavement Functioning

Assessment in the context of bereavement can serve two important functions: identifying suitability for treatment and possible targets of intervention, and measuring progress in those processes and outcomes that permit evaluation of its efficacy. As both are relevant in clinical and research contexts, this section highlights a few instruments that have particular relevance in the assessment of bereaved older adults (for more detailed consideration of the psychometric features of a broad range of grief-specific measures, see Neimeyer & Hogan, 2001; Neimeyer, Hogan, & Laurie, 2008). Exhibit 25.2 provides a summary of recommendations for assessment in the context of a clinical interview with older adults, adapted from a more extensive coverage of such guidelines for bereaved adults in general (Neimeyer & Jordan, 2013). In many treatment settings, interview-based assessment and self-report scales are best used in conjunction to seek an optimal balance between the personalism and depth of the former and the precision and objectivity of the latter in identifying treatment foci and outcomes.

Measures of Bereavement-Related Symptomatology

Depression scales. Several assessment tools for depressive symptomatology have been shown to have validity with older samples, including the Geriatric Depression Scale (Yesavage et al., 1982–1983), the Beck Depression Inventory-II (Beck, Steer, & Brown, 1996), and the Center for Epidemiological Studies Depression Scale (Radloff, 1977). Clinicians should be aware that depression can manifest differently among older adults compared with younger individuals, in that depressed elders often are less likely to endorse affective symptoms, such as depressed mood, and instead exhibit more somatic complaints, anxiety, memory loss, or cognitive impairments (Gottfries, 1998). Given that cognitive impairment may be an indication of depression, clinicians may wish to supplement these assessments with tests of cognitive function to distinguish "pseudo-dementia" (due to depression) from more permanent disease states, such as Alzheimer's disease. In many cases, a cognitive assessment might simply take the form of a brief screening instrument, such as the Mini-Mental Status Examination (Folstein, Folstein, & McHugh, 1975) or the Cognistat Evaluation (Kiernan, Mueller, Langston, & Van Dyke, 1987). Because these brief assessments often are not sensitive enough to accurately and reliably diagnose problems, such as Alzheimer's disease (Galasko et al., 1990), a more refined and thorough neuropsychological assessment likely would be necessary if the goal were to arrive at a differential diagnosis (see Chapter 7 in this volume; for reviews, see Morris, Worsley, & Matthews, 2000).

Prolonged Grief-13. The Prolonged Grief-13 (PG-13; Prigerson & Maciejewski, 2008) is a clinician-rated instrument that includes 13 items that correspond to the empirically derived diagnostic criteria for complicated grief (Prigerson et al., 2009). Primarily used to arrive at a dichotomous diagnosis, this scale may be less useful for assessing a continuum of symptom severity. Further research is needed to assess the psychometric properties of this assessment tool; however, preliminary studies have demonstrated its internal consistency

---

Exhibit 25.2
Guidelines for Interview-Based Assessment of Elders' Response to Bereavement

Guideline	Description
1. Invite the patient's narratives of the death	Discuss patient's account of the illness and death of the loved one, the funeral, and his or her participation in each. Elicit descriptions of any experiences that were particularly difficult or traumatic that may call for therapeutic attention.
2. Explore the meaning of the loss for the patient	Include attention to the role of the deceased in the patient's life; the changes the death has brought about in the patient's psychological and social world; the degree to which his or her assumptive world has been challenged; and the extent to which personal, philosophic, or spiritual beliefs have been helpful in responding to the loss or have been challenged by it in turn.
3. Consider the patient's own evaluations of response to loss	Ask whether there is anything about the patient's response that concerns him or her to reveal less obvious emotional reactions (e.g., guilt, anger) and relational distress (e.g., loneliness, withdrawal) that could be the target of intervention.
4. Assess cultural, gendered, or social class factors that affect the patient's grieving style	Appreciate both the supports and constraints associated with the client's social positioning and the implicit grieving rules to which he or she is striving to conform. Asking how others from a similar community or tradition typically would handle such a loss can open discussion of whether this pattern is (or is not) working.
5. Evaluate social and family support	Inquire about family differences in grieving a mutual loss and norms about the sharing of distress in the family or intimate social context. Focus especially on degree to which patient feels understood by others, her or his skill and willingness to solicit support, and the role of children and others in providing it.
6. Take a psychiatric history of the patient	Because a history of depression, bipolar disorder, posttraumatic stress, and substance abuse can recur in the context of grief and complicate adjustment, they deserve close monitoring.
7. Discuss stability of the patient's life situation	Include assessment of the patient's health, employment, and living arrangements, any of which can buffer the impact of bereavement or be adversely affected by it.
8. Review quality of past relationships	Focus on the security or insecurity of early and subsequent attachments, as these can prime the patient to accommodate the loss resiliently or reinforce a longstanding sense of futility, abandonment, or danger in investing emotionally in another.
9. Observe patient's coping style	Notice the patient's ability to modulate emotion throughout the interview, along with tendencies to overcontrol or undercontrol expression of grief. Inquire about responses to previous losses, and how his or her response to this one compares.
10. Ask about previous experiences of counseling and therapy	Request reactions to past treatment to get an indication of the sort of therapeutic relationship (more professional or personal) and intervention (more directive or responsive) the patient prefers, and thereby avoid potential ruptures in the working alliance.

(Cronbach's $\alpha = .82-.93$) and incremental validity (Delalibera, Coelho, & Barbosa, 2011; Prigerson et al., 2009).

Inventory of Complicated Grief—Revised. The Inventory of Complicated Grief—Revised (ICG–R; Prigerson et al., 1995), a measure of prolonged or severe bereavement distress, was constructed to measure symptoms of grief that form a unified component of emotional distress that is clearly distinguishable from the symptoms of depression and anxiety. Its revised and expanded form, consists of 37 statements

(e.g., "I have lost my sense of security or safety since the death of [name]"; "I feel like the future holds no meaning or purpose without [name]"), which the respondent endorses using a five-point scale to reflect his or her experience over the past month (Prigerson & Jacobs, 2001). The ICG–R yields both a continuous score and a dichotomous complicated grief diagnosis, which has been found to have a sensitivity of .93 and a specificity of .93 in the detection of interview-determined complicated grief (Barry et al., 2002), although the PG-13 might be the better instrument to use for diagnostic purposes. As a self-report measure of grief symptomatology, the ICG–R is best conceived as a dimensional rather than categorical measure, which assesses grief on a scale ranging from normative to complicated and debilitating (Holland, Neimeyer, Boelen, & Prigerson, 2009). It is the most extensively translated grief scale in current use, with versions in a dozen languages, including Spanish, French, Japanese, Dutch, and Arabic.

Core Bereavement Items. The brief Core Bereavement Items (CBI; Burnett, Middleton, Raphael, & Martinek, 1997) represents a distillation of the Bereavement Phenomenology Questionnaire, whose 76 items were drawn from the literature to provide a detailed description of the evolution of the overall bereavement response. The CBI contains 17 questions referring to commonly occurring symptoms (e.g., "Do you experience images of events surrounding [name's] death?"; "Do you find yourself missing[name]?"), which the respondent is instructed to answer on a four-point scale of frequency. Recent exploratory and confirmatory factor analyses supported a two-factor structure, with items tapping into grief-related thoughts and emotional response to loss (Holland, Nam, & Neimeyer, 2013). These factors showed strong internal consistency and unique associations with demographic variables, circumstantial factors surrounding the loss, and the ICG. Its focus on core bereavement phenomena makes it best suited to the study of "normal" grief responses, rather than the more debilitating courses assessed by other instruments. Japanese and Bosnian versions of the instrument are also available.

Theory-Guided Measures of Processing of Loss

In addition to monitoring overt symptomatology relevant to bereavement, recent advances in assessment linked to the conceptual models discussed previously make possible a closer evaluation of those processes theoretically linked to loss accommodation. This section summarizes a few of the measures that have special relevance in the context of grief therapy with older populations.

Continuing Bonds Scale The Continuing Bonds Scale (CBS; Field et al., 2003), unlike more symptom-oriented inventories, concentrates not on bereavement-related problems but rather on one particular dimension intrinsic to grieving, namely, the extent to which the bereaved person feels the lost loved one remains a part of his or her life. Its focus on the maintenance or relinquishment of connection to the deceased is therefore broadly consonant with an attachment theory perspective on grief (Field et al., 2005) and may have special relevance in the context of later life widowhood, when the spouse typically has served a security enhancing function for decades. The CBS consists of 11 rationally derived items, such as "I seek out things to remind me of [name]" and "I have inner conversations with my spouse where I turn to him or her for comfort or advice," which the respondent rates using a Likert-type scale that ranges from 1 (not true at all) to 5 (very true). A principal-components analysis suggests that these items load on a single factor (Neimeyer, Baldwin, & Gillies, 2006).

Inventory of Daily Widowed Life. The Inventory of Daily Widowed Life (Caserta & Lund, 2007), which is grounded in the DPM (Stroebe & Schut, 1999), includes 22 items that operationalize both the loss orientation (e.g., "Thinking about the circumstances or events associated with my spouse's death") and restoration orientation (e.g., "Learning to do new things"), which the respondent rates for their frequency of occurrence on a four-point Likert-type scale ranging from 1 (rarely or not at all) to 4 (almost always). The inventory also permits the calculation of an oscillation balance index, representing the disparity between the frequencies with which the respondent reports the two coping orientations. Both subscales proved internally consistent and related meaningfully to other measures of bereavement outcome, with the more recently widowed showing more balanced access to both orientations, and those farther along in their bereavement demonstrating greater consolidation of restoration. It therefore could be useful to not only index grief responses, per se, but also adaptive emotion regulation and behavior change processes associated with adaptation to spousal loss after a long marriage.

Integration of Stressful Life Experiences Scale. The Integration of Stressful Life Experiences Scale (ISLES; Holland et al., 2010) assesses meaning made of a stressful life event and has been successfully with bereaved individuals (Holland et al., 2010) and older adults (Marquett et al., 2013). The ISLES consists of 16 items rated on a five-point Likert-type scale (ranging from strongly agree to strongly disagree), which tap into both the comprehensibility of a stressful life event (e.g., "I have made sense of this event") as well as one's subsequent sense of footing in the world. Footing in the world gauges the degree of disruption of one's worldviews (e.g., "Since this event, the world seems like a confusing and scary place"), goals (e.g., "My previous goals and hopes for the future don't make sense anymore since this event"), and values (e.g., "My beliefs and values are less clear since this event") by a significant stressor, such as the loss of a loved one. Notably, the ISLES has been shown to uniquely predict (controlling for other known risk factors) referral for mental health treatment (Currier, Holland, Chisty, & Allen, 2011), suicidality and risky behavior (Holland, Malott, & Currier, 2014), psychiatric distress, and workplace burnout (Currier et al., 2013) as well as being sensitive to pre- to posttreatment improvements among older adult psychotherapy outpatients (Holland, Chong, Currier, O'Hara, & Gallagher-Thompson, in press).

INTERVENTION STRATEGIES

For much of its history, grief counseling was treated as a deceptively simple affair (Neimeyer, 2013). It was simple because traditional models suggested that grief work required little more than providing support for the expression of a painful emotion in the context of letting go and moving on, perhaps supplemented by psychoeducation on the stages of grief. It was also deceptive, however, because the complexity of the losses as well as the people suffering them greatly exceeded that of the models guiding the intervention. In contrast, contemporary theory and research have generated a plethora of models and methods of grief therapy, which have gained in precision, creativity, and empirical grounding over the past decade. This section reviews several procedures relevant to the treatment of complicated bereavement in later life and points the reader to further resources for their use.

Behavioral Activation

Especially when the bereaved struggle with persistent depression, they may benefit from basic encouragement to surmount the vicious cycle of withdrawal and avoidance and to help them reengage in a changed social world and adjust to life without the loved one's physical presence. Such efforts can be both general (e.g., scheduling activities to get outside the home several times per week) and specific (e.g., to approach people and places that initially reevoke a sense of loss or to begin or resume an exercise program). Such strategies are congruent with the restoration focus of the DPM (Stroebe & Schut, 2010) as well as with research documenting their efficacy in the treatment of complicated grievers in general (Papa, Sewell, Garrison-Diehn, & Rummel, 2013) and bereaved elderly in particular (Acierno et al., 2012). Holcomb (2012a) and others (Holland & Diliberto, 2012) have offered guidelines for the use of behavioral activation in bereavement.

Emotion Regulation

Growing evidence demonstrates that the ability to modulate painful emotion, not merely express it, is associated with more favorable adaptation to loss (Bonanno, Papa, Lalande, Westphal, & Coifman, 2004). This suggests that techniques that help patients both enter and explore grief and other difficult feelings, and also regulate or distance from them, can play a useful role in treatment. In keeping with the implications of the biopsychosocial dimension of the TTMB (Rubin et al., 2011), such strategies as grief monitoring (Turret & Shear, 2012), mindfulness training (B. E. Thompson, 2012), and yoga (Mitchell, 2012) can help patients develop a capacity to observe and also downregulate their distress. A good deal of research on meditation and breath work support their use in grief therapy (Cacciatore & Flint, 2012), as does the inclusion of grief diaries in evidence-based protocols for the treatment of complicated grief (Shear, Frank, Houch, & Reynolds, 2005).

Challenging Dysfunctional Thinking

Cognitive–behavioral models of therapy offer several methods for challenging fatalistic and self-accusatory patterns of thinking that characterize complicated bereavement, the most basic of which entail some form of rational restructuring of automatic thoughts about the loss. Cognitive features associated with the biopsychosocial track of the TTM may prove responsive, for example, to both behavioral experiments for identifying and disputing catastrophic and absolutistic thinking (Boelen & van den Bout, 2012) and rational–emotive techniques for challenging harsh self-evaluation (Malkinson, 2007) in the context of grieving. Use of such strategies is reinforced by a generally encouraging research literature, although it is not clear that they are more effective than clinical procedures arising from other theoretical perspectives (Boelen, de Keijser, van den Hout, & van den Bout, 2007; Currier, Holland, & Neimeyer, 2010).

Retelling the Narrative of the Death
For many of the bereaved, therapy naturally begins with relating the story of the illness, accident, or act that led to the death of their loved one. What distinguishes a superficial, ruminative or retraumatizing account of the loss from a healing or restorative one, however, seems to lie with the ability to reenter the story, often recounting it in a slow-motion fashion, in a way that helps patients overcome reliance on avoidance coping, process the experience in the presence of a compassionate witness, master the most difficult features of the story, and find a more empowered position as both narrator and protagonist in it (Rynearson & Salloum, 2011). Such narrative work plays a central role in both meaning reconstruction (Neimeyer & Sands, 2011) and DPM models. Evidence for its effectiveness comes from both open trials on restorative retelling interventions (Rheingold et al., 2014) and randomized controlled research on complicated grief therapy that features such "situational revisiting" of the loss (Shear et al., 2005). Detailed procedures for therapeutic retelling of the narrative of the death have been provided by Neimeyer (2012d).

Reconstructing Meaning
With its explicit focus on helping patients find meaning not only in the loss but also in their lives in its aftermath, meaning-based grief therapy (Neimeyer, Burke, Mackay, & Stringer, 2010) is inherently open to the use of a broad range of creative procedures, ranging from analogical listening to probe the felt sense of grief-related emotions in the body (Neimeyer, 2012a) to "virtual dream" stories that permit exploration of themes of loss in the safe context of metaphorical storytelling (Neimeyer, Torres, & Smith, 2011). A meaning reconstruction model perhaps finds its most direct application in journaling protocols that specifically prompt for sense-making and benefit-finding in the wake of loss (Lichtenthal & Neimeyer, 2012). The strong support for such strategies in reducing complicated grief and depressive symptomatology in randomized trials with the bereaved (Lichtenthal & Cruess, 2010; Wagner, Knaevelsrud, & Maercker, 2006) encourages creative extension and evaluation of narrative procedures in future studies.

Reworking the Continuing Bond
In keeping with the emphases of the TTMB (Rubin et al., 2011), attachment theory (Stroebe & Schut, 2005), and the meaning reconstruction model (Neimeyer, 2011b), a variety of clinical techniques now support review and revision of the bond with the deceased, rather than its relinquishment. These include reflective procedures such as facilitated review of the family photo album to access and consolidate positive memories of life with the loved one (Gamino, 2012), encouragement to introduce stories of the loved one to receptive others to resist social banishment of the relationship (Hedtke, 2012), and correspondence with the deceased (Neimeyer, 2012c) or guided conversations with the symbolic presence of the loved one (Jordan, 2012; Neimeyer, 2012b) to address issues in the relationship and reestablish a sense of ongoing connection. Inclusion of such procedures as core components of demonstrably effective grief therapy protocols (Shear et al., 2005) support their use with older adults for whom sustaining bonds with a loved one may be especially relevant.

Life Review
Guided reminiscence and other life review procedures have clear relevance for meaning making in bereavement and later life in general, where they have a good empirical track record in helping elders validate the course of their life journey (Bohlmeijer,

Roemer, Cuijpers, & Smit, 2007). Appreciatively reviewing a lifetime of significant people, stories, challenges, and lessons may have special relevance with seriously ill patients, for whom the recording of such accounts and their dissemination to the family has been found to confer a sense of dignity and meaning at the end of life (Chochinov et al., 2011). In addition to basic life review procedures (Jenko, 2012), loss timelines (Dunton, 2012) and "chapters of our lives" exercises (Neimeyer, 2014) can promote the integration of loss into the patient's self-narrative and the recognition that it punctuates, rather than ends, one's ongoing story.

Goal Work

As the DPM in particular recognizes, adaptation to loss entails not only orienting to grief but also restoring life in the face of a changed reality. Reviewing and revising those long-term life goals that required the physical presence of the loved one (e.g., traveling together in retirement, working only part time in light of a spouse's full employment) therefore plays a critical part in grief therapy, especially once the emotional tumult of early bereavement has subsided. Even in the midst of active grieving, setting proximal goals for self-care (e.g., through conscious attention to diet, sleep, exercise, and social needs) is both feasible and important (Holcomb, 2012b). The prominent inclusion of goal work in evidence-based therapy for complicated grief helps warrant its use with bereaved older adults (Shear et al., 2005).

Expressive Arts Approaches

Music, dance, and the visual arts have played a central role in marking the transition from life to death for bereaved communities from time immemorial, and uses of the expressive arts to register and explore the significance of loss have equal relevance in contemporary meaning reconstruction work in bereavement (Neimeyer & Thompson, 2014). Music therapy, drawing and painting, creative writing, movement, and performance can assist with the articulation, validation, and communication of changing emotions and identities at levels that elude literal verbal expression, and research on their efficacy in facilitating adaptation to loss is

encouraging, if preliminary (Popkin et al., 2011; Torres, Neimeyer, & Neff, 2014). A compendium of such methods with detailed instructions for their use can promote their application to the losses of later life (B. E. Thompson & Neimeyer, 2014).

Psychotropic Medication

For grieving older adults experiencing moderate to severe depression, anxiety, and insomnia, psychotropic medication may be warranted to help manage symptomatology associated with the biopsychosocial track of the TTMB (Rubin et al., 2011). For some depressed mourners, a course of antidepressants may help them engage psychotherapy more effectively, although this assumption is only now being subjected to rigorous research. Professionals should guard against the reflexive prescription of pharmacotherapy in bereavement in light of evidence from randomized controlled trials that antidepressants may fail to ameliorate the core attachment distress that is at the heart of grief, even if they sometimes mitigate depressive symptomatology, per se (Reynolds et al., 1999). Moreover, critics of the recent decision by the American Psychiatric Association to remove the bereavement exclusion in the diagnosis of major depression in the *Diagnostic and Statistical Manual of Mental Disorders, Fifth Edition* (2013) have cautioned that this in effect means that the administration of antidepressants as soon as 2 weeks after the death of a loved one could now become standard practice (Thielman & Cacciatore, 2013). This "medicalization" of grief would be regrettable, insofar as it would obscure recognition that psychosocial interventions should be considered as the evidence-based mainstay in the treatment of this form of suffering, with pharmacotherapy playing an occasional and ancillary role. Practical discussion of the role of medication in the management of bereavement distress, when indicated, can be found elsewhere (Holcomb, 2012c).

SPECIAL ISSUES RELATED TO THE APPLICATION OF BEREAVEMENT INTERVENTIONS

Special Considerations

The most basic issue regarding the use of bereavement interventions is whether they should be offered at all. To a perhaps surprising degree, the answer to this question might be "no." As noted earlier, studies consistently suggest that many of the bereaved are resilient, and a comprehensive review of more than 60 controlled outcome studies suggests that little benefit accrues when professional grief therapy is offered *universally* to anyone who has lost a loved one (Currier, Neimeyer, & Berman, 2008). Indeed, a recent cluster randomized trial of "primary bereavement care," in which family physicians were trained carefully to offer an empirically informed seven-session counseling intervention to widows in the 4th through 13th months of grief found no differences in favor of the intervention relative to a control group of widows receiving standard medical attention. Indeed, control group patients experienced more improvement in somatization, general health, and general emotional outcomes, suggesting that an explicit therapeutic focus on their grief did more to impede their progress than facilitate it (García, Landa, Grandes, Pombo, & Mauriz, 2013). Although negative effects of this sort for bereavement interventions are rare, a "no difference" conclusion is common in controlled studies, as untreated samples commonly improve over time to the same extent as those in active treatment (Neimeyer & Currier, 2009).

The two circumstances in which professional treatment can be appropriate or even essential occur when the circumstances of the death put the bereaved at risk for adverse outcomes (e.g., as when they suffer sudden, traumatic loss or the death of a child), or when the bereaved already have been assessed as having clinically significant distress as a criterion for referral. In these latter cases of *selective* or *indicated* treatment, therapy has been demonstrated to be substantially more effective, in the latter case rivaling outcomes for the efficacy of therapy for other conditions (Currier et al., 2008).

A second consideration in the treatment of bereaved older adults concerns significant cultural differences in grief, which can influence the appropriateness of or receptivity to a given approach to treatment. For example, members of nondominant ethnic groups in the United States, such as African Americans, are at considerably greater risk than Caucasians for violent death bereavement, and the

substantially higher levels of depression, PTSD, and complicated grief symptomatology found to result (McDevitt-Murphy, Neimeyer, Burke, & Williams, 2012). Under such conditions, treatment frequently needs to be multifocal, attending to trauma as well as separation distress in a way that respects and utilizes the greater focus of this community on collective and spiritual styles of coping (Barrett, 2001; Rosenblatt & Wallace, 2005), while also recognizing and addressing the possible adverse effects of loss on these same domains (Burke, Neimeyer, McDevitt-Murphy, Ippolito, & Roberts, 2011). Detailed guidelines for culturally responsive psychotherapy in such cases recently have been formulated (Lau & Kinoshita, 2010).

Case Example

Rosa, the woman described in the opening of the chapter, presented for psychotherapy at the urging of her children, who had grown concerned by her social withdrawal, lack of interest in activities, and persistent clinging to the past following her husband's death. Given Rosa's guarded stance, therapy began by allowing her to tell the story of her loss at her own pace, while at the same time looking for opportunities to probe further and assess the resources that she brought with her into therapy as well as her unique understanding of the death and its implications. As with many older adults, Rosa revealed a vast reservoir of past experiences and accumulated knowledge, and in particular, related a story about the loss of her father nearly 30 years prior. In an initial effort to build trust, instill hope, and focus on strengths, Rosa's therapist initiated a dialogue with her about how she had coped with this earlier loss and ultimately found ways to reengage in life. Recalling how she and her mother had grieved intensely in the weeks and months after her father's death, but later found ways to meaningfully memorialize and celebrate his life, Rosa's therapist began to see a positive shift in her demeanor, as she began to see some flicker of "light at the end of the tunnel" of her suffering.

Building on this momentum and strengthened therapeutic alliance, Rosa and her therapist embarked on more intensive interventions, implementing a flexible behavioral activation plan. In constructing this plan, Rosa was encouraged to consider not only activities that were pleasant (e.g., cooking her favorite meal) but also activities that allowed her to celebrate her husband's life (e.g., organizing and presenting a *fotonovela* of their life together) as well as other tasks that felt important and meaningful, although initially challenging (e.g., attending church again). As the weeks passed and this behavioral activation plan began to take effect, Rosa's mood improved, but she still expressed lingering feelings of guilt and regret regarding her husband's death.

Through the use of two-chair work, Rosa's therapist gently coached her through these difficult imaginary conversations with her husband, as if he were sitting in the room. Initially, these exercises focused on allowing Rosa to express and fully experience negative emotions associated with troubling thoughts, such as "I should have been a better caregiver" and "If I did more, maybe I could have prevented the illness." Because she had been attempting to avoid these painful thoughts and feelings for some time, this expression and gradual exposure to her difficult internal experiences alone provided some relief. As she began to show an increased ability to regulate her negative emotions, Rosa was encouraged to imagine how her husband might respond to these thoughts and feelings of guilt and remorse and speak from his chair. Although she initially had difficulty imagining what he might say, Rosa eventually fully engaged in this role, telling herself (speaking from her husband's chair) that she was a good wife and did everything that she could. Consistent with the protective role he had played in their relationship, she imagined her husband primarily being concerned about her safety and well-being. Although the weight of these words did not immediately sink in, over time, Rosa's guilt and remorse slowly transformed into forgiveness for her perceived mistakes and a strong desire to take good care of herself (as her husband wanted) and celebrate her husband's memory.

CONCLUSION

Given recent demographic trends and baby boomers' generally positive attitudes toward psychotherapy

(Mackenzie, Scott, Mather, & Sareen, 2008), 21st-century psychologists increasingly are encountering grief and death-related issues in their everyday practices. The current state of our readiness for these changes is mixed. On the one hand, few doctoral programs in clinical psychology offer specialized training in gerontology (DeVries, 2005) and licensed professionals report little familiarity with current grief theories and limited training and experience in grief therapy (Ober, Granello, & Wheaton, 2012). Thus, it is not entirely surprising that many trainees express substantial discomfort about working with clients expressing death-related concerns (Kirchberg, Neimeyer, & James, 1998). On a more positive note, most university faculty members believe that training in grief and loss is important and strive to ensure coverage of these topics within graduate curricula (Humphrey, 1993). Given that these more informal efforts to infuse coursework and practicum experiences with some training in grief and loss do not necessarily translate into knowledge and expertise in these areas (Ober, Granello, & Wheaton, 2012), programs may wish to offer more formalized experiences, such as a course on death and dying or an intensive practicum experience in a hospice unit. At a minimum, some training in identifying complicated grief reactions, conceptualizing cases based on current theories of grief, and implementing basic bereavement intervention strategies seems warranted.

From a research standpoint, investigators and funding agencies would do well to prioritize several potentially productive lines of research to fill the gaps in our understanding of grief and loss in later life. First, longitudinal research that aims to examine early predictors of physical health sequelae and mortality in the aftermath of loss could help to identify older adults who are at risk of developing irreversible health problems, which may warrant preventive psychosocial or medical intervention. As mentioned earlier, it is possible that complicated grief, depressive symptoms, and the disruption of daily routines in the aftermath of loss may play a role. Our understanding of this issue, however, would be enhanced greatly by more sophisticated psycho–physiological studies that examine genetic risk factors (e.g., circadian rhythm genes) as well as early biomarkers of declining health (e.g., cortisol dysregulation, telomerase activity, immune functioning). This line of research also would provide opportunities for testing novel interventions that aim to help the bereaved reestablish routines and reduce the physiological stress associated with circadian rhythm disruption. For example, preliminary evidence suggests that a modified version of social rhythm therapy, which addresses lifestyle regularity and sleep hygiene, has great promise for bereaved older adults (Pfoff, Zarotney, & Monk, 2014).

In addition, although a number of interventions have been developed for treating complicated grief, fewer have focused specifically on seniors or attempted to modify interventions to be "gero-friendly." These alterations may parallel those made for the treatment of other psychological problems and may include adjusting the pace of therapy (when there are attention deficits); simplifying abstract concepts (when there are problems with executive function); offering homework, psychoeducational materials, or assessments in large print (when vision is impaired); and making hearing aids available (e.g., a pocket sound amplifier; Holland & Gallagher-Thompson, 2011). Given that a sizable number of elders are homebound or have limited access to transportation, the incorporation of technology that makes these treatments more mobile also would help to improve their accessibility. The efficacy of Internet-based approaches already has been demonstrated (e.g., Wagner et al., 2006). Researchers, however, would do well to expand on this work and develop or test other ways of using technology to make complicated grief treatments more available, perhaps via telephone (for those who do not have a computer) or video-conferencing applications (for those who benefit from having visual cues). Considering that the family is often the most important social context for older adults (Qualls, 1999), the incorporation a family-focused component may be another modification for researchers and treatment developers to examine in the future.

These more superficial modifications may not be sufficient for some older adults, particularly in cases of mild cognitive impairment (MCI) or even more severe cognitive deficits. A growing body of literature suggests that older adults with MCI or problems with executive function may have difficulty engaging in and benefiting from more cognitively focused treatments for depression and anxiety, which often require older adults to think abstractly, make decisions, and separate relevant from irrelevant details of their lives (Caudle et al., 2007; Mohlman, 2005; Mohlman & Gorman, 2005). It has been suggested that in cases of MCI, a more behaviorally focused intervention (e.g., behavioral activation) may be more appropriate (Holland & Diliberto, 2012); however, such a hypothesis has never been tested in the context of bereavement in later life. Thus, research that aims to examine cognitive functioning as a moderator of complicated grief treatment outcomes as well as the development of efficacious interventions for older adults with MCI should be a high priority, particularly given that previous research has identified a link between complicated grief and poorer cognitive functioning among the elderly (Newson et al., 2011).

References

Acierno, R., Rheingold, A., Amstadter, A., Kurent, J., Amella, E., Resnick, H., . . . Lejuez, C. (2012). Behavioral activation and therapeutic exposure for bereavement in older adults *American Journal of Hospice and Palliative Medicine*, *29*, 13–25. doi:10.1177/104.9909111411471

Barrett, R. K. (2001). Death and dying in the Black experience: An interview with Ronald K. Barrett, PhD. *Innovations in End-of-Life Care*, *3*, 1–9.

Barry, L. C., Kasl, S. V., & Prigerson, H. G. (2002). Psychiatric disorders among bereaved persons: The role of perceived circumstances of death and preparedness for death. *American Journal of Geriatric Psychiatry*, *10*, 447–457. doi:10.1097/00019442-200207000-00011

Bartrop, R. W., Luckhurst, E. E., Lazarus, L. L., Kiloh, L. G., & Penny, R. R. (1994). Depressed lymphocyte function after bereavement. In A. Steptoe & J. Wardle (Eds.), *Psychosocial processes and health: A reader* (pp. 166–170). New York, NY: Cambridge University Press.

Beck, A. T., Steer, R. A., & Brown, G. K. (1996). *Beck Depression Inventory–II*. San Antonio, TX: Psychological Corporation.

Boelen, P. A., de Keijser, J., van den Hout, M., & van den Bout, J. (2007). Treatment of complicated grief: A comparison between cognitive-behavioral therapy and supportive counseling. *Journal of Consulting and*

Clinical Psychology, 75, 277–284. doi:10.1037/0022-006X.75.2.277

Boelen, P. A., & van den Bout, J. (2005). Complicated grief, depression, and anxiety as distinct postloss syndromes: A confirmatory factor analysis study. *American Journal of Psychiatry, 162,* 2175–2177. doi:10.1176/appi.ajp.162.11.2175

Boelen, P. A., & van den Bout, J. (2012). Changing catastrophic misinterpretations with behavioral experiments. In R. A. Neimeyer (Ed.), *Techniques of grief therapy* (pp. 125–128). New York, NY: Routledge.

Boelen, P. A., van den Bout, J., & de Keijser, J. (2003). Traumatic grief as a disorder distinct from bereavement-related depression and anxiety: A replication study with bereaved mental health care patients. *American Journal of Psychiatry, 160,* 1339–1341. doi:10.1176/appi.ajp.160.7.1339

Bohlmeijer, E., Roemer, M., Cuijpers, P., & Smit, F. (2007). The effects of reminiscence on psychological well-being in older adults: A meta-analysis. *Aging and Mental Health, 11,* 291–300. doi:10.1080/13607860600963547

Bonanno, G. A., Moskowitz, J. T., Papa, A., & Folkman, S. (2005). Resilience to loss in bereaved spouses, bereaved parents, and bereaved gay men. *Journal of Personality and Social Psychology, 88,* 827–843. doi:10.1037/0022-3514.88.5.827

Bonanno, G. A., Neria, Y., Mancini, A., Coifman, K. G., Litz, B., & Insel, B. (2007). Is there more to grief than depression and posttraumatic stress disorder? A test of incremental validity. *Journal of Abnormal Psychology, 116,* 342–351. doi:10.1037/0021-843X.116.2.342

Bonanno, G. A., Papa, A., Lalande, K., Westphal, M., & Coifman, K. (2004). The importance of being flexible: The ability to both enhance and suppress emotional express predicts long-term adjustment. *Psychological Science, 15,* 482–487. doi:10.1111/j.0956-7976.2004.00705.x

Bonanno, G. A., Wortman, C. B., Lehman, D. R., Tweed, R. G., Haring, M., Sonnega, J., . . . Neese, R. M. (2002). Resilience to loss and chronic grief: A prospective study from preloss to 18-months postloss. *Journal of Personality and Social Psychology, 83,* 1150–1164. doi:10.1037/0022-3514.83.5.1150

Bonanno, G. A., Wortman, C. B., & Nesse, R. M. (2004). Prospective patterns of resilience and maladjustment during widowhood. *Psychology and Aging, 19,* 260–271. doi:10.1037/0882-7974.19.2.260

Bowlby, J. (1980). *Attachment and loss: Vol. 3. Loss, sadness, and depression.* New York, NY: Basic.

Bradbeer, M., Helme, R. D., Yong, H. H., Kendig, H. L., & Gibson, S. J. (2003). Widowhood and other demographic associations of pain in independent older people. *Clinical Journal of Pain, 19,* 247–254. doi:10.1097/00002508-200307000-00008

Brown, L. F., Reynolds, C. F., Monk, T. H., Prigerson, H. G., Dew, M. A., Houck, P. R., . . . Kupfer, D. J. (1996). Social rhythm stability following late-life spousal bereavement: Associations with depression and sleep impairment. *Psychiatry Research, 62,* 161–169. doi:10.1016/0165-1781(96)02914-9

Buckley, T., McKinley, S., Tofler, G., & Bartrop, R. (2010). Cardiovascular risk in early bereavement: A literature review and proposed mechanisms. *International Journal of Nursing Studies, 47,* 229–238. doi:10.1016/j.ijnurstu.2009.06.010

Burke, L. A., & Neimeyer, R. A. (2013). Prospective risk factors for complicated grief: A review of the empirical literature. In M. Stroebe, H. Schut, P. Boelen, & J. Van den Bout (Eds.), *Complicated grief: Scientific foundations for health care professionals* (pp. 145–161). Washington, DC: American Psychological Association.

Burke, L. A., Neimeyer, R. A., McDevitt-Murphy, M. E., Ippolito, M. R., & Roberts, J. M. (2011). In the wake of homicide: Spiritual crisis and bereavement distress in an African American sample. *International Journal for the Psychology of Religion, 21,* 289–307. doi:10.1080/10508619.2011.607416

Burnett, P., Middleton, W., Raphael, B., & Martinek, N. (1997). Measuring core bereavement phenomena. *Psychological Medicine, 27,* 49–57. doi:10.1017/S0033291796004151

Cacciatore, J., & Flint, M. (2012). ATTEND: Toward a mindfulness-based bereavement care model. *Death Studies, 36,* 61–82. doi:10.1080/07481187.2011.591275

Caserta, M. S., & Lund, D. A. (2007). Toward the development of an Inventory of Daily Widowed Life (IDWL): Guided by the Dual Process Model of Coping with Bereavement. *Death Studies, 31,* 505–535. doi:10.1080/07481180701356761

Caudle, D. D., Senior, A. C., Wetherell, J. L., Rhoades, H. M., Beck, J. G., Kunik, M. E., . . . Stanley, M. A. (2007). Cognitive errors, symptom severity, and response to cognitive behavior therapy in older adults with generalized anxiety disorder. *American Journal of Geriatric Psychiatry, 15,* 680–689. doi:10.1097/JGP.0b013e31803c550d

Chochinov, H. M., Kristjanson, L. J., Breitbart, W., McClement, S., Hack, T. F., Hassard, T., & Harlos, M. (2011). Effect of dignity therapy on distress and end-of-life experiences of terminally ill patients. *Lancet Oncology, 12,* 753–762. doi:10.1016/S1470-2045(11)70153-X

Coleman, R. A., & Neimeyer, R. A. (2010). Measuring meaning: Searching for and making sense of spousal loss in later life. *Death Studies, 34,* 804–834. doi:10.1080/07481181003761625

Currier, J. M., Holland, J. M., Chisty, K., & Allen, D. (2011). Meaning made following deployment in Iraq or Afghanistan: Examining unique associations with posttraumatic stress and clinical outcomes. *Journal of Traumatic Stress, 24,* 691–698. doi:10.1002/jts.20691

Currier, J. M., Holland, J. M., & Neimeyer, R. A. (2006). Sense making, grief and the experience of violent loss: Toward a mediational model. *Death Studies, 30,* 403–428. doi:10.1080/07481180600614351

Currier, J. M., Holland, J. M., & Neimeyer, R. A. (2010). Do CBT-based interventions alleviate distress following bereavement? A review of current evidence. *International Journal of Cognitive Therapy, 3,* 77–93. doi:10.1521/ijct.2010.3.1.77

Currier, J. M., Holland, J. M., Rozalski, V., Thompson, K. L., Rojas-Flores, L., & Herrera, S. (2013). Teaching in violent communities: The contribution of meaning made of stress on mental health and burnout. *International Journal of Stress Management, 20,* 254–277. doi:10.1037/a0033985

Currier, J. M., Neimeyer, R. A., & Berman, J. S. (2008). The effectiveness of psychotherapeutic interventions for the bereaved: A comprehensive quantitative review. *Psychological Bulletin, 134,* 648–661. doi:10.1037/0033-2909.134.5.648

Datson, S. L., & Marwit, S. J. (1997). Personality constructs and perceived presence of deceased loved ones. *Death Studies, 21,* 131–146. doi:10.1080/074811897202047

Delalibera, M., Coelho, A., & Barbosa, A. (2011). Validation of prolonged grief disorder instrument for Portuguese population. *Acta Medica Portuguesa, 24,* 935–942.

DeVries, H. M. (2005). Clinical geropsychology training in generalist doctoral programs. *Gerontology and Geriatrics Education, 25,* 5–20. doi:10.1300/J021v25n04_02

Downe-Wamboldt, B., & Tamlyn, D. (1997). An international survey of death education trends in faculties of nursing and medicine. *Death Studies, 21,* 177–188. doi:10.1080/074811897202065

Dunton, A. J. (2012). Loss timelines. In R. A. Neimeyer (Ed.), *Techniques of grief therapy* (pp. 184–186). New York, NY: Routledge.

Field, N. P., & Friedrichs, M. (2004). Continuing bonds in coping with the death of a husband. *Death Studies, 28,* 597–620. doi:10.1080/07481180490476425

Field, N. P., Gal-Oz, E., & Bonanno, G. A. (2003). Continuing bonds and adjustment at 5 years after the death of a spouse. *Journal of Consulting and Clinical Psychology, 71,* 110–117. doi:10.1037/0022-006X.71.1.110

Field, N. P., Gao, B., & Paderna, L. (2005). Continuing bonds in bereavement: An attachment theory based perspective. *Death Studies, 29,* 277–299. doi:10.1080/07481180590923689

Folstein, M. F., Folstein, S. E., & McHugh, P. R. (1975). Mini-mental state: A practical method for grading the cognitive state of patients for the clinician. *Journal of Psychiatric Research, 12,* 189–198. doi:10.1016/0022-3956(75)90026-6

Freud, S. (1957). Mourning and melancholia. In J. Strachey (Ed.), *The complete psychological works of Sigmund Freud* (pp. 152–170). London, England: Hogarth Press. (Original work published 1917)

Galasko, D., Klauber, M. R., Hofstetter, C. R., & Salmon, D. P. (1990). The Mini-Mental State Examination in the early diagnosis of Alzheimer's disease. *Archives of Neurology, 47,* 49–52. doi:10.1001/archneur.1990.00530010061020

Galatzer-Levy, I. R., & Bonanno, G. A. (2012). Beyond normality in the study of bereavement: Heterogeneity in depression outcomes following loss in older adults. *Social Science and Medicine, 74,* 1987–1994. doi:10.1016/j.socscimed.2012.02.022

Gamino, L. (2012). Opening the family photo album. In R. A. Neimeyer (Ed.), *Techniques of grief therapy* (pp. 231–233). New York, NY: Routledge.

García, J. A., Landa, V., Grandes, G., Pombo, H., & Mauriz, A. (2013). Effectiveness of "Primary Bereavement Care" for widows: A cluster randomized trial involving family physicians. *Death Studies, 37,* 287–310. doi:10.1080/07481187.2012.722041

Gottfries, C. G. (1998). Is there a difference between elderly and younger patients with regard to the symptomatology and aetiology of depression? *International Clinical Psychopharmacology, 13*(Suppl. 5), S13–S18. doi:10.1097/00004850-199809005-00004

Hardy, S. E., Concato, J., & Gill, T. M. (2002). Stressful life events among community-living older persons. *Journal of General Internal Medicine, 17,* 841–847. doi:10.1046/j.1525-1497.2002.20105.x

Hays, J. C., Gold, D. T., & Peiper, C. F. (1997). Sibling bereavement in late life. *Omega: Journal of Death and Dying, 35,* 25–42.

Hedtke, L. (2012). *Bereavement support groups: Breathing life into stories of the dead.* Chagrin Falls, OH: Taos Institute.

Hedtke, L., & Winslade, J. (2004). *Remembering lives.* Amityville, NY: Baywood.

Holcomb, L. E. (2012a). Behavioral activation. In R. A. Neimeyer (Ed.), *Techniques of grief therapy* (pp. 111–113). New York, NY: Routledge.

Holcomb, L. E. (2012b). Goal setting for self-care during the grieving process. In R. A. Neimeyer (Ed.), *Techniques of grief therapy* (pp. 289–291). New York, NY: Routledge.

Holcomb, L. E. (2012c). Psychotropic medication for grieving adults. In R. A. Neimeyer (Ed.), *Techniques of grief therapy* (pp. 36–38). New York, NY: Routledge.

Holland, J. M., Chong, G., Currier, J. M., O'Hara, R., & Gallagher-Thompson, D. (in press). Does cognitive–behavioral therapy promote meaning-making? A preliminary test in the context of geriatric depression. *Psychology and Psychotherapy: Theory, Research and Practice*. Advance online publication. doi:10.1111/papt.12030

Holland, J. M., Currier, J. M., Coleman, R. A., & Neimeyer, R. A. (2010). The Integration of Stressful Life Experiences Scale (ISLES): Development and initial validation of a new measure. *International Journal of Stress Management, 17*, 325–352. doi:10.1037/a0020892

Holland, J. M., Currier, J. M., & Neimeyer, R. A. (2006). Meaning reconstruction in the first two years of bereavement: The role of sense-making and benefit-finding. *Omega: Journal of Death and Dying, 53*, 173–191.

Holland, J. M., & Diliberto, R. (2012). Behavioral activation with bereaved older adults: Unique clinical considerations. *Clinical Gerontologist, 35*, 303–315. doi:10.1080/07317115.2012.680685

Holland, J. M., & Gallagher-Thompson, D. (2011). Interventions for mental health problems in later life. In D. Barlow (Ed.), *The Oxford handbook of clinical psychology* (pp. 810–836). New York, NY: Oxford University Press.

Holland, J. M., Malott, J., & Currier, J. M. (2014). Meaning made of stress among veterans transitioning to college: Examining unique associations with suicide risk and life threatening behavior. *Suicide and Life-Threatening Behavior, 44*, 218–231. doi:10.1111/sltb.12061

Holland, J. M., Nam, I., & Neimeyer, R. A. (2013). A psychometric evaluation of the Core Bereavement Items. *Assessment, 20*, 119–122. doi:10.1177/1073191112446656

Holland, J. M., & Neimeyer, R. A. (2010). An examination of stage theory of grief among individuals bereaved by natural and violent causes: A meaning-oriented contribution. *Omega: Journal of Death and Dying, 61*, 103–120.

Holland, J. M., Neimeyer, R. A., Boelen, P. A., & Prigerson, H. G. (2009). The underlying structure of grief: A taxometric investigation of prolonged and normal reactions to loss. *Journal of Psychopathology and Behavioral Assessment, 31*, 190–201. doi:10.1007/s10862-008-9113-1

Holland, J. M., Rozalski, V., Thompson, K. L., Tiongson, R. J., Schatzberg, A. F., O'Hara, R., & Gallagher-Thompson, D. (2014). The unique impact of late-life bereavement and prolonged grief on diurnal cortisol. *The Journals of Gerontology, Series B: Psychological Sciences and Social Sciences, 69*, 4–11. doi:10.1093/geronb/gbt051

Humphrey, K. M. (1993). Grief counseling training in counselor preparation programs in the United States: A preliminary report. *International Journal for the Advancement of Counselling, 16*, 333–340. doi:10.1007/BF01407918

Janoff-Bulman, R., & Berger, A. R. (2000). The other side of trauma. In J. H. Harvey & E. D. Miller (Eds.), *Loss and trauma* (pp. 29–44). Philadelphia, PA: Brunner Mazel.

Jenko, M. (2012). Life review. In R. A. Neimeyer (Ed.), *Techniques of grief therapy* (pp. 181–183). New York, NY: Routledge.

Jordan, J. R. (2012). Guided imaginal conversations with the deceased. In R. A. Neimeyer (Ed.), *Techniques of grief therapy* (pp. 262–265). New York, NY: Routledge.

Keesee, N. J., Currier, J. M., & Neimeyer, R. A. (2008). Predictors of grief following the death of one's child: The contribution of finding meaning. *Journal of Clinical Psychology, 64*, 1145–1163. doi:10.1002/jclp.20502

Kiernan, R. J., Mueller, J., Langston, J. W., & Van Dyke, C. (1987). The Neurobehavioral Cognitive Status Examination: A brief but differentiated approach to cognitive assessment. *Annals of Internal Medicine, 107*, 481–485. doi:10.7326/0003-4819-107-4-481

Kirchberg, T. M., Neimeyer, R. A., & James, R. K. (1998). Beginning counselors' death concerns and empathic responses to client situations involving death and grief. *Death Studies, 22*, 99–120. doi:10.1080/074811898201623

Klass, D., Silverman, P. R., & Nickman, S. (1996). *Continuing bonds: New understandings of grief*. Washington, DC: Taylor & Francis.

Kübler-Ross, E. (1969). *On death and dying*. New York, NY: Macmillan.

Latham, A. E., & Prigerson, H. G. (2004). Suicidality and bereavement: Complicated grief as psychiatric disorder presenting greatest risk for suicidality. *Suicide and Life-Threatening Behavior, 34*, 350–362. doi:10.1521/suli.34.4.350.53737

Lau, A. W., & Kinoshita, L. M. (2010). Cognitive behavioral therapy with culturally diverse older adults. In P. A. Hays & G. Y. Iwamasa (Eds.), *Culturally responsive cognitive-behavioral therapy* (pp. 179–187). Washington, DC: American Psychological Association.

Lichtenthal, W. G., Burke, L. A., & Neimeyer, R. A. (2011). Religious coping and meaning-making following the loss of a loved one *Counseling and Spirituality, 30*, 113–136.

Lichtenthal, W. G., & Cruess, D. G. (2010). Effects of directed written disclosure on grief and distress symptoms among bereaved individuals. *Death Studies, 34*, 475–499. doi:10.1080/07481187.2010.4 83332

Lichtenthal, W. G., Currier, J. M., Neimeyer, R. A., & Keesee, N. J. (2010). Sense and significance: A mixed methods examination of meaning-making following the loss of one's child. *Journal of Clinical Psychology, 66*, 791–812.

Lichtenthal, W. G., & Neimeyer, R. A. (2012). Directed journaling to facilitate meaning making. In R. A. Neimeyer (Ed.), *Techniques of grief therapy* (pp. 161–164). New York, NY: Routledge.

Maciejewski, P. K., Zhang, B., Block, S. D., & Prigerson, H. G. (2007). An empirical examination of the stage theory of grief. *JAMA, 297*, 716–723. doi:10.1001/jama.297.7.716

Mackenzie, C. S., Scott, T., Mather, A., & Sareen, J. (2008). Older adults' help-seeking attitudes and treatment beliefs concerning mental health problems. *American Journal of Geriatric Psychiatry, 16*, 1010–1019. doi:10.1097/JGP.0b013e31818cd3be

Maercker, A., Brewin, C. R., Bryant, R. A., Cloitre, M., Reed, G. M., & van Ommeren, M., . . . Saxena, S. (2013). Proposals for mental disorders specifically associated with stress in the International Classification of Diseases–11. *Lancet, 381*, 1683–1685. doi:10.1016/S0140-6736(12)62191-6

Malkinson, R. (2007). *Cognitive grief therapy*. New York, NY: Norton.

Marquett, R. M., Thompson, L. W., Reiser, R. P., Holland, J. M., O'Hara, R., Kesler, S. R., . . . Gallagher-Thompson, D. (2013). Psychosocial predictors of treatment response to cognitive-behavior therapy for late-life depression: An exploratory study. *Aging and Mental Health*. doi:10.1080/13607863.2013.791661

McDevitt-Murphy, M. E., Neimeyer, R. A., Burke, L. A., & Williams, J. L. (2012). Assessing the toll of traumatic loss: Psychological symptoms in African Americans bereaved by homicide. *Psychological Trauma: Theory, Research, Practice, and Policy, 4*, 303–311. doi:10.1037/a0024911

Meier, A. M., Carr, D. R., Currier, J. M., & Neimeyer, R. A. (2013). Attachment anxiety and avoidance in coping with bereavement: Two studies. *Journal of Social and Clinical Psychology, 32*, 315–334. doi:10.1521/jscp.2013.32.3.315

Mitchell, D. C. (2012). Moving and breathing through grief. In R. A. Neimeyer (Ed.), *Techniques of grief therapy* (pp. 67–69). New York, NY: Routledge.

Mohlman, J. (2005). Does executive dysfunction affect treatment outcome in late-life mood and anxiety disorders? *Journal of Geriatric Psychiatry and Neurology, 18*, 97–108. doi:10.1177/0891988705276061

Mohlman, J., & Gorman, J. M. (2005). The role of executive functioning in CBT: A pilot study with anxious

older adults. *Behaviour Research and Therapy, 43*, 447–465. doi:10.1016/j.brat.2004.03.007

Moon, J. R., Kondo, N., Glymour, M. M., & Subramanian, S. V. (2011). Widowhood and mortality: A meta-analysis. *PLoS ONE, 6*, e23465. doi:10.1371/journal.pone.0023465

Morris, R. G., Worsley, R., & Matthews, D. (2000). Neuropsychological assessment in older people: Old principles and new directions. *Advances in Psychiatric Treatment, 6*, 362–370. doi:10.1192/apt.6.5.362

Murrel, S. A., Norris, F. H., & Hutchins, G. L. (1984). Distribution and desirability of life events in older adults: Population and policy implications. *Journal of Community Psychology, 12*, 301–311. doi:10.1002/1520-6629(198410)12:4<301::AID-JCOP2290120403>3.0.CO;2-I

Newson, R. S., Boelen, P. A., Hek, K., Hofman, A., & Tiemeier, H. (2011). The prevalence and characteristics of complicated grief in older adults. *Journal of Affective Disorders, 132*, 231–238. doi:10.1016/j.jad.2011.02.021

Neimeyer, R. A. (Ed.). (2001). *Meaning reconstruction and the experience of loss*. Washington, DC: American Psychological Association. doi:10.1037/10397-000

Neimeyer, R. A. (2004). Fostering posttraumatic growth: A narrative contribution. *Psychological Inquiry, 15*, 53–59.

Neimeyer, R. A. (2011a). Reconstructing meaning in bereavement. In W. Watson & D. Kissane (Eds.), *Handbook of psychotherapy in cancer care* (pp. 247–257). New York, NY: Wiley. doi:10.1002/9780470975176.ch21

Neimeyer, R. A. (2011b). Reconstructing the self in the wake of loss: A dialogical contribution. In H. Hermans & T. Gieser (Eds.), *Handbook of dialogical self theory* (pp. 374–389). Cambridge, England: Cambridge University Press. doi:10.1017/CBO9781139030434.026

Neimeyer, R. A. (2012a). Analogical listening. In R. A. Neimeyer (Ed.), *Techniques of grief therapy* (pp. 55–58). New York, NY: Routledge.

Neimeyer, R. A. (2012b). Chair work. In R. A. Neimeyer (Ed.), *Techniques of grief therapy* (pp. 266–273). New York, NY: Routledge.

Neimeyer, R. A. (2012c). Correspondence with the deceased. In R. A. Neimeyer (Ed.), *Techniques of grief therapy* (pp. 259–261). New York, NY: Routledge.

Neimeyer, R. A. (2012d). Retelling the narrative of the death. In R. A. Neimeyer (Ed.), *Techniques of grief therapy* (pp. 86–90). New York, NY: Routledge.

Neimeyer, R. A. (2013). The staging of grief: Toward an active model of mourning. In S. Kreitler & H. Shanun-Klein (Eds.), *Studies of grief and bereavement* (pp. 1–18). Hauppauge, NY: Nova Science.

Neimeyer, R. A. (2014). Chapters of our lives. In B. E. Thompson & R. A. Neimeyer (Eds.), *Grief and the expressive arts: Practices for creating meaning* (pp. 80–84). New York, NY: Routledge.

Neimeyer, R. A., Baldwin, S. A., & Gillies, J. (2006). Continuing bonds and reconstructing meaning: Mitigating complications in bereavement. *Death Studies, 30*, 715–738. doi:10.1080/07481180600848322

Neimeyer, R. A., Burke, L., Mackay, M., & Stringer, J. (2010). Grief therapy and the reconstruction of meaning: From principles to practice. *Journal of Contemporary Psychotherapy, 40*, 73–83. doi:10.1007/s10879-009-9135-3

Neimeyer, R. A., & Currier, J. M. (2009). Grief therapy: Evidence of efficacy and emerging directions. *Current Directions in Psychological Science, 18*, 352–356. doi:10.1111/j.1467-8721.2009.01666.x

Neimeyer, R. A., & Hogan, N. (2001). Quantitative or qualitative? Measurement issues in the study of grief. In M. Stroebe, R. Hansson, W. Stroebe, & H. Schut (Eds.), *Handbook of bereavement research: Consequences, coping, and care* (pp. 89–118). Washington, DC: American Psychological Association. doi:10.1037/10436-004

Neimeyer, R. A., Hogan, N., & Laurie, A. (2008). The measurement of grief: Psychometric considerations in the assessment of reactions to bereavement. In M. Stroebe, R. O. Hansson, H. Schut, & W. Stroebe (Eds.), *Handbook of bereavement research: Advances in theory and intervention* (pp. 133–186). Washington, DC: American Psychological Association.

Neimeyer, R. A., & Jordan, J. R. (2013). Historical and contemporary perspectives on assessment and intervention. In D. K. Meagher & D. E. Balk (Eds.), *Handbook of thanatology* (pp. 219–237). New York, NY: Routledge.

Neimeyer, R. A., & Sands, D. C. (2011). Meaning reconstruction in bereavement: From principles to practice. In R. A. Neimeyer, H. Winokuer, D. Harris, & G. Thornton (Eds.), *Grief and bereavement in contemporary society: Bridging research and practice* (pp. 9–22). New York, NY: Routledge.

Neimeyer, R. A., & Thompson, B. E. (2014). Meaning making and the art of grief therapy. In B. E. Thompson & R. A. Neimeyer (Eds.), *Grief and the expressive arts: Practices for creating meaning* (pp. 3–13). New York, NY: Routledge.

Neimeyer, R. A., Torres, C., & Smith, D. C. (2011). The virtual dream: Rewriting stories of loss and grief. *Death Studies, 35*, 646–672. doi:10.1080/07481187.2011.570596

Ober, A. M., Granello, D. H., & Wheaton, J. E. (2012). Grief counseling: An investigation of counselors' training, experience, and competencies. *Journal of Counseling and Development, 90*, 150–159. doi:10.1111/j.1556-6676.2012.00020.x

Onrust, S. A., & Cuijpers, P. (2006). Mood and anxiety disorders in widowhood: A systematic review. *Aging and Mental Health, 10*, 327–334. doi:10.1080/13607860600638529

Papa, A., Sewell, M. T., Garrison-Diehn, C., & Rummel, C. (2013). A randomized open trial assessing the feasibility of behavioral activation for pathological grief responding. *Behavior Therapy.* doi:10.1016/j.beth.2013.04.009

Park, C. L. (2010). Making sense of the meaning literature: An integrative review of meaning making and its effects on adjustment to stressful life events. *Psychological Bulletin, 136*, 257–301. doi:10.1037/a0018301

Parkes, C. M., & Prigerson, H. (2009). *Bereavement* (4th ed.). London, England; New York, NY: Routledge.

Pfoff, M. K., Zarotney, J. R., & Monk, T. H. (2014). Can a function-based therapy for spousally bereaved seniors accrue benefits in both functional and emotional domains? *Death Studies, 38*, 381–386. doi:10.1080/07481187.2013.766658

Popkin, K., Levin, T., Lichtenthal, W. G., Redl, N., Rothstein, H. D., Siegel, D., & Coyle, N. (2011). A pilot music therapy centered grief intervention for nurses and ancillary staff working in cancer settings. *Music and Medicine, 3*, 40–46. doi:10.1177/1943862110391471

Prigerson, H., & Maciejewski, P. (2008). *Prolonged Grief Disorder (PG-13) scale.* Boston, MA: Dana-Farber Cancer Institute.

Prigerson, H. G., Bierhals, A. J., Kasl, S. V., Reynolds, C. F., Shear, M. K., Day, N., . . . Jacobs, S. (1997). Traumatic grief as a risk factor for mental and physical morbidity. *American Journal of Psychiatry, 154*, 616–623.

Prigerson, H. G., Bierhals, A. J., Kasl, S. V., Reynolds, C. F., Shear, M. K., Newsom, J. T., & Jacobs, S. (1996). Complicated grief as a disorder distinct from bereavement-related depression and anxiety: A replication study. *American Journal of Psychiatry, 153*, 1484–1486.

Prigerson, H. G., Horowitz, M. J., Jacobs, S. C., Parkes, C. M., Aslan, M., Goodkin, K., . . . Maciejewski, P. K. (2009). Prolonged grief disorder: Psychometric validation of criteria proposed for *DSM–5* and *ICD–11*. *PLoS Medicine, 6*, e1000121. doi:10.1371/journal.pmed.1000121

Prigerson, H. G., & Jacobs, S. C. (2001). Diagnostic criteria for traumatic grief. In M. S. Stroebe, R. O. Hansson, W. Stroebe, & H. Schut (Eds.), *Handbook of bereavement research: Consequences, coping, and care* (pp. 614–646). Washington, DC: American Psychological Association.

Prigerson, H. G., Maciejewski, P., Reynolds, C. F., Beirhals, A. J., Newsom, J. T., Fasiczka, A., . . . Miller, M. (1995). Inventory of Complicated Grief:

A scale to measure maladaptive symptoms of loss. *Psychiatry Research, 59*, 65–79. doi:10.1016/0165-1781(95)02757-2

Prigerson, H. G., Vanderwerker, L. C., & Maciejewski, P. K. (2008). A case for inclusion of prolonged grief disorder in *DSM–5*. In M. Stroebe, R. Hansson, H. Schut, & W. Stroebe (Eds.), *Handbook of bereavement research and practice: Advances in theory and intervention* (pp. 165–186). Washington, DC: American Psychological Association.

Qualls, S. H. (1999). Family therapy with older adult clients. *Journal of Clinical Psychology, 55*, 977–990. doi:10.1002/(SICI)1097-4679(199908)55:8<977::AID-JCLP6>3.0.CO;2-F

Radloff, L. S. (1977). The CES-D scale: A self-report depression scale for research in the general population. *Applied Psychological Measurement, 1*, 385–401. doi:10.1177/014662167700100306

Reynolds, C. F., III, Miller, M. D., Pasternak, R. E., Frank, E., Perel, J. M., Cornes, C., . . . Kupfer, D. J. (1999). Treatment of bereavement-related major depressive episodes in later life: A controlled study of acute and continuation treatment with nortriptyline and interpersonal psychotherapy. *American Journal of Psychiatry, 156*, 202–208.

Rheingold, A., Asindon, C., Beaddeley, J., Wallace, M., Brown, C., & Rynearson, E. K. (2014). Restorative retelling for violent loss: An open clinical trial. *Death Studies, 38*, 251–258. doi:10.1080/07481187.2013.783654

Richardson, S. J., Lund, D. A., Caserta, M. S., Dudley, W. N., & Obray, S. J. (2003). Sleep patterns in older bereaved spouses. *Omega: Journal of Death and Dying, 47*, 361–383.

Rosenblatt, P., & Wallace, B. (2005). *African American grief*. New York, NY: Routledge.

Rosenbloom, C. A., & Whittington, F. J. (1993). The effects of bereavement on eating behaviors and nutrient intakes in elderly widowed persons. *The Journals of Gerontology, Series B: Psychological Sciences and Social Sciences, 48*, 223–229.

Rosenzweig, A., Prigerson, H., Miller, M. D., & Reynolds, C. F. (1997). Bereavement and late-life depression: Grief and its complications in the elderly. *Annual Review of Medicine, 48*, 421–428. doi:10.1146/annurev.med.48.1.421

Rubin, S. S. (1999). The Two-Track Model of Bereavement: Overview, retrospect and prospect. *Death Studies, 23*, 681–714. doi:10.1080/074811899200731

Rubin, S. S., Malkinson, R., & Witztum, E. (2003). Trauma and bereavement: Conceptual and clinical issues revolving around relationships. *Death Studies, 27*, 667–690. doi:10.1080/713842342

Rubin, S. S., Malkinson, R., & Witztum, E. (2011). *Working with the bereaved*. New York, NY: Routledge.

Rynearson, E. K., & Salloum, A. (2011). Restorative retelling: Revisiting the narrative of violent death. In R. A. Neimeyer, D. Harris, H. Winokuer, & G. Thornton (Eds.), *Grief and bereavement in contemporary society: Bridging research and practice* (pp. 177–188). New York, NY: Routledge.

Schulz, R., Mendelsohn, A. B., Haley, W. E., Mahoney, D., Allen, R. S., Zhang, S., . . . the Resources for Enhancing Alzheimer's Caregiver Health (REACH) Investigators. (2003). End-of-life care and the effect of bereavement on family caregivers of persons with dementia. *New England Journal of Medicine, 349*, 1936–1942. doi:10.1056/NEJMsa035373

Shear, M. K., Frank, E., Houch, P. R., & Reynolds, C. F. (2005). Treatment of complicated grief: A randomized controlled trial. *JAMA, 293*, 2601–2608.

Shear, M. K., Simon, N., Wall, M., Zisook, S., Neimeyer, R., Duan, N., . . . Keshaviah, A. (2011). Complicated grief and related bereavement issues for *DSM–5*. *Depression and Anxiety, 28*, 103–117. doi:10.1002/da.20780

Stroebe, M. (1992–1993). Coping with bereavement: A review of the grief work hypothesis. *Omega: Journal of Death and Dying, 26*, 19–42.

Stroebe, M., & Schut, H. (1999). The Dual Process Model of Coping With Bereavement: Rationale and description. *Death Studies, 23*, 197–224. doi:10.1080/074811899201046

Stroebe, M., & Schut, H. (2005). To continue or relinquish bonds: A review of consequences for the bereaved. *Death Studies, 29*, 477–494. doi:10.1080/07481180590962659

Stroebe, M., & Schut, H. (2010). The Dual Process Model of Coping With Bereavement: A decade on. *Omega: Journal of Death and Dying, 61*, 273–289.

Stroebe, M., Schut, H., & Stroebe, W. (2007). Health outcomes of bereavement. *Lancet, 370*, 1960–1973. doi:10.1016/S0140-6736(07)61816-9

Thielman, K., & Cacciatore, J. (2013). When a child dies: A critical analysis of grief-related controversies in *DSM–5*. *Research on Social Work Practice, 24*, 114–122. doi:10.1177/1049731512474695

Thompson, B. E. (2012). Mindfulness training. In R. A. Neimeyer (Ed.), *Techniques of grief therapy* (pp. 39–41). New York, NY: Routledge.

Thompson, B. E., & Neimeyer, R. A. (Eds.). (2014). *Grief and the expressive arts: Creative contributions to meaning making*. New York, NY: Routledge.

Thompson, L. W., Breckenridge, J. N., Gallagher, D., & Peterson, J. (1984). Effects of bereavement on self-perceptions of physical health in elderly widows and widowers. *Journal of Gerontology, 39,* 309–314. doi:10.1093/geronj/39.3.309

Torres, C., Neimeyer, R. A., & Neff, M. (2014). The expressive arts in grief therapy: An empirical perspective. In B. E. Thompson & R. A. Neimeyer (Eds.), *Grief and the expressive arts: Practices for creating meaning* (pp. 283–290). New York, NY: Routledge.

Turret, N., & Shear, M. K. (2012). Grief monitoring diary. In R. A. Neimeyer (Ed.), *Techniques of grief therapy* (pp. 27–29). New York, NY: Routledge.

Wagner, B., Knaevelsrud, C., & Maercker, A. (2006). Internet-based cognitive-behavioral therapy for complicated grief: A randomized controlled trial. *Death Studies, 30,* 429–453. doi:10.1080/07481180600614385

Wortman, C. B., & Silver, R. (2001). The myths of coping with loss revisited. In M. Stroebe, R. Hansson, W. Stroebe, & H. Schut (Eds.), *Handbook of bereavement research: Consequences, coping, and care* (pp. 405–429). Washington, DC: American Psychological Association. doi:10.1037/10436-017

Yesavage, J. A., Brink, T. L., Rose, T. L., Lum, O., Huang, V., Adey, M., & Leirer, V. O. (1982–1983). Development and validation of a geriatric depression screening scale: A preliminary report. *Journal of Psychiatric Research, 17,* 37–49. doi:10.1016/0022-3956(82)90033-4

Zhang, B., Mitchell, S. L., Bambauer, K. Z., Jones, R., & Prigerson, H. G. (2008). Depressive symptom trajectories and associated risks among bereaved Alzheimer disease caregivers. *American Journal of Geriatric Psychiatry, 16,* 145–155. doi:10.1097/JGP.0b013e318157caec

CHAPTER 26

ELDER ABUSE AND NEGLECT

Laura Mosqueda and Bonnie Olsen

The problem of elder abuse comes to a geropsychologist's attention in a variety of ways. It may be that during a therapy session an older adult reveals he or she has been victimized, although he or she may not even recognize it as such. Or, a perpetrator of abuse may reveal he or she has been an abuser, again without recognizing it as such. Geropsychologists may be asked to examine an elder to determine their cognitive capacity to have made a decision in the past, such as entering into a marriage or signing a document. Or, a geropsychologist may be asked to determine an elder's capacity to decide to stay at home in an abusive situation rather than go to a nursing home. A geropsychologist's clinical expertise may be requested to interpret capacity determinations for judges and juries. These psychologists may even be asked to testify in a trial of elder abuse in a civil or criminal context.

OVERVIEW

The term *elder abuse* is, in itself, controversial; some researchers prefer the term *elder mistreatment*. For clinical purposes, the term elder abuse is sufficient. The authors of this chapter use elder abuse to mean an intentional action or inaction that results in significant physical or emotional harm to a person who is vulnerable because of age-related factors.

Sadly, older adults experience many forms of abuse. Exhibit 26.1 provides a brief description of these types of abuse, including physical, sexual, emotional, financial, and neglect.

Physical Abuse

Physical abuse is an act that causes or is likely to cause physical harm to an older adult (Centers for Disease Control and Prevention [CDC], 2013). This abuse includes a range of activities from hitting, punching, or overtightening of restraints to something such as a "mild" shove. A shove that simply annoys a younger person may result in a fall and hip fracture in an 83-year-old with Parkinson's disease.

Sexual Abuse

Sexual abuse commonly is understood to mean nonconsensual sexual contact of any kind with an elderly person. Sexual contact with an individual who is not capable of giving consent also is considered sexual abuse. It includes, but is not limited to, unwanted touching and all types of sexual assault or battery, such as rape, sodomy, coerced nudity, and sexually explicit photographing (National Center on Elder Abuse, 2013b).

Financial Abuse

Financial or material exploitation is defined as the illegal or improper use of an elder's funds, property, or assets (CDC, 2013). Examples include, but are not limited to, cashing an elderly person's checks without authorization or permission; forging an older person's signature; misusing or stealing an older person's money or possessions; coercing or deceiving an older person into signing any document (e.g., contracts or will); and the improper use of conservatorship, guardianship, or

http://dx.doi.org/10.1037/14459-026
APA Handbook of Clinical Geropsychology: Vol. 2. Assessment, Treatment, and Issues of Later Life,
P. A. Lichtenberg and B. T. Mast (Editors-in-Chief)

Exhibit 26.1
Types of Abuse

Physical and sexual abuse
- Inadequately explained fractures, bruises, welts, cuts, sores, or burns
- Unexplained sexually transmitted diseases

Financial abuse and exploitation
- Lack of amenities victim could afford
- Vulnerable elder or older adult "voluntarily" giving uncharacteristically excessive financial reimbursement or gifts for needed care and companionship
- Caregiver has control of elder's money but is failing to provide for elder's needs
- Vulnerable elder or older adult has signed property transfers (power of attorney, new will, etc.) but is unable to comprehend the transaction or what it means

Psychological and emotional abuse
- Unexplained changes in behavior, such as withdrawal from normal activities, decreased alertness
- Caregiver isolates elder or older adult (does not let anyone into the home or speak to the elder)
- Caregiver is verbally aggressive or demeaning, controlling, overly concerned about spending money, or uncaring

Neglect
- Lack of basic hygiene, adequate food, or clean and appropriate clothing
- Withholding of medical aids (glasses, walker, teeth, hearing aid, medications)
- Person with dementia left unsupervised in dangerous surroundings
- Person confined to bed is left without care
- Home cluttered, filthy, in disrepair, or having fire or safety hazards
- Home without adequate facilities (stove, refrigerator, heat, cooling, working plumbing, and electricity)
- Untreated "bed" sores (pressure ulcers)

---

nonabused counterparts with otherwise-similar profiles (Lachs, Williams, O'Brien, Pillemer, & Charlson, 1998); elders with dementia are far more likely to be abused than those without dementia (Cooper et al., 2009); and family members are the most likely people to perpetrate abuse (Hafemeister, 2003).

Emotional Abuse

Emotional abuse is understood to mean the infliction of mental pain, anguish, or distress through verbal or nonverbal acts (National Center on Elder Abuse, 2013b). Although emotional abuse may be quite subtle, at times, it is actually blatant: The grandson who waves a butcher knife in the face of his grandmother while "suggesting" that she cosign for his car loan, or the daughter who rips up her mother's prized doll collection in front of her because she wet the bed again are two examples. Although emotional abuse is not a mandatory report in most states, practitioners are allowed to report egregious circumstances such as these. Not surprisingly, emotional abuse often is accompanied by other types of abuse, such as physical abuse and financial abuse. So, once emotional abuse is uncovered, it is important to inquire about other types of abuse. The fear and shame experienced by an older adult who suffers from emotional abuse may cause or exacerbate medical problems, such as depression and hypertension (Cornijs, Penninx, Knipscheer, & van Tilburg, 1999). Practitioners must be attuned to the potentially long-lasting emotional and physical health consequences of emotional abuse.

Neglect

When a person assumes caregiving responsibility for an older adult, there are certain givens, including the expectation that rudimentary needs will be met. Neglect is considered if a caregiver, intentionally or unintentionally, does not assure the provision of such basic necessities as food, housing, clothing, and health care (CDC, 2013). Clues to a neglect situation may include the new onset of missed appointments, weight loss, disheveled or dirty appearance, and change in behavior (more withdrawn, depressed, anxious; National Center on Elder Abuse, 2013a).

power of attorney. It is sometimes a fine line between a person's right to make a bad decision and society's obligation to protect. Common lottery scams that ask for payment of taxes or fees upfront, and then never pay out winnings are a good example.

The epidemiology of abuse is not well understood, but a few facts are clear: Abuse is common, affecting 1 out of 10 older adults at some time in their lives (Acierno et al., 2010); elders who are abused are more likely to die when compared with their

Vulnerability to Abuse and Neglect

As people grow older, they are more likely to experience changes in physical and cognitive function that makes them more reliant on others for a variety of tasks and needs. They are also more likely to experience changes in their social situation that make them prone to emotional issues, such as depression, loneliness, and social isolation, which make older adults easy prey for those seeking to take advantage of them.

Several factors are known to be associated with elder abuse. The CDC (2010) examined risk factors for elder abuse by individual (focusing on risk factors for perpetration), relationship, community, and societal levels. Risk factors for victims include having dementia, living in a care facility, and being female. Risk factors for perpetrators, who are often caregivers, include mental illness, alcohol abuse, and hostility. Relationship risk factors include high financial and emotional dependence on the vulnerable elder, past experience of disruptive behavior, and lack of social support. Community-level risk factors include limited, inaccessible, or unavailable formal services, such as respite care. Societal factors include a culture of high tolerance and acceptance of aggressive behavior, and a culture in which health care personnel, guardians, and other agents are given more liberty to make care decisions (Moyer & U.S. Preventive Services Task Force, 2013). See the section Characterizing Elder Abuse for additional information.

Common age-related changes mask and mimic signs of abuse and neglect (Mosqueda, 2012). Because older adults are more likely to have comorbid chronic illnesses than younger counterparts, and because these illnesses typically are accompanied by a growing armamentarium of prescription medications, the physical indicators of abuse and neglect may be confused easily with the notion that "he's just old." For example, a thinner epidermis coupled with increasing capillary fragility, both normal age-related changes, in combination with a common disease such as atrial fibrillation and its treatment with warfarin (a prescription "blood thinner" to reduce the likelihood of stroke) in combination with gait instability may make an older adult likely to have multiple bruises for benign reasons (U.S. National Research Council, Panel to Review Risk and Prevalence of Elder Abuse and Neglect, 2003). How, then, does one determine if an older adult with those characteristics actually has those bruises as the result of an assault?

This chapter is intended to help psychologists understand how to recognize and evaluate the signs of elder abuse, know what to do when they have a suspicion of abuse, and how to respond most appropriately to the possible victim and abuser.

Laws and Reporting Requirements

No federal laws, policies, or guidelines direct the interpretation or definition of elder abuse. Each state has its own interpretation of when a case of abuse rises to a level deemed criminal behavior (American Bar Association [ABA] Commission on Law and Aging 2006a). Some states have age-based criteria, such as that the victim must be over the age of 62 or 65 years. Other states have function-based criteria that outline dependency requirements in activities of daily living (ADLs). Some states use age or function and some use both. Nearly all states mandate a report of elder abuse, as of 2013. Those that do not mandate a report (New York, New Jersey, and North Carolina) still allow a report to be made and have systems for doing so (ABA Commission on Law and Aging, 2006b). According to the ABA, for those states that mandate a report, there is wide variability in who is a mandated reporter and what constitutes a mandated report. Some states, such as California and Illinois, require bank tellers to report suspected abuse and others do not. In most states that have mandated reporting, mental health professionals are mandated reporters. That means that if one has a reasonable suspicion of abuse or neglect, then that person has an obligation to report. Keep in mind that it is not the clinician's duty to investigate or determine whether the abuse actually did or did not occur; a reasonable suspicion requires a report to be made, which then is investigated by the appropriate agency (see the section Reporting Abuse). The states that mandate reporting have a variety of penalties ranging from fines to jail time for failure to report.

Know state laws. It is important for geropsychologists to know the statutes of the relevant state.

Information on state-by-state elder abuse laws can be found on the Center for Elders and the Courts website (http://www.eldersandcourts.org). When in doubt, call the appropriate reporting agency, describe the concern succinctly and clearly, and ask for that agency's opinion as to whether a report is necessary.

Agencies that take reports. Several agencies will take a report of suspected abuse. The practitioner determines the appropriate agency based on the location of the elder and the degree of risk (National Adult Protective Services Association, 2013). The Long-Term Care Ombudsmen Program is responsible for investigating allegations of abuse or neglect of residents of nursing homes, board and care homes, and assisted living facilities. Every state has an Office of the State Long-Term Care Ombudsman, headed by a full-time state ombudsman. At the county level, local ombudsman, many of whom are volunteers, assist residents and their families and provide a voice for those who are unable to speak for themselves. If the suspected abuser is a staff member of the facility, state Licensing and Certification programs investigate the allegations of a facility in conjunction with law enforcement and ombudsmen.

Adult protective service (APS) workers investigate cases of suspected abuse in community-dwelling older adults (i.e., private homes and nonlicensed facilities). APS agencies investigate reports of abuse of elders (ages 65 years and older) and dependent adults (ages 18–64 years) who live at home, in hotels, or hospitals. When an elder is thought to be in immediate harm, it is critical to contact the police to report abuse. Although cross-reporting between the social service agencies (APS and Long-Term Care Ombudsmen Program) is encouraged and done in many jurisdictions, the degree to which it is effective is not known. Some APS agencies require all of their investigators to have degrees in social work or nursing; others have less stringent requirements. No national training protocols, examinations, or requirements specify who may be an APS worker. Some states have rigorous training programs for their APS workers, whereas others do not. Some APS agencies have such high volumes that they have workers who are specialized by geographic area or

type of abuse (National Adult Protective Services Association, 2013). For example, some APS workers may specialize in financial abuse; these people may have relationships with forensic accountants in their local law enforcement or prosecutor's office. Others may specialize in physical abuse and have nursing expertise easily available to them. When APS receives a report of suspected abuse, an APS staff member is assigned to visit the client at his or her home to evaluate the allegation and to recommend or arrange for such services as advocacy, counseling, money management, out-of-home placement, or conservatorship.

Vulnerability Related to Aging

As the saying goes, "Aging is not for sissies"; most individuals experience some change in functioning as they age. All body systems decline, although not at the same rates or with the same consequences. Understanding how different areas of decline can lead to vulnerability is an important foundation for understanding the ways that abuse affects elders in communities.

Physical health. Normal aging is accompanied by a decrease in physiologic reserve. A very healthy 85-year-old has an easily measurable diminution of bone density, renal function, skin elasticity, cardiac output, and the like when compared with a healthy 35-year-old (Kirkwood, 2005). Aging, according to Haber (2013), also is accompanied frequently by such illnesses as diabetes, heart disease, and Parkinson's disease that impair physical function. Together, these normal and common age-related alterations create a physical vulnerability to being victimized and make recovery from the victimization challenging.

Defending oneself from an assault becomes more difficult because of such changes as gait instability, slower reaction time, and declining strength. Physical markers, including bruising, fractures, skin tears, and pressure sores, that may have resulted from abuse or neglect are easily dismissed as unavoidable sequelae of age and chronic conditions (Wiglesworth et al., 2009).

Cognitive decline. The incidence of dementia or more limited cognitive decline in the aging population is enormous, and it increases with each decade; those over the age of 85 years have nearly a 50% risk for dementia (Alzheimer's Association, 2013). Diminished cognitive functioning is the single most common issue that underlies abuse. As such, it is critical to understand how this occurs.

The vast majority of individuals who experience cognitive decline associated with aging notice memory loss first; they have difficulty recalling recent events and information. Impaired concentration may lead to difficulty organizing information into meaningful wholes. Impaired self-regulation and executive functioning results in an inability to follow through on complex multistep procedures until a job is completed. Impaired insight into one's cognitive loss prevents one from engaging in compensatory strategies or to seek assistance. These functions are critical to managing the most complex tasks in everyday life, referred to as instrumental activities of daily living (IADLs; Dodge et al., 2005). Sufficient compromise in any one area can lead to a loss of autonomy and significant risk of abuse.

Memory loss can be used against the victim when someone requests duplicate payments for goods or services. Forgetting to pay rent or mortgage creates opportunity for predatory bank activity. Disorganized recordkeeping allows a predator to manipulate information. Impaired concentration makes it nearly impossible to organize complex medication regimes, let alone remember to take them at the correct time. Poor executive functioning can lead to malnutrition or dehydration as meal preparation becomes overwhelming. Any and all of these situations regularly result in self-neglect, neglect by others, or outright abuse.

Emotional issues.   Aging brings changes, not always welcomed. Spouses may become ill and require extended care, or die. Families may move to distant cities, and friends often move to assisted living facilities. Driver's licenses may be lost when vision is diminished. Fixed incomes buy a lower standard of living. Physical limitations keep one more isolated. Adjusting to these changes requires a strong constitution and emotional reserves that many individuals lack. During these times of adjustment and adaptation, depression and anxiety are

common symptoms. It may be the first time that an individual experiences clinically significant emotional symptoms or it may be a time when subacute symptoms become more pronounced. Those who suffer from life-long psychiatric conditions, such as schizophrenia, bipolar disorder, major depression, and generalized anxiety disorder, are joined by many more who struggle to adjust to the demands that come with advanced age. Any significant emotional symptom or psychiatric disorder can lead to vulnerability to abuse as individuals are less able to address their own needs and may be less able to speak up if they are being mistreated by others.

Contextual stressors.   Stress comes from any number of contextual issues in life, but many can be more debilitating as we age. The stress may be related to financial issues as individuals adjust to living on a fixed income or need to help support adult children who for a variety of reasons are not financially independent. Relationships may become more complex because of a long history of discord or may become disengaged as families expand and shift attention to the generation of grandchildren. Overall role adjustments are necessary when one retires, becomes a widow or widower, can no longer participate as actively in social groups, or loses the ability to contribute to the community in the way one once did. These and many other individual issues—collectively referred to as contextual issues—can contribute to vulnerability to abuse.

Cultural factors.   Our society is multicultural, and all members potentially could be victims of elder abuse. Whatever culture people come from and live within can influence how they perceive, respond to, and understand elder abuse. According to Tatara (1999), minority elders are considerably more vulnerable than White elders when it comes to domestic elder abuse. Some cultural factors, however, may contribute to the risk of abuse, whereas others may reduce the risk. For instance, in some cultures, a family member who has needs is carefully tended to, and responsibilities are shared among all the members. In contrast, some cultures view symptoms of dementia negatively and believe that dementia brings shame to the family (Tatara, 1999). This in turn can lead to neglect or emotional abuse. In some cultures, events that would be considered a reportable instance of abuse are more readily accepted and tolerated, whereas other cultures may have a lower threshold than laws dictate. Clearly, it is important that clinicians incorporate cultural context into their own understanding of abuse and how patients, institutions, and communities perceive and respond to abuse.

Summary

As this section illustrates, vulnerability to abuse arises from a wide variety of factors. Conceivably, any condition that results in a compromise could lead to vulnerability. Clinicians cannot know what an individual's experience of these conditions or limitations may be, but they can be alert to how these conditions may affect an individual's autonomy and ability to respond to adverse situations in their lives.

CHARACTERIZING ELDER ABUSE

Elder abuse cases are complex and diverse, and they occur in a surprisingly large numbers of ways (Brandl et al., 2007). Because of this heterogeneity, investigators have developed a number of strategies to divide the universe of cases into meaningful groups that promote an understanding of the factors contributing to the risk or that help identify meaningful interventions. One strategy is to group cases by the type of abuse. For instance, Jackson and Hafemeister (2011, 2012) described the utility of differentiating between cases of pure financial abuse and cases in which financial abuse occurs along with other forms, such as emotional and physical abuse. Currently, there is no one accepted way to characterize these cases; however, Jackson and Hafemeister found that considering factors that derive from three domains leads to the most meaningful distinctions. The domains include factors related to the victim, the perpetrator, and the context in which the abuse occurs.

Characteristics of the Victim

As noted by Acierno et al. (2010), Beck et al. (2011), and Johannesen and LoGiudice (2013), victims of abuse almost universally have some condition that leads to their vulnerability. The effects of the condition may be to limit the senior's physical functioning, cognitive functioning, sensory loss, or emotional functioning. These may not occur in isolation, but in complex syndromes that overlap. Take, for example, dementia, in which the cognitive impairment ultimately causes individuals to be unable to provide for their own basic needs, such as bathing and toileting, and may include psychiatric symptoms or significant depressive episodes.

Characteristics of the Abuser

There is considerable controversy in the field about how to think about the individuals who abuse elders. Just as the characteristics of the victims cover a diverse array of factors, so too do the factors related to the abusers. For instance, large-scale lottery scams result in financial abuse when vulnerable seniors are unable to recognize the false promises. In other circumstances, the perpetrator may be an unsavory sales person who capitalizes on the elder's inability to process information quickly by pushing the elderly victim to make a quick decision on goods or services that are overpriced or unnecessary. Often the abuser is someone with whom the victim has a personal relationship, such as a neighbor, hired caregiver, attorney, accountant, or minister. By far the most common type of abuser is a family member who may be in a caregiving role they are unable to manage successfully. Often these family members suffer from some form of substance abuse or mental health disorder that appears to contribute to the problem (Jogerst, Daly, Galloway, Zheng, & Xu, 2012).

Contextual Characteristics

Abuse occurs within the context of the older person's life situation, according to Fulmer et al. (2005.) Contextual factors are important to consider because they are often the ones that appear to be the tipping point, the "final straw" that either leads to abuse or protects against it. These factors can be viewed as either risk factors or protective factors. Some of the contextual factors may be financial strain, social isolation, availability of supportive services, and the nature of the relationship between the victim and the abuser (Luo & Waite, 2011; Mosqueda & Dong, 2011).

Common Abuse Profiles

The following are a few examples of how these factors come together in frequently occurring scenarios.

Family caregiver and person with dementia dyad.   One of the most frequent forms of abuse occurs when a family member is in a caregiving role for an individual suffering from dementia (Reinhard, Given, Petlick, & Bernis, 2008). Research suggests that when the caregiver experiences depression or anxiety, has limited skills in caregiving, and perceives him- or herself to be burdened by the caregiving responsibilities, the risk increases (MacNeil et al., 2010). Similarly, when the care recipient needs assistance with basic ADLs and resists this care or displays physical aggression to the caregiver, the risk of abuse or neglect increases (Cooper, Blanchard, Selwood, Walker, & Livingston, 2010; Dunkin & Anderson-Hanley, 1998; Fulmer et al., 2005; Wiglesworth et al., 2010). When this occurs in the context of limited social support, limited financial resources, or poor premorbid relationship, the risk of abuse also increases. In these cases, the abuse can take any form, but it is most typically physical, emotional abuse, or neglect (Cooper et al., 2010). These often are stressed caregivers who do not intend to abuse, but are "in over their head" in the caregiving role and do not or cannot seek help.

Substance abusing or mentally ill caregiver and person with dementia dyad.   Substance abuse and serious mental illness such as schizophrenia, bipolar disorder, or serious personality disorders is debilitating and can result in poor adaptation in many spheres of life (Modestin, Gladen, & Christen, 2001). These individuals may be placed in a caregiving role because family feels this is an unskilled job they should be able to perform or because funds are insufficient to hire a caregiver. Sometimes this can occur because the caregiver recognizes this as an opportunity to take advantage of the person with dementia financially. Not uncommonly, a role reversal occurs, where the elder was once providing care or protection to the impaired individual.

Sadly, abuse in these situations can take any form, including financial, emotional, physical, sexual, and neglect (Jogerst et al., 2012).

Trusted professional and isolated victim.   Taken from the perspective of the victim, this scenario takes many forms, but it largely represents an individual who is made vulnerable by isolation, loneliness, or unmet dependency needs (Luo & Waite, 2011; Podnieks, 2006). Often a widow or widower who needs help sorting out finances, managing medical needs, making home repairs, preparing trust or estate planning documents, selling a home, or other complex life situations comes into contact with a professional (or someone who represents themselves to be a professional). The professional then opportunistically takes advantage of the vulnerability of the victim to gain financially from the relationship. Typically, a contract or other document is signed or funds are transferred that exceed the actual value of the goods or services provided. Although many professionals behave ethically, elder abuse has been perpetrated by mortgage brokers, home repair persons, attorneys, estate planners, physicians, accountants, hired caregivers, realtors, bankers, gardeners, and many others (Kemp & Mosqueda, 2005).

Sweetheart scam.   Community-dwelling older adults often fear that they will not be able to maintain their independence and will end up in a nursing home or other institution. The fear can develop slowly over decades or come on suddenly when a new medical condition creates dependency, or when there is the death of a close relationship. The fear can lead to significant vulnerability. Unsavory individuals who seek to take advantage of others readily recognize these potential victims and set out to ingratiate themselves into the lives of the victim. Abuse can occur in many forms but most often involves some financial abuse. Neglect may be a secondary effect of the isolation that the perpetrator imposes as family and friends are kept at a distance.

Large-scale lottery scams.   Scams are becoming increasingly common and take more and more sophisticated forms. According to the *Consumer Sentinel Network Data Book for January–December 2012*, the Federal Trade Commission (FTC; 2013) reported that the Consumer Sentinel Complaint received nearly 1.7 million complaints of fraud in 2012. Consumers reported paying more than $1.4 billion in fraud complaints in 2012. Consumers age 60 years and over most frequently reported telemarketing calls, government imposter scams, third-party debt collectors, prizes-sweepstakes-gifts scams, and shop-at-home sales. Furthermore, the FTC has reported $1 billion is thought to be lost through foreign lottery scams annually. These elders are common victims for some poorly understood reasons. The inability to recognize and resist false promises or appraise the likelihood of winning a game is a common finding that preliminary research suggests may be related to a specific area of the brain that deteriorates disproportionately in elders (Fein, McGillivray, & Finn, 2007).

Licensed facility.   Many of the aging population are able to live at home or in other independent living settings successfully. However, Murtaugh, Kemper, Spillman, and Carlson (1997) indicated approximately 40% of seniors will spend at least some time in a licensed care facility such as an assisted living facility, board and care home, skilled nursing facility, or long-term care facility. Society should be able to trust that the care they receive is adequate and the patients or residents are protected from mistreatment. Unfortunately, there have been elder abuse cases in which staff, employed by a facility, mistreated residents as well as cases in which one resident mistreated another. The abuse has included physical assault, sexual abuse, emotional abuse, and neglect. These cases are reported through the Long-Term Care Ombudsman Program, which takes appropriate action to protect victims, protect other residents from possible abuse, and coordinate intervention with law enforcement when appropriate.

Domestic violence and family dynamics.   Elder abuse often occurs in the context of the victim's family. Every family has its own culture and expectations regarding roles and values. We have found that in families that have a culture of domestic violence, including bullying, intimidation, suppression, or coercion, the effects often extend to the vulnerable elder in the family system. A common scenario occurs with the death of a dominant, bullying

patriarch. His role may be filled by an adult child who replicates the cycle of power and control over the widow. The widow in turn protects the abusing child, just as she protected her abusing husband. Another common scenario occurs when a long-term victim of domestic violence, as a form of retribution, abuses a demented or physically compromised spouse.

Red Flags and Pink Flags

Some indicators of abuse are quite obvious or distinctive. An elder with severe bruising on the head, face, or neck, for example, is likely to have been abused unless a clear and rational explanation, such as a motor vehicle accident, is offered and verified. An older adult with cuts or bruising in the groin area and tears in the vaginal mucosa is likely to have been sexually assaulted. An older adult who says he or she was beaten or otherwise mistreated should be believed until proven otherwise. See Exhibits 26.2 and 26.3 for a brief description of the most common warning signs of abuse.

More often, however, no red flags are present. Rather, pink flags become suggestive of a reason to be concerned but are not in and of themselves adequate to prove abuse. It is important for the clinician to have elder abuse on his or her differential

---

Exhibit 26.2
Red Flags of Physical and Emotional Abuse or Neglect

Unexplained change in physical appearance
- Weight loss
- Bruising in unusual locations, such as head, face, or neck
- Poor grooming or hygiene

Unexplained change in social functioning
- Withdrawn
- Fearfulness
- Loss of interest in usual activities
- More secretive

Unexplained change in behavior
- Cowering
- Agitation
- Impaired sleep
- Less alert

Exhibit 26.3
Red Flags of Financial Abuse or Undue Influence

1. Medical, pharmacological, psychological, or social problems create vulnerability
2. A person in a position of trust takes advantage of that vulnerability
3. Assets are transferred during the period of vulnerability
4. The older person or the transactions are kept isolated, controlled, or secret
5. A qualified expert did not conduct an appropriate assessment of the older person's capacities and vulnerabilities before the transfer
6. The benefits are not proportional to the value of the assets transferred, or the transfer is not consistent with the older person's prior beliefs, wishes, or behavior
7. Common business or personal ethics are not followed
8. The perpetrator does not give consideration to the effect of the transaction on others, including the victim, other family members, beneficiaries, or the public welfare system.

Note. From "Elder Financial Abuse: An Evaluation Framework and Supporting Evidence", by B. J. Kemp & L. A. Mosqueda, 2005, *Journal of the American Geriatric Society,* 53, p. 1124–1125. Copyright 2005 by John Wiley & Sons, Inc.. Adapted with permission.

diagnosis under a variety of circumstances, so that these pink flags do not go unnoticed. For example, an elder who becomes more withdrawn or depressed ought to be asked about abuse. A person who seems more disheveled or unclean, particularly if a caregiver assists with some IADLs or ADLs, needs to be gently questioned about the possibility of neglect and abuse (Shugarman, Fries, Wolf, & Morris, 2003; Yaffe, 2010).

Understanding who the victims of abuse are and who the potential abusers are is a helpful beginning to developing strategies to reducing the impact of abuse in our communities. When abuse or possible abuse has been identified, agencies often attempt to meet two goals. First and foremost is to protect the elder from any additional abuse, and second is to prosecute the perpetrator when appropriate. Both goals can be extremely difficult to accomplish even under the best of circumstances because of a multitude of factors discussed in the following case.

Case Study

Mrs. JP is a 78-year-old woman who resides alone in her own home. She was widowed about 5 years ago and has 2 adult children who both live out of state. She maintains only telephone contact with them about once every 6 weeks. Mrs. JP had been an active member of her church and once was involved in a local senior center where she attended bridge games but stopped this around the time that her husband become ill. She has a few friends but has stopped going out with them regularly.

About 8 months ago, she was diagnosed with dementia by her primary care physician when symptoms of memory loss became apparent in an office visit. She scored 23/30 on the Mini Mental Status Exam. She did not want to involve her family although her physician strongly encouraged her to bring one of her children to her next office visit. Six months ago, her son, George, moved into her home to help her manage her affairs. Her physician was relieved to see that he was attending office visits with her. George sorted through piles of unopened mail and bills that had not been paid. He took her to the bank where Mrs. JP agreed to have George added to her checking and savings accounts so he could more easily take care of her affairs.

Several weeks ago, Mrs. JP fell in her bathroom and was taken to the hospital by ambulance when her son found her several hours later. She was admitted and treated for a broken hip and discharged to a skilled nursing facility where she is now receiving rehabilitation services. While there, her physician requested a psych consult as she appeared to be more depressed than he had seen in the past. The psychologist saw Mrs. JP and in the course of the interview discovered that Mrs. JP was very sad that she had lost a great deal of independence in recent months and felt overwhelmed with shame that she was becoming incontinent and had difficulty remembering information. The psychologist questioned her further and learned that George often berated the patient when she could not remember information or when she could not get to the bathroom quickly enough. The day she fell, she had had an accident and was trying to clean it up before her son came home. She said to the psychologist, "I can never do anything right and he gets so angry at me. Sometimes he threatens to hit me if I don't do a better job."

The psychologist felt that the information raised sufficient concern that she made a report to the local Adult Protective Services office where a case was opened. A social worker was assigned to the case and began an investigation. Ultimately, it was discovered that George was likely mistreating his mother in a number of ways. He had transferred the title of her home to his name and had provided the paperwork for her to sign on the day after her surgery and when she was still recovering from the confusion caused by anesthesia. He had failed to have her prescriptions filled for the past 3 months because he didn't want to spend the money, although Mrs. JP had over $50,000 in her savings account. Mrs. JP admitted to the social worker that he called her names and had once struck her when she spilled a bowl of soup on the table. The social worker discovered that she had gone to a neighbor asking for something to eat when George left her alone with-

out food in the house for 5 days when he went on vacation.

The case was cross-reported to the local police who also investigated the case. After the police questioned George about the change in the title to the house, he moved out of the home and could not be located, leaving Mrs. JP alone in the home. The social worker helped Mrs. JP arrange for in-home caregiving.

Resistance to Intervention

Cooper et al. (2009) suggested that a common problem that presents for both APS and the Long-Term Care Ombudsmen Program is the resistance of some victims to intervention. There appear to be many reasons that victims may not want intervention. The caregiver–care recipient dyad may have had a long-standing interdependent relationship that the victim is attempting to preserve. Victims often lack insight or understanding that the care they are receiving is inadequate, or deny the possibility that funds were removed from their accounts without their permission or knowledge. As described, seniors often resist any change for fear that it will result in loss of their autonomy. Somewhat related, elders who have limited cognitive functioning often agree to some necessary and helpful changes such as hiring a caregiver or moving to a care facility, only to later change their mind and reject the plan. Resistance to change that is necessary to ensure safety can result in a greater loss of autonomy than would have been necessary otherwise.

Emergency Protective Orders and Restraining Orders

Protecting the victim from the perpetrator is often a complex task that requires legal intervention that may span many months before it is resolved. For instance, when a family caregiver is providing grossly inadequate care resulting in neglect, or there is evidence of physical abuse, one possible response is to seek an Emergency Protective Order or a Restraining Order to keep the perpetrator away from the victim. Alternative care arrangements are then necessary and should be tied to the degree of need of the elder. He or she may need to move to a care facility, perhaps temporarily until medically stable, alternative caregivers can be hired, or family may be able to make arrangements. However, the elder may cling to the caregiver, not wanting the caregiver to leave, or the elder may remain under the care of the perpetrator albeit with increased attention and supervision. Some victims have no family to assist and a referral to the public guardian is made, who in turn applies for a conservatorship of the victim. In some cases, that may be the only viable alternative.

Emergency Shelters

Although emergency shelters commonly are used to protect victims of domestic violence, Heck and Gillespie (2013) suggested that options for emergency shelter of elder abuse victims are not as readily available. Options that do exist for emergency placement vary from state to state. Some states have specific nonprofit or charitable organizations that operate emergency, short-term placement programs for abused elders. These programs utilize available housing options or contract with existing adult care facilities to provide empty beds. APS, in some states, crafts agreements directly with assisted living or skilled nursing facilities for emergency placement or arranges alternative short-term options. Other states are fortunate to have specific elder abuse shelters, adult foster homes, or domestic violence shelters that will accept older adults for emergency placement.

Guardianship or Conservatorship

It is not unusual that elder abuse occurs when individuals have experienced such decline in physical or cognitive function that they are no longer able to make reasonable decisions regarding their own needs. At these times, the lack of awareness of their own needs, sometimes as basic as food, hygiene, and adequate clothing, makes them vulnerable to others who take advantage of their compromised status. Efforts to intervene may fail and ultimately a conservatorship of person or estate is necessary. The mechanism for obtaining this level of protection may vary from state to state, but generally it involves an application to the court, investigation, and ultimately a

hearing to appoint a conservator or guardian. When a capable and willing individual, either family or friend, can act in this role, the court often appoints that individual. Unfortunately, the individuals who do not have someone in their life to act in this regard are the ones who need the most urgent help. In California, a public guardian is then appointed. Although more restrictive than other alternatives, this outcome makes the risk of additional abuse remote.

Protecting Financial Assets

Financial elder abuse is widespread and is the single most common form of abuse (Kemp & Mosqueda, 2005). Once identified, protection of any remaining assets is critical to ensure the welfare of the victim because this will have a direct effect on quality of life moving forward. The protection of assets can occur through some of the previously noted means, such as restraining orders or conservatorship. Less severe mechanisms may include involving a family member or trusted friend by having them receive duplicate bank statements or putting them on the accounts to oversee transactions. Some victims agree to have their mail sent to a post office box or a family member's home so they are not faced with scam solicitations and fraudulent advertising on a daily basis.

Social Programs

Much of the vulnerability to abuse can be mitigated when the elder is engaged in meaningful relationships and others have frequent contact with them. Social connections serve as a protective factor and seem to create somewhat of a barrier to would-be perpetrators who try to ingratiate themselves into the lives of their potential victims. Most communities offer programs that provide social contact in various ways. Friendly visitor programs, senior centers, and adult day care programs are some examples.

Counseling

Elders who have been victims of abuse may need special support, even after they have been removed from harm and their resources secured. They may need professional assistance to understand how the abuse occurred and move forward in their lives. Some may experience posttraumatic stress and develop anxiety symptoms that are masked by other underlying disorders, such as dementia or depression. Addressing these needs quickly once the elder is safe can minimize long-term consequences to well-being. Psychologists who have specialized knowledge and training in geropsychology issues are important resources for this service. Most counties have counseling available for low-income seniors through their social service agencies.

Home Delivered Meals

Some seniors can manage to maintain their autonomy while living alone in all regards other than food. For some, the complexity of getting to the market, managing the transportation and financial transaction, and the meal preparation can be complex and overwhelming. Home-delivered meals can be the only service needed and may function to keep the senior in the community with at least one individual seeing them daily.

Engaging the Family

Family members do not always know how to assess for changes in elders and may miss signs that additional help is needed. For emotional reasons, there may be a bias toward viewing aging parents as more capable of managing their affairs than in fact they are. The vulnerability to abuse and the possibility of neglect sometimes can be reduced significantly simply by helping family to recognize the need for additional support. The support may come in the form of filling medication boxes, attending medical appointments with the senior, helping to pay monthly bills, grocery shopping, or meal planning. It often is helpful for family to hear from a professional when it is the right time to hire a caregiver or to consider moving to a setting where additional help is available, such as an independent living facility or assisted living facility (see Appendix 26.1 for a list of elder abuse resources).

CLINICAL PRACTICE

Psychologists working in clinical practice likely will encounter elder abuse in a variety of ways, some rather unexpected. Regardless of the circumstances,

if one learns of elder abuse in a professional role while working in a state with mandated reporting, one needs to be aware and respond appropriately.

Recognizing Abuse

Clinicians should develop an awareness of the ways in which elders are abused and the typical manner in which it presents. The previous discussion helps to inform these concepts, and it is advisable to be familiar with the most common forms of abuse.

Psychologists may become aware of an incident of possible elder abuse when the elder is not their patient. In fact, it is possible that the perpetrator is their patient. The clinician may learn about an abusive relationship inadvertently in some other role, perhaps through an administrative role in an agency or in a supervisory relationship. Just as in issues related to child abuse, even if the elder is not your patient, if practicing in a state of mandated reporting, the psychologist has the responsibility to report.

Reporting abuse. All clinicians have the responsibility to understand the laws that pertain to clinical practice, including reporting requirements for child abuse, domestic violence, and elder abuse so that they are able to make good decisions and ensure compliance with the law. Mandated reporters must know the format and time frame in which the report must be made. In California, for example, it is mandated that clinical psychologists make a telephone report to APS immediately, or as soon as practicably possible, followed with a written report within 2 working days.

Research suggests that only 4% (1 in 23) of actual incidents of elder abuse are reported (Lifespan of Greater Rochester, Inc., 2011). In part, this could be because clinicians struggle to determine when to report. It is at times difficult to determine whether the abuse actually occurred, whether it reaches the criterion for reporting, or whether it was an isolated incident or part of a larger pattern of repetitive abuse. In all of these circumstances, it is not the clinician's role to make these determinations, but rather it is the suspicion of abuse that triggers the requirement to report. Exhibit 26.4 provides some suggestions regarding how to inquire about abuse issues in the clinical setting. In most states, an APS social worker triages the initial telephone reports, helps the reporter to determine whether the report is necessary, and advises how to proceed. In the author's experiences, no harm is done if a call is placed, the situation is reviewed, and it is determined that it does not require a report. It is generally advisable to error on the side of reporting, to protect patient, self, license, and the public at large.

Maintaining the therapeutic relationship. The impact of a report of elder abuse on the therapeutic relationship is a complex subject with multiple issues that depend on a number of factors. Once the report is made, the clinician should think carefully

about how this will affect their patient so they can anticipate the consequences and be prepared to respond in the most appropriate and therapeutic manner possible.

The impact of a report of elder abuse clearly will be affected by whether the patient is the victim, perpetrator, family member, or other interested party. Making the report fulfills the legal obligation and the clinician is not responsible to identify the remedy to the situation, as this is determined by the APS agency. Depending on the circumstances, APS may request clinical input, but often the clinician will have no knowledge of how they proceed in their investigation and intervention. The clinician, however, has continued responsibility to the patient

---

Exhibit 26.4
Asking About Abuse

Questions for the Older Adult and Possible Victim	Response when the answer is "yes"
Are you afraid of anybody? Has anybody hurt you? Is anyone mistreating you? Is anybody taking or using your money without your permission? Do you always have enough food and water available?	I'm glad you told me and I want to help you now. First, you need to know that it's never ok to hit your father or for someone to hit you. I'm going to call a social service agency so they can come to your home and help you figure out what to do so this never happens again.
Questions for the Caregiver and Possible Perpetrator	Response when the answer is "no"
I can see that you're under a lot of stress. Have you ever gotten to a point where you've hit your mom or thought about hitting your mom? This kind of caregiving is really frustrating. How do you handle it when you've reached your limit?	I'm glad to hear that. You're in a situation where this could happen, so we both need to be alert for it. There's a lot we can do to prevent any abuse from happening so you need to let me know if you're feeling that you're getting too angry or frustrated.
When your wife is resistant to the care you're providing such as with bathing, has it ever gotten physical? Has she ever hurt you? Have you ever hurt her?	Response when the answer is "maybe"
I know your mom is getting up in years and you're probably going to inherit her money. Are you using that money now?	It's good that I know this. I had the sense you were feeling overwhelmed with your or your dad's care needs. Now we need to do something different so that this never happens again.
Do you ever get so tired that you don't take as good care as you'd like to and end up leaving your husband on his own?	

---

despite whether the patient is the victim, perpetrator, or other party involved in the situation. The following issues will help clinicians to clarify their role, limit problems, and provide some direction as they move forward in providing care within the context of an elder abuse report.

Know who the "patient" is. It is important to be absolutely clear who the patient is. When treating elders in a clinical context, it is not unusual for the patient to be the elder individually, the elder as part of a marital relationship, the elder as part of a conjoint relationship with an adult child, or the elder as part of a larger family system. Clarification of the patient is good clinical practice in any regard, but it becomes critical when issues of abuse are present.

Understand the limits of confidentiality. Once the clinician is clear who the patient is, issues of confidentiality should be considered. The report itself is a legally mandated breach of confidentiality. Determining who may be or should be informed, however, requires careful consideration. For instance, if the victim is your patient individually, and he or she does not provide a release of information, the clinician is not permitted to inform family of the abuse, even if this would help to protect the patient and it appears to be in his or her best interest. In contrast, when the patient is the family or couple, it may be appropriate to inform the family of the abuse and that it has been reported.

Know who can make decisions. The issues become even more complex when one or more of the parties involved (victim, perpetrator, patient, or family member) lack the capacity to make decisions for themselves. It is important to be clear who holds decision-making rights for elders who have been deemed incapable of making decisions for themselves; one must also have supporting documentation. In some particularly complex situations, seeking legal consultation regarding confidentiality may be advised.

Will the report remain anonymous? In most states, reports of abuse are made anonymously, and it will not become a therapeutic issue. Often, however, it is clear to the patient or family that the clinician made the report based on the timing of the response by APS or other issues. Thus, it may become known or understood that the therapist reported the incident. It is wise to consider and develop a plan as to how to respond, if this information becomes known.

When to inform patients of elder abuse reports. There are times when it is good clinical judgment to share with the patient or the family that the report was made, assuming there are no limits due to confidentiality. In some situations, this helps to maintain the integrity of the therapeutic relationship and fosters an atmosphere of openness and support. Victims and family respond to learning about abuse in sometimes surprising ways as discussed in the following sections.

When not to inform patients of elder abuse reports. It would be ill-advised to inform the family when the perpetrator of the abuse is a family member, and in particular, when the abuse reaches a criminal level. Informing the patient or the family that you have made an elder abuse report can increase the risk that the patient will be mistreated. It also may make it more difficult for the APS worker to intervene, for instance, when family moves the patient from one facility to another or to another family member's home.

Positive response to elder abuse reports. Victims and family often respond to awareness that abuse has occurred with fear, anger, disbelief, embarrassment, or shame. It often is helpful to guide patients to differentiate their emotional response to the abuse itself from their response to the report and the consequences of the report. Hopefully, patients will experience some relief that it has been revealed, that assistance is available, and that any further harm will be limited or eliminated. Initial hostile reactions sometimes can be softened once patients and families understand that the role of APS is to offer resources and assistance to ensure the safety of the elder.

In some situations, elders are "willing victims" of abuse. This can occur when the elder views the abuse as acceptable because it is better than the alternatives they fear or can imagine—for instance, when a caregiver implicitly threatens a community-dwelling elder by saying, "if it were not for me, you'd be in a nursing home."

Many elderly people have strong emotional attachments to their perpetrators (Jackson & Hafemeister, 2011). They often defend the perpetrator and may not welcome intervention of any manner. Thus, as the reporter, either the victim or the family may view the clinician in a negative light. Again, helping the victim and family to understand that more appropriate alternatives will be explored can help alleviate fear and anger.

Assessment of Capacity and Undue Influence

Psychologists who work in the forensic arena frequently are asked to conduct capacity assessments of elders. As discussed in Chapter 21, this volume, this may involve the assessment of an elders' capacity related to health care and financial decision making. This expanding area of practice often, but not always, relates to issues of elder abuse. Psychologists practicing in the forensic arena should be especially aware of the varieties of ways that elder abuse presents so that they are able to respond appropriately (Wiglesworth, Kemp, & Mosqueda, 2008.)

Capacity to do what and under what circumstances? As with all capacity assessments, the evaluator must be aware of which capacities are in question. This may be unclear and often requires the evaluator to work with whoever is requesting the assessment to clarify what is needed. In most circumstances, the court looks at capacity as an all-or-nothing phenomenon. It is important to frame an opinion regarding capacity in a manner that will lead to the greatest degree of autonomy possible, while maintaining the client's safety and welfare. Thus, it is not unusual to draft an opinion regarding capacity that specifies the conditions that must be present in the environment for the individual to retain a specific capacity.

Components of capacity assessments. As with other capacity assessments, abuse-related capacity assessments should be comprehensive to ensure that the resulting opinion is based on as complete a picture as possible. The joint ABA Commission on Law and Aging and American Psychological Association guidelines (ABA Commission on Law

and Aging & APA; 2008) provided a conceptual framework that indicates the components of an assessment of capacity.

The evaluator must understand the legal standard for the capacity under question, which is the specific legal definition of functions necessary to maintain that capacity. These standards vary by state and often are vague. The medical diagnoses that produce the disability should be documented along with a clear statement as to prognosis and treatment options. An objective measure of cognition is almost always indicated and can be accomplished with standard instruments that measure cognitive functioning or instruments designed specifically for capacity assessment. An evaluation of emotional status and psychiatric symptoms typically is conducted in the course of a clinical interview. The evaluator should assess the individual's functional skills and the ability to successfully engage in basic ADLs and IADLs. This can be accomplished through interview, observation, collateral sources, or tests designed to measure the specific skills in question. The data should be interpreted with the individual's values, preferences, and culture in mind. It is important to understand what efforts have been made to restore the individual's capacity along with the outcome of those attempts. The degree of risk or harm to the victim should be assessed and a statement as to the recommended level of supervision should be made, so that the evaluator recommends the least restrictive alternative possible. Last, the evaluator interprets all of this information through the lens of clinical judgment.

Capacity assessment in the context of elder abuse. A forensic assessment of capacity may be requested as a result of an accusation of elder abuse or neglect. In these circumstances, the psychologist may be asked to evaluate and offer an opinion as to whether an elder was able to both understand the decision and appreciate the consequences of the decision. If that capacity is retained, the event(s) under consideration may not be abuse at all, but rather an instance of an individual making a decision that many would deem to be poor, not in his or her own best interest, or consistent with a long-standing set of values that are not broadly shared.

In contrast, if the resulting opinion is that the individual did *not* retain the capacity in question, that opinion may be a piece of information that leads to prosecution of the perpetrator or the protection of the victim. On occasion, a psychologist may have completed an assessment of an elder who is later abused or mistreated. The psychologist then may be engaged in the legal process that results, as the opinion will be helpful in determining whether abuse occurred, whether the case escalates to the level of criminal prosecution, or how the victim should best be protected. Thus, even when no abuse is apparent at the time of assessment, it is important to keep these concepts in mind in any case involving an elder. Clearly, these assessments have important and widely felt consequences and should be undertaken with utmost care.

Neglect and self-neglect. Neglect, either at the hands of another or oneself, often creates the need for an assessment of the capacity to live independently. These evaluations are often among the most difficult because they concern such a fundamental value—independence—and because the range of skills and abilities that are potentially relevant is so vast (ABA Commission on Law and Aging & APA, 2008). In these cases, the question at hand is whether the elder retains the capacity to make decisions regarding their care needs, and if not, how their needs can best be met (Dong et al., 2010; Mosqueda & Dong, 2011). In many cases, when there is a lack of capacity, the agencies involved arrange to meet the needs against the wishes of the elder, sometimes through the mechanism of a conservatorship or guardianship. In the state of California, when this form of protection is sought, the evaluating psychologist may be asked to complete documentation for the court regarding the capacities in question.

Undue influence. Yet another way in which psychologists are asked to offer forensic opinions relates to the concept of undue influence. As described earlier, some forms of abuse involve perpetrators' efforts to make victims do something that they normally would not do, which is to the benefit of the

perpetrator. Undue influence most often involves financial exploitation and is different than other forms of capacity assessment for two reasons. First, there is no presumption that capacity is diminished in the victim for the abuse to have taken place. Second, the abuse occurs in the context of an unequal but trusting relationship that has been used to pressure the victim. As a direct result of the relationship, the perpetrator uses manipulation, coercion, compulsion, or restraint to effect a monetary transfer (ABA Commission on Law and Aging & APA, 2008).

In any of these roles, the psychologist working in a forensic capacity may be asked to write a report, complete a capacity declaration, respond to subpoenas, participate in depositions, or offer trial testimony. The courts in which these issues are heard span criminal, civil, and probate courts. Before agreeing to be engaged in this form of forensic assessment, as with all areas of practice, the psychologist should ensure that he or she is acting within the limits of education and training as well as have the necessary experience to undertake the task confidently.

Working Collaboratively With Other Disciplines and Agencies

Given their medical, legal, financial, ethical, and social complexity, elder abuse cases are best addressed by working with professionals from other disciplines and agencies (Wiglesworth, Mosqueda, Burnight, Younglove, & Jeske, 2006). The expertise of psychologists make them valuable assets to interdisciplinary teams, and psychologists often serve in leadership roles because of their specialized training in group processes, collaborative treatment planning, and group facilitation. In the field of elder abuse, several models of interdisciplinary teams are in fairly wide practice.

Multidisciplinary teams. Since the earliest days of the field of elder abuse, it has been recognized that no one agency can successfully address elder abuse and neglect (Twomey et al., 2010). Starting in the 1980s, the original elder abuse multidisciplinary teams (MDTs) included professionals from different disciplines who come together, usually monthly, to review cases and address system problems revealed by cases. The teams review cases of abuse, neglect, and self-neglect and provide resources, advice, and new perspectives to the agency bringing the case for review. MDTs typically are composed of representatives from the public agencies that investigate elder abuse, including APS, long-term care, local ombudsmen, law enforcement, city or county counsel, and nonprofit (and occasionally for-profit) agencies that provide services to community-dwelling seniors. Examples of these types of organizations include Meals On Wheels™, care management organizations, home health care organizations, and senior centers. Some teams may invite private professionals, such as attorneys or realtors, to participate. In the decades following the 1980s, MDTs evolved to address specific kinds of abuse, such as financial abuse, and to provide not only advice but also intervention.

Financial abuse specialist teams.   Financial Abuse Specialist Teams are groups of individuals and agency representatives who meet periodically to brainstorm and problem solve particularly complex cases of financial elder abuse. They may have an educational component and often are open to a wide range of interested parties, including representatives from APS, public guardian's office, police, sheriff's department, district attorneys, private conservators, elder law attorneys, private fiduciaries, local ombudsman, financial institutions and brokerage firms, mortgage brokers, care managers, and the like. The team can provide guidance and direction to whomever is working to mitigate the risk and effects of elder abuse in the community.

Elder abuse forensic centers.   An alternative model is the elder abuse forensic center (EAFC). EAFCs developed out of a need to integrate efforts on case investigation, client services, and prosecution. EAFCs are distinct in that these forensic centers provide not only the advice of the traditional MDT but also the intervention and case follow-through. Meeting on a weekly basis, the collective determines a plan of action, and team members assist in actually carrying out the recommendations. The EAFC model reflects a "one-stop-shop" where professionals from APS, law enforcement, or local ombudsman can partner with other agencies to obtain input and action from team members; law enforcement; the medical, mental health, and legal communities; social services; and public guardians. The fact that all of the agencies are together in one place allows for increased efficiency, understanding (and confrontation at times), and eventually trust among agencies.

The psychologist's role in interdisciplinary teams.   Regardless of the specific type of team, it is critical for psychologists to recognize the importance of their role in several respects. First, the psychologist may feel pressure to bias an opinion in forensic assessments to meet the need of an agency or individual, rather than to base the opinion on the facts of the matter. Second, psychologists should strive to model a professional approach that guides others to make decisions that are ethical and within the scope of their expertise. They may help to articulate to the group at large strategies to manage emotional stress that results from working complex cases that often have poor outcomes or those in which little can be done to protect the victims. Psychologists may fill a role of educating team members about relevant research related to elder abuse or related matters and assist in applying the findings to their environment. Last, psychologists may assist the group in maintaining a mutually supportive atmosphere in which no members are held accountable for the inadequate resources or limiting policies of the agencies they represent.

CONCLUSION

Elder abuse is a field that is fraught with controversy. Most clinicians are not comfortable with terms, such as *perpetrator*, especially when working with people who are seemingly well-intended and perhaps ignorant of how to do a better job. For example, the *overwhelmed caregiver* is a real phenomenon; some caregivers are poorly equipped (physically, emotionally, socially) to carry out their responsibility in a way that is nonabusive. For the older adult, however, the motivation does not matter: That person is still being abused or neglected.

The following trends are emerging in the field of elder abuse:

- Functional neuroimaging is being used to determine level of vulnerability to undue influence and financial abuse.

- The needs of a growing number of individuals aging with developmental disabilities, such as Down Syndrome, have changed. Because of advancements in medical technology, many of these individuals now outlive their parents, which is likely to thrust siblings into a situation they did not want. Sometimes the sibling in this caregiving role is not only caring for their disabled brother or sister but also for a parent with dementia or other debilitating disease.

- There appears to be a dangerous intersection of demographics, workforce, and funding. As the size of the middle class shrinks and the number of older adults increases exponentially, more wealth will be concentrated in the older population. This may increase the incidence of elder financial abuse beyond the current levels.

APPENDIX 26.1 ELDER ABUSE RESOURCES

GENERAL

National Center on Elder Abuse. The National Center on Elder Abuse, directed by the U.S. Administration for Community Living, helps communities, agencies, and organizations ensure that elders and adults with disabilities can live with dignity and without abuse, neglect, and exploitation. The National Center on Elder Abuse is based at the Department of Family Medicine, Keck School of Medicine at the University of Southern California. Its website (http://www.ncea.aoa.gov) is the place to turn for education, outreach, and promising practices in stopping abuse.

Ageless Alliance. The Ageless Alliance (http://www.agelessalliance.org) is a national grassroots movement uniting people of all ages and backgrounds to take action against elder abuse locally and nationally. Ageless Alliance's goals include building awareness, providing support, and promoting community action.

Center for Elders and the Courts. The Center for Elders and the Courts website (http://www.eldersandcourts.org) contains an interactive map of state-by-state elder abuse laws, probate laws, and national elder abuse training tools.

FINANCIAL

Elder Financial Protection Network. To better understand financial abuse, the Elder Financial Protection Network website (http://www.elderfinancialprotection.org/what-is-financial-abuse) provides information about common types of elder financial abuse, including warning signs and reporting guidelines.

References

Acierno, R., Hernandez, M. A., Amstadter, A. B., Resnick, H. S., Steve, K., Muzzy, W., & Kilpatrick, D. G. (2010). Prevalence and correlates of emotional, physical, sexual, and financial abuse and potential neglect in the United States: The National Elder Mistreatment Study. *American Journal of Public Health, 100,* 292–297. doi:10.2105/AJPH.2009.163089

Alzheimer's Association. (2013). *Risk factors.* Retrieved from http://www.alz.org/alzheimers_disease_causes_risk_factors.asp

American Bar Association Commission on Law and Aging. (2006a). *Reporting requirements: Provisions and citations in adult protective services laws, by state.* Washington, DC: Stiegel & Klem.

American Bar Association Commission on Law and Aging. (2006b). *Types of abuse: Provisions and citations in adult protective services laws, by state.* Washington, DC: Stiegel & Klem.

American Bar Association Commission on Law and Aging & American Psychological Association. (2008). *Assessment of older adults with diminished capacity: A handbook for psychologists.* Retrieved from http://www.apa.org/pi/aging/programs/assessment

Beck, C., Richards, K., Lambert, C., Doan, R., Landes, R. D., Whall, A., . . . Feldman, Z. (2011). Factors associated with problematic vocalizations in nursing home residents with dementia. *Gerontologist, 51,* 389–405. doi:10.1093/geront/gnq129

Brandl, B., Dyer, C., Heisler, C., Otto, J., Stiegel, L., & Thomas, R. (2007). *Elder abuse detection and intervention: A collaborative approach.* New York, NY: Springer.

Centers for Disease Control and Prevention. (2010). *Intimate partner violence: Risk and protective factors.* Retrieved from http://www.cdc.gov/

ViolencePrevention/intimatepartnerviolence/riskprotectivefactors.html

Centers for Disease Control and Prevention. (2013). *Elder abuse: Definitions.* Retrieved from http://www.cdc.gov/violenceprevention/elderabuse/definitions.html

Cooper, C., Blanchard, M., Selwood, A., Walker, Z., Blizard, R., & Livingston, G. (2009). Abuse of people with dementia by family caregivers: Representative cross sectional survey. *British Medical Journal, 338,* b155. doi:10.1136/bmj.b155

Cooper, C., Blanchard, M., Selwood, A., Walker, Z., & Livingston, G. (2010). Family carers' distress and abusive behaviour: Longitudinal study. *British Journal of Psychiatry, 196,* 480–485. doi:10.1192/bjp.bp.109.071811

Cornijs, H., Penninx, B., Knipscheer, K., & van Tilburg, W. (1999). Psychological distress in victims of elder mistreatment: The effects of social support and coping. *The Journals of Gerontology, Series B: Psychological Sciences and Social Sciences, 54,* 240–245.

Dodge, H. H., Kadowaki, T., Hayakawa, T., Yamakawa, M., Sekikawa, A., & Ueshima, H. (2005). Cognitive impairment as a strong predictor of incident disability in specific ADL-IADL tasks among community-dwelling elders: The Azuchi Study. *Gerontologist, 45,* 222–230. doi:10.1093/geront/45.2.222

Dong, X., Simon, M., Wilson, R., de Leon, C., Rajan, K., & Evans, D. (2010). Decline in cognitive function and risk of elder self-neglect: Finding from the Chicago Health Aging Project. *Journal of the American Geriatrics Society, 58,* 2292–2299. doi:10.1111/j.1532-5415.2010.03156.x

Dunkin, J. J., & Anderson-Hanley, C. (1998). Dementia caregiver burden: A review of the literature and guidelines for assessment and intervention. *Neurology, 51*(Suppl. 1), S53–S60. doi:10.1212/WNL.51.1_Suppl_1.S53

Federal Trade Commission. (2013). *Consumer Sentinel Network Data Book for January–December 2012.* Retrieved from http://www.ftc.gov/sentinel/reports/sentinel-annual-reports/sentinel-cy2012.pdf

Fein, G., McGillivray, S., & Finn, P. (2007). Older adults make less advantageous decisions than younger adults: Cognitive and psychological correlates. *Journal of the International Neuropsychological Society, 13,* 480–489. doi:10.1017/S135561770707052X

Fulmer, T., Paveza, G., VandeWeerd, C., Fairchild, S., Guadagno, L., Bolton-Blatt, M., & Norman, R. (2005). Dyadic vulnerability and risk profiling for elder neglect. *Gerontologist, 45,* 525–534. doi:10.1093/geront/45.4.525

Haber, D. (2013). *Health promotion and aging* (6th ed.). New York, NY: Springer.

Hafemeister, T. (2003). *Financial abuse of the elderly in domestic setting.* Retrieved from http://www.ncbi.nlm.nih.gov/books/NBK98784

Heck, L., & Gillespie, G. (2013). Interprofessional program to provide emergency sheltering to abused elders. *Advanced Emergency Nursing Journal, 35,* 170–181. doi:10.1097/TME.0b013e31828ecc06

Jackson, S., & Hafemeister, T. (2011). *Financial abuse of elderly people vs. other forms of elder abuse: Assessing their dynamics, risk factors, and society's response.* Rockville, MD: National Institute of Justice. Retrieved from https://www.ncjrs.gov/App/Publications/abstract.aspx?ID=255547

Jackson, S., & Hafemeister, T. (2012). Pure financial exploitation vs. hybrid financial exploitation co-occurring with physical abuse and/or neglect of elderly persons. *Psychology of Violence, 2,* 285–296. doi:10.1037/a0027273

Jogerst, G. J., Daly, J., Galloway, L., Zheng, S., & Xu, Y. (2012). Substance abuse associated with elder abuse in the United States. *American Journal of Drug and Alcohol Abuse, 38,* 63–69. doi:10.3109/00952990.2011.600390

Johannesen, M., & LoGiudice, D. (2013). Elder abuse: A systematic review of risk factors in community-dwelling elders. *Age and Ageing, 42,* 292–298. doi:10.1093/ageing/afs195

Kemp, B. J., & Mosqueda, L. A. (2005). Elder financial abuse: An evaluation framework and supporting evidence. *Journal of the American Geriatric Society, 53,* 1123–1127. doi:0.1111/j.1532-5415.2005.53353.x

Kirkwood, T. (2005). The biological science of human ageing. In M. Johnson (Ed.), *The Cambridge handbook of age and ageing* (pp. 72–81). New York, NY: Cambridge University Press.

Lachs, M. S., Williams, C., O'Brien, S., Pillemer, K., & Charlson, M. (1998). The mortality of elder mistreatment. *JAMA, 280,* 428–432. doi:10.1001/jama.280.5.428

Lifespan of Greater Rochester, Inc., Weill Cornell Medical Center of Cornell University, & New York City Department for the Aging. (2011). *Under the radar: New York State elder abuse prevalence study.* Retrieved from http://ocfs.ny.gov/main/reports/Under%20the%20Radar%2005%2012%2011%20final%20report.pdf

Luo, Y., & Waite, L. J. (2011). Mistreatment and psychological well-being among older adults: Exploring the role of psychosocial resources and deficits. *The Journals of Gerontology, Series B: Psychological Sciences and Social Sciences, 66,* 217–229. doi:10.1093/geronb/gbq096

MacNeil, G., Kosberg, J. I., Durkin, D. W., Dooley, W. K., Decoster, J., & Williamson, G. M. (2010). Caregiver mental health and potentially harmful caregiving behavior: The central role of caregiver anger. *Gerontologist, 50*, 76–86. doi:10.1093/geront/gnp099

Modestin, J., Gladen, C., & Christen, S. (2001). A comparative study on schizophrenic patients with dual diagnosis. *Journal of Addictive Diseases, 20*, 45–55. doi:10.1300/J069v20n04_05

Mosqueda, L. (2012). *The role of interdisciplinary teams in elder mistreatment.* Retrieved from http://www.centeronelderabuse.org/docs/TheRoleofInterdisciplinaryTeamsinElder Mistreatment_ppt.pdf

Mosqueda, L., & Dong, X. (2011). Elder abuse and self-neglect: "I don't care anything about going to the doctor, to be honest." *JAMA, 306*, 532–540. doi:10.1001/jama.2011.1085

Moyer, V. A., & U.S. Preventive Services Task Force. (2013). Screening for intimate partner violence and abuse of elderly and vulnerable adults: U.S. Preventive Services Task Force recommendation statement. *Annals of Internal Medicine, 158*, 478–486. doi:10.7326/0003-4819-158-6-201303190-00588

Murtaugh, C. M., Kemper, P., Spillman, B., & Carlson, B. (1997). The amount, distribution, and timing of lifetime nursing home use. *Medical Care, 35*, 204–218. doi:10.1097/00005650-199703000-00003

National Adult Protective Services Association. (2013). *Get help: Help in your area.* Retrieved from http://www.napsa-now.org/get-help/help-in-your-area

National Center on Elder Abuse. (2013a). *Red flags of elder abuse–English (2012).* Retrieved from http://ncea.aoa.gov/Get_Involved/Awareness/Materials/index.aspx

National Center on Elder Abuse. (2013b). *Types of abuse.* Retrieved from http://ncea.aoa.gov/FAQ/Type_Abuse

Podnieks, E. (2006). Social inclusion: An interplay of the determinants of health: New insights into elder abuse. *Journal of Gerontological Social Work, 46*, 57–79. doi:10.1300/J083v46n03_04

Reinhard, S., Given, B., Petlick, N., & Bernis, A. (2008). Supporting family caregivers in providing care. In R. G. Hughes (Ed.), *Patient safety and quality: An evidence-based handbook for nurses* (pp. 341–404). Rockville, MD: Agency for Healthcare Research and Quality. Retrieved from http://www.ncbi.nlm.nih.gov/books/NBK2665

Shugarman, L. R., Fries, B., Wolf, R., & Morris, J. (2003). Identifying older people at risk of abuse during routine screening practices. *Journal of the American Geriatrics Society, 51*, 24–31. doi:10.1034/j.1601-5215.2002.51005.x

Tatara, T. (Ed.). (1999). *Understanding elder abuse in minority populations.* Ann Arbor, MI: Braun-Brumfield.

Twomey, M. S., Jaskson, G., Li, H., Marino, T., Melchior, L., Randolph, J., . . . Wysong, J. (2010). The success and challenges of seven multidiscipliary teams. *Journal of Elder Abuse and Neglect, 22*, 291–305. doi:10.1080/08946566.2010.490144

U.S. National Research Council, Panel to Review Risk and Prevalence of Elder Abuse and Neglect. (2003). *Elder mistreatment: abuse, neglect, and exploitation in an aging America.* Washington, DC: Author.

Wiglesworth, A., Austin, R., Corona, M., Schneider, D., Liao, S., Gibbs, L., & Mosqueda, L. (2009). Bruising as a marker of physical elder abuse. *Journal of the American Geriatrics Society, 57*, 1191–1196. doi:10.1111/j.1532-5415.2009.02330.x

Wiglesworth, A., Kemp, B., & Mosqueda, L. (2008). Combating elder and dependent adult mistreatment: The role of the clinical psychologist. *Journal of Elder Abuse and Neglect, 20*, 207–230. doi:10.1080/08946560801973051

Wiglesworth, A., Mosqueda, L., Burnight, K., Younglove, T., & Jeske, D. (2006). Findings from an elder abuse forensic center. *Gerontologist, 46*, 277–283. doi:10.1093/geront/46.2.277

Wiglesworth, A., Mosqueda, L., Mulnard, R., Liao, S., Gibbs, L., & Fitzgerald, W. (2010). Screening for abuse and neglect of people with dementia. *Journal of the American Geriatrics Society, 58*, 493–500. doi:10.1111/j.1532-5415.2010.02737.x

Yaffe, M. J. (2010). Detection and reporting of elder abuse. *Family Medicine, 42*, 83.

Index